Paul Robeson

'A biography to match the subject, dramatic, detailed, enthralling.
He [Duberman] has an outsider's empathy with Robeson, brings alive
the days of turbulence ... This resolute, generous biography is the first
step towards justice for the memory of a giant of a man.'
SYLVIA CLAYTON, THE GUARDIAN

'Powerful ... Duberman has done an excellent job on a complex
subject ... [He] rates high marks for having seen much that white
biographers of African-American subjects disregard ... [He] weaves
matters private and public into a tapestry that captures both the
greatness and the humanity of a tragic American.'
NELL IRVIN PAINTER, THE BOSTON GLOBE

'In the pantheon of American radicals, Paul Robeson (1898–1976)
holds a high place as a victim of McCarthyite repression. Yet after
reading Martin Bauml Duberman's epic biography, it's hard to say
whether Robeson's rise or fall was more remarkable ... Duberman has
constructed a biography that is a monument long overdue.'
HENRY MAYER, SAN FRANCISCO CHRONICLE

'A bold and accusing acknowledgement of the same virtue in
Robeson himself.'
RUSSELL DAVIES, THE LISTENER

'A monumental biography ... superbly told by Martin Bauml
Duberman.'
THE ECONOMIST

'A tremendous biography, brilliantly attuned to both the greatness and
the complexities of Paul Robeson. It stands along with Richard
Kluger's *Simple Justice* as one of the two best books I have read in the
last fifteen years.'
DAVID J. GARROW, Pulitzer Prize-winning author of *Bearing the Cross*

A distinguished social historian, Professor Martin Bauml Duberman has had unique access to the 50,000 items in the Robeson archive and has carried out research worldwide.
He has previously published a number of books including *In White America, James Russell Lowell, Charles Francis Adams, 1807–1886.*

● MARTIN BAUML DUBERMAN ●

PAUL ROBESON

PAN BOOKS

London, Sydney and Auckland

For Eli Zal
and for my friends in the rooms.

First published in America 1989 by Ballantine Books,
a division of Random House, Inc.
First published in Great Britain 1989 by The Bodley Head Ltd
This edition published 1991 by Pan Books Ltd
Cavaye Place, London SW10 9PG
9 8 7 6 5 4 3 2 1
ISBN 0 330 31385 1
© Martin Bauml Duberman 1989

Printed in England by Clays Ltd, St Ives plc

I have done the state some service, and they know't.
No more of that. I pray you, in your letters,
When you shall these unlucky deeds relate,
Speak of me as I am, nothing extenuate,
Nor set down aught in malice. . . .

Othello V. ii. 339–43

Contents

Contents

Preface

In 1919, when Paul Robeson graduated from Rutgers as valedictorian, the "class prophecy" suggested that by 1940 he would be governor of New Jersey and "the leader of the colored race in America." When 1940 came around, that prophecy had not been entirely realized but—except for the governorship of New Jersey, for which Robeson had no ambition—continued to seem entirely plausible. By then he had added to his undergraduate laurels as scholar and All-American football player, international acclaim as concert artist, stage actor, recording and film star.

Although many white and almost all black Americans in 1940 shared a high estimate of Robeson's accomplishment, their views of what it meant failed to coincide in some important ways. To the white world in general, Robeson seemed a magnetic, civilized, and gifted man who had relied on talent rather than belligerence to "rise above his circumstances." Whites vaguely recognized in 1940 that he was beginning to emerge as a passionate defender of the underclasses, yet the lack of stridency and self-pity in his manner allowed them to persist in the comfortable illusion that his career proved the way was indeed open to those with sufficient pluck and aptitude, regardless of race—that the "system" worked.

Those whites who knew Robeson personally (and he had many white friends) recognized, more than the white world at large did, that his charismatic charm, his grace and generosity, real enough, were hardly a complete accounting of his personality. They had experienced his stubborn reserve, had seen his carefully controlled anger erupt, knew the limits of his gregariousness. By 1940, they also had become aware of his deepening political passion. They had heard him talk with a gravity dramatically different from the unemphatic ease of his usual public self-presentation about the importance of preserving African culture from the corrupting influence of the West. They knew of his deep dismay over the destruction of Republican Spain, his mounting commitment to what he viewed as the anticolonial and egalitarian impulses of the Soviet Union, his mounting anger at the blind ethnocentrism of Europe's privileged classes in their continuing exploitation of colonial peoples.

Black Americans had watched Robeson work his way through the white world with an ease that seemed remarkable—and in moments of optimism provided a ray of hope. Here he was in 1940, son of an ex-slave, risen to be a highly regarded interpreter not only of spirituals but also of the plays of America's foremost white playwright, Eugene O'Neill. He had already starred, as well, in a London production of *Othello* with Peggy Ashcroft and Sybil Thorndike, had sold out concert halls throughout Europe, had been a leading box-office draw in half a dozen films, and had, most recently, been the man chosen to sing on a nationwide radio broadcast—to immense acclaim—the stirring, patriotic "Ballad for Americans." With seemingly equal ease, Robeson had moved beyond artistic recognition to social acceptance—at least in sophisticated white circles in England, where he and his family had resided for much of the thirties.

True, the black actor Ira Aldridge had been hailed for his talent before Robeson, just as the singer Roland Hayes had also filled concert halls. But Robeson had combined both their gifts, had added an outstanding career in athletics, a degree in law, a scholar's ability to summon up wide-ranging points of reference, and a linguist's ability to communicate in several languages. And beyond all these accomplishments, and perhaps more inspiring than any of them to the "ordinary" black American, was Robeson's deepening commitment to improving the lot of people of color around the world. Here was an important black artist who viewed his gifts and his worldly success not as ends in themselves, but as instruments for helping the race.

Most blacks were too open-eyed to believe, as most whites did, that Robeson's success proved that the American system "worked," that it even remotely offset the otherwise prevalent enormities of discrimination. Nor did most blacks interpret (as most whites did) the phenomenon of one exceptionally gifted black man's being allowed through the net as evidence that the net was porous—or even that Robeson's own acceptance was without very real boundaries and qualifications. Still, it was worth knowing, however much white America overemployed the information, that a few supremely gifted blacks did occasionally get the chance to demonstrate their gifts. It was worth even more to know that one such black had become determined to see that others—gifted or not—got their entitlement to a dignified life.

Had the class prophet resumed his duties in 1940 and tried to cast ahead yet another twenty years, he might have justifiably been confident that Robeson's triumphs would multiply and his influence consolidate. This time he would have been woefully wrong. From 1940 to 1960 Robeson evolved fully from an artist with a conscience to an artist committed to political action. He moved from the view that his own accomplishments would open doors for others to the conviction that the doors remained so firmly secured that those who had somehow pushed through them had to see to their permanent dismantling as a *primary* obligation. During the years of Roosevelt's New Deal, Robeson remained reasonably hopeful that white America would itself recognize the worst aspects of institutionalized racism and work to expunge them. But as the democratic impulses of the New Deal drained off into the intolerance of postwar McCarthyism, his real hope fastened on the ultimate transforming power of international socialism. He never ceased being an American patriot—continuing to believe in the inspirational promise of the country's principles, if not her practice— but the more white America failed, in the post–World War II years, to stand up for the rights of people of color, the more Robeson grew into a militant spokesman for the world's oppressed. The country's failure to set its house in order, to ransom its own promise, brought out in him not—as in so many others—weary acquiescence but, rather, uncompromising anger, a dogged refusal to bow.

Robeson's stand endeared him still further to those who shared his politics and his principles, but cost him dearly with the multitude of mainstream Americans who had once been among his admirers. By 1960 his career and health had been broken, his name vilified, his honor—even his good sense—assailed, his image converted by a now hostile establishment from public hero to public enemy. Branded a Soviet apologist, kept under close surveillance by the FBI, his right to travel abroad denied by the State Department and his opportunities to perform at home severely curtailed, deserted by most of the beholden black leadership, Robeson became an outcast, very nearly a nonperson.

This extraordinary turnabout in what had been one of the great twentieth-century careers is a singularly American story, emblematic of its times yet transcending them, encompassing not merely Cold War hysteria during one moment in our history but racial symbolism and racial consciousness throughout our history. That a man so deeply loved all over the world could evoke in his own country such an outpouring of fear and anger may be the central tragedy—America's tragedy—of Paul Robeson's story.

■

CHAPTER 1

Boyhood

(1898–1914)

Princeton, New Jersey, at the turn of the century—and to some extent down to the present day—was known as the northernmost outpost of the Confederacy. Long before the Civil War, Southern aristocrats had enrolled their sons at Princeton University, considering it the only "safe" educational institution for those willing to venture north at all. Some Southern families even sent along—in one of those fits of inadvertent irony in which American history abounds—trusted black servants to insulate their scions from the potential hazards of an alien white culture. And thus from an early time the town of Princeton had a black population—and antiblack attitudes.

Even without the infusion of Southern aristocrats, Princeton had its own native tradition of hostility toward blacks, a hostility found in abundance everywhere in the country. By the early years of the twentieth century, that hostility was resurgent and the explicit Jim Crow principle in schooling, transportation, and restaurants had replaced even the marginal ambiguities of the post-Reconstruction period. Black teachers lost their jobs in integrated schools; black citizens were denied access to hotels; black workers were eliminated from trade unions. Social scientists in the universities (Franz Boas, the anthropologist, was among the notable exceptions) had begun bolstering the old doctrines of innate inferiority with their new "objective" expertise, uniting around the "scientific" doctrine that blacks were a separate species, one step above the ape on the evolutionary scale. Books appeared with such inflammatory, unapologetic titles as *The Negro a Beast* and *The Negro: A Menace to Civilization*. On the eve of World War I, the movie *Birth of a Nation* summarized the accumulated ideology and practice of the preceding two decades by portraying noble-hearted whites reluctantly taking the law into their own hands in order to curb the excesses of savage blacks—and was a resounding popular success. Rural areas of the South added burning at the stake to lynch law's already potent arsenal of terror (there were more than eleven hundred lynchings of Southern blacks in the years 1900–14) and in the cities mob violence edged northward to explode with special ferocity in 1908 at Springfield, Illinois, the home of Abraham Lincoln.[1]

Physical intimidation was matched by political, social, and economic proscription. Between 1896 and 1915 every Southern state passed legislation decreeing white-only primaries, backed up by poll taxes, grandfather clauses, and literacy and property requirements that, taken together, effectively disenfranchised blacks. The federal government added its weight to the campaign to hold blacks in their "place." Both Presidents Roosevelt and Taft, their policies differing in much else, combined in these years to sanction the prosecution and dismissal of black soldiers for responding to the violence directed against them by the townspeople of Brownsville, Texas. Woodrow Wilson, born in the South and elected to the presidency in 1912, continued the policies of his predecessors by extending segregation in federal office buildings and rebuffing black applicants for jobs.

At the turn of the century, Booker T. Washington was chief spokesman for his race, and blacks—at least in public and for white consumption—generally accepted his counsel for accommodation, conciliation, and deference. Washington defined economic rights for blacks as the right to be trained for low-paying jobs in factories and farms, cautioned patience in demanding political rights, and eschewed all interest in social intermingling. In the years immediately preceding World War I, both the militant "Niagara Movement," spearheaded by W. E. B. Du Bois, and the National Association for the Advancement of Colored People would emerge to challenge Washington's views, but in 1900 his philosophy held sway—and the escalation of white violence against blacks served notice that it could be overturned only at terrible cost.

Paul Leroy Robeson was born in the town of Princeton on April 9, 1898. His father, William Drew Robeson, had himself been born a slave, the child of Benjamin and Sabra, on the Roberson plantation in Cross Roads Township, Martin County, North Carolina. In 1860, at age fifteen, William Drew had made his escape, found his way north over the Maryland border into Pennsylvania, and served as a laborer for the Union Army (making his way back to North Carolina at least twice to see his mother). At the close of the Civil War, he managed to obtain an elementary-school education and then, earning his fees through farm labor, went on for ministerial studies at the all-black Lincoln University, near Philadelphia (receiving an A.B. in 1873 and a Bachelor of Sacred Theology degree in 1876). A classmate later described "the 'Uncle Tom' tendencies" among many of the students at Lincoln—but singled William Drew out as "among the notable exceptions."[2]

While studying at Lincoln, William Drew met Maria Louisa Bustill, eight years his junior, a teacher at the Robert Vaux School. Her distinguished family traced its roots back to the African Bantu people (as William Drew did his to the Ibo of Nigeria), and in this country its members had intermarried with Delaware Indians and English Quakers. The many prominent descendants included Cyrus Bustill, who in 1787 helped to found the Free African Society, the first black self-help organization in America; Joseph Cassey Bustill, a prominent figure in the Underground Railroad; and Sarah Mapps Douglass, a founding member of the Philadelphia Female Anti-Slavery Society. Louisa Bustill's own sister, Gertrude, wrote for several Philadelphia newspapers and married Dr. Nathan Francis Mossell, the first black graduate of the University of Pennsylvania School of Medicine (as well as a considerable activist for racial justice). When Louisa Bustill married William Drew Robeson in 1878, the impressive legacy of Bustill achievements, past and current, became part of their son Paul's heritage. But it was not the part he emphasized. He always identified more with the humbler lives on his father's side, often alluding affectionately as an adult to his simple, good North Carolina kin—while scarcely ever referring to his Bustill relatives.[3]

At the time of Paul's birth, his father was fifty-three years old and his mother forty-five. She had already given birth to seven children, five of whom had survived infancy. As the youngest, Paul was the doted-upon favorite, and in later life always spoke of his family with deep affection. The firstborn, William Drew, Jr., later became a physician in Washington, D.C., and died in 1925 at the youthful age of forty-four; Paul later credited him as the most "brilliant" member of the family and his own "principal source of learning how to study." (William's nickname among his contemporaries was "schoolboy.") Marian, the one girl, became, like her mother, a teacher; Benjamin, like his father, went on to the ministry. The fiery Reeve (called Reed) rejected any traditional path or cautionary attitude; he was the family brawler, the boy who reacted to racial slurs with passionate defiance—and became something of an alter ego to his younger brother, Paul. "His example explains much of my militancy," Paul wrote later in life. "He often told me, 'Don't ever take it from them, Laddie—always be a man—never bend the knee.' " As an adult, Paul would look back lovingly on his "restless, rebellious" brother, "scoffing at convention, defiant of the white man's law." But after street fights (Reed carried a bag of small, jagged rocks for protection) and brushes with the police, Reed was packed off to Detroit, became part owner of a hotel, apparently got involved in bootlegging and gambling, and is rumored to have died on Skid Row.[4]

The town of Princeton was a strictly Jim Crow place, with black adults held to menial jobs and black youngsters relegated to the segregated Witherspoon Elementary School (which ran only through the eighth grade; parents who wanted their children to have more education—like the Robesons—had to send them out of town). Emma Epps, a contemporary of Paul's, remembers walking home with a pack of white kids at her heels yelling "Nigger! Nigger! Nigger!" Later in life, Paul scornfully rejected Princeton as "spiritually located in Dixie," and he referred angrily to blacks living there "for all intents and purposes on a Southern plantation. And with no more dignity than that suggests—all the bowing and scraping to the drunken rich, all the vile names, all the Uncle Tomming to earn enough to lead miserable lives." Still, the black community in Princeton was large (15–20 percent of the population) and cohesive, with a sizable contingent from rural North Carolina that continued in its Southern speech and traditions, and with Reverend Robeson's relatives, Huldah Robeson, Nettie Staton, and cousins Carraway and Chance all living nearby. As Paul himself later wrote, blacks "lived a much more communal life" in Princeton "than the white people around them," a communality "expressed and preserved" in the church.[5]

Within that church, Reverend Robeson was an admired figure. He had been pastor of the Witherspoon Street Presbyterian Church in Princeton for nearly twenty years when his son Paul was born in 1898. Of the three black churches in Princeton at the turn of the century, Witherspoon was the largest, the possessor of an auditorium, a parish house, and several additional properties, together valued at more than thirty thousand dollars. As pastor of Witherspoon, Reverend Robeson would later be recalled as having initially "made many improvements in the church methods and church property." He would also be recalled, by blacks, as "ever the defender of justice—standing firmly for the rights of our race." A contemporary commented that "you could move the Rock of Gibraltar" more easily—William Drew Robeson was made of "flintstone, unwilling to compromise on moral principles, even if it meant economic harm."[6]

It did. After twenty years of service, Reverend Robeson was forced out of his Princeton pastorate. The initial charges against him focused on the inability of the Witherspoon Church to become financially self-sustaining. An investigating commission appointed by the Presbytery of New Brunswick reported in January 1900 that no misappropriation of funds had taken place but that there had been "great carelessness" in keeping business records. Finding insufficient improvement six months later, the commission recommended "the dissolution of the Pastoral Relation existing between Rev. William D. Robeson and said Church." No reasons were given, and no charges, or even intimations, were made against Reverend Robeson's character. Seventy-two members of the Witherspoon Church—including all three of its Elders and three of its four Trustees—promptly petitioned against his discharge. Reverend Robeson himself, in a lengthy speech before the Presbytery, "made an eloquent appeal" (according to the local press) in his own behalf. He "intimated that the Presbytery was inclined to be hard on him and his church because colored." The chairman of the investigating commission replied that "if Mr. Robeson had been a white pastor, Presbytery would have dissolved the relation long before this," and declared that "there is a misfit at the Witherspoon Street Church and that it is useless for Mr. Robeson longer to continue in that field."[7]

Further discussion before the full Presbytery "brought out the fact that Mr. Robeson had been kind to his people, administering to the wants of the most needy in times of their suffering out of his own substance, often thereby imperilling his own financial interests and bringing upon himself the very conditions which formed the basis of some complaints made against him." With "neither pastor nor people" asking for a dissolution and with Reverend Robeson's character having been shown to be "above reproach," the Presbytery—for the moment—decided that the commission's suggestion for separation was not "sustained by facts necessary to warrant a recommendation of such grave moment." It voted to recommit the report and instructed the commission to provide concrete reasons for its view that Reverend Robeson's pastoral relations with his church should be severed.[8]

The commission's animus was only momentarily deflected. According to the later testimony of two contemporaries, Reverend Robeson had gotten "on the wrong side of a church fight," having apparently refused to bow to pressure from certain white "residents of Princeton" that he curtail his tendency to "speak out against social injustice" in the town. Many years later, after Reverend Robeson's son Paul (still a toddler at the time of his father's troubles) had himself become the target of public abuse, a family friend from the early days commented on how Paul's "ideas, thoughts and effort were misinterpreted by the white man to keep his black brother in the dark and keep us from making progress," adding, "They did it to his father."[9]

The commission went back into session and in October 1900 issued a "supplemental report" testy in tone and adamant in its recommendation that Reverend Robeson be separated from his pastorate. Forced this time to assign reasons, the commission mostly resorted to vague charges about a falling-off in membership at the Witherspoon Church and a "disrelish" for its services "as at present conducted." In further alluding to "a general unrest and dissatisfaction on the part of others"—meaning white residents of Princeton—"who have been the Church's friends and helpers," the commission tipped its actual hand, for the "lack of sympathy" toward Reverend Robeson that it cited could not have referred to his own black congregation. On the contrary, its members, meeting several times under the independent auspices of a white faculty member from the Princeton

Seminary, spoke out forcefully and voted nearly unanimously in favor of retaining Reverend Robeson as pastor.[10]

That made no impression on the commission. The "welfare and prosperity" of the Witherspoon Church, it announced, would be "greatly enhanced" by Reverend Robeson's departure. Bowing to the commission's intransigence, William Drew Robeson resigned, effective February 1, 1901. His salary (about six hundred dollars a year) and his use of the pastor's residence were continued until May 1. On January 27, 1901, the day of Reverend Robeson's farewell sermon, chairs and benches had to be placed in the aisles to accommodate the overflow crowd, and many stood at the rear of the church. He began by acknowledging that "I have made some mistakes and committed some blunders, for I am human and faulty; but if I know my own heart, I have tried to do my work well." Throughout his speech he made only one oblique reference to those who in the church's "darkest need forsook it," but otherwise advocated "forgetting the things that are behind." With the largeness of spirit that his son Paul would always admire and emulate, Reverend Robeson eschewed any desire "to recriminate and rebuke." "As I review the past," he said, "and think upon many scenes, my heart is filled with love." He closed by urging his congregation, "Do not be discouraged, do not think your past work is in vain." The words would prove emblematic for his son Paul's own life.[11]

Within just a few years of losing his pastorate, Reverend Robeson had to face a second, more devastating tragedy. His wife, Louisa, had long been afflicted with impaired eyesight and ill health. When, on a wintry day in 1904, a coal from the stove fell on her long-skirted dress, she failed to detect it. Fatally burned, she lingered on for several days in great pain. Paul, not yet six years old, was away at the time of the accident, but his brother Ben was home. Throughout Ben's life, according to his daughter, the mere sight of a flame was enough to upset him.[12]

As an adult Paul claimed to have scant memory of his mother—perhaps a predictable effect of trauma. Yet he did several times confide to intimates, "I admired my father, but I loved my mother," and he had a vivid recall of the day of her funeral: "He remembers his Aunt Gertrude taking him by the hand, and leading him to the modest coffin, in the little parlor at 13 Green St.—to take one last, but never forgotten look at his beautiful, sweet, generous-hearted Mother." Otherwise, Louisa Bustill Robeson is barely present in the historical record; a scattered reference or two hint at a woman of considerable intellect and education (she wrote many of her husband's sermons and is also recalled as a "poetess"), generous toward those in need, strong yet gentle—a temperament much as her son's would be.[13]

The Bustill clan showed disinterest in the "dark children" Louisa had left behind (she herself had been light-skinned and high-cheekboned, reflecting the mix of African with European and Delaware Indian heritage), which was perhaps another reason Paul identified deeply with his father's uneducated relatives, who treated him with unfailing kindness. Reverend Robeson, bereft of his pastorate and his mate, struggled to regain his balance. He was occasionally called on to give a sermon in this church or that, but to piece out an income he became a coachman, driving Princeton students around town, and in addition got himself a horse and wagon to haul ashes for the townspeople (the ashes, Paul later recalled, "piled up in the back yard in such mass as if one were looking at a coal heap in the Rhonda [sic] Valley in Wales . . ."). "Never once," Paul remembered, did Reverend Robeson "complain of the poverty and misfortune of those years." He retained "his dignity and lack of bitterness." But for a time he could barely sustain a livelihood. The Princeton *Packet,* wanting in all other news about blacks, printed a notice that William Drew Robeson owed $12.25 in unpaid taxes on his house.[14]

At the time of their mother's death in 1904, Ben and Paul were the only children still at home (Marian, next youngest to Paul, was staying with relatives in North Carolina and studying at the Scotia Seminary for young black women). It wasn't until 1907 that Reverend Robeson managed to relocate himself and his two sons in the town of Westfield, but even then economic hardship continued. Reverend Robeson worked in a grocery store, slept with Paul and Ben in the attic under the roof of the store, cooked and washed in a lean-to attached to the back of the building. Shifting his denominational affiliation from Presbyterian to African Methodist Episcopal, he somehow managed to build a tiny church, the Downer Street St. Luke A.M.E. Zion (Paul and Ben helped lay the first bricks "in this *Pillar* of Zion"), and to hold together its flock of rural blacks from the South. They, in turn, helped Reverend Robeson hold together his family. The woman who ran the grocery store downstairs, along with other church sisters and neighbors, brought food from time to time (supplemented by bags of cornmeal, greens, yams, and peanuts sent up by relatives from Robersonville, North Carolina); and if Reverend Robeson had to visit a parishioner or be away overnight, one of the sisters would take young Paul home, sewing on his buttons, darning his socks, making him rice pudding and chocolate cake. "There must have been moments," Paul later wrote, "when I felt the sorrows of a motherless child, but what I most remember from my youngest days was an abiding sense of comfort and security." The townspeople, in turn, remembered him as a "a nice, open-hearted kind of boy. . . . Made people want to help him, just being what he was." Later the whole town of Westfield would claim him, yet he "was always aware of that subtle difference between my complete belonging to the Negro community and my qualified acceptance (however admiring) by the white community."[15]

In 1910 Reverend Robeson was finally able to re-establish himself in a parish, St. Thomas A.M.E. Zion, in the town of Somerville, New Jersey.

By then Ben had gone off to Biddle University (now Johnson C. Smith) in North Carolina, destined from there to enter the seminary and later to become the pastor of Mother A.M.E. Zion Church in Harlem. That left Paul and his father living alone together. Despite a fifty-three-year gap in their ages, the two were mutually devoted, Paul's respect for his father bordering on awe. The one anecdote Robeson repeatedly recounted as an adult to illustrate his deep regard for his father, and his fear of displeasing him, centered on the consequences of disobeying:

> I remember once he told me to do something which I did not do and he said "come here." I ran away. He ran after me. I darted across the road. He followed, stumbled and fell. I was horrified. I hurried back and helped "Pop" to his feet. He had knocked out one of his most needed teeth. I shall never forget my feeling. It has remained ever present, and I sometimes experience horror, shame, ingratitude, selfishness all over again, for I loved my "Pop" like no one in all the world. . . . Never in all my life afterwards, and this happened in 1908, when I was ten, did he have to admonish me again.

The old man's "rock-like strength and dignity" (in Paul's words) took on added authority from his habit of dressing in the long black coat of the "old school," square-cornered and worn down to the knees—and also by his remarkable speaking voice. Paul later called it "the greatest speaking voice I have ever heard . . . a deep, sonorous basso, richly melodic and refined, vibrant with the love and compassion which filled him." In the mid-twenties in New York, Robeson would sometimes amuse friends with an affectionate imitation of his father, the "voice going down like an organ" as it delivered a soul-stirring sermon.[16]

Reverend Robeson had a passion for oratory—those were the days of Gladstone and Parnell, prime declaimers of the spoken word—and in his youngest son the dream of passing on his vocal powers was realized. He gave Paul speech after speech to memorize, going through them with him line by line, "dwelling on the choice of a word, the turn of a phrase, or the potency of an inflexion." Evenings, Paul would perform his prepared orations for his father's judgment. That done, Reverend Robeson would then often play checkers with his son, and on rare occasions would talk to him about his own early years as a slave. If the tales were infrequent, they were also graphic; later in life Paul would recall how they had haunted his memory and infused his singing of the slave spirituals with a special knowledge and poignancy. He marveled at his father's refusal to remain in bondage and, "in all the years of his manhood," his refusal "to be an Uncle Tom." Though he himself witnessed his father "taunted by the hideous injustices of the color 'bar,' " he never once saw in him a "hint of servility";

Reverend Robeson taught his children that the black man "was in every way the equal of the white man." Paul marveled, too, that his father always acted like "a perfect Christian," rejecting bitterness or even unkindliness. He taught Paul that he had a special responsibility to his race—but also taught him to care "for all people who were unfavorably treated," and never to assume that whites, by definition, were as a group incapable of caring, reminding him "that whites as well as blacks had given him aid and comfort in his trek for Freedom." As if to illustrate his words, Reverend Robeson counted among his friends in Somerville the Woldins, a white family who lived almost directly across West Cliff Street. He and Sam Woldin, who had escaped from czarist persecution of the Jews, would often sit on the porch "puffing contentedly on pipes or little Recruits or sweet Caporals, sharing tales of their respective flights to freedom." As an adult Paul would counsel others in the same theme: neither suffering nor compassion is confined to a single race.[17]

As a parent, Reverend Robeson was loving but demanding, a strict disciplinarian whose perfectionist standards his son eventually internalized ("It was not like him to be demonstrative in his love, nor was he quick to praise," he later wrote of his father). Paul was expected to play an active role in church life, to shoulder a full share of family chores, to turn in a superlative academic performance—and to work at odd jobs to help pay his school fees. He met all the expectations, and then some (beyond the requirements a perfectionist parent articulates usually lies the unarticulated final demand that the child surpass any goal he manages to meet—an insatiable process, once inaugurated, never allowing for surcease). At twelve Paul worked as a kitchen boy, at fourteen on a farm, at fifteen at a man's job in brickyards and shipyards, and then, as an older teen-ager, he became a waiter during the summers at the small Imperial Hotel at Narragansett Pier, Rhode Island.[18]

The waiter's job had its special indignities: the hotel guest list was entirely white, the staff entirely black, and there were no alternate social outlets, no chance to blow off steam in the town. Yet there were compensations. In his "Memory Book" Paul described Narragansett as "wonderful ... plenty of bathing and summer pleasure," and good "chaps" on the staff to hang around with. One of the chaps was Oscar C. Brown, later a Chicago real-estate developer and civil-rights activist. Brown worked in the hotel as a bellhop and part-time secretary, and recalls being pleased that he could take home sixty dollars for the summer's work—"I didn't have to be amused, I was in school." The congenial black staff also included Fritz Pollard; he, like Robeson, would become a storied athlete (in 1916 at Brown, Pollard became the first black All-American football player, named the year before Robeson became the second). The ten or so young black men on the staff enjoyed one another's company, threw a football around on the beach, now and then discussed "current questions," and cheered

Paul on when the hotel sponsored an oratorical contest. (He won.) "Paul didn't know anything about waiting on tables," Oscar Brown recalls, "but he did know everything else—the things we struggled to learn, he could get them just by rote almost." He was a big hit with the rest of the staff. "Everyone loved Paul," another friend from those days remembers, "and wherever we went there was a great demand to hear his beautiful voice."[19]

In school, too, Robeson seems from the beginning to have been the outstanding scholar *and* the most popular boy—a double palm only the most graceful can carry off. On first arriving in Somerville, in 1910, Paul attended James L. Jamison's "Colored School" (Jamison had moved north after the Ku Klux Klan burned down the schoolhouse he had insisted on keeping open during cotton-picking season, when blacks were expected to be in the fields). Paul was one of three graduates from the Jamison School in June 1911, and at the closing exercises, after his father had given the invocation, he "quite captured the audience" (according to the local paper) "by the genuine ring of oratory displayed in his declamation of Patrick Henry's 'An Appeal to Arms.' " Following Paul, one speaker, in "a very practical address to the graduates, . . . urged them to do something." And another (white) encouraged them to continue their education by expressing "his pleasure that a colored boy . . . [had] graduated from the high school this year and he thought others would get through."[20]

Following his graduation from the Jamison School, Paul shifted briefly to Westfield's unsegregated Washington School, graduated at the head of his class, spent eighth grade in a segregated Somerville school, then entered Somerville High in 1912. The town of Somerville had neither Princeton's entrenched racism nor its close-knit black community. By his own later testimony, Robeson "came to know more white people" and made more friendly connections with them than he had when growing up in Princeton. He realized, however, that his own "easy moving between the two racial communities" was "rather exceptional," that "barriers between Negro and white existed," and that his own partial exemption from them was neither typical nor indicative of full acceptance.[21]

Somerville High, reflecting the racial composition of the town, had fewer than a dozen black students in a total enrollment of about two hundred. Robeson and a boy named Winston Douglas were the only blacks in their class of some forty. The "colored fellas," one white classmate asserts, "fitted in very easily." There was "no antiblack feeling in the town," a second classmate insists. "It was a nice small town, very good, and the Robesons were highly respected, really." "There was no prejudice at all," claims a third classmate, "never any mention of any prejudice."[22]

That the youthful Robeson was well liked and widely admired is certain. Those who knew him in high school remark upon his "sweetness and modesty," his "warm, easygoing, laid-back" temperament, his "refined, clean-minded, wholesome" qualities—offering, without irony, a set of attributes that, in their suggestion of constraint and lack of spontaneity, would not be universally regarded as the apogee of adolescent development; and showing, too, no awareness of the psychological costs of always having to appear, and be seen, in so restricted a guise. In the same way, those who knew Paul in Somerville have no trouble citing the astonishing range of his gifts in sports, studies, singing, and debating, but have uniform trouble recalling or crediting any obstacles placed in the way of those accomplishments. They cite the civility of his manner and emphasize the smoothness of his path.[23]

Most of Paul's white classmates apparently believed—at the time and since—that his unfailingly courteous, Christian demeanor reflected the full range of his feelings, and that his penchant for remaining somewhat apart merely reflected a loner's temperament. "Well," Robeson later laconically observed, "I was a good boy, sure enough—but I wasn't *that* good!" And, indeed, one classmate, J. Douglas Brown, remembers that Paul "was so busy with other activities . . . that he was not always fully up on his assignments" and recalls, too, that far from being a joyless ascetic, Paul "was fun to be with." When the two boys put on the funeral scene from *Julius Caesar* (Paul playing Mark Antony) before the entire school, Paul flung off the sheet from Caesar's "corpse" to reveal "a dozen gory splotches of tomato catsup" they had secretly added to heighten the effect. He also took part in an apparently unsupervised theatrical evening filled with songs and jokes so "coarse and of the low variety type" (in the words of the local paper) that the audience "expressed amazement at the audacity of some of the performers," and the Board of Education, after calling a special meeting to consider the grave offense, passed a resolution of "severe censure" on the boys who had participated.[24]

Somerville High also heard the first Robeson *Othello*—a burlesque version. The year was 1915, the occasion a presentation by Miss Miller's English class, before the entire school, of "Shakespeare at the Water Cure," a potpourri of characters from the plays—Romeo and Juliet, Hamlet and Ophelia, Othello, etc.—who meet as contemporaries at a health resort in England. Teacher Anna Miller later recalled her hesitation in asking Paul to take on the parodic role of Othello as a hotel waiter, especially since the performance was designed to raise money for a class outing to Washington, D.C., that Paul could not join because no hotel in the capital would accept a black guest. "But of course Paul was willing" to perform—and proved a huge hit with the audience.[25]

On that evening, and many others, he sang as well. Another teacher at Somerville High, Miss Elizabeth Vosseller, had early spotted Paul's remarkable voice, put him in the school chorus—where he carried the bass section single-handedly—and thereafter took special interest in his progress. Paul's own family had recognized his musical gifts even earlier. As the tale goes—doubtless with the touch of highlighting usual in family lore—

the moment of revelation came when Paul and his older brothers Ben and Bill were "chording up on a few tunes" one day. Sailing through their repertoire—"Down by the Old Mill Stream," "Turkey in the Straw," and "Silent Night"—Paul "bore down with boyish glee" on "one of those minors known only to home-loving groups"—and "put it out of the lot." Brother Bill purportedly yelled, "You can sing!"; Paul purportedly told him to stop making "stupid jokes." According to Ben's later account, the good-natured battle about Paul's talent "raged" for weeks. But mutual encouragement and support were hallmarks of Robeson family life, and the "debate" soon concluded, a consensus emerging that "there might be a grain of truth in Bill's position." Thereafter Paul gave himself "with more attention" to singing in the choir of his father's church and took to entertaining at family gatherings.[26]

Searching their memories many years later, several of Robeson's classmates have ultimately managed to recall some "isolated" instance of bigotry, only to dismiss it as atypical of the prevailing racial harmony in Somerville. In the context of the bitter, often violent antiblack feeling then endemic in the United States, the townspeople are pardonably proud of their record. Somerville was indeed something of an oasis—yet not a utopia. "Your visiting teams, of course," one man recalls, "some of them were a little prejudiced against the colored, you know, and naturally they would endeavor in some way, not to intentionally injure him, but really to take it out on him." But at least once Paul *was* injured in a game: against the much heavier team of Bound Brook, his collarbone was broken. In another incident, Somerville was playing the rival town of High Bridge in baseball, with Robeson catching and Leslie Kershaw pitching. The game had been close until a late inning, when Robeson hit the ball over the center-field fence, giving Somerville the victory. Kershaw claims he heard the High Bridge principal say "big nigger" as Robeson crossed home plate. Whether or no, Paul and everybody else clearly heard shouts of "Nigger!" coming from elsewhere in the stands.[27]

Robeson experienced that kind of overt racism less often during high school than most teen-age black males do, but the subtler variety—the kind that allowed him, through practice and forewarning, to keep his temper under wraps—was more frequent. A distinct social line was drawn. He often walked to and from school with a white girl in his class, but she acknowledges that he never entered her house: "There never really was an occasion to ask him in." Though everyone was "very nice to Paul" and Paul in turn was famously nice to everyone, he and his classmates didn't exactly "pal around" together. As one of his teachers put it, "He is the most remarkable boy I have ever taught, a perfect prince. Still, I can't forget that he is a Negro." Another of his teachers did urge him to attend high-school parties and dances, but Paul himself knew better. "There was always the feeling," he later wrote, "that—well, something unpleasant might happen." Yet a third teacher applauded Paul's discretion: he remained an "amazingly popular boy" *because* "he had the faculty for always knowing what is so commonly referred to as his 'place.' " Early habituated to solitude, Paul would all his life seek it, deeply marked, in the eyes of some, by the melancholy of confirmed apartness. Yet he would never be a true loner. Unwilling ever to live by himself, he would prefer later in life to sleep on a friend's sofa rather than to stay alone. His ideal situation would always be to have loving friends in near proximity, but to be able to retreat at will to an inner monastic fortress.[28]

He learned early that accomplishment can win respect and applause but not full acceptance—although he tried to follow the established protective tactic of Afro-American life in America: to "act right," to exhibit maximum affability and minimal arrogance. Even while turning in a superior performance, he had to pretend it was average and that it had been accomplished offhand, almost absent-mindedly. Any overt challenge to the "natural supremacy" of whites had to be avoided, and on any occasion when whites were surpassed, the accompanying spirit could never smack of triumph. "Above all," Robeson later wrote, as if repeating a litany drummed into his head by his father, "do nothing to give them cause to fear you, for then the oppressing hand, which might at times ease up a little, will surely become a fist to knock you down again!"[29]

This balancing act required enormous self-control. Robeson could safely stay on one side of the exceedingly fine line that separated being superior from acting superior only by keeping the line in steady focus. The effort contributed to the development of an acute set of antennae that he retained all his life—he later told a reporter that he could size someone up immediately, could sense, when introduced to a stranger, "what manner of man he is," regardless of the words he spoke. But having to maintain constant self-control took its emotional toll. "I wish I could be sweet all the time," he once said when under intense pressure, "but I get a little mad, man, get a little angry, and when I get angry I can be awful rough." No young man of Robeson's energetic gifts could continuously sustain a posture of bland friendliness without the effort's exacting some revenge— especially since his father had also taught him to be true to himself. The tension was further heightened by a lifetime conviction that "in comparison to most Negroes" he had had an easy time of it growing up in white America, and complaint might appear, even to other blacks, as ungrateful and unwarranted. He preferred to "keep silent," a tactic for coping with emotional distress that he maintained throughout his life. As an adult he could never reflect with ease on his youth, once confessing to a friend that, when he did recall some of his experiences, they only "aroused intense fury and conflict within him."[30]

Robeson's natural talents were so exceptional that he had to make a proportionately large effort in order to forestall resentment in others. He learned early: even as a boy in Westfield he is remembered as "a shy kid who did everything well, but preferred to keep in the background." Had his warmth and modesty not been quite so engaging, the astonishing record he compiled at Somerville High might well have stirred more fear and envy. Several of his classmates swore he never took a book home at night—even as Paul sat each evening under his father's rigorous eye reviewing the day's lessons in Virgil and Homer. He was wise enough to appear occasionally as less than thoroughly prepared, or to use humor to "take the teachers on a bit, in a nice way." Even so, one classmate confessed, "He used to get my goat, everything seemed so easy to him."[31]

Indeed it did—in athletics especially. Robeson excelled in every sport he attempted. In baseball he played the positions of shortstop and catcher with equal facility, ran fast, and hit well. In basketball—in those days essentially a guarding game—his height and dexterity made him "good at stopping a man." He also ran track and (after school) played a fair game of tennis. But it was his skill as a fullback in football that gained him the most attention. Paul "had such a big strong hand," one contemporary said, that "he could almost wrap [it] around a football" (somewhat rounder than the modern ball) "and throw that thing just like a baseball." Envy of such prowess (especially in someone of his race) did occasionally surface. In a game against the superior team of Phillipsburg High (known as "a rough bunch of kids" and outweighing Somerville ten pounds to a man) the opposition "lay for him" and piled on—but the attack energized him and he scored a touchdown; still, "handicapped by the work of officials" (as the local paper put it), Somerville lost "the greatest game ever played" on the Phillipsburg grounds. Reverend Robeson was often on hand for the games. A contemporary recalls that "he would keep his eyes upon Paul through every second of play. The fellows on the team said he was like a lucky stone. They liked to know he was watching." Far from disapproving of sports, he wanted his son to distinguish himself in that area, as in all others—and stood on the sidelines to remind him that, should adversity arise, he had to resist both the sin of lashing out and the sin of stunting his purpose.[32]

The double injunction to avoid confrontation while simultaneously being self-assertive could in the long haul prove a prescription for paralysis or despair. But for a young man not yet burdened with too great an accumulation of anger, and with a disposition that lent itself naturally to cordiality, the instruction to be proud *and* pleasant does not seem to have been borne with undue strain. Paul's ability for the time being to thrive under rather than succumb to his father's difficult set of standards was illustrated by an episode during his senior year at Somerville. New Jersey had announced a statewide oratorical contest for high-school boys, and Robeson, Somerville's prize debater, entered it. The panel of judges included Frederick K. Shield, then a senior at Rutgers, and the event so

impressed him that seventy years later he remembered it vividly. In addition to Paul, Shield recalls, there were five or six other contestants—all
white boys, all good orators, all well prepared. Each gave his speech, each
performed well, one scarcely divisible in merit from another.[33]

Then, as Shield remembers it, "this handsome big Negro's turn
came." He chose for his text Wendell Phillips's famed oration on Toussaint L'Ouverture, the black Haitian revolutionary who defeated Napo-
leon's troops in a successful rebellion against slavery. Many years later, in
his autobiography, Robeson claimed that he had "had no real appreciation" of the oration's meaning, had given "no thought to . . . the flaming
words." Nonetheless, this was not the sort of topic in 1915 that a black boy
bent solely on being polite would have chosen for public declamation. (In
a similar spirit, during a senior-year debate with another school on the
topic "whether immigration into the United States should be restricted by
a literacy test," Paul's plea for the country to welcome *all* the poor and
downtrodden was "so eloquent and moving"—according to Douglas
Brown, who was also on the platform—"that many in the audience were
in tears.") Nor, had Paul been bent on being *merely* restrained and courteous, would he have invested his Toussaint oration with the passion he did.
"It was as if," Shield recalls, "somebody's life was being saved, somebody
important." So closely did the boy and the subject seem to merge, and "so
great" were the young orator's powers, that Reverend Robeson, sitting in
the front row in an audience of some 250 people, "broke out at times"—
uncharacteristic of that dignified gentleman—"in emotional expression."
Nonetheless, Robeson was awarded only third prize.[34]

In that same year of 1915, the seventeen-year-old Robeson took a
statewide written exam for a four-year scholarship to Rutgers University.
His family preferred all-black Lincoln University, from which both his
father and his brother Bill had graduated, but the strain on the Reverend
Robeson's limited income made the possibility of a scholarship appealing.
Besides, Paul himself did not prefer Lincoln. As his teacher Anna Miller
recalled, "Several of the Negro colleges were suggested to him but Paul
had his heart set on a large school and no hints as to the difficulties he
might encounter on that path could daunt him. . . . 'I don't want to have
things handed to me,' he declared. 'I don't want it made easy.' " The other
students competing for the Rutgers scholarship had previously taken a test
covering their first three years of high school; not knowing of the test in
time, Robeson had to write an exam that included the entire four-year
course of work. Nonetheless, he won the competition. "Equality might be
denied," he later wrote, "but I *knew* I was not inferior."[35]

Like everyone who grows up black in white America, Robeson had
experienced his share of racial abuse. Unlike most, it had not become the
overwhelming fact of his existence. He had been called a nigger but not
consistently treated like one. Accidents of geography, family, and talent

had insulated him from the brutalities of daily life commonplace for black Americans in the pre–World War I years. He would later tell a white reporter—*underplaying* the indignities he had suffered—that his "impressionable years" had been spent "almost entirely in friendly intelligent white society," an experience that kept him "from distrusting the white race as most Negroes do and from having a feeling of forced inferiority." Having grown up among whites, Robeson would find it difficult ever to view them as unredeemable demons—or controlling gods. "I came up an idealist," he once said, "interested in human values, certain that all races, all peoples are not nearly as different one from the other as text books would have it."[36]

His father had passed on to Paul an intricate strategy for survival. He had taught him to reject the automatic assumption that all whites are malignant, to react to individuals, not to a hostile white mass. At the same time, Reverend Robeson knew the extent of white hostility—he had, after all, been born a slave—and he counseled his son to adopt a gracious, amenable exterior while awaiting the measure of an individual white person's trustworthiness. But William Drew was no Uncle Tom; Paul was constantly reminded of his "obligation to the race," constantly reminded of its plight. Taught to be firm in his dedication to freeing his people, Paul was also taught to avoid gratuitous grandstanding. His job was to protest *and* to stay alive; outright rebellion against a slave system was as suicidal as subservient capitulation to it.

The moral precepts of Reverend Robeson coincided with the facts of Paul's youthful experience. His father preached that it was right and necessary to try to get along with whites; Paul's daily life in Somerville had proved that such a strategy was feasible. The lesson was ingrained for life—though in adulthood severe provocation would test and cast doubt on its reliable limit. By talent and upbringing, Robeson had been ideally equipped to bridge both racial worlds, if both would have him, and if bridging was what he wanted to do.

■

CHAPTER 2

Rutgers College

(1915–1918)

Founded in 1766, Rutgers was one of the country's oldest colleges; yet in 1915, when Robeson entered, it was still a private school with fewer than five hundred students, bearing scant resemblance to the academic colossus it subsequently became. Prior to the Civil War, Rutgers had denied admittance to Afro-Americans (Princeton continued to refuse them admission until World War II), and only two had officially attended the school before Robeson—though rumor had it that an additional few had in another sense "passed" through its portals. The year after Robeson entered, a second black student, Robert Davenport, enrolled, and "Davvy" and "Robey" (as they were known during their undergraduate years) became good friends, joining a scattering of other black collegians from the Philadelphia–Trenton–New York corridor to form a social circle. They would need each other.[1]

Robeson's path at Rutgers was centrally defined by his race, though not—thanks to his own magnetism and talent—centrally circumscribed by it. The simple fact of his dark skin was sufficient to bring down on him a predictable number of indignities, but his own settled self-respect kept them from turning into disabling wounds. He further learned at Rutgers what had become almost instinctual knowledge: achievement could win from whites respect and applause, sometimes friendship, but almost never intimacy.

When freshman Robeson walked onto the practice field to try out for Rutgers football, the team had no blacks on it—indeed, like almost every other top-ranked college, Rutgers had never in its history had a black player. In a day when football players typically lacked the mammoth height and girth they have today (five members of the 1917 Rutgers team were five feet, nine inches or shorter), Paul, at six feet, two inches, and 190 pounds, stood some three to four inches taller and weighed some 20 pounds more than most others on the field.[2]

The "giant's" reputation had preceded him. Rutgers coach G. Foster Sanford had seen him play for Somerville and had been duly impressed. The Rutgers first-stringers had also heard about Robey's athletic prowess—and skin color. Several of them set out to prevent him from making the team. On the first day of scrimmage, they piled on, leaving Robeson with a broken nose (which troubled him ever after as a singer), a sprained right shoulder, and assorted cuts and bruises. He could hardly limp off the field. That night (as Robeson described the incident thirty years later) "a very very sorry boy" had to take to bed, and stay there for ten days to repair his wounds. "It was tough going" for a seventeen-year-old and "I didn't know whether I could take any more." But his father had impressed upon him that "when I was out on a football field, or in a classroom, or anywhere else, I was not there just on my own. I was the representative of a lot of Negro boys who wanted to play football, and wanted to go to college, and, as their representative, I had to show I could take whatever was handed out. . . . Our father wouldn't like to think that our family had a quitter in it."[3]

After a visit and pep talk from brother Ben, Robeson went back out for another scrimmage. This time a varsity player brutally stomped on his hand. The bones held, but Robeson's temper did not. On the next play, as the first-string backfield came toward him, Robeson, enraged with pain, swept out his massive arms, brought down three men, grabbed the ball carrier, and raised him over his head—"I was going to smash him so hard to the ground that I'd break him right in two"—and was stopped by a nick-in-time yell from Coach Sanford. Robeson was never again roughed up—that is, by his *own* teammates. Sanford, a white New Englander committed to racial equality as well as to football prowess, issued a double-barreled communiqué: Robey had made the team, and any player who tried to injure him would be dropped from it.[4]

Several of his teammates have subsequently downplayed the amount of racial antipathy Robeson faced on the Rutgers squad—just as whites who knew him in Somerville later minimized town prejudice. One Rutgers teammate, "Thug" Rendall, insisted sixty years later that there had been *no* opposition to Robey's joining the team, and Steve White, a senior when Robeson was a freshman, flatly declared, "There was never any discrimination." Earl Reed Silvers, who graduated two years ahead of Robeson and was later a Rutgers faculty member, claimed to have "attended every football practice" during Robeson's freshman year and did not remember "any untoward incident on the field." Silvers further claimed to have checked his memory with four members of the varsity squad of that season and reported that not one of them could recall a deliberate attempt to injure Robeson. In any case, Silvers felt sure, "Paul would not . . . wish to question the integrity of his college or the sportsmanship of his friends."[5]

A comparable view is held by Coach Sanford's son. He, too, was regularly present at team practices and insists that "a minor incident" has subsequently been blown out of all proportion. Had resentment against Robeson "been that deepseated," Sanford, Jr., argues, it would never have subsided—yet in fact "it never showed its ugly head again." As for Robeson's own reported rage at being mauled, Sanford, Jr., discounts it as not believable because not in character—as "everyone knew," Robeson was "a nice, placid, kind guy" who had "great control of himself; he never blew his top, he didn't have a short fuse."[6]

True enough. Ordinarily, Robeson as a young man did sit on his rage—though even back in Somerville he had been known once or twice to "blow his top," showing, had anyone wished to see, that choosing to muzzle his feelings was not the equivalent of not having feelings, or any guarantee that under special provocation they would not surface. Later in life Robeson told a friend that, although he had never used his hands illegally while playing college football, he did practice breaking up orange crates with his forearm. As for the amount of provocation he actually faced, the bland minimizations of Sanford, Jr., and others are overmatched by countertestimony. Robert Nash, another member of the varsity squad, flatly states that Robeson "took a terrific beating. . . . We gave him a tough time during the practices; it was like initiation. He took it well, though." And Mayne S. Mason, an instructor of physics and one of Robeson's teachers, remembers him coming into his lab one day with his hand bandaged; when Mason asked him what had happened, Paul simply said, "I got hurt." Later, after everyone else had left the lab, he elaborated a bit: someone on the team had spiked his hand that day. He would say no more, but Mason later learned from another student that Robeson had picked the man up over his head as if to throw him to the ground.[7]

The intervention of Coach Sanford prevented *overt* racism from surfacing again on the Rutgers squad, and over time the initial racist reaction to Robeson was gradually replaced by admiration, and in some cases affection (end James Burke even credited him with saving his life: chasing a pass, Burke fell fifty feet over an embankment into the Raritan Canal, and Robeson raced into the water in full football gear to haul him out). Sanford himself developed great respect for Robeson's athletic talent and great liking for him personally, a mutual regard that lasted until Sanford's death. An unusually gifted coach, Sanford took Robeson under his wing and taught him much that honed his game—how to protect himself, how to put his arms chest-high and come up across the body with a forceful elbow (in those days the use of arms in football was restricted), how to employ (no platoon system then existed and members played for sixty minutes) his multiple skills in both offensive and defensive positions, developing particular strength as a pass receiver and a tackler.[8]

By the end of his freshman year, Robeson was in the starting lineup; by his junior year, he had become the star of an exceptionally talented Rutgers team and had gained national prominence—a "football genius," raved one sportswriter, echoing many others, "the best all-round player on the gridiron this season," "a dusky marvel." Twice, in 1917 and 1918, Walter Camp, the legendary Yale coach, put Robeson on his All-American football teams—the first Rutgers player ever named—calling him "a veritable superman." The phrase scarcely seemed overheated; by then, in a superfluity of skill, Robeson had also distinguished himself as center on the basketball team, catcher on the baseball team, and a competent javelin and discus thrower on the track team. By the time of his graduation, he had won fifteen varsity letters in four different sports. On the side, he played club basketball for St. Christopher, a Harlem group that was one of the best in the nation, boasting among its other players the two Jenkins brothers, Harold "Legs" and Clarence "Little Fat," later to become legendary figures in the sport.[9]

All of which suggests, in bald outline, a triumphal procession, inexorable and uninterrupted. The reality was a good deal bumpier. If Coach Sanford had never been bigoted, and if the Rutgers football team was taught not to be, that still left the outside world. One classmate remembers the shouts of "nigger" that would sometimes come from the stands, and Coach Sanford's son recalls that Robeson "was treated very badly by the opponents, not necessarily the Northern opponents but the Southern opponents. . . . Everybody went after him, and they did it in many ways. You could gouge, you could punch, you could kick. The officials were Southern, and he took one hell of a beating, but he was never hurt. He was never out of a game for injuries. He never got thrown off the field; when somebody punched him, he didn't punch back. He was just tough. He was big. He had a massive, strong body, among other things. He felt the resentment but he managed to keep it under wraps." The restraining influence *was* Paul himself, not Coach Sanford. One team member, Donald Storck, remembers that Sanford would sometimes encourage his players to do physical damage to the opposing team; and at least once Storck and Robeson appealed that policy directly to Sanford.[10]

Among Rutgers's Southern opponents in football, William and Mary and Georgia Tech simply refused to play against a black man. A game with Washington and Lee came off only after the Rutgers administration, bowing to pressure from its alumni, ordered Sanford to bench Robeson (Rutgers in 1916 was celebrating its 150th anniversary, and the administration hoped for an outpouring of alumni gifts). Some of the Rutgers players initially protested the decision not to use Robeson against Washington and Lee, but Sanford gathered the squad together outside Kilpatrick Chapel and "explained" that it had been a matter of "courtesy" to accede to a request from the opposing team's coach—courtesy and common sense, he said, for there was a real possibility the Washington and Lee players might gang up on Paul and injure him. Paul gave thought to quitting, but his father told him "he hadn't sent me to college to play football, and vetoed my plan to switch colleges. . . ."[11]

When the news got out that Robeson had been benched, James D. Carr, Rutgers's first (1892) black graduate—a Phi Beta Kappa honor student who had gone on to Columbia Law School and was currently an attorney for the city of New York—angrily protested in a letter to Rutgers President William H. S. Demarest: "Shall men, whose progenitors tried to destroy this Union, be permitted to make a mockery of our democratic ideals by robbing a youth, whose progenitors helped to save the Union, of that equality of opportunity and privilege that should be the crowning glory of our institution of learning?"[12]

The answer was yes. But on a second occasion Coach Sanford held his ground. When "Greasy" Neale, coach of the West Virginia team, also insisted Robeson be dropped from the roster, Sanford adamantly refused to comply. "When we lined up for the first play," Robeson told a friend a decade later, "the man playing opposite me leaned forward and said, 'Don't you so much as touch me, you black dog, or I'll cut your heart out.' Can you imagine? I'm playing opposite him in a football game and he says I'm not to touch him. When the whistle blew I dove in and he didn't see me coming. I clipped him sidewise and nearly busted him in two and as we were lying under the pile I leaned forward and whispered, 'I touched you that time. How did you like it?' " Rutgers held West Virginia, the pregame favorite, to a tie; "the giant Negro" (alternately called by the papers "the big darky") was spotted and held down by the visitors until the final period, when he saved the game with a crucial tackle on the Rutgers two-yard line. After the game Coach Neale purportedly said, "Guts! He had nothing else but! Why that colored boy's legs were so gashed and bruised that his skin peeled off when he removed his stockings." "Every man in the enemy pack," Robeson later told an interviewer, "filed in front of me and shook my black hand!"[13]

In 1917, in Paul's junior year, Rutgers took on the Newport Naval Reserve, an undefeated team headed by Cupe ("Cupid") Black and made up of eleven All-Americans. In a memorable game at Ebbets Field in Brooklyn (with Walter Camp watching from the stands), Rutgers spectacularly outplayed Newport. The Rutgers *Targum* reported that Robeson had seemed to be all over the field, so much so that "the Newport team began to believe that there were, at least, eleven Robesons, and their entire horizon was obscured by him. . . ." More than fifty years later, his performance was still vividly remembered as "brilliant. . . . He led the defense as a linebacker to such success that Newport made only one first down. He also caught a pass on the five-yard line and fought his way over the goal line with three defenders trying to bring him down." And the New York *Tribune* said, "It was Robeson, a veritable Othello of battle, who led the dashing little Rutgers eleven to a 14–0 victory over the widely heralded Newport Naval Reserves."[14]

Because the feats of "the giant Negro" extended beyond football, they could not easily be dismissed as the mere by-products of "animal vitality." Robeson dominated not only the playing fields but the classroom—and the debating hall and the glee club and the honor societies—as well. And he did so with a modesty that further disarmed would-be detractors. "A gentle soul," a man of "great gentleness," is how two undergraduates who knew Robey later described him, and Coach Sanford—who was not given to hyperbole—told a newspaper reporter that Robeson "does not know the meaning of conceit" and is "one of the most likeable fellows I ever met."[15]

Robeson maintained such a consistently high grade average in his course work that he was one of four undergraduates (in a class of eighty) admitted to Phi Beta Kappa in his junior year. A speaker of exceptional force, he was a member of the varsity debating team and won the class oratorical prize four years in succession. His bass-baritone was the chief adornment of the glee club—but only at its home concerts; he was not invited to be a "traveling" member, and at Rutgers sang only with the stipulation that he not attend social functions after the performances.[16]

One reason Robeson tolerated that humiliation was his need for money. Along with doing a variety of odd jobs (including working as a porter in Grand Central Station), he used his glee-club appearances as an advertisement for the private concerts he sometimes gave to augment his scholarship. Ten years later he told a reporter, "I used to hustle around, fix up a concert, and bill myself as a star attraction. It is probable . . . that I attracted my audiences in the first place partly by the fact that my name was already fairly well known as a Rugger man. . . . I would go on the stage, sing a group of songs, orate and flourish for 20 minutes, and then sing again. Usually this procedure brought me in about ten pounds [fifty dollars], and apparently everybody was satisfied. . . . These early ventures were practically the whole of my stage training."[17]

In the same way that Robeson was only partly accepted as a member of the glee club, so, too, was he elected to the Literary Society, Philoclean, without being allowed fully to share in its festivities. On the night the new Philoclean members were inducted, Paul was prevented from participating in the traditional ritual of "standing for a treat" at Bruns (the local ice-cream-and-candy shop) because Bruns would not serve a black man. Paul gave his financial share for the treat to his friend Charlie Bloodgood, but when Charlie said he and some of the others would protest Bruns's policy, Paul discouraged them. He "wanted no trouble," he said, and went home.

"There was a clear line," Robeson later wrote, "beyond which one did not pass"; college life was "on the surface marvellous, but it was a thing apart."[18]

In that same spirit, Paul once let his teammate Donald Storck persuade him to go to a college dance—but positioned himself on the balcony, where, to wild applause, he serenaded the dancers below with "Roses of Picardy." Storck marveled at his friend's calm exterior but recognized that he was "roiling" inside. By others, however, Paul's prudent self-possession was often mistaken for nonchalance. An undergraduate two years behind him sent him myopic congratulations later in life on the attitude he had shown: "I will never forget how much you seemed to enjoy watching, though never participating in any of the social affairs of your contemporaries. . . . This was but one of your most typical, admirable qualities that endeared you to all who knew you. It was in keeping with your modesty. . . ."[19]

Now and then during his undergraduate years, when under unusual pressure, Robeson let whites glimpse a less placid side. One such moment came at the close of his junior year. In May his father suddenly and unexpectedly died at age seventy-three. While lying gravely ill, Reverend Robeson had extracted his son's promise to go ahead with his commitment to compete in—and win—an oratorical contest scheduled for a few days hence. Three days after his father's death, a distraught Paul reluctantly kept his promise and mounted the lecture platform, surrounded by supportive friends. "Paul stood there on the stage," one of them recalls, "gaunt, sombre, obviously steeped in grief as he talked in that beautiful, moving voice." Defenses down, Paul spoke in less measured, benign terms than was his usual style. He pointedly remonstrated with the largely white audience for the inadequate educational opportunities offered blacks—and emphasized, by way of contrast, the distinction with which they continued to fight in the country's wars. In later life, as it became ever clearer to him that white America was unlikely to extend its paper principles of equality (and certainly not without a persistent, militant demand that it do so), Robeson would return often to the paradox of black Americans, denied first-class citizenship, fighting and dying in the nation's armed forces—and he would ultimately counsel them not to.[20]

The following year, his last at Rutgers, Robeson used another public occasion to reiterate his determination to make of his own life a fitting memorial to his father's, a vehicle for helping "the race to a higher life." When it came time to write his senior thesis, he chose for his topic "The Fourteenth Amendment, the Sleeping Giant of the American Constitution"—and proceeded to interpret it in a way that prefigured the eventual use of that amendment as a civil-rights weapon. In his trademark public tone of measured courtesy, and encased in legalistic citation, Robeson entered a plea "for utilizing the potential force of the proviso to ensure equality before the law"; let the amendment "be duly observed," he wrote, and "the American people shall develop a higher sense of constitutional morality." The gist of Robeson's argument was unequivocally a call to work within the system, and its rhetoric was glowingly—some would say, from the vantage point of seventy years later, naïvely—optimistic about white intentions. Yet, once again, beneath the conventional packaging lay some potentially unconventional views. And his white professor spotted them: he penciled across Robeson's thesis *"Extravagant"*—though conceivably he was referring to Robeson's optimism.[21]

In his senior year Robeson was inducted into the Cap and Skull honor society as one of four men who best represented the ideals of Rutgers, and was also selected as valedictorian of the graduating class. President Demarest of Rutgers asked Paul to give the Commencement Oration on six days' notice, after the scheduled student became ill. Demarest called Paul into his office and asked if "he had an old speech" he could give, since six days was scant time for writing and memorizing a new one. Paul said he did, but added that he would prefer to try a new effort that (as Demarest later remembered his words) would "touch upon the racial question" and would "show the dawn of a renaissance for the Negro." Paul explained that this idea was "burning in his soul for expression." Demarest told him to go ahead.[22]

As Paul made his way down the aisle to the speaker's stand on Commencement Day, the board of trustees, the faculty, the many distinguished guests and recipients of honorary degrees all rose, in a rare and perhaps unprecedented tribute, and remained standing until he had reached the platform. He proceeded to deliver a stirring speech, "The New Idealism," in which he carefully alternated patriotic cadences with temperate (yet unmistakable) challenge. In theme and tone the young Robeson sounded far closer to Booker T. Washington than to "upstart" militants like W. E. B. Du Bois and Monroe Trotter. Dutifully praising the nation for having "proved true to her trust," and her soldiers for having successfully preserved her "liberties" in the recently concluded war, Robeson went on to restate Booker T. Washington's familiar doctrines of racial progress through self-help. "We of this less favored race realize," he told the Commencement Day audience, "that our future lies chiefly in our own hands. On ourselves alone will depend the preservation of our liberties and the transmission of them in their integrity to those who will come after us. And we are struggling on attempting to show that knowledge can be obtained under difficulties; that poverty may give place to affluence; that obscurity is not an absolute bar to distinction, and that a way is open to welfare and happiness to all who will follow the way with resolution and wisdom; that neither the old-time slavery, nor continued prejudice need extinguish self-respect, crush manly ambition or paralyze effort; that no power outside of himself can prevent a man from sustaining an honorable character and a useful relation to his day and generation."[23]

But of course it could and did, as Robeson well knew, and as he gently asserted in his concluding remarks. While calling on his own race to practice the "virtues of self-reliance, self-respect, industry, perseverance and economy," he added that "in order for us to successfully do all these things it is necessary that you of the favored race catch a new vision," act according to a new spirit of "compassion" in relieving "the manifest distress of your fellows." It remained true, he emphasized, that "neither institutions nor friends can make a race stand unless it has strength in its own foundation; that races like individuals must stand or fall by their own merit," and he was careful to assure his almost entirely white audience that the new "fraternal spirit" he wished to evoke "does not necessarily mean intimacy, or personal friendship." It implied only "courtesy and fair-mindedness," a willingness to fight for the great principle that "there will be equal opportunities for all." Robeson closed his oration with words closer in spirit to those Du Bois might have chosen, though the tone remained conciliatory rather than militant: ". . . may I not appeal to you . . . to fight for" an "ideal government" whereby "character shall be the standard of excellence . . . where an injury to the meanest citizen is an insult to the whole constitution," and where "black and white shall clasp friendly hands in the consciousness of the fact that we are brethren and that God is the father of us all." The Commencement Day crowd roared its approval.[24]

Robeson's cautious yet challenging valedictory words were as far as he ever went, as a young man, in expressing in front of whites something of the range of his feelings. He talked less guardedly only among his circle of black friends, that small group of collegians, male and female, drawn from the Philadelphia–New York area and (as one of them has put it) from "well-to-do middle class homes. . . . We met regularly for dances, forums, picnics, athletic games, and the usual events that engage college students. There were also profound discussions about the Negro in our society." Sadie Goode, who dated (and later married) Robert Davenport, the black student a year behind Robeson at Rutgers, recalls Paul as distinctly "aware and disturbed" about racial questions. Another young black woman, Frances Quiett, who met Robeson soon after he graduated from Rutgers and dated him seriously for a year, remembers his talking about the prejudice he had encountered growing up in Princeton: "He was race-conscious at an early stage," and "it showed when we met in groups together." Robeson would often draw the others (who were "not as aware") into a serious discussion of racial prejudice, and would describe the hopes he had of someday being able "to do something about it"—though "he wasn't clear at that early age about what he might be able to do."[25]

Of his contemporaries, Robeson was probably closest in these years to Geraldine Maimie Neale, the young black woman with whom he had an intense undergraduate romance. They met when he was a sophomore and Gerry was completing high school in a nearby town; his last two years at Rutgers paralleled her two years at Teachers Normal School in Trenton, where she trained as a kindergarten teacher and also took newly introduced special-education courses for teaching mentally retarded children.[26]

She and Paul did not see each other, according to Gerry Neale, "frequently, as students do today. There were no automobiles among us. We were both serious students." Paul would call on Gerry at the boarding-house in Trenton where she roomed with other students; they wrote letters to each other between visits, and with other friends had song fests in parents' living rooms (Paul never had to be coaxed: "If he was asked to sing, he made no excuse, set no limitations," and sang everything from the Sorrow Songs to love songs. "I Love You Truly" was *their* song, "sending out a shy, tender message"). When together with friends, Paul and Gerry would manage to find "a special grassy spot—a little away from the rest— where we talked, dreamed, created a world of the future where love, romance, happiness would be forever." He gave her "the football he cherished most and the gold baseball which he prized most among his athletic awards"—the one that recorded the savored victory of the Rutgers baseball team over Princeton (savored because it was the first time in fifty years that Rutgers had defeated Princeton in an athletic contest—and because "Proud Princeton" had turned down his brilliant brother William's application for admission out-of-hand).[27]

When Gerry Neale was a young girl, her teacher in the small segregated school she attended in her hometown of Freehold had taught her "pride in African history as well as the history of the Negro in America"— taught her so well that, when she later spoke out time and again in class in Teachers Normal "about the Negro who made this or that contribution," her white history teacher, "with genuine kindly amusement," commented, "Miss Neale will make us all regret we are not Negro." Gerry also insisted, as a young girl, in seating herself on the main floor of the segregated movie theater in Freehold—while her friends went to the balcony as directed. Even so, Gerry felt Paul was ahead of her—and of those few others in their crowd who were concerned with social issues. "His voice got earnest, vigorous (not loud) when speaking about the subject of race discrimination." She adds that she is not implying that Paul's ideas at the time were well formed or that he was a "radical activist" in the subsequent sense of that term: his tone was not militant and his tactics were not confrontational. He cared deeply about the plight of black people, yet as a young man "believed fully that the promises of the Constitution and the Bill of Rights could be realized if people worked hard at it," if they relied on the efficacy of a conciliatory appeal to the nation's conscience. Some fifteen years later Robeson told an English friend that during his adolescence there was "still no questioning of accepted values," and during his college years—a "period of comparative harmony"—his "creative impulses [were] driven underground and interest centered in athletics"; he added, significantly, that it was "a period of apparent triumph, yet not really satisfying."[28]

Robeson's confidence in the essential beneficence of the American system, even when he was a young man, had its limits. Passive reliance on the "inevitability" of progress was, he felt, a chimera and a trap; neither time, patience, nor even reliance on the tender mercies of the Divinity could guarantee desirable social change. That would come about only "if people worked hard at it." When Gerry and her classmate Bessie Moore (Robeson had been close to the Moore family of Princeton since childhood) decided to take some action against segregation in the women's dormitory at Teachers Normal, Paul joined them for planning sessions, encouraging their purpose. After a "very polite but earnest" letter to the college president, Gerry and Bessie pressed their case in a personal interview with him. The president expressed sympathy. He thought he had "the right answer": the school owned an unoccupied house whose basement it used for storing coal. It was a lovely house, he said. He would let the female black students use it for their very own dormitory. Gerry expressed "appreciation for the color scheme he had in mind: black coal, black women students," but said the offer was unacceptable. She and Bessie held out for a change in college policy that would allow any black woman who wanted to live in the regular dormitory to do so. Somewhat to their own surprise, that permission was granted—perhaps in part because it was felt that the black women currently on campus were already settled in private homes and therefore unlikely to avail themselves of the offer. That turned out to be the case; Gerry, who *was* tempted, couldn't afford to move. Still, they had worked hard for a victory, and won it. "Paul was pleased."[29]

But Gerry and Paul did not see eye to eye on all matters. He was more interested in marriage than she: "I was not sure I loved him enough." Her friends were astonished—"Who would ever raise such a question if they could marry Paul Robeson?!" She explained that she did not think her feelings were strong enough to survive the difficulties of marriage to a man who "would be called upon around the world to be Everyman." Gerry, like most middle-class young women of the day, believed that "a good marriage" took precedence over other priorities. Though Paul had been able to persuade her that she was the center of his universe (a charismatic quality that men and women responded to and remarked on all through his life), Gerry was shrewd enough to realize that, as a "man of destiny," he would in time inevitably move on to someone else. So when Paul did actually propose marriage, Gerry turned him down. He refused, however, to accept her decision and for some time longer would continue to try to change it.[30]

In June 1919 they both graduated. The undergraduate "class prophecy" for 1919 confirmed Gerry's instincts by predicting that Paul, by 1940, would be governor of New Jersey, would have "dimmed the fame of Booker T. Washington," and would be "the leader of the colored race in America." That summer Gerry enrolled at Rutgers, to study Shakespeare for her own enjoyment and to take craft courses in preparation for teaching mentally retarded boys in Atlantic City that coming fall. Paul moved to Harlem to prepare for his entrance into Columbia University Law School. Reverend Robeson had wanted him to become a minister, and for a time Paul had felt the inclination himself. From boyhood he had actively worked in his father's church and when Reverend Robeson was indisposed had occasionally deputized for him, "reading and talking a little to keep things going in his absence." But during college Paul decided that he lacked zeal for the ministry and that a career in law better suited his combined wish to make a name for himself and to serve his people. If Reverend Robeson had been disappointed, he never said so—"He made no attempt to upbraid me, or to persuade me to change my resolution." The fact that another son, Ben, was due to become a minister had undoubtedly softened his father's disappointment.[31]

Paul returned to New Brunswick often that summer to see Gerry, but, as she had sensed, his "destiny" was about to unfold, precipitately, taking him off in a variety of new directions.

■

CHAPTER 3

Courtship and Marriage

(1919–1921)

In 1910 more than 90 percent of the Afro-American population still lived in the South, mostly in rural areas; the chief characteristics of daily life were grinding poverty, social segregation, racial violence, and political impotence. The era of Progressivism, heralded then and since as the rebirth of a humane political vision, was not designed to include blacks; white reformers considered the disfranchisement of blacks a necessary corollary of "good government," their degraded status the inescapable consequence of biological inferiority. In 1914 the Supreme Court reaffirmed the rightness of "separate but equal," and President Woodrow Wilson, busy fighting to make the world "safe for democracy," refused to speak out publicly against lynching. He did, however, speak out against what he called "a social blunder of the worst kind"—namely, the effort to appoint black officials in the South, a region without a single black policeman, in a country that could count exactly one black judge, two black legislators, and a total of two thousand black college students.[1]

In search of a better life, blacks for generations had drifted toward Northern urban centers. After 1910 the drift became a tide. The "Great Migration" of the next two decades saw nearly two million blacks leave the rural South, with the black population in cities rising from 22 percent in 1900 to 40 percent in 1930. No promised land awaited the new migrants to the North, yet amid the endemic squalor and discrimination they did manage to make some improvement in their daily lot: decreased death, illiteracy, and infant-mortality rates, a rise in school enrollment and political participation (blacks could vote in the North). Fierce white resistance to residential integration—including bombings and beatings—forced blacks into ghettos, where the development of community institutions like churches and fraternal orders provided some sense of refuge, a potential political base, and a focus for cultural cohesion.

Nowhere were these developments more pronounced than in Harlem. When Paul Robeson arrived in "the Negro capital of the world" in the summer of 1919, it was in transition from an upwardly mobile white enclave to an all-black one, from an outpost of gentility to slumming headquarters for liberated flappers, from a cultural backwater to the cultural center for the self-conscious proclamation of a New Negro—newly militant, newly conscious, newly assertive—and the literary and artistic Renaissance that his emergence brought in train.

Robeson's reputation preceded him. Before he set foot on 135th Street, he had become one of "Harlem's darlings," the personification of the richly talented, unapologetically ambitious New Negro. As an undergraduate football star, he had played at the Polo Grounds, and had become a more conspicuous figure still from his stint on the St. Christopher basketball team; the excitement of those games at Manhattan Centre (later Rockland Palace) had spilled over into nights on the town, the last stop always being Streeter's Chinese Restaurant on 136th Street. Within a few months of moving to Harlem, Robeson had become a familiar figure, strolling down Seventh Avenue on a summer day "with a pretty girl on his arm, greeting friends and admirers all along the way," something of a prince in his kingdom—but an approachable prince, his good-natured modesty deflecting envy, making it possible to think of him, despite all his accomplishments, as "one of us."[2]

It was a heady summer in Harlem, that year of 1919, a summer of dramatic counterpoint. On the one hand, returning black veterans of the much-decorated 369th Regiment, led by Lieutenant James Europe's famed jazz band, were given a high-spirited reception as they wound in triumphal procession up Lenox Avenue. On the other hand, there were daily bulletins about rampaging white mobs shooting, burning, torturing, and lynching black victims—as if to announce that New Negroes would be treated in the same ruthless spirit as had the old. The violence during that "Red Summer" included a two-day riot in the nation's capital that left a hundred people injured and was only aborted when Secretary of War Baker called out the infantry. Paul's older brother William, who had become a doctor and was living in Washington, D.C., at the time, told him vivid stories of how blacks had armed themselves and successfully fought back against their attackers.[3]

Harlem was feistily alive that summer, filled with demobilized officers and men, smart in Sam Browne belts and khaki, and with black students from nearly every state in the Union attending Columbia University's summer session. Very much a part of the scene were Paul Robeson and his two buddies, Jimmy Lightfoot, a young musician with whom he shared an apartment on 135th Street, and Rudolph ("Bud") Fisher, Paul's closest friend at the time, a 1919 Phi Beta Kappa graduate from Brown who was to study medicine at Howard. (Fisher would become a prominent psychiatrist and a major literary figure in the Harlem Renaissance—his two novels, *The Walls of Jericho* and *The Conjure Man Dies,* are still widely admired—before his early death in 1934.) "The pretty girl on Robeson's arm" in those days was often Frances ("Frankie") Quiett, while Fisher's steady date was May Chinn. Frankie had come to New York from Virginia in 1918, worked in a milliner's shop, attended the church of Reverend John Haynes Holmes (the progressive white minister who was one of the interracial founders of the NAACP), and roomed for a time with May Chinn, who introduced her to Robeson. May had probably gotten to know him at Columbia, where she became the first black woman graduate of Bellevue and the first black woman intern at Harlem Hospital—having earlier been discouraged by a racist teacher from going on with her first love, music.[4]

The four spent a lot of time together, and often May would play the piano while Paul sang. As Frankie recalled sixty-five years later, he "had a beautiful, wondrous voice," though in May's opinion an "undisciplined" one, and they pressed him to seek training and to find more opportunities for singing in public. May's struggling mother had somehow managed to buy her a piano, and Paul would practice at her apartment, with May accompanying him—"the lyric type of song, something between opera and the spirituals, the popular song 'Oh Danny Boy' and things of that sort." May's mother let her travel locally with Paul to play for him at the small recitals he began to give in churches, schools, and the private homes of wealthy whites. Occasionally the guest list was racially mixed, but even then, spirituals were not in demand; as Chinn later put it, "The cultured, well-educated Negro in many incidents asked us not to sing the spirituals in audiences in which there would be white people," because they "brought us down" to the level of "the slave people" among whom the songs had originated, and confirmed whites in their assumption that the spirituals "were the only thing in music we could do."[5]

On one of their trips outside of the city, Paul spent all his money buying the two of them dinner on the train; fortunately, May's mother had given her emergency carfare, and their New Jersey hostess loaned Paul his—an episode, in May's opinion, typical of Paul, of his generosity, his "very gentle, very gracious" nature, his "vagueness about time and money: the material things didn't mean anything to him." Spontaneity was part of Paul's good nature. Accidentally running into Frankie on the street one day, he talked her into going up to New Haven with him that same afternoon to see the Yale-Harvard football game. Though afraid she might lose her job (she didn't), Frankie let his enthusiasm catch her up, and the two spent an "exciting" day—she was astonished at how many people in the stadium recognized and greeted Paul.[6]

Robeson's Rutgers coach, Foster Sanford, helped to pay his law-school tuition in return for Paul's traveling to New Jersey every Saturday morning to tutor Sanford, Jr., in Latin. To augment his income further— and in part for love of the sport—Paul continued his football career after graduating. He helped coach at Lincoln University with Fritz Pollard, the black All-American halfback from Brown; he joined the Columbia scrub-team practice against its varsity; and he played professional football for Frank Nied's Akron Pros and for the Milwaukee Badgers. The Pros, with Pollard and Robeson on the 1920–21 teams, had an unbeaten streak of eighteen games, and while on "Bo" McMillan's Badgers squad in 1922 Robeson scored both touchdowns before seventy-five hundred fans in the famed 13–0 duel with Jim Thorpe's Oorang Indians. Akron, a factory town employing many white Southern migrants, was known for its overt, un-apologetic racism. Fritz Pollard later remembered the raucous boos of the fans, the inability to get a hotel room or a meal in a restaurant, and the need to dress for games in Frank Nied's cigar factory. According to another legendary black player, James Milo ("Ink") Williams, who "had the plea-sure of playing with Robeson and the displeasure of playing against him," their relationship with white players was "very poor in some instances." Sitting in a hotel in Green Bay, Wisconsin, Williams and Pollard were "paged out of the dining room," then taken to the office and told, "We don't allow colored people to eat in our hotel." In Canton, Ohio, seated with some white players, Williams was allowed to go on eating—the man-agement simply put a screen around the table. If nothing else, the money was good—as much as a thousand dollars a game, which was top dollar in professional football in the 1920s.[7]

During one game Robeson sustained a serious injury to his thigh muscle and was rushed to New York's Presbyterian Hospital for an emer-gency operation. Henry ("Harry") A. Murray, the young assistant sur-geon on duty (and later known as a pioneer in motivational theory), recalled sixty-five years later that he had been astounded at the extent of the injury—"what was exposed when you looked in there was a great cavern, a hole like an excavation"—and the difficult operation became "a surgical event," the talk of the hospital. The operation was a success, but Robeson had to remain at Presbyterian for several weeks in severe pain. Harry Murray became immensely taken with his patient ("He was like a king, of an ancient civilization, as it were; he had a posture and a look and a presence that were absolutely unforgettable"), and he hit on an idea for making Paul's convalescence more pleasant. Murray had gotten to know and like a young black woman, Eslanda Goode, who was working as a pathology technician in the surgery lab, and he decided to take her to Robeson's bedside for an introduction. What Murray didn't know was that Essie had previously spotted Paul on their mutual rounds of Harlem parties, had met him casually, and had been looking for a chance to extend the relationship.[8]

Eslanda Cardozo Goode, called by everyone "Essie," came from distinguished lineage of mixed racial stock. Her great-grandfather, Isaac Nuñez Cardozo, came from a Spanish-Jewish family of considerable wealth that had emigrated to America in the late eighteenth century. He fell in love with an octoroon slave in Charleston, South Carolina, and married her, though maintaining the fiction—since state law forbade intermarriage—that she was his mistress, an alliance considered socially acceptable.[9]

Essie's grandfather Francis Lewis Cardozo, one of six children of that union, graduated from the University of Glasgow and became pastor of a Congregational church in New Haven. Referred to after the Civil War by Henry Ward Beecher as "the most highly educated Negro in America," Reverend Cardozo, through the American Missionary Association (the most important of the organizations assisting the freedmen), was granted ten thousand dollars to establish a secondary school for blacks in Charleston—which became the famed Avery Institute. Cardozo appealed to the South Carolina legislature for the right to enroll white as well as black children, but was turned down.

Within a few years Cardozo became a prominent racial spokesman and entered state politics. In 1868 he was elected treasurer of South Carolina for two terms, then secretary of state for one, before resuming the office of state treasurer. But his burgeoning career was abruptly halted during the presidential election of 1877. Refusing to abandon the party of Lincoln, and ignoring both physical threats and attempts to bribe him, Cardozo worked strenuously to hold the black vote for the Republican candidate, Hayes. When the latter squeaked into office in a contested (and probably fraudulent) vote count, the state's Democratic leaders indicted Cardozo for embezzlement and jailed him.

Cardozo refused to plead guilty in exchange for a pardon, and only a public campaign in his behalf, and the election of a new governor in South Carolina, finally secured his freedom a year later. President Hayes received him in Washington and, as a token of gratitude for his support during the campaign, offered him a janitorial job in the Treasury Department building. When the scholar-statesman refused it, Senator Charles Sumner of Massachusetts secured him a clerkship. In 1878 he accepted an offer from a committee of prominent black citizens to take charge of the black high school, and in that post he again fought—again unsuccessfully—against segregation.

Cardozo was ahead of his time not only as an educator and a civil-rights activist, but also in encouraging strength of mind in women. His daughter Eslanda (mother to Essie—there was an Eslanda in every generation) was her father's great companion and under his tutelage developed into a forceful, independent, and (so her legion of detractors claim) imperious woman, whom some members of the family nicknamed Queen Victoria. Beautiful as well as clever, the light-skinned Eslanda was popular in Washington's fashionable black circles. That is, until she announced in 1890 that she would marry a dark-skinned War Department clerk named John Goode, who had a degree from Northwestern. Black society expressed its shock: "Essie Cardozo has married a dark man; her children will be dark."

Two of them, John and Frank, were. The third and youngest, Eslanda, like her mother, had cream-colored skin, black hair, and Mediterranean features—with a slightly Oriental look around the eyes that gave her the overall aura of being a foreigner rather than a black. When Essie was only four, John Goode, Sr., died from alcoholism, leaving his family nearly without means. Ma Goode, as Essie's mother was called, attacked the problem of earning money, as her daughter later wrote, with an "almost masculine intelligence." She had taught before marriage, but that option was now closed, because married women were not welcome in the schools. The genteel female trades of dressmaking and millinery did not appeal to her. Finally, she decided to take up beauty culture, and did so with characteristic vigor.

Passing as white, Ma Goode investigated the best beauty shops in Washington, found them "old-fashioned" and "unhygienic," and decided to move her family to New York so she could study "the latest and most scientific methods." There she learned osteopathy from a physician, conferred with chemists about creams and lotions, read the scientific literature in the medical library, put her combined knowledge into the formulation of her own system, opened a private practice at high fees, and promptly became a success, attracting a wide clientele that included wealthy society figures like Mrs. Joseph Pulitzer and Mrs. George Gould.

With energy to spare, Eslanda Goode closely supervised her children's lives. She would hear their daily lessons and, if monthly report cards were good, treated the children to theater or gave them a party. Almost every Saturday night the family played whist together (for money, a family tradition), mother and daughter against the brothers, the two Eslandas (in the daughter's words) fighting "hard to score a feminine victory." Essie went everywhere with her brothers, playing almost exclusively with them and other boys. ("I was freed from the usual inter-sex diffidence. . . . Man, as man, has never made me have dizzy spells, and spots before my eyes.") When her mother asked her why she didn't play with girls, the self-styled "tomboy" impatiently answered, "Oh, who wants to sit on the steps all afternoon and giggle and whisper and play jacks?" When, at age nine, Essie was enrolled for swimming instruction with a lifeguard at Asbury Park, he canceled after the first lesson: Essie had asked to learn how to dive, her apprehensive coach had reluctantly obliged by placing her on a wooden piling to watch him demonstrate the proper technique—and she had impatiently jumped straightaway into the deep water in imitation, giving him a thorough scare.[10]

In 1912 Ma Goode took over a beauty shop in Chicago, and Essie finished high school there, graduating at the age of sixteen. Placing third on the statewide competitive exams, she won a full four-year scholarship, tuition-free, to the University of Illinois. Aminda Badeau (later Mrs. Roy Wilkins) remembers that, when she moved into the rooming house Essie had just vacated, the landlady bored her by endlessly singing Essie's praises as "the ideal young woman." Essie registered at the university in domestic science but soon discovered it was the science part she cared about and became a chemistry major. Deciding she wanted to work in a lab in New York City, thinking she might eventually become a doctor, she transferred to Columbia for her senior year. On graduating in 1917, she accepted an offer as histological chemist at Presbyterian Hospital, becoming the first black employed there in a staff capacity (though the hospital did enjoy a good reputation among black patients for its comparative lack of racial prejudice). She liked to describe herself as "a girl scientist, working in a great white institution," but her job consisted primarily of preparing tissue slides for pathological diagnosis, with no authority to make diagnoses herself.[11]

When the young surgical intern Harry Murray met Essie at Presbyterian in 1920, he was immediately struck by her quick intelligence, her energy and spunk, her "definitely English" air, her superb efficiency (at times "too efficient, too officious, too bossy")—and her beauty. "Well, now, Paul, you really have to see what we have in this hospital," he enthusiastically told the convalescent; "I very much praised her," he remembers, though "I'd known her just a few months." When the two took to each other, Murray became "empathically romantic," even while realizing that the match might not be one made in heaven—depending on whether one believes happiness in a union hinges on the similarity (rather than the complementarity) of the partners. Paul, in Murray's opinion, "gave a definite impression of being natural," while Essie "was contriving. He let things happen, and she tried to make them happen." He seemed "like a Billy Budd"; her essence was that of an "impresario"—the "innocent" versus the calculator. Murray considered Paul deeply sensuous, whereas "there wasn't much sensuousness" about the practical-minded Essie ("In a symposium on achievement versus love, she's on the side of achievement—Paul would be very strong in both of them"). Where he was genuinely warm, she was merely effusive. Paul was interior, self-referring; Essie was more studied and more superficial, concerned with accoutrements and acclaim. Where she was "obvious," meticulous, and purposeful, he was laid back, affable, self-contained—"It was all in the manner. He's not an unnecessary duplicate. He's a unique, separate, superior man. . . . A person could buy everything that Essie had, and couldn't buy anything that Paul had. He had something that's inside."[12]

Essie, like Murray, saw essential differences in temperament between herself and Paul, but regarded them as complementary, rather than as sources of potential antagonism. Ten years later, during a time of hurt and alienation, she expanded on her view of those differences in emphatic, even exaggerated detail:

> His education was literary, classical, mine was entirely scientific; his temperament was artistic, mine strictly practical; he is vague, I am definite; he is social, casual, I am not; he is leisurely, lazy, I am quick and energetic. . . . [He is] genial, easily imposed upon, mildly interested in everybody and very impractical; Essie [is] pleasant to a few people, affectionately and deeply devoted to a very few, and entirely unaware that anybody else existed; she [is] mildly tactful, but if there [is] the faintest suggestion that anyone was to impose on her she [is] distinctly rude. . . . It is doubtful if Paul could be rude or say no to anyone; Essie could relish being rude to anyone who deserved it. . . . He likes late hours, I am an early bird; he likes irregular meals, they are the bane of my life; he likes leaving things to chance, I like making everything as certain as possible; he is not ambitious, altho once having under-taken a thing he is never content until he accomplishes it as perfectly as possible; I am essentially and aggressively ambitious, I like to *undertake* things."[13]

Those words, written in the early 1930s, were designed to rationalize and lessen the pain of a separation which then loomed, its immediate anguish heightening the dichotomies in Essie's description. Still, the personality differences between Paul and Essie were marked and obvious from the beginning—though at the time Essie saw them as essential ingredients of their mutual attraction, "wonderfully ideal complements" for a shared partnership designed (in Essie's phrase) for "shooting the rapids."[14]

Their courtship did not proceed rapidly, although Essie, who was essentially guiding it, did her best to pilot a straight course. She knew what she wanted, he was ambivalent; as she proved all her life, Essie was a systematic and shrewd strategist, clever enough to recognize when caution was called for. Robeson was besieged by attractive young women who had set their caps for him—part of the appeal of Gerry and Frankie, perhaps, was that they had not. Essie (in her own words) "applied her brains to this problem exactly as she applied them to her problems in chemistry; she surveyed the situation as a whole, decided upon a course of action and pursued it religiously." She arranged her dinner hour at the "Y" to coincide with his. She was careful to wear her most attractive clothes if she thought she might run into him. She saw to it that they would "happen" to walk home together from the university, and would meet frequently at Harlem parties. She took care to be well informed about matters that interested him—sports especially; he was surprised and charmed by her knowledge of the comparative strengths of big-league baseball teams, her predictions about the outcome of intercollegiate football games, her attendance at Forest Hills tennis matches, her own skill at swimming, basketball, and ice skating.

By the winter of 1920–21 they were spending long evenings together discussing the law cases he was studying, or the chemistry of nutrition. "She would explain to him what became of the protein and carbohydrates he ate" and the anatomy of the body's muscles and bones—"as an athlete he was greatly interested." Their contrasting habits of mind and temperament produced "deliciously" heated arguments, made more "thrilling" still because (according to Essie) they managed to reach "the same conclusion by widely different paths," usually discovering they "liked the same plays, books, people." As they became more intimate, Essie took care (so she later, unconvincingly, claimed) "to keep the rapidly growing friendship well outside the danger zone of sex"; knowing that Paul and Bud Fisher had been "sowing their wild oats," she wanted "this particular friendship" to be "a little different from his others."

From Essie's perspective, matters proceeded smoothly until the summer of 1921, when Paul stopped coming around with the same frequency. Hurt at his neglect and ascribing it to the sudden appearance at the Columbia Summer School of "some very attractive girls" who "began to vamp Paul first in fun and then rather seriously," Essie decided, with "common sense and directness," to fight fire with fire. She "resorted to the old game"—meaning she began being seen around with a young man named Grant Lucas, and made a conspicuous public display of her apparent interest in him. Due notice was taken; Essie's new attachment (so she later claimed) became the talk of their crowd and within a month a contrite Paul appeared at her door to say he had come to his senses, had been made to realize how much he loved her, and had decided to propose marriage.

Such, at least, was Essie's version of the culmination of their courtship. Possibly it represented all that she knew at the time, more likely all that she was willing to admit. Throughout her year-long campaign to snare Paul, he was apparently playing his own, more concealed game, and was far from being a mere dupe in her plot. Essie liked to think of herself as an irresistibly clever manipulator, but in fact her studied moves were entirely readable. Paul, by contrast, rarely tipped his hand. His easygoing affability served to conceal the actual intricacy of his personality—indeed, encouraged the view that he was merely good-natured. Yet, if Essie could noisily connive, Paul could laconically dissemble, his moves far less detectable than hers. Possibly, in the end, she did force his hand—not by seeing another man but by telling Paul that she was pregnant with his child. In later years he came to believe, or claimed to believe, that he had been tricked into marriage, yet finally the evidence for believing that Essie had resorted to the ruse of a pregnancy is not impressive, let alone conclusive. Besides, nothing in the passionate (and believable) love letters the two exchanged in the first few years of their marriage suggests that they had decided to wed in the summer of 1921 for any essential reason other than love, however much Essie may have plotted its course and outcome and however convoluted were some of the twists and turns it took.[15]

It's unlikely Essie knew *all* the convolutions afoot. Paul had given up seeing Frankie after meeting Essie, but his deeper attachment to Gerry Neale had not only continued but, if anything, intensified. Indeed, the impulsive proposal of marriage to Essie in August 1921 may have resulted not from *her* calculations but, rather, from Gerry's.[16]

In the fall of 1919, Gerry had gone to Atlantic City to teach mentally retarded children. She and Paul corresponded and occasionally he visited her. During her second year there—by this time Paul was seeing Essie—Gerry decided to enroll at Howard University to work toward a degree. Before beginning classes, she returned home to Freehold, New Jersey, for the summer—the same summer that "something happened" (in Essie's words) to deflect Paul's attention. That "something" was Gerry.

In August, Paul went to see her at Freehold, shortly before she was due to leave for Howard University. They talked all day and into the night, and Paul again asked Gerry to marry him. She told him she "was going to have a career and probably might not marry." They discussed Essie briefly. Paul said Essie wanted to marry him, and that he "admired" her, thought her "bright and capable." Mutual friends had already filled Gerry in, telling her that Essie was "brilliant, well educated, successful in her work, aggressive, sophisticated, knew the ways of the world," loved Paul very much—and, yes, they said, "was determined to marry him." Gerry's one direct contact with Essie had been favorable. At a fraternity dance in New York, they had "exchanged pleasantries" and Gerry had seen her do something that she thought boded well for Paul's future: the weather that night was foul, and Essie had gone out in the sleet to find a cab for herself and Paul, leaving him inside the building. The gesture impressed Gerry; she felt Essie was taking the needed precautions "to protect Paul's voice"—and was "devoted" enough "to defy convention." That night in Freehold,

Gerry conveyed her favorable impression of Essie to Paul. He returned to New York.[17]

Essie's account picks up the story. Early on the morning of August 17, 1921, she answered the doorbell to find a "somewhat disheveled" Paul standing there. He said he'd been thinking about "how much he liked her and what a great pal she was" and had realized, after she started to see someone else, "that he was very much in love with her." "He suggested quite simply that they go out and get married that day." Essie "pinched herself" and "with a wildly beating heart calmly told him" that she thought marriage "was an excellent idea." Since Paul still had to finish law school and such a precipitate step might be difficult to explain to their families, they decided not to go to City Hall (since all licenses obtained there were announced the following day in the newspapers). Instead, they headed up to Greenwich, Connecticut, the usual destination for elopers in those days, stopping to pick up Hattie Bolling, Essie's close friend, in case they should need a witness. Told in Greenwich that as out-of-state residents they would have to wait five days, they headed dejectedly back to New York on the interurban streetcar. As they passed through one village, Paul spotted a "Town Clerk" sign, and off they jumped at Port Chester, where, thanks to New York State laws, they were married in fifteen minutes.[18]

Back in the city, they continued their previous bachelor living arrangements. Paul went on sharing a flat with Jimmy Lightfoot, and Essie went on sharing a studio apartment on Striver's Row with her lifelong friend and confidante, Minnie Sumner, a good-natured, tough-minded, dark-skinned young woman who had begun to make her way as a "modiste." When Lightfoot was out of town with his band, Paul and Essie had that place to themselves. When Lightfoot was in town, Essie and Minnie would have Paul over for dinner (Minnie doing most of the cooking), along with a young lawyer recently arrived in the city in whom Minnie was deeply interested (and would briefly marry), William L. Patterson ("Pat"), a future leader of the Communist Party and in later years a close associate of Robeson's. After dinner the four would play whist, which Paul at first disliked. Essie persuaded herself that she eventually managed to interest him in the game by inviting in "another young man to make a fourth," while Paul sat by and studied—an arrangement he "soon tired" of.[19]

Essie took credit for persuading Paul to continue in law school, while she returned to her $150-a-month job at the Presbyterian lab, abandoning thoughts of a career in medicine. Though "uncomfortable about his wife working," Paul agreed reluctantly. By December they decided to make their marriage public, choosing for the occasion the national conventions (to which both were delegates) of his fraternity, Alpha Phi Alpha (the oldest black fraternity in the country), and her sorority, Delta Sigma Theta.

Ma Goode was pleased with the news, but Paul's family, scarcely knowing Essie, gave only guarded approval. (Earlier, Paul's brother Ben had counseled him against marrying Essie; she somehow saw that letter and held it against Ben ever after.) Essie had embossed announcement cards printed at Altman's and sent them out to friends. The couple moved into the top floor of a private house, which they furnished with wedding presents and purchases on installment.[20]

Married life now began in earnest—and its adjustments. With her usual systematic agenda, Essie set about to make "the best and most" of her husband. Since he was already "the sweetest, most intelligent, most gifted and attractive man" she had ever known, she proceeded to implement the needed minor improvements; Essie's attitude toward him, one of her relatives later said, was that "this great handsome hulk of man needs me to refine him." First she "solved" the problem of his appearance. He didn't seem to care about clothes and would absent-mindedly wear the same ones until they wore out, when he would buy new ones—giving him, toward the end of the cycle, a somewhat "untidy" look. Similarly, he would go into an ordinary shoe store, purchase the largest-size shoes in stock, which never proved large enough, and complain vaguely that they cramped his feet. With characteristic thoroughness, Essie set matters right. She went through most of the men's shops in New York until she finally learned that Wallach's and Rogers Peet carried the best selection of extra-large clothing and John Ward stocked size 12½ shoes. She purchased only "lovely and becoming colors"; people told Paul he was "growing handsome," and he pronounced Essie "a miracle worker." She had somewhat less success adjusting their conflicting timetables. Essie's clock ran from 7:00 a.m. to 11:00 p.m., Paul's from noon to 3:00 a.m. She "thought it rather wicked laziness" to sleep after eight in the morning and persuaded Paul to try getting up earlier. He did his best, only to wander around in a daze, kiss her goodbye blindly—and go back to bed. Even Essie could occasionally acknowledge defeat. She relented, calling off at least one of her campaigns.

Their life was busy. Essie worked daily at Presbyterian Hospital; Paul shuttled between full-time law school, part-time athletics, and occasional singing engagements or public appearances (among them a "seat of honor" at the Columbia senior-class dinner at the Hotel Astor). Evenings, they saw an ever-widening circle of friends—Minnie and Pat, Hattie and Buddy Bolling, Essie's old friend Corinne Cook and her new husband, Louis Wright, the brilliant young physician and civil-rights activist who became the Robeson family doctor. Occasionally there would be a trip to one of the cellar cabarets, like Eddie's, that were springing up all over Harlem, or a boat-ride excursion up the Hudson. But for the first year of their marriage, the Robesons were essentially a struggling, upwardly mobile young couple, "primarily concerned with *ourselves,*" as Essie later wrote, "with our own future," not yet at the glamorous epicenter of the Harlem literary renaissance or its burgeoning racial politics.[21]

Back in 1920 Paul had become involved with the Amateur Players, a group of Afro-American students who banded together under the direction of Dora Cole Norman, sister of Bob Cole (one of the great forces in turn-of-the-century black theater). The Players wanted to "attempt to produce plays of their race," a goal that led Mrs. Norman to stage a revival at the Harlem YWCA of Ridgely Torrence's drama *Simon the Cyrenian,* the story of the black man who was Jesus's cross-bearer. She had finally prevailed on a reluctant Paul to play the leading role of Simon; according to an account he gave to a newspaper six years later, his apartment was next to the rehearsal hall and the Players would "waylay him and dragged him in whenever he passed," until he "gave up the fight."[22]

Paul treated the show as a lark, but several whites influential in the theater happened to catch his performance, were impressed, and subsequently recommended him for his first professional role, the lead in a play about voodoo entitled *Taboo.* It was the initial writing effort of Mary Hoyt Wiborg, the fashionable young white socialite "Hoytie," daughter of wealthy financier Frank Wiborg, and sister to Sara (wife of Gerald Murphy of Lost Generation fame). The melodramatic plot of *Taboo* centers on a plantation in antebellum Louisiana. Severe drought conditions threaten the crop, and some of the superstitious plantation slaves, blaming the lack of rain on "a curse" placed on the mistress's mute grandchild, decide to sacrifice the boy. A wandering minstrel, Jim—the part offered Robeson—intervenes, and after several hundred turns in the plot, including an African flashback in which Jim transmogrifies into a voodoo king, rainfall descends at the crucial moment and all ends happily.[23]

Paul was again inclined to refuse the part, preferring to concentrate on law school, but Essie, with Dora Cole Norman backing her up, kept at him. After much discussion, and having determined he could continue his law studies simultaneously, Paul agreed to take on the role: "I knew little of what I was doing, but I was urged to go ahead and try." The production, at the Sam Harris Theater, was an elaborate one. The great black actor Charles Gilpin helped to coach the cast; Augustin Duncan, Isadora's brother, directed; the famed Clef Club Orchestra accompanied; and Margaret Wycherly, most recently associated with the Provincetown Players, starred opposite Robeson. The major critics saw little merit in the play, and nearly as little in the performances. Robert Benchley in *Life* roasted the playwright, and Alexander Woollcott in *The New York Times* roasted the star (Wycherly "gave a monstrously stagy and sepulchral performance"). Robeson's press was generally positive—he "dominates the play," his voice is "rich, mellow"—but Woollcott, though impressed with Robeson's strong presence, advised him that he belonged almost anywhere but on a stage. (Having met Robeson during the play's run, Woollcott later wrote, "I never in my life saw anyone so quietly sure, by some inner knowledge, that he was going somewhere. . . .") Wycherly immediately gave notice, and the production came to an abrupt end after four matinee performances.[24]

Hoytie Wiborg was not discouraged. She had the financial resources and theatrical contacts to back up her self-confidence, and within two months of Taboo's closing in New York had arranged for a production in London. It was to star none other than Mrs. Patrick Campbell, one of the legendary figures of the English stage, who had often stayed at Hoytie's Fifth Avenue home and was given to doing favors for her amateur-playwright friends. Hoytie offered Robeson the chance to re-create his role opposite Mrs. Pat.[25]

He hesitated, but Essie had begun "to set her mind and heart" on encouraging Paul to explore his singing and acting skills further, with a serious eye toward a career in theater as an alternative, or at the least a supplement, to law. She had sat in on every rehearsal of Taboo, carefully going over her performance notes with him, buying them tickets to more and more New York shows, and herself becoming convinced that his race would be less of a hindrance to a distinguished career in the theater than in the law, where at best he was likely to end up, after years of struggle, with "a small political job" or "a good and remunerative practice." Neither prospect, she decided, would be sufficient reward for her husband's extraordinary gifts. Essie was ambitious for something far more spectacular than mere security.[26]

The young black singer Harold Browning further helped to nudge Robeson toward a career in the theater. Browning was a member and the manager of The Four Harmony Kings, a black quartet then playing in the Broadway smash Shuffle Along, the epochal musical that had opened in the summer of 1921—the first entirely black production since the memorable early-twentieth-century contributions by Will Marion Cook, Bob Cole, Bert Williams, and George Walker. When the bass singer of the Harmony Kings unexpectedly left, the quartet's job in Shuffle Along was put in jeopardy. A chance encounter on the street between Harold Browning and Robeson, who had just closed in Taboo and finished his second-year law-school exams, led to Robeson's being hired as the bass replacement. After one day of rehearsal, he joined the cast of Shuffle Along.[27]

His debut performance got off to a shaky start. Jauntily balancing his smart new straw hat and cane, preoccupied with the excitement of the night, Paul tripped over a board while bending to get through the narrow door leading onstage—and nearly fell. Essie, sitting in the audience, "closed her eyes in horror," fearing Paul had stumbled onstage with such force that he had knocked down the three other quartet members "like ninepins." When she opened her eyes, all four were smilingly erect and singing lustily—Paul's trained body had instantly recovered itself. Eubie Blake, the show's composer and conductor, later recalled that for an instant he feared the huge new "King" was going to fall right into the orchestra pit. "That boy will bear watching," Eubie said; "anybody who can nearly fall like that and come up with a million-dollar smile has got *some* personality!" For toppers, Paul's solo rendition of "Old Black Joe" brought down the house. With the omens so auspicious, he decided to accept Hoytie Wiborg's offer to go to England with *Taboo.* [28]

But first he took the occasion of a recital in Washington, D.C., to pay a visit to Gerry Neale at Howard University. According to Gerry's recollection many years later, Paul's visit was unexpected. A call came into the women's dormitory saying a guest was waiting to see her in the reception room. It was Paul. "I was glad to see him. We talked about where his career was going and about what I was doing." To her surprise, he returned the next day. "I somehow shortened the conversation and would not let it get personal." The following evening a friend persuaded Gerry to go to a YWCA dance. "Who was there as big as life but Paul . . . and we danced and talked and danced and talked. He said he believed Essie wanted him to be happy and he was sure she would give him a divorce if I would promise to marry him. I mustered the strength and resolve to say to him that he must go back and work hard to make his marriage work. We said goodbye again."[29]

Paul still wasn't ready to give up, even though Gerry told him she was seriously dating Harry Bledsoe and even though her beau made it clear, when he heard of Robeson's visit to the campus, that "he would be no part of an eternal triangle." In 1924, after graduating from Howard, Gerry and Bledsoe did marry, although, like Essie and Paul earlier, they kept it a secret. Bledsoe went to Detroit to complete his last year of law school, and Gerry went to Bordentown, New Jersey, to teach in the Industrial and Training School. During that year, Paul came to give a concert at the school, and Gerry attended. They talked briefly at the reception, not having seen each other since his visit to Howard. The next day, after assuming Paul had returned to New York, Gerry got a call from the principal's wife asking her to come to their home. Paul was there. When the two were left alone, they "talked and talked" and Gerry again said "he must make his marriage work." Unnerved at his persistence, she decided it was time to send out a formal wedding announcement—and included Paul and Essie on the list. "He wrote me a heartbreak letter saying, How could I do this to him? Why had I not waited?" By now—if not earlier—Essie was aware of Paul's continuing involvement. When their paths twice crossed with Gerry, at a party and a dance in December

1924, Essie confided to her diary that Paul had been "too attentive" to Gerry, "vamping her before my very eyes"—"Paul not loyal to me for first time." Thereafter—whether because of Essie's feelings or her intervention is unknown—the involvement did finally cool. Once in a great while in later years, Paul and Gerry renewed contact, their passion by then having distilled into cordiality.[30]

■

CHAPTER 4

Provincetown Playhouse

(1922–1924)

Paul sailed for England in July 1922 aboard the S.S. *Homeric.* The tentative plan was for him to test the waters and, if the temperature seemed inviting, to send for Essie; if not, to return to the States and rejoin The Harmony Kings; and in either case to return in the fall to complete his last year in law school. On the eve of his departure, Essie took ill and her doctor said an immediate operation for adhesions from an old appendectomy was needed. She kept the news from Paul, not wanting to "worry him to death" and "spoil his work and his trip." At the pier Essie gaily bade him goodbye, postdated twenty-one letters to him, arranged for friends to mail them off at intervals, sent him a cheery cable at sea—and checked herself into Presbyterian Hospital.[1]

The operation went well, but her recovery did not. She developed a variety of postoperative complications, including phlebitis, and was kept in the hospital. Her vitality and courage ebbed in tandem, bolstered only by the arrival of Paul's frequent letters, filled with cheerful news of his experiences—and repeated expressions of his love. The letters are suffused with such extravagant expressions of tenderness ("Sweet I often think of how barren my life would have been had I never seen you"; "I've just been kissing your picture"; "I marvel, Darling, at the strength of our love"; "If ever two were one *we* are," etc.) that we would have to revise our understanding of the ordinary workings of the human psyche in order to believe that the sentiments were wholly counterfeit or that he harbored any substantial doubts about the course of his marriage or any serious grievances about having been "tricked" into it.[2]

Paul's letters also revealed considerable preoccupation with the uncertain course of his career and the likely reception of the play (renamed *Voodoo* by Mrs. Campbell). On first arriving, he was all exuberance—he thought the countryside beautiful, Mrs. Campbell "a really wonderful woman and a marvelous actress" who had "cut the play up" in such a way as to make his part "much better," Miss Wiborg immensely "nice," prospects for the play bright, and his own future so promising that he felt sure he "must stay somehow," and that Essie must come over to join him.[3]

Rehearsals got off to a promising start. From the beginning Mrs. Campbell told him that he "was a good actor" and showed her confidence (as well as the frantic nature of her schedule—she was performing *Hedda Gabler* and rehearsing *Voodoo* simultaneously) by making Paul "one of the directors practically." He didn't think the English cast was on the whole as strong as the American, except for Mrs. Campbell, who was "one thousand times better than Miss Wycherly" and *"really rules,"* being "far better" as a director "in knowing what she wants" than Augustin Duncan had been for the New York production. Early on the play seemed to be "shaping up fine," with firm plans to open at Blackpool, followed by Edinburgh, Glasgow, Liverpool—and, as consummation, London in August. Robeson could hardly wait. "I guess we'll hit," he wrote Essie confidently. "I'm really supposed to knock 'em dead."[4]

He didn't—though he fared better than the production as a whole. The opening in Blackpool proved a disappointment. Perhaps, along with the strained melodrama of the plot, the startling sight of the glamorous Mrs. Campbell, now aged fifty-seven and dressed for her *Voodoo* role as a Louisiana grandmother in braids and crinoline, had something to do with the mixed reception. Paul gamely sent Essie an understated account of the Blackpool performance: "To be truthful things are none too rosy." By Edinburgh, the next stop, he confessed to outright uncertainty about the play's chances: "Really darling I don't know what to do. These folks want to go to London but are not sure." He reported that the state of the theater in general, and the prospects for a black performer in particular, were "not as pictured." The English theater "seems in as bad a state as those in N.Y. or worse. . . . Vaudeville pays better here than the *legitimate.*" The tale "about Negroes making money here," he added, "is bosh." Paul had learned that Will Marion Cook, the pioneering ragtime composer with several successful Broadway credits (including the pathbreaking *Clorindy*), was "wandering around Europe," and his ex-wife, the brilliant singer-actress Abbie Mitchell, "is in Vienna and there's no money there."[5]

Paul was uncertain whether to send for Essie (not having learned yet that she was confined to a hospital bed). He missed her terribly and couldn't bear the idea of being "away from my little girl much longer," but this supposedly laid-back, impractical young man cautioned that they "can't be foolish," must not "take any wild chances." He repeatedly directed Essie to "keep in touch with" Harold Browning and The Harmony

Kings ("If I see things are not breaking I'll get right back with them"), and to find out whether *Shuffle Along* would be coming to London, as rumored (he was sure they'd want him, with "Mrs. Campbell's leading man" tacked on to his name). Should *Voodoo* and all other options fail to pan out, he would head straight back to the States and to law school. "We want to be safe," he wrote her. To that end, he thought he'd perhaps do best to "get down to Law. The sooner I build up, the sooner we'll be on easy street." Even time spent with the quartet and *Shuffle Along* might, in light of those goals, "be wasted and will hold us back." On the other hand, even if he decided to go straight into the law, perhaps it might be better to stay in England and study at Oxford for a year, thereby enhancing subsequent job prospects. The number of possible options and their equal uncertainty "worries me sick." He urged Essie to think things over "carefully from every angle"—"You'll know what to do. . . . You always know."

But Essie, of course, was in the hospital, and her premailed letters, though arriving with routine frequency, never answered Paul's questions or commented on his news. Their obliqueness puzzled him, but for the first few weeks did not overly arouse his suspicion. To relax between performances and bouts of worry over the future, he tried to get about a little. He had taken to England immediately (within a week of landing, he felt he was "getting to be a real Englishman"), and did some standard touring. He also went to the theater frequently (Sir Charles Hawtrey in *Captain Applejack* was "not as good as Eddinger," but Norma Talmadge's movie *Ghosts of Yesterday* warranted an enthusiastic full-page plot summary to Essie). He also took in the tennis matches between Scotland and Sweden ("I enjoyed the atmosphere. Very collegiate you know"). Otherwise, he seems to have made few social contacts, though one proved all-important. In London, Robeson lived for a few days in an extra room in the flat of the black American singer John Payne. (Payne had come to Europe years before with the Southern Syncopated Orchestra and had stayed on to become "Dean" of blacks in London.) Living in the other extra room was a third black musician, twenty-nine-year-old Lawrence Brown, a gentle, charming man of effervescent humor who had come to Europe to accompany Roland Hayes and had stayed to study and also to work on a volume of transcriptions he had arranged of hitherto unknown spirituals. One night at Payne's, Robeson sang a few songs "just for fun," and thirty years later Larry Brown recalled that he "knew at once that it was possible for him to become a great singer." Remembering Robeson's marvelous voice, he later sent him the published volume of spirituals; ultimately he would become Robeson's musical collaborator and friend.[6]

But generally of an evening, so Paul reported to Essie, he stayed home reading ("I like to read good novels of strong love and dream of you"). He reassured her (she had apparently asked) that he was *not* spending any of his time "slumming": he had "too much to think of" and found "no joy in 'slumming' any more" (thereby confirming that he once had). "Dolly [Paul's nickname for Essie] doesn't like and neither do I." She was "not to worry"—about either women or "drugs." "No woman living can make me forget my little wife even for a moment." He promised "always will I remain the noble and fine 'boy' that my little girl has made me. . . . There can be no temptation of any kind." In what may have been an oblique reference to Gerry, Paul reassured Essie that "I have restrained myself all these years in all ways—I've never loved darling until I loved you. All other was mere fancy." Indeed, he reported, "The people in the company have me down as a little prudish," and although he tried "to be nice to all," it could be "so hard"—"I find myself very irritable at times—then I catch myself and be nice like my Dolly would have me." When he got a bad cold—frequent colds were to trouble him all his life—he especially missed Essie: "How I need you to look after me. Yes, Darling, you are the one to spoil me, because I love you." "Sweet," he wrote her on another occasion, "you've spoiled me terribly. I feel absolutely helpless without you. I cried for you when I was sick. If only I could have rested my head on Dolly's breast!"[7]

At Glasgow, their third stop, the play seemed to fare better, and Paul's spirits soared again. Mrs. Campbell had continued to praise his abilities and to encourage him to make a career in the theater. And once she had discovered the beauty of his singing voice, she kept urging him—in keeping with his role as a minstrel and in apparent desperation to call attention *away* from the play—to "sing a lot and long—more—more." By the time they arrived in Glasgow, "the consensus of opinion," Paul wrote Essie, was "that the most enjoyable feature of the show is my singing." (". . . particularly good was Mr. Paul Robson [sic] as the minstrel Jim," wrote one critic. He "sang and acted splendidly . . . a magnificent voice, his singing has undoubtedly much to do with the success 'Voodoo' achieved last night.") At the curtain call, Mrs. Campbell—who "is very unselfish"—pushed him forward ("It's your show—not mine") to "a perceptible outburst of applause." When Mrs. Pat told him she thought he was "a real artist and off-hand suggested I would make a marvelous Othello," he bought a copy of Shakespeare's plays, again started to mull over the possibilities of trying out his luck a while longer in London and having Essie come over to join him: "So anxious for you to see me and criticise. Know you can help me—I feel awkward in certain new positions. I want you, and you only to help me."[8]

But within a matter of days he had to re-evaluate his prospects yet again. Mrs. Campbell, it turned out, wasn't happy playing second fiddle after all. One critic had opened his review by saying, "Mrs. Patrick Campbell is not the dominating personality in 'Voodoo' "—though he did go on to praise her. "She feels the play is more mine than hers," Paul noted, and with him getting "most of the glory," she quickly lost interest in taking the play to London (indeed, Paul reported, she still had not bothered to master her lines). When Mrs. Campbell finally cabled Hoytie Wiborg that she could not continue in the play, Wiborg cabled back, "Your chicken hearted cable just received." "This cable addressed to me!" Mrs. Campbell stormed, having gotten neither good notices nor any salary for her "gesture of friendship." "Hoytie's play," she concluded, "was an ugly business." With Mrs. Campbell defecting, Paul felt "at sea" once more ("I can't trust this bunch here"), even while continuing to feel in his gut that he wanted a year in London, to "start on our little one," to study law, to give "the London people a chance to hear me." What did Essie think? he kept writing. What should they do? As her letters continued to seem maddeningly, puzzlingly indifferent, Paul's concern increased. Finally he telegraphed, "All my questions unanswered. Worried. Is anything wrong. All love, Paul."[9]

By then Essie had been in the hospital for over a month, and her considerable courage had faltered. She decided to cable Paul the truth. Receiving the news, he was "taken absolutely off-guard" and "cried and cried as tho my heart would break—You know how it is when you've passed thru a terrible strain and when its all over—you break down. . . . It is as if I had been at your bedside and saw you come to and go back—and finally safe. I couldn't pull myself together." He was horrified at the thought that she'd gone through the crisis without him and gently chided her for sometimes being "too plucky." He felt like taking the first boat back, but Essie counseled him to remain, thinking she might still make it over. "Rather against my better judgment," he agreed to stay on, but in short order his mounting anxiety about Essie, in combination with the decision to close *Voodoo* before it reached London, put him back on board the S.S. *Homeric*, bound for home. On landing in New York, he went straight from the dock to the hospital. The receptionist, alerted to expect him, greeted him as he entered with "Oh, you're Mr. Goode; I'll take you right up!" Paul rushed into Essie's room and embraced her. "She could only pat his head and laugh and cry," she later wrote, while he whispered "so many sweet things that she felt her heart would burst with happiness." For the next week he barely left her side, except for meals and to sleep. "His very presence, his beautiful sweet strength and love, made it seem absurd for her to be ill." She improved rapidly, and in two more weeks Paul took her home.

In October, Essie was still too ill to return to work, but by late November 1922 they were able to resume occasional socializing, including serving as "guests of honor" at a Harlem affair fancy enough to make the society columns ("Mrs. Robeson wore a flame colored chiffon with brilliants. . . . Fully two hundred and fifty guests were gowned in evening clothes. A dance followed the reception on the third floor. Just a little past 12 o'clock there was a musicale. With Mr. Eube [sic] Blake of the 'Shuffle Along' company at the piano, Mr. Paule [sic] Robeson, Mr. Harold Browning, Mr.

Noble Sissle [Eubie Blake's partner] and Mr. Will Hann [one of The Harmony Kings] rendered musical selections. This was a big surprise and the guests enjoyed the innovation immensely").[10]

But glamour did not pay the bills. Paul gave a few informal concerts, in the fall spent a few weeks at Rutgers assisting Coach Sanford, and in 1923 briefly secured an engagement in the chorus as part of Lew Leslie's *Plantation Revue,* starring Florence Mills (and later Cora Green). The revue was an attempt to cash in on the success with white audiences of the all-black *Shuffle Along;* it simulated a Southern plantation complete with a watermelon moon, an onstage "Aunt Jemima" flipping flapjacks—and Paul, decked out in straw hat, striped coveralls, and a gingham ascot. But with Paul due to start his last year in law school, money continued to be a problem (his salary in *Voodoo* had scarcely covered expenses, and he had had trouble collecting even that small sum). To help them get through the winter, he clerked in a post office and again accepted occasional pro-football engagements, but he didn't enjoy the sport the way he had in college. Two prizefight promoters from Chicago offered to train him as a challenger to Henry Wills and Jack Dempsey, but Paul turned them down. Still, the sportswriter Lawrence Perry, in his column "For the Game's Sake," sent out a story, which was reprinted elsewhere, that Robeson had accepted the offer: he had been "forced to take some radical step," Perry wrote, "whereby he may earn money for his wife and children," since his law practice "has fallen short of paying office space." Thinking the story might have originated with the Rutgers Alumni Office, Robeson immediately wrote to the graduate manager there: "The report of my fistic ambitions . . . was absolutely untrue and unfounded. That matters little. What matters much more is the statement as to my Law Practice. . . . I have not as yet even taken the State Exams, so I couldn't have practised. . . . A report like this can hurt me a great deal. When I settle down to my practice I don't expect to fail—and no few drawbacks at the beginning will discourage me. . . . I cannot see any credit to Rutgers in a prize fighting legal failure." As regarded the report about his "family," Robeson wrote, "I have no family—only a wife . . . and not such a helpless little body at that." The Rutgers graduate manager forwarded Robeson's letter to Lawrence Perry and, in asking for a correction, remarked in a covering letter, "We really expect him to become a power among the Negro race in this Country, and believe that is his underlying ambition." Perry immediately printed a retraction.[11]

Under the double impetus of needing funds and wanting theatrical contacts, Paul finally decided to appeal to the fabled largesse of Otto H. Kahn—"Otto the Magnificent, the Great Kahn," Eugene O'Neill called him in 1924, in mock obeisance to the Provincetown Players' patron. Kahn's generosity was as deep as the range of his benefactions was broad. An immensely wealthy banker—he was head of Kuhn, Loeb & Co., as well as the chief financial adviser to Edward H. Harriman's vast transportation empire—Kahn became one of the great patrons of the arts in America. He bankrolled the Metropolitan Opera as well as the Provincetown Players, and he was known as a sympathetic supporter of black artists.[12]

It was in Kahn's capacity as a trustee of Rutgers, however, that Robeson formally appealed to him in a letter of March 13, 1923. "I am very anxious to get before any theatrical managers and playwrights, especially those who may possibly have Negro roles," Robeson wrote, specifically citing Eugene O'Neill, whose play *The Emperor Jones,* starring Charles Gilpin, had created a sensation in 1920. Referring to his work in *Taboo,* Robeson cited the favorable reviews in both New York and England, enclosed two clippings, and mentioned that Augustin Duncan, Miss Margaret Wycherly, or Miss Wiborg "would be glad" to provide "some definite idea about what I can do." He closed by requesting an interview with Kahn: "I know that you are a power both in theatrical and musical circles and I am hoping that you will be kind enough to use your influence in getting me a hearing." Kahn's reply was perfunctory, though not unfriendly. He promised to keep Robeson's request in mind and invited him to come by his office "any day during business hours," but regretted that "just at present I do not know of any suitable opportunity." A year and a half later, Essie was to approach Kahn with a second appeal.[13]

At the same time Robeson wrote to Kahn, he asked Augustin Duncan, who had directed him in *Taboo,* to approach Eugene O'Neill directly in his behalf. "If you have a Negro part to cast," a complying Duncan wrote O'Neill, "you will find that Mr. Robeson has in my opinion very unusual and extraordinary ability as an actor and most admirable qualities as a student and a man." It would be nearly a year before this avenue, too, opened up; when it did, Robeson was quick to credit Duncan's role in creating an opportunity for him with the Provincetown Players.[14]

With no immediate prospects in the theater, Robeson applied himself to finishing up his law degree. Harold Medina and John Bassett Moore (the international law expert) were among his professors, and William O. Douglas and Thomas E. Dewey among his classmates—but it was Dean Harlan Fiske Stone who caught his imagination, and later in life it was only Stone's name that could conjure up what limited affection Robeson felt for his law-school days. He had, as always, made friends easily, been well liked by his classmates, and been commandeered to play on assorted law-school athletic teams. And, for a time, he did well enough academically to seem a possible candidate for the *Law Review;* its editor-in-chief, Charles Ascher, in later years drew a retrospective sigh of relief that Robeson's broken tenure at the school had made him ineligible—"I had at the time several Southerners on my board, and I could see I would have a bit of a fight to get Paul on." But in fact Robeson's lack of enthusiasm for the study of law

was ultimately reflected in his compiling a mediocre academic record—
in the final count, twenty-four of his course grades (a full two-thirds)
were C's.[15]

After receiving his degree in late February 1923, he let himself drift
for a bit, not actively seeking a job. This worried Essie. "Lolling about"
offended her style of brisk efficiency. She mistrusted introspection as a
form of malingering, a self-indulgent substitute for action—which to her
was a cure for thought rather than, as for Paul, the product of it. Essie was
never sure anything would happen unless she went out there and *made* it
happen. Paul, more secure in his sense of mission, of ultimate purpose,
could afford to wait—a reflection of confidence, not (as Essie was prone
to call it) "laziness." Characteristically, she mistook surface appearances
for the entire truth, equating Paul's outer behavior with his inner attitude
and missing, in her overattentiveness to words, the underlying message of
his feelings. With someone as interior as Paul, this could result in fatal
misunderstanding—in confusing equanimity with idling.

His brother Ben, more cogently, realized that Paul had a habit of
moving by "inner revelation," had the ability to wait confidently until he
felt his path had been illuminated and then "in a moment" to sense it and
to "seize upon it with zest." Until then he was as "stubborn as a mule. He
simply does nothing. He will go for months just hanging on—temptation
after temptation to violate his orders to wait may come, but he lingers. To
the unspiritual soul this is laziness, hardheadedness, the height of folly. To
him it is life, and peace and joy. He will tell you that all of the battles of
his life have been and are waged at this center." Following this intuitive
process, Paul deflected a political-job offer from Tammany Hall, sensing
it would bind him to the wrong kind of loyalties. By June, after three
months of biding his time, he bent his instincts a bit and accepted work
in a law office. "There are times," his brother Ben wrote, in a veiled,
disapproving allusion to Essie's influence, "when for the sake of peace he
is hurried into things."[16]

The offer came from Louis William Stotesbury, a Rutgers alumnus
(class of 1890) and trustee and, at one point in his career, adjutant general
for the state of New York, who had frequently lent a helping hand to the
school's graduating athletes. Still, the offer to Robeson was special: he
would be the only black in the Stotesbury and Miner law office, secretarial
staff included—and in a country where even the handful of Afro-American
banks and insurance companies were loath to hire lawyers of their own
race. The firm specialized in estates and was currently involved in litigation
over Jay Gould's will; Stotesbury assigned Robeson the job of preparing
a brief for it.[17]

He worked away diligently (indeed, when the Gould case came to trial,
his brief was used) but not comfortably. His color (along with his prepos-
sessing physique) made him a conspicuous presence in the office, and it

was commented on, in unfriendly asides, from the first. After a few weeks, the covert mistreatment blossomed into open ugliness: when Robeson buzzed for a stenographer to take down a memorandum of law, she refused—"I never take dictation from a nigger," she purportedly said, and walked out. Robeson took the matter to Stotesbury, who genuinely commiserated. The two men discussed the situation frankly and fully. Stotesbury expressed admiration for Robeson's abilities but told him straight out that his prospects for a career in law were limited: the firm's wealthy white clients were unlikely ever to agree to let him try a case before a judge, for fear his race would prove a detriment. Stotesbury said he might be willing to consider opening a Harlem branch of the office and put Robeson in charge of it, but Paul decided instead to resign. The profession of law, never that inviting, now seemed a decided dead end. (A decade later, after more reflection, Robeson concluded he could never have entered "any profession where the highest prizes were from the start denied to me.") He never took the bar exam, never again practiced as a lawyer. He told Essie that, once more, he would "wait a little. . . . Something will turn up." He had decided on a stubborn retreat to instinct, to hold himself inactive in the presence of things that did not interest him, to await an intuitive signal that some worthwhile opportunity was at hand.[18]

He let himself drift through the fall of 1923—and then came alive. A note arrived, penciled in the margin of a form letter thanking Robeson for subscribing to the Provincetown Players, from its director, Kenneth Macgowan: "I want very much to talk with you about Eugene O'Neill's new play, which we will give in February. Have you a phone?" The new play was *All God's Chillun Got Wings*. Within two days an appointment had been set up. Bess Rockmore, an assistant to the Provincetown director (and the first wife of Robert Rockmore, later to become Robeson's attorney and friend), was present when Paul first read for the Provincetown people. Sixty years later she recalled the impact he made: "All I remember is the audition—and this marvelous, incredible voice. . . . I can tell you, he was a most impressive personality. Even in those days, he was flabbergastingly impressive. . . . He was built so beautifully. He moved so gracefully. He was simply a very attractive man. . . . [There was] something unavoidably present about him." Paul got the part.[19]

The 1923–24 season at the Provincetown was the first under the new leadership of the "Triumvirate"—with Macgowan, O'Neill, and Robert Edmond Jones, the scenic designer, as associate directors. The three men took over from the original group of inspired amateurs headed by George Cram ("Jig") Cook and his wife, the playwright Susan Glaspell, who had founded the Players but retired from the scene following protracted internal bickering that ranged from divisions over artistic purposes to disagreements on casting.[20]

The Triumvirate planned to open with *All God's Chillun*. To foster the entirely professional image at which the new regime aimed, the theater was freshly painted, the tiny stage enlarged, seats numbered for the first time, the "free list" for tickets curtailed, and eight-page playbills substituted for the colored sheets previously used. But *Chillun* had to be postponed briefly; a delay in the play's publication in George Jean Nathan's and H. L. Mencken's *American Mercury* forced the Playhouse, because of O'Neill's contract with Nathan, to await the published version in the magazine's second issue, of February 1924, before producing the play. Paul and Essie now at least had time to mull over the printed version of *Chillun* as it appeared in the *Mercury* (they "reread and discussed it endlessly," according to Essie, "profoundly impressed" with its "beauty"), and also the chance to see the Provincetown's interim production of Strindberg's *The Spook Sonata* ("Didn't know what in hell it was all about," Essie confessed in her diary, salty directness momentarily upstaging elegance—a shift in tone on call throughout her life).[21]

When the Provincetown formally announced a spring production of *Chillun,* press commentary on the play began to build—and with it Paul's notoriety. His period of "drift" gave way abruptly to intense activity. Suddenly he was in demand. A record company approached him. Raymond O'Neill of the Ethiopian Art Theater (organized in Chicago by O'Neill and Mrs. Sherwood Anderson and recently shifted to Harlem) asked Paul to be a "leading man," an offer he turned down after he and Essie saw the troupe's opening night of *Salome* at the Lafayette Theater—"wonderful gathering, terrible, terrible performance," Essie wrote in her diary. Responding to a variety of other invitations, Paul "sang songs by Negro composers and authors" at the Brooklyn YWCA, "sang and made [a] speech" at the banquet of the St. Christopher basketball team, attended a dinner for W. E. B. Du Bois at which he neither sang nor spoke, and went to hear the drama critic Heywood Broun lecture (and "had a nice chat with him after," discovering that he talked the way he wrote—"very witty . . . dry sort of fun"). The Robesons also started to attend NAACP functions, at one of which Paul—at the request of Walter White, one of its officers—sang. In between these proliferating contacts and events, Paul and Essie faithfully continued their round of Greek sorority-fraternity functions and their trips to concerts and the theater: Marian Anderson, Roland Hayes ("Think his voice beautiful in the light lyrical things," Essie wrote in her diary, "but lacking in the robust numbers. . . . Am all inspired now for Paul's voice"), a production of *The Changeling,* and Walter Hampden's *Cyrano.*[22]

In March, shortly before rehearsals for *Chillun* were to begin, Paul acquired additional experience by acting in a revival of *Roseanne,* by the white playwright Nan Bagby Stevens. The play, about a transgressing black preacher in the South saved from his "avenging congregation" by Roseanne, had first been produced in 1923 with a "burnt-cork" all-white cast (despite the acclaim Charles Gilpin had received in 1920 in O'Neill's *The Emperor Jones,* the long-standing practice of whites playing black roles in blackface remained widespread). But the revival at the Lafayette in Harlem in 1924 had an all-black cast, headed by Robeson as the preacher and Rose McClendon in the title role. The Lafayette presented *Roseanne* as one in a series of "colored plays," each for a limited run, designed in part to offset criticism leveled by Harlem intellectuals like Theophilus Lewis, drama critic for A. Philip Randolph's then radical publication *The Messenger.* Lewis had argued that the Lafayette Players—an all-black company founded by Gilpin, and performing before all-black audiences—did the community a disservice by focusing on revivals of popular Broadway shows rather than on producing black plays about black life (though others had countered that few black plays existed and that the Lafayette served the singular function of providing black performers an opportunity to appear in "legitimate" fare and black audiences the chance to see them in something other than musical comedy).[23]

Roseanne played for one week at the Lafayette in Harlem and then for a second week at the Dunbar in Philadelphia. The audiences were small but enthusiastic. A black critic in Philadelphia hailed the performances (but not the play) as being "essentially Negro art, robust, asking for enormous and spontaneous vitality," Robeson's voice rolling "out of him like a vibrant tide." It would be "extremely interesting," the critic thought, to see what Robeson could do with the role of the Emperor Jones, or that of Jim in *All God's Chillun.* He was about to see just that—not merely Jim, but Brutus Jones as well.[24]

The course, though, was not smooth. No sooner had rehearsals for *Chillun* begun than Robeson's costar, Mary Blair (at the time married to Edmund Wilson), fell ill, leading to another month's postponement. The continuing press buildup caused added uncertainty. In the three-month period between the play's publication and its eventual opening in May, negative reaction to the play's theme of miscegenation had mounted, with Hearst's *American* and the *Morning Telegraph* leading the protest.[25]

A full eight weeks before the opening, the New York *American* carried an article headlined "Riots Feared from Drama." Thereafter it printed a succession of comments solicited from the forces of reaction—from conservative church groups, from the Society for the Prevention of Vice, from disgruntled rival playwrights, ex-Confederates, and assorted other champions of Nordic purity—a series so relentlessly inflammatory in its dire predictions of mob violence as to seem designed to provoke it. Producers should not put on plays, the *American* thundered in an editorial, "which are, or threaten to become, enemies of the public peace; they should not dramatize dynamite, because, while helping the box office, it may blow up the business."[26]

Mary Blair was quoted in the Brooklyn *Daily Eagle* as saying, "I deem it an honor to take the part of Ella. There is nothing in the part that should give offense to any woman desiring to portray life, and portray it decently." Her comment was itself considered inflammatory by the manifold legions of racial purists and shortly made still more so when a national news syndicate, emphasizing one transient moment in the script, sent out a rehearsal photograph of Blair entitled "WHITE ACTRESS KISSES NEGRO'S HAND." The photo was republished dozens of times, leading the New York drama critic Burns Mantle to parody the heightening scandal: "Miss Mary Blair, as the wife of a young colored law student, played by Paul Robeson . . . will kneel in gratitude at his feet and kiss his honest but heavily pigmented hand."[27]

As the uproar intensified, so did the demand for official intervention. Initially the licensing commissioner deflected it by pointing out that the Provincetown was an unlicensed establishment open only to subscribers— and therefore beyond the jurisdiction of City Hall. But instead of quieting protest, the ruling rechanneled it; the demand now arose for Mayor Hylan to keep the play from opening in order to prevent a race riot. Eugene O'Neill decided to issue a statement to the press. It began with appropriate truculence: in responding to criticisms of the play, O'Neill said, he was not acknowledging that they "honestly deserve any comment whatever"— since they "very obviously come from people who have not read a line of the play. Prejudice born of an entire ignorance of the subject is the last word in injustice and absurdity." O'Neill was, of course, being disingenuous, knowing as he did that some fair share of the criticism came from confirmed bigots who *had* read the printed version of the play and been directly incited by its indirect appeal for an end to racial bigotry.[28]

"As for the much discussed casting of Mr. Robeson in the leading part," O'Neill went on, "I have only this to say, that I believe he can portray the character better than any other actor could. That's all there is to it. A fine actor is a fine actor. The question of race prejudice cannot enter here." The whole matter was "ridiculous," he continued in fine indignation, for "right in this city two years ago" Robeson had played opposite the white actress Margaret Wycherly in *Taboo,* and in the play's "African scene" he had been cast as the king and she as the queen: "A king and queen are, I believe, usually married." Robeson had then gone on to play the same role in England opposite Mrs. Campbell, and "There were no race riots here or there. There was no newspaper rioting, either." Interviewed a few days before the opening, O'Neill, in a last-ditch effort to quell violence and therefore in a somewhat more compromising spirit, acknowledged, "There is prejudice against the intermarriage of whites and blacks, but what has that to do with my play? I don't advocate intermarriage in it. I am never the advocate of anything in any play—except Humanity toward Humanity."[29]

That was advocacy enough. Far from diminishing, the outcry accelerated. And the Provincetowners became—realistically—fearful. The pile of newspaper articles grew so large that the total bill from the press-clipping service ultimately exceeded the cost of the play's sets. And the mail became so vitriolic at one point that *Chillun*'s director, James Light, decided to withhold the more obscene letters—"the largest part"—from Mary Blair and Robeson. An anonymous bomb threat put a further edge on backstage tension.[30]

In an effort to deflect the public's attention while accommodating the tight schedule caused by Mary Blair's illness, the Provincetown, in April, filled in with a double bill of Coleridge's *The Ancient Mariner* (in a "dramatic arrangement" by O'Neill) and Molière's *George Dandin.* It was not a success, and a planned four-week run had to be cut short. As a substitute, while *Chillun* entered its final rehearsal period, the Triumvirate came up with the idea of reviving *The Emperor Jones* for a week—with Paul Robeson in the lead. *Jones* would open May 6, *Chillun* May 15—an astonishing burden (and of course potential opportunity) for any actor, let alone an untried actor already carrying on his head the curses of one race and the hopes of another.[31]

Rehearsals for *Jones* began in late April—two weeks before its scheduled opening. The seemingly offhand way Paul approached the script alarmed the methodical Essie, though she had begun to realize that what seemed like "downright laziness" in Paul was in fact "a natural repose." He read over the script of *Jones* for what seemed to her "ages," saying innumerable times, "I must commit these lines to memory"—and then didn't. Suddenly one day he "fell to work in earnest," according to Essie, "put his whole heart and soul into memorizing his part; for days and nights eating, sleeping, walking, talking, he would be learning his lines; he even dreamed them." Essie held the script, and the two of them would run lines when they went to bed, when they got up, when they ate—to the point where Ma Goode, who was for the time being living with them, announced that *she* had now memorized half the script. Sometimes the lines came out too much like an oration or a declamation, and Paul went back to work, phrase by phrase, word by word, "digging down to the meaning of every single comma"—until the speech came out sounding natural.[32]

To help the process of memorization, he and Essie would sometimes play games with the lines. Instead of saying, "You can bet your last penny," they substituted the Brutus Jones line "You can bet your whole roll on one thing, white man"; if noise in the apartment woke Paul up, he might be likely to say "Who dare whistle dat way in my palace? Who dare wake up de emperor?"; if they missed a bus or a streetcar and decided to walk, it was to the cadence of "Well, den I hoofs it. Feet, do yo' duty"; in place of the usual goodbye he might substitute, "So long, white man; see you in jail some time, maybe"; and if Essie forgot to kiss him goodbye, "he would drum on the wall with his knuckles, making a sound like the tom-tom in the play, and say 'Well, if dey aint no whole brass band to see me off, I sho' got de drum part of it.' "[33]

"Paul [is] working out splendidly," Essie was soon writing in her diary; indeed, he quickened not only to his new stage role but to the new offstage round of theater talk and theater people as well. Paul (according to Essie) "would listen eagerly for hours, for days, for weeks" to O'Neill's recounting of past ventures and adventures, and Jimmy Light's direction provided another kind of illumination for him. Unlike Paul's previous directors, Light didn't tell him what to do or how to do it; "He merely sat quietly in the auditorium and let him feel his way; he often helped him, of course. When Paul had trouble with a speech Jimmy would sit down on a soap-box beside him on the empty stage, and they would analyse the speech thought by thought, word by word . . . [Paul] working out his own natural movements and gestures with Jimmy's watchful help. 'I can't tell you what to do,' " Jimmy said, in the true Stanislavskian spirit, " 'but I can help you find what's best for you.' "[34]

Essie, who sat in on nearly every rehearsal, was gratified by the way Paul's talent flowered under Light's direction. She was always able to assess her husband's abilities with remarkable candor and objectivity. On the plus side she put his "intelligence, friendliness (sympathy) and beautiful organ voice"; on the negative, awkwardness in moving his six-foot-two-inch frame around a small stage "without seeming to mince" and a lack of technique—timing, pace, "how to pause for effect." Jimmy Light knew how to highlight Paul's strengths and minimize his weaknesses. "Let yourself go, Paul," he'd call out. "Don't hold yourself in; you look as though you're afraid to move." "I am," Paul would answer. "I'm so big I feel if I take a few steps I'll be off this tiny stage." "Then just take two steps," Light replied, "but make them fit you. You must have complete freedom and control over your body and your voice, if you are to control your audience."[35]

Part of learning how to control his body was learning how to be comfortable wearing costumes. Millia Davenport, a young costumer with the Playhouse, remembers the day Jimmy Light brought Paul into her shop. He was wearing old pants, cut off, but Millia, on sight, "knew him to be the most beautiful man I would ever see." Being "a tough little babe," she "did not faint," but Jimmy Light mistook Millia's stunned hesitation for an unwillingness on her part "to touch Paul because he was black" (Paul did not misunderstand; he "very well knew how I was responding to him and I was a cute little trick to whom he was responding in kind"). Light snatched away the tape measure in order to do the job himself. After an embarrassed pause, all came right—at least about the costume. "If I have never had a black lover," Millia concluded some sixty years later, "it's because I saw Paul first." But at the time she decided not to join the "other P.P. women [who] were practically tearing his pants off.

My life had been based on never having anything to do with another woman's husband in a world full of unattached men. I did not much like Essie, but I left Paul alone and good friends we did become." Malcolm Cowley claims that not all the Players shared Millia's scruples. Among others, Nilla Cook, Jig Cook's daughter, "then a buxom sixteen and a juvenile delinquent" (so Cowley describes her with high good humor), airily announced to Cowley "that she had seduced Paul," and he "believed her."[36]

Surrounded by assorted temptations and pressures, Robeson did his best to concentrate on the acting job at hand. He knew full well that the role of Brutus Jones—to be followed within ten days by the world premiere of *Chillun*—was a spectacular opportunity, and for a black actor an all but unimaginable one. Prior to Gilpin's debut in *Jones* in 1920, black actors performing before white audiences had been confined to the comfortable (for whites) and crippling (for blacks) stereotypes of song-and-dance routines. The few straightforward dramas that had appeared about Afro-American life had—like Ridgely Torrence's trilogy of plays—been the work of white playwrights of limited talent and constricted vision (although, before the twenties were out, a few promising plays by blacks had surfaced, notably Garland Anderson's *Appearances* in 1925 and Wallace Thurman's *Harlem* in 1929). A lot was riding on Paul Robeson—and on Eugene O'Neill.[37]

The first dress rehearsal, on May 4, did not go well. "Paul wasn't as good as he has been," Essie wrote in her diary, "still nervous," but—she added confidently—"will work out fine." Her prediction proved accurate. The second dress, next day, went "marvelously"—"Paul easy and natural"—and the opening, on the following night, went better still. The first-nighters, with Gilpin's powerful performance as Brutus Jones in 1920 still fresh in their minds, responded coolly to the early scenes, but by the final curtain (according to Essie's diary) the "applause and stomping and whistling [were] deafening," with Paul called out for five bows.[38]

Charles Gilpin was in the audience that night, and afterward, in the dressing room, he and O'Neill quarreled. It was not the first time. During his long run in the role (204 performances), Gilpin had outraged O'Neill by tampering with the script, sometimes substituting "Negro" or "colored man" for O'Neill's frequent use of "nigger." Gilpin had been venting a long-accumulated fury. Though a brilliantly gifted actor, in the ten years preceding his 1920 opening in *Jones* he had been forced to take menial jobs as barber, porter, and elevator operator. Once more out of work following his triumph in *Jones,* he returned to his marginal existence, tried to make a living as a chicken farmer, and died of alcoholism in 1930 at age fifty-one. "I am really a race man," Gilpin told a New York Drama League dinner honoring him in 1921 (a dinner nearly canceled because of racist objections to it within the League—until O'Neill and others furiously protested);

"I am a Negro and proud of being one, proud of the progress the Negroes have made in the time and with the opportunity they have had. And I don't want the public to think anything different."[39]

O'Neill had been furious with Gilpin for his unpredictable behavior during the first run of *Jones* and had threatened to fire him. "I've stood for more from him than from all the white actors I've ever known—simply because he was colored!" O'Neill wrote his friend Mike Gold in July 1923 in outrage; "Gilpin lived under the assumption that no one could be got to play his part and took advantage accordingly." But O'Neill had decided then and there not to use Gilpin in any revival or in the planned London production. He had, he wrote Gold, "corralled another Negro to do it"—Robeson, that is—"a young fellow with considerable experience, wonderful presence and voice, full of ambition and a damn fine man personally with real brains—not a 'ham'! . . . He'll be bigger than Gilpin was even at the start."[40]

The details of Gilpin and O'Neill's quarrel in the dressing room on the night of Robeson's opening in *Jones* are not known, but a reporter did overhear a "tense exchange of pleasantries" between the two men, followed by Gilpin saying dismissively, and "with a good deal of fervor," that Robeson was "a hard worker. He has studied intensively." As Gilpin was leaving the theater, one of the Provincetowners invited him for a drink. Gilpin said no: "I feel kind of low. I created the role of the Emperor. That role belongs to me. That Irishman, he just wrote the play."[41]

Privately, O'Neill agreed that Gilpin had been better in the role than Robeson was. While Essie was writing in her diary on the night of the opening, "O'Neill and Mrs. O'Neill, James Light and everybody seemed thrilled with Paul's performance," O'Neill was writing in *his* diary: *"The Emperor Jones* opens with Robeson. Big success but Robeson not as good as Gilpin except in last part." And in later years O'Neill told an interviewer, "As I look back now on all my work, I can honestly say there was only one actor who carried out every notion of a character I had in mind. That actor was Charles Gilpin. . . ." Director Jimmy Light, moreover, agreed with O'Neill about the comparative merits of the two actors: "Robeson did the later scenes fine, after the Emperor is in the jungle, but he couldn't do that first scene, that took Charlie. Charlie knew all about that kind of 135th Street humor." Robeson, for his part, modestly wrote six months later, "I recall how marvelously it was played by Mr. Gilpin some years back. And the greatest praise I could have received was the expression of some that my performance was in some ways comparable to Mr. Gilpin's."[42]

But if, in the end, O'Neill preferred Gilpin's performance to Robeson's, many of the critics gave the palm to Robeson. The *Times* called him "singularly fine"; the *World* said his acting "was quite up to that which won Mr. Gilpin high praise"; and the review in the *Tribune*, flecked with racist patronization, declared, "Physically this full-blooded negro fitted the role

better than Gilpin. . . . He sounded the bottom rock depths of terror.
. . . He brings a full measure of understanding to the childlike volatility of
his race. . . ."43

The second-string reviews were at least as good. The critic in the
Evening Graphic announced that "Robeson portrays the part ideally"; the
Evening Post waxed eloquent over his "large and powerful voice—one rich
in shadings and emotion, an organ that should play an important part in
whatever success comes to the young negro actor"; and the *Telegram and
Evening Mail* pronounced him "as fine an actor as there is on the American
stage today." The out-of-town reviewers hailed his performance with
superlatives ranging from a mere "magnificent" to the declaration that it
had been "the kind of evening in the theater that you remember all your
life."44

With one day off after the opening of *Jones,* Robeson was back in
rehearsal for *Chillun* on May 8—while continuing to play *Jones* in the
evenings. (On May 13 *Jones* closed its limited run—to reopen on May 19
and again on June 2 for two additional week-long runs as an alternate
offering to *Chillun.*) A scant five days after the *Jones* opening, *Chillun* was
in dress rehearsal, with various Harlem bigwigs—such as James Weldon
Johnson, executive secretary of the NAACP—there in person to catch the
latest black performing sensation. Essie reported in her diary that the
premiere of *Chillun* would be pushed up to May 15 because Mary Blair,
Paul's costar, "seems quite disturbed about Paul's success in 'Jones,' and
is forcing an early opening. . . ."45

Just as that finally seemed imminent, and only hours before the curtain
was due to rise on the premiere, Mayor Hylan's office announced that it
was rejecting the Provincetown's application—legally necessary in those
days but hitherto routinely granted—for permission to employ child actors
in the first scene of *Chillun* (which depicted white and black children
unself-consciously playing together). No explanation was given—indeed,
none was possible: that same week *Kreutzer Sonata* opened on Broadway
with a child of seven in it, while the youngsters in *Chillun* ranged in age
from eleven to seventeen.46

If Mayor Hylan's announcement was calculated to prevent the play
from opening—rather than serving as a last-minute sop to its racist critics—then it failed. The curtain rose that night on a tense, crowded audience. "When I went on to the stage," Robeson later said, "I half expected
to hear shots from the stalls." Police ringed the theater in anticipation of
disorder—and some steelworker friends of the cast guarded the dressing
rooms (not least, from possible violence by the police). As the lights
dimmed, Jimmy Light stepped in front of the curtain to announce that, due
to the mayor's ban, the opening scene could not be performed—and then
proceeded to read it aloud instead. That hurdle cleared, the performance
proceeded without incident. In his diary that night, O'Neill wrote that the

opening "went over well—none of the expected trouble." And Essie, who under advice had taken an alternate route with Paul to the theater, decided in retrospect that "the average New Yorker, interested in the Experimental Theatre, would have gone to see that play and taken it in stride, had it not been for the deliberate furor created by the press." She noted with satisfaction in her diary that the "audience seemed gripped, moved and tense" and "at any opportunity was generous with applause."[47]

The critics, however, were less so. Most of them were cool to the play, though Robeson's personal reviews were splendid, adding still further to his suddenly enhanced stature. Heywood Broun in the *World* found the play "very tiresome because Eugene O'Neill has no more than outlined his problem [of miscegenation] before he sidesteps it"—the white woman who marries the black student turns out to be suffering from low self-esteem and, ultimately, madness, rather than from a courageous love that is color-blind—but "Caucasian superiority does suffer a little, because Paul Robeson is a far finer actor than any white member of the cast." Alexander Woollcott in the *Sun* felt the play failed to "come to life truly and vividly on the stage," even though Robeson had "superbly embodied and fully comprehended" the role of the student. Robert Benchley announced that Robeson "had taken his place with Charles Gilpin as one of the artists to whom his race may point with pride"; Ludwig Lewisohn pronounced him "a superb actor"; Burns Mantle praised his "dramatically effective" performance; and Laurence Stallings, heaping tribute upon tribute, called him "a genius," "a great actor," a performer who had done "as fine a thing as has been done in the Broadway year."[48]

In *American Mercury*, George Jean Nathan wrote that Robeson, "with relatively little experience and with no training to speak of, is one of the most thoroughly eloquent, impressive, and convincing actors that I have looked at and listened to in almost twenty years of professional theater-going." Why? Because "the Negro is a born actor." Nathan doubted that Robeson understood at all how he created the "beautiful" effects he did with his voice, hands, and "somewhat ungainly body." His acting was "instinctual." His performance in *Chillun* had "all the unrestrained and terrible sincerity of which the white actor, save on rare occasions, is by virtue of his shellac of civilization just a trifle ashamed." It was "not acting as John Barrymore knows acting" but, rather, "something that is just over the borderland of acting, and just this side of the borderland of life and reality." Nathan may have been accurately describing the special power of Robeson's stage presence, but was giving him no conscious credit for creating it. He dismissed the idea that part of Robeson's power as an actor derived from his being an educated and intelligent man. No, educated instincts—*understanding* a role—had nothing to do with it. It was Robeson's *race* that made him a "natural-born actor." In light of condescending praise like this, it becomes easier to understand why, even after Robeson sought further technical training, he would tend to underplay that fact, emphasizing instead—as Nathan had—that he was an untrained "natural."[49]

Nathan's views were hardly unique at the time. Joseph Wood Krutch, also a highly regarded critic, expressed much the same racial interpretation of acting in a 1927 article in the *Nation*. "Ecstasy," he wrote, was the black's—and the black actor's—"natural state"; his "instinctive sense for participation in an emotion larger than his comprehension" gave him "a gift for drama in a form more primitive as well as, perhaps, more purely dramatic than that of our conventional stage." Indeed, the Negro actor "is good only when some utter abandonment is to be portrayed. He may move awkwardly, almost uncomprehendingly, through level scenes . . . but he leaps with an effortless joy into a crisis and surrenders himself to joy, to terror, or to grief, as to a native element."[50]

In making these distinctions, both Krutch and Nathan saw themselves as champions of the black race, endowing it with attractive *innate* qualities. This "liberal" attitude had its roots in the nineteenth-century view that blacks—like women—were *naturally* endowed with childlike emotionalism and a "superior" capacity for affection, personal loyalty, and joy. This deadly confusion between biology and social learning could, by easy re-emphasis, yield a value judgment about *innate* black "childishness" that served as a perpetually self-justifying rationale for proscription and separation.

Though there was scarcely a peep of dissent in the white press about Robeson's performance in *Chillun*, some black reaction both to him and to the play was less favorable. A. B. Budd in *The Afro-American* described *Chillun* as "a hard play to sit through. To see a big, respectable and cultured character as the slave of a slim, depraved and silly white woman isn't the kind of enjoyment calculated to make up a good evening's entertainment." Will Anthony Madden in the Chicago *Defender* praised Robeson and even praised O'Neill for having provided "the Negro the opportunity to show that he is an actor," but he denounced both *Chillun* and *Jones* as "genius productions of subtleness of the most insidious and damaging kind." That indictment was elaborated by William Pickens, field secretary of the NAACP (and dean of Baltimore's Morgan College). Pickens argued that the subliminal theme of *Chillun* was a case *against* racial mixing: in showing how a black boy and a white girl first met in a mixed public school and later fell in love, with disastrous consequences, the play pointed a "dangerous" negative moral—"the Ku Klux would pay to have just such a play as this put on." Nor did Pickens spare Robeson. "Some colored people in it? Oh, that's nothing. Colored people are no better than white people. You can hire SOME of them to do anything that the law allows, if you have money enough."[51]

Other black commentators took issue with this negative judgment—

pre-eminently W. E. B. Du Bois, who chided his fellow blacks for being "tremendously sensitive"—understandably, he acknowledged, since previous portraits of black life had been merely the "occasion for an ugly picture, a dirty allusion, a nasty comment or a pessimistic forecast." But *Chillun*, Du Bois argued, was something different and better—human and credible—and O'Neill deserved applause for "bursting through."[52]

Perhaps taking her cue from Du Bois—whose comments had appeared in the playbill for *Chillun*—but at any rate sharing his opinion, Essie argued that "Mr. Negro-With-a-Chip-On-His-Shoulder," intent on emphasizing the negative implications in *Chillun* of a black from a good family's marrying a "white trollop," ought instead to concentrate on "the important thing"—"that he marries a white girl at all"; "O'Neill has dared to make the Negro fine and chivalrous and ambitious, and the white girl weak and pathetic by contrast." Essie insisted that all blacks "ought to be glad and proud" that Paul had demonstrated to whites that "Negro life is interesting and colorful" and forced them to "see that a Negro can act." She believed that, because of Paul's breakthrough performance, henceforth "plays will be written for us" and black actors "will find themselves on Broadway instead of at the Lafayette." But Paul was less sanguine and far more affected than Essie by the hostile response to *Chillun* from a portion of the black intelligentsia. When his gloom continued, Essie tried to amuse him "by comparing articles in the white press which said the play was an insult to the white race, with articles in the Negro press which said it was an insult to the Negro race."[53]

But Paul was still sufficiently concerned six months later to tell *Opportunity* magazine (the organ of the National Urban League and chief purveyor of the New Negro movement in literature) that he read *Chillun* as the story of "the struggle of a man and woman, both fine struggling human beings, against forces they could not control, indeed, scarcely comprehend, accentuated by the almost Christ-like spiritual force of the Negro husband—a play of great strength and beautiful spirit, mocking all petty prejudice. . . ." He argued that the negative reaction to the play among some blacks was one of "the most serious drawbacks to the development of a true Negro dramatic literature. We are too self-conscious, too afraid of showing all phases of our life—especially those phases which are of greatest dramatic value. The great mass of our group discourage any member who has the courage to fight these petty prejudices." He acknowledged "being damned all over the place for playing in *All God's Chillun*," and also acknowledged feeling annoyed at the criticism: "Those who object most strenuously know mostly nothing of the play and . . . in any event know little of the theater"; nor did they seem to recognize that O'Neill is "a broad, liberal-minded man" who "has had Negro friends and appreciated them for their true worth. He would be the last to cast any slur on the colored people."[54]

Chillun had a profitable run, playing alternate weeks with *The Emperor Jones* through June, then alone through July, and reopening for yet another two months, this time to nonsubscription audiences and standing-room-only crowds in mid-August; it finally closed on October 10, 1924, after a total run of one hundred performances. Robeson's double success had propelled him into the tiny front rank of Afro-American artists, more universally applauded by white intellectuals than by blacks but recognized even by dissenting blacks as superbly gifted. As Augustin Duncan, who had directed him in *Taboo,* wrote to Robeson, "I know you will go on now from one big success to another," adding prophetically, "and I believe your successes will be more than personal successes."[55]

The great point now was, What next? Paul had earned a total salary of only $1,782.15 from Provincetown for the entire year of 1924—and no attractive new vehicle for him was immediately forthcoming. Essie's salary from her job at Presbyterian was still their chief source of income, but she was "sick to death of the Lab," and wrote in her diary in mid-August, "do hope I won't have to go back." Paul began to show renewed signs of restlessness, and began to express anxiety about whether it might not make sense, after all, for him to return to the law. He told a newspaper interviewer in June 1924 that he himself preferred the stage—feeling "as if I were already much farther along in that line than in the lawyer's career" and feeling "sure that I would have more opportunity on the stage to benefit my race." But he acknowledged that many friends, convinced he should be the next Booker T. Washington, had continued mildly to rebuke him for deserting the law, and that he had not yet definitely decided which career choice to make. Essie encouraged him to give the theater another five years before making a final decision, though it would not take that long. In the interlude, the Robesons were able to distract themselves with the assorted pleasures of his newfound celebrity.[56]

■

CHAPTER 5

The Harlem Renaissance
and the Spirituals

(1924–1925)

Antonio Salemmé, a promising young Italian-American sculptor, was at work in his Washington Square studio in Greenwich Village one day when a friend dropped by to tell him he *had* to see "this black actor" doing *Emperor Jones* at a theater only two blocks away. Tony went to a performance the next day. "It was just a little basement theater," he remembered many years later. "And for the first time I see this Paul Robeson, sweating, running away from the drums. . . . I was terribly impressed. I thought, 'My God, this guy is not only a great actor but he's beautiful.' I mean, I saw a statue. All I could think of was a statue."[1]

Salemmé went backstage after the performance, asked Robeson if he would pose for him—and offered him 25 percent of the sale price if he sold the statue. Robeson "was very businesslike, because he needed money" (when Tony later met Essie, he found her "twice as businesslike"—"hard-boiled, absolutely adamant and independent. Drove a hard bargain and didn't make friends"). Robeson said he'd change clothes and go around to Salemmé's studio for coffee with him and his wife, Betty Hardy. "He arrived as if he'd been there a hundred times before. You could see he was collegiate, perfectly dressed, and you could never guess that he'd been sweating, doing *Emperor Jones* less than an hour before. He had this presence, which was both dignified and disarming at the same time. He was very much himself, a very strong presence, but not a presence that would embarrass you or that would make you nervous. He made you feel at home. He himself was at home. That's the point. He had no need to impress, and if he was impressed with you, he didn't show it, didn't make any fuss over it. You knew you had met somebody unusual. There was no mannerism of any sort. Absolute authenticity. He spoke slowly, and he took his time about everything. He never looked at his watch. Paul had this air of not going anywhere, and yet he traveled very fast. That's one hell of a trick to pull off. . . . He was a born gentleman . . . deeply a man of good will."[2]

Before the first visit was over, the two men had agreed to begin work immediately, and Paul came to pose for two hours nearly every day for months. Tony placed him in a standing position, with his hands upraised ("He has wonderful spiritual qualities. . . . His hands upraised [represent his] great healing qualities"). "Now, all right, Paul," Tony would say, "just think of 'Deep River.' " Paul would slowly raise his arms, lost in concentration, and then would start to sing. The voice was so beautiful, Tony didn't know whether to work or just to listen. His first impression held—Paul was a man of dignity, patience, and humor, a "self-contained man, highly evolved, a beautifully clear person, withdrawn in the true sense but without being moody. If there was nothing to say, he wouldn't say anything."

The intermittent sittings ultimately spread over a two-year period due to Paul's other commitments. When the larger-than-life-size statue was completed in 1926, its "spiritual" qualities were not widely appreciated, though Salemmé considered the work "the highest achievement of my art." Philanthropist Otto Kahn came to his studio and sent him a check for five hundred dollars—but did not make an offer for the statue. Ruth Hale (Mrs. Heywood Broun) dropped by and thought the statue so beautiful she cried. The official art world was less enamored. The nude figure stood for a year in the Palace of the Legion of Honor in San Francisco, and in 1930 the Sculptors' Committee of the Philadelphia Art Alliance asked Salemmé to submit it for exhibition. He did—and all hell broke loose. Some worried souls on the executive committee of the Alliance were filled with alarm at the prospect of a naked black man going on public display; the statue was recrated and returned to Salemmé along with a letter explaining that it could not be exhibited because "the colored problem seems to be unusually great in Philadelphia." Asked by the press to comment, Salemmé said, "We sculptors don't sell many statues in Philadelphia." Asked by the Alliance to submit another work in place of the Robeson figure, he sent a plaster Venus.[3]

While the sittings were still in progress, Paul and Tony would sometimes take a break by going off to see an art exhibit together. Tony became something of a guide to Paul in the unfamiliar areas of painting and sculpture, making distinctions that were new for him between work that was "modernist," "realist," or (the term Salemmé preferred for his own art) "classical contemporary." He found Paul "a quick study"—in art and in everything. According to Essie, Paul, on his side, "always remembered those afternoons in the cool quiet galleries. Pictures began to mean something to him." He absorbed additional ideas from the many artists and critics who periodically dropped by Tony's studio—like the sculptor Arthur Lee, who had just won the Widener Medal, or the painter Niles Spencer, or Monroe Wheeler (future curator of the Museum of Modern Art) and his lover, the writer Glenway Wescott.[4]

Before long, the Salemmés and the Robesons began to socialize. Betty Salemmé and Essie became friendly, but Tony never grew close to Essie, continuing to find her too much "on guard" for congeniality—she had "no light touch, no give and take. You didn't become fond of Essie. You became fond of Paul. You got to love Paul." Yet Tony, at least in retrospect, was somewhat sympathetic to Essie's wariness: "Paul was adored by all the women he ever met. Women absolutely swooned over Paul. Paul was pursued, and sometimes caught. You'd have to be a saint not to fool around with a few women who absolutely adored you. And Paul was a saint, in a way. He was never boastful. He was never a show-off. If a woman made it possible for him to go to bed with her, you never heard anything about it. You only—you had to see it. If you didn't, you'd never know it."[5]

Salemmé did see it, and did know it: not only did Paul and Niles Spencer's wife become lovers for a time, but so did Paul and Betty Salemmé. Tony and Betty (who was a famed beauty) had always agreed on an unconventional marriage—indeed, another of her lovers had bought Tony his studio. The couple's close friend Monroe Wheeler sixty years later described Betty Salemmé's enthusiasm for Paul as "boundless," and Wheeler came to share her view, growing "terribly fond" of Paul (on the other hand, he was put off by Essie's "extreme ambition").[6]

While recognizing that Paul would never be confined to a monogamous union, Tony Salemmé nonetheless believed he could not have found a more suitable wife than Essie. "Paul spent money easily, he wasn't penny-pinching, and money went right through him. And so Essie had all the difficulty. She was almost motherly toward him. She fed him. She defended him. He needed Essie to protect him, to sign papers and to call up somebody and make a loan or something like that. Essie didn't make him famous. She merely did some of his business . . . and she was very patient, because she must have guessed that he was attractive to a lot of women. So that was a lot for Essie to bear, wasn't it? She had her dignity. She didn't want to fuss about it enough to lose face. And Paul appreciated Essie. He wasn't going to give her up. He was very smart. He knew people and knew values. And he had a steadiness in himself, which was automatic. He wasn't flighty. I don't think he'd be secure with another woman. He was secure with Essie. That was where he was smart."[7]

Paul and Essie took their new white friends up to Harlem and introduced them to their new friends among black movers and shakers. During the summer of 1924, the Robesons became friendly with Gladys and Walter White (the zesty, charming NAACP officer), who were themselves moving to the center of an interracial network of artists, cultural brokers, partygoers, and political activists. Also part of that circle were Grace Nail

Johnson and her husband, James Weldon Johnson, lawyer, songwriter, editor, diplomat, cultural critic, educator—and the NAACP's executive secretary. Johnson held patriotic and integrationist views that put him at odds with the separatist black leader Marcus Garvey and his followers, and also with some of the attitudes of W. E. B. Du Bois, who placed more emphasis than Johnson did on the need to cherish what was unique in black life (rather than assimilate into white culture).[8]

Robeson would in later years move strongly in the direction of Du Bois, but in the twenties he found the sentiments of James Weldon Johnson congenial. Interviewed by the *Herald Tribune* in July 1924, Robeson told the reporter that he didn't "in the least minimize what I am up against as a negro," but nonetheless stressed opportunities rather than obstacles:

> I may be a bit optimistic, but I think if I'm a good enough actor . . . I can go pretty far. All actors are limited by their physique. A slender five-footer can't play a giant; a buxom heavyweight lady can't play an ingenue. Well, I've got limitations, too—size and color. Same limitations as other actors have, plus . . .

For the present, Robeson believed,

> I can do no better than to do my own work and develop myself to [the] best of my ability. . . . If I do become a first-rate actor, it will do more toward giving people a slant on the so-called Negro problem than any amount of propaganda and argument.

The *Tribune,* of course, was a white-run paper addressed to a white readership, and it might be assumed that Robeson tailored and toned down his views accordingly. Yet he sounded at least as moderate and optimistic when discussing his opinions with a leading black publication—A. Philip Randolph and Chandler Owen's *Messenger.* On the subject of racial barriers, Robeson was quoted in *The Messenger* as saying, "What are the opportunities? Just what I will make them . . . I honestly feel that my future depends mostly upon myself." And in an interview he gave the following year, he is quoted as saying:

> The stories my old dad used to tell me [about slavery] are vivid in my memory; but—well, those bad times are over. What we have got to do is to go forward. There is still too much wild talk about the colour question; some of it wounds me deeply, but I don't let myself get morbid about it. I conserve my energies for my work as an actor. I realize that art can bridge the gulf between the white and black races. . . .[9]

In stressing art as a solvent for racism, Robeson was articulating a characteristic position of Harlem Renaissance intellectuals: racial advance would come primarily through individual artistic achievement, not as the result of political pressure and polemics. As he emphasized in his interview with *The Messenger*, "it is by proving our artistic capacity that we will be best recognized . . . it is through art we are going to come into our own." To the minimal extent he was political at all in these years, he looked to individual cultural achievement—not organized, collective action—as the likeliest channel for the advance of the race. As he told *The Messenger*, "So today Roland Hayes is infinitely more a racial asset than many who 'talk' at great length." (Even Du Bois, who in the twenties was already growing disenchanted with the ideology of art and moving toward the vehicle of direct political protest, continued to sound this common renaissance note of cultural elitism, continued to stress the central role a "talented tenth" would play in advancing the fortunes of the race.) Yet unlike many renaissance figures, Robeson referred at least once in the twenties (as he often would ten years later) to "the culture of ancient Africa" as being, alongside contemporary black achievements, part of the proof of the "artistic stature" of black people—as indeed "above all things" something "we boast of."[10]

Moreover, if he had decided not to "get morbid" about racial slurs, he did not deny that he had felt deeply wounded by them. He even occasionally acknowledged their toll to his white friends. Tony Salemmé recalls that Paul would "sometimes arrive looking depressed." When Tony asked him what was wrong, Paul would quietly answer, "Oh, . . . I went to see an old friend of mine uptown, and I had to take the freight elevator." Once in a while in the telling Paul would get "a little angry," but he had long since learned to keep a lid on his feelings, especially in front of whites, and especially since Salemmé glibly counseled him to take "a philosophical attitude," to "recognize" that little could be done at the moment about racial prejudice.[11]

The Robesons' friendship with the Whites and the Johnsons soon deepened. On one of their evenings together, White confided that his new novel about racism in a Southern town, *Fire in the Flint*, might be filmed, and if so he wanted Paul in the leading role. Soon after, he sent them a copy. Ma Goode read it first and pronounced it "wonderful." Essie came home the following week to find Paul "crying and cursing over Walter's book . . . a supreme compliment, for Paul never cries except when deeply moved. He says the book is very fine and also thrilling." Many literary contemporaries, including Sinclair Lewis, agreed, and Carl Van Vechten, the white writer who was rapidly becoming a spur and spokesman for the black literary renaissance, immediately asked Alfred Knopf, White's publisher, for an introduction to the writer. After the two men spent several hours together, Van Vechten wrote a friend that Walter White "speaks

French and talks about Debussy and Marcel Proust in an offhand way. An entirely new kind of Negro to me." White reported to the Robesons that Van Vechten and his wife, the actress Fania Marinoff, "both feel the novel will make a marvelous play, and suggested Paul would be the ideal man to cast as the hero." "Things look interesting," Essie wrote in her diary.[12]

In January 1925 the Robesons themselves met Van Vechten and his petite, vivacious wife (whom Van Vechten always referred to as "Marinoff") for the first time at the Whites', where the other guests included the Johnsons; Julius ("Jules") Bledsoe, the young black baritone; James Weldon Johnson's brother J. Rosamond Johnson, the musician and singer; and George Gershwin, who played *Rhapsody in Blue* and some of his songs for the group. It was a "wonderful time," Essie wrote in her diary—the first of many with the Van Vechtens and their gifted circle. Van Vechten's genius, disputed in all else, is unchallenged in his role as host; pink-faced and white-maned, exotically gowned in a cerise-and-gold mandarin robe—resembling, in the words of one frequent guest, "the Dowager Empress of China gone slightly berserk"—Van Vechten would pass happily from guest to guest, assuring them that he felt blessed by their talented presence. A shrewd estimate of Van Vechten comes from Lincoln Kirstein, who first met him in 1926: "Carl was a dandy. . . . He understood elegance, a contemporary elegance, in a way no American before him conceived it. . . . Carl saw the fantastic in the ordinary, discovered the natural flair, verbal brilliance, humor and pathos in the so-called 'ordinary' life of Harlem. He was of the tribe of Beau Brummel, of Byron, of Baudelaire, and of Ronald Firbank. . . . Carl adored cats. To me, he always seemed to be an enormous, blond kitty; sometimes he purred; he could scratch. Sometimes he just blinked like a cat whose mysteries and opinions are privately wise. Like a cat, he preferred the cream of life. . . . He did not mind being stroked. . . ."[13]

Two weeks after their initial meeting, the Robesons were back at the Van Vechtens' for another party; this one again included Gershwin, Alfred Knopf, the Johnsons, the Whites, Jules Bledsoe—and also Otto Kahn and dancer Adele Astaire (whom Essie described as having "the friendliest grin and is so sweet and loveable"). Van Vechten wrote a friend that "seven Negroes were present" at the party, "all of them interesting one way or another," and that Robeson "singing spirituals is really a thrilling experience. . . ." The glamorous gatherings alternated between the homes of the Van Vechtens and the Whites, interspersed with somewhat more sedate teas at the James Weldon Johnsons'. Before long the Van Vechtens became the chummily familiar "Carlo and Fania" (she is "quite the sweetest thing I know," Essie wrote in her diary, adding in praise that both the Van Vechtens "seemed devoted" to Ella, their maid). Van Vechten reported to his friend Gertrude Stein, "I have passed practically my whole winter in company with Negroes and have succeeded in getting into most of the important *sets*. . . . One of my best friends, Paul Robeson . . . is a great actor and when he sings spirituals he is as great as Chaliapin. I want you to meet him."[14]

Essie carefully noted in her diary the star-studded lists of guests she and Paul now met regularly on their round of parties. At the Van Vechtens', Theodore Dreiser told Paul he had seen *The Emperor Jones* six times, and took him aside for a long talk. At the Whites', the panoply of glamour included Sherwood Anderson, Ruth Hale and Heywood Broun, Prince Kojo Touvalou Houenou of Dahomey (nephew of the deposed King and a graduate in law and medicine from the Sorbonne, active in publicizing French colonial injustices—Essie found him "a typical African in appearance, but charming and cultured and interesting"), Roland Hayes, the novelist Jessie Fauset, René Maran (the French West Indian author of *Batouala* who had won the Goncourt Prize in 1921), the poet Witter Bynner ("tall and clumsy and very friendly. I never saw anything quite so funny and froglike as he attempts to do the tango with Gladys [White], and his attempts at the 'Charleston' "), Louise Brooks (she "was very late and I couldn't wait for her, but . . . Paul said she was very conceited and impossible"), and the red-haired singer Nora Holt (Ray), half Scottish, half Negro, known for her dalliances. ("Her trail is strewn with bones," Van Vechten wrote H. L. Mencken, "many of them no longer hard"). Essie "couldn't bear her," called her "a red hot mama," and announced that "If she ever went after Paul I'd eat her alive, and I meant it, and they know I did."[15]

Sometimes a group would go from a party to catch a midnight show at a Harlem hot spot like Club Alabam' or to dance to Fletcher Henderson's big band, the Rainbow Orchestra. The covey of celebrities among whom the Robesons now found themselves was further filled out by introductions to the likes of George Jean Nathan, Laurence Stallings, and Mark and Carl Van Doren at Blanche and Alfred Knopf's home, and to Jean Toomer and Countee Cullen at the James Weldon Johnsons'. Paul agreed to sing at a reception given to celebrate Cullen's graduation from NYU—as he sometimes also did at parties—but despite that, Essie, never one to pull punches, found the NYU affair "a fearful bore." Occasionally she even found one of the parties distasteful. The "little gathering" put together by Eric Waldron, the young black short-story writer who was a staff member on *Opportunity,* struck Essie as "a beastly bore—some little insignificant talkative Negroes" (the evening was redeemed only by a quick stop-off at Gladys and Walter White's house en route to the gathering for a fashionable smoke).[16]

Between the rounds of parties with their new acquaintances, Paul and Essie somehow found the time and energy to maintain ties to old pals like Bud Fisher and Minnie Sumner (who remained Essie's closest friend, as well as chief seamstress). The Robesons also kept up with friends they had made among the Provincetown Players, especially Jimmy Light, and occasionally Agnes Boulton and Eugene O'Neill. Essie was particularly fond of Agnes (whom O'Neill divorced a few years later)—"I surely find her more sweet, unaffected and charming every time I see her."[17]

One night in July 1925 Gene O'Neill, accompanied by the Provincetown actor–stage manager Harold ("Gig") McGhee and his wife, Bert—who were to become lifelong friends of the Robesons—went up to Paul and Essie's apartment on 127th Street for what turned into a marathon night of partying. It began with cocktails at the Robesons', dinner at Craig's (the popular hangout for Harlem literati), followed by a trip to see Johnny Nit dance at the Lincoln Theater. Then, to cool off from the hot night, it was back to the Robesons' for more cocktails ("Gene talked a great deal") and an hour of Paul singing (Gene "seemed to enjoy it so much"). Following that respite, they headed out again, this time to catch the midnight show of Eddie Rector's band at the Lafayette. Then it was on to Small's cabaret, where Gene and Essie danced together and Gene treated orchestra and waiters to drinks. He "was royal," Essie wrote in her diary, apparently not knowing that up until that night O'Neill had been on the wagon for the few months preceding, and that his evening tour of Harlem would set him off on a new two-week binge. Essie paid Gene her supreme compliment—a "regular guy"—and at 5:30 a.m. the party moved on to the Vaudeville Comedy Club; since "there wasn't much doing," they didn't go in, instead returning to the Robesons' apartment after stopping off for ice cream on the way. Back home, Gene "talked by the hour—all about his thoughts on 'Jones,' on Paul, on London, himself, etc.—he is simply fascinating." Among the fascinating things he said was that he had a new play in mind—about a "loveable gambler"—and also wanted to write "another play about the 'Emperor Jones' leading up to where 'Emperor Jones' starts in." After breakfast, the party broke up at 9:00 a.m.[18]

By 1925 Bert and Gig McGhee began to figure prominently among the Robesons' friends. Given the proximity of the McGhees' apartment to the Provincetown Playhouse, the two couples would together catch the theater's latest offering—they were especially delighted with Gilbert and Sullivan's *Patience*—or socialize with fellow Provincetowners. One night they dropped into a party at the home of set designer Cleon Throckmorton, but the party was a bit too "wild" for Essie's taste, and they didn't stay long—she "was shocked to see Mrs. Throckmorton and a guest in as near no clothes as I've ever seen a woman in on or off stage." When Jimmy Light directed *S.S. Glencairn,* a cycle of O'Neill sea plays, he had them down to the Provincetown to see it, and on opening night of *Desire Under the Elms,* Light had the O'Neills and Robesons to dinner before the premiere (Essie thought the play "marvelous, powerful, real"); the round of post-theater parties went on until 4:30 a.m. The Robesons had taken to the Village scene, and now that the McGhees were becoming intimates, they talked over the possibility of actually moving there, though nothing came of the idea.[19]

The Robesons were also becoming close friends with the Rumanian-Jewish-gypsy writer Konrad Bercovici and his common-law wife, Naomi, a painter and sculptor deeply involved as well in the Modern School movement. The two couples had met through Walter White, whom Bercovici had gotten to know while writing a series of articles for the *World* on the Ku Klux Klan (when the articles appeared, a bonfire was set on the Bercovici lawn). The Bercovicis' place had become a gathering spot in New York City for artists and intellectuals: "We like simple, fine people with vision," Naomi told a reporter. But their landlords and neighbors did not equate "fine" with "Negro," and the Bercovicis, rather than give up their friends, had to move several times before finally settling at 95 Riverside Drive.[20]

The Bercovicis had their share of famous guests, and the Robesons met most of them—including Georges Enescu, the Rumanian violinist and composer, and Zuloaga, the Spanish painter, who told Essie he would rather paint her than the famously beautiful Gladys White. (Of course he would, the Bercovicis' daughters, Rada and Mirel, remarked playfully many years later—"Essie was a Cardozo.") Usually the Robesons would spend the evening alone with the Bercovicis and their children, Paul often singing to them. Their nineteen-year-old son, "the redoubtable Gorky," might enliven an evening by raging against the falsity of modern life or, as on one night, by taking on the Provincetown Players as "a lot of po-seurs." The daughters do not remember Essie fondly—"cold and very aggressive"—but in Paul, according to Rada, "you sensed depth . . . a presence. . . . It was dark, vast, with shadows." With Mirel, age seven in 1925, Paul developed special rapport: the two would go off to eat ice cream, ride the double-decker bus, and have "long conversations about life"; he made her feel that they "were on the same wavelength."[21]

Paul continued to put in public appearances, perform an occasional concert, mull over suggested new projects, and meet with agents and entrepreneurs. But for a year following his Provincetown triumphs no single offer caught his full attention. The hiatus gave him time for making further professional contacts and for the creative idling characteristic of him. During the year's "lull," he spoke at the Rutgers Freshman Banquet in February 1925 ("It was quite an honor for them to want him," Essie wrote in her diary), appeared as guest of honor at the Rutgers Junior Banquet at the Hotel Martinique in March, and sang at the NAACP's annual conference in 1924 (although he occasionally put in a benefit appearance for the NAACP, he was not connected in any vital way to the organization; as late as 1927, he had not even met Mary White Ovington, chairman of the board). He also did some part-time football coaching at

Rutgers for a few weeks in the fall of 1924, and gave a concert there in December. (Meeting one of Paul's old professors, who commented on his modesty in the face of accelerating fame, Essie laughingly replied that Paul was still "just a big boy.") Paul had opened in a brief revival of *Jones* at the Provincetown only two nights before the Rutgers concert, but they had let him go off to keep the engagement. "Fitzi" Fitzgerald, the company's manager and mother confessor, engaged Gilpin to replace Paul for the night, and advertised his appearance; but (according to Essie) "Gilpin couldn't learn the lines in time," so the performance was canceled.[22]

Paul sang a few other concerts during these same months, both in public halls and at private parties in wealthy white homes. His most notable public appearance—his first formal concert, arranged by the socialite Mrs. Guy Currier—was in early November 1924, at the Copley Plaza Hotel in Boston. Paul and Essie were nervous about the outcome—even though Harry T. Burleigh, the distinguished black composer and arranger of spirituals, lent a hand in running over the music with Paul before the concert. It went well: the ballroom was packed, the applause generous. Paul's private concert, and the reception following, at the Clarence C. Pell home at Westbury, Long Island, dazzled Essie: the Pell limousine met the train, the Pell home was "lovely," and the Pell guests "delightfully appreciative" of Paul's program of spirituals.[23]

Late in 1924 Essie concluded arrangements with the black filmmaker Oscar Micheaux for Paul to star opposite Julia Theresa Russell (Micheaux's future sister-in-law) in the movie *Body and Soul.* Micheaux, a former Pullman porter, had begun making movies a decade earlier and wrote, produced, and directed some thirty-five films, all independently made, all with black casts for black audiences. Essie was delighted to get contract terms from Micheaux that called for 3 percent of the gross after the first forty thousand dollars in receipts and a salary of one hundred dollars per week for three weeks. In this, his cinematic debut, Robeson carried off his double assignment as a fast-talking, pleasure-seeking, corrupt pastor *and* his utterly sincere, good-natured brother with equal assurance—projecting through both portraits a powerfully physical, charismatic film presence. Immediately afterward, in January 1925, Robeson reopened in *The Emperor Jones* for a limited run on Broadway. A new string of well-wishers trooped backstage to offer congratulations, including Roland Hayes, who "raved about the show."[24]

Another visitor backstage was Richard J. Madden of the American Play Company, who was also O'Neill's literary agent. He told Paul that Sir Alfred Butt, the English producer, had seen the show and was interested in negotiating for a London production. Essie was "thrilled" but cautious; only a few months before, she had followed up George Jean Nathan's suggestion of a German production of *Jones* directed by Max Reinhardt, only to have the prospect fall through. Alfred Butt, however, to the Robesons' delight, immediately opened detailed negotiations through Madden. Within a week of their initial contact, Madden and Essie had come to tentative terms that she rightly considered "splendid"—three hundred dollars a week, double ocean-liner passage over and back to Europe, six weeks' guarantee, and 5 percent of the gross over one thousand dollars. Essie, understandably, was "dying to sign the contract," but negotiations continued to spin out for a while longer. In the interim, Paul kept busy sitting for an oil portrait by Mabel Dwight and for a sketch by the Bavarian-born artist Winold Reiss, performing a scene from *Jones* on the radio, consulting Marshall Bartholomew and Paul Draper about vocal problems, and paying frequent visits with Essie to the concert halls and theaters (Essie found Walter Hampden's *Othello* a "beastly bore").[25]

By far the most significant professional development in these months was Paul's reconnection with Lawrence Brown, whom he had met back in 1922 when in England playing *Voodoo*. Larry had already earned a considerable reputation as Roland Hayes's accompanist and as a superlative arranger of spirituals. Arriving back in New York in March 1925, Larry found Paul "the same serious, quiet and pondering young man" he had known earlier and started going over to the Robesons' apartment to sing and play for Paul. Within a few weeks, they decided to work together professionally, and drew up a formal contract that called for joint billing and divided up receipts equally, with 10 percent going to Essie as their agent. When Van Vechten first met Larry in 1925, he was bemused. "He does his best to avoid me," Carlo complained to Essie; "everything considered, his antipathy for me is somewhat inexplicable." Not really, Essie wrote back, not "when you think of his black and white complex—which is very strong." Larry, unlike the Robesons, did not trust whites, or particularly enjoy their company. As a gay man, moreover, he may have had additional grounds for distrusting Van Vechten, who, it was widely rumored, had a special penchant for black men.[26]

Paul and Larry began to practice together nearly every day, "making wonderful progress" from the start, convincing Essie that "they are a perfect combination." She had also become convinced, during her march through the concert halls, that Paul was the equal of the Russian bass Fyodor Chaliapin in dramatic power (though not in experience and confidence)—an opinion that annoyed Paul, who said she sounded like "a silly, adoring wife." Not *even* Chaliapin, Essie persisted, had Paul's indefinable power to "come out onto the stage and immediately enslave an audience before he had opened his mouth. None had his graciousness, his simplicity, his friendliness with an audience." Given the uncertainty of theatrical employment, especially for a black actor, Essie began to cast about for a way for Paul to establish a separate career as a concert artist, so that he could alternate between the two professions as opportunities presented themselves, without being solely dependent on either.[27]

The way, she decided, was through the spirituals—those very songs she herself had earlier dismissed as "monotonous and uninteresting" before hearing Paul interpret them. (Paul, in turn, credited Larry Brown with having "guided me to the beauty of our own folk music and to the music of all other Peoples so like our own.") Essie believed Paul's regal, "typically Negro" physique, his "unspoiled Negro voice . . . full of over and undertones," and its "peculiar husky coloring," enabled him "through some deep racial instinct" to identify more completely with the spirituals than could other black singers of the day, whose overly cultivated technical training and repertoire of European art songs kept them at a distance from those "simple songs." She believed Paul, on the other hand, could bring them to a large interracial audience and to the level of art. Avery Robinson, the white Southerner who had transcribed the Afro-American work song "Water Boy," confirmed Essie's judgment; hearing Paul sing that song, Robinson told him he was the only person who sang it exactly as the black chain gang had when he first heard it.[28]

The hoped-for opportunity opened up through Carl Van Vechten. Larry and Paul performed the spirituals at the Van Vechtens' home one night, and (according to Essie) "Carlo was amazed and just begged for more and more songs," raving "about Paul's voice and Larry's lovely arrangements of the songs." Others at the Van Vechtens' that night included Lawrence Langner of the Theatre Guild, the actress Mary Ellis, and the Knopfs, and all expressed delight; Mary Ellis called Carlo the next day to say it had been "the most thrilling evening she had ever spent." Carlo immediately offered his considerable help in arranging for a public concert. With that backing, Essie went straight to the Provincetowners. They gave her, free of charge, their Greenwich Village theater—its small space perfect for an intimate concert—and Stella Hanau and Katherine Gay, who did publicity for the Players, contributed their services as well, securing newspaper advertisements on credit and defraying the costs of printing circulars, posters, and tickets. Within a week of the evening at the Van Vechtens', a concert date was announced for April 19, 1925. Larry Brown made up a program and coached Robeson "as if," in Paul's words, "we were children he was teaching" (and, he added, "we slept like children all week, not to catch a cold"). Carlo, with additional support from Walter White, personally talked up the concert and mailed out circulars to his friends. On April 18, the day before the recital, Heywood Broun devoted his column in the New York *World* to touting it.[29]

Partly as a result of Broun's friendly press-agentry, "the word" (in the recollection of the Brouns' son) "was all over smart New York that anyone who failed to hear this new young singer had missed out on the music event of the year." By 7:30 p.m. on the night of the concert, even standing room had been sold out, and an excited crowd gathered on the sidewalk clamoring for seats. The capacity audience inside the theater exceeded the fire limit, and hundreds were turned away; part of the overflow stood in the wings offstage, where they could hear if not see the performance. The Provincetowners themselves turned out in a body, dressed, like much of the audience, in formal evening clothes. Paul and Larry were understandably nervous. Millia Davenport, the Provincetown costume designer, remembers that Paul—"the bravest man I ever knew"—stood in the wings "paralyzed with fright," the back of his tuxedo "soaked through"; "with all my strength I [pushed him] onto the stage—to make history."[30]

A roar of applause lasting three minutes greeted them and punctuated every one of the sixteen numbers thereafter. At the end of the concert, the reception was thunderous, with curtain calls and an additional sixteen encores following one after another until finally, exhausted and happy, Paul and Larry brought the evening to a close by having the houselights turned up. "Everybody was wildly hilarious," Essie wrote in her diary, "and we are very, very happy." The Robesons went off to the house of Donald Angus, an intimate friend of Van Vechten's (and rumored to be his lover), to celebrate—along with Carlo and Fania, the James Weldon Johnsons, the Walter Whites, the Salemmés, and a half-dozen other friends. Robeson felt deeply indebted to Van Vechten; two years after the concert, on his way to perform in Europe, he wrote him, "Every time I appear in a strange capital I shall think of that first concert and your unselfish interest and thank you all over again. Because it was you who made me sing."[31]

The next day the critics confirmed the event as a triumph—and for once were able to specify why. The concert marked the first time a black soloist—rather than a choral group, such as the remarkable Fisk Jubilee Singers, who had preceded Robeson by sixty years—had devoted an entire program to spirituals and secular songs. Earlier, artists like Roland Hayes had included one or two groups of Afro-American songs in a concert, but the music had been considered—by many blacks, too—as unsuited to a full evening's presentation because of its supposed monotony. Yet, as arranged by Larry Brown (and, in one of the four sets, by H. T. Burleigh), the actual range of the songs proved a revelation, the "wistful resignation" of "By an' By" or "Steal Away" alternating with the "joyously abandoned" "Joshua Fit de Battle of Jericho," the "proud, tragic utterance" of "Go Down, Moses," and the "sardonic, secular humor" of "Scandalize My Name." As one critic remarked with astonishment, the emotional stretch of the material included "infinite pathos, infinite gaiety, a sort of desperate wildness and an occasional majesty." Brown was praised for the skill of his arrangements, Robeson for the power of "a luscious, mellow bass-baritone" which lent the songs "an overwhelming inward conviction." In summing up the general enthusiasm, one reviewer hailed Robeson as both "the embodiment of the aspirations of the New Negro" and as "destined to be the new American Caruso." Du Bois sent Robeson and Brown a succinct note: "May I tell you how much I enjoyed the fine concert last night. It was very beautiful."[32]

Occasionally a reviewer linked Robeson and Roland Hayes as both singing the spirituals with "parlor manners," but far more typical was the way Carl Sandburg drew a distinction between the two: "Hayes imitates white culture and uses methods from the white man's conservatories of music, so that when he sings a Negro spiritual the audience remarks, 'What technic; what a remarkable musical education he must have had!' When Paul Robeson sings spirituals, the remark is: 'That is the real thing—he has kept the best of himself and not allowed the schools to take it away from him!' " Indeed, a number of critics commented on "the deep racial quality" Robeson manifested—on the combination of simplicity and emotional fervor he managed to convey. To the press, Robeson explained his affinity for the songs as a natural one going back to his childhood: he had "unconsciously absorbed the manner of singing spirituals as they should be sung" while participating in services, with a mostly rural Southern congregation, in his father's church. In taking the songs to the concert stage, Robeson was reported as saying he did not have to force his interpretation. He just let his memory "carry him back to that little church where he had heard them sung so often."[33]

Carl Van Vechten predicted that Paul's success would inspire a rash of new performers singing the spirituals, and he advised Essie not to delay in planning a tour—"For the moment he has the field to himself and consequently will be well known before these and many others get started." Van Vechten's prediction proved accurate. Within six months, five new books relating to the spirituals appeared, most notably Rosamond and James Weldon Johnson's *The Book of American Negro Spirituals,* containing Rosamond's arrangements of sixty-one spirituals and Weldon's fortypage preface, which favorably commented on Robeson's interpretations (both Paul and Essie thought the book "wonderful," and Paul would "pore over it, humming"). In October, Rosamond Johnson and the tenor Taylor Gordon gave several concerts utilizing material from the Johnsons' book, and the baritone Jules Bledsoe, too, included a group of spirituals in his Town Hall concert on October 17. ("This certainly is a spiritual winter," Van Vechten commented.)[34]

"I couldn't possibly ask for anything more," Robeson told a newspaper reporter. Yet more was to come—immediately and in profusion. The concert proved a watershed event in Robeson's career; his reputation was propelled into a stratosphere of acclaim where it would remain for some two dozen years. There was an immediate demand for more concerts, and an immediate assault from concert bureaus eager to arrange them. The agent Howard Kropf wanted to take Paul over for exclusive management and offered as enticement a ten-thousand-dollar advance—astonishing for that day. But Paul and Larry decided instead to go with James B. Pond; his commission (45 percent) was high and he offered no advance, but they liked him personally and he guaranteed Paul time off to appear in plays. They also signed an exclusive one-year contract with the Victor Talking Machine Company for "not less than three double-faced records," and in July began traveling out to Camden to record and do remakes. Paul found time, too, to sit for pictures for *Vanity Fair;* to perform, for fees ranging from $100 to $250, at private homes (at the famed Metropolitan Opera star Frances Alda's, the bathtub was filled with cracked ice and champagne, and she served them lobster salad, sandwiches, cake, and liquor "with her own hands"); and to appear at select public events—at the annual Equity dinner, at the Jewish Women's Committee at the Hotel Astor, and at the swank St. Philip's Protestant Episcopal, the wealthiest nonwhite church in the city ("the best type of colored people," Essie called them). They were concerned in advance about how the St. Philip's congregation would respond to mere "slave" songs, but the reception was enthusiastic.[35]

They also made time to keep up their social life. It ranged in appeal from an evening given by the sculptress Augusta Savage at Villa Lewaro, the mansion of the glamorous party giver A'Lelia Walker (Essie thought it "quite the most stupid party I've been to in a long time") to Chaliapin's farewell concert at the Met, after which the Robesons went backstage; Chaliapin patted Paul on the back, said he'd heard of him and wished him good luck. At an *Opportunity* dinner at the Fifth Avenue Restaurant, Essie disapprovingly noted the presence in their party of Zora Neale Hurston, whom Essie liked "less and less the more I see of her." She didn't specify why, but perhaps Hurston had already articulated the position she later publicly demonstrated, that formal "concerts" of black spirituals, with fixed prosceniums and passive audiences in the tradition of European culture, were a *disservice* to and distortion of the original visceral, communal spirit of the folk from whom the songs had arisen.[36]

Within a month of the Greenwich Village concert, Robeson was honored jointly with Walter White at an Egelloc Club dinner and invited with Larry Brown to attend and sing at one of the periodic luncheons the Dutch Treat Club (a gathering of artists and authors) gave for celebrities, making them honorary members in the process. Robeson and Brown did the entertaining, but were not elected to membership—though the third guest that day, the British explorer Major Forbes-Leith, who had recently completed an eight-thousand-mile motor trip from England to India, was inducted. A front-page article in the *World* the next day revealed that the club's membership had been split and that several were threatening to resign over the insult to Robeson and Brown. (Two months before, Robeson had been denied service at the Algonquin, even though his host had previously notified the management that Robeson would be coming as a guest.) The Dutch Treat's president, George B. Mallon, admitted that it was the "almost invariable" custom to confer honorary membership on guests invited to lunch. He had not done so with Robeson and Brown, Mallon claimed, because he had heard rumors of opposition and didn't want to risk embarrassing them with a less-than-unanimous response of "aye" from the membership. The night before the press storm broke, Essie had written in her diary that Paul and Larry had "had a wonderful time" at the Dutch Treat Club and had been "treated beautifully." Possibly they hadn't told her about the snub. Possibly they hadn't considered it a snub: Paul told the *World* he had not felt "slighted" for the simple reason that he hadn't known precisely what the Dutch Treat Club was—let alone the nature of its peculiar customs; he had thought he "was going down to sing some songs for some newspaper men."[37]

Still waiting to hear whether plans for a London production of *Jones* would go through, Paul mulled over a few other theatrical offers that had come his way. The most tempting was from the producer David Belasco, who wanted Paul, Florence Mills, and Charles Gilpin as the leads in Edward Sheldon's new play *Lulu Belle,* which he had co-authored with Charles MacArthur. A dozen years before, Sheldon's *Salvation Nell* had made him a theatrical lion; he had since been immobilized by a painful case of degenerative arthritis, yet had continued to write plays (though of late with no great success). After mulling over Belasco's offer, Paul decided to turn *Lulu Belle* down, concerned about its "stereotyped format." The play, a melodrama about Harlem street life, opened in February 1926 with a huge cast, featuring the Robesons' good friend Edna Thomas—and with both Leonore Ulric and Henry Hull (in the role that had been offered to Robeson) playing their parts in blackface (according to James Weldon Johnson, their makeup and dialect were "beyond detection"). *Lulu Belle* became a much-discussed hit, helping to propel additional swarms of whites into Harlem nightlife in search of "the real thing."[38]

In June 1925 the London production of *Jones* was finally set, after some protracted negotiations in which O'Neill had held out for Robeson's playing the lead over the original London producer's choice of Charles Gilpin. Robeson was additionally delighted because his old friends Jimmy Light and Gig McGhee were, respectively, chosen to direct and stage-manage. The Robesons booked passage to sail in early August for a September opening at the Ambassadors Theatre. In the meantime, they tried to set their financial situation to rights: a glowing set of future prospects wouldn't pay the accumulated bills at hand. They talked over the problem with Carl Van Vechten. He sounded out his friend, the writer Ettie Stettheimer, about the possibility of arranging a loan (Carlo assured Ettie that Paul was "one of the great artists, as great in his way as Nijinsky, Chaliapin, or Mary Garden. Please heed this!"), and suggested at the same time that Paul and Essie again approach Otto Kahn—and gave them some specific tips on how to proceed.[39]

Essie immediately got off a judiciously worded letter to Kahn. "My husband, Paul Robeson," she wrote, "is at the brink of what we hope will prove to be a very remarkable career. If you could see your way clear to act as his patron and back him for two years, we would surely try to make you never regret it in any way—in fact we would earnestly try to make you feel very proud to have helped him." Essie outlined Paul's immediate prospects—*The Emperor Jones* in London, the contracts with James Pond and Victor records, the one-third interest in Salemmé's statue—and, offering these as security, asked Kahn for a five-thousand-dollar loan. The money, she wrote, would be used for four purposes: to clear up their widely scattered debts (fifteen hundred dollars), to send Larry Brown south while they were in London "so he can collect new songs, compose new songs, and study Negro music, so we will have our material all ready when we begin our concert tour," to publish and copyright all the songs Larry had already composed and arranged (fifteen hundred dollars), and "to be able to live until August" and "study voice all he can" (five hundred dollars). Given the prospects that lay immediately ahead, Essie argued, they "could easily repay the loan at the end of two years," and, to demonstrate their "enormous possibilities," she suggested that Kahn allow her husband and Larry Brown to sing and talk with him at any convenient time, perhaps "at the home of our mutual friend Carl Van Vechten, or at any place you might designate."[40]

Kahn forwarded the letter to Van Vechten, with an appended note: "I know that you are much interested in Paul Robeson." In response, Van Vechten urged Kahn to see Robeson. Kahn knew that Van Vechten's recommendations were not automatic: on another occasion he had urged Kahn to turn down a writer's appeal for financial help with the tart comment "There are altogether too many people in Harlem with 'mouths full o' gimme, hands full o' much obliged' "—an attitude that "should be discouraged." Kahn arranged to have his private yacht, the *Oheka,* waiting at the foot of the East 23rd Street dock on June 28 to pick up the Robesons, the Van Vechtens, and Larry Brown and bring them to the Kahn estate at Cold Spring Harbor.[41]

Because of bad weather, a closed car was substituted for the yacht (and Donald Angus substituted for Fania), but otherwise the day went off without a hitch. Robeson and Brown performed for the Kahns and their half-dozen assembled guests; Kahn provided a tour of the grounds, and, after a long, private talk with Paul and Essie about Paul's career, announced that he had decided to give him the requested loan. The very next day, Kahn sent a check for twenty-five hundred dollars, to be secured by a pledge of the Robesons' five-thousand-dollar life-insurance policy and his contracts with Pond and Sir Alfred Butt in England; in a covering note Kahn assured them of "the pleasure it gave me to see you both yesterday and of my great and appreciative enjoyment of Mr. Robeson's singing." Essie immediately provided Kahn with the stipulated collateral, thanked him for his generosity—"It has all happened so quickly that we are still stunned by our good fortune"—conveyed Paul's offer to sing for the Kahns "at any time you wish him to do so—without charge," opened (with Van Vechten's help) a checking account at the Harlem branch of the Corn Exchange Bank, and requested from Kahn, and got, the second installment of twenty-five hundred dollars. Van Vechten counseled Essie henceforth to write all her business letters on a typewriter and to patronize a clipping bureau, while apologizing for "beginning to sound like a grandpa, always offering advice. Remember that it is the advice of a friend. Reject it when it does not meet your approval. The friendship will remain." In a postscript he added: "I have it in mind to write a letter to Mr. Kahn telling [him] that I have suggested to you—quite unnecessarily, as the idea had already occurred to you—that you keep silent in regard to his kindness at lunch as far as Harlem was concerned—for the present, to prevent his office from being deluged with indigent coloured folk. Further, that in case any such appealed to him, he should feel free to call me up and consult me. Further, I would say frankly that Paul Robeson is the only person, white or black, whom I know at present in which I could make this special plea."[42]

Now that money was no longer a pressing problem, the Robesons moved toward their European trip with assurance. Essie spent the exuberant final few weeks before sailing in shopping and making arrangements, while Paul prepared for a batch of concerts under James Pond's new management. Essie loved to shop but also to find discounts, and went along with Bert McGhee to the Little Jack Horner Thrift Shop to outfit herself with a green beaded gown, a black satin evening wrap, a negligee, and a rose dinner dress—all "wonderful bargains," "cheap as dirt"; she had them cleaned and took them to Minnie Sumner for alterations. Paul was indifferent to clothes—to most things material—but Essie took him off to Rogers Peet for made-to-order shirts, to Wallach's for a steamer cap and ties, and to Racitis for a suit.[43]

Pond arranged for half a dozen concert engagements in the month before departure. Paul and Larry gave two in Peterborough, New Hampshire, where the Cabots "were especially nice" to them—though one of the other socialites annoyed Essie: "She was so stupid, had never heard of O'Neill nor the *Emperor Jones,* and wanted Paul to tell her the plot of *Jones!*" Paul and Essie managed one quiet day together in New York—dinner at the Automat, a stroll down Broadway, a bad movie—and then left for two more concerts in Provincetown, on Cape Cod (both sold out), and a final one at Spring Lake (Paul, rarely punctual, made the train by a second, giving Essie "hysterics," but "the ocean breezes," she wrote Carlo, calmed their nerves). So did a visit with "Shag" Taylor, whom they stopped off to see in Boston after the Provincetown concerts. Taylor, a black graduate of Harvard, ran a famous drugstore on Tremont Street, where he dispensed support and advice to several generations of black students in the area. Shag hired a car, drove them all through Cambridge, and "as usual gave us Boston and the store."[44]

Back in New York, Paul and Essie had a farewell meal with Jimmy Light and the McGhees (who left for England two weeks before them to begin preliminary work on *Jones*), had dinner with the Brouns and Walter Whites, and spent one of their last evenings with the Van Vechtens: Fania gave Essie some felt flowers she'd brought back from Paris, and Carlo gave them a letter of introduction to Gertrude Stein. Up until the eleventh hour before departure, Minnie sewed for Essie and Paul posed for Salemmé. The day before sailing, Paul and Essie raced around to the Victor Company to pick up an advance of $725 for his four (double-sided) completed records, and to Pond's to get paid for the Provincetown and Spring Lake concerts.[45]

August 5 dawned to a steady rain. Last-minute confusion with trunks and taxis made everybody nervous, and their two cabs got inadvertently separated; Ma Goode, "like a trooper," made it down alone with the big trunk and somehow got it on the deck of the *Berengaria*. They made the boat by ten minutes, but then, waiting for the tide, it delayed pulling out for an hour. Minnie, the Salemmés, Walter White, Larry Brown, and a half-dozen other friends waved them off. Five telegrams and letters arrived. Mrs. Guy Currier sent a steamer basket. The stateroom was beautiful. The dining room was beautiful. The food was wonderful. Even the waiter was wonderful. They were off—jubilantly.

CHAPTER 6

■

The Launching of a Career

(1925–1927)

"I was determined," Essie wrote home to Carlo and Fania, "to find a nice cozy place to put my Baby in so he could be free to do his best work." Accompanied by Bert McGhee, she scouted London for three days trying to find a suitable flat. Everything she looked at was either dirty, lovely *sans* toilet, or lovely with toilet but no bath ("just funny tin bath tubs—like our foot tubs—only round!"). She finally found the ideal flat at 12 Glebe Place in Chelsea—the two upper floors of a three-story house, "beautifully furnished in the most exquisite taste," with "fireplaces in all the rooms, geyser bath, electricity, and telephone by the bed," complete with maid service—and all for four guineas. When she took Paul to see it, the landlord "looked at Paul hard," and Essie began to fear there would be "difficulty about us being colored." But if the landlord was upset, he kept it to himself, and Paul and Essie moved in the next day. Jimmy Light and the McGhees insisted "there will be no prejudice" in England. "Here's hoping," Essie wrote in her diary.[1]

Compared with the United States, the Robesons did find England "warm and friendly and unprejudiced." While they were rehearsing *Jones* in Greenwich Village, "the nearest and only place" Robeson could get a decent meal had been up at Penn Station; "the next nearest place was in Harlem." According to Sue Jenkins, Jimmy Light's first wife, "In spite of Greenwich Village's reputation for being so advanced and radical," and in spite of his growing celebrity, Robeson had had difficulty finding a restaurant that would serve him, "so Jimmy and I fed him at our place." In London there were dozens of attractive restaurants near the theater, and none ever raised the issue of race; "the Robesons thoroughly appreciated the fact," Essie wrote, "that here in London they could, as respectable human beings, dine at any public place." They were comparatively free from other humiliations as well. White theaters in New York would sell only balcony seats to blacks, white hotels refused them accommodations, and when Paul and Larry had tried to buy Pullman reservations they were told that only end seats (those over the wheels) were available—the task of buying tickets thereby devolving on the light-skinned Essie.[2]

Still, they (Essie more than Paul) continued from London to take a rather upbeat view of prospects back in the States, too. Perhaps because their own social life had cut across racial lines, and because the hothouse environment of the "Renaissance" had bred optimism, Essie chose to believe that white people were beginning to discover that "the Negro is merely a human being like themselves" and predicted that "prejudice will grow less and less." Unlike Paul, she even argued—in a variation of "blaming the victim"—that "segregation has to some extent been brought about by Negroes themselves," because, like all other ethnic groups, they preferred to congregate with their own; because those few blacks who directly profited from segregation (such as politicians with increased patronage to dispense) imposed it on the rest; and because the average citizen in a black community "could not and would not make a stand against segregation, preferring to shift the burden to the better known members of the race, like petitioning black artists to make the strictly symbolic gesture of not performing before segregated audiences." Whatever the causes and cures of the American malady, the Robesons were grateful for the respite of London.[3]

While Paul rehearsed, Essie toured—indefatigably, as was her style. She methodically attended the London theater "to get a good idea of just what succeeds." She loved Noel Coward's *Hay Fever* but disliked his *Fallen Angels* (Tallulah Bankhead "just pranced back and forth over the stage"), found *The Beggar's Opera* faintly boring, *Charlot's Revue* faintly amusing, thought the modern-dress *Hamlet* a fascinating exercise, and Ruth Draper so wonderful as to warrant a second visit to the theater. But comedies of manner in the Freddie Lonsdale mode, about the minor peccadilloes of the upper class, dominated the English stage of the 1920s, and Essie concluded that theater in London "can't touch New York. These fancy, perfect drawing room nothings can't compare with our virile plays."[4]

The Robesons' socializing, with a few notable exceptions, was largely confined to people they knew from back home—Jimmy Light, the McGhees, "Fitzi" Fitzgerald (the Provincetown's manager), Estelle Healy (the first wife of Lawrence Langner), and—reaching still further back—Paul's old friend, the singer Johnny Payne. Among their new acquaintances, they especially enjoyed Turner Layton and Tandy Johnstone, the black performers who were currently the rage of London, and went to the

Coliseum twice to see them ("It did our hearts good" to hear the galley stamp and whistle its approval, Essie wrote Carlo and Fania).⁵

Their particular new favorite was Emma Goldman. The redoubtable Emma, now aged fifty-six and having already suffered deportation from the United States and disillusionment with what she had seen firsthand of the Russian Revolution, was currently speaking out wherever possible in London against the Bolshevik imprisonment of her anarchist comrades. She and the Robesons initially met through Fitzi, her longtime friend, and they took to one another at once. Of that first meeting, Essie wrote in her diary that Emma "was fascinating—a middle aged Jewess—with a fine mind—but starved for love." In the autobiography she published six years later, Emma, too, recorded her first impressions: "Essie was a delightful person, and Paul fascinated everyone. . . . Nothing I had been told about his singing adequately expressed the moving quality of his voice. Paul was also a lovable personality, entirely free from the self-importance of the star and as natural as a child." With time, Emma became still more glowing about Paul. In the thirties, after their friendship had further ripened, she wrote her intimate friend, Alexander Berkman, "The more I know the man the greater and finer I find him," and in another letter said, "I would not change him for the whole miserable trash in the South. Not only because of his art but because of his splendid fine character, his understanding and his large outlook on life. Frankly, I know few of our A. [American] friends among whites quite as humane and large as Paul."⁶

Within two weeks of their first meeting, Emma invited the Robesons to dinner, and thereafter they frequently exchanged visits. They took her to see Chaplin in *The Gold Rush;* she cooked them a roast goose, gave them her books (and Berkman's) to read, talked about her "disheartening" experiences in Russia and her loneliness in London. "She has a crush on Paul," Essie wrote to Carlo and Fania, "and we like her very much. I like to hear her talk, and tho I often violently disagree with what she says, still it's rather thrilling to hear her—she's so earnest." Carlo agreed, writing back that Emma is "a wonderful woman whom I admire very much." When *The Emperor Jones* bowed at the Ambassadors on September 10, Emma was part of the opening-night audience, and she went back to see Robeson perform a second time.⁷

Along with Emma in the opening-night audience for *Jones* was a glamorous segment of London life—Arnold Bennett, Gladys Cooper, St. John Ervine, Ashley Dukes, Godfrey Tearle, Rose Macauley, Lawrence Langner, and his current wife, Armina Marshall. When the curtain fell, Paul was called back a dozen times, finally forcing him to make a speech. "The audience stood up and cheered and shouted," Essie reported to Otto Kahn—shrewdly including a set of clippings from the London press—and described his performance (and Essie *was* objective about such matters) as "the finest" she had ever seen him give, despite a dispirited dress rehearsal the night before. She also reported to Kahn that a purchase of "the very thinnest pure wool underclothing" at Jaeger's was providing Paul with maximum protection against catching cold. Kahn sent back "cordial congratulations" on "what must have been a veritable triumph," adding his pleasure on learning "that Mr. Jaeger is shielding you and your husband against the vicissitudes of the English climate. . . ."[8]

Robeson's stunning personal reviews brought reporters flocking to the flat—by three o'clock the next afternoon, he had given six interviews. *The New Statesman* called his performance "magnificent," *The Times* "superb," *The Tatler* "singularly fine," *The Saturday Review* "gigantic," *G.K.'s Weekly* "wonderful," and *West Africa* "a tour de force." The theater promptly put Paul's name up in lights on the huge electric sign at Cambridge Circus. "Prettiest thing in London!" Essie wrote the Van Vechtens—"He's an honest to God *Star* now."[9]

But neither play nor production fared as well as Paul. The incessant beating of the tom-tom onstage produced nervous laughter on opening night, apparently fraying some delicate British nerves, while the small space (and perhaps the unfamiliar English-African cast) apparently cramped Jimmy Light's directorial skills (more than one critic found his staging "only moderately effective"). The majority of reviewers did hail the play ("a work of gigantic range, both actual and symbolic," Ivor Brown wrote in *The Saturday Review*), but a minority registered strong doubts about the repetitive "series of anti-climaxes" and O'Neill's tendency toward melodramatic monologue. Ordinarily a set of reviews so heavily weighted on the positive side would draw a strong public response, but *Jones* failed to catch on with an English audience. "They really did not like the play at all," Essie wrote Countee Cullen, although "they did seem wild about Paul and his acting, and said so."[10]

Essie probably put her finger on the failure: "London doesn't want red meat on the table," she wrote Carlo and Fania; "the London audience likes its elegant applesauce on the stage—it does not like to have its neck wrung unless there's sex in the works." To Otto Kahn she characterized the audience as having been "almost exclusively the intelligentsia and the society people—and of course they don't support a play indefinitely." (The play was "too gloomy" for the general public, she wrote James Weldon Johnson.) But perhaps, too, the fact that *Jones* was "a negro play" worked against it. "The sight of a half-naked wretch gradually becoming more demented leaves an English audience cold," one critic commented. Another claimed, "To us, as a people, the negro is unknown." That attitude of bland indifference may have been more characteristic of the attitude of the English intelligentsia than the committed egalitarianism Essie attributed to it; only a single reviewer was inspired by the play to make any comment at all on the questions it raised about the plight of blacks in the United States. Despite hopes for a long run, *The Emperor Jones* closed on October 17, after five weeks, Robeson again getting a prolonged personal ovation.[11]

The Robesons liked London so much they lingered on for two weeks after the play closed. Paul's spreading fame produced a new batch of invitations, and now they had the free time to accept them. The social calendar got jammed once more. They dined with the composer Roger Quilter, the actress Athene Seyler and her guest Hugh Walpole; took tea with the radical American journalist Crystal Eastman and her husband; visited with the widow of the black composer Samuel Coleridge-Taylor (whose cantata *Hiawatha* had impressed the London critics); went to the Russian ballet and to a rugby game; saw Mrs. Patrick Campbell at the King's Theatre and for dinner afterward ("She looked the typical, up to the minute whore house proprietress," Essie wrote in her diary, "but was lovely to us"); spent one afternoon with Miss Amanda Ira Aldridge, second daughter of the great black actor Ira Aldridge (she had written to express her appreciation of Paul's "magnificent performance" and had presented him with the earrings her father had worn on stage as Othello, expressing the hope he would one day wear them when he, too, played the role).[12]

Paul began vocal training with the well-known coach Flora Arnold. Essie described herself as "very jealous of Paul's style and his simplicity of singing" and ready to "fight anybody who tries to make him 'technical,'" but she felt Miss Arnold gave him "just what he needs—and I think when he finishes with her he will have complete confidence in himself." In addition, Essie had begun to cultivate some ambitions of her own. She confided to Van Vechten that she had "quite settled one thing in my mind definitely—as soon as I get home I'm going to make a try to get into the movies—isn't that funny? Of course I shall keep Paul's mark first always. I suppose I'll never get over that! We talked about that particular weakness—or was it strength—on my part one night—remember? Well, anyway . . . I've always longed to act in the movies." She took to wearing her hair "back and a little kinky—something like Nora Ray wears hers." Paul, she reported, thought it looked "interestingly African!," and in combination with long earrings and deep colors it made her feel "much taller and much smarter." Carlo sent back his encouragement: "I'm awfully excited about your movie ambitions. I don't see why you shouldn't realize them."[13]

Essie decided that Paul was "very tired," that "the vocal and nervous strain of *Jones* has been great and the damp climate has taken a toll on his throat and chest," and that he needed a prolonged rest in the south of France. The vacation did prove, in comparison with the social whirl of London, restful—though the six-week stay in France starred its own arresting cast of characters. With introductions from Van Vechten, Paul and

Essie stopped for a week in Paris on their way to the Riviera. They called on Madame Matisse, who showed them the master's watercolors "and some fascinating African wooden carved art"; Paul, in turn, sang, and reduced Madame Duthuit, Matisse's daughter, to tears with his "Weepin' Mary," though she knew scarcely a word of English. Sylvia Beach, proprietress of the Shakespeare and Company bookstore, already counted the Robesons as friends and, "to do a little publicity" for Paul, threw a "port and sandwich" party for him. Among the guests and reporters gathered that day at the Rue de L'Odéon to hear Robeson sing were James Joyce and his wife, the composer George Antheil, the American music publisher Robert Schirmer, Lewis Galantiere, the head of the International Chamber of Commerce, and the Ernest Hemingways.[14]

They also went to have tea with Gertrude Stein. Essie had dropped her a note a few weeks earlier, enclosing a letter of introduction from Van Vechten, which began, "This letter preludes the approach of two of the nicest people left in the world: Essie and Paul Robeson." Van Vechten had already mentioned Paul in three earlier letters to Stein, describing him as "a great actor," "a lamb of God," and someone he liked "better than almost anyone I ever met." "I think you will too and he will love you and you will like his wife just as much."[15]

On the latter count, Van Vechten may have misjudged. Essie made no entry in her diary for November 6—an atypical lapse, given her penchant for recording in detail her meetings with the rich or famous; on her part, Gertrude Stein failed to make a single reference to Essie in her follow-up account of the visit to Van Vechten. But, as Carl had predicted, Gertrude Stein and Paul did take to each other hugely. "There is no doubt about it Carl," Stein wrote him, "you have awfully good taste in friends. . . . Robeson is a dear and he sang for us and I had a long talk with him." That talk, she reported to Carlo in another letter, revolved around "why you like niggers so much Robeson and I had a long talk about it it is not because they are primitive but because they have a narrow but a very long civilisation behind them. They have alright, their sophistication is complete and so beautifully finished and it is the only one that can resist the United States of America." She did not, however, like hearing Robeson sing spirituals. "They do not belong to you," she said to him, "any more than anything else, so why claim them." On a later visit, "a very charming Southern woman" asked him where he was born. New Jersey, he said. Oh, not in the South? she responded—what a pity. "Not for me," he answered. Robeson, Stein concluded, "knew american values and american life as only one in it but not of it could know them. And yet as soon as any other person came into the room he became definitely a negro."[16]

Two years after their first meeting, on the occasion of another talk with Robeson, Stein described him to Van Vechten as "really a perfectly ideal companion, the last time I saw him it was only once and it was in a crowd of people. I liked him then but now after a quiet time alone with him we are really very good friends. . . . He did give charming pictures of you Carl, he does that awfully well makes the people he is talking about very really in front of you and it was nice having that done with you. Thanks for him." Carlo, in turn, reported Robeson's reaction to Stein: "he adores you."[17]

The Robesons also saw a few old friends, like Donald Angus, and took in the much-touted *Revue Nègre*. The *Revue* had been put together by the white producer Caroline Dudley Reagan, an American living in Paris, whom Essie disliked and who was to cause Paul considerable trouble within a few years. Essie reported to Carlo and Fania that the *Revue* was "rotten"—"that is . . . between us," she wrote, "I hate to run down our own stuff." Josephine Baker started out well—"the things she does with her body are amazing"—but she continued to do "the same stuff all evening, and by the end you are slightly bored," especially since her voice couldn't be heard above the orchestra. As for the touted "African scene," the "idea is splendid, and it is all fine until Josephine does this ridiculously vulgar and totally uncalled for wiggling. It would be different if it fitted in anywhere, but it obviously [is] stuck in as an added attraction." The *Revue* in fact marked Josephine Baker's Paris debut—and made her, still a teenager, an overnight sensation.[18]

From Paris the Robesons went to Villefranche on the Riviera. They were immediately taken in tow by Glenway Wescott and Monroe Wheeler, whom they had met in New York at the Salemmés. Both were still in their twenties. Wescott had already gained a reputation as a writer with his first novel, *The Apple of the Eye,* and his lover, Monroe Wheeler (who as a fledgling publisher had printed a book of Wescott's poetry), would later become a highly regarded art curator and critic. Traveling as they did in artistic circles, the Robesons always knew gay men and lesbian women, and counted a fair number among their friends. Paul especially was (in the words of one intimate) "never moralistic or judgmental on that subject but rather wholly accepting," and Monroe Wheeler recalls that when a "fashionable New York dressmaker offered Paul a lot of money to sleep with him," Paul turned the man down with polite disinterest. Essie, in fact, unlike Paul, occasionally showed a bit of superior disdain, once referring to Elsa Maxwell as that "great ugly Lesbian" (adding that she gave "marvelous parties"), and another time reporting having met "a lot of fairies and degenerates" at a cocktail party given by Lady Duff Gordon. But more typically Essie, too, enjoyed the company of gay people. In 1931 she went three times to hear the "down-and-dirty" Gladys Bentley during her engagement at the Clam House, thought her "grand," and wrote the Van Vechtens that she, Essie, would "never be the same." She was also sometime companion and confidante to several gay men, and once expressed disapproving surprise on hearing that one of them preferred to hide his passionate involvement with another man rather than risk being ruined in business and ostracized by French society.[19]

Wheeler and Wescott had a villa in the hills above Villefranche, an unspoiled half-Italian, half-French village situated near Nice. They booked the Robesons into the famed Welcome Hotel (sometime home in 1925 to Cocteau), where the window and balconies of the Robesons' room directly faced the sea in front and the French Alps on the side. They read, wrote letters, ate on the balcony, and during the day strolled along the shore in the sun. Within a week, Paul's congestion began to thaw and Essie's self-described "nervous tension" to ease. It is "the most enchanting spot in the world—so far as we know," Essie wrote Carlo and Fania, "and Paul and I are as happy as can be."[20]

Wescott and Wheeler lived in Villefranche most of the year and had a large circle of friends. Soon after the Robesons' arrival, Wescott invited them to an elegant dinner (three wines plus champagne) with an opium-smoking friend of Cocteau's, the Count de Maleissy, and his wife ("he descended from Joan of Arc," Essie wrote in her diary, "one of the six oldest titles in France, and she a celebrated mistress of everybody, and very difficult with a dreadful inferiority complex")—plus the Count Louis Gautier-Vignal ("His is a papal title"). Paul sang a few songs, and everyone "simply went crazy about him." The Robesons subsequently invited the de Maleissys over to their place on the occasion of a visit from the young writers G. B. Stern and Rebecca West—whom they had met in London and New York, respectively.[21]

Sixty years later Rebecca West's recollection of the Robesons (perhaps retrospectively colored by her Cold War political stand—she, having moved to right of center, thought Robeson "naïve" for remaining on the left) was at odds with that of Emma Goldman and Gertrude Stein, since she distinctly preferred Essie to Paul. Rebecca West described the Robeson of 1925 as having "a proclivity of not getting on with the job. . . . He was too much of a musician to join in with the [political] movements, and too little of a musician to go on with his music." She liked him—he "had such beautiful manners" and was "very sweet"—but liked Essie more. Essie struck Rebecca West as admirably outgoing and lively—she liked parties, "had a great faculty for happiness," and was "very amusing." Monroe Wheeler, oppositely, felt Essie "never got into the spirit" of the festivities; Paul didn't have to be asked twice to sing, but Essie "was very covetous of his voice and didn't like him to give it away." Taking Essie's side, Rebecca West emphasized that it was "very, very hard on her" to have to push Paul all the time, "to bully Paul to keep appointments," and it lent her "a sort of sharpness, a sort of brightness, that offended people"—she was "quick," she "would never think twice before answering." But if she hadn't pushed, Paul "wouldn't have got anywhere so quickly." Rebecca

West and Essie were to see more of each other in London over the next few years.[22]

While on the Riviera, the Robesons also met Frank Harris, the Irish-American writer whose erotic autobiography, *My Life and Loves,* was currently (1922–27) appearing in four volumes in Germany, and who lived at Cimiez, just outside of Nice. Emma Goldman was a good friend of Harris's (she had helped to promote his book *The Bomb,* about the Haymarket anarchists) and had asked him to get in touch with the Robesons when they arrived in the south of France. "He is a nice old man," Essie wrote in her diary, "with the filthiest mouth I ever heard—always talking about your behind and pleasure and breast and filth. . . . He talked dirt all the time till finally we were bored stiff." Harris accompanied them when they went to visit the Jamaican writer Claude McKay and the radical journalist Max Eastman.[23]

Harris had helped to launch McKay as a writer, and Max Eastman had appointed him associate editor of *The Liberator.* But until recently McKay had been out of touch with Harris and for a while had been alienated from Eastman (when he and his sister Crystal withdrew from *The Liberator* in 1921, after a more militant brand of Marxists took control of the magazine, McKay had left, too, gone to Russia for six months—and come back thoroughly repelled by Communism). With the publication of *Harlem Shadows* in 1922, McKay had leapt to the front ranks of black poets. But his blunt denunciation of American *and* English racism—and of white patrons and black patronees—had led him to take up temporary residence in France, where both his health and his finances had suffered. On reading in the newspaper that Robeson was vacationing in the area, McKay wrote to introduce himself as a friend of Walter White's, and to invite him to Nice on the evening he expected a visit from Max Eastman and his wife, Eliena Krylenko.[24]

To McKay's annoyance, Essie, not Paul, answered his letter, accepting the invitation for both of them—"because they just couldn't breathe without each other," McKay commented dryly. In the autobiography he published a dozen years later, McKay describes the visit from the Robesons and Frank Harris as "piquant." Eastman and Harris "detested each other," and on arrival Harris immediately started needling Eastman about his book *Since Lenin Died,* and his "naivete" in ever having thought Lenin or other Bolsheviks gods. McKay got out a bottle of wine, and Harris, after announcing he was on the wagon, proceeded to drink most of it. He then recounted an anecdote by acting out the woman's role on Paul; according to McKay, Essie took him aside and whispered that Harris "was so realistic that I felt afraid for my husband."[25]

Essie saw the visit with less sarcastic eyes. We "dined and spent a marvelous evening with dear Claude McKay and the Max Eastmans," she wrote Countee Cullen, and recorded in her diary that she "found Max Eastman one of the most fascinating men I've ever known" and thought Claude McKay "so sweet—a charming naive West Indian lad, with beauty all through him." Naïve was one thing McKay was not, and his charm, as Essie was shortly to learn, was irregularly exerted. After the Robesons had him over to Villefranche for dinner with the Eastmans, she revised her judgment in stark haste. McKay, she now wrote in her diary, is "a disgusting, black monkey chaser. Was bitterly disappointed in his loudness, commonness and absolute lack of taste, and overwhelming sex conversation." Several days later, after meeting him twice more, she went still further: McKay "is an illbred, horrid nigger, wholly out of place in good society." Such furious distaste was not simply about manners.[26]

In his recent book, *Negroes in America,* McKay had argued that "powerful Jewish syndicates" controlled the American theater. He contended that their baneful influence, in combination with the failure of the genteel black bourgeoisie to respond to any full and honest portrayal of black life, had reduced black artists to limning stereotypes. Resuming this argument with Essie by mail, he conceded that she had debated well—"you made big holes in my argument"—but not well enough. He berated her for having shown a "surprisingly reactionary" point of view in their discussion of the position of the black artist in the United States and chastised her for talking as if "Paul's or Roland Hayes' success" could be taken "as typical of America's attitude to the Negro's artistic struggles." "Negro artists have always gained a finer welcome and appreciation in Europe, and especially England, than in the United States," McKay insisted, and "all the serious-thinking Negro intelligentsia" agreed that it was deplorable that New York had failed to support a black art theater. He did not blame whites entirely for that failure: "Negroes are also to blame because, perhaps, we have not, as the Jews have had, the proportionate cultural background to support and appreciate such a thing. Nevertheless the fact remains that a fine steady appreciation of Negro artistic endeavor in America has always been lacking."[27]

Citing the careers of the black actors Williams and Walker—their "great show ended in vaudeville"—and the failure of *Shuffle Along* to get a road-company production because the Shuberts' manager said "he could not present colored chorus girls to the American public," McKay sought to demonstrate to Essie "how mistaken your point of view is." He reiterated his argument that black artists would "most certainly have developed better" outside the United States, and expressed surprise that she had not learned from Paul's connection with the Provincetown Players "of the difficulties of finer artistic success in America." If Essie still remained unaware of the "radical fight" the Provincetowners had to make to keep alive, McKay sardonically suggested that she "ask Miss Fitzgerald [Fitzi, the manager] when you get back to tell you about it all!" Then he twisted the knife a bit deeper still: "Many Negroes," he wrote—not *just* Essie, was the implication—"do not understand the interest of those radical artistic groups [like the Provincetowners] in their own struggles, because the Negroes' outlook is essentially racial and introspective and not universal and original. . . . So I can quite sympathize with your point of view though it remains unconvincing." McKay closed on a halfhearted note of reconciliation: "It is not necessary to remain a carping sorehead. We are all as Negroes glad of the general new interest in the creative work of Negroes," but, he added, "let us not ignore our historical perspective nor *present facts.*" He was writing to her at length, he explained, because "I am afraid you might have been shocked by my line of argument. My interest in life is universal and curious but intellectually I never deviate from principles and I am always as frank open and intransigent with white people as I am with colored."[28]

McKay wrote a separate, shorter note to Paul, quite different in tone. He assured Paul he would "long remember the interesting and informative talk I had with you" and offhandedly apologized if his own remarks had created "an unpleasant situation"—that had been "farthest from my thoughts." McKay was making a clear separation between Paul and Essie, and Essie knew it. She decided to curtail contact. When Paul returned late one afternoon from a trip to Nice with Monroe Wheeler, Essie greeted them with the news that they had crossed with McKay, who had come in from Nice to visit Paul. Sixty years later Wheeler said, "To this day I can remember Paul's expression when she told him this—he was absolutely crushed that she hadn't kept McKay, that she had sent him back to Nice." After dinner, at 10:00 p.m., Paul went out on his own to look for McKay. Though he had no address for him, he took the tramway into Nice and began a search in the cafés McKay was known to frequent. Eventually he found him, and they talked until the early hours of the morning. By then the tramway had stopped running, and Paul walked the five miles back to Villefranche. "He was so pleased," according to Wheeler, "to have set things right with McKay."[29]

In mid-December the Robesons returned to Paris, where they joined up with the Bercovicis, recently arrived from the States. Daughters Rada and Mirel threw fits of delight at the sight of Paul, and after a three-day reunion, including a birthday party for Essie, the Robesons sailed on the S.S. *Majestic* for New York. "Paul and I are terrifically excited now about coming home," Essie wrote Carlo and Fania a week before leaving Europe. "Paul is sunburned a beautiful ebony, and I am a nice chocolate color. And we feel as tho we could take the world apart, see how it ticks, and put it together again." Paul's voice, she wrote, had never sounded better—"its enormous and round and soft and mellow. Just you wait till you hear your beloved 'Lil David!' " Essie also confided that during their leisure time on the Riviera she'd written a book for a "Negro musical play. . . . The idea has been with me some time—ever since I've been going to Negro shows and disapproving of them." It was "just a simple story . . . nothing at all high brow or intellectual about it all," but Paul had read the script "and thinks it very good!"; Essie cautioned the Van Vechtens not to breathe a word about it—"I want to know what you think of it first."[30]

Within a month of Robeson's return to the States, James Pond's concert bureau had arranged for a series of bookings. Paul and Larry performed eight times in January 1926 (with Essie along as manager), including major concerts in New York, Detroit, Indianapolis, Philadelphia, and Pittsburgh. The inaugural concert, in New York on January 6, got a strongly favorable response, the critics commending the conviction and simplicity of Robeson's singing and the ingenuity of Larry Brown's accompaniment (and also expressing delight at his pleasing light tenor when he joined Robeson in duets). The response in the other cities was equally enthusiastic—though one fatuous reviewer in Indianapolis complained that Robeson "fails to turn 'wild' upon an audience that uncontrolled spiritual something."[31]

Simultaneous with the success of the first mini-tour came the acclaimed release of Robeson's first recordings. Issued both in the United States and England late in 1925, his four double-sided records sold a highly respectable fifty-five thousand copies within four months (the bestseller of the four was "Joshua Fit de Battle" and "Bye and Bye"), bringing Robeson, whose contract was based on a royalty percentage, nearly twelve hundred dollars. The records were well received artistically, too. While Robeson was still in Europe, Van Vechten reported to him that he had taken the new releases along on a weekend visit to the writer Joseph Hergesheimer and with the first one had a roomful of people in tears. In late January 1926, Robeson went back to Camden to make a new batch of recordings for the Victor Company. When they reached Langston Hughes, upon their release later in the year, he wrote Paul to say, "The great truth and beauty of your art struck me as never before one night this summer down in Georgia when a little group of us played your records for hours there in the very atmosphere from which your songs came."[32]

The second round of concerts, in February 1926, did not go as well as the first. The initial stop on the tour, after a twenty-nine-hour ride on what Paul called "a lily" train, was the huge Orchestra Hall in Chicago. Only a small audience had gathered, essentially a turnout of personal friends. Essie blamed the lack of sales on Pond's failure to advertise but reported back to the Van Vechtens that the disappointment fired Paul up—he "just got mad and opened up his lungs and *Sang!*"—"sang better than he ever sang in his life," with the audience shouting for encores, some of the critics remaining to shout along with them. The reviews were unanimously, spectacularly favorable—a rarity for the Chicago critics. "The finest of all Negro voices and one of the most beautiful in the world," wrote the Chicago *Herald-Examiner;* the *Evening American* praised Robeson for his "ideal diction"; the *Evening Post* marveled at his ability to reach "an elemental something that sets the heart strings vibrating"; and the *Daily Tribune* hailed his voice as "something to grow rhapsodic about."[33]

At the next stop, Milwaukee, Pond had leased a sports arena that held ten thousand people—and had then sold the concert to "The Booker T. Washington Social and Community Center," a black lodging house for the blind with about twenty residents. Those "poor ignorant people," as Essie described them, "hadn't advertised, and only our friends (mostly white) made up the audience!" The house was enthusiastic and the reviews decent, but Essie wrote angrily in her diary that "small-towners are not our audience. Callow, silly, ignorant poseurs—not for us."[34]

The third stop, Green Bay, Wisconsin, was unredeemed by either a good audience (the receipts totalled $37.18), a good critical reception, or even a good concert (Essie, never one to pull punches, called it "rotten"). Racial indignities completed the humiliation. Arriving in a snowstorm, the Robesons and Larry Brown went, as prearranged, to the Northland Hotel, only to have the manager inform them that the hotel didn't take blacks. After a phone call to the concert manager, and considerable argument, the hotel partly relented: they were given rooms on the first floor—to prevent them from being seen on the elevator—and told to use the side staircase, to eat in their rooms, and to make themselves "as inconspicuous as possible." The next day, on their way back to Chicago, "some flappers" got on the train at Milwaukee, "stopped and gazed at us in amazement," Essie recorded in her diary, and said in a loud, shocked voice, "Niggers!" "We all got so tickled, we got to giggling and just couldn't stop." Laughter was one way to deal with the indignity; the previous night there had been no laughter, and it had taken some time for Larry and Paul to quiet down "from their fury." "It's a hell of a life!" Essie wrote the Van Vechtens. "Thank God for the theater."[35]

But three months later the same racist specter rose up in the theater world itself—and this time in New York. With no trouble, light-skinned Essie picked up the orchestra tickets for *Bridge of the Lamb* that Jimmy Light had left for them at the box office at the Henry Miller Theater. But, after Paul arrived at the theater and they tried to go to their seats, they were directed instead back to the box office; the man at the booth looked at Paul and asked him—as he handed him tickets for the balcony—if he "understood." Paul said no, he didn't. They refused the balcony seats and left. The managing director of the theater sent Paul a letter of apology, saying it was "a matter of great personal distress" that such a thing had happened and asking him to understand that it had been "merely the stupid operation of a general policy." It was precisely the "general policy" that Paul would come increasingly to protest as he grew less and less comfortable with the individual exceptions made to it—when "mere stupidity" did not intervene—for those few blacks considered sufficiently cultivated or famous.[36]

His New York friends provided some balm. After a well-received benefit concert at Town Hall for a Lower East Side settlement house, Van Vechten gave a party that outshone all but his most spectacular. Sybil Colefax (the English decorator and socialite), who had specifically asked to meet Paul, was the centerpiece, but the sparkling satellites included a sizable theater contingent—Lenore Ulric, Louis Calhern, Rita Romilly, Sidney Blackmer, and Katharine Cornell (Essie found her "very much like she is on the stage, ugly but beautifully spiritual")—along with the Walter Whites, the James Weldon Johnsons, and Rebecca West. Carlo had evidently intended the party as a pick-me-up for the Robesons; in inviting them he'd written, ". . . remember that you aren't the only ones that have terrible experiences. . . . This is a strange country." Paul's trust in Carlo on racial matters during the twenties (later to diminish) is exemplified in his reaction to Van Vechten's controversial novel, *Nigger Heaven*. Many black figures—including Du Bois, Walter White, Countee Cullen, and Alain Locke—strongly disapproved of the book, but soon after its publication, Robeson telegraphed Carlo: "Nigger Heaven amazing in its absolute understanding and deep sympathy. Thanks for such a book. Anxious to talk to you about it."[37]

The worst experience of Robeson's youthful career lay just ahead, at a concert in Boston in March 1926. The city was Larry Brown's hometown, had been the scene of some of Roland Hayes's most memorable concerts, and was known for the coolness of its audiences and critics. Robeson was anxious to perform well there. But a few days before the concert he came down with one of his frequent colds, which did not improve when, on arriving at their mid-range hotel, they were told that it didn't take blacks as guests. Their next try, the Copley Plaza, one of the city's fanciest hotels, received them "with every courtesy." (Boston Brahmins had long prided themselves on their tolerance—toward blacks, that is, not Jews or Irish.) Although Paul went straight to bed and stayed there the whole next day, when he got up that evening to dress for the concert he still felt so poorly that he suggested canceling the performance. Larry and Essie persuaded him to give it a try. He did manage to complete the program, but, as Essie wrote, "It was simply awful, his rich lovely voice was tight and hard and unrecognizable." The audience seemed "embarrassed," but "something of Paul's tenseness and deep sincerity got over to them," and the critics next day were compassionate ("Mr. Robeson's voice is a baritone of not a large range. It is a rich voice, but . . . it is almost harsh at its lower edges, and the fact that its owner was suffering last evening from a cold made the fact more obvious still. Such imperfections, however, seem of minor consequence.")[38]

Paul's confidence was shaken. After a two-year roll of breakneck momentum and unvarying acclaim, he was not used to setbacks. He wondered how other singers dealt with the difficulties of travel and compensated for the toll exacted by nerves and colds (not to mention racism). On Essie's recommendation, he consulted with Teresa Armitage, who had taught music in the Chicago high schools while Essie was a student there. Armitage agreed that Paul had a remarkable voice and recommended that he work with Frantz Proschowsky, a well-known vocal coach. Progress—especially in learning "how to make the most of his low tones"—was at first exhilarating, but Paul soon began to feel that he was marking time, switched to another coach briefly, and then decided to study with Armitage herself. He also consulted a medical specialist, who said his nose and throat were inflamed and treated him for a growth on his vocal cords. Within a month, there was a marked improvement, and in gratitude Robeson went to sing for the doctor's family.[39]

Just as Robeson began to regain confidence in his voice, he had to deal with an acting disappointment. Early in the spring of 1926 the DeMille motion picture office approached him with an offer: "DeMille wants to do a Negro picture" and wanted him for the lead. Negotiations went forward rapidly, and on April 21 Robeson signed a contract to make a picture for DeMille that summer in California. A week later the deal fell through. DeMille decided he had to shoot the film in New York rather than Hollywood, which meant delaying until the fall—and thereby created an unresolvable conflict with Paul's prior scheduling commitments. They were "*so* disappointed," Essie wrote in her diary.[40]

Essie had her own setbacks. She submitted the play she'd written on the Riviera to DeMille and, when Paul's movie with that office came to nothing, sent it to the Shuberts, who told her they were looking for a dramatic piece about black life, not a musical. With characteristic pluck, Essie started on a new script, but the day after completing the first act, she had an unaccountable nose hemorrhage (six months earlier she had mysteriously fainted while attending the theater). Deciding she was "simply dead" from the strain of the concert tours, from trying (as she wrote the Van Vechtens) "to make the boys comfortable, look after everything, and literally sing with them (silently) on the concerts," she took stock and declared "my color was bad, I was too fat, I was sluggish and generally uninteresting—even to myself." ("I haven't had time to pay attention to myself for 4 years—and I find I need it badly.") She decided to devote the summer to staying "very busy with *Essie.*" She went on a strict diet (lamb chops and pineapple), shopped with Minnie Sumner for new clothes, and enrolled in a daily dance class with a Denishawn graduate. She also consulted a doctor for help in getting pregnant.[41]

This flurry of self-improvement was not designed simply to repair the ravages of touring. Essie was feeling insecure in the marriage. On their fourth wedding anniversary, in August 1925, she had written in her diary, "We are so happy." On their fifth, she tersely noted, "Spent it together"—implying they had considered spending it apart. In the retrospective opinion of several of the Robesons' intimates, Paul had never been content in the marriage, but, if so, his tender letters to Essie during the first few years suggest that his discontent was neither sharp nor steady. By 1926 it was. As early as the preceding December, Essie had confided to her diary that she had thought of having an affair with an old beau, the physician Grant Lucas—but immediately gave up the idea when "Baby decided to admire me and be sweet to me, and everybody else looked like two cents." But by March, Paul and Essie went off on separate vacations, he to Atlantic City and she to spend a few days with Minnie at A'Lelia Walker's Villa Lewaro. The change seemed to do them both good: "Paul was home when I arrived—was so glad to see him," Essie wrote in her diary. "He looks so well—clear eyes, etc. I'm sure the rest did him good."[42]

For the next few weeks they went to a round of social events together, with apparent pleasure, including a visit to the art collector A. C. Barnes in Pennsylvania, an evening spent with Claire and Hubert Delany (the lawyer and future judge), two at the Brouns (with Woollcott, William Rose Benet and Elinor Wylie, the Walter Whites, Mabel Normand, Harpo Marx, and Van Vechten's newest favorite, the black singer Taylor Gordon); another with the Knopfs to meet the John Galsworthys (along with Fannie Hurst, H. L. Mencken, and Carlo); an *Opportunity* dinner at the Fifth Avenue Restaurant (Paul, along with David Belasco, Montgomery Gregory, and Stark Young, served as judges for the playwriting prizes); excursions to catch Florence Mills at the Alhambra, to hear Galli-Curci sing, Kreisler play, Al Jolson entertain ("He just is the cheapest kind of music hall artist" was Essie's opinion), and Lenore Ulric perform in the "wonderful" show *Lulu Belle*, which Robeson had earlier turned down.[43]

But the hectic round of events only briefly papered over the underlying tensions. In the beginning of May, Paul's brother Ben (who had disliked Essie from the first) came for a visit, and he and Paul went out alone. Then Paul and Essie quarreled about money. He told her about a friend's note for seventy-five dollars that he had assumed, an act that Essie took to be "a breach of faith" between them and which "so disgusted" her (she always thought Paul's generosity bordered on irresponsibility) that she threatened to turn all their income over to him and let him try handling it himself (a sure recipe, she felt, for self-destruction). A week later they had still another fight. Essie ordered twin beds. Paul began to stay out nights and to drink (Harry Block, a Knopf editor, reported to Van Vechten after one party, "For anyone who is supposed to have had as little practice as Paul, I should say he drinks very well"). Stiff-upper-lipped Essie admitted to feeling "a bit lonely," and turned increasingly to her mother and Minnie for support (she and Minnie also managed to stay drunk for a whole day). As Essie retreated inward, some of her new friends began to worry. "I haven't seen you for ages," Blanche Knopf wrote, and Carlo, too, expressed concern when Paul began to show up at their place without her. When Essie reassured him that she was only "taking care of Essie," he cheerily wrote back, "We had begun to worry about your long absence, but if you're getting thin and chic all at the same time, go to it, kid!"[44]

The storm raged for two weeks. Then, on June 14, Essie wrote in her diary, "Paul returned today. Was so glad to see him. We sort of started life all over again. He is so sweet." He soon became "Baby" and "Angel" once again. Yet Essie knew the reconciliation was fragile. Without consulting Paul, she decided it was time to have a baby.

The immediate tension between them was further relieved by absorption in a new theatrical project. The publisher and producer Horace Liveright (who during the 1925–26 season had presented John Barrymore's modern-dress *Hamlet*) signed him for the lead in Jim Tully and Frank Dazey's new play, *Black Boy,* the story of the rise and fall of a black prizefighter, based roughly on the life of Jack Johnson. Rehearsals began in late August 1926, with the young cabaret performer Fredi Washington (whose name, for some reason, was changed to "Edith Warren" on the playbill just before opening night) cast as Robeson's leading lady. She began rehearsals "in awe" of Robeson, but he was so "kind and helpful" she soon relaxed. According to the rumor mill, they became "an item."[45]

During tryouts it became clear that the play—full of gimmickry and whipped-up emotions, though decidedly not lifeless—was in trouble. A friend of Van Vechten's who saw it in Wilmington reported to him that "half the audience walked out" on the night she saw it—possibly, though she did not say, because of the presence of police and vice reformers gathered in concern over Robeson's appearance in the climactic scene wearing "the few clothes of the ring" and further exercised over a subplot in which Black Boy became involved with a white woman. As the show's tryout progressed, it did seem to be coming together (it was "going ever so much better now," Essie wrote Carlo and Fania two weeks before the scheduled Broadway opening). Edward Steichen took some remarkable photographs of Robeson for *Vanity Fair* ("my little tribute," Steichen wrote Van Vechten), and a dazzling array of celebrities—among them Judith Anderson, Louis Wolheim, Marion Davies, Norma Talmadge, Lee Shubert, Fannie Hurst, the explorer Vilhjalmur Stefansson, and the two boxers Henry Wills and Jack Sharkey—turned out for the New York opening on October 6 at the Comedy Theater. The reviews were mixed to negative (two of the critical heavies, George Jean Nathan and Percy Hammond, turned in the most favorable appraisals), and several were overtly racist. *The Wall Street Journal*'s critic opted for "humor": Robeson "took his fighting amiably just as any colored man of friendly disposition would tackle any job to which was attached a consideration likely to provide pork chops or other dainties favored by those of African descent." Robert Coleman in the *Daily Mirror* wrote, "The authors have cheapened their portrait of the pugilist by introducing the problem of racial antagonism. In our opinion it is always in bad taste to introduce this unpleasant element." Frank Vreeland in the New York *Telegram* went further: "It might as well be confessed by this writer that he is never wrung by great sympathy for negro tragedies or for the misfortunes of prizefighters who omitted brains in their makeup. As figures of fun, both colored folk and pugilists have always interested him, and viewed from that light, he doesn't have to strain to appreciate them. But when they are portrayed as children of sorrow, then this fellow feeling for them oozes out almost imperceptibly. . . . After all, on the stage one's interest in a character who is sorely beset is in proportion to the intelligence with which he can meet his troubles. And the average negro or prizefighter—note I said the average—can never appear sufficiently tragic in adversity to break my heart to the degree that makes a good play. There have doubtless been truly tragic negroes—one thinks of Toussaint L'Ouverture, for one—but they are not really representative of their rather happy-go-lucky race."[46]

Notices for Robeson himself ranged from good to ecstatic. "He towers high above the play," wrote Burns Mantle, sounding a theme reiterated by most of the other critics. Several expressed gratitude that the script called for Robeson to sing twice, allowing welcome relief from having to listen to the authors' words. The worst said about Robeson was that he started slowly; the best outdid even a press agent's vocabulary of superlatives: "A truly great actor"; "A figure of tremendous, Samsonic force"; a performance "perhaps greater than his performance in 'The Emperor Jones,' and that is superlative praise."[47]

But the widely read black paper the Pittsburgh *Courier* regretted that a Broadway show had, yet again, presented a portrait of the Negro as an "ignorant, perverse child . . . [by whites who] evidently know . . . extraordinarily little of the psychology of Aframericans." Robeson himself, a decade later, after his politics had matured, outlined the play's deficiencies as a portrait of black life: "The negro couldn't say in it all that he really lived and felt. Why, the white people in the audience would never stand for it. Even if you were to write a negro play that is truthful and intellectually honest, the audiences, in America at least, would never listen to it."[48]

The play drew poorly and closed within a few weeks, sending Robeson back to the concert circuit. He continued to search for appropriate stage roles, but their scarcity confined him, for the next year and a half, to singing. He told one newspaper interviewer that he dreamed "of a great play about Haiti, a play about Negroes, written by a Negro, and acted by Negroes . . . of a moving drama that will have none of the themes that offer targets for race supremacy advocates." But as he evaluated the serviceability of a given script for meeting such high purposes, Robeson's vision could occasionally be compromised by his desire for commercial success, and further distorted by the sanguine Harlem Renaissance lens through which he viewed his art. When he was offered Paul Green's new play, *In Abraham's Bosom,* late in 1926, he turned it down, fearing it was too negative thematically and too risky commercially: ". . . there's hardly a note of hope in it. I'm afraid it wouldn't be popular and I can't afford to be going into plays that are foredoomed to fail." The play was indeed somber, but so were many aspects of black life. James Weldon Johnson thought the script "closer and truer to actual Negro life" and more deeply probing of it "than any drama of the kind that had yet been produced." Starring Rose McClendon, Abbie Mitchell, Frank Wilson, and Jules Bledsoe, *In Abraham's Bosom* went on to win the 1927 Pulitzer Prize.[49]

In January 1927, two months after *Black Boy* closed, Robeson and Brown set out on another singing tour, this time going as far as Kansas and Ohio. The stop in Kansas City proved unexpectedly eventful. Roy Wilkins, a young black reporter for the thriving weekly the Kansas City *Call* (and later head of the NAACP), was part of a small local group that had organized a black concert company. Robeson was the first performer they had sought to engage, but his standard fee had seemed beyond their means. At the time—according to figures published in *Variety*—Robeson's guarantee for a one-night performance in cities with a population of three hundred thousand was $1,250; in this he ranked twentieth in a listing that put John McCormack at the top ($5,000) and Roland Hayes, the only other black artist to make the list, in the middle ($3,200). That fee was more than the Kansas City group could afford, but, because the organizing group was made up of amateurs with little working capital, Robeson agreed to appear for $750.[50]

Wilkins and friends made arrangements to hold the concert in the Grand Avenue Temple, a large white church in downtown Kansas City. The leading newspaper, the *Star,* agreed to carry an advance notice of the Robeson concert—but without an accompanying picture, for as a matter of policy it did not print photographs of blacks. Since this was coupled with the announcement—again contrary to local custom—that no separate section would be reserved at the concert for whites, advance sales went poorly and the box office threatened to fall short of Robeson's guaranteed fee. The organizers feared he might refuse to perform, but he reassured Wilkins: "Don't worry. . . . I will sing for my people." The concert proved a success—"White folks," Wilkins later wrote, "decided they couldn't stay away." Kansas City saw one of the largest integrated audiences to date, and Robeson got his guarantee, with $300 to spare.[51]

Protest over the concert, however, emerged within the black community. A local music teacher wrote to the *Call* expressing her feelings of "humiliation" as a black at Robeson's confining his program to "slave songs" and omitting "classical" selections, which could have demonstrated a more advanced "musical technique." Her letter set off a lively debate in the columns of the *Call,* which continued into three issues, producing a few additional denunciations of Robeson for "commercializing our backwardness" by devoting his repertory exclusively to Sorrow Songs, but in general leaning toward the opinion that it was time for blacks to end their enslavement to white cultural standards and—like Robeson—to champion the artistic heritage of their own people.[52]

When Paul returned to New York in February 1927, Essie told him that she was pregnant. She later wrote that he "received the news with mixed feelings" and ascribed his ambivalence to concern for her health. When she had earlier broached the subject of having a child, he had said that, "since a child had not just happened . . . perhaps it was best to leave well enough alone." Now that Essie had taken the decision into her own hands and presented Paul with a *fait accompli,* he accepted it, though with a residue of resentment. Essie, by her own account, "grew fat and sparkling, her cheeks flushed with good health and her eyes shining with happiness and eagerness." Six months into the pregnancy she was so large that (as she wrote Van Vechten) "I am not sure whether the person answering to Essie is me or not." With an "immense" baby on the way, she added, "Poor Angel will have to put his shoulder to the wheel."[53]

He did. He signed with Walter K. Varney, the white impresario who had managed the Fisk Jubilee Singers, for a year's concert tour in Europe with Larry Brown, to begin in October 1927. That would put Paul out of the country when Essie was due to give birth, but she strongly urged the contract on him. She even took it upon herself to write to various people, including Frank Harris, Gertrude Stein, and James Joyce, urging them to attend the inaugural concert in Paris on October 29—and asking them to invite their friends. In the summer preceding his departure, Paul and Essie took a cottage for the month of August at Oak Bluffs, the black bourgeois watering hole on Martha's Vineyard, with Paul concertizing locally. "I have a great tan," he wrote Van Vechten, "am really so much *darker*—I'm still visible under a strong light." At the last minute he had a telegram from the Theatre Guild offering him the part of Crown in DuBose and Dorothy Heyward's play *Porgy,* which was due to open on Broadway in October 1927, but to his regret he had to turn it down because of the European tour. That same summer, his old friend William Patterson joined a picket line in Boston to protest the imminent execution of Sacco and Vanzetti, a protest that enlisted a number of others who later became Robeson's friends—Ella Reeve Bloor ("Mother Bloor"), John Howard Lawson, Mike Gold, Rose Baron, and Vito Marcantonio. The event proved a milestone in Patterson's political pilgrimage, and he began to talk to Paul increasingly about Communism and the Soviet Union. For now, "it went in one ear and out the other." Robeson's political milestones still lay ahead.[54]

The impending birth of their baby drew the Robesons somewhat closer. From on board the S.S. *Majestic* on his way to Europe, Paul wrote Essie with a fullness of affection that had recently been missing from their relationship: "So hard to leave you sweet. Seems as tho you are me. . . . You'll never know how marvelous I think you are. Of course I love you more than I love my very self. I just almost melt away with happiness when I think of the beautiful days we have before us. I love you darling with all my soul. . . . So many thanks darling for all you have done for me—for my career—for my better understanding of myself—for your patience and care and devoted love. And know that whatever I achieve shall have been due in great part to your unselfish interest and devotion."[55]

His appreciation of Essie was genuine—but so was his anticipation of meeting in Paris a young woman named Freda Diamond, of whom he had become enamored. They had first met in 1923 at a party for the Chauve Souris, the Russian musical-theater troupe. Paul was stepping into an elevator as the beautiful seventeen-year-old Freda was stepping out of it, accompanied by her sister and mother (the formidable Ida Diamond, a friend of Emma Goldman). Even as a teen-ager, Freda Diamond was a striking presence. She was tall, with dramatic, deep-set eyes—a classic Russian-Jewish beauty—with the forceful, gregarious nature to match. Paul told Essie to continue to their next appointment, while he retraced his steps to the party and danced all night with Freda. Thus began a relationship that lasted, in its many manifestations, and despite the multiplicity of his romantic and sexual encounters, for many years. Despite the conventional demeanor he still chose to show the world, Robeson, emotionally, was already defying official culture, refusing to narrow down his behavior to fit the monogamous norm—to love only one woman forever (or, indeed, even one at a time).[56]

Paul became enchanted with Mama Diamond as well as her daughter, and was closely drawn into the circle of this deeply political family (at age twelve, Freda herself was on the street passing out leaflets against conscription). The circle also included Ida Diamond's sister, Bess Davidoff, her husband, Henry (a schoolteacher who often discussed music with Paul), and their daughter Amy, whom Paul adored (when she died in her early twenties, he was devastated). On occasion in the twenties, Mama Diamond would chide Paul for not being sufficiently committed to politics. One evening (around 1928), Mama Diamond met Paul on the street in front of their building on West 11th Street in Greenwich Village in order to escort him up in the elevator personally. She later explained that the

new doorman had suggested that her black guest would have to go up in
the service elevator and she had stationed herself on the sidewalk to prevent such an indignity. Paul thanked her, but added that her gesture really
hadn't been necessary, since he had learned, as an artist, not to let such
incidents bother him. Mama Diamond lit into him—"We expect plumbers
to have political consciousness, why not artists?". It was a view Paul would
shortly come to share.[57]

CHAPTER 7

■

Show Boat

(1927–1929)

Gertrude Stein had a bad cold and, being "a little afraid of the inside of a Paris theatre," she missed Robeson's inaugural concert at the Salle Gaveau on October 29. Almost everyone else from the American colony, white and black, showed up: Roland Hayes, Caterina Jarboro, Alberta Hunter, Johnny Hudgins, Mrs. Cole Porter, Ludwig Lewisohn, Naomi Bercovici, Michael Strange, and Sylvia Beach—along with James Joyce and some of Paris's own notables, Georges Auric and Baroness Erlanger. Freda Diamond's Aunt Bess and Bess's daughter Amy—soon to become part of Paul's extended family—also turned out for the concert. Although the program had only been routinely advertised, the audience filled the fifteen hundred available seats as well as standing room, and another five hundred were turned away. The enthusiastic crowd called Robeson back at the end of each section of his program of twenty spiritual and secular songs and at the close of the concert gave him an immense ovation, a full half-hour of applause and encores. It was, Alberta Hunter wrote in her diary, "a triumphant success." The critics, like the audience, showered him with praise (*"un baryton magnifique"*; *"L'ensemble n'en fut pas moins fort agréable"*; *". . . y fit valoir la belle qualité d'un timbre naturellement généreux"*); several of the English-speaking critics present who had heard him on earlier occasions commented on the marked improvement in the range and quality of his voice and on the "poise and ease" of his manner.[1]

Robeson himself wasn't pleased. He had come down with a severe cold, and had been in bed for the four days preceding the performance. Yet the reception was so favorable that Varney immediately scheduled a second concert, and this time Robeson agreed with the critics, telegraphing Essie, "Tremendous success. Marvelous critiques. Everything grand." Gertrude's cold was better, too, and she not only attended the second concert but rhapsodized to Paul about the unique quality of his voice. "She had identified him with herself," Essie quoted Paul as saying, "in the unaesthetics—says Paul does with his voice what she does with words—unbroken continuity, etc."[2]

Essie gave birth to a son, christened Paul Robeson, Jr., on November 2, 1927. She had a difficult time with secondary complications, but once again concealed her health problems from Paul. He remained in Europe to continue his concert engagements—and his relationship with Freda Diamond, traveling alone on her first trip to Europe (in those days an unusual act of daring for a young woman). During the four years he had known her, Freda had grown into a confident, fiery, sometimes imperious young woman; after graduating from the Women's Art School at Cooper Union, she was now embarked on additional study in architecture and decorative design and headed toward an influential career as a designer of home furnishings. A radiant, high-spirited twenty-one-year-old, she was Robeson's constant companion in Paris, and was with him when news arrived of Paul, Jr.'s birth. Though Paul expressed minimal enthusiasm for the event to Freda, she urged him to return immediately to New York—and, by the time she left for Italy the next day, thought she had persuaded him.[3]

She had not. Instead of returning home, and oblivious to Essie's actual condition, Paul sent her a series of letters over the next few weeks that presumed her full recovery from the delivery and expressed deep feeling for her. "You see," he wrote, "I really have grown in these two months of separation to love you with a love that seems unbelievable to me. Nothing matters but you—I don't matter—the world doesn't matter and I'm so anxious to see you to show you a new love—a new sweet heart—a new husband—just like the old one but so much sweeter—kinder—more love—more considerate."[4]

He also used his letters to explore career options. He didn't want to stay in Europe for the full year originally planned, and doubted, in any case, whether a profitable tour could be made to stretch that long. Europe was all very well for prestige, as a place that would "appreciate my art—but the money is home. They'll come and rave over our program once or twice—but they really don't get the words—the songs are simple—I do them simply—and they feel well—if he can sing so grandly (like Chaliapin) I should do the things he does—Boris Godunov etc. They say I'm almost wasted upon simple music—no matter how much they enjoy it. So I can't make money doing what I am—I'm sure. I can only attract the concert audience and most discriminating of that. And there aren't enough places to go to. [Roland] Hayes went to Italy for concerts and lost money. He had to cancel his Russian trip." In order to "attain very substantial success financially I'll need other songs—some in the language of the country or classics that they know. . . . There is no money here at usual stuff. The only hope is Opera. . . ."[5]

Only two years before, Robeson had been quoted in the press as saying, "I will not go into opera, where I would probably become one of hundreds of mediocre singers, but I will concentrate on negro music, which has never been properly handled. I may sing a little opera in the morning but only in the bathroom." Though he would periodically be tempted, as he was now, by the prospects of opera, Robeson never moved seriously in that direction. For one thing, his voice, despite its extraordinary warmth and richness, had limited range (in the thirties he sang well down to bottom F, and his high range went to D above middle C—an E-flat range generally; by the fifties he had shifted down about a half-tone)—and this meant that few bass roles in the operatic repertoire would have been comfortable for him. Even if he had been more interested in an opera career than he was, the conservatism of the Metropolitan Opera management in these years would have forestalled it. When Ernst Křenek's *Jonny Spielt Auf (Johnny Strikes Up the Band)* was performed at the Met in 1928, the story of the promiscuous amours of a black jazz leader (which had caused rioting at its Munich opening) was altered so that the leading character did not necessarily have to be black, and then, to confuse matters further, a blackface white singer sang the title role. In a public statement protesting those alterations, James Weldon Johnson noted, "We have in this country colored singers who could masterfully sing that role. I need only name Jules Bledsoe and Paul Robeson." By 1933 the Metropolitan management had progressed to the point where, in producing Louis Gruenberg's opera *Emperor Jones,* it allowed a few minor parts to be played by blacks and confirmed in the program that the leading character had also been written as a black—but again bypassed Robeson for the role and gave it to Lawrence Tibbett to perform in blackface.[6]

Writing Essie from Europe about his newfound conviction that he must broaden his career, Paul concluded that this was "just what you have believed all along but what you have been sensible enough to let me find out myself." Before getting "so excited about my *'art'* etc. I must be the complete artist. There are so many things I would have done to make us money if I had not been afraid of my *'art'*. Black Boy—Vaudeville—Picture houses—pictures—Show Boat—Hammerstein, etc. . . . and it really hasn't been so much *'art'* as thinking what people would say—which of course is silly." From now on, he resolved, he would "turn things over" to Essie— "trust in you and your judgment wholly. . . . You know how to value me—my dignity etc. But we must have money." "I'm in Europe only because you knew I wanted to come. . . . It was so beautiful of you to let me go at the time of your childbirth. I'll never forget that. . . ." But work in Europe, Paul had now decided, could be confined to a few months in the spring and fall, and the rest of the time "ought to be in America." The money, after all, was in America.[7]

That, however, presented problems with Larry Brown, who might not want to return. If that was so, their partnership, in Paul's judgment, ought to be broken up. "I'm a little fed up with having my career handicapped by being tied up with that of another person. . . . If my career can't be built up and maintained by spirituals there is no need in having Larry as a load and carrying him, making every move of mine considering him." If Larry's choice was to stay in Europe and continue with Varney as manager, he couldn't reasonably object to Paul's leaving—"with you in your present condition." By this time, early December, Essie's condition had worsened; Paul was still ignorant of it, but he did feel some vague concern at having received a letter from her mother (of whom he was never very fond) and not from her. Ma Goode had included a description of the baby, and Paul responded somewhat perfunctorily that the baby sounded "grand"; "Won't I be glad to see him." And to see Essie. "I shant touch you," he promised, "until you are completely well. I can get along and seeing you will be so much."[8]

He was to see her, and his son, sooner than he expected. Six weeks after giving birth, Essie developed a breast abscess and a severe case of phlebitis. Over her daughter's objection, Ma Goode finally decided to cable Paul the truth. He immediately wired back, "Darling Coming at once. Wait for me," and booked passage, arriving home in New York the day after Christmas. This time, however, his mere presence was not enough to rally Essie. Recovery proved slow and discouraging. Paul reported to Gertrude Stein that, although the baby was a "wonder"—"much more fun than I ever thought a small baby could be"—Essie had had "a bad time" (but then added, "For any people beside yourself, Essie was just about ready to 'leave this world.' Otherwise my mgr. and Mr. Brown would be very upset. Thanks"). Essie wasn't allowed out of bed until early January, still with a drainage tube in her breast and limping so severely from phlebitis that the doctor warned that her leg might be permanently game. Paul wanted to take her south for a few months to recover her strength, but their money had all but run out. He hoped a nibble from Hollywood would turn into a firm offer, and Essie's doctor endorsed the prospect of California sunshine for his patient. But for the moment plans remained up in the air, and Paul wired Larry Brown, "Essie recovery operation very slowly. Unable return Europe indefinitely. Make your own plans." Essie, though still recuperating, picked up pen and paper to write to Varney and to reestablish ties with Larry Brown; she was soon back in full swing as Paul's manager.[9]

The California movie deal failed to materialize—the producers couldn't find a "suitable" property for Robeson—so, early in March 1928, he agreed to replace Jules Bledsoe as Crown (the role he had been asked to originate) in the successful run of the DuBose and Dorothy Heywood musical play, *Porgy*. He took the role for five hundred dollars per week, Robeson wrote to Larry Brown, "to keep from starving," but it didn't suit him; he had to strain to sing above the full chorus night after night—"My voice would not stand it as I knew it wouldn't." According to his brother Ben, "the raucous shoutings of the play had not only shattered his voice but his nerves." A nick-in-time offer from Florenz Ziegfeld made it possible for Robeson to leave the show six weeks after opening in it. Ziegfeld asked him to sing the part of Joe in the London company of *Show Boat*—which had been a runaway hit in New York—due to open in early May under the personal supervision of Sir Alfred Butt. He would only have to sing one song—"Ol' Man River"—yet, since it would run through the show in three separate refrains, Butt expected Robeson's appearance to generate considerable press coverage. The role would save his voice even while providing him with maximum publicity. Robeson jumped at the chance. The plan was for Essie, who by April had regained her health, to join him in Europe in May, leaving the baby Paul with Ma Goode.[10]

Essie wrote separately to Larry to help smooth the way. She told him that the part in *Show Boat* was "a ridiculously easy one. . . . It wouldn't tax [Paul's] voice as much as a rehearsal," and predicted that if the show "is a hit, as it surely will be, and Paul is the favorite, you and he may easily and speedily become the vogue in London and clean up" doing concerts on Sunday nights, when there were no performances of the play, and private engagements late on any other night. "There is the situation. It seems grand to me." She added, by way of further inducement, "You will have a fit when you hear Paul sing. He has done two months work with Miss Armitage, and he is just too bad."[11]

Paul sent Larry two notes of his own, one from shipboard on his way to England in mid-April, the other immediately on arrival. He apologized for not having written from the States, "but you know how I am—I was so worried for a while and so relieved when Essie improved—that I didn't know just where I was and my plans were so unsettled." But now he was excited by the new prospects. He felt sure the publicity surrounding his appearance in *Show Boat* would open up concert work for them, and he reassured Larry that "My musical career with you is by all odds paramount"—so much so that he was willing to guarantee him "a livelihood out of my salary—which is only fair. . . . I took this job only because it brought me back to my concerts with you and at the same time will give us something to live on while things are taking shape. . . . I'm here to take up our work and keep it up no matter what happens."[12]

Larry was persuaded. But the *Show Boat* rehearsals proved "so trying" that after them Paul would "go home to bed and stay there in order to be able to do my work." He looked forward to Essie's arrival, he told Amanda Ira Aldridge (daughter of the actor, whom he had met three years earlier), "because she'll be able to make me comfortable and take care of me. I'm still rather a 'baby.' " Essie did not arrive until after the opening, but all went well nonetheless. The publicity for *Show Boat,* as promised, *did* feature Robeson, his voice *had* reached a new level of richness, the London reception *did* prove tumultuous—and Robeson became the lion of the hour. As had often happened before, he came off better than the show. The majority of critics hailed the *Show Boat* production as (in the words of one of them) "an overwhelming feast of spectacle, melody and drama"—with its company of some 160, its one thousand costumes, its eighteen scenes (the opulent sets included a rendering of the Trocadero Music Hall and the 1893 World's Fair at Chicago), its luscious score by Kern (along with an unimpressive book by Oscar Hammerstein II), and a cast that included Cedric Hardwicke, Marie Burke, Leslie Sarony, Edith Day, and Alberta Hunter. Some of the leading critics were less than enchanted, complaining about the length of the evening (three and a half hours), the lack of humor, and the confusing side plots. But none complained about Robeson. St. John Ervine in the *Observer* said that throughout the long evening only Robeson "remained superb," and James Agate (perhaps the most prestigious London critic of the day) suggested in the *Sunday Times* that the producers cut a half-hour out of the "inept and clumsy" show—and fill it in with Robeson singing spirituals.[13]

Despite the mixed critical reception, the public made *Show Boat* a huge hit—and moneymaker. That is, the white public. Many blacks who saw the show came away distinctly less enthusiastic. The European correspondent for the New York *Amsterdam News,* J. A. Rogers, reported in an indignant column (reprinted in the Pittsburgh *Courier*) that he had talked to "fully some thirty Negroes of intelligence or self-respect" who expressed "their disapprobation of the play," and he had "also heard many harsh things said against Robeson for lending his talent and popularity toward making it a success." "If anyone were to call him a 'nigger,' " Rogers quoted one informant as saying, "he'd be the first to get offended, and there he is singing 'nigger, nigger' before all those white people." Rogers also objected to the character of Joe's being simply another instance of the "lazy, good-natured, lolling darkey" stereotype "that exists more in white men's fancy than in reality." The obvious solution, he wrote, was for blacks to write their own plays and books, but because he recognized that "it will be a long time before this is done," Rogers felt he could not "join in the indignation against those actors and writers who sell their service to the whites," much as he did regret that *Show Boat* represented a "deliberate attempt on the part of the White American to carry his anti-Negro propaganda into Europe." Even a few whites objected to the show: a cartoonist in *Sketch* portrayed Robeson with the caption "Despite ragtime and jazz music, poor old Joe sings 'Ole Man Ribber' right through the years from 1880 to 1928." *The New York Times* felt called upon—in response, it said, to criticisms by politically minded "negro newspaper editors"—to enter the fray with a defense of "artistic detachment," insisting that "one should not forget that individuals concentrating successfully on their own creations automatically act as leavening agents"—precisely Robeson's own attitude at the time, and that of most Harlem Renaissance figures.[14]

Soon after the opening, Essie went to London, leaving Paul, Jr., with Ma Goode in a rented house in Oak Bluffs, on Martha's Vineyard. Essie and Paul took a furnished flat in St. John's Wood, directly facing Regents Park, and she reported to Van Vechten that "we are very happy" and that "Larry is fine, and in a splendid frame of mind for us—if you know what I mean." Larry was indeed pleased with the flood of new engagements for him and Paul that immediately followed on the success of *Show Boat.* Sir Alfred Butt arranged a matinee concert in the vast Drury Lane theater, where *Show Boat* performed evenings, and considerable private work drifted in as well—including intimate parties given by Lord Beaverbrook, Ruth Draper, Sir Philip Sassoon, and Lady Ravensdale (the daughter of Lord Curzon). Paul went four times in succession to Beaverbrook's house, Cherkley Court, at a fee of £84.10 for each recital—a large sum for those days. Within six weeks of *Show Boat*'s opening, the Robesons had paid off their small debts and (in Essie's words) "are now rolling up our sleeves to tackle the large ones."[15]

The Drury Lane concert on July 3 proved a sensation. The theater was packed and, in Essie's reliable judgment, Paul and Larry had never been better—"Paul took the audience and put it in his pocket with the first song, and kept it there." The critics raved, the Prince of Wales ordained a command performance on July 9 for a dinner party in honor of the King of Spain at York House, and Edgar Wallace, the popular author of "crime" plays (*The Squeaker* was currently a hit in the West End), told Paul he would write a script for him and would himself invest thirty thousand dollars in it. "It looks as tho at last we are at the end of a long journey," Essie wrote Van Vechten. "Paul is so happy he grins and jugs. He is the same sweet modest boy—but is tickled to death and greatly relieved. He really is *nice,* and I *like* him more and more—quite aside from loving him enormously."[16]

In between the succession of public triumphs were an abundance of good times: driving to Maidenhead and Ascot with Tandy Johnstone in his custom-built Daimler; an afternoon in a motor punt gliding up the Thames; nights out at Covent Garden to hear Eva Turner sing *Turandot* and Chaliapin *Faust,* to see the Diaghilev Ballet's *Firebird* conducted by Stravinsky himself ("very beautiful and modern and unique" was Essie's verdict), the Moscow Art Theatre's "splendidly done, raw, red meat theatre diet" of *Powers of Darkness;* to watch Helen Wills defeat Señorita de Alvarez, LaCoste beat Cochet at Wimbledon (Row A, Centre Court—tickets courtesy of Sir Alfred Butt); to cheer on the great cricket star Constantine at Lord's and at the Oval ("When Constantine comes to bat, the opposing fielders spread away out into deep field, exactly as they do for Babe Ruth in baseball. It is thrilling to see this done for a black man"); to hail Layton and Johnstone's performance at the Alhambra, and Coleridge-Taylor's cantata *Hiawatha* at Royal Albert Hall; to attend the several other concerts given by "our folks" in London, pre-eminently Marian Anderson's "glorious" concert at Wigmore Hall accompanied by Sir Roger Quilter; to relax at a party at Maida Vale where the "our-folks" crowd included Turner Layton, Tandy Johnstone, Ella and Leslie Hutchinson, Johnny and Mildred Hudgins, Johnny Payne, Larry Brown, and Marian Anderson.[17]

Then trouble arrived from an unexpected quarter. Back in January, Robeson, desperate for money, had taken an advance of five hundred dollars to appear in a "colored revue" in New York; it was scheduled for a fall opening, with Caroline Dudley Reagan, who had previously brought Josephine Baker in *La Revue Nègre* to Paris, as producer. Late in July, Dudley Reagan read in the New York newspapers that Robeson was scheduled to appear in a second company of *Show Boat* in the States in the fall, and immediately wired to remind him that he was due to open in her revue then. When he cabled back, "All plans indefinitely postponed," Dudley protested to Actors' Equity: Robeson, she said, was refusing to honor his contractual obligations. Equity warned Robeson that if he failed to carry out the agreement with Reagan he would be liable for suspension, and expressed displeasure that he hadn't attempted to seek a release from Reagan before starting production with *Show Boat.*[18]

Essie took passage to the States in order (as she wrote Van Vechten) "to clear up Paul's business affairs in New York, Ahem!" As soon as she arrived, she made appointments with Frank Gillmore, president of Equity, and with Caroline Dudley Reagan. Essie told Gillmore that her husband "does not like the idea of having to sing blues in a revue. He does not think that sort of singing would be good for his voice or his reputation." Gillmore's reply, in essence, was that Robeson should have thought of that before: Dudley Reagan "has done all her work and secured all her backing on the assumption that she would have your husband for the production." Gillmore asked Essie to cable Paul regarding his intentions about returning. She did cable—but her own message: "Equity will cable demanding your return. You tactfully refuse in fairness to yourself and Dudley. Equity will then cable [Sir Alfred] Butt threatening you and him. Equity secretly sympathetic but must make grand gesture. I offered bluffing to buy Dudley contract and pay reasonable damages. She absolutely refused. Take song easy. All love forever." She signed the cable "Cardozo."[19]

When Essie reported that she had had no reply to her cable, Gillmore then took it upon himself to telegraph Robeson, informing him that the Reagan contract was binding—"Do you wish to ruin her and stamp yourself as dishonorable?"—and threatening him with suspension "with its train of publicity and opprobrium" unless he cabled his intention of returning. He did not, instead cabling Essie, "Equity cabled. . . . Cable returning or suspension.' . . . Of course will remain. . . ." On September 6 the Equity Council placed him under suspension for a month, to be changed to "an indeterminate term" should he continue to remain mute in the face of breach-of-contract charges. Equity struck a perhaps gratuitous racial note in asserting that "it would be a great pity if this outstanding member of his race should take such a narrow view of the obligations he incurred when he signed the contract."[20]

As Gillmore predicted, the suspension was widely reported in the press, and the unwelcome publicity included a more-in-sorrow-than-in-anger account in the black *Amsterdam News* expressing the same hope Equity had that "there will be no blot on the career of this outstanding member of the race." Walter White made the same point in a distressed letter to Robeson. Their mutual friend Arthur Spingarn, the white *pro-bono* counsel for the NAACP, had sent White a clipping from *Equity* detailing the case along with a note urging "very strongly"—"as I do," White added—"whatever the immediate financial or other sacrifice which may be involved that to do other than to live up to your contract would be a very great mistake," one that "would react upon all of us." To illustrate the latter point, White recounted a recent exchange he'd had with "a prominent white person" who kept asking him, after White had agreed to do a certain thing, "Now, can I really depend on you?" Irritated, White replied sharply that he "had given my word and that was enough." To which the man said, "Your people are not strong on keeping their promises are they? — Look at what your friend Paul Robeson is doing."[21]

The suspension did not immediately endanger Robeson's role in *Show Boat*, since Britain was outside Equity's jurisdiction, but in early October, Dudley Reagan applied for an injunction in London to restrain Robeson from continuing in the cast. Stage stars packed the courtroom to hear Sir Alfred Butt declare that without Robeson's services the musical might have to close, and to applaud Mr. Justice Maugham's reasoning that if Reagan was granted an injunction "there might be no play started by the plaintiff," making its only practical effect "to drive the defendant out of employment." Accordingly, he refused Reagan's application, though adding that Robeson might still be liable for damages. The following summer (1929), Robeson settled with Reagan out of court. The principals and their lawyers conferred in London, and Reagan accepted payment of sixteen hundred pounds (eight thousand dollars) to be paid in three installments over a six-month period as discharging in full all Robeson's obligations to her. Equity promptly lifted his suspension. "We wanted to avoid a suit here in England," Essie sarcastically wrote Carlo and Fania in explanation of the expensive settlement, "because of Paul's 'noble' reputation!"[22]

The Robesons felt comfortable in England: London's central location made the Continent accessible for concert work, and the English adored Paul. Ethel Mannin, an English writer who interviewed him at the end of the decade, reacted in a characteristic way: "There is a quality of utter sincerity about him . . . [a] complete lack of affectation and self-consciousness"—that is where "the tremendous charm of his personality lies. He is completely unassuming." Mannin thought Essie very different from Paul, but had kind words for her as well: ". . . she has animation, he has repose; she is voluble, he is quiet; she is brisk, he is retiring. She is a brilliantly clever woman . . . her expression [is] animated and cheerful, whereas his face in repose is a little melancholy."[23]

Thus admired, the Robesons decided for the time being to remain in England. Essie collected Ma Goode and Paul, Jr., from the States in September 1928, and they rented a splendid late-Victorian house on Carlton Hill in St. John's Wood from the Countess des Boulletts. It came complete with silver, linen, and servants (cook, maid, gardener) for "an absurdly small" sum, and, to celebrate, they gave a party for the Van Vechtens, who were in London on a visit. The guests included Fred and Adele Astaire, Mrs. Patrick Campbell, Alfred Knopf, Layton and Johnstone, Harold Browning of the Harmony Kings, Alberta Hunter, John Payne, Leslie Hutchinson, Lady Ravensdale, Lady Laski, Lord Beaverbrook, Cathleen Nesbitt, Athene Seyler, Constance Collier, Ivor Novello, and Hugh Walpole. In the States, the black paper the Chicago *Defender* put an elaborate description of the party on page one. Van Vechten described the event and the Robesons' house in a letter to Gertrude Stein: ". . . there are cockney servants and in the dining room large oil paintings of *turks*. Elsewhere whatnots, porcelain, glass and various knick-knacks. The party was lovely. There was a great deal of food and much champagne. . . . Paul sang and was a lamb. It was their first party and a great success. I think you should come to London to go to a party at Paul's. And I'm sure he would give one for you." Hugh Walpole wrote the next day to thank Essie for a "delightful party. . . . Every one radiated happiness!" and, on his way back to the States, Van Vechten dropped her a note to say (somewhat cryptically), "I think you are wise to be so happy and I am delighted that everything is going as well as it is. And hope it will be still better. . . . It was grand seeing you and you were wonderful to us—and let's all go on being wonderful to each other."[24]

News of the Robesons' lifestyle spread. A few weeks after their party, a registered letter from Otto Kahn arrived for Paul, inquiring about his plans for repaying the five thousand dollars he had borrowed in the summer of 1925. At the time Robeson had secured the loan with his five-thousand-dollar life-insurance policy, but had then missed making a premium payment, forcing Kahn to step in to prevent the policy from lapsing. Essie had assured Kahn in 1925 that they "could easily repay" the loan at the end of two years and had formally agreed to a series of step payments (two thousand dollars after the first year, three thousand after the second). But three years had now passed without Kahn's receiving a penny—although he was simultaneously receiving (courtesy of the periodic packets of reviews that Essie herself sent him) continuing news of Robeson's triumphs. On getting Kahn's registered letter, Essie cabled him, "Greatly regret delay. Posted letter today containing full details."[25]

The following day she wrote him that Paul was "very angry with me because he thought I had written ages ago," and she proceeded, in a lengthy letter, to itemize the tribulations and expenses that had kept them from meeting their obligations. Though Paul was getting a healthy six hundred dollars a week salary in *Show Boat*, fifty of that went to an agent and one hundred twenty to British income tax. The furnished house ate up another fifty dollars per week, and a hired Daimler cost an additional thirty-five—necessary because Paul was susceptible to colds and they had found taxis "very cold and drafty, very bumpy, and on foggy and rainy nights" unattainable, while the underground and the buses were "impossible" because "always full of people with colds, sneezing." Running expenses on the house came to another seventy-five dollars a week (heating and food being the major items), and the cost of keeping Ma Goode and Paul, Jr., on Martha's Vineyard had eaten up another large sum. Even so, Essie's apologia continued, she had managed to accumulate a thousand dollars—only to have it used up in the legal fight with Caroline Dudley Reagan.[26]

She went on to detail to Kahn the financial and artistic prospects that were about to open up for Paul and which would allow them to repay the loan imminently. She apologized if they had offended Kahn "by our apparent neglect" and assured him they were "very eager to fully justify" his generosity and trust. Kahn responded promptly and graciously (I "willingly accept your explanation"), but within a month he had to pay another lapsed premium on Paul's life-insurance policy. Eight months after that, Essie wrote again to explain—"By now you must think we are completely impossible"—that the large out-of-court settlement they had been forced to make with Dudley Reagan would mean a further delay in discharging their debt to him. Kahn once more accepted the explanation, but his patience was wearing thin.[27]

The debt to Kahn was still unpaid by December 1930, and his lawyer, Bruce Bromley, finally served Robeson with a summons. The following month, when in New York, Robeson conferred with Bromley and (so Bromley wrote Kahn) "expressed surprise and regret" that previous notices had been ignored and no payments made, stating that "his wife had concealed these facts from him and had told him that she was attending to the indebtedness and making periodical payments on account." He purportedly told Bromley that "he had learned for the first time upon his arrival in New York that his wife had spent all his income and incurred additional indebtedness besides." The two men quickly arrived at an oral agreement whereby Robeson agreed to turn over one-half of the net proceeds of each of his concerts, beginning immediately, until the indebtedness was erased. A year later, hearing that Kahn was coming to London on a visit, Essie invited him to a home-cooked meal for just the two of them: "I should like you to hear the end of the story, which would be better told than written." Pleading prior engagements, Kahn declined.[28]

Following his success in *Show Boat,* Robeson signed on for Lionel Powell's prestigious Celebrity Concert Tour (his other clients included Kreisler, McCormack, Chaliapin, and Paderewski), received concert offers from various places on the Continent, and again started negotiating (again unsuccessfully) for a motion picture in the States. After nearly a year of singing "Ol' Man River," Robeson was "bored to death with it" and "kicking up his heels with glee" at the prospect of a change. He had been taking three voice lessons and three French lessons a week, along with coaching in singing German (which included learning the role of Sarastro in *The Magic Flute*), and was eager to put what he had learned into practice. "There should be a big harvest to be reaped when the show closes," Essie predicted.[29]

The harvest came in immediately. *Show Boat* closed early in March 1929, and by the end of that month Robeson and Brown were singing concerts at Harrowgate and Bournemouth for a hundred pounds each (Paul, Larry, and Essie going thirds, their new arrangement—marking a rise in pay from 20 percent for Essie). Most of April was spent testing the unfamiliar waters of Vienna, Prague, and Budapest. In all three cities the public and critical response were so enthusiastic that second concerts in each had to be scheduled immediately—and they, too, sold out. The American Minister in Prague not only came to the concert, but also invited the Robesons to tea the next day at the legation. They especially appreciated the gesture because the American Ambassador to England had pointedly omitted them from his yearly Fourth of July party—though he invited nearly every prominent white American in London, and though Robeson's immense popularity exceeded theirs. Robeson was pleased, too, when the director of the National Theater in Prague invited him to perform *The Emperor Jones* there in a production planned for the following year.[30]

In Budapest, Robeson was struck by the affinity between the spirituals and Slavonic and Gypsy folk songs; it was the beginning of a keen interest he would develop in charting universal patterns in the folk music of different nationalities. When, a few months later, a reporter asked him how he accounted for the fact that the African people "have an almost instinctive flair for music," Robeson responded with an explanation that linked up the African experience to a universalized view of oppression: ". . . this faculty was born in sorrow. . . . I think that slavery, its anguish and separation—and all the longings it brought—gave it birth. The nearest to it is to be found in Russia, and you know about their serf sorrows. The Russian has the same rhythmic quality—but not the melodic beauty of the African. It is an emotional product, developed, I think, through suffering." While in Central Europe, Robeson also saw something of the poverty of the masses and the plight of the Jews—concerns that would heighten in the years that lay immediately ahead.[31]

Returning to London, Robeson sold out the Albert Hall—the largest crowd ever assembled there except for Kreisler—and swamped the critics. In the tour of English cities that immediately followed, his new manager, Lionel Powell, negotiated the extraordinary fee of 70 percent of the box-office gross (10 percent going to Powell). Essie, in the meantime, had gotten an offer of her own. The London office of Doubleday and Doran Publishing Company approached her to write a book for them "on Paul and the Negro"—a project she had had in mind for some time—offering an advance of a thousand pounds. Essie completed a first draft early in 1929. Miss Moody at Doubleday's found it "so fascinating" (Essie reported to Otto Kahn) that "she read it straight thru without stopping"; but Moody felt that at a mere twenty-five thousand words the manuscript was only half as long as it should be—though she assured Essie that, if she couldn't lengthen it, Doubleday would accept it anyway, using "very thick pages and wide margins" to fill it out. Essie chose to go back to work on it.[32]

When Van Vechten reappeared in London in June, Essie showed him the new draft, saying she would "thoroughly appreciate anything you care to tell me about it—even if it's bad news." It was. Van Vechten laconically wrote Alfred Knopf that he had "read Essie's mss. about Paul and have advised her to do some more work on it," but—a tribute to the honesty of their friendship—to Essie herself he said directly that he thought she had put too much of *herself* into it. Essie agreed with Carlo's judgment: "I re-read the 'book', thinking about what you said about it, and I must confess darling that I blushed for shame at my terrific and unconscious conceit and boasting. I would have been embarassed [sic] to death if it had got out as is! . . . This time I shall try to think how outsiders will take what I write. You are a lamb to help me so much. Really Carlo, you seem to be cast permanently into the role of our Guardian Angel!'' The revised biography would appear the following year, Essie's self-reportage cut back considerably, but with enough patronizing commentary on Paul remaining in the book to anger him—and to contribute to another, this time sharper rupture in their relationship.[33]

For a time it again seemed Robeson might do a motion picture. He signed a contract with Charles Rogers (of the producing firm Asner and Rogers) to begin shooting a film in the States on July 15, 1929. The play *Black Boy*, Julia Peterkin's *Black April*, and Paul Green's Pulitzer Prize–winning play, *In Abraham's Bosom*, were among the properties considered, but, as Essie—implying some element of bigotry—explained to the Van Vechtens, "the producer couldn't get a story which the distributors would accept!" (Nor could Robeson collect a cent on the contract.) The cancellation of the film unsettled his plans to move smoothly into a two-month concert tour of the States. As a filler, Essie tried "to persuade the British talkie people to do a picture with Paul," and the London film columnist Nerina Shute helped her, publishing an article about Robeson's eagerness to make a film under English auspices and his inability to find a satisfactory script. But again nothing suitable was forthcoming (and at the same time, the play Edgar Wallace had been working on for him failed to materialize).[34]

Robeson occupied his time prior to his departure for the States in the fall of 1929 with studying languages, taking voice lessons, doing an occasional concert in the vicinity—and getting teeth extracted (giving him the appearance, in Essie's opinion, of a "scraggly boy," and giving hope that draining an old abscess in his mouth would put an end to his numerous bouts of nose and throat trouble; it did not). He also began to learn the role of Othello.[35]

It had long been in the back of Robeson's mind that he would someday like to play Othello. After his success in *Show Boat*, the idea entered other minds as well. In the end it was the actor-producer Maurice Browne and his wife, the director Ellen ("Nellie") Van Volkenburg, who put together a production. The couple had founded the Repertory Company in Seattle and the Little Theatre in Chicago, and Browne had recently had a huge success producing R. C. Sherriff's play *Journey's End*. The profits from that venture were so great that he became a partner in the purchase of the Globe and Queens theaters. The press reported that Browne had been able to offer Robeson a contract calling for a three-figure weekly salary— "said to equal the largest ever paid in London to an actor in a 'straight' part—though well below the £1,000 a week understood to be commanded by a musical comedy star like Jack Buchanan." Rehearsals were scheduled to begin after Robeson's return from his 1929 American tour, with an opening planned for London in the spring of 1930, followed by a production in the States. "We are really very excited about it," Essie wrote right after Paul formally signed the contract—"Paul is already working on the part."[36]

One month after the press announced with fanfare that Robeson would be playing Othello, it headlined a quite different story about him: he and his wife had been refused service, explicitly as blacks, at the Savoy Grill, the posh watering hole of the supposedly color-blind upper classes. Robeson told reporters he had had nothing to do with making the incident public—"No one was more surprised to see it published than I. I did not agitate the matter and intended to ignore it. Several evenings after the incident I was with an English friend and the question of social barriers in the United States came up. She said that such a thing could not happen to me over here. I realized that it had happened only a few nights before. She was so amazed she took it up with the London papers." (That friend was apparently Sybil Colefax.) In a letter he released to the press, Robeson gave his own detailed version of the Savoy incident:

> I thought that there was little [prejudice against blacks in London] or none but an experience my wife and I had recently has made me change my mind and to wonder, unhappily, whether or not things may become almost as bad for us here as they are in America.
>
> A few days ago a friend of mine . . . invited my wife and myself to . . . the Savoy grill room at midnight for a drink and a chat. . . .
>
> On arriving the waiter, who knows me, informed me that he was sorry he could not allow me to enter the dining room. I was astonished and asked him why. . . . I thought there must be some mistake. Both my wife and I had dined at the Savoy and in the grill room many times as guests.
>
> I sent for the manager, who came and informed me that I could not enter the grill room because I was a negro, and the management did not permit negroes to enter the rooms any longer. . . .

The episode created a stir, and Africans and West Indians living in London called a protest meeting at the Friends' House. Only a month before, Robeson himself had told a reporter that "The colour problem exists only with illiterate English people." But at the protest meeting, the Labour M.P. James Marley (later Lord Marley) and others recounted numerous recent discriminatory actions against people of color—including the inability to find accommodations for two West Indians invited to the country to lecture on art and literature; the repeated barring of Robert S. Abbott, editor and publisher of the Chicago *Defender,* from hotels in London; and the many separate instances when blacks—some of them scholars, solicitors, QCs—were asked to leave dance halls. As for well-known entertainers, Marley said—and he cited Robeson's old group The Harmony Kings as a case in point—they were usually allowed "to stay at first-class hotels, but they stayed there as members of the staff who assisted at entertainments and not as guests." (At exactly this time, the Chinese film star Anna May Wong—a friend of Robeson's—was forbidden by the British censors to kiss an Englishman in a film.)[37]

Marley announced that he would raise the matter in the House of Commons, and to that end wrote to Ramsay MacDonald, the Prime Minister. Although MacDonald had been part of a group of Labour MPs who the previous year had entertained Robeson in the Commons, he straddled the issue, announcing, "It is not in accordance with our British hotel practice, but I cannot think of any way in which the Government can intervene." Other Robeson acquaintances were less ambivalent: one of them telegraphed MacDonald to urge he take action, and Lord Beaverbrook's *Evening Standard* published an article by the novelist Richard Hughes wondering aloud whether the change in London's attitude on the race question was due to "that general Americanization of our capital which so many lugubrious and true-blue patriots seem to find on every side." Hughes called on the leading London restaurateurs to declare their position on the issue of race. Some did, but the response was not reassuring: the managers of the Grosvenor and the Waldorf were unwilling to express an opinion, the manager of the Mayfair announced that, "as in the past, I shall rely solely on my own judgement," and the Savoy Grill itself professed an inability to trace the original incident, while refusing to confirm or deny reports that it would henceforth adopt a "Jim Crow" policy.[38]

In an exclusive interview with the black newspaper the New York State *Contender,* Robeson said that he, too, believed "the influence of American race prejudice was responsible for the affront." That explanation was widely seconded, and not merely by Englishmen eager to shift the blame. When the New York *Journal* asked several prominent Harlem leaders for their reactions, George W. Harris (a former alderman) said, "The American negrophobia has spread to European shores," and Edward A. Johnson (a former assemblyman) claimed that blame for the incident "rested on the shoulders of white American tourists," who within the last few years had been arriving in increasing numbers in England. But, as London's *New Leader* reminded its readers, "It is no new thing for coloured men and women to be treated in this way in the centre of London"—the sense that discrimination was something new resulted from the shock of seeing it extended to embrace a "cultivated, sensitive spirit" like Robeson.[39]

Two weeks later Paul, accompanied by Essie, embarked for his first full-scale American concert tour, under the management of F. C. Coppicus of the Metropolitan Music Bureau. Robeson rarely felt compelled to express himself in writing (though he had the devouring appetite of a scholar for the written words of others), yet while in the States he did keep a kind of shorthand diary for a few days. In it he mulled over the pros and cons of learning additional technique as an artist, remarking that "Water Boy," his "best record," was made "when I was untrained," and he also wrote down his impressions on returning to his native land. They were not favorable. Attending the theater one night, he had a "strange feeling" sitting in the balcony—"I am almost afraid to purchase orchestra seats for fear of insult—when in England my being in the theatre is almost an event. Very curious. I do hate it all so at times. Everything rushes along—not a kind word anywhere. Everyone looking for his own—no sense of peace— calm—freedom as in London. I feel so oppressed and weighted down." On top of everything else, American audiences struck him as "terribly crude," attending for entertainment, not for "love of Theatre."[40]

Robeson's inaugural American concert, at Carnegie Hall on November 5, 1929, did not fare well with the critics, but the large advance sale ensured a box-office success. He no longer felt that the critics were "of great importance" to him; besides, at his second Carnegie Hall concert, five days later, he sang superbly: "To my mind the best recital of my career. I sang evenly and with great variety of mood-color etc. I [did] so because I sang the songs and forgot my voice. The audience responded in great style." And so, this time around, did the critics: "He has improved . . . enormously," wrote *The New Yorker*. A thousand people were turned away, the ushers told Robeson no one had ever filled the hall twice in five days, and Lawrence Tibbett went backstage to tell him "he had never enjoyed a concert so much" in his life.[41]

From there Robeson's two-month tour across the continent turned into something like a triumphal procession. In Pittsburgh he was accorded "one of the greatest ovations ever given a visiting artist"; in Chicago called "the Chaliapin of the moment"; in Wisconsin hailed for "a truly sensational concert"; and on his sentimental return to Rutgers, fifteen hundred people turned out, the "largest crowd they ever had at a concert"—at the close giving "a college yell and cheer for 'Robey.'" The music critic in Toronto epitomized the rhapsodic receptions everywhere:

His voice has all the power of Chaliapin's and practically the same range, but there the likeness ends. Paul Robeson's voice is all honey and persuasion, yearning and searching, and probing the heart of the listener in every tiniest phrase. A rich, generous, mellow, tender, booming voice that you think couldn't say a bitter word or a biting sentence with a whole lifetime of practice. . . .

A voice like his is worth waiting ten years to hear, and an art like his comes once in a generation.[42]

In the face of such acclaim, Robeson continued to harbor a sense, not exactly of unworthiness, but, rather, of mystified awe. Well aware of the technical limitations of his voice, he was yet being received, and by an ever-widening circle of admirers, as the embodiment of vocal perfection. Except for a few minor disappointments and miscalculations, his reputation had spread with a velocity, and his triumphs had proceeded with a regularity, that defied the career pattern ordinarily associated with a profession—or, rather, several professions—in which accidents of luck, timing, and the volatility of popular and critical taste typically undercut any sustained artistic development (or even applause)—not to mention the additional barriers traditionally thrown up to the advance of any black artist. Faced with his unprecedented good fortune, Robeson chose to view it as profoundly mysterious, attributing the steady advance of his reputation not to the inevitable progress of a unique talent, or even to the willed doggedness of his wife, but to the incalculable workings of some higher power. This "I-am-a-mere-vessel" self-image gave Robeson at once a settled inner confidence and an appealing outer modesty. He rarely made public reference to any sense of "mission" and, among the few times he did, added a note of humor: "I don't know what it is . . . that all my life has caused me to succeed whenever I appeared before the public far beyond what my experience, training or knowledge deserved. . . . I shall probably never know my guardian angel, and though once I sought him earnestly, now I don't want to know him!"[43]

Though as an adult Robeson rarely attended church services and gave little demonstration of caring about any formal religious ties, he did, during this triumphal American tour, jot in his shorthand diary some thoughts on "a conception I'm getting about *God*. My career has been so strange and so seemingly guided by some outside influence. And to meet *Essie* who has so clearly guided my career—and to have all the teachers come to me at the right time and the right things to happen—it is simply *extraordinary*." His renewed appreciation of Essie's role in his success was a central ingredient in this meditation. "I had to leave Essie and how I hated to," he wrote in the diary he briefly kept in 1929. "I wanted to talk to her and bring her home and *love* her—but I had promised to say hello to F. [Freda] who had come from Chicago for the concert. She was as beautiful as ever and very glad to see me." Later, still gripped by his feelings for Essie, he wrote in his diary, "In bed and thinking how wonderful my Essie is. I can hardly realize how fine she is and how deeply I love her. If I were quite honest—I would say no one or ones ever meant ⅓ so much as she to me. She understands me *so* completely, and her love is so great. We will do great things together." The presence of Essie in his life seemed part of the "higher plan" for him: "Have wife as scientist who holds me to truth necessary to create *true* beauty. So God watches over me and guides me. He's with me but lets me fight my own battles and hopes I'll win. . . ." Paul's heightened serenity and renewed sense of gratitude were apparent to Essie. Not only was he "singing magnificently," she reported to the Van Vechtens, but the tour had proved "an enormous success in many, many ways. . . ."[44]

■

CHAPTER 8

Othello

(1930–1931)

In the three months between his return to London and the beginning of rehearsals for *Othello* in April 1930, Robeson made two strenuous concert tours—one in the British Isles, the other in Central Europe—acted in a feature-length film in Switzerland, and performed *The Emperor Jones* in Berlin. All three ventures brought continuing acclaim, but only the film extended his range.

The majority of the critics continued to give him splendid reviews, but the sameness in his concert program of spirituals began to create some dissatisfaction. Robeson experimented with several devices for breaking up the format. In Paris he tried singing the spirituals to a full orchestral accompaniment (Pierre Monteux conducting), but it was generally thought—and Robeson agreed—that the effect was artificial, the simplicity of the Sorrow Songs injured, and their impact diluted in so elaborate a context. He also tried sharing the platform with another soloist: at different times the violinist Wolfi and the pianists Vitya Vronsky, Ania Dorfman, and Solomon performed with him. All were received well, but for some critics the problem of "monotony" in Robeson's own program remained bothersome; they were alternately impatient with the "intrinsic" repetitions of the spirituals themselves or disappointed in Robeson's own refusal to branch out beyond them.[1]

The Manchester *Guardian's* critic, representing the one set of complaints, praised Robeson for his "ease and grace" but felt "the music itself is not inexhaustible in its appeal. . . . There is a family likeness about these melodies which reminds us that a small musical vocabulary and a strophic or folk-song style of composition are bound before long to tire the ear. . . ." The Glasgow *Herald* critic, representing the other set of complaints, suggested that Robeson "owed it to himself to embrace the wider field of serious bass music." The demand that he "try something else" grew loud enough for his defenders to answer publicly. The *Daily Express* suggested, "We might as well rail at . . . John Galsworthy because he writes plays but refuses to write revues or musical comedies. . . . Mr. Robeson would not sing Negro songs so well if he had not concentrated all his heart and brain on them. Specialization . . . is the secret of achievement in art, as in other things."[2]

At just the time some critics were growing tired of the spirituals, Robeson was finding new depth in them. His highly successful second tour of Central Europe, where he devoted his concert program entirely to the spirituals, helped further to convince him of their universal qualities: "Slav peasant music has a great deal in common with ours; and in the countries which have for centuries suffered under an alien yoke, I found a more instinctive response, in spite of the bar of language, than in countries like England, who have forgotten what it is like to be conquered." Essie, who went with him to Central Europe, recorded in her diary his enthusiastic reception in Prague, Brno, Vienna, Dresden—everywhere but Bucharest; she thought the Rumanians "a surly lot" (by then Essie was understandably out of sorts, troubled again by a recurrence of phlebitis in her leg and angry after a long, bitter-cold train ride, when they could get a sleeper only for Paul, and she and Larry had had to sit up all night).[3]

Robeson's "fascinating discoveries" about the spirituals during his two 1930 tours deepened his commitment to them still more. A Polish musician "proved" to him that "the melodies of Central Africa have also influenced European music" and "traced its descent through the Moors and the Spaniards until it reached Poland." Robeson's interest in Africa— soon to burgeon—had just begun to emerge, and he dismissed the recently advanced theory that the Afro-American folk song derived from the Scottish folk song—or, indeed, that it derived from anywhere other than Central Africa. He was delighted, in Paris, when talking with Prince Touvalou of Dahomey, to learn that in that land "whole families devote their lives entirely to song." Becoming convinced that "we are on the eve of great discoveries with regard to Negro culture," Robeson was heartened by reports from Germany that "magnificent sculptures" found in the heart of Africa heralded the recovery of "a great civilization." He told one reporter that he hoped to go to Africa "whenever I can get a 'break,' " to study the cultural background for himself; and he told another (who described him as having "the enthusiasm of the true student"), "It is one of my ambitions to make a talkie which will interpret fully the spirit of the Negro race."[4]

At the completion of his two concert tours in March 1930, the Robesons, apparently as a diversion, agreed to spend a week in Switzerland acting in an experimental silent film called *Borderline*. However offhand the Robesons' involvement, the film went on to become something of a classic in experimental cinema, continuing to the present day to have admirers. The so-called Pool Group produced the film: Bryher (Winifred Ellerman), her bisexual husband Kenneth Macpherson, and her lover (and Macpherson's), the poet H. D. (Hilda Doolittle). The Pool Group had previously made three short films. *Borderline* was to be the only feature it would complete before disbanding.[5]

In the film, Robeson plays the part of Pete, a black man living quietly in a shabby Swiss "borderline" town until the arrival of his sweetheart, Adah (played by Essie), ignites a tangled crosscurrent with a white couple (played by Gavin Arthur and H. D., billed under the pseudonym Helga Doorn), disrupting the town and leading, ultimately, to Pete's unhappy departure—a "plot summary" barely detectable when viewing the film and not much elucidated by the elaborate brochure H. D. prepared to accompany it. Macpherson—the film's scenarist, cameraman, and director—concentrated not on narrative coherence but on cosmic psychological metaphors (greatly influenced by the speculations of Hanns Sachs, Bryher's analyst) and on "advanced" experimental cinematic techniques employing complex montage (greatly influenced by the theories of Sergei Eisenstein).[6]

Macpherson meticulously planned camera angles and movement in advance of the Robesons' arrival, hoping to make maximum use of their limited stay by completing enough "one-take" footage to permit later splicing. He spent far less time on the scenario. One did exist (cinematic historians have speculated to the contrary), but only in rough form; Macpherson talked over an early draft with Essie and promised to incorporate her suggestions, yet, when she asked to see the finished version prior to their arrival in Switzerland, Macpherson sent word that he "did not think it advisable to send the scenario as it is not like stage acting—not sustained." He promised to "discuss all the shots with you according as they are taken on arrival." When Essie expressed hesitation about her ability to act, he reassured her: "It is not like the stage, where you simply have to go through with your part without a stop, but a series of, so to speak, snapshots, with waits in between—so that, as I say, the camera is in the end the real actor. Anyhow, I'm quite sure you have a very considerable talent."[7]

The Robesons arrived in Territet on March 20, 1930, and left on March 30—filming completed and a fair amount of sightseeing gotten in on the side. Judging from the casual entries in Essie's diary, the whole experience was in the nature of a lark for them, time out from the hectic pace of touring. They had "great fun," in part because they liked everyone connected with the filming; when they were shooting the interiors, Essie wrote in her diary, "Kenneth and H. D. used to make us so shriek with laughter with their naive ideas of Negroes that Paul and I often completely ruined our make-up with tears of laughter, had to make up all over again. We never once felt we were colored with them."[8]

They danced the tango between takes, and enjoyed the beauty of the countryside, though not the hike up the mountains outside Montreux to get exterior shots—"Paul and I were frightened out of our wits," Essie wrote, although she was mollified by a picnic lunch. In the village of Lutry, they were followed by crowds everywhere they went, Robeson attracting children "as honey does bees." The townspeople filled the streets and hung out of their windows to catch sight of "Monsieur le Nègre." The café did unprecedented business. The fire brigade, alarmed at the new electric installation in the studio (the town hall) for lighting, held a special practice session. The *Tribune de Lausanne* arrived for an interview. Except for an electrician, no one was paid (the total cost of making the film was two thousand dollars), yet, in Bryher's words, "extras had to be dispersed rather than sought, everybody wanted to be in it and every twenty minutes all the lights went out because the tram went by."[9]

When they saw the first three days' work on the screen, Essie reported to the Van Vechtens that they were "surprised to see how well we both filmed." Paul "of course" looked "marvelous"—his "face is so big and mobile and expressive." But Macpherson assured Essie that she, too, was "very good"—and, indeed, two months later, after they had had a look at the first reel of the film, Bryher wrote Essie, "You really are stealing the picture. One knew that Mr. Robeson would be good—every time I see the film it is your acting and your sense of movement that amazes me. Even more than his—if this is not treason."[10]

The Robesons never expected wide distribution for the film. Essie categorized it as "one of those very advanced expressionistic things in the Russian-German manner, so it will probably be shown by Film Societies, etc." She described it in a letter home to A'Lelia Walker as "futuristic"— "We made it up in the Swiss Alps" and "enjoyed every moment of it, though it was hard work." "It's a dreadful highbrow," she confided to the Van Vechtens, "but beautifully done, I think." G. W. Pabst, one of the heroes of the Pool Group—Bryher described his *Die Freudlose Gasse (Joyless Street)*, starring Greta Garbo, as "the one film that we felt expressed our generation"—was given a private showing of the film and declared himself "very enthusiastic"; he offered the use of his own people "to stick the negative and make the exhibition positives"—and also expressed a desire to make a "talkie" with Paul. If the film "is to be 'popular' in the obvious sense, I don't know," H. D. wrote Essie. "It is without question a work of art and that satisfies us."[11]

It had to. The film was not a popular success, and the critics, on the whole, did not think it art. As Essie had predicted, it was booked by cine-clubs and film societies in Europe, and in October 1930 had a showing at the Academy Cinema in London. The British critics were particularly harsh. The reviewer on the *Evening Standard* dismissed the film as "self-conscious estheticism," and the critic in *Bioscope* called it "a wholly unintelligible scramble of celluloidan eccentricity," although adding that it "stimulates one's natural desire to see and hear Paul Robeson in a first-rate British 'talkie' made for the public." That was still a few years off.[12]

The nine days of shooting completed, the Robesons went straight from Territet to Berlin, where Paul had agreed to do two performances of *The Emperor Jones* under Jimmy Light's direction. Light was abroad for a year on a Guggenheim Fellowship, and at his persuading, Essie had "wangled and rearranged and quarreled" in order to piece together the needed three days in Paul's schedule. The terms helped: the Deutsches Kuenstler Theater offered Light and Robeson together 50 percent of the gross receipts. Robeson trusted Light as a director and also liked him as a person, and the experience turned out to be a good one. Hooper Trask, the former actor and correspondent for *The New York Times* and *Variety,* was originally scheduled to play Smithers opposite Robeson, but in the end Light himself assumed the role. (Reviewing the production in the *Times,* Trask confined himself to praising Light's work as a director; Essie described his acting as "not bad.") Audience and critics alike received Robeson warmly, the play much less so. The Berlin critics had earlier seen the great German actor Oscar Homolka in the role, but preferred Robeson; they had unanimous praise for his "childlike originality and naturalness"—he succeeded, as one put it, in "showing the soul of his people to the audience," which no white actor, Homolka included, possibly could. One reviewer congratulated Robeson for having done his best to help a "weak poet" like O'Neill, whose "flat, sociological" play (in the words of another) had little to reveal to "culturally conscious Europeans." Though O'Neill had his defenders, Robeson, not O'Neill, emerged as the star attraction.[13]

The Robesons were "crazy" about Berlin. "It is a marvelous city," Essie wrote home, and recounted the special pleasure they took in hearing, at the Berlin zoo roof garden, Sam Wooding's Negro Band—"I can't tell you how the good old home rhythm sounded to us." There's no evidence that either Paul or Essie saw anything disagreeable or threatening in the political climate during their stay in Berlin. Yet the year 1930 marked a turning point in German history, with massive Nazi rallies throughout the country, with Bruening, a Catholic conservative, succeeding to the chancellorship in March, and with the Nazis emerging in the September election as the nation's second-largest party. All of this went unremarked by Robeson—in much the way he had made no public comment on such recent events as the general strike in Britain in 1926, the phenomenon of women under thirty voting for the first time in that country's 1929 general election, and, in the United States, the Wall Street crash in October 1929. Even after Bruening had been elected in Germany, Robeson told reporters—he was, of course, thinking of the artistic experimentation of Weimar—that his "one great desire" was to return to Germany to study and perform: "Germany is the gateway now of all of Europe," and "on the Continent the colour bar does not exist." As further regards fascism, a reporter from the Jamaican paper *The Daily Gleaner* quoted Robeson as late as 1932 as saying, "If the real great man of the Negro race will be born, he will spring from North America. The Negro Gandhi or Mussolini cannot be begotten but in the land of ancient oppression and revolutionary emancipation."[14]

But it would be a mistake to imply that Robeson was unconscious of or indifferent to political developments. He had long since developed a deep interest in Jewish culture. As early as 1927, to give but one example, he had performed a concert in New York's Town Hall to aid the Women's Committee of the American ORT (the organization devoted to teaching trades to young Jewish people in Eastern Europe seeking to emigrate to Palestine); and he had frequently expressed the view that enslaved blacks had derived inspiration from the Old Testament account of the struggle of the ancient Hebrews. As regards labor unrest in Britain, moreover, Robeson at least once spontaneously offered a gesture of support for the plight of Welsh miners doubly beset by wage cuts and meager unemployment relief, which a Labour government seemed unwilling to ameliorate. To be sure, his political consciousness in 1930 was not yet developed to nearly the extent it would later be, but it was already greater than his near-total silence on public events would suggest. He was inactive (as was his style while awaiting some clear purpose), not unaware, continuing to hold in 1930 to his long-standing view that he could best work against injustice by advancing his own reputation as an artist. But that stance was shifting. Within a few years, Robeson would no longer be content with the view that the enhancement of his artistic stature would somehow produce a generalized improvement for others; he would move instead toward direct participation in organized political efforts to assail oppressive conditions.[15]

The Robesons returned to London in early April, and Paul went directly into rehearsals for *Othello*. He had hesitated about signing on for the production—"Am still afraid of Othello but we can talk it over," he had written Maurice Browne when first approached. Browne later commented, "For eighteen months I wrestled with him," and "my persistence broke down his objections." He overcame Paul's qualms with promises of a first-rate director and a first-rate Iago. He got neither. Browne cast himself as Iago and gave the directing plum to his wife, Nellie Van Volkenburg. Both choices were self-indulgent. Browne had aspirations to act ("I had always itched to play Iago," he later confessed) without being an actor, and Nellie had had scant directing experience since her days with Chicago's Little Theatre, and none in Shakespeare. Robeson did get a first-rate Desdemona in the twenty-two-year-old newcomer Peggy Ashcroft. He had seen her in Matheson Lang's production *Jew Süss,* her first major success, and because his contract with Maurice Browne gave him the right to decide who would play Desdemona, asked Ashcroft to audition. She was terrified: "I can't sing in tune," she remembered years later, "and I had to perform the Willow Song in front of Paul Robeson." Nonetheless, he liked what he heard and she was offered the role. Ashcroft was thrilled at the opportunity; "for us young people in England at the time," she later recalled, Robeson "was a great figure, and we all had his records, and one realized that it was a tremendous honor to be doing this." The supporting cast was also well chosen: Sybil Thorndike as Emilia, the little-known Ralph Richardson as Roderigo, and Max Montesole, an experienced graduate of Frank Benson's famed Shakespeare company, as Cassio. They would prove "supportive" in several needed senses.[16]

At the start, Essie enthusiastically wrote Nellie Van Volkenburg, "I have a feeling that we are going to have a magnificent time with *Othello.*" It proved to be anything but. Robeson realized from the first that his director and his Iago were hopeless, likely to prove actual impediments to his own performance. After the first week of rehearsal, Essie, who had a sharp eye and a short fuse for incompetence, wrote indignantly in her diary, "Nellie doesn't know what it is all about. Talks of 'tapestry,' of the scene, the 'flow,' and 'austere beauty,' a lot of parlor junk, which means nothing and helps not at all. . . . She can't even get actors from one side of the stage to the other. Poor Paul is lost."[17]

Van Volkenburg and Browne were fascinated with the "psychological dimensions" of the play and urged on Paul the theory (both were gay) that Iago's motivation was best explained as the result of his having fallen in love with Othello. When Paul asked for specific direction, he got instead patronization, the more galling for coming from an officious amateur. Nellie had a penchant for standing in the back of the stalls and yelling instructions through a megaphone; one day, while rehearsing the Cyprus scene, Paul paused and asked her a question. "Mr. Robeson," she shouted through the megaphone, "there are other people on the stage besides yourself!" Peggy Ashcroft, horrified at this gratuitous humiliation of Robeson, decided that Nellie was "a racist."[18]

Ashcroft found her entire experience in *Othello* "an education in racism," something about which she had previously been ignorant. "Paul would tell us stories which I could hardly believe. . . . He talked a lot to us, and particularly Rupert [Rupert Hart-Davis, her husband], about his problems in the States," though "he didn't talk politics"—his concern then was with the plight of his people, not with any particular political program for ameliorating it. When queried about "the racial aspect" of the production, Ashcroft was widely quoted in the press as saying, "Ever so many people have asked me whether I mind being kissed in some of the scenes by a coloured man, and it seems to me so silly. Of course I do not mind! It is just necessary to the play. For myself I look on it as a privilege to act with a great artist like Paul Robeson." In fact they were a bit skittish during rehearsals. The press bombardment about "how the public will take to seeing a Negro make love to a white woman" made Robeson somewhat "infirm of purpose"; as he told a reporter fifteen years later, "For the first two weeks in every scene I played with Desdemona that girl couldn't get near to me, I was backin' away from her all the time. I was like a plantation hand in the parlor, that clumsy."[19]

Robeson was sympathetic to Ashcroft's plight under Nellie's direction. While rehearsing the scene where Othello denounces Desdemona as a whore, Nellie insisted Robeson keep slapping Ashcroft to "encourage" her to fall at a particular angle—one that Ashcroft felt "was physically impossible to do in one movement. . . . I think she was a sadist"—bringing her instead to the verge of tears. Without a word, Robeson got up and left the theater. He sent a message to Maurice Browne that he could no longer continue under Nellie's direction, and requested a replacement. When Browne threatened a breach-of-contract suit, Robeson—with the Equity suspension still fresh in his mind—returned to rehearsals.[20]

But thereafter, clear that (in Ashcroft's words) "there was no help, indeed only hindrances, from our director," Robeson, Ashcroft, and Max Montesole—with Sybil Thorndike joining them whenever she could—took to rehearsing together evenings in one another's homes. Montesole, with his considerable experience in playing Shakespeare, provided crucial support; according to Ashcroft, he "was the saving of the production—as far as it could be saved." Jimmy Light also pitched in by coaching Robeson privately. "I think Paul would have given up long ago," Essie wrote in her diary, "if it hadn't been for Jim and Max. They have both been working like blazes over him."[21]

But if the cast members did all they could to help one another, Nellie retained final say over staging, lights, and sets—and made a considerable botch of each. Her staging was at once fussy and remote, long on detail (much of it anachronistic, like the introduction of a quasi-Venetian skirt dance) but short on immediacy (in resorting to a series of ascending platforms, she managed to put much of the stage action at the farthest possible remove from the audience). She cut significant passages from the text in favor of highlighting extratextual diversions like dance, incidental music (including a sailor's ditty as Othello lands on Cyprus), and conspicuous set changes. ("It would not have surprised me," one critic later wrote, "if Mr. Paul Robeson had 'obliged' with a negro spiritual too"—unaware that Robeson and Maurice Browne had had a "terrific row" during rehearsals when Browne tried to insist that Robeson arrive at Cyprus *singing.*) Nellie staged the final scene of the play with the bed tucked away in a corner, creating a remote, frigid mood when precisely the opposite effect was called for. Then, in addition, she allowed set designer James Pryde, a well-known painter (with no experience in scenic design), to include an enormously high four-poster bed, which caused such a racket being hoisted into position behind the curtain as Ashcroft and Sybil Thorndike were playing the preceding Willow Scene that Thorndike—the one cast member to whom Nellie deferred—told the stagehands in no uncertain terms that they could not move the bed until after she had begun her long speech: "*I* can shout my way over it, but Desdemona can't!"[22]

As for the lighting, Nellie kept it dim to the point of inscrutability. The subdued effects were necessary, she explained in her program notes, in order to maintain the integrity of Pryde's scenic "paintings," but as James Agate acidly pointed out in the *Sunday Times,* "The first object of lighting in the theatre is not to flatter a scene-painter but to give us enough light to see the actors by." The actors even had trouble seeing one another, yet when one of them complained to Nellie she snapped, "Switch on the exit lights over the doors"—her sole concession. (Later, with the director no longer on hand after the opening, Ralph Richardson kept a flashlight up his sleeve to light his way across the stage.) To complete her miscalculations, Nellie pasted a disfiguring beard and goatee on Robeson and until the final scene dressed him in unsuitably long Elizabethan garments (including tights, puffed sleeves, and doublets), instead of Moorish robes, which would have naturally enhanced the dignity of his performance.[23]

By opening night, Paul (according to Essie) was "wild with nerves." Her own hair "went gray in a patch" during the final ten days of rehearsal, and she clutched Hugh Walpole's hand throughout the opening-night performance as select members of the gala audience—Baroness Ravensdale, Garland Anderson (the black author of the hit play *Appearances*), Lady Diana Cooper, Anna May Wong—came up during intervals to offer moral support and to compliment her on her white satin gown. Paul, by his own account, "started off with my performance pitched a bit higher than I wanted it to be," but by curtain he was recalled twenty times. The critics, however, responded more tepidly than the audience. Browne and Van Volkenburg got a general drubbing—the production "has little to recommend it"; "Maurice Browne cast himself for Iago, and ruined the play." "They caught the hell they so well deserved," Essie wrote in her diary.[24]

Sybil Thorndike came off well, and Ashcroft got a splendid set of notices, but Robeson's own reviews ran the gamut. The virtues of his performance were sharply contested. At one extreme, he was hailed as "great," "magnificent," "remarkable"; at the other decried as "prosaic" and "disappointing." A number of critics agreed that he had played the role in too genteel a fashion, as if "afraid of losing himself"; Othello became "a thoughtful, kindly man, civilised and cultured," rather than "the sort of great soldier to whom the senators of Venice would entrust their defense." ("Robeson endows Othello with an inferiority complex which is incongruous," wrote *Time and Tide.*) Putting a direct racial gloss on the same complaint, one reviewer ascribed Robeson's caution and geniality not merely to his own personal modesty but to his fear that any "assumption of arrogance might be mistaken for the insolent assumptions of the less educated of his race." Another critic, in *The Lady,* suggested that his "lethargy" was an attribute intrinsic to blacks, and used that as "confirmation" for the view that the hot-blooded Othello had been conceived by Shakespeare not as an Ethiopian but as a passionate Arabic Moor. ("There is not a much closer racial affinity between the Negro and the Arab than between the Arab and the white man, and a far closer cultural affinity between the last two.") In regard to that view, Robeson's own interpretation of the play in 1930 was less pronouncedly racial than it would be by the time of the Broadway production in 1943. Whereas he later argued forcefully that debate over whether Shakespeare intended Othello to be a Negro *or* a Moor was a nonquestion—by "Moor" Shakespeare *meant* "Negro"—in 1930 Robeson told a newspaper interviewer, "There are, of course, two distinct schools on the subject, and it is possible to produce a convincing argument for either side. It is possible to prove from the text that Othello was a Negro, but the same argument applies to a Moor. If, of course, Shakespeare intended definitely to write of a Moor, then I am not the man for the part. This, however, I consider doubtful. Anyway, the Moor is chiefly of negro extraction."[25]

Robeson shared the critics' discontent with his technical abilities, yet attempting the role, he told one newspaper reporter, had nonetheless been liberating: ". . . Othello has taken away from me all kinds of fears, all sense of limitation, and all racial prejudice. Othello has opened to me new and wider fields; in a word, Othello has made me free." Even after the opening, he continued to work with Jimmy Light, steadily improving his performance. "He is much better now than he was at the opening," Essie reported ten days later. "He has been working steadily at his part, and some changes have been made in his costumes, so that he is 100 percent better." The Van Vechtens came over the following month, saw for themselves, and agreed with Essie's estimate. "He is magnificent, unbelievable," Van Vechten wrote Alfred Knopf, and to James Weldon Johnson he reported, "Paul is simply amazing. . . . He completely bowled me over with surprise. I did not expect such a finished and emotional performance. . . . They stood on chairs and cheered him the night we were there." Du

Bois wrote from New York to ask for some pictures for the NAACP's *The Crisis* and to say "how thrilled we are" with his success.[26]

Box-office business was brisk at first, and after Maurice Browne bowed out as Iago (by his own account, he "fled like a frightened rabbit" after the critics drubbed him, turning the role over to his understudy), there was added reason to hope for an extended run. But public interest failed to build, and, given the high production costs—Robeson was paid a reported record salary of three hundred pounds a week—the show closed after six weeks, and then briefly toured the provinces while negotiations proceeded for a transfer to the States. Jed Harris, the American producer who had recently revived *Uncle Vanya* with success, came to dinner at the Robesons', and it was widely announced in the press that he would bring *Othello* to New York the following season with Lillian Gish as Desdemona, Osgood Perkins (who had been hailed in *The Front Page*) as Iago, and Robert Edmond Jones as set designer. It was also rumored that Gish was negotiating to do a film version with Robeson. There were additional soundings from the Theatre Guild and from producers Gilbert Miller and Sydney Ross.[27]

None of this came to fruition. Robeson was under contract for another American concert tour, to run from January to April 1931, which undercut Jed Harris's preferred dates. Apprehension over the likely reception in the States of a black man kissing a white woman also proved dampening. "I wouldn't care to play those scenes in some parts of the United States," Robeson himself told a *New York Times* reporter: "The audience would get rough; in fact, might become very dangerous." One Southern paper editorialized in response, "He knows what would happen and so do the rest of us. That is one form of amusement that we will not stand for now or ever. This negro has potentialities for great harm to his race."[28]

But according to Essie, who carried on the negotiations, it was Maurice Browne who ultimately destroyed the attempt to carry *Othello* to the States. Nobody wanted his production, and he tried to prevent Robeson from appearing in a restaged version by claiming that he alone had the right to "sell" him. He did manage to prevent Peggy Ashcroft from accepting an offer from John Gielgud to appear at the Old Vic, "lending" her out instead—to her anguish—for a Somerset Maugham play. Essie was furious at Browne's manipulations. "He's a rascal indeed. I am surprised he could not play 'Iago' better. He's a real villain."[29]

Paul, too, seems to have blamed Browne far more than Van Volkenburg for the tensions and inadequacies of the production. Once opening night was safely behind him, Paul wrote Nellie a gracious and self-effacing letter thanking her "for the real help you have given me. Under different circumstances you & I would certainly have worked together with much more sympathy. I do feel most of it was my fault, but somewhere in the middle of things Maurice & I suddenly became antagonistic & I'm afraid deep down always will be. . . ." By the time the play closed, in July, Browne (so Essie wrote the Van Vechtens) became "openly nasty," and at the final performance, as Ashcroft remembers it, he gave a curtain speech to the audience in which he "thanked everybody, except Paul and myself."[30]

Career matters soon took a back seat to personal ones. In the middle of the six-week run of *Othello,* the baby fell ill. Paul, Jr. (nicknamed Pauli), at age two and a half came down with a painful and prolonged series of maladies—a bowel fissure, tonsillitis, stomach cramping—that led to a brief hospitalization and a month-long recuperation. Essie thought Paul was insufficiently attentive to the boy during his illness. "The only times you are the least bit interested in him," she wrote him in a summary accusation the following year, "are the rare occasions when you deem it suitable or befitting the artist to mention such prosaic things as children and parenthood; then I suppose you do think of him with pride and with a vague gratification that he is as grand as he is."[31]

On his side, Paul felt renewed anger when Essie's book about him— *Paul Robeson, Negro*—appeared, as timed, the day after the opening of *Othello.* Van Vechten was in London when it was published, and reported to Alfred Knopf (who had turned the book down in the United States) that it is "flopping here"—the book "is *so* bad." It did flop in terms of sales, but the reviews were genial. In general, the book was received as an artless, attractive panegyric to Paul, sprinkled with just enough seemingly candid revelation to make him believably human—for example, Paul's supposed admission that "I have no fatherly instincts about him [Pauli] at all." But if Essie and most of the critics believed her words "humanized" Paul, he did not. He did not appreciate, to put it mildly, being described as "disloyal" to his friends, lazy "with a capital L," and "not in the least sensitive" to racial slurs—agreeing with the one critic who thought the book on that issue had been too bland, had excessively downplayed the "bitter" aspects of trying to make his way as "one of an oppressed race."[32]

Nor was Paul amused at the heroically understanding tone Essie adopted for herself in the book when discussing the subject of sex. She had included a partly fictionalized (and artificially "frank") conversation about infidelity between herself, Paul, and a female friend of theirs—with Essie "forthrightly" pursuing the subject despite Paul's alleged hesitancy and discomfort. The conversation purportedly began with his remark that Essie overdid the "little tin god" version of his character—"she'd never believe I was unfaithful to her, even if the evidence was strong against me"; to which Essie purportedly responded, "We might as well finish this argument, now that we've begun it," and went on to say, "Would it shock you to learn that I might have suspected as much? Of course, I'm not admitting anything, even now. . . . But if I suspected you, I remembered at the same time that in the eight years of our marriage I have been desperately ill three times, with long, tedious convalescences following each illness; that only now am I achieving sound good health and in a position, physically, to be a constant wife to you [this last phrase was taken out of the published version at the last minute by Essie]; I remembered that we have been separated for long intervals by your work. 'Well, darling,' " the book has her saying, while "looking at him tenderly, 'if I ever thought there were lapses, I thought of the possible reasons for them, and dismissed them as not lapses at all. . . . No matter what you may have done in these eight years, there has been no change whatever in your love for me—except perhaps that it has increased. I know that you are faithful to me in the all-important spirit of things; that I am the one woman in your life, in your thoughts, in your love.' " Paul is said to have received this speech with "eyes full of tears, and full of immense relief," and, on recovering himself, to have remarked with admiration, "What can you do with a woman like that?"[33]

Life did not imitate art. Three months after the book's publication, Essie found a love letter from Peggy Ashcroft to Paul—and was instantly furious. She had adored Peggy—"so simple and appealing"—but in her anger, that "lovely girl" now became (in the privacy of her diary) "the little Jew bitch—not even married a year, and after somebody else's husband." Fifty years later, Peggy Ashcroft believed that "what happened between Paul and myself" had been "possibly inevitable"; indeed, it may possibly, in the pertinent, inciting words of Othello himself, have had to do with Shakespeare: "She loved me for the dangers I had passed, and I loved her that she did pity them." For Ashcroft, it was "a lesson to me in the power of drama to encourage a portrayed emotion to become a fantasy of one's own. How could one not fall in love in such a situation with such a man?" Paul had encouraged Peggy by telling her that, although he relied on Essie, he also felt suffocated by her, "that he had to have expression outside" the marriage, and that he already had had such "expression" before.[34]

Essie had previously sent Pauli and Ma Goode to Territet, Switzerland, where she and Paul had filmed *Borderline.* Now she joined them and, once settled there, wrote to Paul (who had embarked on a ten-week tour of the provinces, unsuccessfully trying out a new one-man show consisting of the first act of *Emperor Jones* interspersed with lieder and spirituals). Her letter has not survived, but in the diary entry coinciding with it she accused him of being everything from a dissembling husband to a rotten parent to a dishonest artist. As she had intimated in her book, she had known about some of his "peccadilloes" over the years but not, apparently, their extent. "I am surely a jackass if ever there was one," she wrote in her diary. "Fancy believing his lies right up to the last. He was a smooth one, though. He must have been lying to me for five years, steadily. Well, I'll never let another man know what goes on in my mind and heart. . . . Paul is not any different from any other Nigger man, except that he has a beautiful voice. His personality is built on lies. . . ."[35]

Paul responded to her furious indictment with measured calm. In one of the few long letters he ever wrote, he began by matter-of-factly discussing his financial straits, reviewed work-in-progress on their London flat, and then turned to the Ashcroft episode:

I am very sorry, of course, you read that letter. You will do those things. You evidently don't believe your creed—that what you don't know doesn't hurt you. It makes things rather hopeless. It must be quite evident that I'm likely to go on thusly for a long while here and there—perhaps not. I'm certain I don't know, but the past augurs the future.

I have tried to explain to you that no mail addressed to me—telegraphed, cabled or otherwise—is so important it must be opened. You knew I was coming in Sunday, and you could have held it until then. In fact, if it was Saturday eve, you couldn't have reached me, as I was leaving early Sunday. It's my fault for having mail reach me there, but you were not living there as yet, and I felt that for the time being it was my apt. It makes matters rather difficult, as I must have a certain amount of privacy in my life— and my mail must be inviolate (certainly even this stupid society of today feels that, as tampering with mail is a rather serious offence even legally). So, I see nothing but to leave you the apartment and go to an hotel. I'll keep my front room and come in to see you. I most probably will be at the Adelphi—and you can have the girl live at the house; either that, or we can rent it out and you remain in Switzerland. I could come over for a couple of weeks before going to America.

In our present condition it appears it would be better also for you to remain in England or Switzerland then. (When I go to America.) We'll need every penny, and I'll be so busy with my work, I'll not be able to see much of you—you might feel happier there [in Switzerland] with the boy.

The work on this music must be done, and I can see my way clear if I can concentrate.

As for that letter—I'm sure you haven't destroyed it, and I must not only request but demand that you send it to me. Please send it all, as I shall have it verified. Just how it helps you to do these things, Essie, my dear, I do not know. But I must have the letter. What I feel about this and that I am sure I don't know. I am in a period of transition—where I shall finally finish is of little consequence to me. I would like to get on with my work. To do that I think I need to be alone and to be as far as possible absolutely free. I thought in spite of past misunderstandings it might be possible tho we happened to be in the same apt. But if these things can continually happen, it's quite impossible and will only be bad for you and me. I'd suggest you remain with the mountains and lakes, and I'll come there when I can feel so disposed.

There's no need of beginning something (the apt. scheme) we know will not work out as we wished.

I'm sure that deep down I love you very much in the way that we could love each other. It could not be wholly complete because we are too different in temperament.

But however it is, we haven't helped each other very much. I feel spiritually starved. You became almost a physical wreck. Something's wrong—maybe my fault, maybe yours—most likely both our faults. There's no need rushing ahead and repeating the same mistakes. . . .

I feel that the next few weeks with my rushing from place to place and in the atmosphere of boredom will bring us little as to completer understanding.

I'd love to come to Switzerland for a short while when I am thru and see you, the boy and mother [Ma Goode] before going away. We'd be much more likely to understand each other better there. If you must come to see about the flat and business, all right. If you feel you want the flat—all right. You determine that. But the financial strain must be considered. Love to the boy. Do tell me about him and how he's going along. Of course I'm interested. Write me always as you feel. I often feel extremely close to you and want to see you and talk to you and perhaps weep on your bosom. Let's hope all will come out right. Love, Paul.[36]

Paul's letter made Essie angrier still. She characterized it in her diary as "cold, mean, vindictive." In her view, he wanted her to stay in Switzerland not to save money, as he claimed, but "so he can carry on with Peggy. . . . It would be inconvenient having me in London. . . . It doesn't matter to him that all my clothes are in the flat, all my books, all my work. That I haven't even a coat here for this cold weather. I came here to stay ten days, and only brought clothes for ten days! Yet, if I return to London, he will swear I came to spy on him." She was furious at the suggestion that she had opened the letter to snoop and insisted that "the last thing under the sun" she expected to find was a love letter—especially since he had spoken "very sweetly" to her over the phone from Edinburgh. "Well," she wrote in her diary, "none of it matters. I feel now that he is just one more Negro musician, pursuing white meat. I suppose it's a curse on the race. No wonder white people don't want to let black men into their society. I believe that he would have had a hard time getting in if he hadn't had me to point to, and people felt, 'Oh, he has a wife of his own, and is happy, so I guess he isn't after our women.' . . . He is secret, mean, low. He excuses himself with high sounding words that merely mask a disgusting commonness. We will begin from here."[37]

The affair with Ashcroft was brief; they parted without bitterness, and their feelings of friendship continued (in the late thirties, Paul—with Essie—visited her backstage at the theater). The domestic crisis precipitated by Essie's discovery of Ashcroft's letter was soon eclipsed by another threat to her marital security. Paul had become deeply involved with a woman named Yolande Jackson, a sometime actress whom Essie had known about for at least a year. Paul had even talked to Ashcroft about Yolande, but he did not tell her that their affair was concurrent. Few traces of Yolande Jackson's relationship with Robeson have survived—not the occasion of their first meeting, or details about the early progress of the affair, or any substantial information about her subsequent life. Alberta Hunter has described her as "a wonderful person" (no specifics added), and Rebecca West said she was "vaguely shady—something of a slut" (no specifics added). According to Rupert Hart-Davis, Peggy Ashcroft's husband and a friend of the Jackson family, Yolande was "a large, attractive, flamboyant woman, always with a new enthusiasm and I daresay a new lover," who had been a drama student at the Royal Academy of Dramatic Art but had never pursued a theatrical career with any notable consistency or success. Her father, William Jackson, was a barrister who practiced in India and became head of the bar in Calcutta, where he was known as Tiger Jackson. By the time Rupert Hart-Davis came to know the Jackson family, in the late twenties, they had returned to England and lived in a "small villa on the outskirts of Worthing on the Sussex coast . . . waited on by gigantic Indians in turbans and native dress."[38]

However long Paul had been seeing Yolande Jackson, their love affair now took a significant turn. He developed a consuming passion for her, and ever after described her to close friends as "the great love" of his life, "a free spirit, a bright, loving, wonderful woman." Some time in September, he told Essie about his deep feelings for Yolande, and they may have discussed divorce. Faced with that news, following hard on the revelation of his affair with Ashcroft, Essie had a nervous collapse. As she wrote Carlo and Fania three months later, "I have been terribly ill with nerves, but am gradually getting back to my old self. I really did have a bad time. I had a nervous breakdown that went into paralysis, and lost the use of the whole left side of my face. I was a sight. Well, it's alright again, and I have got the use of the nerves back, and I don't look distorted anymore. It was a close squeak—we thot [sic] I would be permanently paralyzed." During those two months, from October to December 1, 1930, she and Paul managed to reach a temporary *modus vivendi:* she stayed in their flat in London while he remained on tour in the provinces, Yolande sometimes joining him. On weekends he came into London, dividing his time between Yolande and Essie—Yolande getting "most of the time," Essie wrote in her diary. She claimed that Yolande "telephoned, telegraphed, and ran him to earth. . . . I know, because Paul told me so himself."[39]

By December, comparative calm had been restored. Paul spent the early part of the month in the flat with Essie and (according to her) they "had a marvelous time"—theatergoing, dining with the actress Jean Forbes-Robertson (the star of Barrie's *Peter Pan*), supping with Noel Coward (whom they had met earlier in New York). Essie felt that she and Paul had become "better friends than we have ever been, much, much closer." Paul went off to stay with Yolande from December 7 to 19, then joined Essie in Switzerland for Christmas with Ma Goode and Pauli. Essie explained the rapprochement to the Van Vechtens in the vocabulary of an understanding mother chastising her errant boy and in a tone that hovered precariously close to strained nobility: "He's fallen in love with another girl—honest—besides the one he was in love with when you were here—and his life is rather complicated just now. . . . He doesn't quite know where he is himself, so naturally I don't know where I am with him . . . bless him. He's a dear, and I think he's very nice. At first, naturally I was very upset about it all, because with my characteristic dumbness and one-way mind, it never occurred to me that he could possibly be straying. But now that I know he has not only strayed, but gone on a hike, I've turned my mind over and given it an airing—and I feel much better. I certainly hope he gets what he wants, because he has been very sweet to me. If he wants some one else, I shant mind too much. Of course, I'll mind some, but I refuse to be tiresome. Be nice to Paul [he was on his way to the States for a tour]. And Fania, dear, sew on a button for him if he needs it."[40]

Paul and Essie talked outright about divorce just before he left for the States, and momentarily Essie agreed—but soon changed her mind, using renewed anger over Yolande's behavior as an excuse for backing off. Arriving in Paris to see Paul off for the *Mauretania* boat train to New York, Essie became increasingly annoyed at the phone calls from Yolande, still in London, to Paul. Finally Essie flew into a rage. "She knew we were together and that I was saying goodbye to him forever, but still she pursued. . . . I made up my mind that she will never marry him as long as I live, and am able to prevent it. I changed my mind completely, and decided once and for all, if she can't act like a decent sport, and at least treat me with the courtesy that I gave her. . . . God damn it, I'll not get a divorce at all. I'll be damned if I will. She is not a decent person—simply a nymphomaniac, tracking down another man, as she has tried to track down many, and she may have mine—I can't prevent that, but I'll not divorce him—so there." Her resolve was strengthened for the moment by a chance meeting at the Gare Saint-Lazare with Foster Sanford, Paul's football coach from his

Rutgers days and a man he deeply respected. Seeing Sanford "reminded" Essie that if she and Paul were ever divorced, "Sanford and all the men like him would hate [Paul] forever, and that many healthy, friendly doors would be closed to him. Sanford was a symbol, and he helped me to finally make up my mind. I'll sit tight and not move an inch."[41]

She felt confirmed in an opinion she had written into an early draft of *Paul Robeson, Negro:* "A Negro who marries a white woman is promptly ostracized by the majority of his race and the wife is ignored socially. Notable examples of this feeling are Frederick Douglass, that idol of the Negro race, who fell from his pedestal when he married a white woman, and Jack Johnson, the black heavyweight champion of the world and popular hero of both races, who completely lost his popularity when he married a white woman." Clearly this was what Essie wanted to believe—but an idea is not necessarily proved wrong merely because it satisfies a wish. Foster Sanford thought she was right. Soon after their chance meeting in Paris, he himself had a private talk with Paul in New York and (according to Sanford's son) "read him the riot act" about a divorce, warning him that abandoning his wife would offend people of both races, and that doing so in order to marry a white woman would surely cost him the affection of his own people. Bricktop, the famed chanteuse–cabaret owner, apparently spoke to Paul in the same vein.[42]

Essie stayed on in Paris for a few days after Paul left for the States, feeling lonely but determined not to brood. She looked up some old friends, got her hair waved, and set out to see the town, touring the shops and the theaters. On New Year's Day 1931, she had word from Pauli's governess in Switzerland that both he and Ma Goode had fallen ill. Essie spent the next month taking them for medical consultations with physicians in Vienna, where Ma Goode was found to be suffering from an acute abscess of the kidney and Pauli from distorted vertebrae near the base of the spine. He was given artificial sun treatments and massage, and Ma Goode was given injections. Both improved rapidly, and Essie next decided to take herself in hand. "Still a little frightened over the paralysis business," she consulted a Viennese "nerve specialist," who told her the paralysis had been "due entirely to shock" and gave her "a good reconstructing nerve prescription" and a regimen of ten hours' sleep a night. As she, too, began to improve, she queried the Van Vechtens, in her continuing capacity as Paul's business manager, on how his concert tour in the States was going, whether "he actually sang the German and Russian songs, and how they went. I do so hope he had another great success. Bless him. He's a good scout."[43]

The tour, in fact, had not started out well. Carlo and Fania reported to Essie that during the inaugural Carnegie Hall concert the spirituals had gone splendidly but the lieder Paul had added to his program were not well received. Larry Brown, who was accompanying Paul, confidentially cabled Essie that "nothing was going according to plan." "What has happened to the tour?" Essie wrote back. "Is he lying down on it? Or is it really the [economic] depression? I feel the fault must be in him. Even in the worst possible depression here in England, he still drew crowds. . . . Is he fed up, is he bored, is he angry? Has he lost interest in his work? Or is he just lying down as he so often has?"[44]

As Robeson moved across the country—and the tour carried him all the way to San Francisco—he became additionally agitated because of press misrepresentation. The newspapers reported that he had decided to include European songs only because black audiences had demanded them, that the younger "and more intelligent" blacks tended to dismiss the spirituals "as something beneath their new pride in their race," and that, although Robeson himself felt black artists "ought not do anything except their own folk-lore," he had tacked "art songs" on to his repertory to appease the protestors. Robeson complained about this misrepresentation during an interview for the Kansas City *Call* with Roy Wilkins (who was shortly to move to New York to become an officer in the NAACP). Black artists, Robeson told Wilkins, "ought to do as many things as they can do well. Very few singers, perhaps none, can sing German lieder like Roland Hayes. It would be foolish for me or anyone else to say that Roland should not sing German lieder. But I do contend that Negroes should not run off and leave severely alone their own peculiar gifts which none but they can do perfectly." It bothered him, he told Wilkins, "that very little of what I actually say gets into the papers—and I mean great dailies as well as the Negro weeklies." He also told Wilkins that he had decided to live in Europe, where one didn't need friends "to act as 'bumpers' against prejudice."[45]

Meanwhile, in London, according to the rather studied accounts in Essie's diary, she was seeing quite a bit of Noel Coward. She spent the evening of her birthday with him at her flat (his birthday was the following day), and he had become a confidant in her troubles with Paul. Essie may have wanted Paul to think that Coward's "marvelous" attentiveness was a sign of something more than friendship. In a letter to her in January, Paul wrote:

> I had a talk with NC. We talked frankly as he said he knew all the facts. I left my position very clear—that I am very anxious to marry, etc. He thought that rather inadvisable from career angles—but appears to understand. I couldn't gauge him very well. He was non-committal, and rightly so. After all, his business with you is your concern, not mine. He was very nice. I had lunch with him at the Ritz. We had a long chat, he *is* delightful. . . .[46]

In that same letter, written about a month into the three-and-a-half-month tour, Paul reported that it "has been rather trying. . . . What I really need is about 3 months out to do nothing but learn new songs." He was feeling "rather sad and lonely," in part because "I don't like the American scene so much" and in part because "everyone was rumoring over [our] separation. One or two people asked me directly. I denied any such thing. Thought it best for you to handle same as you think best." Essie had already cautioned the Van Vechtens to "let Paul open the conversation about all this. He might be offended if he thot [sic] I had told you, first. I know he will tell you, so all you have to do is sit and wait." But Paul did not, as Essie had expected, confide in the Van Vechtens. When they let her know that he had "said nothing whatever about the situation," simply indicating that she had stayed behind because of health and would be joining him later, Essie chose to interpret that as meaning "definitely I think, that he does not want a divorce, and hopes that I do not," and that "he evidently means" to ask her to come over—"So, it all sounds lovely."[47]

Essie did come to New York in March, but the news immediately leaked out to the press that she was staying not with Paul at the Hotel Wentworth but with her old friend Hattie Bolling at the Dunbar apartments. The *New York News and Harlem Home Journal* in a three-inch headline announced, "ROBESONS SEPARATE," and in the story inside quoted "friends" of the couple to the effect that "a beautiful English woman enamored of Robeson followed him here" and "the battle is now raging . . . between the two women for Robeson's affection." Essie put the issue more casually in her diary, describing her month-long stay in New York as a round of parties and adventures. She went with Minnie Sumner to see Noel Coward in his hit play *Private Lives*, "stopped traffic" at the NAACP annual ball at the Savoy by arriving with Coward as her escort ("Noel danced with me often. He was conspicuously attentive . . . to the confounding of all those present"), went to Washington for two days, where she picked up again with her old beau Grant Lucas ("At last we have had our talk—after ten years—and I find I haven't changed a bit toward him, nor he toward me. . . . He is terribly attractive, and I think he likes me all over again"). She also took a side trip to Columbia, South Carolina, to gather material for a new book she was planning about her family and her early life ("Talking about southern hospitality . . . I've never seen anything like it"). She and Paul did spend his birthday together, going to the theater with the Van Vechtens and spending the night at the Wentworth. But that one evening aside, they scarcely saw each other.[48]

When Essie sailed on the *Leviathan* for England on April 15, her old friend Corinne Wright and Grant Lucas saw her off. At the last minute, Paul, too, came along. "The representatives of the Negro press," Essie wrote Grace and James Weldon Johnson, "looked positively disappointed when they saw Paul arrive with me at the pier, and they solemnly watched him see me off properly. We had to laugh. They insist upon separating us, bless em, but we have other plans!" Yet, a few months later, when drawing up another general indictment of his behavior, Essie rebuked Paul for having appeared at the sailing. "Grant and Corinne were too well bred to show their surprise, but you can imagine how Grant felt." Grant stayed to say a last few words, and after the ship pulled away Essie memorialized his "sweet face" in her diary: "He has done a great deal for me in this last week, has helped me find myself in many, many ways. I shall always be grateful to him for that." From shipboard she wrote the Van Vechtens that she was "still thrilled over the heavenly time I had in America. I can't remember ever having had such a perfect time in my whole life! Honest." She was now convinced that "everything is going to come out beautifully for me"; she still had "no idea what Paul will do, but no matter what he does, we are fast friends, and understand each other better than ever before." Besides, she felt rid at last of "a lot of silly young ideas I used to be boarded up with," and "surprised at the great variety of ways in which I can have a good time. I am having a really good time for the first time in my life. And if I'm happy and he's happy, things are bound to come out right in the end. I'm not at all impatient, because I'm amusing myself."[49]

There matters stood for the next six months. Paul returned to London soon after Essie and immediately went into rehearsal for a revival of O'Neill's *The Hairy Ape*, under Jimmy Light's direction, and with Robert Rockmore (an American lawyer whose wife, Bess, had been a Province-towner) as producer. It was to be a short-lived venture. "The rehearsals nearly killed me," Robeson later told a reporter. "I am supposed to be a strong man. Yet I couldn't stand up to the strain on my physical strength. When I came to the first-night I had no physical reserve left." Essie went to the dress rehearsal and "was a little worried about Paul's voice. He is using much too much voice, and if he keeps on like this, he will strain it."[50]

Yet the opening went off marvelously—for Robeson, not O'Neill. With only two dissents, the critics hailed his portrayal of the shipboard stoker Yank as "splendidly vital," asserting that he had "never been more effective." In a fine display of traditional English homoeroticism, the *Graphic*'s critic devoted a fifth of his review to waxing eloquent over Robeson's physique: "That Mr. Robeson should be stripped to the waist is my first demand of any play in which he appears. Perhaps one of the disappointments of his Othello was its encumbrance with the traditional dress-gown." Most of the reviewers dismissed the play as "sentimental," "grotesque," and already outmoded in its once-fashionable "expressionism." A number of the critics, while exonerating Robeson personally, considered it a mistake to have cast a black in a role originally written for a white. "It upsets the balance or alters the whole direction of the piece," wrote the reviewer in the *Star*. "One cannot help thinking that here is something which has to do with racial consciousness and the oppression of the negro." Essie agreed that Paul had been "magnificent" on opening night but was angered at the presence of Yolande Jackson, who had sat in the front row of the stalls "with a French count—no-account looking. I never saw such nerve in my life," Essie huffed in her diary.[51]

After five performances, the play abruptly closed. "Laryngitis" was the umbrella explanation given out to the press, but Paul's symptoms were in fact more extensive than that. Essie wrote the Van Vechtens that the strain of "a packed concert tour followed immediately by an intense rehearsal period" had exhausted him; he "began yelling, and after opening on Monday night, had to [be] put to bed in a nursing home on the following Friday, suffering from strain, nerves, laryngitis and no voice at all. The doctor kept him in bed a week, treated him with inhalations, etc. and ordered complete rest." This bout of "nerves" conceivably marked the onset—the first symptomatic evidence—of the depressive disorder that twenty-five years later would overtake him.[52]

When reporters asked Robeson about his future plans after the closing of *Hairy Ape*, he alternately replied (or was variously misquoted) that he would not act again for several years, that he hoped to start a repertory theater in London, that he wanted to go to Africa, to return to Germany, to retire for a while to the provinces to learn Russian. He did begin learning Russian in earnest, taking up formal study of it with the composer Alexandre Gambs, and telling the press that he was finding it "extremely easy to learn the language" and that Russian music suited his voice—perhaps, he thought, because "there is a kinship between the russians and the negroes. They were both serfs, and in the music there is the same note of melancholy touched with mysticism."[53]

Essie scorned his "indecision" about implementing plans and announced that she was applying for a Guggenheim to visit Africa on her own. She lectured him that the "inglorious" ending of The Hairy Ape resulted from his typical inability "to make up your mind about things—about your work, about your life. . . . You hadn't the guts to say *no* in the first place—or having said yes, you wouldn't face it and buckle to it and do the thing properly. No—you hem and haw and postpone the evil day, and if something turns up to decide or help or hinder you, you remain quiescent. You only really work or fight if you are pushed back into a tight corner. It's the same about your life. You want Yolande, you don't want me. . . . But do you do anything about it? No. You want us both. Or rather you don't want me, but you don't want to give me up. It's ridiculous and childish."[54]

Essie, as usual, was judging the surface—seeing it lucidly but not penetrating beneath. She was always able to describe behavior accurately but then gauged its meaning narrowly, tending to assume that things *are* what they appear. Judging people by what they *did*, she equated that with who they *were*—it was a major difference between her temperament and Paul's. He was indeed "taking his time," willing to let the appearance of vacillation—a real enough aspect of his behavior, but misconstrued as a summation of it—serve as a useful disguise. To protect himself from Essie's overly zealous scrutiny, her relentless demand to be "up and doing," he found it convenient to cultivate the appearance of irresolution—it kept her, and most of the world, from invading his complex privacy, even though it opened him to charges of being a dawdler. He might have smiled, rather than felt annoyance, at Essie's description of him to Larry Brown as "a very strange person."[55]

Paul moved into bachelor quarters in London, leaving Essie the elaborate flat they had recently taken on Buckingham Street, and, accompanied by Ethel A. Gardner (Larry Brown was in the States), did considerable concert work locally. Essie had to postpone her trip to Africa after suddenly hemorrhaging in June, and she went off to spend the summer in Kitzbühel, Austria, with Ma Goode and Pauli. But she took ill again in August and had to be rushed to a sanatorium for what seems to have been an abortion—or a curettage following an abortion she may have had before leaving London. She and Paul had continued infrequently to sleep together, but she might have gotten pregnant by Grant Lucas while in the States, and she had also been seeing fairly regularly—and possibly having a sexual relationship with—a man named Michael Harrison. In any case, when she went to Austria she went armed with a letter from Paul addressed to a Dr. Lowinger in Vienna in which he refers to Essie's "present pregnancy," expresses concern for her health after the dangerous delivery she'd had with Pauli, and requests Lowinger, if he agrees that it "would be unwise for her to complete the term," to "arrest the pregnancy at once, or as soon as you feel it would be advisable."[56]

Paul wrote her in late August saying he was "really very tired and very unhappy and am very anxious to see the boy and more anxious about your health," sending her money and urging her to see Dr. Lowinger. "If we decided to go ahead with things sometime," he remarked about her pregnancy, "we must be very careful and give every possible chance from the first. Which, I am afraid, during the Period of Possibility will have to exclude foreigners (Verstehen sie)."—perhaps a reference to Michael Harrison—"One can be just so liberal in such important matters." He assured her again that he was "really very devoted"—"love you very much in fact—much more than I ever did and miss you beyond words." Essie wrote the Van Vechtens, once more sounding the patronizing maternal note, "Big Paul isn't very well, and not very happy, bless him. I think he has growing pains. But he is a dear, and we are great friends. When he has quite decided in his own mind what he wants to do, we can come to some sort of decision ourselves, and some plan." Meanwhile, she wrote, she felt "a little guilty being so happy, and so busy." She does seem genuinely to

1. (ABOVE) William Drew Robeson

2. (RIGHT) Louisa Bustill Robeson

3. Somerville High School football team, 1913 (Paul is third from right, second row.)

4. Rutgers track team, 1919

5. Rutgers University baseball team

6. Star players of the Rutgers football team, 1918
(Left to right: Neuschafer, Feitner, Robeson, and Breckley)

7. Robeson playing football against Newport Naval Reserve, Ebbets Field, 1917

8. Rutgers, junior year, 1917–18

Paul's circle of college friends

9. (TOP) Paul is in back row, third from right; Gerry Neale is in front row, second from right.

10. (BOTTOM) Paul is at far left; Robert Davenport is at far right.

11. The Rutgers Varsity debating team

12. Robeson in the first-year class at Columbia Law School, 1920

13. St. Christopher basketball team, Harlem, 1919 (Paul is second from left.)

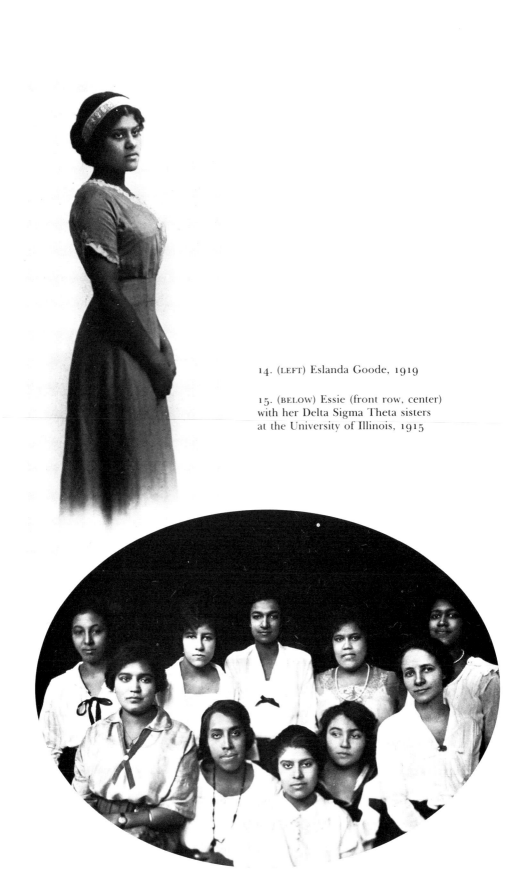

14. (LEFT) Eslanda Goode, 1919

15. (BELOW) Essie (front row, center) with her Delta Sigma Theta sisters at the University of Illinois, 1915

16. Paul (left) in the chorus of *Plantation Revue,* 1923

17. (ABOVE) In the London production of *Voodoo,* 1922

18. (LEFT) Robeson as Jim Harris in *All God's Chillun Got Wings,* 1924

19. Carl Van Vechten, 1930   20. Fania Marinoff

21. The "Triumvirate" of the Provincetown Playhouse:
Kenneth MacGowan, director; Eugene O'Neill, playwright;
Robert Edmond Jones, scenic designer

22. (LEFT) Bronze statue of Robeson, entitled "Negro Spiritual," by Antonio Salemmé, completed in 1926

23. (ABOVE) Portrait of Robeson, by Carl Van Vechten

24. (BELOW) Antonio Salemmé at work on a head of Robeson in the mid-twenties

25. In the 1926 production of *Black Boy*

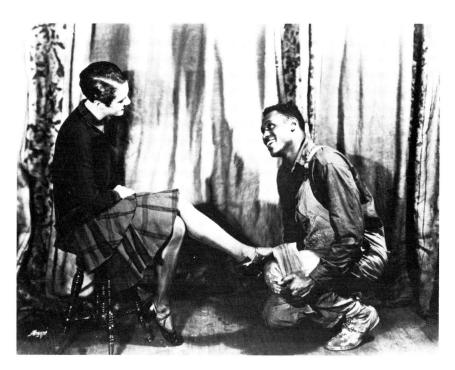

26. With Fredi Washington in a scene from *Black Boy*, 1926

27. (LEFT) In the 1925
London production of
The Emperor Jones

28. (ABOVE) A still from the 1924 film
Body and Soul

29. (RIGHT) Paul on location for the film
Borderline in Switzerland, 1929

30. (LEFT) In *Show Boat*, 1928

31. (BELOW) The London production of *Show Boat*, 1928 (Alberta Hunter is fourth from left, next to Robeson; Marie Burke is fourth from right.)

32. Paul and Essie with friends at Oak Bluffs, Martha's Vineyard, summer of 1927

33. Aboard ship, ca. 1930

34. Essie in London, 1932

35. Paul in London in the 1930s

36. With Peggy Ashcroft as Desdemona in the London production of *Othello*, 1930

37. With Flora Robson as Ella in a scene from the London production of *All God's Chillun Got Wings*, 1933

38. Essie and Paul, 1933

have enjoyed being with Pauli in Kitzbühel, and enthusiastically recorded her son's doings and sayings—he was "so brown," she wrote to Grace Johnson, "with so much red in his cheeks, and perfect teeth, and carries himself like a king." In September she took herself to Vienna for another "procedure"—its exact nature unspecified, even in her diary (suggesting, once again, that it was not entirely designed as a private document).[57]

Essie returned to London in early October. By then Paul had resolved to marry Yolande. While in New York he had seen Freda Diamond—who over the years had become a confidante and an anchor to him—and discussed his feelings for Yolande; she had advised him to go ahead with the marriage if he had his heart set on it. He now wrote Freda to say, "I trust I am going to great happiness, and I miss you dreadfully." That juxtaposition of sentiments was entirely typical: in his emotional life Robeson would not conform to traditional expectations that love (and sex) must be single-minded devotions, that only one person at a time must be the focus of desire. As he further elaborated to Freda: ". . . we must never lose the lovely feeling between us, only strengthen it. . . . Remember that this feeling between us must go on as it always has and will deepen and deepen significantly. You shall never hear things about me—I shall tell you, and nothing can in any way disturb us. I shall tell you . . . because of that in me which is yours." Paul again told Essie that he wanted to be free, and they again discussed divorce. This time Essie finally agreed—"we are both quite happy and pleased over the prospect of our freedom," she wrote in her diary—and they proceeded to see a lawyer. Cordiality reigned. While Paul and Larry rehearsed in the Buckingham Street flat, Essie got together some dinner. Paul scrubbed her back in the tub while she got ready to go out with Michael Harrison, he confiding the hope that Peggy Ashcroft (so at least Essie recorded in her diary) would "stop telling the world she was in love" with him or "it would cause all sorts of upheavals and scandals," she laughing and saying, "It was all due to his devastating charm with the ladies." He left their tub-side tête-à-tête to take Yolande to the theater for her birthday.[58]

A week after that enlightened exercise in togetherness, Paul canceled his Albert Hall concert because of the flu, took to bed in his hotel, and wouldn't let Essie visit. "Paul is behaving very, very strangely," she wrote in her diary, and complained to the Van Vechtens, "It does seem too bad that he won't be reasonable. But I am not allowed to tell him not to go to parties just before a big concert, as I used to, so he just goes and does these things, and gets into trouble." She decided Paul was "certainly degenerating!", having fallen prey once more to irresolution. "He can't seem to make up his mind what to do about his work, about his life, about me, and Yolande, nor anything. He really will have to settle down and get busy, if he wants to hold his place. Poor fellow," she wrote in her diary. "I'm sorry for him."[59]

Essie decided to sketch out a lengthy letter to him. In the no-nonsense manner on which she prided herself (and in which she thought Paul woefully, perhaps morally, deficient), she laid out options, imposed conditions, drew up systematic conclusions. "My dear P," she began. "I don't seem to be able to talk to you any more. We don't seem to speak the same language. So I thought I'd better write." She was now entirely prepared, she continued, to give him a divorce, should he want one. "I shall be infinitely better off divorced from you, than married to you. . . . As your wife, I have rarely had the supposed pleasure and comfort of your company—except at very irregular meals and at odd hours late at night; and of course on those social occasions when you found it convenient or necessary. . . . All I really lose when I divorce you, is a job; and divorces being what they are—I lose the job but keep the salary, with a raise."[60]

She then reiterated her charge that he was a deficient father, uninterested in his own son, and defended herself from his long-standing complaint about her extravagance. "You deplore the number of menages you must keep up," but seem unwilling to forgo separate quarters and conveniently to forget that "the reason we sent Mama and Pauli abroad was because you didn't want your child so much in evidence before your two ladies and before your public. A child is an encumbrance when one is playing the great lover." She then broadly hinted that "Andy" (Joseph Andrews), a Jamaican whom Robeson employed as a valet-secretary but who was really more of a friend, primarily served to abet his adventures. "I must say I feel a little bit embarrassed for you," Essie wrote, "when you identify him as your secretary. Andy can't write a dignified intelligent letter, he can't answer the telephone with dignity and intelligence, and he is inefficient, unpunctual and unreliable. How can he be a secretary, then? When you tell people he is, they think . . . it must be some special arrangement."[61]

As for Yolande, Essie had "thought a great deal about this racial mixing business" and concluded that, "when a white woman takes a Negro man as a lover, she usually lowers him and herself too; white people and Negroes feel rather that she has a bull or a stallion or mule in her stable, her stable being her bed of course, and view the affair very much as if she had run away with the butler or the chauffeur; she is rarely—almost never—a first-class woman, and neither white nor black people think the Negro has won a prize." In her own behalf, Essie objected to the way he had publicly flaunted his affair with Yolande, and his "lack of taste in emphasizing" the gifts Yolande had given him of a cigarette case, a locket, and a seal ring. She compared him in this regard to Leslie Hutchinson, the popular black musician, who took "pride in displaying presents from white women."[62]

"I daresay," she continued, "you will feel I am a stickler for dignity. Well, in a way I am. For instance, there's the matter of Yolande hanging over the railing conspicuously from the stage box at the premiere of Othello; and sitting in the center of the front row of the stalls at the Hairy Ape. In your magnificent selfishness, I suppose it never occurred to you that I might be embarrassed? And that her trying to be conspicuous was in the worst possible taste? . . . Funnily enough, since your audiences are always mostly white, she who wants to be conspicuous is just another white woman, and no one knows the news; when you marry her she will still be just another white woman. . . . You say in your large way, that English women don't know the first thing about how to make love. You are very funny, honey. And you say they haven't suffered! All your intimate information seems to have come from middle class Anglo-Indians—and you know what the English think of them! . . . If you had ever seriously tried to make love to me, I'm sure I don't know what might have happened. But we needn't worry about that—you never did. You made a pass or two at it—took me to a theater and were very pleased with such evidence of your devotion. I was too—which makes it even funnier. [I] seriously doubt if you were ever in love with me. You liked me, were companionable, and I was thoughtful and considerate of you—so you like me. I doubt now if I was ever in love with you—I admired you tremendously, and I was certainly interested in you."[63]

But the past, she concluded the letter, "is behind us. The question is, what should we do with the future? I know what I want to do, and shall do with mine. There is no indecision about me, as you know. But about you—you have a great natural gift, and a magnificent body, neither of which you have done anything to preserve and improve. . . . You also have a terrific charm—but have rather overworked that. You have a fine mind. You have, as I said in 1921, the immediate possibility of becoming the greatest artist in the world—if you want to; and it wouldn't take much work, either—you have so much to start with." Driving home her point, she reiterated her view that if he was ever to realize his potential, he would have to decide what he wanted to do and stick to it. "If you continue to drift along as you are doing now, refusing to face things out, you will degenerate into merely a popular celebrity. Which seems poor stuff when one thinks of being a really great artist, the thrill of having done something perfectly. . . . You can jeer all you like, but I remember vividly your elation when you had given a really fine concert." "Well," she closed, "it does seem that I fall naturally into place in the role of lecturer, doesn't it? All I can say in my defense is that I have decided what to try to make of my own life, and as we part, I should be very happy to know that you have decided upon something for yourself. I do so hate waste. And you will be a wicked waste if you don't step on it."[64]

On the evening of November 28, Paul dropped by the flat to leave a Russian dictionary (Essie had also taken up the study), found she had gone out, and saw the pencil draft of her letter to him. Apparently it moved him, and he returned the next morning to have a talk with her. As she described it in her diary, it turned out to be "a red-letter day for me, perhaps one of the most important days in my whole life. . . . We got closer and more friendly than we have been. He says he wants to see me often, and urgently, and that we have something between us which no one else will ever be able to duplicate. He thinks he wants to marry Yolande, but he isn't sure, but he is sure he wants us always to remain close and friendly. . . . We had a lovely time, slept together, and enjoyed it enormously. I'm so glad things are pleasant and friendly. Most important of all, he has found his feet, so far as his work is concerned, and is through with slacking and sliding and muddling through. Thank God for that!" She sent a high-spirited version of their new arrangements to the Van Vechtens: "He doesn't live here of course, but has reached the regular and often calling stage, which is much more inconvenient. He is a dear, tho, I must say, even tho he is so funny and serious and absurd at times. I think no matter what happens to him, and I'm sure a great deal will happen to him, he'll always be a very nice person."[65]

That same week Essie, on a dare, consulted Madame Maude, a psychic. She liked what she heard. Her marriage, Madame told her, was not a "real" one, but her next one would be—"to a man who has to do with the control of many men . . . in a large building—perhaps in government," and she predicted vast changes in Essie's life within the next few months, changes that would come about as a result of her own "creative work." Essie decided at once to finish up the film scenario she'd been working on, converting it into a novel called *Black Progress,* and to complete her modern-day parody play based on *Uncle Tom's Cabin,* a "comedy with music" about the tour of a black jazz band in Europe. She was still more excited about her prospects after Nell St. John Ervine, a clairvoyante, gave her pretty much the same reading Madame Maude had. "She said she saw me parting with a tall, dark man, turning away for good. . . ." When, two days after that, a third psychic, Mrs. Mohamed Ali, whom Larry Brown set high store by, read her cards and told her yet again that she would divorce Paul, would remarry happily, and would "meet great success" through her work, Essie was elated at the thrice-repeated fortune.[66]

Just before Christmas, Ma Goode and Pauli arrived in London for a visit from Kitzbühel. In a hired Daimler, Paul and Essie went to Victoria Station to meet them, and Paul leapt from the car when the train arrived and hoisted Pauli to his shoulder—they "seemed very happy together," Essie wrote in her diary. On Christmas Day they had a family dinner, and after it Paul took Pauli to the Palladium to see *Peter Pan* with Jean Forbes-

Robertson. On December 29 he again spent most of the day with the boy, then left in the evening to go out with Yolande. The following day Paul sailed alone on the *Olympic* for another tour of the States. He stopped at the flat early in the morning to say goodbye to Essie and Pauli, while Yolande waited downstairs in her car to drive him to the ship in Southampton.

■

CHAPTER 9

The Discovery of Africa

(1932–1934)

Robeson gave his triumphant first recital of the new tour to a packed house in Town Hall on January 18, 1932. Most of the program consisted of familiar spirituals, but for the first time in New York he successfully tried out his increasingly expert Russian with Gambs's "Prayer" and Gretchaninov's "The Captive" (and, as one of the encores, introduced Larry Brown's "Dere's No Hidin' Place Down There"—Brown accompanying). The Russian songs were well received; some Russians in the audience, including members of the Kedroff Quartet, applauded enthusiastically. "I have found a music very closely allied to mine—and emotionally to me as an individual," Robeson explained to a reporter; "in six months I have learned the language, which I also find a more natural means of expression than English. Certainly many Russian folksongs seem to have come from Negro peasant life and vice versa." "He feels he is a kindred soul" to the Russian, Emma Goldman wrote Alexander Berkman the following year, praising him for having "gone into the very spirit of the language. I swear if I had not known Paul as a Negro I should have thought an educated Russian before me. I can't tell you how beautiful he talks Russian." "He's so keen," Essie wrote in her diary. "He feels that he can become an official, and important interpreter of Russian music, and literature. He feels he understands it, and is close to it, and he loves the language."[1]

At Robeson's next tour stop, Boston—his first appearance there in six years—one critic found his voice in "excellent condition," another essentially "untutored." In Des Moines, a request from the audience for "St. Louis Blues" and "Sing You Sinners" brought a frosty response from Robeson's traveling manager: "Mr. Robeson never sings blues!" A reporter's question about the origins of Robeson's singing career prompted him to send Carlo a postcard message saying he had replied "that Mr. Carl Van Vechten had launched me upon my concert career. He's a nice fellow." In Montreal, the sold-out house cheered wildly at the close, and the *Gazette*'s critic packaged the excitement in racialist wrappings: " . . . he looks like an ebony Apollo. He is as tall as a guardsman and carries himself with a royal air. In manner he is as simple as a child, and his beaming face and wide smile, which is sometimes a regular grin, prove him to be, with all his worldly successes, an unspoiled son of mother nature and still close to the earth in which he lives." (The same critic's enthusiasm waned when it came to describing the Russian songs; there, he felt, Robeson was "a stranger in a strange land.")[2]

The two-month tour completed, in March Robeson joined Yolande on the Continent for a brief break before his scheduled return to the States in April for a revival of *Show Boat.* (While in Paris, he discussed with Sacha Guitry the prospects of appearing with him and Yvonne Printemps in a play with an African theme—a project that hung fire while they searched for a suitable vehicle.) Paul was late in sending money to Essie, which annoyed her, and then sent an oblique cable that added mystification to annoyance: "Interesting plans ahead . . . Put flat on market . . . See Paris ahead . . ." "He is a funny boy," Essie wrote in her diary on receiving the cable. "Evidently, he means he wants me to join him in Paris, which is a good one. . . ." Essie, for the moment, was feeling exhilarated over her writing prospects—putting in a lot of hard work on her prospective play, *Uncle Tom's Cabin* ("I honestly think it's good, different, and interesting," she wrote the Van Vechtens. "The role of Tom could be played wonderfully by Paul, but he isn't NECESSARY to the play at all"), and enjoying an independent life in London that included a heady round of socializing and an occasional flirtation. "I mean to PROVE," she wrote exuberantly to Larry Brown, "that I made Paul what he is, by doing the same for myself that I did for him. I mean for little Essie to speak up. And loud, too." She also meant to be prepared in case she and Paul ended up in court. Responding to Larry's sympathetic noises, she tried to enlist him in looking through Paul's pockets or luggage for letters from Yolande, claiming that Paul had "stolen" from her file case the ones she had earlier procured "entirely by accident."[3]

Paul, it turned out, had not been hinting that Essie should join him in Paris. In early April he made his actual intentions clear in a letter: he wanted her to begin divorce proceedings, and to name Yolande openly as corespondent. Essie cabled back that she would proceed immediately. "I'm glad to have it all over with at last," she wrote in her diary. "If he has still the same attitude after two years, that settles it, and we'll call it a day." She was even prepared to put a good face on it publicly, announcing, in contemporary tones of emancipation, that if "this marriage business" was to

survive, it had to be brought up to date, and that divorce was the moderniz-
ing mechanism: "I have been married for eleven years to one of the most
charming, intelligent, gifted men in the world. I am glad that we have
become civilized enough to look at a relationship frankly and say: 'That was
grand. It isn't grand any more. That is enough, Period.' And end it as
happily as it was begun. My husband and I have been exceedingly happy.
I think we are happier now than we have ever been. But we no longer wish
to be married. Not to each other, that is. We want to be friends. I hope
our friendship will grow. This would be impossible, if we have to remain
married to each other for the rest of our lives." In an article, "Divorce,"
that she intended to sell and use to "break into the journalism game," she
wrote "I enjoyed building Paul's career much more than he enjoyed
achieving his success." Paul, on his side, decided to face down public
criticism over a mixed marriage directly, and he sent Essie the name of the
hotel in Paris (the Lancaster) where he and Yolande had stayed and the
specific dates (March 29 to April 6) when they had been in residence there.
Following his instructions, Essie crossed the Channel to obtain the hotel
manager's formal affidavit. Paul left for New York to appear in the revival
of *Show Boat.* [4]

No sooner had he arrived in New York than scandal erupted from an
unexpected quarter. The *Daily Mirror,* a Hearst tabloid, published on May
2, 1932, the sensational story that the British heiress Nancy Cunard had
come to New York in pursuit of Robeson and that the two were staying in
the same hotel in Harlem. Cunard was indeed in New York and indeed
staying at the Grampion Hotel in Harlem—not to pursue Robeson but to
work on her path-breaking anthology, *Negro,* due to appear in 1934. The
two had met briefly in Paris in 1926, and she had twice written to him in
1930 asking him to contribute to the planned anthology, an appeal he had
not answered. That was the sum of their knowledge of each other—there
was no truth to the story of an affair (possibly it had originated as a
transposed version of her involvement with Henry Crowder, the black jazz
musician). Both Cunard and Robeson immediately denied the *Mirror* article, with Cunard stylishly using the opportunity to promote *Negro* and to
call attention to the plight of the nine "Scottsboro boys" being held in
prison under death sentence. [5]

She also wrote directly to Robeson to say she knew "nothing *at all* of
this amazing link up of yourself and myself in the press," to question
whether his choice of the word "insult" in answering the *Daily Mirror* had
been "particularly felicitous," to chastise him for not having answered her
invitations to appear in the anthology, and to suggest that, if the recent
racist remarks attributed to Sir Thomas Beecham (her mother's lover)
proved accurate, it was Robeson's "duty to absolutely boycott all Beecham's musical activities here and in Europe." The story soon faded from
the press, but printed denials could not quite dispel the rumors—the

glamorous lifestyles of both principals were sufficient in the minds of some to sustain suspicion. Wendell P. Dabney, black editor of the Cincinnati paper *The Union,* wrote the Puerto Rican–born bibliophile Arthur A. Schomburg,

> I note that she denies, or rather Robeson denies anything apart from a mere acquaintance with the lady. I understood that she was rather partial to a young orchestra leader from Washington, D.C.—Cromwell [sic] by name. I hope, however, in her zeal to champion the "lost cause," "a forlorn hope," or an oppressed people, she will not get herself inextricably entangled in the meshes of Negroes whose only qualifications are a glib tongue, good clothes and a nice appearance. Verbum Sap.

The black novelist Claude McKay put the blame on Cunard, scorning her as "a very unreliable person and lacking intellectual purpose and balance, mixing up as she does her love affairs with the Negro problem." And the black painter Albert Smith wrote Schomburg, "And so her [Cunard's] Romeo has slipped on his ladder. I have often imagined that that would happen. It was too good to last a long time. For those combinations you need more than flesh to hold them." The "combination" prompted one anonymous white letter-writer to warn Cunard, "Either give up sleeping with a nigger or take the consequences. We will not only take you but we'll take your nigger lover–Robeson–with you."[6]

In this context of romantic rumor—and more was shortly to follow— the opening of *Show Boat* on May 20, 1932, could have been an (unsalacious) anticlimax. But producer Ziegfeld had assembled a powerful cast, retaining most of the members from the original American company— Helen Morgan as Julie, Edna May Oliver as Parthy Hawks, Norma Terris as Magnolia, and Charles Winninger as Cap'n Andy—substituting only Dennis King as Gaylord Ravenal and Robeson as Joe. The show received not reviews but hyperboles—"the greatest musical comedy ever produced," Robert Coleman raved in the *Mirror;* "the most beautifully blended musical show we have had in this country," seconded Brooks Atkinson in the *Times.* Robeson's personal notices soared beyond hyperbole: "celestial" was how Percy Hammond, the famously acerbic, usually reserved *Trib* critic described Robeson's voice. Edna Ferber, author of the book on which the show was based, wrote Alexander Woollcott that the ovation given Robeson on opening night exceeded any she had ever heard accorded a "figure of the stage, the concert hall, or the opera"— the audience "stood up and howled." "Remarkable," James Weldon Johnson wrote Robeson by way of congratulation—and the word was not exaggerated.[7]

Ten days after *Show Boat* opened, the rumor mill began to grind again.

On May 31, in London, a reporter from the *Daily Herald* came to see Essie. Was there truth to the report, he asked, that she had filed suit for divorce, and had named Lady Louis Mountbatten as corespondent? Recently returned from her Paris fact-finding mission (as directed by Paul) to gather the needed evidence for divorce proceedings, Essie, with Paul in agreement, decided to confirm the long-circulating rumor of their separation, though not its purported cause. The marriage, she said, "has gone on the rocks of sheer ennui." In New York, Paul told the press, "Mrs. Robeson and I have been separated for two years, but the separation has been amicable, and I believe the divorce will be." He confirmed that he had been seeing an Englishwoman but, beyond denying that she was either Nancy Cunard or Peggy Ashcroft, refused to reveal her identity; whether they would marry, he told one reporter, "is in the lap of the gods. However, if we do marry, I am prepared to leave the United States if there is any stir about it." "I desire above all things," he told another reporter, "to maintain my personal dignity," and rather than tolerate any racist abuse, "I am prepared to leave this country forever."[8]

And the role of Edwina Mountbatten? In London, Essie, too, refused to name the actual corespondent, adding, "It is most incredible, though, that people should be linking Paul's name with that of a famous titled English woman, since she is just about the one person in England we don't know." But since Edwina Mountbatten was notorious for her multiple paramours (she served as the model for Amanda Prynne in Noel Coward's 1930 play *Private Lives*), the gossip continued to gain ground. The London Sunday paper *The People* headlined a story, "Society Shaken by Terrible Scandal," and suggested that Lady Louis, caught red-handed with Robeson, had been exiled from England for two years by the Palace—"a colored man I have never even met!!!!," the indignant Edwina wrote in her diary. Amused friends brought Essie further elaborations of the gossip—that the Queen had directly asked Essie to discontinue her suit, that Lady Louis had offered her a great sum of money and had had to sell Brook House, her mansion in Park Lane, to raise it. The issue finally came to court in July, Edwina Mountbatten, apparently pressed by Buckingham Palace, having decided to bring a libel suit against Oldham's Press, publisher of *The People*. The British legal system smoothed every path. Norman Birkett, one of the great advocates of the day, represented the Mountbattens, the Lord Chief Justice opened court at the unusual hour of 9:30 a.m. (and without prior notice to the press), and the Mountbattens were accorded the privilege of giving direct testimony themselves. When Edwina took the stand, she denied "the abominable rumours," and the Lord Chief Justice ruled in her favor, compelling Oldham's to make a full apology. *Almost* certainly, "justice" triumphed. No direct evidence exists of an affair between Robeson and Edwina Mountbatten. Yet the writer Marie Seton, who knew all parties concerned, insists that she heard directly from Robeson himself that he and Lady Louis did "go to bed once," that she had been the seducer, and that he had graciously consented to her bringing a lawsuit denying that he had ever been in the house—but that it "jarred inside him."[9]

Fania Marinoff stopped off to see Essie on a trip to London and reported back to Carlo that she had found her, Ma Goode, and Pauli "in a very large Flat very comfortably ensconsed," and "in a high state of excitement about Paul." Essie told Fania that she would give him a divorce, and without naming a corespondent ("she wants to give him everything he wants"), but predicted he was "going to have a horrible time" and claimed to feel "terribly sorry for him." When Essie left the room for a time to try on for Fania the "dernier cri" clothes she had bought in Paris to "knock Paul cold," Ma Goode told Fania that "Essie was forced into giving Paul the divorce, he had not sent her any money for three months, and that she [the mother] and the baby were almost arrested in the Tyrol for the hotel bill. Paul said no divorce no money, et voila; then she said yes and cabled for money for clothes." Fania concluded that although Essie was acting "very gay and frank and free about the whole situation," "au fond, it's really slaying her." Writing in her diary after Fania had left, Essie gloried in the purported news Fania had brought that Paul had been "depressed and unhappy" in New York and in Fania's prediction that "divorce will make a great and unfortunate difference in his whole career." Writing herself to Carlo a few days later, Essie reiterated the view "I hear on all sides that he is very depressed":

> When he gets his divorce he may get himself together. I hope he does, poor lamb. . . . But it seems impossible to please him. I hemmed and hawed, and put off the evil day (divorce) as long as I could, hoping something would happen, but he insisted that he MUST have his freedom, and that I just HAD to give it to him, so I felt I must.[10]

Judging from the one letter Paul wrote to Essie over the summer, his mood was not depressed at all, but upbeat. In going public about his possible marriage to a white woman, he had dared the press to do its worst—and had apparently gotten away with it short of a major backlash. Not only was *Show Boat* proving a triumph for him on Broadway, but a condensed version broadcast over WABC was also acclaimed. His alma mater, Rutgers, awarded him an honorary Master of Arts degree at its annual commencement in June, and he particularly savored the irony of being cited along with the president of Princeton—the university that had barred its gates to blacks. In July he gave a concert at Lewisohn Stadium with the Philharmonic under Albert Coates that was received rapturously:

his voice "is marked by an individual beauty of timbre that sets it apart from the other voices one hears," wrote the *World-Telegram*'s respected critic Pitts Sanborn. "This country is *really* mine," Paul wrote Essie. "And strange I like it again and deeply. After all—this audience understands the Negro in a way impossible for Europeans. Looks as though I'll have to leave, but I am enjoying it all. . . ."[11]

He was seeing very "little of the old crowd," feeling somewhat self-conscious with them, but reported to Essie, "I am still adored in Harlem. They still don't quite understand me"—perhaps because of the perplexing barrage of publicity that reported, almost simultaneously, his titled romances, his performing a benefit for the Harlem branch of the Children's Aid Society, and his attending (in line with his developing interest in Russia) a talk on that country by Walter Duranty, the Moscow correspondent of *The New York Times*. Instead of the old crowd, he saw more of Bess and Bob Rockmore; the latter had produced him in *The Hairy Ape* and would soon become his lawyer. But, Paul wrote to Essie, he had no "new flames"—"Guess I'm really in love this time. . . . Think I'm knocked cold." He also reassured her that he was "really being energetic"—"My French is coming fine—my Russian is unbelievable—and I'm also working at German and Spanish. . . . I have just received your play," he added, "and will read it. Hope it gets placed. I really think you're bound to hit sooner or later. You have such fine understanding of the theatre, and I surely believe you'll strike and hard. So pleased to hear of your doings. . . . You are charming, you know, and different—more power to you. . . . I would often love to see you and talk to you. Many problems could bear that common-sense approach of yours. I do remain *esoteric* at times. Very Russian, I guess. . . . Do know I shall do all I can in this settlement business. I want to be fair, but I don't want to be unreasonable to myself. While working here—swell, but if I transfer my activities to the continent the going will be tough. . . . Remarriage will change things here."[12]

Paul arrived back in England in September 1932 thinking divorce proceedings were well along and his new life with Yolande soon to begin. All did seem to be on an amicable footing with Essie. She wrote Harold Jackman, the West Indian man-about-town, that "Paul and I are great friends, and I think we like each other much better now than we ever did. . . . There isn't any unpleasantness. In fact, Paul is now reading my play, with a view to acting the leading role. Isn't life funny? . . . It's grand fun. To be free, and young enough still to use that freedom." Her particular pals were the gay couple William Plomer and Tony Butts, Michael Harrison and his sister Vi, and the black playwright Garland Anderson. She had a brief flirtation with Helmut Teichner, a young German Jew, until she decided he was "really tiresome and noisy." One evening at Butts and Plomer's house in Kensington, she met Leonard and Virginia Woolf. Essie wrote in her diary, "talked most of the evening with Leonard Woolf about the Negro, and he talked about Africa, and I enjoyed it immensely." Virginia Woolf wrote in *her* diary, ". . . Mrs. Paul Robeson, negroid, vivacious, supple, talking like a woman on the stage: chiefly to L. about negroes."[13]

Essie was not as reconciled to the "new, free life," however, as her public face suggested. Rita Romilly, an actress friend who had crossed on the ship with Paul, brought her news of his finances, which unsettled her surface calm. He had been complaining to Essie about money problems ("Financially of course I'm still struggling"), and, with Bob Rockmore beginning to take over as Paul's business manager, Essie no longer had a detailed accounting of his income. But now, through Rita Romilly, Essie learned that Paul's starting salary in *Show Boat* had been fifteen hundred dollars a week (later cut to nine hundred)—a staggering sum in a Depression year—and that he had turned down a radio contract from "Maxwell House Coffee Hour" for another fifteen hundred dollars a week. "And he has been beefing about paying me $100 a week, and $500 a quarter," Essie huffed in her diary, "and all this summer I have had to cable at least once for every allowance I have had, and I have never received it on time!" She also knew that he had loaned Jimmy Light five hundred dollars, had given money to his sister and brother, Marian and Ben, and had sent Yolande two thousand dollars toward their expenses in the south of France, where they were intending to live for a year. Essie, who in Paris recently had had fashionable fittings at Pacquin's and Lanvin's, immediately called her lawyer, canceled the divorce, and instituted a suit for separate maintenance. "[I'll] see him in hell before I divorce him," she fumed in her diary, "unless he gives me my allowance a year in advance, *and* a contract for 20% of his gross. I was so angry I couldn't sleep, thinking about it all. The swine!"[14]

She had a greater surprise coming. Ten days later Paul told her he would not be marrying Yolande after all. The choice was not his. He had left *Show Boat* prematurely (after only three months) and turned down various opportunities in the States (including that "Maxwell House Coffee Hour") in order to return to Yolande, to live with her in France for a year, and to marry in December—only to have her abruptly call the whole thing off. Under pressure from friends and family—her father, Tiger Jackson, was thought by some to have had a strong aversion to people of color—she "lost her nerve" and (according to Essie), deciding that "it would be too risky an experiment to give up all her friends and stupid, social life to marry Paul," failed to arrive at the appointed place to rendezvous with him. Within a month a public announcement appeared of her engagement to Prince Chervachidze, a Russian aristocrat living in France.[15]

Paul was devastated. Her journalist friend Marie Seton believes he "came very close to killing himself." He tried, however, to keep up a good public front, managing in October to carry out his contractual obligation to appear at the Palladium. And even privately, as time passed, he did his considerable best to blur, or at least transmogrify, the nature of the breakup. He told Freda Diamond that *he* had realized the match was a mistake after Yolande had made amorous advances to him in the back of a chauffeur-driven car and had pooh-poohed his embarrassment at the chauffeur's presence—as if to say that mere drivers didn't matter, didn't really exist as human beings. Her attitude had brought him up short, had reminded him of the way his own people were treated in the South—which is to say, not as people at all. Fifteen years later, in a revised version in which the entire English upper class had been substituted for Yolande, Robeson told an Australian friend that the chauffeur incident (sitting "with Lady So-and-so" in her car) had made him realize for the first time "the affinity between working men and women the world over, that, black and white, we all had a great deal in common." In any case, Paul told Essie to stop divorce proceedings and began to spend time with her and Pauli at the Buckingham Street flat. "I liked the apartment," he wistfully told a journalist friend. Before the year's end, Essie had begun to plan, yet again, for "the beginning of a new life together."[16]

Robeson told friends ever after that he had deeply loved Yolande. What he did not tell them is that for another twenty years at least they stayed in contact, however irregularly, with Larry Brown and the European-based singer John Payne as the go-betweens. A dozen letters have come to light from Payne to Brown, and a half-dozen from Yolande herself to Brown, spanning the years 1932–50, which reveal some sort (on Yolande's part, at least) of continuing attachment. "She is *not* well," Payne wrote Larry Brown as late as 1950, "and *loves* Paul. . . ." Soon after that, Payne reported that she was "greaving [sic] herself to *death* over Paul." Yolande herself wrote Payne, "I am weary unto death, John. What keeps me alive is my love for Paul, my respect for my father, and the life-lines like you—and Larry."[17]

When writing directly to Larry Brown, Yolande was more explicit still, making it virtually certain that she and Paul had not merely stayed in contact, but may have seen each other more than once. "After P. left," she wrote Brown in the summer of 1949 from Monte Carlo, where she was staying with friends, "I lost my mental balance, I think. . . . The cynicism of P. is the thing that has broken me temporarily—and I feel like someone whose legs are badly amputated. It takes time to learn how to walk again." In two additional letters from the same period, she thanked Larry Brown for having been "so loyal a friend to me in every way for many years" and expressed her envy that Larry had "been beside him as the years developed, and no matter how hard the going, could gradually adapt yourself to the vast change. I have had to try to do that in a very few short stolen hours." But Yolande assured Larry that she was "being patient and forcing no issues," even though the situation was *"eating into my soul."* Still, she added, it was "worth any pain—because as far as I am concerned—Paul is Paul. The Alpha and Omega. Therefore if I do not hear from him for long stretches, perhaps *you* could write occasionally. I would not feel so alone then." In an undated note, probably from the same period, she begged Larry to telephone her—"I have no one else who would understand how hard the road is—but I have *got* to accept it, Larry—so even a few minutes on the phone without 'My Lord' knowing—would help enormously. Oh God, Larry—his rules are hard."[18]

Bob Rockmore was apparently the only other person who knew about the continuing contact between Yolande and Paul. On April 22, 1950, she wrote Rockmore an acid little letter that, in its familiar references, confirms both his awareness and her bittersweet attachment to Paul: "Is it against the Protocol to ask whether our mutual friend makes records still—or has he retired to the bosom of his family—or more exhausting still, has taken himself a Female who is prepared to be 'everything' to him? It is so dull not knowing. Dear Bob—how annoying this must all be for you. But to be a lawyer and a friend is always a little trying. . . . I miss the laughter we had together over many subjects, still. . . . I could of course write to him as a fan for an up-to-date photograph signed 'Yours truly,' but as they say in Lancashire, 'Eeh, ah 'avent got the energy, Luv'!"[19]

Yolande told her old friend Rupert Hart-Davis that "she had had a son by Paul, whom she called Little Paul. She said he had been brought up in Switzerland, where he died in childhood." Hart-Davis didn't believe the story, "for Yolande lived as much in fantasy as in real life, and this may have been an unfulfilled wish of hers." In any case, the remainder of her life was, according to Hart-Davis, "chaotic." Her marriage to Chervachidze fell apart and—judging from the few traces of her later life that remain—she led an "unstable and racketing" existence, living in a variety of places, holding down, briefly, a variety of jobs. In a 1950 letter to Larry Brown she wrote, "Life is a lonely affair for me now, and always will be." In 1953, living again in Monte Carlo, she wrote Rupert Hart-Davis, *"slowly* I am finding that a small quotient of happiness can *still* be gained in this rather curious world." Yet a mere three weeks later she wrote him again to say, "depression has seized me by the throat," and to thank him for never having let her down—"& so many people have!" "Perhaps," she added sadly, "something *will* happen one day. . . . I'm so tired of fighting & putting on my clothes as if it were chain armour—I want to *lean* on somebody! Not always to be the prop. Fundamentally, I am so very tired." Thereafter the historical record on Yolande Jackson is blank.[20]

At the end of January 1933, Paul went into rehearsal for a London production of *All God's Chillun,* and Essie sailed for New York. ("I had thought of economizing, and taking second class," she wrote Larry Brown, "but decided against it, as I'm getting too old now to change my habits." She had just turned thirty-six and felt "happier than I have ever been in my life," convinced that she and Paul "understand each other now." She also felt secure in her determination to create a separate career for herself. Both her play, *Uncle Tom's Cabin*, and her novel, *Black Progress*, had been turned down by producers and publishers, but, never one to let grass grow under her feet, Essie rechanneled her ambition into acting. While in the States, she intended to investigate the possibility of enrolling in the American Academy of Dramatic Arts and perhaps as well in Professor George Pierce Baker's famed course in playwriting at Yale. "It's a grand prospect," she wrote in her diary; "I feel as though I shall really be fulfilled, at last. Paul has been sweet through it all, sharing my enthusiasm; advising and helping. I've never seen him so sweet, so understanding, so attractive. I think now I can be happy with him, for the rest of my life."[21]

Essie was not merely indulging a private fantasy. On his own terms—which did not include sexual fidelity or Essie's control over his business affairs—Paul did seem willing to reconstitute some semblance of their marriage. The shock of Yolande's desertion had been profound, the more so perhaps for replaying the childhood trauma of his mother's abrupt death. He would never again actually propose marriage to any of the women he became involved with, though to the more significant among them he would sometimes suggest that external circumstances alone—political and career considerations—prevented him from making a formal, public commitment to them, much to his own regret. For now, the stormy three-year courtship of Yolande still fresh, Paul was content to retreat to a facsimile of domesticity and, above all, to recommit himself to his work. "Am terribly happy at No. 19 [Buckingham Street—their flat]," he jotted down in a few notes to himself at the end of December 1932:

> Henceforth, all my energies will go into my work. . . . Unquestionably, Russian songs are right . . . most right for me. . . . As for languages—Russian—basic; German-French for *pictures;* Spanish; Dutch (as bridge to German); Hungarian along with Turkish (as *bridge* to *Hebrew*). Send for all records at home, then *Swedish.* I *feel so ambitious. Want to work all day* at something. . . .

He told a reporter from the Manchester *Guardian* that his immediate plans included acting in a play by the Hungarian playwright Lengyel, filming *The Emperor Jones,* studying Russian literature, finding theatrical vehicles that would allow him to play such famous blacks as Pushkin, Dumas, Hannibal, Menelik, Chaka, and Toussaint L'Ouverture, and starting a repertory company in a little theater to alternate Shakespeare, O'Neill, and contemporary plays.[22]

First up on his ambitious new agenda was *All God's Chillun.* Robeson referred to the role of Jim Harris, the gentle, sympathetic black law student in *Chillun,* as "still my favorite part," and the London production proved one of his happiest experiences in the theater. He was blessed with a brilliant young costar, Flora Robson, as Ella and a talented director, André Van Gyseghem, a pro-Soviet activist involved with the working-class Unity Theatre. *Chillun* was staged at another laboratory theater, the Embassy. To the surprise and delight of Van Gyseghem and Ronald Adam, manager of the Embassy, Robeson agreed to a salary of ten pounds for the run. As a further gesture of commitment, he personally wrote a check for one hundred pounds when an unexpected demand from O'Neill's agent for an advance in royalties threatened to sink the Embassy's tiny budget and derail the production.[23]

In their later recollections of the rehearsal period, Van Gyseghem's and Flora Robson's memories coincide. Both found Robeson entirely approachable, considerate of others, open to direction. "He was not up on a throne but a real human person that you could contact," Van Gyseghem recalls. Even so, Flora Robson felt at first a little shy of him, afraid that Ella's racist lines would offend him. But after the first week of rehearsals he had put her at ease. She, superbly trained and a brilliant technician, believed that Paul acted from instinct—he either "felt" a role or couldn't perform it—and thereafter she followed Stanislavski's precept that all acting hinges on giving and receiving, and never took her eyes off him while playing. The result was a conflagration of emotion, "something so fantastic," according to Van Gyseghem, "that at times I felt, in those rehearsals, that I ought not to be there. They were stripping themselves so naked, emotionally." Though in his view Paul was "not a finished actor," Paul's technical deficiencies—awkward body movement, a tendency to declaim—themselves fed into the role of the uncertain, desperately sincere Jim Harris, heightening the impact of the performance. The London critics agreed. They gave the edge to Flora Robson, but their praise for Robeson was nearly as unanimous, and the combination of the two was widely hailed as (in the words of *The Observer*'s reviewer, Ivor Brown) "a perfect dramatic partnership." *Chillun* drew enough attention to extend its run for a week at the Piccadilly, but because Robeson had a commitment to film *The Emperor Jones* in the United States, the play had to close after two months.[24]

Essie accompanied Paul to New York for the filming of *Jones,* but the two did not share the same living quarters; Essie again stayed separately with Hattie and Buddy Bolling. On arriving in May 1933, Paul went immediately into production at Paramount's Astoria Studios on Long Island. For his first talkie and first commercial film, he was given a salary (for six weeks' work) of fifteen thousand dollars plus traveling expenses; moreover, his contract stipulated that he not be asked to shoot footage south of the Mason-Dixon line. The film's budget of a quarter of a million dollars was described by *Screenland* as "an almost unheard of sum for an 'independent' production," but in fact the final cost of $280,000 was low, even for 1933. The producers built an artificial jungle and swamp in Astoria, complete with heaters in the water to prevent Robeson from coming down with one of his frequent colds. The chain-gang sequences were shot in New Rochelle, and Jones Beach substituted for a Caribbean island. For the Harlem saloon scenes, director Dudley Murphy decided to serve the cast real liquor instead of the customary tea, in order to "heighten the realism," but the scenes were never printed—the cast got drunk and proved "unmanageable." After the first days of shooting (the entire filming was completed in thirty-eight days), the Will Hays office, the industry's censoring agency, insisted on seeing the rushes. Viewing the passionate footage between Robeson and Fredi Washington, Hays insisted it be reshot, lest the light-skinned Miss Washington come across as a white woman. With Hays warning that the sequences would eventually be cut if the required changes weren't made, the producers reluctantly applied dark makeup to Miss Washington for the daily shoots. The Hays office eventually settled for merely cutting two murder scenes and a shot of a woman smoking.[25]

Reporters visiting the set, aware that the character of Brutus Jones had not been drawn with an eye to pleasing all segments of the black community, asked Robeson for his own opinion of the play. It's a "masterpiece," he told one of them; "O'Neill sounds the very depths of Jones' soul. . . . Coming from the pen of a white man it's an almost incredible achievement, without a false note in the characterization." The black press did not, on the whole, agree. When the film was released in September—a mere two months after completion—it produced considerable controversy.[26]

Some black commentators emphasized their satisfaction at a black man's playing the leading role in a movie that subordinated the importance of whites—that alone, they said, constituted something of a filmic revolution. But others were vocal in complaint. The New York *Amsterdam News* praised Robeson's acting but denounced the use of the word "nigger" in the film as a "disgrace." The Philadelphia *Tribune* pointed out that images derived from stage and screen helped to form the negative view most whites had of blacks, and called Robeson himself on the carpet for perpetuating the stereotype of the black man as "essentially craven, yielding to discouragement as soon as momentary triumph has passed . . . becoming a miserable victim to moral breakdown and superstitious fears." A fellow black actor, Clarence Muse, reported from Hollywood in a private letter to Claude Barnett, head of the Associated Negro Press, that "all agree that [Robeson] gave a great performance but story and direction poor. . . . I think it a damn shame to use such an excellent actor to put over damaging propaganda against the Negro." The white press made no such complaint, but its reception, too, was tepid—if on different grounds. Several critics complained that Robeson was too civilized a man to convey successfully the loutish aspects of *Jones,* but generally they greeted his portrayal as a highly auspicious commercial screen debut, even while expressing contempt for his vehicle.[27]

Robeson himself stressed, at least in the public interviews he gave, the positive benefits he'd derived from acting in the picture. "I was doubtful whether my art could be expressed through the medium of the film," he explained to one interviewer, "but my experience of filming in New York has changed my ideas"; to another he expressed surprise at the ability of the camera to pick up the subtleties in a performance. When asked by an English reporter about the prospects of going to Hollywood, Robeson replied, "I'm afraid of Hollywood. . . . Hollywood can only realize the plantation type of Negro—the Negro of 'poor Old Joe' and 'Swanee Ribber.' " He felt increasingly interested in doing "human stories. . . . A good Negro comedy, if I could find one. Rider Haggard's novels—'Allen Quartermaine,' for example, which has a fine romantic story and an excellent Negro part in Umslopogas. Stories of the great Negro emperors—Menelik, Chaka. America . . . would hardly believe that there had ever been such a person as a great Negro emperor, but in England you know it. You have had to conquer one or two."[28]

Robeson was beginning to expand his indictment of American life and, in a parallel development, to stress the special grace of the black subculture lying within it. To the extent that American culture was distinctive (he told a representative from *Film Weekly* on returning to London after the completion of *Jones*), it derived from Negro culture—most obviously in the area of music. "We are a great race, greater in tradition and culture than the American race. Why should we copy something that's inferior?" he told the *Daily Express.* "I am going to produce plays, make films, sing chants and prayers, all with one view in mind—to show my poor people that their culture traces back directly to the great civilisations of Persia, China, and the Jews." Going much further—publicly—than he ever had before, Robeson described the "modern white American" as "a member of the lowest form of civilisation in the world today." When the rest of the press picked up the remark and Robeson was asked if the attribution had been accurate, he replied, "A trifle exaggerated." His new outspokenness, however, continued for a while longer to be a matter of fits and starts. "I am proud of my African descent," he told an interviewer in 1933, "but I am very far from being color-conscious in the sense in which your true Communist is class-conscious. But then you must remember that I am essentially an artist and a cosmopolitan. . . ."[29]

Newly vocal on themes that had quietly engaged him intellectually for years, his excitement grew, and he began an energetic effort both to broaden his own insights through formal study and to incorporate his emerging new perspectives into his concert work and his future plans. Robeson had always enjoyed the study of language; now it became a passion. He enrolled in the School of Oriental Studies (part of London University) to do comparative work in African linguistics, with the eventual goal (soon aborted) of taking a Ph.D. in philology. He began "haphazardly" by studying the East Coast languages, and then the Bantu group (his own ancestral background), finding in these tongues "a pure negro foundation, dating from an ancient culture, but intermingled with many Arabic and Hamitic impurities." From them he passed on to Ewe, Efik, and Hausa, the West Coast African languages, and immediately found "a kinship of rhythm and intonation with the Negro English dialect" that he had heard spoken around him as a child. It was "like a home-coming"; when he began to study, he felt he "had penetrated to the core of African culture." His hope was "to interpret this original and unpolluted negro folksong to the Western world. . . ."[30]

He supplemented his course work with a close study of phonetics, using gramophone recordings he had collected of the folk songs of many cultures and an intense program of reading. He began to talk not only of visiting Africa but also of settling there eventually. Essie, simultaneously, began work in anthropology at the London School of Economics and University College, specializing in the study of African cultures. "When we get through," she wrote the Van Vechtens, "we will know something about 'our people.' " After she and Paul read Zora Neale Hurston's *Jonah's Gourd Vine*, Essie wrote to Hurston to express their admiration and to describe the African studies she and Paul had embarked on. Hurston wrote back that the news was "thrilling"—"I feel so keenly that you have at last set your feet on the right road. You know that we dont know anything about ourselves. You are realizing every day how silly our 'leaders' sound—talking what they don't know. . . . Harry T. Burleigh [and] Roland Hayes . . . talking some of the same rot. . . . One night, Alain Locke [the black scholar at Howard University], Langston Hughes and Louise Thompson [the black political radical] wrassled with me nearly all night long that folk sources were not important . . . but I stuck to my guns. . . . I have steadily maintained that the real us was infinitely superior to the sympathetic minstrel version. . . . I am truly happy that you and Paul are going to sources. . . . That is glorious. . . ." When W. E. B. Du Bois reminded Essie that her husband "owes THE CRISIS an oft-promised article," she replied, "I told Paul what you said about the article and he laughed and said he was too hard at work finding out about these African languages and learning to speak and read them to stop now. All the better, for when he is ready to talk, he will have a great deal of interest to talk about, I'm sure."[31]

Robeson's interest in African culture did not emerge in 1933 out of whole cloth. At least a decade earlier he had referred now and then to the special gifts and values of black people—to an approach to life that united those of African descent around the world, even as it set them apart from white Westerners. He had occasionally sounded the theme of a distinctive "race temperament," and as early as 1927 had even chastised Roland Hayes and Countee Cullen for abandoning "Negro sources" in their work. This initial discovery of Africa was apparently the result of his contact with African students in London in the 1920s. By the 1930s he had gotten to know such future African leaders as Nnamdi Azikiwe and Jomo Kenyatta (and later Kwame Nkrumah), as well as the radical Caribbean theorist C. L. R. James (and possibly George Padmore). Yet their limited influence on him before 1933 is not sufficient to explain his abrupt and headlong plunge in that year into African themes.[32]

There is no clear-cut explanation for Robeson's pronounced shift of energy and perspective, yet it does seem more than coincidental (if less than conclusively causal) that his re-evaluations followed hard upon the end of three years of emotional turmoil. Walter White, who knew Robeson well in these years, later made an oblique but telling reference to "certain personal and romantic experiences which disabused his mind of the comfortable conception that the people of Great Britain were less prejudiced than the white people of the United States." White may have been referring indirectly to Robeson's affair with Yolande; he was certainly pointing out that Robeson, having attained international fame as an artist, was still subjected to the same indignities—though to a lesser degree—that the white world inflicted upon black people everywhere. Yet Yolande's rejection of him was not insignificant in this regard. Robeson's prolonged involvement with her had not led to the expected consummation, but to unexpected abandonment. To put the psychological matter crudely (and all such formulas tend to be crude), her rejection symbolically portended the likely treatment he could expect from all whites—acceptance up to a point and then, should he assert full entitlement, repudiation. Yolande's abandonment shook Robeson not merely because he had lost a woman he deeply loved, but also because he had to question whether his romance with the white world in general was not set in similar sand. He could never again trust whites to the same degree he once had, nor be quite so sanguine about their ultimate intentions.[33]

As if *one* dam within him had burst, and overflowing with new ideas, Robeson started to jot down notes—a gauge of his excitement, since he rarely committed thoughts to paper. In the Western world, he wrote, in North and South America, the West Indies and the Caribbean, the black man "has become Western for good or for evil, and will contribute to the culture of his respective social milieu. That is, the American Negro will contribute, as he has in the past, to American culture. In fact, he may do most of the contributing." The black man in America *might* have taken his own direction, but "the white man stood in his path and by refusing to stand apart, settled the issue." "Helped immeasurably" by his "most astounding inferiority complex," the Afro-American had become "American to the core"; "his way is settled already." The Westernized black, who heretofore has held center stage in the world's consciousness is, "speaking in the broad sense . . . a decadent, cut off from his source."[34]

In the United States, three possibilities remained. The Afro-American would either, Robeson jotted in shorthand, "in time disappear into great American mass (which Negro prefers frankly) which is simple way—give up and disappear as race altogether," a solution to him "spineless" and "unthinkable"; "or, remain oppressed group, servile—also unthinkable"; or else the black could "become as the Jew before him—a self-respecting, solid, racial unit—with its spiritual roots back in Africa whence he came. Not whining for this or that—but developing his powers to [the] point where there is no possible denial of equality." In formulating these alternatives, Robeson was implicitly rejecting both the brand of black nationalism that sought salvation in a literal (as opposed to spiritual) return to Africa (Robeson never felt any pronounced sympathy for separatist movements like the Garveyites or the Nation of Islam), and also the assimilationist solution then being proposed by James Weldon Johnson and the NAACP he guided.

Robeson had never been a mere assimilationist—one who works for and welcomes the day when cultural variations will disappear. He recognized that what they were marked to disappear *into* was the dominant Anglo-Saxon outlook—and of that he had never been more than a temperate fan. But even in the early thirties, in the flush of his enthusiasm for Africa, he was not merely a "cultural pluralist," either—not parochially insistent on the narrow loyalties and values of one particular cultural or racial group. While rejecting melting-pot aesthetics, Robeson was at the same time attracted to an encompassing, universal vision for mankind. This combined view—ethnic integrity *and* international solidarity—had already been marked out in the early thirties by the New York Jewish intellectuals grouped around the *Menorah Journal.* There is no evidence that Robeson knew any of these men—Elliott Cohen, Lionel Trilling, Herbert Solow, Felix Morrow, Sidney Hook, etc.—or even that he had read any of their publications. But, in a parallelism of development common to the history of ideas, he had begun to share their nonsectarian, cultivated spirit, one that declared itself willing to borrow from many cultures in the name of the ultimate goal of a humane society that was simultaneously anti-assimilationist and cosmopolitan.[35]

In the early thirties, Robeson tilted toward a strong racial identification congenial to the theory of cultural pluralism. But by the end of the thirties, after his experience in Spain and his exposure to the Soviet Union, he would tilt more toward identification with the superseding claims of revolutionary internationalism. Much later, in the fifties, after his cosmopolitan hopes had been trampled by the hostile climate of the Cold War, he would renew and re-emphasize his own black cultural roots. But even then he could never be simply categorized as a "black nationalist." All of Robeson's shifts were subtle, none sudden or complete. For most of his life, he managed to hold in balance a simultaneous commitment to the values (sometimes competing, but in his view ultimately complementary) of cultural distinctiveness *and* international unity.[36]

Like James Weldon Johnson (and in some respects Du Bois), Robeson implicitly accepted the notion of culturally derived "racial traits"—and the importance of taking pride in them; though he located them not, as Johnson tended to, in a large imitative capacity and a love of humor but, rather, in a highly sophisticated sense of community and a primary emphasis on things of the spirit—"the *inner* urge" (as opposed to mere religious "mythology") and a trust in "higher intuition—neither instinct nor reason." Again like Johnson, as well as other leading lights of the Harlem Renaissance, Robeson would continue for a while longer (and to some extent, always) to share the assumption that it was the path of culture, not politics, that best expressed black values and held out the best hope for changing the image of the black man in the white mind—thereby ultimately improving the lot of the black masses. But, while continuing, like most of the black literati, to stress the importance of culture, Robeson was beginning to move beyond them in seeing the "true genius of the race" not in the great deeds of great men but in the accumulated experience and superior wisdom of the *folk,* of the collectivity—in an African cultural heritage that understood the primary importance of spiritual values, in contrast to the desiccated rationalism, and the worship of technology and material accumulation, that characterized the West.[37]

Far from believing, as did many of his contemporaries who considered the issue, that American blacks would and should take the lead in "uplifting" Africa, Robeson argued that it was in Africa itself that the black man's future was to be sought: "From there will come his real contribution to [the] culture of the world." That future, in Robeson's view, was "fraught with danger." The African had been told "he is a primitive," congenitally inferior. A "nonsensical" view, yet one the African might come to believe. The African spirit *was* different—but not inherently inferior, as the history of the resplendent early African empires attested. But, ancient Africa aside, the culture of the contemporary African was itself of "high quality," as exemplified in his intricate music, in a complex tribal development, and in a group of languages capable of expressing the "most subtle ideas" ("It is astonishing and, to me, fascinating to find a flexibility and subtlety in a language like Swahili, sufficient to convey the teachings of Confucius, for example"). In presenting this portrait of the "contemporary African," Robeson was choosing to de-emphasize the many tribal differences that subdivided the continent in favor of stressing a shared set of cultural attitudes and forms.[38]

Africa, in his view, was in danger of being "bludgeoned or persuaded into throwing that equipment away," just as the Afro-American "had—until recently—been taught to hate his own music and folklore." "This is all right with us *decadent* Westernized Negroes—but a halt must be called when the sacred regions of Africa are approached." "Can a whole race of people," Robeson asked rhetorically in his private notes, "spiritually commit suicide? Strange & terrible as it may seem—following the lead of his supposedly advanced American & Caribbean brothers (who incidentally *disown him*) he is on the way.... And I hear no deep protest from black Africa about the destruction of his institutions. Here & there feeble attempts are being made & those often by idealistic Europeans to save them—but on the contrary there should be a positive spirit of positive determination to preserve them as one's very life-blood, which assuredly they are." To avoid the catastrophe that had befallen the Westernized black, young Africans had to reject "with contempt any philosophy or spiritual message—any teaching or instructions as to fundamental values of humanity"—from the West, borrowing its "technique" alone, even while remembering that technique was "mechanical and only fit for certain uses." In this, Robeson advised young Africans to look for a model to China and the East.[39]

The Chinese had always lived

> as artists concerned mainly with [the] inner development of *man*
> ... which we have neglected ... *man* in relation to his fellow man
> as a *"social" being*—not as a kind of "lone wolf" ... have evolved
> a man with much deeper *capacity* for "good life" than our scien-
> tific *man* of West.... Long ago this most ancient of living cultures
> assigned soldier and warrior and glorious *hero* to lowest rank—
> and the scholar stands first—certainly there is no question of
> fundamental rightness of the latter.... [No] need to glorify this
> fighting business as in the West ... leave war in its place. Certainly
> not an ideal of human relations.

China had learned how to borrow from the West without succumbing to it—borrowing applied science, rejecting culture and ideology. "It's my belief," Robeson wrote, "that even an ideology as strong and fanatical as communism may later disappear into the deeper roots of Chinese philosophy." The African, too, must "in his deeper processes ... look Eastward. For the technical and mechanical needs to West."[40]

Yet, in using China as a model, Africans should be neither confined to it nor bound by it, Robeson wrote. Other Eastern cultures, "like those of India and Polynesia," had aspects worth emulating, and the American Negro could use Russian culture "to advantage" as well—because "the history of the Russian peasant closely parallels that of [the] Negro peasant in America." Robeson was not trying to postulate a common origin among these varied cultures and races but, rather, to pinpoint "a common element of centuries of serfdom . . . [and therefore a] common way of looking at life. The Western culture is abstract, from the outside looking in. . . . The Negro and Eastern culture is pure apprehension. . . ."[41]

But finally, Robeson warned, all these examples must be applied with caution. "Even comparison with Chinese only to give him [the African] courage to follow his own way. He can't be Chinese, Arabian, European or anything else. He must be African." The experience of other peoples could at best serve as "a temporary superstructure to help get one's bearings—but only that—and with certain knowledge that as long as that superstructure is necessary—true progress is retarded." Besides, the "human *stem* was one"; "Man's final destiny, when all technique is applied is to live this inner existence—which is close enough to hidden mystery." The African's special destiny—rejecting scientific method, logical thought, and the rules of reason as ultimate values—was to build on "the consciousness of inner spirit," to "look beyond himself" to the "higher apprehension" that "has been his way for untold centuries." "The Negro's whole outlook on life," he told a reporter,

> . . . is one peculiarly his own . . . he does not regard people, things, or incidents in exactly the same way as the European. In many instances, I protect myself in life with weapons entirely different from those used by the white man. . . . When a man comes into my room, the words he speaks, his reasoning, mean little to me. But I can "sense" very quickly what manner of man he is, and there are many other things I "feel" which I can never express entirely through the medium of the English language.[42]

Robeson was not content to work out these views in the privacy of his study. In a series of interviews with the press in 1934, he publicly elaborated his new opinions. "I am more interested in cultures than in politics," he told one reporter when discussing Africa: "Political and economic systems rise and fall, but the soul of a people lives on." Blacks "are a race," he told another, "but not a people. . . . We are as disharmonious as the white race is." Yet blacks "everywhere still feel a bond of unity," even if they do not everywhere recognize that Africa is "their own spiritual centre," but a politically unified—"a national" Africa—was for the time being "so immensely remote that we need not think about it." ("For a long time to come

Africa will continue to be controlled by Europeans.") Robeson felt sure that Christianity, at least "as preached by the missionaries and churches," was the wrong unifying force; it "was not what Africans needed"; it would not heal the enmity between, say, the West African and the Bantu. He did not pretend to know what would, or what kind of leadership was available and desirable. He did know that he personally could not play a leadership role—could not "play Mr. Gandhi for Africa": "I cannot do it. I have been out of touch with the culture and people myself too long. The root of the matter lies in giving the African Negro a pride in himself."[43]

In that cause Robeson felt he did have a contribution to make. "A mighty task confronts us," he said, "to go to Africa and reveal to the blacks their own historical mission. And this task is much more important than my singing." He told the press that he hoped to go to Nigeria soon, "to find some pure African music and songs," to make periodic visits thereafter, to learn the languages, "so that as soon as I arrive I can feel at home," and, eventually, to live permanently in Africa. A disbelieving reporter asked if by that he had in mind some village in the Congo. "Why not?" Robeson replied. "They are my own people, and I would be on my native soil. Among white men I am always lonely." "I am tired of the burden of my race," he told another reporter, a burden that "will be with me so long as I remain here" in the West. "In England I have found perfect freedom and peace, but it has not been so with my friends—companions of my own race. Where I am welcomed they are not."[44]

He did not yet feel ready for repatriation—"Some day I shall go. Not yet; I have work to do here." Part of that work involved trying to restructure his own music. He announced to the press his decision that "classical music" would play "no further part" in his concert programs; he would concentrate in the future on presenting "the folk music of the world." "This is a permanent departure," he said. He no longer had any desire "to interpret the vocal genius of half a dozen cultures which are really alien to me." He had attempted lieder in the past and could speak the German language, but he now concluded that there was "little in the German Romantic school that I feel I can make my own. I cannot sympathize with Wagner, for example. I like him for his general lusciousness of effect, but his music does not stir anything within me." Bach and Mozart, yes; they stood apart for him; the *Art of the Fugue* he found "intoxicating." But henceforth his chief concern would be "trying to find an Art that is purely Negro, that is not dependent on Western and European influences."[45]

In this regard, he rejected jazz as well as Wagner. Jazz "reflects Broadway, not the Negro. It exploits a Negro technique, but it isn't Negro. [It] has something of the Negro sense of rhythm, but only some. . . . The rhythmic complications of [African dialects] . . . make Duke Ellington's hot rhythms seem childish." He elaborated further the following year: "Jazz, which is admittedly negroid in its rhythmical origin, is no longer the honest and sincere folk-song in character. . . . Jazz songs like 'St. Louis Blues' or 'St. James's Infirmary' . . . are actually nearer to their folk-song origin than they are to Tin Pan Alley, but . . . most of it isn't genuine negro music any longer"—and as for a jazz piece like "High Water," it was merely "a vulgarized form of 'Roll, Jordan, Roll.' " ("I would rather get together half a dozen African drummers and listen to them. Their rhythm is so much more complicated.") In dismissing jazz as having "no spiritual significance," and in saying it would have no "serious effect on real music," Robeson was expressing an opinion shared by most "serious" composers and critics of the day. The early explorations of the jazz idiom on the part of Copland, Stravinsky, Milhaud, Weill, Křenek, and others, these critics argued, had just about exhausted its possibilities. Robeson was also echoing an attitude that had existed in the twenties among the black bourgeoisie and some of the Harlem elite—though for very different reasons. Whereas the black upper crust denigrated jazz as the music of their Southern peasant antecedents (an attitude they applied as well to the spirituals), Robeson came to disdain it because it was not a *pure enough* expression of those folk origins. However, just as the Harlem elite had eventually succumbed to the mania for jazz in the late twenties, Paul also seems in later years to have been able to set aside his theoretical arguments with it and to enjoy it for what it was. Throughout the forties, he frequented such legendary jazz joints as the Apollo and Café Society to hear the big bands and some of the jazz greats, like Chick Webb and Ella Fitzgerald. In the fifties he would go "up to the Savoy Ballroom very often to hear Count Basie . . . downtown to hear Don Shirley and back up to Manhattan Casino to hear Charlie Parker and get 'twisted around' trying to dance to those 'off beat riffs', down to the Apollo to hear Dizzy Gillespie take flight. . . . And Thelonious Monk really floored me." And much later, in 1958, Robeson would come around to saying, "For my money, modern jazz is one of the most important musical things there is in the world."[46]

But if, in the thirties, he scorned jazz as "decadent," he had a much higher opinion of the blues, considering them "as much genuine darkie material as the negro spirituals," and was especially admiring of Bessie Smith. The one attempt he himself would ever make at a blues recording, however, had disappointing results. "King Joe," a musical tribute to Joe Louis, recorded in October 1940 with the Count Basie band, demonstrated clearly that Robeson was far more comfortable with a straight melodic line than with the "impure" phrasing, the flattened notes, and the melisma of jazz or blues. John Hammond, the Columbia recording director who was involved in the session, remembered Count Basie's saying in an aside, "It certainly is an honor to be working with Mr. Robeson, but the man certainly can't sing the blues." Robeson would have agreed: his self-knowledge and his modesty about his musical accomplishments were keen. "Boy, if I had known I wouldn't have been thrown off the stage," he once told a reporter after a concert, "I would have come out singing the 'St. Louis Blues.' "[47]

Ultimately, Robeson's inclinations were with folk music. As he said in 1934, folk songs were "the music of basic realities, the spontaneous expression by the people for the people of elemental emotions." It was to such music that he now turned his attention, especially to the folk songs of the Russian, Hebrew, Slavonic, Highland, and Hebridean people, the idioms that in his view held the deepest affinity with the underlying spirit of Afro-American songs. The close kinship he felt with Hebrew culture now led him to declare publicly—his first such declaration—that the current Nazi oppression was "the most retrograde step the world has seen for centuries."[48]

In his periodic concerts in the British Isles during 1934, Robeson did make some innovations in his program offerings—but they met with limited success. In addition to his standard repertoire of spirituals and work songs, he added a group of Russian songs arranged by Gretchaninov, the Welsh "David of the White Rock," the Scottish "Turn Yet to Me" and "Loch Lomond," the Mexican "Encantadora Maria," a Finnish ballad called "The Wanderer," and the English "Oh, No, John, No." Enthusiastic audiences filled the concert halls, but some critics, even the provincial ones who in the past had tended to be almost uniformly worshipful, gently suggested that his greatest affinity was with the songs of his own people. The critic on the Birmingham *Post* was less than gentle: Robeson's voice, he wrote, "is really very intractable"; in the past the force of his personality—unaffected, direct, humane—and not his musical technique had been primarily responsible for his success, his "rather primitive methods" being an ideal match for his material, which he had "always wisely determined by an exact knowledge of his limitations"—thus accounting for "the perfect 'rectitude' of his performance." In expanding his repertory to include the folk songs of other peoples, he was in danger, these critics warned—perhaps uncomfortable with a Robeson they could no longer pigeonhole—of constricting the worth of his musical contribution.[49]

Robeson had still less success when he cast around for a film role that might foster the ideals he had come to espouse. He thought his search was over when, early in the summer of 1934, the Korda brothers offered him the role of the African chief Bosambo in a film they were planning based on Edgar Wallace's book *Sanders of the River*. Zoltán Korda had already spent five months in Central Africa, taking 160,000 feet of film on African life, including music, speech, dancing, and rituals, and Robeson thought the footage "magnificent"—vivid confirmation that Africa "had a definite culture a long way beyond the culture of the Stone Age . . . an integrated thing, which is still unspoilt by Western influence." He was thrilled, too, at the recordings Korda brought back of African music; they revealed "much more melody than I've ever heard come out of Africa. And I think the Americans will be amazed to find how many of their modern dance steps are relics of an African heritage—a pure Charleston, for instance, danced in the Heart of the Congo." Passing up an offer from the Chicago Opera to do two performances of Amonasro in *Aida* (at a thousand dollars a performance and with the certainty of enormous national publicity), he accepted the Kordas' offer to play Bosambo.[50]

A reporter from *The Observer* who came to interview him about the project found him "alight with enthusiasm." "Listen," he said to the newspaperman as he played his records of native African speech on the gramophone—"Listen to this bit of syncopation. No wonder the Negro carries the power to syncopate in his blood. Everything the American Negroes have got they've got directly from Africa—dances and rhythms—movements of the body and ways of walking. Only the original rhythms are a thousand times more complicated." The movie, he told the reporter, promised to be a milestone, the first comprehensive film record of African culture. He found the prospect enormously exciting—"For the first time since I began acting, I feel that I've found my place in the world, that there's something out of my own culture which I can express and perhaps help to preserve—for I'm not kidding myself that I've really gotten a place in Western culture, although I have been trained in it all my life."[51]

Even as the film neared completion, Robeson remained confident of its value. "Every scene and detail of the story is faithfully accurate," he told a reporter visiting the re-created Congolese village the Kordas had built at Shepperton. Some of the music being used was "genuine African melody," and most of the 250 extras in the film were blacks recruited from English port towns who had been born in Africa and came from the actual tribes portrayed (Jomo Kenyatta, cast as a minor chieftain, was one of them). "I am sure," Robeson told the press, that the film "will do a lot towards the better understanding of Negro culture and customs." Essie reported to the Van Vechtens that it was "great fun" working with the Kordas; "they know their business thoroughly and are human beings."[52]

Ultimately, Robeson was bitterly disappointed. It turned out he had lent his talents and invested his hopes in a film that ended up as a glorification of British imperialism. Robeson later told the New York *Amsterdam News* that "the imperialist angle" had been "placed in the plot during the last five days of shooting," and that he had been powerless to protest the shift in emphasis since he had no contract provision for approval of the finished film. (And he told Freda Diamond that he made an attempt to buy back the picture to prevent its release.). But the picture's pro-colonial bias is in fact embedded in its very fabric, including the basic characterization of Bosambo as a loyal lackey dependent on his white master. The African scenes, moreover, though authentically shot on location, are cut and placed in such a way as to signify disparagement, creating an aura made up in equal parts of sentimentality and anachronism. Nor is the film's overarching and explicit theme, of the necessity of a white presence to bring order out of the savage chaos of black Africa, confined to the final reel. The advertising for *Sanders* accurately portrayed its message: "A million mad savages fighting for one beautiful woman! . . . until three white comrades ALONE pitched into the fray and quelled the bloody revolt!"[53]

Robeson may have been misled in part by the Edgar Wallace book from which *Sanders* had been devised. In Wallace's original story, the English District Commissioner is no mere benevolent despot, but a calculating martinet who controls his black subjects through flogging, irons, and hanging. As the Kordas moved gradually away from Wallace's scenario, the changes may have seemed incidental and insignificant—until their accumulated impact was finally felt. It's worth noting, in this regard, that Jomo Kenyatta seems to have felt no qualms about the direction the film was taking, expressing "delight" in "the music and the spirit of the African scenes." Even after its completion, Kenyatta joined in the presentation of a cigarette case to Korda, adding his name to the inscription inside ("With deep admiration and gratitude"), and no one has ever accused Kenyatta of insufficient dedication to the cause of African independence and the integrity of African culture. Kenyatta never again spoke of the film, and Robeson was to speak of it disparagingly; "It is the only one of my films," he said in 1938, "that can be shown in Italy and Germany, for it shows the Negro as Fascist States desire him—savage and childish." In all likelihood, both men were too immersed in their particular segments during the actual filming to get any perspective on the whole—and too emotionally invested in the film's initial promise to see in time that its negative potential was being realized instead.[54]

Most of the leading white critics and nearly all of the black ones had no such trouble. Even those white reviewers who found the paean to British colonialism welcome recognized the picture for what it was. The New York *Daily News* characterized it as "a film glorifying the heroism of one of Britain's noted Empire builders," and the London *Sunday Times* noted, with no trace of irony, that *Sanders* provided "a grand insight into our special English difficulties in the governing of savage races"—it "could not be improved upon for the respect it displays to British sensibilities and ambitions." (The London *Times* daily reviewer added, ". . . it will bring no discredit on Imperial authority.") Less jingoistic critics complained that the film was merely "an imperialistic melodrama," a full-throated panegyric to "the sacredness of British colonial rule," "punctilious in upholding the dignity of the Crown."[55]

Nina Mae McKinney, Robeson's costar, took a particular drubbing. A marvelous talent who as a sixteen-year-old had made a huge hit in the 1929 film *Hallelujah,* she was woefully miscast in *Sanders*—that is, if one assumes the Kordas had ever intended portraying an African woman rather than a commercialized Harlem transplant. Light-skinned, Occidental in features and mannerisms, eyebrows plucked, the sleek, glamorous, American-accented McKinney was disastrously wrong in the role of Bosambo's native wife; as one critic put it, she was far "too cool and sophisticated a figure ever to suggest that she had really lived in the African bush." Robeson himself fared better with the white critics, especially those taken with the film's antiblack theme, with its portrayal of blacks as—at their best—child-like and superstitious. But he was roughly handled by several reviewers, with special mockery made of his "authentic" African singing in the film. The "war-song" reminded one critic "irresistibly of the famous marching song from *The Vagabond King,*" while another dismissed his performance as "half Wallace Beery–Pancho Villa, half concert singer in undress." "Here we have the pathetic spectacle," wrote the American film critic Robert Stebbins in *New Theatre,* "of one of the most gifted and distinguished members of his race placed in a position where in actuality he is forced into caricatures of his people."[56]

During the filming, McKinney and Robeson became, briefly, lovers. The fact was well enough known to reach Ma Goode, who wrote to tell Essie—who already knew. "It all may or may not be true as the stuff Nina Mae said about Paul being her man," Essie wrote back to her mother, and added an elaborate, unconvincing anecdote about how she had decoyed Paul away from seeing McKinney off at the boat train by getting her hair and nails done and putting on a dazzling new outfit for a cocktail party at the Kordas', where she was "an immense success," was asked out to dinner by Robert Donat, and so excited Paul's attention that he took her out for dinner himself instead of going to see McKinney off.[57]

Sanders of the River made money; perhaps *because* it glorified the white man's Empire, it became a popular success. But for Robeson himself it proved an embarrassment. The black press, and even a few friends, took him to sharp account for having lent his name and prestige to a work that disparaged and patronized Africans. According to Frances Williams, the politically active black actress who was working for Katherine Dunham at the time, the two women protested *Sanders* to Essie, who purportedly replied, "Look, we have to make money. And when we're millionaires, the people will notice us"; Williams, in disgust, described Essie as "full of phoneyness." Given Robeson's idealistic intentions, the press indictment was a terrible irony, and a source of grief. In self-defense, and deeply hurt, he lashed back both at his black critics and at the white sponsors who had led him astray. "To expect the Negro artist to reject every role with which he is not ideologically in agreement," Robeson told an *Amsterdam News* reporter—ignoring the fact that when he accepted the role he thought he *was* in ideological agreement with the filmmakers—"is to expect the Negro artist under our present scheme of things to give up his work entirely—unless, of course, he is to confine himself solely to the Left theatre." But subsequently Robeson made a clean break with *Sanders*, accepting full responsibility for his own miscalculation: "I committed a *faux pas* which, when reviewed in retrospect," he told a black-newspaper reporter fifteen years later, "convinced me that I had failed to weigh the problems of 150,000,000 native Africans. . . . I hate the picture."[58]

But in 1934-35 the reorientation in his values, though proceeding rapidly, was still incomplete. He could not disentangle himself from the Western precepts in which he had been reared simply by wishing, or even determining, to do so—certainly not overnight, and never fully. But his experience with *Sanders* helped propel him further in that direction. The white world of filmmaking had proved impervious to his bright new dream of African liberation, but that did not mean to him that the dream had been wrong. On the contrary, given what he had begun to recognize about the world and its ways, it probably proved it had been right; henceforth he would look elsewhere for its fulfillment. In his continuing search for alternatives to a Western culture for which he felt mounting distaste, the next opportunity came from an unexpected source—the Soviet filmmaker Sergei Eisenstein.

Using as a go-between the English journalist Marie Seton, whom he had met two years before in Moscow, Eisenstein sent Robeson a letter inviting him to the Soviet Union as the guest of the Administration for Films, to discuss making a picture together. "I never had an opportunity to meet you and I was allways [sic] sorry of it," Eisenstein wrote Robeson in his rudimentary English, "because you are one of the personalities I allways liked without knowing them personally!" He went on to say that he was

> extremely pleased to hear from Mary [sic] that you get really interested in our country and the problems which run around it all over the world. And I am enthusiastic to see you here. As soon as you'll be in this country we will have an opportunity to talk (at last!) and we will see if finally we will get to do something together.[59]

Eisenstein had long been an admirer of black culture and interested in making a film about Toussaint L'Ouverture, the liberator of Haiti, and his successor, Christophe, a subject long dear to Robeson's heart as well. Eisenstein had already talked over the project with Boris Shumyatsky, whom Stalin had appointed head of the Soviet film industry. Shumyatsky was a man of little experience with cinema, and he had already begun "disciplining" Eisenstein by refusing to allow the completion of his Mexican film, *Que Viva Mexico*. Still, he let Eisenstein feel somewhat encouraged about the Haitian project, going so far as to list it in the export catalogue of Intorgkino. And so, accompanied by Marie Seton, Paul and Essie left London for Moscow on December 20, 1934.[60]

■

Berlin, Moscow, Films

(1934–1937)

Because there was no through train to Moscow, the Robesons and Marie Seton had to lay over in Berlin for the whole day of December 21. It proved to be a nightmare. Berlin was not the city Robeson remembered from almost five years before, when he had played *Emperor Jones* there and marveled at its vivacity and freedom from color discrimination. The Nazis were now in full charge, and he felt the change immediately. On the walk from Friedrichstrasse Station to the hotel, his dark skin drew instant attention—surreptitious glances from passers-by, contemptuous stares from storm troopers. On arriving at the hotel, he turned silent, lying on the bed and staring at the ceiling. Essie put in a call to a Jewish friend they had known in 1930, a "highly-cultivated" man they had liked. He came by the hotel, furtive and frightened, and told them of the horrors of the mounting persecution. He looked like "a living corpse, skeleton head, haggard eyes," Essie wrote in her diary; he was "terrified." After the man left, Paul, upset and angry, decided they should stick close to the hotel until time for the train departure.[1]

When they made their way to the station that evening, Paul and Marie went to find the train while Essie went to look after the luggage. An older woman stared in angry disbelief at the sight of a black man and a white woman together, then took her complaint to three uniformed men standing on the platform. When they looked over in Paul's direction, he "could read the hatred in their eyes"; it reminded him of a lynch mob. He had been conditioned all his life to maintain a calm exterior, but he also remembered what his brother Reeve used to tell him: "If you have to go, take one with you." "I took a step forward," Paul told a reporter many years later, and "they could read something in my eyes." For whatever reasons of their own, the men moved off. When Essie joined them a few minutes later, there was still (as she wrote in her diary), "a terrible feeling of wolves waiting to spring," but they managed to board the train without further incident. "For a long time after the train moved out of Berlin," Marie Seton later wrote, "Paul sat hunched in the corner of the compartment staring out into the darkness."[2]

A very different reception awaited them in the Soviet Union. At the frontier, the customs house walls were covered with the slogan "Workers of the World Unite!" (in several languages) and with huge murals of scenes from farm and factory. The customs inspectors, enchanted with Paul's fluent Russian, let Essie through with all her trunks and bags. ("Paul's Russian is even more practical than he had hoped," Essie wrote the Van Vechtens, "and everyone is astounded and delighted when he speaks. I do what I can with my German, and get pretty far with it.") On the train that night they contentedly drank wineglasses full of vodka before dinner, watched a heavy moon rise over the steppes, and listened to "some lovely gypsy music" on the radio. Next morning, at the Moscow railroad station, an entire delegation greeted them—Sergei Eisenstein and his cameraman, Edward Tisse; the head of the Society for Cultural Relations with Foreign Countries (VOKS); the Soviet playwright Alexander Afinogenov (whose *Fear* had recently been a sensation) and his mulatto American wife, Genia; and several black Americans living in the U.S.S.R., including Essie's two brothers, John and Frank Goode. The Goodes, sympathetic to the Soviet experiment, had decided to try living in a socialist land and thus far were enthusiastic over the experiment. John had gotten work as a bus driver at the Foreign Workers' Club garage, and Frank, more recently arrived, had—as a towering, powerfully built man—the prospect of being billed as a "Black Samson" in a wrestling troupe tour of circuses and carnivals. He "is already acclimated," Essie wrote her mother, but she didn't like the looks of John—"cold, and worn, and old." During their stay, Essie loaded him up with warm underwear and a heavy leather coat, paid rent for six months on a room he could have to himself, and left him enough foreign money to buy scarce eggs, meat, and vegetables till spring (while they were still there, John turned "from gray to pink," Essie contentedly reported to Ma Goode).[3]

Following their initial reception at the railroad station, the Robesons were taken to their suite in the National Hotel near Red Square. They found a "magnificent" set of rooms, four huge windows overlooking the square, parquet floors, fine, heavy furniture, a marble bath, a white bear rug—and a grand piano. Interviewers and reporters poured in as soon as the Robesons arrived. "I've come to the USSR on a holiday," he told them, to visit the theaters ("the most interesting in the world"), hear the opera, see the country. His chief interest, he said, would be to "study the Soviet national minority policy as it operates among the peoples of Central Asia." (As he told the London *Observer* in the spring of 1935, "I'm not interested in any European culture, not even the culture of Moscow—but I am interested in the culture of Uzbekistan.") Eisenstein stayed for lunch that first day, and he and Paul quickly discovered that they liked each other immensely.[4]

The next two weeks were a whirlwind of activity and of rising enthusiasm, Robeson for the Russians, the Russians for Robeson. Nights at the theater and opera, long talks with Eisenstein, gala banquets, private screenings, trips to hospitals, children's centers, factories—events tumbled one after another, a heady mix of new, confirming experiences, all in the context of a warm embrace ("The people have gone mad over him," Essie wrote home). Christmas Eve was spent at the home of Maxim Litvinov, the Soviet Foreign Minister, and his English wife, Ivy. The Robesons drove out to the Litvinovs' with Eisenstein, Marie Seton, and the conductor Albert Coates along the Leningrad Highway, the air bitterly cold, the roads full of ice, the car skidding from side to side. On arriving, they found a broad white-columned house set in the midst of a stunning pine forest, a feast complete with chocolate ice cream—and two Red Army generals for dinner companions. The redoubtable and cultivated General Tukhachevsky (executed in 1937 for "plotting" against Stalin) sat next to Essie, and the two chatted along amiably in German.[5]

After dinner there was exuberant dancing; the Foreign Minister cut up with something that resembled an Irish jig, and Eisenstein demonstrated—to general hilarity—the dance steps he *thought* he had learned at the Savoy Ballroom in Harlem. After exhaustion set in and the guests had been refortified with a monumental Russian tea, Paul, simply and gently, said he wanted to sing some of his people's songs. When he finished, Litvinov put his hand on Robeson's arm and told him how glad they were he had come to the Soviet Union, that they understood the plight of blacks in the United States and "were one" with them. Litvinov, Essie wrote Ma Goode, was "grand" (though she thought Ivy "extremely ordinary and disappointing"—"Don't repeat this, for heaven's sake"). She also described to her mother, offhandedly, how at one point during the day she had "cried with the cold." Marie Seton remembers the tears, but accounts for them differently:

> Paul got such intense warmth and affection from everybody.
> . . . She didn't get the same enthusiastic love and affection. And
> it's the only time I ever, ever saw her break down and cry. . . .
> I think Sergei [Eisenstein] and I were the only two people who

actually saw her. . . . She defended herself by saying it was the cold.[6]

Back in Moscow that evening, the Robesons went to spend an hour with William Patterson, whom they had known from the early twenties, when he had been married to Essie's closest friend, Minnie Sumner. In the interval Pat had become a committed Communist, and was deeply involved in political work, most recently with the International Labor Defense organization that was spearheading protest against the imprisonment of the Scottsboro boys (the nine black youths accused in the South of raping two white women). Worn down by his efforts, and suffering from tuberculosis, Pat had come to Moscow for treatment and lay seriously ill. The Robesons found him in bed in a dingy, sparsely furnished room—but talking "as enthusiastically as ever." Essie and Pat had never liked each other, and four days later Robeson went back to see him alone. Pat later told Marie that on the second visit he encouraged Paul to return home and participate actively in the black struggle, but that Paul, though fully agreeing with the importance of the struggle, simply could not see himself living in the States.[7]

On New Year's Eve, the great filmmaker Pudovkin collected the Robesons for a private showing of *End of St. Petersburg* and *Storm over Asia.* That was followed by a midnight celebration with Eisenstein at Dom Kino, the House of the Cinema Workers, where the revelries got boisterous and the dancing frenzied—Essie, uneasy at the "brutal kicking and knocking about," decided that the Russians "are a rough people." That impression was confirmed the following day. Stopping off briefly during their New Year's Day rounds at John Goode's garage, Paul sang and got a raucous welcome—but Essie was a little put off by the "vicious shoving" and the "sickening smell of cabbage" everywhere. Still, Essie was on the whole impressed with what she saw in the Soviet Union—with the improved status of women, the quality of care in the hospitals, the diet and preventive injections given the children in nurseries, and the psychology of childrearing Alexander Luria expounded on during the private tour he gave her (and the visiting left-wing American Muriel Draper) of his Twin Nursery Kindergarten (Luria also told them there was "no room" for psychoanalysis in the Soviet Union—"everyone was too busy").[8]

Paul was more impressed still, above all with what he found out about "the minority question." Far into one night, he and Eisenstein discussed the so-called primitives of Central Asia—the Yakuts, Nentses, Kirghiz, Tadzhiks. Eisenstein said he disliked the unfair implications of inferiority which the term "primitive" conveyed—which was why, he explained, the Soviets had preferred to use the phrase "national minorities." On another day, Eisenstein came by with Alexander Luria, who told Robeson that one of his best students was a Yakut, a man who performed "magic rites" alone in his room, yet had "no difficulty whatever" with scientific and conceptual ideas. On a visit to the Technical and Theater School of the National Minorities, the Robesons were intrigued at the mix of faces and colors, at the excellence of the work produced, and at the declared purpose of the training—to send graduates back to their own peoples to form theater groups. Nearly thirty years later, Robeson himself referred, in a speech, to coming in contact during his 1934 trip with "a people called the Samoyeds. . . . They had come from the northern country, from the so-called Eskimo peoples. 'Samoyed' in Russian means 'self-eater.' 'Self-eater,' that was their own name in 1917, which certainly presumed that they were a backward people. . . . In 1934 I found out, in the Soviet Union, that there was no such thing on earth as a backward people."[9]

He also found strong sympathy for his own "national minority." At dinner with the theater director Alexander Tairov, Robeson was impressed at how widely the talk ranged over African art, music, and culture. And when he went to see a Children's Theater production, the play turned out to be about how life in an African village was disrupted by greedy white hunters. At intermission, a little boy rushed up to Robeson, hugged him around the knees, and begged him to stay in the Soviet Union—"You will be happy here with us." Not surprisingly, Essie wrote the Van Vechtens that "We both love it here, and are profoundly interested in what they are doing."[10]

The Robesons talked with some of the "minorities" themselves. They spent a lively evening with Jack and Si-lan Chen, whose father, Eugene Chen, had been the first Foreign Minister of the Chinese Republic under Sun Yat-sen, and whose combined ancestry of Trinidad black, Chinese, and English struck Robeson as an ideal blend of cultures. The beautiful Si-lan, a dancer married to Eisenstein's American student Jay Leyda, did not at first take to Robeson: he went "rambling off on an endless comparison of Chinese and African sculpture," seemed unsure of "the genuineness of his Soviet welcome," and "determined to be cautious with all new acquaintances." Si-lan was herself fierce in her devotion to the Revolution. Her art, she said, was designed to be "nationalist [Chinese] in form, and socialist in content"—a precise expression of Paul's emerging wish to combine the integrity of ethnic cultural forms with a humane cosmopolitan vision, and after their first encounter, Si-lan found him "much more relaxed and normal."[11]

Robeson also talked at length with American blacks resident in the Soviet Union. VOKS threw a banquet for the Robesons to which most of the black community in Moscow came; Robert Robinson (an Afro-American toolmaker who had come to the U.S.S.R. in 1930 in search of a job—but not out of any ideological sympathy) remembers the reception as excelling "by far" any such occasion he had attended—formal attire, "exquisite" food, elaborate entertainment. On another evening, the black community itself fêted the Robesons. Essie thought the expatriate Afro-Americans had chosen to marry "very third rate" Russian women; Robert Robinson, in turn, thought Essie more than a little vain and arrogant. According to Essie's diary, all the black Americans expressed deep contentment with life in the Soviet Union, a society, they told the Robesons, that was entirely free of racial prejudice. Robeson became convinced that the Soviets had solved the minorities question—"in the only way it can be solved, by granting self-determination to all nations within its boundaries."[12]

Robeson realized "how much my shy, sensitive Pauli would enjoy" the "sincere friendliness" of the Soviet citizenry toward people of color, and he and Essie began to consider the idea of resettling Pauli for a few years in Russia. He had occasionally stayed with his parents in the Buckingham Street flat in London, but essentially he had continued to live with and be raised by Ma Goode. Currently the two were living in New York, where Pauli, just past his seventh birthday, had finally found some children of his own age to play with. Essie was content with that arrangement for the time being, but she didn't want Pauli to "get like those other niggers in New York," and she warned Ma Goode not to take him "to any nigger beach" and "to keep him up to scratch"—"The more careless his surroundings are, the more sloppy the children, the more important it is to keep his manners perfect, and charming. . . ." For his part, Paul had paid scant attention to his son's upbringing ("I have no fatherly instincts about him at all," Essie quoted Paul as saying; "I'm busy with my work and he has people to look after him"), interfering only when he felt Essie and Ma Goode were too incessantly drumming "manners" into the boy—"The poor little fellow has enough to learn, anyway, without being taught a lot of unimportant stuff." But Paul did want his son "to go to America at regular intervals, so he will know his own people. . . . I want him to have *roots*. I want him to know Negroes. . . . I don't want him to be prejudiced. I want him to know and feel that he is a Negro." Yet for now, having had the idea of placing Pauli in a Soviet school for a few years, Paul actively investigated the possibility. He decided that, if a spring concert tour in the U.S.S.R. worked out, they (in Essie's words) would "go thoroughly into the question of living conditions here" and, if those passed muster, would bring Pauli and Ma Goode over for two years. They felt Pauli would adjust easily, since he was already fluent in German, a language widely spoken in the Soviet Union.[13]

During his two weeks in Russia, Robeson saw more of Sergei Eisenstein than anyone else. The two men were together on nearly a daily basis. Eisenstein arranged introductions, accompanied the Robesons on visits, took them on a tour of the film institute (GIK) where he taught, and introduced Paul to a packed audience of artists at a special party for him at the Dom Kino. Essie reported home that Eisenstein was "marvelous company"—"He is young, and great fun, with brains and a sense of humor." Eisenstein also screened his own films, *General Line* and *Potemkin*, for them—Robeson later told a reporter that he thought *General Line* "easily the finest film I've seen"—and many a time the two men talked far into the night about the possibility of working together on a picture. Eisenstein had been trying for a long while to make a film about the Haitian revolution, and he had tentatively entitled it "Black Majesty" (earlier he had offered it to Paramount but was swiftly turned down). At the moment, Shumyatsky was considering the proposal, and if it went through, Eisenstein hoped to cast Robeson as Christophe (or possibly Dessalines) and the Yiddish actor and director Solomon Mikhoels as Toussaint. Eisenstein hoped to use Robeson in several other projects as well—over the next two or three years, they would consider doing a film together based on a Pearl Buck novel, a stage production of the American working-class play *Stevedore*, and, after civil war broke out in Spain, a film on that conflict. All these projects would have to wait for official approval from the Soviet authorities.[14]

Toward the end of his stay, Robeson sat down beside Eisenstein and talked quietly about the gratitude he felt for the warmth of his welcome. He had hesitated to come, he said, had not really been convinced that the Soviet Union would be any different for him from any other place. But he was leaving filled with enthusiasm for what he had seen and heard—and deeply moved at his personal reception, at "the warm interest, the . . . expression of sincere comradeship toward me, as a black man, as a member of one of the most oppressed of human groups." In the Soviet Union he had felt "like a human being for the first time since I grew up. Here I am not a Negro but a human being. Before I came I could hardly believe that such a thing could be. . . . Here, for the first time in my life, I walk in full human dignity."[15]

Still, Robeson was not yet ready entirely to commit himself to a socialist—or, indeed, any other—political vision. Soon after he returned to London, he told a reporter that his interest in the Soviet Union "was, and is, completely non-political," perhaps deliberately exaggerating his lack of interest in public so that in private he might be better able to mull over options. Three years later, after he *had* become fully engaged politically, Essie wrote William Patterson that "Paul, in his quiet easy way, has apparently been fundamentally interested for a long time, but has been taking it easy," delaying overt public commitment until his instincts and his understanding could become consonant. Robeson's deeply disturbing exposure to fascism in Berlin had been immediately followed by his strongly affirmative exposure to communism in the Soviet Union. (Stalin's forced collectivization programs were already well advanced, and famine was already raging in the Ukraine—but of all this Robeson saw and heard nothing.) Emotionally linked in his experience, they would thereafter be centrally connected in his psyche. Nazi fascism and Soviet communism became opposite, symbolic representations of evil and good, shorthand explanations ever after for opposing forces in the universe. The Soviets, understandably, helped along the courtship; Ivan Maisky, the Soviet Ambassador in London, henceforth regularly invited the Robesons to Embassy events, including lunch with George Bernard Shaw.[16]

"Paul is extraordinarily happy these days," Essie wrote her mother in February 1935, a month after their return, "and it seems permanent." Fania Marinoff lunched with them at the fashionable Ivy and reported to Carlo that "they both looked marvelous and Essie seems very happy," though "Paul was full of himself as usual." Part of his new agenda was to earn enough money in the next eighteen months to free himself from financial worry, allowing more time for political activity. The plan was straightforward: a two-month concert tour of the English provinces, then tryout openings in small theaters for two new plays with politically promising themes: *Basalik,* about an African chief who resists white encroachment, and *Stevedore,* a play of racial and trade-union conflict that had already successfully debuted in New York. If the two plays went well, Robeson planned to tour them in repertory theaters for six months in the provinces. Having "made a fortune," he would then take a year off and go to Africa and back to the U.S.S.R. Not everyone, however, was prepared to believe in Robeson's conversion to a more politically conscious role. When Nancy Cunard heard that he had agreed to appear in *Stevedore,* she wrote Arthur Schomburg, "The news that Robeson wants to act in it is encouraging. But there, between you and I, my dear Arthur, with R. it is more uncertain. It is a strange 'case,' in fact. He has given his talent for the German victims of Hitler; he has never, as far as I know, done a thing for his race, anyway in England. So, we shall see."[17]

The concert tour went according to plan. In February and March, Robeson sang seventeen times in the English provinces, Scotland, Ireland, and Wales. He drew large crowds everywhere, despite the economic depression and even though he essentially sang his old program, making few additions to his repertory from that body of world folk music to which he had recently felt drawn. Perhaps he recognized that his ability to hold a popular audience hinged to some extent on the familiarity of his offerings. In any case, the warm welcome reassured him that his recent political outspokenness had not cost him his audience. After two standing-room-only concerts in Belfast and Dublin, Essie wrote her mother, "Everybody tells him he mustn't say this, and he mustn't say that, or the public will be angry with him and desert him. Well, see how they desert him."[18]

The critics, recognizing that he had become a popular idol in Britain, tended to applaud the charm of his personality, his modesty, deep feeling, simplicity, and sincerity of manner—rather than to belabor technical points of musicianship. Where they did, the advice offered was contradictory. Some of the critics continued to express the hope that Robeson would expand his repertory; others chided him for the songs he had already added, finding them unsuited to his "Negro" voice. Robeson paid the press scant attention. The distorted newspaper accounts of his trip to Russia had taught him to discount the accuracy of their coverage. "They have twisted what I say about the Soviet Union around so badly that now I give them written statements," he told a reporter from *Soviet Russia Today*. [19]

The three-performance tryout of *Basalik* (step two of Robeson's agenda) faltered at the Arts Theatre Club. The play's strong ideological appeal to Robeson was not buttressed by much artistry. Basalik, chief of an African country bordering on a British protectorate, carries off the British governor's wife as a hostage—treating her subsequent sexual advances with royal disdain—in a successful effort to extract a promise that his people will be left in peace. The formula of the Noble Savage dictated that Robeson, as Basalik, would do little more than stand around in regal silhouette, making majestic, monosyllabic noises. The critics handled him sympathetically, commiserating with his inability to find a vehicle suitable to both his gifts and his political integrity, but they gave no encouragement to any notion of extending the play's run beyond three performances.[20]

The following month, May 1935, Robeson appeared in the play *Stevedore*, directed by André Van Gyseghem (who had directed the London production of *All God's Chillun* in 1933). *Stevedore* had had a considerable success the year before in New York at the Theatre Union (a group which had come together to stage plays with working-class content and at inexpensive box-office prices): Brooks Atkinson had hailed it in the *Times* as "a swift and exciting drama of a race riot seasoned with class propaganda." In London the play was performed mostly with nonprofessional actors; Mrs. Marcus Garvey and George Padmore (the influential West Indian Marxist) helped recruit black cast members from various social strata, ranging from medical students to African seamen recently departed from their tribal villages. Robeson's old friend John Payne supervised the singing in the play, and Larry Brown appeared in the supporting role of Sam Oxley. The script exemplified Robeson's hope of fostering socially useful art. It tells the story of Lonnie Thompson, a black worker falsely accused of raping a white woman, who eludes a lynch mob, rallies his fellow blacks, wins the support of a group of white union members, and routs the rampaging mob—though Thompson himself is shot dead. Frankly propagandistic, the play combined the theme of the oppression of American blacks with a message of hope: the ability of a confederation of like-minded workers of every race and creed to unite against injustice.[21]

The play's good intentions were embedded in a melodramatic structure that lent it a certain vigor, but at the cost of complexity. As James Agate complained in the *Sunday Times,* the play "presents an ungraded picture of the virtuous savage and his vile oppressor," useless as a contribution toward solving a social problem because "its simplistic stereotypes did not match up with real life." Some of the other critics were more impressed with the play than Agate was, but almost all (including Agate) applauded Robeson's performance. Given the handicaps of an obvious script and an overcharged production, the consensus was that his "extraordinarily vivid and arresting personality" had been shown to advantage. Nancy Cunard, who had been skeptical of Robeson's intentions, not only liked the play ("extremely valuable in the racial-social question—it is straight from the shoulder") but also wrote in *The Crisis* that Robeson "is much more real than in such other parts as 'Othello' (which does not suit him)."[22]

Because the play did not draw enough of an audience to extend its run, Robeson's plans for doing both *Basalik* and *Stevedore* in repertory for six months in the provinces had to be canceled. He continued, though, to get a variety of attractive offers. Soon after *Stevedore* closed, the German director G. W. Pabst offered Robeson the leading role of Mephisto in a film adaptation of Gounod's *Faust.* "This picture will be in no sense a Hollywood picture," Pabst wrote him, but, rather, "an attempt to make [an] artistic product of the highest kind." To that end, he had asked George Antheil to arrange the score and Fritz Reiner, then of The Curtis Institute of Music, to conduct it. Antheil, who knew Robeson, also wrote to urge him to accept the role ("I am sure that it will be a great production"). But he decided to pass on the offer, shying away from European opera, which he felt ill-suited to his voice and unsympathetic to his temperament. Pabst let him know that he thought he'd made a mistake—"I am sure we could have done a marvelous thing together." The previous year Robeson had turned down an opera closer to his vocal and personal needs—Gershwin's *Porgy and Bess.* Gershwin had offered Robeson the part of Porgy and told him he was "bearing in mind Paul's voice in writing it." But, despite additional pleading from DuBose Heyward, who was doing the libretto, Robeson decided against the role.[23]

He also declined an offer of quite another sort that came to him from a group of students at Edinburgh University. They wanted to nominate him for the Lord Rectorship, an honorary position decided upon by student election and involving no obligation other than a speech at investiture. It was, one of the students wrote him, "a gesture toward yourself and toward your race which for its national and international importance, ought to be encouraged." Robeson declined with "grateful thanks," saying that he expected to be spending a great deal of time abroad during the next three years, "some of it in Africa and some in Asia."[24]

He did accept two other offers: to portray Toussaint L'Ouverture in a stage play by the radical Trinidadian C. L. R. James, then residing in London, and to re-create his role of Joe (for a forty-thousand-dollar salary) in the film version of *Show Boat*. Having been unable to combine socially significant work with commercial success, he temporarily split them apart: the Toussaint play would satisfy his political needs, *Show Boat* his financial ones. (He had hoped that by now Sergei Eisenstein would have succeeded in pushing through their proposal to do a film on Haiti together, but Eisenstein's letters contained no encouragement.) *Show Boat* was first up. At the end of September 1935, the Robesons left for Hollywood.[25]

They stopped on the way in Pittsfield, Massachusetts to see Pauli. He had remained under the tutelage of his grandmother, to whom the Robesons sent eighty pounds a month. Ma Goode's own theories on childraising included the peculiar notion that touching or cuddling a child was tantamount to spoiling him. Essie attempted at least indirect supervision through long letters—of instruction to her mother and of exhortation to Pauli (Paul occasionally appended for his son a brief "Hello Fellow!" note, and at one point wrote him, "... I love you very, very much and I'm making a New Year's resolution that I'll see a great deal of my boy the next year and all years thereafter"). Essie commented to her mother at length about everything from Pauli's schooling to his wet bathing suits. She wanted Pauli brought up, she wrote, in the same way she had been:

> to feel perfectly at home and at ease, in any company . . . to consider myself a pretty swell human being, and to look for human beings everywhere, in any walk of life . . . to open up my mind and to think with it . . . to do impossible things . . . to be as good as I could . . . never . . . to think I am being looked down upon. I unconsciously feel I'm top dog. That's the reason I am at home in any society. I want Paul to have that. It saves a lot of hurt feelings, imaginary slights, etc.[26]

To Pauli, Essie tried to convey egalitarian values she wasn't always able to live up to in her own life, cautioning him against snobbism in any form, and encouraging an effort at self-assertion she herself had never needed. She did not want him deferring to any authority, including that of parent or teacher, or ever obeying without question ("if and when he comes under my control," she wrote her mother, "[I] will teach him to question everything and everybody"; she wanted him "to speak up for his rights"). She especially did not want Pauli internalizing any disparage-ments thrown at him as a black child. Hearing that a classmate had called him a "nigger," Essie wrote him a long letter about the importance of being proud of his color:

> We, too, were called "nigger" when we were young. But we didn't mind very much. . . . I honestly think that white people call us all niggers, because they are jealous of us. They only call us nigger, when we do something better than they do, or when they are angry. . . . All white people, or nearly all white people, have no colour at all. They are just white. Some of them have rosy cheeks, but that is all. . . . We think the colour is beautiful, and much more interesting than just plain uninteresting white.

Hearing that Pauli had called another boy a "sissy," Essie chastised him for indulging in equally unjust name-calling: "There are a lot of very nice children who are not well and strong, and who cannot play games. It may not be their fault at all. I don't want you to hate them, and fight them. That is horrid. . . . I'd much rather you didn't hate anybody. Hating people makes you nasty, yourself. Don't hate him, don't fight him. If you don't like him, just leave him alone." Along with the detailed comments on his behavior, she reassured Pauli that "It is a great sadness to us that we cannot have you with us to live," promising that "some day, soon, I hope we will all settle down together."[27]

The Robesons also stopped for a brief time in New York—to take in some theater, to see the Van Vechtens and other friends, and to confer with Oscar Hammerstein II about the *Show Boat* film. Then they headed out to the coast, stopping off in Chicago so that Essie could interview Joe Louis (who had recently defeated Max Baer) for a collection of "Negro portraits" she hoped to do as a book. "I found him charming, and very very simple and natural," she wrote back to the Van Vechtens. "He only goes clam when you take him out of his field. He's as sweet as he can be, and crazy about the RACE." What with Joe Louis's victory and the arrival of Robeson in Hollywood, Van Vechten predicted to Alfred Knopf that "there is going to be a great deal of talk again about Negroes this winter," citing Mussolini's invasion of Ethiopia and the premiere of Gershwin's *Porgy and Bess* as two additional reasons. By November the Robesons, along with Larry Brown, were settled in a "grand flat" in Pasadena, each of them in his or her own bedroom "so we can all live happily and comfortably, without getting under each other's heels," lemon trees in the backyard, orange trees outside the kitchen window, and enormous poinsettias lining the walk from the street to the house. "Its all rather picture post cardy," Essie wrote Hattie Bolling, "and you're never quite sure its real, but its lovely."[28]

The filming proved a happy experience; the relationships were good all around (possibly excepting Allan Jones—"If you saw the Four Marx Brothers in A Night at the Opera," Essie wrote home, "you have seen our Ravenel, who is Allan Jones"). Robeson especially liked Helen Morgan, who played Julie, and was delighted with James Whale's direction. He felt he learned a great deal from Whale about how to work in front of a camera and how to use his vocal strengths to maximum advantage. He was in marvelous voice and spirits throughout the filming; when he finished singing "Ol' Man River" through the second time, the members of the orchestra applauded, and members of the technical crews frequently crowded the set to watch him ("We are proudest of the enthusiasm and interest of the property men and the electricians," Essie wrote. "If you can interest them, you're good").[29]

The shoot was condensed into a two-month period so Robeson could get back to London in time for rehearsals of C. L. R. James's play about Toussaint. Given Show Boat's cast of three thousand and the lavish production settings, that meant hectic scheduling; Whale shot nearly two hundred thousand feet of film in little more than six weeks. Essie had no trouble keeping busy on her own, spending much of her time wandering around the film sets and reporting back impressions to her friends (Carole Lombard—who was shooting Spinster Dinner with Preston Foster—is "a gorgeous bitch . . . and as unrestrained as the air"). Newly trained in anthropology, Essie regaled Hattie Bolling with the strange customs of the natives: "The former studio manager of Universal City made it a rule that the employees who punched a time clock had to get off the sidewalk when stars, or people who 'Got screen credit' came along. They were just like the niggers of the place."[30]

When the shooting was over, James Whale wrote Robeson to say, "Your 'Joe' is really magnificent," and to express the hope that "I will have the pleasure of directing you in a starring vehicle soon." The likely vehicle for a time seemed to be the C. L. R. James play, Black Majesty (it had the same title as Eisenstein's proposed film). Whale, as well as Jerome Kern and Oscar Hammerstein II, became excited about the script after Robeson showed it to them, and they immediately bought the film rights. "What we all three want to do," Whale wrote Robeson, "is to get you going in 'BLACK MAJESTY,' " and Hammerstein thought the film "must be done on a very broad scale or not at all." The picture would cost less to make in England, and Hammerstein (perhaps momentarily forgetting Sanders of the River) felt "such an unusual undertaking will have a better chance with Korda who is a man of taste and courage, untrammeled by the superstitions and the conventional convictions of Hollywood producers." Besides, Hammerstein wrote Robeson, "Popular as you are here, you are even more popular in England." But three months later, Hammerstein's interest had waned, and he wrote Essie that "it would be better to keep BLACK MAJESTY in abeyance." The postponement became permanent.[31]

While the film languished, Robeson tried out the stage version. Arriving back in London late in January 1936, he went directly into rehearsals for the James play. (For the unknowing, the *Sunday Times* identified Toussaint as "the subject of one of Wordsworth's sonnets.") Sponsored by the Stage Society, the play was given on several Sunday evenings in March 1936. The critics thought Robeson made the most of his material but didn't think much of the material, denigrating it as a "careful prose record" while elevating his performance above it. "By the rules that apply to others," *The Times* wrote, his acting "is clumsy, but his appearance and voice entitle him to rules of his own." The critic on the *Evening Standard* lamented that "Japhet in search of a father was not a more forlorn figure than Mr. Paul Robeson in search of a play."[32]

Still, it was an experience Robeson valued, not least for the opportunity it gave him to broaden his friendship with C. L. R. James. The two men had been acquainted before the production, but they got to know each other much better during it and remained in contact over the years. James recalls that Robeson's power onstage was primarily due not to his acting skills *per se* but to the immensity of his personality: "He was a man not only of great gentleness but of great command. . . . The moment he came onto the stage, the whole damn thing changed. It's not a question of acting. . . . The physique and the voice, the *spirit* behind him—you could see it when he was on stage. . . . But he wasn't a John Gielgud. No. And I say that not with any desire to discredit him but to place him historically."[33]

James had the impression that Robeson was a man of deep "reserve" and was "detached" from any interest in the glamour or material rewards of a theatrical career—though not, in James's opinion, because it had as yet been superseded by any profound political commitment. James—who was himself a committed Trotskyist—never felt that Robeson became political "in the sense that Richard Wright did"—that is, "a revolutionary political person, whose whole life was spent, wherever possible, in striking blows at capitalist society." James felt that Robeson came to be "on the side of the revolution; he was on the side of black people; he was on the side of all who were seeking emancipation. But that wasn't his whole life." Where Richard Wright, in James's opinion, "would have stopped doing anything to strike a serious political blow," Robeson "was not that type." He was, rather, "a distinguished person giving himself to revolutionary views"—which was why George Padmore, "a hundred-percent Marxist," always felt "a certain reserve" toward Robeson, even while he "admired and thought very much of him."[34]

Because Robeson kept his own counsel until he had taken whatever amount of time he needed to digest a given issue, his behavior could be characterized from the outside according to the viewer's own script. At exactly the time when James was doubting Robeson's temperamental ability to commit himself to Marxism, Emma Goldman—who as an anarchist had as early as 1922 expressed her disillusionment with the Soviet system as a betrayal of the Revolution—was expressing concern that he might have already overcommitted himself. In response to a letter from Essie describing how happy her brothers were in Russia, Emma replied that the Soviets might have done away with "the barbarity of racial differences," but much else in their system was deplorable. She had heard "the claims of the Communists that Paul has become a full fledged Communist," but whether the reports were true or not, and she hoped not, "I love and admire Paul's genius so much that [the claims] . . . could have no effect on me. . . . Politics and politicians come and go, they rarely leave a ripple on the surface of the human struggle. But creative genius goes on for ever. Besides, I never believe what the Communist press writes about anybody." Emma's long-standing commitment to anarchism and Paul's growing attachment to socialism did not get in the way of their cherishing their relationship. According to Freda Diamond, Paul told her that Emma once picketed a political event in which he was participating; he walked off the platform, took Emma's sign out of her hand, gave her a hug, handed her back the sign, and then returned to the platform.[35]

Robeson, meanwhile, continued to educate himself. Essie reported to the Van Vechtens that Paul had become so excited over Sidney and Beatrice Webb's 1935 book, *Soviet Communism: A New Civilization?* (a work full of glowing predictions and devoid of criticism), that he read bits aloud to her, "marked it all up with pencil marginings," and "turned down pages everywhere." He also read most of the leading Africanists of the day—Westerman, Oldham, Willoughby, de Groot, Soothill, Levy-Bruhl, and Hornbustel—and he wrote Melville Herskovits, the pioneering anthropological authority on Africa, with whom he had briefly roomed in the early twenties when both were graduate students at Columbia, asking for additional reading suggestions; Herskovits sent a long bibliography and a large envelope full of reprints. Robeson joined Jomo Kenyatta, Z. K. Matthews, and other guests at gatherings at the West African Students Union, receiving "prolonged applause" when he spoke, at one such event, about the need for Africans to "wake up and do something for themselves." He asked Langston Hughes for some of his "left poems" for possible conversion to songs, and Hughes sent him three about lynching and four about the Revolution ("Breaking the bonds of the darker races, Breaking the chains that have held for years . . ."). When Mei Lan-fang, the famous male interpreter of female roles for the Peking Opera, arrived in London, Robeson sought him out to discuss Chinese culture. When Charles Spurgeon Johnson, the Fisk University sociologist who had been one of the guiding spirits of the Harlem Renaissance, came to London (he had written ahead to ask Paul about hotel accommodations, wanting, for the sake of his wife, to avoid "embarrassment"), he and Robeson had a long talk about the prospects of "race war."[36]

Robeson also sought out Norman Leys, a white doctor and a committed socialist who had lived in various parts of East Africa from 1902 to 1918, written the influential book *Kenya,* and spent a lifetime pleading the African cause in Britain. Leys recognized the cultural richness of the African past but felt that colonialism had already destroyed its most vital aspects and that traditional African institutions had not, in any case, reflected an intrinsically different set of human needs and aspirations. He saw African tribalism as a source of weakness, a hereditary form of division that had facilitated European exploitation, and he believed Africa should modernize along Western lines. He and Robeson disagreed on many matters, yet respected each other's opinions. Leys thought Robeson judged "aesthetically rather than morally or rationally"—admitting he was "a Westerner" even while claiming that "all American Negroes have kept much of their inherited African culture." In his view, Robeson wished to keep alive "a specifically African philosophy and way of life" where it existed and revive it where it did not, even while recognizing that he "is a heretic, for his own people want to be 100% Americans and deny their possession of racial characteristics" that he asserts they still have—and although, further, he recognized that "Negrophobes are delighted with the doctrine of a special racial character" (which didn't in itself disprove its existence). Leys was putting his finger on real ambivalences within Robeson's evolving views. Even in his own notebooks for 1936, Robeson continually veered back and forth, now emphasizing that the Afro-American was "essentially decadent" and would be "happy if tomorrow he could disappear as a group into the American conglomerate mass," now emphasizing instead that, "emotionally, the modern American Negro would find himself quite at home in Africa," insisting that "the bond is one not only of race but more important of culture—of attitudes to life, a way of living."[37]

Robeson attempted to resolve his own ambivalence by thinking of the assimilationist black as "deluded" in insisting upon his "European heritage to the exclusion of his African one"—in ignoring the "fact" that "in every black man flows the rhythm of Africa; it has taken different forms in America, in the Caribbean, in South America, but the base of all these expressions is Africa." The assimilationist was also deluded, Robeson believed, in thinking that the way out of bondage lay in "deliverance by some act of a God who has been curiously deaf for many centuries; for certainly if prayer and song and supplication could effect a release, the Negro in America would long ago have been free." Robeson offered as his "humble opinion that we can get nowhere until we are proud of being black—and by the same token demand respect of other people of the world. For no one respects a man who does not respect himself."[38]

When talking to Leys, Robeson spoke repeatedly of his belief in some unique essence that blacks carried with them from their African past. Finding his ideas "vague and confused," Leys pressed Robeson as to whether he thought this "essence" was inherently racial or traditionally cultural in origin. He could not extract an answer that satisfied him. (Perhaps because Robeson did not wish to give it. In his private jottings at just this time, he wrote: "I base nothing on distinctions of race. They are too vague. But color distinctions cannot be avoided. Neither can cultural differences.") If African "differentness" was inherently racial, Leys was prepared to agree with Robeson that some tangible basis existed for asserting the future possibility of unifying all Africans under one cultural banner. But Leys found "no evidence extant so far to prove the existence of special racial mentalities." If, on the other hand, Robeson believed the African was different because of his special tribal heritage, Leys was prepared to argue that the past had no automatic claims on our loyalty: "If there is such a thing as a body of African tradition, I see no reason to think it deserves a higher place in African life than the O.T. [Old Testament] or the Sagas or the Vedas." He deplored the destruction by foreigners of Kikuyu or Zulu social life, but not when the abandonment of old values resulted from exposure to new ideas: "No-one of us has the right," Leys argued, "to keep others away from the fruit of that tree" from which they had themselves imbibed, with the usual mixed results of bringing death in one hand and abundant new life in the other—"they have the same right to face the danger as we have."[39]

As against Robeson's wish to preserve and foster the African "essence," Leys protested that such "deliberate exaltation of a group is bad" in the same way nineteenth-century nationalism was bad: it sanctioned and glorified "exclusiveness." It did so, moreover, on the assumption that the exposure of Africans to Western ways would inescapably result in a diminishment for Africans. But Western scientific thought—the great bugaboo—was not, in Leys's view, inherently evil, and could only be portrayed as such when science was misconstrued as mere information rather than a process of discovery; the study of scientific "truth itself cannot be other than a wholesome discipline." Just as Leys claimed his own "right to the full human heritage," so he claimed it for Africans:

. . . if an African finds his personal ideal best fulfilled outside African life he ought to be free to leave it. . . . World citizenship means in practice maximizing both liberty and variety *inside* every human group, whether it be family or any larger one not excluding nation and race. Liberty must obviously diminish or destroy characteristics *peculiar* to the group.

To Robeson such views represented the familiar Western tendency to assign primary value to the needs of the individual rather than the community. He agreed with the ideal of *enabling* Africans "to become world citizens"; but he continued to hope Africans would employ their opportunities *selectively,* choosing—as the Chinese had—to incorporate only those aspects of the "newness" that would better help them sustain their traditional emphasis on the needs and values of the collectivity. Robeson wanted to protect an invaluable heritage, Leys to create a still "better" synthesis.[40]

Through interviews and co-authored articles, Robeson further clarified and expanded his views. He did not doubt, he wrote, that Western science "worked miracles" and through its accumulated knowledge allowed growing power over "the *external* world." But that kind of material power had come to be considered the only source of "good," the "measure of all things." In his view, the ultimate questions lay not in the realm of knowledge "but of ethics"—which is what Leys had meant in calling his approach "aesthetic" and "unrealistic." Robeson felt the African heritage, with its concern for the inner life and for community values, had much to recommend it. He could not accept "wealth and luxury as the ultimate goal of human activity"—or the apparent equanimity of a man like H. G. Wells in suggesting (in *The Work, Wealth, and Happiness of Mankind*) that spiritual needs, the "mystery" of ultimate truths, were outside the bounds of everyday life. Robeson realized that many of his own people admired him, ironically, precisely to the extent that he had become successful on Western terms and had accumulated Western-prized luxuries. "They think I must be happy and proud," but "deep down inside me I am African, and for me the African life has a much deeper significance."[41]

On the other hand, Robeson did not want to be construed as advocating a narrow nationalistic view that equated artificial geographical boundaries with the parameters for maximum human happiness. "I am not a Nationalist," he asserted; "this belief, I know, has taken firm root in India, and the Near East, and is perhaps spreading. As for the people in that part of the world it may be a natural transition. I, however, am more profoundly impressed by likenesses in cultural forms which seem to transcend the boundaries of Nationality. Whatever be the Social and Economic content of the culture—Archaic, Clan and Tribal organization, Feudalism, Capitalism, or Socialism—this cultural Form seems to persist, and to be of vital importance to the people concerned. I realize that I am one of the very few who persists in suggesting that the African cultural form is in many respects similar to the old Archaic Chinese (Pre-Confucius, Pre-Lao-tse). . . . This comparison may seem much clearer if you will contrast this old Chinese form with an African form of a high level, namely, that of the Yoruba (Benin), Ashanti, Zulu or Boganda. . . . So, I am in no way exclusively 'nationalist' in pursuing my line of inquiry, and I am as interested in the problems which confront the Chinese people, as well as in those which concern, for example, Abyssinia. To me, the time seems long past when people can afford to think exclusively in terms of national units. The field of activity is far wider."[42]

As he became increasingly attracted to the socialist vision, Robeson moved somewhat away from his preoccupation with preserving African culture and toward an international perspective—from urging the primary need of asserting *black* values to emphasizing the overriding importance of *human* values. As he wrote in his notebook, he felt "certain that all races, all Peoples are not nearly as different one from the other as textbooks would have it. . . . Most differences [are] only superficial. History of Mankind proves this. No pure race. No pure culture. No people has lived by itself." In the voluminous private notes he jotted down during 1936, he complained that "even in as advanced and friendly a country as Russia," stereotypes of "savage" Africa remained, yet at the same time he was coming to believe that the concern of American Negroes "should be to make America socialist." Moving somewhat in the direction of Norman Leys, he now began to champion the view that, "if the world is to prosper," it must be "broadened to transcend national boundaries," toward the "possible synthesis of, and on the other hand, constant interplay between related cultural forms." Africa's geographical location, he felt, "appears to have symbolic significance. She stands between East and West, and in the future must take from both."[43]

C. L. R. James has emphasized two additional corollaries to Robeson's developing world-view. Though blacks had "special qualities" as a result of their special experience, they were "able to participate fully and completely in the distinctively Western arts of Western Civilization"—a black man might bring unique attributes to the role of Othello, but that did not disqualify him from performing Macbeth or Lear. Similarly, blacks might see the world from a somewhat different perspective from whites, but that did not make it impossible "for whites to understand blacks, or blacks to understand whites." The "human stem"—as Robeson had written in 1934 and would continue to emphasize for the rest of his life—"was one." Lopped off and set in separate soil, the branches of the tree would die; fastened to a common trunk and nourished equally, all would thrive.[44]

At the same time that Robeson was trying to formulate a theoretical position, he was trying on a practical level to incorporate his new values into his work as an actor. Early in 1936 he agreed to record a prologue and theme song for Joseph Best's *Africa Looks Up* (released as *My Song Goes Forth*), a documentary film about South Africa, and to make two movies with African themes, *Song of Freedom* and *King Solomon's Mines*. He could only hope—and did his best to ensure, through contract guarantees—that these new cinema projects would better fulfill his social ideals than the earlier ones had. He worked hard on revising the prologue to Best's documentary and in the final draft has himself as narrator say, "Every foot of Africa is now parceled out among the white races. Why has this happened? What has prompted them to go there? If you listen to men like Mussolini, they will tell you it is to *civilize*—a divine task, entrusted to the enlightened peoples to carry the torch of light and learning, and to benefit the African people. . . . Africa was opened up by the white man for the benefit of himself—to obtain the wealth it contained." The mainstream reviewers gave *My Song Goes Forth* a middling reception; the London *Daily Worker* thought it too bland to serve a militant liberationist purpose.[45]

Even as he signed for his two new films, *Song of Freedom* and *King Solomon's Mines,* his most recent one, *Show Boat,* was released. Robeson had tried to get "final-cut" approval but had been turned down (as Carl Laemmle, Jr., cabled Universal Studios, "Impossible let him okay takes. Garbo doesn't have this privilege nor anyone else"). The picture as shown rearranged and diminished the original dimension of his role—described in the ad campaign as the "lazy, easy-going husband" of the showboat's cook (played by Hattie McDaniel). In the States most reviewers hailed the film as (in the words of the *Trib*'s critic) "opulent, spectacular and generally enchanting." But the British notices were generally tepid and in some cases sardonic: James Agate in *The Tatler* suggested that enough money had been spent on the picture "to build and support a National Theatre," with artistic results on the level of "oleographs on a cottage wall. . . . It has been said that we shall see nothing like it again for a hundred years. I sincerely hope not." Segments of the black press, moreover, continued to berate Robeson for portraying (in the words of the California *News*) yet another "shiftless moron," and Marcus Garvey's monthly magazine, *The Black Man,* denounced him for using "his genius to appear in pictures and plays that tend to dishonour, mimic, discredit and abuse the cultural attainments of the Black Race." (In a lighter vein, the dancer Bill Robinson wrote Essie, "Tell Paul that we saw Show Boat twice; just to hear him sing and to get the new way of shelling peas.") To add to Robeson's discomfort, friends whose opinion he valued highly told him they thought little of *Show Boat.* Emma Goldman (commenting on the 1935 revival, not the film) wrote to say she thought him "magnificent," but didn't care for the theme. Eisenstein, commenting on the film, conveyed his continuing belief that Robeson was "a marvel," but added that

> only in two or three shots is his face, figure and personality treated in the way it ought to: there is so much to be made out of him! Picture pretty poor, considering all possibilities in it. Illustrating "Ol' Man River"—not the best taste: would prefer

realistic treatment of Paul singing—song and singing being so marvellous by themselves.[46]

Robeson had reason to hope his new screen venture, *Song of Freedom*, would appease his critics—and his own conscience. Based on Claude Williams and Dorothy Holloway's *The Kingdom of the Zinga*, the film began shooting in the spring of 1936. It tells the story of John Zinga (played by Robeson), a London dockworker whose glorious bass voice is accidentally discovered, launching him into international success as a concert singer. In one of those remarkable coincidences on which film plots turn, Zinga learns that the mysterious carved disc he has always worn around his neck reveals him to be the legendary King of Casanga. Abandoning his concert career to return to his people, he is met with scorn and abuse from them until he bursts into sacred song, thus persuading them of his royal heritage. The film ends with Zinga's resuming a part-time concert career in order to raise needed revenue for his people. Though inane as narrative, the film held strong appeal for Robeson. In its dockside scenes especially, it showed blacks coping within the context of ordinary life—a welcome switch from the previous stereotypes of shuffling idiot, faithful retainer, happy-go-lucky hedonist, or menacing con man. Zinga himself is portrayed in the film as a natural aristocrat, a man of charm and intelligence (as is his wife, played by Elizabeth Welch). *Song of Freedom*, Robeson told a reporter, "gives me a *real* part for the first time," and he continued to refer to it in later life as one of only two films he made (the other was *Proud Valley*) in which he felt he could take any pride.[47]

Elizabeth Welch remembers talking politics with him on the set—or, rather, declining to. Coming from a varied racial and ethnic background, she considered herself nonpolitical, and when Robeson talked to her about "doing something to help her people," she responded that "all people are my people." He let it go at that, unwilling to crowd her with polemics. Far from remembering him as insistently political, she retains the image of an affectionate, good-humored man, "modest about his acting," satisfied with his life, content with *Song of Freedom*. Even the black press, this time around, agreed he should be satisfied: the Pittsburgh *Courier* welcomed *Song of Freedom* as the "finest story of colored folks yet brought to the screen . . . a story of triumph." Langston Hughes wrote Essie, "Harlem liked 'Song of Freedom.' "[48]

Nineteen thirty-six was to prove the busiest year in Robeson's film career. He had only a few months' interval between the completion of *Song of Freedom* and the commencement of work on *King Solomon's Mines* for Gaumont British. The interval was so brief that he decided not to accompany Essie and Pauli on their long-hoped-for trip to Africa that same summer, especially since "both the British and South African authorities opposed his going." According to Essie, he was also concerned about protecting his voice: "He has to have the best conditions only—the best hotels and the best traveling facilities in trains." Instead, Paul went on a short vacation alone to the Soviet Union, intending to improve his Russian, and Ma Goode traveled separately to Moscow to check on living conditions for herself and Pauli, with the possibility in mind of his attending school there.[49]

Another marital crisis may additionally have contributed to Paul and Essie's heading off in separate directions. According to Marie Seton, tension between them became so great in 1935 that Marie advised Paul to make a clean break, saying outright that Essie "was poison to him." Political differences may have played a central role in creating the tension: Essie was trying to serve as a brake on Paul's accelerating commitment. As regards South Africa in particular, an (aborted) effort was made in 1935 to involve Robeson in the affairs of the Industrial and Commercial Workers' Union (ICU), which Essie did her best to resist. The effort involved a circle of interested whites that included Norman Leys, the Yorkshire novelist Winifred Holtby, her friend Vera Brittain (author of *Testament of Youth*), William Ballinger (the Scottish trade unionist who went to South Africa to help organize the ICU), his wife, Margaret Hodgson (who became a white representative for blacks in Parliament), and Ethelreda Lewis, later well known as the editor-writer of the *Trader Horn* books. When Ballinger told the press that Robeson had become more "politically minded" and was giving thought to a trip to South Africa to find out about conditions there, Essie reacted angrily, writing Winifred Holtby that her husband "was an artist and not a politician." Holtby reported to Margaret Hodgson that "Robeson is not indifferent. . . . I feel that Mrs. Robeson is our real antagonist." Vera Brittain put the matter more pointedly—"Pretty sure the annoyance, & indeed the whole attitude, is Mrs. Robeson's, not Paul"— and described Essie as "an aggressive little woman really, determined to fight for Paul's material interests & angry when he is led away from his purely artistic—& commercially profitable career." Summing up to Norman Leys, Holtby described Essie as "a bit too slick & American for my taste."[50]

Essie kept Paul closely posted on the details of her African adventure. She and Pauli were gone three months, stopping at Madeira on their way down the West Coast to Cape Town (where Essie barely managed to gain entry) then working their way upcountry into Swaziland, Basutoland, Uganda, and the Belgian Congo. They went armed with letters of introduction stressing that Essie would be engaging in anthropological field work, thus easing the problem of visas and travel restrictions, which might otherwise have curtailed her freedom of movement. She was further aided by African friends who met her and Pauli at many stops, passed them through a network of loving hands, and provided them with experiences not ordinarily available to foreigners.[51]

Along with attending a political convention at Bloemfontein and seeing the "frightful conditions" of the mines in Johannesburg and the slums in Cape Town, Essie at one point in the trip met and was housed by Max Yergan. Articulate and personable, Yergan was a 1914 graduate of Shaw University in North Carolina; he had been in Africa under the auspices of the International Committee of the YMCA for seventeen years and had made a brilliant career working with the Bantu of South Africa to improve educational facilities (he was awarded the NAACP's prestigious Spingarn Medal in 1933). Yergan would shortly return to the United States, would become an intimate of the Robesons, and would figure conspicuously in their lives.

Wherever they went, everyone seemed to have heard about "Robeson," and when the ship landed at Cape Town the newspaper reporters crowded around to insist (as Essie wrote Paul) "you were assuming leadership—world leadership of Negroes, and were now beginning to do something constructive about it. What measures were you taking to lead your people? Was I here to start your campaign? And so on." Essie tried to be cautious and diplomatic in her answers. "I said you were young and healthy and entirely normal and not particularly spiritual, and that you were naturally interested in the Negro everywhere. We are Negroes ourselves and as Negroes, are interested in our people, and in conditions which affect our people." The white paper, Cape Town *Argus*, translated that into "My husband has never been interested in politics. . . . He holds no fanciful ideas about Africa for the Africans. . . . He is not yet 40 and has no romantic ideas about devoting his time and energies to his people." The African trip, Essie wrote after she had returned,

> was one of those grand dreams come true. It is certainly the most interesting thing I have done, and I will always be grateful for the opportunity. Its quite a different world and I think every Negro who can, should go and look & listen and learn. We have a grand heritage from Africa, as a race, and it is shameful that we are not interested in it, and almost wholly ignorant of it.[52]

Paul and Ma Goode returned from their respective trips to the U.S.S.R. equally full of praise for the life they had found there. Paul had stayed for a few days with friends on film location at a collective farm and had had an "idyllic" time, "astonished" at how well informed the village children were about "the American Negro problem"—and how free of racial prejudice. That had been precisely Ma Goode's impression, and Paul now made the final decision that she and Pauli would go to live there at the end of the year. Peggy and Eugene Dennis (a leading figure in the

Communist Party, U.S.A.), who had left their older son, Tim, in school in Moscow and then been denied permission to take him out, warned the Robesons to leave Pauli with maximum publicity. They did exactly that: Paul announced widely to the press that they had decided to educate their son in the Soviet Union so that he would not have to undergo the discrimination his father had faced growing up in the United States.[53]

On his return from the Soviet Union, Paul went to work immediately on *King Solomon's Mines.* It was one of those no-expenses-spared productions—twenty-seven thousand natives in "authentic" animal skins! grass huts! erupting volcanoes!!—and replete with a corresponding number of stereotypes and anachronisms. Based on Rider Haggard's novel, the film tells the story of Umbopa (Robeson), servant to the white man, who ultimately reveals his true identity as an African chief, regains his throne, saves the lives of his treasure-seeking white friends (Cedric Hardwicke, Roland Young), and sings his way into the inspirational sunset. Robeson sang beautifully, but the music was composed and placed with fatuous disregard for authenticity, succeeding only in confirming the cinema's inability fully to use the range of his gifts and to respect his dignity. The black New York *Amsterdam News* expressed its gratitude that the film "at least doesn't reek with the imperialistic theory of British superiority" (most viewers today find that reek palpable), but the black Pittsburgh *Courier* was wholly negative: Robeson "is made to sing childish lyrics to dreary tunes in the most unlikely circumstances."[54]

His luck did not improve with his next film venture, *Big Fella,* which followed almost immediately and involved essentially the same team that had put together *Song of Freedom:* J. Elder Wills as director and Elizabeth Welch as costar. Welch, in retrospect, remains puzzled as to why Robeson agreed to do the film: her guess is that he accepted the poor script—based on Claude McKay's *Banjo*—out of a sense of obligation to Hammer–British Lion Productions for having given him the opportunity to do *Song of Freedom.* Possibly, too, he wanted to have a crack at a lighter role; he had told a reporter two years before that he wanted to try his hand at a comic part—as long as it was not some shuffling stereotype. It may also be that Essie applied a bit of leverage: she was eager to play the role of the café proprietress, which the producers offered her (they also cast Larry Brown in a secondary part), and she hugely enjoyed being in the film. "I spoke some French & wore false hair à la Pompadour!" she wrote a friend. "Larry was magnificent. Paul was *very pleased* with my work, and so was the Director."[55]

Big Fella tells the story of Banjo, a dockside worker and an itinerant balladeer (justification for having Robeson burst yet again into song), who locates a lost boy, sees him unwillingly returned to his home, is called in by the boy's family to help rear him, but ends up preferring the easygoing life of the docks. The scriptwriters did, under pressure from Robeson, make it clear that Banjo was "a steady, trustworthy sort of fellow," who worked for a living and did not participate in the "roguery" of the dockside life. They also voluntarily agreed to change the film's title from *Banjo* to *Big Fella* to avoid leading "the audience to expect a sort of 'Uncle Sambo' of the cotton plantations." Robeson was thus enabled to make a racial statement about an ordinary but admirable black man, functioning well in a contemporary, European setting. But, that virtue aside, the picture had little to recommend it.[56]

Between the completion of *Big Fella* and the immediate onset of yet another film project, *Jericho*, Robeson managed a month's trip to the U.S.S.R. He gave a four-city (Moscow, Leningrad, Kiev, Odessa) concert tour, and he and Essie helped settle Ma Goode and Pauli in for a nearly two-year stay. The concerts were well received—Essie described the audiences as "marvellous . . . wildly appreciative. I have never heard Paul & Larry better." The English language Moscow *Daily News* hailed his December 16 concert in the Large Hall of the Conservatory as "brilliant"— precisely because Robeson "is a 'mass singer', simple, natural and human." His friend Eisenstein, reviewing the concert in *Workers' Moscow*, congratulated Robeson on the "pure Russian" of his "hello" and "thank you" to the audience, regretted that no translations were provided for the English-language songs, and commented on how Robeson's "every gesture conveyed irony toward his formal dress, to which he had been condemned by world concert conventions." Pauli entered a Soviet Model School, with Stalin's daughter and Molotov's son among his schoolmates, and he took at once to the kindliness of his Russian teachers and to (in Essie's report home) "the complete lack of colour consciousness among the students." On New Year's Eve the family gathered together in Moscow—Ma Goode, Pauli, Paul, Essie, Essie's brothers, John and Frank, Larry Brown, and William Patterson. They had "a high old time"; three days later Essie felt "still full of vodka, caviar, champagne and Russian cigarette smoke."[57]

In contrast to the economically depressed West, Essie sent back a glowing report of a U.S.S.R. with "thousands of well stocked shops. . . . Everyone well fed & warmly dressed. Books everywhere, outrageously cheap & everyone reads." Six months earlier, referring to his prior trip to the Soviet Union, Robeson had told Ben Davis, Jr. (the black American Communist who was to become a Robeson intimate), that everywhere he went he had found "plenty of food," that he had made a point of visiting workers' homes and "they all live in healthful surroundings"—would that "the Negroes in Harlem and the South had such places to stay in." Apparently the Robesons had still heard nothing, or chose not to credit the few rumors that might have come their way, about Stalin's forced collectivization of agriculture, a policy that produced widespread famine, cost millions of lives (hitting the "national minority" population in Kazakhstan especially hard), and in the case of the Ukraine was deliberately designed by Stalin to crush the notion of an autonomous culture.[58]

In mid-January the Robesons left Pauli and Ma Goode "happily settled" in the Hotel National, and returned to London. Essie and Paul had only a four-day layover there before they had to leave for Egypt to film exteriors for *Jericho*. The shooting lasted a month. They stayed just outside Cairo and wandered its streets between takes, struck at the extreme contrasts in wealth and poverty, at European chic side by side with ancient tradition. "Cairo is a wonderful place," Robeson told an interviewer; "it is such a queer mix." In a letter to the Van Vechtens, Essie expressed fascination "that the Egyptians are pure coloured folks, science notwithstanding"—"we can find a double in Harlem for everyone we've seen here. It's great fun to see an enormously rich country like this, where the coloured folks are the bosses!" She reported, too, that "Paul is in fine form— bigger, sweeter, dearer than ever, interested in his work, interested in me, interested in Pauli, and all is very very well."[59]

Along with liking Cairo, Robeson enjoyed working on the film itself. "It's the best part I have ever had for a picture," he told one reporter. To another he revealed that he had "become very interested in Egyptian films" and expected to make one soon with Om Kalsoun, the noted Egyptian singer, as his female lead. The *Jericho* experience also confirmed Robeson in his fondness for cinema as a vehicle for his voice. He felt he could use it in a "perfectly natural" way while filmmaking, without having to strain for volume and projection, as he sometimes had to onstage or in concert; "I can sing best when I'm natural. I don't like posing or raising my voice or strutting about."[60]

One of his costars in the film, Henry Wilcoxon, became friendly with the Robesons and often shared meals with them. He found Essie "very sharp . . . the kind of person you don't push around," but he thought Paul an immensely appealing human being, at once modest and charismatic, having "a natural stage presence," and conducting himself on the set like "a pro." Robeson talked to Wilcoxon in a low-keyed way about the rising threat of fascism in Spain and gave him a book to read on socialism, offhandedly suggesting he have a look at it.[61]

The location shots for *Jericho* were made fifteen miles out in the desert at a studio site across the road from the Pyramids. One day Robeson, Wilcoxon, and Wallace Ford, another of the film's stars, inspected the Great Pyramid of Giza. With the help of a dragoman, they worked their way into the King's chamber at the geometric center of the pyramid, their path lit every hundred feet or so by a low-watt bulb. Inside the chamber they discovered "the most incredible echo" and Wilcoxon got the idea that Robeson should try singing. The first note "almost crumbled the place," as Wilcoxon remembers, and when Paul followed with a triad, "back came the most gigantic organ chord you have ever heard in your life. This was Paul Robeson plus!" Then, "without any cue from anybody Paul started to sing 'Oh Isis und Osiris' from *The Magic Flute.* . . . When he finished and the last reverberation had gone away . . . I was crying, the dragoman was crying, Wally Ford, bless his heart, who was usually doing nothing but laugh, he was crying, and Paul was crying. . . . There were tears going down our faces. And we almost daren't breathe to break the spell of the thing." Hardly saying a word, the three men drove back to Cairo.[62]

The good feeling carried over into the filming. *Jericho,* in the opinion of some, is one of Robeson's better pictures (which is not, to be sure, among the higher compliments one can pay to his career). The picture's story line, certainly, is the least conventional of his films. Jericho Jackson (Robeson) is a medical student drafted to serve in the army, who rescues some fellow soldiers from a torpedoed troop ship, then flees an unjust court martial to wander across North Africa until he marries the daughter of a Tuareg chieftain (played by the real-life Princess Kouka, discovered in the Sudan—and then cosmeticized), becomes leader of the tribe, and, after avoiding recapture by the white authorities, lives out his life as a benefactor of his people. Robeson, as always, was called upon in the film to break periodically into incongruous song and to behave with unswerving heroism, but in comparison with most of his other movie roles, the part of Jericho Jackson did enable him to move several steps away from the standard stereotype of servile childishness (even if it kept him firmly rooted in an alternate caricature of simplistic nobility). The press—perhaps still hankering after the servile stereotype—was lukewarm. In London the critics were polite. In New York (where the film played under the title *Dark Sands*) the response ranged more widely but not more enthusiastically: Bosley Crowther in the *Times* suggested that "out of respect to Paul Robeson and his magnificent baritone voice the less said about *Dark Sands* the better." The film was not a commercial success.[63]

On returning to London from Cairo in the early spring of 1937, Robeson lent his support to various political causes. In April, he appeared in concert at the Victoria Palace to aid homeless women and children in Spain. In May, he contributed fifteen hundred dollars to forward the work of the International Committee on African Affairs (a new organization in New York headed by Max Yergan, who had recently housed Essie and Pauli on their visit to South Africa). Also in May, Paul and Essie returned to the Soviet Union for another visit.[64]

They stayed in Russia for most of the summer, the first long holiday they had ever taken. They found Pauli and Ma Goode "very well" (except that Pauli had developed an intestinal problem calling for a special nonfat diet, which necessitated finding them a flat with kitchen facilities for preparing his special meals). Pauli had been promoted with honors; "He adores the children," Essie wrote the Van Vechtens, and Mama "loves Russia." The National Theater of Uzbekistan was currently in Moscow and Paul and Essie took Pauli to the Uzbek folk-dance-and-song matinee; he was "thrilled to death" and "nearly danced in his seat."[65]

For Paul himself, it was the Uzbek Opera that provided the special thrill. The two performances he and Essie saw were (in Essie's words) "vivid and vital, and a striking cross between Chinese, Arab and African— the whole with a definite and instantly recognizable African rhythm. . . ." Paul saw in the Uzbek Opera the fruit and confirmation of the success of Soviet policy toward its national minorities. As he put it, the Uzbeks, "a rather dark Mongolian people of Southern Asia who had enjoyed a brief period of glory under the famous Khans" and had then become "an oppressed and subject people," were, under socialism, being encouraged to preserve their cultural identity even while being welcomed on equal terms into the fellowship of Russian citizenry. He rejoiced to find leaders of the Soviet state in attendance at the opening-night performance; they were lending the weight of their presence, as he saw it, to the recent promulgation of Article 123 of the Soviet Constitution, which had declared as "irrevocable law" the equality of all citizens of the U.S.S.R., "irrespective of their nationality or race, in all fields of economic, state, cultural, social, and political life."[66]

To Robeson, Article 123 was "an expression of democracy, broader in scope and loftier in principle than ever before expressed." It stood in sharp contrast to the official policies and unofficial practices that characterized the rest of the contemporary world, where doctrines of "the inferiority of my people are propagated even in the highest schools of learning." The Uzbeks, unlike blacks in America, were not being counseled "to suffer endless misery silently, comforted by the knowledge that by 'divine decree' they are the 'hewers of wood and the drawers of water.' " They were not being told that their language and culture were "either dead or too primitive to develop" and had to give way before the "superior" utility of alien forms. In its treatment of the Uzbeks and other national minorities, the Soviet Union, Robeson believed, had uniquely placed itself in opposition to cultural tyranny and racial oppression—an achievement, to him, that "shines with special brilliance."

It stood in particular contrast, he felt, to what was currently happening in Spain. In that sundered country, beset by civil war, Franco's fascist forces of reaction were mobilizing to destroy the Republican government and to keep the Spanish people, "poor, landless and disfranchised," from claiming the right to control their own destiny. Robeson saw the mounting conflict as crucial in "the world-wide fight of the forces of democracy against reaction," and he called upon people of color everywhere to participate in the Spanish struggle "against the new slavery"—"it is to their eternal glory that Negroes from America, Africa and the West Indies are to be found fighting in Spain today on the side of the republican forces, for democracy and against those forces of reaction which seek to land us back to a new age of darkness."

To demonstrate his own commitment to the Republican cause, Robeson interrupted his holiday at the Soviet health resort of Kislovodsk to fly back to London for a mass rally in aid of the Basque refugee children at the Albert Hall on June 24, 1937. He had originally intended to broadcast his remarks from Moscow, but as soon as he learned that the Albert Hall management might not allow the broadcast to be heard (with a simultaneous threat from Germany that it would jam the relay), he rushed back to London to appear personally. The group of sponsors included W. H. Auden, E. M. Forster, Sean O'Casey, H. G. Wells, and Virginia Woolf, and the meeting was a huge success, as judged by the overflow crowd and by the number of contributions that poured onto the platform table. Robeson not only sang but also spoke, and the newspapers described his speech as the most striking of the evening. His words were impassioned:

> Like every true artist, I have longed to see my talent contributing in an unmistakably clear manner to the cause of humanity. I feel that tonight I am doing so. . . . Every artist, every scientist, every writer must decide *now* where he stands. He has no alternative. There is no standing above the conflict on Olympian heights. There are no impartial observers. . . . The battle front is everywhere. There is no sheltered rear. The artist must take sides. He must elect to fight for freedom or for slavery. I have made my choice. I had no alternative. The history of this era is characterized by the degradation of my people. Despoiled of their lands, their culture destroyed, they are in every country save one [the USSR], denied equal protection of the law, and deprived of their rightful place in the respect of their fellows. Not through blind faith or coercion, but conscious of my course, I take my place with you. I stand with you in unalterable support of the government of Spain, duly and regularly chosen by its lawful sons and daughters. . . . May your meeting . . . rally every black man to the side of Republican Spain. . . . The liberation of Spain from the oppression of fascist reactionaries is not a private matter of the Spaniards, but the common cause of all advanced and progressive humanity.[67]

Returning from his Russian holiday in August, Robeson broadened his political activity. He spoke out in opposition to Japanese aggression against China and appeared at benefits for the *Daily Worker* and the Friends of the Soviet Union. In the fall of 1937, he told the British press that he could not "portray the life nor express the living interests, hopes and aspirations of the struggling people from whence I come" in "commercial films and in the 'decadent' " West End theater and would instead do his next performance at Unity, the "workers' theater." He elaborated further to an interviewer from the *Daily Worker:*

> This is not a bolt out of the blue. . . . Films eventually brought the whole thing to a head. . . . I thought I could do something for the Negro race in the films; show the truth about them and about other people too. I used to do my part and go away feeling satisfied. Thought everything was O.K. Well, it wasn't. Things were twisted and changed—distorted. . . . That made me think things out. It made me more conscious politically. . . . Joining Unity Theatre means identifying myself with the working-class. And it gives me the chance to act in plays that say something I want to say about things that must be emphasized.

Stafford Cripps, the leading socialist politician, sent Robeson "my most sincere congratulations upon the action that you have taken. It is a splendid gesture of solidarity with the workers and I know how deeply it will be appreciated throughout the country." Just as Cripps's letter marked the beginning of a friendship, Robeson's increasing public advocacy marked his full emergence as a political spokesman.[68]

The escalating civil war in Spain now became Robeson's primary concern. In the month of December alone, he made four appearances in behalf of the Republic. He participated in the Third Spanish Concert at the Scala Theater; made a broadcast appeal for the Loyalists (receiving over four hundred letters in response); sang at a concert sponsored by the Left Book Club (which had been founded in 1936 by Victor Gollancz, John Strachey, and Harold Laski and quickly burgeoned into a real political force) in support of the International Brigadists fighting on the Republican side in Spain; and appeared on the stage of a huge rally in the Albert Hall to raise funds for victims of the war (it met on the same night that government troops, by the glare of searchlights, attacked Franco's forces at Teruel). The Albert Hall rally was an emotional high point. Clement Attlee, leader of the Opposition, spoke out forcefully against the betrayal of Spain by the so-called democracies of the West, whose governments, he argued, were in fact devoted to protecting class interests. Ellen Wilkinson, the member of Parliament who had recently been in Spain with Attlee and had shared in the attacks made on him in Parliament for his "partisan" trip, made a moving appeal for funds and succeeded in raising three thousand pounds. And Herbert Morrison further aroused the crowd by urging the Labour Party in Britain to work against the "treacherous and vacillating"

Chamberlain government then in power. But it was Robeson's appearance, according to newspaper accounts, that created a furor of enthusiasm. He galvanized the rally when he sang "Strike the cold shackles from my leg"; and when he altered the lyrics in "Ol' Man River" from "I'm tired of livin' and scared of dyin' " to "I must keep fightin' until I'm dyin'," the hall went wild.[69]

CHAPTER 11

■

The Spanish Civil War and
Emergent Politics

(1938–1939)

"I want to go to Spain," Paul announced early in December 1937. Essie, who thought of herself as the adventurous member of the family, afraid only of cats, demurred. "I am essentially a practical person," she wrote, "and I thought: Paul is doing some very good work for Spain, here in England . . . singing at important meetings . . . speaking and writing quite frankly, and enthusiastically, about his great interest in the struggle. . . . Why need he go into the war area, into danger, perhaps risk his life, his voice?" She fought the idea but it soon became clear that Paul was determined to go whether she accompanied him or not. He tried to clarify for her the importance of the trip. "This is our fight, my fight," he told her (in Essie's paraphrase). She decided to accompany him.[1]

Initially the U.S. Department of State denied them a visa, but, "after a lot of worrying and cabling," it was issued. The Spanish Embassy sent them two "safe-conduct" orders, Paul spent the afternoon of January 21 recording songs from *Porgy and Bess* at Abbey Road, and that night they caught the ferry train for Paris, accompanied by Charlotte Haldane, wife of the left-wing scientist J. B. S. Haldane. The Robeson party arrived at the Spanish border on January 23. A government army lieutenant drove them across the frontier, where they were "greeted by everyone, with a smile of welcome, and 'Salud!', with the raised, clenched fist." From there a militiaman took them in a car directly to Barcelona.[2]

On arriving at the Majestic Hotel, they were met by the press. The Afro-Cuban writer Nicolás Guillén found Robeson "blockaded by a crowd of people hanging on his most insignificant gestures. Robeson pays attention to everyone, smiling. He poses repeatedly for photographers, answers the most diverse questions without tiring. . . . When he talks, he talks passionately, his enormous hands contracted and palms turned up, an invariable gesture of his when talking. . . . His solid personality projects great attractiveness, and his body moves with the elasticity of an athlete." Asked by Guillén why he had come to Spain, Robeson replied, "It is dishonorable to put yourself on a plane above the masses, without march- ing at their side, participating in their anxieties and sorrows, since we artists owe everything to the masses, from our formation to our well-being; and it is not only as an artist that I love the cause of democracy in Spain, but also as a Black. I belong to an oppressed race, discriminated against, one that could not live if fascism triumphed in the world." As militant and as Marxist as the Guillén interview makes Robeson sound, for contrast there is the Manchester *Guardian* account, which quotes Robeson as saying, in moderate terms far more reminiscent of his earlier formulations, "In the democracies the Negro has to struggle against prejudices, but not against an actual crushing law. He finds opportunity if he has the initiative to seek for it and the courage to fight for it." Very likely Robeson did alternately sound a militant and a moderate note, accurately reflecting some linger- ing ambivalence which would very shortly solidify in the direction of militance.[3]

After the interviews, the Robeson party was taken to see the effects of an air raid that had taken place that very morning—residential apartments, schools, and even hospitals bombed by Franco's planes. It was a point in the war where Republican hopes were alive but fading. The Loyalist offen- sive against Teruel would culminate in success on January 8, 1938, but the Franco forces would retake the city on February 22, form a government, and by spring reach the border of Catalonia (on March 9, Hitler would occupy Austria). Faced with the "absolute savagery" of the bombings of Barcelona, Robeson told the press that he could not "understand how the democracies of Britain, France and America can stand by inactive."[4]

In that first evening, Robert Minor and his wife, Lydia Gibson, visited. Minor was a singular figure—a Communist from Texas, a talented cartoon- ist, he had been active in the early thirties in the League of Struggle for Negro Rights and would later be the Party's Southern representative. Essie thought Minor "the warmest, most human, delightful man—Imagine a Texas man really understanding Negroes. But he did and could." Minor told them that Earl Browder, the Communist Party/USA general secretary, might be in Barcelona when they got back at the end of their trip. They went to bed that night carefully arranging dressing gowns, slippers, and torches for a quick escape in case the warning sirens went off.[5]

For their tour, a seven-passenger Buick was put at their disposal and an army captain, Fernando Castillo, was assigned to them as escort and guide, along with a driver. The Robesons warmed immediately to Castillo. He had studied in London, spoke English fluently, and, Essie wrote, had "a delightful sense of humor"—"our dignified military captain, and our dignified, serious Paul, became two, mischievous, small boys. There are stories, and jokes, to which Charlotte and I contribute occasionally. Paul sings softly, by the fire, and our captain hums with him." On the long drive to Benicasim, Castillo told them that his father, a physician, had been an elected member of the assembly that had drawn up the Spanish Republican Constitution of 1931, and had been killed by the fascists in 1936. Five of his brothers were fighting at the front.[6]

Benicasim, once a summer resort for wealthy Spaniards, was now the base hospital nearest the front line, and the roads to it were thronged with wounded and convalescent soldiers. Robeson sang at three different places in and around Benicasim, all within an hour. As their car came to a halt at one spot, he saw a young black soldier stare in disbelief at him. Robeson spoke to the soldier and found that he was a Spanish black from Harlem who had been fighting in Spain eleven months and had just been wounded at the battle of Teruel. They were soon surrounded by other volunteer soldiers, the International Brigadists, from Britain and the States. Two days later, at Albacete and Tarazona, they "were delighted to meet many of 'the brothers'"—Andrew Mitchell from Oklahoma, Oliver Charles Rose from Baltimore, Frank Warfield from St. Louis, Ted Gibbs from Chicago, and Claude Pringle, a coal miner from Ohio. They "talked at length with them all, and gave them the latest news from America. The men were all keen, and aware, and sturdy spirited"—the Lincoln Brigade was the first U.S. unit ever integrated up to and including command positions.[7]

The most celebrated of the black volunteers was Oliver Law, a thirty-three-year-old regular-army man from Chicago who had never been promoted above the rank of private but had risen to be commandant of the Lincoln Brigade and had died on the Brunete front. The more Robeson heard about the "quiet, dark brown, strongly built, dignified" Law and how he had kept up the morale of his men by personally undertaking any assignment he asked of them, the more Robeson determined to do a film that would center on Law, but also tell the story of "all of the American Negro comrades" (in Robeson's words) "who have come to fight and die for Spain." The project never got off the ground; "the same money interests that block every effort to help Spain," Robeson wrote, "control the Motion Picture industry, and so refuse to allow such a story," preferring to produce profitable films of "mediocre entertainment."[8]

Everywhere he went, Robeson was immediately recognized by the troops. They had read about him, seen his films, heard his songs. Astonished to see him in Spain, they crowded around him at several stops, and at each he sang without accompaniment, the soldiers calling out favorite songs. At the International Brigade training quarters in Tarazona, he was warmly welcomed by soldiers from a dozen countries—some fifteen hundred men packed the church, after passing in review and saluting the Robeson party, to hear him sing and Charlotte Haldane talk—so movingly, her own eyes full of tears, that the men stood up and cheered her at the close. Two of the British volunteers still remember the impact Robeson himself made. The soldiers "were thrilled to bits to see him," George Baker recalls—that is, once they believed he was actually there. "You don't get people like that every day of the week running into a war to see how things are going," says Tommy Adlam, then a sergeant in the medical corps, recalling that at first most of the men discounted the rumor that Robeson was in the vicinity. After it was established as fact, "the whole place lit up." Robeson was so "alive and vivid," he had an instantaneous effect—"it was just like a magnet drawing you . . . as if somebody was reaching out to grasp you and draw you in." After he sang and talked with the men, they felt they had been with "a friend of lifelong standing."[9]

From Tarazona the party drove to Madrid, finishing the last part of the trip in darkness and at a crawl because that stretch of road was within range of the fascist artillery and was regularly bombed. Madrid itself had been shelled on a nearly daily basis since 1936, and no women and children were being allowed to enter the city; the Robesons got through only because they had special government papers. Driving directly to the Presidencia, they were received by the acting governor of Madrid, Dr. F. Grande-Covian, and went from there to luxurious accommodations in the Palace Hotel, "astonished" that such facilities were still available. They were only a few miles from the front line and could hear artillery fire clearly.[10]

The next day, from the observation tower in the former royal palace, they could see the trenches, government troops on one side, the insurgents on the other. While they were still in the tower, a shell whizzed over and burst into a nearby building; another landed on a nearby bridge, destroying it. They took refuge in the staff room and were entertained on the guitar by a young lieutenant, as other soldiers joined in singing flamenco songs (Robeson told Nicolás Guillén, "the Flamencan song is Black in its rhythm and its sad depths"). Robeson, in turn, sang for the soldiers—the Mexican folk song "Encantadora Maria" and spirituals ("My songs," he told the *Daily Worker* reporter in Spain, "came from the lips of the people of other continents who suffer and struggle to make equality a reality"). The soldiers seemed as absorbed in the singing as if there were no war at all. On the streets, too, the Robesons had been impressed with the remarkable capacity of the people to remain cheerful and to carry on, between shellings, with daily life. It was Essie's impression that they harbored little bitterness against the adversary, were optimistic that Franco would be defeated and anxious not to sully their own cause by adopting the barbarous tactics of the enemy (the Robesons were elated when news came over the radio that the government had successfully bombed Saragossa—only to hear their Spanish friends disapprovingly comment that the government had resorted to "murderers' weapons," had mistakenly adopted Franco's antilife values).[11]

The Robeson party was welcomed everywhere in Madrid. They met the remarkable Communist leader Dolores Ibarruri (La Pasionaria), the press came for interviews, Robeson broadcast to the nation, and Dr. Grande gave a party for them at which the great Pastora Imperio danced and Paul sang. At a performance of Cervantes's *Numancia,* Paul was recognized in the audience; the cast then performed some special folk songs and dances in his honor—and he in turn sang from the stage while the audience stomped and shouted its approval. On January 29 the Robesons went to the barracks where soldiers from the front lines were resting, and then to the parade grounds, where he talked and sang to the men; the soldiers called out requests to him in various languages, and a motion-picture crew shot him "from every possible angle" with the troops; Robeson later dubbed in two songs as sound background for the film—choosing the militant "Joshua" and Rosamond Johnson's "Singing wid a Sword in Ma Hand, Lord!"[12]

From Madrid the Robeson party drove to Valencia, stopped all along the road by earnest young militiamen "armed to the teeth" who recognized the official car but nonetheless insisted on the precaution of checking their papers. A fierce air raid on Valencia had preceded them by only a few hours, and they saw the terrible devastation on all sides. After resting for the night, they moved on to Barcelona by way of the coast road; they were again fortunate in their timing, and arrived there just after two morning air raids. In Barcelona, Essie thought the reporters "depressing, rather like vultures. Not sympathetic at all . . . I doubt if they really care who wins or loses." They saw Robert Minor again and had lunch with Earl Browder, who had just arrived from Toulouse. "Browder was a quiet middle-aged man, very sympathetic and interesting," Essie wrote in her diary. "We had a good talk over lunch, and afterwards over coffee. . . ." The Commissioner of Information of Catalonia, Jaume Miravitlles, and the well-known folklorist and musician Joan Gols i Soler also paid visits; with both of them Robeson discussed the music of Catalonia, and Gols promised to send him a collection of songs.[13]

After another overnight, they headed out of Spain to the French border, stopping at Figueras to pick up their driver's brother. During the trip he told them that the Spanish people "lack all sense of color prejudice and are actually proud of whatever Moorish blood they have"—perhaps deliberately broadening his own Republican principles to cover a less than spotless historical record. Lieutenant Conrad Kaye, a popular New York volunteer, had earlier told them that they had had "quite a time at first with some of the southern white Americans and the British on this Negro question . . . the really difficult ones [having been] the British. They refuse to eat in dining rooms with the Negroes, etc., and have to be drastically educated, because neither the Spaniards nor the International Brigade will tolerate such heresy." Essie, for one, "never felt any barrier because of Race or Color with the Spaniards." As they drove toward the French border, mingling political talk with a song fest (the Robesons teaching the others the words to "I'se a Muggin'"), Captain Castillo unpinned the medal he had won for heroism in 1936 from his uniform and handed it to Essie with the simple words "I give you this." At the border there were fond farewells and embraces. The Robesons got into a small sedan and crossed over into France; they arrived in Paris on the morning of February 1.[14]

Robeson later called the 1938 trip to Spain "a major turning point in my life"—in the sense of intensifying his already well-developed political sympathies. "I have never met such courage in a people," he told a reporter. He disliked the notion of turning to war to solve problems, but felt the Spanish people could not stand there and "be just murdered." In his notebook Robeson wrote, "We must know that Spain is our Front Line. . . . We are certainly not doing anywhere nearly enough. We don't feel deeply enough. . . . If we allow Republican Spain to suffer needlessly, we will ourselves eventually suffer as deeply." He deplored the failure of the Western democracies to aid the Loyalist cause in Spain. In contrast, Robeson felt, Communists had proved themselves enthusiastic allies in the fight against Franco, and the Soviet Union's support of the antifascist struggle confirmed for him—and for many others—that it stood in the forefront of the struggle for democratic liberties everywhere. On Essie, too, the trip to Spain had a profound effect. "Hitherto," she wrote William Patterson, she had not been "fundamentally interested" in politics, but now felt she was rapidly "catching up" with Paul's commitment. Less than a week after returning to London, Paul and Essie left for Paris so he could sing for the exiled delegates of the Cortez (the Spanish Parliament) on their way back to their respective countries. From Paris, Essie went on to Moscow to discuss with Ma Goode whether she and Pauli should return to London because of the worsening international situation, and Paul went back to London. They stayed in touch for many years with Captain Castillo, subsequently put him up with his family, and financed an exhibition of the paintings of his father-in-law, Don Cristobal Ruiz, in London (Freda Diamond took on the job of getting him an exhibition in New York), and then essentially supported the family until it could resettle in Mexico.[15]

Disgusted and alarmed at political developments, Robeson felt he could not simply "stand by and see it happen." He began to consider returning to the States, where he could speak out without being dismissed as an "alien." In England, as a noncitizen, he had to try to remain "reasonably discreet," but, as Essie wrote William Patterson, the "attitude and behaviour" of the "ruling classes" in England "has soured us, and we despise them openly." Essie also conveyed to Patterson her approval of the recent purge trials in the Soviet Union. They had given her "a bad scare," she wrote, because they brought back to mind the personal contact she had had with Ignaty N. Kazakov, the doctor who had just "confessed" to murdering OGPU Chairman Menzhinsky. Kazakov had asked Essie, when she and Paul left Kislovodsk after their 1937 vacation, to bring him "some compound of tungsten" for his laboratory when she returned to Moscow. She had managed to secure the tungsten from her London physician, but, being unable to learn what it could be used for—other than in light bulbs— she had decided to return the tungsten to her doctor; she did not want to "be responsible for importing anything I didn't understand myself." On returning to the Soviet Union, she had gone to explain to Kazakov—and found that he was in prison. "Can you imagine my being so dumb??" she wrote Patterson. "It develops that he used this marvelous clinic of his for poison, as well as for more constructive work." She thought the treachery of the "conspirators" "a very terrible thing" and was "glad they have been punished."[16]

There is no record of Paul's reaction to the 1936, 1937, or 1938 Moscow trials, but as early as 1936 he had given an interview to Ben Davis, Jr., in which he is quoted as saying that the U.S.S.R. had dealt properly in the trial of the "counter-revolutionary assassins" of Kirov—"They ought to destroy anybody who seeks to harm that great country" (and while saying it, according to Davis, he looked "as if he could strangle the assassins with his own hands"). Marie Seton recalls a far less histrionic and apologetic version. Paul, she says, acknowledged to her in 1937 that "dreadful things" had taken place in the Soviet Union, implying sympathy for those who had "confessed" to an antigovernment "plot" but blanketing his doubts with the extenuating argument that rapid social transformation comes with an inevitable toll. That was a view common in the ranks of pro-Soviet intellectuals everywhere, exemplified in Britain by John Strachey's influential 1936 book, *The Theory and Practice of Socialism,* in which he could "find no meaning in the allegation" that Stalin had made himself a dictator and hailed the Soviet system for producing a "far wider measure of democracy than do parliaments or congresses."[17]

The Robesons' alarm over the world situation made them anxious about leaving Pauli, now age ten, in school in the Soviet Union. It had become difficult to reach Moscow except through German-controlled territory (even the Scandinavian air route stopped at Hamburg), and with Spanish and Russian stamps on their passports guaranteeing German hostility to them, the Robesons finally decided to send for Pauli and Ma Goode. They did so reluctantly, knowing how happy the pair had been in Moscow; indeed, Pauli agreed to return only because (as Essie wrote the Van Vechtens) "we PROMISED to spend a lot of time with him, and after all, he hadn't seen his parents enough." Ma Goode went to the States for a prolonged visit, and Pauli was able to live with his parents on a daily basis for the first time since their summer vacation together in 1937. He was also happy when they immediately enrolled him in the Soviet School in London, maintained for the children of U.S.S.R. officials, an arrangement that allowed him to continue his studies without interruption (and to continue to be shielded from some of the rawer daily manifestations of racism— "Russian children don't look at you as if they hated you," Pauli told a newspaper reporter).[18]

Robeson stepped up the pace of his political appearances in London. He sang at a variety of rallies—the International Peace Campaign at the Royal Opera House, a Save China assembly at Covent Garden (with speakers including Edouard Herriot and Madame Sun Yat-sen), the Basque Children's Committee, and the British Youth Peace Assembly. He also contacted experts on Spanish music, with the aim of learning more about the *cante jondo* style, and was involved in preliminary discussions for setting up a foundation called International Theatres of the People. And for a brief time it looked as if he and Sergei Eisenstein might finally get together on a film project: Eisenstein wrote from Moscow in April 1938 to say that "all my troubles are over. New people are running the film business"; he was completing "one of the most important pictures to be made this year" *(Alexander Nevsky),* was "thinking in the direction of the brotherhood of nations and races," and suggested that if Robeson had "some fine ideas in that direction to be made together," he should let him know immediately. But although Eisenstein was to receive the Order of Lenin on February 1, 1939, and was soon to be made artistic head of Mosfilm, his projects would again run into roadblocks, and he and Robeson would never make the film they had long hoped to.[19]

Once again Robeson was warned that his political activities might hurt his artistic career, this time by Harold Holt, his London agent, who admonished him to curtail his outspokenness or face the likelihood of losing concert bookings. "It is my duty, as your representative," Holt wrote, "to point out that your value as an artist is bound to be very adversely affected. . . . You are doing yourself a great deal of harm." Robeson ignored Holt's warning and—for the time being—suffered no loss in public popularity. His first concert in more than two years at the Albert Hall was packed, and the applause greeting his entrance was so prolonged that, before the concert could proceed, Larry Brown had to play a piano introduction through twice, and Robeson had to give a little speech thanking the audience for its welcome. In the same month (June 1938) that Holt admonished Robeson about his political appearances, he was—perhaps in a gesture of deliberate defiance—particularly active, singing the Soviet anthem at a huge rally organized by the Emergency Youth Peace Campaign, and appearing at two other public meetings.[20]

Instead of retreating from his political commitments, Robeson was establishing their primacy. He explained to the press that "something inside has turned"; long-standing discontent over the stage and film roles he had played had finally crystallized into a coherent vision of how he wanted to employ his talents in the future. He would never again, he said, do a part like that in *Sanders of the River*—a film he now saw as "a piece of flag-waving . . . a total loss." Even the movie version of *The Emperor Jones* he now regarded as "a failure": the changed order of the scenes had destroyed the play's psychological integrity, and its director, Dudley Murphy, had misused him in the title role—rushing him through whole sequences lest his "mood" change, on the "fool notion that negroes had moods and could only play" when they were in the proper one. For the future, Robeson vowed to appear only "in stories that had some bearing on the problems" ordinary people faced in their daily lives (and at a box-office price they could afford). He no longer believed, he told another reporter, in the once-prevalent notion—held by most of the major figures in the Harlem Renaissance—that a "talented tenth" of the black people could or should, through their own demonstrated achievements, lead the black masses out of bondage. In line with his new convictions, Robeson chose for his next stage appearance the Unity Theatre production of *Plant in the Sun*.[21]

Political theater in Britain, as well as in the United States, had taken on new life in the early thirties. A group of British actors, encouraged by André Van Gyseghem and Herbert Marshall (who was then studying filmmaking with Eisenstein), had performed at the First International Workers' Olympiad in Moscow in 1933. On returning home, they formed the Rebel Players and, after a striking success in 1935 with Clifford Odets's *Waiting for Lefty*, had reconstituted themselves as the Unity Theatre, renovating a large hall that had once been a derelict mission, in Goldington Crescent. In a wave of enthusiasm, they declared themselves "a people's theatre, built to serve as a means of dramatising their life and struggles, and as an aid in making them conscious of their strength and of the need for United action."[22]

Plant in the Sun was the third play performed in the new Unity building. Written by a young American, Ben Bengal, it was directed by Herbert Marshall, who had gotten to know Robeson during his 1934 visit to the Soviet Union. The two men had talked over Robeson's difficulty in finding politically astute material that would not be mutilated during production by commercial managers, and Marshall had suggested he read the script for *Plant in the Sun*. Robeson was immediately attracted to its forceful advocacy of trade-unionist principles, its story line about the irresistible success that follows when white and black workers combine their forces in a sit-down strike. He also liked the idea of playing a lead role that had originally been written for an Irishman. He found additionally appealing the Unity Theatre's policy of having everyone in the cast—which included a full complement of real-life carpenters and clerks—appear anonymously. Robeson decided to accept the role.[23]

Word spread rapidly of Robeson's pending appearance in the play, and the limited, month-long run immediately sold out, fashionable West Enders vying with Unity's usual working-class audience for seats. *Time and Tide* noted that Robeson, "who can fill any great hall in London on his own," had not only given his services free to Unity, but was also prepared to make a personal plea to Parliament for support of a theater that "should put on plays of working-class life."[24]

Rehearsals had to take place on weekends and on evenings, because most of the amateur cast held daytime jobs. Neither the evenings nor the amateurs fazed Robeson. Enthusiastic, he would arrive early for rehearsals, and would sit outside in front of the theater chatting with Vernon Beste, Unity's chairman. (Robeson told Beste he didn't like doing concert tours— they made him feel too lonely—and recalled the deep kinship he had experienced talking with mill workers on the Isle of Man; in general, he seemed to Beste "greatly worried by the worsening political situation.") Rehearsals were run along the lines of a pep rally. The actors discussed the social significance of the play, watched documentary films about "stay-in" strikes in France, made a special study of the dialect of the East Side of New York (where the play's candy factory was set), visited two British confectionery factories, and even heard a formal lecture on "spontaneous struggles and their expression in strikes." Robeson's rapport with the amateur cast was complete. The actor Alfie Bass, who had been connected with Unity from the beginning and worked with Robeson on *Plant,* measured him against the other "stars" he'd known and decided, "Nobody I've ever met for intelligence, humanity and so on would ever come up to this man—and I tell you I'm not easily fooled, I look with contempt on people that are supposed to be 'big' people."[25]

Robeson, for his part, was delighted to be working in a setting and on a script that suited his political vision. Before the Unity experience, he told a reporter, he had felt himself "drying up . . . acting in plays and films that cut against the very people and ideas that I wanted to help. For me it was a question of finding somewhere to work that would tie me up with the things I believe in, or stopping altogether. It was as strong as that." Robeson's satisfaction with *Plant in the Sun* found considerable echo among the critics. They were generally respectful of the "compact little study" and widely admiring of the "dignity and gentle strength" of Robeson's own performance. "It was a melodrama of course," the Manchester *Guardian* commented, "but with reality in it."[26]

Even during the run of *Plant,* Robeson managed to fit in a few political appearances—notably at a large rally for Loyalist Spain held at the Granada Cinema, and at a meeting to protest conditions in Jamaica ("I have appeared on many platforms for various causes. Tonight I am appealing for, as it were, my flesh and blood"). It was also in 1938 that Robeson made the acquaintance of another leader of another oppressed people— Jawaharlal Nehru, the foremost figure in the Indian National Congress. Nehru came to London in June, directly from a five-day tour of Spain with Krishna Menon, the dominant force in the India League and the man who had earlier enlisted Robeson's support in behalf of Indian independence. Robeson gladly accepted the League's invitation to appear at a public meeting welcoming Nehru to London, and in turn Nehru and Krishna Menon were taken to see Robeson's performance in *Plant in the Sun.*[27]

The rally to welcome Nehru drew a large crowd to Kingsway Hall on June 27, 1938. The Dean of Canterbury, Stafford Cripps, Harold Laski, Ellen Wilkinson, R. Palme Dutt (the Communist Party's expert on colonial affairs), and Robeson were among those who spoke to the gathering. Dutt gave the chief address, emphasizing that "the Indian problem" could not be solved within the framework of British imperialism and hailing Nehru's success in raising the membership of the Indian National Congress within two years from half a million to over three million. Robeson's welcoming remarks stressed the indivisibility of the struggle for freedom, and called for an "even greater measure" of unified action by "democratic and progressive forces" to combat the "common onslaught by reactionary forces" in Abyssinia, Spain, China, Austria, and the West Indies. He claimed, with perhaps a touch of wishful thinking, that black Americans "have closely watched the Indian struggle and have been conscious of its importance for us."[28]

Within a few days of the rally, the Robesons lunched with Nehru, accompanied by his sister, Vijaya Lakshmi—"Nan"—Pandit (she would remain a lifelong friend, particularly of Essie's), and Essie followed up the luncheon by sending Nehru a copy of her book, *Paul Robeson, Negro.* He responded cordially ("It was such a delight to meet you and Paul Robeson. I am looking forward to a repetition of that experience"), and a friendship quickly blossomed. Within a few months of their first meeting, Nan Pandit was writing Essie to say "I feel as if we were old friends—it seemed so easy to establish contact with you," and Essie was adding to Nehru's reading list a gift of Richard Wright's first (1938) published work, *Uncle Tom's Children* (a book she and Paul were so taken with that he wrote a foreword to it when Victor Gollancz published it in England: "Wright is a great artist, certainly one of the most significant American authors of his time. . . . Would that everyone who has read *Gone with the Wind* would read *Uncle Tom's Children!!*").[29]

The Robesons and Nehru began to meet frequently, and Nehru later remembered that Essie "would dash in occasionally into my flat and announce, in the American way, that she was feeling like a million dollars. I am sure she has that capacity of feeling that way whatever happens." Nehru clearly became fond of Essie, describing her as "one of the most vital and energetic women I have ever met. She is overflowing with an exuberant vitality." Essie, in turn, told Marie Seton that she thought Nehru immensely attractive. There is even a hint that she and Nehru moved to the edge of having an affair—and that Essie was the one who backed off.[30]

When *Plant in the Sun* closed, Robeson and Larry Brown went off on a concert tour of the provinces while Essie made a brief trip back to the States to tie up some loose business ends surrounding the release of *Jericho* and to have a look at the successful WPA production of W. E. B. Du Bois's *Haiti* as a possible vehicle for Paul in London (the decision was negative). Paul's provincial tour was the most successful he had ever had. Far from abandoning him for his outspoken new political stance, audiences embraced him with fervor. At Eastbourne hundreds of would-be ticket purchasers were turned away; at Swansea a large throng waited to cheer him outside the theater after the concert; at Torquay police had to be called in to restore order when a "surging mass of people" carried Robeson into the concert hall "to the accompaniment of tremendous cheering"; and at Glasgow the papers reported "amazing crowd scenes"—people forming a line four deep and a quarter of a mile long outside the concert hall. Robeson had succeeded in his new aim of "reaching the people"—the "ordinary" people who sat in the galleries. They had always loved him—more uncritically than the professional arbiters of taste; now that he had become a self-identified "people's artist," they adored him. The London paper *The Star* reported that Robeson was among the ten artists whose recordings sold best, and in a *Motion Picture Herald* popularity poll he came in tenth among British film stars—though he did not place among the top ten in the United States.[31]

Robeson, of course, had his detractors. Between 1936 and the 1939 signing of the Nazi-Soviet pact, criticism of the Soviet Union was rarely heard in Harlem intellectual circles—even among such bitter later critics as A. Philip Randolph and Roy Wilkins (the NAACP journal, *The Crisis,* edited by Wilkins, carried not a single article critical of the Soviets during this four-year period). Yet within black ministerial circles "anti-Communism" had already surfaced. Claude A. Barnett, director of the Associated Negro Press, wrote Robeson from Chicago to report a recent visit to his office "by the president of a great religious association," bearing a huge placard designed to portray black celebrities in commemoration of the forthcoming seventy-fifth anniversary of emancipation. During the ensuing conversation, he told Barnett that Robeson's name had been suggested for a place on the placard but the suggestion had led to "quite an argument" among members of the anniversary committee—one minister insisting that Robeson had made "a disparaging comment relative to the Negro church, which he attributed to certain acquired communistic views," and another insisting "that no man who sang spirituals" as Robeson did could do so "without loving them or believing in them." Barnett asked Robeson a few queries of his own: "Are you planning to relinquish your American citizenship? Are you planning to become a citizen of Russia? Would you be interested in making Russia your home?"[32]

Robeson ignored the detractors. In his very next public statement, in September, soon after returning to London from his provincial tour, he further consolidated his populist image. In more forceful terms than ever before, he told the press about his disenchantment with commercial film-making. "I am tired of playing Stepin Fetchit comics and savages with leopard skin and spear," he told one reporter. The film industry had refused to give him the kind of roles he wanted to play—the life of the black composer Coleridge-Taylor, say, or a film based on the Joe Louis story. As a result he was determined, he said, to try to make pictures independently—at the time he still hoped to do a film with Eisenstein—or to get a picture off the ground based on the life of Oliver Law, the black American soldier who had died in Spain. It was not an unrealistic path: documentary films had recently come into prominence, and such talented film personalities as Robert Flaherty, Paul Muni, and Leslie Howard had washed their hands of the film industry proper and gone their independent ways.[33]

Meanwhile, he agreed to sing as many as three shows daily in a few of the popular cinema palaces—Gaumont State, the Trocadero, the Elephant and Castle. He was willing to work harder and at reduced fees—eighteen performances at one of the giant cinema houses brought him a salary equivalent to the fee for one performance on the Celebrity Concert series at Queen's Hall—in order to reach the people he now considered to be his "natural" audience, and at a price they could afford. But Robeson could never be a "pop" singer in the Frank Sinatra mode, and whenever he tried to stretch his voice and repertoire in that direction he invariably stumbled. Essie wisely counseled him to return to what he did best, the spirituals, and he quickly heeded her advice.[34]

Simultaneously, Robeson maintained a hectic pace of political appearances, lending his name and presence to a plethora of organizations and events—the Spanish Aid Committee, Food for Republican Spain Campaign, the National Memorial Fund (for the British members of the Brigade), the Labour and Trade Union Movement, the National Unemployed Workers' Movement, the League for the Boycott of Aggressor Nations, the Coloured Film Artists' Association, the Society for Cultural Relations, and, in December 1938, the Welsh National Memorial Meeting at Mountain Ash, to commemorate those "men of the International Brigade from Wales who gave their lives in defence of Democracy in Spain."[35]

The Mountain Ash meeting in Wales held special meaning for him. Ten years earlier, a much less political but nonetheless instinctively egalitarian Robeson had impulsively joined a group of Welsh miners demonstrating in London when he ran into them while coming out of a posh affair dressed in a dinner jacket. In the years since, his identification with the Welsh had grown—with their ethnic insistence, their strength of character, their political radicalism. His strong bonds with the people of the Rhondda Valley would endure for the rest of his life, and the film he was soon to make about the Welsh miners, *The Proud Valley,* would always be the one in which he took the most pleasure. In 1938 at Mountain Ash, seven thousand people gathered to commemorate the thirty-three men from Wales who had died in Spain. Veterans of the International Brigade marched behind the flags of Wales and Republican Spain onto a platform filled with one hundred black men, women, and children from Cardiff, as well as a group of orphaned Basque children. The speakers included the Dean of Chichester and Arthur Horner, president of the South Wales Miners' Federation, who introduced Robeson to the audience as "a great champion of the rights of the oppressed people to whom he belongs." Robeson sang, recited two poems Langston Hughes had composed in Spain, and told the audience, "I am here because I know that these fellows fought not only for Spain but for me and the whole world. I feel it is my duty to be here." The audience gave him a standing ovation.[36]

Robeson had next planned a trip to Australia for a recital tour, but it had to be called off because of the uncertainty of the political situation in Europe. In April 1939, though, he and Larry Brown did manage a brief Scandinavian trip, performing in Oslo, Copenhagen, and Stockholm, where enthusiastic crowds turned the concerts into anti-Nazi demonstrations. Then, in May, Robeson sailed for a two-month stay in the States, perhaps at the prompting of his lawyer, Robert Rockmore—increasingly his confidant and business manager—who felt concerned that he "has been away so long that I am afraid that he may lose his so-called American audience, which, as you know, at best is a very fickle one." Robeson had wanted to make a trip to New York anyway to discuss with Oscar Hammerstein II the possibility of doing the play *John Henry,* and while there he agreed to do some concert engagements and also to appear in what turned out to be a well-received week-long revival of *The Emperor Jones* (directed by Gig McGhee) at the Ridgeway Theater in White Plains.[37]

Soon after arriving in New York, he told the *Sunday Worker* that,

> Having helped on many fronts, I feel that it is now time for me to return to the place of my origin—to those roots which, though imbedded in Negro life, are essentially American and are so regarded by the people of most other countries. . . . It is my business not only to tell the guy with the whip hand to go easy on my people, . . . but also to teach my people—all the oppressed people—how to prevent that whip hand from being used against them.

Robeson was besieged by requests for additional interviews and public appearances, but hid out at the McGhees' apartment. No one could find him—and everyone seemed to be trying. Alexander Woollcott wanted to take him to lunch, Max Yergan wanted to discuss a pending conference on Africa, NBC wanted to discuss the possibility of radio dates, and Walter White wanted him to speak at the thirtieth annual conference of the NAACP. What *Robeson* wanted was to conserve his energy and call his own shots. "Nobody can find you," Essie wrote in consternation from London—which was precisely how Paul had planned it. But his inaccessibility did ruffle some feelings. Carl Van Vechten was so put out over Paul's failure to contact him that Essie had to write a lengthy apology, diplomatically claiming that Paul "feels terrible" about "the mess he made of things while he was in America."[38]

He did not. And Carlo knew he did not. "There is no word from Paul that HE is sorry," Van Vechten wrote his wife, Fania, "It's pretty obvious that Paul doesn't want to see *us* very much, or *most* of his old friends." "There is only one thing to do," Carlo decided, "and that is refrain from flattering them by letting them think we are MAD." Two days later, still smarting despite his resolution not to, Carlo returned to the subject in another letter to Fania,

> The point about Paul is that he only wants to talk about himself and how he's improving and how he is working on new songs and he can't talk to his old friends that way because they've heard this story so long: so he hunts up new ones to listen. . . . There is no earthly use in going into all this because it is a matter of indifference whether we see him or not. . . . If they want to call up and come round in the fall, why let them. I don't think they will bother us much. Essie's whole idea is to keep us from getting sore, because she knows that would do Paul harm, but the other people he has treated like this will do him more harm.

In reply, Fania, who shared her husband's distaste for being ignored, let go with an accumulated backlog of venom against Paul:

> [He is] weak, selfish, indulgent, lazy—really if it were not for his meagre talent and his great charm he would be just the traditional "lowdown worthless nigger"—is in spite of himself thoroughly ashamed of his failure to function as a worthwhile and fine human being when he was on his own, without needing Essie to "remind him" and prod him along. I feel sorry for him in a way. But I think it's about time Essie "reminded" him that even HE can't treat his friends with large doses of indifference and neglect and expect to keep them. *We* understand him. Besides we don't give a dam [sic].

But his other American Buddies perhaps won't take his behavior so lightly. In any case, they will *talk* about it, and HOW we will keep silent; as you say, in the Fall it's *all* up to *them*. More and more I admire Essie. . . . He's utterly consumed with his own importance. Nobody else matters. I say to HELL with people like that![39]

Paul, having established his own set of priorities, went about meeting them. One was to contact Angelo Herndon, the black Communist who had been arrested in Atlanta in 1932 for leading a biracial demonstration of the unemployed and been sentenced by an overtly racist trial judge to eighteen to twenty years on a chain gang. In 1935 the Communist Party—after the Supreme Court had refused to hear Herndon's appeal—had led a petition drive in his behalf that attracted "united-front" support from Communists and non-Communists alike, and had led in 1937 to the Court's narrowly overturning Herndon's conviction. Benjamin Davis Jr., the black Harvard graduate and the son of a wealthy Atlanta real-estate operator, had served in the 1932 trial as Herndon's attorney (and would himself later rise into the CPUSA hierarchy). Reading of the trial in the London papers, Robeson resolved "to learn how a man did that in the heart of Georgia." He and Davis had at least met in the early twenties, but as he wrote him many years later, after the two men had long been close friends, "Your courageous example in the Herndon case was one of the most important influences in my life." During his trip to New York, Robeson not only saw Ben Davis but also volunteered his services to Herndon in support of the Negro Youth Congress's current drive to place five hundred new black voters on the county list in Birmingham, Alabama. Herndon was unable to take up Robeson's offer to help raise money because, as he wrote him, "the people who would make such an affair a success" could not be contacted on short notice.[40]

While in New York, Robeson also scouted for suitable new properties. Prior to leaving London, he had turned down the lead in Maxwell Anderson and Kurt Weill's *Eneas Africanus*, reacting negatively to the patronizing story of an ex-slave's eight-year effort to locate his former plantation—and to the condescension of Anderson's covering letter, which referred to the slave as never having been "obliged or encouraged to make an ethical decision for himself" or having "to worry about" any "responsibilities." Robeson had been more excited by a possible new play by DuBose and Dorothy Heyward (authors of *Porgy* and *Mamba's Daughters*) about the black insurrectionary Denmark Vesey; from London, Essie seconded his enthusiasm: "I like the Vesey conception because I feel it IS what you think and feel, and you could therefore go for it in a big way."[41]

While in New York Robeson met with Langston Hughes and heard part of his blues opera, *De Organizer*, which Labor Stage planned to put on in the fall. He also checked out the Harlem Suitcase Theatre, affiliated with the International Workers Order (the CP's fraternal society), whose first production, Langston Hughes's agitprop drama *Don't You Want to Be Free?*, had opened in 1938 and attracted an enthusiastic following in Harlem. Essie thought that play "ineffective" and "definitely amateur," but she agreed that soundings made to Paul about plans (which never matured) for a Langston Hughes–Duke Ellington musical, *Cock o' the World,* were "very intriguing." As Paul considered various prospects, Essie supported his determination not to accept a trifling role: "You are now too aware, too definite minded, too militant. . . . You couldn't do a small person, because you are too big, inside and out. Amusing, mischievous, rascally trifling— yes. But permanent inherent trifling—no."[42]

The new project that finally crystallized carried no danger of being trifling. Michael Balcon, head of Ealing Studios, announced in the spring of 1939 that he had persuaded Robeson to return to films. He would play the lead role in a fictionalized story about the life and plight of the Welsh miners, as told through the eyes of David Goliath, an unemployed American black who, through a series of plausible accidents, goes to work in the Welsh mines and becomes centrally involved in the miners' struggle for a better life. The youthful Pen Tennyson, hired as the film's director, told the press that Robeson would not be used as "a negro or a famous singer"; he would play the role of a penniless man who lands a job in the Welsh mines and shares the life of a poor Welsh family—"It is a real life story showing Robeson as a simple, likeable human being, who has to take the rough with the smooth, the same as all of us." The prescription was ideally suited to Robeson's political vision. It remained to be seen whether good politics could be translated into good art.[43]

Shooting on *David Goliath* (the title was later changed to *The Proud Valley*) was due to begin in August. To trim off some pounds before going in front of the cameras, Robeson entered a "nature-cure" rest home as soon as he returned to London in July. His weight, as he reached age forty, had been gradually increasing until, in Essie's view, "all semblance of that grand figure has long since disappeared under bulk." She had been pestering him to go on a diet, but he ignored her until friends in New York who hadn't seen him in years joked about how he had lost his figure and become "an Ox." He stayed in the rest home—a mansion with 150 acres of grounds—for a full four weeks, subjecting himself to a repetitive round of electrical baths, massages, fasts, and colonic irrigations, and emerged "feeling like a million."[44]

He also emerged into a full-scale European war. The news in August 1939 that Stalin had signed a nonaggression pact with Hitler proved shattering to some believers in the revolutionary purity of Soviet ideology, but Robeson publicly stated that the pact "in no way whatsoever" "weakened or changed" his convictions. He saw the Nazi-Soviet agreement as having been forced on Russia by the unwillingness of the British and French governments "to collaborate with the Soviet Union in a real policy of collective security"—in his notes he recorded his certainty that an Anglo-Russian pact "would have stopped Nazi aggression"—leaving the U.S.S.R. with no alternative way of protecting its borders from a German attack. But if the pact provided the Soviets with some security, it provided the Nazis with more. On September 1, 1939, Hitler's battalions moved into Poland, plunging Europe into war.[45]

Essie, with typical efficiency, had been stocking up on supplies for a year. Now, with the sky full of barrage balloons, civilian police manning clogged traffic points, anti-aircraft guns going up on building tops, sandbags against windows, the Robesons decided it was time to return home. They delayed passage only until the shooting on *The Proud Valley* could be completed. Essie drove Paul out to the studio early each morning, and he came home in the dark every evening by underground. The routine was exhausting, tension compounded because of air-raid precautions and blackouts, and because Paul, between takes, had to squeeze in recording sessions for His Master's Voice. Even so, he pulled no star turn on the set, indulged in no histrionics. On the contrary, his fellow actors found him (in the words of one of them, Rachel Thomas) "so easy to work with, so easy to get on with. No temperament at all." In the view of another cast member, Roderick Jones, Robeson's concern centered on his fellow actors, not himself: when his stand-in was kept hanging around for hours under hot lights while the technical people made their adjustments, Robeson—without raising his voice or losing his temper—told them, "Now look, this has got to stop. You can't keep these people waiting around like this all the time."[46]

On September 25 the film was completed; on September 28 Robeson saw a rough cut and was delighted with it; on September 29 Essie sent off twenty-four pieces of luggage to the boat train; and on the morning of September 30, Pauli in tow, the family bid goodbye to London.[47]

■

CHAPTER 12

The World at War

(1940–1942)

When the Robesons docked in New York in mid-October 1939, their old friends Minnie Sumner, Bob Rockmore, and Bert McGhee were waiting for them. So was a small battalion of reporters. Robeson had prepared a written statement—suggesting his high level of concern for being quoted accurately—but the statement itself was anything but cautious. He referred contemptuously in it to "those Munich men" (Chamberlain and Daladier) whose supineness had served to abet fascist aggression in Spain, Czechoslovakia, Austria, and Ethiopia; still in power, they were prosecuting a war, *in the name of democracy,* that was in fact aimed at saving Germany from her own leadership, in order ultimately to secure her support for a crusade against the Soviet Union. ("The gentlemen of Munich," Robeson wrote in his private notes, "are seeking to preserve . . . a Nazi Germany with one exception—without Hitler. . . . It is interesting in this connection to note the campaign in the pro-Munich conservative press, to build up Goering by pointing out that he is a gentleman—not a proletarian sign painter like Hitler, that he hunts . . . that a Germany headed by Goering could get peace terms.") A Western triumph in a subsequent conflict with the Soviet Union would, in Robeson's opinion, mean the continuing dominion of a colonial spirit scornful of Asians and Africans and devoted to maintaining oppressive foreign control over their countries. He could see no reason, therefore, for blacks anywhere, or for the United States as a nation, to take part in a dispute that was lining up as fascist versus communist.[1]

Robeson's remarks were reprinted in the British press and infuriated, among others, Lord Beaverbrook, the press magnate. Though an acquaintance of the Robesons, Beaverbrook let it be known that his newspapers would refuse to advertise or review Robeson's forthcoming picture, *The Proud Valley*. The London columnist Hannen Swaffer, also a Robeson acquaintance, joined in the denunciation of him, prophesying that his ill-timed remarks—"after all, this country is now fighting for its existence"—would mean the end of his career in Britain. Undaunted, Robeson in the next few months repeated and expanded his views to reporters. In his opinion, the massing of Western imperialists (calling themselves "democracies") for a showdown against the Soviets warranted Russia's decision to march into Poland and Finland. He characterized the Soviet moves as "defensive," a response to the "reactionary" influence Britain had been exerting in Scandinavia and to the pending alignment of Western Europe—including the "purified" new regimes expected to replace Hitler and Mussolini in Germany and Italy—against the "threat" of Bolshevism. The Soviet Union's subsequent peace treaty with Finland, Robeson insisted, proved that the Russians had been interested only in securing strategic border points. Robeson was not alone in holding "the men of Munich" in contempt. English socialists with whom he said he had "discussed causes and conditions of the European conflict," such as Harold Laski, J. B. Priestley, H. G. Wells, and George Bernard Shaw, shared that estimate. Robeson's views were also shared by Captain Eddie Rickenbacker, the World War I ace, who in a speech at the Engineer's Club made exactly the same prediction Robeson had about the pending political realignment in Europe—though, unlike Robeson, he applauded the coming crusade against Communism.[2]

Robeson insisted that in making his remarks he was speaking neither as a Communist nor even as a fellow traveler, but, rather, as someone who subscribed to the philosophy of "real democracy" and spoke "from the point of view of the son of a slave," aware and concerned about issues affecting the fate of millions of subject black people in the world. But his views did parallel those of the Soviet leadership, and one black reader wrote to the New York *Amsterdam News* in protest: "No, Paul old boy, you can't expect right thinking people whether they be black or white to denounce Hitler and Mussolini for their sordid deeds, and acclaim Joe Stalin for his depredatory acts." Claude McKay also rebuked him. McKay had been to the Soviet Union ten years before Robeson and, like him, had, as a black man, been fêted and acclaimed; unlike him, McKay had become rapidly disenchanted. He now took to print to chastise Robeson publicly for not seeing "beyond the pleasantries with which the Soviets deluge a much wanted guest," for his uncritical approach toward a Soviet state grown "mindlessly cruel and powerful," persecuting its own peasantry, suppressing its trade unions, sentencing "its intellectual minorities to a death purge"—and setting out to destroy "the cooperative and semi-social democratic regime of its little neighbor Finland." It was nonsense, McKay claimed, for Robeson to defend Russia because it was "a land free of prejudice against Negroes." There had never been any such prejudice, McKay argued, not even under the czarist regimes—"Before the Revolution an American Negro was the popular proprietor of the most fashionable cabaret in Moscow." The true "minority parallel," McKay insisted, was between the American treatment of blacks and the Russian treatment of Finns: "Stalin's attack upon Finland is as vicious as Crackers lynching Negroes under the assumption that they are all rapists." Hailing Finland as "a valiant fighting minority nation," McKay called upon the Afro-American minority to lend its support to the Finnish cause.[3]

Robeson would not budge. In follow-up interviews he reiterated his conviction that the Soviet Union was fighting a "defensive war," and he refused to participate in theatrical benefits to raise money for the Finns. "According to my reasoning," he said, "aid to the Finns is aid to reactionary forces"; the Chamberlain and Daladier governments, and Mannerheim's in Finland, did not represent "the progressive" segment of public opinion in their own countries. He could not see, he added, why blacks— "millions of whom are victims of a British Empire" that maintained its oppressive rule in South Africa and of a British government that continued to refuse independence to India and Jamaica—could possibly believe that Chamberlain was fighting in any sense for them. Anyone genuinely interested in freedom for colonial minorities, Robeson insisted, would do better to applaud "the Soviet action in freeing the Western Ukrainians and White Russians" by moving their armies into those regions. Van Vechten, still brooding over Robeson's neglect, relished the opportunity to assail his politics. "I see Paul has come out in favor of Russia against Finland," Carlo wrote Walter White. "This is very bad business, indeed." To another correspondent Carlo waxed philosophical about how "One-third of America may be enslaved, but everybody in Russia is a slave, with no hope of ever climbing out of it. Here there is that possible chance for any one. . . ." To Robeson's old acting friend Dorothy Peterson, Van Vechten was more succinct: "I spit on Russian sympathizers."[4]

Within six weeks of their arrival home, the Robesons had settled into a five-room apartment in the Roger Morris, a fashionable Harlem building at 555 Edgecombe Avenue. Ma Goode and Pauli were installed in a separate three-room penthouse in the same building. Initially Pauli had been interested in the Soviet school in Brooklyn, but after Essie "went back and back" to the Russian Consul, she "finally realized it was no go, but they didn't want to say so," and Pauli was enrolled in Fieldston, the Ethical Culture school. Robeson himself, within three weeks of landing in New York, participated—almost inadvertently—in a radio broadcast that reaped him nationwide acclaim, erasing (or at least neutralizing) whatever distaste his initial remarks to the press had created.[5]

The composer Earl Robinson had written music for a number of WPA-sponsored shows during the Depression, including a revue called *Sing for Your Supper* with the poet John LaTouche that had featured as its finale "The Ballad of Uncle Sam." After the revue closed, Robinson suggested the ballad to his friend Norman Corwin at CBS for his new series of half-hour programs called "The Pursuit of Happiness," an upbeat salute to democracy that had already featured Ray Middleton singing Maxwell Anderson's "How Can You Tell an American" and Raymond Massey reciting from *Abe Lincoln in Illinois*. Robinson sang his ballad at the piano for Corwin, who liked it and had him perform for the CBS brass—Vice-President Bill Lewis's reaction was "Wouldn't Robeson knock the Hell out of this!"[6]

"Pursuit of Happiness" had already approached Robeson to appear on the series, but his asking fee of a thousand dollars had been considered too high. Corwin now decided to pay the fee, and in late October—just weeks after Robeson's arrival in New York—Robeson and Robinson set to work. Commenting on the rehearsal experience years later, Earl Robinson said, "I have never had such a cooperative person to work with—*never!* There was nothing of the prima donna about him, nothing of arrogance. We had only one argument—about pitch." Robeson's voice was richer in the lower keys, and when recording he could use a microphone to avoid having to reach for the extra volume needed to produce the low tones— volume that he sometimes had trouble creating in a concert hall. He "would insist," according to Robinson, "on moving pitch down, three, four, five keys down. And I argued with him. I said, 'Paul, you've got those notes up there. It's no problem for you.' And he said, 'Yes, but I don't like them. I'm a folk singer. And I sing in my key.'" Then he added, with a twinkle, "The Russians transposed Boris Godunov down for me." Robinson gave in. "It was a wrench, especially since I knew he could sing it in E if he wanted to."[7]

During rehearsals, Norman Corwin rechristened the piece "Ballad for Americans," and the broadcast took place on November 5, 1939. It created an instant sensation. The six hundred people in the studio audience stamped, shouted, and bravoed for two minutes while the show was still on the air, and for fifteen minutes after. The switchboards were jammed for two hours with phone calls, and within the next few days hundreds of letters arrived. Robeson repeated the broadcast again on New Year's Day, then recorded "Ballad" for Victor and watched it soar to the top of the charts. Norman Corwin congratulated him on "making radio history." Brooks Atkinson, the *Times* theater critic, wrote him directly to say what a "deep impression" "Ballad" had made on him and to thank him "for your voice, which God gave you, and especially . . . for the fortitude and honesty of your character, which are qualities for which you are responsible yourself." More unpredictably, Robeson's friend Robert Minor, the Texas Communist he had met in Spain in 1938, wrote to say that he had heard the broadcast "with wet eyes and wonder," hearing in it the death knell of "an age old slave system" and rejoicing that it had been sung by one "whose inner fire is generated by the fight to overthrow it." Minor— and Robeson—had been stirred by those LaTouche lyrics which acknowledged the dark side of the American dream ("the murders and lynchings . . . the patriotic spoutings"), and proclaimed

> *Man in white skin can never be free*
> *While his black brother is in slavery*

Other Americans, coming in on their own terms, thrilled to the rapturous patriotism of

> *Our Country's strong, our Country's young*
> *And her greatest songs are still unsung.* [8]

With something for everyone, "Ballad" stampeded the nation. It was a time when the United States, in a crescendo of patriotism, was offering itself double congratulations for having emerged from the Depression and for having kept out of a European war. Tin Pan Alley spawned a batch of hit tunes catering to the national mood—"I'm a Yank Full of Happiness," "Defend Your Country," "I Am an American"—of which "Ballad for Americans" became the favorite. When the Republicans opened their 1940 national convention with Ray Middleton and a chorus singing "Ballad" (the Democrats offered Irving Berlin's "God Bless America"), a groaning Earl Robinson predicted, "Next thing you know boy scouts will be singing it." Presto! Thirty-six Boy Scouts *did* sing it—in Gimbel's basement, as a seasonal come-on.[9]

After the second broadcast, also a huge success, Paul and Essie went to lunch with Marie Seton, who was visiting from England. It was served upstairs in Marie's hotel room at the Elysée. Only years later did she tell the Robesons why: the hotel had informed her in advance that they would not serve Robeson in the public dining room. Nationally acclaimed one day, on the next he could eat in a hotel only if kept out of sight of its other guests. Earl Robinson, too, realized "the tremendous irony, the marvelous contradiction," of Robeson's being all at once a second-class citizen and CBS's choice as *the* spokesman for the All-American Ballad.[10]

At the end of November, Robeson—home only a little more than a month—went into rehearsal for *John Henry,* a Roark Bradford play based on the valorous feats of the legendary black folk hero. He had been considering the role for some time, against the advice of Larry Brown and Essie, who thought the script inadequate. But Robeson told Ben Davis, Jr., that he would do the play "because I want to get back to American folk life. I want to work with my people with whom I belong." The project went poorly from the start. The talented cast included Josh White and Ruby Elzy—and a member of the chorus named Bayard Rustin who remembers having been "absolutely taken" with Robeson: "He was so large, so full of life, so warm, and so totally respectful of everybody on the stage and in the play. . . . He didn't play superstar. . . . Anybody could knock on his door and go in and sit down and talk to him." Essie was less popular, by a considerable margin. She ran "interference in every respect for Paul," "bulldozing her way" through all obstacles with "a kind of arrogance"—or so it appeared, Rustin cautions, to people unfamiliar with an "I-don't-take-any-shit-from-anybody" attitude from a black person, let alone a woman. After opening to mixed notices in Philadelphia, the production returned to New York for additional rehearsals, substantial rewrites, and a new director. Yet the Boston opening that followed went no better. Arriving on Broadway—Robeson's first appearance there since the revival of *Show Boat* in 1932—on January 11, 1940, the play failed to move either critics or public, and closed after a mere seven performances.[11]

The following week, Paul collected an honorary Doctor of Humane Letters degree from Hamilton College, in upstate New York, presented at the instigation of Alexander Woollcott, a Hamilton alumnus. In accepting the award, Robeson cautioned that the "future reorganization of civilization" that so many now heralded would, if it was to represent a true synthesis, include elements of African and Asian cultures. Referring to "Ballad for Americans," which he read from, he said it represented "how naturally wide in human terms is our civilization" and declared that he himself, on returning to America, felt "so much a part of all America." Acknowledgment from the mainstream did not deflect Robeson from his commitment to the margins. He lunched at the Soviet Embassy in Washington with Ambassador Oumansky (with whom he established a personal friendship) and the Russian colony, and arranged for Pauli to take special lessons at the Soviet school in New York to keep up his Russian, and to attend the Soviet summer camp upstate.[12]

In 1940 Robeson could still openly display his friendship for the Soviet Union without the American public's taking any notable affront. There were, to be sure, some occasional ripples. His appearance on a Kraft radio program was delayed because, as the Columbia Management Bureau explained to Fred Schang, Robeson's American concert manager, Kraft officials "are a little leery about Robeson as they understand that he is a Communist." When the Dies Committee of the House of Representatives held hearings in the spring of 1941 on "Un-American Activities," its research director, J. B. Matthews, cited an interview with Robeson five years earlier in *Soviet Russia Today* as proof that "he has made his choice for communism." And Columbia Masterworks, when drawing up a 1941 recording contract with him, specified that he had "the right to record with another firm those selections which, for political reasons, we find unsuitable for our catalogue." Schang himself warned Bob Rockmore, "If it gets around that Paul is endorsing Stalin against the Finns he can kiss his concert tour goodbye." But in fact that was not the case. Robeson's support of the Soviet Union did raise some incidental murmurs against him, but in a man otherwise considered so exemplary a figure, and in a country still debating the wisdom of entering the war as an ally of England and France, his views remained within the acceptable range of political dissent.[13]

That Robeson's popularity with the general public remained at a high level is evident in the reception he got when *The Proud Valley* opened in 1940. The prominent black trade-unionist A. Philip Randolph expressed his private doubts to Walter White (who was now executive director of the NAACP), saying he feared the picture would exert a "bad influence" "because the Negro worker [Robeson] in the film was excluded from consultations with management," and was shown as a "mendicant" whose death failed to produce a "collective expression on the part of the workers of sympathy and remorse." But, although the film in general got lukewarm notices, Robeson himself emerged unscathed. Not a single reviewer—not even in Britain—rebuked him for what some had earlier called his "dangerous" new tendency to dilute art with politics.[14]

His stage work and concertizing also met with near-uniform applause. In May 1940 he appeared in a star-studded (John Boles, Norma Terris, Helen Morgan, Guy Kibbee) revival of *Show Boat* with the Los Angeles Civic Light Opera Association, in which whites and blacks had to use separate dressing rooms and (as Edwin Lester, the producer, later recalled), "We had to be very careful that no black man on the stage ever touched a white girl." Oblivious to such contradictions, the gala first-night audience greeted Robeson's appearance on the stage with an ovation, and the critics, even while expressing some doubt about the cohesion of the production, singled him out for special praise. In the ultimate accolade, one of his costars literally swooned with admiration: Bertha Powell, the great Hall Johnson singer who played Queenie, was relatively inexperienced in theater and, toward the end of the dress rehearsal, during her scene with Robeson, broke into a fit of sobbing. When she seemed unable to stop, Robeson took her in his arms and helped her offstage. She later explained that she'd simply become overwhelmed at the realization that she was actually playing opposite him.[15]

Robeson's singing tour in 1940 met with a comparably rapturous reception. He opened it with a Lewisohn Stadium concert in New York dedicated to democracy and notable on several counts. It marked Robeson's first appearance at the famed outdoor concert series and featured, along with his now obligatory singing of "Ballad," a double premiere: Roy Harris's "Challenge 1940," and "And They Lynched Him on a Tree," with words by Katherine Garrison Chapin (Mrs. Francis Biddle, wife of the U.S. Solicitor General), music by the black composer William Grant Still, and the lead role sung by the black contralto Louise Burge. But it was Robeson, according to the reviewers, who carried off the honors, and proved the crowd pleaser; welcomed with a "rousing" ovation, he closed to the applause of an audience "gone wild." Afterward he and Essie met with Eleanor Roosevelt, who had come up from Washington to cheer Katherine Chapin on; Essie recorded in her diary that they found Mrs. Roosevelt "charming but tired, and very gracious."[16]

In the cross-country tour that followed, Robeson was everywhere accorded the same rousing reception. In Chicago tens of thousands packed into Grant Park—the management estimated the crowd at 160,000—and, after (in the words of the critic Claudia Cassidy) a "deeply satisfying" performance, "roared" for more and refused to go home until Robeson sang an "indescribably moving" "Ballad for Americans," without orchestra or chorus, only Larry Brown accompanying him. August saw him in a two-week stock-company revival—directed by his old friend Jimmy Light—of *The Emperor Jones,* one reviewer hailing his performance as even better than the riveting version of some fifteen years earlier; it so impressed Lawrence Langner, head of the Theatre Guild, that he sent Eugene O'Neill a laudatory account and for a time considered the possibility of moving the production to Broadway.[17]

Perhaps the apex of the summer successes was Robeson's performance of "Ballad" in the Hollywood Bowl, the sold-out crowd estimated as the largest ever to attend an event there. The public honors, however, were not matched by private ones. When "Ballad"'s composer, Earl Robinson, appeared by invitation at a breakfast thrown by the Hollywood Bowl Association, he was surprised not to find Robeson there. On the assumption that Robeson had simply been too busy to attend, Robinson quickly put the matter out of his mind. Later in the day he asked Paul why he hadn't seen him at the breakfast. "Why?" Paul answered evenly. "Because I wasn't invited." On top of that, Earl Robinson recalls, Robeson's agent was at first unable to get him a hotel in Los Angeles. The Beverly Wilshire finally agreed to take him—at a hundred dollars a day for a suite and on condition he change his name. It was idiocy for the hotel to think a pseudonym would prevent Robeson from being noticed, but, just to be sure, he "made it a point to sit in the lobby of that hotel two hours every afternoon." When Robinson asked him why he bothered, Robeson replied, "To ensure that, the next time black singers and actors come through, they'll have a place to stay."[18]

When Robeson gave a concert that same month at the Robin Hood Dell in Philadelphia, Essie went down for it, noting cryptically in her diary that "Freda was there too." Freda Diamond was now the wife of Alfred ("Barry") Baruch, an industrial engineer, and well launched in her career as a designer and home-furnishings consultant. Before she and Barry Baruch had married in 1932, they had agreed on a marriage that, although conventional enough by other standards, would eschew hidden affairs and the guilt that usually attends them. No questions were to be asked about past or present relationships. Barry also encouraged Freda to use her maiden name professionally and to pursue her career. Freda says in retrospect, with a formidable sense of independent identity not characteristic of women of her generation, "I was rarely Mrs. Alfred Baruch until after five p.m. That was my second identity. I was Freda Diamond. Both Paul and Barry loved me over the years—and I loved them—in very different ways: Barry in a constant, happy marriage for thirty-two years, Paul in an enduring relationship despite his extensive travels and long absences. Sometimes we saw each other seldom while he lived abroad or during his other intimate relationships, but we kept in touch, and our love and friendship for each other continued until he died."[19]

Robeson was most consistently attracted to strong and intelligent women. Several of his relationships went on for years in one way or another; some began in friendship; some transmuted to friendship. It was inevitable that a few of these women were married to men he knew well. The husbands, for the most part, seem to have been aware of these affairs (some of the men were not themselves monogamous and may have been better able therefore to accept Paul's presence in their lives). None seems to have objected, or left any record of objection, opting instead for a cordiality compounded in unmeasurable and varying degrees of denial, disinterest, resentment, discreet compromise—and genuine pleasure in Paul's company.

Barry Baruch was friendly but not close to Paul. They shared an enthusiasm for sports, played chess, and occasionally argued about politics. Barry was a political liberal, not a radical, and as Paul's public commitment to the Soviet Union grew during the forties, their discussions sometimes turned to serious disagreement. Paul and Freda were much closer in their political identification; indeed, one of the strengths of their long-standing relationship was its political aspect, with Freda an active participant in several organizations—particularly, in the postwar years, the American Labor Party, the Progressive Party, and the National Council of American-Soviet Friendship—with which Paul was affiliated.

Even though Paul and Barry were less politically sympathetic, the two men were friendly enough to take a studio together briefly in the early forties in Greenwich Village (Paul rehearsed, Barry sculpted). Soon after, Paul came to live with Barry and Freda. For the better part of three years in the early-to-mid-forties, first in a townhouse on Charlton Street in the Village and then in Murray Hill, Paul had his own separate floor within their household, which he occupied between his travels. Freda prided herself on making it a genuine home for him—"We didn't use Paul as bait," she later said, "or as a social lion around which to build our lives."

Freda also became a good friend to Essie, listening to her troubles, encouraging her to believe in her own gifts and to become independent. Early on, Essie was describing Freda as "very lovely. I always thought she was attractive in the old days, but now she seems to have 'jelled.' " By the fifties, she was introducing Freda (in a letter to Nehru) as "a very dear friend of ours." And she was. Over the years, Essie grew genuinely fond of Freda and appreciative of her friendship—even though, in the forties, she still suffered periodic alarms that Freda might someday officially displace her. "If Essie had these qualms," Freda has since said, "they were completely unfounded because she knew first-hand that I would never divorce Barry. Once, when the subject came up between us, I assured her that as far as I was concerned she would always be Mrs. Paul Robeson—and she knew I meant it."[20]

Essie, for her part, had learned to compromise since the stormy scenes over Peggy Ashcroft and Yolande Jackson a decade earlier, and to adopt tactics more commensurate with worldly-wise middle age. If Essie wanted to remain Mrs. Paul Robeson (and she did), she had to accept—not only tolerate—the needs of Paul's nonmonogamous nature. If she felt reassured that her marriage would, formally, be maintained, she continued to feel dismay at the erosion of her actual role within the partnership. On returning to the States, Robeson gave his lawyer, Bob Rockmore, complete control over the management of his affairs, removing business and artistic matters alike from Essie's jurisdiction. He had steadily grown to trust Rockmore, even though the lawyer's politics leaned to the conservative side. Valuing Essie's opinion, Paul sometimes still consulted her, but she felt this transferral of power as a wounding and humiliating blow, one she would thereafter periodically protest. The blow struck her the harder because her own attempts at a separate career were not going well. Her novel, *Black Progress,* had still failed to find a publisher, and her screenplay, *Uncle Tom's Cabin,* had failed to interest a film studio. Never one to accept defeat, Essie gamely tried other career options. During the spring term of 1940, she registered at Columbia for courses in radio writing, film writing, playwriting, and elementary Russian, and worked at them with her usual commitment and intensity, enjoying especially her work with Erik Barnouw, the well-known radio figure. To pursue her interest in photography, she went off in August 1940 on a trip to Central America, vowing, "I will make the most of myself these next six months and see what happens." An admiring Nehru wrote her, "Your mental energy is something amazing."[21]

Paul, meanwhile, continued his occasional concertizing, interspersed with considerable political activity. He agreed to serve on a board of eight (including Richard Wright, Edna Thomas, Max Yergan, and Alain Locke) for the Negro Playwrights' Company, launched in the summer of 1940 to help fill the void left by the demise of the Federal Theatre, and he sang at an inaugural celebration for the company that drew five thousand people (three-fourths of them white; Ben Davis, Jr., ascribed the lack of attendance by blacks to the high admission price).[22]

Additionally, Robeson went on the radio to introduce songs of the International Brigade during the Spanish Civil War, appeared at a rally in behalf of the China Defense League, helped to dedicate the Children's Aid Society in Harlem, and, along with a host of other celebrities, appeared at a mass meeting sponsored by the Committee to Defend America by Keeping Out of War, to protest conscription and other preparedness measures. There he argued, yet again, that under their present leadership Britain and France were essentially engaged in a struggle to protect the profits of plutocrats, not the rights of the people. As late as March 1941, Robeson told a reporter that he was against aid for Britain because he believed the mobilization was primarily aimed at saving the British Empire. According to the reporter, Robeson spoke "angrily" and "stormed" over the refusal of the British ruling class to do anything "about giving India and Ireland and Africa a taste of democracy." But after Nazi Germany invaded the Soviet Union in June 1941, the war would become, in Robeson's eyes, an unimpeachable and united struggle against fascism.[23]

Starting out on another concert tour in the fall of 1940, Robeson took along with him as "associate artist" Clara Rockmore, the pert, feisty, attractive second wife of Bob Rockmore, and the world's leading theremin player (an instrument whose tone and dynamics are created by the juxtaposition of the hands in an electromagnetic field). Clara Rockmore had begun her musical life as a prodigy (as had her pianist sister, Nadia Reisenberg), winning admittance at the unprecedented age of five (Heifetz had been eight) to the conservatory in Petrograd to study violin with the famed Leopold Auer, teacher of Heifetz, Zimbalist, and Elman. An injury to her arm forced her, at age nineteen, to give up the violin and turn to a career with the theremin. She and Paul were already good friends before their tour together in 1940, when they became *'just* good friends," affectionately addressing each other as "Clarochka" and "Pavlik."[24]

They were to do three tours together in the forties, and during their long months on the road Paul would sometimes confide in Clara, shedding the everyday cordiality that had become second nature to him (and which, along with being an expression of his genuine warmth, had long served as protective coloration as well, as a guard against unwanted intrusion). Paul's generosity of spirit showed itself, Clara Rockmore recalls, in his delight at *her* success with the reviewers. It was not some undefined "charisma"—so often remarked upon—that set Robeson apart, in her opinion; it was "a weight of concern"—the sense he transmitted of concentrated interest in others.[25]

He also let Clara see more of the depth of his hurt and anger in the face of racial discrimination. When they played the college towns there was rarely a problem, but elsewhere racial incidents did occur, despite Robeson's celebrity and his presumed immunity from discrimination. Clara Rockmore recalls "the indignity of having to go through a different door than Paul and Larry did, of coming into a railroad station with signs marked 'For Whites Only.'" She remembers, too, once impulsively throwing her arms around Larry in public, only to have him gently reprove her: "I'd better teach you the facts of life"; when she persisted—"I don't care what *they* think"—Larry replied, "I know you don't care, but do you want to get me lynched?" To deflect intrusion—and hostility—Paul and Clara would usually talk to each other in Russian when in public places, amused at the stupefaction on onlookers' faces at the sight of a giant black man and a diminutive white woman chatting away in some unintelligible tongue. (She found his Russian "beautiful"; he spoke it "almost too well," having learned, from his reading, the literary language of Pushkin and Dostoevsky.)[26]

Following a concert in San Francisco one night in November 1940, famished after the performance and high-spirited from its success, Clara and Paul (still dressed in evening gown and tails) went with friends to get some food at Vanessi's, a well-known spot in the cosmopolitan North Beach area. Their party included Revels Cayton, the black labor leader (then an official of the Maritime Union of the Pacific), who was becoming a good friend of Robeson's; his wife, Lee; Louise Bransten, the wealthy white left-wing supporter (a devoted friend of Robeson's, and a sometime lover); and John Pittman, black foreign editor of the San Francisco *People's World.* The light-skinned Pittman, first to enter the restaurant, was told by the headwaiter that *he* was welcome but that big guy behind him—pointing to Robeson—was not. They left quickly and went back to the Fairmont Hotel, "made quite a joke" of the incident, ordered food in the room, and had a party. On the surface Robeson reacted "philosophically"—but he was angry. Friends of his in San Francisco subsequently brought suit against Vanessi's for discrimination, but it never came to trial.[27]

The episode, including the way Robeson handled it, was characteristic. His polite exterior was no accurate gauge of the intensity of his inner feelings—and now and then the geniality gave way and his rage poured out. Once, in the privacy of the Rockmore living room, he stormed around in such indignation over a racial slur that Clara, in alarm, tried to soothe him with some folksy parable about "being careful when cleaning a chicken not to let the bile touch the sweet meat, because just pricking that bile would embitter it"; Paul laughed and allowed himself to be mollified. But, as Clara herself recognized, "When he was insulted, he knew he was being insulted. When he wasn't, he knew that he wasn't. He knew where he was welcome, and why, and for what reason. Or not. He was a very wise man who would not only hear what you asked, but would know why you were asking it." (However, a close friend describes him as being, by the end of the decade, in a controlled rage "most of the time.")[28]

Paul also confided to Clara his doubts about the quality of his musicianship. He worried about his lack of training and the fact that he had never led a musician's life—he did not go frequently to concerts, did not travel in musical circles, was not familiar with various instruments and with musical literature, was not able to sight-read. These were serious deficiencies, he told Clara. His sense of inadequacy in part reflected his high regard, as an instinctive scholar, for those who had thoroughly mastered all aspects of a given subject over those who proceeded on the basis of natural gifts alone. But he "made too much of it," had, in her view, "an exaggerated respect for musicians who were trained classically." She would scold him for belittling himself, for internalizing a negative, patronizing evaluation of his gifts by musicians who were in fact envious of the unique quality of his voice—a specialness their academic training had failed to provide. Besides, Clara did not believe that his lack of training had actually hampered his development. Even with the requisite background, he would not, in her opinion, have wanted to perform operas or oratorios. She never sensed a strong temperamental inclination on his part toward opera, or any significant frustration at being denied (as a *black* singer) the opportunity to perform it. "He was not dreaming about operas. If he had all the equipment under the sun, I doubt that he would want to sing opera. It didn't make him less, it didn't make him more. He was what he was. He was an actor-singer, carrying a message in the song. I don't think that with some training he would have been any greater a Paul Robeson. He might have been less. There will not be another Paul Robeson. There'll be people with as good a voice, but they won't have as much heart."[29]

While Paul, Clara, and Larry toured, Essie was not thriving. Her weight soared to 153 pounds; her socializing narrowed to a few old friends like Corinne Wright and Minnie Sumner; her writing was still unpublished, her photography unrecognized. She turned her restless energy to attending parents' functions at Pauli's school and to taking lessons in jiujitsu. She sent letters to Paul reporting her prowess in learning the hip throw and—in pointed detail—her excursions with Pauli, such as buying him his "first young man's clothes" at De Pinna's ("I said they were your present, because you had always said YOU were going to give him his first grown up clothes"). Her efforts at retaliation—"Pauli was thrilled with your wire. I'm so glad you did send it. It was a little confusing, with the signature Paul Robeson. Pauli could not understand why it wasn't signed Daddy?"—did nothing to narrow the growing gulf between them.[30]

In the early spring of 1941, bowing to Essie's importunities, willing to indulge her stylish fantasies if simultaneously they would serve to remove her and her overbearing mother from his proximity (and give him, as well, the tax advantages of an out-of-state residence), Paul agreed to purchase an imposing two-and-a-half-acre, twelve-room Georgian-Colonial house in Enfield, Connecticut, for nineteen thousand dollars. Complete with servants' quarters, a swimming pool, and a separate recreation building that had a bowling alley and billiard room, the house was so large and in such disrepair that one of the workmen hired to fix it up told a reporter, "He's gonna hafta sing alotta songs to heat this place." Essie did some of the manual labor herself, including painting much of the house (Freda's brother, on a visit, was "shocked to come upon her balanced on a scaffold while putting a coat of paint on the staircase ceiling")—though Bob Rockmore's sense of fiscal propriety was nonetheless jarred by her expenditures. On May 1, 1941, Essie, Pauli, and Ma Goode were able to move into the Enfield house. "We are all simply crazy about the country," Essie wrote the Van Vechtens, adding that "Big Paul loves the quiet and low gear of the place, and flies home for every moment he can spare even when on tour." She was adamantly putting the best face on it, as her concluding comment—"it is all much too good to be true"—inadvertently acknowledged. Paul did occasionally spend time there, but his primary residence alternated between the Freda Diamond/Barry Baruch household and the McGhees', and the focus of his life was in New York, not at Enfield. Which is not to say Paul did not still have an occasional burst of affection for Essie. While in Los Angeles in August 1941, he wrote her a letter that began, "I miss you terribly and would so like to nestle [you] on my nice shoulder and be patted and called Sweetie Pie and oh so many things," went on to give her news of mutual friends, and then teased her good-humoredly with having met Hollywood celebrities:

> And most exciting of all, at a British benefit (swanky) I met all the stars, and had a special chat with—breathe hard—*Mr. Charles Boyer.* . . . I told him of you and he's waiting, he says. He came to my recital and told Morros [the producer] that he has all my records. So the ground is laid. I said the *ground!* I feel grand, completely relaxed and am sleeping thru anything.

He then went on to ask about Pauli: ". . . How's my boy. Everyone, everywhere asks about him and I tell them how sweet, intelligent and thoughtful he is, what an athlete—and a few other things. They conclude I like him enormously and am very proud of him. I think they are perhaps right about that." He ended the letter with as sweetly tender a message as any he ever sent her: "I love you very, very much and miss you until it hurts. I do like my place so much both in Conn. and in your heart—and I feel I'm camping out until I get back to both." Although Paul was capable of dissembling, this does not seem such an instance. More likely, this complicated man was having a genuine spell of nostalgic affection for Essie. On her side—never one to indulge introspection or wallow in self-pity—Essie plunged into the maelstrom of painters, plumbers, and pipe fitters with renewed zest (Freda Diamond visited her frequently and helped her choose furnishings), establishing a home in which she knew she would, for the most part, live without Paul.[31]

The years from 1935 to 1939 had been the heyday of the Popular Front, a time when a substantial consensus was reached internationally on the left. The Communist Party/USA (CPUSA) refocused its sights away from revolutionary bellicosity and toward cooperation with mainstream liberalism in a combined effort to resist the rise of fascism abroad and to work at home in behalf of trade-unionism and racial equality. CP leader Earl Browder's declaration in 1936 that "Communism is 20th Century Americanism" plausibly affirmed this solidarity—and also signaled the marked influence Communism had come to have in American life: CP membership rolls dramatically lengthened, hundreds of new Party units formed, and Communists were welcomed to affiliate in large-scale coalitions with "radical democrats." The Nazi-Soviet pact in August 1939 effectively ended this antifascist unity.

In the two-year period following that pact, and until Hitler's invasion of the Soviet Union in June 1941, Robeson took his position on the CP side of the sundered left-wing coalition. He sounded the themes and advocated the policies simultaneously being endorsed through the linked voices of the Communist Party, the newly powerful National Negro Congress (NNC), and some of the left-wing unions in the recently emergent Congress of Industrial Organizations (CIO). The particular fortunes of the National Negro Congress illustrate the shifting general pattern of left-wing alliance and Robeson's own role within it.[32]

The Communist Party had played a prominent but not a controlling role in the creation of the NNC, joining forces with a diverse spectrum of black-activist organizations and leaders. At the first NNC convention, in 1936, eight hundred delegates representing a wide range of civil-rights organizations, church groups, fraternities, and trade unions gathered to form a broad coalition dedicated to struggling against fascism and for civil rights and unionism. John P. Davis, a black economist and Harvard Law School graduate (and possibly a secret CP member), was the leading figure in the NNC from the beginning, but its notable supporters initially included Ralph Bunche, A. Philip Randolph, Lester Granger of the Urban League, and Adam Clayton Powell, Jr. This pluralistic combination held at the NNC's second convention, in 1937, but strains had already appeared. The affiliated mainstream liberals were beginning to be unnerved by the fact that increased funding for the NNC was coming from the Communist Party and from the left-wing unions. When John P. Davis launched an antilynching drive in 1938, the coalition was further rent: the leadership of the NAACP had been working for years on securing federal antilynching legislation and deeply resented this "encroachment" on its territory. The Nazi-Soviet pact in 1939 drove off additional legions, and by the time of the NNC's third convention, in April 1940 (it had held no national meeting either in 1938 or 1939), numerous non-Communists had drifted away. After a blistering speech to the 1940 convention, in which he equated the Soviet Union with Nazi Germany, A. Philip Randolph resigned the presidency and was succeeded by a rising figure in left-wing circles, Max Yergan.[33]

Still, over five hundred delegates from twenty-nine states did show up for the third convention—a concert engagement prevented Robeson from attending—to hear NNC speakers emphasize, as had Robeson in his own recent public appearances, that the current European conflict was a struggle between rival imperialist powers—and to call upon American blacks to focus their energies instead on the struggle for rights within the United States. That message made sense to many blacks. World War I, they remembered, had also been fought with noble slogans about making the world safe for democracy—and had resulted in the colonial powers' extending their control over people of color; more recently, protestations of democratic fervor had not extended to concern over Mussolini's rape of Ethiopia. As Robeson had been arguing for a year, dark-skinned people could not be expected to believe the British claim that they were "fighting for freedom" when they continued contemptuously to deny it to the people of India.[34]

Following the Nazi-Soviet pact, the CPUSA, too, reversed its call for collective security against fascism and revived its historic insistence that the working class of the world refuse participation in an "imperialist" war. Using that same line of argument, Robeson spoke out continually against American involvement in a European conflict ultimately aimed, in his opinion, at destroying the threat of Soviet-inspired peoples' revolutions. He also played an energetic public role in protesting the American government's 1940 sentencing of Earl Browder, the Party leader, to four years in prison on the pretext of having violated passport regulations. Claiming that the real animus against Browder related to his antifascism, Robeson in March 1941 joined the labor hero Warren K. Billings, New York Labor

Party Congressman Vito Marcantonio, the Communist leader Elizabeth Gurley Flynn, Max Yergan, and the Spanish Civil War veteran Conrad Kaye (now of the American Federation of Labor) in a rally in Madison Square Garden to "Free Earl Browder." Gurley Flynn announced at another public meeting that Robeson had contributed more money to help free Browder than had any other single individual. When Robeson was introduced at an antifascist fund-raising dinner in March 1942 as "America's leading anti-fascist," he declined that title to bestow it on Browder (who was finally released from prison in May 1942).[35]

In regard to trade-union issues, Robeson typically advised black workers to defy their employers and to join the CIO, declaring his belief—one shared by the NNC and the CPUSA—in a biracial trade-union movement as the most promising vehicle for extending American democracy to blacks. In May 1941 Robeson put in a dramatic appearance in Detroit in behalf of the United Automobile Workers' CIO organizing drive, just days before its successful showdown with Henry Ford. Three months later he told reporters, "The future of America depends largely upon the progressive program of the CIO," and he claimed that "the Negro people, for the most part, understand that the CIO program is working for all laboring groups, including their own minority."[36]

In making this hopeful assertion, Robeson chose to minimize some disfiguring realities. In the mid-thirties, the CP had abandoned "revolutionary unionism" based on proletarian rule in order to cooperate, under a Popular Front banner, with trade-unionism. By the late thirties, the logic of that decision had forced the CP to make some accommodation to the racism that characterized even such left-leaning CIO unions as the Transport Workers or the Hotel and Restaurant Workers (though these unions were light-years ahead of most AFL affiliates in accepting blacks for membership). Mike Quill of the TWU never made any substantial effort to fight for expanded job opportunities for black workers, placing priority instead on issues of union recognition and the protection of the rights of those already enlisted in its ranks. Other left-wing labor leaders did have strong convictions about the need to change patterns of racial discrimination within industry, but were sometimes reluctant to push their more conservative memberships in a direction that might split their unions and jeopardize their own positions of leadership. And the CP did not exert much pressure in that direction on labor leaders sympathetic to its ideology. Preoccupied with the international crisis, the CP by the late thirties placed more emphasis on maintaining its alliances than on pushing aggressively for the kind of action against job discrimination that might shake those alliances. In choosing to "Americanize" the Party, in other words, the CP's leaders had inescapably become enmeshed in the contradictions of American life: to maintain its influence within the labor movement, it had to compromise somewhat on its vanguard position regarding black rights. The CP and CIO's comparative inaction against racial discrimination during and after World War II (when measured against their earlier clarion calls) would lead black militants, in the late 1940s and early 1950s, to press for "black caucuses" within each union. Robeson's friend Revels Cayton would play a central role in that movement—and Robeson, who would never sanction a back-seat role for blacks for long, would also become involved.

The dilution of the CP's mission to press the issue of job rights for the economically depressed black working class, in combination with the CP's aggressively secular scorn for Christian institutions and values so central to the culture of Afro-Americans, seriously constricted its appeal to the black masses. But if Communism failed to ignite the enthusiasm of any significant segment of the black working class—the agency on which it theoretically relied for producing social change—it did turn out to have a broad appeal for black artists and intellectuals. When emphasizing the class struggle in the years before the Popular Front, the Party as a corollary had downplayed the specialness of black culture. But during the Popular Front years, with the centrality of class struggle deemphasized, the Party threw itself into pronounced support for black arts, helping to sponsor a variety of efforts to encourage black theater, history, and music. Robeson was hardly alone among black artists in welcoming this uniquely respectful attitude toward black aesthetics. Here was an "Americanism" that exemplified *real* respect for "differentness" rather than attempting, as did official mainstream liberalism, to disparage and destroy ethnic variations under the guise of championing the superior virtue of the "melting pot"—which in practice had tended to mean assimilation to the values of white middle-class Protestants.[37]

Symbolizing this appreciation of black culture, the fraternal organization International Workers Order sponsored a pageant on "The Negro in American Life" (with the Manhattan Council of the NNC as cosponsor) dramatizing major events in Afro-American history. Robeson enthusiastically offered his services. The pageant, written by the black playwright Carlton Moss, proved weak in its dramaturgy but strong in its emotional appeal. Its dedication "to the Negro People and to Fraternal Brotherhood Among All" roused a racially mixed audience of five thousand to an ovation—and then to an ecumenical frenzy of cheering when Robeson called for all minorities to unite in making "America a real land of freedom and democracy."[38]

Another event cosponsored by the NNC led—for the very reason of its sponsorship—to a major controversy. Robeson had already given his support on several occasions in 1941 to benefits for Chinese war relief when the Washington Committee for Aid to China put together a gala

"Night of Stars" and asked him to headline it. He quickly agreed—but the Daughters of the American Revolution did not. Approached by the China Committee with a request to lease Constitution Hall, the DAR flatly refused, reiterating its policy of barring the hall to black artists, despite the uproar that had attended its denial of the hall two years earlier to Marian Anderson (which had led Eleanor Roosevelt to resign her DAR membership and personally to welcome Anderson to a huge alternative concert on the steps of the Lincoln Memorial).[39]

The China Committee appealed to Cornelia Bryce Pinchot for help. A friend of Mrs. Roosevelt and wife to Gifford Pinchot, the former governor of Pennsylvania, the patrician Mrs. Pinchot was nationally known as an activist supporter of human rights (Marian Anderson had stayed at her house while in Washington for the Lincoln Memorial concert). She responded to the committee's appeal by taking on the concert chairmanship herself and organizing an illustrious sponsorship committee that included Mrs. Roosevelt, the Chinese Ambassador Hu Shih, Mr. and Mrs. Archibald MacLeish, Senator Arthur Capper, Oscar L. Chapman, and the wives of Francis Biddle, Hugo L. Black, Louis D. Brandeis, and William O. Douglas—the "left wing" of the New Deal establishment. The DAR's ban created additional publicity for the concert and, due to the heightened demand for tickets, Mrs. Pinchot rented the seven-thousand-seat Uline Arena.[40]

At that point she discovered that the NNC was cosponsor of the concert and that it had made an agreement to provide money and services in advance of the event in exchange for 50 percent of its proceeds—a proportion initiated by the China Committee, not the NNC. Mrs. Pinchot protested the "diversion" of funds to the NNC and notified the committee that she could not sanction any arrangement that did not call for the entire proceeds from the concert to go to the advertised cause of aid to China. John P. Davis, the leading figure in the NNC, offered to terminate his organization's contract with the committee if two conditions were met: reimbursement for the NNC's expenses, and a guarantee that the Uline auditorium, which had agreed to suspend its Jim Crow policy for the single night of the Robeson concert, not discriminate in the future. The Uline management refused to provide such a guarantee, and since that meant the NNC would not retract its cosponsorship, Mrs. Pinchot announced that she—along with Mrs. Roosevelt and Ambassador Hu Shih—were withdrawing support, saying that "the ramifications from the original errors have spread too far to be corrected."[41]

The only "ramification" Cornelia Pinchot mentioned in the telegram she sent Robeson—signed also by Mrs. Roosevelt, and simultaneously released to the press—to account for their withdrawal was the refusal of the Uline management to give a pledge against future discrimination. She alluded in the telegram to "a number of other reasons which it is unnecessary to burden you with," explaining their resignations wholly on the grounds that they were unwilling "to ask a great Negro artist to appear in any place which is believed to discriminate against members of his race." But the telegram was at the least disingenuous. The condition that Uline agree not to discriminate had, after all, been set by John P. Davis, not Cornelia Pinchot, so it alone could hardly account for the sum of her discontent. More likely, that hinged instead on nervousness at being publicly associated with the Communist-leaning National Negro Congress. The nervousness may have been compounded by the fact that both Walter White of the NAACP and A. Philip Randolph had broken with the NNC in 1940, and those two men (unlike John P. Davis) had the ear of the administration; because of Randolph's January 1941 call for a March on Washington to protest federal job discrimination, he had its decided attention as well.[42]

Robeson, sympathetic to the NNC, was not swayed against performing by Mrs. Pinchot's solicitous refusal to ask a "great Negro artist" to appear under such clouded circumstances. Not only did he appear, but he sold out the house. The National Negro Congress remained on the program as cosponsor, and John P. Davis spoke words of welcome from the platform. An estimated crowd of six thousand gave Robeson an ovation that one reporter likened to "the Willkie gallery at Philadelphia," and the organizers later wrote to thank Robeson for his "magnificent" contribution to the event's success.[43]

Hitler's invasion of the Soviet Union on June 22, 1941, and the Anglo-Soviet pact that followed soon after, created an international realignment that abruptly brought Robeson's views into greater consonance with mainstream patriotism. The Soviet Union was now hailed among the Western democracies—as Robeson had hailed it all along—as the front line of defense in the struggle against fascism. The image of the bullying Russian bear bent on aggression quickly gave way in the West to the image of a heroic homeland battling to preserve the integrity of its borders against fascist incursion. The Communists and their pro-Soviet allies in the NNC and the left-wing CIO unions were no slower in repainting their political canvases. A year before the Nazi invasion, CP leader William Z. Foster had branded the British Empire "the main enemy of everything progressive," but after the invasion the main enemy rapidly became Hitler's Germany—so much so that, out of its concern for a unified war effort, the Party would support a "no-strike" pledge by labor and dilute its protest against racism in the armed forces, thereby partly compromising the vanguard position in the civil-rights struggle that it had earlier staked out for itself.[44]

Robeson, too, shifted his advocacy from nonintervention to massive aid for the Soviet Union. He urged the Roosevelt administration to help arm the now combined forces of antifacism—to support the Allies against the Axis (as the struggle soon came to be called, once the Japanese completed the diametric symmetry by bombing Pearl Harbor at the end of the year). He freely lent his voice in concerts and his presence at rallies in support of an all-out effort to assist the Soviets, Britain, and China, alternately joining fellow artists like Benny Goodman in presenting an evening of Soviet music, or cosigning a letter that deplored the "strikingly inadequate" information available in America about the Soviet Union and offering to make up the deficiency with free copies of *The Soviet Power*, a book by Reverend Hewlett Johnson (the "Red" Dean of Canterbury). At a time when Soviet military fortunes were at a low ebb and predictions of the U.S.S.R.'s collapse widespread, Robeson insisted in statements to the press that the Russian masses, convinced they had a government that offered them hope, would never succumb to the Nazis.[45]

With the Soviet Union now a wartime ally, the cause of Russian War Relief became so entirely respectable by 1942 that, in a rally at Madison Square Garden on June 22, Robeson was joined on the podium by a full panoply of American life—Supreme Court Justice Stanley Reed, Mayor La Guardia of New York, William Green (president of the AFL), Harry Hopkins, U.S.S.R. Ambassador to the United States Maxim Litvinov, the Jewish leader Dr. Stephen S. Wise, Jan Peerce, and Artur Rubinstein. The shift in public opinion from antagonism to approval of the "heroic" Russian ally became dramatically complete over the next few years, with the mass-circulation magazines illustrating—and fostering—the changing image. *Collier's* in December 1943 concluded that Russia was neither Socialist nor Communist but, rather, represented a "modified capitalist set-up" moving "toward something resembling our own and Great Britain's democracy," while a 1943 issue of *Life* was entirely devoted to a paean to Soviet-American cooperation. Wendell Willkie's enormously popular *One World* contained glowing praise of Soviet Russia—and Walter Lippmann, in turn, praised the astuteness of Willkie's analysis. A nationwide poll in September 1944 asking whether the Russian people had "as good" a government "as she could have for her people" found only 28 percent replying in the negative. By 1945 no less a figure than General Eisenhower told a House committee that "nothing guides Russian policy so much as a desire for friendship with the United States."[46]

None of this diluted the suspicion of Bolshevik intentions harbored by the right wing—and notably by its chief champion in the federal bureaucracy, FBI director J. Edgar Hoover—or its rising conviction that Robeson was playing a sinister role in Soviet councils. As early as January 1941, special agents were reporting to FBI headquarters in Washington that Robeson was "reputedly a member of the Communist Party" (which he was not, and never would be). Three months later a zealous agent in Los

Angeles sent a brown notebook to Hoover, "apparently belonging" to Robeson, that "contains Chinese characters"; the Bureau's translation section examined the notebook and concluded it was "clearly of significance to no one other than its owner." In the summer of 1942 an agent was present when Robeson visited Wo-Chi-Ca, the interracial camp for workers' children, and portentously reported that Robeson had signed "Fraternally" to a message of greeting and that "tears had rolled down his cheeks" when a young camper presented him with a scroll.[47]

As Robeson stepped up his activities in behalf of the Allied war effort, Hoover stepped up surveillance of him. By the end of 1942, the Bureau had taken to describing Robeson as a Communist functionary: "It would be difficult to establish membership in his case but his activities in behalf of the Communist Party are too numerous to be recorded." The FBI began to tap his phone conversations and to bug apartments where he was known to visit. Special agents were assigned to trail him and to file regular reports on his activities. By January 1943 Hoover was recommending that Robeson be considered for custodial detention (that is, subject to immediate arrest in case of national emergency); such a card was issued on him on April 30, 1943—the same month that he was being hailed in the press for a triumphal concert tour and just before he starred in a giant Labor for Victory rally in Yankee Stadium. By August 1943 "reputedly" was being dropped in special-agent reports to Hoover, with Robeson now being straightforwardly labeled "a leading figure in the Communist Party . . . actively attempting to influence the Negroes of America to Communism." From this point on, the FBI fattened Robeson's file with "evidence" to support its view that he was in fact a dangerous subversive. During the war years, Robeson's secret dossier and his national popularity grew apace—their collision was still half a dozen years off.[48]

For the time being, national and personal priorities coalesced. President Roosevelt's reaffirmation of democratic values on the home front, in tandem with the country's joining hands internationally with a Russian ally Robeson believed free of racial and colonialist bias, meant that national purpose coincided with his own special vision more fully than he had ever imagined would be possible in his lifetime. The juncture galvanized him, releasing in him a torrent of energy and resolve. Over the next three years—until the death of Franklin Roosevelt, in April 1945—Robeson operated at the summit of his powers, in an escalating spiral of activity and acclaim, and in the glow of a political optimism that would be as brutally shattered as it had been, briefly, unexpectedly plausible.

Even at its height, Robeson's optimism was not unblinkered. Roosevelt might now speak kindly of his "heroic" Russian ally, but Robeson hardly took that to mean the President had converted to socialism. In the same way, he did not regard New Deal domestic policies, promising though he found them, as signifying the imminent attainment of social justice. The Roosevelt administration did much to excite the hopes of black Americans: it opened itself to the counsels of such notable black figures as Mary McLeod Bethune, Robert Weaver, William H. Hastie, and Walter White; it issued the President's 1941 Committee on Fair Employment Practices (FEPC) order; it included blacks in the AAA-sponsored voting on cotton-control referendums. Yet, as Robeson well knew, the Democratic Party remained tied to its racially unreconstructed Southern wing, and the actual execution of policy had produced only marginal changes in the oppressive pattern of daily life for the black masses. In the mid-forties Robeson told a friend that he thought Roosevelt's reformism would have as its chief result the guarantee that capitalism would exist for another fifty years.[49]

As Robeson crisscrossed the country in a whirlwind of rallies, concert appearances, meetings, dinners, and testimonials, he tempered his enthusiasm for the nation's wartime mission to defeat fascism with reminders about its obligation to combat oppression at home. The CP opted for primary attention to the war overseas, downplaying the black struggle at home; Robeson did not. He encouraged blacks to support the war effort, warning that the victory of fascism would "make slaves of us all"—but he simultaneously called on the administration to make the war effort worth supporting for blacks by destroying discriminatory practices in defense industries and the armed forces. "Racial and religious prejudices continue to cast an ugly shadow on the principles for which we are fighting," he told a commencement audience at Morehouse College in 1943. At the prestigious and widely broadcast annual *Herald Tribune* Forum that same year, he devoted most of his speech to warning that continuing economic insecurity, poll-tax discrimination, and armed-forces segregation were arousing "the bitterest resentment among black Americans"; they recognized that under Roosevelt some progress was being made but rightly felt that the gains thus far had been "pitifully small" and that their own struggle for improved conditions was intimately bound up with "the struggle against anti-Semitism and against injustices to all minority groups."[50]

Robeson insisted that "The disseminators and supporters of racial discrimination and antagonism [appear] to the Negro and *are*, in fact, first cousins if not brothers of the Nazis. They speak the same language of the 'master race' and practice, or attempt to practice, the same tyranny over minority peoples." He called on the Western democracies to match the Soviet Union in the explicitness of their stated war aims: "abolition of racial exclusiveness; equality of nations and integrity of their territories; the right of every nation to arrange its affairs as it wishes." He gave the same two-pronged message to trade-unionists, applauding the breakthrough efforts during the war of left-wing CIO unions to lower racial barriers, but reminding his audiences of how many barriers still remained before any biracial trade-union movement worthy of the name could come into being. Robeson raised his eloquent voice everywhere in praise of the national purpose, singing for the troops, appearing at war-bond rallies. But he also sought to universalize the struggle against oppression, linking the cause of black Americans with that of Spanish Americans, Asians, Africans, and underprivileged white Americans: "this is one of the great ends of this war—that the very concept of lower classes, colonial or backward peoples, disappear[s] from our minds and actions. For Fascism means degradation and inferior status. A people's war is fought for dignity and equality." And everywhere he went Robeson kept his incomparably sharp ears and eyes open for continuing signs of racial bigotry.[51]

In Kansas City, Missouri, in 1942, those eyes scanned the concert audience gathered to hear him sing and saw that blacks had been seated in the top balcony. When he reappeared on the platform after the intermission, Robeson abruptly announced to the startled audience that he was continuing with the second half of the program under protest. "I have made a lifelong habit," he told them, "of refusing to sing in southern states or anywhere that audiences are segregated," and had accepted the Kansas City engagement on the assurance there would be no segregation in the auditorium. He agreed to finish the concert, but only because "many local leaders of my own race have urged me to." Robeson then proceeded to sing a group of Russian songs, followed by the "Jim Crow" song, delivering it, as a local critic reported, "with stronger feeling that he had put into any other number." At that point several whites in the audience left; a hundred more trickled out before the close of the concert.[52]

The very next day, a hotel in Santa Fa canceled Robeson's advance reservation. When the chairman of the Santa Fe concert series at which he had been due to appear justified the hotel's policy by citing "New Mexico's proximity to the southern states," Robeson promptly refused to fulfill his upcoming concert date. The Kansas City and Santa Fe incidents were widely reported in the national press. Lucile Bluford, news editor on the black Kansas City paper, the *Call*, wrote to thank Robeson "for the stand you took against segregation in the Municipal Auditorium here. I think that your protest has spurred the Negro citizens here to wage a campaign against discrimination in our tax-supported buildings. You have given us a good start." The black columnist Joseph D. Bibb wrote in the Pittsburgh *Courier* that by his action Robeson had "held himself out in bold relief to the majority of 'shoot crap, shortening bread Sambos' of radio, screen and stage."[53]

Max Yergan was one of several who reported to Robeson that everyone was "tremendously pleased and proud" of the stands he had taken. Yergan had resigned his YMCA post in South Africa in 1936 and returned to the United States, gradually becoming an influential public figure as an officer in the National Negro Congress, a sympathetic adherent (though not a member) of the Communist Party, and the executive secretary of the Council on African Affairs. By 1942 Yergan had become Robeson's political liaison to the same pronounced degree that Rockmore had become his artistic one. Yergan filtered requests for political appearances, Rockmore for concert ones, the two comparing notes to avoid scheduling conflicts. As regarded the CPUSA, however, Robeson maintained an independent liaison through Ben Davis, Jr., who was in the Party's highest councils and whom Robeson trusted as fully as he did anyone—which is to say, with only minimal reservation. The only other direct channel to Robeson during most of the forties was Essie, though her centrality had been greatly reduced since their return to the States in 1939. She sometimes had to fall back on her close personal friendship with Yergan to exert influence (which she could not do with Rockmore; the two disliked each other, even while maintaining formal appearances of friendship).[54]

Yergan's own public prominence had come to hinge increasingly on his role in the Council on African Affairs (CAA). The Council had been founded in 1937, and by 1941 Robeson had become chairman and Yergan executive director; in 1943 Alphaeus Hunton (a Marxist who had taught at Howard University) became its educational director. The Council's central purpose was to "provide a sound basis of accurate information so that the American people might play their proper part in the struggle for African freedom." Pan-Africanism—"the conviction that all persons of African descent are commonly oppressed by a common enemy"—can be traced in the United States to such early-nineteenth-century proponents as Martin R. Delany and Alexander Crummell, but in the twentieth century the view is centrally associated with W. E. B. Du Bois, who was arguing its tenets for two decades before World War II. By the end of the war, though, concern with the fate of black Africa—and the linkage of its fate to that of black America—had become a commonplace among Afro-American intellectuals and organizations. The Council on African Affairs was designed as a clearinghouse of accurate information on Africa and as a lobbying force for African interests, not as a mass organization. Although Hunton periodically argued for conversion into a mass-membership organization, in the early forties the Council had fewer than two dozen members and met only three times a year, with subcommittees convening somewhat more frequently and with Hunton and Yergan carrying out most of the daily administrative work. Robeson involved himself far more with the actual organizational mechanics of the Council—though rarely on a day-to-day basis—than with any of the other manifold groups that counted him as a supporter. The CAA—as Alphaeus Hunton later put it—"was the one organizational interest among many with which he was identified that was closest to his heart."[55]

In its fusion of anticolonial and pro-Soviet sentiments, the Council did accurately reflect Robeson's basic perspective. Because the United States was relatively unencumbered by a history of colonialist activity in Africa, Robeson and the CAA hoped that the United States might spearhead the drive among the Western democracies to apply the principle of self-determination to the African continent. Even before Roosevelt's death (which shattered that hope), the brilliant West Indian theorist George Padmore, less sanguine than the CAA, had argued that the United States would emerge from the war not as a liberating force but as the dominant imperialist power, using dollar diplomacy rather than outright annexation to control the key commercial and strategic routes on the African continent. By 1942 the FBI had decided that the CAA was not just a Communist front organization, but first among those groups "presently active in creating considerable unrest among the negroes by stressing racial discrimination. . . ."[56]

Soon after the Kansas City and Santa Fe episodes, Robeson made his first trip into the Deep South to attend a convention of the Southern Negro Youth Congress, which was dominated by CP activists. The SNYC gathering at Tuskegee of over five hundred representatives from twenty Southern states, Mexico, and British Guiana heard a message from President Roosevelt calling for unity in the fight against fascism and declaring his conviction that out of victory "will come a peace built on universal freedom such as many men have not yet known." The conference responded with a unanimous pledge of "the full and unswerving loyalty of Negro youth," coupled with a letter of reply to the President expressing concern about the extent to which "discriminatory barriers remain against our fuller participation in our democratic way of life."[57]

The SNYC conference marked Robeson's initial contact with a number of future Party activists, including Howard "Stretch" Johnson, Ed Strong, Louis Burnham, and James Jackson. Stretch Johnson recalls the vivid impression Robeson made on him: "He was awesome. He exuded magnetism and charm and charisma. And then he was so gentle and nonegocentric. He had the . . . common touch. You know, you felt you could communicate with him directly. There was no screen. He was available to you." Five years later, at another SNYC convention, another rising young figure in the Party, Junius Scales, had much the same initial reaction to Robeson: "He strode onto the crowded stage with a combination of dignity, grace and responsive enthusiasm. . . . When the gentle thunder of his greeting broke over them, it was as though each person there had been struck by the lightning of that smile, the grandeur of that presence. There were no formal phrases; he spoke straight to the hearts of all present.

. . . Robeson was as genuine and magnetic socially as he had been on the stage. He managed to listen to every word spoken to him and to reply graciously. When I was introduced to him he made me feel like the guest of honor."[58]

Leaving the Southern Negro Youth Conference in Tuskegee, Robeson went directly to the Southern Conference for Human Welfare at Nashville. The short-lived SCHW, concerned with both economic and civil rights in the South, was denounced by conservatives as a Communist front, but in fact, like so many liberal organizations of the period, it was conceived and controlled by progressives of varying affiliations. Mrs. Roosevelt joined Robeson on the SCHW platform, presenting awards for "service to the South in 1942" to Mary McLeod Bethune (the black director of the National Youth Administration and president of Bethune-Cookman College in Florida) and to Dr. Frank P. Graham (president of the University of North Carolina and a leading white advocate of black rights); in her remarks, Mrs. Roosevelt spoke of the need to accept responsibility for the "miniature world of all races right here in America." Robeson, in turn, repeated his call for "full integration" and again added an appeal for the release of Earl Browder. According to H. L. Mitchell, a founder of the Southern Tenant Farmers Union, who was in the audience when Robeson spoke, his appeal to free Browder "was enough to convince the southern liberals that they were being used to advance the cause of the Communist Party and they abandoned the Southern Conference for Human Welfare"—but it is at least as plausible to believe that they were driven out by Robeson's demand for "full integration." In her "My Day" column the next morning, Mrs. Roosevelt wrote that hearing Robeson sing "Ballad for Americans" at the conference had been "a thrilling experience. . . . It always stirs me as a ballad, but last night there was something peculiarly significant about it."[59]

Robeson's reputation as "hero of the race" was slightly dented in May 1942 when *Tales of Manhattan,* a film he had made in Hollywood the previous year, was released for public showing. The picture follows the trail of a dress coat as it passes from owner to owner, spinning a vignette about each in turn, until finally the coat, stuffed with money, drops from an airplane into the hands of a group of sharecroppers who divide it up and "praise de Lawd." Robeson, Ethel Waters, and Eddie ("Rochester") Anderson played the resident sharecroppers—and the film's vignettes were peopled with an array of stars that included Ginger Rogers, Cesar Romero, Rita Hayworth, Charles Boyer, Henry Fonda, Charles Laughton, and Edward G. Robinson. This glittering gallery of co-workers may have been part of the film's attraction to Robeson, but the more potent appeal lay in a chance to depict the plight of the rural black poor, shown in the film, additionally, as investing the bulk of their windfall in communal land

and tools, and as believing in share-and-share-alike, with "no rich an' no mo' po'."[60]

Some black reviewers, focusing on the film's depiction of sharecropping, came out in its favor. But the majority did not, with the New York *Amsterdam Star News* headlining its negative review "Paul Robeson, Ethel Waters Let Us Down," and declaring, "It is difficult to reconcile the Paul Robeson, who has almost single-handedly waged the battle for recognition of the Negro as a true artist, with the 'Luke' of this film . . . a simple-minded, docile sharecropper." The left-wing white-run paper *PM* was no less brusque, denouncing the film's "utter failure to visualize Negroes in any realer terms than as a *Green Pastures* flock in a Thomas Hart Benton setting." The black actor Clarence Muse spoke out in Robeson's defense, claiming that the "ideological" words spoken by Luke in the film gave the lie to dismissals of the character as a mere Uncle Tom; and from Hollywood came reports of a "secret meeting" at Eddie Anderson's home to deny that "the human interest sequence of rural Negro life" was in any sense "disgraceful."[61]

Still, the outcry against the film was sharp, and when it opened in Los Angeles, the militant *Sentinel and Tribune* organized pickets to demonstrate. Robeson threw in his lot with the demonstrators, declaring he would join any picket line that might appear during the film's New York showing. In a widely publicized series of interviews, he explained how his initial hopes for the film had been dashed during production, the portrayal of a Negro sharecropper degenerating into just one more "plantation hallelujah shouter," into a simple-minded, docile darky mistaking money dropped from an airplane for a gift from the Lord. Robeson denied that he'd made the picture for money—correcting his reported fifty-thousand-dollar salary to an accurate ten thousand, and pointing out that he had recently turned down more lucrative offers. He had been led to believe he would be able to make script changes; when they were rejected, he could not afford to buy his way out of the contract. This was a familiar enough result—indeed, with a few changes in detail, it could stand as a paradigm for most of Robeson's career in films.[62]

This time around, Robeson drew the line. Calling a press conference, he announced that he was quitting Hollywood for good. A New York *Daily News* reporter ascribed Robeson's discontent to "a way of feeling" Communists have "about any play, book or movie that was not engineered by a Communist." He had, in truth, tried the only options available to a black performer and had found all of them wanting. He had acted in a "race movie" (Micheaux's *Body and Soul*), had tried making an experimental film (*Borderline*), and had used his limited leverage to change the roles and the scripts available from the major studios. None of these routes had proved satisfying; none had offered him the chance to play parts commensurate with his sense of political responsibility. Reflecting on Robeson's film career, Sidney Poitier, a leading figure in the subsequent generation of black performers, speaks sympathetically of the mix of "uneasiness" and admiration he feels when seeing Robeson on the screen: "None of that generation of black actors—Robeson, Louise Beavers, Ethel Waters, Hattie McDaniel, Rochester, Frank Wilson—was given anything to play that did not characterize 'minority roles.' They were appendages to the other actors, the white actors. They were there almost as scenery. To have them as full-blooded individuals with the ability to think through their own problems and to chart their own course—American films were not into that. Difficult as it is today, it is nowhere near as impossible as it was for Robeson."[63]

In announcing to the press his retirement from films, Robeson said the only solution to big-budget stereotyping was for the federal government to impose standards of "honest treatment"—and for filmmakers to turn to low-budget projects not reliant on a reactionary Southern market for profits. *Native Land* was exactly the sort of alternative cinema Robeson had in mind. Directed by Leo Hurwitz and Paul Strand, with a score by Marc Blitzstein and with Robeson narrating off-camera, *Native Land* was a feature-length documentary that re-enacted scenes of civil-liberties violations as actually revealed in testimony before the LaFollette Senate Committee during its investigation into infringements against the Bill of Rights. Robeson accepted the minimum fee AFRA allowed—and then made a gift of the fee to the nonprofit, progressive producers, Frontier Films. Because of financial stringency, the film took nearly five years to complete (as early as 1939 Robeson had been one of several celebrities to join in sponsoring a benefit screening of rushes), and was finally released in New York in May 1942. The timing proved inauspicious. Frontier Films had by then disbanded, and in a wartime climate stressing the need for national unity, some viewed *Native Land* as impolitic, others as subversive. An FBI report labeled the film "obviously a Communist project," and Texas Congressman Martin Dies, head of the House Committee on Un-American Activities, included Robeson, along with Frontier Films, on the list he presented to Congress in September 1942 of people and organizations he considered "Communist." In 1942 that accusation was aberrant; within a few years it would be commonplace.[64]

Tales of Manhattan did not seriously compromise Robeson's image in the black community: even if he had not patiently explained his reasons for accepting the role and freely confessed to his error, blacks knew that the odds against a black man's making his way necessarily made him something less than a free agent. In the face of those odds, many blacks in the comparatively optimistic, patriotic climate of the early forties were heartened by any evidence that one of their own could still come through, yielding to the momentary comfort of tokenism even as they (and Robeson) decried its inadequacy. To the minimal extent that Robeson's image had been tarnished by his appearance in *Tales,* this would be forgotten and then some in the wake of the new project he embarked on in the summer of 1942—an American production of *Othello,* a triumph that would mark the apogee of his career.[65]

■

CHAPTER 13

The Broadway *Othello*

(*1942–1943*)

Margaret Webster, the Shakespearean director, had seen Robeson's youthful 1930 performance of *Othello* in London. "Frankly," she told an interviewer fifteen years later, "I hadn't thought he was very good. But he said to me that he himself didn't think he was very good and that now he had studied and restudied the role and he thought he was ready to play it." Early in 1942 Webster and Robeson decided to work together, but every New York management Webster approached was afraid of a production in which a black man made love to and murdered a white woman. "Everyone was scared," Webster later wrote; "a few fell back on the scholastic argument . . . that Othello was a Moor, not a Negro, or expressed doubts about Robeson's technical equipment as an actor. But mostly they were just plain scared of the issues which the production would raise."[1]

Rather than give up the idea entirely, they turned to the summer-theater route, themselves offering to assemble the cast and pay all freight costs in exchange for a tryout. Most of the summer leasers turned out to be as cautious as the Broadway managements, but two finally came forward who were not: John Huntington of the Brattle Theater in Cambridge, and the team of Day Tuttle and Richard Skinner of the McCarter Theater in Princeton (the town where Robeson had been born). The contracts called for an opening at the Brattle and then a brief run at the McCarter. Only a two-week rehearsal period was allotted, one week in New York for the principals, the second in Cambridge, where the principals would be joined by pickup members of the Brattle Theater's own company in the secondary roles.[2]

Webster, who had had a considerable career as an actress, decided to play Emilia herself; ordinarily she avoided taking on the dual function of actress and director—though it was more widely done at that time than today—but she did so now to simplify the tight rehearsal schedule. Two crucial roles remained to be cast: Desdemona and Iago. At the urging of her close friend Eva Le Gallienne, Webster offered the parts to the husband-and-wife acting pair, Uta Hagen and José Ferrer. Both had had recent successes, Ferrer in *Charley's Aunt* and Hagen as Nina in the Lunt's 1938 star-studded production of *The Sea Gull* (in which Webster herself had played Masha). Though they were already hailed as rising stars, Ferrer had never played Shakespeare and Hagen was still in her early twenties and comparatively inexperienced. Webster's judgment, seconded by Robeson, was to go with them.[3]

The company worked ten hours a day, ardor matched by anxiety. "Robeson is going to be *very* bad," Hagen wrote her father, "but he's an angel." Webster agreed with Hagen's estimate of Robeson's acting but not of his beatitude, deciding early on that he was "difficult to direct," a "special problem." His ability to "seize on an idea like lightning," she believed, was due to his energy and intelligence, not to his acting craft. "Not only has he no technique," she wrote, "which *he* knows, but no conception of 'impersonation'. He can only do it if he can get a kind of electric motor going inside himself and this has to be started by some feeling—not Othello's feeling, but Robeson's. Fortunately his tremendous vocal resources protect him. . . ." (Robeson himself acknowledged that a device he used to excite his nightly rage onstage was to imagine his trusted friend Ben Davis betraying him.)[4]

Tickets for the week-long run at the Brattle sold out within hours of the first announcement, and debate over the production's prospects took no longer to heat up. Scholars quickly checked in with opinions about whether the casting of a black man in the role of Othello was a betrayal or a realization of Shakespeare's intentions. Broadway veterans argued over the commercial chances of the venture, whether American audiences would ever turn out in sufficient numbers for a Shakespearean play, let alone one with a racially mixed cast. Theater buffs debated the extent of Robeson's talent: Had his career up to now been the triumph of personal magnetism over aptitude? Did he, at age forty-four, have the experience and skill necessary to carry off such an assignment? Given the handicaps of an insufficient rehearsal period, a director who did not trust her star's talent, and, for good measure, an August heat wave in Cambridge so intense that Robeson had to wring out his robes between scenes, the prescription seemed set for opening-night disaster.[5]

But in the theater, intensity—the charged edge of nervous uncertainty—is more often rewarded than composed confidence. In one of those peculiar "miracles" in which theatrical lore abounds, every element on opening night fell into near-perfect place. When the curtain fell, the audience erupted in ovation. The contingent of Harvard undergraduates ritually pounded its heels and clapped its hands by way of offering Alma Mater's ultimate accolade. Wave after wave of "Bravo!" accompanied the curtain calls, the clamor so thunderous a reporter marveled that "the staid old walls didn't burst from the noise and enthusiasm." Pacification was finally achieved only after the entire company joined the audience in singing the national anthem. Flora Robson, who had costarred with Robeson in 1933 in the London production of *All God's Chillun,* was in the Cambridge audience that night and reported to Margaret Webster's parents (the illustrious actors Ben Webster and his wife, Dame May Whitty), that the evening had been "a tremendous triumph for Peggy and Paul. . . . It went without a single hitch. . . ."[6]

Next day the Boston critics weighed in with a favorable verdict equal in fervor to the audience's. "A great artistic achievement," wrote one; an "abundantly deserved" ovation, declared another. *The New York Times* and *Variety* also covered the event and competed with the local critics for superlatives. The *Times* magisterially reassured those who had been concerned in advance of the opening as to whether "a Negro actor is acceptable, both academically and practically," that Robeson's "heroic and convincing" performance had indeed captured all the facets of Othello's layered personality. *Variety* went further: "no white man," its critic wrote, "should ever dare presume" to play the role again.[7]

The critics were not, of course, above caviling. Louis Kronenberger, writing in *PM,* found Robeson's performance "uneven"; another chided Ferrer for insufficiently conveying Iago's "charm"; a third raised questions about the "comparatively small and limited color" of Uta Hagen's voice. Some doubts were expressed, too, about the effectiveness of the production, with one critic complaining that Margaret Webster's telescoping of the play into two acts and four scenes had made Iago's already "implausible machinations" still more incomprehensible. But such incidental complaints were lost in the general huzzahs. Kronenberger, despite his doubts, expressed the hope that, "after further polishing," the production would "come to Broadway this winter." Should it do so, the *Variety* critic predicted, it "would hurl Broadway on its practically invulnerable ear."[8]

But the production would not make it to New York for another fourteen months. This time it was not for want of managers—as soon as the reviews appeared, producers swamped Margaret Webster with offers (ultimately she gave the nod to the Theatre Guild). Robeson himself, however, was not available for a quick transfer to Broadway. He was able to follow the Brattle performances with a two-week run at the McCarter Theater in Princeton, but after that he had to meet a variety of prior commitments. The company temporarily disbanded, to reconvene a year later for a scheduled Broadway opening in October 1943.[9]

Ten days after *Othello* closed at McCarter, and with scant rest, Robeson resumed his hectic schedule of concerts and political appearances. On September 2 he spoke at a mass rally in Manhattan, sponsored by the Council on African Affairs, in support of the Free India movement, a cause dear to him since the 1930s, when, in London, he had come to know several future leaders of subject nations—including Nehru. "Many of these boys and I found we had much in common," Robeson wryly told the September rally. What they "had in common," he went on to explain, was the conviction that the era of colonialism in Africa, Asia, and Latin America had to be brought to a close. The current war against the Axis powers, Robeson told the crowd, "is not a war for the liberation of Europeans and European nations," but "a war for the liberation of all peoples, all races, all colors oppressed anywhere in the world." The righteous Allied cause should not be contaminated, Robeson argued, by repressive policies historically linked to the constituent Allied nations. He credited President Roosevelt with seeing "very clearly" that the war was one for universal liberation—unlike Winston Churchill, Robeson said—but did not absolve the President or the country of blame for archaic policies and distorted attitudes; colonialism and racism, he insisted, compromised the moral integrity of the struggle against fascism and potentially diluted the commitment to it of oppressed people everywhere. Yet Robeson insisted, too, that blacks had a *greater* stake in the war than did whites, for an Axis victory "would mean a thousandfold intensification" of their present submerged status, given the "vicious doctrine of race hatred" associated with Italian, German, and Japanese fascism. The FBI agents at the Free India rally summed this up simply by reporting to headquarters that "the Communists" had met.[10]

Robeson continued to sound his interconnected themes in rallies that same month of September 1942 in California. Speaking and singing before thousands of CIO aircraft workers at the North American Aviation plant and at mass meetings in Los Angeles and San Francisco, he emphasized over and over the connection between "the problems of the Negro today and the problems of oppressed people all over the world, in the Balkans, among the Welsh miners, in the London slums"—and stressed that the common solution to those problems "lies in the overthrow of Fascism." Apparently the vision was too abstract for one reporter, who asked him to be more precise about the present attitude of blacks toward the war effort. "Some feel the war is theirs and some feel it isn't," Robeson answered; "I feel it is ours." Though he didn't minimize the persistence of Jim Crow, he felt heartened at "the progress, great progress," being made against it. A month later, speaking before the nonsegregated audience he had insisted on in the Booker T. Washington School auditorium in New Orleans, he gave a somewhat different emphasis: "I had never put a correct evaluation on the dignity and courage of my people of the deep South until I began to come South myself. . . . I had imagined Negroes of the South beaten, subservient, cowed. But I see them now as courageous, and possessors of a profound and instinctive dignity, a race that has come through its trials unbroken, a race of such magnificence of spirit that there exists no power on earth that could crush them." Like many progressives during the war years, Robeson was sounding a fuller note of optimism than he would ever again feel. Yet, all his life, even in the discouraging years that followed the war, he would always emphasize his conviction that blacks had come through the duress of their historical experience with redoubled dignity and spiritual vigor. Unlike many black leaders of the subsequent generation, such as Malcolm X, Robeson continued to stress the success rather than the pathology of black life—a reading as much from his own sanguine temperament as from history.[11]

In October 1942, accompanied by Larry Brown and Clara Rockmore, Robeson set out on the longest concert tour of his career to date—some seventy performances, one every two to three days, concentrated in the Far Western states but stretching from New Hampshire to Montreal to Pocatello, Idaho. It ended up on April 5, 1943, in Mansfield, Ohio; thirteen hundred people jammed into an auditorium to hear what the local paper called "a sort of United Nations tribute"—a program of songs and folk tunes from Russia, France, England, and China, culminating in "Ballad for Americans" and "The Star-Spangled Banner"—and earning Robeson thirteen encores. He returned to New York after the six-month tour, nagged by a persistent cold, overweight by twenty-five pounds (his normal weight of 230 had ballooned to 255), and underexercised (like many athletes, Robeson disliked mild forms of exercise and at the most might throw around a basketball). He promised himself a period of recuperation—a promise he did not keep—before the onset of rehearsals of *Othello*.[12]

Instead, May saw him addressing a giant Labor for Victory rally at Yankee Stadium, along with Mayor La Guardia and Joseph Curran, president of the National Maritime Union. In June he traveled to Morehouse College in Atlanta to receive an honorary Doctor of Humane Letters degree, to deliver the seventy-sixth commencement address, and to hear Morehouse President Benjamin E. Mays laud him as "truly the people's artist," a man who had experienced and expressed "a common bond between the suffering and oppressed folks of the world" and become champion of their cause, who "perhaps more than any other person" had "made Negro music accepted as first rate art by the world at large," and whose performance as Othello had "rendered the Negro race and the world a great service" by demonstrating "that Negroes are capable of enduring interpretations in the realm of the theatre as over against the typical cheap performances that Hollywood and Broadway too often insist on Negroes doing." These words were special balm to a man who had come to resent and regret bitterly some of his own performing history.[13]

In July, Robeson joined Robert Shaw's Collegiate Chorale, with Alexander Smallens conducting the Philharmonic Orchestra, for a concert that filled Lewisohn Stadium's twenty thousand seats. From that triumph it was out to Chicago to sing and speak at a Production for Victory rally at the Apex Smelting Co. plant, then back to Los Angeles in early August to participate in a rally to benefit the Joint Anti-Fascist Refugee Committee and to San Francisco to address a CIO-sponsored conference on racial and national minorities. At the Apex plant he confessed himself "a little discouraged" with aspects of the domestic scene after traveling through the West and seeing the extent of opposition to "giving everybody a fair chance"; and in San Francisco he told the crowd that "the temper" of black people in the United States had changed during the war and that if there was to be a solution to the race problem, "Labor will have to rally and understand these problems": white allies within the CIO would have to help push for more integrated opportunities in the job market.[14]

By August 1943 Robeson had cleared his calendar to begin rehearsing for the scheduled Broadway opening of *Othello* on October 19. But just prior to the start of rehearsals the show's producers, the Theatre Guild, decided to replace Ferrer and Hagen. The Guild objected mainly to Ferrer: his draft status was uncertain, he had received the weakest reviews of the three principals during the tryouts, and, most important, he was insisting on star billing and on substantial salaries for himself and Hagen—while also making it clear that neither would work without the other. Robeson and Margaret Webster took their side. Robeson argued that he worked well with the couple and that their talent warranted their demands; Webster argued that Ferrer simply needed more rehearsal time. When no agreement could be reached, the Guild decided to hire Stefan Schnabel for Iago, and Virginia Gilmore for Desdemona. Margaret Webster had her doubts about Gilmore but was pleased with Schnabel, and wrote her mother, May Whitty, that "Paul—who, as usual, was not to be found for several days while everything hung in mid-air—is delighted with him" as well.[15]

Hardly. Paul confided his unhappiness over the cast changes to Freda Diamond. There simply wasn't the same magic, he complained, that he had previously felt when performing with Uta and Joe, and he wished there was some way Bob Rockmore could manage to overcome the contractual stumbling blocks to their continuing. Freda told him to do it himself—*he* was a lawyer, he didn't need Rockmore's intercession. Why didn't he just get on a train to Ossining (where the Ferrers had a house) and work things out directly with Uta and Joe? Freda says that Paul took her advice, went up to Ossining that same evening, and settled it.[16]

After smoothing over terms with Uta and Joe, Robeson laid down the law to the Theatre Guild. Flexing the combined muscle provided by his star status and his contractual rights, he declared his refusal to continue unless the Ferrers were rehired. His adamance infuriated Margaret Webster. "Against his inarticulate but immoveable resolve, pleas, arguments, threats, reason broke in vain," she reported to her mother. "No Ferrers no Robeson, no Robeson no show. And I, as usual, left to straighten it out." She did, negotiating to buy out Schnabel's contract (Robeson agreed to pay half of the four thousand dollars), soothing the cast's alarm over the escalating rumors, persuading the Ferrers to forgo equal billing with Robeson in exchange for being "prominently featured in all display advertising," and having their salary demands met fully. All the while, she wrote her mother, she behaved "as if I loved them and didn't want to pitch them off the balcony into 52nd St."—in order to "get a show out of that big, black jelly-fish and those two conceited little asses and make us all happy and bursting with harmony and enthusiasm!" Robeson later succeeded in getting the Ferrers costar billing as well—in smaller type than his own name, but featured above the title. That, in turn, engendered renewed rage in Webster; she felt, with some justification, that costar status did not accurately reflect the comparative drawing power of the Ferrers as measured against Robeson's and was, in the bargain, an insult to her own worth as an actress (she had again cast herself as Emilia). To which Robeson responded—at least so Webster reported—that she "had 'got' plenty out of it as the producer-director and in effect took the attitude that if [she] didn't want to be billed below Uta but would prefer to leave the cast that was all right too!!" Webster's indignation may have been fed by having previously miscalculated Robeson's temperament. She now recognized, belatedly, that "This sweet, unassuming, dear, big bear of a man could crush us all." It would seem, she wrote her mother in icy fury, "I have not been playing Svengali to his Trilby, but Frankenstein to his monster." Expressions of high dudgeon in the theater, particularly during the tension of a rehearsal period, rarely survive as final verdicts. Passions rise and fall, and antagonism quickly transmutes into felicitation when a project culminates in success. To that end all hands now bent their efforts.[17]

At Robeson's insistence, a six-week rehearsal period was scheduled—in contrast to the two weeks allotted the cast before the Brattle tryout the preceding year. The praise of the Boston critics in 1942 had seemed to him excessive, even unwarranted. He, more than anyone, acknowledged—indeed, tended to exaggerate—the inadequacies of his tryout performance. He had not yet gotten to the bottom of his role, and he knew it. "It's not right," he told Uta Hagen; "I don't have it." Forty years later, Hagen admiringly recalls his attitude. "He had judgment about himself that was astonishing," she said. "He didn't fall for praise—other people's accolades never went to his head." Along with an "enormous capacity for self-evaluation" went unusual modesty about the work. He was determined to get it right, was determined to acquire the needed additional technique to rid his performance of the traces of self-consciousness, tonal monotony, and deliberateness some of the critics had pointed to. He was angry that he had been denied the needed coaching in the past, that he had had directors regard him as a great "natural" talent—the soulful primitive—who should not be tampered with for fear of destroying his instincts, diluting his force.[18]

Surveying his past experience as an actor, he told one interviewer that at the Provincetown Playhouse during the 1920s, "no one told me anything. They didn't want any 'actor's tricks.' So I was the former college athlete, playing on muscle." Growing up in the oratorical tradition of the black church, he had, naturally enough, turned to declamation when in doubt. Throughout the 1930s, "directors assumed that I knew what I was doing, when the fact was that I had no technique at all. They no more questioned my 'technique' than they would that of a Hindu dancer." It was an attitude characteristic of the time: the art of the Negro was pure, instinctive, unique, and would be spoiled if any effort was made to guide or train it.[19]

Robeson had not been immune to that attitude himself. Throughout the early 1930s he had spoken fervently of the need for Africans to keep their cultural heritage unsullied, to stand apart from the contaminating influences of the West, to eschew imitation. But that was not quite the whole story, either. Robeson sometimes *deliberately* cultivated the image of a "natural actor who had been deprived of technical training." He did so, typically, to cover all bases; he let others think he was stumbling through his roles on instinct as a hedge against being judged by standards he himself, with almost knee-jerk modesty, felt unable to meet; should he be found wanting when measured against those standards, he could fall back on his "noble-savage" disguise. In regard to his singing, too, he sometimes adapted this same double-edged defensive posture, on the one hand studying lieder diligently, on the other allowing the view to take hold that "Joshua Fit de Battle of Jericho" marked the outer limit of his range. In truth, Robeson had considerable training over the course of his life both as actor and singer—more at least than he was always ready to acknowledge—and, had he determined to, he could have had still more.[20]

With the Broadway opening looming, he did turn for help to Margaret Webster. And she did try to provide it. But Webster was accustomed to giving actors line readings; she conceived of the craft of acting as the process of shaping outer form. Her strong points, as a fellow director has said, "were picturing, pacing and energizing a show"—entertainment values, with theatricality stressed over poetry, the well-composed stage composition stressed over the well understood. Typically she would tell an actor where to stand and how to speak—hows, not whys—trusting that her own understanding was a sufficient guide for the others. She was willing to discuss the meaning of a line in a one-on-one huddle—but would then announce her conclusion: "What the old boy meant by that was . . ." When the meaning seemed transparent to her and an actor's hesitations incomprehensible, she would simply command impatiently, "Well, just look at what Shakespeare *says.*" Webster's skill and intelligence were of a high order, and consequently her line readings were rich. But the external process she encouraged was antithetical to Robeson's need to move away from outer effect and vocalization.[21]

Early in rehearsals Webster concluded that Robeson "lacks the quality of real rage." Of his anger over racism, she said, "he could not bring it onto the stage with him; he could not recapture it. . . ." In her view, he "was at his best in the gentle passages" and wooed Desdemona "with tenderness and loving humor." But he "never matched at all" the frenzy and passion the role called for in the later scenes, substituting instead the speech of the pulpit, "sonorous and preachy," with admixtures of "the slight artificiality of an opera singer." Robeson acknowledged that he had trouble unearthing his rage on demand—he had been brought up, as a survival tactic, to keep it carefully interred.[22]

Webster, in turn, acknowledged that, if Robeson lacked the "emotional and nervous concentration which Othello required," the fault may have been her own. "Had I been more of a 'Method' director," she was later to write, "perhaps I should have been better . . . about releasing the pent-up emotions in Paul"—thus granting that the essential problem was not Robeson's lack of emotional resources but his inadequate technique for uncovering and utilizing them. Webster, by her own admission, turned to "tricks to help him—speed above everything; if he slowed down, he was lost." She gave him accelerated line readings, and she tried to "mask his heaviness of movement by having him stay still, while the other actors moved around him." "My job," she wrote, "is to jockey him into some approximation of Othello, and then make a kind of frame round him which will hold the play together. It's very difficult—like pushing a truck up-hill— yet sometimes when he catches fire (from me) he goes careening off at eighty miles an hour and leaves all the rest of us standing. But he's so undependable." His performances showed "immense variation": "Sometimes they are filled with his own personal quality; sometimes they are an empty house with nobody home."[23]

In short, Webster superimposed surface effects, and what Robeson most needed and wanted was inner exploration. Her formalistic gifts and perceptions came out like prose essays, the content impressive and difficult for an actor to dispute—but equally difficult to translate into performance skills. Webster didn't purposefully withhold her help—she gave it in the only way she knew how. It was not, for Robeson, a fruitful way. "I don't think she ever helped Paul with *anything,*" is Uta Hagen's opinion. "Margaret Webster was a brilliant woman," but she "belonged in a university."[24]

Hagen herself was not able at the time to offer him anything more. She was still in her early twenties and in retrospect feels that she began to learn about acting for the first time only after she met Harold Clurman in 1948.

At the time of the *Othello* production, "I thought I knew more and was better than Paul—and he encouraged me to think so—but I wasn't." Robeson did turn to her for coaching, but she says, "I wasn't equipped to teach anybody" then and wouldn't have known whom to recommend for training. Prior to the late forties, "training" usually meant the American Academy of Dramatic Arts or the Royal Academy—"terrible then and terrible now," in Hagen's judgment. Otherwise there were only limited options available to actors: pre-eminently, Sanford Meisner, Erwin Piscator, and Herbert Berghof at the Neighborhood Playhouse (in 1947 the Actors Studio was founded). For *established* actors to seek further training was not then a common phenomenon; once a performer had been "recognized," the product tended to be considered finished—signed, sealed, and approved.[25]

By all accounts, Robeson got along beautifully with his fellow actors; the cast became "like a family," and rehearsals were marked by warmth and mutual respect. Robeson knew everybody's name, even the spear-carriers with no lines or only the obligatory "What ho!" John Gerstadt, a youthful cast member who served as general factotum—making lightning changes for his roles as messenger, servant, and Cypriot—marveled at Robeson's ability to make him—and everyone—feel "special," to convey focused concern for him.[26]

Gerstadt never felt that Robeson's attentiveness was calculated or compulsive—the star doing a *noblesse oblige* turn to elicit kudos for egalitarian virtue or to create a patina of backstage solidarity. Robeson's friendliness was not overemphatic or in any way suspect. He made no special point of asking cast members to call him "Paul"; his easy accessibility made that, in time, seem natural—though this was still a period in the American theater when stars were addressed as *Mr.* Paul Muni, *Mrs.* Priestly Morrison, or *Miss* Katharine Cornell. Nor did Robeson seal himself off in the star's traditional isolation, to be fussed over by dressers, fawned over by fans. (Gerstadt remembers that Robeson showed up one day to play on the cast softball team in Central Park—producing a storm of mock protest from the opposing team: "This is for cast members only! *That man's* obviously a ringer! You're not Paul Robeson!" "If I'm not Paul Robeson," he called back, "I learned all those lines for nothing." The *Othello* team won the game 24–3.) Robeson kept his dressing room at the theater open, except when he was onstage or making a change. The cast was otherwise welcome to hang out there, a gesture the nonfeatured players particularly appreciated, since the play was housed in the Shubert Theater, a musical house whose communal dressing rooms were quite a distance from the stage—a distance that could barely be covered before the next entrance cue.[27]

Gerstadt, still in his teens and "full of outrage at the world's injustice," remembers bursting in on Robeson with regularity to share his latest breathless enthusiasm. One day he appeared in Robeson's dressing room to announce his fury over the continuing segregation of black troops in the armed forces—and his solution. "Wouldn't this be a terrific time to say the hell with your army, your navy, we're not going to fight if the Negro isn't treated better! — Wow! what a perfect time!" Didn't Robeson agree? "No," Robeson responded gently, "no, I don't, John. First things first, Hitler first." Robeson "didn't go on about it," Gerstadt recalls. He never went on about it, James Monks, another young cast member, adds. He would neither initiate political topics nor, if they did come up, indulge in political harangue; he would give his opinion, but not attempt to over-power in argument or to convert. "He didn't put you down because you differed with his opinion"; his characteristic comment would be along the lines of "Well, that's possible, but have you considered the alternative argument that . . ."[28]

"Powerfully cool" is how one associate from those years describes him. Robeson's benign, shrewdly calibrated forbearance contributed to the unheated way the company was able to approach the "black-white" issues within the play itself. No one recalls any semblance of self-consciousness about race—whether among members of the company themselves or in regard to the potential controversy for an audience in a black Othello's playing opposite a white Desdemona. "I don't recall anyone saying 'we might get in trouble here, do we dare?'" Gerstadt says, no attempt to evade or deliberately to titillate.[29]

Whether tactics or temperament played the larger role in Robeson's posture of outward equanimity cannot be measured with assurance. This was, after all, an otherwise all-white cast in a nearly all-white profession, and Robeson, at age forty-five, had long since learned the likely limits and durability of white folks' empathy. Robeson the man was not unlike Othello the character in the surface composure that overlay his interior passion and which, under duress, could give way to the warrior's strength. As he would demonstrate before the decade of the forties was out, Robe-son could give vehement public vent to his sense of grievance, but the event had to warrant the feelings; he picked his occasions for calm, and his occasions for anger. In regard to *Othello,* he kept his manner cool in order to avoid jeopardizing the broader impact he intended: to make of his portrayal a political statement beyond the purview of art—while preserving the integrity of his performance as art. "I like to feel," Robeson told a newspaper reporter, "that my work has a farther reach than its artistic appeal. I consider art a social weapon." And he told the black journalist P. L. Prattis, "Not simply for art's sake do I try to excel in *Othello,* but more to prove the capacity of the people from whom I've sprung and of all such peoples, of whatever color, erroneously regarded as backward." To Uta Hagen he said, "I do the singing and I do the acting because it helps me make a statement, gives me a platform to say what I believe."[30]

"Othello kills not in hate but in honor," Robeson once said: "It wasn't just the act of infidelity" that led Othello to take Desdemona's life, "it was the destruction of himself as a human being, of his human dignity." In a number of interviews Robeson gave while preparing the role, he expounded his view that Othello was a great—and persecuted—"Negro warrior," and that his own responsibility was to convey the tale of a man who had managed to rise to a position of leadership in an alien culture—only to be destroyed by it. To make Othello's jealousy believable—since "under ordinary circumstances" he could have dispelled it with a word to his wife—Robeson felt the foundation had to be laid early in the play by stressing the cultural as well as racial differences that set the Moor apart: his values as well as his appearance accounted for his distinctiveness.[31]

Robeson, in his own words, "listened carefully to directors and Shakespearean authorities, but in some cases their Othello didn't think and act exactly as I believed a great Negro warrior would do, and in those cases I played it my way." He made those decisions with great care. His own style in preparing a role always entailed close analysis and cautious unfolding. As a man of erudition, moreover, he approached Shakespearean scholarship with familiarity and respect—and was well aware that both academic and theatrical tradition provided weight for his own chosen interpretation.[32]

For a century and a half after the play's first presentation, Othello *had* been portrayed as black. Edmund Kean first broke with this tradition when he offered Drury Lane a coffee-colored version—one hailed by Coleridge as a most "pleasing probability." So well did it please, that tawny half-castes thereafter streamed forth from the stage, with such luminaries as Henry Irving and Edwin Forrest playing a range of rainbow-tinted Othellos. (A Maryland woman in 1868 was so delighted with one of the lighter versions that she felt able definitely to declare, "We may regard, then, the daub of black upon Othello's visage as an EBULLITION of fancy, a FREAK of imagination. . . . Othello was a WHITE man.") From the mid-eighteenth to the late nineteenth century, *Othello* had been popularly performed in the United States as an animated lecture on, alternately, the sin of jealousy, the evils of drink, or the perils of lust—as a Moral Dialogue on any number of questions, excluding only the question of race. A host of famed actors had offered the role in a host of hues—excluding only black.[33]

But at least once notably before Robeson, and several more times passably, a black actor had played Othello as a black hero. The great Ira Aldridge first opened in the role in 1827 in Liverpool, with Charles Kean as his Iago. For four decades thereafter, Aldridge toured *Othello* to acclaim throughout Britain and the Continent, and in the 1860s was received with particular enthusiasm in Russia. Théophile Gautier was in St. Petersburg when Aldridge performed there in 1863. He had gone expecting an "energetic, disordered, fiery, rather barbaric" portrayal, but found a "quiet, reserved, classic, majestic" one—"Othello himself, as Shakespeare has created him, with eyes half-closed as if dazzled from the African sun, his nonchalant, oriental attitude, and that Negro free-and-easy air that no European can imitate." Aldridge, Gautier reported, was the lion of the hour. The United States, however, did not believe in a black Othello. Aldridge never played the role in his native land.[34]

Margaret Webster agreed with Robeson's insistence on an Othello of unambiguous racial identity. Only with "a great man," she wrote, "a man of simplicity and strength [who] also was a black man" playing the role, could an audience believe he could command Venice's armies while remaining a stranger in its midst; only then could the sources of Iago's hatred and the extent of Desdemona's courage be adequately measured; only then could the depth of Othello's vulnerability and resentment, his wary susceptibility to tales of the betrayal of his honor, be fully laid bare.[35]

Webster hired the great stage designer Robert Edmond Jones—who had designed the last previous *Othello* on Broadway, in 1937, and had known the Robesons since their days together at the Provincetown Playhouse in the 1920s—to do sets and costumes. She essentially retained her staging ideas from the Brattle production, but in the interim had further streamlined the script. On his side, Robeson prepared for the role by growing a beard and trimming his weight back down to 230. His fifteen-hundred-dollar-a-week salary was a fraction of what he earned singing concerts (two thousand to twenty-five hundred a night), and the demands of the role were greater. He was later to say that playing Othello took the equivalent energy of three concerts; only *Emperor Jones*, twenty years before, had involved a comparable effort.[36]

He concentrated particularly during rehearsals on bringing more fluidity to his physical movements—an added challenge in a small playing space that heightened the static impression created by his large build. He also worked hard at overcoming his self-acknowledged tendency "to be too loud, too big," worked to bring his voice down to the level where he could get the full tonal value out of it and "to be constantly careful not to make my lines too musical, not to sing my lines, but to SPEAK them MUSICALLY." At the end of a day's rehearsal he typically needed ten to twelve hours' sleep to recuperate, and when not rehearsing he stayed close to his book-filled apartment in New York (rarely going up to Enfield), reading, studying languages (at the moment he was plugging away at Chinese), and spending long hours listening to his huge record collection.[37]

For four and a half weeks prior to the October 19 Broadway opening, the company tried the show out on the road, first in New Haven on September 11 for one week, then in Boston for two weeks, and finally in Philadelphia (". . . we eat and drink like pigs," Uta Hagen wrote her parents, "talk until all hours, get up around twelve or one in the afternoon"). Although the three-city tour brought in an exceptionally high gross of $103,000, its progress was not one of unalloyed triumph. Some of the out-of-town critics showered the production with superlatives, but an equal number (and the better-known ones) registered more reservations than had greeted the Brattle tryout of the previous year. In Boston, the best-known theater town, the respected critics Elinor Hughes and Elliott Norton turned in sharply divergent verdicts, representing the generally split decision of their colleagues.[38]

Hughes served up praise for all hands, but above all lauded Robeson, for a performance that had "deepened and simplified since last summer" and was now wholly convincing; his "tremendous magnetism, splendid size and bearing, rich voice," and powerful emotional conviction successfully conveyed—for the first time in Hughes's long experience—a believable hero: "At last the tragedy becomes inevitable, not arbitrary." Elliott Norton turned in a directly contradictory verdict. Aside from a few "breathtaking" moments (for which he mostly credited Uta Hagen), Norton thought the production unconvincing. And for the worst of it he blamed Robeson himself: "His acting does not fulfill the promise of that tentative week at Cambridge." When Robeson could call on his own experience, Norton felt, he "walks with the great men of the stage"; when he could not, he fell back on strained tricks, vocalizing and declaiming to merely "artificial" effect. Anyone familiar with the vagaries of theater reviewing in the daily press knows that disparate judgments are commonplace, that what passes for considered critical opinion is as likely the product of an ill-digested dinner, rushed deadlines, or the psychological safety of reiterating a prior view. Still, the divided out-of-town verdict necessarily heightened the company's anxiety as opening night on Broadway finally drew near. "We're getting ourselves keyed up," Uta Hagen wrote to her father. "Hold your thumbs."[39]

On the day of the opening, veteran theatrical commentator Sam Zolotow led off his *New York Times* column by declaring that the Theatre Guild was launching its twenty-sixth season that evening with a production of *Othello* that the "theatrical pundits say has all the earmarks of a rare occasion in the annals of the Broadway stage." The prediction was especially notable—and a gauge of the excited anticipation—for being made in a Broadway season that saw the premiere of *Oklahoma!*, Katharine Cornell and Raymond Massey in *Lovers and Friends*, Margaret Sullavan and Elliott Nugent in *The Voice of the Turtle*, and, during the same week *Othello* was due to open, saw the Frank Fay–Ethel Waters–Bert Wheeler vaudeville show *Laugh Time* move to the Ambassador. This wasn't just another opening of just another show. Margaret Webster later wrote, "I have never been so paralytic with fright," adding that "for the first time in the United States a Negro was playing one of the greatest parts ever written . . . and [the occasion] was trying to prove something other than itself. . . ."[40]

It did. When the curtain came down that night, the audience erupted into an ovation that (as *Newsweek* reported) "hadn't been heard around those parts in many seasons. For twenty minutes, and half as many curtain calls, the applause and the bravos echoed from orchestra pit and gallery to give Forty-Fourth Street the news of something more than just another hit." Burton Rascoe, theater critic for the *World-Telegram,* wrote in his column the next day, "Never in my life have I seen an audience sit so still, so tense, so under the spell of what was taking place on the stage as did the audience at the Shubert last night. And few times in my life have I witnessed so spontaneous a release of feelings in applause as that which occurred when the tragedy was ended." "The ovation opening night was so tremendous we all cried like babies," Hagen wrote to her parents. The next day Margaret Webster wrote her mother, "They yelled at us through a long succession of calls and fairly screamed at Paul and finally I had to make a speech to finish it up. . . . Then they cheered the roof off again. The notices are better than we are—it was just one of those nights. Magic happened—not so much to the performance which, as far as I could judge, was very good but not more so than it has been before, but to the audience, who just got drunk." A Soviet journalist reported home that "many American writers and journalists" with whom he spoke "consider the 19th of October, 1943"—the day of the *Othello* premiere—as the moment when "the doors of the American theatre opened for the Negro people." All hands adjourned to Freda Diamond's house on Thirty-eighth Street for a gala party that night, the theatrical celebrants joined by Paul's sister, Marian Forsythe, who came up from Philadelphia, and his brother Reverend Ben Robeson and his family, who came down from Harlem.[41]

Contrary to myth, the New York critics were nearly as divided in their verdict as their Boston counterparts had been—though in New York the split was not among the daily reviewers, but between the dailies and the weeklies, with the former nearly all favorable, the latter variously mixed (the disparity perhaps best explained by the fact that the daily reviewers had seen what all agree was the magical first-night performance). The outright panegyrics came from the lesser daily critics—Robert Coleman in the *Daily Mirror* ("the most absorbing" production of *Othello* "ever to command the attention of your drama reporter"), Robert Garland of the *Journal-American* ("in all my nights of attendance on the world of make-believe, there has been nothing to equal it"), and Burton Rascoe of the *World-Telegram* ("one of the most memorable events in the history of the theater. . . . It is unbelievably magnificent").[42]

The five other dailies (whose reputation for critical astuteness was collectively somewhat higher than the other three) were only a shade more subdued. Praise for Margaret Webster's production was all but unqualified; she was uniformly hailed for simultaneously satisfying the needs of Shakespeare and the needs of the modern stage—and for doing so with blazing, melodramatic theatricality. All five critics were nearly as positive in estimating the three principals, shading their preferences a bit for one over another and in entering this or that minor reservation about the work of the two also-rans. By a hair, praise for Robeson lagged behind that for Ferrer and Hagen. All five critics agreed that his performance was "memorable" and "towering," but three of the five felt his "deep organ tones became a trifle monotonous," the "anguish" coming out as strained declaration, or as "song." The two major trade papers, *Variety* and *Billboard*, had comparable reactions, both lauding Robeson ("a great 'Othello' "; "a tremendous performance"), both expressing reservations about his occasional tendency "to concentrate more on vocal tones than on acting," to "expostulate rather ponderously in a monotone."[43]

The weeklies, priding themselves on printing more considered judgments than were possible in the deadline-ridden daily press, weighed in with less glowing accounts. They included five of the most respected critics of the day: Stark Young *(The New Republic)*, Louis Kronenberger *(PM)*, Wolcott Gibbs *(The New Yorker)*, Margaret Marshall *(The Nation)*, and the Shakespeare specialist Robert Speaight. Of the five, Kronenberger was the most enthusiastic about Robeson's performance. He credited him with a "magnificent presence," in bearing, in voice, in manner fully conveying Othello's heroic dimensions; yet he regretted Robeson's "tendency to confuse solemnity with grandeur" and felt that ultimately his success hinged on being "a great personality" rather than a great actor. The other weekly critics were somewhat less impressed. Gibbs lamented that Robeson sometimes employed his "majestic voice" for "meaningless organ effects" (though he doubted if "this matters very much. His reading is admirably clear . . . and he is ideal pictorially"). Stark Young found him "moving and intense" but lacking in an undefined quality he called "tragic style." Speaight complained that Robeson's voice had not been trained for the Bard's verse, Marshall that his "monumental and inert" body was not the supple instrument of a trained actor.[44]

Robeson's own costar concurs. In Hagen's retrospective estimate, Robeson's "*humanity* onstage is what made him a tremendous success as Othello; everyone melted at his *personality,* even though it came through a rather vocal, verbal, conventional, ordinary shape of a performance—the human presence was so big that they went for it anyway." Adding his estimate, the acting coach Sanford Meisner recalls Robeson as "impressive physically" onstage, his voice "beautiful and rich." But, in Meisner's view, Robeson "couldn't act the demands of the part, only recite them—very eloquently, like a good reciter, but not emotionally alive." Impressive as a man in life, as an actor Robeson conveyed to Meisner merely "impressive emptiness."[45]

But many whites and almost all blacks would have regarded such measurements as possibly inaccurate and certainly insignificant when placed against the overriding importance of Robeson's *Othello* as a racial event of the first magnitude. Many years later James Earl Jones, about to attempt the role himself, paid tribute to the importance of Robeson's performance (which Jones had seen): ". . . it was essentially a message he gave out: 'Don't play me cheap. Don't *anybody* play me cheap.' And he reached way beyond arrogance . . . way beyond that. Just by his presence, he commanded that nobody play him cheap. And that was astounding to see in 1943."[46]

Most of the black press hailed the production as a milestone in race relations, but almost none of the white press did—although one or two referred to Robeson's blackness as an asset in heightening the play's plausibility, and one or two others latched on to the production's success as a happy gauge of the country's progress toward racial equality. It was left to Robeson's old costar Fredi Washington (who for lack of decent roles was currently serving as theatrical editor for the Harlem paper *The People's Voice*) to sound a somewhat different note. She interviewed Robeson backstage before the opening and lauded him in her review for having taken "onto the stage his ideals, beliefs and hopes," for having created "a great social document." But she stopped short of hailing the event as a tribute to American democracy. It was only *possible* to hope, she wrote, that "the dynasties of the far-reaching picture world will become adult enough to shoulder their full democratic responsibilities" and to make a *film* of *Othello* "for all the small-minded unjust elements of our country . . . to see, digest and become enriched thereby." That hope would not be realized. Robeson had been in demand for a decade to portray black stereotypes in film, but he would never be given the chance to portray Othello.[47]

■

CHAPTER 14

The Apex of Fame

(1944–1945)

J. Edgar Hoover was among the few Americans unimpressed with Robeson's triumph in *Othello*. The director had already received numerous reports from FBI agents in the field that Robeson had: lent his name to a dinner at the Hotel Commodore in New York "celebrating the 25th Anniversary of the Red Army"; included in a concert several songs originally "sung by Loyalist soldiers during the Spanish Civil War"; made "a speech pertaining to the common man"; been seen in the company of "a wealthy woman [Louise Bransten] extremely active in Communist Party Front organizations"; "pointed out the similarity of the Russian serfs prior to the 1860s and the Negro of the United States"; recorded "the new Soviet National Anthem." By 1943 J. Edgar Hoover was quite prepared to believe the opinion of his agents that Robeson "is a confidant of high officials of the Party" and "is undoubtedly 100% Communist."[1]

Hoover aside, letters of congratulation poured into Robeson's dressing room, awards multiplied, requests for personal appearances avalanched. "I take pride in your reflected glory," wrote William L. Dawson, the black Congressman from Illinois, as the box-office line for *Othello* stretched in double file out to Broadway and the advance sale within two weeks of opening night climbed to an astronomical (for Shakespeare) hundred thousand dollars. Old friends joined in the chorus of praise. Walter White wrote Lawrence Langner of the Theatre Guild, "It is one of the most inspiring and perfectly balanced performances I have ever seen," and added that "the playing of a Moor by a Negro actor" "has given [blacks] . . . hope that race prejudice is not as insurmountable an obstacle as it sometimes appears to be." Even Van Vechten, recently estranged, wrote Essie to say, "Paul's success is terrific. I think it will turn into a record for a Shakespeare run, judging by the advance sale." Noel Coward, who had been out of touch for some time, sent a telegram inviting the Robesons to a cocktail party. W. E. B. Du Bois requested a photograph of Robeson in costume for publication in the journal *Phylon.* [2]

Among the major honors that came Robeson's way in the immediate aftermath of *Othello,* and from a host of different constituencies, were the Abraham Lincoln Medal for notable services in human relations, election (along with Sumner Welles and Max Lerner) to the editorial board of *The American Scholar,* a testimonial dinner tendered by the national black fraternity Alpha Phi Alpha, the First Annual Award of Kneseth Israel, the Donaldson Award for "outstanding achievement in the theater," a citation from the National Negro Museum "for courage and devotion to the ideal upon which American democracy was founded," the Page One Award from the New York Newspaper Guild (for his "distinguished performance in *Othello*"), and election (along with twenty-one others) to the Chicago *Defender*'s Honor Roll of 1943 for having "contributed most to mutual goodwill and understanding" in the battle against racial prejudice. He was also the subject of an article in *The American Magazine* entitled "America's No. 1 Negro" and the recipient (only the tenth in twenty years) of the Gold Medal from the American Academy of Arts and Sciences for the best diction in the American theater. Willa Cather, Samuel S. McClure, W. E. B. Du Bois, and Theodore Dreiser were honored at that same AAAS ceremony—"a really dreary demonstration," Dreiser wrote H. L. Mencken afterward; "the best bit of the whole show was Paul Robeson—an outstanding personality who in my judgement dwarfed all the others."[3]

His acceptance of honorary membership in a number of CIO-affiliated unions produced some fallout. The *Tribune* reported Robeson saying during an interview that the CIO "is by far the most progressive section of the labor movement. It goes on record as giving Negroes equal opportunity for jobs and upgrading. . . . On the other hand . . . there is great discrimination in A.F. of L. unions." It was not an attitude AFL President William Green appreciated. He remarked at the AFL convention that Robeson and others were hindering the Federation's efforts to organize black workers by throwing their weight behind "a rival labor body." When Robeson continued to accept memberships in CIO unions and to encourage black workers to enlist in its ranks, the AFL accelerated its attack on him. The Central Trades and Labor Council, the ruling body of the AFL, demanded he either resign his honorary membership in two CIO unions (the Longshoremen and the Municipal Workers) or face expulsion from Actors' Equity Association, an AFL affiliate. When Robeson refused, Equity declined to press charges.[4]

Along with honors came appeals—would Robeson sit for a portrait, read a script, listen to a song, contribute an essay, issue a statement, sign a petition, meet a delegation, join a rally, support a strike, protest an outrage, declare, decry, affirm, affiliate—polite requests and peremptory demands combining to create an unmanageable deluge. Robeson's inclination was too often to say yes, and even with Yergan and Rockmore running interference, he sometimes took on more than his energy could accommodate, leading to temporary exhaustion and retreat. After a whirlwind of political appearances in behalf of Roosevelt's re-election in 1944, he told Yergan, ". . . I must have been somewhere every five minutes. . . . [It] just murdered me. . . . Of course it was worth it, you know, for the elections. . . ."[5]

As it was, he managed—while playing seven performances of *Othello* a week—to put in a nearly nonstop string of appearances, lending his voice time and again against fascism, racism, and colonialism, and constantly reiterating the same themes: the first requirement for realizing a democratic America was to win the war against fascism; the best hope for blacks lay in an alliance with progressive (CIO) forces in the labor movement; the continued denial of full rights to black Americans was "the argument of fascism"—the exaltation of a "Master Race"; the fact that blacks continued to be "hurt and resentful" was "for good and sufficient reasons"; the remedy was for blacks everywhere to continue to demand the abolition of the poll tax, the end of segregation, the right of equal access to upgraded jobs; the Soviet Union had already provided a concrete example to the world of how racial prejudice could be eradicated within a single generation; the right of African peoples to self-government had to be high on the agenda of the postwar world, necessitating a worldwide coalition of progressive-minded people to combat the "new imperialists" who were using the argument of caution in dismantling the colonial systems as a blind for maintaining the *status quo*. Given the continuing bigotry, the seemingly endless blasting of hopes, Robeson marveled over and over again at the patience and patriotism of his own people: "They may not be allowed to vote in some places—but they buy bonds. They cannot get jobs in a lot of places—but they salvage paper and metal and fats. They are confronted, in far too many places, with the raucous, Hitleresque howl of 'white supremacy'—but they are giving their blood and sweat for red, white and blue supremacy."[6]

Of Robeson's public efforts, his participation in the campaign to desegregate major-league baseball brought him special satisfaction. The pressure created by the long-standing arguments of the Negro Publishers Association and other groups for the desegregation of baseball was heightened in 1943 when Peter V. Cacchione, Brooklyn's Communist councilman, introduced a desegregation resolution. Kenesaw Mountain Landis, the high commissioner of baseball, agreed to let eight black newspapermen and Robeson attend the annual meeting of the club owners in December 1943 and plead their case. Rumors spread that Landis was preparing to recommend that the owners immediately sign black players, but Landis had avoided the issue before, allowing the negative arguments of Larry McPhail, president of the Brooklyn Dodgers, to carry the day.

Robeson took along to the meeting two friends, William Patterson and the Chicago-based Ishmael Flory (who was executive secretary of the left-wing Negro People's Assembly and managing editor of its newspaper, *The New World*)—but both were kept cooling their heels in the anteroom. Robeson, however, was allowed to address the club owners. "I come here as an American and former athlete," he told them. "I come because I feel this problem deeply." For twenty minutes he used his own history to make an impassioned appeal, citing his earlier experience in college football and his current performance as Othello as arguments against the assumption that racial disturbance automatically follows desegregation. When Robeson finished, the owners applauded him vigorously but did not ask questions. Speaking to the press later, Landis reiterated for the record his previous position that no law, written or unwritten, existed to prevent blacks from participating in organized baseball—again tossing the issue back into the laps of the owners, who were not prepared, for the moment, to move. Still, a step in that direction had been taken: for the first time the owners had listened in person to the pleas of black representatives—and applauded them. As the New York *Amsterdam News* put it, the meeting "had a cleansing, if not wearing, effect." Although the color barrier in baseball was wobbling, it would not fall until two years later, when Branch Rickey would ease Jackie Robinson onto the Dodgers' squad. Four years after that, Jackie Robinson was to take the stand in Washington before the House Committee on Un-American Activities and disparage Paul Robeson to the country.[7]

Robeson's efforts in behalf of Ben Davis, Jr., were more immediately successful. Davis, a Communist, decided to run for a City Council seat in a campaign marked by a black alliance with progressive labor; this was precisely the coalition Robeson had been urging, and he enthusiastically lent support to the campaign. At the Golden Gate Ballroom two weeks before the election, he performed a scene from *Othello* in an all-star Victory Rally organized by Teddy Wilson, the pianist and band leader, at which an ecumenical range of black performers—Coleman Hawkins, Hazel Scott, Billie Holliday, Pearl Primus, Mary Lou Williams, and Ella Fitzgerald—contributed their talents. On election night, bedlam broke loose in the Harlem Lincoln-Douglass Club when the official count confirmed a Davis victory, and Robeson joined the celebrants at Smalls' Paradise, happily partying away the night. (In thanking Robeson for his help in the campaign, Teddy Wilson wrote him, "You have endeared yourself more than ever in the hearts of our people.") Davis's victory marked a point of considerable recovery for the CP's Harlem Section from the loss of support following the 1939 Nazi-Soviet pact. As early as the preceding April,

Ben Davis had reported cheerfully that the Harlem Section "is beginning to break records. We have doubled our membership (securing 400 new members in three months)." With the Harlem CP back up to Popular Front levels and Ben Davis's victory symbolizing the Party's renewed ability to forge alliances with influential Harlem trade-unionists and intellectuals, there was reason for Davis and Robeson to believe (in Davis's words), "We've just begun." An FBI informant reported soon after Davis's victory that Robeson would run for Congress on an independent ticket in 1944, but there is no evidence he had any impulse in that direction.[8]

Life was not all hardworking politics and performing. During the forties Robeson was a regular at Café Society, where he would often drop by after the evening performance of *Othello*, often with a group of friends. It had been opened in 1938 by Barney Josephson as the first mainstream nightclub in a white area to cater to a mixed-race audience (earlier "Black and Tan" cabarets had been in black neighborhoods), and soon became a gathering spot for the left. Café Society also pioneered in offering a career boost to a host of performers—including Lena Horne, Hazel Scott, Josh White, Jimmy Savo, Pearl Primus, and Zero Mostel. But even as Robeson enjoyed himself, he was aware of the fledgling performers struggling in front of the Café Society microphone against the double obstacle of stage fright and noise from the boisterous clientele. Lena Horne remembers well his soothing encouragement; Pearl Primus recalls how he came up to dance with her in order to calm her jitters; and Sarah Vaughan, about to be drowned out by the din of clinking glasses and laughter, was rescued when Robeson stood up in the audience and silenced the crowd with a polite "Ladies and gentlemen, quiet, please! I came to hear the young lady sing." Even in Café Society there were occasional racial incidents. Barney Josephson remembers the night an out-of-town couple, seeing Robeson dancing with a white woman, called Josephson over to the table to protest. He told them that if they didn't like it they could leave. They did. Uta Hagen remembers that one particularly ugly incident caused Paul to "really lose his cool" in public for the only time she could remember. A white Southerner at another table—"drunk as a skunk"—called out to Paul that *his* name was also Robeson and said, "Your daddy was probably one of my daddy's slaves. You probably belong to me." According to Uta, "Paul jumped up and started shouting, 'You Bastard!'" and Barney Josephson, who was very fond of Paul, intervened.[9]

The affection Robeson inspired, the extent of endearment felt for him, was made clear in a mammoth celebration of his forty-sixth birthday on April 16, 1944, which also commemorated the anniversary of the Council on African Affairs. Under the auspices of the Council, twelve thousand showed up at the Armory at Thirty-fourth Street and Park Avenue—four thousand were turned away for lack of space—for five hours of entertainment and tribute. The list of performers was a veritable who's who from stage, film, music, and radio—including Mildred Bailey, Count Basie, Jimmy Durante, Mary Lou Williams, and Duke Ellington. Dozens of letters and telegrams poured in from various walks of life and from around the world: Vice-President Henry A. Wallace, Sidney Hillman (president of the Amalgamated Clothing Workers), Edward G. Robinson, Earl Browder, Babe Ruth, Eugene Ormandy, Vito Marcantonio, Pearl S. Buck, Andrei Gromyko, W. C. Handy, Harry Bridges for the Longshoremen's Union, Canada Lee, Walter Damrosch, Oscar Hammerstein II, André Maurois, Rockwell Kent, Charles Boyer, Theodore Dreiser, Rabbi Stephen S. Wise, Thomas W. Lamont, Lillian Hellman, and, from the playwright Marc Connelly, perhaps the most memorably eloquent message: "I suppose by that dreary instrument, the calendar, it can be contended that you are the contemporary of your friends. But by more important standards of time measurement, you really represent a highly desirable tomorrow which, by some lucky accident, we are privileged to appreciate today."[10]

Mary McLeod Bethune, in her message, hailed Robeson as "the tallest tree in our forest," and Joseph Curran, Max Yergan, Ben Davis, Jr., the author Donald Ogden Stewart, and Vicente Lombardo Toledano, president of the Confederation of Mexican Workers, were among those who spoke at the celebration itself. Robeson responded briefly, his voice choked, tears on his cheeks—"Save your voice, Paul!" someone in the crowd yelled—calling for unity among the world's progressives, paying tribute to the African masses, and emphasizing the need to win self-determination for colonial peoples.[11]

As the crowd joined an all-black soldiers' chorus in singing "Happy Birthday, Dear Paul," Army Intelligence agents scanned the audience for familiar faces and forwarded a detailed report, which was shared with the FBI. The agent covering the rear floor observed the arrival of Raissa and Earl Browder, and noted that "Browder, who did not speak, was seated in a front row and was observed placing his arm around Zero Mostel in a very friendly fashion." The government agents also noted that they had been unable to locate Adam Clayton Powell, Jr., Roy Wilkins, or "other leading figures in the National Association for the Advancement of Colored People or the Urban League" in the crowd, and that no mention was made of their names during the course of the celebration. The significance, according to the intelligence report, was that "a rift may be developing among the Negro leaders due to possible rivalry between Robeson, Powell, and A. Philip Randolph for the national leadership of the American Negro"—and the report added, portentously, that Robeson was not scheduled to participate in a forthcoming gathering to present A. Philip Randolph with an award. The intelligence reports exaggerated a "rift"—that was still a few years off—but did accurately spot a growing unwillingness on the part of established black leaders to associate with "Communist sympathizers."[12]

Three months after the birthday celebration, *Othello* ended its Broadway run in preparation for a national tour. At the time of the show's closing, it was still playing to standees, had taken in nearly a million dollars at the box office, and had set an all-time Broadway record for a Shakespearean production with 296 performances. After a two-month vacation, the show embarked on a thirty-six-week coast-to-coast tour of the United States and Canada, beginning in Trenton, New Jersey, in September 1944 and ultimately taking the company to forty-five cities in seventeen states, covering nearly fifteen thousand railroad miles. The tour proved a personal as well as a professional milestone: on it Robeson and Uta Hagen intensified a love affair that had begun during the New York production.[13]

The striking young actress was an appealing combination of innocence and high spirits, of ebullient humor and serious purpose. Her European background (in Germany, her mother was an opera singer, her father a distinguished academic) gave her a bedrock of traditional values, which played off in easy tandem against the enthusiastic ardor acquired during an American girlhood; she was a woman simultaneously passionate, proper, and strong-willed. Hagen had not initially thought of Robeson romantically or sexually—"I thought of him as a fabulous older friend," she later recalled. Then one night they were standing in the wings waiting for an entrance and joking together. Suddenly, with total boldness and confidence, Robeson "took his *enormous* hand—costume and all—and put it between my legs. I thought, What *happened* to me?! It was being assaulted in the most phenomenal way, and I thought, What the hell, and I got unbelievably excited. I was flying! Afterwards I looked at him with *totally* different eyes. He suddenly became a sex object." In retrospect Hagen is convinced that her initial *lack* of sexual interest in him had been a challenge; pursued all his life by white women, Robeson by his mid-forties found indifference a stimulant. Up to this point in her life, Hagen had seen herself as utterly conventional; sex and love for her were inseparable, and the idea of a spontaneous sexual response to someone, let alone an extramarital affair, had seemed entirely foreign.[14]

As Paul and Uta began to spend more time together, and as rumors of their liaison spread, Joe Ferrer, according to Uta, seemed indifferent. He was himself seeing a member of the *Othello* touring company, and he seemed to Uta "unbelievably happy to pass me off onto Paul." Joe proved altogether cooperative, and even took to whistling outside a closed door to avoid surprising the couple. He would later claim not to have known of the affair initially, but both Uta and Paul believed he was well aware of it from the beginning.

When in New York, the Ferrers continued to live together, and Robeson continued to stay at the home of Freda Diamond and Barry Baruch. Since Uta and Paul sometimes rendezvoused there, the idea never crossed Uta's mind that he and Freda were themselves involved (though he did talk to her often about how much he had loved Yolande Jackson). "I was naïve enough to think," Uta said years later, "that this only happened if one was deeply in love. In other words, that it was a consequential relationship. That it was just 'a fling' never occurred to me. To just 'do it' for fun, I'd never done in my life. I had no idea he was doing anything with Freda. I had no idea he was doing anything with anybody!" When she finally realized that Paul and Freda were lovers as well as friends, she confronted Paul. He not only acknowledged the truth but expressed surprise that Uta had not known. He also agreed to stop seeing Freda—which he did not do. Uta moved him into her house, maneuvering Joe Ferrer into issuing the invitation on the pretext that Paul had had a fight with Barry and Freda and could no longer live with them.

Paul had not, up to that point, ever mentioned marriage to Uta—on that score he had been scrupulous. He did tell her that he "despised" Essie, that he never saw her except from necessity (Uta met her only three or four times in the two years she and Paul were together), and he constantly denigrated her, mocking what he saw as her pretentions, expressing scorn, for example, for the white-pillared "Southern mansion" at Enfield in which she took such pride. Uta was persuaded that he "loathed Essie," but sometimes wondered whether his unaccented negativism wasn't partly calculated for her benefit. It may have been. On occasion he certainly did loathe Essie—and she him, a condition not unknown even to the most devoted pair-bonders (which Paul and Essie were not). But residual affection, intertwined with dependency, could sometimes resurface as well. He was still capable of sending off a loving note to her as late as 1942, while preparing *Othello:* "Love me—Hug me often. I adore you—Love you."[15]

But, whether he did indeed "loathe" Essie, Paul made it clear that he would never leave her, and particularly not for a white woman; he knew that the outcry against him in the black community would be too great, destroying his effectiveness as a public figure. Although this was true enough, Uta got the additional sense that Essie had come to serve Paul over the years as a convenient cover: he could sleep around freely while using his "unbreakable" ties to her as a plausible device for avoiding any binding commitment to a new partner. And he did sleep around, as Uta gradually came to realize: "He had many, many that I know of personally. There was a girl in every port. When we went around to these homes on the tour I had the feeling that every hostess we went to he'd had a thing with. I think there were many, many, *many* women." But, he told Uta, there were relatively few black women (and they tended to be light-skinned)—though perhaps, too, there were not quite so few as he suggested.[16]

All this dawned on Uta slowly—these were all the "questions I had after I grew away from him." During most of their two years together, "I loved him so much that I kind of passed it off," persuaded that their importance to each other was profound, of a different order from his frequent flings. And Paul encouraged that view; though he avoided any serious discussion of marriage, he would sometimes talk passionately, romantically, of "running off together—to Russia maybe, to anywhere." Uta later came to realize that he was uninterested in committing himself permanently to any one woman—"I wanted to marry Yo [Yolande Jackson]," she quoted him as saying many times; "she's the only woman I ever wanted to marry"; he talked about Yolande "continuously, with tenderness, with enormous respect, with nostalgia"—and told Uta that she and Yolande were a lot alike. Uta tried not to prod him into agreeing to a permanent arrangement he did not authentically want, tried to stay satisfied with the apparent intensity of his devotion.

The nine months on tour with *Othello* were, from Uta's perspective, particularly "wonderful." Joe Ferrer carried off his side of the arrangement with contented aplomb, sharing like a true comrade in the tense adventures of a racially mixed traveling company. And the adventures were many.

Although there was a steady flow of hate mail, no actual performance was disrupted—no catcalls, no titters, no incidents. But outside the theater the story was different. Early on in the tour, the tone was set for much of what followed. In Boston, the Ferrers went out one night with a classmate of Joe's from Princeton who was then a vice-president of the Statler chain. Complimenting him on the liberality of Statler hotels in admitting people of all races, they expressed puzzlement over their inability to get served in a Statler restaurant when they were with Paul. "You can go into any restaurant you want," their friend replied. "Here's what will happen. You'll ask for dinner, and if the dining room is empty, you'll be told there are no tables. If you complain, you will wait. Finally they will seat you. Next to the kitchen. Then you will wait forty-five minutes for a menu. Then you will wait forty-five minutes for your first course. And it will be burnt. And before long you will leave, and you won't come back again." His tone, as Hagen remembers it, was utterly matter-of-fact. But, as she soon learned, racism in Boston did not always wear a bland face. One day she and Paul were descending in the hotel elevator, her arm linked through his, when the door opened and a woman got on, took one look at them, and actually spat in Uta's face—"It was so unexpected that I didn't do anything about it, and neither did Paul."[17]

Soon after, the company manager announced that he was canceling an upcoming stop in Indianapolis. He had been unable to get Paul a hotel reservation, and complaints were being made there about desegregating the theater. Paul had a clause in his contract barring any performance in a Jim Crow house, so the Indianapolis engagement had come to seem like more of a hassle than it was worth. Paul intervened; he told the company manager to forget about the hotel—it was more important that Indianapolis see the play. Then a mixup with plane tickets raised a new obstacle. After the rest of the company had gone ahead from Dayton to Indianapolis, the Ferrers and Robeson found themselves still in Dayton with only two available seats on the flight out. Joe volunteered to take the train, but Paul insisted that *he* stay behind—it would be unwise for him to travel alone to Indianapolis with a white woman. Paul won the argument, but the Ferrers felt nervous about leaving him. Dayton was not a hospitable town for blacks—Paul had told them about a racial incident when he had last been in Dayton, some twenty-five years earlier, playing professional football— and, besides, the only available transportation for him to Indianapolis turned out to be a 4:00 a.m. bus.[18]

The next morning the Ferrers sat around the bus depot in Indianapolis anxiously awaiting Paul's arrival. When the bus finally did pull in, the exhausted trio went off to a hotel where desegregated facilities had finally been found—except that Paul's room turned out to be nonexistent: the hotel had put him into a back office, hastily assembling a dresser, a fan, and a cot. Joe told the desk clerk that the room was unacceptable—which set the clerk to grinning with pleasure: "Then Mr. Robeson will not be staying here?" Paul immediately accepted the room. After a few hours' sleep, all three moved out to stay with friends of Paul's, but they did so with a flourish: the Ferrers gave Paul their key, announcing to the desk clerk that "Mr. Robeson is taking our room." None of them slept in it again, but once a day Paul would arrive at the hotel, check in, use the toilet, wash his hands, come out again—and return to his friends. Occasionally racism took a comical turn. In Sacramento, after yet another snarl with room reservations had finally been cleared up, the bellboy, who had been pleasant and sympathetic, came in to where Joe, Paul, and Uta had been waiting, looked at their luggage, and said, "I beg pardon. How would you like me to segregate the luggage?" "Son-of-a-bitch," Paul said, as the three of them broke up with laughter, "now they're doing it to the luggage."[19]

When the tour reached Montreal, Uta was startled at how respectfully people treated Paul, and the difference it made in him—"It was like some-body took the weights off his shoulders; he was like an open, free, normal human being, without having to prove himself, without being 'charming.' He just *was.*" But tension did not entirely subside. One night at the Royal Alexandra Theatre in Toronto, panic developed onstage when it suddenly seemed that part of the audience had risen from its seats and was moving *toward* them—not to commit mayhem, it turned out, but to escape from smoke, which was seeping into the theater from a faulty furnace. In Winnipeg, Canadian hospitality reached its apogee: after they missed a connection, the mayor arranged for the royal railway car to be attached to a troop train passing through, and they sailed across the continent in high style— only to "regain our racial tensions in Seattle."

Uta was intrigued by the way Paul handled the race issue. He seldom lost his temper, and in public almost never. Faced with bigotry in a social situation, he would alternately turn on the charm or the "old jigaboo stuff"—enjoying the spectacle of confusion on the perplexed white faces unable to decide if Robeson was putting them on or putting them down. "He had eighteen roles that he played on different occasions, totally aware of what he was doing," of the impression he was creating, doubling Uta up with silent laughter at his expert performances. He could play a variety of roles among blacks, too. When the company performed in Cleveland, they were entertained by the wealthy black community—"unbelievable snobs," in Uta's opinion—and Paul alerted her in advance to watch how he handled them; he played their own game, as if he were one of them, but later mocked their pretensions. ("It was certainly never boring," Uta added.) On the other hand, at a postperformance party in Indianapolis at the home of Ted Cable, with attorneys Charles Chandler, Henry J. Richardson, Jr. (later an attorney for the NAACP), and (in Richardson's words) "other satellites of intellect and culture," Paul became genuinely absorbed in the conversation, sitting around until the early hours of the morning talking "in a communitive social session . . . [about] the fundamentals of our social order. . . ."[20]

Robeson's need to test himself, to rise to the challenge of dislike or disdain, to win over *everybody* through charm, sometimes became compulsive. For example, the Ferrers had a black woman from the South named Frances working for them who, on first hearing Robeson was coming to dinner, slammed the door and retreated to her bedroom. When finally coaxed out, she refused to cook or serve during Robeson's visit: "We niggers don't wait on each other!" Good as her word, Frances stayed in her room the whole time Robeson was there, and Uta cooked the dinner. Subsequently, on a train trip to Boston, Frances was part of the traveling group that included Paul, the Ferrers, and their baby daughter, Letty. When they reached the station stop, Paul walked up to Frances, took her bag and Letty's toys, and carried them down onto the platform. "It had become his cause to win her around," Uta believed, and he succeeded: "Frances was hooked. By the time we left Boston, he was her idol!"

Uta was hooked, too. The more time she spent with Paul, the more deeply she fell in love. She idolized him without idealizing him. He was "brilliant and exciting—but no saint, that's for sure." At times he could be "unbelievably selfish," "insanely possessive," downright "cruel." At one low ebb, frightened and guilty about her own infidelity, depressed that her relationship with Paul was not going anywhere, missing her daughter on the road and wanting another child, Uta briefly reunited with Joe and became pregnant. According to Uta, Paul "went insane," got very drunk, and in a room in Seattle hit her—which, in her view, contributed to her eventual miscarriage. Afterward, she says, he wept with remorse and begged Uta to understand that he had lost his head because he loved her so much and couldn't bear the thought that she might be carrying another man's child. (Perhaps he "went insane," too, because being told of a pregnancy might have brought to mind Essie's announcement in 1921—or at least the fear of being "trapped" into marriage.) Uta forgave him, but not without wondering whether he did accept full responsibility for his behavior or was using the excuse of "passion" as a rationalization. It was not the kind of question, she decided, that Paul was likely to ask himself. For all his unorthodox ways, he was a "traditional male" in his expectations of his mate—she was supposed to be there for *him:* "He wouldn't have said it, but if I was going to be with him, that would have been my life."

It was a decision that Uta at the time was perfectly willing to make. She realizes in retrospect that she would "never have had my own life" if she had stayed with Paul, but nonetheless, not being conventionally ambitious, she would "definitely" have "gone anywhere and done anything" to be with him, would have been willing "to follow him around." She had never known a more enchanting man, for all his faults. "There was nothing smug or arrogant or know-it-all" about him. He had an insatiable curiosity and a scholar's passion for knowledge, and lost all interest in mere one-upsmanship when any true discourse was possible; if he enjoyed charming people, he preferred convincing them (and in Uta's words, he "was as persuasive as a Jesuit.") He and Uta would spend hours together reading Pushkin and Chekhov, listening to music, studying the etymology of language, his "wonderful ear for sound" and his ardor combining to make those times magical for her. When he didn't know something, he "was always the first to acknowledge it, dying of curiosity to find out more"; she found his open eagerness "unbelievably endearing." And, always, he made you feel that *"you* were the center of his mind and his imagination." He had the "remarkable ability to concentrate on you at the seeming expense of everybody around," confirming the fantasy that no one else mattered, or mattered nearly so much. *"That* was his power."

At Chicago, the last stop on the tour, Essie came out from New York with Bob and Clara Rockmore to see the opening and to celebrate Paul's forty-seventh birthday. It was not a happy occasion. News of President Roosevelt's death came during the Chicago run. The cast dedicated a performance to his memory, and Robeson made a curtain speech that night that, according to Studs Terkel, moved many to tears; the President's death, Robeson predicted, would alter things, and not for the better, for many years to come. Until Chicago, the production had been receiving brilliant reviews; Uta thought Paul was better on tour than he had been on Broadway, working more internally, less for outer form. But in Chicago the show was off—perhaps because of distress over Roosevelt's death—and the critics were merely lukewarm. Essie's indignation focused on the *offstage* show.[21]

She had only agreed to go to Chicago, she later wrote Paul, at Bob Rockmore's suggestion: "He thought Freda might be there [she was not], and I would be a bulwark." But on arrival Essie found herself first put in "a travelling salesman's bedroom" in the Sherman Hotel and then shifted to "a back apartment with a fire-escape, from which I was robbed," while Bob and Clara had "a lovely corner suite" and Paul was "elegantly housed in the penthouse apartment with Joe and Uta." Taking the high ground, she admonished Paul for the damage to his own public image: "Your white lawyer and his wife were elegantly housed. Your colored wife was put in first one dump, and then another. What do you think the hotel personnel thought of that one? I was embarrassed for you, Honey, because that sort of thing is beneath you. The few dollars you saved weren't worth the loss of general dignity, nor the personal insult to me." Henceforth, she wrote Paul, she would reserve—and pay for—her own room. She would also make "a careful note" of the fact that Paul had not invited her to Chicago, that she therefore "had no right to be there at all, at all," and would "never make that mistake again." Perhaps, she concluded, "I'm unduly sensitive. I doubt it. Could be I take my dignity, and your dignity, too seriously. I doubt it, but could be. Anyway, that's the way I am." She shared a private laugh about *his* dignity with Larry Brown: "I love the new title for the Boss. His Moorship. That's very good."[22]

Essie was feeling her worth. Over the previous two years she had been holed up in Enfield, eschewing the glamorous life she had previously clamored for, in order to attempt, once again, to make an independent career for herself. It had not been an easy time. Paul, Jr. (as he was now known), had gone off to study engineering as an undergraduate at Cornell, and she had been left alone at Enfield with her aging and ever-more-querulous mother. Within a few years, Ma Goode would become increasingly delusional, and Essie would have to put her into a nursing home in Massachusetts, but even now, as she wrote her son, "She is proving more and more difficult. . . . No, she hasn't cracked up, but is just 'more so' of everything she was, if you know what I mean." Nonetheless, Essie found enough leftover energy to make a major effort in her own behalf and to turn out a considerable body of work. Late in 1943 she had enrolled in the Hartford Seminary Foundation (where Paul's Rutgers classmate Malcolm S. Pitt was dean) as a candidate for a Ph.D. in anthropology, attending classes on Africa, India, and China three days a week ("You are a born academician," Van Vechten wrote her). By the end of 1944 she had not only completed her doctoral thesis, but was also revising Goodbye Uncle Tom, the play she had labored over intermittently for ten years (and earlier called Uncle Tom's Cabin), and reworking the notes she'd taken during her trip to Africa in 1936 for publication as a book.[23]

For a time she had high hopes her play would finally find a producer, her spirits soaring each time a favorable reading suggested a possible production—but none materialized. Her book on Africa had quite a different outcome. When she finished the manuscript (initially called *African Material*, then changed to its publication title, *African Journey*) she sent it around widely for comment—including a copy to Earl Browder. "I would not like—however inadvertently"—she wrote Browder in a covering note, "to say anything about my favorite subjects (Africa, and the Color Problems) which would in any way contradict what we all believe." She asked him to let her know "privately, not for quotation in any way, what you think about its possible implications or repercussions." Browder read the manuscript immediately, found it "not only interesting, but sound," and advised her to publish it. "What a grand relief," she wrote back—and included for his further scrutiny her doctoral dissertation *and* the script of her play ("I know this is a terrific nerve on my part . . . [but] I feel you are interested in these problems, and would not like me to make any mistakes in my handling of them"). Published in August 1945, *African Journey* (illustrated with photographs Essie herself had taken) was well received by the critics and quickly sold out its first printing. Reading *The New York Times'* review ("an extremely attractive and natural book") in an airport, Paul called Essie and told her he'd "got the thrill of his life" from the review; "He's a Sweetie-Pie," Essie commented to the Van Vechtens.[24]

She was thrilled at the book's reception and at the follow-up requests for public appearances, and made no bones about her excitement. "Quite frankly," she wrote Larry Brown, "I don't know whether I'm coming or going," and thanked him for "having been my loyal fan for lo these many years. And especially because you always encouraged me when I was down, and nobody paid me any mind." To the Van Vechtens she reported that even Ma Goode had taken to deferring to her "with incredible respect." Adding still further to Essie's sense of worth was the active role she began to play locally in politics. Speaking widely in the Connecticut area on race relations, she proved highly effective, and quick, sharp, and forthright in spontaneous question-and-answer exchanges with her audiences. After hearing Essie speak on one occasion, a close friend of Larry Brown's wrote him, "Mrs. Robeson was a tremendous hit here. The only lecturer able to hold students in their seats during the entire lecture series. She was terrific. *And stunning.* Improved 100% in appearance." In 1945 the National Council of Negro Women selected her as "one of twelve outstanding women in American life." Bob Rockmore had a different view of Essie's accomplishments, speculating archly in a letter to Larry Brown as to whether Paul had conferred with Essie about "competing" with her as a public lecturer and whether having two rival speakers "within one hearth" might "disturb the family harmony. (Ha ha)." Rockmore's patronization of Essie further fed her well-established dislike of him.[25]

In the 1944 presidential campaign, Paul and Essie had both stumped for Roosevelt, Paul on the national level, Essie on the state one. On radio station WHK on election eve, Paul had praised the President as one who "rightly believes the rights of man more important than the rights of private property." On election day, Essie had written Earl Browder, "I've just come home from casting my straight Democratic vote, and feel very elegant indeed." In both her pre- and postelection appearances she expressed political views closer to those of Paul than had earlier been the case. In "The Negro and Democracy," one of her standard talks, she praised the lack of discrimination in CIO unions like the National Maritime Union, characterized the Soviet Union as having "solved" ("thoroughly, completely and very successfully") the minority problem, and in strong terms decried the continuing prejudice against blacks in the United States; she even expressed the view—an advanced one for the mid-forties—that only "legislation and force will settle this thing." When Essie wrote Ben Davis, Jr., about a "practical plan" she and Pearl Buck had started to work on for federal guarantees of civil rights, he responded that her activity "was confirmation of my long-held view of your capacity to make independent contributions to the people's movement in this country." And when she subsequently sent Davis some unspecified "information . . . in regard to Paul," he replied, "It seems a confirmation of your course of action. Don't be provoked into deviating from that course, for every sort of provocation is bound to rise. It is the penalty for being the wife of a great man—one of the great men of the day. And he is fortunate to have such a strong and realistic mate."[26]

. That cryptic exchange almost certainly referred to one, or several, of Paul's concurrent affairs. The Communist Party apparently advised Robeson at several different points in his life—the word carried through Ben Davis, Jr.—that it felt his divorce from a black woman to marry a white one would be a mistake, that it would inflame his black constituency, alienate his white one, decrease his prestige and political clout. As a close friend, Davis probably knew the usual course of Paul's love affairs at least as well as Essie did, and realized that, since Paul's breakup with Yolande in the early thirties, he had not again seriously contemplated divorce and remarriage, preferring his freedom to a binding relationship, however lonely that freedom sometimes made him. But just in case Paul might once more be tempted to remarry, Davis probably thought it wise to confirm Essie in her already well-settled intention to rise above Paul's affairs, to pursue an independent course—and to remain married to him. It was a strategy she had adhered to from the mid-thirties on, though now and then, under special provocation (such as when given "inferior" accommodations in Chicago), she would take to lecturing Paul about her entitlement and the danger of his compromising his public image.[27]

For the time being, that public image continued to shine brightly, the luster further enhanced in 1945 by two additional honors: Howard University conferred on him an honorary degree, and the NAACP awarded him its prestigious Spingarn Medal. Established in 1914 by the late Joel Spingarn, then chairman of the NAACP board, the medal was presented annually "to the man or woman of African descent and American citizenship, who shall have made the highest achievement during the preceding year or years in any honorable field of human endeavor." The Spingarn Medal carried more prestige in the black community than any other award, and in winning it in 1945 Robeson edged out Channing H. Tobias (New Deal official and member of the NAACP board of trustees) and Joe Louis. The participating members of the nominating committee—A. Philip Randolph, Dr. John Haynes Holmes, and Judge William H. Hastie—had split in a close vote: two first places and one second to Robeson, one first and two seconds to Tobias, and three third places to Joe Louis. Because of the near-tie, the absent members of the nominating committee were polled, and Robeson emerged the winner. When his name was presented to the full board, it was approved—though, in the memory of one of its members, the record producer John H. Hammond, there was some expression of dissent. Because of Robeson's commitment to *Othello*—the tour ended late in May 1945, but the show had then reopened in New York for a three-week run at the City Center—he would be unable to accept the Spingarn Medal until October. That occasion would prove a political milestone for him.[28]

■

CHAPTER 15

Postwar Politics

(1945–1946)

In the closing days of World War II, Robeson had continued to feel broadly optimistic, as he told several interviewers, that "the forces of progress are winning," that Jim Crow in the United States was on the run, that the days of colonial rule in Africa were numbered, and that international acceptance of the Soviet Union's right to exist was assured. But within months of Truman's accession to the presidency in April 1945, and the shifts in policy that his administration inaugurated, Robeson's optimism was shaken, and his mood gradually darkened.[1]

The first major setback to his hopes came at the United Nations Conference in San Francisco in April–May 1945, when the Western powers adopted a set of resolutions on the colonial issue that, from Robeson's perspective, raised the specter of continuing exploitation of Africa and other parts of the world. He had been hopeful that the United States would lead the way in establishing the principle that all colonial possessions—not merely those wrested from the defeated Axis powers—would be placed under United Nations trusteeship as a guaranteed route to effective independence. Robeson, and the Council on African Affairs he headed (which by the mid-forties was the most important American organization dealing with Africa) considered the trusteeship issue of crucial importance for the postwar world.

Instead, the United States introduced a set of proposals at San Francisco for a trusteeship system that fell woefully short of what the CAA had desired: no firm limits set on the length of supervision, no insistence that the Allied powers put their own territorial possessions on the path to self-government, no provision for the representation of colonial peoples themselves in trusteeship administrations—and no guarantee that the Soviet Union would have a voice on the Trusteeship Council. With the call of American naval authorities in the summer of 1945 for permanent U.S. control of strategic Pacific islands like the Marshalls and the Carolines, the future of the underdeveloped world seemed once more thrown into doubt—and white-supremacist imperialism once more thrust to the fore. Robeson began to fear that the United States would throw its weight not behind freedom for dependent peoples but for maintaining the prewar colonial systems of France and Great Britain—a move concealed behind politics of confrontation with the Soviet Union. The columns and editorials in *New Africa,* the influential monthly bulletin of the CAA, measure the gradual decline in expectations: from enthusiastic congratulations to President Roosevelt for refusing to postpone the UN conference (Roosevelt died just before the San Francisco sessions convened), to sadness and anger over the actual trusteeship proposals and resolutions that emerged from there. By the close of the UN conference, *New Africa* was writing, "The hope and faith which the people of Africa and Asia had in America when Roosevelt was alive is now at low ebb."[2]

In his capacity as chairman of the CAA (which the FBI had already begun to brand a "Communist" organization), Robeson wired President Truman and Edward R. Stettinius, chairman of the U.S. delegation to San Francisco (and soon to become its chief delegate to the UN), urging more clear-cut "expression to and support [for] the principle of full freedom within [a] specified time for all colonial peoples." Stettinius replied belatedly and evasively; John Foster Dulles, also a member of the U.S. delegation, wrote to Robeson the following year on the specific issue of incorporating South-West Africa into the Union of South Africa, declaring, "I did not feel that the United States, in view of its own record, was justified in adopting a holier-than-thou attitude toward the Union of South Africa." To Robeson, the UN conference in San Francisco, and the subsequent defense of its decisions by U.S. officials, signaled a dangerous revival of imperialist ardor both at home and abroad.[3]

A USO overseas tour that Robeson undertook in August 1945 heightened his uneasiness. He had planned to take *Othello* to Europe immediately following the close of its American tour to perform before black troops, but when it proved impossible to clear in time all the necessary channels—diplomatic and theatrical—he and Larry Brown decided to accept the USO offer as an alternative arrangement, especially since they would be part of the first interracial unit to be sent overseas (it included as well the violinist Miriam Solovieff and the pianist Eugene List). The month-long trip involved thirty-two appearances, taking Robeson to Germany, Czechoslovakia, and France, and the black paper the Chicago *Defender* reported that his presence overseas proved "a boost to the colored troops' morale who needed it badly." He did bring the black troops an essentially optimistic message about the increased economic opportunities they would find on returning home, but in other regards he warned them that they would "find an America not greatly altered in terms of their position."[4]

But he did not share with the troops the full extent of his concern. In fact, what he saw and heard overseas profoundly disturbed him. The "unwillingness" of American authorities to proceed with de-Nazification seemed to Robeson a deliberate strategy for restoring German power as rapidly as possible, to serve as a counterweight to the influence of the Soviet Union. This interpretation was confirmed in his mind on hearing American army officers in Germany—in particular, officers in Patton's Third Army, in Bavaria—talk glibly and ferociously of "pushing straight on to Moscow and destroying the Bolshies while they're weak." In Czechoslovakia, Robeson's observations persuaded him that the American military would support only those Czechs who had been "collaborationists and Sudeten soldiers" (the Sudetenland, a part of western Czechoslovakia on the German border, had been strongly pro-Nazi).[5]

As soon as he got home, Robeson asked Max Yergan to arrange through the auspices of the CAA a private meeting of seventy-five to a hundred people in which he could "unburden himself" about his experiences in Europe and, he hoped, raise ten thousand dollars to go on the air for one or two national hookups so he could get his message of concern across to a large audience. The meeting took place on October 21, 1945, at the home of Frederick V. Field, the wealthy white left-wing sympathizer whose wife, Edith Field, served as CAA treasurer. A somewhat disappointing forty or fifty people showed up. The FBI had bugged preparatory phone conversations between the organizers, and the reports reveal that the effort to gather people to hear Robeson may have been hampered by a growing distrust of Yergan among progressives—a distrust that would erupt into bitter confrontation on the Council of African Affairs within two years.[6]

Disappointing though the turnout was—only four thousand dollars was raised, not enough to put Robeson on the air—he delivered a strong message to the people gathered in the Fields' living room. He stressed two points: the continuing, even flourishing existence of the Nazi spirit and leadership in Germany; and the determination among the traditional European power elite to maintain colonialism in Africa and the Far East. He specifically connected these developments with Truman's assumption of the presidency, his appointment of Southern segregationists to his cabinet, and the immediate falling away thereafter from Roosevelt's concern with the plight of the underclass around the globe. Among Truman's advisers, Robeson held Edward L. Stettinius, Jr., and Secretary of State James F. Byrnes particularly responsible for the shift in policy emphasis. And overseas he held Winston Churchill predominantly accountable for resurgent imperialism.[7]

Robeson and the Council on African Affairs had distrusted Churchill's intentions while the war was still on. They had hailed the statement on colonies that had issued from the opposition Labour Party's 1943 conference on postwar policy as "a serious and detailed document" notable, despite its weaknesses, for demanding that the "color bar" be immediately abolished in all territories subject to Parliament. When the British Labour Party, led by Clement Attlee, won a sweeping election victory over Churchill and the Tories in July 1945, Robeson cabled Attlee his congratulations, choosing to see in the results a defeat for imperialism which would open the way to positive action on independence for colonial peoples.[8]

But within months Robeson had to revise that estimate, as evidence quickly mounted that the new British government was adhering to the same old Tory policies in regard to Java, India, and Africa. The CAA published in *New Africa* a series of articles decrying the "indecent haste and anxiety" of Attlee to "re-establish British authority in Hong Kong and other possessions liberated from Japan"—"exactly what might have been expected of a Churchill government"—and expressed its grief in an editorial at the "revolting and base" spectacle of American troops being used to assist the British, French, and Dutch in their "coercive restoration of the colonial system" in Indonesia.[9]

At just this time, the fall of 1945, the postponed Spingarn award ceremony took place, and Robeson decided to use the occasion to express his mounting concern over world developments. The NAACP, on the other hand, had expected to use the occasion for its own purposes. When planning for the event had begun the preceding spring, Roy Wilkins had telegraphed Walter White that the presentation ceremony "offers chance to place Association before many persons attracted by Robeson but unaware of our work." Since Wilkins believed that the "downtown audience will follow Robeson anywhere," he suggested the affair be held in either of Harlem's three-thousand-seat auditoriums—the Golden Gate or the A.M.E. Zion Church, where Robeson's brother Ben was pastor. (Ultimately the Hotel Biltmore was decided upon, the seven hundred guests straining its ballroom to capacity). Wilkins suggested Helen Gahagan Douglas, Fredric March, or John Mason Brown to make the presentation to Robeson. Walter White was attracted to the possibility of Lawrence Tibbett, but that name was scratched when Clara Rockmore, among others, let it be known that Tibbett's selection would "rankle" Paul because of Tibbett's "envy and resentment of Paul's success" in the past. Bob Rockmore suggested to Walter White that Robeson's own preference would be either Mayor La Guardia, Marshall Field, Henry A. Wallace, or Henry Morgenthau. The name of Harold Ickes was later thrown in, and Orson Welles was briefly considered—until word arrived that he would ask the NAACP to pay his expenses from Hollywood ("I don't think it worth that," was White's comment). Scheduling conflicts finally took most of the contenders out of consideration, and the NAACP settled on Marshall Field, publisher of the Chicago *Sun,* to make the presentation.[10]

Walter White officiated at the gala ceremony. Marian Anderson, Louis T. Wright (Robeson's old friend and himself a Spingarn Medalist), J. J. Singh (president of the India League of America), playwright Marc Connelly, Arthur B. Spingarn (president of the NAACP), and Essie were among those seated on the dais; and Mrs. Roosevelt, Judge William Hastie, and Henry Wallace were among those who sent congratulatory telegrams. In his presentation, Marshall Field settled for rather bland and sonorous phrases, citing Robeson's "broad human sympathies."[11]

But in his response Robeson struck a far more overtly political note than was traditionally associated with the august Spingarn event, and in the process "shocked" (according to a headline in the Pittsburgh *Courier*) many of the notables in attendance. Venting his concern over the drift of events in the six months since Roosevelt's death, and what he perceived as a shift in emphasis away from civil-rights reform on the domestic scene and toward renewed colonialism on the international one, Robeson warned against abandoning the ideals for which the recent war had purportedly been fought. "The people of Asia, China and India want to realize promises made to them," he said, and black Americans, too, expected the "fight for democracy" to be realized at home. Further, Robeson denounced renewed signs of hostility from the United States and Britain toward the Soviet Union as symptomatic of a resurgent fascism (leading the FBI in its report on the dinner to note ominously that Robeson had said "full employment in Russia is a fact, and not a myth, and discrimination is non-existent. The Soviet Union can't help it as a nation and a people if it is in the main stream of change").[12]

Six years later, at the height of the Cold War, when Walter White and Robeson had become estranged, White wrote a bitter account of Robeson's performance at the Spingarn dinner. The NAACP's initial intention, White claimed, had been to present the medal at Town Hall, with admission free, but Rockmore—despite Robeson's strenuous "espousal of the 'little man' "—had insisted on a " 'good downtown hotel,' " thereby excluding all but the reasonably affluent (no evidence in the NAACP papers or elsewhere supports White's claim). After faithfully promising to be prompt for a photographing session at 6:30 p.m., Robeson, according to White, arrived at 7:45—at the conclusion of the reception and after the platform party had moved to the dais (this part of White's charge, given Robeson's tendency to be late, is credible). Robeson refused to submit the text of his speech in advance for the press, claiming that he planned to speak from notes, but, as White told it, just before Robeson started, Max

Yergan purportedly came to the speakers' table and began to "whisper earnestly" to him—in a voice loud enough to be overheard—that "They say" and "they want you to say" such-and-such in the speech ("they" being, in White's view, the CPUSA). White described the speech Robeson did give as "a lengthy and vehement attack upon all things American and indiscriminate laudation of all things Russian," thereby missing a "magnificent opportunity to make converts," "stunning" the audience and producing only scattered, tepid applause—an overstatement more heated in its choice of words than Robeson's speech had been.[13]

The Spingarn Medal marked both the apex of Robeson's public acclaim and the onset of his fall from official grace. Henceforth his own disillusion with the promise of American life would proceed in tandem with his ejection from it.

A few weeks after the Spingarn event, at a World Freedom Rally in Madison Square Garden on November 14, 1945, Robeson reiterated his fears about postwar developments. He forcefully assailed the role of the American government "in helping British, French and Chiang Kai-shek governments to crush the peoples' struggles toward democracy, freedom and independence," reminding the audience that while "millions of Africans faced unnecessary starvation" and "the tragic plight of Europe's anguished Jewish people has still to be solved," it was premature to talk of "world peace and security"—a goal that would not be advanced by "reliance upon mighty armaments, military bases and atomic bombs." At the end of November, at a two-day "institute on Judaism and race relations" convened by the Central Conference of American Rabbis, Robeson again spoke out bluntly against the "active counter-revolution" that had abruptly arisen, calling upon American public opinion "to bring to task our State Department and President Truman for their part on the side of reaction" and specifically warning that blacks are "not only miserable, but . . . determined not to continue miserable." Six months earlier an FBI report had hawked the false rumor that Robeson had joined the Communist Party; a Bureau agent now insisted that, although "his Communist Party membership book number is not known"—for a time the FBI believed he had become a member under the name of John Thomas— "his actions, connections and statements definitely classify him as a Communist."[14]

Simultaneous with Robeson's developing distress over Western policies came the disarray within the American Communist Party following the release of the "Duclos Letter." Published in the April 1945 issue of *Cahiers du communisme* (the organ of Communist Party theory in France), the article by Jacques Duclos, a leading French Communist, denounced Earl Browder for having made the unorthodox suggestion that the time had come for capitalism and socialism to coexist peacefully and to collaborate in the United States. Browder had first presented those views, the culmination of his long-standing Popular Front efforts to "Americanize" the Party, to the national committee of the CPUSA in January 1944. He had recommended the dissolution of the Party and its replacement with a new organization, the Communist Political Association; with only William Z. Foster among the leadership dissenting, Browder's views had been adopted. But Duclos now took Foster's position, denouncing Browder for "a notorious revision of Marxism, an acceptance of the possibility of class peace in the postwar period which was tantamount to nothing less than a rejection of the inherent disharmony in the struggle between labor and capital." Browder for a time tried to sustain the notion that Duclos's viewpoint was peculiar to the French Communists and had not emanated from Moscow. But that proved not to be the case, and when the National Committee of the CPUSA met from June 18 to 20, 1945, "Browderism" was routed and William Z. Foster emerged as the Party's new head.[15]

Despite his personal friendship with Browder, Robeson agreed that Browder had been moving the CP in the wrong direction. The FBI monitored a phone conversation between two unidentified parties immediately before the meeting of the National Committee in which one of them reported having had an extended discussion with Robeson that same day; during it Robeson purportedly said he hadn't paid much attention in the past to Browder's new strategy, thinking of it "as purely something tactical," figuring that at some later time the CP would regroup under the old banner. He had been surprised in reading Duclos's article to learn how far the Party had gone in Browder's direction—"too far," he now believed, given the resurgence of imperialism and of anti-Soviet animus. He credited William Z. Foster with having foreseen these developments, which Browder had not. He said he was going to try to get in touch with Browder.[16]

These political developments further dampened Robeson's mood as he set off on an extensive concert tour with Larry Brown late in September 1945. What he saw and heard on the tour concerning the deteriorating circumstances of black Americans put him into a worse humor still—the sight of wretched housing and declining job opportunities, the tales of police brutality and a sharp increase in the number of lynchings in the South. The tour was the longest Robeson and Brown had ever made, lasting seven months (with a brief break for Christmas), covering thousands of miles, including 115 engagements and, according to the Pittsburgh *Courier*, grossing two hundred thousand dollars. In Brown's opinion, Robeson was at the peak of his power as a singer and, as the tumultuous reception proved, still very much a popular favorite. And yet Brown reported that Robeson was in a foul mood for much of the tour, and "more difficult to work with than during all the years before." His energy depleted by the round of concert commitments, Robeson nonetheless made frequent political appearances (or, as the FBI agents who reported on his activities preferred to put it, he continued to lend "his presence and influence to various meetings sponsored by known [Communist] front groups"). Among the "subversive activities" the FBI agents noted was Robeson's defense of the right of actors to appear at rallies sponsored by the Joint Anti-Fascist Refugee Committee, his endorsement of the "known pro-Communist" Michael J. Quill, head of the Transport Workers Union, in his race for re-election to the New York City Council, and his appearance while in Toronto at a gathering of the Labour Progressive Party ("similar to the Communist Party in the United States"), at which he "sang the American Left Wing Song, 'Joe Hill,' " and "made a MARXIST speech"—namely, reporting that on his recent USO trip to Germany he had found many American army men anti-Russian and pro-German and alarmingly willing to place ex–Nazi leaders back into positions of influence.[17]

Winston Churchill's speech on March 5, 1946, in Fulton, Missouri, did nothing to improve Robeson's state of mind—nor did his public response to it improve his reputation with the FBI. After being voted out of office in 1945, Churchill had come to the United States to lobby for support of British intervention in Greece on behalf of the monarchy. Churchill and Truman conferred together in the White House and then journeyed to Fulton, where the President introduced Churchill and sat on the dais while the former Prime Minister delivered a searing indictment of the Soviet Union—his celebrated "Iron Curtain" speech—warning that "the Dark Ages may return" if Communist expansionist policies were not firmly resisted.[18]

Robeson was on tour in San Francisco when Churchill delivered his speech. He and Yergan immediately got on the phone to discuss a public response, their call monitored by the FBI. Yergan read Robeson a draft statement he had prepared over Robeson's signature, denouncing Churchill's speech "as both a slander upon the Soviet Union" and—because Truman's presence had seemed to give assent to the slander—"an affront to the American people," and calling Churchill's characterization of Soviet policy a "warmongering" distortion designed "to sow dissension" between the wartime allies. The real contrast between British and Soviet policy, the statement went on, was between the Soviet attempt to build "a strong Federation of equal peoples advancing together toward a common goal" and the British determination, exemplified by Churchill's speech, to preserve "the Imperialist System and to secure America's help in order to do so." It was Churchill's policy, not the Soviets', that pointed to "a path of war and disaster." "The negro people in this country . . . will never consent" to an American commitment to such a policy.[19]

"That's all right," Robeson said when Yergan finished reading the statement, "I feel like you . . . [though] I probably personally wouldn't sit down and say it, that's all." Picking up on Robeson's hesitation, Yergan assured him that he had "consulted a lot of our friends here and their view was . . . that a pretty sharp statement is required." "Yeah, sure," Robeson responded—he could become laconic when pushed—but "it ought to be I say a little more than a personal blast at him." Perhaps the problem could be solved, he added, simply by appending "Chairman of the Council on African Affairs" after his signature—"I just always want to make it as modest as I [can]. . . . I don't want to sort of obviously attack the President and get a lot of notice, you know and all that sort of thing."[20]

Yergan got the message. The letter to Truman as sent went out from the Council on African Affairs, signed by Robeson as chairman and co-signed by Max Yergan as executive director. The wording, moreover, was somewhat softened. Churchill was still accused of aiming at "preserving the British imperialistic system with the help of the American troops and military power," and Truman's presence on the platform was still charac-terized as an "affront" that "makes Americans question whether Mr. Churchill was speaking not only for himself and the British Government but the Administration of this country as well." But the remaining lan-guage was modified to sound more tentative ("we are confident" that black Americans, "who know from bitter experience the oppression and suffer-ing which Fascists and near-fascists can impose," will refuse consent to a policy in support of imperialism). And while the letter called upon Truman to "keep faith" with the views of his "illustrious predecessor," it also contained the compliment and reminder that he, Truman, had himself "made high commitments as to the rights of all peoples."[21]

Even with its modifications, the letter was sharp enough, and Robeson further honed its edge in some of his public comments during the ensuing weeks. At a mass meeting in support of famine relief for South Africa, he declared that the basic cause of hunger was the withholding of freedom: "Let the colonial peoples . . . govern themselves and they will no longer suffer from landlessness and labor exploitation which are the reasons for their present starvation"—and he denounced Churchill's recent speech as exemplifying a scheme for "Anglo-Saxon world domination," which would continue to deny the suffering of subject peoples. In April, Robeson was elected by the seven hundred delegates to a Win the Peace Conference to cochair the national organization, along with Colonel Evans Carlson, the Marine Corps hero who had led the famed Carlson's Raiders; in accepting, Robeson warned the convention that the world was facing the prospect of a continuance of colonial tyranny under a "more highly developed kind of benevolent Anglo-American imperialism." In a speech at Temple Israel in May, he contrasted the "dither" over the presence of Soviet troops "in a country directly on the borders of the Soviet Union" with the "silence" over the "continued presence of British and American troops in country after country all around the world far removed from either Great Britain or the United States."[22]

Robeson was by no means isolating himself on some narrow sectarian margin. On the contrary, his sentiments were still widely shared, and he was joined in his various public efforts by a broad range of American opinion. The sponsors of the Win the Peace Conference, for example, included three Senators and twenty Congressmen and was addressed, among others, by Congressman Adolph Sabath, dean of the House of Representatives; Mordecai Johnson, president of Howard University; and Senator Claude Pepper, who reiterated the very theme Robeson himself stressed: "War is a danger that can be avoided only if that unity of the Big Three molded by Roosevelt is not lost." In 1946 it was still acceptable, even popular, to decry the direction of Anglo-American policy and to insist on the benign, essentially defensive strategy of a Soviet Union exhausted from its devastating war toll. It therefore seemed perfectly appropriate, when Harry Hopkins died, for his widow to invite Paul Robeson to sing the "Battle Hymn of the Republic" at her husband's funeral. And when Edward R. Stettinius, Jr., U.S. representative to the UN, was laid up with an acute sinus infection and could not meet with representatives of Win the Peace, he troubled to write personally to Robeson to apologize for his absence.[23]

Nor did Robeson isolate himself by denouncing renewed outbreaks of racial violence at home. Between June 1945 and September 1946, fifty-six blacks were killed in a reinaugurated reign of terror highlighted by a particularly brutal lynching in Monroe, Georgia, and a white police riot against blacks in Columbia, Tennessee. In South Carolina, a man named Isaac Woodward, a black soldier who had served fifteen months in the South Pacific, was falsely arrested on disorderly conduct charges and blinded in a vicious beating at the hands of a South Carolinian police chief who was later tried and acquitted. The NAACP had, all through the thirties, battled against antiblack violence but had never managed to convince President Roosevelt to commit himself to a federal antilynching bill, though he had periodically leaned in that direction. The latest tide of violence seemed aimed at "uppity" black veterans who had returned from the "struggle for democracy" overseas determined to struggle for it at home as well. Robeson was indignant at the silence of the federal government in the face of the resurgent barbarity: "This swelling wave of lynch murders and mob assaults against Negro men and women," he angrily told a Madison Square Garden rally on September 12, 1946, "represents the ultimate limit of bestial brutality to which the enemies of democracy, be they German-Nazis or American Ku Kluxers, are ready to go in imposing their will. Are we going to give our America over to the Eastlands, Rankins and Bilbos? If not, then *stop the lynchers!* What about it, President Truman? Why have you failed to speak out against this evil? When will the federal government take effective action to uphold our constitutional guarantees? . . . The leaders of this country can call out the Army and Navy to stop the railroad workers, and to stop the maritime workers—why can't they stop the lynchers?"[24]

But instead of taking action, the United States waxed vocal in the UN about its determination to spread "the blessings of democracy" to the four corners of the globe, and Taft Republicans and Rankin Democrats in the Congress succeeded in filibustering the Federal Employment Practices Committee to death and in preventing any action from being taken against the poll tax. Robeson and W. E. B. Du Bois decided, along with the liberal white lawyer Bartley Crum, to issue a call for a gathering in Washington, D.C., on September 23, 1946—timed to coincide with the anniversary of Lincoln's Emancipation Proclamation—to launch "an American crusade against lynching," to demand that killers be prosecuted and that the Congress enact a federal antilynching law.[25]

The NAACP leadership was angered by the Robeson–Du Bois call. Walter White wrote Robeson privately to say that he would not attend and—trusting that "our friendship is such as to permit me to speak very frankly"—to deplore what he characterized as a duplication of effort. The NAACP had already held a meeting of what White called a "broadly representative group" to discuss unified action against lynching, and to work "in cooperation with the NAACP" on antilynching legislation (a struggle which the NAACP had "pioneered for many years"). Robeson's call, a mere month later, would, in White's view, "create confusion in the public mind and would also give comfort to our enemies who would believe that there are rival groups fighting for anti-lynching legislation." Not only did White personally refuse to cooperate, but the National Office of the NAACP also advised its branches, by special-delivery letter, not to participate. In a memo directly to Dr. Du Bois (who was still officially connected to the NAACP), White expressed his displeasure at the old warrior's having lent his name: "It would be most helpful on issues which are an integral part of the Association's work like the fight against lynching if inquiries could be made by you on such matters inasmuch as the calling of this conference has tremendously complicated and overburdened the office." Du Bois sent back a sharp note claiming that White's memo was the first he had heard about "your new Anti-Lynching movement. My cooperation was evidently not needed. It was certainly not asked. If I had been notified, I would gladly have cooperated. On the other hand I have been fighting lynching for forty years, and I have a right to let the world know that I am still fighting. I therefore gladly endorsed the Robeson movement which asked my cooperation. This did not and could not interfere with the NAACP program. The fight against mob law is the monopoly of no one person, no one organization." In reply White wrote, "The tone of your memorandum was distinctly surprising in its tartness." There the matter rested for the moment between the two men—their dispute would reach a climax two years later in Du Bois's dismissal from the NAACP.[26]

Ultimately, Robeson's American Crusade proved only a partial success. On September 23, three thousand white and black delegates gathered in Washington, D.C., officially to launch the Crusade. Scheduled as a one-hundred-day intensive campaign for federal action, it drew the support of dozens of celebrities, headed by Albert Einstein—but it also drew the scorn of Gloster Current, NAACP director of branches, who insisted Robeson had brought "extraneous issues" into the antilynching campaign, thereby confirming that "responsible organizations such as NAACP" had been wise not to affiliate with "groups which merely use the Negro issue as an opportunity to foist their opinions on other matters on the unsuspecting public."[27]

Immediately following the gathering in the capital, Robeson led a seven-person delegation to the White House to petition Truman's support for antilynching legislation. Meeting with the President in the Oval Office, Robeson had barely finished reading aloud the first paragraph of the delegation's prepared statement when Truman irritably interrupted him. He was concerned about lynching, the President said, but the time was not propitious for passage of a federal bill; for an issue so fraught with potential political repercussions, timing was all-important. Mrs. Harper Sibley, president of the United Council of Church Women and a member of the delegation, suggested that the principles currently being enunciated at the Nuremberg trials were inconsistent with the American government's refusal to punish lynchers. Truman retorted with a "reminder" to the delegation that the United States and Great Britain represented "the last refuge of freedom in the world." With that Robeson took direct issue. The British Empire, he said, was in his view "one of the greatest enslavers of human beings," and added that the temper of black people was changing. A snappish Truman asked him to elaborate. Robeson—who later told reporters he had felt it was important to be polite, but not "excessively polite"—said that if the federal government refused to defend its black citizens against murder, blacks would have to defend themselves. Truman declared the interview at an end.[28]

Within two weeks Robeson was called to testify before the Joint Fact-Finding Committee on Un-American Activities in California, chaired by Senator Jack B. Tenney (and informally known as the Tenney Committee). Robeson took the stand on October 7, 1946, and remained under questioning for several hours. Chairman Tenney and his committee counsel, Richard E. Combs, were polite, and at moments the hearing took on a tone of outright cordiality—a friendly disputation among rival philosophers. Robeson was not yet a pariah to be publicly whipped and displayed, not even by congressional investigators. That would come later.[29]

In the course of the unhurried discussion, a number of pointed questions did get posed—and answers made. Directly asked if he was a member of the Communist Party, Robeson suggested that Tenney might just as well have asked him if he was a registered Republican or Democrat—since the Communist Party was not less legal in the United States. But in fact, he continued, he was "not a Communist," and if he had to characterize himself it would be as "an anti-Fascist and independent." He added, though, with precision, "If I wanted to join any party I could just as conceivably join the Communist Party, more so today than I could join the Republican or Democratic Party"; after all, "the first people who understood the struggle against fascism and the first to die in it, were Communists"—so he had "no reason to be inferring communism is evil."

But had not the Soviet government purged some of its own intellectuals and officials? Counsel Combs asked. Was not that "evil"? Were the purges not comparable to lynchings in the United States? No, Robeson answered, they were not. Russia had been living for a long time under a state of siege—England "has been determined to destroy the Soviet Union since 1917"—and also under conditions of "civil strife," beset by internal enemies at odds with the government's goal of "giving life to the common people." Disliking the Soviet system, having "no faith in the potentiality of the Russian people," these dissenters "ought to get out of there or get shot." Did not the democracies of the West shoot traitors during wartime? Had not even the Norwegians—those "nice people"—shot Quisling?

It was important to understand, Robeson emphasized, that ordinary Russians backed their government, felt it represented "their leadership." He likened the situation to his experience as a football player—"The coach tells you what to do and we do it"; it was not a question of being under a "dictatorship" but of agreeing to work for a common goal believed to be in the interest of all. If you wanted to talk about such matters as "freedom of speech," Robeson suggested, you might better turn to the American South, where blacks were being "shot down" for speaking their minds, for asserting their right to the supposed guarantees of American citizenship ("The Negro people," he added, "are no longer willing to be shot down").

"You don't find that sort of thing in California, do you?" Chairman Tenney asked. "Yes, in California," Robeson replied, and recounted a recent experience in Fresno. He had gone into a restaurant with friends and been told they were not serving. "But you are serving," Robeson said, seeing people sitting around eating. He was asked what he meant by "coming in here with your hat on with white folks." "I started for the guy," Robeson said, but a friend saw the man reach for a gun and warned Robeson to hold back. "I could have been dead" in Fresno, California, he said, "exactly like I would have been dead in Georgia. I am not saying the state of California wouldn't have done more [about] it, but I would have been good and dead." Plenty of white workers were "just as bad off" in California, Robeson added; moreover, he'd gone into the fields and seen the abominable conditions under which Mexican laborers suffered. The struggle against inequality, he believed, was a "unified struggle [of] . . . Negro and white workers, both divided because the fellows at the top keep them divided; but their essential interests are the same." Still, in his view, neither this internal struggle at home nor the worldwide struggle between competing American and Soviet systems necessitated violence. He himself believed that "the only way people can get back on their feet is to national-ize the means of production," but he also believed "there is still plenty of room for private enterprise" in the world—"we shouldn't have to go to war with Russia because they haven't got free enterprise." Revels Cayton, the black union leader, who had accompanied Robeson on a series of political appearances in California just preceding the Tenney hearing, reported to Max Yergan that "This red-baiting outfit took the shellacking of their life. Paul made a tremendous talk . . . extremely timely and to the point."[30]

Cayton and Robeson had known each other earlier but had drawn close together after Cayton's arrival in New York City in the summer of 1945 to become executive secretary of the National Negro Congress. An exuberant, earthy, outspoken man, Cayton was the grandson of Hiram Revels, the black Senator from Mississippi during Reconstruction, and the brother of the distinguished sociologist Horace Cayton. A veteran trade-unionist (he had for years been chairman of the California CIO's state committee on minorities), Revels Cayton was also a CP stalwart who was rambunctiously independent of the Party when it came to black issues.[31]

In 1946 Cayton was intent on orienting the work of the NNC around the needs of the black working class and the trade unions, challenging the domination of "the NAACP and the other conservative organizations." That much was fine with the Party. But when, in the late forties, Cayton came to argue for the necessity of forming separate black caucuses within the industrial unions, part of the CP leadership would balk—even though these early attempts, in Cayton's own view, never amounted to more than "a quiet gathering of blacks to talk things over." Nonetheless, Cayton would continue to insist that the caucuses were needed in order to push for more job opportunities for blacks, an effort that, by the early fifties, even the left-wing unions had become reluctant to undertake—and the Party became reluctant to press them for fear of jeopardizing its influence. By the fifties, the Party leadership came to distrust, in varying degrees, what it viewed as a resurgence of black nationalism and of dual unionism—divisive threats to its continuing and overriding concern for black-white unity based on shared class interests. It was the character of the unity—integration without equality—that Cayton would challenge in the early fifties. In practice, he argued, "unity" had meant whites leading blacks and putting the interests of whites first. In the United States, Cayton under-stood, divisions based on race were often a more important determinant of behavior than commonalities based on class. Like any good Marxist, Cayton believed that class unity would *ultimately* be the instrument of liberation—but in the interim, he insisted, injustices based on race could best be attended to by the unification of blacks.[32]

Cayton came to have an important influence on Robeson. Increasingly in the postwar years, they shared political platforms, and Paul would often stay over at Revels and Lee Cayton's apartment, sharing meals, crooning their baby to sleep, arguing political points into the night. He came to agree with Cayton that the black working class had become the central agency in the struggle for black rights. The black trade-unionists who had gotten a toehold in industry during World War II were (like Robeson) strongly connected to the black churches and strongly identified with black culture—but otherwise had scant patience with any form of black nationalism (whether it be Marcus Garvey or the Nation of Islam) that called for a separatist political solution. In the early thirties especially, Robeson had stressed the importance of preserving a black cultural identity, but he had never sought to preserve its integrity through political separation. He remained committed all his life to a strategy of political coalition and, after his exposure to socialism in the late thirties, had vigorously supported alliance with the white oppressed.

Robeson believed the Party emphasis on "Black and White Together" represented a genuine commitment to the ideal of brotherhood, but by the late forties he recognized, too, that this could serve some of the less racially enlightened whites in the Party with a rationale for ignoring black aspirations and for maintaining their own control. As early as 1946 Robeson brought Ben Davis, Jr., over to Cayton's house one night, "just to see," according to Cayton, "if Ben and I would get into an argument." Cayton and Davis never got along more than passably well; Ben represented Party orthodoxy, Cayton represented the mavericks. That night, running true to form, Davis accused Cayton of "petit-bourgeois nationalism" in pushing for black power within the unions, of forgetting that the Party, not a separate group of black trade-unionists, was the vanguard of struggle. As Cayton recalls it, he told Davis to "just look at the facts: the white working class is supposed to be leading us, and where the hell are they going?! God help us if we follow their lead. They're not doing a goddamn thing for blacks! When are they going to start leading, Ben? Our folks are really moving, and if I have to decide between the two, I'm going to go with my people." Robeson had brought the two men together to let them argue it out, and for most of the evening he simply sat quietly and listened. Then he took off the month of October 1946 to stump with Cayton on the West Coast in behalf of the National Negro Congress.[33]

Cayton reported back to the NNC staff in New York that he and Paul were "pounding away on the need of building" that organization, speaking on the radio, at community meetings, in churches and to a variety of union gatherings: to striking maritime workers on the San Francisco waterfront, to a luncheon gathering "of practically every ranking official of the CIO in San Francisco," to Dishwashers I ocal 110, to Cayton's own local union (the Shipscalers and Painters Local 10 in Seattle), to the Marine Cooks and Stewards Union in Los Angeles, and in that same city to Harry Bridges's International Longshoremen and Warehousemen union. They met everywhere with "tremendous good will and enthusiasm," but also, in Cayton's view, "the circle of followers was growing smaller, due in part to the deepening of the Cold War; not only was there a basic lack of understanding of the Congress' program," but the black working class was preoccupied with pending "economic annihilation" due to the closing down of wartime industry. Indeed, the heralded "rebirth" of the NNC never materialized. In Cayton's words, "We didn't have a base, we didn't have any credentials in the black community." With no significant growth in membership, the NNC, in less than two years, folded into the newly formed Civil Rights Congress—for which another Robeson friend, William Patterson, would become the chief spokesman. Patterson was more of a doctrinaire Party man than Cayton, who over the years would become estranged from the CP and would eventually leave it.[34]

At several times during the fall of 1946, Uta Hagen had flown out to be with Paul as he crisscrossed the country filling political and concert engagements. By Christmastime he was back in New York briefly, and Uta planned a festive holiday. She and Joe Ferrer had recently separated—he went to stay at their country place in Ossining, she kept the New York town house—but had remained on friendly terms. On Christmas Eve, Uta went to Joe's dressing room (he was performing *Cyrano*), put up a German Christmas tree complete with candles and a little music box, left gifts from herself and their daughter, Letty, and told the cast seamstress to light the candles just before Joe came in. Then she went home to wait for Paul's arrival at her house for their planned Christmas Eve dinner together.[35]

It was a cozy evening. Paul and Uta exchanged gifts, had dinner, and curled up—Paul in an armchair, Uta on the sofa—to talk (sex was out: "I was having a bladder attack and was in pain," Uta later said; "The Lord was with me—we weren't doin' nuthin' "). Uta suddenly thought she felt a draft. At the door to the room, she had put a high screen which stood about six inches off the floor. Glancing over to see where the draft was coming from, her eyes fixed on a man's feet showing under the screen. She jumped up, went to the door, found Joe there, and impulsively threw her arms around him—"Oh! You came to wish me a Merry Christmas!" As she hugged him, she found herself face to face with two men standing in the doorway. One was a lawyer, the other a detective. Joe strode into the living room. "I'll never forget it," Uta recalls. "Joe looked so little and Paul so big. He looked up at Paul and said something like 'You son-of-a-bitch!' All

Paul said, in a quiet, sorrowful voice, was 'Oh, Joe, no.' It was just awful. Finally Joe got embarrassed, and the lawyer got very embarrassed," and the detective just stood there—and then all three walked out.

Paul, in Uta's view, "had a most peculiar reaction, and got very paranoid. He panicked. He called all his friends. He had them come—I forget who they all were—they came in a limo, they came with guns. . . . One of them was a pale black man with light white hair. I remember him vividly. And I'd never seen any of them before. They went off in a big limo. It was like a Chicago gangster movie." Indeed it was. "They" may well have been members of the "Black Mafia," lieutenants of the famed Ellsworth "Bumpy" Johnson, a friend—and devoted protector—of Robeson's. The "panic" can only be guessed at, assuming in the first place that Uta read it right, that Paul was not to some significant degree consciously embellishing his distress for secondary gains (such as perhaps wanting to disentangle himself from Uta anyway). Yet, if Hagen's further details are reliable, panic is what it certainly sounds like: while awaiting his friends—they didn't arrive until two o'clock in the morning—Paul paced up and down the room "in a sweat," "talking himself into more and more fear," mumbling that if Joe would raid them he was capable of anything, that he might even then be waiting outside with a gun. "I still think it was *unreal*," Uta said some thirty-five years later, "to assume Joe was going to do him bodily harm, that he needed an escort to get out of my house. . . . It was *paranoid*. What would they shoot him for?"—though she does agree that in those years a black man found with a white woman could easily be accused of rape, especially a famous black man who had recently defied the President of the United States and was a plausible target for an FBI setup.[36]

Ferrer's behavior was grounds enough for shock; the affair between Uta and Paul was, after all, two years old, and Ferrer seems up to then to have treated it with exemplary understanding—indifference, even. He had never done or said anything to suggest outrage, or even shown any diminution of his affection for Paul. To this day Uta finds Joe's motives for the raid puzzling. They probably hinged, she thinks, on the fact that divorce proceedings were in progress and Joe wanted to avoid paying alimony. But, beyond the shock at Joe's behavior, Paul must have been reacting to the certain knowledge that publicity about being "caught with a white woman" could be used to ruinous effect—to his career, to his credibility as a political spokesman, to his standing with the black community. The raid did become common gossip, and some accounts did appear in the press; but the only overtly sensationalistic—and wholly garbled—version appeared in *Confidential,* and then not until 1955.[37]

The raid marked the end of the affair between Paul and Uta. "It was like suddenly the relationship had become a threat," as Uta recalls, "and he had to end it. But he did not say so in so many words." After that night, through the intercession of the actress Rita Romilly, they exchanged a few letters and met a few times—"maybe six times after that"—but when they did get together Paul made no attempt to explain his remoteness other than to say that they "had to be careful until the whole thing calmed down." In short order the "silences got longer and longer." Paul soon stayed away entirely, and the affair "just disintegrated." Between her husband's raid and her lover's disengagement, Uta "was mad at men for a long time." Mad, and flat broke. Ferrer refused to give her a nickel of alimony, and Paul volunteered only a couple of hundred dollars now and then for a short time; it wasn't until her starring role in *A Streetcar Named Desire* a few years later that she got back on her feet, financially and professionally. The last time she saw Paul was in Chicago in 1949, when he came to see her in *Streetcar.* They had dinner afterward and, according to Uta, it was "unbelievably nostalgic," Paul "making a very big pitch towards me again." She felt "rather objective about it all—I still adored him, but the spell was broken, completely broken that one night."[38]

Paul and Essie's life together had become so attenuated that, whether or not she knew of the raid, she had long since learned that any attempt to interfere with Paul's privacy could only jeopardize her standing with him. It was a time in her life, in any case, when her newfound success as writer and lecturer had given her a sense of independence. She had spent May through November 1946 in French Equatorial Africa and the Belgian Congo, was writing a book about it, and was collaborating with Pearl Buck on another. Feeling riskily outspoken, she wrote Paul a thirty-five-hundred-word letter in December 1946—just before the raid—on the subject of money, her lack of it and Bob Rockmore's "vindictive" withholding of it. The letter had been triggered by a recent episode involving Paul, Jr. Inducted into the Air Force in the spring of 1946, he had been stationed in Spokane, had found a girlfriend out there and needed a little extra money. When he wired Essie for forty dollars from his own savings, she used the occasion—to Paul, Jr.'s dismay—to sit down and write Rockmore, asking him to send Paul, Jr., a hundred dollars. According to Essie, Rockmore got "very angry" and reluctantly agreed to send him an additional fifty. Essie decided to use the episode as an occasion for challenging Rockmore's stewardship—which she had always resented—over her own finances.[39]

Rockmore feels, Essie wrote Paul, Jr., that "you should behave like a modest little colored boy, efface yourself, play it low," dutifully applying to him as a supplicant so he could feed his "power complex"—he "wants to run everybody"—and his "VERY patriarchal attitude toward Negroes"; it seems we have "a lot of folks among our friends who will always TELL you what to do, and how to do it. YOU must always be the last word for YOU. Even against me and The Papa. And I mean that." As for herself, she refused to be patronized any longer; she intended to be polite to Rockmore "but that's all." None of this, she stressed to Paul, Jr., had been Paul,

Sr.'s fault—"The Papa is too generous, he has never been tight in his whole life."[40]

Yet, when she wrote to Paul, Sr., herself a day later, she felt the need to expound again on the subject of finances. Her set of grievances turned out to be much broader than that, but she started with a restatement of her money problems—"to get it off my chest," so that "the few times we do meet," money would not have to be discussed. "I've never had a personal allowance of any kind ever since we've been back in America," she wrote, "and I've never had enough to run the house properly"; on occasion she had been reduced to cutting the grass herself after Rockmore announced they couldn't afford a gardener. The breaking point had come when she came back from Africa late in 1946 and had had to put Ma Goode into a nursing home; Rockmore's reaction had been to cut her allowance from ninety dollars a week to eighty. "I suddenly saw the light: He'd never have dared to do that to a white woman. Never. But I'm colored folks, and so I can take low. . . . I really don't believe, in all fairness to Bobby, that this kind of explanation has ever crossed his mind. (He tries consciously, VERY consciously, to be pretty liberal). . . . Suddenly, I've had my stomach full. I feel at 50 [her upcoming birthday was December 15] . . . I'm going to start a new life altogether. I'm going to get myself settled and straightened out, so I'll know where I am, where I'm going, and how."

That said, Essie advised Paul to "heave a deep breath. . . . I'll take you further along the garden path and prepare yourself, because its going to be rough walking." She had a couple of questions she needed to ask. First and foremost: "Am I to continue to be Mrs. Robeson? Yes or No." The last time she'd been in Rockmore's office, he'd confided "that you had been going to marry Freda, and proved to me that you were." That news, Essie continued in her letter, "set me back. Maybe I wasn't even Mrs. Robeson any more." She wanted to know. And she also wanted a guaranteed personal allowance ("I should have had one ever since we returned to America. Otherwise I'm being your wife for my living, only, and am merely a paid housekeeper. I feel I rate better than that. Anyway, good housekeepers come high, these days"). The assured income would allow her "to do something on my own. . . . I may even be able to make myself independent, so if ever you want to shed me, it should be easy. . . . My wings are itching, and I think I'm going to fly. But I want good visibility before I take off." Having had her say, Essie promised not to bring up "my personal business" again; "I've said everything that's been on my mind for some time, and I feel better for saying it, no matter how it comes out."[41]

Essie knew how to tough it out, but Paul knew when and how to acknowledge the din—in order to neutralize it and to be better able to proceed on his own unencumbered way. He told Essie (as she reported to Paul, Jr.) that he "couldn't imagine anything more reasonable" than her insistence on a hundred dollars a week for the house and a hundred a month for her personal allowance, and said that in the future, if she needed more, she should come to him directly, immediately. Just two months after sending her husband what read like a firm ultimatum, Essie was confessing to her son that she herself wasn't "clear" about what was going on. "Bobby does his ground-work dirty. He tells me one thing, and The Papa another. And what with all the misunderstanding, and inefficient (deliberately so) interpreting, The Papa and I get more and more distant." Essie may to some degree have decided against greater clarity with Paul, Jr., to spare him—he had apparently expressed concern over the possibility of a formal split between his parents—for when she did allude to additional complications it was in a protectively evasive way: "Of course, bad news is bad news, but if its well delivered, it isnt as bad as it could be. Maybe this is over your head. And anyway, there may be no bad news at all. . . . Anyway, you make plenty of sense when you say: If the three of us cant work everything out, we ought to give up. That's my sentiments. And I too, think its high time the three of us DO work it out."[42]

Essie, quick to flare, knew how to back down when it appeared her belligerence might threaten her own vital interest in remaining Mrs. Robeson. She knew that Paul, ordinarily less quick to react, capricious about the details of ordinary life, had a powerful will. If he came to feel that *his* essential interests were at stake, he could prove by far the more intractable of the two, difficult to turn from any course of action upon which he had decided, insistent, ultimately, on doing exactly what he wanted and telling others only precisely what he wanted them to know. "Nobody tells me anything," Essie complained to Revels Cayton, aware somewhere in her depths that the brash appurtenances of command she liked to flaunt were pale shadows of her husband's quietly powerful authority (and no match for it). Having openly broadcast her complaints, she now wisely decided, "once and for all, to close ranks with him."[43]

■

CHAPTER 16

The Progressive Party

(1947–1948)

Henry A. Wallace, Roosevelt's Vice-President and now Truman's Secretary of Commerce, began to speak out against administration foreign policy in 1946. He, like Robeson, deplored Churchill's "Iron Curtain" speech at Fulton, Missouri, and counseled Truman to adopt a more flexible attitude toward the Soviets in order to control atomic energy and to maintain peace. Truman ignored him. On September 12, 1946, Wallace delivered a crucial speech at a meeting sponsored by two groups (Robeson was affiliated with both) that later that year were to merge into the Progressive Citizens of America; in it, Wallace forcefully attacked the emergent Anglo-American "get-tough" policy toward Russia, arguing that nations with different economic systems could and must live in peace together (the same argument Robeson employed when testifying before the Tenney Committee three weeks later in California). Wallace's speech caused an uproar, with Secretary of State Byrnes threatening to resign and the foreign-policy hard-liners in both parties repudiating it. On September 20 Truman requested and received Wallace's resignation from the Cabinet. The rift had been opened that would lead to Wallace's third-party Progressive race in the presidential election of 1948, but throughout most of 1947 he explicitly refrained from declaring his candidacy. Robeson, meanwhile, remained primarily absorbed in fighting political battles on his own front.[1]

They began to multiply. As early as the spring of 1946, local right-wing forces had succeeded in banning various Win the Peace meetings at which Robeson had been scheduled to appear, or in forcing him to shift concert halls. Embarked on yet another four-month, cross-country concert tour with Larry Brown in January 1947, Robeson arrived in St. Louis,

Missouri, to find himself in the middle of a controversy about segregated facilities in the city's theaters. When the Civil Rights Congress of St. Louis called for a demonstration in front of the American Theater, Robeson joined the picket line of about thirty people. At a press conference the next day he created another flurry by announcing that at the conclusion of his current tour in April he intended to abandon the theater and concert stage for two years in order to "talk up and down the nation against race hatred and prejudice. . . . It seems that I must raise my voice, but not by singing pretty songs." For the immediate future he would sing only "for my trade union and college friends; in other words, only at gatherings where I can sing what I please." A few days later the left front wheel came off a car in which Robeson was riding on a highway near Jefferson City. Fortunately the car had been moving at a moderate speed and no one was hurt. The Pittsburgh *Courier* did not hesitate to report the episode as "a prejudice-prompted attempt on the life of Paul Robeson." The driver of the car told the *Courier* that "the wheel showed definite signs of having been tampered with."[2]

Both the FBI and the gossip columnist Hedda Hopper, on their respective fronts, took due note of Robeson's announced intention to devote himself to political activity. J. Edgar Hoover, in an apparent decision to formalize charges against him, had already ordered the New York Office to "prepare a report in summary form" setting forth "only such information of a legally admissible character as will tend to prove, directly or circumstantially, membership in or affiliation with the Communist Party, and knowledge of the revolutionary aims and purposes of that organization." Hedda Hopper rushed to her own set of barricades. When Robeson came to California in March, she devoted most of her column to lambasting him for having sung the Russian "People's Battle Song" and for remarking in public on the effort "in America today to kill the liberal movement, to crush the labor movement, to stifle the cries against reaction." Such talk, in Hedda Hopper's view, was an example of Robeson's "abusing the precious heritage of freedom given us by our Constitution in flaunting the preaching of our most dangerous enemy. . . ."[3]

When Robeson reached Peoria in April, the sniping against him mushroomed into a full-blown public confrontation. From the first announcement of a Robeson concert in Peoria, there had been rumblings of opposition. Then, two days before the concert, the House Committee on Un-American Activities cited him, along with nearly a thousand others (including Henry Wallace, David Lilienthal, and Harlow Shapley, the Nobel Prize–winning astronomer from Harvard), as one "invariably found supporting the Communist Party and its front organizations." Edward E. Strong, organization secretary of the National Negro Congress, gave vent to the anger felt by many progressives: "The Un-American Committee in Washington has allegedly been carrying on an investigation of un-

American organizations and subversives. Whom have they attacked? The C.I.O. but not the Ku Klux Klan; Paul Robeson but not Theodore Bilbo; not a single group guilty of burning Negroes, gouging out the eyes of veterans, and subverting the Constitution throughout the South . . . have been called to the stand. . . . The un-American forces . . . in the name of 'patriotism' would deny the great Robeson the right to sing in Peoria, while the supporter of fascism during the war, Flagstad, is singing and being acclaimed at Carnegie Hall in New York."[4]

When word of HUAC's citation reached the Peoria City Council, it immediately passed a resolution opposing the appearance of "any speaker or artist who is an avowed propagandist for Un-American ideology." A group of local citizens protested this affront to civil rights, declaring that "there are few progressive independent thinking people who have not been branded 'red' at some time or other since Hitler developed this technique to destroy democracy and bring Nazi-fascism to Europe." Peoria Mayor Carl O. Triebel agreed momentarily to make City Hall's assembly room available to the citizens' group so it could hold a reception for Robeson. But Triebel held to his promise for only one day, rescinding it under a barrage of pressure from "patriot" groups on the following after-noon—the day Robeson, accompanied by Max Yergan, arrived in Peoria. He came despite rumors of impending violence and although William Patterson had reported that he had seen more guns in Peoria "than he ever had before." Denied a place to sing, and refused time to present his case on the local radio station, Robeson was reduced to meeting with a handful of people in the living room of Ajay Martin, a union official and the president of the Peoria branch of the NAACP.[5]

Interviewed by the local press, Robeson declared, "I have been all over the world and the only time I have seen hysteria reach these heights was in Spain under Franco and Germany under Hitler." (Mayor Triebel responded that he and the City Council were only trying "to prevent bloodshed.") Asked by the reporters for the fiftieth time that week whether or not he was a Communist, Robeson responded with the same formula he had used when testifying before the Tenney Committee: "There are only two groups in the world today—fascists and anti-fascists. The Com-munists belong to the anti-fascist group and I label myself an anti-fascist. The Communist Party is a legal one like the Republican or Democratic Party and I could belong to either. I could just as well think of joining the Communist Party as any other. That's as far as you'll get in any definition from me." Robeson put it more succinctly still to a reporter from Marshall Field's liberal paper, the Chicago *Sun:* "If Communism means pointing out to the people that their lives are being dominated by a handful, I guess I'm a Communist." He vowed that he would return to Peoria, and swore to "fight this violation of civil liberties."[6]

The repercussions within Peoria itself centrally involved Clifford

Hazelwood, commander of the black Roy B. Tisdell American Legion Post in the city, and also local vice-president of the NAACP. Hazelwood had spoken out against the anti-Robeson campaign, and the executive board of Tisdell had then accused him of "communistic activities and ideologies." It did so without first consulting the membership, and a fight within the Tisdell post ensued; the membership voted against the executive board's denunciation of Hazelwood, which in turn led the Legion's state commander to revoke the post's charter, to padlock its meeting house, and to confiscate its material assets. The word was spread that the entire Tisdell post was "communistic." Hazelwood had in the meantime appealed to his friend Senator Everett M. Dirksen for FBI information about the validity of the accusations against Robeson, and Dirksen sent the letter on to J. Edgar Hoover. Simultaneously Hazelwood appealed to the national offices of the NAACP for help in clearing his name, and Roy Wilkins supported his request for an FBI investigation, emphasizing in a letter to Hoover the need to refute "the misguided (or deliberate) attempt to use Hazelwood's connection with the NAACP to imply in some manner that this Association is engaged in spreading communistic ideology"; Wilkins made no protest or appeal in Robeson's behalf. J. Edgar Hoover turned over the entire Dirksen-Hazelwood-Wilkins correspondence to the Attorney General's office for further action, and eventually all parties were notified that neither the FBI nor the Justice Department felt empowered —in the absence of any "violation of federal law"—to proceed with an investigation.[7]

"The Peoria affair," Robeson told the Chicago *Sun,* "is a problem bigger than just me." He characterized "the situation in America" as "much more serious than people realize" and predicted that the incident would be a signal to other localities to proceed against him. Within weeks, the Albany, New York, Board of Education announced that it was canceling permission for him to give a scheduled concert at Livingston High School. Albany's Mayor Erastus Corning II proudly took credit for being the moving spirit behind the cancellation. But this time around, local protest proved substantial, and the black sponsors of the recital (an affiliate of the Israel A.M.E. Church) brought legal action to restrain the Board of Education from barring Robeson.[8]

In the ensuing hearing, Albany's corporation counsel argued before the court that neither the Board nor the city "will subsidize Communism or anything having to do with Communism. The color of Paul Robeson's skin has nothing to do with this case, but the color of his ideologies has." But Supreme Court Justice Isidore Bookstein ruled that Albany could not bar Robeson from singing because of his alleged sympathies with Communism and issued an injunction restraining the Board of Education from interfering with the concert. Bookstein did stipulate, however, that Robeson confine himself to his musical program. According to the newspapers, he did just that, "speaking only to describe some of the songs he was about to sing as encores." But to the Army Intelligence agents covering the event, he "complied with the letter of the law" while defying its spirit; in singing encores relating to Republican Spain, the Soviet Union, and the Chinese antifascists, Robeson had, the intelligence agents insisted, "managed to further the CP line by means of his songs."[9]

The following month, the police commissioners in Toronto also issued Robeson a permit to sing only on condition that he not talk at his concert. Angered by the escalating restrictions on him, Robeson spoke out at a Council on African Affairs rally in New York. "This could happen," he said, "to any American who believes in democracy and says so fearlessly. This is the heart of the issue. Whether I am or am not a Communist or Communist sympathizer, is irrelevant. The question is whether American citizens, regardless of their political beliefs or sympathies, may enjoy their constitutional rights. If the government is sincerely concerned about saving America from subversive forces, let our officials . . . stop worrying about the Communists whom they *suspect* of subversive activities and start doing something about the fascists who are openly parading their disdain of civil rights and democratic procedures here in America today." He concluded by saying, "I, however, am going to function exactly as I have tonight, at other times. . . . I come from the people, and from the side of the people. . . . I want nothing back but the kind of affection that comes to me tonight, the kind of feeling that you're there—that's what allows me to do what I do—because you are there! I want no political office of any kind, nor will I ever seek one. . . ."[10]

Two weeks later *Newsweek* published a sardonic article entitled "Paean From Pravda," reporting that the Soviet Union had recently expressed "gratitude" for its American friends, listing among them Henry Wallace, Albert Einstein, Professor Ralph Barton Perry of Harvard, former U.S. Ambassador to Moscow Joseph E. Davies—and Paul Robeson. The nationally syndicated conservative columnist George E. Sokolsky followed through with an article holding Robeson himself responsible for the Peoria incident: "If Robeson chooses to be both singer and propagandist, that is his risk. Those who favor causes must risk the consequences of opposition. Better men than Paul Robeson have been thrown to the lions." (J. Edgar Hoover liked Sokolsky's column so much he wrote on the bottom of it, "A good summary on Robeson so don't let it get lost." It wasn't.)[11]

When Robeson made a brief trip to the Panama Canal Zone at the end of May, the FBI monitored his movements. The agent covering Robeson's concert in Panama City sounded crestfallen that "In spite of predictions the concert was free from any Communist or union propaganda." But if Robeson held his tongue while in the Canal Zone, he immediately aired his views on returning to the States. Speaking in Miami under the sponsorship of the Southern Negro Youth Congress, he "stunned" the assembly with the vehemence of his views on U.S. policy in the Zone. Blasting the U.S. government for "keeping the black masses in ignorance and pitiful poverty," he excoriated as well the powerful clique of local politicians who cooperated with U.S. officials. He devoted the proceeds from several subsequent concerts to setting up a Canal Zone scholarship fund for the education of black teachers, and in 1948 he joined Du Bois, Charlotta Bass (publisher of the California *Eagle*), and Charles P. Howard (lawyer and publisher) in establishing a committee to fight Jim Crow social and economic discrimination in Panama.[12]

Despite the mounting harassment, Robeson remained a popular public figure during the summer and fall of 1947, and very much in demand. In a Gallup Poll released in June, he was one of forty-eight runners-up in a survey of the public's "ten favorite people." That same month he sang to a capacity house at Symphony Hall in Boston "while scores outside vainly sought admission," and in July he sold out Lewisohn Stadium in New York City. Dozens of left-wing organizations vied for his presence as guarantor of a large turnout; he gave preference to the Civil Rights Congress, the Joint Anti-Fascist Refugee Committee, and, as the prospects of a Wallace campaign increased, to the Progressive Citizens of America. He agreed to become one of the PCA's host of notable vice-chairmen, and on September 11 shared the platform in Madison Square Garden to hear Wallace, on the first anniversary of his dismissal from Truman's Cabinet, tell the crowd of nineteen thousand that the country was suffering from a "psychosis about communism, which has been carefully nurtured by men whose great fear is not communism but democracy."[13]

The battle lines for the coming presidential election were forming rapidly, and the jockeying for position becoming intense. In June 1947, heeding the advice of the liberal wing of his party, Truman vetoed the antilabor Taft-Hartley Bill—arguably his most important single move in cutting away the support of organized labor from Wallace and assuring his own re-election. In 1946 A. F. Whitney, president of the Brotherhood of Railway Trainmen, had vowed to spend his union's entire treasury to defeat Truman after the President had threatened to draft railway strikers; following Truman's Taft-Hartley veto, Whitney declared that a third party was "out of the question." At the same time, Secretary of State George C. Marshall announced the administration's commitment to underwriting the economic rehabilitation of Western Europe (the so-called Marshall Plan)— a move that proved popular in the nation but split the progressive ranks. Wallace and Robeson came out vigorously against it. They argued that, in combination with the Truman Doctrine of three months earlier—which had called for aid to Greece and Turkey to prevent those nations from going "communist"—the administration was making a deliberate attempt to circumvent the United Nations and to "hem Russia in."[14]

Additionally, the progressives were divided over whether to accept proffered support from the Communist Party. In the first half of 1947 the CPUSA still remained on the sidelines, but its reasons for supporting the new progressive organization were mounting. When Congress passed the Taft-Hartley Bill over Truman's veto, that bill's Section 9H, which required all labor unions wishing to use the collective-bargaining procedures of the National Labor Relations Board to file non-Communist affidavits, became the law of the land. Section 9H threatened, alternatively, to destroy the left-wing unions or to lead them to sever all connection—even all signs of friendship—with the CPUSA. Simultaneously, Wallace's cross-country tour in June 1947 revealed unexpectedly high enthusiasm for the progressive cause, further confirmed by favorable showings in the Gallup Polls. Meeting that same month, the CPUSA's national committee heard William Z. Foster hail the emerging divisions within the American ruling class, and Eugene Dennis, the Party's general secretary, warn against the Party's taking precipitous steps of any kind. That same mood of cautious commitment continued to characterize the Progressive movement itself throughout the summer and fall of 1947, with Wallace still resisting the formation of a third party and any overt declaration of his own candidacy, and with the CIO left wing still flirting with the strategy of trying to revitalize the Democratic Party (while a simultaneous trend was developing toward compliance with the required affidavits of Section 9H).[15]

In this clouded and volatile atmosphere, Robeson lent his name to a move to coordinate an agenda for outlawing lynching and the poll tax and for restoring the Fair Employment Practices Committee. Essie seems to have played a large role in the effort, possibly stimulated by her earlier attempt with Pearl Buck to come up with a set of propositions for federal action in behalf of blacks. The initial invitation to meet with Essie and Paul in October brought a sparse response; only Louis T. Wright, Dr. Marshall Shepard (the recorder of deeds in Washington, D.C.), and Alphaeus Hunton showed up. The meeting was brief and politic; it stressed that their effort to coordinate a black agenda "would not interfere or compete with the fine work which many organized groups had already accomplished." The decision was made to invite an additional hundred or so black leaders to gather in November. Essie cast a wide net in trying to enlist support for that meeting, inviting, among others, Walter White, Mary McLeod Bethune, Lester Granger, A. Philip Randolph, and Adam Clayton Powell, Jr.[16]

Walter White responded to her invitation with a lengthy private letter illustrative of the divisions within the black leadership—current and future. During the war years the NAACP, following the trend in the black community itself, had become militantly anticolonialist (Walter White's denunciation of Churchill's "Iron Curtain" speech had been as uncompromising as Robeson's). The organization had shown a dramatic increase in membership from 1940 to 1946, its branches tripling in number and its rolls going up nearly ten times over. After 1946 the pace of growth slowed, in tandem with the national shift toward Cold War confrontation and away from any willingness to grapple with domestic problems. With the NAACP's values and organizational fortunes in flux, Walter White was in no mood to broach opposition, to take kindly to a political project that might circumvent established lines of power in the black community—especially not if it emanated from Dr. Du Bois, a longtime personal antagonist of White's who, on returning to his association with the NAACP in 1944 in the role of director of special research, had already begun to threaten White's authority.[17]

Robeson and Walter White were no longer on the terms of personal intimacy they once had been. "Although Paul and I have not seen eye to eye on some points—political and strategic—during recent years," White began his letter to Essie, "I have had much more respect for him in that he has spoken out frankly about his views instead of wiggling and wobbling as so many other people do who favor Communism but take to cover when the going gets hot. I have the same respect for Ben Davis." Nevertheless, White continued, he had to "very frankly question that the kind of conference you suggest would do what you want it to do. . . . I think it would promptly be smeared as being just another 'united front.' " He believed organizations were already in place to combat the various ills the conference planned to address, and expressed his personal view that no such legislation had a hope of passage "until the Senate rules are amended" to prevent filibustering. He declared his preference for channeling efforts in that direction.[18]

Only eighteen people convened for the November meeting at the Harlem branch of the New York Public Library; except for Du Bois, none of the established black leadership attended. Essie, who chaired the meeting, opened it by declaring that the general idea behind the gathering was to try "to find some kind of basic program behind which all Negroes, organized and unorganized, could unite" in order to exert mass pressure on Congress for some kind of constructive legislation. Paul then spoke of his conviction that "division" was the "greatest weakness" keeping blacks from winning their rights. He had been pleased in his travels around the country, he reported, to find that "the rank and file of the Negro people everywhere, especially in the South, are anxious to see and know and hear their Negro leaders and artists; if they can hear their voices," he insisted, "they will follow and support these voices." He suggested that those present form themselves "into a loose, temporary organization to unify the Negro people." Discussion thereafter was desultory and repetitive. Du Bois argued that "there was already unanimity of opinion among Negroes on such fundamental issues as the poll tax, FEPC and anti-lynching," to which Essie replied that "unanimity of opinion" now required "unanimity of action." First Robeson, and then Du Bois, declined nominations to chair future meetings (the nod then went to Reverend John Johnson of New York City). Another gathering was tentatively planned, "to work out a concrete program."[19]

Ultimately the group did manage to launch the "National Non-Partisan Mass Delegation to Washington" on June 2, 1948, to demand passage of civil-rights legislation. But it caught on with neither the black masses nor the black leadership. The organizers were able to add to the list of cosponsors a few nationally recognized names—Benjamin J. Davis, Jr., Earl B. Dickerson, Ewart Guinier, Dr. Benjamin E. Mays, William L. Patterson, Mary Church Terrell, and Coleman Young—but the front-rank black leadership remained aloof. And with Walter White and the NAACP, an uneasy politeness prevailed—for the moment.[20]

In December 1947 Henry Wallace formally declared his candidacy for the presidency on a third-party ticket. Robeson announced for Wallace immediately, stood on the platform with him in Chicago in mid-January 1948—heard the crowd shout, "Robeson for vice-president!"—and became one of five cochairmen of a national Wallace for President committee. At the Progressive Party nominating convention in July, Robeson took his name out of consideration early in the planning sessions for any headline role. But he gave himself over entirely to electing the Progressive Party ticket and prepared to appear at rallies ranging from the anonymity of high-school gyms to the hoopla of Madison Square Garden—and in every section of the country.[21]

In anticipation of Wallace's candidacy, Clark Clifford, part of the liberal wing in the Truman administration, had presented the President in November with a lengthy confidential memo outlining a strategy for the 1948 campaign. In it, Clifford not only predicted that Wallace would run but laid out a plan for destroying his candidacy, a plan that Truman carefully—and successfully—followed. The strategy was shrewd and prescient. "Every effort must be made," Clifford wrote, "to identify [Wallace] in the public mind with the Communists," even though, as Clifford acknowledged, the Progressive Party movement could not legitimately be dismissed as Communist-inspired. As a necessary corollary, Clifford further recommended that Cold War tensions with the Soviet Union be maintained at a taut level of unease. Truman himself should remain above the fray, leaving it to "prominent liberals" to attack Wallace directly—a job that the recently formed Americans for Democratic Action (ADA) took on with aggressive zeal. Arthur Schlesinger, Jr., led the way with *The Vital Center*, a book linking liberalism to anticommunism and indulging in an inflamed red-baiting rhetoric that prefigured the McCarthy years.[22]

The Communists, both at home and abroad, made their own profound contribution to the Progressive Party's problems when the CPUSA decided formally to declare for Wallace. He honorably refused to disavow their support, though he did suggest in one speech that if the CP would run a separate candidate, his new party would lose ten thousand votes but gain three million; still, he insisted on defending the CP's right, as a legal political entity, to participate fully in American life. He made it clear that he himself was neither a Communist nor a Marxist, but added that he could find "nothing criminal in the advocacy of differing economic and social ideas, however much I differ with them."[23]

International developments, meanwhile, further undermined Wallace's credibility. The Progressives could mount a strong argument that American belligerence had done much in the crucial 1945-46 period to initiate the Cold War, but by 1948 the Soviet Union had severely compromised its aura of injured innocence. The expulsion of Tito's Yugoslavia from the Communist bloc, the coup in Czechoslovakia and the death of Masaryk, and the blockade of Berlin followed hard one on another, making the earlier argument for the Soviet Union's essentially defensive posture in reaction to American bellicosity ever less persuasive. As Soviet policy, in tandem with ADA belligerence, combined to make a shambles of Wallace's foreign-policy position, Truman himself took the high road, radiating bonhomie and dispensing rhetorical largesse to special-interest groups—particularly to the black community. Though he put little emphasis on civil rights during the campaign, and though he was later to ignore or renege on almost all that he did promise, he made some shrewd and large concessions, issuing one executive order calling for desegregation of the armed forces and another creating a Fair Employment Practices Committee—and made the gesture of choosing Harlem to deliver his one major civil-rights address.[24]

This end play on civil rights ultimately wooed black voters into Truman's column—where the only real opportunity for legislative progress resided. But early in the campaign Wallace's strength among blacks was high (a poll in Minnesota in March showed 54 percent of black voters leaning to Wallace), and even at the end he got a much higher proportion of the black vote than the white (17 percent in Harlem, but only 8 percent of the total vote in New York State). Most of the prominent black leadership—pre-eminently Lester Granger and Walter White—did what they could to foster allegiance to Truman, with only Robeson and Du Bois among the front-rank figures working actively for Wallace.[25]

The Wallace campaign generated considerable excitement and respect within the black community. The Progressives nominated proportionately more black candidates—including Eslanda Robeson to run for secretary of state in Connecticut—and for a wider variety of offices than did the other two parties. And Wallace called repeatedly for equal justice everywhere he went, South as well as North; in the South he took the unprecedented step of refusing to speak before segregated audiences. His defiance of local Jim Crow ordinances—with attendant cross-burnings and egg-splatterings at his rallies—generated considerable emotion on both sides of the racial divide, stirring black enthusiasm and white racism alike.

Robeson himself campaigned in the Deep South, and at no little risk, especially since he put the chief emphasis in all his speeches on the struggle for black rights, not on a defense of Soviet (or an attack on American) foreign policy. Representing in his person the doubly unpopular image of black *and* red, he was an open target for the aggression of bigots and superpatriots, and it took considerable courage to invade their territory repeatedly. In Memphis, Boss Crump tried to prevent a planned Progressive Party rally featuring Robeson, but a black minister offered a meeting space, and two to three thousand people, white and black, showed up. Much the same happened in Savannah: after being denied the right to appear by the authorities, Robeson and Clark Foreman (the Party's treasurer) found a warm welcome in a rally sponsored in the black district of the city. On one occasion, traveling in the club car of a train with George Murphy (the radical member of the family that owned the *Afro-American* newspaper chain) and Wallace, Robeson was slouched down out of sight when they heard two white men discussing with satisfaction the violence they expected the integrated Wallace campaigners to run into south of the Mason-Dixon line; Robeson "got out of his chair by stages, like a djinn coming out of the bottle, and said in this very deep, soft voice, 'Something's likely to happen to other people *before* we get to the Mason-Dixon line.' " Both men got up and left.[26]

Robeson was deeply moved by the courage of his own people everywhere in the South. The protective cordon they formed around him gave him "a sense of great safety" but, beyond that, he marveled at their refusal to buckle under to terroristic threats against their own persons. At Tampa he met a black preacher whom the Klan had threatened to kill for openly supporting the Progressives; the preacher announced from a sound truck that he wasn't going "to get out of a party that is fighting for my people . . . and if anybody wants to find me my address is 500 such-and-such an avenue." During a Progressive Party meeting at Columbus, Georgia (as Robeson later described it),

> the Klan drove up actually in cars, opposite the building, their lights trained on it, and [James] Barfoot, running for governor, says he didn't know what was going to happen. He walked up to the building, and he saw about a hundred Negroes around, sort of standing around, smoking and saying hello. He invited them up to the meeting, and they said, "No, we'll stay down here." And they stayed there, and it was a very fine meeting, and the Klan didn't move. Now, Barfoot told me . . . he found out a little later that there was a very good reason why the Klan didn't move in: because each one of the boys had a gat in his back pocket. There was going to be no disturbance of that Progressive Party meeting.

And it's extremely interesting that these were not Progressive Party Negroes; they were just Negroes who understood that this party was fighting for them. . . .

In Georgia, too, Larkin Marshall, the black editor of the Macon *World*, running as the Progressive candidate for the U.S. Senate, reacted to the Klan's burning a cross on his lawn by putting an advertisement in the paper asking whoever was responsible to come and get the remains; when no one did, he left the charred cross on his lawn for months. "They won't run me out," he told Robeson. "They might carry me out, but they'll never run me out." Robeson found this spirit all over the South. It gave him hope for the future, regardless of how the '48 election itself came out—even as the outright murder of other blacks (including several who merely tried to vote) continued to feed his anger.

Robeson ran into personal hostility outside of the South as well. In St. Louis he was denied accommodations at the Statler Hotel. In Indianapolis the state police had to be called out in force to forestall a threatened riot. He was denied the use of a high-school auditorium in Chicago and of university facilities at Ohio State and Michigan State, where the dean of students told reporters that he had checked with the FBI and learned that Robeson "was a known Communist." Interoffice FBI memos during these months were repeatedly reporting that (in the words of one) Robeson "consistently follows the Communist Party line." There was apparently frustration at the Bureau at the inability of its agents to turn up "any positive evidence" that Robeson was actually a CP member—but it nonetheless continued to insist that "there is every reason to believe that he may well be."[27]

The FBI's inability to find evidence was not for want of trying. When Robeson made a week-long tour of Hawaii in March 1948 under the auspices of the Longshoremen's Union, J. Edgar Hoover directed the special agent in Honolulu "to closely follow his activities while he is there to determine if he contacts any Communist Party members or representatives of allied organizations." Because Larry Brown intensely disliked flying, Earl Robinson, the composer of "Ballad for Americans," agreed to accompany Robeson on the Hawaiian trip. It was "one of the beautiful times in my life," Robinson recalls, working and living closely for a week with a man "so loaded with love—the love he gave out, it was beyond belief." Rapturously received in his concerts, Robeson responded by performing three songs in the language of the islands, having learned them in twenty-four hours, and by telling his union-packed audiences (as Earl Robinson remembers his words), "I stand by you and with you, and as for the Big Five [the companies that controlled sugar production in the islands], I ask you to give them no quarter." These unabashedly political remarks were not quite what the FBI had been looking for; the special agent had to report back to J. Edgar Hoover that "no information has been developed during the period of his stay that would indicate that Robeson was in Hawaii on a special assignment on behalf of the Communist Party."[28]

After returning from Hawaii in late March, Robeson spent April campaigning in Iowa with Charles P. Howard, the Des Moines black attorney and NAACP leader. On arriving in Sioux City, they learned that the superintendent of schools would agree to let Robeson use a high-school auditorium only if he signed an affidavit promising not to make any "un-American statements." He "politely refused," Howard wrote in his diary, adding, "It was interesting to observe the dignity with which Robeson handled this situation. He stated simply that he had no objection to signing anything that other speakers were required to sign, but refused to subscribe to any treatment that other American citizens under similar circumstances were not required to subscribe to." Robeson and Howard took their campaign to a local union hall, but one of its top officers managed to bar its use, and they were likewise frustrated in their efforts to arrange alternate facilities with city officials. Finally, as often before, a black minister came through, offering the use of his church; neither the source of the rescue nor the routine nature of the prejudice that necessitated it came as any particular surprise to Robeson.[29]

Late in May 1948, he took time out from the campaign to testify before the Senate Judiciary Committee, which was holding hearings on a pending bill (Mundt-Nixon) that would require all Communist and "Communist-front" organizations to register (the bill's significant features would subsequently be incorporated into the McCarran Act of 1950, providing the government with its official rationale for proceeding against "subversives"). Henry Wallace and the Progressives had taken the lead in denouncing the Mundt-Nixon Bill, Wallace characterizing it as an effort "to frighten all the American people into conformity or silence," and insisting that "our present laws against treason and sabotage are adequate for a democracy, but they aren't adequate to establish a smoothly functioning police state." The House passed the bill by a lopsided vote on May 20, and the Senate Judiciary Committee began hearings on it the following week. Wallace appeared before the committee two days before Robeson and in a blistering statement called the bill "the most subversive legislation ever to be seriously sponsored in the United States Congress." Referring to Hitler's campaign against the Communists, Wallace warned that "the suppression of the constitutional rights of Communists is but the prelude to an attack upon the liberties of all the people."[30]

Taking the stand on May 31, Robeson reiterated Wallace's warnings and added some pungent remarks of his own. He testified for an hour and a half; Republican Senator Homer Ferguson of Michigan did most of the questioning, with occasional assistance from Chairman Wiley of Wisconsin and periodic jabs from Republican Senator Moore from Oklahoma. Robeson was asked to define what the American Communists "stood for." "For complete equality of the Negro people," he shot back—emphasizing his own paramount reason for supporting the Party's position. He went on to deny that American Communism "is an offshoot of Russian Communism"—other than in the sense that Russian Communism itself could be called an outgrowth of and reaction to the desperate social conditions prevalent in nineteenth-century Europe. And "Are you an American Communist?" Senator Ferguson asked. "That question," Robeson responded, "has become the very basis of the struggle for American civil liberties," representing an invasion, among other things, of the constitutional right to a secret ballot—since the CPUSA was a legal entity. Robeson therefore refused to answer the question, though he volunteered the information that he had "many dear friends who are Communists" and he thought "they have done a magnificent job."[31]

The Senators were neither pleased nor persuaded. Moving along to the next item in what had become a familiar litany of accusations, they asked Robeson if it wasn't true that American Communists owed primary allegiance to the Soviet Union. Robeson parried with an end run: "I don't think they do have as much allegiance to Russia as certain Americans seem to have today, say, to fascist Greece or to Turkey." And what did he mean by "fascist"? Two things, Robeson replied: a belief in racial superiority and a monopoly of resources in the hands of the few. At the heart of Communism, he said, was an interest in representing the interests and alleviating the suffering of the have-nots.

Would he comply with the Mundt-Nixon Bill, if it were passed? Robeson replied with a question of his own: during World War II, was a Frenchman faced with a law passed by the Vichy government curtailing civil liberties obligated to observe it? No, was his implied answer—he would be obligated to join the Resistance. "I would violate the law," was Robeson's spoken response. The Senators preferred their own analogy: surely the American people were better protected in their rights than the Russian people, who faced "liquidation" if they dissented from official policy. Well, said Robeson, "I have been threatened with death two or three times," and "my sharecropping relatives" in North Carolina faced the daily threat of lynching if they dared assert even their minimal rights.

Did he believe he could "best carry out" his ideals by backing the third party? "I certainly do," he answered. Did that mean he was "disloyal to the United States"? No, it made him feel "infinitely more loyal to the United States," since the starting point of the Progressives was "the suffering and the needs of millions." But "the Communist Party is supporting Wallace," one of the indignant Senators interjected. "I think they should," Robeson replied, "because he represents the struggles of the people in this country, as they do. That doesn't make Mr. Wallace a Communist, though." Did Robeson think "Communism a better system of government than our own system"? "There are many ways to enlighten the world," Robeson said, "Socialist systems, Communist systems, our so-called private enterprise systems. Well let's see which can work better. . . . We should be able not to think that we have got to wipe something else off the face of the earth." He believed the Mundt-Nixon Bill was "part of that hysteria"; it would encourage the American people—who today "are extremely confused"— to sacrifice their own civil liberties in the name of a needless holy crusade against Communism.

When the session ended, the gathered reporters questioned the Senators on the committee. Senator Moore told them that "Robeson seems to want to be made a martyr. Maybe we ought to make him one." Wiley made the comment, "I'm not interested in whether Robeson is a Communist or not. I am interested in the dignity of the committee." Ferguson added that, since a quorum of the committee was not present, a contempt citation might run into legal problems. Robeson stayed in the capital long enough to join five thousand pickets at the White House protesting the Mundt-Nixon Bill. He told the press that Truman could not justifiably "pass the buck" on civil-rights legislation to Congress and brought the protest to a close by singing "Ol' Man River" at the foot of the Washington Monument. The Pittsburgh *Courier* called the racially integrated demonstration "the most impressive 'march-on-Washington' since the Bonus March," but *Time* insisted it had "so riled some Senators that they angrily trumpeted their determination to push the Mundt-Nixon bill through—although it had been headed for the shelf. That was O.K. with the Communists," *Time* asserted. "If the bill became law they would be martyrs. If it didn't, they could chortle triumphantly that they had killed it." Robeson returned to the campaign trail.[32]

Serious divisions opened within the black community over the continuing accusations of "communism" being leveled at the Progressive Party. In September, Lester Granger, head of the Urban League, declared that "Communist decision established the Wallace party, Communist support has given the campaign such impetus as it maintained and Communist strategy determines Progressive party policy." The division was further accelerated by a momentous rupture in the Council on African Affairs.[33]

As anti-Communist fervor had mounted nationwide, Doxey Wilkerson, third in command at the Council, noticed that Max Yergan, its executive director, "began to sort of shift with the winds." Wilkerson also helped to edit *The People's Voice*, the militant Harlem weekly Yergan part-owned and published (Adam Clayton Powell, Jr., had been its editor-in-chief until 1946, when he severed connection with it as "Communist-dominated"). After Attorney General Tom Clark released his list of subversive "Communist-front" organizations in November 1947 (which included the Council), Wilkerson and Yergan got into a mounting number of disputes over policy pronouncements on both the paper and the Council, and

Wilkerson finally went to Ben Davis, Jr., and Henry Winston, two other black members of the Party in leadership positions, to warn them of Yergan's growing disaffection. As Wilkerson remembers it thirty-five years later, "they sort of discounted" his assessment—"it was almost unthinkable that Max Yergan would be turning."[34]

Yet he was. At a meeting of the Council members on February 2, 1948, Yergan argued that the organization should publicly declare its "nonpartisan character," should openly avow that it was not "identified with any partisan ideology." Robeson and others insisted that such a statement would play into the hands of "reactionary red-baiters and would not help the Council." After prolonged debate, Yergan's suggestion was tabled by the close vote, including proxies, of thirty-four to twenty-nine. The matter was referred to a policy committee, headed by Du Bois, to report its recommendations to the full Council.[35]

As the policy committee began its deliberations, Yergan first denied its authority and then, that failing, tried to circumvent it. He so obstructed its working that Du Bois finally resigned the chairmanship in protest. Yergan, on his own authority, called a meeting of the full Council for March 12, prompting Alphaeus Hunton, the educational director, to warn the other members that Yergan was planning a "coup" at the meeting and urging them to be present. Robeson telegraphed Yergan asking for a postponement of the meeting until March 25, when he could fly in from the campaign trail to attend.[36]

The March 25 meeting marked a decisive defeat for Yergan. When a report from the finance committee containing censure of some of his financial transactions was adopted, Yergan and his supporters stalked out of the meeting, claiming that no quorum existed. It did, but barely: twenty-one of the sixty-nine members attended, with sixteen proxies having been sent in—fourteen of them assigned to Robeson—for a bare majority of thirty-seven. William Jay Schieffelin, a white member of the Council, accused Robeson of being "absolutely unfair" in disqualifying Yergan's proxies—and walked out. The next day Yergan fired Hunton, and on April 5, deciding to go public with his case, called a press conference. That act sealed his fate with the Council's membership. Yergan told the reporters—and the story was widely printed—that a struggle had broken out "between Communist and anti-Communist factions," that the Communist faction, led by Robeson, Hunton, and Wilkerson, had become determined to capture the organization as a lever "to swing the Negro vote to the support of Henry A. Wallace," and that he intended to fight back against their unlawful seizure of power at a meeting of the Council he was calling for April 21.[37]

Under Robeson's name, a counterstatement immediately went out to the press, denying (accurately) that the Wallace issue had ever come up at a Council meeting, describing Yergan's bolt from the previous meeting, rejecting his authority to call a new one, and expressing surprise that "for reasons of his own, and quite in contrast to his former position, Dr. Yergan is now unwilling to challenge the imperialist policy of the U.S. State Department."[38]

The schism was now in the open, the skirmishing intense. Yergan persisted in his call for another meeting, Robeson hotly protested the date (fixed for when Yergan knew Robeson would be out of town), and Essie joined the fray by circulating a letter to fellow Council members in which she stressed that "Max Yergan has not—until now—ever challenged the political opinions of Paul Robeson." She did not, she wrote, know whether any or all of her fellow members were, as Yergan charged, Communists, nor did she consider it any of her business: "I find it surprising that it is now suddenly of such grave concern to Max Yergan, because . . . it was in his home on Hamilton Terrace that I first met Earl Browder; this very well known Communist was the guest of honor there" (perhaps forgetting she had met him in Spain in 1938). It seemed to her that the sudden eruption of charges of Communism was "a recognizable part of the frightening and very un-American pattern," currently abroad in the land, of trying to discredit dissenters. "When we bring up the normal relevant questions of American intervention abroad, high prices, lack of housing, discrimination, political corruption at home, we are met with the irrelevant answer, Communism." Yergan's comment to the press that he was "determined to restore" the Council's "true function" of working to improve conditions in Africa wrongly implied that it had ever been diverted from that function. "If the Council has ever been used for any other purpose, Max Yergan himself has so used it, for he has kept the political, financial and social direction of the Council's affairs exclusively in his own hands, and we have not been able to say as much as we would like about them."[39]

On April 21 the Council members met again in what proved a near-rerun of the March 25 meeting. When Robeson and nine other members arrived at Yergan's office at the appointed hour, his secretary told them that Yergan was not in and that the meeting would be held downstairs in the library. Yergan never appeared in the library, and so the assembled members proceeded to hold an informal meeting, which was interrupted when Yergan was spotted leaving the building. Robeson and two other members went after him, stopped him on the sidewalk, and demanded an explanation. He told them he had been waiting for them in his office, and since they had failed to appear, the meeting was canceled. In fact, they later learned, Yergan had conducted his own rump gathering with two of his supporters, "elected" a new set of officers to replace everyone except himself, and "dropped" twenty-three Council members from the organization.[40]

Outraged at this attempt to "thwart a democratic resolution of the problems facing the Council," the executive board suspended Yergan from the office of executive director on May 26, 1948. Further maneuvers, including legal threats on both sides, continued throughout the summer, with the members of the Council unanimously resolving in its September meeting to discharge Yergan from office and expel him from membership. In his capacity as chairman, Robeson issued a press release expressing gratification that the disruption was at an end and the way clear for the Council "to go forward with its work" in behalf of colonial peoples.[41]

But in fact the organization had sustained heavy damage. Several of its members, including Mary McLeod Bethune, simply stopped attending. Six formally resigned, including some of the most prestigious—Judge Hubert T. Delany, Adam Clayton Powell, Jr., and Channing Tobias. Whether or not "Communist control" was chiefly responsible for the resignations, Yergan's charges to that effect, widely publicized as they were, seemed confirmation of the Attorney General's "subversive" listing for the Council, and under continuing government pressure it slid into decline, finally disbanding in 1955.[42]

Yergan himself emerged within a few years as an enthusiastic, full-blown Cold Warrior, moving far away from the principles espoused by the Council that he had helped to found. In 1953 he went on assignment to Africa for *U.S. News & World Report* and then wrote a lengthy article entitled "Africa: Next Goal of Communists" in which he argued that it was necessary to cultivate a "sympathetic and constructive" attitude toward the white government in South Africa, and characterized the Mau Mau uprising in Kenya as "a criminal, conspiratorial movement." Robeson responded in print: "If one did not know that Yergan was a Negro (no insult intended to my folk—I'm just stating the hard fact of life!), [one] would have to assume that the article was written by a white State Department mouthpiece assigned to working out a formula for maintaining white rule throughout Africa." In the early sixties, Yergan joined the conservative black columnist George Schuyler in forming a right-wing lobby called the Katanga Freedom Fighters in support of Moise Tshombe's separatist movement in the Congo, and then in 1966 served as cochair with William A. Rusher (publisher of *The National Review*) of the American-African Affairs Association, a group designed to "save" Africa from Communism by propping up the breakaway, segregationist regime of Ian Smith in Rhodesia.[43]

The same charges of "Communism" that split the Council grew loud in the country at large as the Progressive Party campaign neared its conclusion. On July 20 the FBI raided the national headquarters of the CPUSA and, under the Smith Act, indicted a dozen of its leaders for "advocating forcible overthrow of the government and membership in organizations which did same." The ensuing trial was to carry over into the next several years. Robeson, Du Bois, Charles P. Howard, and Roscoe C. Dungee (editor of *The Black Dispatch* of Oklahoma City) immediately sent out a letter to black leaders warning that the "round-up" of national Communist leaders "reminds us all too much of the first step fascist governments always take before moving to destroy the democratic rights of all minority groups." Unless an aroused public put a halt to the government's campaign, the letter warned, "we Negro Americans will lose even our right to fight for our rights." They solicited signatures to an enclosed statement emphasizing that "we raise here no defense of the principles of the Communist Party"; the concern instead was to protect "the right of all minorities to fight for the kind of America they consider just and democratic. Unless this right is protected, the Negro people can never hope to attain full citizenship." Eventually the statement got nearly four hundred signatures, but the "Negro leaders" listed as endorsing it were in fact a relatively obscure collection of Progressive Party congressional candidates, trade-unionists, clergymen, businessmen, artists, and miscellaneous others—with the actor Canada Lee perhaps the single name, other than the original four sponsors of the statement, that might have drawn national recognition.[44]

The dwindling base of support for the Robeson–Du Bois position was further highlighted in September, when the NAACP board voted to sack Du Bois from his position as director of special research. The action was widely deplored in the black community, and Robeson devoted nearly his entire speech at a Progressive Party rally in Chicago on September 14 to denouncing the summary dismissal of "this patriarch of the Negro people," this man who had refused to permit the NAACP "to be utilized as a tool for the Truman Administration in the prosecution of a foreign policy that would enslave Negro peoples throughout the world while paying lip service to democracy at home." But the dismissal stuck. And so did the red label to the Progressives. By late summer the lesser-of-two-evils theory had come to hold sway with many liberals; they preferred to believe in the authenticity of Truman's newly acquired Rooseveltian rhetoric, because the prospect of the election of Republican Thomas E. Dewey was abhorrent. The persistent charge that the Progressives were "reds," in combination with the fear that Dewey would waltz through any division in liberal ranks, drove off large numbers of Progressive Party adherents. The only remaining question was just how severe its electoral defeat would be.[45]

Robeson maintained an optimistic stance, at least for public consumption, up to the end of the campaign. In a radio broadcast with Henry Wallace on October 29, he described himself as full of "tremendous hope," and in strong language denounced Truman's civil-rights program as "a program on paper—of words—it has nothing to do with the background of terror, the atmosphere of horror in which most Negroes live. . . . No, Truman is with Dewey—words, only words: empty lies, vicious lies. Truman is with the Dixiecrats in deeds."[46]

On election night Robeson sang to the hundreds of campaign workers and supporters who gathered at Progressive Party headquarters in New York to await the returns. They proved even more disheartening than expected. Wallace's popular vote was only slightly over one million—less than the total given to J. Strom Thurmond, presidential candidate of those Dixiecrats who had bolted the Democratic Party in protest over its promise to extend civil rights to blacks. In electing Harry Truman, the nation seemed to be giving sanction to his "get-tough" policy with Communists abroad and at home—and their "sympathizers" as well. Truman was to waste no time in exercising that mandate.

■

CHAPTER 17

The Paris Speech and After

(1949)

"I do not fear the next four years," Robeson told a reporter ten days after the election. Talking to the *National Guardian* (the new non-Communist left-wing paper, which Un-American Activities instantly labeled "notoriously Stalinist"), he elaborated, "I do not foresee the success of American reaction. I see only its attempt and its failure. By 1950 there will be no fascist threat in our land." Exuding public confidence, he immediately set off on a concert tour through Jamaica and Trinidad. The FBI set off with him, its agents alerted to watch for any evidence of "non-musical function." They found none. Robeson himself found his "first breath of fresh air in many years." Although Jamaica and Trinidad were still under British rule, "for the first time I could see what it will be like when Negroes are free in their own land. I felt something like what a Jew must feel when first he goes to Israel, what a Chinese must feel entering areas of his country that are now free." Robeson's gratis, open-air concert at the Kingston race course was so jammed (estimates range from fifty thousand to eighty thousand) that a small building crowded with spectators collapsed. In Port of Spain, Trinidad, he laid the cornerstone for Beryl McBurnie's Little Carib Theater, an attempt to use "the music and dance of the people to arouse a national consciousness and pride of heritage." His concert in Port of Spain was greeted with "a spontaneous demonstration of hero worship [that] has never been equalled in this community." As Robeson told the *National Guardian,* "If I never hear another kind word again, what I received from my people in the West Indies will be enough for me."[1]

He would need the remembered solace. By December, when he returned to the States, the forces of reaction, whose ultimate success Robeson doubted, were moving into high gear. A threatened Dixiecrat filibuster in the Senate seemed likely to block any action on civil rights. The Mundt-Nixon Bill, with strengthened provisions, was reintroduced in Congress. The Truman "loyalty-oath" program for civil-service employees was fully operative. In Trenton, New Jersey, an all-white jury, on transparently trumped-up charges, condemned six blacks (the "Trenton Six") to death for murder. And in New York, the Smith Act trial of the twelve Communist Party leaders began its initial skirmishing. *Life* magazine took the occasion to applaud the Yale football squad's election of a black captain, Levi Jackson, as proof that the American Way "worked" and that the "extremist" tactics of a Paul Robeson were as unnecessary as they were misguided. On January 17, 1949, J. Edgar Hoover specifically requested that the New York FBI Office update its files on Robeson: ". . . it is felt that in view of the tense international situation at the present time, a new report should be submitted setting forth the extent of the subject's present activities in connection with the Communist Party and related groups. . . ."[2]

Robeson maintained his political activity on all fronts. At the end of January 1949 he joined six hundred eighty delegates to the legislative conference of the Civil Rights Congress (his old friend William Patterson was now its national executive secretary) in Washington, D.C. The night before the gathering, Walter Winchell warned the American people in a national broadcast that the delegates were coming armed with baseball bats. Government officials needed no inducement to bar the doors. President Truman refused to see a group of CRC delegates that included Bessie Mitchell (whose brother and two relatives sat in Trenton's death house) and the widow of Isaiah Nixon, who had been killed when he tried to vote in Georgia. Vice-President Barkley, cornered in a corridor by another group of CRC delegates, expressed the view that nothing could be done about Jim Crow in the capital, and, when asked what measures the government would take to prevent further lynchings, turned his back and returned to the Senate chamber. Carl Vinson, chairman of the House Armed Forces Committee, told the delegation that came to see him, "The only reason Negroes are segregated is because the army's so big." Representative McCormick of Massachusetts remarked to the group of delegates who visited his office to protest the Smith Act trials that "Communists are not Americans—they're outside the law."[3]

Returning to New York, Robeson put in an appearance at the Foley Square courthouse in New York, where the trial of the Communist leadership was about to begin. He shook hands with each of the defendants, announced, "I, too, am on trial," explained that he was there not only as a private citizen but as cochairman of the Progressive Party, as a leader of the Civil Rights Congress, and as chairman of the Council on African Affairs, and stated that Communists had risked their lives for his people as early as the Scottsboro case.[4]

Attempting to get a postponement of the trial on the assumption (incorrect, it turned out) that with sufficient time a mass movement could be mobilized to protest the indictments, the CPUSA leaders launched a challenge to the court's system of jury selection. Robeson joined the challenge. Along with forty others (including Dashiell Hammett, William Patterson, Vito Marcantonio, Muriel Draper, Fur Workers union President Ben Gold, and Howard Fast), he called an emergency conference to demand reform of a nonrepresentative jury system that precluded the prospects of a fair trial. The protest succeeded in demonstrating that handpicked juries overrepresenting white male professionals and underrepresenting minorities, the poor and women, did not afford—as the Constitution guaranteed—a jury trial by one's peers. But Harold Medina, the judge sitting on the case—a brilliant jurist who on the Communist issue tended to be alternately flippant and abrasive—ruled that they had not demonstrated the *deliberate* exclusion of the underrepresented, and after six months of skirmishing turned down all further defense motions for postponement. Medina ordered the trial to begin on March 7, 1949, at Foley Square. *The* symbolic judicial battle of the Cold War was about to begin. Robeson, by then, was in Europe on an extended concert tour, but he publicly announced that he would return to testify at the trial whenever needed.[5]

The overseas tour was a replacement for eighty-five concert dates within the United States that had been canceled. Robeson's agents, Columbia Artists Management, had had no initial trouble in booking the engagements at top fees after Robeson decided, in the fall of 1948, to return to the professional concert stage. But following the presidential election, and in the wake of the furor surrounding the indictment of left-wing filmmakers subsequently known as the "Hollywood Ten," the entertainment industry took a quick dive to the right; local agents caved in and canceled Robeson's bookings. The symptoms of reaction were growing ominous, but the unexpected offer of an extended European concert tour temporarily took Robeson away from the heat.[6]

Starting in the British Isles late in February 1949, he and Larry Brown began a four-month tour that demonstrated that in Europe, at least, Robeson's popularity had not diminished. It had been nearly a decade since his last appearance in Britain, but he had not been forgotten—the tour was "something like a triumphal procession," Desmond Buckle (a black member of the British CP) reported to William Patterson. The concerts were sellouts, and, as Larry wrote Essie, "the English public seems as fond if not fonder of Paul than ever." ("Felt almost like Frank Sinatra," Robeson later said.)[7]

Despite his reception, Robeson felt disquieted, for the first time in his memory "homesick." It had "never even occurred" to him before that "such a thing was possible—but I really am. This will remain for me the outstanding fact of this tour. A truly qualitative dialectical change. I think it has much to do with the Struggle—my being so much a part of it—it is the most important in the world today—I'm sure of that— But it also has something to do with people who have become very dear to me."[8]

Robeson wrote those sentiments to Helen Rosen, a woman he had first met when playing Othello on Broadway. She had been doing volunteer work for the Independent Citizens Committee for the Arts, Sciences and Professions (a forerunner of the Progressive Party), and Paul used to drop in to ASP headquarters, which were just around the corner from the theater. Helen invited him home to dinner one night, and the Rosens ultimately became close friends. She was a fifth-generation New Yorker of the Portuguese-Dutch-Jewish van Dernoot family (Paul used to call her teasingly "Miss van Der Snoot"). Both her parents were lawyers, and she herself had been educated at the Ethical Culture School and Wellesley College. In 1928 she married Sam Rosen, who became a well-known ear specialist at Mount Sinai Hospital in Manhattan. Sam was warm, perceptive, and outgoing; Helen, the driving force behind the couple's political commitment, was dynamic, beautiful, immensely shrewd about people, and indomitable, a woman whose integrity, emotional and political, could not be breached (Sam once said she "had a whim of steel"). In every way she was the kind of woman to whom Robeson was drawn. The Rosens would both be devoted to Paul for the rest of his life. Helen would become one of his few intimates.[9]

But Robeson was not writing to Helen Rosen of his "homesickness" merely to signal his growing attachment to her. In several letters written to Freda Diamond at the same time, he confided to her, too, that "for the first time, I can't transfer and function." He "had been going every moment," and he was eager to come home. "This time," he wrote her, "I've no desire to see anyone here in general or particular. Have many friends but it's so hard to get started. I just want to get concerts done (these are very important) and return. . . . About the first time that this has happened. I evidently—whatever the difficulties—pressures, etc.—like my life back there—and I'm afraid I like the whole pattern—whole mosaic—so to say. . . ." He also acknowledged to Freda in a subsequent letter that "somewhere, at most unexpected times, I do something to destroy much of your security. I've stopped trying to figure it out. But I know that I love you very deeply and know that you are certainly one of [the] people dearest to me in this world. . . ." Indeed, Robeson would never lose his deep affection for Freda Diamond, but increasingly, after his return to the States, his emotional life would come to be centered more and more on Helen Rosen.[10]

During the four-month tour in Britain, Peter Blackman, a left-wing West Indian writer living in London, helped Desmond Buckle look after Paul's arrangements, serving as general aide to him. Blackman was appalled at the "creative chaos" of Paul's habits—a suitcase full of unanswered mail, an obliviousness to the mechanics of daily living—and wrote Ben Davis, Jr., to complain that the Party, in not helping Paul to organize himself better, was showing insufficient appreciation for his unique importance. Davis wrote back genially, reminding Blackman that the entire leadership of the Party was currently fighting for its life in court and reassuring him that Paul was recognized as "one of the brightest jewels of the international working class movement," though "the magnitude of the man is so overwhelming that it is difficult to contain him."[11]

Robeson made several political appearances while in Britain, most notably at a conference called in London by the India League to protest Premier Malan's apartheid "revolution" of 1948 in South Africa. The Coordinating Committee of Colonial Peoples sponsored the event, and Krishna Menon, later India's controversial delegate to the United Nations, and Dr. Yussef M. Dadoo, the Communist Indian leader of the African National Congress in South Africa, organized it. An East African student in the audience described Robeson's oratory as "thrilling . . . the great voice was low and soft but with the suggestion of enormous power behind it. . . . The audience sat intent and still. . . . This was no trickster. . . . There was emotion in his voice all right . . . but all that he said was carefully reasoned. . . . There was forcefulness indeed but no arrogance. Instead, there was humility, combined with a deep pride in his race. . . . [But] he did not confine himself to the struggle of his own race for freedom. He is evidently a man who has got beyond mere racialism. He told us about the Chinese. He described white people of English descent he had seen living in appalling conditions in America. In many parts of the world there were black spots of Fascism, whatever name it might be called by locally and [he said] it was his business and the business of freedom-loving people everywhere to combat it. . . ." Following the meeting, the South African government—about to become a loyal U.S. ally in the Cold War, in return for Washington's working to postpone any direct UN action on South-West Africa—announced that henceforth the playing of Paul Robeson's records on the radio would be banned. Robeson told the Manchester *Guardian* that the only parallel he could think of was when the Nazi gauleiter of Norway banned his records during the war—"But the Norwegian underground still played them right through the occupation."[12]

Robeson was not deflected from giving outspoken support to the liberation movements in South Africa and Kenya. In the fifties, mostly through the auspices of the Council on African Affairs, he would keep his unintimidated voice raised in behalf of his "African brothers and sisters

. . . jailed by the Malan Government for peacefully resisting segregation and discrimination" and tried and imprisoned in Kenya "for insisting upon the return of their land." Invited by Oliver Tambo in 1954 to send a message to the African National Congress at its annual conference, Robeson forcefully linked arms with its struggle:

> I know that I am ever by your side, that I am deeply proud that you are my brothers and sisters and nephews and nieces— that I sprang from your forebears. We come from a mighty, coura- geous people, creators of great civilizations in the past, creators of new ways of life in our own time and in the future. We shall win our freedoms together. Our folk will have their place in the ranks of those shaping human destiny.[13]

In April 1949 Robeson went to Paris to attend the Congress of the World Partisans of Peace. Tensions and suspicion were running high on both sides of the Cold War. The Chinese Communists had captured Nanking and were advancing to the outskirts of Shanghai, *the* symbol of Western influence in East Asia. *The New York Times* termed the Commu- nist advance "a cataclysmic development" which "doomed the first buds of a Chinese democracy that sprouted under Chiang Kai-shek's rule." The imminent Communist victory in China, the *Times* warned, had re- sulted from the "fatal miscalculation" of trying to negotiate with Com- munists; "all Asia" was now threatened "with a similar fate" unless "more effective steps" were taken "to insulate" the Chinese Commu- nists. Simultaneously, hearings were in progress before the Senate For- eign Relations Committee on passage of the North Atlantic Treaty, a mutual-defense pact among the Western powers that the Soviets de- nounced as yet another harbinger of (in the words of Frédéric Joliot- Curie, the French Communist atomic scientist) "a new war they are preparing."[14]

In this heated international atmosphere, two thousand delegates from fifty nations gathered in Paris for the World Peace Congress. Du Bois headed the American delegation; Picasso, Louis Aragon, and J. D. Bernal were among the celebrated figures in attendance; and Robeson and Joliot- Curie were the most prominently featured speakers. The State Department denounced the gathering in advance as "part of the current Cominform effort to make people think . . . that all of the Western powers are governed by warmongers." By the time Robeson stepped up for his turn at the podium, Du Bois, Joliet-Curie, Pietro Nenni of Italy, and the British left- wing leader Konni Zilliacus had already ignited the delegates, Zilliacus saying, "workers of Britain will not fight or be dragged into fighting against the Soviet Union." Robeson sang to the gathering and then made some brief remarks, most of them unexceptional echoes from a dozen previous and more elaborate speeches in which he had spoken out for colonial peoples still denied their rights. But then he tacked on a less familiar refrain. The wealth of America, he said, had been built "on the backs of the white workers from Europe . . . and on the backs of millions of blacks. . . . And we are resolved to share it equally among our children. And we shall not put up with any hysterical raving that urges us to make war on anyone. Our will to fight for peace is strong. (Applause.) We shall not make war on anyone. (Shouts.) We shall not make war on the Soviet Union. (New shouts.)" Though Robeson could not know it at the time, those comparatively innocuous words (scarcely different from those Zilliacus as well as others had just used) were to reverberate around the world, marking a fateful divide in his life.[15]

An Associated Press dispatch purporting to "quote" from Robeson's speech was picked up and reprinted across the United States:

> We colonial peoples have contributed to the building of the United States and are determined to share in its wealth. We denounce the policy of the United States government, which is similar to that of Hitler and Goebbels. . . . It is unthinkable that American Negroes would go to war on behalf of those who have oppressed us for generations against a country [the Soviet Union] which in one generation has raised our people to the full dignity of mankind. . . ."[16]

Robeson had not spoken the words the AP dispatch ascribed to him. But almost no one paused to check its accuracy. And no one seems to have noticed that, even if Robeson *had* said the offending words, it would not have been the first time a prominent black figure had angrily asked whether blacks should fight in the country's foreign wars; during World War II, A. Philip Randolph's *Messenger* had thundered in an editorial, "No intelligent Negro is willing to lay down his life for the United States as it presently exists." But Robeson's (alleged) words were treated as if they were the unprecedented, overwrought excesses of a single misguided "fanatic."[17]

The outcry was immediate, the denunciation fierce. The white press rushed to inveigh against him as a traitor; the black leadership hurried to deny he spoke for anyone but himself; agencies of the U.S. government excitedly exchanged memos speculating about possible grounds for asserting that he had forfeited his citizenship. Robeson was perceived as having stridden across—not merely crossed—an impermissible line. For many years his success had served white America doubly well: as proof that a "deserving" black man could make it in the system; and as one who, during the New Deal years anyway, had talked with appropriate optimism and patriotism about the country's democratic promise. In the four years since Roosevelt's death, Robeson's increasingly disenchanted public pronouncements had steadily eroded his assigned image; the AP account from Paris suggested that he had now wholly discarded it. The showcase black American had turned out not to be suitably "representative" after all—and it became imperative to isolate and discredit him.[18]

Eager applicants for the job appeared on all sides. Anyone who could hold a pen—quite a few of whom had apparently learned to wield it like a machete—seemed impelled to comment. The gloating of the right-wing press (Robeson "may hereafter be dismissed and forgotten") came as no surprise. Less predictable were the swiftness and severity with which the black establishment moved to distance itself. Black leaders, in the forties, were supposed to "act nice" and "not make a lot of noise," not call militant attention to a militant set of goals, however much they might in fact be in sympathy with them. Most of the black leadership believed at the time that hope for accomplishing even a modest civil-rights program hinged on placating the white power structure, convincing it that blacks had benign and patriotic aims.

Walter White, responding to a request from the State Department, immediately issued a statement. He cautioned that white America "would be wise to abstain from denunciation of the Paul Robesons for extremist statements until it removes the causes of the lack of faith in the American system of government" that Robeson exemplified. White even acknowledged that "many Negroes will be glad he [Robeson] spoke as he did if it causes white Americans to wake up to the determination of Negroes to break the shackles which race prejudice fastens upon them." But White then went on to reaffirm that "Negroes are Americans. We contend for full and equal rights and we accept full and equal responsibilities. In event of any conflict that our nation has with any other nation, we will regard ourselves as Americans and meet the responsibilities imposed on all Americans." Walter White's voice turned out to be the *moderate* one in a nationwide assault on Robeson that became instantly vituperative (Robeson "is just plain screwy," the black columnist Earl Brown wrote in the New York *Amsterdam News*).[19]

Bayard Rustin, A. Philip Randolph's chief lieutenant, later remembered "very distinctly" Roy Wilkins's phoning Randolph and asking him to convene a meeting of black leaders. According to Rustin, Randolph himself "had no objections whatever to calling upon blacks not to participate in the military" (soon after, during the Korean War, he successfully threatened to call for a black boycott of the armed services if Truman failed to issue an executive order dismantling segregation, and Rustin acknowledged that Robeson "had sort of helped lay a radical approach to this matter"). But Randolph and other black leaders did object, according to Rustin, to Robeson's stressing "politics" (the Soviet theme) over "principle" (the issue of a segregated armed forces). "Paul was saying they shouldn't go into the army to fight against Communists"; Randolph was

saying they shouldn't go into a segregated army "to fight against anybody." In Rustin's view, Robeson had further compounded the risk that
blacks would be branded "black *and* red" by making his announcement on
foreign soil—"There's a sort of unwritten law that if you want to criticize
the United States you do it at home; it's a corollary of the business where
you're just a nigger if you stand up and criticize colored folks in front of
white folks—it's not done. . . . We have to prove that we're patriotic."
Besides, Rustin added, there was resentment against Robeson's assuming
the posture of political leadership when in fact he "did not ever take any
organizational responsibility for what was happening in the black community. . . . Here is a man who is making some other country better than ours,
and we've got to sit here and take the gaff, while he is important enough
to traipse all over the country, to be lionized by all these white people,
saying things for which he will not take any responsibility."[20]

Rustin himself made arrangements for the "meeting of black leaders,"
and according to him "most" of the civil-rights establishment showed up,
a total of about twenty people, including both Randolph and Roy Wilkins.
The meeting was designed to create "a united front to make sure that
America understood that the current black leadership totally disagreed
with Robeson." There was no thought of approaching Robeson himself:
"The general theory was that he was being used, and anybody who had to
barter with him on these issues was going to end up being used, too, if not
by the Soviets, by Robeson himself." The meeting decided that the most
effective strategy would be *not* to issue a joint statement—"That's the habit
in the black community," Rustin explained, "not to look as if there's been
an organized effort" but, rather, to have a group of similar statements
emanate from what would appear to be a variety of quarters.[21]

In a statement read at all services of the Abyssinian Baptist Church,
of which he was pastor, Congressman Adam Clayton Powell, Jr., proclaimed, "By no stretch of the imagination can Robeson speak for all
Negro people." Mary McLeod Bethune, president of the National Council
of Negro Women, told the press, "American Negroes have always been
loyal to America, they always will be"; Robeson "does not speak for the
National Council, and I am not aware that any other national Negro organization has appointed or designated him to speak for them in Paris."
Charles H. Houston, the prominent Washington attorney and chairman of
the NAACP legal staff, said, "We would fight any enemy of this country,"
Robeson's view to the contrary. Edgar G. Brown, director of the National
Negro Council, characterized Robeson's speech as "pure Communist
propaganda." Channing Tobias, who had recently become head of the
Phelps-Stokes Fund, declared that Robeson's statement marked him "not
only an ingrate but a striking example of disloyalty." And Bishop William
Jacob Walls of the A.M.E. Zion Church insisted that, in defense of "religious liberty in the greatest adventure in self government in the world—

the American nation," the "colored race" would move "at the command of the American republic." Du Bois, scheduled to give the June commencement address at Morgan College, received word from the college president begging him "frantically not to come" because he had " 'been present' when Robeson spoke in Paris."[22]

And so it went, with the designated leaders of every major black organization stepping forward—without waiting to learn whether Robeson had been quoted accurately in Paris—to declare their loyalty to the nation and to cast out the reprobate son. But what the black establishment felt it had to do publicly did not represent the full range of its reaction to Robeson. "It is very difficult to know what black leaders and others think from what they say," Rustin cautions. It was important, he feels, for "the public to see that Robeson was completely isolated," but in fact it was recognized that the radically outspoken position he had taken "was ultimately a positive thing to have done." His "wild" statement helped to make their demands, by comparison, appear reasonable and even modest; his implied threats of future disorder made the passage of their "responsible, middle-of-the-road" program seem more urgently necessary. As blacks would analogously say in the sixties, "First we had to have the riots; then we got the Great Society."[23]

In denying Robeson's "fantastic and presumptuous" claim (which in fact he had never made) to speak for blacks, the black leadership in turn never hesitated to assert its own summary of "the general feeling of the Negro masses" (in Adam Clayton Powell, Jr.'s phrase). Yet it is not at all clear that their representations were either more legitimate or more accurate than Robeson's. Indeed, the popular reaction in the black community to his alleged remarks in Paris did *not* fully coincide with the black leadership's presentation of it.

"Ordinary" black citizens had long known that allies are always imperfect and that conservatives are always fond of linking the black struggle with Communist subversion—and accordingly had been far more indifferent than whites to the official description of the Cold War as a Manichaean contest between good and evil. As one editorial letter put it, "a person does not have to be a Communist, a fellow-traveler, or 'to echo the Communist line' in order to be conscious of the thousands of indignities suffered daily by Negroes." "There is hardly a Negro living in the South," a black newspaper in North Carolina editorialized, "who, at some time or another, has not felt as Robeson expressed himself as being unwilling to lay down his life for a country that insults, lynches and restricts him to a second-class citizenship, whether it be in a war against Russia, Germany or Great Britain." And in the Pittsburgh *Courier* the columnist Marjorie McKenzie wrote, "Paul's remark that Negroes in the U.S. will refuse to fight an imperialistic war against Russia burns along the edges of the American conscious [sic] like sagebrush in a forest fire. . . . I think the vitality of Paul's remark lives on because it suggests, though it does not articulate, a deeper question. . . . He must see the present political and economic context as an impossible vehicle for Negro aspirations. Else he would not advocate that Negroes should, not predict that they will, react in so drastic a fashion. If our situation is truly hopeless at the hands of a Truman administration and its successors, [the] revolt against selective service for a war makes sense. . . . The Government ought to regard the exaggerated response to Paul's statement as a storm signal."[24]

Such views were directly at variance with the contentions of Max Yergan. In a lengthy letter he fired off to the *Herald Tribune* (which was printed in full), he denounced Robeson's statements as having had "as their purpose the vicious and cynical effort which Communists in America have for a long time been putting forth to drive a wedge between American Negroes and their fellow American citizens. . . ." He also denounced Robeson's actions on the Council on African Affairs as "disgracefully unfair and undemocratic" and condemned him for his "slavish following of the Communist instructions with regard to the organization. . . ." In his own view, Yergan added, "this country is moving forward on all fronts and in all of its geographical areas in bringing about social well being, democracy and a realization of constitutional guarantees for all of its citizens."[25]

The black columnist (and Communist) Abner Berry angrily disputed the right of "the cold-war boys" like Yergan to repudiate Robeson in the name of fifteen million blacks, doubting whether their "breast-beating declarations" of patriotism could succeed in tying most Afro-Americans to a "my country right or wrong" stand. A black technical sergeant wrote to the New York *Age*, "As a vet who put in nearly five years in our Jim Crow Army, I say Paul Robeson speaks more for the real colored people than the Walter Whites and Adam Powells. . . . I saw the U.S. bring democracy to Italy, while white officers kept informing the Italians that the [black] 92nd Infantry men were rapists and apes." Ben Davis, Jr., believed that blacks had "gotten pretty sick and tired of Truman's empty talk and Republican lies about civil rights, and are not in any mood to die in a jimcrow war," particularly not to fight against the colonial peoples of Africa, Asia, and the West Indies to safeguard the profits of a minority of whites. But Du Bois probably struck the bottom-line note in declaring, "I agree with Paul Robeson absolutely that Negroes should never willingly fight in an unjust war. I do not share his honest hope that all will not. A certain sheep-like disposition, inevitably born of slavery, will, I am afraid, lead many of them to join America in any enterprise, provided the whites will grant them equal rights to do wrong."[26]

With Paul still in Europe, Essie decided to join the debate. At a Progressive Party dinner at the Hotel Commodore in New York, she directly took on "the professional Negro leaders" who had "rushed into

print" to deny the mere suggestion that black Americans might not enthusiastically take up arms in defense of the republic. Even if the black
establishment did speak for the "theoretical 2 million" of their followers,
who, she asked, spoke for "the other 12 million unorganized Negroes—the
vast majority of the Negro people?" She believed the large majority of
blacks *would* rally to the defense of the country if it were invaded, but that
was not the same as going off "to fight a war in Greece for a King the
Greeks don't want, to fight a war in China for Chiang Kai-shek whom the
Chinese people don't want." She claimed that "every sensible Negro in
this country—professional leaders notwithstanding—feels that if he must
fight any future war for Democracy, the proper place to begin such a fight
is RIGHT HERE." Why? Because "our country keeps telling us, time after
time, in heartbreaking ways, that we have no rights and privileges as
American citizens—except those it chooses to grant us when it feels
indulgent."[27]

Paul was angry at Essie for not having consulted with Alphaeus Hunton before presuming to quote "exactly" words he in fact had not said at
Paris. But William Patterson, still believing, apparently, that the quote was
accurate, wrote Paul that Essie had dealt skillfully and effectively with
those—among their own people—who were "crawling on their bellies
trying to prove worthy" of the esteem of the very people who were assailing their constitutional rights. Congressman Vito Marcantonio was so impressed with Essie's speech that he read it into the *Congressional Record,* and
the Progressive Party stalwart Charles P. Howard wrote her that he
thought it was "tremendous"—"the finest answer I have ever heard to the
question of the Negro's loyalty." Howard himself was among the few
nationally prominent blacks to defend Robeson publicly. He took the lead,
along with Ben Davis Jr., when a venomous editorial in the May 1949 issue
of *The Crisis,* official organ of the NAACP, pushed the debate to a still
more strident level.[28]

The unsigned editorialist (Roy Wilkins) was not content to insist that
in his Paris speech Robeson "was speaking for himself." The column went
on to imply that "his record of service to his race" hardly entitled him to
even a personal opinion. The sum total of Robeson's contribution, Wilkins
asserted, was to have "inspired them by his singing and given them a 'great
one' to cite in their briefs for better treatment." As for the rest, Robeson
had simply concentrated on making money and keeping his fellow blacks
at "a safe distance. . . . While Negroes in Dixie were struggling to do
something about conditions here and now, Mr. Robeson was lavishing his
attention on an outfit called the Council on African Affairs, long ago
labeled a Communist front by the Department of Justice." In truth, the
Crisis editorial concluded, "Robeson has none except sentimental roots
among American Negroes. He is one of them, but not with them."[29]

The editorial is "one of the dirtiest, gutter attacks upon Paul that I've ever seen," Ben Davis Jr. wrote Essie, and "from a source that considers itself progressive and decent." He correctly guessed that it had been the work of Roy Wilkins, not Walter White. Ben Davis believed that other members of the NAACP board—like Louis Wright, the chairman, and an old friend of the Robesons'—agreed with "the mild liberal tendencies of Walter" and, unlike Roy Wilkins, "would not stoop to such a malicious slander." He therefore advised against attacking the whole NAACP, though he himself did write directly to Walter White, denouncing Wilkins's editorial as "one of the most shocking personal attacks upon a great American leader I have ever seen."[30]

But Charles P. Howard felt otherwise. He had toured the country, sometimes with Robeson, for the Progressive Party, and was smarting at the NAACP for having extolled the virtues of Truman in the recent election—even while claiming to be a nonpartisan organization. Writing directly to Wilkins, Howard exploded with anger at the *Crisis* editorial in particular and the NAACP in general: "The NAACP is no longer best serving the people whom it was organized to serve, but has been sidetracked into serving the very interests it was organized to fight." "It is inexcusable," he continued, for a publication like *The Crisis* to assault Robeson: "Nobody may have ever heard it around NAACP Headquarters, but Paul Robeson is recognized by the great masses of the Negro people as more nearly their ideal leader than all of the Walter Whites and Roy Wilkinses in the country and he doesn't get a dime for doing it, only the kicks of Negroes who ought to be appreciating him." How dare *The Crisis* defame the man as having only "sentimental roots" among black people—a man who had given up his concert, radio, and stage career for a year "to go out and sing and fight for the common people"? "Even school children know that fact."[31]

Wilkins also had at hand Ben Davis's letter to Walter White, which White had passed on to him with a notation: "This letter . . . will make your ears singe if they haven't been singed already by some of the other comrades." He suggested to Wilkins that "it would be a good idea for it to be placed before the Board, if it meets with your approval, and then let the Board go on record as backing your position." But that did not meet with Wilkins's approval. "I do not favor bringing it to the Board," he wrote back to White. "I have a few letters hitting the Robeson editorial and just as many praising it. The Davis letter is all in the day's work of running a magazine."[32]

But although the issue did not come before the NAACP board, Roy Wilkins did agree to meet with what he called "the leading members of the Robeson front." He told them he had received a total of fourteen letters of protest about the editorial, thirteen of them from miscellaneous "left-leaners." (Mary Church Terrell, the distinguished community leader and reformer, may have been the fourteenth; she had already written Alphaeus

Hunton to say she held Robeson "in the highest esteem" and to denounce the attempt to "belittle" his sacrifice and contribution.) Wilkins did not, he said, consider leftist displeasure to be "a very representative sample of support" for Robeson, and if his friends wanted to make an issue of the editorial, he "would simply cite the letters" as additional proof that Robeson was the spokesman for a tiny clique, not for all black people. "The Robeson matter died right there," Wilkins later claimed. For good measure, he took an indirect swipe at Robeson in his speech at the fortieth annual convention of the NAACP that July: "We do not cry out bitterly that we love another land better than our own, or another people better than our own."[33]

But of course the controversy did not end there. *The New York Times*, probably echoing a widely held view among whites, commented in an editorial that Robeson was "mistaken and misled" in deciding to "devote his life to making speeches" and suggested that he return to using "his great gifts" as a concert artist: "We want him to sing, and to go on being Paul Robeson." He did remain abroad for two months after his Paris speech, completing his concert tour. But additional developments in Europe further fed the dispute. Robeson had flown to Stockholm on the evening of April 20, immediately following his speech in Paris, and performed there the next day before an overflow crowd, part of which booed when he sang a Soviet song (irritating Robeson, according to an FBI report, "beyond control" and launching him into a speech "extremely critical of the treatment of the American Negro in America"). At a hostile press conference following the Stockholm concert—and not yet having heard about the instantaneous uproar his Paris speech had set off—he asked should blacks "ever fight against the only nation in the world [the U.S.S.R.] where racial discrimination is prohibited and where the people live freely? Never!" he answered, and then, using words he had avoided in his Paris speech (though they had been ascribed to him), he sounded as if he *was* claiming to speak on behalf of all black Americans: "I can assure you they will never fight against the Soviet Union or the People's Democracies." A few days later, Alphaeus Hunton, by telegraph and telephone, brought Robeson up to date on the outcry he had produced. On May 1 Paul wrote Freda Diamond (in his usual shorthand style), "This has been such a long, long ache that I'm numb. . . . I have read much of stuff from home. Distorted—but let it rest. There is just one thing I will stress: I said: 'Negroes would fight for peace, would become Partisans of peace rather than be dragged into a war against the Soviet Union and East where there is no prejudice.' I said: 'Take a questionnaire and give Negro sharecropper an honest appraisal—peace with nations who are raising their former minorities, or war in interest of those who just refused him his civil rights.' " Then he added, "I can understand their using Walter, but Max!!! I'm ready enough."[34]

Hunton translated verbatim a French newspaper account of Robeson's actual words in Paris, and as early as May 2 part of that text was printed in the *National Guardian* (and subsequently by limited portions of the black press—but *not* by establishment newspapers). Arriving in Copenhagen, Robeson gave an interview in which he issued a second denial, telling the reporter, "what I said has been distorted out of all recognition." When he referred to "Negroes," he had been thinking, besides Afro-Americans, of the 40 million West Indians and 115 million Africans, who obviously had no stake in a war against the Soviet Union—or any other designed to foster imperialist interests. In an accurate summary of the actual words he had used, he declared, "The emphasis in what I said in Paris was on the struggle for peace, not on anybody going to war against anybody." Again no one seemed to be listening: his corrective remarks were not widely reprinted.[35]

Robeson's two concerts in Copenhagen had been arranged by the Liberal paper *Politiken.* When he learned that the paper advocated Denmark's joining the North Atlantic Treaty Organization, he asked to be released from his contract. *Politiken* complied, and Robeson sang under the auspices of *Land og Folk,* the Danish Communist paper. In Oslo, his next tour stop, *Friheten,* the chief organ of the Norwegian Communist Party, arranged a mass meeting at Youngstorget that drew a huge crowd and was climaxed by a singing of the "Internationale." In addition to his regular concert, Robeson spoke five times while in Oslo—including talks to the Norwegian-Russian Society and the World Federation of Women for Peace. From Oslo he returned for another round of concerts in England, then embarked on the final leg of the tour, which called for stops in Prague, Warsaw, and Moscow.[36]

Larry Brown decided against participating in the East European part of the trip, so Robeson brought along Bruno Raikin as his accompanist. Only recently arrived in England, Raikin was a white South African who had been involved in left-wing politics and been a personal friend of Dr. Yussef Dadoo, the South African Communist leader of Indian descent. Dadoo had introduced Raikin to Robeson, and the two men had quickly taken to each other. Fortunately Raikin could transpose music at sight, so he wasn't unnerved by Robeson's periodic request, sometimes five minutes before a performance, to "put it down, put it down"—to transpose to a lower key (Robeson was trying to save his voice, as he grew older, by shifting to a key closer to an extension of his speaking voice). Raikin still considers the trip with Robeson a high spot in his life—"He was a man of enormous generosity . . . a big man, not in size but in character. There was nothing puffed up about him."[37]

The hospitality that greeted them in Prague was lavish—luxurious suites of rooms, adoring crowds for the concerts, extravagant receptions hosted by the country's highest dignitaries (including Czechoslovak President Gottwald). Arriving at the National Theater one night to hear Smetana's *The Bartered Bride,* Robeson entered just behind a British Communist leader who mistook the enormous applause as meant for him and—to general amusement—smilingly acknowledged the crowd. But not every segment of Czech opinion welcomed Robeson or thought well either of his musical tastes or his political friends. Josef Škvorecký, a young writer, jazz aficionado, and anti-Stalinist, later wrote bitterly of Robeson's image among his circle:

> In place of [Stan] Kenton, they pushed Paul Robeson at us, and how we hated that black apostle who sang, of his own free will, at open-air concerts in Prague at a time when they were raising the Socialist leader Milada Horáková to the gallows, the only woman ever to be executed for political reasons in Czechoslovakia by Czechs, and at a time when great Czech poets (some ten years later to be "rehabilitated" without exception) were pining away in jails. Well, maybe it was wrong to hold it against Paul Robeson. No doubt he was acting in good faith, convinced that he was fighting for a good cause. But they kept holding him up to us as an exemplary "progressive jazzman," and we hated him. May God rest his—one hopes—innocent soul.[38]

Desmond Buckle, on the other hand, told Peter Blackman that Prague Party circles were full of rumors that Robeson was a U.S. spy, an agent, and that he had no political judgment. Robeson never hinted to Blackman that he was aware of such a rumor—or aware that some young Czechs like Škvorecký resented his presence. Robeson spent his last evening in Prague talking with a group of blacks who had sought him out—perhaps having heard that earlier in his visit he had told a political rally that "ninety-five percent of United States Negro leadership is corrupt" (a remark reprinted in several black newspapers in the States). After the group left, Robeson went on talking to his old friend Marie Seton, whom he had unexpectedly met in the city, into the early morning hours:

> " 'You know, I have no illusion,' he said, 'I know how hard it's going to be in America. I don't know if I'll live to see the end of the struggle. . . . I've overcome my fear of death, I never think about death now. Tomorrow morning, I'm going to Warsaw and then to Moscow. I'm going to the people I love. It's my great wish to live among the Russians for a time before I die, but can you understand it? Even at this moment I'm homesick. Even this very night I'd rather be in America than any place on earth. I'll go back. I'll never leave America as long as there is something I can do.' "[39]

Peter Blackman joined Robeson and Raikin in Warsaw. The city was unseasonably hot and (along with two factory concerts) Robeson sang in an outdoor stadium before a huge gathering. Though warned not to risk Polish resentment by singing in Russian, he did sing the Soviet "Fatherland Song"—after explaining to the crowd that he regretted not knowing enough Polish to communicate fluently with them in their native language. At the close, the audience gave him a standing ovation. After a moving tour of the field of brick once known as the Warsaw Ghetto, Robeson flew to Wrocław, where he sang first in a factory and then, in the evening, in Liubdova Hall—to the same warm welcome: deputations of townspeople with flowers followed in a seemingly unending procession.[40]

On June 4 Robeson arrived in Moscow in time for the celebration of the one hundred and fiftieth anniversary of Pushkin's birth, accompanied by Blackman but not Raikin. The anti-"Zionist" campaign was in full swing in the Soviet Union, and Raikin—perhaps because he was Jewish—had been denied a visa. Raikin was not only surprised but "also a little bit shocked" that the Soviets would refuse to admit Robeson's official accompanist (and at the last minute, to boot). But if Robeson took that as an insult, or a portent, he never showed it: he shrugged and told Raikin how sorry he was that the visa had failed to come through. Peter Blackman was at least as shocked—and angry—when the customs officials thoroughly searched Robeson at the Moscow airport. Again he shrugged the incident off, saying he was no more entitled than anyone else to preferential treatment. However, *The New York Times* was soon reporting that Robeson was being received in Russia with "greater acclaim than had been given in recent years to any United States visitor" (and reporting, too, that during a concert he had dedicated the song "Scandalize My Name" to "the international bourgeois press"). The Moscow press brimmed with laudatory interviews, and *Komsomolskaya Pravda,* journal of the Communist youth movement, published a series of articles by and about him. Addressing a concert crowd in Gorky Park, Robeson said he found it difficult to express "how deeply touched and moved" he was to be "on Soviet soil again" and declared in ringing tones, "I was, I am, always will be a friend of the Soviet people."[41]

But at the same time, Robeson himself felt some uneasiness over his inability to locate Jewish friends from previous visits to Moscow. Eisenstein had died in 1948. Solomon Mikhoels, the actor-director Robeson had known, admired, and played host to when he, along with the Jewish writer Itzik Feffer, had visited New York in 1943, had been found brutally murdered on January 13, 1948 (on Stalin's personal order, it later turned out), his body smashed and mutilated. At the time, Mikhoels's "mysterious" death had been widely mourned in the Jewish community, and the following month Robeson had participated in a memorial meeting for him in New York. But where was Itzik Feffer? Finally, on the eve of Robeson's departure, his persistent inquiries produced Feffer (who, unbeknownst to Robeson, had been arrested on December 24, 1948). Feffer was brought, unaccompanied, to Robeson's hotel. Paul later told his son—pledging him to silence during his lifetime—that Feffer, through mute gestures, had let him know that the room was bugged. The two kept their talk on the level of superficial pleasantries, while communicating essential facts through gestures and a few written notes. Mikhoels, Robeson learned, had been murdered by the secret police; other prominent Jewish cultural figures were under arrest; there had been a massive purge of the Leningrad Communist Party and of many in the Moscow Party, and Feffer's own likely fate (here he drew a hand across his throat) would be execution (three years later he was shot). According to Peter Blackman, in the days that followed, Robeson never once verbalized any distress but—in perhaps an indirect signal—he did ask Blackman to "stick around" during the rest of their stay in Moscow, saying he wanted someone he knew with him. Blackman also recalls Robeson's cautioning him to "watch what you say because they"—the Soviet Party—"think you are a nationalist." "Nationalism," like "Cosmopolitanism" and "Zionism," had become a term of slander.[42]

Robeson decided to conclude his last Moscow concert program with a direct reference to Feffer. Asking the audience for quiet, he announced that he would sing only one encore. Then he expressed with emotion the sense he had of the deep cultural ties between the Jewish peoples of the United States and the Soviet Union, and of how that tradition was being continued by the present generation of Russian-Jewish writers and actors. He then referred to his own friendship with Mikhoels and Feffer, and spoke of his great joy in having just come from meeting with Feffer again. Robeson then sang in Yiddish, to a hushed hall, "Zog Nit Kaynmal," the Warsaw Ghetto resistance song, first reciting the words in Russian:

> . . . *Never say that you have reached the very end,*
> *When leaden skies a bitter future may portend,*
> *For sure the hour for which we yearn will yet arrive,*
> *And our marching steps will thunder: we survive! . . .*

After a moment's silence, the stunned audience, Great Russians and Jews alike, responded with a burst of emotion, people with tears in their eyes coming up to the stage, calling out "Pavel Vasilyevich," reaching out to touch him.[43]

Having made that public gesture in Moscow in behalf of Feffer and other victims of Stalin's policies—all that he could have done without directly threatening Feffer's life—Robeson clammed up on returning to the United States. He told a reporter from *Soviet Russia Today* that the charges of anti-Semitism being laid against Russia in the Western press failed to square with what he had himself observed: "I met Jewish people all over the place. . . . I heard no word about it." He reiterated his belief that the Soviets "had done everything" for their national minorities and recalled that while in Moscow he had attended the Kazakh Art Festival and had thought it "a tremendous thing that these people could be there with their literature, music, theater—not after a thousand years, but in hardly one generation." To those who would say the Soviets had no black problem because they had no blacks, Robeson answered, "There are of course tens of millions of dark peoples there who would be vigorously Jim Crowed in the United States. Take the peoples of Georgia. The people you see in Tiflis; they are very dark, like the Puerto Ricans and Mexicans; and there are millions of yellow people—I have seen how the Chinese are treated in San Francisco."[44]

Robeson had come to believe so passionately that U.S. racism and imperialism were the gravest threats to mankind, including the real possibility in 1949 that the United States would launch a pre-emptive war against the Soviet Union, that he felt public criticism of anti-Semitism in the U.S.S.R. would only serve to play into the hands of America's dangerous right wing. If his judgment on that point ever wavered, he never revealed it. To the end of his life he would refuse to criticize the Soviets openly, never going further than to make the barest suggestion in private, to a few intimates, that injustice to some individuals must always be expected, however much to be regretted, in an attempt to create a new world dedicated to bettering the lot of the many. He continued to believe that the best chance for reaching his primary goal—improving the condition of oppressed peoples—lay with the egalitarian impulses originally unleashed by the Russian Revolution. Convinced in the thirties of the Soviets' unique freedom from racial prejudice, and seeing no major Western power in the ensuing years developing a comparable commitment to the welfare of its minorities, he resisted every pressure to convert any private disappointment he may have felt in the Soviet experiment into public censure.[45]

Robeson touched down at La Guardia Airport on June 16. Some sixty friends (including Rockmore, Patterson, and Hunton) waited on the one side, two dozen police on the other. According to *The New York Times*, "twenty uniformed policemen [was] a routine number for the arrival of prominent personages at La Guardia," but Robeson didn't think so, and laconically contrasted leaving Eastern Europe surrounded by well-wishers with being greeted in New York by a grim police squad. FBI agents were present during the careful search made at customs of his luggage—the officials reporting that "no documents or papers were found that would indicate subversive activities." Paul, Jr., having arrived home the week before with a B.S. degree in electrical engineering from Cornell, greeted his father first. (Essie had planned to meet the plane, too, but Paul's last-minute shift in arrival dates had meant she was addressing the National

Conference of Social Workers in Cleveland.) Robeson then turned to the waiting array of reporters and photographers.[46]

Hunton had suggested to Robeson that he say nothing more at the press conference than that he was glad to be back, had had a marvelous tour, and would save further comments for the Welcome Home rally planned in his honor three days hence. Robeson turned in an altogether more sizzling performance, blasting the American press for having distorted his overseas statements. When a reporter objected that no conspiratorial "higher-ups" had given them instructions to "distort," Robeson shot back, "You don't need them." When another reporter asked whether a story that quoted him as loving the Soviet Union "more than any other country" was accurate or not, Robeson replied, "I happen to love America very much—not Wall Street and not your press. I love the working classes of Britain and France and the people of the Soviet Union. I love them for their struggles for the freedom of my people and the working white people." Asked if he planned to testify in defense of the Communist leaders on trial in Foley Square, he gave an unequivocal yes: "I consider the trial a complete test of American civil liberties." Then, contrasting the scene at home with what he had found in Europe, he said, "No one is hysterical except in America." Robeson, clearly, had not arrived home in a compromising mood.[47]

His mood had not softened three days later. June 19 began with a major personal event and concluded with a major political one. Paul, Jr., and Marilyn Paula Greenberg, who had been a fellow student at Cornell, both aged twenty-one, had decided to marry. Marilyn Greenberg came from a lower-middle-class Jewish family; her mother (but not her father) had been involved with the politically active left-wing community of Sunnyside. Paul and Essie were both entirely supportive of the marriage—Essie told the press, "our new daughter-in-law is a darling, and we are awfully glad to get a daughter"—but Marilyn's father would not attend the wedding; he was (in her words) "very resistant to the idea of my marrying a black man." The young couple made all plans for the wedding themselves, choosing the progressive minister Reverend John Whittier Darr, Jr., to officiate at an ecumenical ceremony in his own apartment, with only immediate family present. If they had also hoped thereby to avoid any public hullabaloo, that hope was thwarted. Turning the corner into Reverend Darr's block, they saw (in Marilyn Robeson's words) "the street filled with hundreds and hundreds of people, standing there and screaming all kinds of hostile things at us as we got out of the cab. We had to push our way through people to get into the house, and as we went up the stairs, photographers kept running up and down, getting ahead of us and sticking their cameras in our faces . . . just swarming all over us." Paul, Sr., according to the *Herald Tribune,* told the newsmen that he "resented their presence, as the wedding was private. This would cause no particular excitement in the Soviet Union," he supposedly commented. According to Essie, he "nearly punched an impertinent reporter."[48]

Coming back downstairs after the brief ceremony, the wedding party faced a rerun of the earlier scene—reporters crowding around for a statement, onlookers taunting bride and groom, photographers poking cameras in their faces. When they tried to pull away in cabs, one photographer stuck his head into the taxi carrying Marilyn's mother and Paul, Sr. When Robeson lifted his hand toward the man, the photographer bumped his head against the window frame and dropped his camera on the sidewalk as he tried to extract himself—an incident the press delighted in playing up as an "assault." Carl Van Vechten, long disaffected from Paul's politics, wrote Essie: "I have observed that anyone who quarrels with the press usually gets the worst of it. Would you quarrel with Pravda, which certainly misrepresents people by the wholesale?" He also wanted to know, "Why werent we asked to [the] wedding?" Essie answered him on both counts: "I wouldnt quarrel with PRAVDA because Russia is not my country and I dont know all the ins and outs of their situation. . . . But this IS my country . . . and I insist upon sounding off . . . when I reach boiling point. That's what keeps me from bursting. . . . You weren't asked to the wedding party, My Dears, because it wasnt OUR party, it was Marilyn's and Pauli's." "Our friends," she reminded him, "are our friends. . . . If you are not political, that's alright too. . . . We are still friends, and have faith in and affection for each other. That's the way I feel about it, anyway, and I hope you do too." But in fact the Robeson–Van Vechten friendship, already attenuated, from this point effectively ceased.[49]

"What a disgrace to us all," Pearl Buck wrote Essie a few days after the wedding, having read accounts of the crowd's behavior. "How such stupidities and crassness drag the honor of [our] country down, before other peoples!" She added: "I like to see these good marriages between superior people. They blaze a trail. . . ." Eleanor Roosevelt, asked to comment on the wedding at a press conference, refused: it was, she said, "a marriage of two Americans and completely personal." The arriving hate mail struck a quite different note. "Congratulations on marrying your son to a white girl (tho she is only a kike)," read one representative letter. "Now you have achieved the ambition of all niggers, to mix with white blood. Enjoy your future black and tan grandchildren." As if all this was not difficult enough, Essie's mother, Ma Goode, unhappily ensconced in a Boston nursing home, wrote her daughter a string of querulous letters advising them all to leave the country for Russia (where she, Ma Goode, would open an orphan home for black children and then send them around the world as "missionaries" to demonstrate "the mentality of those who [are given] the opportunity").[50]

The "go-back-to-Russia" theme was soon sounded by parties who saw in that prospect not (as did Ma Goode) a refuge from cowardly racists but, rather, a deserved perdition. The chorus went into full cry as a result of the words Robeson spoke that same day, June 19, at a Welcome Home rally staged for him by the Council on African Affairs at the Rockland Palace in Harlem. The wedding party, with only a few hours' respite, went directly from the hostile mob scene at Reverend Darr's to the cordial frenzy of forty-five hundred political fans, roughly half of them white, gathered at the Rockland Palace.

The rally ran for four and a half hours, replete with a dozen speeches and again as many announced messages of greeting. Du Bois gave a lengthy, formal address, declaring, "American Negroes have lost their world leadership of the darker people," and Charles P. Howard gave a brief and impassioned personal defense of Robeson in which he denounced the attacks on him as "the basest kind of character assassination" and lamented the "shameful" truth that "some of the lowest, meanest attacks upon Paul have come from our own press, the Negro press." But it was Robeson himself who provided the real fireworks. His anger already aroused by the shenanigans at the wedding ceremony, he threw the full weight of his enormous emotional gravity into one of the most powerful polemics of his career, the passionate eloquence of his voice washing over the occasional patches of rhetoric.[51]

"I defy any part of an insolent, dominating America, however powerful," he said, "I defy any errand boys, Uncle Toms of the Negro people, to challenge my Americanism because by word and deed I challenge this vicious system to the death. I'm looking for freedom—full freedom, not an inferior brand." He insisted that most black Americans, unlike some of their leaders, were "not afraid of their radicals who point out the awful, indefensible truth of our degradation and exploitation. . . . What a travesty is this supposed leadership of a great people! And in this historic time, when their people need them most. How Sojourner Truth, Harriet Tubman, Frederick Douglass must be turning in their graves at this spectacle of a craven, fawning, despicable leadership. . . . You stooges try to do the work of your white bourbon masters, work they have not the courage to do. Try it, but the Negro people will . . . drive you from public life!" Defending his personal record, Robeson recounted how he had had to go to Europe to renew a singing career after his scheduled concerts in this country had been canceled because of his political activities in behalf of civil rights. In thunderous tones he denounced the "vicious" Atlantic Pact ("American big business tells all of Western Europe what to do"), the continuing enslavement of colonial peoples, the betrayal of the American worker by labor leaders like Reuther, Murray, Carey, and Townsend. He hailed those progressives he had met in Europe—"in great part Communists"—who had been "the first to die for our freedom." Just as they had defended his people, black people, he would continue to defend the CPUSA leaders on trial in Foley Square.[52]

"I am born and bred in this America of ours," he said. "I want to love it. I love a part of it. But it's up to the rest of America when I shall love it with the same intensity that I love the Negro people from whom I spring, in the way that I love progressives in the Caribbean, the black and Indian peoples of South and Central America, the peoples of China and Southeast Asia. Yes, suffering people the world over—in the way that I deeply and intensely love the Soviet Union. That burden of proof rests upon America." Black Americans, he insisted, "must have the courage to shout at the top of our voices about our injustices and we must lay the blame where it belongs and where it has belonged for over three hundred years of slavery and misery—right here on our own doorstep, not in any faraway place."

Then, deliberately employing a subtle modification of the words which had been falsely ascribed to him in Paris (but actually said by him in Stockholm), Robeson converted the earlier version—a prediction that black Americans *would* not fight their friends—into urging that they *should* not fight: "We do not want to die in vain any more on foreign battlefields for Wall Street and the greedy supporters of domestic fascism. If we must die, let it be in Mississippi or Georgia. Let it be wherever we are lynched and deprived of our rights as human beings. Let this be a final answer to the warmongers. Let them know that we will not help to enslave our brothers and sisters, and eventually ourselves." Kay and Aubrey Pankey (the black singer who later expatriated himself to Europe) drove Paul and Essie home after the rally. He was "strung out," Kay Pankey remembers nearly forty years later, "and soaked right through his suit. And he was irritable. Essie was being overprotective—and it was the last straw, Essie being so nice." In spite of the tensions, the difficult day ended with a large and happy wedding party for Paul, Jr., and Marilyn at Freda and Barry's home.[53]

"Loves Soviet Best, Robeson Declares," blared the headline on *The New York Times* story the following morning. "An Undesirable Citizen," ran the heading on a front-page editorial carried by Hearst newspapers all over the country—the editorial going on to declare, "It was an accident unfortunate for America that Robeson was born here." (That statement so impressed Representative Thomas J. Lane that he had it read next day into the *Congressional Record.*) In answering the Hearst editorial, and the dozens of other vitriolic anti-Robeson articles that poured out, the Pittsburgh *Courier*, though not often sympathetic to Robeson, defended his "right to become angry. . . . He is joined by millions of other real American citizens of every racial, religious and economic group, who have felt the sting of segregation and discrimination."[54]

On the whole, though, the black press was not kind to Robeson. *The*

Afro-American ran a story headlined, " 'I Love Above All, Russia,' Robeson Says," and the New York *Amsterdam News* printed a feature (picked up from the *Sunday Express* in England and entitled "Why Doesn't Paul Robeson Give More to His Own Negroes Instead of Russian Reds?") that described Robeson as the "world's richest artist," who had changed his politics because his son had been denied admittance to a public school in England. Lester Granger, head of the National Urban League, published a column in the *Amsterdam News* lambasting Robeson's "predictably hackneyed statement" and adding: "He is probably the biggest personal asset the Communist Party possesses today. . . . The Communist leaders here in America, when they say their prayers at night and turn their faces toward the Moscow god whom they worship, must assuredly say a special prayer for the continued health and vitality of their current star attraction. They'd better, for he's the last bit of glamor their raggedy party can produce these days." At a press conference, President Truman was quoted as using the word "gang" in denouncing Robeson, Wallace, and Clifford J. Durr, president of the National Lawyers Guild (the three had jointly called for an FBI investigation of the Klan). Did you say "gang"? an incredulous reporter asked. Yes, "gang," the President replied, brusquely adding that he had taken care of them in the last election.[55]

Worse soon followed. The House Un-American Activities Committee decided it wanted to hear testimony—pledges of loyalty, the cynics said—from prominent Afro-Americans in response to Robeson's statement that American blacks would or should not fight in a war against the Soviet Union. The NAACP telegraphed Representative John S. Wood, chairman of HUAC, protesting the hearings on the ground that "There never has been any question of the loyalty of the Negro to the United States of America" and stating that the "NAACP fails to see the necessity of holding hearings to be assured of what is already known to be true by our government." Wood replied that HUAC was not undertaking an investigation of the loyalty of the black citizenry but, rather, graciously responding to "requests [that] have been received by this committee from members of his [Robeson's] race that a forum be afforded for the expression of contrary views" to the "disloyal and unpatriotic statements" he had made. "This is a privilege which the Committee feels should be granted."[56]

The hearings opened in mid-July. Alvin Stokes, a black investigator for HUAC, testified on the stand that the Communists planned to set up a Soviet republic in the Deep South and that "Robeson's voice was the voice of the Kremlin." Manning Johnson, the black anti-Communist (and professional informer) who had previously testified in numerous loyalty cases, declared unequivocally and falsely that Robeson was a member of the Party, had "delusions of grandeur," and was "desirous of becoming the Black Stalin." (Asked by a reporter two months later whether he had such ambitions, Robeson dryly replied that he "was in no way trained for political leadership.") And a disabled black veteran pledged his loyalty to the United States.[57]

Next to testify were some heavyweights. Charles S. Johnson, president of Fisk University and earlier a friend of Robeson's, limited himself to saying on the stand that he saw no evidence of Communists' trying "to impregnate Negro schools." Thomas W. Young, president of the Guide Publishing Company in Norfolk, Virginia (publishers of the newspaper *Journal and Guide*), declared that Robeson had broken the bond he once had with black people and had "done a great disservice to his race—far greater than that done to his country." Lester Granger of the Urban League, who had already published a column attacking Robeson, used his opportunity in front of HUAC to suggest that it investigate the activities of such organizations as the KKK, "to reassure Negro leadership that while it is fighting against one enemy of this country, Communism, our Government is helping to fight off the other, Racism."[58]

Now came HUAC's final and star witness, Jackie Robinson, whose entry into major-league baseball Robeson had worked to facilitate. With movie and television cameras grinding away and the committee room packed, he read a prepared statement apparently written for him by Lester Granger. He had been urged, Robinson began—and "not all of this urging came from Communist sympathizers"—not to show up at the hearing. But he had, out of "a sense of responsibility," decided to "stick my neck out." He made it clear that he believed black Americans had real grievances, and "the fact that it is a Communist who denounces injustice in the courts, police brutality, and lynching when it happens doesn't change the truth of his charges"; racial discrimination in America was not "a creation of Communist imagination." Robeson had written Robinson just before his HUAC appearance to warn him that the press had "badly distorted" his remarks in Paris, and Robinson commented that "if Mr. Robeson actually made" the statement ascribed to him about American blacks' refusing to fight in a war against Russia, it "sounds very silly to me. . . . He has a right to his personal views, and if he wants to sound silly when he expresses them in public, that is his business and not mine. He's still a famous ex-athlete and a great singer and actor." As for himself, Robinson continued, as "a religious man" he cherished America as a place "where I am free to worship as I please"; "that doesn't mean that we're going to stop fighting race discrimination in this country until we've got it licked," but it did mean "we can win our fight without the Communists and we don't want their help." Three members of the committee joined in complimenting Robinson on his "splendid statement." He left the capital immediately for New York, thereby escaping, as the black newspaper *New Age* pointed out, "being Jim Crowed by Washington's infamous lily-white hotels." That same week, Republican Representative Kearney of New York, a former national commander of the Veterans of Foreign Wars, recommended that Robinson receive the VFW's medal for good citizenship.[59]

The New York Times put Robinson's testimony on page one, printed his HUAC statement in full (claiming that at the completion of his testimony a voice had called out "Amen" from the audience), and for good measure ran an editorial the same day declaring, "Mr. Robeson has attached himself to the cause of a country in which all men are equal because they are equally enslaved." Joining the denunciation of Robeson and the praise of Robinson in her nationally syndicated "My Day" column, Eleanor Roosevelt wrote, "Mr. Robeson does his people great harm in trying to line them up on the Communist side of the political picture. Jackie Robinson helped them greatly by his forthright statements." The New York *Amsterdam News* was equally supportive of Robinson, reporting that in its survey of 239 Brooklynites "not one person disagreed" with his position—"Jackie Robinson apparently batted 1,000 percent in this game."[60]

But black reaction, in fact, was far from unanimous. The Council on African Affairs predictably issued a statement that "The Un-American Committee is out to smear Robeson because he challenges and refuses to accept any brand of second-class Jim-Crow Americanism." And the following week, at a Bill of Rights conference sponsored by the Civil Rights Congress, the twelve hundred delegates gave Robeson a standing ovation at the conclusion of his militant address—"I am a radical. I am going to stay one until my people are free to walk the earth"—and three hundred and sixty black delegates passed a resolution declaring that Paul Robeson "does indeed speak for us not only in his fight for full Negro democratic rights, but also in his fight for peace." But, discounting the views of such interested parties, some black establishment voices were also sounded in Robeson's behalf. *The Afro-American* ran a cartoon depicting a frightened little boy labeled Jackie Robinson with a huge gun in his hand, uncertainly tracking the giant footprints of Paul Robeson, with the caption "The leading player in the National Baseball League is only a tyro as a big-game hunter." The respected black columnist J. A. Rogers expressed agreement with many of Robinson's sentiments but disapproved of the auspices under which he had delivered them; he was convinced, Rogers wrote, that Robeson was "as loyal an American as any other" and convinced, too, that "Negroes are responding to him." And *New Age* reported that "Harlemites . . . split sharply on the issue of whether the popular ballplayer should have gone before the committee. . . . Opinion was both congratulatory and condemnatory."[61]

Robeson's own reaction to Robinson's testimony was muted. He assailed the HUAC proceedings in general terms as "an insult to the Negro people" and an incitement to a terrorist group like the Klan to step up its reign of mob violence; he also challenged the loyalty of HUAC to the ideals of the republic, because it maintained an "ominous silence" in the face of the continued lynchings of black citizens. But he refused to "be drawn into any conflict dividing me from my brother victim of this terror," insisting that he had only respect for Jackie Robinson, that Robinson was entitled to his opinion, and—realizing that, in the context of the day, Robinson's statement had actually been mild—that there was "no argument between Jackie and me." When reporters tried to draw him out further, he refused the bait, saying only, "We could take our liberties tomorrow if we didn't fight among ourselves." Though Jackie Robinson became more active in the civil-rights struggle after he retired from baseball in 1956, he campaigned actively for Richard Nixon in 1960 and stated in his 1972 autobiography that he had no regrets about the remarks he'd made before HUAC. But in fact he did. Disillusioned himself in his final years with the conservative leadership of the NAACP and the seeming impasse over improving the lot of the average black person, he also wrote in his autobiography:

> . . . in those days I had much more faith in the ultimate justice of the American white man than I have today. I would reject such an invitation if offered now. . . . I have grown wiser and closer to painful truths about America's destructiveness. And I do have increased respect for Paul Robeson who, over a span of twenty years, sacrificed himself, his career, and the wealth and comfort he once enjoyed because, I believe, he was sincerely trying to help his people.[62]

The cauldron, in any case, was aboil. When a black man in Knoxville, Tennessee, refused to move to the rear of a bus, a cop shouted at him, "You're just like Paul Robeson!"[63]

■

CHAPTER 18

Peekskill

(1949)

The deep animus against Robeson that the HUAC hearings disclosed did not serve to slow his activities. Opposition, typically, emboldened him; pressure brought out his intransigence. And he could be profoundly intransigent, surface geniality notwithstanding. His powerful will and his ardor for principle, combined with his ingrained optimism, allowed him all at once to proceed in the face of resistance, to close his mind to counter-arguments, and to feel confident of ultimate results. In a talk at the left-wing People's Songs Conference on August 13, he told the crowd, "In Europe and since I've come back . . . I've thrown down the gauntlet, and it's going to stay."[1]

Four days after Jackie Robinson's HUAC appearance, Robeson, as good as his word, publicly assailed the "machine politicians" who had entered an alternate candidate against Ben Davis, Jr., in his re-election bid for the New York City Council. The following week he joined a hundred people picketing the White House in protest against discriminatory hiring practices at the Bureau of Engraving and Printing (the demonstration had been called by the United Public Workers of America, CIO—of which Robeson was an honorary member). The next day he denounced President Truman's appointment of Attorney General Tom Clark to the Supreme Court as a "gratuitous and outrageous insult to my people," for Clark had listed multiple organizations fighting for civil rights as "subversive." The day after that, from a loudspeaker truck in Harlem, Robeson addressed a rally demanding the freedom of Henry Winston, the black Communist leader, who had been jailed by Judge Medina for contempt of court in the ongoing trial of the Communist leaders at Foley Square. That same day,

J. Edgar Hoover received photostats of Robeson's federal income-tax returns for the years 1939–47, part of the "documentary evidence" he had been soliciting from Bureau agents which would prove "suitable for cross-examination" should Robeson, as expected, testify at the trial of the Communist leaders.[2]

In that same week in mid-August 1949, People's Artists Inc., a left-wing New York theatrical agency, announced a Robeson concert at the Lakeland Acres picnic grounds, outside of Peekskill, for August 27, the proceeds to go to the Harlem chapter of the Civil Rights Congress. (It would be the fourth Robeson concert in the Peekskill area; the preceding three had all been successful.) The Peekskill *Evening Star* immediately ran a front-page story on Robeson's upcoming appearance with a three-column headline: "Robeson Concert Here Aids 'Subversive' Unit—Is Sponsored by 'People's Artists' Called Red Front in California." The *Star*'s editorial, on the inside page, insisted, "The time for tolerant silence that signifies approval is running out," and it printed a letter from an American Legion officer (headlined "Says Robeson and His Followers Are Unwelcome") that declared, "Some of the weaker minded are susceptible to their [the "Communists"] fallacious teachings unless something is done by the loyal Americans of this area"; "I am not intimating violence," he added, "but I believe that we should give this matter serious consideration. . . ." The *Star*'s coverage set off a rash of activity. The president of the Peekskill Chamber of Commerce issued a statement attacking the concert; the Junior Chamber of Commerce called it "un-American" and called for "group action" to "discourage" it; the town supervisor of Cortlandt, where the Lakeland picnic grounds were located, said he was "deeply opposed to such gatherings"; the Joint Veterans' Council urged its members to join the anti-Robeson demonstration.[3]

The town of Peekskill, in New York's Westchester County, was a typically mainstream blue-collar place, set apart from ten thousand others by the pockets of left-wing sympathizers in surrounding areas, mostly Jewish and mostly summer residents. The year-round citizens had long felt distaste for these "rich, radical outsiders," and a potentially volatile tension had long existed. Sam and Helen Rosen were part of this world, often journeying up from their apartment in Manhattan to their house in the estate area of Katonah, about fifteen miles from Peekskill. On Saturday, August 27, the day of the scheduled concert, Paul called Helen Rosen from Grand Central Station, where he was about to board a train for Peekskill, to say he'd heard rumors of possible trouble. Sam—confined at home with a broken leg—turned on the radio and, sure enough, reports came over that various groups, including the Veterans of Foreign Wars, the American Legion, and St. Joseph's, the Catholic high school, were mobilizing. Helen told Paul she'd meet his train. She then phoned a friend in Croton, Sydney Danis, and asked him for backup help. He agreed "to get two stalwart fellows" and meet her at the Peekskill station. Helen set out with her fourteen-year-old son, John, who insisted on accompanying her. ("Nobody's going to hurt our Paul." His eighteen-year-old sister, Judy, shared his sentiments; as soon as she heard the news of trouble, she flew home from California, where she had been vacationing, and arrived in Katonah the following day.)[4]

At the train station, as Helen recalls it, "it was just like any Saturday afternoon, with people coming up for the weekend" and cars lined up to greet them. While awaiting Paul's arrival, Helen heard on the radio that protesters were massing at the picnic grounds. Paul got off the train without incident, but it was decided that he should go in Danis's car, with Helen and John driving in front of them in their station wagon. As they neared the picnic grounds, it was immediately apparent that a brawl was in progress. A truck was deliberately parked in the middle of the road, effectively blocking it, forcing traffic to a crawl, allowing marauding groups of young men to check the occupants of each car, yanking some of the passengers out while a jeering crowd on the sidelines yelled "Dirty Commie" and "Dirty kike," tossing rocks, mauling suspicious strays. Police were visible on the sidelines, some smiling, none making a move to interfere with the mob; although the identities of the townspeople were familiar—St. Joseph's School had proudly unfurled its banner—the police arrested no one. Helen saw a burning cross on the hill. She got John down on the floor of the station wagon and ran to the car behind her, where Paul was. He was enraged and, according to Helen, "We had a hard time keeping him from getting out of the car." "Get him the hell out of here!" she yelled to Danis and his friends. "Get the hell out of here! Get him to New York!"[5]

Somehow Danis managed to back out of the line of cars and drove Robeson first to the Danis house in Croton and then to the Rockmores' summer place in Ossining, thirty minutes from Peekskill. Helen and John inched their way home while the anti-Robeson mob moved on to attack the concertgoers, smash the stage, torch the camp chairs set up around it—and put a dozen Robeson supporters in the hospital. Clara Rockmore remembers that when Paul arrived he was more agitated than angry, not quite able to believe the awful reality of what had happened. He put in a call to the Rosens to tell them he was safe; then he and the Rockmores sat up most of the night on the porch overlooking the lake. In the morning a car came to take him back to New York City. He went straight to a press conference at the Hotel Theresa in Harlem, where he called for a Justice Department investigation, characterized the rioting as "an attack on the whole Negro people," and suggested that a boycott of Peekskill merchants might prove an effective way to put pressure on those decent but indifferent souls who deplored violence but did nothing to prevent it.[6]

That same afternoon, the Rosens opened up their place in Katonah for a protest meeting. Already inundated with hate calls, Helen asked the state police for protection. "They promised to be there, but nobody came." John Rosen owned a .22 for target practice; after he strapped it on, he and a friend booby-trapped the driveway with wire fencing and then personally patrolled it. Fifteen hundred people showed up at the Rosens', formed the Westchester Committee for Law and Order, and invited Robeson to return to Peekskill. Representatives from several left-wing unions—the Fur and Leather Workers, the United Electrical Workers, the Longshoremen—pledged to mobilize their members to serve as a cordon of defense for a rescheduled concert—"come what may," as a statement signed by union leaders put it. Ten union men bedded down right then and there on the Rosens' porch to guard the family.[7]

The following day—Monday, August 29—the first newspaper accounts of the riot hit the stands. "Robeson: He Asked for It," headlined the *Daily Mirror.* The *Daily Worker,* in contrast, reported its story under the lead "Lynch Mob Runs Amuck at Robeson's Concert." While the press furiously debated who had provoked whom to do what, the FBI's own agent, in a teletype message sent the night of the riot, acknowledged twice that it had been "started by vets." That was to prove the outer limit of official candor. The FBI dutifully brought the matter to the attention of the Justice Department, but J. Edgar Hoover decided he would "conduct no investigation unless requested."[8]

By now statements, charges, and protests flooded the media. The Joint Veterans Council of Peekskill disclaimed any involvement in a "riot," describing its activities as a "protest parade . . . held without any disorder and . . . peacefully disbanded." The national commander of the Veterans of Foreign Wars also denied any responsibility for the lawlessness, acknowledging only that the local post had engaged in "a spontaneous demonstration." The Peekskill police chief said the picnic grounds had been outside his jurisdiction; a spokesman for the state police said he had never received a request for troopers. The commander of Peekskill Post 274 of the American Legion disdained excuse or apology: "Our objective was to prevent the Paul Robeson concert and I think our objective was reached."[9]

On the other side, the American Civil Liberties Union, in a statement signed by John Haynes Holmes, Roger Baldwin, and Arthur Garfield Hays, declared it was "unfortunate and inexplicable that during the three hours of rioting which took place, a sufficient number of law enforcement officials . . . did not appear on the scene." The music critic Olin Downes and the novelist Howard Fast led a protest meeting of the New York State Council of the Arts, Sciences and Professions. Vito Marcantonio accused Westchester County officials of direct complicity. The state commander of the Jewish War Veterans, denouncing the riot as "a shameful blot," denied that local officials could be relied on for an unbiased report and called for a special investigator. A large number of concerned individuals added their voices—among them Henry A. Wallace, Lindsay H. White (president of the New York NAACP), and Rabbi Irving Miller (chairman of the American Jewish Congress). The FBI carefully noted the names of those speaking out in Robeson's behalf.[10]

Governor Thomas E. Dewey at first refused to comment on events at Peekskill, but as calls for an investigation mounted, he bowed to the pressure and ordered Westchester County District Attorney George M. Fanelli to make a report to him. Fanelli immediately announced that he had studied pictures of the mêlée and was subpoenaing prints of one "particularly revealing" photograph published in the New York *Daily News:* a black holding a knife in his hand. Fanelli also portentously announced that in the litter on the picnic ground a pamphlet entitled *Political Economy in the Soviet Union* had been retrieved, as well as a cardboard coin container bearing the label "1949 Lenin Memorial."[11]

On Tuesday, August 30, an overflow crowd of three thousand gathered at the Golden Gate Ballroom in Harlem in response to a call put out by the Emergency Committee to Protest the Peekskill Riot. The turnout was so large that speakers at the rally repeated their remarks to those who waited outside the hall. The New York *Amsterdam News* described the huge crowd as "composed of Robeson fans, Communist Party leaders . . . rank and file Harlemites and the curious representing all shades of political opinion." Robeson handled the crowd masterfully, interjecting into his long speech singing, talking, and confidential asides. He began by emphasizing that "It's been a long struggle that I've waged, sometimes not very well understood," and he reiterated, as so often in his public statements, that the struggle was not just by and for Communists and blacks but included an alliance of the oppressed everywhere. Then he launched into a political polemic as fierce and telling as he ever delivered: "I will be loyal to the America of the true traditions; to the America of the abolitionists, of Harriet Tubman, of Thaddeus Stevens, of those who fought for my people's freedom, not of those who tried to enslave them. And I will have no loyalty to the Forrestals, to the Harrimans, to the Wall-Streeters. . . ." Calling the Peekskill riot "a preview of American storm troopers in action," he added, with perhaps calculated optimism, that it also meant "a real turn in the anti-Fascist struggle in America." Peekskill had opened people's eyes. "We are a part of a very historic departure. This means that from now on out we take the offensive. *We* take it! We'll have our meetings and our concerts all over these United States. That's right. And we'll see that our women and our children are not harmed again! We will understand that . . . the surest way to get police protection is to have it very clear that we'll protect ourselves, and good! . . . I'll be back with my friends in Peekskill. . . ." As the crowd cheered, a special detail of more than a hundred police and detectives kept an eye out for trouble. None came. When the meeting ended, at midnight, the police escorted the

Robeson supporters in a torchlight parade down Lenox Avenue to 135th Street.[12]

According to Howard "Stretch" Johnson, a second-echelon CP leader who at the time was the Party's New York State educational director, "There was a big debate in the Party as to what kind of reaction we should have" to the Peekskill riot. A segment of the Party leadership was already annoyed at Robeson for his "nationalistic" speech in Paris (the rumor was that Ben Davis, Jr.'s vigorous defense of Robeson had imperiled his own position for a time), and so when Peekskill erupted, "the dominant white [New York State] leadership," particularly Robert Thompson, wanted to "follow the path of least resistance" and confine protest to the Harlem rally. But Johnson and others successfully led the opposing group in arguing that they had to "beard the lion in his own den and go back to Peekskill." Robeson agreed. He announced that he would give a rescheduled concert on September 4.[13]

When it was learned in Peekskill that Robeson would return, tension quickly mounted. The Associated Veterans' Group, representing fourteen posts, announced that it would stage a mammoth protest parade on the day of the concert. Flag salesmen appeared on the streets of the town, and most businessmen—for fourteen dollars—prudently bought one for display. Signs and car stickers began to appear everywhere with the slogan "Wake Up America—Peekskill Did!" To deal with the rash of threatening phone calls coming in to pro-Robeson supporters, the Peekskill telephone company had to hire extra operators. The New York *Compass* reported that, under the threat of the anonymous calls, vacationers were closing up their houses and returning to New York. Helen Rosen, determined to go to the market in order to feed the union men guarding her house, discovered that nobody in town would talk to her. (One neighbor did, though: he came over with an offer to buy the Rosen place. It's yours, Helen told him—for a million dollars, to be paid *now*. He declined.) The Fur and Leather Workers Union and several other left-wing groups organized a security force to protect the concertgoers (the FBI lumped all such activity together as "Communists . . . endeavoring to recruit delegations"). The Westchester Committee for Law and Order spent the forty-eight hours preceding the concert, largely without sleep, contacting state and local officials in an effort to ensure a peaceful outcome. Two effigies of Robeson were hanged on the night before the rescheduled concert.[14]

At 6:00 a.m. on September 4, the first union guards arrived to set up defense lines at the concert site at Hollow Brook Golf Course, three miles outside of Peekskill. The state police, under the direction of Superintendent John Gaffney, set up a command post in a nearby area. Overhead a police helicopter circled. Four ambulances stood by. As some twenty thousand concertgoers began to arrive at midday, a veterans' protest parade—only about eight thousand strong rather than the thirty thousand the

Associated Veterans' Group had called for—marched outside the grounds under the eyes of state and local police, yelling anti-Semitic and anti-black remarks and taunting the arrivals with shouted threats: "We'll kill you!," "You'll get in but you won't get out!"[15]

Robeson, under the advice of the security men, remained in his car. Promptly at two o'clock the concert began. Union guards, Revels Cayton among them, ringed the platform. Pete Seeger sang. Pianists Ray Lev and Leonid Hambro played Bach and Chopin. There were no speeches, political or otherwise. At four, Robeson, accompanied by an admittedly terrified Larry Brown, performed, ringed around by fifteen or so union men; after opening the concert with "Let My People Go," he brought the crowd to its feet with a rendition of "Ol' Man River" that emphasized his earlier change in lyrics: "I must keep fightin' until I'm dyin'." Helen Rosen noticed several men with guns on the ridge surrounding the hollow; Paul, an easy target in full view, was clearly taking his life in his hands. (Cayton had predicted before the concert that, "With so many people watching, they wouldn't dare go for him," that Robeson "was going to be like the safest man in New York." For years afterward, when setting off on some chancy engagement, Robeson would laughingly say, "I guess I'll be the safest man in the country.") The security force flushed two men with high-powered rifles out of a nest in a hill overlooking the hollow. The uneasy truce held throughout the concert. When it was over, Robeson was taken out in a convoy of cars whose windows were shaded with blankets; Robeson himself lay on the rear floor, while two of the trade-union bodyguards covered him with their bodies.[16]

Then the crowd started home. Or tried to. As the line of buses and cars crawled along the steep road winding out of the hollow, it ran into a gauntlet of enraged locals. Some hurled rocks from the embankment; others stopped cars, dragged out the occupants, and beat them. The police did nothing to intervene. Some of the troopers joked with the anti-Robeson forces on the embankment; others joined the attackers below. One eyewitness saw the driver of a car in front of him hit in the kidneys by a cop; another was clubbed by a group of fifteen to twenty policemen; a third was dragged face down in the dirt and then told to "Get going, you red bastard!," "Go back to Jew town, if we catch you up here again we'll kill you!" Before long the scene was "a nightmare of crashing rocks, flying glass, blood, and swerving cars."

Hundreds of the volunteer union guards were trapped in the hollow, surrounded by the stone-throwing mob and by a thousand state policemen who refused to let the union men return to their buses. Leon Strauss, vice-president of the Fur and Leather Workers, who was in charge of the defense force, later insisted that Superintendent Gaffney and District Attorney Fanelli had done nothing to clear away the threatening crowd or to restrain some of their own men, who encircled and then charged the trapped guards, beating them with their clubs. Twenty-five of the guards were arrested. Called at his home and asked to intervene, Henry Wallace tried to get through to Governor Dewey on the phone but could get no further than James C. Hagerty, the governor's press secretary, who told him it was "just a bunch of Communists who had started violence." The mêlée went on until 1:30 a.m. By the time it was over, dozens of buses and cars had had their windows smashed and been overturned, and a hundred and fifty people were injured seriously enough to require medical treatment (among them Revels Cayton and Irving Potash, who nearly lost his eye from flying glass and appeared the next morning as a defendant at the Foley Square trial wearing dark glasses). District Attorney Fanelli congratulated the police on having done "a magnificent job."[17]

The next day Robeson held a ninety-minute press conference in the library of the Council on African Affairs. Newsmen jammed the room to hear fifteen witnesses, several bandaged from injuries, give eyewitness accounts, and to hear Robeson explain that the concert had ended in violence because the "police who were supposed to protect us, attacked and assaulted us." He called the marauding state troopers "Fascist storm troopers who will knock down and club anyone who disagrees with them," charged Governor Dewey with complicity, and demanded federal intervention to restore law and order. When he added that "we Negroes owe a great debt to the Jewish people, who stood there by the hundreds to defend me and all of us yesterday," tears started from his eyes. In Albany, James C. Hagerty said the governor would not comment until he had full reports from District Attorney Fanelli and State Police Superintendent Gaffney. In nearly the same breath, and with no hint of irony, Hagerty announced that Governor Dewey had ordered a full police mobilization to take immediate action against an "outbreak of lawlessness" among UAW strikers at the Bell Aircraft plant near Niagara Falls.[18]

Fanelli made his report to the governor on September 7. It exonerated veterans' groups and police from responsibility for the violence: "Every precaution possible was taken to insure the safety of all present. All police departments that took part in the plan should be commended for their excellent work." After meeting with Fanelli and Gaffney, Dewey issued a statement the following week that went the D.A. one better. Characterizing the concertgoers as "followers of Red totalitarianism," Dewey asserted that the "Communist groups obviously did provoke this incident." He sounded as his only note of regret that the demonstrators, in responding, had given "the Communists effective propaganda." In the same spirit, *Life* magazine stated flatly that the Communists had aimed for "the calculated, purposeful incitement of racial conflict" at Peekskill and that Robeson had "baited the Communist trap." *Newsweek,* similarly, declared that "with the aid of anti-Communist hot-heads, the Communists had won a smashing propaganda triumph." Bombarded from many quarters—the ACLU, labor unions, the National Committee of the Progressive Party, the American Jewish Congress, the National Lawyers Guild, groups of clergymen, law professors, and a fair portion of the press—with the demand for an impartial inquiry, Dewey did finally order a grand-jury investigation. But he carefully hedged the bet, charging the jury with instructions to inquire whether the breach of peace had been "a part of the Communist strategy to foment racial and religious hatreds" and placing in charge of the investigation none other than D.A. Fanelli.[19]

Back in Katonah, the Rosens hung on for another few weeks but then, in the face of a torrent of hate mail and obscene phone calls, temporarily closed up their house (to return in the late fall, with Paul as a frequent though hidden guest). In Manhattan, Sam Rosen's medical practice dramatically dwindled, despite his superb reputation as an ear specialist. (Undaunted, Sam undertook basic research and in 1953 invented stapes surgery, a major breakthrough in the treatment of deafness.) In the immediate aftermath of Peekskill, the vigilante spirit was not confined solely to hobbling the Rosens. The Peekskill *Star* editorially compared the recent "incident" to the Boston Tea Party. Stickers reading "Communism Is Treason, Behind Communism Stands—the Jew!" were pasted on cars (and in the neighboring village of Harmon, the only Jewish home was stoned, its windows smashed). The American Legion requested that books by "known Communists" be removed from the Peekskill library. Veterans from fourteen posts in Westchester and Putnam counties held a "patriotic rally," and in Cortlandt town officials announced an anti-"disturbance" ordinance so loose—imposing fines and jail sentences for those "disturbing the public peace"—that it threatened to destroy the right of assembly. Among the residents active in resisting the wave of repression, one local man stood as a bulwark; it later turned out he was a plant—during subsequent grand-jury proceedings he fingered the very people he had professed to be working with.[20]

Impaneled in October, the grand jury held lengthy hearings, listening to the testimony of some two hundred and fifty witnesses. At the close it issued a report that read as if dictated by D.A. Fanelli, with a few embellishments peculiar to the jury itself—like the reference in its report to the union security guards as "goon squads," the claim that the colonies of summer residents in the Peekskill area harbored active Communists, and the assertion that *the* underlying cause of the outbreak had been Robeson's own inflammatory statements "derogatory to his native land" during 1949. The grand jury concluded that the Communists had deliberately fomented "racial and religious hatred" on September 4 and at the same time insisted that the violence "was basically neither anti-Semitic nor anti-Negro in character." "The fundamental cause of resentment and the focus of hostility was Communism . . . and Communism alone." Given the provocations, the grand jury commended the police for not having used "any more force than was justified."[21]

The other legal and quasi-legal proceedings following on the riot likewise ended in defeat for the Robeson forces. Three months after Peekskill, Robeson and twenty-seven other plaintiffs filed a two-million-dollar damage suit against various veterans' organizations and county officials—including Fanelli and Gaffney—charging personal injuries, property damages, and deprivation of constitutional rights guaranteed by the Fourteenth Amendment and the provisions of the 1870 and 1871 civil-rights acts. Walter Winchell, who had already blasted Robeson in a radio commentary, announced, "It is too bad the law doesn't allow a counter-claim by the veterans of 1 billion dollars—for service rendered in defending the U.S. Constitution and the privileges of the plaintiffs to abuse it." The action dragged on through various delays and rulings until New York Supreme Court Justice James W. Bailey dismissed the suits fifteen months later.[22]

In the immediate aftermath of the "battle of Peekskill," defense attorneys for the Communist leaders on trial in Foley Square moved for a mistrial, on the grounds that the riot had been "a conclusive manifestation of the prejudice existing" against the eleven defendants. Judge Medina characterized the events at Peekskill as an "outrage," but denied the motion as irrelevant to the trial at hand. When the defense attorneys pressed their demands for an investigation of Peekskill, Medina exploded—such tactics were "part and parcel of the endeavor to launch a counter-attack on society instead of meeting the issues of the trial." He ordered testimony to continue. Ten days later Robeson took the stand facing Medina, his old law professor from Columbia.[23]

He was on the stand about twenty minutes. Every time the black defense attorney, George W. Crockett, Jr., asked Robeson a question, U.S. Attorney John F. X. McGohey objected—and each time Judge Medina sustained the objection, ruling the question irrelevant (among the questions Crockett asked Robeson was whether his father had been born in slavery). Robeson managed to make only two points: that he personally knew all eleven defendants (but had not been allowed to serve as a character witness) and that he had studied under Judge Medina. Unable to get the testimony he wanted from Robeson, Crockett withdrew him. "I don't think you should have called him." Medina remarked.[24]

Stymied in court, Robeson held a press conference at the Federal Court House. He blasted Medina's rulings. He had wanted to say, he told the newsmen, that "the Communist Party has played a magnificent role in fighting for the freedom of the American Negro," and he hadn't gotten the chance to because "they don't want the truth." "Are you a Communist?," a reporter asked. "That question is irrelevant," Robeson replied. That same week, the black columnist Lem Graves, Jr., printed an exclusive interview with Robeson in the Pittsburgh *Courier* during which he asked Robeson if he wanted "a new kind of economic and political system in America." Robeson is quoted as replying that he wanted "any kind of system the people want. . . . I don't want America to adopt a system for which it is not ready. . . . This country is not ready for either the socialization which was adopted in England or the system which is in operation in Russia. But it is ready for the extension of democratic principles. . . ." He also called for a redistribution of wealth "to eliminate the situation where 1 per cent of the people own 60 per cent of the wealth." Asked if he would approve of a revolution in the United States, "he answered that he did not think a physical revolution would be successful and added that he disliked physical violence."[25]

The day after Robeson testified at the Foley Square trial, New York Congressman Jacob Javits spoke briefly in the U.S. House of Representatives, deploring the Peekskill riot as a violation of the constitutional guarantees of freedom of speech and assembly. That brought Representative John Rankin of Mississippi storming to the microphone. "It was not surprising to hear the gentleman from New York defend that Communist enclave," Rankin shouted, but he wanted it known that the American people are not in sympathy "with that N—— Communist and that bunch of Reds who went up there." On a point of order, Representative Vito Marcantonio of New York protested to speaker Rayburn that "the gentleman from Mississippi used the word 'nigger.' I ask that the word be taken down and stricken from the RECORD inasmuch as there are two members in this House of the Negro race, and that word reflects on them." Rayburn said he understood the gentleman from Mississippi to say "Negro." "I said 'Niggra,' " Rankin yelled, refusing to let Rayburn off the hook, "just as I have said since I have been able to talk, and shall continue to say." Marcantonio insisted Rankin had said "nigger." Standing at his place on the floor, Rankin shouted back, "If that N—— Robeson does not like this country, let him go to Russia, and take that gang of alien Communists with him."[26]

Speaker Rayburn ruled that "the gentleman from Mississippi is not subject to a point of order. He referred to the Negro race, and they should not be ashamed of that designation." Thus encouraged by the Speaker, Representative Gene Cox of Georgia took the floor to denounce Robeson as a "Communist agent provocateur," demanding to know why he, too, was not on trial in Foley Square. Two days after that, Representative Walton W. Gwinn, whose district included Peekskill, made extensive remarks about "the Communist military raid" on Peekskill, ending with the peroration that "Our people need to awake to the danger in their midst, from soft shilly-shallying compromises, in the name of tolerance." The AP reported that in at least two places—Tallahassee, Florida, and Birmingham, Alabama—effigies of Robeson were tied to trees and burned.[27]

For Essie, who was fearless, the threats became so numerous that she had an alarm system installed in Enfield and took to sleeping at night with a hunting knife next to her pillow (the police having turned down her request for a gun permit). "If anyone I don't know enters this house, I will kill him first and find out afterwards why he came here," she told a reporter. She went on to say that she was "in complete harmony" with her husband "on major issues," though they disagreed about "a million things," and she was convinced an effort was being made to silence him because "he personifies the resistance of the colored man to enslavement and repression."[28]

The national debate on Peekskill raged for many months. Eleanor Roosevelt struck perhaps its most recurrent note when, in one of her syndicated "My Day" columns, she simultaneously expressed her dislike for "everything that Paul Robeson is now saying" and denounced the "lawlessness" of the anti-Robeson forces at Peekskill as "quite disgraceful." When the American Civil Liberties Union asked for Mrs. Roosevelt's signature on a public statement deploring current efforts "aimed at putting penalties upon political opinions," she declined, declaring herself in disagreement with the part of the statement that called for "every encouragement" to be given "to the fullest freedom of expression by Communists as by all others in order that the American people may determine through public debate of all issues, the road to progress." Her reluctance to assert the importance of preserving the right of free speech for Communists represented the "liberal" view.[29]

In the black community, Mrs. Roosevelt's counterpart was A. Philip Randolph. In a lengthy letter to *The New York Times*, Randolph, too, adopted a pox-on-both-your-houses posture. He deplored the violence at Peekskill but also deplored the willingness of "Robeson and his followers . . . to seize upon, capitalize and even aggravate the situation. . . ." Above all, Randolph expressed concern with "dissociating this whole affair from the cause of the Negro and his fight for liberation." The Peekskill riot, he wrote, "was not racial," and Robeson was not a spokesman for black people. "Men must earn the right to become the responsible voice of an oppressed group," and Robeson, Randolph asserted—in much the same way Roy Wilkins had earlier—had been insufficiently engaged in "struggle, suffering and sacrifice and service for said group" to qualify. Taking quite an opposite tack, the black sociologist E. Franklin Frazier praised Robeson for refusing to play the white-assigned role of "humility and forgiveness," for insisting instead on "represent[ing] the Negro man in the masculine role as a fearless and independent thinker"—thereby earning the enmity of white America. Langston Hughes asked in print "why a concert singer cannot have political opinions, too—even if he is colored." And in response to hostile editorials on Robeson, the black reporter Alice Dunnigan wrote Claude Barnett, head of the Associated Negro Press, that instead of "blasting Robeson because the white newspapers blast him," Afro-American papers should be "praising Robeson for his courage to speak what 99 and 44/100 percent of our population thinks."[30]

At the end of September 1949 Robeson, true to his public pledge after the first Peekskill incident, set out to carry his voice and message across the country, expecting—and meeting—resistance, but also meeting with redoubled proof that his ability to draw an audience, especially among black people, continued to be considerable. The Council on African Affairs handled the arrangements for the rapid cross-country trip, in cooperation with local sponsoring committees (the bulk of the work being done by Louise Thompson Patterson, William Patterson's second wife, who had joined the Council a few months before as organizational director after having been vice-president of the International Workers Order).

Robeson told the press with a smile that, along with singing, "I'll also be saying a few words about things." The musician Larry Adler, though himself an outspoken progressive, told Robeson he didn't approve of putting political content into a professional performance; as Adler recalls it, "Robeson smiled that wonderful grin of his, and said, 'You do it your way, Larry, I'll do it mine.' " But even before he set off on the tour, some of the places Robeson planned to visit let it be known that his words were not wanted. American Legion officials led a fight to ban his proposed peace rally in Pittsburgh, and in Ohio local officials in both Akron and Cincinnati denied the use of facilities for Robeson concerts (his supporters in Cincinnati pointed out, in a public statement that the newspapers of the city refused to print, that the Board of Education denying Robeson its facilities had never had a black representative on it). Robeson himself canceled a scheduled appearance at Oberlin College after its president insisted he would have to share the platform with a black minister who opposed his views; the right of a citizen to be heard, Robeson said, was not a proper subject for debate (the Chicago *Defender* preferred to draw the implication that Robeson had "cold feet"). In the end, Robeson's sole appearance in Ohio took place in Cleveland. That city's mayor, supported by the state's largest black weekly, had publicly suggested a boycott (rather than a ban), but the black population poured into the Paradise auditorium in the heart of the Cedar-Central ghetto to hear him.[31]

In Chicago, all the major civic halls refused the use of their facilities to Robeson's sponsoring host, the Civil Rights Congress. He sang instead at the Bakers Hall on the North Side, and the following night at the Tabernacle Baptist Church on the South Side (where the bulk of Chicago's black population lived). Dr. Louis Rawls, pastor of Tabernacle Baptist, a man of deeply conservative religious and political values, had not hesitated to open his church to Robeson. "I saw no reason," Rawls recalls, "why this church that serves the community should not allow *these* people to come in. Who are we to judge? They say Robeson 'believes in Communism.' Now, he never told me that. He said he wants freedom." Rawls not only agreed to lend his church, but also reduced the usual fee from $150 to $75. On the face of it an unlikely candidate to provide Robeson with an outlet, Rawls to that exact extent represents the fact that no substantial segment of the black community was actively against Robeson—some prominent black pastors and national leaders, yes, but few among "ordinary" blacks.[32]

And they turned out for Robeson. At both of his Chicago appearances the audience was largely black, and at both, the crowd overflowed to the streets. In a welcoming statement, Bishop W. J. Walls of the A.M.E. Zion Church compared Robeson to "the noble Frederick Douglass," who also refused "to bask in the sunlight of his great advantages without always bringing to the front the cause of his enslaved people. . . . You have gone the second mile." When Robeson attended a White Sox baseball game in Chicago, he was surrounded by autograph-seekers—but when he tried to get a meal at the Hotel Sherman, he was refused service. Veterans' organizations had advised the FBI that there would be no protest pickets at Robeson's appearances, disdaining to provide his "Communist followers with an excuse for disturbances." Taking no chances, the FBI—plus the local offices of Naval Intelligence, Army Intelligence, and the Office of Special Investigations—were all on the alert, but no incidents were reported.[33]

The prospects for trouble in Los Angeles seemed greater. The City Council dubbed Robeson's coming concert "an invasion" and unanimously passed a resolution urging a boycott. (The Council then directed its attention to a bill designed to set up a municipal Fair Employment Practices Committee, and defeated it eight to six.) One councilman, Lloyd G. Davies, went out of his way to "applaud and commend those [in Peekskill] who had the courage to get out there and do what they did to show up Robeson for what he is. I'd be inclined to be down there throwing rocks myself." An FBI agent reported to J. Edgar Hoover that "the Communist Party logically might endeavor to foment an incident at the concert in order to arouse the crowd." Hollywood gossip columnists Louella Parsons and Jimmy Fidler fanned the flames with rumors of violence, and the Motion Picture Alliance for the Preservation of American Ideals published ads red-baiting Robeson. Charlotta Bass, publisher of the California *Eagle,* the black newspaper that sponsored Robeson's Los Angeles appearance, was swamped with threatening phone calls and denied insurance coverage.[34]

Robeson's supporters fought back. The Los Angeles NAACP Youth Council passed a resolution calling on all young people, black and white, to attend the concert. The prestigious national black fraternity (Robeson's own), Alpha Phi Alpha, announced that it would host a luncheon in his honor the day following the concert. His supporters deluged the City Council with angry protests over its call for a boycott, and they turned out in force for the event itself. A tiny group of race-baiters did go to hear a local realtor call for the expulsion of all blacks and Jews from Los Angeles—but fifteen thousand went to hear Robeson. And the rally came off without incident. A special force of black police officers (among them future Mayor Thomas Bradley) was assigned to protect Robeson. He thanked them from the podium and asked that the L.A. police force protect "every colored boy, every Mexican-American boy, every white boy on the streets of Los Angeles." He thanked the Jewish people of Peekskill for having turned out in numbers to protect him in that town. And he thanked the crowd in front of him for having turned out to defend its own liberties. He would continue, he said, "to speak up militantly for the rights of my people"; he told the rally that when asked the question "Paul, what's happened to you?" he replied, "Nothing's happened to me. I'm just looking for freedom." Then he sang "We Shall Not Be Moved," and the last verse, "Black and white together, we shall not be moved," brought the crowd to its feet.[35]

Much the same pattern prevailed on the remaining stops of the tour. The opposition chose the tactic of boycotts over demonstrations, the authorities wavered between banning the rallies and guarding them, and supporters turned out in large numbers to fill the auditoriums to overflowing. The crowd at the Forest Club in Detroit was so great that Robeson had to give a repeat performance in the Shiloh Baptist Church that same evening. In Washington, D.C., seventeen of Washington's black leaders, including Charles H. Houston, Mary Church Terrell, E. Franklin Frazier, Adam Clayton Powell, Jr., W. H. Jernagin (past director of the Fraternal Council of Negro Churches), Rayford W. Logan, and Reverend Stephen Gill Spottswood (president of the local NAACP) issued a statement in advance of Robeson's arrival declaring that, although "many of us find ourselves in sharp disagreement" with the public positions he has taken on certain issues, "we are united in affirming his inalienable right to speak and sing to all who wish to hear him." A second group of black supporters, including his old friend Joseph L. Johnson, dean of the Howard Medical School, gave him a dinner at the Dunbar Hotel.[36]

On the night of Robeson's D.C. concert, police lined up three feet apart for a block on both sides of Turner's Arena and on every corner for a radius of six blocks. Robeson told the mostly black audience in the packed auditorium that there could be "no question about my loyalty to America. I will give all I have for my country and my people. But I will have nothing to do with the Dewey and Dulles fascists and the Rankins." He insisted that he stood for peace and predicted that because the Soviet Union now had the atomic bomb, war was *less* likely, since "people don't want to be blown up for the Duponts and Anaconda." Richard L. Strout, staff correspondent for the *Christian Science Monitor* (and for three decades thereafter the highly respected "T.R.B." columnist on *The New Republic*), did not like the fact that he saw "Communist literature . . . openly on display with that of non-Communist books" in the lobby of Turner's Arena. Nor did he like what to his "practiced eye" was the compelling evidence of the "fellow-traveler or outright Communist direction" of the event, "and the evident Communist effort to fan a racial conflagration." Still, when Robeson appeared on the platform to a roar from the crowd, even Strout confessed himself impressed; Robeson gave "every appearance of profound sincerity and deep consecration," spoke not with "inclusive bitterness, but with a certain massive magnanimity regarding injustices to his race," and gave the impression "as one listened of a tremendous new force unleashed among American Negroes by the presence of this powerful personality"—even though "this great new power was running on a transmission belt from Moscow." The Washington *Post,* in an editorial following Robeson's appearance, congratulated the residents of the capital for having avoided "a violent clash which would have enabled [the Communists] to pose as champions of civil liberties." "Whatever the hostile press and our so-called leaders may say or fail to say," Robeson wrote Franklin Frazier, he felt his reception "from east to west served to confirm the correctness of the stand I have taken and the people's support of my stand. . . . Facts are facts: no wishful thinking can dissipate or explain away the reality of what the Negroes down below are at present feeling and thinking."[37]

Energized by the tour, Robeson returned to New York to find an additional wellspring of support in the letters and invitations that had arrived from overseas. The World Convention of Religions solicited his help in the interests of international peace; Joliot-Curie of France invited him to attend a conference in Rome; the Swedish Committee for the Defense of Peace telegraphed their solidarity with him; the All-India Peace Congress notified him of his selection as president of its forthcoming meeting in Calcutta; and Nan Pandit, currently serving as India's Ambassador to the United States, wrote Essie with a private message from her brother, Nehru. Now Prime Minister, Nehru was coming to Washington on a state visit. Because he would be an official guest of President Truman, Nan Pandit wrote, "his engagements are checked up by the State Department," but "He has written to say he wants to see you and Paul privately for a good talk" on November 6 in New York, where he would be arriving "incognito" after having officially left the country on the 5th. Robeson refused the invitation to see Nehru. In the continuing political strife in India, the Communist Party there had come under attack, and Robeson felt that Nehru had been responsible for the large number of deaths among the Communists. Essie exploded in anger at Paul for what she called the worst kind of dogmatism, blamed the Party for applying pressure on him, and determinedly went off on her own to greet Nehru. He was deeply hurt at Paul's refusal to meet with him. Subsequently, however, the two men were reconciled, and Nehru would play a decisive role in the late fifties in the struggle to get the U.S. government to issue Robeson a passport.[38]

In mid-October Ben Davis, Jr., and the other Communist leaders on trial at Foley Square were convicted. Judge Medina handed out prison terms of five years to all but one of the defendants, sentencing Robert Thompson to three years (in deference to his having received the Distinguished Service Cross in World War II—prompting a protest from Thompson, who said he took "no pleasure" in receiving special favors from a "Wall Street judicial flunky"). In response to his own five-year sentence, Ben Davis wrote, "One thought crowded everything else out of my mind—in the whole history of the United States, with more than 5,000 brutal and monstrous lynchings of Negroes, not one perpetrator had received a sentence of five months—to say nothing of five years." Congressmen ranging from the South Dakota conservative Karl Mundt to the New York liberal Jacob Javits hailed the fairness of the verdict. The national press made Medina into the lion of the hour—with lone and muted dissenting voices from *The New Republic,* the *St. Louis Post-Dispatch,* and the American Civil Liberties Union. The Court of Appeals, however, did allow for bail, and after the Civil Rights Congress posted the required two hundred sixty thousand dollars, the Communist Eleven were temporarily set at liberty.[39]

The news that Ben Davis was free on bail touched off a large rally in Harlem, and Robeson stood by Davis's side as he was welcomed back. Toward the close of the rally, a brief skirmish broke out between bystanders and police. The *Journal-American,* in a banner headline, tried to blow up the marginal event into "360 Extra Police Ordered to Harlem After Red Riot," seconded by the *Daily News* ("6 Arrested as Pro-Reds Fight Cops"), but in fact the clash, such as it was, developed over the issue of police brutality in Harlem and (as the New York *Post* reported) was in no sense planned or abetted by "Communists." Davis, despite his indictment, had been renominated to the City Council, and his opponent in that contest, the conservative black columnist Earl Brown, immediately accused the CP of having incited the skirmish, charging that the Party had imported its workers "from all over the country specifically to start trouble." In the few days remaining before the election, Robeson worked hard for Davis's campaign but his bid was lost at the polls by a three-to-one majority. At a rally that night in Harlem, Davis's campaign manager, Ollie Harrington, couldn't figure out why Robeson hadn't shown up as promised. Calling "downtown" to CP headquarters, he told them a no-show on Robeson's part would be "a terrible mistake." Within twenty minutes Robeson appeared at the rally and sang his heart out to the waiting crowd, but the incident upset Harrington; he saw it as a typical example of how the Party sometimes misused Robeson "and compromised his image with the black masses." Yes, Revels Cayton concurs, "they used Paul in a kind of way that made him unacceptable to the masses of Negroes. This giant—they had not the slightest idea of how to work with him." But on the issue of being "used," Robeson himself deserves the final word: "The Communists use the Negro," he once said with a chuckle, "and we only wish more people would want to use us this way."[40]

■

CHAPTER 19

The Right to Travel

(1950–1952)

In October 1949 Andrei Vyshinsky, Foreign Minister of the U.S.S.R., responded to charges at the United Nations that the "anti-fascist" trials in progress in Eastern Europe were in fact suppressions of civil liberties, by declaring that the United States had "no moral qualifications" for such a discussion; incidents like Peekskill, Vyshinsky retorted, suggested that "under the guise of freedom of expression" the United States allowed "pro-fascist" hooligans to break up peaceful assemblies. The following month Robeson appeared at a Waldorf-Astoria dinner in honor of Vyshinsky (and of the thirty-second anniversary of the Soviet state) sponsored by the Council of American-Soviet Friendship, a group that had been founded in the last years of the war with prominent mainstream Americans like Averill Harriman as participants but whose membership had narrowed with the onset of the Cold War.[1]

Welcoming Vyshinsky at the dinner, Robeson spoke of the peoples of Eastern Europe as "masters of their own lands," of Tito—who had recently moved his country out of the Soviet sphere—as "disguising" himself as a revolutionary, and of Truman as an "imperialist wolf disguised as a benevolent watchdog." He also denounced the "insolence" of those who questioned his love for his own country, asserting that "ONLY those who work for a policy of friendship with the Soviet Union are genuine American patriots." This was not language designed for conciliation (or even entire accuracy). In his determination to avoid appearing cowed, in his anger at being caricatured, Robeson was taking on some of the polemically simplistic tones of his adversaries, trading in slogans. The brutality of the public attack on him had hardened his own rhetorical arteries, brought out the obstinacy that was always one of the constants (though usually better concealed) in his personality. The danger was that the suppleness of his inner process would be permanently affected, that opinionated and oracular defiance would become a reflex mannerism, that he would imitate and come to resemble his own dogmatic persecutors.[2]

A similar ideological-emotional constriction is apparent in the position Robeson took on the civil liberties of the Trotskyist Socialist Workers Party. At a Bill of Rights Conference in New York City in late July 1949, a resolution was introduced calling for freedom for eighteen Trotskyists convicted in 1941 under the same provisions of the Smith Act currently being used against the leaders of the CPUSA. The chairman of the conference, Paul J. Kern, argued forcefully before the convention that free speech should never be denied because of a difference in political opinion—a view seconded by Professor Thomas Emerson of the Yale Law School. An impassioned Robeson took the platform to denounce the Kern-Emerson position. Like most pro-Soviets, Robeson had long blamed the followers of Trotsky for spreading exaggerated "slanders" about Stalin's "police state." Adherents of the Socialist Workers Party, Robeson exclaimed, "are the allies of fascism who want to destroy the new democracies of the world. Let's not get confused. They are the enemies of the working class. Would you give civil rights to the Ku Klux Klan?" *NO,* the delegates roared back. They defeated the resolution and passed a substitute that simply called for the defense of "all anti-fascist victims of the Smith Act." It was not Robeson's finest hour.[3]

Even some of the leaders of the CPUSA thought he ought to tone down his rhetoric. They had no trouble with the content, but did worry about the timing. On trial as "subversives," a segment of the Party leadership feared that Robeson's "refusal-to-fight-the-Soviets" line had inadvertently painted them as disloyal. Paul Robeson, Jr., recalls that one evening late in December 1949 his father asked that he accompany him to a West Side apartment. On entering, Paul, Jr., recognized several leaders of the Party, including Henry Winston. After some cordial talk, Winston suggested to Robeson that perhaps for the time being he might consider confining himself to singing—which to Paul, Jr., implied that Winston was urging his father to accept a rumored State Department "deal" to call off its surveillance if he returned to "art." Paul, Jr., "felt" his father's body stiffen; "I instinctively started to raise my right hand to block a blow which I thought he might direct at Winston's head." Robeson gripped the arms of his chair and, eyes narrowed, simply stared at Winston. "There was this dead silence, with everybody frozen. And he said, 'No, Winnie, I don't think that would be too good an idea.' He sounded like a lion growling." Then he rose and, his son following, went out the door. In Paul, Jr.'s view, Henry Winston and Elizabeth Gurley Flynn actually led a movement within the Party to issue some kind of disclaimer of Robeson's Paris statement, but Ben Davis succeeded in derailing it. Paul, Jr., believes his father disliked Winston but was fond of Gurley Flynn. Politically, he felt close to neither; his own sympathies lay more with the Ben Davis–William Z. Foster "left-wing" faction in the Party, and sometimes with the centrist Eugene Dennis, whom he liked greatly. But finally, in the words of Doxey Wilkerson, Robeson "was bigger than the Party. He was an institution, if you will. He managed to deflect the kinds of jealousies that would ordinarily be leveled against a person of great magnitude. Everybody knew he was straight, honest, and what he wanted to do. He was universally respected."[4]

That same week of December 1949, Robeson joined Du Bois, Patterson, Alphaeus Hunton, Ben Davis, Doxey Wilkerson, and others in cabling greetings to Joseph Stalin on the occasion of his seventieth birthday. The New York *Amsterdam News* commented that "when these 'left wing Negro leaders' go on record with expressions of love for the arch enemy of America, then we can expect the boys who run this country to suspect their motives . . . plac[ing] them even further on Uncle Sam's black list." Indeed, Army Intelligence reported to the FBI that "the Communists plan to shuttle Paul Robeson to rallies throughout the United States with the express intention of provoking riots and spreading propaganda to the effect that the Communist Party is 'shedding blood' in the interest of racial equality." FBI surveillance became so constant that Robeson got to the point where he recognized plainclothesmen—though he did not let on, to avoid alarming his friends.[5]

Robeson did continue to travel and speak out, but his outlets were narrowing. He gave his first major address of the new year, 1950, at the Progressive Party national convention in Chicago in February. At meetings just prior to the convention, the Progressive Party leaders agreed to disagree about the Tito-Stalin split (Robeson sided with Moscow), to unite behind a call for pardons for the eleven Communist leaders prosecuted under the Smith Act, and to emphasize commitment to the black struggle for civil rights. In his own remarks to the convention, Henry Wallace gave a speech that bordered on being anti-Communist (a few months later he would break with the Progressives over the issue of the Korean War, offering his support to the Truman administration). When Robeson's turn came to address the delegates, he confined himself almost entirely to the issue of civil rights, barely alluding to the Soviet Union. He excoriated the two major parties for keeping blacks in a condition of second-class citizenship and praised the "magnificent role" of the Progressive Party in battling for civil rights, in having "proven to the Negro people that we mean what we say." The delegates elected him cochairman.[6]

The country was in no mood for an appeal to tolerance. "Bad news" had begun to arrive with regularity, fraying nerves, souring the national disposition. Judith Coplon, a Justice Department employee, was arrested by FBI agents during an alleged rendezvous with a Soviet official and charged with espionage. Russia exploded an atomic device. The British scientist Klaus Fuchs was arrested and charged with passing nuclear secrets to the Soviets. The State Department released its White Paper on China, conceding "the unfortunate" victory of the Communists. (When the news of Chiang Kai-shek's defeat came over the radio in October 1949, Paul and Helen and Sam Rosen headed out into the street on their way to an appointment and then, in a burst of high spirits, linked arms and sang "Cheelai," the Chinese Communist song, at the top of their lungs—to the general astonishment of passers-by.) Late in January 1950, a New York jury found Alger Hiss guilty of perjury. Richard Nixon charged the administration with suppressing evidence of Hiss's Communist connections. The right-wing press came close to labeling Secretary of State Dean Acheson a traitor. Senator Joe McCarthy journeyed to Wheeling, West Virginia, to deplore American impotence in the world and to hint darkly about the infiltration of the "enemy" into the highest echelons of the State Department.[7]

In the midst of this crescendo of alarm, Eleanor Roosevelt's son Elliot announced that Paul Robeson would appear on his mother's Sunday afternoon television show, "Today with Mrs. Roosevelt," to debate with Representative Adam Clayton Powell, Jr., and the black Mississippi Republican committeeman Perry Howard on "the role of the Negro in American political life." He might just as well have announced the imminent appearance of the devil. NBC at once received hundreds of hostile phone calls; the state commander of the American Legion told the press that Robeson's purpose would be to incite "hatred and bigotry"; the Catholic War Veterans demanded that the networks protect "decent Americans" from exposure to anti-American propaganda; and the Hearst paper the New York *Journal-American* put its front page anti-Robeson story right next to an article hailing Senator McCarthy for having "named" two "pro-Communist" State Department employees.[8]

Less than twenty-four hours after Robeson's appearance had been announced, it was canceled. An NBC spokesman told the press that Mrs. Roosevelt had been "premature" and Paul Robeson would not appear on her program—indeed, would *never* appear on NBC as long as the network could help it—thereby making him the first American to be officially banned from television. Robeson told reporters that he hoped "Mrs. Roosevelt and Elliot Roosevelt will struggle, as I am sure they will, for the civil rights of everyone to be heard. . . . I cannot and will not accept the notion that because someone is accused of being a Communist or a 'Communist sympathizer' that he has no right to speak." (This was precisely the right he had argued against extending to Trotskyists eight months earlier.) Howard Fast challenged Mrs. Roosevelt to speak out against censorship at a Robeson concert scheduled for the following week, but Mrs. Roosevelt declined any comment except for the *non sequitur*—after reporters pressed her—that the television discussion was to have been a "general" one and Robeson would not have had "unlimited time to express his point of view." When a private citizen wrote to ask her why she had not publicly objected to cancellation of the program, Mrs. Roosevelt replied, ". . . because I was away and in any case, the National Broadcasting Company has the final say on these programs. I can, of course, think of several other negro Americans who are better qualified to speak than Mr. Robeson because they are more objective. However, I would not be afraid of anything Mr. Robeson might say."[9]

Refraining from any attack on the Roosevelts, Robeson aimed his fire at NBC. The banning was "a sad commentary on our professions of democracy," he said, but he was not surprised that the network had balked at a candid discussion of "the Negro in politics"—it had always balked at any but stereotyped presentations of blacks (while freely opening its airways to white supremacists) and had consistently refused to hire any skilled blacks in its army of technicians. Support for Robeson came from limited quarters only. *The Afro-American* printed an editorial censorious of the NBC action—and soon after named Robeson to its 1950 National Honor Roll— but most of the black press remained silent. Adam Clayton Powell, Jr., registered a protest, but it was lukewarm, leading the CP trade-unionist Ferdinand Smith to denounce Powell as "pussy-footing." Roy Wilkins, speaking for the NAACP, delayed so long in issuing a statement that his lieutenant Henry Lee Moon sent him a memo expressing anxiety that the NAACP had failed to speak out expeditiously. The Progressive Party and the American Civil Liberties Union did back Robeson's right to appear, and a few members of the left-wing Harlem Trade Union Council did picket NBC. But dominant opinion was represented by an editorial in the New York *Telegram-Sun:* Paul Robeson had been "publicly and rightly censured."[10]

From abroad came a small flood of invitations asking Robeson to appear at peace gatherings. The peace movement (anti-Communists charged that it was sponsored by pro-Communists) had been gathering international momentum, and activists from around the world requested Robeson's presence at their various meetings. He sent greetings to all— and recorded statements to several—but he had a raft of promises to fulfill at home. His bicoastal appearances within just a few months included benefit concerts for the Progressive Party, anniversary celebrations for the *Morning Freiheit* and the Jewish Peoples' Fraternal Order, a fund-raiser for the California *Eagle,* speeches at the New York May Day parade and the National Non-Partisan Committee to defend the Communist leaders, an FEPC vigil in front of the White House, conferences with black trade-unionists in Chicago and California, and half a dozen testimonial dinners.[11]

Essie, meanwhile, was carrying out a full agenda of her own. Her politics had by now moved closer to Paul's—though he rarely trusted her to speak in his behalf. Her style of public debate was less combative than his, her commitment less instinctive, but she was nonetheless an effective speaker. Returning in January 1950 from a three-month trip to China, she embarked on a well-received national speaking tour. The FBI agent who monitored her speech in St. Louis reported that she had denied the existence of slave camps or of anti-Jewish discrimination in the Soviet Union; when asked from the audience what the difference was between Western colonialism and the Russian satellite system, she purportedly replied, "colonialism meant controlling and exploiting while a satellite was just influenced." By temperament an ingrained pragmatist, impatient with doctrinal dispute in any form, Essie devoted the central portion of her standard stump speech on "Communism" to redefining it under the blandly accessible rubric of "land reform." Further expounding her loose approach to doctrine, she won over a group of conservative black ministers and their wives in Detroit by stressing their *theological* duty to take up issues of social justice. Her audiences were apparently less persuaded by her increasingly explicit—and in 1950 decidedly "premature"—feminism; in her speech "Women and Progressive America," for example, she declared, "I think it is high time that women had some say in the running of their governments, and in the running of the world." The FBI decided in August 1950 that Essie was, after all, a "concealed Communist" and once again issued a Security Index Card for her.[12]

In May, Paul made a quick trip to London to attend a meeting of the World Peace Council, of which he was a member. More than twenty thousand Londoners packed Lincoln's Inn Fields to hear the leaders of the international peace movement, but saved their greatest applause for Robeson, who sang Chinese, Soviet, and American songs and told the crowd— once more calling on his reserves of optimism—that the working class in America was awakening to the realization that *it* (and not just those who were avowed Communists) was in danger of losing civil liberties; this awakening meant that fascism "will never be" revived in America. George Bernard Shaw, who had met Robeson two decades earlier, dropped him a humorous note demurring to a request for support of Progressive Party candidates: "If you connect my name and reputation with your campaign . . . you will gain perhaps two thousand votes, ten of them negro, and lose two million. . . . Keep me out of it; and do not waste your time courting the handful of people whose votes you are sure of already. Play for Republican votes and episcopal support all the time; and when you get a big meeting of all sorts, don't talk politics but sing Old Man River." Sympathetic though he was to Robeson, Shaw was not above a bit of well-meant patronization.[13]

Back in the States by June, Robeson went to Chicago to address a thousand delegates to the National Labor Conference for Negro Rights, many of whom were black packinghouse workers. To Marie Seton, who attended the meeting, "Robeson was never so much himself" as that night, "in the midst of his own to whom he spoke of all the world." He exhorted black trade-unionists to "exert their influence in every aspect of the life of the Negro community" and "to accept the fact that the Negro workers have become a part of the vanguard of the whole American working class. To fail the Negro people is to fail the whole American people." He spoke movingly of the need to end the persecution not only of black Americans, but of Jews and of the foreign-born as well, and asked the audience not to be deflected from that goal by divisive calls from press and politicians to save the world from the "menace" of Communism. "Ask the Negro ministers in Birmingham whose homes were bombed by the Ku Klux Klan what is the greatest menace in their lives. . . . Ask Willie McGee, languishing in a Mississippi prison. . . . Ask Haywood Patterson, somewhere in America, a fugitive from Alabama barbarism for a crime he, nor any of the Scottsboro boys, ever committed. Ask the growing numbers of Negro unemployed in Chicago and Detroit. Ask the fearsome lines of relief clients in Harlem. . . . Ask any Negro worker receiving unequal pay for equal work, denied promotion despite his skill and because of his skin, still the last hired and the first fired. Ask fifteen million American Negroes, if you please, 'What is the greatest menace in your life?' and they will answer in a thunderous voice, 'Jim-Crow Justice! Mob Rule! Segregation! Job Discrimination!'—in short White Supremacy and all its vile works. Our enemies," Robeson concluded, "are the lynchers, the profiteers, the men who give FEPC the run-around in the Senate, the atom-bomb maniacs and the war-makers," those who sustain injustice at home while shipping arms— here Robeson was surely prescient—to "French imperialists to use against brave Vietnamese patriots." His black audience gave him a prolonged ovation.[14]

Two weeks later the daily press blazoned in screaming headlines that "COMMUNIST IMPERIALISTS FROM NORTH KOREA" had invaded their "PEACE-LOVING BROTHERS" to the south. The victors of World War II had put an end to Japan's colonial rule in Korea and split that country into two, the North, under Kim Il Sung, claiming to build socialism, the South, under Washington's puppet Syngman Rhee, proceeding to bolster capitalism. From the first there had been constant sniping across the border, each side threatening to "liberate" the other, but when Sung's well-equipped army finally crossed into the South, Rhee's troops were unprepared and ill-equipped. Though Truman had in the past shown contempt for Rhee, he felt he couldn't risk—not so soon after the Communist victory in China and the sensational publicity surrounding the fall of Hiss and the rise of McCarthy—having the Republicans charge that he was soft on Communism. The U.S. Ambassador to the UN, Warren Austin, secured a resolution condemning North Korea, and a week later Truman dispatched ground troops. Americans of almost all persuasions—including Henry Wallace—rallied around the President. Congress opened debate on passage of a new Internal Security Act, the infamous McCarran Act, which equated dissent with treason and established concentration camps to detain subversives in time of national emergency. When it passed in September, Truman vetoed it, at some political risk, but the veto was overridden. The days when Robeson could count on at least minimal sufferance had passed.[15]

Yet he refused to trim his sails to any degree. Speaking out at a Civil Rights Congress rally at Madison Square Garden at the end of June 1950 to protest Truman's action in sending troops to Korea, Robeson excoriated the President for tying the welfare of the American people "to the fate of a corrupt clique of politicians south of the 38th parallel in Korea." The meaning of Truman's order, Robeson predicted, would not be lost on black Americans: "They will know that if we don't stop our armed adventure in Korea today—tomorrow it will be Africa. . . . I have said it before and say it again, that the place for the Negro people to fight for their freedom is here at home. . . ." When Robeson had "said it before," in Paris in 1949, he had brought on a national debate; those same words, repeated in 1950, marked its foreclosure. The climate had changed. The government decided to muzzle him.[16]

He had planned to return to Europe at the end of the summer, but the State Department planned otherwise. It issued a "stop notice" at all ports to prevent Robeson from departing, and J. Edgar Hoover sent out an "urgent" teletype ordering FBI agents to locate Robeson's whereabouts. Going first to Bert and Gig McGhee's apartment, where Robeson had recently been staying—as a result of which the FBI had taken out a Security Index Card on Gig—they were told he was not at home. The agents waited outside the building through the night and, when Robeson failed to appear, contacted the Council on African Affairs. Through Louise Patterson, Robeson made arrangements to meet with the Internal Security agents sent out to confiscate his passport. When they arrived, he had an attorney with him, Nathan Witt of Witt & Cammer. Witt checked the agents' credentials, and Robeson said he would have the passport for them in the morning. But when the agents called the next day, Witt informed them that on his advice Robeson had decided not to surrender the passport after all. The State Department immediately notified immigration and customs officials that Robeson's passport was void and that they were "to endeavor to prevent his departure from the U.S." should he make an attempt to leave.[17]

Robeson now joined other radicals whose right to travel had been or was soon to be restricted—Rockwell Kent, Charlotta Bass, Corliss Lamont, the writers Howard Fast and Albert Kahn, and Reverend Richard Morford (head of the National Council of American-Soviet Friendship). Historically, the State Department, when denying passports, had given concrete reasons, chiefly citing lack of citizenship, the need to protect applicants from going to danger spots abroad, and the need to intercept criminal elements attempting to flee the country or to engage in drug trafficking. But increasingly in the early 1950s, the State Department gave no reason for lifting a passport other than the vague catchall explanation that travel abroad by a given individual would be "contrary to the best interests of the United States," a cover for monitoring left-wing political dissent. The passport weapon had occasionally been used against dissenters in the past—anarchists and socialists in particular—but now it became widely employed, and directed pre-eminently at "Communists" (even though the U.S. government had previously protested the refusal of totalitarian governments to let their citizens travel freely as the denial of a fundamental human right).[18]

Witt wrote directly to Secretary of State Acheson requesting an explanation. A reply came from the chief of the passport division: "the Department considers that Robeson's travel abroad at this time would be contrary to the best interests of the United States." That, Witt responded, is not "a sufficient answer"; it presented "a conclusion" but gave no justification for it. He requested a meeting either with Acheson or his representatives. Word came back that passport officials would meet with Robeson and Witt on August 23, though "the Department feels that no purpose would be served."[19]

The department was as good as its prediction: the August 23 meeting accomplished nothing. Along with Nathan Witt, Robeson was attended by four black attorneys, including William Patterson (who two weeks before had been called a "black son of a bitch" by Representative Henderson Lanham of Georgia during a hearing before the House Lobbying Committee; Essie, in a letter of protest, cleverly denounced the name-calling as "an all too typical incident illustrating UnAmerican behavior today"). When Robeson and his attorneys requested clarification as to why it would be "detrimental to the interests of the United States Government" for him to travel abroad, they were told that his frequent criticism of the treatment of blacks in the United States should not be aired in foreign countries—it was a "family affair." Unless he would give a signed statement guaranteeing not to make any speeches while abroad, there could be no reconsideration of his passport application. When his attorneys protested that this amounted to an unconstitutional violation of the right of free speech, they were told that they were at liberty to take the matter up in court. Robeson's lawyers prepared to do just that.[20]

There was no national outcry against the State Department's lifting of Robeson's passport. The minuscule left-wing press (led by the *Daily People's World,* the *Daily Worker,* and the *National Guardian*) wrote editorials against the action; a number of European peace organizations telegraphed their indignation to Acheson; and scattered left-wing groups like the Progressives and the Committee for the Negro in the Arts registered their anger. But no important black leader joined the protest; as Bayard Rustin puts it, "I don't know whether the leadership was sufficiently anti-Robeson or sufficiently intimidated. . . ." Robeson himself denounced the passport action as one more attempt by the Truman administration "to silence the protests of the Negro people"—but his statement was not widely carried in the press. He was being effectively isolated, which became clear early in September when, on the first anniversary of Peekskill, Madison Square Garden refused to rent its space to the Council on African Affairs for a planned concert rally in protest of the passport ban. The *Daily Worker* announced a demonstration outside the Garden, but only fifty people showed up.[21]

There was a much larger turnout in Harlem—the *Daily Worker* estimated the crowd at six thousand—on September 9, when Robeson supporters held an outdoor rally in Dewey Square, under the auspices of the Harlem Trade Union Council. Joined by Patterson, Ben Davis, Leon Strauss, and half a dozen other speakers, Robeson told the assembled crowd that he had definitely decided to bring suit against the State Department, denounced the action of the Madison Square Garden corporation as "an arbitrary edict in violation of the right of free assembly," and described the various "security" proposals under discussion in the Congress—the Wood, McCarran, and Mundt-Nixon-Ferguson bills—as "police state" proposals. "There has not been a single bit of federal legislation passed to guarantee the economic, civil and political rights of the Negro people; but . . . we see such Congressmen as Rankin of Mississippi spearheading the hysterical drive to jail and muzzle Negro and other Americans who engage in . . . criticism of government policy."[22]

Two months earlier it had also been possible to gather an audience in Harlem for a Hands Off Korea rally; the "red menace" did not strike most Harlemites as notably more invidious than the white one. Even after the Cold War climate deepened, Harlemites could not be stampeded into an automatic anti-Soviet response. Annette Rubinstein, state vice-chairman of the American Labor Party, remembers using a sound truck all over New York to gather signatures against the execution of the Rosenbergs: "We were in every neighborhood, and people were terrified. . . . Even in the Jewish neighborhoods on the Lower East Side, people would say, 'Well, where there's smoke, there's fire. There must be something to it.' . . . But in Harlem we didn't have to argue or prove that it was a frame-up."[23]

But Harlem's mood was not the country's. No longer friendly with Robeson, Carl Van Vechten commented with some satisfaction in a private letter on Paul's fall from "the top of the heap" to "the dog house." And the nationally syndicated columnist Robert C. Ruark expressed his double pleasure that Robeson, "the Negro press agent for the Communist Party, has finally been hanged high as Haman," and that Negro troops in Korea had been acquitting themselves so well—thereby giving the lie, Ruark believed, to Robeson's prior insistence that blacks would not fight against Communists. (Wasn't it interesting, the black sociologist Horace Cayton— brother of Revels—noted, to see press attention being given to the exploits of black troops in Korea: could it be, Cayton asked, that the United States was "embarrassed" that "there have been no [other] non-white people fighting on their side?")[24]

It did nothing for Robeson's public image when it was announced that Moscow intended to present a play depicting scenes from his life. At the same time, his old friend Josh White—who had performed with him in *John Henry* in 1940—went before HUAC to express his "sadness" that Robeson was giving aid to people who "despise America" and to declare his own fervid willingness "to fight Russia or any enemy of America," regretting that earlier he had allowed certain "subversive" organizations to "use" him. Robeson had in fact been forewarned—by Josh White himself. According to Revels Cayton, the two men talked it over in a bathroom in his house, turning on the tap water as a precaution against bugging. "They've got me in a vise," White purportedly told Robeson. "I'm going to have to talk." "Do what you have to but don't name names," was Robeson's response—just as he generously warned others (like Dizzy Gillespie, Harry Belafonte, and Sidney Poitier) to avoid being seen or connected with him lest their own careers be damaged.[25]

Disparagement of Robeson at home began to alternate regularly with tributes to him from abroad. In October came word that Mayor Hynes of Boston had barred the display of Robeson's picture in a touring exhibition of portraits of famous blacks—and nearly simultaneously the Second World Peace Conference in Warsaw announced that Robeson had been chosen to share the $14,300 International Peace Prize with Pablo Picasso. (In defending his action, Hynes announced, "We are not glorifying any avowed Communists, whether white, Negro or yellow," and the Boston *Post* backed the mayor's decision, declaring it unthinkable that, while "boys of every color and racial strain are today giving their life's blood in far-off Korea, in a war inspired by Mr. Robeson's friends in Moscow," Boston could "in decency" honor such a man.) On November 6 the Associated Negro Press reported that in Alabama one James T. ("Popeye") Bellanfont, a black school-bus driver, had begun a "crusade" to "stop Robeson from speaking for the Negro," claiming to have already enrolled twelve hundred members in seventeen states—and on November 18 the ANP carried a bulletin that the town council in Lvov, Poland, had voted to name a street after Paul Robeson. That same week *Life* magazine published two pictures side by side: one of the black cadet Dave Campbell leading the graduation parade at the navy's preflight school in Pensacola, the other of Robeson—"who has long been used by Reds to exploit the color line"— attending a party at the Soviet Embassy in Washington, D.C., to celebrate the thirty-third anniversary of the Bolshevik revolution; Robeson, *Life* reported, "came early, stayed late, seemed delighted to be there."[26]

Robeson was now increasingly linked, in the press and in the public mind, with another black dissenter, W. E. B. Du Bois. The two had been working closely together since 1948, when Du Bois moved his office from the NAACP to the Council on African Affairs, and Du Bois had been elected along with Robeson to serve on the new World Peace Council. Now, in October 1950, Du Bois—as fit as he was venerable at age eighty-two—decided to run on the New York American Labor Party ticket for a seat in the United States Senate, opposing the popular incumbent, Herbert H. Lehman. Most of the black leadership came out for Lehman; A. Philip Randolph, Mary McLeod Bethune, Channing Tobias, and the powerful Tammany Hall trio of New York black politicians, Hulan Jack, Joseph Ford, and J. Raymond Jones, all endorsed Lehman on the basis of his substantial civil-rights record. Those lining up for Du Bois were far less influential: the actress Fredi Washington, Ollie Harrington, Nina Evans (president of the Domestic Workers Union), and Bishop William J. Walls, head of the Second Episcopal District of the A.M.E. Zion Church. And, of course, Robeson.[27]

At a rally for Du Bois at Harlem's Golden Gate Auditorium, Robeson introduced him as "the elder statesman of our oppressed people," a man who stood against the determination of monopoly big business "to run the world, to make it over in the American Jim-Crow, 'free enterprise' image— or ruin it." At a second rally just before election day, threats of violence led to the stationing of a 150-man police detail on rooftops and streets in the area. But there was no trouble, and in his speech to the gathering Robeson congratulated the American Labor Party for turning to Du Bois for leadership, "and not to the sycophants and flunkies of monopoly wealth and plantation power that clutter up the tickets of the twin parties of reaction." (According to *The New York Times*, Robeson left the rally with seventeen bodyguards.) When the vote was in, Du Bois ran ahead of the rest of the American Labor Party ticket, tallying a respectable—indeed, in the deepening freeze of the Cold War climate, a remarkable—13 percent of the five million votes cast. Three months later the Justice Department indicted Du Bois as an "unregistered foreign agent." His trial was scheduled for November 1951.[28]

In the interim, Du Bois and Robeson moved still closer together in cooperating on a new journal, *Freedom*. The publication was edited almost single-handedly in the beginning by Louis Burnham, former executive secretary of the Southern Negro Youth Congress and Southern director of the Progressive Party—and an unusually able journalist. Burnham had to cope not only with deficient financing and an intransigently conservative national climate, but also with the "special ways" of his star contributor, Dr. Du Bois. The actress-writer Alice Childress, who worked on *Freedom*, recalls that, when Burnham requested an article from Du Bois, telling him frankly that they had no money to pay him, the Doctor reared up. He could not, he indignantly explained, work for nothing. Childress put in a placating phone call to say, "Somehow we'll get you some money. What do you want?" Fifteen dollars, Du Bois replied, explaining to a relieved Childress that he had been offended merely by the notion that he was somehow "on call" to do the magazine's bidding.[29]

With an article by Du Bois, the first issue of *Freedom* appeared in December 1950. It also carried a column, meant to inaugurate a regular feature, by Robeson. He worked out the columns with Lloyd L. Brown, a left-wing black writer (who would later collaborate with him on his autobiography); Brown wrote up the columns, and Robeson checked them over. "The people of America," the first column read, "can save their land if they will. But this means the saving of every precious life. . . . I am not making great sacrifices which need fanciful explanation. I am simply fulfilling my obligation—my responsibility, as best as I can and know, to the human family to which I proudly belong." Inadequately financed, *Freedom* struggled along for a few years, relying heavily for support on a national "Freedom Fund" established at the same time as the magazine—and was promptly labeled "a Communist Party front organization" by the FBI. To aid the fund, which never raised money commensurate with the need, Robeson lent his name and presence to a publicity campaign that included mailings and benefit appearances. He (and Essie, too) worked hard for the success of *Freedom*, which managed to hold on—barely—through 1955.[30]

The same month that *Freedom* began publication, December 1950, Robeson's lawyers instituted in the United States District Court a civil action for the return of his passport, against Secretary of State Acheson "in his representative capacity" as head of the State Department. The complaint described Robeson as "a loyal, native-born American citizen" and insisted that the cancellation of his passport had not only deprived him of his constitutionally guaranteed rights of freedom of speech, thought, assembly, petition, association, and travel, but would also prevent him from practicing his profession and earning a living. The State Department's lawyers responded by filing a motion to dismiss the suit, contending that historically the Secretary of State had always exercised the discretionary power to issue or refuse a passport and emphasizing that the United States was technically still at war (the state of national emergency proclaimed at the start of World War II had never been officially terminated). The Robeson passport case had begun its tortuous way through the courts. "In the modern emergency," Robert C. Ruark wrote in his syndicated column, "Mr. Robeson is as worthy of internment as any Jap who got penned away in the last, since . . . he is an enemy of his own country and a passionate espouser of those people who are now declared enemies. . . . He goes to the court to have his passport restored so that he may rend America further abroad. . . ." Across the FBI copy of Ruark's article, J. Edgar Hoover wrote, "certainly well said." Panic momentarily seized the Passport Division when a U.S. customs agent reported that Robeson had booked passage on the Cunard ship S.S. *Media* for Liverpool. After much alarmed scurrying about, an embarrassed correction came through: the "Robeson" in question was a white member of the British equestrian team on his way home after competing in the international horse show in Madison Square Garden.[31]

The new year began with two more public assaults on Robeson from well-known black figures. Returning from a successful boxing tour of Europe, Sugar Ray Robinson told the *Herald Tribune* that "America provides opportunity for everyone, regardless of race, creed or color" and declared that assertions to the contrary were simply "Communist propaganda" put out by Paul Robeson. A more considered and substantial attack came from Walter White in his *Ebony* article, "The Strange Case of Paul Robeson." Utilizing private information gleaned from twenty-five years of friendship, and employing a tone of sympathetic puzzlement ("Robeson is a bewildered man who is more to be pitied than damned"), White, in urbane words, put a high gloss on a set of conventional Cold War accusations. He portrayed Robeson as having a penchant for luxury and a neurotic oversensitivity to discrimination, a man who for some "mysterious" reason had always harbored "deep resentment" over racial slights and therefore been particularly susceptible to the propaganda the Soviets put out about their bias-free society. "It has been inexplicable to Mr. Robeson's friends," White claimed, that he could be "so generous" toward Russia and yet have done "so little toward helping movements to correct the flaws in American democracy." White further embellished his suave indictment by referring to Robeson as having lived in "magnificent" style in London's "exclusive Mayfair section." The Robesons had never lived in Mayfair, and Robeson's impressive record of involvement in movements designed to "correct the flaws in American democracy" had included the Progressive Party, the trade-union movement, and the Council on African Affairs—all unmentioned by Walter White.[32]

Just before White's article appeared, the American public-affairs officer in Accra, the Gold Coast, had sent a memo to the State Department suggesting that a piece be "specially written" about Robeson for use throughout Africa; it should be "told sympathetically, preferably by an American Negro devoted to his race, as the tragedy which in fact it is. . . . Much more with regret than rancor, it must detail Robeson's spiritual alienation from his country and from the bulk of his own people . . . his almost pitiful (for so robust and seemingly dignified a person) accommodation to the Communist line. . . ." There is no evidence that Walter White had written to specification, but his article did at least obviate the need for the State Department to plant one of its own. Perhaps unwittingly, Walter White had done his Cold War service.[33]

Furious at White's article, Essie dashed off an angry rebuttal to *Ebony*. She began by acknowledging that Paul "always went stubborn when anyone (including me) *told* him what to do; you could *ask* him, maybe *persuade* him, but you couldn't *tell* him. . . . He doesn't side-step the challenge, but goes right in, swinging." But being stubborn in defense of one's rights was neither "oversensitive" nor "neurotic"—unless one wanted to argue that an uncompromising insistence on equality was in itself a symptom of "disturbance" (would one then include as "neurotic" Gandhi and Nehru because of their intransigent fight for Indian independence against the British?). Perhaps, Essie suggested, it was time for a hard look at the assumptions of the current crop of black leaders in America. None of them pretended that "Negroes are *satisfied* with their present situation in the U.S.A. . . . that they like being lynched, attacked, abused . . . that they like being unjustly treated in our courts . . . that they like being segregated and discriminated against. . . . What, then, do these Negro leaders say?" They don't dare claim, she went on, that Russia is responsible for the discrimination against blacks in the United States; instead they "go out of their way to insist that American democracy, with all its faults, is the best there is and therefore we must all fight if need be die for it. Since most of the *faults* and few of the *benefits* of this democracy apply directly to Negroes, these Leaders find themselves in the very strange position of insisting that Negroes fight and die for the faults of our democracy. Paul Robeson is far too clear-sighted . . . to be maneuvered . . . into such a position. *He* is *fighting the faults* of our democracy. That's what all the fuss is about." *Ebony* declined to publish Essie's rebuttal; it finally appeared in the sympathetic black newspaper the California *Eagle*.[34]

White's article was all the more effective because, unlike most black leaders, he had not previously participated in a direct personal assault on Robeson. Those who had led the earlier attacks, like Roy Wilkins, continued to do their bit to fan the accumulating animosity. When a New Jersey doctor wrote Wilkins asking if the written record proved that Robeson was a Communist, Wilkins replied, "Mr. Robeson is known far and wide as a Fellow Traveler of the Communist Party. . . . He is one of the few American Negroes who has been permitted behind the Iron Curtain and received enthusiasm [sic] in Moscow." For two consecutive months, November and December 1951, the NAACP's official organ, *The Crisis*, printed savage Cold War articles. The first, "Paul Robeson—the Lost Shepherd," signed "Robert Alan"—purportedly "the pen name of a well known New York journalist" (Paul Robeson, Jr., believes it was Earl Brown)—directly attacked Robeson as a "Kremlin Stooge" who "spouts

Communist propaganda as wildly as Vishinsky." The second ("Stalin's Greatest Defeat"), under Roy Wilkins's own byline, denounced the CPUSA in terms comparable to those disseminated by the FBI: "The latest tactic of the party is infiltration into established organizations. Having failed under its own name, it seeks to operate under other labels, but in this it has been soundly rebuffed, particularly by the National Association for the Advancement of Colored People, a prime target of party strategists. . . ."[35]

In that same month of December 1951, the New York *Amsterdam News* listed previous winners of the NAACP's coveted Spingarn Medal and omitted Robeson's name (he had won in 1945). Soon after that, Don Newcombe, the black Dodger pitcher, nearly came to blows with Robeson at the Red Rooster Tavern in Harlem. A woman in Robeson's party recognized Newcombe and asked Robeson to go over to his table to get his autograph for her. According to newspaper accounts, Newcombe was blunt and rude, and when Robeson tried to smooth things over, Newcombe purportedly shouted, "I'm joining the Army to fight people like you." At that Robeson lost his temper, and the two men had to be separated by bystanders. In response to one of the newspaper accounts, Essie posed a series of rhetorical questions: "Does [Newcombe] think Robeson is responsible for having kept him and Campanella and Robinson out of big league baseball for so many years? Does he think Robeson is responsible for making him and the majority of the Negro people live under segregation and discrimination and persecution?" "All I can say," she went on, "is Don Newcombe had better begin to talk and think for himself, if he ever wants to be more than a pitcher." W. E. B. Du Bois had a more succinct response to the general assault on Robeson: "The only thing wrong with Robeson is in having too great faith in human beings."[36]

On April 9, 1951, messages of greeting arrived from around the world for Robeson's fifty-third birthday. A few even arrived from the United States. But more emblematic of his country's regard was notification that Federal Judge Walter N. Bastian had upheld the State Department and dismissed Robeson's suit for the return of his passport. His lawyers immediately filed a notice of appeal; the next round in the protracted fight was not to come up for some five months.[37]

For a man with restricted travel rights, Robeson managed to keep exceedingly busy. He spoke in behalf of the Harlem Trade Union Council, participated in several peace crusades to the capital, attended numerous rallies, and helped organize appeals relating to the Willie McGee and Martinsville Seven cases (the latest in a lengthy series of legal outrages against blacks). He spoke at celebrations in honor of William Patterson's sixtieth and William Z. Foster's seventieth birthdays, and at the release from prison of three of the Hollywood Ten (John Howard Lawson, Dalton Trumbo, and Albert Maltz); and he gave the eulogy at the funeral of the ancient agitator herself, Mother Bloor. On May 5 Robeson celebrated a different event—the birth of a grandchild, David Paul Robeson. In June the Supreme Court upheld the Smith Act convictions. Four of the eleven CPUSA leaders immediately went underground, and without delay the government inaugurated a drive against second-echelon Party officials. On June 20 a federal grand jury in New York returned Smith Act indictments against an additional twenty-one CP leaders, seventeen of whom were arrested. The daily press debated whether the administration planned prosecutions in the thousands, or merely the hundreds.[38]

Robeson declared himself "one hundred percent on the side of the condemned and arrested leaders." At the mammoth Chicago Peace Congress at the end of June, he spoke out forcefully against the threat to civil liberties: "The First Amendment today lies temporarily gutted as a result of the validation of the Smith Act and the jailing of the Communist dissenters from American foreign policy. No other dissenter, whatever his politics, can feel safe in the exercise of the historic American right to criticize and complain so long as the Smith Act stands on the statute book and the Supreme Court decision remains unreversed." Chatman C. Wailes, one of the young black organizers for the Chicago rally, was present in the lobby of the Persian Hotel when the jazz musician Charlie Parker spotted Robeson and went up to him. "I just wanted to shake your hand," Wailes heard Parker say. "You're a great man."[39]

In Robeson's mind, the domestic civil-liberties issue was inescapably linked to the international question of peace. He saw repression at home as a direct consequence of a pathological fear of the Soviet Union. "We affirm the undeniable fact," he argued, "that the American people can live side by side with many different ways of life to achieve higher standards of living and eventual freedom for all." He applauded the resolution introduced by Colorado Senator Edwin C. Johnson for an end to the Korean War as a first step in detoxifying Soviet-American relations, and unfavorably contrasted the warm reception Jacob Malik, U.S.S.R. representative to the UN, had given him in his capacity as a representative of the World Peace Council, with the blanket refusal of Warren Austin, chief U.S. delegate to the UN, even to receive him. Robeson released to the press a letter of protest he sent Austin in which, among other sharp remarks, he lectured him on the United Nations: "far from representing the hopes and aspirations of the greater portion of mankind, [it] just remains what it has tended recently to become—the parroting whisper of powerful American corporate interests which many officials in positions of public trust happen to represent."[40]

Nonetheless, Robeson and other militant black leaders decided to turn to the United Nations to protest the recent rigged trial of Willie McGee, the case of the Martinsville Seven, and the conviction of the Trenton Six as confirmation of the institutionalized oppression of blacks in the United States. William Patterson spearheaded the drive to present a formal petition—"We Charge Genocide"—to the UN as a means for publicizing the terrible toll of racism in the United States. A number of prominent blacks—including Bishop W. J. Walls of Chicago, Reverend Charles A. Hill of Detroit, Du Bois, Charlotta Bass, Ben Davis, Jr., and Mary Church Terrell—supported the petition, but white liberals refused to endorse it. They, along with the established black leadership, balked at the petition's "exaggeration," its equation of official violence against blacks with a systematic governmental decision to wipe them out; institutionalized oppression, they argued, was not the same as institutionalized murder, though the one could sometimes spill over into the other. Robeson dismissed this distinction as a semantic one, and spent long hours with Patterson drawing up the UN petition. They insisted that their use of the term "genocide" was sanctioned by the United Nations' own definition of the term, as established in its Genocide Convention (which in 1951 remained unratified by the U.S. government). The UN definition had gone beyond the usual understanding of genocide as referring to *state*-sanctioned *mass* murder to emphasize instead the doing of "serious bodily and mental harm" to individual members of a national, ethnic, racial, or religious group. In its final form, the Patterson-Robeson petition went beyond even this elastic definition to embrace what it called "economic genocide," the "silent, cruel killer" that reaped its harvest from the deprivations of daily life. In mid-December the two men presented the petition simultaneously: Robeson to the UN Secretariat in New York, Patterson to the UN General Assembly in Paris. Both were formally received—and informally circumvented; the United States successfully used its influence behind the scenes to prevent the Human Rights Commission of the UN from discussing the genocide charge.[41]

Robeson's defiant words and actions continued to find far more response outside the United States. Word came from Bombay that he had been enthusiastically applauded *in absentia* at the All-India Peace Convention; from Paris that his was one of four huge pictures (FDR, Abraham Lincoln, and CP leader Eugene Dennis were the other three) carried by the crowd in the Bastille Day parade; from London offering a concert tour; from Aberdeen asking him to stand for election as rector of the university. (In responding to one of the Aberdeen students who had expressed concern that Robeson might misinterpret the invitation as support for Communism rather than, as intended, a protest against political persecution, Robeson repeated the theme he had already sounded several times in public that "the essence of my world outlook is that it is entirely possible for men and women of different political viewpoints to join hands in the common search for peace, equality and freedom.") At home his reputation was faring far less well. Some union halls and some black churches continued to keep open their doors, but the announcement of his appearance in an American city now routinely produced a wave of opposition. The

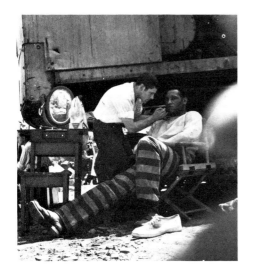

39. & 40. Robeson on the set of the film *The Emperor Jones*, 1933

41. With Dudley Digges in a scene from the film *The Emperor Jones*

42. (ABOVE) Arriving
in Moscow, December
1934. Paul (in hat,
rear) is flanked by
Herbert Marshall (left)
and Sergei Eisenstein
(right). Essie is in
the front row, second
from right; Larry
Brown is in the
front row, far left.

43. (LEFT) Leaving
Waterloo Station
on the boat train
The Majestic, 1935

44. (RIGHT) Paul and Paul, Jr.,
in London, 1936

45. (BELOW) With Larry Brown
in a December 1936 concert
at the Moscow Conservatory

46. On the set of *Show Boat*, 1935

47. James Whale (seated) directing a scene from *Show Boat* with Robeson and Hattie McDaniel

48. (ABOVE) Robeson as Bosambo, with
Nina Mae McKinney, in *Sanders of the River*

49. (RIGHT) With Jomo Kenyatta on location
for the film *Sanders of the River,* 1934

50. In *Song of Freedom* with Elizabeth Welch (right), 1936

51. (LEFT) Robeson as
Umbopa in *King Solomon's
Mines*, 1937

52. (BELOW) With Essie
in a scene from *Big Fella*,
1938

53. *The Proud Valley,* 1939

54. With Ethel Waters in *Tales of Manhattan,* 1942

55. Robeson singing to the Loyalist troops in Spain, 1938

56. Robeson (center) talking with two American volunteers in Spain
(photo from a scrapbook concerning the tour of the Negro People's
Ambulance for Loyalist Spain)

57. With Ruby Elzy (seated at right) in *John Henry,* 1940

58. After receiving the Medal for Good Diction on the Stage from
the American Academy of Arts and Letters, 1944 (From left to right:
Samuel S. McClure, Willa Cather, Theodore Dreiser, and Robeson)

59. (ABOVE) With Uta Hagen
as Desdemona in the Broadway
Othello, 1944

60. (RIGHT) With *Othello* co-stars
Uta Hagen and Jose Ferrer

61. (BELOW) With Margaret
Webster as Emilia in *Othello*

62. Hagen and Robeson in Desdemona's death scene

63. (LEFT) Ma Goode at the Robeson house in Enfield, 1940s

64. (BELOW) Freda Diamond

65. Paul, Jr., Freda Diamond, Essie, and Barry Baruch at Enfield, 1941

66. Max Yergan

67. Revels Cayton

68. Larry Brown

69. Essie in 1948

70. & 71. Robert and
Clara Rockmore

72. (ABOVE) Robeson
(with Earl Robinson
behind him) picketing
Ford's Theatre in
Washington, D.C., 1947

73. (LEFT) Robeson with
Henry Wallace during the
1948 Wallace Campaign

74. (LEFT) Robeson
speaking out against
the Taft-Hartley bill
in Washington, D.C.,
August 1948

75. Robeson with W. E. B. Du Bois and New York Representative Vito Marcantonio

76. Singing a duet with Larry Brown at a recording session in the late 1940s

Harvard Dramatic Club delighted in sending him an invitation to play in *Othello,* but a letter more typical of the climate of fear came from a white former supporter who now suggested "you refrain in the future from contacting me."[42]

The State Department moved to close down still further Robeson's access to his foreign fans. Receiving word that he planned to give a concert in Vancouver, British Columbia, in late January 1952, under the auspices of the United Mine, Mill and Smelter Workers Union, the State Department took steps to prevent Robeson from leaving U.S. soil. The means for doing so were not obvious. No U.S. citizen needed a passport to travel to and from Canada, so access for Robeson could not be denied on those grounds. Nor could reliance be placed on Canadian Immigration to prevent his crossing over the border from Seattle to Vancouver: the Canadian authorities disclaimed any authority to inhibit such passage. And so the State Department fell back on legislation originally passed during World War I and amended during World War II allowing the U.S. government— "during the existence of the national emergency"—to prevent the entry or departure of its citizens. State notified U.S. Immigration and Naturalization Service officials in the Vancouver area to prevent Robeson from leaving U.S. soil. Instructions were also given to detain Vincent Hallinan, who had been scheduled to appear on the platform with Robeson at the Mine, Mill convention. Hallinan was defense counsel for longshoremen's union leader Harry Bridges (currently appealing a perjury conviction that Robeson had protested); he was also the future standard-bearer of the Progressive Party in the 1952 election.[43]

Hallinan was removed from a Great Northern passenger train en route to Vancouver. Two hours later Robeson arrived by car at Blaine, Washington—the crossover town at the border—and was stopped by INS officials, who told the press that the action was taken on authority of the State Department. Hallinan boarded a southbound train after angrily accusing the immigration officers of "false arrest." Robeson courteously accepted the ruling and returned to Seattle. When a delegation from the miners' union protested to the U.S. Consul General, the official told them it was pointless to discuss the case, since redress, if any, lay in Washington. The miners, in consultation with Robeson, hit upon a more satisfying way to register their indignation.[44]

Through the device of a long-distance telephone hookup relayed to the public-address system, Robeson sang and spoke for seventeen minutes the following day directly from the Marine Cooks and Stewards Hall in Seattle to the miners' convention, two thousand strong, in Vancouver. He began by singing "Joe Hill"—the song about the Western Federation of Miners' organizer framed on a murder charge in Utah in 1915—and ended with a stirring speech. The government, Robeson told the miners, seemed determined to keep him in "a sort of domestic house arrest and confinement" because of his "passionate devotion to the full liberation of the black and brown peoples" of the world, and because of his insistence, toward that end, that the Western powers stop devoting their energies to preparations for war and try recommitting them to the notion that "all peoples can live in peace and friendly coexistence." He emphasized that in his view the INS move had been "an act of the U.S. administration, not of the American people." In response, the convention approved the suggestion of militant union leader Harvey Murphy that an across-the-border Robeson concert at the "Peace Arch" be arranged for that spring, and unanimously passed a resolution condemning the action of the State Department. The lack of a dissenting vote, Murphy announced—to a roar of laughter—meant that the representatives of the Royal Canadian Mounted Police and the FBI who were present were in support of the resolution.[45]

The Peace Arch concert did take place, as planned, in May, but not without considerable effort. From New York, the *Freedom* Family (as the associates of the publication affectionately called themselves) worked hard to arrange the Vancouver concert as the centerpiece for a two-month Robeson tour designed to bring in revenue for the United Freedom Fund—a joint endeavor for the newspaper, CAA, NNLC, and the Committee for the Negro in the Arts. But neither the engagements nor the revenue proved easy to come by. The group started its work without a penny, and was able to begin planning for the tour only after borrowing a thousand dollars from *Freedom* newspaper, itself desperate for money. That was only the initial hurdle. It remained to be seen whether people—even progressives—would run the risks of political ostracism and possible physical injury by coming out to hear Robeson sing.

The most successful single stop on the tour, from both a political and a financial point of view, was at the Peace Arch itself—largely because of the response from the Canadian side of the border. Thanks to the efforts of the Mine, Mill trade-unionists, twenty-five to thirty thousand Canadians turned up on the Vancouver side for the concert; no more than five thousand mobilized on the American side (the American press estimated *total* attendance at five thousand; the Canadian press put the figure seven times higher). The FBI, predictably, was also there. While the Border Patrol took license-plate numbers, FBI agents filmed and photographed the event itself. Nonetheless, there were no incidents, and the sponsors laid plans for making the Peace Arch concert an annual event.[46]

Seattle, the next stop, proved an altogether more complicated affair. Robeson's experience in that city in mid-May 1952 illustrates, in microcosm, the specific difficulties he encountered throughout the tour, the sources of support and opposition generated by his presence, and the general state of his reputation at the time.

In Seattle, as everywhere else on the tour, the groundwork was done by the *Freedom* staff in New York—Louis Burnham; the newspaper's general manager, George B. Murphy, Jr.; and its business manager, Bert Alves—in combination with local sponsoring groups, pre-eminently left-wing unions and black churches. In Seattle, Terry Pettus, head of the Northwestern Bureau of *People's World,* the militant (the FBI said "Communist") newspaper, was the key coordinating figure. A month before Robeson's scheduled arrival, Pettus reported glumly to the *Freedom* people in New York that the city authorities had abruptly canceled their agreement to lease the civic auditorium for Robeson's concert on the grounds that it would "tend to cause antagonism to the Negro race." The *Freedom* staff responded with a double-pronged plan for counterattack: initiate court action and mobilize the local black community.[47]

The Seattle organizers did precisely that. They sent out special-delivery letters to leaders of black clubs, churches, and political organizations stressing the importance of giving the lie "to the white supremacy statement of the city officials" that Robeson's appearance would create racial antagonism; and, for shrewdly calculated extra effect, they enclosed a recent editorial on Robeson and Du Bois from the *Star of Zion,* official organ of the A.M.E. Zion Church, praising the struggle of the two men in behalf of black people. Simultaneously, Pettus and the other organizers filed for a court injunction to prevent the city from canceling the contract for the civic auditorium. In New York, the *Freedom* staff got busy on its own phones, enlisting support from Coleman Young and the National Negro Labor Council in Detroit, Reverend Charles Hill, and black newspaperwoman Charlotta Bass.[48]

The combined efforts paid off. Though attorneys for the city scoured the black community, they were able to persuade only one person—a black police officer—to testify that Robeson was held in low esteem. According to a newspaper account, the officer appeared "obviously embarrassed" on the stand and let it be known that he had been called out of bed to testify that morning by the white officer who headed the local "red squad." A number of Seattle's black leaders—Vincent Davis, Lester Catlett, and James McDaniels—followed the officer on the stand and, contradicting his view, described Robeson as "recognized and loved by the overwhelming majority of the Negro people because of his consistent fight for full equality, political and economic, for his people." When asked if he was a member of the Communist Party, Catlett scornfully refused to answer: "We don't ask people their political affiliation. I don't know yours. . . ." In reference to the same issue, McDaniels responded, "I have heard more about that in this courtroom the past two days than I have heard among my people the past 20 years." At the end of the three-day hearing, it was ruled that the city had failed to prove that Robeson's appearance would engender racial antagonism. The judge instructed that the civic auditorium be made available for the concert.[49]

The moral victory did not translate into a financial one. Seventeen

hundred people paid admission to the concert, and there was no disturbance of any kind, but the organizers had hoped for an attendance of
twenty-five hundred. When expenses were paid, only $250 was left over for
the Freedom Fund. Worse, there were local reprisals. Within three days
of the concert, Jack Kinzell, one of its white organizers, was let go from
his job as a popular radio announcer at station KIRO, and Vincent Davis,
who had defended Robeson on the stand, was fired from his department-
store job on direct order from management headquarters in New York.[50]

The events in Seattle set the tone for much of what followed on the
rest of the tour. San Francisco, the next stop, was nearly an exact replay.
Mayor Elmer E. Robinson had said he would refuse to let Robeson sing
in the Opera House because he "has seen fit to vilify the United States of
America at Communist sponsored gatherings at home and abroad." The
Oakland authorities simultaneously denied Robeson the use of Oak Auditorium—a facility opened to the fascist leader Gerald L. K. Smith that same
month. Again, the local citizenry came to the rescue. Bill Chester, regional
director of the longshoremen's union, led the fight, with the black leadership taking a strong stand in support of Robeson—Chester reported to
New York that 98 percent of the black community stood behind him
—while in Berkeley twelve hundred people turned out for a town meeting that voted by a margin of four to one in favor of Robeson's appearance. As a result, he gave two concerts in the area—one at the largest
black-owned church hall—which together drew more than five thousand
people.[51]

The rest of the tour—some fifteen cities in all—saw a repetition of
official harassment, but not of aroused local support for Robeson's appearance. In St. Louis a black minister withdrew his Prince of Peace Baptist
Church as the site for Robeson's concert after city officials warned him that
"vandals" would be likely to wreck the church in reprisal. In Milwaukee the
black churches stood firm, but their audiences did not, despite a house-to-
house canvass for ticket sales. The tepid response perhaps accounted for
the particular tone and emphasis of the speech Robeson gave that night:
he pointed out that if he was indeed a Communist he would have been
hauled before a congressional committee or a court long since, and he
emphasized that, although he admired the Soviet Union for its support of
minority rights, "the real core of my fight is not political but is based on
. . . sympathy for my people and for all colored people of the world.
. . . The only thing we must concern ourselves with is Negro liberation."
At the University of Minnesota the Young Progressives organization took
up sponsorship of his concert and initially obtained approval from the
authorities, but after the tickets were already printed President Morrill
denounced Robeson as "an embittered anti-American, anti-democratic
propagandist" and the university revoked its approval. In Pittsburgh the
authorities outdid themselves in efforts to intimidate potential Robeson

supporters: they condemned the concert building as unsafe and then, for good measure, prohibited "mixed occupancy." The local sponsors repaired an exit door and a fire escape, thus permitting the concert to take place, but two FBI agents took motion pictures of the arrivals from an adjoining apartment. Not surprisingly, only 350 people turned up. Even a public celebration of Robeson's fifty-fourth birthday had to be canceled after New York City's Manhattan Center broke an oral agreement to rent its hall.[52]

When receipts were tallied at the end of the tour, the United Freedom Fund had grossed a little under fifteen hundred dollars. The sum was so small that the four cooperating organizations voted to put it toward organizing a possible 1952–53 tour instead of dividing the proceeds, contenting themselves for the moment with the notion that "politically and culturally" the tour, in reaching some seventy-five thousand people, had been a success. Robeson himself had averaged a three-hundred-dollar fee per concert—as compared with the two thousand dollars he had once commanded—but even that money he tried to turn over to *Freedom*. The tough-minded Bob Rockmore placed himself squarely in the path of Robeson's magnanimity and for Robeson's own good. Though recording royalties and investments continued to bring in substantial sums—Robeson's income never fell to a level of serious hardship—he no longer had the extra cash to support his many generosities.[53]

■

CHAPTER 20

Confinement

(1952–1954)

Following the close of his tour, Robeson turned full attention to the 1952 Progressive Party campaign for the presidency, speaking widely in behalf of its national ticket. It was an unpropitious time for a left-wing campaign: "subversion" had become a national preoccupation. The Korean War had turned into a bloody stalemate, and when Truman dismissed General MacArthur rather than yield to his call for escalating American military commitments, Senator McCarthy loudly blamed the "Communists" for having led a "smear campaign" against the general. In McCarthy's view—and the polls showed him strongly supported in the country—the continuing indictments of second-level Communist Party leaders under the Smith Act would not be sufficient to expose and contain the enormity of the Red Menace. His pursuit of the Asian expert Owen Lattimore as Alger Hiss's "boss," though fantasy, proved an effective headline-grabber; and when Julius and Ethel Rosenberg were arrested and charged with conspiracy to transmit atomic secrets to the Soviets, the ensuing hysteria in the country finally seemed a match for McCarthy's own inflamed imagination. There were air-raid drills in the urban centers and calls in Congress for a preventive first strike against Russia (an option seriously considered for a time as realistic). Dwight D. Eisenhower, the Republican candidate for president, was thought by some to be quietly antagonistic to McCarthy's wilder tactics, but the force of public opinion seemed so strongly mobilized behind the Senator that Adlai Stevenson, the Democratic candidate and a purported liberal, began moving to the right, announcing support for the Smith Act convictions, for loyalty programs, and for the firing of "Communist" teachers.[1]

Tweedledum and Tweedledee: in Robeson's view the two national candidates and their parties were near–carbon copies of reaction. He and Essie attended the Progressive Party national convention in Chicago in July, she as a delegate from Connecticut and a member of the platform committee, he as one of the Party's national leaders and a member of the nominating committee which chose Vincent Hallinan for president and Charlotta Bass for vice-president. Both Essie and Paul went on to play active roles in the campaign, Paul going as far as California to participate in a Culver City Stadium rally that drew ten thousand. During one California stop, Charlotta Bass, who was lighter-skinned than Robeson, was asked by an audience member, "Why don't you look like Paul?" "Honey," Mrs. Bass replied, "I should, but I've been tampered with." Robeson's appearances rarely produced so lighthearted a note. Local opposition to him from veterans' groups surfaced frequently, and in Ann Arbor, Michigan, they attempted to get a court injunction to prevent him from speaking in public. Everywhere he went Robeson told audiences that 1952 "has been a fateful year" and, for black people particularly, "one of gathering crisis," epitomized by the all-white jury in North Carolina that had tried the black tenant farmer Mack Ingram for "leering" at a white woman dressed in men's clothes and standing seventy-five feet away: "The United States," Robeson commented, "is certainly making a unique contribution to the jurisprudence of the so-called 'free' nations of the West."[2]

In Cleveland, speaking to the National Negro Labor Council and deliberately echoing yet again the words ascribed to him at Paris in 1949, he asked whether black youths should "join with British soldiers in shooting down the brave peoples of Kenya" or in firing on the crowds in South Africa currently engaged in a civil-disobedience campaign. Of course not, Robeson replied: "I say again, the proper battlefield for our youth and for all fighters for a decent life is here . . . where the walls of Jim Crow still stand and need somebody to tear them down." Despite his starkly spoken opposition to the reactionary drift in American life, Robeson was still occasionally able to strike a hopeful note: he told his audiences that, although the Republican and Democratic conventions had evaded civil-rights planks, the issue had at least moved toward the center of the nation's attention.[3]

But that hopefulness found scant confirmation in the election results. In a record-breaking turnout, Eisenhower won a landslide victory, while the Progressive ticket polled an abysmal nationwide total of under two hundred thousand votes—about a fifth of their minuscule count in 1948. Meeting for a postelection rehash, the Progressive Party national committee (of which Essie was a member) managed to find a ray of hope in the outcome of some state contests—in Corliss Lamont's receiving nearly a hundred thousand votes on the Progressive line in his New York run for the Senate, and in the trailing of McCarthy's vote in Wisconsin behind

Eisenhower's. But this was a desperate clutching at straws. The Progressives had suffered a crushing rejection at the polls, and the Party never again ran a national ticket (or many local ones).[4]

A month after the election, Moscow announced that Paul Robeson was one of seven recipients—and the only American—of the 1952 International Stalin Peace Prizes. Established three years earlier in honor of Stalin's seventieth birthday and carrying an award of a gold medal and a hundred thousand rubles (about twenty-five thousand U.S. dollars), the prizes had been established as a kind of counter-Nobel, to honor citizens of any country of the world for outstanding service in "the struggle against war"; Soong Ching-ling (Madame Sun Yat-sen), Frédéric Joliot-Curie, Pietro Nenni, and Jorge Amado had been among its distinguished previous recipients. The award carried the mark of great prestige among Communists—Stalin had not yet been revealed to them as a mass killer—and the mark of enduring infamy among anti-Communists. The reaction to Robeson's designation as a Stalin Prize medalist varied according to one's allegiance. Rockwell Kent telegraphed him, "In you, Paul, we greet a hero." Oppositely, José Ferrer, who had had his own trouble with the "red" label, told the press that in accepting the award Robeson would do "irreparable harm" to his race. The right-wing columnist George Sokolsky applauded Ferrer for having "served his country well" by "pinpointing" Robeson's "unforgiveable sins against his native land."[5]

In accepting the prize, Robeson told the press he did so "not merely as an individual, but as a part of the growing peace movement in the United States, a peace movement that has been honored by the leadership of the great scholar, Dr. W. E. B. Du Bois." As Robeson had already said during a speech at Reverend Charles Hill's Hartford Avenue Baptist Church in Detroit, "I'm very proud that somewhere people understood that I'm struggling for peace, and that I shall continue to do [so]." He announced that he would again apply for a passport in order to be able to receive the prize in person. The State Department, in turn, announced—within a week—that Robeson's application was denied. "We see nothing to indicate," a spokesman said, that Robeson's "attitude has changed." The Passport Division also notified him, with no hint of irony, that its reluctance to sanction American citizens' visits to the Soviet Union was based on an inability "to assure them in that country the degree of protection which it likes to afford to American citizens traveling abroad."[6]

The State Department was accurate in one particular: Robeson's "attitude" had not changed. His whole point was that the right to a passport did not and should not hinge on a citizen's politics. Under the Constitution, "attitudes" were not actionable; they were instead at the core of the country's protected heritage of free speech. The government's case rested on dubious interpretations of the President's war powers, the Secretary of State's discretionary power in issuing passports, and the actual state of the current "national emergency." Not only were the State Department's justifying arguments cloudy, but its underlying racist animus was revealed with startling clarity in a footnote to one of the briefs it used when arguing the Robeson case before the Court of Appeals in March 1952: ". . . he has been for years extremely active politically in behalf of independence of the colonial peoples of Africa. Though this may be a highly laudable aim, the diplomatic embarrassment that could arise from the presence abroad of such a political meddler, traveling under the protection of an American passport, is easily imaginable." The State Department was apparently admitting, however inadvertently, that advocating the independence of the colonial peoples of Africa was not in the best interests of the United States—a revelation reported in the *Daily Worker* and in *Freedom*, but ignored by the national press.[7]

Two months later, Joseph Stalin was dead. The new leaders in the Kremlin soon began speaking openly of détente with the West, a possibility heightened by Eisenhower's nomination of Chip Bohlen, a known proponent of "peaceful coexistence," to the ambassadorial post in Moscow—a nomination fought fiercely by Senator McCarthy. When an armistice in Korea in the summer of 1953 officially ended hostilities there, another element for the easing of Cold War tensions fell into place. But an actual thaw was still in the future, as the execution of the Rosenbergs in June 1953 pointedly illustrated. Robeson had worked hard for the commutation of the Rosenbergs' sentence, telling one rally, "My people are not strangers to frameups—they know what to expect from the courts of this land." He called upon those present to work for "the possibility of restoring to the American people their social sanity, their democratic bearings, their dedication to justice and due process."[8]

Thwarted politically and circumscribed artistically, Robeson relied more and more during the fifties on his restorative relationship with Sam and Helen Rosen. At their apartment in New York City, and more especially at their house in Katonah, he found with the Rosens a needed family atmosphere of deep bonds of affection and congeniality, a respite from political tensions, a chance to relax. He talked sports for hours with Sam, taught the Rosens' son John football plays on the rug, and sang while their daughter Judy accompanied him on the living-room piano. He would curl up for hours reading or studying Chinese calligraphy, taking time out to consume mammoth portions of chocolate ice cream and peanut brittle. Mornings—which for Paul usually started at noon—he would beguile Odessa, the housekeeper, into making him pancakes, plus biscuits with honey, while she was trying to plan lunch. He was an astonishing eater. He and Sam would have "corn races," demolishing two dozen ears of Wallace Hybrid (developed by the former Progressive Party candidate) during its August glory; Paul invariably won, and Sam invariably accused him of cheating by not finishing each ear. At 2:00 a.m., or 4:00 a.m., Paul would coax Helen into cooking him a hamburger or fried eggs over lightly—"You know," he'd say, laughing, "not hardly."[9]

Paul disliked cold weather, and in wintertime Helen would manage to find him a size 12½ snow boot and an extra-large lumber jacket; he would then tramp happily through the clean country snow, tossing snowballs at family members who mockingly protested his "professional" throwing arm. Summers, Helen would try to teach him to swim in the pond. He was always a bit frightened of the water, even after she bought him a size 50 life jacket and a pair of water wings besides—"we used to launch him," Helen remembers. She remembers, too, that he preferred to walk with her in the secluded stand of large fir trees right near the house. They were always careful, but when they were alone in the woods he would put his head on her lap and drowsily sing her favorite, "The Riddle Song." During their quiet talks, the political issues that concerned them both often came up, as they conjured images of a world without bigotry and war, and Paul would say—"It will be, it must be." When they were sitting among the sweet pines, everything still seemed possible.[10]

His own son, Paul, Jr., had been having a difficult time professionally. Though he had graduated in engineering from Cornell in the top 10 percent of his class, he had found himself blocked from employment opportunities in his field. A number of firms, including GE and Westinghouse, gave him interviews, but none followed through. He finally landed a job with a physics lab in Long Island City, but the next day the FBI was on the phone to the prospective employer, warning that the firm would lose defense contracts if it hired him. For several years, he taught electronics at private technical schools, and then became a free-lance translator of Russian scientific journals. Despite Paul, Jr.'s restricted opportunities, he does not describe himself as "suffering greatly" in those years: he was a happily married family man, with his second child, Susan, born in 1953, and was deeply engaged with his CP organizing activities in Harlem.[11]

For two of those years, 1953–55, Paul, Jr., ran Othello Recording Company, which he and Lloyd Brown set up to provide an artistic outlet for his father after professional recording studios closed their doors to him. For want of any other available space, one of the recording sessions was held in the Rosens' New York apartment, with their daughter Judy accompanying on the piano (alternating with a professional accompanist, Alan Booth). The walls were hung with rugs to muffle outside noise, and the "boy genius" in the apartment next door—who invariably began practicing his piano every time they got ready to record—was eventually silenced after Helen made a diplomatic appeal to his parents.[12]

The first of the three albums Robeson made with the Othello Recording Company, *Robeson Sings*, was the only one recorded in a commercial studio. Performed with orchestra and chorus, based on arrangements by Don Redman, it had a slick sound throughout which made it musically undistinguished. Still, the album sold well. Released in December 1952 and publicized through small ads in the left-wing press, the record within four months sold some five thousand copies at five dollars each. That brought Robeson a net royalty (computed at 15 percent) of about four thousand dollars, hardly a munificent sum for a man who at the height of his fame had earned that amount of money in two nights of singing. Fortunately, Bob Rockmore's shrewd investments continued to provide Robeson with a comfortable if diminished income. Without Rockmore's loyal services Robeson would have suffered severe financial stringency, since by 1953 new opportunities for him to earn money from singing or acting had evaporated.[13]

In June 1953 he set off on a second tour to benefit Freedom Associates, but overall it failed to meet even the moderate expectations of the previous year. It was decided this time to aim his appearances more than previously at the black community ("not artificially excluding the white community, but the balance must be on *our* side rather than the other way around," wrote one *Freedom* staff member). But resources in the black community were limited, and the reservoir of good will toward Robeson, while profound, was neither inexhaustible nor uncontested. The central Washington office of the NAACP threatened its Oberlin chapter with the removal of its charter if it sponsored Robeson in a concert (when he heard about that decision six years later, Robeson said with a grim smile, "Yes, those were the people who did the final hatchet job on me"). "The Negro masses love him," Bert Alves of *Freedom* wrote to John Gray, another staff member. "The Negro middle class admire him but are fearful of his hold on the masses," and frightened that "the disapproval of white leaders will injure the special position of leadership and privilege these middle class folk enjoy." The black paper the San Francisco *Sun* agreed: "The working class Negro feels that Robeson says the things which they would like to say." He had, Stretch Johnson adds, "a Teflon coating in the black community."[14]

The coating was thinnest, though, among the black bourgeoisie. Aaron Wells (who became Robeson's doctor in 1955) remembers an evening in 1950 when he invited a few of his Harlem neighbors in the Riverton Apartments to meet Paul: "One happened to have been a banker; the other was a prominent lawyer. I'll never forget how they rode me the next day—'How dare you invite us to your home when Paul Robeson is there?'" (Many whites, of course, including some who called themselves political radicals, were afraid to be in Robeson's company. Helen Rosen recalls that Lillian Hellman upbraided her fiercely for having Paul as a fellow dinner guest, insisting his presence put them all in danger since the FBI was known to be following his movements.) A few years later Wells went with Robeson to a meeting on St. Nicholas Avenue of the Alpha Phi Alpha fraternity of which they were both members. Several of those present reproved Robeson to his face for "not having been with us when you were at the height of your career," and one lawyer (later a federal judge) openly attacked him on the issue of Communism. Robeson simply responded (as Wells recalls his words), "You know, brothers, you are really hitting at the wrong enemy. I am not your enemy. You're hitting in the wrong direction."[15]

The churchgoing black masses were not automatically put off—as so many white churchgoers were—by accusations that Robeson was a "godless" Communist. He didn't *sound* godless. He personified the spirituals in his music, and nothing about his presence when he sang them suggested an antireligious man. Nobody who didn't "have God in him" could sing "Deep River" the way Robeson sang it; even if he himself didn't know it, or consciously denied it, he "had God in him." But in fact he didn't deny it. His own family—with both his father and his brother Ben pastors of A.M.E. Zion—gave him impeccable credentials in the black church, and Robeson himself had turned to it in times of trouble. If he never showed any particular devotion to the institutional church or the literal pronouncements of Scripture, he never expressed even the remotest allegiance to "materialistic atheism." If he was not a religious man in any formalistic sense, he was nonetheless an intensely spiritual one, convinced that some "higher force" watched over him, and drew fundamental strength from a deep cultural identification with his people and their religion.

Even if Robeson was a "communist" with a small "c," believing in a society where a larger number of people could share in its opportunities and rewards, he was no "subversive." Blacks were well aware that if there had been any proof he was a "Communist" with a capital "C"—a registered member of the Party—J. Edgar Hoover would have long since had him hauled into court under the Smith Act. To the average black churchgoer, working for civil rights was an integral and proper part of the church's business. The black church had been in the forefront of the freedom struggle from its inception, and it was assumed that the church was a natural recruiting ground and fount of strength for *that* kind of political work in the world. Robeson was seen primarily as a champion of black rights—not as the agent of a foreign power—and to that large extent it was not doubted that he was a proper church person. "We are convinced," the black Methodist minister Reverend Edward D. McGowan said in a 1953 speech before the National Fraternal Council of Churches, "that we must come to the defense of all Negro leaders who are attacked. We will not succumb to the enemies of the Negro people who would divide us by name calling and smear tactics. For we know that a better life for our people will not be achieved by a divided people. And so . . . I will come to my own conclusions about Paul Robeson—no one else can tell me what I must think or believe about this great leader of the Negro people."[16]

This is not to say that every black church automatically opened its doors to Robeson; those dominated by the black bourgeoisie, or its values, were not receptive; nor were those closely identified with a politically ambitious and self-protective minister—Adam Clayton Powell, Jr., for example, never invited Robeson to his influential Harlem church. Yet the basic contrast holds. When Robeson appeared in the black churches of Detroit in 1953, the enthusiastic response suggested a revival meeting rather than the stiff atmosphere of a concert. But when he appeared for the second annual Peace Arch concert in Blaine, Washington, an essentially "white" event, he drew only half the crowd he had the preceding year—and almost all of that from the Canadian side of the border. Yet his defiance was not dampened: "I want everybody in the range of my voice to hear, official or otherwise, that there is no force on earth that will make me go backward one-thousandth part [of] one little inch."[17]

While in Seattle as part of his tour, Robeson took the occasion (duly noted by FBI agents) to put in a public appearance at the U.S. Federal Court. Six defendants—including Terry Pettus, the editor of *People's World,* who had helped to arrange Robeson's tour the previous year—were on trial under the Smith Act for conspiracy; during recess, Robeson made a point of talking with the defendants, and because one of them was under a contempt citation and not permitted to leave the courtroom, Robeson met with him in the U.S. marshal's office. It was hardly the first time, of course, that Robeson had insisted on publicly identifying himself with those under federal indictment. From the first round of Smith Act arrests back in 1949, he had played an active role on committees and at rallies to defend the victims and their families. At one point the FBI had even speculated that Essie and Paul had turned their house at Enfield into a secret hideout for CPUSA leaders who had gone underground. An overzealous neighbor had excited the Justice Department with tales about an unfamiliar Dodge parked near the Robeson home; in the retrospective opinion of the Enfield chief of police, the mystery vehicle more likely belonged to FBI agents themselves; their presence around the Robeson house had become a commonplace.[18]

The Enfield property was put on the market. Bob Rockmore's careful management had allowed Robeson to maintain a comfortable lifestyle, but as his income shrank and his legal fees mounted, some belt-tightening did become necessary. For two years Rockmore had been exerting pressure on Essie to put the house up for sale; as he saw the financial picture worsening, he wrote her that "something" had to be done "to get Enfield off Paul's back." She dragged her feet for a while: she had loved the house, and it had also served—even if rarely—as the one domestic meeting ground she still shared with Paul. But as his relationship with Helen Rosen deepened in the early fifties, any real domestic life he had was with the Rosens, and he had stopped coming to Enfield altogether. In New York City he based himself at the McGhees' apartment (where he paid a regular monthly rent) and sometimes stayed at his brother Ben's parsonage in Harlem. Even after Essie came around to the idea of selling Enfield, it became difficult to get a buyer. It wasn't until the spring of 1953, after dropping the asking price from thirty-five to twenty-two thousand—with only six thousand down—that Rockmore was able to dispose of the property. Essie tried hard to persuade Paul that they should build a small house in Norwalk, but he gladly deferred to Rockmore's insistence that such a project would be beyond his means. Just at this time, Ma Goode died, after many years in a Massachusetts rest home. Essie, bereaved and uprooted, reluctantly took up hotel life in New York, while Paul continued to stay with the McGhees and to spend much of his time at the Rosens'.[19]

Essie's mind was temporarily taken off her displacement by a summons to appear before McCarthy's Senate Investigating Committee on July 7, 1953. The Senator had recently "discovered" that the Voice of America and the Overseas Library Program were hotbeds of sedition, and while trampling through those vineyards a McCarthy staff member's eyes lit upon this statement in Essie's 1945 book, *African Journey:* ". . . the one hopeful light on the horizon . . . [is] the exciting and encouraging conditions in Soviet Russia, where for the first time in history our race problem has been squarely faced and solved. . . ." Eslanda Robeson was summoned to Washington to explain, if she could, her traitorous words. Short of bagging Robeson himself—and the lack of government evidence had thus far made that impossible—this seemed a delicious prospect for the red-baiters.

But Essie denied them the triumph. Accompanied by her lawyer, Milton H. Friedman, she gave a feisty account of herself, turning the session, if not into the rout she later claimed, nonetheless into an impressive draw. She set a tone of charming belligerence with her very first response on the stand: "You are Mrs. Paul Robeson, is that correct?" counselor Roy Cohn asked her. "Yes," she answered, "and very proud of it, too." She then surprised the committee by pleading the Fifteenth as well as the First Amendment in refusing to answer whether she was a member of the Communist Party. Witnesses had routinely been citing the First Amendment (and after 1950, the Fifth Amendment against self-incrimination), but no one before Essie had called upon the Fifteenth. "The Fifteenth Amendment?" the surprised McCarthy asked. "This solely deals with your right to vote. You cannot refuse to answer questions about a conspiracy to destroy this nation because you have the right to vote. . . . Before this committee we do not have Negroes or whites. . . . We have American citizens. They all have the same rights. . . ." He repeated his standard warning that witnesses would be cited for contempt if they based their refusal to answer a question on any grounds other than self-incrimination.[20]

Essie was not intimidated. "I don't quite understand your statement," she said, "that we are all American citizens. . . . I am a second class citizen now, as a Negro. That is the reason I claim this fifteenth amendment. I would be very happy if we didn't have to discuss race, and I hope we will at some point get to a place where we don't have to. But in the meantime you are white and I am Negro and this is a very white committee and I feel I must protect myself. I am sorry it is necessary." "The only person who has been discussing race today is yourself," McCarthy shot back. Senator Symington tried to inject a conciliatory note: "Would you be more willing to answer questions with respect to Communism and the possibility of your being a Communist, if you were more satisfied with your position in this country as a Negro?" Essie did not bend: "The reason I refuse to answer the question is because I think that . . . my opinions are my private personal affair. . . ." But did not the government, Symington persisted, "have a right to ask you whether you are dedicated to an organization which in turn is dedicated to overthrowing the American government by force and violence?" Essie refused to bite: "I don't know anybody that is dedicated to overthrowing the government by force and violence. The only force and violence I know is what I have experienced and seen in this country, and it has not been by Communists."

McCarthy then defended his all-white committee on the grounds that the people had not chosen to elect any black senators, a sloppy argument that Essie punctured by pointing out that most blacks lived in the South, where they were commonly denied the right to vote. When he tried to trap her into telling whether she had ever attended Communist cell meetings, Essie insouciantly asked him to define what a cell was; when he shifted to the word "unit," she professed not to know what a unit was either. McCarthy remained polite, perhaps even impressed. He pronounced Essie "very charming" and "intelligent." "I am not going to order you to answer those questions and cite you for contempt. . . . You are getting special consideration today. . . . I do not propose to argue with a lady." Essie thanked him, announced she was "a very, very loyal American," and stepped down from the stand. It was "hilarious," she wrote Marie Seton, "all sweetness and light, very clear, very respectful and reasonable." "Paul is VERY pleased, the Children are very proud, and all our friends are simply delighted. So."[21]

Paul's pleasure in Essie's performance was momentary. As the number of rebuffs continued to mount and as government surveillance intensified, the cracks in his public good spirits, and even in his health, became more discernible. It's "tough sledding," he wrote Helen Rosen's daughter Judy from the road. "Whole weight is thrown against us—in every city, town & hamlet." He added, though, that when in St. Louis he had gone to the last session of the NAACP convention "and the whole audience recognized me (I also was in the audience) and I was hour & half getting away—signing autographs etc.— Gave top brass (White & Co) a fit. . . ." To Helen Rosen he wrote, "I miss you terribly. Miss the quiet and sweet-warm response of chatting about this & that—of reading as a kind of lovely communion—of philosophizing—and the ever recurrent theme of life and being. . . . I have grown to love you ever so deeply. . . . I have almost no defenses where you are concerned."[22]

By late 1953 rejections and disappointments were arriving in bunches. Invitations from England to perform *Othello* and from Wales to sing at the Eisteddfod festival—as well as a host of additional requests for overseas appearances at peace conferences and political events—had to be turned down for lack of a passport. At home, the governing board of the Brooklyn Academy of Music refused to honor its contract with ASP (National Council of the Arts, Sciences and Professions) for a cultural festival when it learned that Robeson would be participating—his presence would create a "danger of disorder." At Hartford, Connecticut, he was belatedly allowed to appear onstage—protected by a police detachment of 250 men—only after the local Board of Education had successfully resisted the demand of the City Council to bar the concert. Baited by reporters afterward for "hurting your cause by allying yourself with Communists," Robeson lashed out in anger: "Is this what you want?" he asked them, pretending to bend at the waist. "For me to bend and bow and shuffle along and be a nice, kindly colored man and say please when I ask for better treatment for my people? — Well, it doesn't work."[23]

The government was determined to scotch the notion that militancy would work, either. The Attorney General put the Council on African Affairs on its list of "Communist-front" organizations and ordered it to appear for a hearing before the Subversive Activities Control Board in Washington. The CAA categorically denied the allegation that it was Communist-controlled but acknowledged that in the current climate, where parallelism of ideas was considered a sufficient basis for establishing guilt, it was powerless to exonerate itself: "the only defense we have is to *get rid of McCarthyism and the McCarran Act!*" That, the Council stressed, was "the prime task of the hour." But the hour was not at hand. *Freedom* magazine also began to feel the heat. With subscriptions and revenues declining, Robeson had to extend a personal loan—which his straitened finances could ill afford—to keep the publication going. (For the first three months of 1954, Robeson took only three hundred dollars in artist's fees from Freedom Associates, even as the *Amsterdam News* was reporting, "Don't go feeling sorry for Paul Robeson, he still makes $600 at each left-wing rally he appears at.") The prolonged, accumulated stress on him began to show. FBI headquarters in Washington received a report from a field agent that Robeson was "suffering from heart trouble." That specific rumor was unfounded, but Robeson did have to enter a strictly supervised diet program for several weeks in Washington, D.C., to control his ballooning weight. "It's been really restful," he wrote Helen Rosen. "I've taken off some 18–20 lbs. . . . I was around 278 when I arrived here. I had no idea."[24]

It was the briefest respite. The new year opened with *Jet* magazine's republishing a rumor that columnist Cholly Knickerbocker had originated in the conservative *Journal-American* that Robeson "would like to break with the Communist Party, but is being hindered by his wife and his son." A year earlier a "confidential informant" had supplied similar information to the FBI, claiming that Robeson "is still a Marxist, but is disillusioned with Stalinism. . . . He is primarily a Negro Nationalist and secondarily a Marxist." The rumor of his disillusion—without any known basis in fact—persisted. From a second source entirely, the FBI received another report several months later that Robeson "is about to make a public break with the Communists," and on May 2 Drew Pearson, in his regular Sunday-evening broadcast, climaxed the accumulating hearsay with the assertion that Robeson had been meeting with black leaders and becoming persuaded "to change his left-wing views."[25]

Robeson categorically and publicly denied all such reports. In a lengthy reply to *Jet,* he strenuously reasserted his respect for the "many fine, sincere, great-hearted radicals" he knew in this country, as well as his own devotion to the Soviet people and "the building of their new magnificent society." He reiterated his belief that the "socialistic" countries of Eastern Europe and Asia were actively working to abolish racial discrimination and to help "former colonial peoples to reach full dignity," and were thereby continuing to highlight the hypocrisy of "the so-called Free Western imperialist nations. Please tell me why I should . . . attempt to lay hands upon these friends from across the seas? My reason tells me that if I am going to get rough, I know just where the enemy is, close at hand"— Messrs. "Byrnes of South Carolina, Talmadge of Georgia, McCarran, McCarthy and their ilk." "Am I expected," he asked in a formal statement issued through Freedom Associates in 1954, "to ignore the continuing massacre of my brothers in Kenya? And here in America, is Jim Crow dead and buried? Has Congress passed the Anti-Lynching Law and the F.E.P.C.? Have my people's demands for economic, political and social equality been granted? If not, why should Paul Robeson, who has dedicated his life to the struggle for these goals, change his mind about them now?"[26]

In asserting his "respect and affection" for the people of the Soviet Union, Robeson rarely made any distinction between them and the government that ruled them—an equivalence that was common parlance in the world Communist movement of the time, yet has opened him ever since to alternating charges of naïveté or rigidity. *The New Statesman and Nation* echoed the view of many in 1955 when it wrote, "Paul is courageous but not sophisticated about politics. . . . His personal warmth and generosity, his bigness and his kindness, made him everybody's friend—and many of those friendships have lasted despite the naivete of his political activities in recent years. Even today, when Paul makes some outrageous statement, one which would seem silly or vicious in the mouth of a hard-boiled party official, one feels more embarrassment than anger." But Robeson, in the words of Stretch Johnson (the entertainer and second-echelon black CPUSA leader), was "not so much naïve as trusting." He deeply believed in human nature, even though he had learned deeply to distrust human beings—his faith was in the potential, not in current distortions of it. He had seen, and come to expect, the world's every mean trick—yet in his heart he continued to believe that people were good and that socialism would create an environment that would allow their better natures to emerge. The world has never had much tolerance for those who persist in arguing unseen possibilities against the abundant evidence of their eyes, for the champions of what might be as against what is. The powers that be, bent on inculcating narrow-gauged formulas about the "necessities" of human nature and human society—on the acceptance of which the continuation of their hegemony depends—must always vilify those purveying a more sanguine message. This is not to say that Robeson never dealt in simplicities but, rather, that those making the charge usually did so on the basis not of greater sophistication, but of competing simplicities.[27]

Robeson did refuse, adamantly, to engage in direct criticism of the Soviet government for mistaken or malignant policies. Perhaps in reaction, he sometimes overweighed the indictment against the government of the United States. Thus, in presenting his 1951 petition to the UN, Robeson had come close to equating institutional oppression of blacks with a policy of official genocide against them. It was an equation that stuck in the craw—then and since—of some of those who otherwise admired Robeson. Even Essie, who leapt to his political defense in public, confided privately to Marie Seton that "Paul is inclined to be a bit arrogant sometimes when people don't agree with him, especially politically. Not in any other field, as I think of it now. Only politically." He always strenuously insisted that his indictment of the American government was not an indictment of the American people, and he constantly reiterated his view that the "real" America was a progressive America, that the American people, good in their hearts, ultimately would set everything to rights. But this faith in the American people, his detractors felt, was as rhetorically overdrawn in the one direction as his indictment of their government was in the other. Besides, they asked, why did Robeson find it possible to distinguish between the American people and *its* rulers and yet so resolutely refuse to make any comparable separation in regard to the Soviets?[28]

Even in private, even among intimates, Robeson would not dwell on that distinction. When Khrushchev revealed the full extent of Stalin's crimes at the Twentieth Communist Party Congress, early in 1956, Robeson read the complete text in *The New York Times* and put down the newspaper without comment. As Paul, Jr., recalls, "He read it, he knew it was true," but "he never commented on it to my knowledge in public or in private to a single living soul from then to the day he died"—not to Helen Rosen, or to Freda Diamond, or to Revels Cayton. As early as the thirties Robeson had had some knowledge of the purges, and in the late forties some of his friends—Itzik Feffer, for one—had disappeared. He possibly regarded the trials of the thirties, as did many of those who were pro-Soviet, as necessary reprisals against the malignant "intrigues of the Trotskyists," believing that subsequent reports on the extent of the purges were exaggerations designed to discredit the Revolution. He adopted the standard argument "You can't make an omelet without breaking eggs," justifying the purges as *occasional* injustices, as the inevitable excesses inherent in any effort to create a new society, the excesses to be excused, if not justified, on the principle that collective welfare takes precedence over the rights of individuals. Robeson would have approved the analogy offered by André Malraux: though Christianity has had its murderous inquisitions, few have demanded that Christians abandon their religion because of its past depravities. Paul, Jr., says that his father told him and Lloyd Brown that "it was incomprehensible to him that American Communists would leave the Party over what happened in the Soviet Union." Still, Khrushchev's revelation of the sheer number of Stalin's crimes, his policy of *systematic* murder, shook the faith of many in the eggs-omelet analogy; and it suggested to some that brutality may have been endemic to the centralized authoritarianism that had come to characterize the Soviet system, displacing its earlier, visionary ideals.[29]

There is no evidence that Robeson either disputed the accuracy of Khrushchev's revelations or discounted reportage of them in the Western press as exaggerated. His reaction *probably*—this must remain a "best guess," given the lack of concrete evidence—fell into the middle ground of disappointed acceptance: disappointment that the socialist experiment in which he believed had been derailed by the acts of an unsound leader, acceptance (and continuing faith) that in the long run the derailment would prove temporary and that socialism, still humanity's best hope, would triumph. Even this much he could have said had he wanted to clarify his position publicly. But he chose not to, chose silence instead, preferred to be called a stubborn dupe—naïve at best, criminal at worst—rather than join the growing legion of Soviet detractors, rather than become himself (as he saw it) an obstacle to the eventual triumph of socialism.

However naïve his continuing faith may have appeared to the world at large, it was an accurate reflection of one strain in his complex personality. While he essentially trusted no one, Robeson had, at the same time, a fundamental belief in the decency of most people, and held to the sanguine view that they were potentially as generous, as aware and as concerned about the sufferings of mankind as he was. He expected much of others—as he did of himself. He had never learned as a youngster, as had almost all black Americans, to deal in limited expectations; treated in his own family like a god, he had met in the outside world far fewer institutional humiliations than afflict most blacks attempting to make their way. Ingrained optimism had become a characteristic attitude; he expected *every* set of hurdles, with the requisite hard work and determination, to be cleared as handily as those of his youth had been.

But Robeson was hardly naïve. Even as a young man he had experienced enough discrimination in his own life, and seen enough desperation everywhere around him in the black world, always to have carried with him the knowledge that society was cruel and individuals frail. When awareness of the brutalities of daily life further deepened in adulthood, however, and disappointments over political attempts to mitigate them continued to mount, Robeson could somehow never entirely digest the world's bad news. "He was a softie," the black trade-unionist Sam Parks remembers with reproving admiration. "He never wanted to hurt anybody—it used to make me mad at him." With time, Robeson came to temper his faith only to the degree of accepting the view that social transformation would be a longer process than he had originally thought—simply because human nature had been more disabled than he had once assumed. But he did remain full of faith—faith that one day humanity would rise to its better nature, that a cooperative social vision would supplant a ruthlessly competitive one, that human beings would somehow turn out better than they ever had, that the principle of brotherhood would hold sway in the world. There was no other attitude—with disappointments on every hand—that would have allowed him to persevere. Nor one, resting as it did on accumulated denial, more likely in the long run to produce an emotional breakdown.[30]

Robeson's political identification was primarily with the Soviet Union in its original revolutionary purity, and not with its secondary manifestation, the American Communist Party. On the most obvious level, he was never a member of the CPUSA, never a functionary, never a participant in its daily bureaucratic operations (he told Helen Rosen that its internecine warfare and rigidity made him miserable). He was a figure apart and above, his usefulness to the Party directly proportionate to the fact that his stature did not derive from it. The Party, as Eugene Dennis's widow, Peggy Dennis, has put it, "was just a small part of Paul's life." "I have a hunch," Dorothy Healey, the ex-Communist leader in California, has added, "that 90% of the inner-C.P. stuff was either unknown to Paul or, if known, considered unimportant." He had aligned himself with the Soviet Union by the late thirties because it was playing the most visible role in the liberation of American and colonial peoples of color; he had aligned himself with the principles of black liberation and socialism, not with national or organizational ambitions. From his early visits to the Soviet Union, he

had taken away the overwhelming impression of a nation devoted to encouraging the independent flowering of the cultures of different peoples—
including nonwhite people—within its borders, a policy in basic opposition
to the "melting-pot" view for which the United States officially stood. The
socialist principle could in practice be sabotaged or misdirected—as it was
in the Soviet mistreatment of the Crimean Tatars—but to Robeson the
principle remained uniquely attractive.[31]

Despising American racism and viewing the Soviets as the only promising counterbalancing force to racism, Robeson was inclined to look away
when the U.S.S.R. acted against its own stated principles, to look away
fixedly as the perversions multiplied over the years, discounting them as
temporary aberrations or stupidities ultimately justified by the long view,
the overall thrust, the "correct" direction. Explaining Robeson's view (and
her own), Dorothy Healey describes him as "well aware" of the Soviet
Union's "terrible weaknesses" but nonetheless convinced that "it's going
in a direction that you think is a proper direction. . . . You never settle it
once and for all," but "you're not going to get caught in the company of
the anti-Sovieteers." In ex-CP leader John Gates's comparable if more
bellicose version, Robeson took "the classic point of view that all of us did.
. . . This is a revolution, and you have to fight all kinds of people in
revolutions, and sometimes innocent people get killed. It's a war."[32]

In refusing to vent any direct or sustained public criticism of Soviet
or CPUSA policy, Robeson did not always agree with its twists and turns.
When in disagreement, he followed his own counsel, rarely stating his
disagreement publicly; to do that, in his mind, would have meant giving
comfort to conservative-minded bigots, as well as involving him more
than he wanted in the temperamentally distasteful daily routine of factional infighting. Instead, he simply went his way. During World War II,
when the CP staked everything on the struggle against fascism, downplaying all "secondary" issues such as black demands for a fair employment commission and for the elimination of the poll tax and of
segregation in the armed forces, Robeson continued to function with
black issues at the center of his activities, calling everywhere in his
speeches around the country for a *double* victory—against fascism abroad
and racism at home. When British tanks, late in 1944, crushed Communist-led resistance to the monarchy in Greece, the Soviet Union remained
silent, and Browder, for the CPUSA, cautioned against "shallow agitation"—but Robeson spoke out against what he viewed as the suppression
of a democratizing impulse. When, in the postwar period, under William
Z. Foster's leadership, the CPUSA emphasized the "imminence" of economic depression, the triumph of fascism in the United States, and a
coming World War III, Robeson—though generally sympathetic to the
Foster left wing—sounded an optimistic counternote about the possibil-

ity of peaceful coexistence between socialism and capitalism far more reminiscent of the discredited Browder, whose removal from CP leadership Robeson agreed had been necessary.[33]

In 1948, similarly, he threw all his energy into the Wallace movement, not because the CP told him to but because, despite internal dissension within the CP over the wisdom of supporting the Progressive Party, *he* was convinced that it offered the best current vehicle for championing black rights in the United States. And when, under the tutelage of Revels Cayton, Robeson came to believe in the necessity for black caucuses within the left-wing trade unions, he campaigned widely for them among black workers—even though the CP leadership tended to view the caucuses with uneasy suspicion as representing a resurgence of deviationist black "nationalism" and dual unionism.

In the fifties, according to Stretch Johnson, Robeson believed the Party "could do more in the struggle for Negro rights" than it was doing, and felt that he himself "was not being used enough in the black community"—that being featured as *the* American figure in the world peace movement had diminished his specific stature as a spokesperson for black and colonial peoples. Rose Perry, the wife of Pettis Perry (the black executive secretary of the Party's National Negro Commission from 1948 to 1954), recalls that at one point, around 1950, Robeson's concern with being isolated from his own black constituency became so acute that he would talk far into the night with Pettis Perry about possible ways to solve his public-relations problem with Harlem—a problem partly met by the establishment in 1950 of *Freedom* magazine, and by Robeson's increased number of appearances at his brother Ben's A.M.E. Zion Church and at black gatherings elsewhere.[34]

But by the fifties Robeson no longer had the luxury of independent maneuver; he felt it was a matter of conscience to declare solidarity with the victims of the Smith Act, voluntarily binding himself to their plight. To the extent that he did still harbor disagreements with CP policies—and his disagreements had always been marginal—he felt as a matter of principle bound in loyalty to maintain his commitment to the persecuted Party leadership. In 1951 he even offered to join the Party as a public gesture of solidarity, just before its leaders were jailed. The gesture was rejected, out of hand. All four of the leaders (Eugene Dennis, Ben Davis, Jack Stachel, and John Gates) present when Robeson made the offer at a small private meeting refused even to entertain the idea, considering it a personal disservice to Robeson—it would have further reduced his influence in the black community—and thereby a disservice to the Party as well. "Nobody hesitated," is how John Gates remembers the occasion; "we were smart enough to say no. And without any hesitation. All of us."[35]

Robeson functioned in relationship to the CPUSA primarily through the Party leadership—not through participation in rank-and-file activities. The pre-eminent leader of the CPUSA during the early forties, when Robeson initially became a prominent ally, was Earl Browder. Studious, strong-willed, intensely private, he and Robeson had much in common temperamentally, and the two became personal friends, even though Browder, like most of the "right wing" of the Party, was closer to mainstream liberalism on the black question than William Z. Foster and Ben Davis, Jr. In those years Browder and Ben Davis were Robeson's main contacts with the Party. During World War II, when black issues took a back seat to the struggle against fascism, Robeson privately expressed annoyance—especially to his closest friend in the Party, Ben Davis—over the CP's quiescence on issues like anti–poll-tax and antilynching legislation or the passage of an FEPC. But Robeson never criticized the Party or Earl Browder in public—nor did the Party ever caution him to tone down his strenuous public advocacy of black issues. Yet, when the Duclos Letter appeared in 1945, Robeson did let it be known within CPUSA leadership circles that he sided with the opposition to Browder, going along with most of the black rank-and-file leadership in support of the Dennis-Foster coalition.

When Eugene Dennis supplanted Browder as the Party's pre-eminent leader, Robeson continued in close contact with the top echelon, for he and Dennis were also personal friends, Robeson admiring Dennis's intelligence, his deep commitment to black equality, and his low-key, unimperious exercise of authority. When Dennis was on the eve of going to federal prison, Robeson asked him and his wife, Peggy, to attend his Carnegie Hall concert as his personal guests, and installed them in a box near the front of the stage; just before singing Blitzstein's "The Purest Kind of Guy," Robeson leaned into the microphone and announced he was dedicating the song to his dear friend Eugene Dennis; the spotlight went up on the Dennises' box, and Paul sang the song directly to Gene. According to Peggy Dennis, the relationship between the two men involved considerable give-and-take: "Paul had his own very definite ideas, whether it was on the black question or on socialism or on the Soviet Union or on the Progressive Party or whatever else." He was held in immense esteem by the leadership and the rank-and-file alike as "the voice of the black people," as an artist who insisted upon being political. He also caught the imagination of some of the younger cadre, like Peggy Dennis herself, who had ambivalently learned "to smother all personal aspirations," sublimating private passions into serving Party dictates; Robeson's insistence on *self*-expression in combination with political responsibility released "a kind of subtle envy." But although Robeson was widely regarded as a figure apart, "a very special human being in a very special relationship to the Party," on the top level—where discussion took place, say, between Eugene Dennis and Robeson—Peggy Dennis believes that "no one was in awe of Paul as an artist"; the rule of thumb instead was an open give-and-take among equals.[36]

Robeson never joined in any outright factional dispute within the Party. His characteristic style was to discuss his views with the few leaders with whom he felt closest, personally and politically—Dennis, Pettis Perry, and, above all, Ben Davis, Jr. (though he sometimes thought Davis too abrasively sectarian)—and to let those men serve as a conduit for conveying his views. To protect his independent standing further, he would sometimes hide behind the calculated disclaimer that he was "only an artist, after all, and not a political leader," shrewdly sidestepping organizational responsibility and factional attachments. He remained privy to what was going on factionally, and his sympathies often leaned toward the "left-wing" (Foster-Davis) grouping in the Party. But though admiring Foster, he found him too dour for intimacy; besides, Robeson's commitment to the left wing was a tendency only, not a firm adherence; his "outwardness and breadth" (in Peggy Dennis's words) prevented him from taking any rigidly sectarian stance.[37]

Robeson's role essentially resembled that of a foreign ambassador to an allied country—to a close ally in time of war. His primary allegiance remained with his home base—with black people—but he believed that the Soviet Union, alone among the world's political powers, was a genuine deterrent to Western imperialism (and thus an ally of black and colonial freedom struggles) and he therefore worked hard to champion the interests and to ensure the survival of the Communist movement. Still, deeply sympathetic and committed to close collaboration though he was, he functioned as an emissary to that movement, not as a citizen of the realm, not a participant either in the householder's daily chores or in the quarreling discord of its officialdom. Like every good ambassador, Robeson could be most devious when appearing most open (he was not so invariably direct in his dealings as myth would have it). Like every good ambassador, too, he knew the region well and could accurately assess the shifting fortunes of the local players, even while standing aloof from their squabbles. He did, of course, have his preferences among the players, and sometimes disapproved their specific moves. But he picked his friendships from among all wings of the Party, much preferring, according to his son, the company of the centrist Eugene Dennis to that of left-wing black leaders James Jackson and Henry Winston. Despite the fact, moreover, that there was considerable ill-feeling between his closest associate, Ben Davis, Jr., and Gene Dennis, Robeson maintained friendships with both. He always remained adept at separating someone's plausible political line from what he felt in his gut about the person's human reliability. By the mid-fifties, for example, he began to distance himself from William Patterson, grateful for his devoted work on the passport case but increasingly wary of Pat's self-glamorizing assumption of the Robeson mantle.[38]

Except for a few brief meetings with Khrushchev in the late fifties, Robeson remained remote from the sources of real power in the Soviet Union and exercised no direct influence. Yet through the years he did come to know many of the Soviets' most prominent ambassadors (Litvinov, Maisky, Malik, Feodorenko, Zarubin) and, in regard to one, Panyushkin, he bluntly told Paul, Jr., "that the SOB talked like a Nazi about the Jews. . . . He sounded like Goebbels at times." But Robeson was careful not to express such views in public, and only rarely in private. He did not transfer his dislike of particular leaders into a condemnation of the cause they represented, however poorly, or the political entities they headed. His commitment to socialism and to black liberation took automatic precedence over his occasional trouble with particular individuals who happened temporarily to represent those causes to the public.[39]

But that is not quite the whole story, either. Robeson also sat on his personal opinions *because* the individuals in question were designated leaders—endowed with the mantle of liberation, invested with the hope and authority of a revolutionary world movement. One generation removed from slavery himself, he knew that the success of a *collective* struggle took automatic precedence over the comparatively trivial tastes and preferences of any individual. He felt that by acceding to his father's authority, he had been able successfully to navigate the shoals of white indifference and intimidation; if his people as a whole were to navigate the same treacherous waters, invested faith in the new father of international socialism would have to be sustained in public in the same obedient spirit—even if one harbored in private independent judgments of individuals and events. John Gates believed that Robeson's "commitment to the leadership" was so complete that "he thought anything we proposed was wise"—but Gates did not realize that Robeson had also learned from his father that if he did not express his every feeling, he could thereby preserve his inner integrity.[40]

Robeson's unswerving loyalty to the CPUSA was not always reciprocated in kind. In general the Party leaders accepted his support on its own uniquely independent terms, but now and then, in times of unusual pressure, a segment of the leadership would try to convert a treaty of alliance into a condition of vassalage. According to Ben Davis, Jr., Henry Winston (supported by Elizabeth Gurley Flynn) strongly suggested that Robeson, following his 1949 Paris speech, "tone down" his "nationalistic" utterances or face public party criticism—to Robeson's fury. And in 1951 Winston was enthusiastic about Robeson's suggestion that, as an act of solidarity with the Smith Act victims, he join the Party; Winston apparently felt that Robeson's personal prestige would help rescue Party fortunes and bowed reluctantly to the counterview of Eugene Dennis, Ben Davis, Jr., and others that the far more likely result would be to destroy Robeson's own standing. At around this same time, Robeson discovered that one of his bodyguards, Walter Garland (a black American hero during the Spanish Civil War), had been planted by "a certain group in the top echelons of the Party" to report on his activities. He became livid, told Garland to get lost "and to tell those so-and-sos downtown, 'Don't ever pull that on me.' " Robeson complained directly to Ben Davis—who temporarily supplied him with his own bodyguard.[41]

Robeson never allowed the occasional discontent he felt with his allies to mitigate the public contempt he expressed for his enemies—not the American people or the American experiment, but the "racist oligarchy" in control of the U.S. government. "I have shouted," he told a reporter of *The Afro-American* in March 1954, "and will continue to shout at the top of my voice for liberation, full emancipation." And he did just that. That same month, March 1954, he denounced U.S. intervention in Guatemala, loudly protested continuing persecutions under the Smith Act and the move by the Justice Department to have the Council on African Affairs register under the McCarran Act, and, in regard to events in the colonial world, raised his voice angrily against the imprisonment of Kenyatta and the effort to discredit the movement for Kenyan independence. "Is it 'subversive,' " he asked reporters, "not to approve our Government's actions of condoning and abetting the oppression of our brothers and sisters in Africa and other lands?"[42]

Against equally imposing odds, he continued the fight for the return of his passport. Another round was inaugurated in the spring of 1954, with coordinated campaigns simultaneously launched from England and the United States to drum up petitions, letters, and cables to the State Department deploring Robeson's continuing "domestic arrest." The response from abroad was extensive, far more so than at home. Messages in support of Robeson arrived from around the world—from, among many others, Charles Chaplin, Sylvia Townsend Warner, Ivor Montagu, Laurence Housman, René Maran, Pablo Neruda, Yussef Dadoo, J. D. Bernal, and peace groups from places as distant as Uruguay, Austria, Israel, South Africa, Iraq, and Finland.[43]

In England a major "Let Robeson Sing" campaign was launched. It began when John Williamson (the American Communist Party leader who had been deported back to the land of his birth under the Smith Act) proposed a resolution at the Scottish Trade Union Congress in support of returning Robeson's passport. A committee still in existence from the campaign to save the Rosenbergs from execution was activated by Franz and Diana Loesser in Robeson's behalf. Centering their efforts at first in Manchester, the Loessers organized a meeting in the Free Trade Hall that featured the black boxer and CP member Len Johnson as a speaker and drew a spill-over crowd, with the local Labour Party and the strong Jewish community in Manchester turning out in particularly impressive numbers. An approach was made to Aneurin Bevan, the Labour Party leader, to lend official support to the campaign for Robeson's passport, but, according to Diana Loesser, "Labour Party proscriptions against being associated with Communists—and several were sponsors of the campaign—kept Bevan necessarily at arm's length"; he did, however, "make sympathetic noises" and avoided taking any steps against rank-and-file involvement. From this beginning, the British "Let Robeson Sing" campaign would grow by leaps and bounds; by 1957 it would be a considerable embarrassment to the U.S. government.[44]

In the United States, the campaign focused on a "Salute to Paul Robeson" from his fellow artists—including Thelonious Monk, Pete Seeger, Leon Bibb, Alice Childress, Julian Mayfield, Karen Morley, and Lorraine Hansberry—at the Renaissance Casino on May 24, 1954. The casino was packed, with an overflow crowd of a thousand accommodated in an adjoining church. For a brief time it seemed, in the words of an enthusiast, as if "now we are really ready for a campaign that can in fact force the return of Paul's passport."[45]

But the optimism was short-lived. Permission for a follow-up Robeson concert in Chicago was canceled at the last minute by the local Board of Education. And at the end of July, barely two months after the new passport campaign had been launched, the State Department announced that it was again denying Robeson's application. Scores of protests followed, and Robeson told the press he would appeal the decision to the Supreme Court. He hired new lawyers: the black Washington, D.C., attorney James T. Wright, and the white left-wing activist Leonard Boudin, who was himself shortly to be denied the right to travel. The State Department remained adamantly indifferent: as long as Robeson continued to refuse to execute an affidavit stating his relationship to the Communist Party—which he adamantly refused—his appeal for a passport was "precluded." There the issue held fire for the moment, both sides immovable.[46]

Robeson continued his piecemeal activities—singing again at the Peace Arch in August (to a still smaller crowd than the previous year), working to win amnesty for the Smith Act defendants and to provide succor for their families, attending the fourth annual National Negro Labor Council convention, allowing himself to be fêted, along with Essie, at a *New World Review* fund-raiser (where he spoke movingly of her contributions to his own development and her efforts "in behalf of first-class citizenship for the Negro people"), giving an occasional concert when the doors could be opened, and, when they could not, making additional recordings for distribution through the Othello Recording Company, to which Paul, Jr., was now devoting full time. But the accumulated stress was telling on him. Mary Helen Jones, the left-wing black community leader in

California, reported to John Gray at *Freedom* in New York that, following an appearance by Paul on the West Coast, Essie had implored her to try to "keep him out here . . . for ten days incognito for a rest. She suggested a hospital but he prefers a private home where he can go on a diet and get some rest and get away from the crowds." Jones discussed it with him, and initially he was "in favor of it," but he then decided it was "out of the question." "Frankly," Jones reported back in New York, "I can't understand why he 'seemed' to be receptive to the idea when I discussed it with him and then 'froze' after I left. . . . He is a very *stubborn* person when it comes to not looking out for himself. . . . Many people out here are thinking about Marcantonio [who had recently died of a heart attack] and that he left here at the age of 51. . . . Paul needs a rest. . . ."[47]

The closest thing he could manage was a change of address. Following the sale of the house in Enfield in 1953, Essie had moved into the Hotel Dauphin in New York City—after staying with Paul, Jr., and Marilyn. Paul had continued on at the McGhees' on East 89th Street, sometimes staying around the corner with Helen and Sam Rosen or with the Caytons, or with his brother Ben at the parsonage. But by the end of 1954, with FBI agents holding him under constant surveillance, Paul decided he would find more privacy and security in Harlem—a move also dictated by his fear of having become, through residing in the heart of white Manhattan, too isolated from the black community. The concern was not new. As early as 1947, leaders from the United Negro and Allied Veterans of America had called a private meeting with him in Washington, D.C., to express, "deferentially," "how all of us feel about you, and how we love you. Well, we think you're a great artist and a great man and all that, and while it may be true that you are a 'Citizen of the World,' we'd like you to let our folks know a little more strongly, that you are *first* a part of us and then *'Citizen of the World.'* " According to George Murphy, Jr., who attended the meeting and recorded the vets' words, "Paul listened very carefully, told the vets he thought they were eminently correct, especially in thinking enough of him to come to him and say what they thought." By 1949 columnist Dan Burley in the New York *Age,* a black newspaper, was remarking that Robeson "has been away from Harlem so long that people only know him by what they have read or heard. . . ." His close friend Revels Cayton urged him to do something about the continuing criticism, and that same year of 1949 he took over the St. Nicholas Avenue apartment of the black singer Aubrey Pankey and his wife, Kay (the couple had by now settled in Europe). But, according to Kay Pankey, Robeson moved back downtown within the year, "pestered too much" by the constant invasion of his privacy.[48]

By 1954 the security and warmth of a Harlem haven had become more important than solitude, and when his brother Ben and his wife, Frankie, suggested he move into the parsonage of the Mother A.M.E. Zion Church at 155 West 136th Street, where Ben was pastor, Paul accepted. He would never have asked Ben to take him in, unwilling to subject his brother's family to possible obloquy, but when Ben volunteered the invitation, Paul gratefully took him up on it. Ben and Paul had not seen much of each other during the forties, and Ben's family thought Essie—with whom they did not get along—might have deliberately kept Paul away from the parsonage. But in fact Paul's long absences were a characteristic pattern in all his relationships, and did not necessarily reflect how important those relationships were to him. Paul always moved in and out of personal commitments, the pattern perhaps in part reflecting the childhood trauma he'd suffered at his mother's sudden death, forever imprinting on him the lesson not to become overly attached. But the pattern also reflected the expansiveness of a nature that could never be content for long interacting exclusively with one other individual. Robeson's middle-class white friends had particular trouble dealing with his in-and-out-again commitment to them. They tended to interpret the long stretches of time between visits, and his failure to stay in touch through letters and phone calls, as somehow a judgment on the quality of the friendship, a sign of its insignificance to him.

Ben, sharing the same family culture as Paul, had the same view as he of the etiquette of relationships. Like Paul, he didn't need the reassurance of constant declarations of concern in order to believe in its reality. The dutiful little attentions crucial to middle-class definitions of the proper contours of friendship and family were not given the same weight of importance—closeness was not measured by how often one saw someone or how much one revealed to him. Between Ben and Paul, as with Paul and his sister Marian, a profound sense of assurance that their ties were lasting and deep precluded any need for constant verification. Though Marian's house in Philadelphia was always a haven for Paul—and he often retreated there—between visits he rarely communicated. What might be called a secure passivity—"I don't need to *make* it happen"—best characterizes his attitude. The ties were there—or were not—and no amount of verbal reassurance or attentiveness would change that essential fact. Robeson's belief in the ebb-and-flow of friendship, combined with his ingrained respect for the privacy of others, meant that he rarely commented on and never tracked the lives of his friends. The quality of intrusiveness—the need to keep talking about a bond in order to establish its validity—was foreign to Robeson's sense of the natural history of relationships. He felt no need to analyze intimacy in order to reassure himself of its presence.[49]

The level of trust between Paul and Ben Robeson, despite the long periods of absence, had never wavered. The two men were entirely comfortable with each other. When Paul moved into the parsonage in the winter of 1954 (where he would remain for about a year), he felt in a real sense that he was coming home—back into the bosom of his immediate family and back into the larger family of the black community. Robeson always enjoyed sitting around—black people only—and talking "colored talk." Howard Fast remembers his astonishment once when he tried to find Robeson at a party they had gone to in the late forties in a fashionable black suburb of Detroit. Directed to the basement, Fast opened the door to find half a dozen prosperous, middle-aged black men smoking good cigars, jackets off, all attention on Robeson, who was holding forth in a "raw, black, Deep-Southern language," telling "rich, earthy stories with no restraint, no polite talk like upstairs." It was the only time, Fast felt, that he ever saw Robeson "with his wall down." Helen Rosen remembers coming upon the same sort of earthy talk at the parsonage, with brother Ben—despite his staid outward appearance—joining in with equal gusto.[50]

Among much else that the two brothers shared was a profound concern for the welfare of black people. Ben—a registered Republican (he was a friend and an admirer of Nelson Rockefeller), sedate and traditional in manner—worked out his commitment through the church. Paul's was expressed through art and politics, but in Paul, too, the family "preacher" temperament was ingrained. His "calling" seemed so obvious to Bishop Stephen Gill Spottswood of A.M.E. Zion, after he heard Paul's passionate platform delivery once in a black church, that he wrote and begged him "to give the remaining years of your life to the work of the ministry," reporting that Bishop Walls of Chicago was also "enamoured of the idea."[51]

Comfortable though Paul felt at the parsonage, it was not the tranquil environment it outwardly appeared to be. There was a lot of drinking, and at times—when Ben and Frankie's daughters periodically returned home, in retreat from their difficult marriages—considerable family friction. Paul was fond of all three of his nieces, but eventually the increasingly frequent storms at the parsonage proved too much for him. He needed a respite from the turbulence he encountered in the outer world, not a recapitulation of it. Throughout his life, he could never stay for long in an unquiet home. His domestic requirements, ultimately, were for solitude, stability, and protection.

■

CHAPTER 21

Breakdown

(1955–1956)

On the national scene, scattered signs were emerging to indicate a thaw in the conservative deep-freeze. The army-McCarthy hearings in the spring of 1954 precipitated a Senate censure vote against McCarthy on December 2. Cold War tensions, too, began to dissipate by 1955: the long-standing Russian-American deadlock over a treaty with Austria was finally broken, a United Nations Conference on Disarmament produced some positive results, and an Eisenhower-Khrushchev summit meeting eased relations so notably that "the Geneva spirit" became a tag reference for every intimation of international cooperation. Simultaneously, the Supreme Court pendulum took a swing toward the liberal side; the Justices modified a host of loyalty-security laws, reasserted concern with protecting the rights of political dissenters, and, in the landmark *Brown* v. *Board of Education* decision, struck down segregation in the nation's public schools. Such developments, of course, were auguries only, not automatic guarantors of a new day.

Robeson hailed these "tokens of sanity," these "hopeful signs that the commonsense of rank-and-file America will yet prevail," but he was not ready to discount the power of the "atom-maniacs in Washington." He noted that one of the immediate effects of the Supreme Court's shift to the left was to produce a countervailing shift to the right, uniting Southern Democrats and conservative Republicans behind a defense of segregation and militant anti-Communism. He was therefore not surprised when the black Communist Claude Lightfoot in Chicago, and Ben Gold, the Communist leader of the Fur and Leather Union, drew jail sentences, when William Patterson was remanded for contempt, and when Ben Davis, after serving nearly four years in the penitentiary, was rearrested. Robeson spoke out at public rallies in their defense and in the 1954 fall elections supported the American Labour Party in New York State, which ran John T. McManus, general manager of the *National Guardian,* for governor. Robeson did not know it at the time, but the Justice Department was giving thought to indicting him as well. Despite its best efforts, however, the FBI was still unable to come up with any "specific information from any source" directly linking him to the Communist Party.[1]

Early in 1955, however, Robeson was subpoenaed to testify before a joint state legislative committee. It had been empowered to investigate alleged misappropriations in philanthropic fund-raising charged against three "Communist-front" organizations with which he was closely affiliated: the American Committee for Protection of the Foreign Born, the Joint Anti-Fascist Refugee Committee, and the Civil Rights Congress. The prosecution claimed that "millions of dollars given by public-spirited citizens for a variety of causes" had been "diverted to subversive uses." Dorothy Parker, the economist George Marshall, and Dashiell Hammett (who had headed the New York State Civil Rights Congress from 1946 to 1951, when he went to prison for six months for contempt of court) were among the witnesses called during the three-day hearing; Hammett testified that "Communist to me is not a dirty word. When you're working for the advancement of mankind it never occurs to you if a guy's a Communist or not." Robeson's turn on the stand proved stormy. He said he was "very proud" to be a national director of the Civil Rights Congress and, when asked for specifics about how the CRC raised and dispensed funds, replied, "I sing for Hadassah and the Sons of Israel and any number of worthwhile causes and no one asks me how much money they raise." *The New York Times* pronounced his answer evasive, and an editorial in the *Herald Tribune* fulminated against "Red-fronters" whose "refusal to give accounting" of their "dangerous . . . double-dealing . . . charity rackets . . . cannot be tolerated." No, Robeson decided, the Cold War had not yet evaporated, any more than the national climate had been miraculously purged of unbalanced suspicion.[2]

He remained wary. Delighted though he was with the Supreme Court's desegregation decision—he characterized it as "a magnificent stride forward in the long battle of colored Americans for full equality"— he noted the white South's negative reaction and warned of the need for black vigilance and firmness in equal measure. "As might be expected," he wrote in *Freedom,* "the Dixiecrats have responded with howls of anguish and threats of retaliation. . . . The planters have organized a new Ku Klux Klan. They have laundered it a bit, given it a face-lifting, and called it White Citizens Councils. But no Negro in Mississippi will be fooled. He knows the Klan when he sees it, by whatever name it's called." Robeson hailed Mississippi's "heroic" black people for the "stirring chapter" they were writing in the history of resistance and, four months after the Supreme Court decision, called on blacks everywhere to "fight to see that it is enforced"; he warned, in the face of spreading white opposition, that the decision could turn out to be merely "a token gesture," yet another paper promise falling far short of the "full freedom" he continued to demand. Robeson's health might be weakening, his outlets for singing and speaking all but gone, but his tenacity, his galvanizing sorrow held.[3]

He used the occasion of a concert booking in California early in 1955—his earlier hope for a full-scale tour of the state had been dashed by a lack of response—to express enthusiasm about the unity movement developing between black organizations to break Jim Crow barriers in television and radio, and about the recent election of the radical Norman Manley to head the government in the British West Indies ("a powerful voice for dignity and equality of colored peoples everywhere"). While Robeson was in Los Angeles, the front wheel twice came off the car in which he was being driven by Frank Whitley. There had been a similar incident in St. Louis in 1947, and there would be two more in 1958. Whitley's conclusion was that the wheel had been tampered with, but if so, the uncertain evidence makes it impossible to say by whom—whether racists, red-baiters, or even, conceivably, federal agents (who had both Robeson and Whitley under close surveillance in L.A.), acting either under orders or on their own.[4]

When the conference of Asian and African nations—denounced in advance by Secretary of State Dulles as a misguided form of self-segregation—assembled in Bandung, Indonesia, in April 1955 Robeson sent a message hailing the gathering as a certain sign of "the power and the determination of the peoples of these two great continents to decide their own destiny." Prior to the Bandung gathering, William Patterson wrote directly to Prime Minister U Nu of Burma appealing for a statement from Asian and African leaders deploring the continuing "persecution" of Robeson by his own government. Instead, at Bandung, Adam Clayton Powell, Jr., took it upon himself to rebuke Robeson and to dismiss "Communist propaganda" that no progress was being made in the United States toward equality for its black citizens. Essie sent an angry response to *The Afro-American* in which she accused Powell of exaggerating the amount of progress made, but Robeson himself continued to sound a positive note. Invited to sing and speak at the City College of New York (having been barred four years earlier) and also at Swarthmore, he expressed delight at the overflow crowds, at "the stirrings of new life" among students, at the "fresh breeze of free expression beginning to filter into the stale atmosphere of the cold-war classrooms."[5]

Robeson's often reiterated public optimism was a function both of temperamental expansiveness and of a proud refusal to let the enemy know he had been hit, to concede the toll taken from a decade of being followed by agents, of having his mail intercepted, his phone conversations bugged, his public appearances monitored and reported. Years of downplaying, perhaps even to himself, the wearing negative effects of his confinement and of refusing, as well, fully to acknowledge the profound psychic costs—in one so naturally affirmative—of having always to maintain a stance of opposition, contributed to building up a potentially explosive amount of anguish and rage. The crunch—the moment when anguish overwhelmed affirmation—finally came in late 1955, triggered by a particularly bruising round in the ongoing fight to regain his passport.[6]

The receipt of several unusually appealing offers from abroad became the occasion for going back once more into court. From Prague had come an invitation to appear in concert at the National Opera House, from the British Workers' Sports Association the prospect of doing a series of concerts in celebration of the association's silver jubilee, from the leading cultural agency in Tel Aviv an inquiry about coming to Israel, and from Mosfilm Studios in the Soviet Union the offer to star in a planned film version of *Othello*. Singly each invitation presented a notable opportunity; taken together they held out the real promise of a restoration of Robeson's international career. There was reason to believe, this time around, that the courts might finally rule favorably on his application. In February 1955 a U.S. district court had returned a passport to Otto Nathan (Albert Einstein's executor), and in subsequent legal actions passports had been given back to Clark Foreman, Joseph Clark (foreign editor of the *Daily Worker*), the atomic scientist Dr. Martin Kamen, and others previously refused on security grounds. On May 10, 1955, with Robeson's hopes higher than they had been for years, his attorneys, Leonard Boudin and James T. Wright, started up the judicial process again by making application to the Passport Division of the State Department. The application was immediately denied; Robeson was again told he had to sign a "non-Communist" affidavit before a passport for him could even be considered.[7]

Late in June, the U.S. Court of Appeals ruled in the case of Max Schachtman—whose organization, the Independent Socialist League, was on the Attorney General's "subversive" list—that "the right to travel is a national right" that could not be withheld except by due process of law. The ruling was widely hailed as historic and also as presenting an exact precedent for justifying the return of Robeson's passport. Following that logic, Robeson's attorneys reapplied in mid-July. "In view of recent court decisions," his application read, "and the granting of passports to others whose passports were previously refused, I insist that my right to travel be granted at once." He and his attorneys were called to Washington for a conference.

In the course of the seventy-five-minute meeting on July 18, the State Department officials promised "careful and prompt" attention to Robeson's passport request, and he left Washington feeling buoyed. His spirits got a further boost a few days later, when official word arrived that he would henceforth be allowed to travel to Canada—though still not to other places where Americans normally went without a passport, like Hawaii, Jamaica, and British Guiana. Singing his fourth annual Peace Arch concert at the Canadian boundary line the following week, Robeson told the crowd that he was jubilant at the partial victory and predicted he would soon be granted the right to travel anywhere.[8]

He was wrong: the State Department quickly announced that it had decided not to issue Robeson a passport. His attorneys immediately took the matter before Judge Burnita S. Mathews in a hearing on August 16 at the district court in Washington. Judge Mathews had recently returned a passport to Clark Foreman (for whom Boudin had also been counsel), but in the Robeson case she decided that the plaintiff "had not exhausted his administrative remedies"—meaning he had not signed a "non-Communist" affidavit. Leo A. Rover, the federal district attorney representing the State Department, argued that the Robeson case was different, that "this man" (he was called "Mr. Robeson" only once during the hearing) was "one of the most dangerous men in the world." In Leonard Boudin's recollection, Rover addressed the court in "stentorian tones," passionate in his conviction that Robeson was a direct threat to the security of the United States. In accepting Rover's argument and denying Robeson his passport, Judge Mathews blasted his raised hopes. The effect on him, in Boudin's opinion, was "traumatic"—he keenly felt that he had been singled out for unjust treatment.[9]

So did the black press. "Why is the State Department more afraid of Robeson than of the whites to whom it is giving passports?" asked J. A. Rogers, the Pittsburgh *Courier* columnist. The obvious answer was echoed widely in black newspapers: racism. As Rogers put it, "it's getting to the point where to prove you're not a subversive you must be a Ku Kluxer, a McCarthyite, or some other 'thousand percent American,' that is a Fascist at heart." The conservative New York *Amsterdam News* stood apart from most of the black press in calling on Robeson to sign the affidavit: "We think he should level with all of the necessary facts in the case, if he is really in dead earnest." In response, Robeson issued a public statement thanking the black news media for their support and taking issue with the *Amsterdam News* for ignoring two important facts: that the affidavit was not a standard requirement demanded of other Americans, and that he was not being charged with membership in the Communist Party or accused of any illegal act, such as espionage, for which he would be subject to indictment. An affidavit had been demanded of him, Robeson argued, because he had refused to keep silent about the treatment of blacks in America and of people of color throughout the colonial world. He suggested the State Department stop persecuting him for advocating better conditions for blacks and start prosecuting those in Mississippi "who have unleashed against our people a reign of terror and bloodshed." He was a "threat" (a security risk) because he told the truth.[10]

The State Department had openly acknowledged the accuracy of Robeson's interpretation as early as 1952 when, in a legal brief submitted to the Court of Appeals, it had argued that the revocation of his passport was justified because his activity in behalf of independence for the colonial peoples of Africa was potentially a "diplomatic embarrassment." At the August 1955 hearing, U.S. Attorney Rover had reconfirmed that Robeson's interest in colonial liberation abroad and equality for blacks at home constituted the basis for the animus against him. In explaining to Judge Mathews why Robeson was peculiarly "dangerous," Rover had pointed directly and solely to his speeches and writings: "During the concert tours of foreign countries he [Robeson] repeatedly criticized the conditions of Negroes in the United States," and in his message to the Bandung conference he had asserted—as, indeed, he had—that "the time has come when the colored peoples of the world will no longer allow the great natural wealth of their countries to be exploited and expropriated by the Western world while they are beset by hunger, disease and poverty."[11]

To deny black Americans the right to disclose their grievances abroad was tantamount to denying them one historic means they had always employed for winning their struggle at home. As early as 1830 the black abolitionist Reverend Nathaniel Paul had gone to England to promote the antislavery cause, later followed by Charles L. Remond, William Wells Brown, and Frederick Douglass, who in 1845 had said, "So long as my voice can be heard on this or the other side of the Atlantic, I will hold up America to the lightning scorn of moral indignation. In doing this, I shall feel myself discharging the duty of a true patriot; for he is a lover of his country who rebukes and does not excuse its sins." This historical point was forcefully made the following year in an *amicus curiae* brief that a group of black Americans submitted in support of Robeson's passport claim. The brief further pointed out that Robeson's views were in fact wholly in accord with *officially* declared U.S. opposition to colonialism and with its formal ratification of the Charter of the Organization of American States, which, among other things, supported the right to work and the right to free speech. Had Secretary of State John Foster Dulles (the brief went on) once raised his voice to denounce the persecution of black people in the South— for example, over the recent murder of Emmett Till—Afro-Americans would feel less need to look overseas for support. Instead Dulles had spoken out in support of the Portuguese claim to Goa and—exercising *his* constitutional right to utter unorthodox views—had issued his notorious "brink-of-war" statement, bringing down on his head the rebuke of Governor Harriman of New York, Senator Hubert Humphrey of Minnesota, and ex-President Harry Truman, who said Dulles had "brought dishonor to our national reputation of truth and honesty." No one, however, had suggested that Dulles's passport be revoked.[12]

The powerful voices and arguments raised in Robeson's behalf failed to budge the State Department. And so, after a brief period of high hopes, Robeson was flat up against the fact that he remained, in his words, "a prisoner in his native land." Because his expectations had soared, his ensuing disappointment was proportionately great. Six weeks after Judge Mathews's decision returned him to square one in the passport fight, Robeson noticed that he was passing blood in his urine. He consulted the young black physician Aaron Wells, who was on the staff of Sydenham Hospital in Harlem, had occasionally treated Essie, and was also physician to the Ben Robeson family. Paul confided to Wells that he thought the trouble might be the result of gonorrhea he had had as a younger man, but Wells told him the trouble was a degenerative condition of the prostate and recommended surgery with McKinley Wiles, a urologist at Sydenham. Nearing his fifty-eighth birthday, Robeson had only been in a hospital once (for a football injury) and, as both his son and Helen Rosen remember it, was "frightened stiff." His nerves were already raw from the passport fight, and the accumulated strain of years of surveillance by the FBI fueled his fear of what might "be done" to him in the hospital, a fear given a certain plausibility by the government's demonstrably malignant attitude toward him. He decided that he had cancer and was going to die. The last few days before entering Sydenham, he kept telling Paul, Jr., "If something happens to me, please do this, and that," and revising his will.[13]

He did have a difficult operation—some friends thought it had been "botched"—and suffered considerable pain in the postoperative period (both the white and the black press reported he had been operated on "for an abdominal obstruction"). His three-week stay in the hospital, with round-the-clock private nurses for most of that time, proved a grim experience. Released early in November, he decided not to return to Ben's parsonage but to take up life again with Essie. Since he and Essie had gone almost entirely separate ways after the sale of the Enfield house, his agreement to let her buy 16 Jumel Terrace in Harlem and his decision to take up his own residence there surprised many of his friends. Lee (Mrs. Revels) Cayton recalled in bemusement a joking remark Paul had made earlier: "I'll never be in *that* rocking chair."[14]

But the decision had its own logic. Essie had herself been ill that summer, and the diagnosis had turned out to be cancer, leading to a radical mastectomy. She kept the news a tight secret, determined, with her usual grit, to live out her life at full steam and without the pity of others. In fact she made a good recovery and it would be several years before she would have a recurrence, but at the time the prognosis was chancy and Paul felt he owed it to Essie to go back and live with her again. Besides, he needed her, needed the approval of black public opinion which a return to her side would create, and needed, too, beset by the debilitating effects of political repression and physical decline, her competent, efficient ministrations. It had been convenient in the forties, for a man bent on avoiding an exclusive commitment to any one woman, determined to lead several lives simultaneously, to be able to point to the existence of a formal marriage that actually made no difficult demands on him. Now, during the mid-fifties, older, unwell, and unnerved, less interested in romantic attachments and sexual adventures, he was tired of living in other people's homes, and his primary need was for comfort and stability. He knew Essie wanted—had always wanted—him back again, even if only in name. He knew she would manage and organize his life as no one else could, protecting him completely while being careful not to impose any requirements other than his formal presence in the same house. Paul needed to be taken care of again, and Essie was happy to work hard again at the job.

Besides, she was far more of a political creature than in her youth. Her views on the Soviet Union now closely coincided with Paul's, and over the years she had become powerfully engaged with the struggle for black freedom and against colonialism. She remained more elitist than Paul, less alienated from the white power structure, less profoundly identified with the working-class poor, white and black, less ideological and theoretical, less responsive to Party discipline, but was nonetheless, in her awareness and commitment, a more acceptable political mate than she had once been.[15]

In 1955 Essie was accredited to the UN as correspondent for *New World Review,* but in between her journalistic chores she delighted in having a new house to fix up. Resuming her role as world-beating shopper, she raced off to auctions looking for bargains, and her close friend Freda Diamond often came up to Jumel Terrace to give her professional help with decorating. At one point Essie saved money by buying up parachute material to use for draperies; at another, deciding they couldn't afford new carpeting on a much-reduced income, she located miles of thick used beige and taupe carpets, bought them for a song, and, after "scientifically" studying printed instructions, consulting a local Armenian tradesman, and purchasing the necessary tools, laid them herself. In her spare time she supervised Paul's diet and welcomed her grandchildren for occasional Saturday-night sleepovers.[16]

Even so, Paul's recovery was slow. In December 1955 he consulted Dr. Morris Pearlmutter, whose partner, Ed Barsky, had performed the mastectomy on Essie. Pearlmutter found elevated blood pressure and a "somewhat enlarged" heart, but when Robeson returned for a second visit, in January 1956, both conditions had disappeared. Pearlmutter therefore decided that it was all right for Robeson to keep a concert date in February in Toronto, where he had been invited by his old friends the Mine and Mill workers after the State Department restored his right to cross the border into Canada. On February 7, along with Alan Booth, his temporary accompanist, and Lloyd L. Brown, who had been helping out in a general managerial capacity, Robeson left the United States for the first time in six years. He went straight to the national Mine, Mill convention in Sudbury, Ontario, telling the delegates that "no attacks from any quarter will force me to tread backward one inch," and then stayed on in Canada to fulfill other engagements until the end of the month. For his Toronto concert in Massey Hall, every one of the twenty-eight hundred seats was filled, and he was given a standing ovation when he stepped onto the stage. The critics commented on how much thinner he was—"almost frail"—and lamented that his pacing seemed off and his vocal color dimmed; still, they hailed the continuing power of his "magnetic" presence. Robeson ended the concert with a dramatic reading from *Othello* and from Pablo Neruda's *Let the Rail Splitter Awake,* then spoke a few words to the adoring audience: he had, he said, but one purpose in life, "to fight for my people that they shall walk this earth as free as any man."[17]

The trip did not mark, as Robeson had hoped, a restoration of his health. No sooner had he returned to the States than he was hit with a serious blow: a U.S. Court of Appeals decision not to overrule the State Department's refusal to grant him a passport. Then, four months later, Khrushchev's revelations about Stalin's crimes at the Twentieth Party Congress were published in *The New York Times.* In contrast to the many white Communists who went to pieces over the Khrushchev report, deserting the CPUSA in droves, few black members left the Party, preferring to read Khrushchev's revelations as a sign of renewed hope, an indication that the U.S.S.R. was about to return to the purity of its earlier revolutionary goals. Even so, it would be the calculus of phony heroics to claim—as some of Robeson's intimates do—that the Khrushchev report had no impact on him. Such an interpretation would reduce a greathearted man to a wooden warrior. He was, demonstrably, mortal—susceptible to disappointment, weariness, despondency—if anything, more susceptible than most, given his enormous capacity for empathy. He did, however, make the decision not to comment on his reactions to anyone, instead maintaining silence and outward equanimity, and even managing, on March 10, to show up at a party celebrating William Z. Foster's birthday. But within the week he suffered a recurrence of urinary-tract infection, this time followed by an emotional collapse as well.[18]

His dream had been closing down with an abrupt vengeance of late: some nine months before the Khrushchev revelations, and simultaneous with the failure of his 1955 passport appeal, both *Freedom* and the Council on African Affairs had suspended their operations. Then had come the prostate surgery, which, especially when coinciding with a set of external pressures, does frequently bring on depression. In Robeson's case, however, his initial bout of what would later be called "bipolar disorder" was primarily manic (though it turned to severe depression two months later). At first, instead of confusion, fatigue, paralysis of will, lack of motivation, inability to concentrate or conceptualize—the classic symptoms of depression—he became, according to his son, "a dynamo of intellectual energy," much of it going into compulsive and vocal elaboration of what he claimed was a universal music theory based on the pentatonic scale. The universality of the pentatonic scale (what amounts to the five-note harmonics of the black keys on a piano) in folk music around the world is a "discovery" as indisputable as it is unoriginal—it is a scale, as Pete Seeger has said, "as natural to music as making a basket is once you've learned how to twist a thread." Musicologists do disagree, however, as to whether the harmonic scale is built into the sound of wind and string instruments or has been historically transmitted primarily through human contact—a point of disputation in which Robeson had scant interest and to which he made no theoretical contribution. *His* concern—to the point of obsession when in an agitated state—was in the proven *universality* of the pentatonic scale and in the case that could be extrapolated from that proof for the commonality of human experience. He would tell Helen Rosen and others that in solving the riddles of Bach he would somehow succeed in solving the problems of the world; and once thrillingly announced to Freda Diamond that he saw similarities between cantorial liturgy and some parts of Bach's masses, therefore "proving" that Bach was a converted Jew.[19]

Helen Rosen, one of the very few people allowed to see him during these months, confirms the obsessive zeal with which he went "on and on" about the pentatonic interconnection of practically everything (trying out his theories on the composer Marc Blitzstein, Robeson got angry when it became clear that Blitzstein, attempting to be polite, was in fact "astonished and appalled"). When Paul stayed overnight at the Rosens' place, Helen would sleep with one ear cocked, concerned about what he might do. At four o'clock one stormy winter morning she discovered him trying to leave the house; when she asked him where he was going, he said he had to get a book to track down an idea he'd just gotten about his pentatonic theory. "He didn't know *what* he was doing," in Helen's opinion. On another day he seemed so "disheveled" to her when she visited Jumel Terrace that, coming downstairs from his bedroom and finding Revels Cayton and Ben Davis in the living room, she couldn't restrain her tears. "I can't bear to see him like this," she said. Revels and Ben tried to persuade her that Paul would be all right. Although he did improve—indeed, judged by externals, would soon appear entirely normal—in Helen's opinion he was "never again quite the same."[20]

His physician Dr. Aaron Wells listened to him rattle on about pentatonics and how he intended to learn more languages in order to prove additional similarities between seemingly disparate cultures, and decided he was "off the wall." Wells prescribed sleeping pills; they didn't work. Dr. Pearlmutter suggested a psychiatric consultation, and a psychiatrist friend of Ed Barsky's did come to see Robeson, who refused to cooperate. Wells believed Robeson was in "deep trouble" psychologically but that the problem might have an essential organic component as well, perhaps the onset of some form of "early senility triggered by underlying arteriosclerosis." Pearlmutter thought otherwise, believing his condition had resulted from the combined stress of prostate surgery and the accumulated pressure built up from years of harassment and confinement—though warning that medical diagnosis, particularly after the fact, is not "an exact science."[21]

By the middle of May, Robeson had lapsed into a deeply depressed state. With the doctors in disagreement and with Robeson refusing to see a therapist, he simply stayed in his room at Jumel Terrace and remained almost totally inactive, going nowhere and seeing almost no one except family. Then, just as he seemed to have reached rock bottom, word arrived from Washington that he had been subpoenaed to appear before the House Committee on Un-American Activities as part of its investigation into "passport irregularities by Communist sympathizers."[22]

The doctors advised him not to go, and even wrote letters to HUAC declaring him unfit to give testimony without serious risk to his health (Wells, in his letter, overplayed Robeson's minor cardiac condition in order to downplay rumors of an emotional collapse, but the prostate surgeon, Dr. Wiles, did emphasize in the letter he wrote that "stress" had produced Robeson's "weakened condition"). HUAC granted Robeson a two-week postponement but did so reluctantly and hoped to use the delay as a way of trapping him. Don Appell of HUAC phoned Wick of the FBI to say "it occurred to the staff of the Committee" that if it could be shown Robeson left his house between May 29 (when he had been scheduled to appear) and June 12 (his new date), "it will be possible for the Committee to cite him for contempt"; HUAC asked the FBI to inform the committee of "his movements." (A note on the memo, in what appears to be J. Edgar Hoover's handwriting, reads, "I don't think we should be making investigations for the House Committee.") Beyond the two-week postponement, Robeson refused to request a further delay. He "insists upon making a trip to Washington, D.C., which he considers urgent," Wells wrote in disapproval to Milton Friedman (whom Robeson had retained to represent him before HUAC), and was disregarding Wells's opinion that "at this time he should not make any public appearances."[23]

Essie and Paul, Jr., along with Milton Friedman, Lloyd Brown, and William Patterson, accompanied Paul to Washington. Just before he entered the hearing room, he appeared so depressed and his eyes looked so vacant that it was doubtful he could go on. Friedman got Paul to agree that on prearranged signal he would ask for time out to consult with counsel. Essie told Freda Diamond that she had decided to pull a fainting spell if Paul's testimony seemed to be going haywire. But, to everyone's surprise, he performed with élan. His steady, even caustic testimony was all the more remarkable because the committee did what it could to unnerve him further—refusing to let him read the prepared statement he had brought (he had accurately predicted in the statement that "those who are trying to gag me here and abroad will scarcely grant me the freedom to express myself fully in a hearing controlled by them") and, ignoring all pretense of discussing the purported focus of its investigation on passports, took every opportunity to goad him into answering whether he was a member of the Communist Party.[24]

The hour-long session proved stormy, the committee members gunning throughout for an angle to justify throwing the book at him, taunting him with implied accusations, and reading into the record previous and tainted testimony from professional informers like Manning Johnson. Robeson, on his part, at first cagily parried blows, then, toward the end, bellowed at his tormentors in full defiance. "Are you now a member of the Communist Party?" asked Representative Gordon Scherer (Republican, Ohio), not two minutes into the hearing, and implying that Robeson's membership *now* was the only unresolved question. "What is the Communist Party?" Robeson responded, then added, "As far as I know it is a legal party . . . a party of people who have sacrificed for my people. . . ." HUAC Counsel Arens persisted, "Are you now a member of the Communist Party?" This time Robeson gave a tart reply: "Would you like to come to the ballot box when I vote and take out the ballot and see?" Pressed yet again, he took the Fifth Amendment and told the committee to "forget it."[25]

Arens moved on to the tired accusation, which the FBI had failed for ten years to prove, that Robeson's Communist Party name was "John Thomas." Robeson burst out laughing—as Essie later wrote, "the idea of this world-known giant with the fabulous voice trying to hide himself under an assumed name" was absurd. Recovering his gravity, Robeson replied, "My name is Paul Robeson, and anything I have to say or stand for I have said in public all over the world—and that is why I am here today." The committee was neither amused nor impressed. Chairman Francis Walter— one of the architects of the McCarran-Walter Act—took up the cudgels, doing his best in a series of questions to assert Robeson's friendship with a variety of Soviet espionage agents. Feigning not to recognize Walter, Robeson asked if he was "the author of all of the bills that are going to keep all kinds of decent people out of the country." No, Walter replied, "only your kind." "Colored people like myself," Robeson shot back. Arens then confronted Robeson with the 1948 testimony of Max Yergan: "It

440

became clear to me that there was a Communist core within the Council [on African Affairs]. . . . Paul Robeson was . . . certainly a part of that Communist-led core." Robeson replied: "I am not being tried for whether I am a Communist, I am being tried for fighting for the rights of my people, who are still second class citizens in this U.S. of America. . . . You want to shut up every Negro who has the courage to stand up and fight for the rights of his people. . . ." Walter cited Jackie Robinson's disparaging testimony about Robeson from 1949 as proof that he did not represent his people, and when Robeson replied "that in his heart" Robinson "would take back a lot of what" he had said about him, Arens countered with the flat assertion of Thomas W. Young (the black editor of the conservative Guide Publishing Company) that Robeson "does not speak for the masses of the Negro people whom he has so shamelessly deserted."[26]

When Robeson asked to read from other black publications and to quote from other black leaders about his reputation, he was denied permission; Representative Kearney (Republican, New York) suggested that instead he read "from some of the citations you have received from Stalin." He had been cited, Robeson retorted, for his efforts for peace, and he asked, "Are you for war, Mr. Walter?" Then he repeated a new variation of his own 1949 Paris statement that "it was unthinkable to me that any people would take up arms in the name of an Eastland [Senator James Eastland, chairman of the Senate Judiciary Committee and a rabid segregationist], to go against anybody." That, in turn, induced various committee members to scoff at his notion that blacks would not fight against the Soviet Union, to which Robeson in turn retorted that in 1956 it was still "perfectly clear" that, taken as a whole, the nine hundred million colored peoples of the world would *not* go to war in defense of Western imperialism.[27]

From there, what remained of civility gave way. Scherer asked Robeson why he had not remained in Russia. "Because my father was a slave," he responded, "and my people died to build this country, and I am going to stay here and have a part of it just like you. And no fascist-minded people will drive me from it. Is that clear?" Why had he sent his son to school in the Soviet Union? To spare him from racial prejudice, Robeson answered. "What prejudice are you talking about?" Walter asked. "You were graduated from Rutgers." Robeson tried to explain that "the success of a few Negroes including myself or Jackie Robinson" did not atone for the fact that thousands of black families in the South had a yearly income of seven hundred dollars, living still in a kind of semislavery. "I'm glad you called our attention to [the] slave problem," Arens quipped. "While you were in Soviet Russia, did you ask them there to show you the slave labor camps?"[28]

That was as close as the committee came to landing a body blow, but Robeson refused it. This deeply stubborn, angry man would neither denounce nor defend Stalin's crimes, choosing instead to place them in the context of the United States' crimes against black people. The Soviet Union's problems were its own problems, he thundered: "I'm interested in the place I am in, the country where I can do something about it." He pounded so hard on the table, Milton Friedman feared his fist might go through it. As far as he knew, Robeson insisted, the Soviet slave camps were occupied by "fascist prisoners who had murdered millions of the Jewish people and who would have wiped out millions of the Negro people could they have gotten hold of them. That is all I know about that." He would not discuss the camps further, he added, "with the people who have murdered 60 million of my people"; back "among the Russian people some day singing for them, I will discuss it there. It is their problem." After a few more exchanges of insults and Robeson's shouted insistence that the committee members were the true "un-Americans, and you ought to be ashamed of yourselves," a furious Chairman Walter banged down the gavel and adjourned the hearing. Robeson got in the last word: "you should adjourn this forever, that is what I say."[29]

The indignant committee members immediately retired behind closed doors, and within minutes voted unanimously to recommend that Robeson be cited for contempt. "There was no contempt," Robeson told a reporter outside the building. "I answered every question. I was just standing my ground." His counsel, Milton Friedman, noted that only the House of Representatives had the power to vote an actual contempt citation and predicted that Congress would not act on the committee's recommendation. Robeson had indeed shown contempt, blistering contempt for the committee. But the legal grounds for a contempt citation were narrow: failure to appear or failure to answer questions. Trying to get around that limitation, Chairman Walter argued that Robeson's "entire conduct" at the hearing, his "personal attacks on the Committee," and in particular his "smear" of Senator Eastland were sufficient grounds for a citation. The House disagreed, refusing, finally, to take any action against him.[30]

Back in New York that same day, Robeson got on the phone with Ben Davis (the FBI got on the phone, too) and told him he thought that it had gone "fine." Davis had received an eye-witness report from William Patterson and agreed that Robeson had done "a grand job." So did a host of political fans and supporters. Du Bois and his wife, Shirley Graham, sent their "congratulations," and Mary Helen Jones reported from California that her phone "rang all night" with "people expressing their admiration for you. . . . You made such fools out of them. . . . The Negro Community is strictly in your corner." James Aronson, executive editor of the *National Guardian,* wrote Robeson that he had "cheered the reports of your exchanges. . . . Keep yourself whole; you are sorely needed," and Aubrey Williams of *Southern Farmer* congratulated him "on one of your finest performances, and God knows you have given some great performances in your life time." The black press was also warmly supportive. "Mr.

Robeson Is Right," headlined the editorial in *The Afro-American*, agreeing with him that House members "could more profitably spend their time passing civil rights measures and bringing in for questioning" white supremacists. Thomas Flemming in the San Francisco *Sun Reporter* wrote that Robeson "says the things which all [blacks] wish to say about color relations," while Horace Cayton in the Pittsburgh *Courier* challenged the government either to prosecute Robeson if it actually had any evidence he was engaged in a "Communist conspiracy" or, if not, to restore his right to travel.[31]

The confrontation did wonders for Robeson's spirits. A month later he was able to make a three-day visit to New Jersey, where Ernest Thompson, a black officer in the United Electrical, Radio and Machine Workers of America, arranged a successful series of get-togethers with black groups, deliberately keeping interested whites and CP functionaries at a distance—Thompson, among others, felt the CP had misused Robeson in the past by keeping him too distant from blacks. A few weeks later Essie was writing Rockmore that Paul was "well and happy." (By the early fall, he was even back to the point where he once again had a concert canceled for political reasons, this time in Newark.)[32]

In November, with the U.S.S.R.'s occupation of Hungary in process, Paul and Essie attended the Soviet Embassy party in Washington, D.C., to celebrate the thirty-ninth anniversary of the October Revolution; except for the surprise appearance of Justice and Mrs. William O. Douglas, official Washington boycotted the affair. One week later Robeson again thumbed his nose at prescribed behavior—and this time was directly attacked for it. Arriving to attend a peace rally sponsored by the National Council of American-Soviet Friendship, he was greeted by a furious crowd of two hundred egg-and-tomato-hurling hecklers, mostly of Hungarian descent; carrying placards denouncing "Communist Barbarians," they shouted their anger at the "murderers" arriving to attend the meeting. A large detail of police kept the demonstrators in check and escorted Robeson into the building. Somebody in the crowd tossed a bottle of ammonia at him, but it splattered harmlessly on the ground close by.[33]

Inside the hall, a small crowd of about five hundred heard Dr. Harry F. Ward, professor emeritus of Christian ethics at Union Theological Seminary, counsel against gearing up hysterically for the "inevitability" of a third world war. It then listened in surprise (and silence) as Reverend William Howard Melish of the Trinity Episcopal Church in Brooklyn deplored the Soviet "error in judgment in resorting to armed coercion" in Hungary; Melish softened his reproof by pointing out that "all of us have compromised with our ideals"—as witnessed by the U.S. imperialist venture in Guatemala and the British-French-Israeli invasion of Egypt. When Robeson's turn came to speak, he left out the reproof—subsequently he suggested that "somebody" had fomented trouble in Hungary, probably the same somebody who had been at work in Egypt. According to the New York *Post*, Robeson told a reporter on leaving the hall that "The Hungarian revolution was brought about by the same sort of people who overthrew the Spanish Republican Government." William Z. Foster wrote to congratulate him on his "militant stand": "In view of the wobbling and confusion to be found in our ranks, it is good to see someone showing clarity of understanding and fighting spirit. . . . This is a moment when steadiness is especially necessary in Left ranks. Undoubtedly there has been much confusion and vacillation caused by this Stalin affair, especially the tragedy in Hungary. It is one of those great obstacles that the movement has to overcome in its historic march ahead. It is a crisis of growth."[34]

Robeson's negative view of the Hungarian "freedom fighters" found considerable echo in the black press. "The cynicism of America's Negro citizens in respect for the Hungarians' 'fight for freedom' is thick enough to be slashed with a knife," the Pittsburgh *Courier* editorialized, "and solid enough to be weighed on scales. . . ." Where, the *Courier* wondered, was any comparable expression of concern for the victims of the savage bombings of Port Said and Cairo? And where was the comparable outrage at the mob violence against the young black student Autherine Lucy as she tried to attend classes at the lily-white University of Alabama? "How can America, in good faith," chimed in the San Francisco *Sun Reporter*, "blow such loud horns about the freedom of the Hungarians, when such a large portion of her own population is deprived of freedom guaranteed by the Constitution of the United States?"[35]

A few days after the American-Soviet Friendship rally, Robeson elaborated his views on current affairs in an interview with *The Afro-American*. Commenting on the results of the recent presidential election, in which Eisenhower had again swamped Adlai Stevenson, Robeson said he found them both "pretty lax" on civil rights and expressed the hope that Eisenhower would use his mandate "to be much firmer on the question of carrying out the Supreme Court's school desegregation decision." He also took the occasion to deplore the invasion of Egypt (though not of Hungary) as proof of Western reluctance to accept a changed status for third-world people. He saw the action as a particular affront to the Bandung Pact nations of Asia and Africa, crediting the Soviet Union's defense of their rights to independent nationhood as the chief counterweight on the international scene to Western efforts at maintaining the old colonial system.[36]

The Supreme Court, meanwhile, announced its refusal to hear arguments appealing the Appellate Court decision on Robeson's passport—even though it granted, on the very same day, a new trial in Pittsburgh to five defendants convicted under the Smith Act. The decision further isolated Robeson, seeming to confirm his status (in William Patterson's indignant words) as "the only living American against whom an order has been issued directing immigration authorities not to permit him to leave the continental confines of the United States," not even to go to Mexico, the West Indies, Hawaii, or other areas that "demand only proof of American citizenship as a means of entry." In public, Robeson tried to put the best face on it. He told *The Afro-American* that since the Supreme Court claimed he had not exhausted all "administrative remedies" available, his lawyers would once again request an administrative hearing from the State Department—though he would continue to refuse, he emphasized, to sign the kind of "non-Communist" affidavit the State Department had previously insisted would be necessary before they would consider any such hearing. If the government stuck by that policy, Robeson said, he would then ask for a rehearing in the Court of Appeals on the grounds that he *had* "exhausted all administrative remedies" currently open to him. Since a rehearing on those grounds was unlikely, Robeson was in fact acknowledging a stalemate. His personal Cold War had not eased.[37]

■

CHAPTER 22

Resurgence

(1957–1958)

The enforced inactivity in Robeson's life coincided, ironically, with an upsurge of movement for black Americans in general. The beaching of a man who had spoken out for two decades against the paralyzing oppression of black life now stood in stark contrast to the quickened hope that swept black communities across the nation. Not that the Supreme Court's 1954 *Brown* decision had in itself marked the swift demise of Jim Crow. Far from it. The court's own implementing decision rejected the notion of rapid desegregation in favor of a "go-slow" approach, which itself proved too radical a notion for President Eisenhower; initially he refused to endorse the *Brown* ruling, remarking, "I don't believe you can change the hearts of men with laws or decisions," and calling his own appointment of Earl Warren to the Supreme Court "the biggest damn fool mistake I ever made."[1]

The caution of official Washington was matched on the state level by fierce white resistance. On March 12, 1956, 101 Southern members of Congress issued a "Declaration of Constitutional Principles," which called on their states to refuse implementation of the desegregation order. Defiance became the watchword in the white South, massive resistance the proof of regional loyalty. Every item in the white-supremacist bag of tricks—from "pupil-placement" laws to outright violence—was utilized to forestall integration of the schools. The Ku Klux Klan donned its masks and hoods; the respectable middle class enrolled in White Citizens' Councils; the press and pulpit resounded with calls to protect the safety of the white race. A tide of hatred and vigilantism swept over the South. Some blacks knuckled under in fear; many more dug in, prepared once again to endure—and this time overcome. On December 1, 1955, in Montgomery, Alabama, Rosa Parks, a forty-two-year-old black seamstress, stubbornly refused to give up her bus seat to a white man—thereby launching the Montgomery bus boycott, energizing black resistance, catapulting Martin Luther King, Jr., and his strategy of nonviolent direct action to the forefront of the movement. An epoch of black insurgency had been ushered in.

Robeson, of course, applauded it—but from the sidelines, where he had been shunted. Confined by the white ruling elite, ostracized by the black establishment, he and his influence had been effectively neutralized. His limited access to the media, in combination with his disinclination to write, meant that he had few public opportunities to express his support for the burgeoning civil-rights movement. When one did present itself in July 1957, during a rare series of engagements in California, he told the press that he "urged the Negro people to support Reverend Martin Luther King—the strength of the Negro people lies within their organizations and churches, as demonstrated by the magnificent Montgomery, Alabama Bus Boycott and other activities conducted by the Negro people in the South." And in September 1957, when the National Guard in Little Rock, Arkansas, under orders from Governor Orval Faubus, prevented nine black students from enrolling in Central High, Robeson issued a statement calling for a national conference to challenge "every expression of white supremacy."[2]

But no one much was listening. Only one black paper, *The Afro-American*, printed his statement in full—and his call for a national conference was ignored. Not only was Robeson's name no longer instantly recognized, but, to the extent that he was still known among the new activists, his pro-Soviet stance was regarded as something of an irrelevance, even a hindrance. Anne Braden, who with her husband, Carl, was active in the civil-rights struggle in Kentucky, remembers that most of the *young* black activists "really knew nothing about Paul Robeson," and those who had heard of him "would have been scared to death if he'd shown up at one of their meetings." That would change somewhat by the early sixties; by then young blacks would be more militant, would have learned more about their own history and learned, too, that their white "friends and protectors" in Washington, who had been advising them against associating with "Communists," might not after all have their best interests at heart.[3]

When Paul, along with Essie and Paul, Jr., went to Washington in May 1957 to take part in the Prayer Pilgrimage, he was largely ignored: the organizers asked Robeson antagonists Roy Wilkins and Adam Clayton Powell, Jr. (who had bolted to Ike in 1956), to speak, but not Robeson. (A month before the Pilgrimage, struck by how little organizing had been done, Essie speculated that Wilkins and A. Philip Randolph were actually trying to sabotage the event, and she wrote George Murphy, Jr., "The more I think of the NAACP the more dangerous I think it is. They always calm the waters when something concrete and really good is cooking.") At about this same time, ironically, the head of the FBI's New York Office was confidentially advising J. Edgar Hoover that Robeson's recent California trip "had been conducted for the purpose of determining whether he had enough of a following to attempt to take over the National Association for the Advancement of Colored People on a national scale." A few weeks later that allegation had been transmuted into a CPUSA takeover of the NAACP, and Hoover directed the New York Office to "follow Robeson's activities." Robeson and Roy Wilkins would have been equally astonished at the news of a pending coup. Though the FBI apparently did not realize it, the government and the media had, over nearly a decade, done its work better than it knew in making Robeson invisible to a new generation of black youth, in moving him to the margins of the black struggle.[4]

During the first half of the fifties, Robeson could take some solace from the fact that his isolation had been imposed by white authorities in response to his militant stand in behalf of the rights of the world's colored peoples. During the second half of the fifties, as a mainstream black protest movement emerged within his own country and seemed uninterested in his presence, his sense of isolation became more acute and painful. In contrast to his former wide-ranging public life, he now spent his time engaging in pentatonic musical studies and pursuing his passport fight. They did not absorb his energies. He read over Marie Seton's manuscript for a book about him and worked with Lloyd L. Brown on an autobiographical volume, but these were retrospective activities; he was, for the time being, not living fully in the present. Nor could continuing recognition from the peace movement overseas and periodic visits from Ben Davis, Jr., or William Z. Foster compensate for the deafening lack of interest in his services at the Prayer Pilgrimage and the failure of any call for consultation from the Montgomery boycotters or from Martin Luther King, Jr. As if to assuage his own hurt, to compensate for being bypassed, Robeson's public statements occasionally became boastful and overweening, traits in jarring contrast to his once characteristic modesty. The dissonant strain of braggadocio—and an occasional penchant for the imagery of martyrdom—marked a poignant bid for the attention and affirmation that he had never before had any need to summon up.[5]

A reporter picked up the false new note during Robeson's six-week trip to California in the summer of 1957 (he traveled with Revels Cayton) to perform several concerts that left-wing friends had finally managed to arrange—the only series he gave that year. Understandably expansive in the glow of a rare chance to sing in public, and delighted at his well-attended and well-reviewed concerts in the black community ("a welcome far beyond anything I could have expected," he told a reporter), Robeson held a two-hour press conference in Los Angeles, which left the black journalist Almena Lomax of the *Tribune* with an overall impression of "total self-absorption." Even while declaring admiration for Robeson's "gifts and the richness of personality of the man," Lomax expressed disquiet at his nearly nonstop discourse about his own accomplishments—"a sort of antic quality, overall." Possibly Robeson, basking in the now unaccustomed light of publicity, was having nothing more than a cheerful and perfectly human burst of vanity. Possibly it had been triggered by a mild clinical recurrence of mania. Whatever the cause and combination of circumstances, his personality seemed to have lost its once-characteristic emotional centeredness, the solidity and surety of purpose that had long given him such easy, magnanimous grace.[6]

Some sustenance came from overseas. His many friends in England, mobilized as the National Paul Robeson Committee, accelerated their campaign for the return of his passport. By the spring of 1957 the list of notables in support had grown to include twenty-seven members of Parliament and such distinguished—and in many cases nonpolitical—figures as the classicist Gilbert Murray, Leonard Woolf, the economist Barbara Wootton, Augustus John, Julian Huxley, Benjamin Britten, Pamela Hansford Johnson, the historian Sir Arthur Bryant, Sir Compton Mackenzie, Kingsley Amis, John Betjeman, the Shakespearean scholar J. Dover Wilson, and Robeson's old acting partner Flora Robson. (Clearly, Tom Driberg wrote in his regular column for *Reynolds News,* this movement in Robeson's behalf "is not, as some Washington bureaucrats pretend, a mere political stunt.") In late April 1957 British Actors Equity in its annual meeting—after some heated exchanges, during which the actress Helena Gloag suggested that the resolution had originated from "an international subversive movement, Communism"—voted a resolution in support of efforts currently being made to enable Robeson to perform in Britain.[7]

To cap off the campaign, Cedric Belfrage, editor-in-exile of the *National Guardian,* organized a concert which Robeson sang via transatlantic phone circuit to an audience assembled in a London theater—in ringing symbolic defiance of the passport ban. It came off wonderfully. At an all-day Robeson celebration before the concert, actress Marie Burke shared her recollections of Robeson in *Show Boat,* followed by speeches from Gerald Gardiner, QC, the miners' leader Arthur Horner, black Labour parliamentary candidate David Pitt, and the Kenyan Joseph Murumbi of the Movement for Colonial Freedom. That same evening, with one thousand people crowded into St. Pancras Town Hall to hear the "live" Robeson concert, the actor Alfie Bass took the stage to entertain while everyone excitedly awaited the hookup. After a few false starts ("We all thought Somebody was starting to sabotage the show," Belfrage later wrote Essie), they succeeded in making connection with New York just five minutes before the event was scheduled to begin.[8]

The stage now empty except for an enormous blowup photo of Robeson on the back wall, the Union Jack on one side, Old Glory on the other, his resonant bass suddenly flooded the hall. He sang six songs in all, with the audience "jumping out of their seats" to shout approval. The reception—over the new high-fidelity transatlantic telephone cable—was superb, and the audience (according to Belfrage) went home "spiritually 'high.'" Press coverage, though, was minimal: Belfrage had invited all U.S. papers with representatives and agencies in London, but none came. Except for an unexpected article in the Manchester *Guardian*—which said the concert had succeeded in making "the United States Department of State look rather silly"—only a few small items appeared in British papers. Still, Robeson was profoundly grateful to his British friends. He was "so deeply moved," Essie reported to Belfrage, that by the end of the concert "he was close to tears," thrilled at the prospect of "a new means for communication from the jailhouse."[9]

Three months later, and perhaps to some unmeasurable degree influenced by the mounting Robeson campaign abroad, the State Department finally made a partial concession on his right to travel. For the better part of a year, Leonard Boudin had sought in vain to get a hearing from the Passport Division, which had alternately delayed any response to his letters and then, when it did reply, stipulated still more procedural requirements not asked of other passport applicants. But just as Boudin had become convinced that they would have to go back into court in order to get any action, the State Department granted Robeson an administrative hearing.[10]

Boudin and Essie accompanied him to Washington on May 29 for what turned into a six-hour marathon session. As Robert D. Johnson for the Passport Division relentlessly posed loaded questions and presented hearsay evidence about Robeson's purported CP membership, Boudin consistently refused to allow his client to respond, on the grounds that personal and political associations were irrelevant to the issue of the right to travel. When the lengthy charade was over, Johnson declared that Robeson's refusal to "make a full disclosure" automatically halted the administrative processing of his passport application (Johnson reported to the FBI that, although he had "thrown the book" at Robeson, the hearing had been a "'wash out' inasmuch as Robeson did not admit any Communist connections or activities"). Allowed to make a statement at the end, Robeson repeated his view that the real reason his passport was being withheld concerned his outspoken protests over the condition of black people at home and abroad. "My Negro friends," he said, "tell me I am a little too excited about it. I don't see how you can get too excited about it—not so much whether one has even bread to eat at a certain point, but the essential human dignity, the essential human dignity of being a person."[11]

The passport stalemate seemed unbroken. The government refused to reconsider unless Robeson first signed a "non-Communist" affidavit, and Robeson refused to yield on a point he considered central to his constitutional rights (fearing, too, that if he did say he had never been a CP member, the Justice Department could then call out its stable of informers to swear, falsely, that he *had* been—thereby allowing an indictment against him for perjury). But then—the jockeying completed, the mutually contradictory positions laid out—in August 1957 the State Department unexpectedly made its first concession to Robeson in seven years: though still refusing him a passport, State announced that henceforth he would be allowed to travel to Alaska, Hawaii, Puerto Rico, the Virgin Islands, Guam, and American Samoa—places in the Western Hemisphere where a passport was not required of U.S. citizens. It had become an embarrassment, at a time of easing Cold War tensions and mounting black protest, to have Robeson remain the *one* citizen of the United States (excepting only Dave Beck, indicted president of the Teamsters Union, who had been placed on travel restriction at the specific request of the Senate's McClellan Investigating Committee) against whom an interdiction to nonpassport areas of the Western Hemisphere remained—restraints that had already been removed by national committee members of the CPUSA. When rumors immediately began to circulate that Robeson would shortly visit the West Indies, U.S. Naval Intelligence in Trinidad telegraphed Washington that it doubted the British would allow him to enter—though doubtless the "Communist" husband-and-wife team, Prime Minister Cheddi Jagan and his American-born wife, Janet, would "welcome him with open arms" to British Guiana.[12]

Robeson's sights, however, were leveled not on the West Indies or on South America but on England. Hard on the heels of the State Department's refusal to lift the passport ban came an alluring invitation from Glen Byam Shaw, general manager of the Shakespeare Memorial Theatre at Stratford-upon-Avon: would Robeson be available during the 1958 season to star as Gower in *Pericles,* the production conceived by Tony Richardson, a young director who had recently won acclaim in both London and New York for his staging of John Osborne's *Look Back in Anger?* (Shaw sent the additional word that Peggy Ashcroft—Robeson's Desdemona in the 1930 *Othello*—had been "overjoyed" when told of the invitation to him.) With rehearsals due to begin in June 1958, and citing this "very great opportunity," Boudin immediately asked the State Department to reconsider its recent refusal and issue Robeson a passport of limited duration and purpose so he could accept the engagement in England.[13]

Flattering though the offer was, and potentially serviceable in his passport fight, Robeson in fact viewed it with some trepidation. He accepted the role immediately—pending, of course, State Department acquiescence—but after reading the play began to have doubts (as Essie wrote Shaw) whether he had "the traditional classic Shakespearean background and experience and style and accent, to play this role in the midst of an experienced and beautifully trained English cast in the shrine of the Shakespeare tradition." Othello was the only Shakespearean role he had ever undertaken, and that more than a decade ago; Othello, moreover, had called for (in Essie's words) "a foreigner, dark, different from the rest of the cast, and it was a foreignness which he thoroughly understood and actually *was.*" Tony Richardson was in New York to stage *The Entertainer,* and met with Robeson to encourage him. Shaw, moreover, sent a long letter "begging" him to have no doubts that he would do the part of Gower superlatively well: "Gower is, as it were, detached from the rest of the play. . . . He is the great storyteller. . . . It doesn't matter what nationality he is provided the actor has a compelling power of personality, the feeling of deep understanding of humanity and, of course, a wonderful voice with which to tell his story. All these qualities you possess in a degree that no other actor does." Robeson thanked Shaw for the kind words, and said he felt reassured.[14]

The London press played up Robeson's pending arrival as big news (contrarily, the development was entirely ignored by the major media in the United States). The *Daily Herald* carried an eight-column headline, "I'm-a-Comin', Says Robeson," with a subheading that proclaimed "And Paul's Head Will Not Be Bendin' Low Here in Britain." However, the British press was not unanimous in hailing him; Beaverbrook's *Daily Express,* predictably, announced that he "would be a most unwelcome visitor"; with an unforgiving memory, the *Express* recalled that "In the dark days of the war," Robeson had said that Britain's reactionary influence had inspired Finland to attack the Russians, and later had called Britain "one of the greatest enslavers of human beings in the world." Still, additional British offers quickly came in: to star in England's biggest television show, "Val Parnell's Sunday Night at the Palladium," and also to perform on a "Spectacular" for Associated Television. London's Royal Festival Hall offered him a concert, and Harold Davison, the theatrical agent, started making preliminary arrangements for a tour. "Excitement and anticipation," Tony Richardson reported, were keen. Essie replied that "The spread in the British press . . . has had great effect here. The State Department is frantically defending itself. . . ."[15]

That was wishful thinking. The State Department refused to budge, coolly notifying Boudin that it continued to deem it necessary for Robeson to "answer the questions with respect to Communist Party membership before consideration can be given to his request for passport facilities." Two other passport cases—those of Walter Briehl and Rockwell Kent—pending before the Supreme Court and involving the constitutional issue of the right to travel, held out the hope of establishing a precedent favorable to Robeson, but the court was unlikely to hand down a decision in those cases until June. While awaiting that verdict, the State Department remained obdurate; even had it wanted to, it could not have given Robeson a limited passport without weakening its case against Briehl and Kent. By late February, with no hope of an immediate break in the situation, Robeson felt obliged (and perhaps relieved) to notify Glen Byam Shaw that he would have to withdraw from the role of Gower. "You can imagine how we hate to say this," Essie wrote Shaw, "but fair is fair, and plans are plans, and we know we are not going to make it." The news, Shaw wrote back, was "a bitter disappointment. . . . It would have not only been a great joy but also an honour for me if he could have appeared at this Theatre during the time of my directorship."[16]

The offer was aborted, but not the impulse it represented. As if a signal had been given, some attractive invitations within the United States began to trickle in, themselves a reflection of a decline of McCarthyite influence on the national scene. In reaction to these first "mainstream" opportunities offered him in a decade, this prospective armistice, Robeson showed at least a bit more circumspection, a modicum of prudence when addressing the public—especially the black public. Still vigilant about his integrity, still loyal to past friends and his own past opinions, he nonetheless responded with a subtle new regard, around the edges, for the prospects of rehabilitation. He would to no degree compromise with the John Foster Dulleses—the white power structure, which he continued to regard as racist, militarist, and colonialist—but, to enhance his reputation with mainstream *black* America, he began to downplay his "Communist" image and revivify his black one. He would not leave the mountain, but he was willing to take a few sideways steps to avoid the direct path of the lava flow.

Early in 1958 he made a discernible shift away from *public* pro-Soviet activities. In the last two months of 1957 he had been as outspoken and conspicuous as ever in defense of the U.S.S.R., traveling to Washington in November to celebrate the fortieth anniversary of the Revolution at the Soviet Embassy, speaking at American-Soviet Friendship's annual event at Carnegie Hall on November 10, 1957, wiring congratulations to the Soviets on the orbiting of Sputnik. The FBI reports from late 1957 even have him privately saying "that people who are losing courage should get out of the way," and characterized him as "solid as a rock . . . with the 'supers' (super left) all the way." But in the opening months of 1958 Robeson fell *comparatively* silent, confining his public statements to a set of perfunctory "New Year's greetings" to the peoples of China, Eastern Europe, and the U.S.S.R. (not omitting the Albanians, whom he hailed for their "demonstration of what a Peoples Socialism can do to transform a whole land").[17]

His retreat from a high level of *open* commitment to the Soviet Union was a reflection not of disillusion but, rather, of a conscious determination to restore his reputation as a spokesman for black people. When, for example, Tony Richardson sent him a script for consideration, he rejected the suggested role of an unsavory West Indian as unsuitable, as "not constructive at this time." Black people, Essie wrote Richardson, "would resent it" if Paul should appear in such a role, given their intense interest currently "in the coming independence of a Federated West Indies; he could not afford to consider only artistic angles." In that same spirit of mending ties in the black community, Essie broadened her New Year's greetings list to include such one-time friends as Fritz Pollard and such new heroines as Daisy Bates, the NAACP organizer who had coordinated the effort to integrate Central High in Little Rock, Arkansas. And when boxing champion Archie Moore sent Paul a fan letter ("I'm not a hero worshipper by a long shot but there are men I admire and you are one of the few"), Robeson telephoned to thank him.[18]

In a comparable spirit, he took care, when filling his first commercial concert dates in years in California, Portland, and Chicago early in 1958, to present a less belligerent public image. In Sacramento a critic commented on his "new gentleness." In San Francisco he told a reporter, "I am sorry now that I quit the concert stage because of politics. . . . Any 'politics' in the future will be in my singing," leaving the surprised reporter—who apparently could not distinguish a tactic from a conviction—to conclude, prematurely, that Robeson was now "more interested in musicology than in politics." In Portland, perhaps to avoid such simplicities, he told an interviewer, "I'm here as an artist"—but was also careful to add, "My political position is precisely the same now as it has always been."[19]

The FBI understood this better than the press. Far from believing—as part of the press kept announcing—that Robeson was retiring from politics, the FBI theorized that he was bent on trying to restore his influence in the world of black politics. Its agents dutifully reported the occasional rumors adrift that Robeson was about to defect from Communism, but the Bureau recognized that no proof existed to support them. It preferred to believe in its own previously floated fantasy that Robeson's effort to present an image of himself more acceptable to mainstream blacks was in the name of capturing the NAACP for his own nefarious (i.e., Communistic) purposes.[20]

The FBI's special agent in Los Angeles even reported to J. Edgar Hoover that Robeson might in fact be the "real leader" of the left-wing Foster-Davis faction of the CPUSA and may have designed his trip to California in 1958 as an effort to sway that "right-wing" CP stronghold to the left. The L.A. agent passed on his informants' opinion that Robeson "is much more dangerous to the security of this country than those who have taken the position of extreme 'right.' " Hoover did not doubt it. He advised the Bureau's L.A. Office to explore fully and attempt to corroborate its information, noting that the FBI lacked "recent evidence" (actually it had never had evidence) that Robeson "has taken a direct part in the policy or other affairs of the CP." The best that the L.A. agent could do was to report back that in California Robeson had seen "a great deal" of black CP leader Pettis Perry, and that subsequent to his visit to the state, the left-wing faction had succeeded in gaining new prominence. The recollections of Rose Perry, Pettis's widow, are a good deal more mundane: Pettis and Paul spent most of their time talking about black issues, and she and her husband spent most of theirs "terribly afraid that something might happen to Paul physically." According to Paul, Jr., their fear was justified: the left-front wheel came off of the car that Paul had been riding in. Although he was not a passenger at the time, and no one was hurt, it was a disturbing reminder of the incidents in St. Louis in 1947 and in Los Angeles in 1955.[21]

The California music critics gave Robeson's 1958 comeback concerts enthusiastic notices. One of them remarked that "it would be too much to expect the velvety smoothness of that magnificent bass voice to continue as consistently as of old," but the larger number expressed amazement that "the years have done virtually nothing to the greatest natural basso voice of the present generation"; and there was unanimous agreement that his dramatic, gracious personal presence remained singularly powerful. The audience response was also keen, with most of the concerts selling out in advance to enthusiastic crowds. More important to Robeson, off the concert stage he succeeded once again in drawing reinvigorated support from the black community. Attending the twentieth anniversary of the founding of *People's World* (the FBI attended as well), he heard Pastor Livingston introduce him as "a champion fighter" for his race; in response Robeson reaffirmed his belief in socialism but did not mention Communism or the Soviet Union or the CPUSA. Even the FBI reports stressed that Robeson had been "increasingly effective . . . among the Negroes and especially among some of the Negro clergymen," his appearances in their churches helping them to raise "a considerable amount of money."[22]

In Pittsburgh two months later, his reception in the black community was again heartening. The management of the Soldiers and Sailors Memorial Hall canceled his announced concert, but two of the leading black churches, Central Baptist and Wesley Center A.M.E. Zion, opened their doors to him, and the packed assemblies gave him deafening receptions. After the concerts, the local chapter of his own powerful Alpha Phi Alpha fraternity entertained him, and P. L. Prattis of the *Courier* sent Essie a private report of the combined events:

> Your "man" came, saw, conquered and knocked their eyeballs out—even mine. . . . But you would never have known he was proud, for as they applauded him, he applauded them. His pride was in them, not himself, for they had come to bring him comfort and he had lain himself on their bosom. . . . The Alpha boys tell

me that he stormed their place for two hours, his eyes sparkling, never tiring. He defined himself, laid himself on the line, so to speak. And with all his greatness, he was modest.

A relative in Pittsburgh reported to Paul's sister, Marian Forsythe, that "Paul acts rejuvenated once more. He had seemed so quiet for a while, but it all seems to be in the past now."[23]

By the time Robeson reached Chicago in April, his spirits had soared, and the reception in that city further cheered him. Essie had written in advance to Margaret Burroughs (schoolteacher, political activist, and later founder of the DuSable Museum of African American History), "Paul wants you, if you will do so, to coordinate whatever he can do in the Negro community. He does NOT want any of this to go through the manager, Mr. [Paul] Endicott, who is white. . . . He would like the people to know that he wants to sit down with them." Essie facilitated matters by herself sending letters accepting invitations for Paul to a local black minister and to the Chicago chapter of Alpha Phi Alpha, which had offered to give him a smoker (introducing Robeson to the Alphas, Oscar Brown, Sr., told them, "Brothers, you are looking at immortality").[24]

Margaret Burroughs, angry at the "black bourgeoisie" in Chicago for having earlier, in her opinion, turned its back on Paul, and sharing his commitment to a socialist vision, felt "it was an honor to open my home to him." For her straightforward advocacy, she was called before the Board of Education and questioned about whether it was true that she was "sympathetic to that red, Paul Robeson." Yes indeed, she responded, she was sympathetic, she was even downright proud of him—since, from everything she could gather, he was "a fine artist and a fine human being"; Burroughs kept her job, but by a hair. Julia and Metz Lorchard (he was editor of the Chicago *Defender*), who were also friendly with Robeson and had housed him on several visits to Chicago, were likewise threatened with reprisals. Julia Lorchard worked for the Cook County welfare office, and for a time her job was in serious jeopardy; one neighbor even denounced the Lorchards for playing Robeson records in their own home.[25]

On this trip to Chicago, Robeson spent the first night with Cathern and Ishmael Flory, the black Communist whom he had known from the forties, when Flory was the international representative for the Mine, Mill union. Robeson, Flory recalls, was "a very considerate man" who warned them that he was a late riser and "wasn't much good" until after 2:00 p.m. But he was good for a late-night talk, and he and the Florys stayed up discussing the "change for the better" they all saw taking place in the country—"I think I'm on my way back among the people," Robeson told the Florys. On the second night Robeson went to stay with Johnnie Mae and Sam Parks. Johnnie Mae was a master "downhome" cook, and Paul had gotten friendly with the earthy, outspoken Sam when he headed the predominantly black Packinghouse Workers local in the late forties and when the two worked together in the early fifties on the National Negro Labor Council. (Parks contrasts himself with Revels Cayton: "I was a worker who attained some intellectual understanding; he is an intellectual who became a worker.")[26]

Sam Parks was exactly the kind of man in whom Robeson had come to invest high hopes, a man with strong ties both to the black church and to the black trade-union movement, and he showed Parks a side of himself that he did not reveal to Flory. Talking again late into the night, Robeson acknowledged to Parks that left-wing white trade-unionists had not proved, under the pressure of the conservative Cold War climate, as staunchly committed to the welfare of the black working class as he had anticipated. He acknowledged, too, that the "worldwide coalition" represented by *Freedom* magazine had not sufficiently addressed the specific needs of American blacks—that the "internationalist view" had too often bypassed rather than incorporated the black perspective. Robeson's disappointment in the failure of the trade-union movement to remain a militant force at home was paralleled by his sense (as Parks recalls) "that the rose beds he'd seen in other countries weren't rose beds but beds of thorns." He expressed no word of disillusion with the Soviet Union but, rather, a generalized grief that the "world movement" for liberation seemed in disarray, and his eyes filled with tears when he talked about his "mistake" in having let "whites front me off to my own people," keep him at a distance from his own grass roots. Still, he believed he had begun to repair that damage, had made significant strides in the past year in restoring his image as "a race man" *and* an artist.[27]

His stay in Chicago confirmed that estimate. Flory arranged a public meeting for Robeson at the Parkway Ballroom, and the turnout—five hundred people "from all over the county"—exceeded expectations. So did the enthusiasm. People clamored to say hello, including some who, in Flory's compassionate phrase, "had gotten scared and lost their way"—not so much people on the street, who had never gone as far as the black leadership in renouncing Robeson, but rather some recalcitrant members of the black bourgeoisie. One such member, a prominent black physician in Chicago and a fellow Alpha, on this visit described Robeson as "one of the heroes of our fraternity." (The reception among whites in Chicago was far less favorable: when a local public-affairs television program announced that Robeson would be a guest, negative popular reaction forced cancellation of his appearance.) In April, *Jet* magazine reported that both Robeson and Du Bois "suddenly are enjoying popularity sprees," and George Murphy, Jr., wrote Essie, "With the two biggest Negro papers in the country [*The Afro-American* and Pittsburgh *Courier*] behind Paul . . . and with the Negro church, our most important political institution increasingly behind him, and, with Sister Essie Robeson in there methodically pitching every day . . . how can our Paul fail?"[28]

Nothing did more toward refurbishing Robeson's image than the publication, early in 1958, of *Here I Stand*, the 111-page manifesto-autobiography he wrote with Lloyd L. Brown, who had collaborated with Robeson earlier on speeches and writings. The book amounted to a subtle yet clear declaration to black America that Robeson viewed his primary allegiance as being to his own community and not to international Communism. The very first line of the Author's Foreword read, "I am a Negro." On the second page he added, "I am an American." In addition, he tried to demystify his continuing refusal, ever since his 1946 Tenney Committee statement, explicitly "to give testimony or to sign affidavits" as to whether or not he was a Communist: "I have made it a matter of principle, as many others have done, to refuse to comply with any demand of legislative committees or departmental officials that infringes upon the Constitutional rights of all Americans." He made it clear that he would continue to refuse, but pointed out that "my views concerning the Soviet Union and my warm feelings of friendship for the peoples of that land . . . have been pictured as something . . . sinister by Washington officials. . . . It has been alleged that I am part of some kind of 'international conspiracy.' . . . *I am not and never have been involved in any international conspiracy or any other kind, and do not know anyone who is*." He insisted that "my belief in the principles of scientific socialism, my deep conviction that for all mankind a socialist society represents an advance to a higher stage of life—that it is a form of society which is economically, socially, culturally, and ethically superior to a system based upon production for private profit . . . have nothing in common with silly notions about 'plots' and 'conspiracies.' "[29]

Without making any apology for his own past actions, without acknowledging any "lapses" in the integrity of Soviet policy—like all proud-spirited people, he lacked the habit of berating himself in public—Robeson looked forward, not back. He did reaffirm his friendship for the Soviet Union and for individuals like Ben Davis, Jr. (who hold "nonconformist or radical views"), but his own primary allegiance, he made clear, was to the interests of black people. In the struggle for those interests, he cited black trade-unionists and the black church—not the Communist Party—as the vanguard institutions, and also as the wellspring of his own personal strength. He advised black leaders, moreover, that they "must rely upon and be responsive to no other control than the will of their people"; allies—"important allies among our white fellow-citizens"—were welcome, but "the Negro people's movement must be led by *Negroes*. . . . Good advice is good no matter what the source and help is needed and appreciated from wherever it comes, but Negro action cannot be decisive if the advisors and helpers hold the guiding reins. For no matter how well-meaning other groups may be, the fact is that our interests are secondary at best with them."

In publicly declaring independence from the CP, Robeson was also distancing himself from accusations of white domination in general. He put his faith in "aroused and militant" black mass action, siding with what he perceived—long before most prominent blacks did—as "a rising resentment against control of our affairs by white people, regardless of whether that domination is expressed by the blunt orders of political bosses or more discreetly by the 'advice' of white liberals which must be heeded or else." In contrast to well-intentioned white liberal and establishment black leaders alike, Robeson rejected the notion of "gradualism" in the struggle for civil rights as "but another form of race discrimination: in no other area of our society are lawbreakers granted an indefinite time to comply with the provisions of law." The insistence that progress must be slow was, he argued, "rooted in the idea that democratic rights, as far as Negroes are concerned, are not inalienable and self-evident as they are for white Americans." How long? he asked rhetorically. *"As long as we permit it."* Black people had the "power of numbers, the power of organization, and the power of spirit" to "end the terror"—*now*. Robeson's concept of "mass militancy, of mass action," was an appeal for coordination that he knew "full well . . . is not easy to do. . . ." But, "despite all of our differences," he felt a "nonpartisan unity" among blacks was nonetheless possible, because there was "a growing impatience with petty ways of thinking and doing things." Robeson was attempting to heal divisions within the black community by a transcending appeal to move beyond them—and somehow to transcend as well the powerful resistance to change within the dominant white culture. If he slighted practicalities, his clarion call for black unity in *Here I Stand* at once prefigured the language and vision soon to be taken up by militant young blacks, and served to announce his own primary commitment to the black struggle in the immediate present.[30]

Except for the minuscule left-wing press, white publications wholly ignored *Here I Stand* (*The New York Times* failed even to list it in its "Books Out Today" section, a courtesy extended to some of the most obscure publications). But the black press not only reviewed the book widely, but also got its message: "I Am Not a Communist Says Robeson," blared a headline in *The Afro-American* (hailing it in an editorial as a "remarkable book"). "Paul Robeson States His Case," ran the front-page article in the Pittsburgh *Courier,* its chief editor, P. L. Prattis, declaring in a separate column that he had been "deeply stirred" by Robeson's words. The Chicago *Crusader* expressed delight that Robeson had finally answered those calling him a Communist and a traitor—his "refusal to defend himself has isolated him at a time when we sorely need the type of courageous leadership he represents"; the *Crusader* now hailed him as "one of the mightiest of all Negro voices raised against world oppression of people based on race, color, national origin and religion." The only negative review in the black press came, predictably, from Roy Wilkins in the NAACP's magazine, *The Crisis*. Wilkins repeated his decade-old assertion that blacks had "never regarded" Robeson as a leader, and dismissed him as a man who "imagines his misfortunes to stem, not from his own bungling, but from the persecution of 'the white folks on top.'" With no help from Wilkins or from the general press, the first edition of *Here I Stand* was exhausted within six weeks, and by May 1959, without benefit of a commercial distributor, twenty-five thousand copies had been sold. Robeson, after a decade in the wilderness, was re-emerging into prominence and favor.[31]

Just prior to Robeson's successful California-Chicago trip, the mainstream black magazine *Ebony* had somewhat prefigured his re-emergence by publishing an interview with him by the respected journalist Carl T. Rowan. Entitled "Has Paul Robeson Betrayed the Negro?," Rowan's article concluded that he had not: "even Negroes who consider Robeson politically naive and tactically dumb find reasons to sympathize with him. . . ." The Rowan piece was not entirely laudatory (George Murphy, Jr., characterized it as "collaborationist"), describing Robeson at one point as looking like "a sad-voiced martyr," and at another—when Rowan asked him directly about Khrushchev's denunciations of Stalin as a murderer —as acting like "a singer who has forgotten his lyrics; he mumbles vaguely. . . ." Rowan subsequently amplified his reaction to Robeson on the popular "Tex and Jinx" radio program. Though complaining that Robeson had never answered his question about Stalin, and while disagreeing with him "greatly on a great many issues," Rowan said, "when he's talking about what's happening to Negroes or when he's crying out for freedom of Negroes or when he's talking about a constitutional issue like the freedom to travel, I find it very difficult to disagree with him."[32]

At the same time the *Ebony* piece appeared, Robeson began to be rediscovered by the recording industry. Thanks to the valiant efforts during the early fifties of Paul, Jr., and Lloyd Brown, Robeson's voice had found a marginal outlet through their Othello Recording Company. But in the beginning of 1958 Vanguard put him back in a commercial studio for the first time in seven years. According to Essie, "Paul was nervous as a cat," but everyone deemed the sessions a success—"Paul was never in better voice. The sound technicians were amazed, and the Vanguard folks were simply thrilled, and so was Paul, of course." Then, in April 1958, another breakthrough came in the form of an Actors' Equity resolution. Following the lead of their British counterparts, the quarterly membership meeting on March 28 voted 111–75 to urge the State Department to issue Robeson a passport (Equity President Ralph Bellamy was one of the negatives).[33]

It was a nice present, arriving just before Robeson's sixtieth birthday, on April 9, 1958. That occasion provoked many additional tributes. Before the birthday rites were concluded, no fewer than twenty-seven countries had held celebratory events of one kind or another, with Peggy Middleton, the London County Council member from Greenwich and executive secretary of the London Paul Robeson Committee, coordinating the assorted arrangements as if from a command post. In Mexico City, twenty leading figures in the arts sponsored a concert; in South Africa, a group of students and faculty at Cape Town University arranged a recital of Robeson recordings; in East Berlin, a Robeson song-film made on direct commission to Earl Robinson especially for the occasion premiered in the city's biggest hall; in Stockholm, the literary magazine *Clarté* put out a special Robeson issue; in Hungary, commemorative concerts were performed throughout the country; in Japan, Radio Tokyo broadcast Robeson songs and speeches; in Port-au-Prince, the celebrants gathered at the Société Nationale d'Art Dramatique; in Peking, a rally was staged in the new Capital Theatre that lasted over three hours, preceded by two days of Robeson songs on national radio; in Moscow, the celebration took place in the enormous Hall of Columns—and in New York the Soviet representative to the UN, A. Sobolev, hosted a dinner for Robeson.[34]

The festivities in India threatened for a time to produce serious political repercussions. Prime Minister Jawaharlal Nehru himself issued a proclamation hailing the planned celebration of Robeson's sixtieth birthday as a fitting tribute, "not only because Paul Robeson is one of the greatest artists of our generation, but also because he has represented and suffered for a cause which should be dear to all of us—the cause of human dignity." The American press, which ignored all other birthday tributes to Robeson, did publicize Nehru's comment—disturbing U.S. Embassy officials in New Delhi, especially Ambassador Ellsworth Bunker, and briefly threatening to damage diplomatic relations between the two countries.[35]

Attempting to exert pressure on the Indian government to cancel plans for the celebration, Ambassador Bunker found a sympathetic ear in Secretary General Pillai, who purportedly told him that he, too, was "very concerned" about the Robeson affair: he was himself "continually having difficulty with 'woolly headed Nationalists' who were easy dupes of Communists." American Chargé d'Affaires Turner in Bombay called on M. C. Chagla, Chief Justice of the High Court, to express "puzzlement" at the decision to honor an American "who is currently engaged [in a] lawsuit with [the] U.S. government, who is critical of his own country and has compared it unfavorably with [the] USSR." Turner warned that "Americans would certainly interpret [the] celebration as Communist-inspired and even anti-American and that many would regard" it "as evidence that India was going Communist." Unintimidated, Chagla "stoutly defended" the purpose of the celebration, and added with dignity that his own presence on the committee "was guarantee against political flavor or Communist inspiration." In Washington, India's Ambassador Mehta stood up just as strongly. Called in by the State Department, he pointed out that Robeson was not a "convicted Communist" and that Prime Minister Nehru, Judge Chagla, and others involved in the birthday event were not Communists—"he didn't understand why anyone was concerned about this celebration in India."[36]

Nehru slightly modified his tribute to Robeson in a subsequent statement but refused to withdraw it. He did, however, leave additional planning and comment to his daughter, Indira Gandhi, who actively promoted the birthday celebration. Unable to budge the Indian government, Secretary of State Dulles and Ambassador Bunker, as a fallback protest, instructed all U.S. officials to refuse invitations. The elaborate festivities climaxed in simultaneous events in Bombay, Delhi, Calcutta, and Lucknow, with Chief Justice Chagla presiding in Bombay—and with no U.S. officials present. Essie sent thanks to both father and daughter: "There are just no words," she wrote Nehru, "to express how deeply grateful we are for your statement. . . . It was beautifully said, and at exactly the right time for maximum effectiveness."[37]

The following month Robeson logged another milestone on the road to restoration. After more than a decade's absence from the New York City concert stage, he reappeared at Carnegie Hall for what turned into a jubilant occasion. Fifteen policemen were stationed at the hall for the sold-out concert, but not even the whisper of a disturbance occurred. The crowd cheered Robeson on his arrival, rose to its feet three times during the concert to cheer him again, and at the conclusion shouted and whistled its approval. The critics were almost as kind. Those who felt his voice had "lost much of its old glow" (in the words of one reviewer) charitably focused instead on his undiluted power over an audience—his "incomparable vigor of presentation and limitless charm." Sonorous and playful, Robeson treated his listeners to a recital that mixed song with comments, laughter, reminiscence, even a bit of dancing. He was delighted to be performing again and gratified by his reception; the success of the concert, he told Ben Davis, opened up "entirely new vistas." His only disappointment was that the hall had mostly been filled with whites. To remedy that, he scheduled a second concert and saw to it that hundreds of tickets were distributed through Micheaux Bookstore and other Harlem outlets. That one, too, sold out. (Still, when Edith Tiger, who had known him well during Progressive Party days, went backstage, she found him feeling "awful." He told her his kidneys were causing him trouble. Then he said that it was his "nerve endings," that he had shingles and couldn't wear clothes comfortably. Edith thought something else was wrong: "His eyes were terrible.") Two weeks later, Robeson gave a memorable concert at Mother A.M.E. Zion, his brother Ben's church. Alan Booth had been accompanying him for most of his few concerts of recent years, but for the

A.M.E. Zion event Robeson was reunited with Larry Brown. "I want the folks of Mother Zion to know," Robeson told the overflow crowd, "that a lot of the hard struggle is over and that my concert career has practically been reestablished all over this land. . . . I've been waiting for this afternoon just to come back to give my thanks here. . . ."[38]

The best news of all finally—incredibly, when measured against the years of deflating delays—came in June. The Supreme Court, in a 5–4 split decision (William O. Douglas writing for the majority) on the related Rockwell Kent and Walter Briehl cases, announced that the Secretary of State had no right to deny a passport to any citizen because of his political beliefs. The court added that the Passport Division had no right to demand that an applicant sign an affidavit concerning membership in the Communist Party. Suddenly it was all over.

The State Department (in Leonard Boudin's words) "immediately capitulated," acknowledging that the Kent-Briehl ruling encompassed the Robeson case as well. Two weeks later Robeson was in Boudin's office, smiling broadly, holding up his passport so photographers could get a good shot of it, telling them he would soon be traveling, that the victory was not just a personal one but, rather, "a victory for the 'other America,'" and illustrative of the "change of climate in the United States." In private, Robeson expressed some trepidation, concerned that, at a time when his people were at last in motion, he would be leaving the struggle behind if he traveled abroad—and concerned, oppositely, that if he did not go he would disappoint those all over the world who had worked for his release and had been waiting to see and hear him. His friends, anyway, were jubilant. An FBI tap of a phone call between Ben Davis and Lloyd Brown memorialized Davis's high-spirited remark that as a result of the court's decision *he,* Davis, should now be able to "go to New Jersey"; in a second call a few weeks later the two men exulted that "the Negro from the chain gang made it." "We keep pinching ourselves," Essie wrote, "wondering if we'll wake up and find it all a dream."[39]

It must have seemed that way, after eight years of stalemate and confinement, as congratulations poured in from around the world and as a stack of glamorous offers began to accumulate. Glen Byam Shaw instantly telegraphed asking Robeson to open Stratford's 1959 season—its historic hundredth anniversary—in the role of Othello. *The Observer* wanted to publish a "Profile"; Pablo Neruda asked him "to sing for the Chilean people"; others invited him to Berlin, to Paris, to Tokyo, to Sydney, to New Delhi. Dream or no dream, the Robesons started packing their bags, sorting out music, getting medical and dental checkups. "It will be good to hear applause again," Paul told Freda Diamond, "but it won't mean anything." The Robesons decided to plan no further than London; once there, they would sit down and leisurely sort through the pile of offers. Essie was very much back in the role of coordinator for Paul's schedule. "I want him to take his time," she wrote Indira Gandhi, "and not rush headlong into a back-breaking schedule of work."[40]

On July 10 Paul and Essie drove out to Idlewild Airport along with his brother Ben (who accompanied them to London), Lloyd Brown, Paul, Jr., and Marilyn, and their two grandchildren, David and Susan. Television, radio, and the press were all out in force. To avoid them, Paul lingered in the parking lot until the last moment. He had already told the press that he expected to be overseas for a considerable time but intended to return to the States at intervals. He would not, he said, discuss politics; he was going to Europe "as an artist." No, he added, he harbored no bitterness. But James Aronson (coeditor of the *National Guardian*) recalls a small farewell dinner party at the Rosens' a few nights before the Robesons left the country at which Paul expressed such a depth of anger that Aronson was "shocked and touched"; as he remembers it, Paul said he "owed this country—or at least its leaders—nothing." He insisted on a BOAC plane, rather than an American carrier. When friends chided that the U.S. government was not about to sabotage a commercial plane in order to "get" him, Robeson grinned sheepishly and said he just didn't trust them.[41]

The plane took off for London at 5:30 p.m. As Paul settled in the seat beside her, Essie jotted down a few quick notes: "It has been an 8 yr pull, struggle all the way, for this trip. Paul is . . . quiet, happy, relaxed, 'on his way' at long last. He is humming, singing softly, trying out his voice. It's there, alright. . . ."[42]

In a send-off column, Robert Ruark, Robeson's old antagonist, wrote that he was "willing to bet" the British would meet him in the same spirit of hooting derision with which they had greeted that other "anti-American," Charlie Chaplin, the year before.[43]

The British had something quite different in mind.

Return to Europe

(1958–1960)

Two hundred friends and fans gathered behind police barricades at the London airport. The exultant group included Cedric Belfrage; Tom Driberg, chairman of the Labour Party National Executive; the agent Harold Davison; the eighty-one-year-old Labour peer, Viscount Stansgate; Dr. Cheddi Jagan, Minister of Trade in British Guiana; the deported American Communist leader Claudia Jones; Glen Byam Shaw; London County Councillor Peggy Middleton; and Harry Francis, assistant secretary of the musicians' union (who would become a good friend). When Robeson's plane touched down at 11:00 a.m. on July 11, they burst into "Hip, hip, hooray" and "For he's a jolly good fellow." Crowding around the Robesons after they cleared customs, the well-wishers, some of them weeping, pressed in with bouquets and hugs.[1]

Reporters from all the major British papers, and many foreign ones, were waiting, too. Robeson paused only for brief remarks—and a few spontaneous bursts of song—and then in the afternoon held a full-scale press conference at the Empress Club in the West End. The hostile Lord Beaverbrook, who had never forgiven Robeson for his anti-British remarks during World War II, boycotted the event, but the turnout was nonetheless full. A reporter from the *News Chronicle* called the press conference "the most remarkable I have ever attended," describing Robeson as "full of gaiety and excitement about his future." Yet not all the reporters were charmed. Twice asked whether he was a Communist, Robeson twice refused to reply—the second time Essie chimed in to say, "It is not a friendly question"—and referred the press to his statement in *Here I Stand*, insisting that he had come to England as an artist. "He behaved like a royal personage," an angry reporter wrote in the *Daily Sketch*. "I pointed out I hadn't time to read his book. 'Then you'll have to wait,' he announced autocratically." Tom Driberg, disgusted at the "ignorant questions," turned away to keep his temper. (When asked the same question under less trying circumstances a few months later, Robeson responded, "My politics are to free my people.") Generally, though, the press coverage was sympathetic and extensive; nearly every paper splashed the story of Robeson's arrival, with pictures, over the front page. Back in America, news of his welcome was either ignored or distorted ("Robeson, in Britain, Balks at Red Query," headlined the New York *Herald Tribune*).[2]

The British public received Robeson with an uninflected enthusiasm. James Aronson was in London at the time and described for the *National Guardian* how the welcome translated into heartwarming daily gestures: "A charwoman greets him on an early morning walk; people on their way to work rush up to shake his hand; a cab driver refuses with indignation to accept payment. . . ." Robeson was "euphoric," Aronson recalls, "at the reception he was getting, seeing old friends, realizing that he hadn't lost his power and, just the simple joy of living in a society where he was respected, loved, and where he could be as free as he wanted to be, without qualms." You had to be there, Aronson added, to understand the full symbolic weight of the reception—"to understand how Europe feels about Robeson . . . how through him they express their love of good culture and contempt for the philistinism of American policy."[3]

Overnight Robeson became a "hot" show-business property once again. Within twenty-four hours of his arrival, Harold Davison had arranged three half-hour TV appearances at a thousand pounds each, had begun putting together a British tour for the fall, and was helping him sift through concert offers from around the globe. Robeson signed with Glen Byam Shaw to open the hundredth-anniversary season at Stratford in *Othello,* took tea at the House of Lords with Lord Stansgate and his son, Anthony Wedgwood Benn, lunched at the House of Commons with Manchester MP Will Griffiths and Aneurin Bevan and his wife, Jennie Lee, and dined with Philip Noel Baker and Peggy Ashcroft. Over the following few weeks, he held a book-autographing party for *Here I Stand* at Selfridges and was guest of honor at a variety of celebrations at embassies and private homes—including, notably, an affair at the Café Royal hosted by Indian journalists and a dinner given by the Nigerian Minister of Internal Affairs.[4]

The exhilarating—and exhausting—round was topped off by several formal concerts. The first, on July 26, marked Robeson's initial appearance on television: "Paul Robeson Sings"—a half-hour program for ATV. He was so nervous prior to the filming that arrangements were made to clear the studio during his performance ("I've never seen such a quiet neat perfect job done," Essie wrote Lloyd Brown), and as a result Paul was relaxed and in excellent voice. Bruno Raikin, who accompanied him, felt that in general Robeson was "not the same man any more," but that the TV broadcast stood out as an exception—"He sang beautifully," and toward the end spontaneously discussed with the TV audience, without any prior preparation and with enormous charm, his pentatonic-music theories. "We find with relief," wrote the London *Times,* "that he is one of those whom age shows no signs of withering. . . . He still talks to us quietly and good-naturedly, and breaks into a smile that is the quintessence of friendliness; he still sings with a huge delight in his songs." "Paul is very heartened," Essie wrote Freda Diamond, "and I realize he has a whole new career open to him." Paul added a note at the end of the letter: "Just a little too much excitement. In spite of all this miss the home fires."[5]

Larry Brown arrived from America by ship in time to accompany Robeson in a formal concert at the Albert Hall two weeks later. Robeson could do no wrong with the sold-out audience. Several of the critics rejoiced that his "magnificent" voice remained intact, but others complained about his narrow range and said that his use of a microphone had made it impossible to assess the real condition of his voice. Through the medium of Tom Driberg's sympathetic column in *Reynolds News,* Robeson explained that he had used a mike for many years, usually concealed in the footlights, and that had he not he wouldn't be singing well at age sixty. The young American sensation Harry Belafonte was making his English debut on the same night as Robeson's concert, performing three miles away at the Gaumont State Theatre, and the tabloids tried to turn a coincidence into a competition: the young contender bidding for Robeson's crown. Robeson put a stop to that particular nonsense: he showed up for one of Belafonte's performances at the Gaumont, warmly applauded him, and later chatted amiably backstage. When a reporter commented to Belafonte that his singing was more lighthearted than Robeson's, Belafonte responded, "It is because Robeson made his protest bitterly that we can be more light-hearted now."[6]

On August 15, after a month's stay in London, Paul and Essie flew to Moscow. If his British reception had been cordial, his Russian one was tumultuous. At Vnukovo Airport, a jostling, eager crowd gave them a rapturous welcome, sweeping Paul away from Essie, burying him in bunches of gladioli, preventing Soviet Minister of Culture Mikhailov and the official delegation of artists and dignitaries from making any formal presentation. When the Robesons finally reached the Metropole Hotel, another crowd awaited them in the street, yelling *"Droog"* ("Friend") and *"Preevyet, Pol Robeson"* ("Welcome, Paul Robeson"), applauding wildly, pressing forward still more bouquets. The pushing and shoving at one point proved too much for him—he "was actually in a state," Essie reported to the family, and needed a police escort to reach his car.[7]

On the evening of August 16, Soviet television broadcast a live twenty-minute conversation with Robeson, preceded by a narrated film about him.

On camera, he described his life in the United States since his last visit to the U.S.S.R. and expressed his joy at being back. The U.S. Embassy in Moscow reported to the State Department that his remarks had been distorted in translation by the television commentator, giving as an example the transposition of Robeson's saying, "We still have trouble in America, but things have become a lot better," into "Life in America is very hard." The Embassy characterized the television program as "Soviet exploitation of an obviously politically illiterate (but very charming, warm, and sympathetic) Robeson for its own propaganda purposes. . . ."[8]

That same "exploitation," according to the Embassy, continued the following day at Robeson's public concert—his first in the U.S.S.R. in nine years—in the Lenin Sports Stadium, with eighteen thousand people filling it to capacity. The event was televised, and Robeson was shown as "visibly affected" by his reception, weeping openly, and, immediately after being introduced, bursting into the Russian patriotic song "Shiroka Strana Moya Rodnaya" ("My Broad Native Land"), singing twice the refrain, "I know no other land where people breathe so free," opening his arms wide to the audience in a bear-hug embrace. Next came all the old favorites—"Ol' Man River," "Joe Hill," "John Brown's Body"—followed by folk songs from many lands and a little speech in which he thanked the Russian people for the strength they had given him and his family to persevere, promising that "the fight for freedom goes on" ("He did not specify what freedom or whose," the Washington *Post* acidly wrote—almost alone among the American press in reporting to the States on Robeson's Soviet reception).[9]

The morning of August 19 was spent (according to Essie's summary account) "with the Negroes in Moscow, who came in a body to the hotel to greet and welcome Paul." That afternoon they left by jet for Uzbekistan, in Soviet Central Asia, to attend the opening of the International Festival of Films of African and Asian Peoples. "We were literally laden with flowers," Essie wrote of their welcome, "staggering happily under their bulk. . . . When our motorcycle escort stopped momentarily so that the way could be cleared, people peered into the car and the shout went up . . . 'Pol Robeson is here!' And crowds seemed to materialize out of nowhere to shout 'Preevyet!' Welcome."[10]

But it was not all cheers and flowers. The heat in Tashkent was brutal, with clouds of flies everywhere. Vasily Katanian, a film director, came out with a crew to make a documentary on Robeson and found him "prostrate from heat and exhaustion . . . glumly silent," pouring sweat. Katanian accompanied the Robesons the following day to visit a famous local collective farm outside the city headed by Khamrakul Tursunkulov. The roadway out was primitive, and (according to Katanian) they arrived two and a half hours late, "absolutely beat from bouncing over the potholes through the dust and heat," while their hosts, dressed in full welcoming regalia, melted in the sun. Tursunkulov, who was deaf, kept forgetting Robeson's name.

Raising his glass to propose a toast to "our best friend, that dear man whom we have known so long and loved so well," Tursunkulov was forced to pause, lean down to Katanian, and ask, "What's his name?" Pleased with having finally managed to navigate the first attempt, Tursunkulov later proposed another toast—only to forget Robeson's name a second time. After they returned to Tashkent, the Robesons had to sit in a stuffy film-festival hall watching "unbearable two-reel Indonesian films that were dubbed in Uzbek." Regaining his spirits somewhat in the cool of the evening, Robeson enjoyed an official supper and even did "a strangely quiet, simple, dignified Asian jitterbug" with one of the dancers. The next day he was down with a fever and had to go to bed.[11]

His cold did not improve, but the schedule was relentless ("This is a rat race," Essie wrote home, "a marvelous one, mind you, but very very hectic"). After arriving by jet at Tbilisi, the capital of Georgia, the Robesons decided to continue straight to Sochi to get some rest, but the Georgian Minister of Culture came out to the Tbilisi airfield to insist they stop over in the capital for two days, as originally planned, saying, "There can be no discussion that you just fly past us." Robeson "sleepily, but decisively" refused, and Essie flashed her bright smile while saying no ("You know me when I put my big foot down, especially wearing my Murray Space shoes"). At Sochi, exhausted, Robeson did little for three days except sleep and let himself be filmed in various positions of relaxation. Then, on August 26, still accompanied by Katanian's camera crew, they boarded a steamship to Yalta for a leisurely cruise along the Black Sea coast.[12]

At Yalta, Robeson revived. The government rest house, Orianda, with its elegant cuisine, luxurious suites, and an elevator down to the sea, became home for two weeks. He made a few side trips, including a visit to Chekhov's house (where, according to Katanian, "Paul looked with disinterest at all of the memorabilia," but which Paul later diplomatically told the Moscow *News* he had found "awe-inspiring and heart-warming"). He and Essie spent a little time with the British journalist Paul Delmer, and with Sally and Rockwell Kent, who were passing through (Sally Kent thought him decidedly out of sorts—he "couldn't sit still or stop talking," full of uncharacteristic boasting about his own achievements). The Yalta doctors ordered more rest, so the Robesons mostly sat about while the film crew memorialized them. Katanian had to fend off the constant interference of Raisa Timofeyevna, wife of Mikhailov, the Soviet Minister of Culture. She objected to the suggestion that Ilya Ehrenburg write the film script ("No, he lisps") and tried to persuade Katanian to film Robeson in a variety of artificial settings (discussing sports with athletes, discussing production schedules with workers, etc.).[13]

Katanian held his ground against Timofeyevna, but one day nearly had his comeuppance. On the spur of the moment the Robesons were asked to come to the nearby Khrushchev lodge, where the Premier, his family, and assorted officials were vacationing. They joined a lively and informal group to watch a volleyball game in progress (at one point Khrushchev called out to a Cabinet minister who had missed several plays, "We will support the minister, but he should play better!"). When the *Pravda* correspondent began shooting the scene with his camera, a distraught Katanian realized belatedly that *his* camera equipment was sitting back in the hotel at Yalta ("I might as well lie down and die"). Mikhailov and Raisa Timofeyevna were aghast: "What do you mean we won't have Nikita Sergeyevich in our picture?" The situation was saved a few days later when Khrushchev invited the Robesons to dinner and the camera crew was allowed to tag along. Paul and Essie were driven for half an hour to a hunting lodge in the hills above Yalta, where they were greeted by the Khrushchevs, the Voroshilovs, the Mikoyans, Tupolev (the airplane designer), and others, and then proceeded in a line of cars up to a further retreat another twenty minutes into the hills. There they met the rest of the company—the current "leaders of the German, Italian, Rumanian, Bulgarian, Polish, Czech, Hungarian governments and their wives, and in some cases, their children" (as Essie described the gathering in a letter home)—and went out on a shooting party ("Kadar won the shooting, bringing down every single bird. He is quiet, a very nice friendly gentle man"). At dinner, toasts were made all around—Paul's was so moving, Essie reported, that it produced tears—and then the Robesons were returned by car to Orianda.[14]

After leaving Yalta on September 12, they spent two final days in Moscow, making appearances and seeing Essie's brother Frank Goode, who had remained in the Soviet Union. Then they returned to London to prepare for a three-month concert tour of Britain, with Larry Brown accompanying and Bruno Raikin as soloist. As in the past, Robeson could do no wrong in the British provinces. But this time, at age sixty, the tour took its toll. After every concert, as Raikin remembers it, Robeson would swear he was going to give up singing. "I'm a nervous wreck," he told Raikin, who decided not only that Robeson's voice had deteriorated—to be expected in a performer of his age—but also that "he wasn't as happy a person, as fulfilled a person, as he had been in 1949."[15]

Robeson refrained from making political comments during the tour, though he continued to sprinkle his concerts with talk—this time almost exclusively talk about the universality of folk music. The chief exception came at the start of the tour, when he told reporters that he felt so much at home in London, and so pleased to be among people anxious to hear him, that he planned to make the city his headquarters, traveling back and forth to the United States as the occasion warranted. He stressed that this did *not* mean he was "deserting the country of my birth," yet *The New York Times*, picking up the remark, headlined a story, "Robeson to Quit U.S. for

London"—and other American papers followed suit. Essie tried to smooth the waters, fearful that black America, especially, would take umbrage. "Paul says a man may live and work in many countries," she wrote Carl Murphy, president of the *Afro-American* newspaper chain and Robeson's chief supporter in the black press, "but a man's HOME is where his family is, where his people are, and where his roots are. All these, for Paul, are in the United States. Period." Murphy wrote back to reassure her that "None of us took seriously press reports that he had or would make his permanent home in England."[16]

On October 11 Robeson took part in a historic service at St. Paul's Cathedral. Church officials departed from custom and authorized a collection for a South African defense fund and then broke further with tradition by inviting Robeson to give a half-hour recital during Evensong—the first time either a secular artist or a black would sing in the cathedral. Four thousand people, including many nonwhites, crammed into an Evensong service that ordinarily drew four to five hundred. Standing where John Wycliff had been tried for heresy and Bishop Tyndale's New Testament had been publicly burned, Robeson read the First Lesson, ". . . and let there be war no more." After the sermon, he returned twice to the lectern to sing spirituals, with Larry Brown accompanying. Peggy Middleton, who sat with Essie in the first row, afterward wrote that "there were tears on many faces" at the poignancy of the occasion and the compassion and nobility of Robeson's presentation. The London papers widely reported the event as a historic one.[17]

When Paul went back on tour, Essie returned to the United States for two weeks to cover the UN General Assembly sessions and to consider renting out the Jumel Terrace house (but in fact she did not). In December she flew to Accra to attend the All African People's Conference, about which she did a syndicated series of articles for the Associated Negro Press. Back in London, she and Paul attended a party for Krishna Menon, had tea with Nan Pandit at the Indian Embassy, and dined with Marie Seton to celebrate the publication of her book about Paul. In between, they collected clothes and packed for a trip to Prague, Moscow, and India scheduled to begin on December 23.[18]

When word got out that Robeson was planning to visit India, Val Washington, a black member of the Republican national committee, got on the phone to Acting Secretary of State Christian Herter. He relayed to Herter the concern voiced by P. Chakravarty (a UN delegate from India and also permanent secretary of the Congress Party) that the Indian Communists were planning to lay "great stress" on Robeson's trip and to acclaim him "as the greatest and most important negro leader in the United States." Chakravarty had further told Val Washington that Robeson would "do great damage among the darker Indians if [he] gets away with the kind of propaganda he wants, allowing the already powerful Communist Party in India to attract still more converts." Chakravarty "wondered," Val Washington reported to Herter, "if there were not steps we could take to counteract the impact of Robeson's visit." Herter replied that he "would look into the matter immediately."[19]

Picking up on the concern, U.S. Ambassador to India Ellsworth Bunker let it be known that Robeson's visit, like the celebration of his sixtieth birthday which had preceded it, would not be viewed kindly in the United States. The U.S. Information Agency sent out material on Robeson "for discreet but widespread placement with Indian newspapermen," emphasizing that "he was not being persecuted as a champion of the Negro." Bunker reported to Secretary of State Dulles that he had told American officials in India to boycott any political function in which Robeson was involved but advised that "a few official Americans be permitted to attend Robeson concerts"—"to walk out unobtrusively," however, should Robeson indulge in any "tirade against U.S. and American democracy." Dulles telegraphed back, "Assume walkout would be extreme last resort since publicity gain for Robeson resulting from publicized walkout would be considerable and possibly detrimental U.S. interests." One heavily censored CIA dispatch contained suggestions on how to prevent Robeson's forthcoming visit from being used as an occasion for attempting to desegregate a local swimming pool.[20]

Ultimately, and for other reasons entirely, Robeson's trip to India did not come off. On the day the Robesons were due to leave London, Essie, packing up Paul's suitcases, went to get his passport—and discovered it was lost. She spent hours searching the flat without finding it, and became "panic-stricken"—a rare state for the unflappable Essie. She decided to wake Paul. He took the news calmly, called Harold Davison to see if he had forgotten to return the passport (he hadn't) after taking it to secure a work permit. Paul then helped Essie search the flat again, without success. By then it was time to leave for Prague, where Paul was booked for television and radio performances on Christmas Eve. They telephoned Prague for advice and were told to forget the passport and to try to make it through. British Immigration officials at the London airport cooperated, letting them board the plane after hearing their tale of woe.[21]

Then, an hour into the flight, fog descended, closing the Prague airport and forcing the plane to land in Zurich. Swiss Immigration agreed to let the Robesons spend the night, but by the next morning the fog had thickened and all airports in Czechoslovakia were shut down. Getting on one of the few planes leaving for London, they landed—after a hair-raising trip—at Southend, outside London. Immigration officials recognized Paul and gave him an emergency entrance permit. The next day Essie took the flat apart room by room, drawer by drawer, file by file—and finally found the precious passport. She sat down in the middle of the floor and cried. On December 29 the weather cleared and the Robesons—too late for his engagements in Prague—took off by jet, along with Du Bois and his wife, Shirley Graham, for Moscow. Du Bois, aged ninety, had also gotten his passport back and had begun to travel extensively. When he had arrived in England (where he and Shirley had stayed for a time with the Robesons) in August 1958, the *Daily Worker* had reported that Du Bois viewed "his own persecution with a calm detachment. But as he speaks of Paul Robeson his face becomes angry. 'What they have done to Paul has been the most cruel thing I have ever seen,' he said."[22]

New Year's Eve in Moscow was a formal affair, with engraved invitations to dinner at eleven in the Kremlin. In the tapestry-hung reception room, Khrushchev and other Presidium members greeted the guests, who were then ushered into the marble Georgian Hall, where long tables had been spread for a feast. Robeson spotted Du Bois and Shirley, who were habitually early and already seated. Both men stood up, and as they made their way toward each other, weaving through the crowded tables, people stopped talking to watch them. When they embraced in the middle of the banquet hall, the entire crowd, including Khrushchev, stood and applauded; after a moment of stunned surprise, as if noticing for the first time where they were, Robeson and Du Bois broke into laughter. At exactly five minutes before midnight, Khrushchev proposed a toast, the lights dimmed, and suddenly—as Shirley Du Bois described it—"all around us snow seemed to be falling, the Christmas tree of many colors gleamed, and then far up in the Kremlin tower we heard the solemn, slow striking of the clock. . . . When the last stroke died away, the orchestra played, all the lights blazed and an array of butlers bearing large, silver trays began plying us with food. Ulanova danced, the Oistrakhs, father and son, played, and when the performing artists appeared together on stage for the finale, two of the opera stars unexpectedly went out into the audience to where Robeson was sitting and led him back up to the stage. The orchestra struck up 'Fatherland' and Robeson's voice 'boomed out as he led the chorus.' "[23]

A few days later Robeson came down with yet another cold. This time there was an added complication: unexplained bouts of dizziness. Simultaneously, Essie began to have uterine bleeding and went in for a curettage. It revealed "an irregular arrangement of cells" that the doctors diagnosed as a "precancerous condition of the mouth of the uterus." They recommended that she enter the Kremlin Hospital for treatment, but before doing so she persuaded them to let her return to the hotel to collect her things and to help Paul pack for his scheduled trip to India on January 12. She found him not only feeling a lot worse, but also having failed to call a doctor as he had promised. "I was waiting for you to get home," he told her—"Can you imagine?!" an indignantly pleased Essie wrote Marie Seton. Essie promptly got a physician to look him over. A consultant was then called in, and the doctors told Paul he had to be hospitalized immediately.[24]

He refused. He was scheduled to perform in concert that same day, and in the evening was due to leave for New Delhi; he wanted, characteristically, to honor his commitments. ("Paul has the duty idea in a very bad form," wrote a disapproving Essie; "he has a very great dread of disappointing people, and once he promises anything, he will do it or drop dead.") The next day he felt still worse, becoming "frightfully dizzy" whenever he tried to get up. He confessed for the first time to Essie that he had often been dizzy before and had had spots before his eyes at concerts. He also confessed that he had been feeling under "continuing strain," concerned that he might not be able "to do all the things he finds himself agreeing to do"; the worry "has got him down." Fearing a stroke, Essie suggested it was "the perfect time for us to step off the merry-go-round, and collect ourselves and re-organize our lives, especially our health."[25]

Another consultant was called in and also insisted that Paul go to the hospital. "Scared," he "listened meekly" and finally consented. And so, on the morning of January 12, 1959—the day they had intended to leave for India—Paul and Essie were both admitted to the Kremlin Hospital, he into a private room on the fourth floor, she into similar accommodations on the second. When it was announced that Paul would not be performing his scheduled concert that day in Moscow, rumors flew that he had somehow been injured. A crowd gathered at the Metropole Hotel, where the Robesons had been staying, anxiously inquiring about his health, asking what might be done to help, dispersing only after officials reassured them that Robeson was in good hands. Paul cried when told of the crowd's distress and concern.[26]

He was given a battery of tests. Initially there was some worry about a possible heart condition, but finally his low blood-pressure readings and continuing dizziness were ascribed to an "acute state of exhaustion." The doctors insisted on a total rest for a minimum of ten days, probably longer, which precluded the trip to India. Paul turned "mulish," Essie reported home, but the doctors, seconded by Essie, finally managed to persuade him that the changes in climate and water, "not to say anything about the enormous strain of another National Welcome," would affect his health for the worse. On January 14 Essie herself began therapy, having radium inserted into the mouth of her uterus, requiring that she lie still for twenty-four hours after each treatment. For the first two days of hospitalization, she had gone up in the elevator to visit Paul; now, when she was prostrate, he came down and watched television with her (including the sessions of the Twenty-first Party Congress). On the days she was allowed up, Essie worked away at her typewriter—eventually turning out no fewer than ten articles during her hospital stay.[27]

Next came the problem of what to do about *Othello,* scheduled to begin rehearsing at Stratford in mid-February. Robeson had had reservations about playing the role from the beginning, apprehensive that after so long an absence from the stage he would fail to measure up to what was being widely billed as a "historic" event and the "jewel in the crown of his career." As bouts of dizziness continued in the hospital, Essie reminded him that *Othello* demanded "sudden, vigorous brave moves and strides" and insisted it was "madness" for him to undertake the part. Paul finally agreed to cancel, and Essie so notified Glen Byam Shaw, who at first tried to recast the role but then cabled Robeson begging him to reconsider ("I implore you Paul to help me or [the] Stratford season will be ruined"). He promised to adjust rehearsal and performance schedules in such a way as to minimize all strain on him.[28]

By then Paul was feeling considerably better, and getting restless. On February 5 he left the hospital for a month's stay at Barveekha Sanatorium, the plush rest home for government officials and distinguished foreign visitors, while Essie stayed behind for continuing radium treatments followed by a gamma-ray series as an additional precaution. At Barveekha, ice skating and a careful diet further increased Paul's zest (though failing actually to reduce his weight). Mulling over Shaw's offer, he began to view it as an opportunity to get back into harness on terms that would minimize risk to his reputation. He would be able to concentrate—with due advance warning to colleagues and the press—on the vocal aspects of the role, the aspects he felt most comfortable with, and to minimize the physical movement, with which he did not. With the burden now "on other shoulders, not his," as Essie explained it, the essential responsibility would be "with them, and they will be very grateful if he just appears." Paul wired Glen Byam Shaw his acceptance. Shaw was ecstatic; he even promised that special light costumes would be designed so that Paul would not "have to carry a lot of weight." Paul now looked forward to the engagement, "not with dread, as before, but with anticipation and interest."[29]

On March 9 Robeson left Barveekha for London. "I think everything will be fine," Essie wrote Sam and Helen Rosen, "if he just doesn't beat his brains out with the extra curricular activities." Always eager to spare him whether he wished it or not, Essie put off telling him until the last minute that she would have to stay behind in the Kremlin Hospital; the doctors were pleased with the results of the radium and gamma treatments, but wanted her to complete the series before joining Paul in Stratford later in the month. Met at the London airport by reporters—who noted his weight loss and thought he looked older than his years—Robeson took the occasion to say that he thought his performance as Othello would now have to be a "muted" one, and to thank the able team of Soviet doctors who had looked after him and the many well-wishers who had sent encouraging messages. He added good-humoredly that "many people seemed to be more worried" about the effect of the illness "on my voice than about me," and apparently "wouldn't have minded if I had to crawl back from Moscow on crutches, just as long as I can still sing." Essie, writing privately to Paul, Jr., struck a less wry and more overtly angry note: "I mean to begin to preserve the Robesons first, and then do what I can for everybody else. If that's not political maturity, then write me down as an INFANT, period. Everybody else nearly got us killed once, and I say NEVER NO MORE. Which does not mean I am signing off, but it does mean I'm cautious, as from now. . . . People!!! I'm thoroughly disgusted. Not even an 'if you are well enough,' or 'if you are not tired,' merely please, please, please, you owe it to the cause, etc. And there are about ten causes. Sheer disgusting exploitation."[30]

With the April 7 opening less than a month away, Robeson went straight to Stratford to begin rehearsals. He was accompanied by Joseph ("Andy") Andrews, who since the early days in England had served him both as valet and friend. At Stratford, Robeson moved into a suite of spare rooms in a large converted farmhouse in Shottery, on the outskirts of town. It was owned by Mrs. Whitfield, described by her son-in-law Andrew Faulds (an actor who later became a Labour Party member from Stratford) as "a very old-fashioned sort of English lady, conservative with a small 'c' and totally unaware politically." Unexpectedly—to her family—she became "devoted to Paul," enamored of his "extraordinary courtesy and good manners"; she developed immense "respect for this man, and she had had no knowledge of him, either as an artist or a politician." When Robeson was not rehearsing, he lived as a member of the Whitfield clan, wandering into Mrs. Whitfield's sitting room for a chat, relaxing in the garden with Faulds and his wife and the two other Whitfield daughters, Mary and Thisbe. When Faulds talked politics with Robeson, he got the sense of, "well, 'melancholy' is the only word, of disappointment, of profound disappointment in how things had happened in the world . . . an immense awareness of the intractable bloody problems of the world at large." But "the overall feel of Paul in Stratford was of personal happiness." Among other things, he had a brief affair during these months, which he remembered with great tenderness. Robeson was, in several ways, enjoying a restoration.[31]

The twenty-seven-year-old director, Tony Richardson, had won instant fame for his vivid, brisk staging of John Osborne's path-breaking play, *Look Back in Anger.* In turning his hand to *Othello,* Richardson cast in a contemporary spirit, choosing Osborne's wife, Mary Ure, to play Desdemona, and the American actor Sam Wanamaker for Iago, but he interpreted the text conservatively. Ignoring the revisionist and iconoclastic views of the critic F. R. Leavis that *Othello* is the story of a self-dramatizing narcissist, Richardson settled instead for the traditional view of Othello as the Noble Moor brought down by the machinations of an alien world. This romantic Moor—steadfast, dignified, honorable, put-upon, loving—is almost certainly the only kind of Othello Robeson had any interest in play-

ing, or could play. And it was in the mainstream tradition of recent Stratford Othellos—of Godfrey Tearle in 1948, Anthony Quayle in 1954, and
also the portrayals of Richard Burton and John Neville in alternating
performances of Othello and Iago at the Old Vic in 1956. Not until 1964,
at the National Theatre of Great Britain, would Laurence Olivier attempt
a "Leavis" Othello—and triumph.

Since Robeson was the kind of actor who majestically played an aspect
of himself and could not (like an Olivier) inhabit a variety of characters
foreign to his being, Tony Richardson was obliged to tailor his conception
of *Othello* to his lead player. The logical path—if the goal was consistency—
would have been to opt for a production style consonant with Robeson's
own. Instead, Richardson mounted a production basically at odds with his
star's gravity and reserve, filling the stage with flashy special effects that
called maximum attention to his own lively powers of invention—rock-
and-roll drumbeats, Great Danes dashing across the footlights, a deathbed
scene enacted on an elevated platform. Moreover, he allowed Sam Wanamaker to play Iago with the Midwestern twang and strut of a slick confidence man, and Mary Ure to portray Desdemona as if she were acting in
an Arnold Wesker kitchen-sink drama. (The supporting cast included a
remarkable number of future stars: Albert Finney as Cassio, Roy Dotrice
as the second Montano officer, Zoe Caldwell as Bianca, and—lost in a
crowd of anonymous Venetian Citizens—Diana Rigg and Vanessa Redgrave.) All this made for moments of immense vivacity—but at the expense of emotional coherence, and with the additional danger of making
Robeson, with his sonorous tones and serious demeanor, look like an
anachronism.

The critics, an old-fashioned lot on the whole, voted for tradition,
praising Robeson and decrying the gimmicky production that had threatened to swamp him. A few—including the prestigious *Times* and Manchester *Guardian* reviewers—lumped production and star together, dismissing
the entire evening as a tricky failure; several others expressed concern that
the subtleties of the verse continued—as in his 1930 performance of the
role—to elude Robeson, declamation too often displacing feeling. But the
critical majority succumbed to the authority of his stage presence, and
congratulated him for having risen above the circumstances of the production. W. A. Darlington, dean of the London critics, ranked Robeson's
Othello among the best he had ever seen, the *News Chronicle* hailed it as
"superb," and even Lord Beaverbrook's *Daily Express,* which for years had
conducted a political vendetta against him, praised his "strong and stately"
portrayal (though suggesting it was a triumph of "presence not acting").[32]

Robeson was more than pleased; he was grateful. Given the obstacles
of an uncongenial production, a recent illness, and the many years that had
elapsed since his last appearance in a play, he felt lucky to have extracted
some power from the role. It was doubtless with real relief that he told a

reporter from the London *Daily Mirror*, "I am overwhelmed by the reception I have been given." He was gratified, too, at the public response. The play immediately sold out its seven-month run, and long lines formed nightly in the hope of last-minute tickets. On opening night itself, the audience gave him an ecstatic fifteen curtain calls (Sam Wanamaker pushed Robeson forward and led the cast in applauding him). Essie, who arrived in Stratford at the end of March in good time for the opening, wrote Freda Diamond that it had been a "terrific personal triumph." Helen Rosen, who had also arrived for the opening (the Rosens and Robesons had intended to rendezvous in India in January), found him undismayed by the few negatives: "He had never claimed that he was a great actor," she recalls, and had always tended to agree with critics who pointed to his incomplete technical mastery. Peggy Ashcroft, too, was on Robeson's side. Disappointed with what she saw in 1959, she put the blame in equal parts on "a production that did not suit his particular genius," on a "technique that had not developed," and on the fact that he was "surrounded by actors of a more modern style."[33]

Once the hectic first few weeks were over, Robeson settled into a more relaxed stride. His schedule called for four, then three, then two performances a week for the rest of the play's seven-month run, leaving him considerable free time for interim engagements. Requests came thick and fast, and at almost every performance friends and admirers crowded backstage to offer good wishes. Essie alternated with Andy in deciding who got through the net; among those who made it were Du Bois and Shirley Graham, Bob and Clara Rockmore, the lawyer Milton Friedman, Oginga Odinga of Kenya, Peter Abrahams of South Africa, Joshua Nkomo of Rhodesia, Reverend and Mrs. Stephen Fritchman (the left-wing minister who had hosted two of Robeson's 1957 concerts in California). In late May, Sam Rosen arrived from the United States to join Helen for a few days; in July, Paul, Jr., and Marilyn brought their two children over. Robeson lived in the village several days a week, but Essie increasingly stayed in London, at their Connaught Square apartment. She was having trouble getting her strength back and needed rest; besides, she and Paul were not getting along well—the FBI even picked up a rumor that the couple would soon formally separate.[34]

Between performances of the play, he pursued an active schedule, though "he tires greatly" (Essie wrote the Soviet filmmaker Katanian) and occasionally had to cancel an engagement because of exhaustion. Only two weeks after opening night, he joined Peggy Ashcroft, along with various foreign diplomats and the company of actors, in a procession through the town of Stratford to commemorate Shakespeare's birthday. Ashcroft remembers that twenty or thirty young people suddenly broke from the curb on the pavement to join Robeson in the procession—"following him as if he were the Pied Piper." She thought that "in the year of the Sharpeville Massacre" in South Africa, they saw in Robeson, even though he "was no longer a household name, the symbol of black and oppressed people with whom they were in sympathy. . . . It was very moving." But on the train ride together back to London, Ashcroft found him "withdrawn and sad." Possibly the reaction of the young reminded him of the civil-rights struggle going on back home, which was proceeding without him and which he yearned to join.[35]

That same month, Robeson joined another old friend, the deported American Communist Claudia Jones, at the West Indian Caribbean Festival in London, and subsequently spoke in support of the West Indian *Gazette,* which she had helped to found (and even promised he was "going to do something for her paper)." With the weight of the *Othello* opening behind him, Robeson began to make other political appearances and pronouncements. In April he took part in the African Freedom Day concert sponsored by the Movement for Colonial Freedom. He told the rally, "The struggle is not one of individual people; it is a collective struggle," and credited the Soviet Union—emphasizing his point "with a clenched fist," according to the report from the U.S. Embassy to the Secretary of State— with being a positive force in the fight for African freedom. Only the *Daily Worker* on the left and Lord Beaverbrook's *Daily Express* on the right covered Robeson's Africa Day appearance, each reporting in predictable style: the *Express* blasted him for abusing British hospitality by spending his day off taking part "in a rally whose object was to denounce the British Empire."[36]

The *Express* was hardly mollified when, that same week, Robeson sang to a huge disarmament rally in Trafalgar Square—and followed that in June with yet another appearance at a tumultuous ban-the-H-bomb gathering. That same month he made a forty-eight-hour trip to Prague to attend the Congress of Socialist Culture, and in early August joined Paul, Jr., and Marilyn at the World Youth Festival in Vienna. The U.S. Embassy in London notified the State Department of Robeson's Continental travels, and American legal attachés abroad alerted J. Edgar Hoover. U.S. press representatives were also present when he strode to the platform at the Youth Festival in Vienna on August 3 to be greeted by a roar of applause, a deluge of flowers, and, at the close, some "anti-Communist" catcalls from members of the American delegation, which were relayed back home on CBS television and reported in *The New York Times.*[37]

In his speech in Vienna, Robeson reflected on the disappointment many American blacks felt at the rising tide of white resistance to desegregation in the South, and on the fact that "eighteen million of us do not have full freedom." But *The New York Times* chose to relegate that portion of his speech to a parenthetical clause and to focus instead on what it called his "general attack on his country's foreign policy," headlining its article "Robeson Sees Rise of Fascism in U.S." The *Times* further reported that when delegates critical of his stand tried to question his views, they were "shouted down or ruled out of order by the Communists, who control the program." It was not the sort of publicity likely to make Robeson seem (as he very much wished) a desirable comrade-in-arms to the black leaders of the civil-rights struggle; whether or not the *Times* was deliberately attempting to keep the "radical" Robeson distanced from the movement, it made a decided contribution to that end.[38]

Returning from the festival, Robeson used the few hours during a plane change in Budapest to give a speech and an interview to the Hungarian Telegraph Office. The gesture created a delicate situation, and on two counts: Robeson had publicly supported Soviet intervention during the Hungarian uprising of 1956; plus, his American passport was clearly stamped "Not Valid for Travel in Hungary." By making himself visible in Budapest, he risked offending the people of one nation and the authorities of his own. He minimized the first danger by confining his remarks while in Budapest to generalities. Never once mentioning the U.S.S.R. by name, he instead spoke glowingly of his belief in Socialist Man and his personal feelings of affection for the Hungarian people. The second danger was not so successfully navigated. In defying the ban on travel to Hungary, Robeson had given the State Department an opportunity to invalidate his newly won passport—especially since he had alluded to an intention to go to China soon, also a forbidden travel area.[39]

Frances G. Knight, head of the Passport Division, sent an airgram to American posts in Budapest and elsewhere requesting additional information on what Robeson had said and what his prospective travel plans might be. The State Department directed the U.S. Embassy in London to contact Robeson for direct verification of whether he had visited Hungary and if so what he had said there. After the Embassy had sent him two registered letters, and after he had had a chance to confer with Bob Rockmore in the States and D. N. Pritt (who had been counsel to Jomo Kenyatta) in England, Robeson confirmed that it had indeed been his "privilege and deep pleasure" to find himself in Budapest on a regular stopover made by the Dutch KLM plane on which he had been traveling. He pointed out, by way of mitigation, that American athletes had recently competed in Hungary "in a very friendly atmosphere" and that American businessmen and artists had been in the country as well. Since Robeson had technically been in transit only, and since he had been "getting less and less publicity" of late, Frances Knight argued it should be kept that way, and the State Department decided to delay passport action against him until his intentions with regard to a trip to China were made clear. The State Department was about to play out yet another war of nerves.[40]

The British continued to treat Robeson as a beloved celebrity, not a potential subversive. The BBC decided to feature him in a series of ten

Sunday-night radio broadcasts and also to offer on the Home Service "The Paul Robeson Story," featuring Ronald Adam, Marie Burke, and Dame Sybil Thorndike ("The radio series is going like a house-a-fire," Essie wrote Helen Rosen, "and the fan mail is fabulous"). On television, Robeson was first paired with Yehudi Menuhin for a conversation about music that *The New Statesman,* not given to overpraise, found so stimulating that it absolved television for the "hours of muck" that made up its ordinary fare (a gratifying dividend for Robeson was Menuhin's apparent expression of interest in his musical theories). A second television program, with the British jazzman Johnny Dankworth sharing the billing, was not nearly so well received: "too many mutual compliments, too much nebulous waffle," was the opinion of *Variety.* That one misfire aside, Robeson's radio and television appearances produced so much favorable comment and such a deluge of fan letters that the BBC decided to schedule yet another series, for 1960. Essie periodically expressed concern that Paul might not be getting enough rest, but, after nearly a decade of enforced silence, he seemed willing to run the risk. Although white America rarely reported on Robeson, the Pittsburgh *Courier* headlined to black America, "Paul Robeson Great Success in Britain."[41]

On October 13, 1959, Essie wrote Claude Barnett of the Associated Negro Press, asking for accreditation as a roving reporter so she could cover Khrushchev's planned visit to Africa in January. "Have had quite a struggle with my health," she wrote Barnett, "but am finally beginning to get back my energy." Barnett immediately sent her a press card, but soon after, she came down with "terrific and blinding pain"—and Essie was not a complainer. She wrote the truth to Sam and Helen Rosen, whose discretion and intelligence she had come to trust (though, given Paul's involvement with Helen, a certain distanced politeness remained the rule). To the Rosens she confessed that she had "pain everywhere," but begged them to "keep mum, please, please," since "Paul has no idea how very bad things are with me. . . . He already has his own affairs to cope with, and there is nothing he could do, anyway." Essie feared that her cancer had recurred, and the Rosens recommended that she see J. B. Blaikely, a leading gynecologist who had headed a team of British doctors cooperating with Soviet physicians on radiation treatment. Blaikely put her in the hospital for exploratory surgery. He found no sign of a recurrence and assured Essie that the doctors in Moscow had "done a wonderful job." Her pain, he decided, was from an ulcer on the front wall of the rectum, a common aftereffect of radiation therapy, and advised her that if she maintained a bland diet it would heal itself within six to nine months.[42]

Paul took Essie home from the hospital on November 14, and she arranged for her friend Peggy Middleton to come in twice a week and help with her letters. Essie reported to Freda Diamond, "Paul is *so* relieved and happy that it isn't cancer, that he is quite thoughtful and useful." To the Rosens she sent a less glowing version of domestic life: "I give him full run of the living room and his bedroom, while I have my bedroom and the dining room. It works out very well." On November 26 Paul made his last appearance as Othello and was called back for ten curtain calls. He had not missed a single performance in seven months, but the grind had been far more difficult than he publicly acknowledged. "It's been wonderful but a constant hazard," he wrote Helen Rosen near the end of the run, "the going has been tough—and I've resorted to all means of self hypnosis between performances—languages—music—sleep—investigation of the ways of various nationalities—travel. . . . Have done fairly well in some regions." Yet at one point, he confessed, he had become so lonesome for her that he had "debated flying over (really) in between engagements." When his old theatrical friend Flora Robson came to see his performance, he confided to her that he was having great difficulty remembering the lines and had to have a prompter on hand all the time. With the show now finally closed, he decided on a complete rest before beginning a three-month British concert tour with Larry Brown in mid-February.[43]

In January 1960 Paul and Essie went for a three-week stay in Moscow to complete their rest cure and to have medical checkups. The Moscow doctors put Essie in the hospital to evaluate her continuing pain and to give her a blood transfusion. After a week of exhausting procedures, they told her the location of the ulcerated area, high on the wall of the rectum, made it difficult to treat, but assured her they could help; she settled in for a period of outpatient therapy that would continue long after Paul had returned to London. *His* health was found to be "very fine." Essie reported home that "he is in excellent shape, considerably overweight, and a little tired. No exhaustion as before and they are all very pleased with him. . . ." She also reported that he was "very happy." He made radio and television appearances, spoke and sang at a mass meeting in his honor at Ball Bearing Plant No. 1, attended the Chekhov hundredth-anniversary celebration, met with the *Izvestia* staff, participated in sessions of the World Peace Committee, and in between took out a week to rest at the Barveekha Sanatorium. He is "having a ball," Essie wrote, though "nobody likes his [Othello] beard and mustache, which he still wears and still likes—says it makes him look Abyssinian!" The U.S. Embassy in Moscow also reported on his activities: his "television appearance and press statements were notably uniform in including laudatory mention of the Soviet troop reduction announcement, in mesh with the current Soviet propaganda exploitation of this item."[44]

Paul returned to London on February 7, while Essie remained for additional treatments. John Pittman, a black American Communist who had come with his family to live as a correspondent in the Soviet Union, had an apartment a few doors down from Essie, and the writer Albert Kahn was also nearby. "So between her American and Russian friends," Paul wrote Helen Rosen, "she'll be all right." He, however, was far less resourceful than Essie about ordinary daily matters and within a few weeks of returning to London was writing to Helen, "The apartment is rather lonely these days. No one to get breakfast and no peanut brittle." The new British tour, beginning on February 21 and lasting until May 15, took up the slack.[45]

He had avoided giving concerts in the Soviet Union because the sound arrangements were rarely adequate, but in England most of his concerts were booked in acoustically sophisticated cinemas. Nor did he have to worry about the provincial reception. In a thirty-two-city tour that led up to Manchester, Edinburgh, and Aberdeen and back down through Hull, Liverpool, and Birmingham, he was greeted with nearly unanimous praise, though the actual turnout proved disappointing (he grossed about eighty-five hundred pounds). Bob Rockmore, who had been expecting substantial sums from Paul's overseas earnings to pay off his commitments at home and to provide a nest egg for later years, began to complain again about "the expenditure of too much money by everybody concerned," and was hardly appeased when Paul cabled him to give the proceeds of his share ($1,650) from the sale of some property to his brother Ben.[46]

In talking with reporters during his tour stopovers, Robeson struck something of a valedictory note: having succeeded at Stratford, he said, "I can now relax, feel that my artistic life has been fulfilled and hope to continue at a good level without any startling plans." Though he pretty much avoided discussing politics with the press, he didn't hesitate to attend the thirtieth anniversary of the London *Daily Worker* or to celebrate May Day with the Scottish miners, telling the assembled crowd, "You will need all the strength you have got to see that you who create the wealth of the country have a chance to enjoy it." But even in Glasgow, with people calling out warmly on the streets, "Paul, stay with us!," he continued to show signs of erratic mood swings. One man who had known him before couldn't get over "how much he'd aged and how tense he was," once losing his temper with his well-regarded accompanist Harry Carmichael— a lapse in courtesy unthinkable for Robeson at any previous point in his life.[47]

On his return to London, Robeson spent most of the next month making a second series of radio broadcasts for the BBC to release the following year, and then, on June 18, went to East Berlin for two days to participate in the third annual press festival sponsored by *Neues Deutschland*, official organ of the Communist Party. It was a considerable gesture, with the GDR unrecognized in the West and thought to be near collapse (soon after, the Berlin Wall went up). In appreciation, the East Germans built Robeson a special bed big enough for his huge size, and assigned him both a private doctor and a bodyguard (he was a small man, but he reassured

Robeson, "Never mind, Paul, I can just cover your heart"). Robeson appeared as the featured artist during the ceremonies officially opening the festival and held a press conference at which he said that in the autumn he hoped to make an extended visit to the East European socialist countries; he also said he planned to return to the United States. Indeed, his homesickness had been growing. During the run of *Othello,* Andrew Faulds had sensed "a keen desire on his part to get back to America," to "get back with the folks"—though his wish to be part of the burgeoning civil-rights struggle he had helped to inaugurate alternated with the realization that the NAACP and even Martin Luther King, Jr., would be reluctant to share a platform with him.[48]

Otto Nathan saw him in London and reported to Robeson's lawyer Leonard Boudin that he "is not very happy, he does not look well." Paul himself confessed as much to Helen Rosen. While still on tour he had written her, ". . . desolate without you—crying for you—Got de *Blues* and too damn *mean* to cry—No! I'm almost weepin—Tell Odessa [the Rosens' housekeeper] to come over here and get me and bring me back. . . . That's the 'blues' or 'secular' side of my personality talking. . . ." Five days later he wrote her that everything was going "fine" but that it "all gets a little desolate now and then—no matter how wonderful things are in general." Then he uncharacteristically spelled out his new priority of needs: ". . . I never thought that friends would one day out-weigh the seemingly all-powerful social and political drives. . . . All the *slogans* in the world can't replace even *hours* of concern and tenderness—let *alone* years and years. Funny how that complete 'inner security' springs up when surrounded and 'encircled' as in Katonah . . . somehow loses some of its power when surrounded without question by the respect and deep affection of thousands and thousands. Strange but true."[49]

Two months later he was still writing Helen frequently and still sounding the same desolate themes: "I'm so lonely. Doesn't seem to improve at all . . . Suppose you'll head to the country [Katonah]. Boy! What a few weeks there would do! What you say!" "If only those 'blokes' could *improve* the atmosphere," he wrote her yet another time, "a trip [home] might be possible." American artists like Nat King Cole, Sammy Davis, Jr., and Diahann Carroll were "jumping back and forth" from the States to England—"Why can't I do the opposite? . . . makes one really homesick." (While making a speech during these same months in which he referred to "my country," Robeson blurted out, ". . . any time my folks say they need me, if it's tomorrow morning, I'll get back there don't worry, bet your life I will.") Helen was startled to get Paul's letters: both their frequency and their content were highly atypical. It made her wonder what special pressures might be working within him. At just this time, ironically, the FBI was reporting that Robeson "has taken up permanent overseas residence," and the Washington *Post* headlined a rare U.S. report on him, "Robeson Tours as 'Exile' " (*self-*exiled, the article went on to claim).[50]

As much as Robeson yearned for home, the signals he got from the States were mixed. Old friends like Earl Robinson wrote that "the climate really does seem more favorable than negative for peace and progress." Daily headlines described the spread of sit-ins and the birth of the Student Non-Violent Coordinating Committee (SNCC), marking a more militant phase in the black struggle and generating, in the growing circle of liberal, labor, religious, and campus support, a more sympathetic Northern white response to it. By 1960, too, a dozen African nations had gained independence, led by Ghana's successful revolution in 1957. Yet the newspaper accounts also made clear that the actual pace of progress in the white South remained slow and uncertain. Six years after the Supreme Court's desegregation decision, only 6 percent of Southern schools were integrated, and the rate of compliance in ending disenfranchisement was still so glacial that fewer than one in four blacks of voting age in the South could register.[51]

When the Democrats named John F. Kennedy and Lyndon Johnson to head their 1960 presidential ticket, some saw it as harbinger of vigorous federal commitment to civil-rights legislation, but Essie and Paul were not among them. The ticket "is really American," Essie sarcastically wrote Freda Diamond. "Millions, Irish Catholic Boston background, and the South. What a combination. I will be deeply interested to see if Negroes will vote for THAT combination. If they do, shame on them. I also will be interested to see what The Left will do in this dilemma: they simply cannot vote for Kennedy-Johnson, equally they simply cannot vote for Mr. War Tricky Dicky [Nixon], so perhaps, if they have any principle at all, they will just NOT vote. I wouldn't pollute my vote by casting for either of that stink." Just before Kennedy narrowly won the election, Robeson was asked at a press conference in East Berlin whether he thought the Democratic nominee represented "the other America." "Maybe you'd better define what you mean by the other America," Robeson replied. "The other America for me is Jefferson, Lincoln, Harriet Tubman, Frederick Douglass, Franklin D. Roosevelt. Kennedy is just about as dangerous as anybody else. He does not represent the Democratic Party's great traditions, but is, like Nixon, a firm supporter of NATO and he wants more bases, not fewer."[52]

Essie, unlike Paul, felt no particular pull to return to the United States. After four months of treatment in Moscow, she arrived back in London in May, but her recovery continued to be erratic—"just when I think I've turned a corner for the better," there is "blood, pain, etc." She tried to live from day to day and characteristically pushed herself to maximum activity with minimal self-pity. She had hoped to attend the African Women's Conference in Ghana, but had to forgo the trip. Paul, on the other hand, was again feeling energetic, and accepted a new batch of invitations to attend functions on the Continent. But before embarking on yet another round of what Essie called his "rat race" of commitments, he decided to take off some weight. He had gone up to 282 pounds, and Essie alternately described him as a "walking mountain" and an "over-stuffed divan." Taking an injection of gonadotropine every morning to "break up the entrenched fat," and sticking to a diet of five hundred calories a day, he lost forty pounds in forty days. He "looks and feels like a million dollars," Essie reported.[53]

In his trim new appearance, his mood swing once more heading upward, Robeson set off for Paris early in September to participate in a festival for the fortieth anniversary of the Communist paper *L'Humanité* in the working-class suburb of La Courneuve. The huge throng that turned out for the festival gave him a thunderous greeting, and privately he was entertained by *L'Humanité* editors Etienne Fajon, René Andrieu, and André Carrel, who brought him together both with French Communist officials and with visiting Soviet artists. From Paris he went to Budapest (the State Department had recently made travel to Hungary legal for American citizens) and then, after a two-week break back in London, returned to East Berlin for a four-day visit. Feeling much improved by then, Essie accompanied him to the GDR for what proved a series of stately ceremonials.[54]

At Humboldt University's 150th anniversary celebration, Robeson was awarded an honorary Doctor of Philosophy degree. After the ceremonies, standing on a balcony overlooking the massed crowd on Unter den Linden, Robeson sang "John Brown's Body" and "Ol' Man River"; the stiff German professors surrounding him on the balcony, as a gesture to their honored guest, broke uneasily into their own *very* special accompaniment version of "John Brown's Body." Aware that the evangelist Billy Graham was conducting meetings across the border dividing East and West Berlin, Robeson commented, "Why doesn't he go down to Alabama instead and preach about brotherhood?" Later in the day the Robesons were individually awarded prizes by the East German peace movement. That evening the honors were completed at a gala that called for "full medals." Surveying his assorted awards, Robeson asked Franz and Diana Loesser with dismay which one he was supposed to wear. "I'm afraid all of them," Franz said. Robeson grimaced and said he would wear only one—picking out a handmade medal given him by the students of Humboldt. At the Central Youth Club that same night a performance of folk songs and dances was put on in his honor in a hall jammed to capacity with five thousand people and graced by the presence of Walter Ulbricht and Otto Grotewohl, leading members of the government. Robeson spontaneously joined a group of African students from Leipzig in a dance, then later spoke and sang to the crowd. It was, he told them, "one of the most moving days of my sixty-two-year-old life." As the climax of the evening, Helene Weigl, the widow of Bertolt Brecht, presented Robeson with a silk cloth bearing a reproduction of Picasso's peace dove—symbol of the Berliner Ensemble—and Chairman Ulbricht pinned on him the Order of the Star of International Friendship; Robeson was the first person given the award.[55]

"In a socialist country," Robeson told a reporter on his return to London, "I give my services free. In a capitalist country I charge as much as I can." He put that principle to work in deciding whether or not to take up a lucrative offer to tour New Zealand and Australia for ten weeks. He didn't want to go; he was tempted to visit Ghana instead, and was also homesick for the States. Offered more than a hundred thousand dollars for twenty concerts in Australia and New Zealand, with additional sums to be added for television appearances, Robeson reluctantly decided to accept. For two or three months' work, Essie wrote to Freda Diamond, they could "clean up some fast money, and then he can retire, and do only what he wants to do, when he wants to. Which means television, radio, and occasionally a concert. And some writing." (Paul still hoped to do a book about his musical theories.) With Essie and Larry Brown, Robeson arrived in Australia on October 13.[56]

The tour did bring in the expected income and generated some incidental pleasures as well, but, far from being a piece of cake, it proved a grueling ordeal. In Robeson's opening press conferences in Sydney and Brisbane, several hostile reporters prodded him with sharp-edged questions, and Robeson rose angrily to the bait. Had the Hungarian uprising been justified? Robeson pointed his finger at the questioner and told him the uprising had been inspired by "fascists"—encouraged by Voice of America broadcasts to Hungary—and was not a revolt of the people. Had not the condition of blacks in the United States greatly improved of late? It had *somewhat* improved, Robeson shot back, primarily because blacks had become militant in demanding their rights and because the U.S.S.R. had supported the black struggle. Was he bitter about the way the U.S. government had treated him? Bitter? Robeson echoed, and then launched into what one newspaper later described as an "emotional outburst" and another as a "nauseating" political "tirade." "If someone did something bad to me I wouldn't be bitter—I'd just knock him down and put my foot into his face" (crashing his foot down on the floor to illustrate his point). He then went on—at least, so the press reported—to say that the Russians would "hammer out the brains" of any country, including America, who took arms against them, and to declare that, in the event of such a conflict, he would side with Russia. Paul "is angrier than ever," Essie reported ruefully to Freda Diamond, "and it makes me shudder, because he is so often angry at the wrong people, and so often unnecessarily angry."[57]

Paul's anger reflected not the momentary logic of events but stored-up griefs, a nature unraveling. Behind the reporters' hostile questions—which had been thrown at him now for two decades—he heard the smug, unspoken subtext: "Come on, Robeson, *confess,* confess that your hopes have run aground, confess that human beings *stink*, confess that the rest of us have always been right, that we're perfectly entitled to go on leading the narrow, hardened, opportunistic lives you silly idealists once so righteously scorned." He told Nancy Wills, an Australian woman he had first met in London in the forties, that he was afraid to walk the streets in Australia—"He didn't believe that the people here loved him." When Essie, in front of Wills, mentioned the possibility of stopping off in the Philippines on their way back to London, Paul flew into a rage, declaring that U.S. agents would kill him if he ever set foot in the Philippines—"It was frightening," as Wills remembers the scene, "to see and hear anyone so distraught, so angry."[58]

Australia had not fully emerged from its own McCarthy-like deep-freeze, and the current Menzies government was, at the very moment of Robeson's arrival, debating an anti–civil-libertarian Crimes Act Amendment. Having set him up with a string of loaded political questions, the Australian press proceeded to lambaste him for being too political. The *Herald* and *Sun* chain of newspapers headlined their stories of Robeson's initial press conference, "Would Back Russia in a War," and "Robeson Bitterly Critical of U.S." while the *Telegraph* weighed in with "I Wish He Was Still Bosambo." D. D. O'Connor, the sponsoring agent for Robeson's tour, wrote Essie that the headlines "aroused a certain amount of resentment, particularly in official circles and of course in the wealthy and rather snobbish section of concert patrons." Since tickets for the tour were scaled rather high, O'Connor expressed concern for its commercial success, a concern heightened when the director of adult education in Hobart promptly canceled Robeson's scheduled appearance in that city ("My Board is reluctant to be identified with Mr. Robeson's public statements, and cannot co-operate with you as previously arranged").[59]

Things simmered down once the tour itself began. The next three weeks were spent in New Zealand, and there the press was altogether more civil than in Australia. At a typical concert appearance Robeson (continuing his recent practice) would eschew a formal program and present instead an informal combination of talk and song. One reporter vividly caught his platform manner:

> Robeson treated the normal procedures . . . with something like kindly indifference, putting on thick-rimmed glasses to read the words of a song from a copy of the printed program, and commenting on many of his songs in the light of his own view of social justice ("If they call that politics, I plead guilty"). With a small lectern beside him, to hold notes and reminders, there were times when he stripped his glasses off at the end of a song and challenged his audience with the optical and vocal intensity of a preacher delivering a spiritual ultimatum. . . . This cosmic

belch of a voice still has the power to astonish by sheer, carpeted magnificence.

Not only did the music critics hail Robeson's artistry, but the news reporters skirted political questions (according to one reporter, Robeson's New Zealand agent phoned in advance to request that political topics be avoided). When his plane set down at Whenaupai Airport in Auckland, he was given a traditional Maori welcome, and he later visited the Maori Community Centre. "The Maoris are a wonderful people—beautiful copper colored," Robeson wrote Clara Rockmore. They "have accepted us as of them and [are] very proud of our success. . . . Am over the dumps (the bad spots)—and riding high." Despite his agent's worry, and although local Catholic schools were instructed not to support Robeson's concerts because he was a "Communist," they in fact sold out.[60]

Still, the fireworks, if dampened, continued to smolder. The New Zealand *Woman's Weekly* reported that Robeson at times seemed "edgy" when speaking to the press—"A quick answer, an impatience at any sidetracking. . . ." It also quoted him as saying he had no further musical ambitions and was now only ambitious "as a scholar"; he wanted "to be so fluent in one other language—any one—that I can find myself dreaming in that language, so that I am not forced, as I am now, to do all my thinking and talking in the tongue of my oppressor. That sounds bitter, I guess." Robeson sometimes talked politics to the reporters even when they did not goad him into doing so. In Auckland he told the press he was "here to sing" and was "through with missions for the moment"—and then proceeded to criticize the United States for supporting Franco and Chiang Kai-shek. He declared himself still "a rigid Marxist," expressed concern about mistreatment of the Maoris and the suppression of their culture, and even volunteered sardonic disappointment that blacks back home seemed wholly wedded to a prayerful, nonviolent struggle: "They say to me: 'Paul, you're black like we are but you don't pray so much. You're more likely to break a few heads. So you stay overseas where you are.' " The reporter from the conservative New Zealand *Herald* concluded, "He is a man who quite openly wears a chip on his shoulder." Robeson further alienated conservative New Zealand opinion by singing to the waterside workers in Wellington, who were out on strike, and accepting membership in their union. Essie gave a few interviews in her own right and saw her function as being "especially gracious and pleasant, though always forthright, to try and counteract some of the anger." But by the end of the tour, Essie was fed up with trying to pacify Paul and the press simultaneously. She let out her feelings to the Rosens: "Your Boy is full of bile and tension, and remains ANGRY at the drop of a hat. I'm very tired of coping with it. I've developed enough patience to last me the rest of my life, so there is no need to develop any more. You can have him. He's tired out, but keeps on doing everything on the horizon, and so hereafter, I just don't want to look at it. I'd rather not see it. Then I won't need to protest, and try and save him, and try and fob off pests. He resents everything I do, no matter what. So, I'm up to here. Period."[61]

The U.S. Consul in Auckland was pleased to report back to the State Department that "no civil reception or other formal type of welcome was tendered to Robeson during his stay." Peace groups took up the social slack. In both New Zealand and Australia, the Robesons were welcomed in every city by delegations drawn from the trade unions, the Communist Party, Soviet and Chinese friendship societies, peace committees, and the Union of Australian Women. In Sydney, the Soviet Ambassador came down from Canberra to attend a peace reception in the Robesons' honor, and the Tass representative in Australia solicited an article from Paul (written by Essie) about their impressions of the country. In that article, and frequently elsewhere as well, Robeson spoke out against New Zealand's discrimination against the Maoris and Australia's more overt brutality to its own native population, the aborigines. There were about seventy-five thousand aborigines in a total Australian population of ten million, driven off their land into a desert interior scarce in food and water and nearly devoid of the game they had traditionally hunted and lived on. Without the vote or representation, the aborigines roamed the Outback, a desperately abused people, Australia's "niggers."[62]

The more Robeson learned about the condition of the aborigines as his tour progressed through the country, the more his indignation grew. Through Faith Bandler, an aboriginal activist, the Robesons saw a private showing of a fifteen-minute film made in the late 1950s on the plight of the aborigines in the Warburton Ranges. As she remembers it, "The tears started to stream down his face"; but when the film showed thirsty children waiting for water, his sorrow turned to anger. Flinging to the floor the black cap he had taken to wearing on his head for warmth, he swore aloud that he would return to Australia and help bring attention to the appalling conditions in which the aborigines lived. He repeated that promise a few days later to the press, and again at a large peace reception for him at Paddington Hall in Sydney. "There's no such thing as a 'backward' human being," he told the crowd. "There is only a society which says they are backward." He cited the case of his own family: his cousins in North Carolina who worked the cotton and tobacco fields were also called "backward"; that meant they hadn't been allowed to attend school. "The indigenous people of Australia," he roared, "ARE my brothers and sisters."[63]

Arriving at the Perth airport in Western Australia toward the end of his tour, Robeson was met by Lloyd L. Davies, a lawyer and longtime aboriginal activist. Davies remembers that a throng of well-wishers was on hand at the airport to welcome Robeson but when he spotted a group of local aborigines shyly hanging back, he instantly headed for them, moving through the crowd "like a fullback." When he reached them, "he literally gathered the nearest half dozen in his great arms," and when he moved toward his waiting transport, the aborigines moved with him. Davies heard one of the little girls say, almost in wonder, "Mum, he likes us." In his speech to the West Australian Peace Council, Robeson referred to his "darker brothers and sisters" whom he had seen at the airport—"they're good stockmen, they tell me, know how to handle those horses and sheep; they ain't too dumb for that. Not too dumb to labor for nothing." Robeson went on to say, "I wish I could be sweet all the time. . . . Sometimes what you read in the paper sounds a little rough. You're right, it was rough. That's right. I said it." In Davies's view, Robeson's gestures and words during his visit to Australia "gave a tremendous boost to the Aboriginal cause."[64]

The Robesons returned to London in early December 1960, their bank balance improved, their pockets stuffed with excellent artistic notices and mixed political ones—and thoroughly exhausted from the effort. "Had a really wonderful—moving tour," Robeson wrote Clara Rockmore right after they returned, "surely need no more *'Proof'* of anything"; the tour "fulfilled its mission in a most complete way. The audience took me up at my own valuation and responded nobly." Still, he felt "just tired out— *Bored*—to put it truthfully." From one angle, he was "just not too interested in what comes up—will do what does as well as I can—but in a 'normal world'—I'd just quit—retire in general—and do just enough to keep going *well* above water." But "there is little excuse not to function without seeming very difficult and *shirking,*" and so he would try to be "philosophic." Of one thing, though, he felt certain: "that's the *last tour,* as such. I'll sing at benefits as far as concerts are concerned—and professionally will do what I have to do." Additional plaudits meant nothing to him; to be "perfectly honest," he wrote Clara, they had become entirely overshadowed by "the *absolute vacuum* (emptiness) in my personal life." He felt "terribly, terribly lonely. . . ." It was "almost unbearable." "We are just beginning to feel the strain," Essie wrote in innocent imitation of Paul's freighted lines, "so we are taking time out for a couple of months, just to sit here with NOTHING to do!!" Essie, who was "feeling much better generally," went to work on a new book about blacks and American politics, while Paul continued desultory work for a book on folk music and held occasional sessions with Larry Brown to prepare recital material for future concerts.[65]

No one saw more of Robeson in these months than Harry Francis, the left-wing assistant secretary of the musicians' union, who had become a friend and an intermediary. Francis told Paul, Jr., twenty years later that his father had returned from the Australian trip so depressed that he took to lying on the bed in a darkened room with the curtains drawn. Francis dropped in frequently, and also brought over Harry Pollitt's (the leader of the British Communist Party) bodyguard, who played pinochle with Robeson by the hour. During one of Harry Francis's visits, the phone rang and he answered it. Fidel Castro—so Francis tells it—was on the other end, calling from Havana, asking to talk with Paul Robeson. As the FBI was well aware, Robeson had been giving thought to a trip to Cuba (and to China and Africa as well); indeed, his uncertainty about whether to undertake another strenuous journey had contributed to his debilitating anxiety. He told Francis to explain to Castro that he couldn't come to the phone at the moment. Only a few weeks later, anti-Castro forces, mobilized by the government of the United States, made their landing at the Bay of Pigs.[66]

In early January, Essie and Paul gradually started to get around socially again, spending evenings at the Soviet and East European embassies, attending the Oistrakh (father and son) concert at the Albert Hall as guests of the Soviet Ambassador, and having a private hour-long visit with Kwame Nkrumah, the President of Ghana, who was in London for a Commonwealth prime-ministers' conference (Essie did a series of articles on the conference for the Associated Negro Press). In addition, Paul put in an appearance on the television program "This Is Your Life" to honor his old acting partner Flora Robson (". . . myself in Person very dignified," he wrote self-mockingly to Clara Rockmore; thanking him for appearing on the show, Flora Robson wrote, "It was *you* who taught me to be kind"). He closely followed political events, watching in alarm as President-elect Kennedy tried to justify American involvement in Laos, reacting with fury to Lumumba's assassination in the Congo, protesting vigorously against the continued imprisonment of his old friend Jomo Kenyatta in Kenya ("Let him be free, NOW, AT ONCE," Paul wrote, "to take his rightful and dearly-won place; to give his courage, knowledge and perception to his too long-suffering folk").[67]

Deciding on plans for the future entailed additional strain. Essie was against traveling to regions restricted for U.S. citizens for fear Paul would lose his passport and they would be forced to leave England, where she preferred to live. Attractive offers arrived in abundance but had to be sifted through with one eye aimed at conserving energy and the other at fulfilling political obligations that might, ideally, combine with plausible career opportunities. Paul toyed with the idea of accepting an invitation to return to Australia in *Othello,* and he waited to see if Herbert Marshall, his colleague from Unity Theatre days, would be able to bring off a Russian film on the life of Ira Aldridge (for which Robeson would do the narration, not play the lead)—but he immediately turned down a proposal from the British producer Oscar Lewenstein that he appear as Archibald in Jean Genet's *The Blacks;* returning the script, Essie wrote Lewenstein, "I'm sorry neither Paul nor I like it at all."[68]

Within a few months of having returned to London from Australia, the Robesons had consolidated their plans for the rest of the year. Paul would go alone to Moscow for a visit in late March; in April he would attend the Scottish Miners' Gala in Edinburgh; late May and part of June would be given over to the Prague Music Festival, with a return in between to participate in the Welsh Miners' Gala in Cardiff; part of July would be spent in East Berlin; August was reserved for a much-delayed trip to Ghana; and then, in the fall, there would be return visits to Rumania, Hungary, Bulgaria, and the U.S.S.R. It was a full schedule but, given its emphasis on visits rather than concerts, seemed not overly exhausting. In a letter to Clara Rockmore, of uncommon length and explicitness, Paul explained that he had changed "a great deal," had had a chance "to find out *'who'* was *'who'*—to see some of the way things work":

> In those years, [late fifties] I came very close to many of the Negro *People*—not "generally" only—but felt their warmth & generosity. I'm talking of the simple folk on the [West] Coast—etc.—not the "big shots."

He also recalled with affection "great sections of the American Jewish community who not only were close in many phases of the Peace struggle, etc. but also . . . were very warm & human." Still, at this point he felt "completely desolate." Summarizing his current mood, he explained to Clara why, despite his homesickness, he had no immediate plans to come home:

> I'm convinced that if I should return to America—I'd never get out again—within any time that was pertinent. Even that would be thinkable—in the light of the way I felt—but I'm also convinced they'll not rest until they've gone much further. In one way I would welcome the struggle, if my closest allies could understand my point of view.
>
> For I'll get off the plane calling the Pentagon, etc. the *bastards* they are—the upholders of Fascism & Nazism the world over—and dangerous to all of human-kind. If that's Treason—let's have it out.
>
> But I'm *not* prepared to come back to "retire" from the scene & keep my mouth shut, etc.
>
> If there's any crowd I can't take its those guys who gave me such a bad time over all those years—and my very pride would never let them get hold of me again.
>
> For I'm one Negro, who means to take some *one* or I hope *"some over"* with *me* of the *"enemy"* if I must go.
>
> Sounds a little "cloak & dagger"—but really—the "double talk" about the Negro question in America—and the way its *"swallowed"* by Negroes themselves—is just too awful to behold.

So feeling that way where can one go—I still play with Canada [but he feared, as he had written Clara earlier, that HUAC "might try to reach into Canada" after him]—they might refuse me entry or demand I do concerts under a regular Impresario. . . . The West Indies seems to be out. They're making a deal with the "Big Boys" in Washington & wouldn't trust them.

Maybe Cuba will be in the picture once the relations are again normalized—I shall certainly get there at some time—normal relations or not.

But Canada seems the best bet. . . .

Am planning to work at television, recordings etc—but with no heart in it. But I'll work—because the money is there—and I'm sure I'll need it.

Sure all will go well because I've really turned into a *"Pro"* and if it must be done—it must be done. . . . Will come up into the "World" again & start swinging—

In two follow-up letters he reassured Clara that he was feeling "much better" and cautioned her not to take his earlier, "very discouraging epistle too literally"; he even felt more optimistic politically: "Kennedy seems to be at least realistic and some of the people around him *are* decent. Let's hope."[69]

Clara took Paul's reassurances in stride, but Helen Rosen did not. She, too, received an uncharacteristically lengthy letter from Paul, ten days after the one he had written to Clara:

I've been feeling very "down" but feel much better now and see some daylight. . . . From television (we get Kennedy's television interviews etc.) things seem to have taken not a bad turn. No one can be too optimistic but someone's got to face reality. . . . The Negro group seems to be moving way ahead according to their own light. Revels sent me a marvellous tape of a Negro gathering or conference of . . . middle-class Negroes on the Coast.

The conference treated . . . questions precisely from that point of view. "We are middle class trying to integrate—and all must aid us—as for these 'Peasants' from the South—They embarrass us—but we must get them to understand that this is *our* not their day."

As Revels said on the tape—nothing could be franker.

As a matter of fact—this seems to me most "American" at this juncture. . . . It's not easy to see this firm *basic* turn in Negro life—which is clearest to me.

They see themselves as Ambassadors to Africa etc.—and helping America win "cold war"—& minds of men etc. And there seems no way to really function in the Negro Community without real "Red-Baiting"—even now. If not "baiting" a deep refusal to be caught anywhere in the deep *"left."*

Weaver (Housing) case is typical [Robert C. Weaver; under Kennedy, he became the first black to head a major federal agency, Housing and Home Finance].

And of course this is so more or less for the whole country. Castro & Cuba seem to have "cut across" some areas— But again that's across the Borders.

This makes difficult the "coming over for a time" which might be possible in a truly "artistic" setting or at least if one would or could "pipe down" for a while.

Quite frankly—the day is long gone for any quiet "double-talk" or reticence, I feel—so being as realistic as possible—I see hanging in for a while here but eventually looking Eastward near & far. We'll see.

If the tension subsides as well it might—then there's a different story. Hope so.

As far as our conversation [Helen had been in London briefly in early February to recuperate from an illness she contracted while in Africa], you have a right, certainly to see things as you always do—very realistically— But there are others who will for better or for worse pursue their lifelong direction—especially at this historic moment of Real Triumph over much of the World whatever the domestic Picture.

And the whole history of America—certainly testifies to the need of that advanced group—whatever the difficulties involved.

It remains a source of deep wonder to me that these folk are there—in every corner of the world—and in much worse conditions than the U. States. But there they are—and when a Cuba suddenly?? erupts—the Patience & Labor seem well worth the effort.

However one individual or the other views these things—modern history has evolved this ideology and that group to actualize the theory. And pretty well they're doing as I said before.[70]

Paul's political comments, though in spots even more enigmatic than usual, didn't seem any cause for alarm to Helen (much as she regretted his seeming change of mind about coming home, as she had long advised and as he had seemed on the verge of doing). But the comments he made, both in the long letter and in shorter follow-up notes, on his emotional state did arouse her active concern. "Terribly lonely," he wrote, "but just doing the best I can. Have altogether failed to find friends over here. Guess I'm to blame—but also a little *'set'* in *'ways'* I guess." Soon after that downcast note, he wrote twice in one day to reassure her (as he had Clara) that he was "feeling fine" again; since he rarely wrote at all, this heightened rather than diminished Helen's concern, especially since he added: "I can't wait to see Sam again. He's so sweet about me—and so disturbed when I'm raging and ranting. Both he and you are right— It means some 'inner' disturbance— But know that I 'dig' into it without 'mercy'—and come up at last with the 'needed' adjustment." He closed a note of February 24 with words that sounded suspiciously manic, however tender: " 'Thank you Lord.' Thank you! . . . Thank you Lord! for such a lovely family [the Rosens] and you thank them too for taking me in. . . . I *do* love you—*adore* you—*cherish* you—"[71]

Relying on her own well-honed instincts, Helen concluded that Paul was in emotional trouble. She first told her fears to Sam, and then the two of them contacted Paul, Jr., and also Ed Barsky, the left-wing doctor whose medical partner, Morris Pearlmutter, had treated both Essie and Paul. The four of them huddled. Helen explained her strong conviction that Paul was having serious difficulty and should come home, and it was decided she should go over to London and check on his state of mind firsthand. She did, a few weeks later, and seeing him convinced her more than ever that in fact he did desperately want to return to the States but did not feel well enough. She did everything she could to persuade him to follow his inclinations. Essie, however, was adamantly opposed to a return and, realizing the purpose of Helen's mission, did her considerable best to keep them apart. They managed, toward the end of Helen's visit, to spend an afternoon alone together in the apartment of Andy (Robeson's valet and friend). The next day Helen arrived at the Connaught Street flat by prearrangement for lunch, only to be told that Paul had left by plane for Moscow. Essie was "jubilant" and Helen "stunned"—to this day, she says, she "doesn't understand what happened," doesn't know whether Paul, on sudden impulse, took off for his planned trip to Moscow earlier than he had originally intended, whether Essie played any role in encouraging that impulse (and, if so, how—by getting some of his Moscow friends, like Boris Polevoi or Mikhail Kotov of the Soviet Peace Committee to call? by promising a return to the States after the Moscow trip?).[72]

On Paul's arrival in Moscow, the Soviet press reported him busy and happy ("The telephone rang constantly. . . . Robeson smiled and clapped his hands in astonishment. He wanted to be everywhere"). The editorial staff of *Izvestia* consulted with him; he dined at the Grand Hotel; he conferred about radio and TV appearances; Georgi Zhukov, chairman of the State Committee for Cultural Relations with Foreign Countries, welcomed him on a visit to the Patrice Lumumba Friendship University, and Zavadsky of the Mossovet Theater invited him to play Othello. On the night of March 23 Paul and Essie talked by phone. They chatted about plans and friends: Essie reported that Peggy Ashcroft was asking if he would be available for a poetry reading with her; Paul reported that Galya and Boris Lifanov's baby had been ill. Essie wrote him the next day to say how pleased she was that he "sounded so happy on the telephone, it must be good news all round."[73]

On March 27 Essie had another call from Moscow. Paul had slashed his wrists.

CHAPTER 24

Broken Health

(1961–1964)

They couldn't tell Essie much when she arrived in Moscow. There had been a noisy party in Paul's hotel room the night before; at 2:00 or 3:00 a.m. students had still been asking for his autograph; he had retreated into an inner room. His translator, Irina, had found him in the bathroom, his wrists slashed with a razor blade. (Two years later Robeson told a doctor treating him in the GDR that in Moscow "people whose parents or whose relatives were in jail had approached him—'Can't you help me?'—this sort of thing had put him into conflict.") Who had been at the party? When had Paul slashed his wrists? At what hour did Irina discover him? How close was Paul to death? All this remained unanswered (as much of it still is) when Paul, Jr., arrived in Moscow a few days later. Deeply suspicious, he sought a logical explanation from officials. Some of the guests, he was told, "were not Soviet people"—enough innuendo to feed his suspicions but not to clarify them. If there was anything mysterious, or possibly sinister, in the circumstances surrounding Robeson's attempted suicide, those who had had recent contact with him provided scant elucidation. Harry Francis expressed surprise that Robeson had left London without a word to him. Ivor Montagu, who had by chance ended up on the same plane to Moscow with Robeson, recalled his surprise at the sudden agitation he had shown during the flight—earlier he had seemed "fine"—when a Good Samaritan sitting behind him (and a stranger to Robeson) had offered him his over-coat against the cold weather.[1]

A team of Soviet doctors headed by Dr. Snezhnevsky offered the diagnosis "depressive paranoic psychosis generated by an involutional form of arteriosclerosis," and prescribed Largactyl and Nosinan, commonly used tranquilizers. According to Paul, Jr., the doctors told him that his father "had been so paranoid when first admitted that he thought they were spies and were going to kill him, and was yelling that Essie was a spy, too. For the first few days that Essie tried to visit him, Paul wouldn't see her." By the time, Paul, Jr., saw his father, Robeson was able to converse with clarity. But he chose, as was his style with matters of deepest import, to say nearly nothing. Paul, Jr., later ventured to ask him why he had done it; the guarded, mysterious answer he got—according to Paul, Jr.—was that "someone close to me had done irreparable damage to the U.S.S.R."[2]

A rumor has persisted, alternately, that Robeson himself had become disillusioned with the Soviet Union. But those who knew him best stoutly deny that intepretation, and, indeed, scant evidence has surfaced to support it. Robeson's disillusion, such as it was, was not with the U.S.S.R. per se but with the way the world worked, its refusal to adhere to a historical process that had seemed predetermined. His sense of blighted hopes, personal and historic, is readily documented, but was generalized—not reducible to any specific disappointment with Soviet policy or development. Robeson's forlorn sense of loss was more encompassing, and one contributing factor may well have been "chemical"—a bipolar depressive disorder that fed on political events and largely expressed itself through them but was finally more than their sum. On the other hand, without the accumulated pressures of government harassment and worldly disappointments, any underlying depressive tendency might never have become manifest. Further, almost anyone subject to the kinds of pressures Robeson was—even without an organic "predisposition"—might have become susceptible to breakdown. It may well be that all Robeson himself knew about his deepening sense of malaise was what, accompanied by tears, he had once told his Chicago friend Sam Parks: his moorings had slipped— abroad he now felt himself a stranger in unfamiliar territory, at home he felt himself bypassed by a civil-rights movement he had done so much to forge.[3]

Paul, Jr., continued to search for clues to corroborate his own view that his father had been "neutralized" by malignant unknowns, possibly CIA agents, at the "wild party" preceding the suicide attempt. He used his connections within the CPUSA to gain access to someone on the Soviet Central Committee and to a representative from the Security Division; his frantic pursuit produced only circumstantial clues, but did dangerously increase his own level of anxiety. Twelve days after arriving in Moscow, he himself broke down. Terror-stricken, hallucinating, he heaved a huge chair through the plate-glass windows of his hotel room and nearly threw himself after it. Himself hospitalized, in his view a second victim of those responsible for his father's collapse, he assigned the same cause to his own: chemical poisoning by the CIA.[4]

Within a few weeks both father and son were doing notably better—

playing chess, taking long walks, following (Paul, Sr., reluctantly) the prescription of the Soviet doctors for regularized calisthenics (a prescription Sam Rosen, for one, thought lamentably inadequate). In consultation with Essie—who as always had responded to crisis by redoubling her energies and burying her doubts—they decided to give out minimal information. Even to intimates like his brother Ben, his sister Marian, Helen Rosen, Freda Diamond, and W. E. B. Du Bois, Essie sent the same message (embedded in lighthearted letters otherwise full of casual chitchat and breathless excitement over Yuri Gagarin's recently completed mission into space): after years of overwork, compounded by "a slight heart attack," Paul's health had given way; he had fallen "flat on his face with exhaustion" and his doctors had bedded him down for a long rest; Paul, Jr., had been sent for as a precautionary measure, because of his father's "heart attack." As to Paul, Jr.'s own condition, no elaborate word was necessary, since no elaborate rumors had leaked out; not even his wife, Marilyn, was informed of the full extent of his collapse, and his uncle Ben and the others were merely told he had come down with "a stomach upset." Essie delayed sending out most of her letters for over a month—until Big Paul was feeling well enough to append a few reassuring lines of his own ("Feeling much better. Soon back to normal"), thereby, it was hoped, giving further weight to the official version they had concocted. To those making business or professional inquiries, Essie merely replied that, because of overwork, Robeson's doctors had insisted on a rest period of several months.[5]

And, indeed, within a month of the attempted suicide he was feeling much improved and the doctors were much encouraged. Both Pauls, with Essie in attendance, were transferred to the Barveekha Sanatorium for further rest, and by early May, Paul, Jr., was writing Marilyn that his father was "in a relaxed and even carefree mood," their shared cottage luxurious, and the surrounding grounds lovely. Essie took advantage of the medical facilities to have a complete checkup of her own, and the doctors found no signs of any recurring cancer. By mid-May, Big Paul was occasionally trying out songs on a piano and was feeling well enough to receive the Chinese Ambassador to the U.S.S.R. for a brief visit. By the end of May, Essie felt able to fly to London to pick up needed clothes, supplies, and typewriter from the flat; when she returned to Barveekha ten days later, she found both men so improved that the doctors decided to push forward their discharge dates. Paul, Jr., flew home to the States on June 2, and the following week Essie and Paul, Sr., were allowed to return to London on the promise of a prolonged rest free from commitments.[6]

After arriving back at Connaught Square on June 10, Robeson began working for an hour or so a day with Larry Brown on their music ("The Voice sounds unimpaired," Essie wrote Helen Rosen), and gave some renewed thought to a trip to Africa, bolstered by a personal letter from Kwame Nkrumah inviting him to assume the recently created chair of music and drama at Ghana's University of Accra (he also got an invitation from Cheddi Jagan to come to British Guiana, in South America, as his personal guest). The good cheer lasted less than two weeks. Robeson's mood took an abrupt turn downward, and Essie made a split-second decision to get him back into the hospital in Moscow. A worried Shirley Du Bois reported to Freda Diamond that mutual friends had seen Paul "being *carried* from the plane," on landing in Moscow, "by two whitecoated male nurses, one on each side." Essie again put the best face on it to correspondents: they had been "hasty" in returning so soon to London and for caution's sake had now gone back to Moscow to ensure an absolutely "solid" convalescence. "Hearts are strange things," she wrote Shirley Du Bois in one of the emblematic lines of her life, "and I respect them." Hearing of Robeson's setback, Dr. Du Bois wrote him a charming letter explaining that he had been in Rumania for a month getting (at age ninety-three) rejuvenation treatments from the famed Dr. Aslan, but was getting "bored"; he asked Robeson to kiss the stones of Moscow and greet all his friends, announcing himself "fed up" with an "impossible" America and expressing the hope that he would soon see Robeson in Ghana (where Du Bois was shortly to take out citizenship). Essie at first admitted to Paul, Jr., and Marilyn that she was "seriously discouraged," yet within two weeks was again sounding a positive note ("All is very well now, and on the way UP"). Bob and Clara Rockmore asked Essie, with considerable heat, to let them know "in plain English just what's what," promising not to divulge to anyone what they were told. She would not, continuing instead to send chatty, uninformative notes that reaffirmed her ability to keep a confidence—and to enjoy the secondary satisfaction of being in absolute control of an incapacitated Paul.[7]

The same tactics failed to work on Helen Rosen. Receiving a note from Essie on July 31 that the doctors were "VERY much pleased with [Paul's] progress" and that they would be at the Barveekha Sanatorium for another month or so to consolidate his improvement, Helen and Sam decided to have a look for themselves. They were already in nearby Rumania to attend a medical conference. (Sam's now renowned stapes surgery had brought him international attention, and Helen had trained in audiology in order to assist him in the operation; they were traveling widely to demonstrate the procedure.) In mid-August they arrived at Barveekha for a four-day stay. Helen was appalled at what she found. Paul was utterly lethargic and passive, as if drugged, and Essie's singsong attempts to rouse him—"Let's show Helen and Sam how nicely we do our exercises"—only added to the poignancy. "They gave one look at him and guessed," Essie reported back to Paul, Jr., and Marilyn—that is, guessed "SOME of the story." Essie encouraged the Rosens to believe that the breakdown had happened only after the second trip to the Moscow hospital, that it duplicated "the 1956 experience" (his first breakdown), that it was the byproduct of "nervous exhaustion and tired heart"—and said nothing at all about "the ideas" (as she cryptically referred to them to Paul, Jr.) he had expressed during his least lucid days. The Rosens resented not having been told the truth before, but after Essie assured them that Big Paul had been "adamant" about not letting anyone but himself tell his story, they said they "understood." When they left, four days later, Essie wrote home that Paul was "so sad . . . I may have to bury him tomorrow. . . ."[8]

By the second week in September, after a three-month stay, Robeson was again improved, and the Barveekha doctors decided to risk letting him go back to London, urging that if all went well he should eventually return to his own country. "So hold onto your hats," Essie wrote the Rosens just before boarding the plane for London. Her augury proved all too apt; Robeson had barely been in London forty-eight hours when he again relapsed, this time suffering his most serious episode yet. The usually unflappable Essie put in a panic call to Helen Rosen in New York: could she come at once to London? Helen dropped everything, took the next plane, and arrived in London the following morning. She found Paul huddled in a fetal position on the bed, tangled up in the bedsheets, "positively cowering" in fear. Essie, in consultation with Paul's agent Harold Davison, made arrangements for Paul to enter the Priory, a private facility that had the reputation of being the best psychiatric hospital in England.[9]

The Priory sent out a five-passenger car and two orderlies, one of whom, a Mr. Williams, "beguiled and soothed" Paul into the back seat, with Essie and Helen on either side of him. They drove out from London toward the Priory in Roehampton, hoping he would stay calm during the half-hour trip. But when the car approached the Soviet Embassy and Paul (according to Helen) "thought we were driving in there," he started muttering, "You don't know what you're doing, you don't know what you're doing"; then, as they drew opposite the Embassy, he frantically signaled them to "get down!!"—implying, Helen felt, "that great danger was at hand." He pushed her down on the seat, leaning over her with his body as they drove past. "He was frightened," Helen recalls, "cowering himself and trying to protect me." She didn't know which building they were passing until Essie told her it was the Soviet Embassy, without adding any other comment. To this day Helen remains "astonished" that Paul knew where he was, given the terrible shape he was in—"He just suddenly came to."[10]

At the Priory he was put under the care of Dr. Brian Ackner, assisted by Dr. John Flood, both highly regarded specialists. Ackner, co-author of a classic paper on insulin coma, has been described by a contemporary specialist as "a first-line authority" on mental illness at the time. It was Ackner's view that Robeson suffered from "one of those somewhat rare chronic depressions which fail to respond to any therapy or continue to relapse but which in the long run have a good prognosis." He was supported in that view by Professor Curran of St. George's Hospital, who was later called in for consultation, and by Dr. Flood, who chose the words "endogenous depression in a manic depressive personality" to describe Robeson's underlying condition. Examining Robeson on the day of his admission, September 15, Ackner found him "in a depressed, agitated state with many ideas of persecution," expressing "ideas of . . . unworthiness which, although they may have had some basis of reality in the past, were quite delusional in the degree to which they were held." Ackner decided to begin a course of electroconvulsive therapy (ECT)—brain seizures triggered by electric currents—immediately. In Western medicine in the early sixties, ECT was the preferred treatment for "major depressive" illness. Twenty-five years later, it remains a standard weapon in the medical arsenal, but the doubts of some experts about its possible culpability in memory impairment and even brain damage have made ECT more controversial than it once was; the development of alternate drug therapies since 1965 has further reduced it to the status of one among several possible—and hotly debated—treatment options.[11]

Essie did not tell Paul, Jr., home in New York, about the decision to give his father shock treatments. When he later learned about them, he was outraged, insisting that if he had known at the time he would have raced to Europe and brought his father home. Essie, accustomed to "sparing" her men, believed she had to shield Paul, Jr., from the news, given his own recent breakdown. Paul, Jr., believed she acted to deceive him, concerned only to prevent interference with her own willful plans. He believed, too, that there had been "foul play" at the Priory and that the "wrongly administered" ECT treatments had "damaged his father's brain." Once aroused, Paul, Jr.'s suspicions of his mother were never to quiet.[12]

Helen Rosen, who was on the scene, does not doubt that the decision to proceed with shock treatments seemed inescapable, given the lack of medical options at the time and Paul's desperate condition. Even today, after the development of a much larger arsenal of drug therapies than existed in 1961, several specialists have suggested that, should a "Robeson" arrive at their offices with his presenting symptoms, he would still be a likely candidate for ECT. But it is also almost certain that today they would first attempt to treat his symptoms with medication, probably a course of lithium (which first came into use in some research centers in the late 1960s). If any criticism can be made of the way Ackner and his staff at the Priory treated Robeson, it would center on the speed—two days after his admission—with which they moved to ECT. Eventually, in the course of Robeson's long stay at the Priory, he did get a full course of treatment with the few drugs then available, but "without much benefit" from any. To the criticism that this drug therapy should have preceded the ECT series, Ackner would probably have responded that Robeson's suffering was too acute to await a delayed and problematic response to a limited arsenal of chemicals. Besides, Robeson did respond well enough to ECT—at least in the immediate aftermath of treatments—to reaffirm Ackner in his choice of therapy and in the cautious optimism he had felt from the beginning about Robeson's long-term prognosis. The positive short-term effects of ECT treatments in bringing Robeson out of a "down" cycle encouraged his doctors to continue with them even though in the long term the treatments provided no cumulative benefits.[13]

Helen decided to stay on in London until the initial crisis had passed; in the end she stayed a month, living at the Connaught Square flat with Essie, joining her on the daily trek to the Priory. The difficult trip required a change of buses—not made easier by Essie's insistence on carting out the meals she prepared at home for Paul after he felt well enough to start complaining about the Priory's food. Of an evening, the two women were often exhausted, which precluded the probing exchange of intimacies neither wanted. Helen mostly read and Essie mostly kept up her voluminous correspondence. One evening Helen blued Essie's hair for her and brushed and combed it into a chignon; Essie had long since given up taking fashionable care of herself, lapsing into dowdy overweight and practical Murray Space Shoes; after the hair styling she expressed delight at her improved appearance. The two women went to bed early almost every night, Helen in Paul's bedroom. She found it almost impossible to sleep, because his bed was next to the elevator shaft and the noise was horrendous. She couldn't understand how Paul could have abided such discomfort on a regular basis.[14]

Once again, explanations—or, rather, a formula for avoiding them—had to be made to friends. Most seem to have accepted Essie's blandly reassuring words about "recurrent exhaustion . . . improving steadily . . . is now really recuperating . . . real progress . . . well on the way to recovery. . . ." But Clara and Bob Rockmore continued to protest Essie's vague and (as they wrote her) "transparently not valid" descriptions. Essie placated them with a few additional details, yet basically held them at bay with abstractly rounded phrases like "Everything is going VERY well." She wrote to Paul, Jr., that Rockmore "is furious because he does not know everything," and barely concealed her satisfaction at turning the tables, at being able to write to the man who in her view had kept her under patronizing financial control for years, "You will know everything in due course."[15]

She told Paul, Jr., in New York very little more. He did know the truth about the suicide attempt and the actual depth of his father's depression, but, fearing that he would overreact, Essie kept him only partly informed about the course of his father's treatment and progress. She filled her frequent bulletins to him and Marilyn with reassuring generalities, relaying details about the "up" cycles, avoiding news of the down side ("Progress, real progress, is being made," she wrote three weeks after Paul had been hospitalized; "It was quite a business, to make an understatement"). Instead of lingering on negative or uncertain medical developments, she chatted on about how Shirley and W. E. B. Du Bois had visited the flat; how Helen had made a "great success" cooking breakfast for them all; how Larry Brown had "dropped by to pay his respects"; how Martin Luther King, Jr., at a reception in London that she attended, had had "very warm and sweet and respectful" things to say to her about Paul.[16]

In mid-October, Helen Rosen returned to New York; two weeks later Sam Rosen looked in on Paul. After talking with the Priory doctors, he came away feeling that they "were taking good care" of him. By November, Dr. Ackner decided to allow Robeson an occasional day visit back to the Connaught Square flat: "He watched rugby on TV," Essie reported, "we had tea, he had a nap, then supper, then watched [on] TV the Gracie Fields show, which was a marvellous half hour and just the kind of thing he could do." To Paul, Jr., and other family and friends, Essie continued to send these vague, generally upbeat reports, sometimes in the form of daily diary "entries." But to Helen and Sam she sent a considerably more complicated set of truths about Paul's condition. When he had a setback in early December, she reported to the Rosens that Dr. Flood says "it is a chronic depression"; when Paul rallied, she wrote, "IF he were a radio set, we could say he is now RECEIVING, but not yet SENDING."[17]

In a separate letter to Helen, Essie confided—perhaps because Helen had been present when Paul got frightened riding past the Soviet Embassy—that he "is back on his round of thoughts, which worry him." Harry Francis—the British trade-unionist who was the only person besides Essie allowed to visit Paul on a regular basis—"insists," Essie wrote Helen, "that none of his thoughts have foundation, none whatever, and is going to try to persuade him so. H. says everyone is shocked that he should have such ideas, and just cannot understand why. Except that he is exhausted and ill. . . ."[18]

Essie never specified the contents of Paul's "thoughts," and Helen has never understood his fear while passing in front of the Soviet Embassy. According to Paul Robeson, Jr., "the 'thoughts' were of suicide." But the fact that Harry Francis was made privy to them and passed them on to "shocked" others—who could only have been people as politically reliable as himself—also suggests that the "thoughts" may have related, too, to some subterranean fears Robeson had regarding the U.S.S.R., or possibly his own standing with the Soviets. There is no surrounding evidence for believing that those fears centered concretely either on dismay at the course of Soviet history or, oppositely, on concern that he himself, or someone close to him, might be thought to have done harm to the Soviet cause—or even some murky combination thereof of treachery and disillusion. In an interview ten years later, Harry Francis recalled that he had spent "many hours with Paul during the period that he was in the nursing home and we used to discuss all manner of subjects. The propaganda that was put around that he had become disillusioned with the Soviet Union was completely without foundation. . . . Our association was such that if he had had doubts, he could have expressed them to me. Paul was certainly convinced that the reports that we had all had about the Stalin regime were justified—as big a shock to him, of course, as they were to all of us who had gotten no idea of what was happening. But he did not accept it in any sense of disillusionment with socialism or the Soviet Union as such." If the fantasies Robeson manifested when acutely ill did reflect some interior reality (in however distorted a form) that he otherwise repressed, the road map for understanding it is lost.[19]

Essie also conferred with the Rosens about the advisability of letting Paul, Jr., come over to London to see his father. Helen sent Essie some details about Paul, Jr.'s emotional state, which so upset Essie that she was sick in the bathroom. She successfully discouraged her son from making the trip to England, but she knew that would increase his resentment of her, and she warned Helen that he would also be angry at her and Sam for having spent time with his father when he could not. "Yours has been help," she wrote the Rosens, "when help was desperately needed."[20]

Early in February, Essie confided to the Rosens that Paul had become "VERY depressed" and had begun talking again of finding a "short, fast way OUT." The doctors decided on a second series of eight ECT treatments (completed in mid-April) to add to the sixteen he had already had. "I have said nothing about treatment to anyone else, to NO ONE," Essie wrote the Rosens. "You understand these things, but there's no point in alarming or confusing the others—Bobby or Pauli, or anyone." To the Rosens she gave a full account, repeating a conversation with Paul in which he insisted "it wasn't worth it. Nobody could help, they tried their best, but he was sick to death of the struggle. If I was loyal, I would help [him die]. I agreed, but said first I must be sure there is no help. We must be sure we have tried everything. He agreed to that. . . ."[21]

The second series of ECT treatments did again produce momentary relief. Within ten days the improvement was so pronounced that Paul was asking for the newspapers, sleeping better, and once more eating the filet steaks Essie brought out on the bus. He told Essie he was glad to read in the paper that Jackie Robinson had been elected to the Baseball Hall of Fame. He himself wrote a note to the Rockmores to say he was "feeling much much better . . . might jump over that way soon . . . have turned the corner—am sure will be all right from here on in." By early March he was feeling so much better that, when Essie told him she was going to see Ella Fitzgerald's show with Coleman Hawkins at the Hammersmith Gaumont, he surprised her by saying he would like to go along. Harold Davison managed to come up with a second ticket at the last minute; the two seats were separated, but had a clear view of each other in case a problem developed. Along about her third song, Ella Fitzgerald came forward and quietly announced that she wanted to dedicate her next number to "her fellow-artist and a very great man, Paul Robeson, wherever he may be sitting." There was a hush, and everyone strained to locate Paul in the audience, but thanks to the darkness of the house only his immediate neighbors recognized him (he surreptitiously gave them the autographs they asked for). With the aid of ushers, he was quickly removed from the auditorium at the end of the concert, before a crowd could gather around him. He then asked, to everyone's renewed surprise, to go backstage to greet and thank Ella Fitzgerald. Ella, according to Essie, was "thrilled," hugged and kissed him, said it was "a big day" in her life, and expressed joy that he seemed to be so much better. Davison got the Robesons into a car back to the Priory. Since he had had "no bad reactions" to the outing, they repeated it four days later with a trip to the Aldwych to see Peggy Ashcroft and John Gielgud in *The Cherry Orchard.* Paul again went backstage; Peggy cleared her dressing room of other visitors and they caught up on news, promising to do a poetry reading together the following year. Paul was especially touched when the stage-door man, an old acquaintance, told him "the whole of the theatre world would be glad to hear he was up and about and getting well." He told Essie that, although he felt fine, he wanted to go back to the Priory—he didn't want people to think he was again "available," or everyone would start "having plans for him again."[22]

The pattern of shuttling back and forth between the Connaught Square flat and the Priory was to go on for many, many months, with the time spent at the flat lengthening during periods of apparent improvement—and also varying with Robeson's tolerance for being cooped up with Essie. Her unlimited presence was at times a contributing source of unease. Devoted to him she undoubtedly was, but it was devotion encased in control. To be dependent on Essie for his daily needs was a lifetime habit, but to be *confined* to her was a lifetime's nightmare; the man with "a thousand pockets" had been slipped into a thin topcoat, and Essie held out the sleeves. For thirty years he had avoided being locked away with her, had strained against any arrangement that threatened to curtail his need for a rich variety of contacts. Now, in his sixties and desperately ill, he had to rely on her judgment about the advisability of a nap. He was lucky to have her—yet on another level this was his definition of defeat. Open antagonism between them, however, was on a back burner; sick and dependent as he was, being "cooped up" with Essie was no longer the worst imaginable fate. She was devoted to his comfort and did everything in her considerable power to prevent any demands from being made on his limited ability to cope, turning away callers and telephone calls, rejecting all requests on his time. But in fact the demand for his public services had become negligible, and Essie strictly limited the private traffic in friends to Harry Francis, occasionally Harold Davison, and rare, select visitors from overseas like the Rosens, the Du Boises, the Rockmores, or an old political chum like John Abt or Charles Howard.[23]

Larry Brown, who had known Paul for over thirty-five years, was allowed to drop by two or three times, but he was not in the best of shape himself, and Essie had grown impatient with what she felt was his lachrymose passivity. When the Home Office refused Larry a labor permit, he "talked about THE END, suicide, wept, and said he'd go to Paris." But (as Essie wrote the Rosens), "I said a four-letter word in disgust, and it shook him. He said, well, what then? . . . I told him he had never written down most of his stuff, that he owed it to the RACE, what with all this Rock and Roll, and other corruptions out of which people were making fortunes, and still he kept putting off writing down the original, wonderful, historic stuff. He was definitely jolted . . . gave up the liquor . . . and bought some manuscript paper." When it came time for him to return to the States, Larry wanted to see Paul for a last time. Essie hesitated, but finally decided that if he didn't get to say goodbye he "would feel badly" and "wouldn't know how to explain at home, etc." So she arranged a half-hour visit, and Larry was "gratified." He lived for nearly another decade back in the States, short of funds, reliant on friends, never able to commit most of his music to paper. If, on their last visit, Paul had been too unwell to summon up appropriate words of farewell, he had at least once, when introducing Larry to an audience back in 1949, done so publicly: ". . . he's here tonight, and he's with me all the time. And I can't ever tell him—I try to tell him once in a while, never sort of face to face, but to audiences like you, who love him, that I know our lives have been close. He knows how I feel—that as long as I can sing a note, as long as we're going along, we're going to be there together."[24]

Though the world left Paul alone, it had not entirely forgotten him. His sixty-fourth birthday, on April 9, 1962, brought greetings and letters both from old friends and from distant admirers. And from Kwame Nkrumah came a touching invitation to Ghana: "It is impossible not to flourish in this land of sunshine and friendliness and, as one of our truly dear friends, you will receive an abundance of both." ("One of the greatest anxieties and frustrations Paul has," Essie wrote Nkrumah, "is that he has not yet been to Africa.") Helen called from New York, thrilled that his voice sounded "so deep and quiet," and the East European, Chinese, and Cuban legations, as well as the Movement for Colonial Freedom, all sent their "warm fraternal greetings."[25]

Perhaps encouraged by the loving response to his birthday, Paul began to take a more consistent interest in things, to read a little, and occasionally to discuss events ("When he is depressed," Dr. Ackner wrote in a report, "he loses all interest in the question of Negro rights and segregation in the U.S.A., but when he becomes more cheerful he regains his interest"). He was able to approve the draft Essie drew up for him of a brief preface to a book on singing, and in his own hand he sent a few lines of greeting to Waldemar Hille, who had accompanied him for some of his West Coast concerts. More promising still, Robeson was able to go in person to the U.S. Embassy when the renewal of his passport once again threatened to become an issue.[26]

The FBI had continued to keep Robeson on its Key Figures and Top Functionaries list, though aware of his debilitated condition—indeed, its agents had been alerted that his "passing" would be "exploited" by the "international communist movement." When the Robesons applied to have their passports renewed, what could have been a routine matter was prolonged to the point of harassment. Well aware that without a valid passport Robeson could not renew his residence permit in England (which was also due to expire shortly) and that a forced departure from England at this stage of his recovery could prove ruinous, the State Department had no scruples about jeopardizing his life. No evidence has come to light suggesting that agencies of the U.S. government were directly complicitous—as his son has long maintained was probable—in the breakdown of Robeson's health, but once it did deteriorate, they proved perfectly willing to assist in its further decline.[27]

Essie took advantage of the presence of Clara and Bob Rockmore in London for help in bringing Paul by car to the U.S. Embassy so he could make application in person, as required, for the passport. Harry Francis and Harold Davison met them at the door to the Embassy, providing—as Essie reported to the Rosens—"a feeling of great security." And all the clerks, with the exception of the consul, were British, and "most sympathetic and interested." The American passport consul, Helen Bailey, turned out to be a Robeson fan and was "very considerate" (she reported to her superiors that "he appeared to be a very frail and subdued old man"). Essie had made a trial run to the Embassy the week before to make sure no unforeseen obstacles would develop, and the applications were quickly filed without a hitch. The preliminaries successfully navigated, everyone breathed a sigh of relief and went home to await the passports.[28]

They did not come. What arrived instead, six weeks after application had been made at the Embassy, was notification from Helen Bailey that the State Department had decided to invoke Section 6 of the Subversive Activities Control Act—which denied the right of any member of a Communist organization to apply for a passport. The Robesons were requested to submit sworn statements indicating whether they were or were not members of the CPUSA currently or at any time in the preceding twelve months. Furious, Essie dashed off to the Embassy in a cab. "Sheer harassment," she angrily told a startled and embarrassed Helen Bailey: the State Department, the FBI, and everybody else knew perfectly well that they were not Party members. She herself immediately swore an affidavit to that effect:

"I hereby state categorically and without reservation whatsoever that I am not now, and never have been, in all my life a member of any Communist Party in the United States, or in any other country. *Never!*"[29]

Paul was another matter. He had always refused to sign any "non-Communist" affidavit, viewing it as an intolerable abridgment of his constitutional rights. Ill though he was, he again refused to sign—"no matter what," Essie reported; with the Party in disintegration at home, he felt "very strongly that he won't let anybody down, especially now that they are under pressure." What to do? Essie hit on a clever strategy. She wrote immediately to John Abt and Ben Davis, Jr., and enlisted their help in persuading him to sign. "Remembering his still very belligerent conscience and principles," she wrote them, "he MAY be persuaded" on their say-so. She added for emphasis that "he is frantic with worry about it. He will begin all that persecution complex all over again, and with reason, which was distantly related to his illness. I hate to think of what will happen. . . ."[30]

John Abt (speaking for Ben Davis as well) came up with exactly what was needed. "We unanimously and emphatically recommend," he at once wrote back, "that Paul sign the requested affidavit." He spelled out the reasons. There could not possibly be any legal consequences for Paul; the affidavit only required him to swear that he had not been a CPUSA member for the past year and was not one currently; since he had been abroad for four years that was "a simple, self-evident and unassailable truth." (By implication, Abt was suggesting the oath might have been assailable if interpreted to cover a previous period—because, as in the past, someone could always be found to swear, for financial or political considerations, that Robeson, or anyone else, *had* been a Party member earlier). As for the moral and political implications of signing the "non-Communist" oath, Abt provided a soothing if not entirely persuasive rationale. Paul, he argued, had done his share: his "long, heroic and successful fight for a passport" had made travel possible "for hundreds of people." But the Supreme Court decision ordering the CPUSA to register, and the authorization under the McCarran Act to deny passports to CP members, had pushed the legal battle to a different level: it had now become a struggle by *admitted* CP members to prove their constitutional right to a passport nonetheless, a struggle already commenced by Elizabeth Gurley Flynn and Herbert Aptheker. "Paul's strong right arm is still needed for a host of battles, but the second round of the passport fight is not one of them." Abt ignored the point—one Robeson himself had always stressed—that to sign a "non-Communist" affidavit was automatically to compromise constitutionally guaranteed rights. But, reassured by Abt that "if we had any reservations . . . we would not hesitate to say so," Paul finally agreed to sign. He and Essie were issued new passports forthwith.[31]

Despite the resolution of the passport problem, Robeson's spirits began to sink again. He talked of his own condition as "hopeless"; given the repetitive ups and downs, he "didn't see how he could ever recover, [and] just expected to wither away." The return of the Rosens in late summer temporarily improved his mood. Accompanied by their daughter Judy, her husband, Al Ruben, and their two young children—all of whom adored "Beep" (their private nickname for him, based on the initials for Big Paul, B.P.)—the Rosens stayed in London for several days and interspersed a number of short visits with Beep. Helen managed to spend some time alone with him; she reported to the others that he had been "very communicative" and had smiled often. His terrible bouts of sleeplessness eased somewhat: for several nights in a row he was able to forgo a second dose of Seconal when he awoke after a few hours. Essie began to hope against hope—and for public consumption to predict yet again—that "we are nearing the end of this nightmare, and in a month, or two at the most, he will be really well again. . . ."[32]

A few additional people were allowed to come for brief visits. Philip Lebon (Harold Davison's doctor, and the man who had put Essie in touch with the Priory) got his first look at Paul in many months, and Essie reported excitedly that he had succeeded in engaging Paul in animated talk about music, even leading him to sing a few excerpts to illustrate a point: "It was rather thrilling to see him first really interested and enjoying himself, then participating, then contributing." Essie's friend Peggy Middleton went to the Connaught Square flat for tea while Paul was there. "He seemed better than he had been for two years," she wrote Cedric Belfrage. "He had never since the collapse been able to talk about world situations and people or in fact to talk to me for more than 5 *minutes*. This time we gossiped for almost an hour and I felt happy about it and he seemed gay and made jokes. . . . Essie felt the breakthrough had been made. . . ."[33]

Four days later he was back in the Priory, heading down into another low. On top of that setback came the shocking news of Bob Rockmore's sudden death from a heart attack. Essie could not decide how to tell Paul, and the doctors suggested she wait. It wasn't until a month later, in mid-March 1963, when he was once again on an up cycle, that she felt able to risk it. Hearing the news, he "just put his head down, put his hand over his eyes, and went RIGHT DOWN," Essie reported to Clara. He just sat there, sad and apathetic until—at least as Essie told it—she said "very firmly: No, YOU, dont just sit there, DO SOMETHING. Write NOW to Clara, and send your love and sympathy. Hold her hand by mail. Bobby would like that. . . . And I gave him a pad and pen, and addressed and stamped an envelope for him, then went back to my knitting. After another hour, he picked up the pen and said: What shall I write? I said write what is in your heart and in your mind, period. So he did. And I sealed and mailed it on the way home. . . . After he wrote the letter he immediately felt better, because he had done something constructive. On Sunday he was fine, but sad. But he didn't DESCEND, if you know what I mean." Paul's note to Clara that day was simplicity itself: "Do so wish I were with you to talk and talk and talk. It seems I could write pages and pages about what dear Bobby meant to me. . . ." Two months later, writing to her again, Paul struck a more inclusive, elegiac note: "Seems such a strange world already. . . . I'll do the best I can. . . ."[34]

In the hope of accelerating his progress, Essie decided to orchestrate plans for his approaching sixty-fifth birthday in order to ensure an enthusiastic response. She mailed out a form letter ("Dear Dear Friends") soliciting greetings ("I would like him to receive an avalanche of Birthday Cards") and even outlining the sentiments she wanted expressed: ". . . wish him health and happiness, say you are so glad to hear that he is recovering and thank him for his example and courage and integrity during a very tough period. . . . Knowledge that he is remembered and understood . . . will be a major contribution to his permanent recovery, which seems to be in the very near future." Paul would have been horrified at the letter, having all his life avoided any crass bid for attention. But crassness did produce the desired avalanche.[35]

On the day of his sixty-fifth birthday, April 9, 1963, Essie was able to take a small mountain of congratulatory messages and presents out to the Priory. But Paul's reaction was not at all what she had anticipated. The more he read the letters, the more agitated he became, until finally, pushing them aside, he angrily got up and started shouting about the demands being made on him. People were beginning to expect too much from him again—writing that they hoped he would return to Australia, sing again in Prague, speak here there and everywhere—didn't they understand he would never sing again, never return again, never see any of them again? Essie tried to quiet him: "People didn't want him to do a damn thing at the moment, except to get well," she insisted. *You* don't understand, he shot back, "I'll never be well. . . . I'll just sit in a corner . . . until maybe something can happen to me like happened to Bobby [Rockmore], and that will be fine. Or maybe some sympathetic understanding doctor will give me something." "He was so angry," she reported to Helen Rosen. Essie told Dr. Ackner what had happened. "Not to worry," Ackner purportedly told her, "it's all a part of the picture. . . . He cant go too far back now, just setbacks temporarily."[36]

The birthday hurdle over—if not quite cleared—Essie promptly turned to the next task: replying to spreading reports that Paul had become disillusioned with the U.S.S.R. In its fullest form, the rumor had appeared in January 1963 as a two-part article purported to have been written by Robeson himself in a fly-by-night sheet called *The National Insider*. The style of the articles wasn't remotely close to Robeson's own, and the content was almost comically foreign to his actual history (". . . at times I have been a Socialist and a Fascist. . . . [My father's sermons] were really powerful, but none of them appealed to the intellect. Most of the congregation didn't really have any intellect to begin with"). Yet, as farfetched as the articles were, and as disreputable as the publication in which they appeared was, the section in which Robeson purportedly rejected Soviet-style Communism (though not the dream of a classless society) was reprinted in *Le Figaro* and then picked up elsewhere. It therefore required rebuttal.[37]

Essie drafted a reply and sent it off for comment and correction to Paul, Jr., Ben Davis, D. N. Pritt, Lloyd Brown, Harry Francis (and through him John Gollan, head of the CP in Great Britain), Carlton Goodlett of the peace movement, and Alexander Soldatov, the Soviet Ambassador to Britain. She made revisions according to their suggestions—particularly Pritt's—and got off a strong statement, under her own name, denouncing the articles as "pure fabrication" and declaring that "None of us has seen any indication that 'he has changed his political views' in any way, as has been alleged in the articles. On the contrary, there has been no interruption in his warm friendship and close contact with our Soviet and Socialist friends." (In a letter to Cedric Belfrage, Peggy Middleton provided a private gloss on that view: ". . . so far as I know Paul has never repudiated the SU, but I can well believe he said something angry and incoherent that got misconstrued. Essie says that he does.") The Associated Negro Press issued a release based on Essie's statement, and for the moment the matter died, neither the original allegations nor the denial receiving widespread circulation. (Several months later, Essie released a further statement in Paul's name calling talk of his recantation "completely absurd"; *Time* announced that "The phrasing sounded suspiciously Eslandic.")[38]

By then, Essie had become fierce about press intrusions. She "still treats the whole thing [the illness] as confidential," Peggy Middleton wrote Cedric Belfrage in bemusement. And Essie herself wrote Mikhail Kotov in the U.S.S.R. that the press had become a "serious worry" to her. She was not merely being her usual overprotective self, for at one point in late 1962 reporters had actually come out to the Priory to try to get a statement from Paul about Castro; the authorities at the institution had effectively blocked access, and Paul himself had had no idea a press hunt for him had been on. But now, in mid-1963, with more than two years having passed since his collapse in Moscow, the newspapers (according to Essie) had decided to renew their efforts "to smoke Paul out, interview him, and see exactly what was what." Their only real interest, she felt, was in whether he had changed his political views, and she "determined NOT to permit" a question that "would so infuriate him, and offend him . . . I dare not risk his cursing them out." In the summer of 1963, however, a confrontation with the press appeared imminent when Essie decided to make a shift in Paul's medical treatment.[39]

Peggy Middleton—according to her account—had been protesting for some time against Paul's ECT treatments at "a rich man's hideout where," she felt, "the emphasis was on the social situation and not on general health." Her constant needling, in combination with the growing length of Paul's stay at the Priory and the uncertainty of his progress, lay the groundwork for doubt that an unexpected arrival further activated. Claire ("Micki") Hurwitt, wife of the New York surgeon Elliott Hurwitt and herself trained in psychiatric nursing, had known Paul a little from Progressive Party days, and when she arrived with her two small children in England, she dropped off an introductory note from Helen Rosen at the Connaught Square flat. Essie invited Micki up for tea and took an immediate liking to her (as did Micki to Essie), finding her combination of left-wing and medical credentials irresistible. When Essie told her about the course of Paul's treatment at the Priory, Micki expressed surprise at the large number of shock treatments—by then a documented fifty-four—confessing an instinctual distrust of ECT. Essie suggested she come out to the Priory and have a look at Paul directly.[40]

Micki did not like what she saw. As soon as she walked into Paul's room, she was overwhelmed by the smell of paraldehyde, a "knockout" drug she associated with only the most desperate and uncontrollable psychiatric cases. A nurse at one point beckoned Micki aside and showed her Paul's medication chart; Micki was horrified at the number and high dosage of drugs he was getting every day—"enough to kill a horse," she told Essie. "Get him out of there," she said. Her husband arrived from New York several weeks later and agreed with her estimate. Peggy Middleton had recently spent a day at the famed Buch Clinic in East Berlin and had been particularly impressed with Dr. Alfred Katzenstein, an American-trained clinical psychologist who had served with the U.S. Army during World War II and had experience dealing with survivors of the concentration camps. Essie flew over to Berlin to have a look around, was impressed with what she saw, and made preliminary arrangements for a September 1 consultation for Paul, if he was willing.[41]

Initially he was not. Then he said he would go, but only if he could go at once. Franz and Diana Loesser, who several years before had initiated the Robeson passport campaign in Manchester and now lived in the GDR, were enlisted to make quick arrangements. A flight on Polish Airways was booked for its regular nonstop Sunday flight to East Berlin on August 25. Somehow the British press got wind of the plans, and several reporters congregated outside the Connaught Square flat and rang Essie's phone at all hours of the day and night. Peggy Middleton advised a statement to the papers, but Essie felt "there was always the chance that he would refuse to go at the last minute" and feared most of all that if Paul himself was accosted, he might break down. Determined to avoid the press, she hit on an elaborate set of ruses worthy of Agatha Christie.[42]

Late Saturday night, Peggy Middleton, Diana Loesser, and other friends collected eleven pieces of baggage from the Robeson flat and deposited them at Paddington Station. Sunday morning, the *Telegraph* hit the stands with an article reporting that Robeson, who had "broken with Moscow," was about to be spirited behind the Iron Curtain to keep him silent, and that his wife was denying all access to him in the interim. "Paul is no longer a public figure," the *Telegraph* quoted her as saying over the phone, "He is not in the public domain." The article set the press to salivating, and a horde of reporters now moved into Connaught Square. Essie was ready for them.[43]

While Harry Francis got Paul out of the Priory—on the floor of a car under the noses of reporters waiting at both entrances—Essie concocted a scheme for getting herself out of Connaught Square. She enlisted Micki Hurwitt and another friend, Nick Price; Nick collected Micki in his car and parked it near the Robesons' flat. Micki got out, casually strolled past the reporters, rang the Robesons' doorbell, and was admitted, Essie having been watching from the window. Essie gave her the key to the flat, a piece of hand luggage, and her big traveling purse; with Essie's two overcoats draped over her arm, Micki went back out into the street, trying to appear elegantly calm. When she'd gotten a block away, one of the reporters ran after her and asked if she was Mrs. Robeson; Micki gave him "a withering stare" and he backed off.[44]

On returning to the car, she gave Nick Price the apartment key, and he in turn went up to the flat, casually letting himself in as if he lived in the building. Essie gave him the rest of the hand luggage, draped Paul's overcoats over his arm, and arranged to meet him and Micki at the Lancaster Gate underground stop. Nick got back to the car without incident, but when Essie prepared to leave the flat herself, she discovered she'd sent off all her money in the handbag with Micki. But her luck held. Though it was a Sunday in the summer, she found one neighbor at home and borrowed ten shillings. Taking a deep breath, she then stepped out of the building, a plastic cover over her hair, a pile of letters in her mouth for posting at the corner (*Punch* later had a good time with the letters, recommending them to its readers as the latest word in ingenious disguise). No one recognized her; a heavy rain and her lack of luggage helped. She made it safely to the Marble Arch underground and within minutes met Nick and Micki at Lancaster Gate. Nick had already picked up the heavy baggage from Paddington.[45]

They made it to the Priory in twenty minutes. If they had been daring, Paul had been lionhearted. After being removed from the Priory, he had remained in the hands of Harry Francis and the "British left" (Hurwitt's phrase) in a car parked in the nearby woods, awaiting the rendezvous with Essie. He had not been in the best of shape recently, but somehow held together—"He had all kinds of guts," was Hurwitt's laconic summary. After speeding to the airport, they found the director of the Polish airways waiting for them, apprehensive at the lateness of the hour. Having cleverly directed the press to the VIP lounge, he quickly led the Robesons and Hurwitt through the regular gate onto the first-class section of the plane. The three other passengers in the compartment paid them no attention. Within minutes the plane took off, and they settled back with a sigh of relief. Essie, laughing, handed Paul the *Telegraph* article about his pending "abduction."[46]

At that moment, a pleasant-looking young man got up from his seat, came over to the Robesons, smiled, and handed Paul his card. Paul smiled back, read the card, scowled, and handed it to Essie. Printed on the card was "John Osman, Foreign Correspondent for the *London Daily Telegraph.*" (Reuters News Agency, they later learned, had planted a reporter in tourist class as well.) Essie jumped up and insisted Osman return to his own seat, eventually forcefully accompanying him, expressing her indignation that the British press would harass a sick man ("The thing I resented most," she later wrote Marie Seton, "was that it was so *American* at its worst, and this I did not expect from the British. Well, we live and learn"). To make sure Osman would stay in his seat, Essie parked herself next to him and talked him right into Berlin.[47]

To her surprise, he "seemed nice" and had been to Africa, so, as Berlin came into view, she agreed to let him ask Paul two and only two brief questions: What did he think of the *Sunday Telegraph* story, and what did he think of the recent March on Washington? Paul had been monosyllabic up to that point, but he somehow, remarkably, summoned up the energy to answer, and did so eloquently. He said the *Telegraph* article was vicious and, worse, wishful thinking—not having been able to establish that he had changed his political views, and disappointed that he was voluntarily returning to a socialist country, the press had decided to make a mystery of it. As for the March on Washington, Robeson called it "a turning point," said he was proud of the black strength and unity it showed—and sent his congratulations. Osman tried to continue the interview, but Essie cut him off. In his article in the *Telegraph* the next day, Osman described Essie as "a formidable 'protector' " who had threatened him with judo at one point. He accurately printed Paul's replies to his two questions and described him as looking "haggard and worn. His features were thin and his stooping gait bore little resemblance to his public image."[48]

The doctors at the Buch Clinic thought so, too. Dr. Katzenstein found him "completely without initiative," his depressive moods "very low," his ups "not high enough to be called manic"—the reverse of his breakdown in 1956. The doctors immediately took him off all sedation (though adding Librium subsequently) and expressed considerable doubt—even anger—about the "high" amounts of barbiturates and ECT that had been given him. "I don't think anyone would have argued with ten or twelve ECT treatments," Dr. Katzenstein said more than twenty years later, but fifty-four such treatments was not only "very unusual" but "a very doubtful procedure unless immediately followed by psychotherapy." He believed fifty-four shocks could theoretically produce "considerable changes within the brain"; though in fact he found no such evidence, he felt that at the least they had shaken Robeson's confidence—"just the process of being grabbed and hit, you lose the sense of being in control of your own life." Katzenstein freely acknowledges, however, that "here in the GDR we generally consider British psychiatry to be superior to ours." Indeed, the literature on ECT since the early sixties does not as a whole support Katzenstein's views. For quick alleviation of *acute* depressive symptoms (as in Robeson's case), ECT remains the preferred initial treatment. But disagreement does still exist about whether improvement from ECT is temporary and can or should be built upon with additional courses, and also about the extent to which psychotherapy can prove a useful adjunct for those who are severely disoriented. A successful outcome in the treatment of mental illness seems centrally to depend on careful adjustments tailored to the individual needs of the patient at hand. Such adjustments require intuitive skills of the highest order. Which is to say, one part of medical care, perhaps the greatest part, is an art. Robeson was not fortunate enough to have been treated by artists.[49]

After a comprehensive set of tests, the Buch clinicians found a heart "insufficiency"—not unusual, they said, in a man of sixty-five—a slightly enlarged liver (possibly a toxic reaction to drugs), and "a secondary colitis with incipient ulceration," perhaps also drug-related. Additionally (and peripherally), the GDR doctors diagnosed Paget's disease, a condition—of unknown etiology and no psychiatric import—involving an abnormal amount of bone deformation and known to be fairly commonplace. Katzenstein did not feel he could rule out some underlying organic cause for Robeson's condition—since little was (or is now, for that matter) known about the chemistry of the brain—but felt that ultimately the extraordinary pressures he had been under for a decade were themselves sufficient to explain his collapse. Castor oil with every meal quickly put Robeson's digestive system in good order. And getting off sedatives not only made him immediately more alert and talkative but also *improved* his ability to sleep (as is now well known, a prolonged use of sleeping medication can produce a reverse effect). Passing through East Berlin two weeks after the Robesons' arrival, Elliott Hurwitt was impressed with Paul's improvement (as was Sam Rosen a few days later, though he was not impressed with Dr. Katzenstein himself). Hurwitt wrote Essie soon after that he felt sure "Paul is in what is, for him, the best possible medical environment that could be found." Coming to the Buch Clinic has "turned out to be a very fine move," Essie reported home. To Helen Rosen she wrote that Paul "now enters into discussion. He stammers, and is slow on the up-take, but on the beam, right on the beam."[50]

But she did not report that Dr. Katzenstein had suggested that "what is left of Paul's health" would have to be quietly conserved. Nor did Essie tell anyone—including Paul—that she had been given bad news about her own health. Explaining why she was flat on her back in the hospital, she wrote home airily about "a bad flu," "an infected gall bladder," and "general exhaustion from the long siege." But in fact the diagnosis was a good deal worse. Although the London and Moscow doctors had continued to give her a clean bill after her periodic checkups, the Buch doctors found evidence of recurring cancer and in fact told her it was terminal. Determined to live out her life at full tilt, Essie went off to collect a "peace" medal she had earlier been awarded; the ceremony had been delayed until she could appear in person.[51]

Paul was not told about Essie's condition, or about his own prognosis; he was encouraged to believe they were both on the road to full recovery. And certainly he seemed greatly improved, able to participate in more socializing within a period of a few weeks than had previously been possible over many months. It was protected socializing—a few friends, like Stephen Fritchman, Joris Ivens (the filmmaker), Earl Dickerson (the black executive and activist), Henry Winston (the CPUSA leader), Vladimir Pozner (of *L'Humanité*), and Helen and Scott Nearing, would drop by for carefully limited visits. Sometimes Dr. Katzenstein would take Robeson to feed the ducks in the park, or on supervised outings with himself and his wife to the park, the zoo, to shop, or to drop in briefly at the Soviet-German House of Culture. Diana and Franz Loesser visited Robeson at Buch several times, and had him out to their house twice for tea; Diana noted with delight the gradual improvement—when he first arrived in the GDR "he looked very strange and ill, burnt out," but within a few months he "was talking to people and you got the feeling he could cope, though a very sick person." A few expeditions were more elaborate still. Paul took an accompanied trip downtown to be measured for a new overcoat, and on one notable occasion not only took tea at the Soviet Ambassador's residence but stayed for an extended chat about grandchildren, the "Negro Revolution," and the hockey match between Russia and Canada. Essie described the visit (with her usual optimistic overelaboration) as fluent and lighthearted.[52]

The Robesons had Thanksgiving dinner with Kay and Aubrey Pankey and their other guest, Ollie Harrington, the black American cartoonist, now living in Berlin. Pankey had left his singing career in the States in search of wider opportunities and had found them in Eastern Europe, regularly performing in concert and settling in the GDR. The Pankeys hadn't seen Robeson in a dozen years, and Kay Pankey recalls her shock on opening the door: "I saw a tall, gaunt, thin man; he was all eyes. My heart just went out." Ollie Harrington, who had also been living in Europe for a decade, was equally stunned at the sight of Robeson: "I'd never seen such a change in a man." But Harrington, a warm and witty storyteller, decided to try to break through to Paul—"Intuitively I knew he was there, somewhere," so "I started telling anecdotes we used in our 'special times' back in Harlem, tales about 'the stupidity of Charley' alternating with 'the ridiculous reaction of the Brothers.' " Robeson slowly responded: his eyes gradually came alive, and he even laughed out loud a few times. "I haven't seen Paul throw back his head and laugh so heartily for a very long time," Essie later wrote the Pankeys in thanks. "It was like a visit home in the old days, with none of the bad past." To Harrington, the evening showed that Paul "*was* there; he was not a brain-damaged individual; communication could be established—but on *his* terms." On his way out of the door, having already lapsed back into melancholy, Paul impulsively grabbed Ollie's hand. "Thank you, thank you," he said over and over.[53]

Yet Paul's ability to go out more exacerbated his unease in one sense: the very fact that he could see improvement and enjoy himself unleashed deep fears of incompetence; the accelerated activity itself fed his anxiety about being once more asked to "perform." Dropping in one day with Dr. Katzenstein to visit the Soviet-German House of Culture, he roamed around comfortably and had coffee in the restaurant, and was even able to tolerate a few people staring at him as if to say, "Is *that* Paul Robeson?" But then an official did recognize him, gathered others around and persuaded Paul to sign the visitors' book. He seemed to take it all in stride, but the next day, according to Essie, "he was in a bit of a tizzy," and she finally found out why: he was worried about whether he had written something "really adequate" in the visitors' book. When he told Essie and Dr. Katzenstein what he had written, they assured him that it was fine and that, besides, nobody expected instant wisdom on such an occasion. Paul seemed only partly comforted.[54]

Essie, who was still keeping the outside world at bay, had withheld from Paul for months the sad news that his beloved brother Ben had died of cancer of the esophagus in July. She finally told him in November, after Paul had written his brother a little note. She left no record of how he took the news of the loss of someone who had been such a loving anchor to him. Probably it was without much outward reaction, for, as Essie had once written to Helen Rosen, ". . . nobody knows what is in . . . Paul's mind." However, in mid-November he headed into another down cycle, and Essie reported to the family that he told her he "just cannot make it any more. . . . I am too tired. I haven't got the energy. Maybe the voice is still there, but I haven't the energy, and it takes energy and nerves. And I just haven't got them anymore." He had felt "exhausted," he told her, as far back as 1956, following prostate surgery, and had never really mended. He had been able to make a "supreme effort" now and then—California in 1957, Carnegie Hall in 1958, *Othello* in 1959, Australia in 1960—but only with "great fear and worry." (During the run of *Othello*, he now confessed to her for the first time, "every performance was an ordeal": he always expected to forget his lines and once did.) He dreaded any prospect of yet another "come-back," yet at the same time he worried over the fact that he had never managed to get to Africa or China and still felt he "should make some kind of contribution and gesture of respect" to them. He told Katzenstein he had "failed" his own people, had been "unable to bring forth the victory," "could not help them any more." Essie conveyed his fearful questions back home to the family: "Will people understand? Will they think he has changed, as the Western Press insists? What can he say? What can he do???? And last and most important, he feels he should be home participating in the Negro struggle. But how??? He isn't up to personal appearances. . . ."[55]

Essie tried to ease Paul's mind, joined in the effort by the Buch clinicians, and seconded by friends back home like Helen Rosen. Together they urged him to retire, in body and conscience; he had done his share, and more; it was better to end on a dignified note; now was the time for a younger generation of black leaders to shoulder responsibility; perhaps after he had recovered his health he might again consider an active role, but for the time being he should set his mind at ease by formally announcing that the public phase of his life was completed, by medical command. Paul said he agreed—and went on worrying. He could not shake a lifetime of trying to live up to those perfectionist demands his father had placed on him in childhood, and which he had long since internalized as his own, to live up to the dictum that he should always do better and more. He could never quite believe that he had done *enough* to allow him to retire with honor from the field. Particularly, he could not shake the wish to rejoin in a significant way a black-rights movement he had done so much to inaugurate, could not give up the hope that the new generation of black activists would make some request for his services that he would be able to fulfill, that together they might establish some continuity of purpose, some mutual acknowledgment of interconnection between the generations.[56]

Paul seemed unable to leave it alone, continuing to fret about whether he had a future, and if so whether he wanted one. Essie (at least as she reported to the family) told him *he* had to make the decision, had to tell her what he wanted to do, where he wanted to go. She drew up a list for him of the possible places they could live and the pros and cons of living there. On the morning of December 7, 1963, he told her he had made a decision. He wanted to go home—home to the States, to Jumel Terrace, to his grandchildren, to his people. Essie had several more go-rounds with him, but he held to his decision: "This is what he seems to want," she reported to the family, "so we are going to have to go, as the British say." She added, "I have a VERY good feeling about it myself. . . . I know your welcome, and your concern will warm his heart, and relax him very much. He knows you wont expect him to DO anything, just BE. That's what everybody here wants, and hopes, but HE doesn't leave it at that. He feels he should be doing something, saying something." Dr. Katzenstein felt Paul's decision to go back to the States was the right one. He was pleased that his effort to "treat the whole person" had led to some improvement, that Paul had gained weight and appeared more animated in manner; yet Katzenstein felt "there was no way of knowing if he stayed longer whether he would improve more." He hoped Robeson "would find a peaceful home."[57]

On December 17 Paul and Essie flew nonstop to London to collect some of their things from the Connaught Square flat and to take their leave of friends. On December 22 they boarded a BOAC jet for Idlewild Airport, New York.

Robeson was going home, as he had wanted to for years.

■

Attempted Renewal

(1964–1965)

Three Port Authority policemen ran interference through the reporters as Essie on one side and Paul, Jr., on the other escorted Paul to a waiting car. As newsmen tried to throw questions at him, Robeson smiled away in benign silence. Only twice did he respond. When a television reporter stuck a microphone in his face, Robeson whispered that he had nothing to say for now but might "later on." Asked by another reporter if he was going to take part in the civil-rights movement, he said, "I've been a part of the civil rights movement all my life." As the repetitive question "Are you disillusioned with Communism?" continued to resound, Essie jumped in to say, "No, he thinks it's terrific—he always has and he always will" (thereby further feeding rumors that her function was to muzzle him).[1]

A "Muted Return," headlined the New York *Post*. "Native Son Robeson Back Without a Song," chorused the *Daily News*. The conservative black New York *Amsterdam News* referred to Robeson in its lead sentence as "apparently disillusioned" and predicted he faced a congressional probe into his politics and a snubbing from black civil-rights organizations. Dorothy Kilgallen reported in her syndicated column that she had "received hundreds of letters protesting the fact that he was allowed to return"; she herself favored it as "a propaganda victory for our way of life." Congressman William S. Mailliard protested Robeson's return directly to the FBI; the Bureau replied that as a citizen he was entitled to come home. This did not mean that J. Edgar Hoover was ready to give up his pursuit of Robeson: he instructed the New York Office of the FBI to "ascertain the extent of his activities." The office wired Hoover that, "not being certain" of Robeson's attitude toward Communism, it "is not making any recom-

mendation for an interview by newsmen upon his arrival back in the US"—
an open declaration that it would and *could* manipulate the press. *The New
York Times* featured Robeson's return on the front page, described him as
"much thinner and not his old vociferous self," accounted for his illness
as due to "a reported circulatory problem," and reported that his "comfortable income" was still secure. To a separate profile piece the *Times*
affixed the headline "Disillusioned Native Son."[2]

Such polite indirection did not suit the purposes of the *Herald Tribune*,
which opted for a frontal attack. In a lead editorial, the conservative
paper—having never played any role itself in the civil-rights struggle—
blasted Robeson for having "run away" when "the going got rough." "He
abandoned the battle, as well as his country, to indulge a juvenile's taste
for Marxist idealism, leaving it to others to stay at home to fight the war
for civil rights. . . . Now that the back of the opposition to civil rights has
been broken, Robeson returns anxious to jump on the bandwagon. . . .
[He] always has and always will be a juvenile, with a big voice but a small
mind . . . [and] would be more of a hindrance than a help to the civil-rights
movement. His countrymen have proved that they can manage without
him." The attack could hardly have been phrased in a more hurtful way,
fueling Robeson's own nightmare fears that he had lost touch with the
black struggle and that his earlier contributions to it would be forgotten
or distorted.[3]

But not everyone had forgotten or felt malevolent toward him. As one
indignant letter-writer to the *Tribune* put it, "Robeson jumping on the
bandwagon now? Hell, man, he built that wagon—that's John Henry himself you're insulting." In the Pittsburgh *Courier*, J. A. Rogers protested the
Tribune's "rough going-over," accusing it of "sheer ignorance of the influence for good Robeson's career and accomplishments have had on the race
situation here." And when W. E. B. Du Bois died at age ninety-five in Accra
and Essie made her first public appearance, two months after arriving
home, at a Carnegie Hall tribute to him, she got a standing ovation that
lasted for minutes, clearly in the nature of a warm welcome home both for
herself and for Paul.[4]

He himself could do little to respond to those who falsified his past
accomplishments and gloated over his present disability. Having minimal
energy and fearful of another relapse, he was unable to give interviews, let
alone face the barrage of a formal press conference. Dr. Morris Pearlmutter,
once again taking over as Robeson's physician (he had treated him in
1955–56), found him on arrival "emaciated . . . not very communicative,
and . . . having severe insomnia. His appetite was quite poor and he
complained of marked fatigue." Pearlmutter put him on Elavil and Librium
and at bedtime chloral hydrate to induce sleep. He advised Robeson to
remain quietly at home for the time being.[5]

"Home" alternated between his sister Marian's in Philadelphia and the house at Jumel Terrace in Harlem that he shared with Essie. Marian provided the deeper level of comfort, though he did feel secure at Jumel, with its privacy and its considerate neighbors. "Paul roams freely from floor to floor," Essie wrote Harold Davison in England, "retires any moment, bounces up and around as he feels like." To make Paul more comfortable still, Freda Diamond sent over a reclining chair; Ben Davis and Lloyd Brown dropped by to visit; and Paul, Jr., arrived most mornings, bringing his work (translating technical journals), thus freeing Essie to resume her job as a United Nations correspondent several days a week. Paul, Jr., arranged to take him to see a matinee showing at a neighborhood theater of Sidney Poitier's film *Lilies of the Field.* "It went off beautifully," Essie reported, "with no strain or worry, and just enjoyment, and feeling that this could be done more often!!" Their grandchildren were a source of particular delight: Essie ("Nana," as David and Susan called her) was a doting and effusive grandmother, describing the children to friends as "so gay and healthy and normal and busy and interested and interesting." "Grandpa Paul," in his contrasting style, took pleasure in being around the children, but (in Marilyn's words) "was more of an observer."[6]

Early in March, some two months after returning, Big Paul ventured out to the apartment of his old friends John Abt (the lawyer) and Jessica Smith (the editor of *New World Review*) for a quiet dinner. It turned out to be less quiet than expected, yet Paul managed to hold his own. John Abt began "a terrific discussion" (in Essie's words) by saying he had been disappointed in the Carnegie Hall tribute to Du Bois because only Lorraine Hansberry among the speakers had mentioned that he had joined the Communist Party. Having given one of the speeches at the tribute, Essie felt a bit aggrieved at Abt's criticism until the others assured her that anything more would have been inappropriate for *that* meeting. Besides, she wrote George Murphy, "Just between you and me, we should not brag too much about his joining. It was a fine gesture, and wonderful. But it was at the end, and then he left. So, easy does it, record it with due respect and justice, but we should not BRAG."[7]

Though fully aware of her advancing cancer, the irrepressible Essie was on the move again. She made up a "plan-of-action," a list of things "To Do" and "Not To Do" for the rest of her life, "so as not to waste what I had left but use it to best advantage." Following the success of her initial appearance at the Du Bois tribute, she agreed to take part in a panel at the American Institute for Marxist Studies organized by the historian Herbert Aptheker, to speak at the annual *National Guardian* luncheon, and then to embark on a two-week lecture tour to the West Coast. While she was away, Paul managed to take himself by train to Marian's house in Philadelphia. By June he was feeling improved enough to go with Paul, Jr., to a baseball game, and Dr. Pearlmutter noted with satisfaction that he was sleeping and eating better and had steadily put on weight. "The results so far have exceeded my best expectations," Pearlmutter wrote Robeson's previous doctors in the U.S.S.R., England, and the GDR. "He is again the Paul Robeson with a lively interest in life, people, and the world around him."[8]

Pearlmutter's own case records show a somewhat less euphoric result, but Robeson had indubitably improved. By mid-June he had put on thirty pounds and was near his normal weight of 250. "Paul is so much better," Essie wrote a friend, "but he still says and feels he isn't," and still fretted that "people will not understand his idleness." Pearlmutter felt confident enough to reduce the medication, cutting out two Elavil and one Librium a day. Robeson's energy level rose; he was less lethargic, more interested in his surroundings, better able to watch and enjoy television. He began to talk for the first time about possible activity, cautiously considering some limited public appearance. "He is now PLANNING, no less," Essie wrote the Rosens. "On a low level, but never mind."[9]

The right opportunity, though a sad one, came at the end of August. Ben Davis, Jr., died of pancreatic cancer on August 22 at age sixty. The loss of his great friend and comrade was compounded by the recent death of Du Bois, and the passing of his beloved brother Ben the previous year while he was incapacitated in Europe and unable to return home for the funeral. In making the effort to attend Ben Davis's memorial, Robeson was saying goodbye to his brother and to Dr. Du Bois as well. He managed to say a few words, writing them out himself and delivering them without any hesitation or stumbling. A throng was waiting on the sidewalk outside when the two hundred mourners emerged from the chapel. Catching sight of Robeson's still-towering figure, the crowd surged toward him; people called his name in admiration, reached over to pat him on the back or squeeze his arm. For a few moments he seemed trapped in the sea of well-wishers, and the police were unable to clear a path to him. But he finally edged his way to the curb and got into a cab—apparently none the worse, despite the sorrow and tension of the occasion.[10]

Indeed, he felt so encouraged that a few days after the funeral he issued his first public statement since returning home, directing his words exclusively to the black press. In it he spoke of his recovering health but said for the time being he would be unable to resume public life. He wanted it known, however, that "I am, of course, deeply involved with the great upsurge of our people. Like all of you, my heart has been filled with admiration for the many thousands of Negro Freedom Fighters and their white associates"—he had never veered from the vision of an integrated struggle, and world—"who are waging the battle for civil rights throughout the country, and especially in the South." He took pride in pointing out that, when he had written in *Here I Stand* in 1958 that "the time is now," some people had thought "that perhaps my watch was fast (and maybe it was a little), but most of us seem to be running on the same time—now." He was also pleased that the call he had sounded in the book for unified action and mass militancy among blacks was no longer deemed "too radical." Most black people, he felt, had finally come to agree with his 1949 Paris statement calling upon them to eschew foreign wars and to conserve their strength for the struggle at home, a struggle that black artists as a matter of course had now joined—though in his day he had been told to sing, not talk. "It is good to see all these transformations."[11]

Emboldened, Robeson was willing for the first time to cast a wary eye on a writing project that he had previously dismissed out-of-hand as beyond his capacity. Three publishing firms had asked him to write some sort—any sort—of memoir, and offered him contracts. For a time (in Essie's words) Paul was "absolutely adamant about being unable and unwilling to undertake this. . . ." But as he improved, Essie put out some documents and clippings from her voluminous files for him to read if he felt up to it, and before long he was browsing through them, asking questions to refresh his memory. He agreed to let his old friend Earl Robinson (composer of "Ballad for Americans") bring a young Macmillan editor named Alan Rinzler over to the house. Rinzler, though white, was on the steering committee of SNCC and a devoted admirer of Robeson's. He was shocked at the condition in which he found him. Instead of the vigorous, charismatic figure he had grown up admiring, he found a man who "seemed very faint and hesitant, as if brain-damaged. Both his speech and movement were slow. . . . He looked weak and frail. He seemed like he was eighty. I was stunned by his appearance." Essie, on the other hand, struck Rinzler as charming and vigorous, deeply considerate of Paul—and definitely in favor of Paul's writing the book. They talked for three hours. Rinzler offered a guarantee that the publisher would do no "doctoring" of the text and encouraged him to try "some conversations" with Lloyd Brown, his co-author on *Here I Stand,* as a way of generating a manuscript. Paul promised to think about the possibility further. "We were all surprised and delighted, and I think Paul surprised himself," Essie wrote a friend.[12]

In October, during Robeson's monthly office visit, Pearlmutter found him "a little more restless," but made no changes in his medications and no effort to discourage the light activity he'd begun. In November, perhaps overeager to capitalize on these limited gains, Robeson attended a U.S.S.R. reception at the United Nations, a National Council for American-Soviet Friendship celebration at Carnegie Hall, and a seventieth-birthday fête for John Howard Lawson, one of the Hollywood Ten—all within a week's time. He got a tumultuous reception at each of the events. At the Soviet affair people kept coming up to him in disbelief, wanting to see for themselves if he was really there. At the Carnegie Hall occasion he got a standing ovation that lasted for a full five minutes when he put in a surprise appearance, telling the crowd how very good it felt to be there and how "very gratifying to see the remarkable growth and development on many levels" in the Soviet Union, a remark that may have struck some as curious, since the admired reformer Khrushchev had recently resigned under pressure. At Lawson's birthday party Robeson gave a short speech in praise of the "dean of the Hollywood Ten," which led Lawson later to write him that "words cannot express" the joy he had felt at Robeson's presence.[13]

That round of activity temporarily slowed him. Essie wrote a friend that Paul "is thoroughly exhausted. . . . Although he is very happy that he has been able to do it all . . . the effort tires him because he does pay close attention to what everyone says to him, and so many people speak to him." "Essie says 'he's depressed,'" Pearlmutter recorded in his notes when he saw Robeson at the end of November, and he prescribed a repeat dose of medicine if he awakened at night. Even so, Robeson managed to begin work on a brief reminiscence of Du Bois for the militant new black magazine *Freedomways.* When the celebratory issue containing Robeson's short article appeared in March, he not only attended the *Freedomways* party to celebrate publication but also chose the occasion to sing in public ("Jacob's Ladder") for the first time in nearly four years; he was given a standing ovation. At the beginning of the new year, 1965, there were two more deaths of prominent left-wing figures—the black Communist leader Claudia Jones at age forty-nine, and the gifted playwright Lorraine Hansberry, who had worked with Robeson on the newspaper *Freedom,* of cancer at thirty-four. These poignant losses called out Robeson's reserves of strength, and he decided to respond to both publicly. Against the continuing processional of death, he continued to test his ability to rejoin life.[14]

Claudia Jones had died at her home in London—having been deported from the United States under the Smith Act some years before—and Robeson made a tape recording for her funeral. On it he spoke of her as "one of the victims of the dreadful McCarthy period" and rejoiced that after her deportation she had found her place in London's West Indian community helping to found and develop the West Indian *Gazette.* At Hansberry's funeral, Robeson not only appeared personally—despite a blizzard—but also delivered a eulogy. Speaking in a voice the *Times* called "still compelling . . . his eyes cast downward, his hands moving restlessly," he paid tribute to Hansberry's "feeling and knowledge of the history of our people . . . remarkable in one so young," and, as if encouraging himself to heed the advice, reminded the crowd that she "bids us to keep our heads high and to hold on to our strength and power—to soar like the Eagle in the air."[15]

At the Hansberry funeral, Malcolm X let it be known through an intermediary that he would like to meet Robeson. A little more than a year before, Malcolm had praised Robeson's "brilliant stand" in questioning as early as 1949 "the intelligence of colored people fighting to defend a country that treated them with such open contempt and bestial brutality." Paul, Jr., talked to Malcolm at the back of the funeral parlor and then relayed the invitation to his father. Robeson felt no affinity for the religious austerity of the mainstream Black Muslim movement and its leader, Elijah Muhammad, nor for their emphasis on separation from whites, the confinement of women, and the importance of black entrepreneurship. But toward Malcolm personally he felt high regard, especially after Malcolm had begun to sound an internationalist note following his seminal journey to Mecca. Still, it was decided to delay a meeting between the two men until a less stressful moment. A month later Malcolm was assassinated.[16]

With the approach of Robeson's sixty-seventh birthday, the editors of *Freedomways* asked if they could use the occasion to stage a "salute" to him, which might simultaneously be a moneymaker for the magazine. Given Robeson's improved condition (he had been going regularly on extended visits to his sister Marian's in Philadelphia, sometimes on his own), he gave *Freedomways* the go-ahead. Not everyone invited responded with enthusiasm. Some of those who sent regrets, like Coleman Young and John Howard Lawson, clearly did lament their schedule conflicts. But Roy Wilkins's cold reply to the request that he serve as a sponsor of the event (he had "overextended" himself, he wrote, and NAACP projects now required his undivided attention) was matched only by David Susskind's outright hostility: "My only reaction is that you must be joking—and what a bad joke it is."[17]

However, James Baldwin, Ossie Davis, Earl Dickerson, Dizzy Gillespie, John Coltrane, Paule Marshall, Linus Pauling, Earl Robinson, Pete Seeger, and I. F. Stone were among the sixty illustrious sponsors who did offer their names. More than two thousand people flocked to the ballroom of the Americana Hotel on the night of April 22, to be entertained during the four-hour celebration by Morris Carnovsky, Diana Sands, Roscoe Lee Browne, Howard da Silva, M. B. Olatunji, and Billy Taylor. The crowd was predominantly white and middle-aged, but made up in warmth what it lacked in diversity. John Lewis, chairman of SNCC, had been invited as a keynoter (the black activist lawyer Hope R. Stevens was the other) in the hope that he would serve as a symbolic bridge between Robeson and the new generation of black activists, but it turned out Lewis "knew so little" about Robeson that he turned to his fellow SNCC member Alan Rinzler, the editor who had been trying to coax Robeson into doing a memoir, to write his speech for him. Rinzler gave Lewis a "series of notes" and was "then appalled when Lewis read it word for word." Still, the words rang out with comradely flair—"We of SNCC are Paul Robeson's spiritual children. We too have rejected gradualism and moderation. We are also being accused of radicalism, of communist infiltration"—and they gladdened Robeson's spirit. When Bob Moses, a legendary SNCC leader, also showed up for the event and personally paid his respects to Robeson, it was possible to believe that generational continuity—and a sense of indebtedness—was as much fact as reverie.[18]

When Robeson himself took the platform, the crowd, uncertain whether he would speak, greeted him with a near-pandemonium of cheers, waves, and tears. Deeply moved, he thanked the artists "who have taken time out from their busy lives to come here this evening." Then, sticking closely to his prepared text, his voice firm and resonant, he sounded once again the themes that had been central to his life: art as the reflection of "a common Humanity"; the "great variety," in combination with "the universality," of human experience—its unity, "the one-ness of many of the people in our contemporary world"; the importance of letting people "decide for themselves" between the contending systems of social organization—and his personal pleasure that so many of the "newly emancipated nations of Asia and Africa" were moving in the direction of a socialist arrangement; the importance of the FREEDOM NOW struggle for the liberation of black people in the United States—*and* as an arena for finding and building "a living connection—deeper and stronger—between the Negro people and the great masses of white Americans, who are indeed our natural allies in the struggle for democracy."[19]

"A lot of love went towards him"; "a memorable occasion"; an "inspiring" night—almost everyone at the event found it "thrilling." The notable exception was the *Liberator,* one of the prominent organs of the new black militants. "Those who attended to welcome home a *leader* found themselves paying respects to a *legend,*" the *Liberator*'s columnist impatiently reported. "Even Robeson's own speech at the end of the evening was a disappointment in this respect." Yet the *Liberator*—apparently knowing nothing of Robeson's recent incapacity—did not entirely dismiss what it graciously acknowledged to be his leadership *potential.* In *Here I Stand,* the *Liberator* wrote, Robeson "foresaw and dealt with many of the problems which have come to a head since then"—the struggle for civil rights as a minimal necessity, not a maximum fulfillment; the moral right of the black community, threatened in life and property, to defend itself; the need for blacks to wrest control of their lives—and their movement—from white domination; the insistence that black leaders be single-mindedly dedicated to their own people's welfare. Yes, the *Liberator* solemnly concluded, the new generation of black activists had "the right and duty" to ask a man of Robeson's proven stature and insight to rejoin them "in battle." Robeson probably never saw the *Liberator*'s comments, but if he got wind of them he might have found solace for the impudence and forgetfulness of the young in remembering a letter Azikiwe of Nigeria had sent him nearly ten years earlier. Sensing that his own reign as national liberator and hero was coming to an end, Azikiwe had philosophically written, "Although we have spent a greater part of our fortune and our lives in the struggle, the lilies of the field who neither toil nor spin are now in the vanguard to reap where they have not sown. The result is a conflict of interest between those we had stimulated all these years to look forward to a new day and those who have arisen from among them to lead them to a Canaan of our dreams."[20]

The *Freedomways* event had gone off so well that it was decided to proceed with plans for a trip to California, with Essie accompanying Paul and—so it seemed in the planning, anyway—with careful protective measures to safeguard his health. The decision was made over Paul, Jr.'s strenuous objection, for he was convinced that his father was not up to the trip. Alice Childress also begged Essie to cancel plans for California. Childress had attended the event at the Americana, had seen "the sweat just popping out" on Paul's face, the hands trembling. But Essie told her, "He can't stay out of sight. He's a public figure. People want to know, where is Paul Robeson. We have to do it."[21]

The trip started out well enough. At Kennedy Airport in New York they got the red-carpet treatment because, as Essie wrote the Rosens, "the head Negro porter recognized Paul and went straight to the top guy and alerted him. He was having no nonsense about HIS idea of a VIP. And so the seats were cleared for us to have no immediate neighbors, and we were very comfortable." At the Los Angeles airport they were met by Steve Fritchman as well as Chuck Moseley and Homer Sadler, two black left-wing activists assigned as bodyguards ("I have never seen such security," Essie wrote home; "I at once was taught how to use a 15 repeater rifle, and found it easy and great fun"). Moseley and Sadler also kept guns hidden under the quilt on the car seat, but, unlike earlier years, there was no incident of any kind involving Paul's personal safety. The Robesons went directly to the home of their old friend Frankie Lee Sims of the National Negro Labor Council, with whom they were staying in the black community of Watts, and rested all the remainder of that day and the following day until time for a celebration in their honor at Fritchman's First Unitarian Church. Robeson was interviewed at the church by a friendly reporter from the Los Angeles *Times* whom Fritchman had okayed in advance (and, indeed, the sympathetic story was headlined "Robeson Cherishes His U.S. Heritage"), and then had dinner privately with Fritchman and church officials before joining the packed festivities. After Martha Schlamme performed a group of songs and a church choir sang, Paul himself was introduced to the gathering. He gave essentially the same speech he had at the Americana, but also sang without accompaniment a Hebridean song and "Jacob's Ladder," and at the close recited in Yiddish two verses from the song of the Warsaw Ghetto rebellion. "This is the first time," he told the adoring crowd, "I'm sort of playing around much with the singing, but I guess the voice is still around somewhere." Essie thought it sounded better than that—"full, complete with overtones, and under very firm control." He "seems to feel very experimental," she wrote home to the family. "He wants to try things. I am keeping clear watch, so no one can push him, and that he gets rest."[22]

Indeed, she guarded him so closely, screening out friends and strangers alike, that she aroused resentment at the time and suspicion since. According to Dorothy Healey, CP people "could not talk to him, see him, or have any kind of communication with him. . . . We were told that he was very sick." Rose Perry confirms that she and Pettis got an unexpected call from Essie enlisting their help. "I don't want the Party coming near him," she remembers Essie saying, and "If they call I'm going to tell them that you're arranging his meetings." Yet local Party leader Bill Taylor did have access to him, and when the top Party leader Gus Hall came through California he, too, was allowed to drop by; that alone aroused factional jealousy. When some old friends who were not Party people also found themselves barred, the resentment escalated into a conspiratorial view of Essie's intentions. Geri Branton, active in the civil-rights struggle and instrumental in arranging Robeson's previous appearances in California in 1958, found herself stopped at the door by Essie and not even invited to participate in the event at Fritchman's church. It seemed logical to assume that Essie was lending herself—and, through her control over his schedule, Paul—to some partisan maneuver; rumors flew that she was taking orders from the Gus Hall wing of the Party or even (having "turned") from the FBI. But logic, as is often the case, was not truth. A dying woman, always overzealous by temperament and especially when contending for undisputed control over Paul, had simply overstepped a few boundaries here, failed to flatter a few egos there.[23]

The frequency as well as the nature of Paul's appearances further fed antagonism toward Essie. Paul, Jr., for one, became irate when he discovered—belatedly—what he felt to be the irresponsibly hectic and overcrowded schedule Essie had subjected his father to. After Paul's appearance in Fritchman's church, it seemed to Paul, Jr., that one engagement was allowed to spill directly into the next. On one day, a morning breakfast in the black community was followed by a packed meeting at Mt. Sinai Baptist Church, in turn followed by an evening gathering at the home of a black physician in the Compton area. At all three events Robeson spoke, albeit briefly, and at one he sang. The remaining week in Los Angeles was more leisurely, but at least one meeting and usually two were scheduled for every day—gatherings in black homes, a fund-raiser for *People's World,* a meeting with a group of black businessmen who were starting a credit union—and at nearly every stop Paul spoke and occasionally sang a song or two.[24]

Arriving in San Francisco on May 24, the Robesons were met by the left-wing figure Mary Helen Jones and whisked away for rest to the Marin County home of Ruby Silverstone, a white liberal. When Paul, Jr., later heard of the arrangements, he became furious at Essie, claiming that the sprawling "estate" in the wealthy, protected white enclave where Silverstone lived was designed to remind his father of nothing so much as the grounds of the Priory sanatorium—and on top of that was devoid of the welcoming warmth he would have found from old friends in the area like Lee and Revels Cayton, who had expected to be contacted but somehow never were. But in fact Ruby Silverstone was very much a known quantity to Robeson, and her purported "estate" was nothing more than a modest two-bedroom house. She had first met Robeson in the early forties; Robeson had stayed with her for a few nights during the *Othello* tour, and again when he had been out on the Coast in the late forties; they had many friends in common, including the Caytons, Louise Bransten, and Vivian and Vincent Hallinan.[25]

When Paul and Essie arrived to stay with Silverstone in 1965, she gave him her own bedroom and Essie slept in the dressing room just off it. Silverstone also made it clear that all casual callers would be barred from her house and that as far as she was concerned Paul should appear as much or as little as made him feel comfortable. But by that time trouble was already brewing. Paul "began to wake up, day after day, TIRED," Essie reported home, and she herself came down with severe back pain, which a local doctor diagnosed as "either kidney or bladder"—at least that was all Essie was willing to tell; Paul showed alarm at her being incapacitated and she had to keep up a good front for him. Somehow they both managed to show up for a Du Bois Club fund-raising dinner organized by the Hallinans, their associates from Progressive Party days, and two days later they let their old friend John Pittman, foreign affairs editor of *People's World*, collect them for lunch at his house.[26]

But that was it. By the time June 4 rolled around—the evening of a long-planned and elaborately organized Salute to Paul Robeson at the Jack Tar Hotel—both Essie and Paul were incapacitated beyond the point where mere will power could continue to stand in for health, and had to forgo the event. They had intended to stay in the area for at least another ten days, but gave up the struggle and flew home to New York. Paul felt he had "let the folks down," and once home, he quickly slid into depression: moody, uncommunicative, uninterested in food or people or events, he sat lethargically around the house in pajamas.[27]

On the evening of June 10 Essie came upon Paul "holding a scissors to his chest"; he managed to inflict a superficial wound before she could control the situation "with difficulty." Later that same day Paul, Jr., walked into the bedroom and found his father, his face blank with terror, holding a double-edged razor blade in his hand. "Put it down," Paul, Jr., said quietly; not getting any response, he took it from him. After settling him back down, Paul, Jr., went around the house hiding other sharp objects, but he and Essie realized Paul could not safely be kept at home. Pearlmutter, Barsky, and Sam Rosen, who came up to the house in response to their emergency call, agreed with them. The decision was made to admit Paul immediately to Gracie Square psychiatric hospital, under the supervision of Dr. Nathan S. Kline, the psychopharmacologist whom Pearlmutter called into the case. Kline had helped to develop the drugs reserpine and mar-salid, winning the Lasker Award for the latter accomplishment—though another clinician later successfully challenged his claim as primary re-searcher. Kline was additionally controversial in the eyes of some of his fellow professionals because of his penchant for emphasizing drugs to the near-exclusion of psychotherapy, and for his assembly-line treatment of patients.[28]

Robeson was admitted to Gracie Square on June 11, 1965, under the pseudonym Frank Robertson. Because of the suicide attempt, he was given special nurses around the clock and separated from the other patients. The admitting physician recorded Robeson's general health as "satisfactory" and, despite his "recurrent depression," found him "polite" and respond-ing to questions with "appropriate affect" and coherence, though "little spontaneity." His nurses the first few days described him as pleasant but noncommunicative; "at times he mutters to himself and prefers to sit in a chair most of the day." But three days after his admission, another staff doctor found him "cooperative and friendly. Speech was coherent and relevant, memory was not impaired. No delusions or hallucinations were elicited," though he did admit "to feelings of depression as well as occa-sional feelings of hopelessness and suicidal thoughts." By then, June 14, Dr. Kline had been in to check on Robeson's progress—Kline did not believe in seeing patients often—and decided that he was "definitely im-proved." Still, he made no substantive changes in medication, even though Pearlmutter, after examining Robeson on the day he was admitted, wrote on his chart, "He will need more potent anti-depressant medication now. . . ." Dr. Kline, contrary to his general reputation, was proving to be a restraining influence. That is, for the time being.[29]

Robeson continued to make progress; he asked for reading materials from home, and his appetite and sleep improved—though his nurses fret-ted at his continuing refusal to leave his room, his occasional "confusion" (packing up his suitcase one night, he said "the car was waiting"), his reluctance, alternately, to take his pajamas off during the day or to put them on at night. But the momentum toward becoming more alert, cheer-ful, and talkative continued, and on July 1, three weeks after his admission, the doctors decided to let him go home.[30]

Kline was away for most of the summer, and a young psychiatrist who shared an office with him, Ari Kiev, temporarily took over Robeson's case. Thirty-two years old at the time, Kiev had recently returned from a year's residency at the Maudsley, a psychiatric teaching hospital in London (Brian Ackner, Robeson's physician at the Priory, was one of the attendings at Maudsley). Robeson would (in his son's words) "go stiff as a board" in the presence of the mellifluous, silver-haired Dr. Kline, but he *liked* Ari Kiev. Over the next two months he agreed to go to Kiev's office, accompanied by Paul, Jr., perhaps six to eight times in all, for a kind of "monitoring" psychotherapy, primarily a check on how he was reacting to the drug treatment, not the kind of intensive psychotherapy that Dr. Katzenstein at the Buch Clinic had considered necessary.[31]

Kiev was struck above all by Robeson's great sadness. He felt "unappreciated," anguished at not having received recognition from the current generation of black activists as one of the civil-rights movement's forerunners. Robeson "never gave a speech about it," Kiev says, but he had the clear impression from incidental remarks that he suffered a great deal from not having had his contribution acknowledged. Kiev saw Robeson as an "innocent" in the best sense, a man not naïve but "pure"; his motivational spring was "compassion, not ego," and therefore he felt devastated when others, less "purely" motivated, cast him aside; he was a man "fundamentally puzzled" at how his humane instincts and vision had run aground. Kiev was saying what Du Bois had said earlier: "The only thing wrong with Robeson is in having too great faith in human beings."[32]

The injury had been compounded by the loss of his audience. Robeson's temperament centrally craved contact with other people—even as it intermittently craved solitude and concealment—and his success in reaching out over the years through words and songs had built up in him an almost automatic dependence on human responsiveness. But in place of the sanctifying affirmation he had grown used to from his audiences had come, from his government, castigating banishment. He had been marked and isolated—classically punished with ostracism from the beloved community. The wonder to Kiev was not that Robeson broke down under the punishment, but that he had not broken down sooner.[33]

Yet his physical deterioration, in Kiev's view, was not wholly due to psychological causes. Robeson, he believes, suffered from "a combination of depression and some underlying organicity . . . some kind of underlying cerebral arteriosclerosis." But it might be said that everyone has some sort of "underlying organicity," some "biochemical imbalance" or potentially malignant physical condition—and that these do not commonly manifest themselves without extrinsic triggering events, "nonorganic" in nature. In short, had Robeson not been harassed and excluded, a "bipolar depressive" disorder or arteriosclerotic degeneration might have claimed him anyway; but they might not have, either, or might have done so only at a much later point in his life, merging softly, leniently, into the aging process itself. Kiev, in any case, decided there was no treatment for Robeson's organic condition; for the depression he believed the so-called tricyclic drugs (Elavil, Tofranil, etc.) were likely to produce the most relief, and he was pleased that during the two months he saw Robeson, his patient did become "more communicative and cheerful."[34]

Now it was Essie's turn on the grimly alternating cycle. Seized with terrible pain, she was hospitalized at Beth Israel, and a series of cobalt treatments began. To general astonishment, Paul himself took Essie to the hospital. Yet, despite that show of strength, Paul, Jr., feared his father would do poorly if left alone at Jumel Terrace and suggested to the doctors that he take him down to Marian's in Philadelphia. Pearlmutter told Paul, Jr., he was behaving like a mother hen. So, as a substitute, Paul, Jr., went up to Jumel each evening to cook dinner for his father. Four days after Essie's hospitalization, he arrived at Jumel to find ashtrays full of cigarette butts, an unmistakable sign (since Paul, Sr., rarely smoked) of his father's growing unease; he decided to enlist Helen Rosen's help. She drove in from Katonah to collect Paul and took him back up to her house, a spot he had always loved.[35]

By the middle of the day, with Paul seemingly in revived spirits, Helen decided to have a swim, and asked if he wanted to walk down to the pond with her. He said yes; Helen had her dip and then came up and sat on the grass with him. Suddenly Paul got up and walked over to the twelve-foot-high dam, which had steps going down into the pond. He put his foot on the top step, looked over at Helen, and with "a devilish laugh" (as Helen recalls it) put his foot down on the next step. Helen knew she had to do something; Paul could not swim. Trying to stay calm, she walked casually over to him and joined in his laughter. "What are you going to do," she said, smiling, "get your shoes all wet, and that nice suit? Come on off of there." She took his arm and he let her lead him back to the grass. She acted as "natural" as she could, got him back to the house, made him his usual hamburger, and then—because Sam was away—went in and called Paul, Jr.[36]

He and Marilyn drove straight up to Katonah. Both Pearlmutter and Kline were out of town on vacation, but Paul, Jr., managed to reach Ari Kiev, still covering for Kline. He advised them to bring Paul back to New York immediately so he could have a look at him. After seeing him in the office, Kiev decided that he belonged in the hospital and readmitted Robeson to Gracie Square. Paul offered no resistance; his attitude was compliant—"I'll do whatever you think best." On the day of admission, August 7, 1965, Kiev wrote on Robeson's chart: ". . . depression, *suicidal thoughts* and agitation in setting of wife's admission to hospital." Kiev added the antidepressant Niamid and a second tranquilizer (Phenergan) to Robeson's medications.[37]

For a few days he held his own, with no basic change in symptoms. The staff noted his reluctance to talk or leave his room but when they questioned him directly found him generally coherent and responsive. Dr. Kline dropped by once and Dr. Kiev daily, noting on the third day, "Depression seems less." The following day, August 10, Essie was operated on at Beth Israel and "invasive carcinoma" was discovered everywhere. Her doctors told Paul, Jr., that she probably had only a few months to live. Visiting his father that same day, Paul, Jr., was apparently so persuasively reassuring about Essie that even an attending physician wrote on Robeson's chart, ". . . his wife's surgery was successful. This was a hysterectomy for a carcinoma which was limited to the endometrium." But Paul himself "wasn't much cheered" by his son's report, according to the notes made on his chart by the special-duty nurse.[38]

The following evening, August 11, Robeson became, in the words of his private nurse, "dispirited and very apprehensive," and she decided to ask the doctors on duty to check him. Several of them had a look, and the *least* alarmed reported elevated blood pressure and some "muttering"; one resident suggested that Robeson's multiple medications were the possible, though unlikely, culprit, and another described him as "almost catatonic," sitting "rather rigidly," smiling "rather inappropriately"—"in general considerably more depressed than on admission." The next morning Robeson continued to be uncommunicative, "muttering and only rarely expressing himself in an intelligible way," and still "smiling inappropriately on occasion." Dr. Kiev was contacted and discussed the case with Dr. Pearlmutter. That same afternoon, August 12, Kiev wrote on Robeson's chart, "Will continue drug regimen as before." But because the symptoms had still not abated by evening, and Kiev was hoping to make Robeson more comfortable, he started him on ten milligrams of Valium four times a day, and the following morning on a small dose of Thorazine.[39]

Paul, Jr., noted these developments with mounting alarm. On each daily visit his father seemed worse—"drugged, nodding like a junkie." He was not specifically aware at the time that the doctors had added Valium and Thorazine. Investigating later, he was told the Thorazine had been for "restraint"; but since Big Paul was not at the time showing manic, unruly symptoms, the question has always remained in his son's mind: "restraint from *what??*" His suspicions, then and since, were further fed by one of the special-duty nurses, who strongly implied, without explicitly saying so, that his father was being overmedicated and that Paul, Jr., should "do something." He did. Enraged, he created a scene in the hospital; it brought the residents running, but their hospital doublespeak failed to soothe his nerves—or dull his intuition that his father was in deep trouble.[40]

When Big Paul's condition continued to deteriorate—by the afternoon of August 16 his temperature had shot up to 103, and his nurses reported that he was "muttering to himself and perspiring profusely" and had started "making a speech on social conditions, with a very anxious expression on his face"—Paul, Jr., put in a desperate call to Sam Rosen. Sam in turn managed to reach Pearlmutter, who was vacationing in the country. Pearlmutter declined to return to New York and told Sam to contact Dr. Richard Nachtigall, the physician covering for him. Nachtigall hurried to the hospital, with Sam close behind. They found Robeson "stuporous," "muttering incoherently, not responding to verbal stimuli." Nachtigall ordered a battery of tests, including a spinal tap, blood cultures, and chest X-rays, started him on intravenous fluid with antibiotics, put him on the critical list, and wrote in his report that he suspected pneumonia, possibly induced by phenothiazine toxicity—dehydration due to drugs. Dr. Kline was notified; he dropped by two days later. Dr. Pearlmutter did not come in.[41]

The X-ray results and tests over the next several days confirmed double pneumonia and kidney blockage. Robeson was near death—his temperature had gone to 105 and neither the addition of Chloromycetin nor the application of an alcohol-and-ice-water sheet had made any difference. Sam Rosen and Nachtigall decided on the spot to transfer Robeson to the superior medical facilities at University Hospital. The decision saved his life. Described on admission as "acutely ill, tremulous," Robeson's initial course at University Hospital was "stormy," but treatment with hypothermia for the high fever, and intravenous fluids for what had probably been a bacterial bronchopneumonia, produced gradual improvement, the fever subsiding, the symptomatic trauma retreating. Yet throughout Robeson's time at University Hospital the doctors noted that "he retained elements of an organic mental syndrome" even as he became "more lucid mentally." When they discharged him on September 9, after a three-week stay, they suggested as a final diagnosis "psychosis" with "toxic metabolic encephalopathy probably secondary to combined drug therapy." The pneumonia, in other words, had been a transient (if nearly fatal) episode; though it was successfully resolved, Robeson nonetheless remained seriously ill.[42]

In early September, Paul and Essie were brought home from their respective hospitals within days of each other, Essie dying, Paul uncertainly involved with life. She lay upstairs in bed; he, brooding and melancholy, passed unpredictably from room to room. Frankie Lee Sims, their old friend from California, and Marie Bowden, a union secretary, moved into Jumel to take care of them. Paul, Jr., and Marilyn shuttled between a physically shattered mother still keenly alert and an emotionally disconnected father seemingly indifferent to anyone's struggle for survival, including his own. Paul's inability to connect was not markedly different, except in style, from the separate solitudes into which Essie and Paul, Jr., were locked as well. Essie was unreconciled to finding herself in a situation at last that she could not somehow "manage." Paul, Jr., still bitterly blamed both her and Dr. Kline for having taken the "wrong" step, thereby bringing on his father's collapse, protracting his anger through an obsessive insistence that somehow catastrophe could have been avoided.

By early October, Big Paul seemed headed further downhill. Agitated and restless, he continued to roam the apartment anxiously. On the evening of October 15 Paul, Jr., noticed that his pacing had narrowed to the hall leading to the front door, and he told Frankie Sims to keep an eye on his father while he went upstairs for a bath. Frankie had to attend to another chore momentarily, and Paul, Jr., sitting in the tub, heard the front door slam. When he raced downstairs with a towel around him, he discovered his father was gone. He dressed quickly and dashed outside to search the neighborhood. No Paul. It began to rain lightly. He phoned Lloyd Brown, who lived nearby and owned a car, and together the two men searched in a wider perimeter. No Paul. They called friends, just in case he had stopped off at somebody's house. No one had seen him. By midnight, frantic, they phoned the police to report Paul missing. The police, in turn, put out a missing persons bulletin. Early the following morning an anonymous phone-caller to the Wadsworth Avenue station house reported that while walking his dog he had come upon a man lying in a clump of bushes near Highbridge Park, a few blocks from Jumel Terrace. Conscious but incoherent (fortunately it had been a warm night), Paul was taken to the Vanderbilt Clinic at nearby Presbyterian Hospital, treated for facial lacerations and a bruised right hip and ankle, and then transferred to University Hospital. When Paul, Jr., Lloyd Brown, and Essie (who somehow managed to get out of bed) arrived, Big Paul told them he had no recollection of leaving the house, or of anything else: "What happened to me?" he kept repeating, "What happened to me?" A spokesman for the Vanderbilt Clinic told the press Robeson had been mugged, but after the police reported no evidence of assault, Essie issued a formal statement saying her husband had been ill and occasionally suffered from loss of balance and dizzy spells. Released from University Hospital several days later, he was taken by Paul, Jr., to Marian's house in Philadelphia.[43]

Essie's symptoms, in the meantime, had intensified. Beset with nausea, vomiting, and diarrhea, she was readmitted to Beth Israel by Pearlmutter on November 23. The cancer had metastasized throughout her body. By the first week in December she was having trouble breathing, but despite severe discomfort continued to see visitors, including Freda Diamond and Helen Rosen. On December 12 she was put on the critical list. That day a friend from the UN arrived with an armful of holly, "thinking it wise to begin celebrating the Holidays a bit early. Essie smiled with her eyes, but she could no longer speak." At five-thirty the following morning, two days before her seventieth birthday, she died—her unquiet, tenacious spirit stilled. Paul, Jr., went down to Philadelphia to bring his father the news. Big Paul signed the death certificate and, without saying a word, turned away. The funeral was private, with only Paul, Jr., Marilyn, and their two children, Susan and David, present. Paul Sr. did not attend.[44]

■

CHAPTER 26

Final Years

(1966–1976)

Marian Robeson Forsythe, a retired schoolteacher, widowed in 1958, was seventy-one years old in 1965 and lived in a comfortable, unpretentious house on Walnut Street in Philadelphia with her daughter Paulina. With-drawn since childhood, Paulina was a silent presence in the house, a re-sponsibility of, rather than a companion to, her mother. Marian took on the second responsibility of Paul without a murmur of protest; she had always worshiped her younger brother, and the two had always felt entirely comfortable, if not intimate, with each other.[1]

Marian was an intensely private person with deep nurturing instincts; she saw it as her duty and privilege to protect Paul from unwanted intru-sion and believed that with enough loving care he could be nursed back to health; she was the last in a long line of women willing to devote their energies to him. Since Marian lived on limited means, she accepted a small monthly sum for Paul's keep from Lee Lurie (who on Rockmore's death had taken over as Paul's attorney and financial manager), but no amount of money could have bought such total devotion and uncompromising optimism. Seeing Robeson a month after Essie's death, Lee Lurie was only willing to say, "Paul is doing better, but it is pretty rough." Marian, more sanguine, reported he was "fine" and had thoroughly enjoyed two the-ater outings, to see *Carousel* and *The Sound of Music* in their Philadelphia revivals.[2]

There were others, including Helen and Sam Rosen, who occasionally allowed themselves a spell of optimism about the possibility of Paul's eventual recovery, but his son believes to this day that his father's second stay in Gracie Square Hospital in August 1965 was decisive for the course of his illness thereafter, that the toxic reaction to unwarranted drug treatment had produced organic brain damage, which made any real hope for improvement chimerical. "My father was never the same after Gracie Square," Paul, Jr., still says. "Every once in a while he'd have a good day, but basically he wasn't there." Yet Paul, Jr., and Marilyn, no less than sister Marian, did everything they could to coax a more positive outcome.

On the assumption—Big Paul did not ask—that he would rather live in New York than Philadelphia, Paul, Jr., and Marilyn decided to bring him back from Marian's and arranged to move into Jumel Terrace with him, along with their two children, in February 1966. Perhaps having an uneasy sense from the outset that the arrangement would not work, Paul, Jr., and Marilyn held on to their old apartment. Though Big Paul was not visibly mourning Essie, he was reluctant to leave the house. Once in a great while he would go to dinner at the homes of old friends, but, as Jim Aronson remembers one such evening (at Vita and Ed Barsky's), Paul stayed "very much removed; it was very difficult to pull him into the conversation." With Paul, Jr.'s help, he did manage to attend one public event—a benefit dinner for SNCC in March 1966. Seated, at the family's request, at an inconspicuous table, he was nonetheless given a big ovation by the crowd. John Lewis came over to his table and said, "Paul, this all started from you." James Forman, chairman of SNCC, paid tribute to him in his speech and wrote him afterward to say, "We all know of your part in the struggle for Freedom and it was a great privilege to be able to tell you how much you mean to all of us." "It's fine finally for a prophet to be honored in his own country," an admirer later wrote Robeson. Still, by the end of the evening, Big Paul was "laid out" with exhaustion.[3]

Occasionally other requests came in for an appearance, a statement, a sign of approbation. He was asked to attend testimonial dinners for the poet Gwendolyn Brooks, the historian Herbert Aptheker, his old comrade William L. Patterson (on the occasion of his seventy-fifth birthday); he was invited to the Rutgers New York Bicentennial dinner-dance at the Hilton, to be one of three subjects (along with Robert Kennedy and Stokely Carmichael) for a documentary film on American politics, to accept an award from the Czechoslovak Ambassador for having promoted "friendship and co-operation with the Czechoslovak Socialist Republic"; he was asked by A. Philip Randolph to join him as a sponsor in the campaign of the Committee of Conscience against apartheid in South Africa. To each, Paul, Jr., fulfilling a function Essie had performed for decades, replied that his father's health made it impossible for him to meet the request. The FBI, which continued to receive desultory reports from its agents about Robeson, got the same message from the field: "the subject was seriously ill."[4]

Anna Louise Strong, the eighty-year-old radical firebrand, then residing in China, was one of many refusing to believe that the oaken warrior they had earlier known could have any organic disorder, or at least not one that couldn't be set to rights. "I personally have always felt," Strong wrote Steve Fritchman, "that Paul's trouble had a deep psycho-somatic cause in the shock and trauma he suffered from the Sino-Soviet split [of 1957]. . . . Paul had a very deep love and devotion both for the USSR and for China's revolution and . . . consequently the split must have been especially hard for him, since his devotions have always been through passionate allegiance rather than through theory." He must come to Peking, she urged—with the simplistic vigor that had always been part of her charm, and her limitation. She had "made inquiries"; Paul would be "extremely welcome," surrounded by love, soon made well again.[5]

Caught between the needs of a dependent father and the demands of growing children, Paul, Jr., and Marilyn began to feel the strain. But Paul, Jr., was unwilling to accept defeat; if the experiment at Jumel had failed, perhaps in another setting they might all be able to live together. He took Big Paul back to Marian's in Philadelphia temporarily in the late spring of 1966, while he and Marilyn set about finding and then refurbishing an apartment that might meet all their needs. A spacious place on West Eighty-sixth Street in Manhattan seemed to fit the bill, and they spent the summer of 1966 renovating it so that Big Paul would have a separate suite of rooms within the larger space of the apartment. In the fall of 1966 he was again collected from Philadelphia to make another effort at togetherness in New York.

This one, too, proved short-lived. In Marilyn's words, "Life very much centered around Big Paul and his needs. . . . He was almost wholly gathered up into himself." He had always taken for granted that others would provide for his practical daily needs—but now he could no longer reward them with warmth and charm. He stayed very much to himself in the private little wing Paul, Jr., and Marilyn had constructed for him within the larger apartment, but was not notably more present when he joined the rest of the family. Marian, up from Philadelphia for a visit, was "shocked" that he had become "so withdrawn he couldn't understand what I was saying." "I'll never understand what happened," she wrote Lee Lurie. "He was in fine condition when he left here with Paul Jr. to go to New York." She strongly suggested he once more come and live with her. Dr. Alvin I. Goldfarb, a Mt. Sinai geriatric psychiatrist, concurred: since he was not "impressed by any organic component to the illness," Goldfarb believed "Mr. Robeson's condition can be controlled" and "he will ultimately be responsive to therapeutic efforts"—but advised that "at present residence with his sister . . . is indicated." Paul, Jr., acknowledged that the experiment in living together had failed, and only a few months after it had begun, Paul was back with Marian in Philadelphia, this time to remain.[6]

Just a little vain about her own superior nurturing skills, Marian was immediately reporting back to New York that Paul "is getting better. . . . He is eating and sleeping well and most of the time relaxed. He is talking a little, understands what you say and answers your questions though not initiating conversation." Marian secured part-time help (Lee Lurie sent seventy-five dollars a week to cover all expenses), took Paul around with her to the bank to open an account, went with him to his new doctor and had a piano-teacher friend of hers come in on a regular basis to try to rekindle his interest ("I think it will help him with his speech and get him to talking again," Marian wrote Lee Lurie). She was confident that "Paul is well taken care of and has very little to annoy him." By the spring of 1967 she was reporting that he had been taking walks in the neighborhood and had "really enjoyed" an outing to see the film *The Taming of the Shrew.* "Weather permitting," she expected to "really have him stepping out" before long. In August 1967 the house at Jumel Terrace was sold for a little under eighteen thousand dollars.[7]

Paul now settled down to the life of a cherished—and haunted— invalid. His every need was attended to with devoted alacrity, his every momentary sign of vivacity greeted with hope and applause—yet the gigantic figure remained a shadow behind the arras, obscurely brooding on the perplexing continuation of his own days. Word arrived late in 1967 that *Who's Who in American History* had finally deigned to include his biography and that a student group at Rutgers had pressed the university, after fifty years of omission, to submit his nomination to the National Football Hall of Fame. Told the news, Robeson smiled and shrugged.[8]

In December 1967 he was admitted to University Hospital in Philadelphia. The *Evening Bulletin* reported that he was suffering from "a skin ailment." The FBI's informants were closer to the mark, reporting that he "had been very ill and has been inaccessible to anyone for the last couple of months." Yet, only a few weeks after that, Peggy Middleton, on a trip to the United States, impulsively put in a phone call to Paul at Marian's house and "He sounded so like himself that I became tongue-tied." It was one of those occasional "good days" that continued unaccountably to occur.[9]

Robeson was now approaching his seventieth birthday, and preparations for the event took on considerable proportions, particularly in Britain and in the GDR (where Essie, in the last few months of her life, had managed to help arrange for the establishment of an official Paul Robeson Archive). *The Worker* devoted a five-column spread to detailing the celebrations, and an FM radio station in New York kicked off the festivities with a two-hour tribute to Robeson on April 9, 1968. Speakers at the Moscow affair included Robeson's old friends Boris Polevoi and Mikhail Kotov, and the CPUSA celebration featured an address by William L. Patterson. In advertising it, Claude Lightfoot and Charlene Mitchell of the Black Liberation Commission of the CPUSA noted that "The white power structure has generated a conspiracy of silence around Paul Robeson. It wants to blot out all knowledge of this pioneering Black American warrior. . . . Because of this there exists a young generation of freedom fighters who are unaware of this great man and his outstanding contributions to their struggle. . . ."[10]

In the GDR, the elaborate celebration spread over several days (at one point the participants stood at their seats out of respect for the memory of Martin Luther King, Jr., who had been assassinated in Memphis, Tennessee, on April 4). In London on April 8 an evening of music, poetry, and drama was staged at an annex of the Royal Festival Hall, with a number of distinguished artists participating. Comedian Bill Owen shared his anecdotal memories of days at Unity Theatre in the 1930s, old friends Alan Bush and Bruno Raikin contributed their musical talents, and Robeson's two British Desdemonas, Peggy Ashcroft and Mary Ure, read in tribute to him (as did Peter O'Toole and Michael Redgrave). Many who could not attend sent in moving recollections of earlier, happier days—Marie Burke, Sybil Thorndike, John Dankworth, John Gielgud, Yehudi Menuhin, Flora Robson, André Van Gyseghem, Alfie Bass, and Elizabeth Welch. Speaking for the new generation, Oliver Tambo, who would one day serve in exile as leader of the militant African National Congress, wrote in honor of "a universal idol and a friend dear to all who know him or have only heard his priceless voice."[11]

As the days and years of being out of the public eye lengthened and the world inexorably changed its shape, as Kennedy gave way to Johnson, then Nixon in the White House (and sectors of the white working class rallied to the banner of George Wallace, whose antiblack campaign amassed ten million votes), as SNCC declined into warring sects and then disappeared, and the police brutally dispersed poor people encamped in protest of their plight on federal property, Robeson became a faded memory to one generation and an unknown name to another. People over forty wondered what had ever become of him (the rumor spread that he had gone into self-exile in Russia), and many people under forty had no idea he had ever existed.

But old devotions did not entirely die, and in the early seventies it was even possible to think that a Robeson "boomlet" was on the horizon. In 1970 Rutgers dedicated a lounge—and then in 1972 elevated the honor to a student center—in Robeson's name; the New York chapter of the Association for the Study of Negro Life and History gave him its coveted Ira Aldridge award; the radio station WQXR devoted several programs to Robeson's records; Canadian Broadcasting, as well as the PBS station in New York, aired programs on his life; and the Black Academy of Arts and Letters cited him for his "immeasurable contribution to our society." In 1971 alone, *Freedomways* devoted an entire issue to him ("The Great Forerunner"), the GDR held a two-day symposium in his honor, and Beacon Press reprinted *Here I Stand*. In 1972 the boomlet looked as if it might escalate into a full-scale boom as the number of awards mounted—the

Association of Black Psychiatrists cited him as "a model and inspiration" to black youth, the New York Urban League gave him its Whitney M. Young, Jr., Award, and the Hollywood NAACP added an Image Award for his contribution to "brotherhood"; as well, he was designated in the first group elevated into the Theater Hall of Fame. Press attention also grew: *Sports Illustrated* carried a story about his athletic prowess, *Ebony* named him among the "10 Greats of Black History," and the Sunday Arts and Leisure section of *The New York Times*, daring to ask the question "Time to Break the Silence Surrounding Paul Robeson?," answered "Yes."[12]

The public's interest, though, was occasional, erratic, and confined to limited circles. Yet if Robeson's name did not evoke the instant recognition that had once greeted it, he did not cease to be deeply loved and attended by those who had been closest to him. The number of people who wanted to visit Paul was always greater than the number who were allowed to. Paul, Jr., asked even intimate friends to check with him before going down to Philadelphia, but basically people like the Rosens, Lloyd Brown, Clara Rockmore, and Freda Diamond had unimpeded access—limited only by their own sense of appropriateness. The same was decidedly *not* true of everyone else. Paul, Jr., and Marian made a combined and largely successful effort to bar visits from mere acquaintances and to hold at fierce bay the idly curious. In taking on the role of public protector, Paul, Jr., proved at least as adept in guarding his father's seclusion as Essie had earlier been. He, again like Essie before him, thereby opened himself to accusations of being overprotective and to the resentment of those who thought of themselves as Robeson intimates and who, in their anger at not being confirmed as such, spread a host of tales about the son's "devious" purposes. Paul, Jr., was alternately denounced as his father's jailor, censor, and uncrowned surrogate, his motives variously ascribed to the demands of politics (to prevent word from getting out of Big Paul's purported change of heart about the Soviets) or personality (to come at last into uncontested control of his father's legacy).[13]

Robert Sherman of WQXR, for example, once drove his aunt Clara Rockmore down to Philadelphia and came away from the visit with the impression that physically Robeson was "stronger, healthier" than the rumor mill suggested. But Sherman thought his "mental condition" was abysmal. Although he seemed glad to see them, there were long gaps in the conversation—"We were under injunctions from Paul, Jr., not to talk politics of any remote stripe"—and Sherman was stunned that a man of such diverse intellectual interests, and such a fabled commitment to engagement with the problems of the world, now seemed content merely to sit. Nothing seemed to interest him: "He just didn't care." Sherman acknowledged that it was probably Robeson's own choice to live in complete isolation, but he nonetheless blamed Paul, Jr., for cooperating with his father's wish, for not surrounding him with more stimulation. Going still further, others concluded that Paul, Jr., had his own reasons for letting his father remain in near-total seclusion: he did not want it known that Paul Robeson the legendary fighter had lost interest in the world; he did not want his father's historic image compromised or shattered. "I think Paul, Jr., was ready to go to any lengths," as Robert Sherman puts it, "to preserve the image that he wanted, of a politically active man," to allow him to go on saying, "No, he didn't recant anything, he didn't regret anything, he was politically concerned till the very end."[14]

Helen Rosen, who went to Philadelphia with Sam about once a month, confirms that Paul did *not* want to see most people, that often he was "sort of sleepy," but that on his better days she and Paul talked theater and he and Sam talked football—"and he'd come alive." His main physical problem, "heart block," with its attendant symptoms of dizziness and lethargy, was essentially solved by the installation of a pacemaker in the early seventies (though he did have to enter the hospital several times so it could be adjusted, and one time replaced). A steady and mild maintenance dose of a mood elevator (Tofranil) further reduced his symptomatic discomfort. Nonetheless, his internist, Dr. Roger Good, described him in 1970 as "semivegetative," and when the cardiologist Dr. Herbert E. Cohen took over Robeson's case in 1973, he found him "in sad shape, not a normal seventy-five-year-old," but a man "extremely withdrawn." On the other hand, only once in all the years Robeson lived in Philadelphia with Marian did his doctors consider him severely enough withdrawn to weigh the advisability of yet another set of electroshock treatments (ultimately they decided against it), and on that occasion, following the familiar alternating pattern of his illness, Robeson soon improved. Visiting him in the hospital several weeks after his admission, Lloyd Brown "found him to be more like his old self than at any time since he returned ill from California" in 1965.[15]

But Robeson's doctors, unlike some of his friends, did not mistake temporary improvement for any prospect of permanent rehabilitation, nor did they recommend a reinvigorated routine as a first step toward some imagined notion of ultimate recovery. He would not recover; he could only be made comfortable. And, to that end, Paul, Jr., and Marian's prescription for limiting visitors seemed a humane design for keeping demands from being made on Big Paul that he could not meet, and which would only reawaken his sense of inadequacy. Marian took care never to *discourage* his interest in the world—indeed, she would eagerly report whenever he felt "more alert," up to talking on the telephone, taking a walk, occasionally even writing a note—but neither she nor Paul, Jr., would allow any mistaken notion to develop that Paul Robeson—if only encouraged to *try* harder—could yet make a significant public contribution.[16]

Marian and Paul, Jr.'s overriding concern was to safeguard Big Paul's privacy, to prevent a mischievous reporter or ogling sightseer from dis-

turbing the regularity of a daily routine that had created at least a semblance of serenity, minimizing his mood swings, keeping him safely this
side of heroic medical interventions. In his zeal to be protective, Paul, Jr.,
now and then did overstep the line, did reject supplicants roughly. "He was
a dictator, he had to have control," one woman has indignantly remarked.
Still, it was difficult to strike the right balance—to ascertain the exact extent
of a potential visitor's previous connection, the precise degree of Big
Paul's receptiveness on a given day, the definable effect on him of an effort
at conversation. Marian's impulses were more elastic. Now and then she
would even allow some friend passing by to come inside for a brief visit;
visitors would then trumpet the news of having gained access (sometimes
trumpeting as well what "wonderful shape" they had found Robeson to be
in, not realizing Marian had only decided to admit them because he was
having one of his uncommonly good days), thereby further feeding the
rumor mill that had put Paul, Jr., down as arbitrary and even malignant in
his choices.[17]

As Robeson's seventy-fifth birthday approached, Paul, Jr., worked
around the clock for months on a Carnegie Hall event that would simultaneously serve as a salute to his father and as a benefit to help establish
a Paul Robeson Archive in the United States. The response was gratifying,
the hall jammed on the night of the gala, April 15, 1973. Yet, in the absence
of the guest-of-honor himself, grounds were again found for faulting the
son; his father had been up to attending, the malcontents insisted, and
should have been encouraged to make the effort ("Paul, Jr., didn't want him
at the concert," is how one of them puts it, "didn't want them to see a thin
and weakened man"). Robeson's taped message to the gathering seemed
to some to strike one suspiciously false note after another: his insistence
that "I am the same Paul, dedicated as ever to the worldwide cause of
humanity," sounded to them like mere bravado, uncharacteristic self-
puffery; and his devoting a full minute on a mere two-minute tape to a
series of exaggerated political greetings to colonial liberationists, socialist
"partisans for peace," and heroic anti-imperialists seemed outlandishly
unconnected to the actual insularity of Robeson's life and his steady drift
away from polemical involvement. When Angela Davis hailed Robeson as
"above all, a revolutionary," "a partisan of the Socialist world," the largely
middle-class, middle-aged crowd (of both races) joined the malcontents in
responding with merely tepid applause.[18]

Still, for most of the evening and for most of the audience, the Carnegie Hall celebration of Robeson's seventy-fifth birthday was a joyful occasion, a chance to express admiration and affection for the man and to draw
symbolic sustenance from his life. A multi-media scripted show with live
actors integrated with recordings, slides, and movies depicting highlights
from Robeson's career met with tumultuous applause; Ramsey Clark, the
former Attorney General, drew a few tears when he spoke of Robeson's

embodying "the grace and beauty" that America was "afraid of"; Pete Seeger got the crowd singing along with him on "Freiheit" (one of the Loyalist songs from the Spanish Civil War that Robeson had often performed); and Dolores Huerta, vice-president of the Farm Workers Union, elicited roars of *"Viva Robeson!"* and *"Viva la causa!"* when she linked his name to the cause of migrant farm laborers.[19]

Many notables from the black community attended and participated in the Salute—including Odetta, Leon Bibb, Sidney Poitier, Harry Belafonte (who also produced the show), James Earl Jones, Roscoe Lee Browne, Ossie Davis, and Ruby Dee. Coretta Scott King spoke of Robeson's having been "buried alive" because, earlier than her husband, he had "tapped the same wells of latent militancy" among blacks; Mayor Richard G. Hatcher of Gary, Indiana, referred to him as "our own black prince and prophet." An even larger number of notables sent in tributes. Andrew Young wrote from the House of Representatives to thank him for his "beautiful life" and to say that, had he not "kept alive a legacy of hope through some of the darkest days of our history . . . our accomplishments in the 60's would not have been possible." The same note of acknowledgment was picked up and broadened by a host of leaders from third-world nations. Julius K. Nyerere, President of Tanzania, expressed sentiments very close to those of many others (Prime Minister Michael Manley of Jamaica, Cheddi Jagan, L. F. S. Burnham of Guyana, Lynden O. Pindling of the Bahamas, Errol W. Barrow of Barbados, and the President of Zambia, Kenneth Kaunda) in thanking Robeson for having "used his great abilities and great gifts" to draw attention "to the evils of oppression and inequality." Sounding a more personal note, Indira Gandhi recalled "the wonder," on meeting him, "of finding such gentleness in such a powerful frame." And a Mr. Guy Warren of Ghana wrote this from the heart: "If I told you that I LOVE you and that you are simply gorgeous, won't that bring a smile to your glorious lips?"[20]

A few additional honors came during Robeson's seventy-sixth year—his alma mater, Rutgers, held a symposium on his life (and his father's alma mater, Lincoln University, awarded him an honorary degree), his old friend C. L. R. James lectured at the University of Massachusetts on "Mr. Robeson and the International Struggle for Freedom and Independence" as part of a series set up in Robeson's honor, and the Black Sports Hall of Fame cited him for his athletic achievements. But essentially the hurrahs were over with the Carnegie Hall event. Definitive closure came from the FBI—early in 1974 it dared to conclude that "no further investigation is warranted." Such milestones as remained tended to be sorrowful ones. Larry Brown passed away just months before Robeson reached seventy-five, and at a memorial concert in remembrance of Brown's gentle, whimsical spirit, recordings of some of the songs the two men had performed together in their thirty-year collaboration were played over an amplifier to end the service. A poignant note of another kind was struck by Max Yergan, Robeson's one-time political associate and then bitter political adversary. Himself ill, Yergan wrote Robeson a brief letter late in 1974 to say, "I am at times deeply pained that a long and cherished friendship with you was interfered with," and "to make it clear that it is my deep desire to withdraw, wipe out and apologize for anything I ever said or did which could interfere with our friendship."[21]

Robeson's life was drawing to a close. Stephen Fritchman, now retired as minister of L.A.'s First Unitarian Church, stopped by to see him in September 1975, their first meeting in nearly a decade, and Fritchman reported to the congregation that, when he entered Marian's house, "there was Paul," dressed (as always when receiving visitors) in coat and tie, "rising from the sofa to his great height, his countenance beaming, his deep-set eyes twinkling, his hand extended. . . . He embraced me with a bear hug and a kiss on the cheek and the years fell away as we talked of many things. . . ." Fritchman apparently arrived on a *very* good day, but Freda Diamond, too, recalls that Paul often spoke during her visits, and once even sang: "When a question came up about a particular spiritual, he reminded me that it was *that* spiritual he was singing as the curtain rose in *All God's Chillun Got Wings*"; he seemed surprised that *she* didn't remember the song—and sang it through for her. After visiting Robeson in his seventy-seventh year, Lloyd Brown reports talking with him for a little bit about his great-great-grandfather Cyrus Bustill—"though [he was] obviously relieved to get back to his restful chair. His strength is now only in his spirit." When Brown asked him directly about his health, Robeson replied, "Just kickin' along."[22]

A month after Lloyd Brown's visit, on December 28, 1975, Robeson was hospitalized with what was thought to be a mild stroke. After a setback he had always physically rebounded to his previous baseline. Not this time. To his cardiologist's surprise, there was "an abrupt onset of weakness," and then a final stroke. On January 22, Paul, Jr., and Marilyn visited his father. On January 23, Helen and Sam Rosen arrived at the hospital and were told that Paul had died an hour before. They were shown into his room and left alone to say their private goodbyes. As Helen recalls the moment, "Sam drew back the curtain surrounding Paul's bed, leaned over, and kissed his forehead. He lay still and gray, dressed in a suit. I held his hand, and the dam of years of restraint in me broke, and I sobbed. Then Sam and I went to fetch Marian and to call Pauli. He came and took over. . . ." A hospital spokesman announced to the press that the cause of death was "complications arising from severe cerebral vascular disorder." No autopsy was done: his son decided against it, willing to trade the additional knowledge an autopsy would have yielded on his father's medical history in favor of being able to let the black community view the body at the funeral home, of letting his father "go out in style."[23]

Condolences came in from around the world, from those who had stood beside him, near him—and apart from him. Old, old friends—among them Fritz Pollard, Peggy Ashcroft, André Van Gyseghem, and Flora Robson—sent their sorrowful messages of loss—and Roy Wilkins, who had been his adversary, characterized him as "a man of strong convictions." (Coretta Scott King, unstinting, deplored "America's inexcusable treatment" of a man who had had "the courage to point out her injustices.") The white press, after decades of harassing Robeson, now tipped its hat to "a great American," paid its gingerly respect in editorials that ascribed the vituperation leveled at Robeson in his lifetime to the Bad Old Days of the Cold War, implied those days were forever gone, downplayed the racist component central to his persecution, ignored the continuing inability of white America to tolerate a black maverick who refused to bend. The black press made no such mistakes. It had never, overall, been as hostile to Robeson as the white press (though at some points in his career, nearly so). Now, at his death, one paper—in a paroxysm of atoning grief—splashed "GOODBYE PAUL!" in its headlines, and others spoke in editorials of this "Gulliver among the Lilliputians," this life that would "always be a challenge and a reproach to white and Black America." A black prisoner in the Marion, Illinois, penitentiary perhaps summed it up as well as anyone in a poem:

PAUL ROBESON

They knocked the leaves
From his limbs,
The bark
From his
Tree
But his roots
were
so deep
That they are
a part of me. [24]

A cold rain fell all day outside Mother A.M.E. Zion Church in Harlem on January 27, 1976. Despite the rain, thousands, mostly black, gathered on the sidewalks and slowly moved inside the historic church where Paul's brother Ben Robeson had presided for twenty-seven years: Old Left and New, theater people and trade-unionists, white and black, Communists and conservatives, dear friends, old adversaries, complete strangers. A. Philip Randolph and Bayard Rustin showed up; so did Harry Belafonte; Uta Hagen; Malcolm X's widow, Betty Shabazz; and Paul's Rutgers sweetheart, Maimie Neale Bledsoe; so did Steve Nelson of the Abraham Lincoln

Brigade and Henry Winston, national chairman of the CPUSA; so did Helen and Sam Rosen, Clara Rockmore, Eubie Blake, Revels Cayton, and Freda Diamond; so did hundreds of Harlem's so-called ordinary people. As they filed in, Robeson's voice came out over the loudspeakers, singing the spirituals and songs most closely connected to him. His closed casket at the foot of the pulpit was draped in black, covered with red roses.[25]

Bishop J. Clinton Hoggard, a boyhood friend, delivered the eulogy. He commended the family for the decision "to bring Paul home" to Mother Zion and used a verse from Galatians—"Henceforth, let no man trouble me"—to recount the history of a man who had tried to live "with dignity" and who for his persistence "bore on his body marks of vengeance"; he ended with a paraphrase from a line Robeson used to sing at the close of "Joe Hill"—"Don't mourn for me, but live for freedom's cause." Lloyd Brown and Sam Rosen spoke next, spoke of how fortunate they felt that Paul had graced their lives, of how (in Sam's words) "his warmth and love and humor and wisdom" would always remain a precious memory.[26]

Lastly, his son rose to pay his tribute. His words the more eloquent for being spare and unsentimental, he thanked the "great and gentle warrior" who was his father for the example of his compassion and his courage, for his legacy of "special memories that will always sustain us." When he concluded, they carried the coffin out into the rain. The mournful strains of "Deep River" flooded the Harlem street.

Acknowledgments

The many Robeson friends who allowed me to interview them, the correspondents who shared firsthand anecdotes, and the owners of privately held manuscript materials who shared them with me are cited in the Note on Sources. That still leaves a large number of acknowledgments to make for a large variety of assists in preparing this book.

For help with translation, transcription, and research, I am grateful to Jules Cohen, Tim Couzzens, Anita Feldman, Martin Fishgold, Eric Garber, Eric Gordon, Rosalyn and Terrence Higgins, Michael Lipson, Laura Mayhall, Peter Osnos, Grace Palladino, Susan Palmer, Anne Lise Spitzer, Carol Shookhoff, Laurie Winer, Nancy Wonders, and Zina Voynow. During the first year, Terry Collins labored with special diligence; during the last year, Janet Jones showed special resourcefulness in locating material on William Drew Robeson.

A number of specialists—medical, legal, and scholarly—have given me the benefit of their advice: Edward Allsworth, Stan Arnold, Nicholas Barber, Stephen F. Cohen, Thomas Cripps, Richard Dyer, Candace Falk, Donald Gallup, Edward Greer, Judith Mara Gutman, Barbara Haber, Frances Kean, Stanley I. Kutler, Ellis Levine, David Levering Lewis, Lawrence Mass, Michael S. de L. Neill, Robert Millman, Arnold Rampersad, Judith Stein, and Theodore Tyberg. For a wide assortment of other favors, assists, supports, and leads, I particularly want to thank: Dennis Altman, Joyce Easton Ashley, Neal Basen, Theresa Bauml, Rosalyn Baxandall, Kathy D. Beckwith, Sally Belfrage, Jolanta Benal, Alan Bennett, Esme E. Bhan, Alison Boyle, Susan Brownmiller, John Bynoe, Annette Cameron, Nancy Clements, Louise A. De Salva, Cecilia Drury, Joellen El Bashir, Bill

French, Frankie Gillette, Saskia Grabow, Larry Gross, Barbara Heinzen, Jean Herskovits, Howard Johnson, Bruce Kellner, Randall Kenan, Michael Kimmel, Seymour Kleinberg, William A. Koshland, Gara La Marche, Hollis R. Lynch, William S. McFeely, August Meier, Ralph Melnick, Emily Miles, E. J. Montgomery, Frank Morris, Vance Muse, Marc Myers, Alan Newland, Mary Martin Niepold, Gil Noble, Kent Paul, Isabelle Powell, Thomas Powers, Shephard Raimi, David Richards, Judy (Rosen) Ruben, Rose Rubin, Irene Runge, D. A. Sachs, Kate Sharpe, Susan Sheehan, William Stampus, Dorothy D. Storck, Sarah McKinley Taylor, Mike Wallington, Steven Watson, Sule Grey Wilson, Laurie Winer, Melvin T. Wolfe, and Anne T. Zaroff.

The following archivists and librarians have been particularly resourceful and generous in aiding my research: Yuri Afanasyev (Moscow State Institute of History and Culture), Whitney Bagnall (Columbia Law School Archives), Brigid Bogelsack (Robeson Archiv, Berlin), Susan L. Boone (Sophia Smith Collection), James A. Cavanaugh (State Historical Society, Wisconsin), Toni Costonie (DuSable Museum), Rudolph De Jong (International Institute of Social History), Anne Engelhard (Schlesinger Library, Radcliffe), Linda Evans (Chicago Historical Society), David Farneth (Kurt Weill Foundation for Music), Jackie Goggins (Library of Congress), Cathy Henderson (Ransom Humanities Center), Charles J. Kelly (Library of Congress), Diana Lachatanere (NYPL/Schomburg), R. Russell Maylove (Northwestern), Judith Mellins (Harvard Law School Archives), Eleanor Mish (American Museum of the Moving Image), Christine Naumann (Robeson Archiv, Berlin), Marjorie F. Nelson (Robersonville Public Library), Hans E. Panofsky (Herskovits Library of African Studies), Randy Penninger (Atkins Library, UNC, Charlotte), Kathleen Reed (Special Collections, University of Pennsylvania), Sheila Ryan (Southern Illinois University, Carbondale), Betsy Sandoz (UCLA Special Collections), David E. Schoonover (Beinecke Library, Yale), Ruth Simmons and Ed Skipworth (Rutgers University Archives), Richard Strassberg (Catherwood Library, Cornell), Edward E. Weber (Labadie Collection, University of Michigan), Richard J. Wolfe (Countway Medical Library, Harvard), and Mary Yearwood (NYPL/Schomburg).

I owe a special debt to the dedicated staff at the Moorland-Spingarn Research Center of Howard University, the repository of the Robeson Archives; I am particularly grateful to Thomas C. Battle, Maricia Bracey, and Karen Jefferson for easing my path in a multitude of ways.

Finally, I'm greatly indebted to those—some of them participants in the events described, others "objective" scholarly observers—who read drafts of this book in whole or in part. Though occasionally I've had to resist the special pleading of certain participants (or, alternately, the ideological disagreements of certain scholars), these early comments have helped me to correct any number of errors. My thanks for their efforts to:

Acknowledgments

Geraldine (Maimie) Neale Bledsoe, Angus Cameron, Revels Cayton, Frances Quiett Challenger, Peggy Dennis, Freda Diamond, Max Fink, Uta Hagen, Alfred Katzenstein, Ari Kiev, David Machin, Richard Nachtigall, Sam Parks, Rose Perry, Martin Popper, Paul Robeson, Jr., Helen Rosen, and Fredi Washington (Bell). I want to offer Eric Gordon, David Levering Lewis, and Eli Zal special thanks: they gave me immensely useful readings of the entire manuscript, catching everything from misplaced commas to fuzzy conceptualizations.

Barbara Bristol, my editor at Knopf, has patiently sat with me while —day after day, line by line—we fine-tuned the final manuscript; along with a superb set of editorial suggestions, which improved the manuscript immeasurably, she provided endless psychic balm. Frances Goldin, my agent and friend of long standing, amazes me more than ever: I know of no one else whose capacity for hard work is matched by such a capacity for caring. Eli Zal was a great comfort and support to me while I was finishing this book; he reminds me that there will still be life after it.

Note on Sources

This biography has been written almost entirely from manuscript sources. In this regard, the Robeson Family Archives has proved by far the most important single collection. The Archives has been deposited since 1978 at the Moorland-Spingarn Research Center at Howard University, in Washington, D.C., but has not previously been open to scholars.

It is a vast archive. Totaling some fifty thousand items—with a diary counting as a single item—it was originally amassed by Eslanda ("Essie") Goode Robeson and subsequently added to and organized by Paul Robeson, Jr. It was he who came to me late in 1981 offering unrestricted access to the Family Archives as an inducement to undertake his father's biography. I needed no inducement, but I did feel it necessary to attach one condition before accepting Paul Robeson, Jr.'s offer: a formal legal agreement in which he eschewed approval of the final manuscript. I felt the need to put in writing what every scholar takes as a guiding principle: the refusal ever to write to specification, to allow any interested party to interfere with the process of historical inquiry. Paul Robeson, Jr., has been of great help in introducing me to some of his father's friends, and has also given generously of his time in sharing his own recollections, but he and I have had sharp disagreements throughout. We evaluate some of the historical evidence differently, and hence have come to see certain segments of his father's history quite differently. Sons and scholars often have separate agendas. The conclusions in this book are mine alone.

Ultimately those conclusions must undergo the scrutiny of other scholars, and soon will, when the Robeson Family Archives has been opened to general use. To facilitate that evaluation, I have made my notes unusually full, using them to cite gaps or contradictions in the evidence, to point to relevant secondary sources as well as manuscript materials—and in general to do all that I could to alert other scholars to the possibility of variant interpretations. I do so in recognition that Robeson's history has previously been uncharted and is an emblematic story of black achievement and struggle. As such, it belongs to future generations, and awaits their evolving verdict.

Rich though the Robeson Family Archives is, it has one serious drawback: the materials represent Essie Robeson far more than Paul. Herself a voluminous letter-writer and diarist, Essie tended to save, even to hoard, every scrap. Paul was the temperamental opposite. He had no instinct for "collecting" and scant interest in recording his own thoughts and feelings. To a remarkable—and, for a biographer, disheartening—degree, he avoided putting pen to paper. Except for some brief shorthand notes made at a few points in his life, he kept no diary. And he disliked writing letters; indeed, his avoidance of correspondence became something of a joke (and occasionally a source of recrimination) to his friends. The Archives contains hundreds and hundreds of pages of Robeson's musical notations, his markings on film and theater scripts, and, for the period of the mid-thirties, some lengthy, valuable discursive ruminations on Africa. But of more private matters there is almost nothing, no substantial enough record of his personal response to individuals (or even to such critical public events as Khrushchev's revelations to the Twentieth Party Congress) to allow a scholar to track his emotional life with retrospective confidence.

His antipathy to keeping a personal record has been the chief stumbling block to this biography, and especially to any effort at probing his inner life. Time and again, the material in the Robeson Archives consists of Essie's, rather than Paul's, jottings and musings. Since they were very different people, often at odds emotionally and politically, her account can hardly be taken as an accurate reflection of his. Yet, in the absence of other material, I have sometimes had to use Essie's letters and diary (especially for the period of the twenties) as the chief sources for a given event. In doing so, I've tried to remain alert to the danger of equating her attitude with his—and have periodically alerted the reader as well (see, for example, note 43, page 601; note 38, page 624; note 41, pages 644–45). Robeson's refusal to leave behind a detailed record of his own is consonant with his temperament. Accurately described by one of his close friends as "a man with a thousand pockets," he disliked the notion of anyone's being able to rummage through them all, to pierce the secretiveness he came to regard as necessary protection.

Since the Robeson Archives is heavily weighted with material Essie Robeson herself accumulated or wrote, I've attempted to leaven that bias by interviewing some 135 friends and associates of Robeson's and by reading widely in other manuscript collections. Finally, nothing can substitute for Robeson's own voice (nor can any amount of scholarly diligence invent one), but the interviews have thickened the number of perspectives on him, and the supplementary manuscript sources have yielded much additional material about him (and even a few supplementary letters by him)—as well as enriching the general contextual background. Below is a full listing of interviewees, followed by the manuscript sources consulted other than the Robeson Family Archives itself.

People Interviewed

James Aronson
Peggy Ashcroft
Etta Moten Barnett
Cedric Belfrage
Mirel Bercovici
Rada Bercovici
Eubie Blake
Charles L. Blockson
Leonard Boudin
Anne Braden
Geri Branton
Fredda Brilliant
Oscar Brown, Jr.
Oscar Brown, Sr.
Margaret Burroughs
Alan Bush
Angus Cameron
Lee Cayton
Revels Cayton
Frances Quiett Challenger
Si-lan Chen
Alice Childress
Herbert E. Cohen
Gertrude Cunningham
Peggy Dennis
Freda Diamond
Earl Dickerson
Hazel Ericson Dodge
Bess Eitingon
Inger McCabe Elliot
Emma Epps
Howard Fast
Andrew Faulds

Max Fink
Ishmael Flory
Moe Foner
Harry Francis
Milton Friedman
Indira Gandhi
John Gates
Nina Goodman (Mrs. Ben
　Davis, Jr.)
Sally Gorton (Mrs. Rockwell
　Kent)
Joseph Gould
Victor Grossman
Bonnie Bird Gundlach
Uta Hagen
John Hammond
Ollie Harrington
Dorothy Healey
Jean Herskovits
Lena Horne
Micki Hurwitt
Jean Blackwell Hutson
C. L. R. James
Ruth Jett
Howard Eugene ("Stretch")
　Johnson
Barney Josephson
Alfred Katzenstein
Ursula Katzenstein
Larry Kerson
Ari Kiev
Bernard Koten
Joseph Lederer

Harold Leventhal

Elma Lewis

Jay Leyda

Marian Liggins

Diana Loesser

Sanford Meisner

Herbert Marshall

Josephine Martin

Carl Marzani

Jan Mason

Ivor Montagu

Chuck Moseley

H. A. Murray

William Mutch

Richard Nachtigall

Kay (Mrs. Aubrey) Pankey

Sam Parks

Graham Payn

Morris Pearlmutter

Theodora Peck

Thelma Dale Perkins

Rose Perry

William Pickens III

Sidney Poitier

Martin Popper

Louis Rawls

Edward Rettenberg

Milton Rettenberg

Jim Richards

Alan Rinzler

Marilyn Robeson

Paul Robeson, Jr.

Earl Robinson

Robert Robinson

Flora Robson

Clara Rockmore

Ted Rolfs

Helen Rosen

Norman Roth

Rose Rubin

Annette Rubinstein

S. A. Russell

Bayard Rustin

Homer Sadler

Antonio Salemmé

G. Foster Sanford, Jr.

Junius Scales

Sylvia Schwartz

Pete Seeger

Jean Seroity

Marie Seton

Sadie Davenport Shelton

Robert Sherman

Frederick Shields

Julius Silverman

Ruby Silverstone

Abbott Simon

Anita Sterner

Michael Straight

Alexander Taylor

Studs Terkel

Edith Tiger

Chatman Wailes

Ruth Walker

Fredi Washington (Bell)

Elizabeth Welch

Aaron Wells

Rebecca West

Monroe Wheeler

Mrs. Harry White

Henry Wilcoxon

Doxey Wilkerson

Aminda Badeau (Mrs. Roy) Wilkins

Addie Wyatt

Asa Zatz

In addition, I have had access to Paul Robeson, Jr.'s interviews with: Peter Blackman, Bruno Raikin, and Marie Seton; and to Anita Sterner's interviews (done for a 1978 BBC program on Robeson) with: Tommy Adlam, George Baker, Frank Barnes, Alfie Bass, Alan Booth, Dave Bowman, Lord Brockway, J. Douglas Brown, May Chinn, George C. Crockett, Jr., Ossie

Davis, Ruby Dee, Leonard de Paur, Dai Francis, John Gerstadt, Leo Hurwitz, Emlyn Jenkins, Roderick Jones, Armina Marshall, James Monk, Mrs. Northcote, Will Paynter, "Princeton Old People," Philip Stein, Phillip Thomas, Rachel Thomas, André Van Gyseghem, Otto Wallen, Charles Wright, Ellsworth Wright, Coleman Young.

Manuscript Sources
(other than the Robeson Family Archives)

AKADEMIE DER KÜNSTE DER DDR, PAUL ROBESON ARCHIV: assorted manuscript letters, first-person reminiscences of Robeson, extensive newspaper and photo collection.

AMISTAD RESEARCH CENTER: Fredi Washington Papers; Countee Cullen Papers

CHICAGO HISTORICAL SOCIETY: Claude A. Barnett Papers

COLUMBIA UNIVERSITY: Robert Minor Papers; Oral History Research Office (some two dozen pertinent interviews including especially those done with: Charles Ascher, Eric Barnouw, A. Philip Randolph, William Jay Schieffelin, Carl Van Vechten, Roy Wilkins, and Henry Agard Wallace); Paul Robeson Law School Records

COUNTWAY MEDICAL LIBRARY, HARVARD: Louis Wright Papers

DUSABLE MUSEUM, CHICAGO: Metz Lorchard Papers; Margaret Burroughs Papers

FDR LIBRARY, HYDE PARK: Eleanor Roosevelt Papers

INTERNATIONAL INSTITUTE OF SOCIAL HISTORY, AMSTERDAM: Emma Goldman Papers

KURT WEILL FOUNDATION FOR MUSIC: Weill/Eslanda Robeson Correspondence

LIBRARY OF CONGRESS: Nannie H. Burroughs Papers; NAACP Papers; Mary Church Terrell Papers; Margaret Webster Papers

MOORLAND-SPINGARN RESEARCH CENTER, HOWARD UNIVERSITY: Bustill-Bowen-Asbury Collection; E. Franklin Frazier Papers; George Murphy Papers; William L. Patterson Papers; Jessica Smith Papers; Jacob C. White Collection

NEW YORK PUBLIC LIBRARY, MANUSCRIPT DIVISION: Paul Kester Papers; Vito Marcantonio Papers; Joel E. Spingarn Papers; Carl Van Vechten Papers

NEW YORK PUBLIC LIBRARY, SCHOMBURG COLLECTION: Lawrence Brown Papers; Civil Rights Congress Papers; Melville J. Herskovits Papers; Alberta Hunter Papers; National Negro Congress Papers; Papers of the Black Academy of Arts and Letters; Pettis Perry Papers; William Pickens Papers; Paul Robeson Collection; Arthur Schomburg Papers

NEW YORK UNIVERSITY, WAGNER ARCHIVES: Actors' Equity Association
Records
NORTHWESTERN UNIVERSITY LIBRARY: Melville J. Herskovits Papers; Ira
Aldridge Collection
PRESBYTERIAN HISTORICAL SOCIETY: Records of New Brunswick Presbytery
PRINCETON UNIVERSITY: Sylvia Beach Collection; Otto Kahn Papers
RUTGERS UNIVERSITY ARCHIVES: assorted Paul Robeson–related material
SCHLESINGER LIBRARY, RADCLIFFE: Charlotte Hawkins Brown Papers;
Margaret Cardozo Holmes interview
SMITH COLLEGE, SOPHIA SMITH COLLECTION, WOMEN'S HISTORY ARCHIVE: Ella
Reeve Bloor ("Mother Bloor") Papers
SOUTHERN ILLINOIS UNIVERSITY, CARBONDALE, SPECIAL COLLECTIONS: Herbert Marshall Papers
STATE HISTORICAL SOCIETY, WISCONSIN: Eugene and Peggy Dennis Papers
SYRACUSE UNIVERSITY: Earl Browder Papers
UNIVERSITY OF CALIFORNIA, LOS ANGELES, SPECIAL COLLECTIONS: R. Golding
Bright Papers; Oral History interviews with Edwin Lester and Ed
Biberman; Ralph Bunche Papers; George Johnson Film Collection
UNIVERSITY OF MASSACHUSETTS, AMHERST: W. E. B. Du Bois Papers
UNIVERSITY OF CALIFORNIA, BERKELEY, BANCROFT LIBRARY: Noel Sullivan
Papers
UNIVERSITY OF MICHIGAN, LABADIE COLLECTION: Maurice Brown/Ellen Van
Volkenburg Papers
UNIVERSITY OF TEXAS, RANSOM HUMANITIES CENTER: Maxwell Anderson
Papers; Frank Harris Papers; Alfred and Blanche Knopf Papers
YALE UNIVERSITY: James Weldon Johnson Memorial Collection of Negro
Arts and Letters; Laurence Langner Papers; Eugene O'Neill Correspondence; Gertrude Stein Correspondence; Theater Guild Papers;
Carl Van Vechten Papers

Additionally, a number of people have given me access to privately held
manuscript material:

Peggy Ashcroft (ms. memoir)
Cedric Belfrage (Belfrage–Peggy Middleton correspondence)
Maimie Neale Bledsoe (ms. memoir and speeches)
Leonard Boudin (files on Robeson passport case)
A'Lelia P. Bundles (ms. letter)
Revels Cayton (ms. letter, biographical materials)
Tim Couzzens (Robeson materials in William Ballinger and Winifred
Holtby Papers)
Gertrude Cunningham (Nathan F. Mossell papers)
Lloyd L. Davies (ms. letters, reminiscences)
Freda Diamond (ms. letters)

Paulina Forsythe (ms. letters to Robeson during the dozen years, 1965–76, when he lived with her and her mother, Marian Forsythe, in Philadelphia)
Milton Friedman (court briefs)
Walter Goldwater (ms. letters)
Nina Goodman [Mrs. Ben Davis, Jr.] (ms. letters)
Rupert Hart-Davis (ms. letters)
Marie Jones (ms. letters)
Corliss Lamont (ms. letter)
H. A. Murray (ms. letters)
Kay [Mrs. Aubrey] Pankey (ms. letters)
Juliet [Mrs. Malcolm] Pitt (ms. letters)
Paul Robeson, Jr. (hospital records; book manuscripts ("With Malice Toward One," "Gideon's Journey"); Washington, D.C., FBI files)
Clara Rockmore (Rockmore-Robeson correspondence)
Helen Rosen (Rosen-Robeson correspondence)
Junius Scales (ms. memoir)
Marie Seton (ms. letters, book ms.)
Louis Shaeffer (interview notes)
Anita Sterner (tapes and transcripts of three dozen interviews for 1978 BBC program on Robeson)
Leonora [Pat] Gregory [Stitt] (ms. memoir and draft of book started with Robeson)
Studs Terkel (tape of others reminiscing about Robeson)
Nancy Wills (ms. memoir)

A number of people I corresponded with added further to the stock of primary materials through their anecdotes and personal recollections of Robeson (as well as by providing leads to others with firsthand accounts). In this regard, I owe special thanks to Kathryn Cavan Avery, Paul Avrich, Edward Biberman, Charles L. Blockson, George Breitman, Harry Bridges, Bob Cohen, Malcolm Cowley, Millia Davenport, Michael H. Ebner, Veit Erlmann, Kim Fellner, Bernard Forer, Joseph Gould, James Frederick Green, Judith Green, John Devereux Kernan, Ralph Kessler, David Randall Luce, Luretta Bagby Martin, Ruth C. McCreary, Jim Murray, Paul G. Partington, Robert Richter, Naomi Rogers, Irene Runge, Stanley Schear, Athene Seyler, Harry Slochower, George Spector, C. A. Tripp, Jules Tygiel, Mrs. William A. P. White, Nancy Wills, and Jane Wright.

Finally, additional documentation about Robeson was secured under the Freedom of Information Act. Some time ago, when access under the FOIA remained comparatively open, Paul Robeson, Jr., got considerable material from the Main Office files of the FBI (as well as some CIA and State Department documentation). Some of that material, however, consisted of condensations sent from the FBI's New York Field Office, the originating branch for surveillance of Robeson. I felt it was urgent to secure the New York files themselves—especially after I discovered that surveillance had been so continuous and intense that the field office file had generated its own internal index (a so-called Correlation Summary, developed only for the very largest FBI collections). Unfortunately, by the time I began this biography in 1981, open access under the FOIA was a policy of the past. When I applied for Robeson's New York file, I did get some material from the early forties, but for the later period I received little more than page after page of inked-out reports. In denying me access, the Bureau cited the now catchall justification of "national security."

Given the persistent rumors that the FBI (as well as other government agencies) had had a direct hand in causing the deterioration in Robeson's health during the fifties, I felt it was essential to try to extract additional materials from the recalcitrant Bureau. To that end, I initiated a formal lawsuit against the FBI through Edward Greer, the Boston lawyer with special expertise in FOIA files. Litigation dragged on for nearly three years. Ultimately, running out of money and nearing completion of the book, I had to agree to an out-of-court settlement that did secure for me some additional documentation, but not enough either definitively to corroborate or to disprove the rumored involvement of the FBI in Robeson's physical and emotional collapse. None of the limited amount of material I received as a result of the court case contains any suggestion of FBI (or other governmental) complicity. Still, the issue must be considered unresolved. The mere existence (apparently unique, according to Ed Greer) of an FBI "Status of Health" file on Robeson remains unexplained, and there are enough other loose ends in the available evidence to make it impossible at this point in time either wholly to absolve or clearly to indict U.S. government agencies for playing a role in Robeson's decline. Final judgment must await the release of *all* pertinent material. Unfortunately, that day may never come: during the course of litigation, the FBI lawyers told Greer—their tone sardonic—that some 56 volumes (out of a probable 103) in the Robeson file of the New York Field Office had "unaccountably disappeared."

Notes

CHAPTER 1 BOYHOOD *(1898–1914)*

1. It would serve no useful purpose to list the voluminous literature on race for this period—expecially since August Meier and Elliott Rudwick's excellent *From Plantation to Ghetto* (Hill and Wang, 1970) summarizes the pertinent evidence and sources. For an updating, see Louis R. Harlan, *Booker T. Washington: The Wizard of Tuskegee, 1901–1915* (Oxford, 1983).

2. WDR obituary in the Somerset *Messenger,* May 22, 1918 (year of degrees). The classmate (and subsequent relative by marriage) was Nathan F. Mossell. His comment on Lincoln University is in his ms. autobiography (which also includes part of his correspondence), generously loaned to me by a descendant, Mrs. Gertrude Cunningham. She also gave me a number of other documents of special value in reconstructing the history of the Robeson family; these are too scattered and numerous to list in full. Besides the Cunningham documents, I have found of special value, despite its distortions, Eslanda Robeson, *Paul Robeson, Negro* (Gollancz, 1930), hereafter ER, *PR, Negro*; Robeson's own autobiography, *Here I Stand* (Beacon Press, 1970), hereafter PR, *Stand*; the Jacob C. White and Bustill-Bowser-Asbury ms. collections at the Moorland-Spingarn Research Center at Howard University, hereafter MSRC; Anna Bustill Smith, "The Bustill Family," *Journal of Negro History,* Oct. 1925; and the collection of ms. letters given me by Paulina Forsythe, daughter of Marian Robeson Forsythe (Paul's sister).

3. Gertrude Bustill edited the Women's Department of the New York *Age* and the Indianapolis *World,* worked for Philadelphia's most influential newspapers, the *Inquirer,* the *Press,* and the *Times,* and was active in a wide variety of women's and public service organizations in the black community (they are detailed in *Twenty 19th Century Black Women,* a publication of the National Archives for Black Women's History and the Mary McLeod Bethune Memorial Museum). Her book,

The Afro-American Woman (George S. Ferguson Co., 1894) surveys the accomplishments of black women, giving due attention to the social conditions that limited their options; it contains as well some "advanced" views on the plight of women in general.

Anna Bustill Smith (cited in note 2) was yet another noteworthy member of the Bustill clan. Cousin to Maria Louisa Bustill Robeson, Paul's mother, she published "Reminiscences of Colored People of Princeton, New Jersey" in 1913, recently rescued from oblivion by the Princeton History Project (see Fred Ferretti, "Black History in Princeton," *The New York Times,* March 5, 1978), which reprinted it in *Princeton Recollector,* vol. III, no. 5 (Winter 1977), with a biographical sketch of Anna Bustill Smith by Gledhill Cameron. Anna Smith's father, Joseph Cassey Bustill, the grandson of Cyrus Bustill, is credited by Cameron with being the youngest member of the Underground Railroad, and her mother, Sarah Humphrew, a Chippewa Indian, with being the first black graduate of the Girls' Normal School in Philadelphia. Paul Robeson personally knew both Gertrude Bustill Mossell and Anna Bustill Smith; all three of them gave speeches at the Eighth Annual Re-Union of the descendants of the Bustill family, June 21, 1918 (the invitation and program are in the Robeson Archives—henceforth RA).

The ms. autobiography (courtesy of Mrs. Gertrude Cunningham) of Gertrude Bustill's husband, Nathan F. Mossell, gives a detailed account of his own noteworthy career. Having surmounted the color bar to medical training, in 1895 he founded with other black doctors what became the famed Mercy-Douglass Hospital in Philadelphia (its history is recounted in Elliott M. Rudwick, "A Brief History of Mercy-Douglass," *Journal of Negro Education,* vol. 20 [1951], and also in the hospital's *Annual Reports,* given to me by Mrs. Gertrude Cunningham). Mossell remained active in the protest against racial injustice throughout his long life.

His ms. papers contain a large number of speeches, letters, and petitions that attest to his activism, including correspondence with William Jennings Bryan about racial "amalgamation" and protests about racial issues to both the Presidents Roosevelt.

4. Gertrude Cunningham documents; PR, ms. notes (written May 2, 1956), RA (rocks; militancy; Laddie); PR, *Stand*, pp. 12–13, 21–22; interview with Marian Liggins (Ben's daughter), Nov. 21, 1982; interview with Rada and Mirel Bercovici, July 7, 1985 (Reeve); multiple interviews with Helen Rosen (recalls PR saying Reeve had ended on Skid Row). Since blacks were not permitted in the Princeton high school, William had to travel to Trenton to get an education (PR, *Stand*, p. 10; Epps interview, Aug. 11, 1987). Alexander ("Ting") Taylor is the source for William's being called "schoolboy"; Taylor (b. 1891), and his family lived opposite the Robesons on Greene Street (interview with Taylor, Aug. 11, 1987). Emma Epps (b. 1900), also a neighbor, believes Reeve became a mortician in Washington, D.C., before going to Detroit (interview with Epps, Aug. 11, 1987). Both Taylor and Epps confirm that Reeve always stood up for his rights ("Wouldn't take nothing from nobody," in Taylor's words). Paul Robeson, Jr. (henceforth PR, Jr.), is the source for Reeve's being part owner of a hotel, but denies that there is any truth to the rumor that he died on Skid Row (PR, Jr., ms. comments). In a heated speech in 1949, PR referred to Reeve's answering "each insult with blows that sent would-be slave masters crashing to the stone sidewalks, even though jail was his constant reward" (press release, Council on African Affairs [hereafter CAA], June 19, 1949).

5. *Princeton Press*, March 26, 1906 (size of black population). Both Taylor and Epps stressed to me (interviews, Aug. 11, 1987) the cohesiveness that existed in Princeton's black community in the early decades of the century, and also the "large number" of black-owned businesses and property. PR, *Stand*, pp. 10–11; Pearl Bradley, "Robeson Questionnaire" (twelve-page interview for Bradley's M.A. thesis), RA (NC contingent); Anita Sterner interviews with Bishop Clinton Hoggard and J. Douglas Brown (PR contemporaries) for 1978 BBC program on PR, tapes courtesy of Sterner (hereafter "Sterner interviews"). PR's later remarks on Princeton are from a June 19, 1949, CAA press release summarizing a speech he had given, and also a handwritten ms. reminiscing about his youth (in ER's hand), RA. In later life PR often referred with special fondness to his Aunt Huldah (e.g., *Freedom*, April 1952); according to Epps (interview, Aug. 11, 1987), Huldah Robeson was married to Rev. Robeson's brother Ben (a second brother, John, apparently also lived in Princeton). PR's childhood playmates included Bessie and Christine Moore, whose mother was white and whose father made considerable money running a cleaning establishment for Princeton students and also a boardinghouse; Christine Moore (later Howell, who lived until 1972) remained close friends with Marian Robeson Forsythe through the years. (I'm grateful to her daughter, Paulina Forsythe, for sharing with me Christine Moore Howell's letters).

6. Rev. Robeson had had a brief pastorate in Wilkes-Barre, Pa., before being called to Witherspoon (obituary, Somerset *Messenger*, May 22, 1918). Anna Bustill Smith, "Reminiscences of Colored People of Princeton, New Jersey"; Sterner interview with Hoggard; Somerset *Messenger*, May 22, 1918. Blacks had originally been listed in the rolls of the First Presbyterian Church and had successfully resisted efforts to set them apart until 1846, when the First Presbyterian Church of Color was organized; its name was changed in 1848 to Witherspoon Street Presbyterian Church (Arthur Link, *First Presbyterian Church of Princeton* [Princeton University Press, 1967], pp. 32–36; V. Lansing Collins, *Princeton, Past and Present* [Princeton University Press, 1945]; Thomas Jefferson Wertenbaker, *Princeton 1746–1896* [Princeton University Press, 1946]).

7. Records of the New Brunswick Presbytery, Jan. 30, June 26, Sept. 19, 1900, The Presbyterian Historical Society (PHS); Trenton *Times*, June 28, Sept.

20 ("eloquent"), 1900; Princeton *Press,* Sept. 22, 1900 ("misfit").

8. Records of the New Brunswick Presbytery, Sept. 24, 1900, PHS; *Daily State Gazette* (Trenton), Sept. 25, 1900; Princeton *Press,* Sept. 29, 1900.

9. Sterner interview with Hoggard; Grace Doman Willis to Marian Robeson Forsythe, Feb. 21, 1976 ("did it to his father"), courtesy Paulina Forsythe. One false rumor that circulated about Rev. Robeson's forced departure centered on "mischief with one of the girls in his congregation." Alexander Woollcott printed that rumor in his New York *World* column for May 20, 1928, adding, "Years later, they tell me, a divinity student, who had helped to bring the accusation, confessed that it had been an invention fabricated by someone who wanted to occupy that pulpit himself." In a second article, Woollcott referred to "some skulduggery on the part of two scheming divinity students" as being responsible for Rev. Robeson's ouster (*Hearst's International Cosmopolitan,* July 1933; conceivably Woollcott's source was Paul, since the two were friendly at the time).

10. Records of the New Brunswick Presbytery, Oct. 17, Nov. 12, PHS; Princeton *Press,* Nov. 10, 1900 (Seminary meeting).

11. Princeton *Press,* Feb. 2, 1901. The six-hundred-dollar salary is an estimate based on a report in the Princeton *Press,* June 30, 1906, that the salary of the pastor of Witherspoon Church had, after a recent increase, reached seven hundred dollars. The statement issued by the Church Session of Witherspoon Street Presbyterian (printed in the Princeton *Press,* Feb. 16, 1901) makes no reference at all to a dispute, merely commending Rev. Robeson for his eloquence as a speaker and for his continuing efforts for "social and moral reform and Christian union." The records of the Witherspoon Street Church might contain additional information about the reasons for Rev. Robeson's departure, but in response to my inquiry the church archivists reported that they could not locate the records for the period in question. One hopes those records are only temporarily mislaid.

12. Interview with Marian Liggins,

Nov. 21, 1982. The fullest account of Louisa Robeson's death is in ER, *PR, Negro,* pp. 23–24, but additional information about her is in PR, *Stand,* pp. 14–17, 21-22, and Rev. B. C. Robeson, ms. "My Brother Paul," RA, subsequently reprinted as "My Brother—Paul Robeson—An Appraisal," with a "Comment" by Bishop W. J. Walls, in *The Quarterly Review of Higher Education Among Negroes,* Oct. 1954, and as appendix A to PR, *Stand.*

13. The "intimates" quoted are Helen Rosen and Clara Rockmore, in multiple interviews with each. The recollection of his mother's funeral is in PR, ms. notes, written May 2, 1956, RA. John H. Johnson, whose mother, Harriet Howard, was a good friend of Louisa Bustill Robeson, described her, in one of the few accounts that are even secondhand, as "a beautiful woman . . . in all ways a most admirable person." (Johnson to PR, June 5, 1975, courtesy Paulina Forsythe). The *Sunday Times* (New Brunswick), June 8, 1930, referred to her as a "poetess." Emma Epps (interview Aug. 11, 1987) described her as "very brilliant," "a beautiful person—most of us never got over it."

14. Epps interview, Aug. 11, 1987 (preaching); Princeton *Packet,* Jan. 2, 30, 1904; Sergeant, "A Portrait of Paul Robeson," *The New Republic,* March 3, 1926 (dignity); PR, ms. notes, written May 2, 1956 (ashes). In the latter source, PR also wrote that his brothers Reed and Bill would help their father out as coachmen, driving the Princeton students "to earn a few quarters"; but the work, PR added, was "often hazardous— Many of the students being from the deep south and imbued with Platonic ideas of the 'Elite' and the superiority of Anglo-Saxon over African—and especially if the wine had flowed in abundance." The original ms. version of Marie Seton's *Paul Robeson* (Dennis Dobson, 1958) contains PR's handwritten comments and deletions in the margins (ms. courtesy Seton—hereafter "Seton Ms."). In the ms. Seton made two separate references to the Bustills' doing "nothing to aid Maria Louisa's dark children" after her death, seeking Paul out "only after he became a famous

man"—"he was too black to be accepted as one of them. . . ." Seton based her book primarily on talks with Robeson himself, but when he went over her ms. he cut out the references cited above, and they do not appear in the printed version. Further evidence of the Bustill attitude is in an FBI report which quotes Robeson as saying that "his mother's family looked down on his father's people" (FBI Main 100-12304-7), and in a *World Telegram* interview with him (Oct. 5, 1935). Paul's identification with his father's family was so strong that at times he may have exaggerated the extent of his actual contact with them. In a 1948 speech, for example (the tape is in RA), he mentions in passing that "I was in the South a lot as a boy." In point of fact, he was not. Apparently his mother did take him on a visit to North Carolina when he was an infant (PR, "Here's My Story," *Freedom*, April 1952), but that was the only time he spent there. Yet his 1948 claim may well represent, in a symbolic sense, how deeply he felt attached in spirit to his North Carolina roots (and may also reflect the Southern "feel" of Princeton).

15. Rev. Robeson was formally "dismissed" by the Presbytery of New Brunswick to the A.M.E. Zion New Jersey Conference in April 1906 and appointed two months later by the bishop to A.M.E. Zion in Westfield (Princeton *Press*, April 28, June 1906). PR later wrote that his father "reluctantly moved on from Calvinism to the Church of John Wesley" (PR, ms. notes, written May 2, 1956, RA—also the source for laying first bricks). Somerville *Courier-News*, April 20, 1973 (Sam Woldin, Arthur Van Fleet, and Donald M. Pearsall's recollections of PR, including the years in Westfield); interview with Hazel Ericson Dodge (a Somerville classmate), Nov. 7, 1983; Sterner interviews with Hoggard and Brown, plus her tape marked "Discussion at Old People's Meeting in Princeton"; PR, *Stand*, pp. 12–15; New York *Herald Tribune*, Oct. 17, 1926 (overnights); Seton Ms. (church sisters; most of this section does not appear in Seton's printed version); *The New Yorker* profile of PR, "King of Harlem," Sept. 24, 1928 (sewing buttons, etc.). The comment

about "a nice, open-hearted boy" is from Langston Hughes, New York *Herald Tribune*, June 29, 1930, in which he reviews ER, *PR, Negro,* and recounts his own talks about PR with his neighbors in Westfield (where Hughes was living in 1930). PR's comment on qualified white acceptance in Westfield is from the ms. of his column in the first (Dec. 1950) issue of *Freedom,* PR Coll., New York Public Library, Schomburg Collection (hereafter NYPL/Schm). In the same ms. he recalls sometimes taking meals in "one of the few colored restaurants" in town, "rushing from school to get my favorite dish and my nickname, a 'thousand on a plate.' "

16. Scattered information on Reverend Robeson's activities as pastor in Somerville are in the *Unionist-Gazette* (Somerville) for Jan. 23, Feb. 20, April 17, May 1, 1913, April 30, 1914, Jan. 7, April 29, May 13, 20, June 24, July 1, 1915; they include references to his hosting and attending church conferences, welcoming the Colored Boy Scouts for a concert held at St. Thomas, and a successful carnival to raise money for church expenses; two of the news items (Jan. 23, 1913 and April 1, 1915) refer to two week-long revivals and "religious awakening" at St. Thomas during which "many were reclaimed." The obituary in the local paper when Rev. Robeson died reported that, "During the first three years of his pastorate a debt of $1,600 on the parsonage was liquidated" (the Somerset Messenger, May 22, 1918). Condolence letter from "Lawrence" to PR, May 20, 1918 (devoted), RA; PR, *Stand*, p. 9. Ben Robeson was appointed to his first pastorate in the A.M.E. Zion Church, Bayonne, N.J., in 1914. His thirteen months of overseas service as a chaplain in World War I left him, in his daughter's opinion, with jangled nerves thereafter, despite a calm exterior. He was appointed to Mother A.M.E. Zion Church in 1936 and remained its pastor until his death in 1963. He married Frances Cline in 1915 and they had three daughters, Marian Liggins, Vivian Reynolds, and Bennie Ryan (program for Memorial Service, Dec. 5, 1963; Philadelphia *Tribune,* Sept. 22, 1962; interview with Marian Liggins, Nov. 21, 1982). The version

quoted in the text about Rev. Robeson's fall is from Seton, *Robeson,* p. 18—a variant of the anecdote is published in PR, *Stand,* p. 9; yet a third version is in an undated thirteen-page ms. speech by Geraldine (Maimie) Neale Bledsoe, PR's girlfriend during his undergraduate years, recounting the story as she had heard it from Paul (ms. courtesy Bledsoe). H. A. Murray was one friend who heard PR's imitation of his father in the twenties; Murray thought it "too good for words" and prevailed on PR to give a repeat performance at the bedside of ailing playwright Ned Sheldon (interview with Murray, Feb. 6, 1985).

17. PR, "From My Father's Parsonage," *Sunday Sun* (London), Jan. 13, 1929 (inflexion). In *Stand,* p. 13, PR wrote that his father "never" talked about his years as a slave. I have substituted "rarely" for "never" on the basis of PR's own testimony at other points in his life—for example, in interviews he gave to the *Messenger,* Oct. 1924, and to the *Methodist Times* (London), Jan. 3, 1929. The *Methodist Times* interview and *Stand,* pp. 11–13, along with Jerome Beatty, "America's No. 1 Negro," *The American,* May 1944, are the sources for the quotations, except for the one about "trek for Freedom," which is from Maimie Bledsoe to me (April 4, 1985) and as repeated by her in a twenty-one-page speech (the ms. of which she sent me) that she delivered in the 1970s about Robeson. The Woldins gave Rev. Robeson a plot of ground in their backyard on which to grow vegetables, since his own soil was not suitable (Sam Woldin, ms. reminiscences, RA).

18. PR, *Stand,* p. 9.

19. Interview with Oscar Brown, Sr., July 2, 1986; Joseph H. Nelson to me, Dec. 14, 1982, with his ms. enclosure, "Paul Robeson: Citizen of the World," dated Feb. 1981 ("beautiful voice"). Brown emphasized to me that on the whole he and the rest of the black staff were well treated at the hotel. In his autobiography, *By a Thread* (Vantage Press, 1983), p. 25, Brown writes, "Most of the boys were able to get a suit out of their summer work." Fritz Pollard is mentioned in PR's "Memory Book" for "Summer 1916," RA. In her diary for

Dec. 30, 1924, ER mentions seeing "dear old Oscar Brown" (RA).

20. Somerset *Messenger,* June 29, 1911 (Jamison graduation).

21. PR, *Stand,* pp. 17–18. Unlike Paul, his wife, Essie Robeson, later seems to have equated the town's surface acceptance with equality. In her 1930 book on her husband, *Paul Robeson, Negro,* she exaggerates community acceptance, painting a near-cloudless picture of race relations in Somerville (e.g., "He played with the sons and daughters of the most cultured white people in the town. . . . Apparently no one thought about the mixing, and certainly no one resented it. . . . He himself never thought about it" (ER, *PR, Negro,* pp. 30–31). Paul deeply disliked ER's book (see pp. 139–40).

22. Interview with Hazel Ericson Dodge, Nov. 7, 1983; Sterner interviews with Frank Barnes and Leslie Kershaw, 1977. Barnes told Sterner that Winston Douglas later became principal of a school—"to me a more satisfying life than Paul. . . . He [Robeson] could have done more had he remained in maybe the teaching profession." See also the interview with Kershaw in the *Democrat* (Flemington, N.J.), Feb. 5, 1976.

23. Interviews with Ericson, Barnes, Kershaw; "refined, clean-minded, wholesome" is a phrase from ER, *PR, Negro,* p. 31; J. Douglas Brown, three-page typed reminiscence of PR at Somerville High, dated April 4, 1976 (hereafter Brown, "Somerville"), in the Special Collections of the Rutgers University Library (hereafter RUA). When PR returned to Somerville in 1926 to give a concert, ER wrote in her diary, "So many people, colored and white, came backstage afterwards to welcome Paul back. Paul remembered all about their sons and daughters, and what they were doing, etc., and tickling the people to death" (ER Diary, Jan. 14, 1926, RA).

24. PR, *Stand,* p. 17; Brown, "Somerville" (Caesar), RUA; *Unionist-Gazette,* Feb. 19, 26, 1914 ("coarse . . . censure").

25. *Unionist-Gazette,* Feb. 11, March 4, April 1, 1915 ("Water Cure"); interview with Hazel Ericson Dodge, Nov. 7, 1983; Sterner interviews with Kershaw, Barnes, Brown; Brown, "Somerville,"

RUA; Mina Higgins, "Paul Robeson, Bright Star . . ." in *Sunday Times* (New Brunswick), June 27, 1924, for which PR supplied the basic data (Jennings to PR, Feb. 27, 1924). The *Sunday Times,* June 15, 1924, and the Somerset *Messenger Gazette,* April 19, 1972 (reminiscences of five PR contemporaries) also have references to the "Water Cure," but the fullest account, one that draws on the recollections of Anna Miller, is in the *Sunday Times,* April 1, 1934. The *Unionist-Gazette,* April 18, 1915, *does* list PR as part of the senior class trip to Washington; perhaps, finally, he did not go (as his classmates' accounts listed above attest), but this contradiction in the evidence remains unresolved.

26. PR, *Stand,* p. 19; Kershaw interview in the *Democrat* (Flemington, N.J.), Feb. 5, 1976 (Vosseller); Rev. B. C. Robeson, ms. "My Brother Paul," RA.

27. In an interview with Kershaw in the *Democrat* (Flemington, N.J.), Feb. 5, 1976, he claimed (with what I would guess is only marginal plausibility, given PR's restraint) not only that the High Bridge principal called PR "big nigger" but also that it caused Paul "to vent his anger for the only time" Kershaw could remember: "He grabbed the principal by the back of the coat and pants and marched him out in front of the stands," finally restrained from doing him further injury by three or four of his fellow players. In *Stand,* pp. 20–21, PR recounts the racial bigotry of the supervising principal of the Somerville system, Dr. Ackerman. It's possible Kershaw, keen to defend Somerville's reputation, transposed that hostility to the neighboring principal in High Bridge.

28. *Sunday Times* (New Brunswick), June 15, 1924 (teacher), April 1, 1934 (place); interview with Hazel Ericson Dodge, Nov. 7, 1983; PR, *Stand,* pp. 19–20. Several of his male contemporaries, however, recalled that their families had "entertained and dined" him in their homes (as interviewed in the Somerset *Messenger Gazette,* April 19, 1973).

29. PR, *Stand,* p. 20. The 1924 article on PR (Mina Higgins, "Paul Robeson, Bright Star . . . ," *Sunday Times* [New Brunswick], June 15, 1924) contains some interviews and reminiscences by PR's contemporaries at Somerville High, which provide additional confirmation both of the "subtle" racism to which he was subjected and of the "affable" way he reacted to it. One woman quoted in the article, for example, compared him favorably with the other black student, Winston Douglas, who was characterized as "bossy": "Paul isn't a bit. He's not nearly so good looking . . . but Paul is so exceptionally nice. I never really think of him as black—do you?" Paul is also referred to in the article as "appreciative"—"he can understand the white point of view as well as he can the black. He belongs to the human race first of all."

30. *Pearson's Weekly* (London), Oct. 20, 1934 ("manner of man"); "awful rough" is from public remarks PR made in Australia in 1960, tape courtesy of Lloyd Davies. The quotes about "in comparison to most Negroes" and "intense fury" are from the ms. of Seton's *Robeson;* they were cut from the printed version at PR's own insistence. According to Seton, he asked her to delete "additional examples of hurtful acts of discrimination" because "he suffered less than virtually all black people" (Seton to Geoffrey Baines, Nov. 30, 1978, courtesy Seton).

31. As pieced together from the following five interviews, the first four conducted by Sterner: Barnes, Brown, Hoggard, Kershaw, Ericson (with me, Nov. 7, 1983); and also from the reminiscences by Woldin, Van Fleet, and Pearsall in the Somerville *Courier-News,* April 20, 1973, and from the interview with Kershaw in the *Democrat* (Flemington, N.J.), Feb. 5, 1976 (books home).

32. The largest amount of material on Robeson's high-school athletic career is in the *Unionist-Gazette* (Somerville); for baseball, the issues of May 12, 1913, April 16, May 28, 1914, May 13, 20, 1915; for track, May 28, 1914; for football, Oct. 23 (Phillipsburg), Nov. 6 (Bound Brook) 1913. Somerset *Messenger Gazette,* April 19, 1973 ("rough bunch"); *Sunday Times* (New Brunswick), June 8, 1930 (Rev. Robeson). Brown writes about the Phillipsburg game, "The local toughs urged their players to get Paul. The rest of us

protected him on every play" ("Somerville," RUA). Donald M. Pearsall, who knew PR in Westfield, recalls that he played on the high-school baseball team while he was still in the seventh grade (as interviewed in the *Courier-News* [Bridgewater, N.J.], April 20, 1973). PR was also "athletic editor" of the *Valkyrie,* the student paper (*Unionist-Gazette,* June 17, 1915).

33. Phone interview with Frederick K. Shield, Nov. 8, 1983.

34. PR, *Stand,* pp. 25–26; Brown, "Somerville," RUA; Shield interview, Nov. 8, 1983. Shield's retrospective enthusiasm for PR's performance led him, in our interview, to remember that PR had been awarded first prize. That memory is contradicted not only by PR's own account in *Stand,* but also in the contemporary newspaper account (*Unionist-Gazette,* April 29, 1915). Shield may have been remembering the preliminary round to choose Somerville's contes-

tant—which PR did win—but for that contest Shield is not listed in the paper as having been a judge (*Unionist-Gazette,* April 22, 1915). Additional information on debating events in which PR took part is in the *Unionist-Gazette,* Feb. 4, 11, (literacy test), 18, March 11, 1915.

35. PR, *Stand,* pp. 24–25; *Sunday Times,* New Brunswick, April 1, 1934 (Anna Miller). The Class of 1915 closing ceremonials—Banquet, Class Day Exercises, and Commencement—are described in the *Unionist-Gazette,* May 13, June 17, 24, July 15, 1915. PR played the role of a gypsy in the Exercises and at commencement recited "a splendid oratorical analysis" of Elijah P. Lovejoy, the abolitionist martyr.

36. Profile of PR, "King of Harlem"; PR, "Notes: 1936," RA ("idealist"). He had been brought up "more like an English schoolboy than an American one," he once remarked (Seton Ms., courtesy Seton).

CHAPTER 2   RUTGERS COLLEGE (*1915–1918*)

1. Interview with Davenport's widow and son, Sadie Davenport Shelton and Robert Davenport, March 26, 1985 (PR, Jr., participating).

2. The team measurements are recorded on a piece of paper in RA.

3. PR interview with Robert Van Gelder, "Robeson Remembers," *The New York Times,* Jan. 16, 1944.

4. Van Gelder interview, *The New York Times,* Jan. 16, 1944; *New Yorker* profile, Sept. 24, 1928; Sterner interview with Kershaw.

5. Sterner interview with Rendall. White's comments are in " 'Robey' at Rutgers," Rutgers *Daily Targum,* April 10, 1973), an article by Ronald Dean Brown containing interviews with PR's classmates. Earl Reed Silvers, *Rutgers Alumni Monthly,* Nov. 1930, p. 44. Silvers also wrote to James M. Nelson, associate editor of *The American Magazine* (April 3, 1944), protesting the accuracy of "the recurring appearance in newspapers and magazines of the story to the effect that Paul's teammates attempted deliberately

to injure him during his first weeks as a member of the squad."

6. Interview with G. Foster Sanford, Jr., April 12, 1983.

7. Interview with Angus Cameron, July 15, 1986 (orange crates); Mason's version was told to me by his daughter Jan Mason in a phone interview, March 5, 1985; Nash's comment is in the Rutgers *Daily Targum,* April 10, 1973. Additional confirmation has come to me from William E. Mutch, Rutgers 1920 (interview Feb. 25, 1987), and from Bernard Forer, who later taught with Alfred Neuschafer, a guard on the Rutgers team, and reports that Neuschafer told stories about the varsity's "conspiring" to pound Robeson "unmercifully" (Forer to me, Aug. 12, 1982). See also Forer's account in the *Rutgers Alumni News,* Spring 1988, p. 21.

8. New Brunswick *Sunday Home News,* Oct. 16, 1965 (Burke); this episode is also recounted in Larry Pitt, *Football at Rutgers, 1869–1969* (Rutgers, 1972). Five years after graduating, Paul and Essie had dinner with Sanford (ER Diary, Feb. 7, 1924,

RA), and when a special memorial meeting was held honoring Sanford's induction into the football Hall of Fame, Robeson sent his greetings (the message is in RA). Sanford, Jr., also recounted (interview, April 12, 1983) how his father championed PR to the extent of physically threatening train conductors and hotel managers who refused accommodations to PR when the team was traveling, but I've found no outside confirmation of those events. According to Sanford, Jr., Robeson was "very conscious of his social strata," as demonstrated by the fact that, when he found himself on the same ship with the Sanfords on returning from Europe once in the twenties, he chose to eat in his stateroom rather than "embarrass" the Sanfords by coming into the dining room and possibly being seated at their table (interview with G. Foster Sanford, Jr., April 12, 1983).

9. According to the account based on interviews with contemporaries in the *Sunday Times* (New Brunswick), June 8, 1930, PR got his first break as a freshman as a result of Budge Garrett's being hurt in one of the early games of the season. A large collection of newspaper clippings, ranging from the Rutgers *Targum* to the national press, chronicling PR's athletic career in detail, is in RA; they are too numerous to cite. George Daley of the New York *World* (Nov. 28, 1917) is the sportswriter quoted above; Walter Camp's comment is in *Collier's Weekly,* Jan. 4, 1919. PR's compiled athletic record is in J. C. Hilliard to PR, April 25, 1923, RA. PR's "Memory Book" (RA) contains the references to St. Christopher. PR later reminisced warmly about "St. C," which he referred to as "the boy's club of St. Philips Parish" in *Freedom,* Nov. 1951. Seven years after graduating from Rutgers, PR is quoted as saying that, after the first two years of playing football, "the games lost much of their pleasure for me. It became too much a case of thinking that winning the game was its only object. . . . Instead of playing for the love of it you then were playing only to win" (Boston *Evening Globe,* March 13, 1926). William E. Mutch was on the baseball team with PR and

remembers that the coach, "General" Frank Cox, always took the room with Robeson when the team had to sleep away from the campus on an overnight (interview with Mutch, Feb. 25, 1987).

10. Interviews with Sanford, Jr., April 12, 1983, and Mutch, Feb. 25, 1987 ("nigger"). Storck's comments are as reported to me by his daughter, Dorothy D. Storck (phone interview, May 5, 1987). Storck entered Rutgers in 1916 and was later an All-American from West Point.

11. Interview with Mutch, Feb. 25, 1987 (Kilpatrick); Boston *Traveler,* Aug. 14, 1942 (quitting).

12. The Carr letter, June 6, 1919, is in RUA. It has been reprinted by George Fishman in *Freedomways,* Summer 1969, and by Peter Mazzei, "James Dickson Carr: First Black Graduate of Rutgers College," *The Journal of the Rutgers University Libraries,* vol. XLVII, no. 2, Dec. 1985. The Mazzei article contains additional details of Carr's career at Rutgers and also reprints Pres. Demarest's brief and evasive reply to Carr's letter of protest.

13. Boston *Traveler,* Aug. 14, 1942; New York *Tribune,* Nov. 4, 1917; Cincinnati *Post,* Oct. 25, 1929; undated [1944?] clipping from a Westfield, N.J., paper, RA.

14. *Targum,* Dec. 19, 1917, *Rutgers Athletic News,* Oct. 4, 1969 (p.12), L. L. Arms writing in the New York *Tribune* (as quoted in the *Scarlet Letter,* 1919, p. 165 ("Othello"), The *Sun,* Nov. 25, 1917.

15. The comments on PR's gentleness are by Rudolph Illey (Rutgers '20), who also described PR as "a loner," and Robert E. Galbraith (Rutgers '24); they are part of a collection of reminiscences about PR in RUA.

16. A list of PR's course grades is in RA. His worst grade, a D in Physics Lab, was given him by Prof. Mayne Mason, who nonetheless referred to him as "*extremely* bright" (interview with Jan Mason, March 5, 1985). Among his teachers, PR had particularly fondness for Dr. Charles H. Whitman, a professor of English who took him to New York to see his first Shakespeare play, *The Merchant of Venice* (Bradley, "Robeson Questionnaire," 1944, RA). In a later newspaper interview

(*Sunday Times* [New Brunswick], June 8, 1930), Whitman said he encouraged PR to become an educator "among the people of his own race." After graduation, Robeson returned to speak at Whitman's contemporary drama class.

The ms. of Seton's *Robeson* (courtesy Seton) contains several sentences about the glee club that were subsequently cut from the printed version; one of them reads, "These rules were that no Negro student would be welcome because there were white girls present," but Robeson crossed out the words following "welcome" and wrote in instead "to social events. Not social equality. Please."

The same pattern of social discrimination is apparent in PR's room assignments. The Rutgers College Catalogues (RUA) list him as living alone in Winants Hall during both his freshman and sophomore years—though only a few single rooms are available in Winants, and upperclassmen traditionally have preference on them. In his junior year PR was assigned a room with Robert Davenport, the only other black student at Rutgers, and Leon Harold Smith, a white freshman described in these words in his yearbook: ". . . even *he* claims he's really stupid." In his senior year PR was put in a room with another white freshman, Herbert Lewis Miskend from Brooklyn. There is no certain evidence that PR accepted these room assignments; several fragmented references suggest that he lived at least part of the time with black families off-campus. According to J. Douglas Brown and Clinton Hoggard, PR did at first live in a campus dormitory, but then stayed with the Cummings family in New Brunswick (Sterner interviews with Brown, Hoggard). Confirmation that PR did live in Winants is in a set of ms. reminiscences by undergraduates who knew him at Rutgers (in RUA), one of whom (Charles T. Dieffenbach, '22) recalls living in the room just below Paul's—"will always remember his booming 'Pipe down, freshmen!' aimed at the three of us more than a few times." William E. Mutch, a year behind PR at Rutgers, remembers Robeson's room in Winants as being on the ground floor and essentially bare except for desk, bed, and chair. Mutch distinctly recalls Davenport as Robeson's roommate, but doesn't remember any white student living with them. Additionally, Mutch remembers that PR would participate in "sings" on the steps of Winants or outside of the Beta Theta Phi fraternity house—though no fraternity at Rutgers would admit a black to membership inside the house. According to Mutch, PR's performance of "Gopher Dust" at the "sings" became so popular that whenever he appeared the shout "Gopher Dust!" would go up (interview, Feb. 25, 1987). In the *Sunday Times* (New Brunswick), June 8, 1930, an unidentified man who played varsity football with PR is quoted as saying that, during the steak suppers the team would be treated to after a game, PR "used to sing his own little Negro songs" between courses, and also "college songs and the popular tunes of the day," and before the games he "came over to the fraternity house often . . . and sang."

17. Rev. Robeson "stinted and got help from influential people" (Seton Ms.). Among the latter, apparently, was Lena Horne's grandmother Cora Horne (as told in 1983 to the Washington *Post* drama critic David Richards, who kindly passed the information on to me). Audreen Buffalo's interview with Lena Horne (*Essence*, May 1985) repeats that same story. Lena Horne's daughter, Gail Lumet Buckley, claims that Cora Horne "helped Paul apply for the scholarship he won at Rutgers" (*The Hornes: An American Family* [Knopf, 1986], p. 50). According to Sanford, Jr. (interview, April 12, 1983), PR may also have gotten some money from a group of "gentlemen underwriters," a syndicate of Rutgers alumni formed to ensure that their alma mater "became a major football power"; the practice of paying college players was then legal and commonplace, and Sanford, Jr., feels certain that PR received some assistance; one fifty-dollar letter of credit for PR, signed by a John P. Wall of New Brunswick, is described in Faulk to Wall, June 24, 1919, RUA.

18. The Philoclean episode is in Charles E. Bloodgood to Hans Knight, Aug. 21, 1975, carbon courtesy of

Paulina Forsythe. "A thing apart" is from ms. of PR's column in *Freedom*, Dec. 1950 (PR Coll., New York Public Library, Manuscript Division, henceforth NYPL/ Ms. Div.).

19. Storck's recollections are as reported to me by his daughter Dorothy D. Storck (phone interview, May 5, 1987); Charles N. Prickett to PR, Dec. 8, 1969, RA ("watching").

20. Geraldine (Maimie) Neale Bledsoe, mss. of three unpublished talks about PR, undated (1970s), courtesy of Bledsoe. For more detail on these mss., see note 26.

21. New Brunswick *Daily Home News*, June 5, 1919; Dorothy Butler Gilliam, *Paul Robeson, All-American* (New Republic, 1976), p. 20. PR's thesis is printed in Philip S. Foner, ed., *Paul Robeson Speaks* (Citadel, 1978), pp. 53–62.

22. *Sunday Times* (New Brunswick), June 8, 1930 (Demarest).

23. PR's valedictory speech is in RA and was also printed in full in the Rutgers *Targum*, June 1919; Charles E. Bloodgood to Hans Knight, Aug. 21, 1975, carbon courtesy of Paulina Forsythe (audience standing).

24. In my reading of PR's valedictory speech, I find Sterling Stuckey's characterization of it as showing "an essentially nationalist stand" off the mark. (Stuckey, " 'I Want To Be African': Paul Robeson and the Ends of Nationalist Theory and Practice," *The Massachusetts Review*, Spring 1976). At the other extreme, Harold Cruse has argued that Robeson never developed a nationalist perspective (*The Crisis of the Negro Intellectual* [Morrow, 1967]). Stuckey and Cruse have tangled extensively over this question in print, but since the controversy focuses on the 1930s, the bulk of my discussion of the issues will be found in the chapters on those years. Suffice it to say here that in my view both men, though coming at the question from opposite perspectives, adopt a static analysis, failing to detect the *developmental* aspect of Robeson's thought, and failing also to make a crucially needed distinction between the public words Robeson spoke as a young man to white or mixed audiences and the private words he spoke (and the inner emotions he felt) with black friends—a distinction I have tried to draw in this chapter. For the Stuckey-Cruse controversy, see also Stuckey, "The Cultural Philosophy of Paul Robeson," *Freedomways*, First Quarter 1971; Cruse, "A Review of the Paul Robeson Controversy," *First World*, vol.2, no.3, 1979; and Stuckey, "On Cultural Nihilism," ms. copy, RA.

25. Interview with Sadie Goode Davenport Shelton and her son Robert Davenport, March 26, 1985 (PR, Jr., participating); interview with Frances Quiett (Challenger), Dec. 7, 1983. Sadie Goode only met PR and the "Trenton crowd" a few times; her husband was closer to them. After graduation, Davenport went to teach at Slater (Winston-Salem) and then in Texas, but kept in occasional touch with PR. Though he died young (1939), before PR became a controversial figure, Davenport was, according to his widow, always quick to defend him against slurs of any kind. When Davenport died, PR was unable to attend the funeral, but was moved enough to ask his brother Rev. Ben Robeson to represent him. As late as 1952, when in the New Jersey area, PR stopped by to say hello to Sadie Davenport's father, a Montclair chauffeur on whose porch PR had sometimes slept as an undergraduate if he missed connections back to New Brunswick (he slept on the porch, not inside, because "it was late and he didn't want to disturb anyone in the house"). In PR's "College Scrapbook" (RA), Davvy wrote, " 'In you I see more and more the qualities of my ideal'—Selected. Oh! Boy!"

26. The Neale quotations which follow to the end of this chapter are taken from some eight to ten letters from her to me, three of which (July 17, Aug. 6, 1983, April 14, 1985) are lengthy memoirs totaling about fifty pages. She also kindly sent me six unpublished speeches that she delivered over the years about PR, which I also quote from in this and subsequent paragraphs. Since this batch of materials is privately held, I will not attempt precise citations here; suffice it to say that all quotations in this section are drawn from the private collection—un-

less otherwise noted. In PR's fragmentary "College Scrapbook" and "Memory and Fellowship Book" (RA), there is one definite mention of "Gerry" and three other probable references to her.

27. "Wish my family in Freehold had not discarded mine," Gerry Neale Bledsoe wrote me (July 7, 1983) in regard to their exchange of letters. Neither side of the correspondence exists in RA, either. The 1919 baseball game had also marked the very last time PR would play in any athletic event for Rutgers. As the newspaper accounts in RA make clear, he played "in wonderful style," and Rutgers won the game 5–1. A jubilant PR told Gerry, who attended the game, that he was "thrilled" to have beaten "Proud Princeton," which "up to that time had never played a team with a black player on it" (unpublished Bledsoe speech).

28. The "English friend" is Leonora ("Pat") Gregory (now Stitt). She co-wrote several of PR's articles (including the well-known "Primitives") in the thirties. She has described the composition and ramifications of the articles in a series of letters to me (for more, see note 43, p. 625). PR was so pleased with the articles that he and Gregory began discussing the possibility of doing a book together, a project interrupted by PR's 1939 return to the States. The book did reach the stage of a written "draft plan," which Stitt kindly shared with me. The quotations about adolescence and college are taken from this "draft plan."

29. This account is taken from two of the dozen letters previously cited from Gerry Neale Bledsoe to me, those of Aug. 6, 1983, and April 14, 1985. PR and Gerry Neale possibly met through the well-to-do Moore family; the two daughters, Bessie and Christine, had become Gerry's closest friends, and Bessie was a classmate at Teachers Normal. There are letters from Christine Moore to Paul's sister, Marian, right up to CM's death in 1972 (letters courtesy of Paulina Forsythe).

30. Bledsoe's version of these events, as described in letters to me, has been confirmed by Sadie Davenport Shelton (interview, March 26, 1985—"Gerry turned him down").

31. The "class prophecy" is in the Rutgers *Targum*, June 1919, which in an accompanying editorial expressed the hope, "May Rutgers never forget this noble son. . . ." Evidence of Paul's "deputizing" for his father is in the Somerset *Messenger*, Nov. 1, 1916, where he is recorded as delivering the "response" after welcoming addresses at a district missionary convention held at St. Thomas A.M.E. Zion. PR's flirtation with the ministry is described in an article and an interview from the twenties: PR, "My Father's Parsonage . . . ," *Sunday Sun* (London), Jan. 13, 1929; interview with Rev. Robertson Ballard, *Methodist Times*, Jan. 3, 1929; Charlotte Himber, *Famous in Their Twenties* (YMCA, 1942), p. 98 for "zeal" (as told to Himber by Ben Robeson).

CHAPTER 3   COURTSHIP AND MARRIAGE *(1919–1921)*

1. For these and other details on the condition of the black masses, see the convenient summary in ch. 1 of Harvard Sitkoff, *A New Deal for Blacks*, vol. I, *The Depression Decade* (Oxford, 1978).

2. Ms. of PR's column for the first (Dec. 1950) issue of *Freedom*, PR Coll., NYPL/Schm. (Streeter's). The quotations in this and the following paragraph are from an unpublished autobiographical account, of roughly thirty-five thousand words, by Eslanda Goode Robeson in RA. The ms. was meant to be part of

her 1930 book, *Paul Robeson, Negro*, but only a segment of the section dealing with 1922–28 ever appeared in print (hereafter Ms. Auto.)

3. Multiple conversations with PR, Jr. (D.C. riot).

4. Interview with Frances Quiett (Challenger), Dec. 7, 1983; Sterner interview with May Chinn. Chinn may have first met Robeson when they performed together; a program from July 1919 in the RA lists Chinn, Robeson, and Rudolph Fisher as appearing on a "public presen-

tation of music and speeches featuring outstanding young Negro collegians"; Robeson repeated his speech on the "New Idealism," May Chinn accompanied on some songs, and Fisher spoke on "The Emancipation of Science."

Details of Fisher's life are in *The Negro History Bulletin*, vol. II (Dec. 1938), p. 19. For current, highly favorable assessments of his work, see Jervis Anderson, *This Was Harlem* (Farrar, Straus and Giroux, 1982), p. 210, and David Levering Lewis, *When Harlem Was in Vogue* (Knopf, 1981), p. 229. Additional information on May Chinn is in George Davis, "A Healing Hand in Harlem," *New York Times Magazine*, April 22, 1979.

5. Interview with Frances Quiett Challenger, Dec. 7, 1983; Sterner interview with Chinn.

6. Ibid.

7. Interview with G. Foster Sanford, Jr., April 12, 1983 (tuition). Gene Sumner, a cousin of ER's friend Minnie Sumner and in 1917 manager of Lincoln University's football team, apparently was responsible for first inviting Robeson to Lincoln: "Hard pressed for a coach (World War I had drained off so much) Paul came down on my invitation and spent two days from Rutgers, where he was a star, teaching the boys 'big league' football." In 1919, Paul came "for a concert at a church . . . and he spent his two nights with me" (handwritten reminiscences by Gene Sumner are in the collections of the DuSable Museum for Black History and Culture, hereafter DSMC). The James Mayo ("Ink") Williams quotes are from an interview with him by Studs Terkel in 1969 done as part of a round-table discussion of Robeson with prominent blacks in the Chicago area (Margaret Burroughs, Judge Sidney Jones, Etta Moten Barnett, Earl Dickerson, "Ink" Williams, Charles V. Hamilton), recorded as a seventy-second birthday tribute to him. It was first played on WFMT Chicago on May 8, 1970, then later rebroadcast. I'm grateful to Terkel for letting me copy the tape. A friend of Frank Nied's quotes him as saying, "Robeson is a gentleman—than which there isn't . . . Also that Paul was amazingly game, refusing to quit when he was hurt, and that no

amount of the terrific ganging naturally administered by the white (Nordic?) professionals could make him lose his head" (quoted in Nat Lewers to Alexander Woollcott, Nov. 29, 1933, RA). The account of Robeson's professional football career is compiled from newspaper clippings in RA. In her Ms. Auto., ER refers to the "big money" he was paid in pro ball. For more on PR and Thorpe, see note 11, p. 584. Robeson stayed in peripheral contact with Fritz Pollard through the years. As late as 1933, ER recorded in her diary, "Saw Fritz Pollard, of all people, and we talked old times over" (ER Diary, Feb. 22, 1933, RA). Pollard's quote about Akron is from an interview *The New York Times* did with him in 1978, as quoted in his obituary (*Times*, May 31, 1986).

8. Interview with Henry A. Murray, Feb. 6, 1985. Because of the overall accuracy of the rest of his testimony and the specific detail (usually a sign of veracity) with which he described this episode, I've accepted Murray's account, although he was ninety-three years old at the time of our interview (yet entirely lucid as well as witty, I should add)—and although ER has left variant versions of her initial meeting with her future husband. In one newspaper interview (New York *Amsterdam News*, Aug. 6, 1938), she recalled first seeing him one day as she was going into DeVann's popular restaurant; in another (Birmingham *Post*, May 7, 1959), she recalled first *meeting* him "at a party in Harlem." In her Ms. Auto. in RA, she recalls being first introduced to him—casually—when both were strolling with friends down Seventh Avenue in the summer of 1919. "Her alert mind," she writes, "marked him, and stored him away. She saw him frequently that summer at parties, dances, tennis matches, and in the dining room of the Y.W.C.A., where all the young people congregated for meals; but she did not do more than to idly note that she must inquire about this young man. He seemed so universally popular. . . ." Possibly ER *asked* Dr. Murray to introduce her to his patient, having already "marked him out." (One such combined version of their meeting, though with almost all the significant details

askew, can be found in Shirley Graham, *Paul Robeson: Citizen of the World* [Julian Wenner, 1946], pp. 119–20.) Among the other claimants to having introduced the couple, Judge Raymond Pace Alexander insists he did so when the two were guests of his at a picnic on a Hudson River Line steamer (Alexander to SALUTE committee, March 14, 1973, RA). Murray and the Robesons stayed marginally in touch over the years. ER wrote in her diary on Jan. 17, 1926 (RA), "Went to a party at Harry Murray's . . . and had a beautiful time. . . . Harry Murray and his wife are as sweet as ever." As late as 1957, they sent him an affectionately inscribed Christmas card (the card courtesy of Eugene Taylor, archivist to H. A. Murray; also Murray to PR, 1925?, ER to Murray, Aug. 12, 1942, RA).

9. In reconstructing the history of the Cardozo family, I've relied chiefly on two ms. sources: a twenty-page handwritten account (apparently set down for her daughter's edification) by Eslanda Cardozo Goode ("Ma" Goode, mother to Eslanda Goode Robeson); and Eslanda Goode Robeson's lengthy Ms. Auto. Both documents are in RA and are in general accord (but some of the variances are an illuminating index of their respective personalities), with Eslanda Goode Robeson's account the fuller one, combining her mother's version with additional source material. Unless otherwise cited, the family background described in the following pages is taken from these two mss. (with a few details filled in from printed sources, especially Euline W. Brock, "Thomas W. Cardozo: Fallible Black Reconstruction Leader," *The Journal of Southern History*, May 1981).

10. All the quotes continue to be from the two mss. previously cited (Ma Goode's twenty-page account and ER's lengthy Ms. Auto.), but the swimming anecdote is from ER Diary, Nov. 23, 1941, RA.

11. Interview with Aminda Badeau (Mrs. Roy) Wilkins, March 12, 1985; "girl scientist" is from ER, Ms. Auto.; the analysis of her job derives from my interview with Henry A. Murray, Feb. 6, 1985. I haven't been able to verify Essie's claim to have been the first black of either gender on staff. By her own account (ER Diary, Nov. 4, 1931, RA) she once referred to "all the colored girls I had known at P and S [Physicians and Surgeons: Presbyterian] . . . and colored men"—though she didn't specify in what capacity they'd been there. Whether she was first or fifth, of course, her accomplishments remain considerable—the only point at issue is the extent to which she felt it necessary to embroider on an already considerable achievement. Near the end of her life, Essie herself referred to having worked at Presbyterian "at its most progressive stage" (ER to Helen Rosen, Oct. 15, 1963, courtesy Rosen).

12. Interview with Henry A. Murray, Feb. 6, 1985. Dr. Smith Ely Jelliffe (the well-known psychoanalyst who edited the *Psychoanalytic Review*, was on the Presbyterian staff, and had a number of theatrical and literary patients including at various times Robert Edward Jones and Eugene O'Neill) thought well enough of Essie to remain her personal friend (ER Diary, Feb. 16, 1933, RA). She listed Jelliffe as one of her six referees when applying for a Guggenheim in 1931 (the application form is in RA).

13. ER, Ms. Auto., RA.

14. ER, Ms. Auto., RA. Before meeting Paul, Essie had seriously dated Oscar Brown, Sr., who had worked with Paul at Narragansett Pier (interview with Oscar Brown, Sr., July 2, 1986); see pp. 11–12.

15. When Essie finally did become pregnant, she had to undergo corrective surgery in order to conceive. This by itself, however, proves nothing about what Essie did or did not tell Paul in 1921. Even if she had told him that she was pregnant, she herself may have been legitimately mistaken or misinformed.

In one letter (undated, July 1922, RA) Paul does say, "How happy I am that in choosing, I chose right. My Sweet helped me to choose and I'll be grateful to her always"—implying that Essie *had* to some extent forced his hand. But not, it would seem, to any significant extent, for in another letter (Aug. 10, 1922, RA) he harks back to "a year ago. I was in heaven. Just a-wooing my Dolly [his nickname for ER] and saying 'She must be mine for life' "—a year ago meaning just prior to their marriage. A third reference, moreover (PR to ER, Aug. 23, 1922, RA), bears directly and importantly on the suggestion that Essie forced him into marriage by falsely claiming to be pregnant: "Yes, sweet, I do hope we may be able to have a child. For your sake most of all—you do love them so. But you remember, sweet—when we married—I knew that perhaps it might not be our lot—no child can ever mean as much as my Dolly— And if there is any danger to be undergone beyond the normal— never." This suggests Essie told him at the time of their marriage either that she might not be able to get pregnant—or that she *was* pregnant and had to abort for health reasons. One piece of evidence suggesting the latter interpretation comes from Essie's diary for March 4, 1931 (RA). In it she wrote: "I am off for New York today, on the Olympic. I've got to do a 'job' and I think Dr. West, who did my other one more than 10 years ago, is the best bet. And also Presbyterian will be close to hand if anything goes wrong." The "job" does sound like an abortion (or a curettage—see p. 150) and "10 years ago" would be 1921, the year Paul and Essie married. Further evidence of a pre-marital pregnancy comes from Freda Diamond (in multiple interviews). In later years Paul told Freda that Essie had come to him in 1921 with the claim that she had become pregnant but had aborted after a doctor warned her that she would be at high risk in giving birth (and had produced some sort of "proof" that she had actually had the abortion); according to this version, Paul remained skeptical but, out of his sense of "honor" at having made Essie pregnant, decided to marry her. Moreover, the possibility of deception on Essie's part can't be discounted because, by her own account, she was determined to marry Paul and by almost all other accounts was in active pursuit of what she wanted. Finally, the specific question of an actual versus a faked pregnancy may be insignificant, since it comes down to trying to prove or disprove a matter of degree: Essie *was* willing to deceive to get her way; the particular strategy she hit upon for that purpose becomes a secondary issue.

16. Frankie did not see Paul again for more than twenty years, until she went backstage at *Othello* on Broadway. "He kissed me, he hugged me, and he was very glad to see me." That was the last time they met (interview with Frances Quiett Challenger, Dec. 7, 1983).

17. This account (including the quotations) is taken from letters from Gerry Neale Bledsoe to me, July 7, 1983; April 14, 1985. Commenting on Essie's protectiveness, Langston Hughes recalled that "Harlem wits have a story about a great public ball after one of Paul's concerts, where she went around the hall closing all the windows so 'her baby' wouldn't catch cold! Then she took him home—on time!" (Hughes in New York *Herald Tribune,* June 29, 1930.)

18. The quotations in this and subsequent paragraphs describing the marriage are from ER, Ms. Auto., RA. However, the quote from Essie's relative on p. 42 is from the transcript of an interview with Margaret Cardozo Holmes in the Schlesinger Library, Radcliffe. Hattie Bolling remained a loyal friend of Essie's, once writing her appreciatively, ". . . your promises are as true as gold" (HB to ER, Oct. 6, 1934, RA). Hattie's husband, William ("Buddy"), had apparently known Paul since 1912—so at least, he stated on a June 27, 1922, passport affidavit (FBI NY 100-25857).

19. ER, Ms. Auto., RA; William L. Patterson, *The Man Who Cried Genocide* (International Publishers, 1971), pp. 53–58. A description of living arrangements in Striver's Row is in Patterson, but in Essie's account she lists her address as 225 Seventh Avenue, which is not Striver's Row. Minnie's sister Sadie also remained a lifelong friend of Essie's. Patterson spells Minnie's last name "Summer," Essie as "Sumner," which is correct. Patterson (p. 53) describes Essie at the time as having "lively and searching" eyes and being, unlike Minnie, "deeply concerned with social problems," "acutely aware of the racial issue"; judging from other evidence, Patterson's judgment was *ex post facto,* a description of Essie's political awareness as a middle-aged woman. One of the "fourths" for cards was Gene Sumner,

Minnie's cousin (handwritten recollections, DSMC).

20. According to later FBI sources, Essie "attempted unsuccessfully in 1918 to enter Columbia University, College of Physicians and Surgeons" (FBI Main 100-12304-11). May Chinn claims that she left her job at the Presbyterian lab in Sept. 1920 to study medicine at Columbia but "had several small illnesses during the first year and stayed away one day longer than they allow you." They "gave her the chance of repeating the year," but she decided not to, having by then met Paul (Sterner interview with Chinn). Essie's salary at Presbyterian is listed on her Guggenheim Fellowship application of 1931 (RA). The announcement card and the marriage license are in RA. According to Ben Robeson's daughter, Marian Liggins, Paul wrote to his older brother asking for permission to marry Essie, "and Daddy wrote back giving him all the reasons why he thought he should not marry her" (interview with Marian Liggins, Nov. 21, 1982). Robeson's fraternity, Alpha Phi Alpha, was founded at Cornell in 1906. Its members have included Thurgood Marshall, Martin Luther King, Jr., and Andrew Young.

21. The Columbia class dinner is described in the New Brunswick *Daily Home News*, Feb. 25, 1921, and is included here somewhat out of chronological order. ER's remark about *"ourselves"* is from ER ms. "Introduction to I Want You to Know" (July 1961, RA). There is intermittent correspondence from ER to Louis and Corinne Wright (including a letter of condolence to Corinne on Louis's death in 1952) in CML: Wright.

22. This account of the impetus behind the production of *Simon* is from Mina Higgins, "Paul Robeson, Bright Star ... ," *Sunday Times* (New Brunswick), June 15, 1924, an article for which Robeson himself apparently provided the basic data (Kenneth Q. Jennings, of the *Sunday Times* staff, to PR, Feb. 27, 1924, RA); and from Percy N. Stone's interview with PR in the New York *Herald Tribune*, Oct. 17, 1926 ("dragged him in").

Torrence, who was white and well regarded at the time as a lyric poet, had caused a considerable sensation with the original production on Broadway of *Three Plays for a Negro Theater* (of which *Simon* was one) in April 1917. James Weldon Johnson hailed the opening as "the most important single event in the entire history of the Negro in the American theater. . . . The stereotyped traditions regarding the Negro's histrionic limitations were smashed" (*Black Manhattan* [Atheneum reissue, 1977], p. 175). Johnson emphasized that Torrence had gotten his way in insisting on a black cast. For additional details see Eugene Levy, *James Weldon Johnson* (Chicago University Press, 1973), pp. 302–4, and Edith J. R. Issacs, *The Negro in the American Theatre* (Theatre Arts, 1947), pp. 54–60. For more information on the Amateur Players, see Johnson, *Black Manhattan*, p. 179.

23. Honoria Murphy Donnelly with Richard N. Billings, *Sara and Gerald* (Times Books, 1982). In a newspaper interview three years later, Robeson said, "I was broke at the time and it was far better than working in the Post Office for a month or so" (*World*, May 3, 1925). My reference to "several whites" is deliberately vague. Essie (Ms. Auto., RA), specifically names them as Robert Edmond Jones and Emilie (Mrs. Norman) Hapgood, respectively the set designer (he later designed the 1943–44 *Othello*) and producer of the 1917 Broadway version of *Simon*, and Kenneth Macgowan, who in 1923 would join the Provincetown Players. Recent commentators have gone on to elaborate (as Essie did not) the consequences of their attendance. David Levering Lewis, for example (in his otherwise fine book *When Harlem Was in Vogue*), has them, in 1920, dashing backstage after the curtain "to offer him the lead in something called *The Emperor Jones,"* which Robeson (as Seton further advances the tale in *Paul Robeson*, p. 23) turned down: "I went home, forgot about the theatre, and went back next morning to Law School as if nothing had happened." Thanks to O'Neill's biographer, Louis Sheaffer, who generously put certain unpublished manuscript materials in my hands, I do have some peripheral confirmation of the *Emperor Jones* offer to Robeson, but, like Sheaffer, have concluded it rests on uncertain memories

(Sheaffer to me, Sept. 29, 1982, July 28, 1986) and is finally not persuasive. The materials in question are recollections by Jasper Deeter and Cleon Throckmorton, two Provincetown Players stalwarts, as given to Sheaffer in interviews.

Deeter, who played Smithers in the 1920 *Jones* production, told Sheaffer that he did approach Robeson about doing the lead role, but "Robeson stood up with self-aware dignity: 'You may know this kind of person, and Mr. O'Neill may know this kind of person; but I don't.'" Although such an exchange may have taken place, most likely it was in regard to the 1924 revival, since Deeter refers to Robeson as having been recommended to him (by *Crisis* magazine, not by fellow Provincetowners) as currently "the best Negro actor"—and in 1920 he was not so regarded.

The second testimony comes from Cleon Throckmorton, who designed the sets for both the 1920 and 1924 productions of *Jones*. He told Sheaffer that the following dialogue ensued when they approached Robeson in 1920: "We'd like you to be in a play by Eugene O'Neill." "Never heard of him." "Well, we think he's America's coming playwright and we think *The Emperor Jones* is a fine play." "What sort of part is it?" "A railroad porter from a lowly background becomes emperor of a tropic island and then, under terror, slips back." "Good day, gentlemen. I think you know more about that sort of life than I would." This dialogue—pompous, rude, and surly—sounds wholly uncharacteristic of Robeson and throws the reliability of the entire testimony into question.

As Sheaffer wrote me (July 28, 1986), "Regardless of what Deeter and Throckmorton told me, I now feel most doubtful that Robeson was ever considered to play Jones in its first production. What stage experience did he have then? None. It seems absurd that anyone in the Village group would think for a moment of entrusting such an all-important part to a total novice." I concur with Sheaffer's judgment. He added, though, that since both men "recall something about Robeson standing on his dignity when offered

the part, there may be something to it, but exactly what?"

Though the evidence remains contradictory, it suggests, on balance, that if Robeson was considered at all for the first production of *Jones*, it was only by some lower-echelon Provincetowners, which is not the same as asserting—as others have—that an actual offer was made to him. What finally persuaded me that some *marginal* soundings might have taken place is the number of times Robeson himself makes reference to such an event in various interviews he gave over the years. He even went so far as to include a reference to it in the program notes for his Nov. 1929 Carnegie Hall recital (RA). Especially persuasive in this regard is the detailed (and otherwise uncommonly accurate) interview with Percy N. Stone printed in the New York *Herald Tribune* on Oct. 17, 1926 (the fact that it appeared in the widely read *Tribune* further suggests Robeson would have taken the utmost care to present his prior history accurately). In regard to the 1920 *Jones*, the Stone interview reads as follows: "From way down in the village came eager scouts when the little shows [*Simon the Cyrenian*] were put on. They saw Robeson perform and when *Emperor Jones* was booked for the Provincetown Theater, up ran one of the attachés of that place with the script. He did not show O'Neill's play to Robeson; he sat down and read it through to him. At that time Robeson was quite sensitive about the Negro question. It was his first year in New York and the problems he faced made him race conscious. As the play was read, Robeson got madder and madder until, when that final line was reached, he wanted to throw the man out of the window. Instead, he just refused the part, much as he needed the money." (Yet another persuasive piece of testimony to the same effect is Robeson's article "My Father's Parsonage . . . ," *Sunday Sun*, London, Jan. 13, 1929.)

What we do know for certain is that Macgowan, for one, did see Robeson in *Taboo* and did like him "tremendously" (Macgowan to PR, Dec. 21, 1923, RA). And in Mina Higgins's 1924 article, "Paul Robeson," she states that not only were

Macgowan and Emilie Hapgood in the audience, but Eugene O'Neill as well. O'Neill was sufficiently impressed, says Higgins, to offer Robeson a reading for the role of "Brutus Jones," but Robeson turned it down, since at that time he was thinking "of nothing but perfecting himself in his chosen profession" of law. Emilie Hapgood and her husband, Norman, were friends of Mrs. Patrick Campbell's, which is another link in this network of friendships perhaps responsible for Robeson's progression of theatrical roles. (See Margot Peters, *Mrs. Pat: The Life of Mrs. Patrick Campbell* (Knopf, 1984), p. 300; Michael D. Marcaccio, *The Hapgoods* [University Press of Virginia, 1977], p. 25.)

24. Benchley, *Life*, April 20, 1922; Helen Deutsch and Stella Hanau, *The Provincetown* (Russell and Russell, 1931, reissued 1972) (Gilpin); Woollcott, *The New York Times*, April 20, 1922; Anatol I. Schlosser, "Paul Robeson: His Career in the Theater, in Motion Pictures, and on the Concert Stage," doctoral thesis, New York University, 1970 (hereafter Schlosser). Some of the other critics were kinder to Wycherly and even more so to Robeson. Charles Darnton thought his playing had "something of the Gilpin power," and Burns Mantle felt all "the colored players" gave "veristic and technically artistic characterizations." Several singled out Fannie Belle de Knight for praise; she, like Robeson, was to perform the play in England—and to "pester" Robeson with unwanted attentions (see his letters to ER, summer 1922, RA). There is considerable correspondence from Woollcott to the Robesons throughout the thirties in RA, and in her diary (Dec. 22, 1932, RA) Essie described him as "the most entertaining man I ever met."

25. Margot Peters, *Mrs. Pat*, p. 381 (friendship with Hoytie Wiborg).

26. ER, Ms. Auto., RA. In RA there is one whole notebook (1920s) headed "Essie's notes on theater and cinema from professional standpoint," which attests to the rigor and diligence with which she pursued her goal. The notebook consists entirely of her handwritten comments on costumes, production, lighting, etc., copied out of source books, apparently as an aid for Paul.

27. For more on *Shuffle Along* in particular and black theater history in general, see the previously cited books by Edith J. R. Isaacs, James Weldon Johnson, David Levering Lewis, and Jervis Anderson, plus Theodore Kornweibel, Jr., *No Crystal Stair: Black Life and "The Messenger," 1917–1928* (Greenwood, 1975).

28. ER, Ms. Auto; in PR's recollection, given to a newspaper reporter three years later, he had remained disconcerted a bit longer: "I was so nervous that for the first two songs my voice was absolutely gone" (*World*, May 5, 1925). Interview (PR, Jr., participating) with Eubie Blake, March 12, 1982 (he was then ninety-nine years old). Blake recalled having met Robeson before he entered the *Shuffle Along* cast—when he heard his "wonderful" voice singing in Strep (John) Payne's apartment in Harlem. Blake also remembered that Robeson always called him "Hubert" (his full name was James Hubert Blake), though nobody else did; Blake felt it "was a mark of respect" to have been called by his real name rather than his nickname. He remembered Robeson fondly as being "the same all the time"—success "didn't change him. That's the great thing. . . . His head never got swollen. . . . He was a master gentleman." The Harmony Kings continued as a group at least into the early thirties, and with considerable success (The Kent and Sussex *Courier*, May 17, 1929, and the Dundee *Evening Telegraph*, March 5, 1930). In 1932, PR referred to The Harmony Kings "at present enjoying a sensational European success" (PR, "Notes: 1932," RA).

29. In placing this meeting in the spring of 1921 I'm following the chronology of Gerry Neale Bledsoe herself, as outlined to me in a series of letters, having decided (through outside verification of other portions of her testimony) that she is a scrupulous, reliable witness. Even she, however, has expressed some uncertainty (in a letter to me of July 7, 1983) about the precise dating of this episode: "It was late in my first year at Howard or possibly into my second year there." But even if the visit from Robeson took place

six months later than the spring of 1921, its meaning and importance—as a gauge of his tenacity, as a comment on his marriage—remain the same.

30. ER Diary, Dec. 26, 30, 1924, Jan. 1, 1925, RA. Gerry and her husband had a happy marriage and distinguished joint careers working in the labor movement and for civil rights. Bledsoe became prominent in Democratic Party circles in Michigan, and when the American Bar Association refused to admit blacks, he helped to found the National Bar Association. Some of Gerry Bledsoe's public activities during World War II are described in Dominic Capeci, *Race Relations in Wartime Detroit* (Temple University Press, 1984), pp. 46, 83, 133. Her many organizational activities culminated in election to the Michigan Women's Hall of Fame in 1983.

After 1924, Paul and Gerry apparently didn't see each other again for many years (Gerry caught a performance of *The Emperor Jones* in 1925 but did not go backstage), until the late forties, when he made several public appearances in Detroit and spent time with the Bledsoes in their home. Gerry and her husband made a point of going to his Detroit concerts (she served on the Nellie Watts Concert Series sponsoring committee for some of them) as a public act of support at a time when he was being criticized for his involvement in Henry Wallace's presidential campaign and again in the 1950s, when he was being widely denounced as a Communist. On one Detroit visit, Robeson spent a few days at the University of Michigan and took Gerry Bledsoe's daughter, Geraldine, a first-year student at the university, as his companion to many of the events. Both mother and daughter visited him in Philadelphia during the 1970s (see note 25, p.763).

Gerry's later recollections of Essie are less cordial. In the mid-forties, Dorothy Roosevelt, sister-in-law to Eleanor and a friend of Gerry's, invited her and half a dozen other women to a small dinner for Essie. Gerry describes the event: "I was taken aback when Essie brought up the subject of Paul and me and said that she had taken him away from me. One of my friends shot back in not a very gentle voice: That's *not* the way I heard it! I said nothing. I was a little embarrassed for Essie." Later, at the University of Michigan, Gerry's daughter, Geraldine, went up to speak to Essie. "She turned away. Geraldine was stunned"—knowing nothing at the time of her mother's previous involvement with Paul. (These quotations are taken from the dozen letters from Gerry Bledsoe to me.)

CHAPTER 4   PROVINCETOWN PLAYHOUSE *(1922–1924)*

1. ER, Ms. Auto., RA; R. R. Roberts to PR, April 10, 1973 *(Homeric)*, courtesy of Forsythe.

2. The quotations are from two of his undated (but definitely July 1922) letters to ER, RA. Essie's letters to him are not extant, but Paul quotes from one in a letter of his own and it leaves no doubt that Essie was as impassioned as he: "I love you Dubby [his nickname was "Dubby," hers "Dolly"] Darling—across the sea—across the Land—if you go to the end of the earth—my love will follow my precious and bless him and keep him the angel husband he is to me" (quoted in PR to ER, Aug. 2, 1922, RA).

3. PR to ER, undated (week of July 17, 1922), RA.

4. The quotations in this and subsequent paragraphs describing Robeson's stay in England are pieced together from his twenty-two letters to ER (RA). Since the quotes are so scattered, I won't attempt to link each one to a given letter.

5. Peters, *Mrs. Pat*, p. 381, says the opening was a disaster, with the audience pelting the stage with oranges, scattering the cast, but I've found no corroboration for that in the Blackpool newspaper reviews.

6. Marie Seton, "Lawrence Brown: Musician Who Honors Music," *Freedom*, April 1952 (first meeting at Payne's).

7. In perhaps another reference to Gerry, he wrote, "I could never have loved any other woman as I love you.

Never. Love like mine could not have been given to two persons" (RA).

8. The newspaper clippings are in RA. Several of the British reviews had racial overtones. One said the play "gave one an idea of the horrible rites practiced by negro tribes in the heart of the jungle"; another valued it for insight into "coon humour" and a third saw the soppy, denigrating melodrama as "a brilliant study in the psychology of the negro."

9. Peters, *Mrs. Pat*, p. 381 (Wiborg).

10. This quote is from one of two unidentified, undated (but, from internal evidence, definitely Nov. 1922) newspaper clippings in RA.

11. The fact that Robeson assisted Sanford in the fall of 1923 is established in the reminiscences of Jules A. Kaiser and in PR to William P. Garrison, Jan. 16, 1923 (both in RUA). A newspaper photograph of the *Revue* cast is in RA. Details on the *Plantation Revue* are from Lewis A. Erenberg, *Steppin' Out, New York Nightlife and the Transformation of American Culture 1890–1930* (Greenwood, 1981), p. 254. In the very first entry of the diary Essie began to keep at this time (Jan. 1, 1924, RA) she wrote, "Paul had to learn to sing at the Plantations, but came [home?] each morning about 1 a.m." Paul must have been part of the revue while Mills was still in it, for he later wrote, "I donned some overalls and a straw hat and warbled 'Lil Gal' to a Chorine. . . . How thrilling it was to listen to Florence Mills sing nightly— 'Down Among the Sleepy Hills of Tennessee.' . . . The only columnist who spotted me in those days was S. Jay Kaufmann then on the Telegram" (PR "Notes: 1932," RA). When Mills died of appendicitis in 1927, Paul wrote Essie, "I weep every time I think of it. It really is heartbreaking" (PR to ER, Dec. 12, 13, 1927, RA). He is quoted in a newspaper interview as saying that, next to Bessie Smith, he considered Florence Mills "the greatest Negro artist he has ever heard" (*Daily Herald*, London, May 4, 1935). As for Bessie Smith, late in life, the writer Laura Riding wrote Robeson to reminisce about "how we talked of Bessie Smith, and you demonstrated her moving presence when she sang to people!"

(Riding to PR, May 9, 1972, RA.) Riding and her lover, Robert Graves, got to know the Robesons somewhat in London in 1928–29.

New York *Herald Tribune*, Oct. 17, 1926 (post-office clerk job). Perry's New York *Herald Tribune* column had been reprinted in the *Daily Home News* (New Brunswick) Jan. 8, 1923. PR to William P. Garrison (graduate manager), Jan. 16, 1923; Garrison to PR, Jan. 18, 1923; Garrison to Perry, Jan. 23, 1923, are all in RUA. (PR to Garrison was printed in the *Rutgers Alumni Monthly*, Feb. 1923). Additional newspaper reprints of Perry's column are in RA, along with a personal letter of regret from Perry to PR. The "prizefighting episode" may not have been so clear-cut as my description of it suggests. In the ms. of Seton's *Robeson* she writes that he *"sought* [italics mine] the advice of the sports writer, Lawrence Perry" about the prizefighting offer, and "it was Perry's opinion that Robeson could never become a leader of the Negro people if he was associated with prizefighting," a view that tied in with Robeson's own. These lines were cut from the printed version of Seton's biography, *perhaps* at Robeson's request— since they imply that he was uncertain enough about the offer to have sought Perry's advice, and that the consultation between the two men might have been the source for Perry's original column suggesting that Robeson was interested in it; in the same way, Perry's subsequent denial may have been made specifically at Robeson's request. Alexander Woollcott confirms Robeson's aversion to the prizefighting offer, and offers *an* explanation for what brought it about. According to Woollcott, in one of Robeson's professional football games, playing for the Milwaukee Badgers against Jim Thorpe's Oorang Indians (see note 7, p. 577). he got into a nasty fight with Thorpe while defending himself (so Woollcott tells it) from an eye-gouging: ". . . the story of his quality as a fighter spread over the country before nightfall. Drooping fight promoters were galvanized into sudden action. Within a week, more than a million dollars had been confidentially pledged to back him as the prospective heavyweight champion of the world" (Alexander Woollcott, *While Rome Burns* [Grosset and Dunlap, 1934], p. 127). Many years later the dean for student affairs at MIT wrote PR to say, "Unless I am making up memories, I recall that at my boarding school one day, by sheer chance, I found myself sitting next to a guest, Gene Tunney. . . . I recall his saying that the next heavyweight boxing champion of the world could be, if he wanted it, a young man named Paul Robeson" (William Speer to PR, Sept. 24, 1972, courtesy of Paulina Forsythe).

12. *DAB*, suppl. I, vol. II (Scribners, 1944), pp. 457–58. Additional information on Kahn's generosity to black artists is in Lewis, *Harlem in Vogue.*

13. PR to Kahn, March [Feb.?] 13, 1923; Kahn to PR, March 12, 1923, William Seymour Theatre Coll., Kahn Papers, Princeton University (hereafter PU: Kahn).

14. This, incidentally, throws further doubt on the theory that O'Neill himself had offered to read Robeson for *Emperor Jones* back in 1920 (see note 23, p. 580). Nothing in Robeson's letters to Kahn or in Duncan's letter to O'Neill refers to any prior contact—which surely would have been mentioned if it had in fact occurred. Duncan to O'Neill, Feb. 23, 1923, RA; Duncan to PR, May 10, 1924, RA (in which he thanks Robeson for having credited him in a recent letter—not, so far as I know, extant). On still another occasion, Duncan notified Robeson that a new play was about to be produced with "a very unusual Negro part in it" and suggested he drop by to see him about it (Duncan to PR, Sept. 14, 1923, RA).

15. For classmates and professors, see William O. Douglas, *Go East, Young Man: The Early Years* (Random House, 1974), pp. 138–39. Interview with Martin Popper, Jan. 17, 1987 (Stone); Columbia University Oral History interview (by Tom Hogan, 1971) with Charles Ascher, CU. PR's academic record in law school is in CU, Law Archives. Interview with Edith Tiger, June 17, 1985, for the view that Robeson never took to law; the same view is expressed by Woollcott in *While Rome Burns*, pp. 127–28.

16. Essie's remark is in *PR, Negro*, p. 70; his brother Ben's comments are from his ms. "My Brother Paul" (1934), RA; Tammany Hall is from Seton, *Robeson*, p. 26. Once, when Essie was teasing Paul about his inactivity, their close friend and physician, Louis Wright, told her that Paul "was the most intelligently lazy man he had ever known."

17. This account of Robeson's law-firm tenure is taken from the following sources: ER, *PR, Negro*, pp. 70–72; ER, Ms. Auto., RA; interview with G. Foster Sanford, Jr., April 12, 1983; phone interview with S. A. Russell, July 31, 1982. Russell got to know Robeson through the writer Philip Van Doren Stern, also a Rutgers alumnus and the brother-in-law of Freda Diamond, later one of Robeson's intimates. Russell was recounting to me the version of his law-firm experience that Robeson gave him at a dinner party in the mid-1950s. The information on Stotesbury comes from the files on him at RUA.

18. ER, *PR, Negro*, p. 72; PR, "My Father's Parsonage . . . ," *Sunday Sun* (London), Jan. 13, 1929. Sounding a "proper-young-man" (rather than a racial) note, which he perhaps calculated to appeal to the British, Robeson is quoted as telling a newspaper reporter two years later, "I have studied law, but law in New York is not a dignified profession as it is in London: it is too mixed up with politics" (*Star*, Sept. 11, 1925). Still later Robeson said, "I could never be a Supreme Court judge; on the stage there was only the sky to hold me back" (*Time*, Nov. 1, 1943).

19. Macgowan to PR, Dec. 19, 21, 1923, RA. An undated note from O'Neill to PR in RA, which from internal evidence seems to have been written in Nov. 1923, suggests—*if* I've correctly dated it—they were in touch shortly before Macgowan contacted him about reading the new play. O'Neill's letter refers to Hopkins (Arthur Hopkins, the Broadway producer, who presented some of O'Neill's plays in London) as having been "extremely favorably impressed by your talk with him," advised "you will like being associated with him I know," and reported that Hopkins "agreed with me

before he left that 'Jones' would be best to follow 'A.C.' [*Anna Christie*] if it could be so arranged with Cockran over there" (in the spring of 1923, Hopkins had opened *Anna Christie*, to a positive reception in London); O'Neill promised to let Robeson know "whatever information I get." In other words, it seems PR had been contacted no later than Nov. 1923 about doing *Jones* (in London, apparently) and then in Dec. was asked by Macgowan to have a look at the new *Chillun* script as well.

Interview with Bess Rockmore (Eitingon), March 30, 1982.

20. For background on the Provincetown Players, see Sheaffer, *O'Neill, Son and Artist* (Little, Brown: 1973), and the still-useful book by two Provincetowners, Helen Deutsch and Stella Hanau, *The Provincetown*.

21. Deutsch and Hanau, *The Provincetown*, pp. 101–2, for details on redoing the theater; Sheaffer, *O'Neill*, 123, for the *Mercury;* ER, Ms. Auto., RA, for "profoundly impressed"; ER Diary, Jan. 8, 1924, RA *(Spook)*.

22. ER Diary, Jan. 21 (record company), Feb. 1, 21, March 3 (Ethiopian), Feb. 10 (YWCA), Jan. 23 (St. Christopher), April 13 (Du Bois), April 10 (Broun), Feb. 10, 19, 26 (NAACP), Jan. 20, 26, 30, Feb. 4, 9, 10 (Greeks), Feb. 18, April 25 (Anderson), Jan. 3 (Hayes), Jan. 4 *(Changeling)*, April 11 *(Cyrano)*—all 1924, RA. Apparently there were two nibbles from record companies at the same time; ER, in her diary for Jan. 21, mentions an appointment with the Brunswick Co., and in RA there is a letter to PR from J. Mayo Williams of the Chicago Music Publishing Co. (Feb. 7, 1924, RA). Williams mentioned that he got PR's address from Fritz Pollard, his old football buddy. Nothing seems to have come of this contact immediately, though there was additional correspondence the following year (Williams to ER, March 14, 1925, RA). Robeson had heard Du Bois for the first time in 1918 at a banquet for Assistant District Attorney F. Q. Morton at Terrace Garden. "Fine speeches," he wrote in his notebook ("School and Social Functions," RA), "A real insight into political life of New York City."

23. Johnson, *Black Manhattan*, p. 192; Sheaffer, *O'Neill*, p. 135; Anderson, *This Was Harlem*, p. 112; Benjamin Brawley, *The Negro in Literature and Art in the United States* (Duffield and Co., 1930), pp. 130–32; *The New York Times*, May 7, 1924. Gilpin had opened in the role of the preacher in the revival of *Roseanne;* PR subsequently replaced him. For more on the Lafayette Theater, see Sister M. Francesca Thompson, O.S.F., "The Lafayette Players, 1917–1932," in Errol Hill, ed., *The Theater of Black Americans* (Prentice-Hall 1980), vol. II, pp. 13–32. For more on Theophilus Lewis, see Theodore Kornweibel, Jr., "Theophilus Lewis and the Theater of the Harlem Renaissance," in *The Harlem Renaissance Remembered*, essays edited with a memoir by Arna Bontemps (Dodd, Mead and Co., 1972); another version of the essay is in Kornweibel, *No Crystal Stair.*

24. Philadelphia *Record*, April 1, 1924.

25. There is reason to believe that Helen MacKellar was originally offered the part of Ella but withdrew when she learned she would be playing opposite Robeson (*Evening Star* [Washington, D.C.], Feb. 22, 1924; Syracuse *Herald*, July 14, 1929; PR, "My Father's Parsonage . . . ," *Sunday Sun* [London], Jan. 13, 1929).

26. Johnson, *Black Manhattan*, pp. 193–94; Arthur and Barbara Gelb, *O'Neill* (Harper and Row, 1962), pp. 547–57; Sheaffer, *op. cit.*, pp. 134–40; Deutsch and Hanau, *The Provincetown*, pp. 107–13; the newspaper clippings are in RA.

27. Brooklyn *Daily Eagle*, Feb. 22, 1924; New York *World*, May 18, 1924.

28. Extended portions of O'Neill's statement are printed in Gelb and Gelb, *O'Neill*, and Sheaffer; a shorter version is in Deutsch and Hanau, *The Provincetown.*

29. Sheaffer, *O'Neill*, p. 141.

30. Deutsch and Hanau, *The Provincetown*, p. 108 (press-clipping bill); Sheaffer, *op. cit.*, p. 140 (Light quote); Gelb and Gelb, *O'Neill*, p. 552 (bomb).

31. Sheaffer, *O'Neill*, pp. 137–38, 140; ER, Ms. Auto., RA.

32. ER, Ms. Auto., RA.

33. Ibid.

34. ER Diary, April 28, 1924, RA; ER, *PR, Negro,* p. 75.

35. ER, *PR Negro,* p. 75; undated (early 1930s?) two-page handwritten manuscript in RA, simply titled "Paul, Theatre."

36. Millia Davenport to me, June 7, 1982; Malcolm Cowley to me, Nov. 5, 1982.

37. For more on the precursors of "black theater" and especially on the pivotal role played by Alain Locke and the Krigwa Little Theater Movement, see Abiodum Jeyifous, "Black Critics on Black Theater in America," *The Drama Review,* vol. 18 (Sept. 1974), pp. 37–39.

38. ER Diary, May 4, 5, 6, 1924, RA; Sheaffer, *O'Neill,* p. 140 (cool response). According to Sheaffer's sources (p. 141), at the opening night party held at set designer Cleon Throckmorton's apartment, O'Neill spent most of the evening playing the tom-tom that had been used in the play. At one point during the party, Robeson, Throckmorton, and Light took their shirts off to compare physiques, a tourney O'Neill joined at his wife's urging.

39. ER Diary, May 6, 1924, RA (quarrel); Brawley, *Negro in Literature,* pp. 130–31; Sheaffer, *O'Neill,* pp. 32–36 (League).

40. *Telegram and Mail,* May 7, 1924 (O'Neill/Gilpin); O'Neill to Mike Gold, July 1923, courtesy of Louis Sheaffer (see note 42).

41. Sheaffer, *O'Neill,* p. 37.

42. ER Diary, May 6, 1924, RA. O'Neill's letter to Mike Gold July 1923, and the entries from his "work diary" were kindly sent to me by Louis Sheaffer, whose splendid biography of O'Neill has been indispensable in my reconstruction of Robeson's opening night (see Sheaffer, *O'Neill,* especially pp. 32–37). Jimmy Light's opinion was given in an interview with Sheaffer, who passed its contents on to me. *Opportunity,* Dec. 1924, pp. 368–70 (PR on Gilpin). O'Neill did use Gilpin in *Jones* again. Over the next few years, the Provincetowners periodically revived the play, usually with Robeson, but in 1926 with Gilpin again assuming the lead. Apparently he continued to change lines in 1926 as he had in 1920. Essie and Paul went to see his performance twice, and Essie expressed "shock" in her diary at Gilpin's "sacrilege and blasphemy" in rewriting lines—and at his generally "ordinary" performance (ER Diary, Feb. 24, March 1, 1926, RA). Despite his preference for Gilpin, O'Neill's admiration for Robeson's talent was keen. In 1925, on the flyleaf of a presentation copy to the Robesons of the collected edition of his plays, O'Neill wrote: "In gratitude to Paul Robeson in whose interpretation of 'Brutus Jones' I have found the most complete satisfaction an author can get—that of seeing his creation borne into flesh and blood! And in whose creation of 'Jim Harris' in my 'All God's Chillun Got Wings' I found not only complete fidelity to my intent under trying circumstances but, beyond that, true understanding and racial integrity. Again with gratitude and friendship" (the presentation copy is in RA; Essie referred to the inscribed volume as "one of the Robesons' most valued possessions" [ER, Ms. Auto., RA]). For additional commentary on *Jones* as a play, and the contrasting strengths Robeson and Gilpin brought to it, see John Henry Raleigh, *The Plays of Eugene O'Neill* (Southern Illinois Press, 1965), pp. 108–10; Arnold Goldman, "The Culture of the Provincetown Players," *American Studies,* vol. 12, no. 3 (1978), pp. 291–310; and Dr. Nick Aaron Ford's denunciation of the play (*The Afro-American,* April 23, 1955) as merely another stereotype: Brutus Jones, "the superstitious dupe, egotistical braggart, razor-toting crapshooter."

43. *The New York Times,* New York *World,* New York *Herald Tribune*—all May 7, 1924.

44. New York *Evening Graphic,* Dec. 16, 1924; New York *Evening Post,* May 7, 1924; New York *Telegram and Evening Mail,* May 7, 1924; Dallas *Herald,* June 1924 ("magnificent"); Cleveland *News,* May 18, 1924 ("all your life").

45. ER Diary, May 11, 12, 1924, RA.

46. Sheaffer, *O'Neill,* p. 142.

47. Interview with PR, *Star* (London), Dec. 28, 1929 ("shots"); O'Neill, "Work Diary," May 15, 1924 (courtesy of Sheaffer); ER ms., "Paul, Theater," undated (probably early 1930s), RA; ER

Diary, May 15, 1924, RA. Clara Alexander Weiss, of the Provincetown Players' office staff, told Louis Sheaffer that everyone was so relieved when *Chillun* went off without violence that the party afterward was "particularly jubilant," and Robeson sang spirituals and other songs "for hours" (interview courtesy of Sheaffer).

48. New York *World*, May 16, 1924 (Broun); New York *Sun*, May 16, 1924 (Woollcott); *The Nation*, June 4, 1924 (Lewisohn); New York *Daily News*, May 17, 1924 (Mantle); New York *World*, June 21, 1924 (Stallings). The casting of two of the secondary roles in *Chillun* was noteworthy. Dora Cole (no longer Dora Cole Norman), who had been responsible for urging Robeson into the theater in her production of *Simon* (see p. 43), played the role of Hattie, sister to Jim Harris (the Robeson role), and the fine black actor Frank Wilson, who had earlier appeared in O'Neill's *The Dreamy Kid* and would later star, with great success, in Paul Green's *In Abraham's Bosom* and in Gershwin's *Porgy and Bess*, played the role of Joe. Both Cole and Wilson received excellent notices in *Chillun*.

49. Essie, interestingly, proudly reprinted Nathan's review in *PR, Negro* (pp. 76–77) without taking any issue with its sentiments.

50. Krutch, *The Nation*, Oct. 26, 1927.

51. The "peeps" of white dissent included Arthur Pollock, in the Brooklyn *Daily Eagle*, who found Robeson "a sad disappointment"—an earnest, hardworking amateur and nothing more; Burns Mantle, who in a second column on the play, noted "the awkwardness of the amateur" in Robeson's performance; and Percy Hammond in the *Times*, who was caustic about the play, and referred to Robeson as "a dignified and handsome negro of the earnest type."

The Afro-American, May 23, 1924; Chicago *Defender*, May 24, 1924; the clipping of Pickens's newspaper column, undated, is in RA. Sheaffer (*O'Neill*, p. 138) cites two additional negative comments from black leaders: Rev. A. Clayton Powell, pastor of the Abyssinian Baptist Church (and father of the Congressman) called the play "harmful because it intimates

that we are desirous of marrying white women," and Rev. J. W. Brown of A.M.E. Zion Church felt the play would do his people "only harm." But both these comments were made to—and perhaps distorted by—Hearst's *American* (March 15, 1924), which had been doing its best for months to stir up trouble. Johnson, *Black Manhattan*, pp. 195–96, also deplored the play as "shifting the question from that of a colored man living with a white wife to that of a man living with a crazy woman," claiming it had "failed to please coloured people." In regard to *Emperor Jones*, Langston Hughes wrote an account (quoted in Jeyifous, "Black Critics," p. 42) of a somewhat later production of that play in Harlem that the audience "hounded with laughter"; it "wanted none of *The Emperor Jones*"—"that was the end of *The Emperor Jones* on 135th Street."

52. The playbill, with Du Bois's comments, is in RA.

53. ER, Ms. Auto., RA.

54. *Opportunity*, Dec. 1924, pp. 368–70. The magazine had a peak circulation of ten thousand, about 40 percent of it white. In an interview the following year, when he was playing *Jones* in London, Robeson told a newspaper interviewer: "O'Neill has got what no other playwright has—that is, the true, authentic negro psychology. He has read the negro soul, and has felt the negro's racial tragedy" (*Reynold's Illustrated News*, Sept. 20, 1925).

55. Duncan to PR, May 10, 1924, RA. By Aug., Mayor Hylan had lifted his ban against children's playing in *Chillun*. In mid-Sept., Dorothy Peterson replaced Mary Blair, and Essie thought she "did very well" (Diary, Sept. 15, 1924). Peterson (whose father, Jerome Bowers Peterson, had founded the black paper, *New York Age*) remained a long-time friend of the Robesons. During the summer, Robeson gave two open-air performances of *Jones* in the Mariarden Theater, Peterboro, N.H., where it was well received (newspaper clippings, RA).

56. ER Diary, Aug. 15, 1924, RA. The salary total is in a receipt to PR in RA, signed "M. Eleanor Fitzgerald"—the manager of the Playhouse. Some sketchy

evidence suggests that Robeson was offered the position of assistant district attorney of New York some time before 1925, but turned the offer down (program notes for his Dec. 17, 1924, Rutgers concert, RUA).

CHAPTER 5 THE HARLEM RENAISSANCE AND THE SPIRITUALS *(1924–1925)*

1. Interview with Antonio Salemmé, March 31, 1983. Salemmé had been born in 1891, in Gaeta, Italy. He came to the U.S. at the age of eleven and studied at the Boston Museum of Fine Arts, with George L. Noyes (a pupil of Monet's) and later with William Paxton, the neoclassicist.

2. Interview with Antonio Salemmé, March 31, 1983. Essie later worked out the formal agreement with Betty Salemmé, whereby Tony got two-thirds and Paul one-third of the sale price. Betty had suggested a fifty-fifty split, but Essie decided that was too generous: "Tony had had a great deal of experience and training, and should therefore get more than Paul, who had the beautiful body and gave his time" (ER Diary, May 14, 1925, RA).

3. Newspaper editorialists, North and South, had a field day chastising Philadelphia. If such action had been taken by a Southern city, a North Carolinian wrote, "It would have been condemned as just another manifestation of Southern nigger hate," and the New York *World* suggested that "Perhaps the average Pennsylvanian, secretly a little ashamed of the civic and political record of his State, becomes a bit hysterical at the thought that some one may conceive the notion of a statue of Pennsylvania in the nude. That would be appalling. There are some people and some States that need all the concealment possible." The Brooklyn Museum put the statue on display for a few months, cataloguing it as *Negro Spiritual*. The French showed it in the Salon des Tuileries, and the jury for the Art Institute of Chicago initially awarded the statue a prize but then, not wishing to over-emphasize the representation of a "colored man," demoted it to honorable mention. The Union League Club of New York invited Salemmé to exhibit the statue but then decided not to show it, out of deference to "the ladies."

Salemmé dutifully applied a plaster figleaf as a poultice but that, too, failed to please and the statue was removed. When Dr. George F. Kunz, chairman of the club's art committee, was asked if the statue had been ruled out on racial grounds, he replied indignantly that the question was absurd: "Do you know of any other club that employs all Negro waiters and servants?" he asked (*Time*, Dec. 1, 1930; *Express*, Jan. 4, 11, 1980; *Sunday Bulletin*, Feb. 8, 1976). The statue thereafter disappeared, never to be recovered. Philadelphia's racial problem was not solved. Interview with Antonio Salemmé, March 31, 1983; interview with Salemmé, Pittsburgh *Courier*, Nov. 20, 1926 (highest achievement); ER to Otto Kahn, Aug. 21, 1925, PU: Kahn; ER Diary, Aug. 4, 1925, RA (Ruth Hale); New York *Herald Tribune*, May 23, 25, 1930; Raleigh, North Carolina, *News Observer*, May 24, 1930; New York *Evening World*, May 23, 1930. According to Salemmé (unpublished ms.), Leonor Loree, president of the D & H Railroad, at one point planned to buy the statue with Otto Kahn and donate it to Rutgers. Loree agreed to Salemmé's price of $18,000 for the sculpture in bronze, but the sale fell through when the Rutgers Board of Trustees decided that Robeson was too young to be honored with a statue. Salemmé later (1927) made a head of Robeson, which still exists (he shipped the head, in bronze, to Robeson in London for exhibition and sales—asking $700–1,250 per head (Antonio Salemmé to ER, March 24, 1930, RA). When I interviewed Salemmé in 1983, he was—at age ninety-three—back to work on a new version of the life-size statue.

4. ER, *PR, Negro*, pp. 82–87; ER Diary, Sept. 23, 1924, RA (Arthur Lee); interview with Monroe Wheeler, Nov. 12, 1985. Rebecca West, for one, thought Salemmé was a "very bad influence" on Robeson. She met them both in the mid-

twenties in New York through Walter White and decided Paul was "basically lazy," unwilling to become "a dedicated musical worker"—for which she in part blamed Salemmé's influence (interview with Rebecca West, Sept. 1, 1982).

5. Interview with Salemmé, March 31, 1983.

6. Interview with Monroe Wheeler, Nov. 12, 1985. John Hammond (interview, Aug. 8, 1985) is the source for PR and Betty Spencer's being lovers.

7. ER Diary, May 20, June 28, Nov. 12, Dec. 29, 1924, RA; interview with Salemmé, March 31, 1983. I've strung Salemmé's remarks together, omitting some of the pauses and ellipses in our conversation; but I've neither invented any words nor rearranged them in a way that would change their essential emphasis and meaning.

8. Among the large number of works on these and other renaissance figures, I've found the following especially useful (along with Levy, *James Weldon Johnson;* Huggins, *Renaissance;* Lewis, *Harlem in Vogue;* Johnson, *Black Manhattan;* and Anderson, *This Was Harlem*): Bruce Kellner, *Carl Van Vechten and the Irreverent Decades* (University of Oklahoma, 1968); James Weldon Johnson, *Along This Way* (Viking, 1933); Robert E. Hemenway, *Zora Neale Hurston* (University of Illinois, 1977); Lawrence Langner, *The Magic Curtain* (Dutton, 1951); Emily Clark, *Innocence Abroad* (Knopf, 1931); Edward G. Leuders, *Carl Van Vechten* (Twayne, 1955); Blanche Ferguson, *Countee Cullen and the Negro Renaissance* (Dodd, Mead, 1966).

9. New York *Herald Tribune,* July 6, 1924; *Messenger,* Oct. 1924, p. 32; undated clipping [late 1925], RA ("morbid").

10. *Messenger,* Oct. 1924, p. 32; *Journal News* (Ithaca, N.Y.), April 23, 1926; *Evening Globe,* March 13, 1926. Lewis, *Harlem in Vogue,* pp. 192–93, plus his fine discussion, passim, of cultural elitism (see especially pp. 108–15, 157–62, 211–19).

11. Once in a great while, Salemmé did hear Paul sound a more bitter, less resigned note—and when he did was quick to blame it on the baneful influence of Dr. Smith Ely Jelliffe, the well-known psychoanalyst whom Paul and Essie had met at Presbyterian Hospital (see note 12, p. 578), and especially on his Southern-born wife, Bea, who in Salemmé's view "was very pro-Negro" and had "a chip on her shoulder." She "wanted to help Paul, and she used . . . to sort of goad him into rebelling. She brought out the bitterness in him, and I told her she shouldn't do that, but she did" (interview with Salemmé, March 31, 1983). Ten years later Essie was still in touch with the Jelliffes; she mentions dining with Bea Jelliffe in her diary for Feb. 16, 1933 (RA). During our interview Salemmé referred approvingly at one point to Ethel Waters's autobiography, *His Eye Is on the Sparrow,* as another example of a black artist he had known who eschewed bitterness, but he showed no awareness of the actual depth of anger in her book. After Robeson became more political and more outspoken on racial questions, he let his friendship with Salemmé dissolve; when Salemmé was in Europe on a Guggenheim in 1934, Robeson failed to show up for a scheduled appointment and never got in touch to explain. Salemmé suspected that politics was at issue, but nonetheless resented Robeson's way of breaking off (interview with Salemmé, March 31, 1983).

12. ER Diary, July 27, Aug. 26, 29, 1924, RA; CVV to Edna Kenton (Aug. 1924), Bruce Kellner, *Letters of Carl Van Vechten* (Yale, 1987), p. 69 (hereafter Kellner, *Letters CVV*).

13. ER Diary, Jan. 3, 1925, RA; Langner, *Magic Curtain,* p. 1964 ("Empress"); Lewis, *Harlem in Vogue,* pp. 180–89. Walter White had also been responsible for introducing Van Vechten to James Weldon Johnson, Langston Hughes, "and ever so many more" (Carl Van Vechten to Alfred Knopf, Dec. 19, 1962, Knopf Papers, Ransom Humanities Center, University of Texas (henceforth UT: Knopf). The Walter Whites and the Knopfs had "drifted completely away from each other" (in Alfred Knopf's words) by the late forties (Knopf to Van Vechten, Sept. 22, 1948, UT: Knopf). Lincoln Kirstein's analysis of Van Vechten is from a five-page typed description of him headed "For Fania: De-

cember 23, 1964," written by Kirstein on the occasion of Van Vechten's death. The manuscript is in UT: Knopf and continues, in part: "I met Carl first in the Spring of 1926 at an evening-party in Muriel Draper's old stable-loft on East Fortieth Street. He was wearing a red fireman's shirt. I was a freshman introduced into New York's High Bohemia, so it seemed perfectly natural that at Muriel Draper's one would meet, along with Mr. Gurdgieff [sic], Edmund Wilson, Gilbert Seldes, Paul Robeson or Mary Garden, a fireman. . . . Carl made Harlem real to me; it was not the tragic Harlem we now know. It was a Harlem far more secret, parochial, more remote, less dangerous, at least seemingly, and in our ways of thought more Parisian. . . ."

14. ER Diary, Jan. 17, Feb. 13 (Fania), 1925, RA; CVV to Scott Cunningham (circa Jan. 1925); CVV to Gertrude Stein, June 30, 1925, Kellner, *Letters CVV*, pp. 74, 80.

15. ER Diary, Aug. 17, 1924 (Touvalou; Maran), Jan. 27, 1925 (Bynner), Feb. 12, 1925 (Anderson), March 25, 1925 (Brouns), April 5, 1925 (Dreiser), April 21, 1925 (Brooks), June 8, 17, 1925 (Nora Holt), RA; CVV to Mencken (circa 1925), Kellner, *Letters CVV*, p. 87. The Robesons saw Prince Touvalou several more times during the following month. He spent two afternoons in their apartment; during one they "had lots of fun explaining our American slang to him. He has a marvelous sense of humour" (ER Diary, Sept. 12, 1924, RA). On the second visit, the Prince told Essie she ought to study for the stage—she had "such an expressive face and such a mischievous manner." "We'll see," Essie wrote expectantly in her diary—and told Paul the Prince wanted to "write something African" for him, since voodooism had "originated in Dahomey, his home, and he knew so many stories about it" (Sept. 16, 1924). The very next day, they bumped into Touvalou when they went backstage after seeing *Chocolate Dandies* to chat with its creators, Sissle and Blake (Sept. 17, 1924). There is a touching reminiscense of Robeson by Heywood Broun and Ruth Hale's son, Heywood Hale Broun, in his memoir *Whose Little*

Boy Are You? (St. Martin's, 1983), pp. 55–57, in which he describes Paul as "the greatest container for love and affection" he had ever met: "After you had spoken with him for a few minutes you realized that he was finding your wonderful hidden qualities, and after a few more meetings you were trying to think of ways to tell him how much he meant to you." In the early thirties, Robeson was involved, along with Walter White and Zora Neale Hurston, in an opera based on Maran's *Batouala*, to be conducted by Leopold Stokowski (White to PR, May 31, 1932). Stokowski also approached Robeson about appearing with the Philadelphia Orchestra (Schang to PR, March 11, 1933). After the outbreak of World War II, Robeson lent his efforts to helping Maran and his wife get emergency visitors' visas to the U.S. (PR to Jane Sherman of Exiled Writer Committee, Oct. 18, 1940; Rockmore to Walter White, Oct. 18, 1940; Sherman to PR, Oct. 23, 1940—all NAACP Papers, LC).

16. ER Diary, Nov. 5, 24, 28, Dec. 2, 24 (Henderson), 1924; Jan. 4 (Toomer), Jan. 30 (Alabam'), March 11, 27, 29, April 10, June 10 (Cullen reception)—all 1925, RA. Johnson, *Along This Way*, pp. 378–81. Additional examples of PR singing at friends' parties is in FM to CVV, Jan. 1, 14, 1927, CVV Papers, NYPL/Ms. Div. The Robesons and Countee Cullen stayed in intermittent but peripheral contact. When Cullen came to Paris on a Guggenheim Fellowship in 1928, he wrote Paul asking if it would be possible for him to arrange "a few reading and lecture engagements" to help "take care of my expenses," and reporting that his father and Harold Jackman (the West Indian man-about-town rumored to be Countee's lover), who had gone backstage in London after seeing a performance of *Jones*, "came back to Paris with glowing reports of your London success" (CC to PR, Sept. 5, 1928, RA). In 1940, Cullen tried to interest Paul in appearing in a play of his, but Essie responded, in one of her "brisker" notes, that she thought the first part "real, natural, moving in spots," but the second "nagging, whining, uninteresting and depressing" (Cullen to ER, Feb. 5, 1940, RA; ER to

Cullen, April 10, 1940, Cullen Papers, Amistad Research Center [henceforth ARC: Cullen]). In a cryptic, handwritten note, n.d. (1956?) in his Music Notes, RA, PR refers to Cullen as "perhaps . . . closer than Langston [Hughes] to African bards." The Robesons and Eric Waldron maintained some limited contact. When Waldron published an article, "Growth of the Negro Theater," in *Opportunity* (Oct. 1925), Essie complimented him on it; Waldron replied that he appreciated her praise but he considered the article "a pot-boiler" and *some time* hoped "to have the poise and restraint and the power to say what I have in mind to say about goings on in the Negro Theater" (Waldron to ER, Nov. 15, 1925, RA).

17. ER Diary, Aug. 28 (Minnie Sumner), Sept. 12 (Agnes Boulton), 26, 27 (Fischer), Nov. 4, 16, 1924, April 27, May 8, 10, 22, July 3, 21, Aug. 11, Sept. 11—all 1925, RA. They also saw something of May Chinn; when *The Emperor Jones* opened yet once more, this time for a brief run at a Broadway house, they took Chinn to the packed last showing in the old theater (ER Diary, Dec. 27, 1924, RA).

18. ER Diary, May 15, 20, June 14, 22, 28, July 10 (O'Neill), 29, Aug. 23, Nov. 27, Dec. 4, 1924, and May 12, 30, 1925, RA. Isaac Don Levine records another "memorable night in 1925" when he, O'Neill, and Robeson went on a tour of Harlem. Levine had recently returned from the Soviet Union, and he claims O'Neill and Robeson "plied" him with questions about "the dramatic struggle for power then taking place in the Kremlin" (Isaac Don Levine, *Eyewitness to History* [Hawthorn Books, 1973], pp. 84–89). Gig McGhee had played Smithers opposite Robeson in the Peterborough, N.H., showing of *Jones*. On May 4, 1925, Essie and Paul had a party at their place for about thirty of the Provincetowners; the Walter Whites, the James Weldon Johnsons, Zora Neale Hurston, and a Mrs. Carson were, she noted, "the only colored guests."

19. ER Diary, Sept. 12, 28 (McGhees' apartment), Nov. 4 *(Glencairn)*, 11 *(Desire)*, 1924, Feb. 6 *(Patience)*, March 21

(Throckmorton), May 19, June 3 *(Elms)*, 18, July 13, 25, 1925, RA.

20. ER Diary, Feb. 12, 1924, RA; article on Bercovicis in New York *Evening Journal*, April 8, 1925; interview with the Bercovicis' two daughters, Rada and Mirel, July 7, 1985. In his book, *It's the Gypsy in Me*, Konrad Bercovici says that he and his wife Naomi were introduced to PR for the first time backstage after a performance of *Emperor Jones*, by director Jimmy Light. For background information on the family, I'm grateful to Rada and Mirel Bercovici for a variety of materials they shared with me. They credit their father with having originally suggested the use of a nonstop tom-tom beat in *The Emperor Jones*. In *It's the Gypsy in Me* (p. 194), Konrad Bercovici recalls that when the Robesons first came to dinner "the colored maid shed her apron, declared that she wouldn't 'serve no "Niggers," ' " and left. When Paul came to see them again, "the colored elevator man refused to take him up." Following those insults, "the agent of the house informed us that the other tenants threatened to cancel their leases unless I ceased having colored men go up in the same elevator with them." At that point the Bercovicis bought the townhouse at 81st Street and Riverside Drive.

21. Interview with Rada and Mirel Bercovici, July 7, 1985; ER Diary, Sept. 27, Dec. 28, 1924, Jan. 17, Feb. 1 (Zuloaga; Gorky), Feb. 5, 26, March 1, 6, April 12, 20, May 8, June 2, 9, 16, 20, 21, 1925, RA. Robeson often sang to the children of his friends, sometimes giving them private concerts. From some dozen people (including Peggy Dennis, Cedric Belfrage, and Rose Perry) I have heard near-duplicate tales of Robeson's singing to their mesmerized offspring.

Rada and Mirel Bercovici (interview of July 7, 1985) cast doubt on the accuracy of a few details in Essie's diary. In regard to that diary, I've come to the overall conclusion that Essie *is* given to exaggeration and dramatic highlighting (though almost never to outright invention) and especially in one area—when recording the doings of "glamorous" people and events as they intersected with the Robesons' own lives. Rada and

Mirel Bercovici characterize her as more attracted to the "high life" than Paul (she tended to "costume things a bit," as Rada put it) and was (in Mirel's words) "posthumously conscious"—meaning she was self-consciously aware of posterity's evaluations, and not likely to scribble away in a diary with entire spontaneity. She may have kept a diary in the first place in order to glamorize her life retrospectively. It's significant, in this regard, that she started her diary only in January 1924—just as Paul was being catapulted to fame. Still, Essie's pridefulness only occasionally comes across as wildly overblown; on the whole her diary remains a reliable, valuable resource.

22. ER Diary, Feb. 2 ("honor"); March 26 (Junior Banquet), 1925; Dec. 17 (Rutgers concert; Gilpin), 1924; NAACP and Nazarene appearances from newspaper clippings in RA; Mary White Ovington to PR, Jan. 19, 1927, RA. The professor to whom ER made her remark (which is in the *Sunday Times* [New Brunswick], June 8, 1930) was Charles H. Whitman; for more on Whitman and PR, see note 16, pp. 573–74. The *Jones* revival moved—again for a brief run—to the Punch and Judy Theater on Broadway in mid-Jan. 1925.

23. ER Diary, Aug. 25, Oct. 17 (Burleigh), Nov. 1, 2, 1924 (Copley), Dec. 12, 1924, Jan. 12, 1925, for other concerts; Mrs. C. C. Pell to PR, Oct. 15, 1924, RA; ER Diary, Dec. 6, 1924 (Pells), RA.

24. ER Diary, Oct. 17, 1924 (Micheaux), Jan. 27, 28, 30, 1925 (Hayes), RA; *Variety*, Nov. 26, 1924 (Russell); Daniel J. Leab, *From Sambo to Superspade: The Black Experience in Motion Pictures* (Houghton, Mifflin Co., 1975), has more detail on Micheaux's career. The film critic J. Hoberman has called Micheaux's *God's Step Children* (1938) an account of self-directed racism "as profound and powerful an embodiment of American racial pathology as D. W. Griffith's *The Birth of a Nation* or John Ford's *The Searchers* and as amazing a movie as either of them"; according to Hoberman, *God's Step Children* was "temporarily forced out of circulation by the Harlem chapter of the Communist Party" (*Village Voice*, June 12, 1984). In her diary for Nov. 3, 1924, RA,

Essie wrote, "Micheaux made storm scene out on Corona today. What with the wind machine, fire hose, etc., it was the most realistic thing I ever saw." The day before Hayes appeared backstage at *Jones*, Paul had journeyed to Philadelphia to hear Hayes at the Academy of Music; and two days after Hayes's visit, Paul and Essie again returned the compliment by attending Hayes's concert at the Brooklyn Academy of Music as soloist with the Boston Symphony (Essie thought it "very fine" but "didn't like the robust things he did").

25. ER Diary, Sept. 24, Oct. 2, 20, Nov. 12, 20, 22, 24, 1924 (Germany); Dec. 7 (Reiss), 8, (Bartholomew), 24; Jan. 23, 18, 1925 (Madden); Dec. 1, 8, and passim, 1925 (Dwight portrait); April 25, 1925 (radio), Jan. 28 (Hampden), Feb. 19, 22, March 4, 10—all 1925, RA. Marshall Bartholomew to PR, Dec. 24, 1924, RA.

26. ER, Ms. Auto., RA; ER Diary, March 20, 24, 1925, RA; Seton, "Lawrence Brown" ("pondering"). Larry Brown's father had also been born a slave. The contracts are in RA. Carl Van Vechten to ER, n.d. (1925), RA; ER to CVV, Sept. 28, 1925, Yale: Van Vechten. The black singer Taylor Gordon is among those rumored to have been Van Vechten's lover. A collection of nude photographs Van Vechten took of black men is in Yale: Van Vechten.

27. ER, Ms. Auto., RA.

28. ER, Ms. Auto., RA; PR, Music Notes (1956?), RA (Brown "guided"). For a fine background discussion of the spirituals, see Lawrence W. Levine, *Black Culture and Black Consciousness* (Oxford, 1977), pp. 30–55 (and for the ambivalence some educated blacks felt toward the spirituals, pp. 167–69).

29. ER Diary, March 27, 29, 1925, RA; ER, Ms. Auto., RA; Van Vechten to PR, March 30, 1925, RA; PR, Music Notes (1956?), RA (children; Brown "guided").

30. Heywood Hale Broun, *Whose Little Boy*, p. 56; Millia Davenport to me, June 7, 1982.

31. ER, Ms. Auto., RA; ER Diary, April 19, 1925, RA; Frank B. Lenz, "When Robeson Sings," *Association Men*,

July 1927 (sixteen songs and encores); PR to Van Vechten, postmarked Oct. 21, 1927, Yale: Van Vechten ("unselfish interest"). Monroe Wheeler gave it as his opinion that Van Vechten and Donald Angus *were* lovers (interview with Wheeler, Nov. 12, 1985). The program for the concert is in RA. It was repeated twice more—on May 3, in the same Greenwich Village theater, and on May 17, in the 48th Street Theater. Three drafts of a blurb Van Vechten wrote for the second concert are in Yale: Van Vechten; in it he hailed Robeson and Brown for having restored "the spirit of the original primitive interpretation to these Spirituals . . . which apparently no other public singer has hitherto entertained. . . ."

32. Van Vechten, draft of a blurb for the second concert ("wistful," etc.), Yale: Van Vechten; New York *World*, April 20, 1925 ("infinite"); New York *Evening Post*, April 20, 1925 ("luscious"); *The New York Times*, April 20, 1925 ("conviction"); Edgar G. Brown in New York *News*, April 25, 1925 (Caruso); Du Bois to PR and Larry Brown, May 4, 1925, U. Mass.: Du Bois. (Du Bois attended the second concert.) Essie, Paul, and Larry wrote and thanked both Walter White and Van Vechten: "Your untiring work in our interest certainly brought very tangible results" (April 25, 1925, Yale: Van Vechten). White, who went along with them when they made their first test record for Victor (ER Diary, April 21, 1925) two days after the concert, wrote back (April 28, 1925, RA): "I have never in my life been so pleased—and moved—as I was by your joint letter of thanks. . . . You can always count on me to the limit. The best of all thanks and the thing that'll make me most happy will be an overwhelming success which will come and which the three of you so richly deserve." PR had in fact given several earlier concerts devoted mostly to Afro-American music. Accompanied by Louis Hooper, he performed such a program on Nov. 2, 1924, in Boston, to warm praise from the reviewers (Boston *Transcript* and Boston *Post*, both Nov. 3, 1924), and again (still accompanied by Hooper) at Rutgers on Dec. 17, 1924, and at the Highland Park

Reformed Church on Jan. 9, 1925 (the latter two programs are in RUA).

33. Interview with Percy N. Stone in New York *Herald Tribune*, Oct. 17, 1926. The remark linking Hayes and PR is in the New Orleans *Item*, an article by Hudson Grunewald on Edna Thomas (a friend of Robeson's) lauding *her*, in contrast to the two men, as a purveyor of the real thing. Sandburg's remarks are in the Chicago *News*, Sept. 29, 1926.

34. Carl Van Vechten to ER, Oct. 9, Nov. 19, 1925, RA; ER to Van Vechten and Fania Marinoff, Oct. 8, 20, Yale: Van Vechten; ER to James Weldon Johnson, Nov. 1, 1925 ("pore"), Yale: Johnson. In his Oct. 9 letter, Van Vechten reported that H. T. Burleigh, the black composer and arranger of some of the songs Paul and Larry had used, "is in a frightful stew and does not hesitate to show it. Meeting Larry and Rosamond on the street he abused them roundly, saying that neither of them knew anything about Spirituals or even music itself and that the book was a botch. . . . He threatened to talk to certain critics and promised them bad notices. 'If you knew anything about Brahms and Debussy,' he added, 'your harmonizations would be far different.' " In his Nov. 19 letter, Van Vechten reported that "Bledsoe recently sang to a half-full listless house. He will not put his very real personality into his concerts and he sings Spirituals worse than any one I know."

35. New York *World*, May 3, 1925 ("anything more"); James B. Pond to PR, May 29, 1925 (two separate letters), RA; ER Diary, May 4, 23, 26, 1925, RA. The contracts with Victor are in the RA. ER Diary, April 21, July 16, 27, 30, Aug. 4, 1925 (recordings); May 11 *(Vanity Fair)*; May 7, 11, 21, June 1 (Alda); May 3 (Equity); May 25 (Jewish Committee); June 19 (St. Philip's), 1925, RA. At the private program sung for Mrs. W. Murray Crane and her guests, Essie seemed inordinately pleased that they "were all asked into the drawing room and introduced to everybody" (ER Diary, May 11, 1925, RA). The photo of Robeson appeared in the July 1925 issue of *Vanity Fair*. In the issue of Feb. 1926, Van Vechten, in his article "Moanin' wid a Sword in Ma

Han'," wrote: "Paul Robeson is a great artist.... I say great advisedly, for to hear him sing Negro music is an experience allied to hearing Chaliapin sing Russian folksongs."

36. ER Diary, May 10 (Chaliapin); May 1, 2 (Hurston); June 8 (Savage), 1925, RA. Claire and Hubert Delany, the lawyer, were also part of the Robesons' party at the *Opportunity* dinner. Essie and A'Lelia Walker were more than acquaintances, less than friends; they occasionally corresponded, and in the twenties occasionally played bridge together (ER to Walker, April 8 [1930], courtesy of A'Lelia P. Bundles). Chaliapin's daughter, Marfa Hudson Davies, later wrote Robeson to tell him "how much my father in turn admired you" (Davies to PR, Oct. 8, 1960, RA). Hurston's views on black spirituals are in Hemenway, *Zora Neale Hurston*, pp. 54–55. Hemenway (pp. 54, 184–85) quotes from a comment Hurston made in 1934 specifically on Robeson as a singer of spirituals: " 'Robeson sings Negro songs better than most, because, thank God, he lacks musical education. But we have a cathead man in Florida who can sing so that if you heard him you wouldn't want to hear Hayes or Robeson. He hasn't the voice of either one. It's the effect.' " In 1933, at Rollins College, Hurston produced a successful concert that implemented her view of the proper uses of folk art. Though the evidence is limited, it's possible to argue that Robeson's views on the spirituals in fact coincided with Hurston's. On the occasion of the Hampton Singers' performing in England, Robeson is quoted as telling a reporter that they would demonstrate "how Negro spirituals should be sung. I cannot possibly interpret them properly . . . when I sing them as solos. It is not recognized in Europe that singing spirituals is a social act, a group affair, in which there must be both the solo and the chorus. There are many spirituals such as 'Go Down, Moses' which I absolutely refuse to sing alone, for it is nothing without the rolling refrain, 'Let my people go' " (*The New York Times*, April 26, 1930).

37. New York *World*, April 30, 1925 (the New York *Sun* also carried an article about the incident on April 30); ER Diary, Feb. 18 (Algonquin); April 28, 29, 1925, RA. Fifteen years later Robeson was involved in a second incident with the Dutch Treat Club. The New York *World-Telegram* reported (Jan. 20, 1940) that he had failed to appear for an engagement at the club and had "deliberately" not notified it—retrospective retaliation for his mistreatment in 1925. Essie wrote to the club denying that his action had been deliberate, but the possibility nonetheless remains. (Ray Vir Den, vice-president of Dutch Treat, to ER, Jan. 25, 1940, enclosing copy of his letter of protest to Roy W. Howard, president of *World-Telegram*, also dated Jan. 25, 1940, RA).

38. "Ned" Sheldon was also famed for the remarkable serenity of spirit with which he dealt with his illness, continuing to receive friends in the confines of his apartment—among them many of Robeson's previous theatrical associates, Emilie Hapgood, Hoytie Wiborg, and Mrs. Patrick Campbell (and, back in 1922, at the behest of H. A. Murray, Robeson himself—see note 16, p. 570). ER Diary, June 12, 1925; Johnson, *Black Manhattan*, pp. 205–6. Charles MacArthur later apologized to Robeson for some of the language used in the play—like "tarbaby," "musta'd colored snake charmer," and "real nigger style" (Jhan Robbins, *Front Page Marriage: Helen Hayes and Charles MacArthur* [Putnam's Sons, 1982], p. 37). At the time Robeson told an interviewer, "There is a wealth of material in the Negro's past," and he feared "the stereotyped format of plays that will imitate 'Lulu Belle' and even the play he now appears in"—meaning *Black Boy* (Wilmington, Delaware, *Press*, Oct. 4, 1926). Though Robeson turned down the role in *Lulu Belle* and had let his disapproval of its stereotypes be known, Essie records a pleasant evening spent with Ned Sheldon six months after the play opened: "Dined with Edward Sheldon. . . . He is fascinating. The dinner was delicious. Paul sang for Sheldon, and read some scenes from 'Emperor Jones' and 'All God's Chillun.' We stayed three hours, and enjoyed every minute of it" (ER Diary, Aug. 5, 1926, RA).

39. ER Diary, June 17, 1925, RA; Van Vechten to Blanche Knopf, June 30,

1925, UT: Knopf. Van Vechten to Ettie Stettheimer, June 18, 1925, NYPL Ms. Div.: Van Vechten; "I want to raise $5,000 (or at least $3,000)—not for myself!—as a loan, to be repaid with interest in one or two years for an extremely worthy cause. . . . I might add, however, that it is not for starving Belgian babies, but would constitute you a patron of the arts!" In his catalogue for this NYPL collection (p. 37), Van Vechten later wrote, "The request for money was in behalf of Paul Robeson. I secured the full amount for him from Otto Kahn."

40. ER to Otto Kahn, no date but filed June 22, 1925, PU: Kahn.

41. Van Vechten to Kahn, Sept. 9, 1925 ("'gimme'"); Kahn to Van Vechten, June 19, 25, 1925, PU: Kahn.

42. ER Diary, June 28, 1925, RA; Kahn to ER, June 29, 1925; two letters, ER to Kahn, filed July 3 and July 30, 1925—all in PU: Kahn; Van Vechten to ER, July 1, 1925, RA. If Van Vechten did write the suggested letter to Kahn, it is not in PU: Kahn. In a draft legal agreement (RA), Robeson agreed to start repaying the loan by Jan. 1, 1926—two thousand dollars during the first year, three thousand during the second.

43. ER Diary, July 13, Aug. 2, 4, 1925, RA.

44. ER Diary, July 4–6 (Peterborough), July 15 (quiet), July 18–19, July 21–24 (Provincetown), Aug. 3 (Spring Lake), 1925, RA; ER postcards to Carl Van Vechten, July 6, 19, 24, Aug. 4 (plus one undated), 1925, Yale: Van Vechten. Rita Romilly, "Concerning a Singer and an Actress," *New Age,* Sept. 10, 1925. ER Diary, July 24, 1925 (Taylor)—also March 15, 1926, RA for another visit to him.

45. ER Diary, July 3, 13, 19, 26, Aug. 2, 4, 1925, RA. Van Vechten was currently trying to persuade Alfred Knopf to publish Stein's *Three Lives.* Knopf wrote Van Vechten (May 18, 1925, UT: Knopf) that he was "entirely willing" to publish her book "if you feel sufficiently strongly about it but there is no use my trying to read this lady for I simply can't in my present mood at any rate, get through more than fifty to a hundred pages."

CHAPTER 6   THE LAUNCHING OF A CAREER *(1925–1927)*

1. ER to CVV and FM, Sept. 7, 1925, Yale: Van Vechten; ER Diary, Aug. 13, 14, 15, 1925, RA.

2. Louis Sheaffer interview with Sue Jenkins (courtesy of Sheaffer); ER, Ms. Auto., RA; Ruth C. McCreary to me, June 11, 1982 (restaurant discrimination). When performing in *Black Boy* on Broadway in 1926, Robeson and Horace Liveright (producer of the show) attempted to lunch at the Café des Beaux Arts in New York City, but were turned away at the door (Cleveland *Plain Dealer,* Oct. 17, 1926). Robeson had even had trouble getting his teeth fixed. After several dentists had refused to take him as a patient, Lewis Dicksteen (contacted by an artist friend in Greenwich Village) agreed to treat him. In gratitude, Robeson sent the Dicksteen family free tickets to *Emperor Jones.* (The incident was related by Lewis Dicksteen's son, the Queens Democratic committeeman Abbott Dicksteen, to Jules Cohen, who passed it on to me.)

3. ER, Ms. Auto., RA. ER's views on race in this period are further set forth in *PR, Negro,* pp. 52–63.

4. ER to CVV and FM, Oct. 8, 1925, Yale: Van Vechten; ER Diary, Aug. 13, 14, 17, 20, 24–27, Sept. 1, 4, 15, 28, Oct. 10, 1925, RA. ER took a brief side trip to Paris with Bert McGhee and reported to the Van Vechtens on her theater adventures there. She singled out Racquel Meller as "a great artist," deplored the Follies Bergère (except for Benglia), and thought the show at the Casino de Paris "terrible" (ER to CVV and FM, Aug. 28, 1925, Yale: Van Vechten). She expands on her Paris impressions in her diary for Aug. 24–27, 1925, and later wrote a set piece about the trip (Jan. 29, 1931, RA).

5. Essie was intrigued with John Payne's home ("the electric light Buddha in his drawing room is weird and beautiful"), but disliked a recital of his that she and Paul heard ("His Negro songs were his worst. He got a sort of Charleston

rhythm into them, that was jazzy and terrible") (ER Diary, Sept. 19, Oct. 2, 1925, RA). ER to CVV and FM, Sept. 7, 1925, Yale: Van Vechten.

6. ER Diary, Aug. 22, 1925, RA; Emma Goldman, *Living My Life* (Knopf, 1931; Dover reissue, 1970), vol. II, p. 980; EG to Alexander Berkman, Feb. 5, 1933, Feb. 28, 1936, Berkman Archive, International Institute of Social History, Amsterdam (courtesy of Paul Avrich), hereafter IISH.

7. ER Diary, Aug. 22, Sept. 5, 10, 13, 23, 25, Oct. 5, 15, 1925, RA; ER, *PR, Negro*, p. 93 ("disheartening"); ER to CVV and FM, Sept. 7, 1925, Yale: Van Vechten; CVV to ER, Sept. 27, 1925, RA. In another letter to the Van Vechtens (Sept. 28, 1925, Yale: Van Vechten), Essie wrote that Emma "is another *real* person to add to our short list. We see her very often and like her more and more."

8. ER Diary, Sept. 10, 1925, RA; ER to Otto Kahn, Sept. 17, 1925; Kahn to ER, Sept. 29, 1925, PU: Kahn.

9. *Statesman, Review,* and *Africa* are Sept. 19; *Weekly,* Sept. 26; *Tatler,* Sept. 30, 1925. A dozen other reviews were raves. The sole negative seems to have been from the American correspondent from *Billboard* (Sept. 19, Oct. 31, 1925), who found Robeson merely "talented." Robeson, retrospectively, agreed: "I knew nothing about the technique of acting" (Seton, *PR,* p. 40). ER Diary, Sept. 23, 1925, RA; ER to CVV and FM, Sept. 28, 1925, Yale: Van Vechten *("Star").*

10. The effects of the tom-tom came in for considerable discussion (e.g., Cicely Hamilton in *Time and Tide,* Sept. 25, 1925). The negative comments on Light's production are in *G.K.'s Weekly,* Sept. 26, 1925, and *The Saturday Review,* Sept. 19, 1925. Seton, quoting from an interview with Jimmy Light, refers in her book (*PR,* p. 38) to the African members of the cast being dockworkers and some of them "illiterate." In the ms. of her book, Robeson had crossed out "illiterate" and substituted "uneducated in English language." Curiously, the printed version retains "illiterate," though in most other cases Seton adopted Robeson's corrections. Negative comments on

the play are from the *Daily Sketch,* Sept. 11, 1925; the Birmingham *Post,* Sept. 12, 1925; *Vogue,* early Oct. 1925; *The Outlook,* Oct. 3, 1925; and *The New Statesman,* Sept. 19, 1925. ER to Countee Cullen, Nov. 22, 1925, ARC: Cullen.

11. ER to CVV and FM, Sept. 28, 1925, Yale: Van Vechten; ER to Otto Kahn, Oct. 9, 1925, PU: Kahn; ER to J. W. Johnson, Nov. 1, 1925, Yale: Johnson; ER Diary, Oct. 17, 1925, RA (closing). The comments about "a negro play" are from the Birmingham *Post,* Sept. 12, 1925, and *The Gentlewoman,* Sept. 26, 1925. Alan Bott, in *The Sphere,* Sept. 19, 1925, is the one reviewer to discuss "the tragedy of the negro."

12. ER Diary, Oct. 14, 15, 18, 19 (Aldridge), 20 (Quilter), 24, (Campbell), 26, 30 (Eastman), 30 (Taylor), 1925, RA; Jessie Coleridge-Taylor to ER, Oct. 13, 1925; Athene Seyler to ER, Oct. 9, 1925, RA. PR probably met Quilter through Larry Brown, who had earlier become his friend. There are several letters from Quilter and three from Miss Ira Aldridge from this period in RA ("magnificent," etc., is from the Aldridge letters). In the Ira Aldridge Collection, Northwestern University Library (henceforth NUL: Aldridge), there are two letters from Paul to Miss Aldridge and one (signed in Paul's name) from Essie. In Essie's letter to Aldridge (Oct. 19, 1925) she asked for a copy of "Summer is de Lovin' Time," which Aldridge had played for them that afternoon, for possible use in concerts and recording. Sixty years later Athene Seyler recalled "one intimate conversation" with Essie: "I asked her if there was any real difference between black people and white, as I felt one could talk to her freely on any topic and would respect her opinion. She replied that there was no essential difference at all—but that black men found white women irresistible. This was said quite impersonally but with perhaps a hint of wistfulness" (Athene Seyler to me, Jan. 1, 1983).

13. ER Diary, Aug. 9, Sept. 30, Oct. 6, 1925, RA; ER to CVV and FM, Aug. 10, Sept. 7, Oct. 8, 11, 20, 1925, Yale: Van Vechten.

14. ER to Otto Kahn, Oct. 9, 1925 ("very tired"), PU: Kahn. She was ex-

plaining "all this" and their plans for a recuperative vacation, Essie wrote Kahn, "because I don't want you to think we are being extravagant. I do hope you will approve of my plans." He did, writing back to assure her that it was "quite right" to take a rest before returning to America and expressing the view that, although the play was closing prematurely, "the main purpose of your European adventure has been fully achieved, and its effects ought to be of lasting value" (Otto Kahn to ER, Nov. 4, 1925, PU: Kahn). Otto Kahn is "awfully nice," Essie wrote to Carl and Fania (Oct. 11, 1925, Yale: Van Vechten). ER Diary, Aug. 28–29, Nov. 2–8 (Paris), Nov. 7 (Matisse), 8 (Beach tea), 1925, RA; ER to CVV and FM, Sept. 7, Nov. 16 (Beach, Matisse), 1925, Yale: Van Vechten; ER to Otto Kahn, Nov. 17, 1925, PU: Kahn. Sylvia Beach to her mother, Oct. 30, Nov. 10, 1925, PU: Beach. Robeson's visit to Sylvia Beach was duly noted in "Latin Quarter Notes" for Nov. 13, Dec. 11, 1925, in the Paris *Tribune* (Hugh Ford, ed., *The Left Bank Revisited: Selections from the Paris "Tribune" 1917–1934* [Penn State University Press, 1972], p. 103). The *Tribune* also quoted Robert Schirmer as announcing that "in all likelihood" he would issue "an edition of spirituals as interpreted by Robeson." Essie may have met Beach earlier, when she and Bert McGhee dropped into her bookstore on an excursion to Paris, to purchase a paperbound copy of *Ulysses* for Paul. It had cost her sixty francs (three dollars), and she had smuggled it back to London "between my bath towel and my douche bag—I figured no gentleman would rummage thru these 2 articles—not even a customs man"; they hadn't, and Paul had been "tickled to death" with the gift (ER Diary, Aug. 28–29, 1925; ER to CVV and FM, Sept. 7, 1925, Yale: Van Vechten).

15. ER to Gertrude Stein, two undated notes (Oct. 1925) referring to the enclosed letter of introduction and the date for the tea, Yale: Stein. CVV to GS, June 30, July 10, Aug. 1, 1925, printed in Edward Burns, *The Gertrude Stein–Carl Van Vechten Letters: 1913–1946*, 2 vols. (Columbia University, 1986),

originally a 6-vol. dissertation at CUNY.

16. Stein to CVV, Nov. 9, 1925, Aug. 11, 1927, printed in Burns, ed., *Letters of GS and CVV;* Gertrude Stein, *The Autobiography of Alice B. Toklas* (Vintage, 1933, 1960), pp. 237–38 (spirituals; Southern woman); in her memoir, Alice B. Toklas supplies her own version of the initial meeting with the Robesons and the encounter with the Southern woman, both very close to Stein's recollections (*What Is Remembered* [Holt, Rinehart and Winston, 1963], pp. 117–18). In the same passage of the *Autobiography* cited above, somewhat repeating what she had privately written to Van Vechten in 1925, and prefiguring what Ralph Ellison was to say about "invisibility," Stein "concluded that negroes were not suffering from persecution, they were suffering from nothingness. She always contends that the african is not primitive, but he has a very ancient but a very narrow culture and there it remains. Consequently nothing does or can happen."

17. Stein to CVV, Oct. 26, 1927 ("ideal companion"); CVV to GS, Jan. 8, 1928 ("adores you"), printed in Burns, ed., *Letters of GS and CVV.* Essie did write Stein a note from the Riviera to say they were "happily settled," that "Paul's nose and throat have already cleared up," that they didn't like Nice ("Atlantic City-ish . . . a sort of toy place"), and that Paul joined her "in thanking you again for that delightful afternoon at your house in Paris" (ER to GS, Nov. 22, 1925, Yale: Stein). Stein had invited the painter Marsden Hartley to the party for the Robesons, but he'd been out of town; he later wrote to tell her that he had met the Robesons and had found him "a most attractive person" (Donald Gallup, ed., *The Flowers of Friendship: Letters Written to Gertrude Stein* [Knopf, 1953], p. 183; Gallup also reprints CVV's letter of introduction on p. 179).

18. ER to CVV and FM, Nov. 16, 1925, Yale: Van Vechten; Bricktop describes the sensation Baker created in her memoir, *Bricktop,* written with James Haskins (Athenaeum, 1983), pp. 107–8. Though Essie refers to her as "Josephine," I've found no evidence that they

were personally acquainted at this point—though they were later (see note 8, p. 754).

19. ER Diary, Jan. 26, Feb. 9, 18, June 3 (Maxwell), 5 (French society), July 4 ("degenerates"), Sept. 27, 1932, Feb. 24, 1933, RA; ER to CVV and FM, April 20, 1931 (Bentley), Yale: Van Vechten; interviews with Helen Rosen and Monroe Wheeler. Rebecca West, on the other hand, recalls Robeson's being "very much upset" when a man tried to pick him up in Germany (interview with me, Sept. 1, 1982). Essie's occasional ambivalence is reflected further in her reference to girls at school who fell in love with other girls "with alarming frequency" (ms. of her essay "Divorce," RA), although she has two young men in one of her unpublished plays discuss homosexuality with insouciance ("Leave Them Alone . . . ," ms., RA). For discussion of the unsubstantiated rumors that Robeson himself was bisexual, see note 15, p. 631.

20. ER Diary, Nov. 10, 11, 12, 1925, RA; ER to CVV and FM, Nov. 16, 1925, Yale: Van Vechten; interview with Monroe Wheeler, Nov. 12, 1985. An interview with Glenway Wescott ("Remembering Cocteau") by Jerry Rosco is reprinted from *Sequoia* in *The Body Politic*, July 1986.

21. Interview with Monroe Wheeler, Nov. 12, 1985; ER Diary, Nov. 12, 16–19, 1925, RA; ER to Countee Cullen, November 22, 1925, ARC: Cullen. The Robesons also spent an afternoon with the opera star Mary Garden (ER Diary, Nov. 15, 1925, RA). Wheeler told me (interview, Nov. 12, 1985) that he had been with Robeson in New York when a restaurant refused him service, but felt Robeson had grown "used to" rebuffs and had no anger about them; indeed, according to Wheeler, Robeson spoke only in the "kindliest" terms of his treatment at Rutgers. Wheeler, like so many others, was here mistaking Robeson's decision to keep a calm and modest face about racial slurs for an inner indifference to them. It is not insignificant that Robeson chose never to discuss racial questions with Wheeler. Wheeler and Wescott fell out of touch with the Robesons subsequently,

but a charming letter exists from Wescott to PR (undated, but 1927, RA) in which, having heard him in recital for the first time, he wrote to say, ". . . when I think of America as a place of poetry, it is your intonation I hear—when I think of art we must have in the future—beyond all this fear and muddle—it is your musicianship I compare it with." G. B. Stern (1890–1973) is best known for her "The Rakonitz Chronicle," of which the first, *The Matriarch*, had in 1924 just been published.

22. Interviews with Rebecca West, Sept. 1, 1982; Monroe Wheeler, Nov. 12, 1985. For additional details, of uncertain reliability, about the visit from G. B. Stern and Rebecca West, see ER, *PR, Negro*, 102–3 (in which she records a much more favorable opinion of Paul by Rebecca West). For later expressions of friendship, see Rebecca West to ER, June 18, 1929, Sept. 25, 1933, RW to ER and PR, Dec. 30, 1932, RA, ER to CVV and FM, postmark June 11, 1929, Yale: Van Vechten. In another letter to the Van Vechtens (Dec. 25, 1932, RA), Essie recounts unexpectedly running into Rebecca West in Brussels and crossing with her to London: "Seems much kinder and gentler than of old. Maybe its because she's happy." Essie recorded the same opinion in her diary: "Rebecca seems to have changed since her marriage—not so sarcastic and bitter; she seems more mellow, and friendly, less catty." In adding, "I actually liked her," Essie suggests their friendship had not been as pronounced as Rebecca West later remembered it. At the time, West publicly wrote in far more favorable terms about Robeson than she spoke in private many years later (in the New York *American*, April 25, 1933, she described his performance in *Chillun* as "thrilling," and in *While Rome Burns*, p. 131, Woollcott quotes from a letter he received from Rebecca West soon after she saw *Chillun:* "Both were monstrously superb. I couldn't have believed Paul could rise to such heights of poetry. . . . He seems to be just beginning").

23. Frank Harris to PR, Oct. 21, 1925; Frank Harris to ER, "Friday 1925," RA.

24. ER Diary, Nov. 21, 1925, RA; St.

Clair Drake, Introduction to the 1970 reissue of McKay's *A Long Way from Home* (Harcourt, Brace and World, 1970; original ed., Lee Furman Inc., 1937) for biographical information on McKay; see also the excellent discussion in Lewis, *Harlem in Vogue,* especially pp. 50–58. The fullest account of McKay, with a detailed reconstruction of his relationship with Eastman, is Wayne Foley Cooper, "Stranger and Pilgrim: The Life of Claude McKay, 1890–1948," Ph.D. thesis, Rutgers, 1982 (since published as *Claude McKay: Rebel Sojourner in the Harlem Renaissance* [LSU, 1987]). McKay's letter to PR, undated ("Monday"), is in RA.

25. McKay, *Long Way,* pp. 266–67.
26. Cooper, *McKay,* pp. 438–40 (in thesis); ER Diary, Nov. 21, 28, Dec. 1, 3, 1925, RA. ER to Countee Cullen, Nov. 22, 1925, ARC: Cullen. In her printed version (*PR, Negro,* p. 100) of the meetings with McKay, Essie is blandly true to her initial rather than her revised impression of him: she merely refers to the "eager talk and laughter" that characterized their time together.
27. Claude McKay to "Eslanda," no date (probably written between December 4 and 9, 1925, since he refers in the letter to "Thursday night's talk" and it was a Thursday—December 3—when their meeting had taken place), RA.
28. McKay to ER, no date (December 4–9, 1925), RA.
29. McKay to PR, Dec. 14, 1925 (with a postscript written Jan. 14), RA; interview with Monroe Wheeler, Nov. 12, 1985. In his autobiography (*Long Way,* pp. 267–68) McKay makes some additional nasty remarks about Essie.
30. ER Diary, Dec. 13, 14, 15, 1925, RA; ER to CVV and FM, Dec. 6, 1925, Yale: Van Vechten. Before leaving Nice, the Robesons had one last dinner party of note: with the director Rex Ingram, who had recently opened his own studio outside Nice (and given work to Claude McKay as an extra and a reader). Ingram, who was interested in Africa, took them to his studio (MGM) and to his villa, where he "played lovely Egyptian records for us" (ER Diary, Nov. 27, RA). The next day, through "Rex Ingram Productions" at MGM, Ingram sent them some "Afri-

can music" (H. Lachman to PR, Nov. 28, 1925, RA).
31. Sample reviews are in *The New York Times,* Jan. 13, 1926, the *American, Sun, Tribune, Telegram, World,* and *Post*—all Jan. 6, 1926; the Indianapolis *Times Star* and *News*—both Jan. 21, 1926; the Detroit *News,* Jan. 21, 29, *Free Press* and *Evening Times*—both Jan. 29; the Philadelphia *Inquirer,* Jan. 23, 1926; and the Pittsburgh *Gazette* and *Chronicle Telegraph*—both Jan. 28, 1926.
32. The royalty statement (up to May 31, 1926) from Victor Talking Machine Co. is in RA. Hergesheimer's reaction is in CVV to ER, Oct. 27, 1925, RA; Hughes to PR, Oct. 11, 1927, RA. A sample of the favorable reviews of the recording is in *Record,* March 31, 1926, and *Singing,* July 1927. Additional information on the success of the records is in ER to Otto Kahn, Nov. 17, 1925, PU: Kahn; and CVV to ER, Oct. 8, 1925, RA. The new recording session is described in ER Diary, Jan. 25, 1926, RA. Paul presented the first records to Carl, and Larry Brown dedicated his "L'il David"—CVV's favorite—to him (ER to Fania Marinoff, postmarked June 26, 1925, Yale: Van Vechten).
33. ER Diary, Feb. 8 ("a lily"), 9–11, 1926, RA; ER to CVV and FM, postmarked Feb. 16, 1926, Yale: Van Vechten; all the newspaper reviews are from Feb. 11, 1926.
34. ER to CVV and FM, postmarked Feb. 16, 1926, Yale: Van Vechten; Milwaukee *Journal,* Feb. 13, 1926; ER Diary, Feb. 12, 1926, RA.
35. ER Diary, Feb. 13, 14, 1926, RA; ER to CVV and FM, postmarked Feb. 16, 1926, Yale: Van Vechten.
36. Arthur Hornblow, Jr., to PR, May 27, 1926, RA.
37. ER Diary, Feb. 18, 1926, RA; *The New York Times,* Feb. 19, 1926; CVV to ER, Feb. 16, 1926, RA; PR telegram to CVV, Aug. 12, 1926, Yale: Van Vechten. PR repeated the compliment in public, telling a newspaper reporter soon after that he thought the novel "was excellently written and judicially presents life in Harlem" (Wilmington, Delaware, *Press,* Oct. 4, 1926).
38. ER Ms. Auto., RA; ER Diary,

March 14, 1926, RA; Boston *Transcript,*
March 15, 1926.

39. ER Diary, March 16–19, April 5,
6, 9, June 1, July 23, 1926, RA; ER Ms.
Auto., RA; ER Diary, April 21, May 21,
1926, RA; John Devereux Kernan (son of
the doctor of the same name) to me, June
6, 1982.

40. ER Diary, April 1, 15, 21, 29,
1926, RA. The DeMille film was announced in the press, with PR, Gilpin,
and the Club Alabama star, Alma Smith,
rumored for the leads (*Variety,* May 26,
1926).

41. ER Diary, April 6 (diet), 7 (play),
24–25 (play), 26 (hemorrhage), May 5
(doctor), 1926, Sept. 28, Oct. 8, 1925
(fainting); ER to CVV and FM, postmarked July 21, 1926, Yale: Van Vechten.

42. ER Diary, Aug. 17, Dec. 26, 28,
1925 (beau), Aug. 17, 1926, March 3–11,
1926 (separate vacations), RA. Essie may
also have been hinting at an affair (and/
or marital problems) when she wrote the
Van Vechtens, "There's so much I want
to tell you" (postcard, postmarked Jan.
18, 1926, Yale: Van Vechten)—a line
more or less repeated three months later
("Have some interesting things to tell
you when we get home": ER postcard to
CVV, April 23, 1926, Yale: Van Vechten).

43. ER Diary, March 20, 21, 31
(Barnes), April 2 (Broun), 3 (Kreisler), 8
(Ulric; Knopf), 20 (Jolson), 21 (plays),
May 1 *(Opportunity),* 2 (Mills), 3, 4, 5
(Broun), 1926, RA. Though Essie found
Lulu Belle "wonderful," Paul objected to
its stereotypes (Wilmington, Delaware,
Press, Oct. 4, 1926). Since Essie kept a
diary and wrote voluminous letters—and
Paul did neither—there is an inherent
danger of assuming that the opinions
Essie expressed were those of Paul as
well; in the absence of material that can
be directly ascribed to Paul, the danger
cannot always be avoided, nor the dis-
crepancies in their opinions charted. For
a discussion of PR's turning down *Lulu
Belle,* see p. 83 and note 38, p. 595. Essie
found A. C. Barnes "completely impossible," though "dear" Eric Waldron came
home with them and "a lovely chat"
saved that particular day. A fair sample of
why Essie found Barnes impossible is in
the letter he wrote her the next day (April

1, 1926, RA), a high-flown, hectoring,
and patronizing discourse on "the negro
soul." Robeson had wanted to give Frank
Wilson's "Sugar Cane" first prize and
"Blood" second, but the other judges
preferred John Matthews's "Cruiter" for
second prize (as had Essie), reducing
"Blood" to third. They gave Zora Neale
Hurston an honorable mention (New
York *Herald Tribune,* May 2, 1926, New
York *World,* May 9, 1926).

44. ER Diary, May 8, 23, 30, June
4–15, 1926, RA. Block to CVV, postmarked Aug. 4, 1926, NYPL: Van
Vechten; Blanche Knopf to ER, n.d. (but
March 1926); CVV to ER, June 24, 1926,
RA. In late July, Paul went by himself to
spend a weekend in Brewster, New York,
with Fitzi and other Provincetowners (ER
Diary, July 31, 1926, RA); Malcolm Cowley to me, Nov. 5, 1982; Millia Davenport
to me, June 7, 1982; Slater Brown to me,
postmarked Dec. 18, 1982. In her letter,
Davenport recounted a sample set-to
about money that she once overheard between Paul and Essie: "Essie took care of
all money and doled out $5.00 a week
to Paul. Once he begged and begged
for more. Essie was obdurate. Finally
Paul said: 'Oh be all nigger—give me
$10.00' "; variants of that same exchange
have been told me by several others, and
also dated variously.

45. Tully had been a prizefighter
himself, and also a professional hobo; his
Outside Looking In is based on hobo le-
gends. Dazey, whose father had written
the famous melodrama *In Old Kentucky,*
had co-authored an earlier play, *Peter Wes-
ton.* The colorful lives of both men are
detailed in a *New York Times* article for
Oct. 10, 1926. Burns Mantle describes
the unsuccessful search for an actress to
play opposite Robeson in an article in the
New York *Daily News,* Oct. 17, 1926. According to Fredi Washington, it was the
producers' idea to change her name, for
reasons she never understood (phone interview, Feb. 22, 1987; Fredi Washington
[Bell] to me, March 4, 1987). Etta Moten
Barnett (phone interview, April 18, 1985)
is the source for PR and Fredi Washington's becoming "an item."

46. Phoebe Gilkyson to CVV, Oct.
15, 1926 ("audience walked out"); ER to

CVV and FM, postmarked Sept. 21, 1926; Steichen to CVV, n.d., NYPL: Van Vechten; CVV to Gertrude Stein, Sept. 30, 1926 (photos), printed in Burns, ed., *Letters of GS and CVV*. In his opening night telegram to PR, Frank Dazey cabled, "I cannot tell you how fine you have been in every way about this play. Your acting has been an inspiration. Your very presence has given all the rest of us strength" (RA). In retrospect, Essie blamed the failure on the rewrites done during rehearsals, turning the script into "a rather ordinary popular play" (ER, Ms. Auto., RA). One of the three Wilmington reviews was in fact laudatory, and the other two mixed, with PR winning high praise from all three (Wilmington *Morning News, Evening News,* and *Evening Journal*—all Oct. 1, 1926. New York *Telegraph,* Oct. 2, 1926 (subplot). *Mirror,* Oct. 7, 1926 (police; subplot); *Telegram,* Oct. 9, 1926; *Wall Street Journal,* Oct. 8, 1926; Percy Hammond's review is in the *Herald Tribune,* Oct. 7, 1926, Nathan's in *The American Mercury,* Dec. 19, 1926. Nathan's review was also contrary to the mainstream reaction in that he thought PR less than perfect; his performance was "picturesque" but "he permitted himself an occasional platform manner. . . ." Among the other leading reviewers, Brooks Atkinson (*The New York Times,* Oct. 7) found the play "cheap and meretricous," and he, too, modulated his praise of PR (he "gradually settles down to a revealing portrait," and, though "perhaps a trifle heavy in his meteoric, cloud-skimming role," did distinguish himself through his "artlessness"—"His own personality crosses the footlights without dilution"). E. W. Osborn (*Evening World,* Oct. 7) thought the play "a piece of theatrical sounding brass," and *Time* (Oct. 18) dismissed the "triteness" of the plot. More favorable evaluations (along with those by Hammond and Nathan) are in the *Evening Graphic* (Oct. 7) and the New York *Sun* (Oct. 7).

47. The reviews quoted on PR's performance are: New York *News,* Oct. 7, 1926 (Mantle), *Evening Graphic,* Oct. 7 ("truly great"), New York *American,* Oct. ("Samsonic"), *Morning Telegraph,* Oct. 7, 1926. *Life* (Oct. 28, 1926) thought he was slow to warm up (whereas *The New Yorker,* Oct. 16, 1926, oppositely, thought that in the climactic scene he "does an utmost which is yet not sufficient"). Alexander Woollcott thought the play "raucous, vehement, cheap, yet not unentertaining," but was one of those who welcomed Robeson's "pushing it aside" while he sang and who thought he towered in stature above the proceedings (*New York World,* Oct. 7, 1926).

48. Pittsburgh *Courier,* Nov. 6, 1926 ("child"); *The Era* (London), June 17, 1936 (PR's view).

49. Wilmington *Evening News,* Oct. 4, 1926 (Haiti); New York *Telegraph,* Nov. 28, 1926 *(Bosom);* Johnson, *Black Manhattan,* p. 207 *(Bosom).* Fania Marinoff thought only McClendon "any good": "Bledsoe had a magnificent part. But he got worse and worse" (FM to CVV, Jan. 17, 1927, CVV Papers, NYPL/Ms. Div.).

50. *Variety,* Feb. 2, 1927. The story of the Kansas City concert is in Roy Wilkins (with Tom Mathews), *Standing Fast: The Autobiography of Roy Wilkins* (Viking, 1982), pp. 71–72, and was confirmed to me in an interview with Aminda (Mrs. Roy) Wilkins, March 12, 1985. The same version is in Wilkins's Oral History interview at Columbia University, done in 1962 by William Ingersoll.

51. Wilkins, *Standing Fast,* pp. 71–72; interview with Aminda (Mrs. Roy) Wilkins, March 12, 1985.

52. *Call,* Feb. 18, 25, March 4, 1927. As late as 1932 PR told an interviewer, "Some people expect me to take up Italian opera. In fact, in Philadelphia the people of my own race won't come to hear me sing because I limit my programs to the Negro folk songs. They would pay to hear me sing opera but not the simple things" (New Bedford, Mass., *Mercury,* June 16, 1932).

53. ER, Ms. Auto., RA; ER to CVV, postmarked Aug. 14, 1927, Yale: Van Vechten.

54. The contract with Varney, dated "September 1927" (RA) had, compared with PR's earlier contracts, rather stiff restrictions on his right to do outside performances of any kind. Apparently there had been a row with James Pond when Robeson decided to do *Black Boy,* and he

had had to consult Arthur Garfield
Hayes—precipitating a break with Pond
and perhaps alerting Varney to the need
for binding terms (ER Diary, Jan. 26, Feb.
1, 1926, RA). ER to Frank Harris, Oct.
12, 1927, UT; ER to Gertrude Stein (one
note undated, the other dated Aug. 28,
1927), Yale: Stein; ER to James Joyce,
Oct. 13, 1927, PU: Beach; ER postcard
to CVV and FM, postmarked Sept. 5,
1927; PR to CVV, postmarked Aug. 18,
1927, Yale: Van Vechten; Patterson, *Genocide*, ch. 5; interview with Paul
Robeson, Jr. (March 3, 1984), for "in one
ear."

55. PR to ER, Oct. 16, 1927, RA.
56. Multiple interviews with Freda
Diamond; also letters and telegrams
courtesy of Diamond.
57. Multiple interviews with Freda
Diamond. Years later PR inscribed in the
copy of *Here I Stand* that he presented to
Ida Diamond, "To dear, dear Mama Diamond, with much, much love and many,
many thanks for your help and encouragement over the years" (copy courtesy
of Freda Diamond). The elevator episode
happened some time during the years
1928–30, when the Diamonds lived on
11th Street.

CHAPTER 7 *Show Boat (1927–1929)*

1. Stein to CVV, postmarked Oct. 26,
1927, printed in Burns, ed., *Letters of GS
and CVV*; Alberta Hunter diary, Oct 29,
1927, Hunter Papers, NYPL/Schm; *La
Presse*, Nov. 1, 1927; *Le Courrier Musical*,
Dec. 1927; *Comoedia*, Oct. 31, 1927; *The
New York Times*, Oct. 30, 1927; New York
Sun, Nov. 22, 1927; Baltimore *American*,
Nov. 19, 1927; *Daily Mail* (London), Oct.
31, 1927.
2. On the ms. of Seton's *Robeson*, PR
wrote, "In Paris at first concert I had a
severe cold and was a disappointment.
The second concert was a tremendous
success." ER to CVV and FM, Nov. 11,
1927 (quotes telegram), Nov. 17, 1927
(Stein's comment, as rephrased by Essie),
Yale: Van Vechten. Robeson and Stein
began to see each other with some frequency (PR to GS, two undated notes
[but late 1927]), Yale: Stein.
3. PR to ER, Dec. 10, 12, 1927, RA;
multiple interviews with Freda Diamond.
According to Jean Blackwell Hutson,
Essie's friend Hilda Anderson was with
her when Paul, Jr., was born and, according to Hutson, she and others tried frantically to locate Paul to tell him about the
birth of his son (interview with Jean
Blackwell Hutson, Sept. 21, 1983).
4. PR to ER, Dec. 10, 12, 1927, RA.
5. Ibid.
6. Montreal *Gazette*, Sept. 12, 1925
(singing in bathroom); New York *Graphic*,
Jan. 19, 1929 (Johnson); *The Afro-American*, Feb. 11, 1933; New York *Sun*, June

16, 1932 (in which Karl K. Kitchen advocates Robeson over Tibbett). *The New
York Times* panned the Křenek opera
(April 15, 1928). Essie saw the production of *Jones* at the Metropolitan twice,
describing it as "foul" and Tibbett as
"strutting, and cocky, and absurd" (ER
Diary, Feb. 8, 11, 1933, RA). Interview
with Alan Bush, Sept. 3, 1982 (PR's
voice); Bush, a professor in the Royal
Academy of Music from 1925 to 1978,
knew Robeson in the thirties and worked
with him in 1939 on the Festival of Music
for the People. For an additional discussion of Robeson and opera, see pp. 120;
179; 193; 245; note 43, p. 615; note 22,
p. 642.
7. PR to ER, Dec. 12, 1927, RA.
8. PR to ER, Dec. 12, 13, 1927, RA.
9. ER, Ms. Auto., RA; PR to Stein,
n.d. (February 1928), Yale: Stein; ER to
Larry Brown (hereafter LB), Jan. 8, 1928;
PR telegram to LB, Jan. 8, 1928, NYPL/
Schm: Brown. In late December, Essie
described her health as "at present . . .
about at zero" (ER to Lawrence Langner,
Dec. 22, 1927, Yale: Johnson).
10. ER to LB, March 20, 1928; PR to
LB, April 19, 1928, NYPL/Schm: Brown;
Ben Robeson, "My Brother Paul" (1934),
ms., RA; FM to CVV, Feb. 29, 1928
($500), CVV Papers, NYPL/Ms. Div.
Two years later, Robeson told the English writer Ethel Mannin "He would like
to have played the title role [of Porgy] but
it was generally considered that he was

too big to play a cripple" (Ethel Mannin, *Confessions and Impressions* [Jarrolds, 1931], p. 159).

In the comparative leisure time after Essie began to improve and before rehearsals for *Porgy* began, Robeson found time to sing at a birthday dinner for Oswald Garrison Villard, and to participate in a Provincetown Playhouse jubilee to celebrate its thirteenth birthday—and to try to raise money. He probably also went to Theodore Dreiser's for one of the informal at-homes the writer started in 1928; in inviting Robeson to drop by, Dreiser wrote, "Mostly, these days, when I get tired writing—I put on one of your records—Mt. Zion or Witness or Waterboy—and let your sympathetic voice revive my failing spirits" (Dreiser to PR, March 5, 1928, RA). For more on Dreiser and PR, see notes 34 and 35, p. 652; p. 281; and note 3, p. 665.

The motion-picture nibble involved Frank Dazey, co-author of *Black Boy*, and his screenwriter wife, Agnes Christine Johnson, in conjunction with the producing team of Asner and Rogers. Dazey warned Robeson, apparently because of his known preference for "art" over "commerce" (see PR to ER, pp. 111-12), to concentrate on ensuring that his first film would be "sound commercially. An 'artistic failure' may be all right on the stage, but it helps no one in pictures" (Frank Dazey to PR, July 9, 1928, RA; also Agnes Christine Johnson to ER, June 6, 1928, RA).

11. ER to LB, March 20, 1928, NYPL/Schm: Brown.

12. PR to LB, April 10, 19, 1928, NYPL/Schm: Brown.

13. PR to Amanda Ira Aldridge, n.d. (April-May 1928), NUL: Aldridge. *Empire News*, May 6, 1928 ("feast"); Agate, *Times*, May 7, 1928. After seeing Paul and Essie together, Ethel Mannin made a comment similar to the sentiment Paul himself had expressed to Aldridge: Essie "gives the impression of managing him as she might a big child who cannot look after himself; and he gives the impression of complete childlike submission to her management" (Mannin, *Confessions and Impressions*, p. 160). Among the dozens of reviews, the most prestigious of those

that expressed doubts about the show (but none about Robeson) include: *Daily Sketch, Star,* and the *Evening Standard*—all May 4, 1928—and *Queen,* May 19, 1928. John C. Payne, the European-based black singer who had known Robeson earlier (see p. 49; note 28, p. 582) and was to continue to play a role in his life (see p. 164), was hired as chorus master of *Show Boat* (John C. Payne, "Looking Back on My Life," *Negro,* ed. Nancy Cunard [London, 1934; reissued in New York by Negro Universities Press, 1969]). Robeson often attended and sometimes sang at Payne's open-house Sundays in London, a gathering place for European-based black artists.

Alberta Hunter has suggested (Sterner interview) that Robeson was "so powerful" in his role, "a little feeling of jealousy between the stars" developed, plus envy at the way "the carriage people would roll up and walk right up to Paul Robeson's dressing room"—the tension, she suggested, contributed to the closing of the show. Frank C. Taylor and Gerald Cook (*Alberta Hunter* [McGraw-Hill, 1987], p. 102) quote Hunter as saying that the only time Robeson's voice failed during the run of *Show Boat* was the night King George V and Queen Mary attended: "Paul started singing off-key and stayed off-key the whole night. Later he cried like a baby." She also made this poignant comment on his voice: "There was something about [it] . . . that was most alarming. Sometimes when he'd hum to himself, he'd sound like a moan, like the resonance of a bell in the distance."

14. New York *Amsterdam News,* Oct. 3, 1928; Pittsburgh *Courier,* Oct. 6, 1928; *Sketch,* May 10, 1928; *The New York Times,* April 15, 1928. Though Robeson in 1928 did sing the lyrics as written—"Niggers all work on the Mississippi"—by the thirties he had changed "Niggers" to "Darkies" and then, by the time of the film *Show Boat* in 1935, had substituted "There's an ol' man called the Mississippi; that's the ol' man I don't like to be." Freda Diamond says she suggested the change, "I'm tired of livin' and scared of dyin' " to "I must keep fightin' until I'm dyin' " (for its reception, see p. 214), but her second

suggestion for a substitution in lyrics had some unintended results. When Robeson first sang "You show a little spunk" (substituted for "You get a little drunk") in New York, it was greeted with tremendous applause—but in London with dead silence. Robeson later learned that to the English "spunk" means semen, and promptly changed the line again, substituting "grit" (multiple interviews with Freda Diamond). In regard to Robeson's changes in his lyrics, Oscar Hammerstein II is quoted as saying, "As the author of these words, I have no intention of changing them or permitting anyone else to change them. I further suggest that Paul write his own songs and leave mine alone" (New York *Age*, June 18, 1949). On the other hand, Dorothy Van Doren recalls Hammerstein's deep human sympathy with Robeson: "Well," she quotes Hammerstein as saying on television in response to a question about Robeson's having "turned Communist," "if I were a tall, handsome man, member of the All-American football team, Phi Beta Kappa from the University of Pennsylvania [sic], a world-famous actor and concert singer, and if I couldn't get a hotel room in Detroit, I don't really know what I'd do" (Lakeville *Journal,* Aug. 1972).

15. ER to CVV, June 14, July 8, 1928, Yale: Van Vechten; ER Diary, "May 1928," RA; A. J. P. Taylor, *Beaverbrook* (Simon & Schuster, 1972), p. 235. Lady Ravensdale's guests (as reported in the *Daily Sketch,* June 16, 1928) included the Duchess of Marlborough, Mrs. Samuel Courtauld, Mrs. Phipps (Lady Astor's sister), and Lord Allington.

16. Philip Sassoon to PR, June 28, 1928; Barry O'Brien (Wallace's agent) to PR, Aug. 13, 1928; Edgar Wallace to PR, Aug. 16, Nov. 12, 1928, RA; ER to CVV, June 14, July 8, 1928, Yale: Van Vechten. At the Prince of Wales's party, the press reported that the King of Spain had been "enormously impressed" with Robeson's singing, which was part of a general cabaret offered that evening (*Sunday Dispatch,* June 13, 1928). Robeson told a reporter (*Star,* Nov. 28, 1929) that he was "tremendously pleased at the prospect of starring in a Wallace play; he had thought

The Squeaker "really splendid." Except for the incidental wish expressed by two or three reviewers to hear Robeson in an expanded repertory ("It would be interesting to hear what the singer could do beyond the modest range of these Dixieland ditties" [*Daily Mail,* July 4, 1928], the notices of the Drury Lane concert were uniformly excellent. One stands out for raising the question "What is the secret of his mastery?" and for its provocative answer that the "trance" Robeson created in his listeners hinged on more than his greatness as an actor and a singer—"He is a great man, who creates the soul of a people in bondage and shows you its true kinship with the fettered soul of man. We became like little children as we surrendered to his magical genius" (James Douglas, in *Daily Express,* July 5, 1928).

17. ER Diary, "May 1928," RA.

18. I've pieced together the story of Robeson's Equity suspension from a combination of newspaper accounts and ms. sources. The latter will be cited in the notes that follow, but the newspaper accounts are too numerous, and I've drawn from them too piecemeal, to bear individual citations; suffice it to say that the most important are: New York *Amsterdam News,* Sept. 12, 19, 1928; New York *World,* Sept. 5, 18, 25, October 4, 1928; *Equity,* Sept. 1928; London *Times,* Oct. 4, 1928; *Variety,* Oct. 17, 1928; and *Star* (London), Oct. 3, 1928.

19. ER to CVV, Aug. (?), NYPL/Ms. Div.: Van Vechten; quotes from the conference with Gillmore are in "The Tangled Affairs of Paul Robeson," *Equity,* Sept. 1928; ER cable to PR, Aug. 26, 1928, RA.

20. PR, undated cable, RA; *Equity,* Sept. 1928. Langston Hughes may have played some role in the affair, judging from two oblique references in his letters to Van Vechten: "I may have to see Mrs. Reagan" (LH to CVV, Aug. 18, 1928); "I hope Mrs. Reagan really puts on a show" (LH to CVV, postmarked Aug. 28, 1928)—both in the NYPL/Ms. Div.: Van Vechten. Hughes had been working on lyrics and sketches for a Reagan revue at least as early as 1926 (see Arnold Rampersad, *The Life of Langston Hughes* [Ox-

ford, 1986], vol. I, especially pp. 133, 135, 154).

21. New York *Amsterdam News*, Sept. 19, 1928; Walter White to PR, Sept. 20, 1928, RA.

22. "Law Report," Oct. 3, London *Times*, Oct. 4, 1928; the settlement papers are in RA; ER to CVV and FM, Aug. 5, 1929, Yale: Van Vechten.

23. Ethel Mannin, *Confessions and Impressions*, p. 160.

24. Fred and Adele Astaire to "Mr. and Mrs. Robeson," n.d. (1928), RA (the entire note reads: "We would love to come to your party"); Chicago *Defender*, Jan. 5, 1929; CVV to Stein, Nov. 27, 1928, printed in Burns, ed., *Letters of GS and CVV;* Walpole to ER, Nov. 27, 1928, RA; CVV to ER, Dec. 12, 1928, RA.

25. Kahn's registered letter, Dec. 21, 1928, went astray and had to be traced; Otto Kahn to ER, Dec. 18, 1925 (lapse), ER to Kahn, Jan. 20, 1929, RA.

26. ER to Otto Kahn, Jan. 21, 1929, PU: Kahn.

27. Otto Kahn to ER, Feb. 1, June 15, 1929; ER to Kahn, Jan. 21, March 12, May 23, Oct. 7, 1929—all in PU: Kahn (as is a series of letters between the offices of Kuhn, Loeb and Co. and Metropolitan Life detailing the payment of Robeson's life-insurance premium).

28. Bromley to Otto Kahn, Jan. 31, 1931; ER to Kahn, Dec. 21, 1931, PU: Kahn. Tony Salemmé told me he thought Kahn had been "very mean" in asking them to pay back the loan (interview with Salemmé, March 31, 1983).

29. ER to Otto Kahn, Jan. 21, 1929, PU: Kahn; ER to LB, Feb. 15, 1929, NYPL/Schm: Brown. When he first opened in *Show Boat,* Robeson had been worried, not about his own possible boredom but about how to keep the repetitive rendering of "Ol' Man River" from becoming monotonous for the audience. When Essie arrived in May, she had helped him work out a "nice variety" of delivery (ER to CVV, June 14, 1929, Yale: Van Vechten).

30. ER to Larry Brown, March 6, 1929, NYPL/Schm: Brown; ER to Otto Kahn, May 23, 1929, PU: Kahn (Vienna, Prague). A full set of the Vienna, Prague, and Budapest reviews is in RA; the

Vienna reviews frequently referred to him as the "Coloured Mitterwurzer"—an allusion to the famous Viennese interpreter of folk songs. The flavor of Robeson's press reviews in Central Europe is accurately captured in the description Essie sent Kahn: "I am sure you would think I was exaggerating if I told you what the finest critics in the German, Austrian, Czech, Hungarian newspapers said about his production, the beauty of his voice, and his great artistry, so I would rather you read them yourself" (ER to Kahn, May 23, 1929, PU: Kahn).

31. PR interview with R. E. Knowles, Toronto *Daily Star*, Nov. 21, 1929 (African-Russian); Seton, *Robeson,* pp. 48–49 (poverty).

32. ER to Kahn, Jan. 21, 1929, PU: Kahn. PR told Ethel Mannin that the echo in the Albert Hall "worried him and when I asked him if he did not think it a dreadful, dreary place, he laughed and agreed" (Mannin, *Confessions and Impressions,* p. 159).

33. ER to CVV, postmarked June 4, 20, 1929, Yale: Van Vechten; CVV to ER, June 16, 1929, RA; CVV to Knopf, June 25, 1929, UT: Knopf. I have, as it turns out, inadvertently confirmed my agreement with CVV's estimate of ER's first draft by referring to it in these notes as "ER, Ms. Autobiography"—a form of citation I've decided to retain as illustrating my own view of it, though the ms. is in fact the first draft of her biography of PR. The contracts, along with considerable correspondence about editorial changes, are in RA. See pp. 139–40 for the effects the published book had on Robeson.

Van Vechten seems to have avoided making further comments on Essie's ms. (ER to CVV and FM, Dec. 6, 1929, March 25, 1930, Yale: Van Vechten). After Alfred Knopf turned the book down, Essie decided not to bother Van Vechten again about trying to place it, sending it out herself to other publishers. She also decided not to pursue an offer Van Vechten had made to write a preface to the book (ER to Otto Kahn, May 23, 1929, PU: Kahn; ER to CVV and FM, March 25, 1930, Yale: Van Vechten). She instead asked Eugene O'Neill, who turned her down: ". . . I long ago, in self-defense, made an absolute rule to write no introductions under any circumstances. . . . I know you will understand" (O'Neill to ER, April 10, 1930, RA). The book appeared without an introduction. (Additional correspondence on the subject, especially between ER and her editor at Harper and Brothers, Eugene F. Saxton, is in RA.) In summarizing the twists and turns, Essie gracefully let Van Vechten off the hook: "But Carlo, my dear, it would take more than a book—or two books—to make me quarrel with you. My friends are my friends, no matter what they do—or don't do" (ER to CVV and FM, March 25, 1930, Yale: Van Vechten).

34. The canceled film contract, dated Feb. 28, 1929, is in RA; Frank Dazey to PR (1929), RA; Louella O. Parsons's syndicated column for June 17, 1929, Denver *Post;* ER to CVV and FM, Aug. 5, 1929, Yale: Van Vechten; Nerina Shute, "Robeson Talkie Search," *The Film Weekly,* vol. 2, no. 45 (Aug. 26, 1929). The British producer Herbert Wilcox was interested in making a film with Robeson and tried, among other possibilities, to get the rights to *The Emperor Jones*—but O'Neill refused to relinquish them. Avery Robinson was also involved with PR in trying to put together a film project (AR to PR, Sept. 19, 1929, RA).

35. ER to Otto Kahn, Oct. 7, 1929, PU: Kahn; ER to Larry Brown, March 15, 1929, NYPL/Schm: Brown (dentistry); Sir George Henschel to PR (scheduling voice lessons), Oct. 13, 1929, RA. During these months Essie supervised their move (in late March 1929) from St. Johns Wood to a house in Hampstead, priding herself on her ability to locate the best shops and the best prices (interview with Rebecca West, Sept. 1, 1982; interview with Fredda Brilliant, July 20, 1985).

36. Philip Merivale to PR, June 6, 1928 (Othello offer); Merivale to ER, June 22, 1928; Maurice Browne to PR, Feb. 14, 1929, RA; PR to Maurice Browne, Oct. 6, 1928, Browne and Van Volkenburg Papers, University of Michigan Labadie Collection (henceforth UM: Browne/Van Volkenburg). Browne had had the financial backing of Dorothy Straight and Leonard Elmhirst (the innovative couple who had founded Darting-

ton Hall), and they were his partners in the theater purchases as well (Michael Young, *The Elmhirsts of Dartington* [Routledge and Kegan Paul, 1982], pp. 217–19; interview with Michael Straight, April 3, 1985). *Daily News* (London), Sept. 4, 1929 (contract); ER to Stella Hanau, Sept. 10, 1929, courtesy of Richard Hanau ("very excited"). "We all feel that it will be a great event," Essie wrote to Kahn (ER to Kahn, Oct. 7, 1929, PU: Kahn). Ten years later Merivale again approached PR about an *Othello* production, with himself as Iago (Merivale to PR, Feb. 17, 1940, RA). Robeson told a reporter that Othello was "one role I have always wanted to play. . . . This may be because most of the Othellos I have seen, with blacked faces, have been unsatisfactory to me" (*Lantern,* Ohio State University, Dec. 13, 1929).

When *The New York Times* announced that Robeson's portrayal of Othello would "probably" mark the first time a black had done the role, James Weldon Johnson wrote the *Times* to say the news came as a surprise to a group of American blacks who had "recently subscribed $1,000 to endow a memorial chair in the Shakespeare Memorial Theatre" at Stratford to Ira Aldridge, who had played the role in London and on the Continent, with Edmund Kean (among others) playing Iago (JWJ to The Editor, *Times,* Sept. 6, 1929).

37. Interview with PR, Ceylon *Morning Leader,* Sept. 13, 1929 ("illiterate"); reports of the protest meeting, as well as PR's letter, were widely printed in the English press; among the fullest accounts are: *African World,* Nov. 21, 1929; Manchester *Guardian,* Oct. 23, 1929; Liverpool *Post,* Oct. 30, 1929. Long accounts also appeared in the American press, including *The New York Times* (Nov. 17, 1929) and the *Herald Tribune* (Oct. 29, 1929), from which the quote from PR about "ignoring" the incident comes.

38. Seton, *Robeson,* pp. 50–52; *The New York Times,* Nov. 18, 1928 (PR visit to Commons), Oct. 24, 1929 (Hughes), Nov. 17, 1929 (other cases of discrimination; hotel reactions); Knoblock to PR, Oct. 22, 1929, RA. In Feb. 1929 the Robesons had been guests of the Na-

tional Labour Club, Ltd., of which the Rt. Hon. J. Ramsay MacDonald was president (Fred O. Roberts to PR, Feb. 19, 1929, RA). The Robesons' solicitor, Philip Cox, personally conducted an inquiry at the Savoy and reported to the Robesons that the manager of the Grill Room "denies having spoken to you at all and he says that so far as he is aware no one referred to a colour bar or to any restrictions whatsoever!" (Cox to PR, Nov. 8, 1929, RA.)

39. *Contender,* Oct. 28, 1929; *New Leader,* Oct. 25, 1929.

40. PR Diary, Nov. 8, 1929, RA.

41. PR Diary, Nov. 9, 10, 1929, RA. Among the unfavorable critical responses to his Nov. 5 Carnegie Hall concert, Pitts Sanborn (New York *Telegram,* Nov. 6, 1929) found "excessive reserve" in PR's performance and suspected "there has been some unhappy tinkering with a naturally easy tone production"; Noel Straus (New York *Evening World,* Nov. 6, 1929) thought PR showed "a decided loss of bloom and power" and also denigrated the program as "too little differentiated in treatment"; Samuel Chotzinoff (New York *World,* Nov. 6, 1929), perhaps the most scholarly of the critics, based his objections on technical matters, on PR's inability to vary his "tone color and musical artifice." The far more favorable reception of the second (Nov. 10) Carnegie concert was exemplified by *The New Yorker*'s review (Nov. 16, 1929)—though *The New Yorker*'s critic sounded a cautionary note that was frequently heard:

". . . it is a pity for an artist of Mr. Robeson's gifts and intelligence to appear only as an intoner of racial airs." Among the few unfamiliar songs Robeson added to his repertoire was "Exhortation" by the black composer Will Marion Cook—but of all the numbers on the program, that one fared the worst with the critics; ". . . it has a hollow and artificial ring" was one representative comment (Detroit *Evening Times,* Dec. 7, 1929). "Exhortation" was again excoriated—this time by English critics—when Robeson performed it on his 1930 tour of the British Isles (Birmingham *Post,* March 9, 1930; Yorkshire *Post,* March 15, 1930).

42. Pittsburgh *Courier,* Dec. 7, 1929; Chicago *Herald and Examiner,* Dec. 10, 1929; Rutgers concert program with ER's handwritten comments ("college yell"); Toronto *Musical Courier,* Dec. 7, 1929.

43. *Evening News* (London), July 19, 1928.

44. PR Diary, Nov. 10, 12, 1929, RA. ER to CVV and FM, Dec. 6, 12, 26, 1929, Yale: Van Vechten. Among the highlights of the two months in the States were a reunion with many of the Provincetowners at a kind of vaudeville show (in which PR participated) to raise money to sustain their recent move to the Garrick Theatre ("Fitzi" to PR, Nov. 21, 1929, RA; Arthur L. Carns to Otto Kahn, Nov. 25, 1929, PU: Kahn), and a midnight buffet supper at the Otto Kahns' at which the guests danced till daybreak (Seattle *Times,* Dec. 14, 1929, report of the party).

CHAPTER 8   *Othello (1930–1931)*

1. "R.L." to PR, Feb. 22, 1930, RA; *Musical Courier,* April 5, 1930 (Paris); interview with PR, *Radio Times,* April 18, 1930 (agreement about orchestra).

2. Manchester *Guardian,* March 17; Glasgow *Herald,* Feb. 18; *Daily Express,* March 11, 1930. Other papers registering complaints included the Eastbourne *Gazette,* July 24; *The Times,* Feb. 14; the *Daily Telegraph,* Feb. 17; the Bristol *Evening Times,* Feb. 26, all 1929; and the Newcastle *Weekly Chronicle,* March 15, 1930. The single most scathing (and prestigious)

negative came from Ernest Newman, who wrote in the *Sunday Times* (May 5, 1929) that the spirituals "mostly bore me almost to tears," insisting their current vogue could be explained by "causes external to music *qua* music—a sentimental background of emotion derived from our nineteenth century religiosity, dim childhood memories of Uncle Tom and Topsy," etc.—and took Robeson to task for exercising his gifts on such "wretched material."

3. Interview with PR, *Radio Times,*

April 18, 1930 (Slavs); ER Diary, Jan. 18, 21, 24, 1930, RA. Paul Bechert reported in the *Musical Courier* (March 15, 1930) that Robeson's return to Vienna had been "a feast for all," and that Robeson was given "a royal welcome."

4. *Musical Standard*, March 22, 1930 (Polish musician); Glasgow *Citizen*, March 3, 1930 (Scottish); *Observer*, Feb. 16, 1930 (Dahomey; trip to Africa); Edinburgh *Evening Dispatch*, March 8, 1930 (talkie). While in Edinburgh, the Robesons saw Joe Washington, a young black from Brooklyn Paul knew, who was studying medicine at Edinburgh University (ER Diary, March 9, 1930, RA; also, Washington to PR, Jr., Jan. 26, 1976, RA).

5. By far the fullest account of the history and impact of *Borderline* is Anne Friedberg's Ph.D. thesis, "Writing About Cinema: Close Up, 1927–1933," New York University, Oct. 1983. Thomas Cripps, *Slow Fade to Black* (Oxford University Press, 1977), has also been useful, as was my interview with the film historian Jay Leyda on May 26, 1985.

6. Friedberg, "Writing About Cinema"; Cripps, *Slow Fade;* R. H. (Robert Herring, one of the core group of *Close-Up*–Pool writers), "Filming with Paul Robeson," Manchester *Guardian*, May 22, 1930.

7. Kenneth Macpherson to ER, Dec. 26, 1929 (scenario), Feb. 12, 1930 (acting); Macpherson to ER, March 16, 1930 ("not sustained"), RA.

8. ER Diary, March 20–29, 1930, RA. H. D.'s biographer, Barbara Guest, has identified as Robeson the character Saul Howard in "Two Americans," a story H. D. wrote in 1930: "His least movement was so gracious, he didn't have to think things out. Nevertheless with an astonishing analytical power, he did think. . . . He had a mind, a steadfast sort of burning, a thing that glowed like a whole red sunset or like a coal mine, it was steady, a steady sort of warmth and heat, yet all the time intellectual; he thought not as a man thinks. Paula Howard, his wife, thought more as white folks, consistently, being more than half white" (Barbara Guest, *Herself Defined: The Poet H. D. and Her World* [Doubleday, 1984], pp. 198–99).

9. ER to CVV and FM, March 16, 20,

27/8 (Montreux), 29, April 22, 1930, Yale: Van Vechten; Bryher to ER, May 26, 1930, RA. Gavin Arthur seems to have stood outside the general friendliness; Bryher thought him "rather lost and silly," though "nice under all" (KM to PR and ER, n.d. [April/May 1930], RA). Herring, "Filming with Paul Robeson" (honey bees, etc.); Bryher, *The Heart to Artemis* (Harcourt, Brace, 1962), pp. 250, 262. The good feeling all around is exemplified in the subsequent letters they sent each other. "We missed you so much," Bryher wrote Essie, and Macpherson wrote Paul, ". . . thanks for the great week, about which we still grow maudlin on the set, putting on Robeson discs, and pretending it's him in person at the piano!" (Bryher to ER, April 7, 1930; Macpherson to PR, n.d. [April 1930], RA.) H. D. wrote Essie (n.d., RA), "We talk of you still just as if you left yesterday."

10. In my own viewing of the film, I was struck by Essie's strength and assuredness—and by her powerful gaze. Ultimately Bryher gave the acting palm in the film to Blanche Lewin, "a retiring gentlewoman from the British colony whom we called Mouse," who in her opinion stole the show (Bryher, *The Heart to Artemis*, p. 262).

11. ER to A'Lelia Walker, April 8, 1930, courtesy of A'Lelia P. Bundles; ER to Eugene F. Saxton, n.d., RA ("Russian-German"); Bryher, *The Heart to Artemis*, p. 250 (*Joyless Street*); Bryher to ER, May 26, July 1 ("very enthusiastic"), 23 ("exhibition positives"), Aug. 31, 1930, RA; Macpherson to PR and ER, Aug. 9, 1930 (talkie), RA; ER to CVV and FM, Aug. 3, 1930, Yale: Van Vechten; H. D. to ER, May (?) 1930 ("art"), RA. Initially Macpherson had planned to have a private showing of the completed film for press and friends, and Bryher wrote to Essie "wondering whether it would be possible—without involving great expense—to get a small Negro orchestra for the one performance?" (May 2, 1930, RA.)

12. H. D. to ER, Feb. 10, 1931, RA; *Evening Standard*, Oct. 20, 1930; *Bioscope*, Oct. 25, 1930.

13. ER to Light, Feb. 18, 1930; Light to ER, two undated letters (Feb.-March

1930), RA; *The New York Times,* May 25, 1930 (Trask); ER to CVV and FM, March 25, April 22, 1930, Yale: Van Vechten. I am grateful to Christine Naumann of the Paul-Robeson-Archiv, Akademie der Künste, East Berlin, who during my research trip to the GDR sat with me to summarize and translate the 1930 Berlin reviews of *Jones;* the specific citations quoted from the Berlin critics come from *Neue Berliner Zeitung,* April 1, 1930, and *Berliner Volkszeitung,* March 31, 1930. O'Neill wrote Essie, "Jimmy told me Paul knocked them dead! I am tickled to death. I knew darn well he would" (O'-Neill to ER, April 10, 1930, RA). Dr. Robert Klein, head of the Kuenstler Theater, gave a luncheon_for the Robesons which the playwright Ferenc Molnár and his actress wife, Lili Darvas, attended; Molnár failed to pass Essie's critical muster— "he's an ass," she wrote in her diary (April 1, 1930, RA), "conceited, abnormal, vulgar, a glutton," though she found Darvas "lovely-looking, very distinguished, aristocratic, intelligent."

14. ER to A'Lelia Walker, April 8, 1930, courtesy of A'Lelia P. Bundles: (Wooding); *Daily Express,* June 4, 1930 ("colour bar"); New York *Herald Tribune,* June 15, 1930 (gateway). The *Daily Herald* (Nov. 23, 1923) carried a shortened version of the *Daily Gleaner* interview (Oct. 31, 1932) headlined "Paul Robeson Looks for a Negro Mussolini."

15. New York *American* (May 12, 1927) is among the newspapers that reported on PR's ORT concert; the *Jewish Tribune* (July 22, 1927) is among the papers that printed a statement by PR linking the spirituals with Old Testament inspiration. Passing through Poland on their 1930 trip, the Robesons met an Austrian Jew who was a Rumanian subject; while serving for two years in the Rumanian Army, he told them, "they made him a servant, beat and kicked him, and . . . they are really terrible to the Jews. . . . Poor fellow" (ER Diary, Jan. 22, 1930, RA). For the plight of the Welsh miners, see Arthur Horner, *Incorrigible Rebel* (Macgibbon & Kee, 1960), pp. 103ff.

16. PR to Browne, Oct. 6, 1928, UM: Browne/Van Volkenburg ("afraid"); Browne, "My Production of *Othello,*" *Ev-*eryman, May 15, 1930; Maurice Browne, *Too Late to Lament* (Gollancz, 1955), p. 323 (itched); *Daily Express,* May 21, 1930. Hannen Swaffer, the influential *Daily Express* columnist, who knew Robeson personally, offered an intriguing anecdote about the reaction Paul and Essie had to *Jew Süss:*

"Paul Robeson and his wife had one of their little arguments.

"The only thing I found them disagreeing about, hitherto, was Marcus Garvey, the Negro spell-binder, who was in London not long ago. Paul believes in him. His wife does not.

"It was when they saw 'Jew Süss,' however, that the other argument began. When they came out Mrs. Robeson said, 'Now, don't agree with me this time. I hope you do not think what I thought.'

"'I thought that Peggy Ashcroft ought to play Desdemona,' said Paul.

"'That is what I thought,' said his wife, 'but I hoped you would not see it.' That is how Peggy was chosen."

Outside of this brief mention by Swaffer, there is no other evidence that I have found of PR's having any interest in Marcus Garvey (see note 36, p. 623). Swaffer, of course, may have gotten it wrong. In her unflattering portrait of him, Ethel Mannin accuses him of being "savagely intolerant" toward blacks and, specifically, "patronising" toward Robeson (*Confessions and Impressions,* pp. 153–56). Interview with Dame Peggy Ashcroft (PR, Jr., participating), Sept. 9, 1982 (hereafter Ashcroft interview); and a four-page typewritten memoir of the production which Dame Peggy kindly prepared for me, Aug. 1984 (hereafter Ashcroft Memoir).

17. ER Diary, April 15, 16, 1930, RA; ER to Van Volkenburg, n.d. (May 1930), UM: Browne/Van Volkenburg.

18. Ashcroft interview, Sept. 9, 1982; Ashcroft Memoir, Aug. 1984.

19. Ashcroft interview, Sept. 9, 1982; *Daily Sketch,* May 21, 1930 (kissing); *The New York Times,* Jan. 16, 1944 ("clumsy"). "This in itself made it more than a theatrical experience, it put the significance of race straight in front of me and I made my choice of where I stood" (Ashcroft Memoir, Aug. 1984).

20. Ashcroft interview, Sept. 9, 1982.

21. Ashcroft interview, Sept. 9, 1982; Ashcroft Memoir, Aug. 1984; ER Diary, May 13, 1930, RA.

22. *Daily Telegraph,* May 20, 1930 (skirt dance). *Time and Tide,* May 31, 1930 (spiritual); the "terrific row" was told by PR to Vernon Beste and described in a letter from Beste to Ann Soutter, May 14, 1985, courtesy of PR, Jr.

23. Agate, *Sunday Times,* May 25, 1930. The reviewer for *West Africa* (May 24, 1930) took particular exception to Robeson's costume, pointing out that when he was finally allowed to wear the flowing white Moorish robes in the last scene, he not only looked but also sounded his best; Ashcroft Memoir, Aug. 1984 (Richardson); Ashcroft interview, Sept. 9, 1982 (costume).

24. ER Diary, May 19, 20, 1930, RA; *The World* (New York), May 21, 1930 ("started off"); *Illustrated London News,* May 31, 1930 ("little to recommend"); *Truth,* May 28, 1930 (Browne). Browne and Van Volkenburg were additionally drubbed in the *Evening Standard,* the *Daily Mail,* the Manchester *Guardian,* the *Daily Telegraph*—all May 20, 1930; *The Saturday Review,* May 24, 1930; *Everyman,* May 29, 1930; *Time and Tide,* May 31, 1930; and *Sphere,* May 31, 1930. Hannen Swaffer recorded a touching episode in his *Variety* column (June 4, 1930): "I think Paul performed a very kindly act the other night. He called to see me at my flat to ask me to say that the actor who played Cassio [Max Montesole] had been unfairly criticized by some of the critics, who did not know that his part had been cut on the afternoon of the performance, and that, indeed, he had been going out of his way for days to help Robeson, perhaps to the detriment of his own job." Swaffer also reported that "One London editor walked out during *Othello* because there were Negroes around him in the stalls."

25. *Week-End Review,* May 24, 1930 ("great"); *Daily Mail,* May 20, 1930 ("magnificent"); *Evening News,* May 20, 1930 ("remarkable"); *News of the World,* May 25, 1930 ("prosaic"); *Daily News,* May 20, 1930 ("disappointing"); *Christian Science Monitor,* June 2, 1930 ("losing"); *The New Statesman,* May 24, 1930 ("kindly"); *Reynolds News,* May 25, 1930 ("great soldier"); *Time and Tide,* May 31, 1930 ("inferiority complex"); *Country Life,* May 31, 1930 (arrogance); *The Lady,* May 29, 1930 ("affinity"). Also *The Tatler,* June 4, 1930: "the Moor was not an Ethiopian." Two additional examples of laudatory reviews are the *Daily Telegraph,* May 20, 1930 ("a fine presence, a beautiful voice") and *The New Yorker,* June 21, 1930 ("a great personal triumph for Paul Robeson"). As *The New Yorker*'s summary comment indicates, the New York press reported capsule versions of the London reviews and, surprisingly, leaned with inaccurate one-sidedness to the positive view of Robeson's reception (e.g., *Herald Tribune,* May 21, 1930). Moreover, the American critics who attended the performance praised him more fully than did their English counterparts (e.g., G. W. Bishop, *The New York Times,* May 20, 1930; *Christian Science Monitor,* June 2, 1930; Richard Watts, Jr., New York *Herald Tribune,* May 29, 1930). *Pearson's Weekly,* April 5, 1930 (PR's view of play). It's possible that *Pearson's* misrepresented PR's views of the play. Either that, or his views soon evolved. In two subsequent statements he sounded less ambivalent. "There are very few Moors in Northern Africa without Ethiopian blood in their veins," he told *The Observer* (May 18, 1930), and in a radio broadcast in June entitled "How It Feels for an American Negro to Play 'Othello' to an English Audience," he asserted, "In Shakespeare's time . . . there was no great distinction between the Moor and the brown or the black. . . . Surely most of the Moors have Ethiopian blood and come from Africa, and to Shakespeare's mind he was called a blackamoor. Further than that, in Shakespeare's own time and through the Restoration, notably by Garrick, the part was played by a black man" (as reported

in the New York *Herald Tribune,* June 8, 1930).

26. *Daily Express,* June 4, 1930 (liberating); ER Diary, May 20, 1930, RA; ER to CVV and FM, May 29, 1930, Yale: Van Vechten. CVV to ER, June 22, 1930, RA ("Paul's performance is still with us"); CVV to Knopf, June 27, 1930, UT: Knopf; CVV to Johnson, June 21, 1930, Yale: Van Vechten. Essie had gotten hold of a pair of opening-night tickets for the Van Vechtens—"All London is trying to buy them"—but they couldn't get over in time (ER to CVV and FM, March 25, 1930, Yale: Van Vechten). Du Bois to ER, July 10, 1930, RA.

Roger Quilter congratulated PR on his "great achievement" (Quilter to PR, June 22, 1930, RA). Aldous Huxley wrote that, after seeing his "beautiful and illuminating performance," he often found himself thinking back on it "with the most profound satisfaction" (Huxley to PR, July 5, 1930, RA). The writer William Plomer was so moved by his "splendid Othello, in spite of the handicap of bad costume and lighting," that he was "hardly in a fit state" to come backstage (Plomer to PR, May 21, 1930, RA). The explorer Vilhjalmur Stefansson was a bit more backhanded in his compliment— "Shakespeare is stilted and hard to believe but you got more out of your part than any actor whom I have seen" (Stefansson to PR, July 6, 1930; RA)—and Bryher was downright truculent: "I see no reason for acting Shakespeare now. Still I forgot these very strong views whenever I was listening to Othello last week and they only emerged into consciousness during the other sections of the play. I hope this is a road to your working in plays linked to modern consciousness." Bryher also reported in her letter that she had "had a severe shock over Bantu." She had begun studying the language but had found it "far worse than Chinese. . . . No wonder Negro Music has evolved such wonderful forms. If you have nine declensions and they are all differentiated by TONES what else is to be expected? I am abandoning sadly all attempts at Bantu" (Bryer to PR, May 26, 1930, RA).

In retrospect at least, Peggy Ashcroft

was one of the enthusiasts of Robeson's performance. Given the fact that he "had to endure great difficulties," she feels "his performance was indeed very, very memorable" (Ashcroft interview, Sept. 9, 1982). "He was a natural and instinctive actor, with imagination, passion and absolute sincerity, and those factors made up for what he lacked in technique" (Ashcroft Memoir, Aug. 1984).

27. Browne, *Too Late to Lament,* p. 323; *Time and Tide,* June 7, 1930; *Morning Post,* June 18, 1930 (salary); ER to CVV and FM, May 29, 1930, Yale: Van Vechten. *Othello* drew large audiences on its brief tour, due in part to reduced prices (*Sunday Express,* Oct. 13, 1930). ER Diary, May 13, June 3, 1930 (Harris), RA; *The New York Times,* June 8, 1930 (Harris); *The Film Weekly* (England), June 7, 1930 (film). A telegram from Walter White to PR in RA, March 25, 1930, apparently at the behest of Harris, conveyed the offer, adding, "Miss Carrington, who coached Barrymore, to coach in Diction." Noel Sullivan, the wealthy San Franciscan liberal who was a sometime patron to Langston Hughes and who Robeson and Larry Brown had stayed with during their 1931 cross-country stop-over in San Francisco, was apparently also involved in efforts to bring Robeson's *Othello* to the U.S. (PR telegrams to Sullivan, Feb. 14, March 13, April 14, 1931, Noel Sullivan Papers, Bancroft Library, University of California, Berkeley [henceforth BLUC]).

28. *The New York Times,* May 22, 1930; *Times Enterprise* (Thomasville, Ga.), May 27, 1930; Ashcroft interview, Sept. 9, 1982; interview with PR in the Leeds *Mercury,* Nov. 21, 1930: "In New York one is quite safe, but touring the country one visits spots where shooting is a common practice."

29. ER Diary, June 10, July 7, 1930, RA; ER to CVV and FM, July 8, 1930, Yale: Van Vechten. Apparently there was also talk of filming *Othello,* but Robeson turned Browne down on that score. "He feels," Essie wrote Browne, "as I do, that a film will be made forever, and all its faults will mock us in the future, and so he must be careful. . . . He says his performance must be much better than it is now for a permanent record, and I think per-

34. ER Diary, Sept. 1, 1930 (discovery of letter), "October, 1930" ("bitch"), RA; Ashcroft interview, Sept. 9, 1982; Ashcroft Memoir, Aug. 1984. According to Marie Seton (in a letter to me, Nov. 23, 1982), when Essie discovered that Paul had given Ashcroft a piece of jewelry, "she went straight out and bought herself (charging it to P) a far more expensive jewelry item." On three different occasions Essie had expressed her admiration for Ashcroft to the Van Vechtens (ER to CVV and FM, March 25, April 22, May 29, 1930, Yale: Van Vechten). Within six months of discovering the letter, and having had a chance to recover her equilibrium, Essie sent Ashcroft a good-luck telegram for a theatrical opening, and Ashcroft responded with a thank-you note expressing the hope that "I may come & see you one day" (Ashcroft to ER, March 7, 1931, RA). When she subsequently met Essie a few times during the mid-thirties, Essie was gracious to her—and Ashcroft was shocked to hear from me of the bitter things Essie had recorded about her at the time in her diary. When Ashcroft later saw PR in the 1950s and 1960s, their meetings were cordial and warm (see pp. 478–79, 507).

35. ER Diary, "October, 1930," RA. When a newspaper reporter asked Robeson what would happen if his vocation came into conflict with his "duty to his family," Robeson is quoted as replying, "Then my family must suffer." "That's rather hard saying," the reporter replied. "It is," Robeson said. "But it's the truth. The artist gives joy to hundreds of thousands, perhaps to millions. He consoles, he inspires. He must consider his responsibilities to this multitude rather than to those few" (*Daily Herald*, July 11, 1930).

PR opened his one-man show at the Savoy in late Aug. 1930, with Max Montesole playing the Cockney role in *Jones.* It was not well received by most of the critics; they complained that the first act of *Jones* did not successfully stand alone (*The Star*, Aug. 26, 1930; *Everyman*, Sept. 4, 1930; *Sunday Dispatch*, Aug. 31, 1930), that a "modernist" London theater like the Savoy was an inappropriately "sophisticated" setting for the spirituals (*The Times*, Aug. 26, 1930), and that Robeson

haps he is right" (ER to Browne, June 28, 1930, UM: Brown/Van Volkenburg). For a more positive view of Browne, see Maurice Evans, *All This . . . and Evans Too!* (University of South Carolina Press, 1987); in reference to the 1930 *Othello*, Evans merely comments, "the less said about that the better" (p. 43).

30. PR to Ellen Van Volkenburg, n.d. (June/July 1930), UM: Browne/Van Volkenburg; Ashcroft interview, Sept. 9, 1982.

31. ER Diary, June 12, 30, July 2–9, RA; ER to PR, pencil draft (Nov. 1931), RA.

32. Eslanda Goode Robeson, *Paul Robeson, Negro* (Victor Gollancz Ltd., London, 1930 [published in the United States by Harper and Brothers]). The dedication of the book reads "For Our Son." William Soskin's review, the New York *Evening Post,* June 25, 1930 ("bitter"); also W. Keith in *The Star,* May 20, 1930; and *The Observer,* March 23, 1930. Rose C. Field in *The New York Times* (July 13, 1930) wrote that "In the light of literature, this book will not cast lengthy shadows but as a homely picture of a colorful individual it has much to recommend it." Langston Hughes in the New York *Herald Tribune* (June 29, 1930) spent most of his review recounting recollections of Robeson and then ended simply by saying, "Mrs. Robeson has written a chatty, informing and naively intimate book that couldn't have been bettered by the best press agent."

33. ER, *PR, Negro,* pp. 132–34. The omitted phrase is in "Changes in Manuscript" sent by ER to her publishers. The woman friend was identified in the English version as "Martha Sampson," and in the American version as "Marion Griffith"—but was in fact Martha Gruening, sister of Ernest Gruening (later Senator from Alaska). The name changes came about because Gruening, having originally agreed to be quoted, subsequently decided the section put her in an indelicate light, denied the authenticity of the account, and threatened legal action if necessary. To avoid that, Essie substituted the pseudonyms. The dispute is summarized in ER to Saxton, May 8, 1930, RA.

did not sing lieder well (*Evening Standard,* Aug. 26, 1930). During the ten-week tour of the provinces that followed the Savoy opening, Robeson attempted considerable experimentation with the format. He dropped the lieder, added some Stephen Foster songs, tried substituting a one-act play by Stanley Houghton, *Fancy Free,* and, toward the end of the tour, seems to have turned to a full-scale vaudeville format, including a ventriloquist, "feats of strength by the Three Cressos," an impressionist, and a dancing sequence by Marinek and Constance. None of these experiments met with much favor, though the reviews of the tour were somewhat better than those at the Savoy (Birmingham *Post,* Oct. 21; Birmingham *Mail,* Oct. 21; Sheffield *Independent,* Oct. 28, 1930; ER to CVV and FM, Sept. 2, 1930, Yale: Van Vechten).

36. PR to ER, Sept. 29, 1930, RA.

37. ER Diary, "October, 1930," RA.

38. The evidence for Yolande being a sometime actress is from Rupert Hart-Davis to me, June 6, 7, 1987, and in John Payne to Larry Brown, June 3, 1945 (NYPL/Schm: Brown): reporting on a visit from Yolande, Payne wrote, "She looks very well, has been with the 'Erisa' Concert party doing Shakespears [sic] plays. . . ." Ironically, Ashcroft first met Robeson through Yolande's brother, Richard (a barrister who was later with Scotland Yard and was knighted in 1963)—he and Ashcroft's husband, Rupert Hart-Davis, were good friends. She only met Yolande once and had no clear impression of her (Ashcroft interview, Sept. 9, 1982; Ashcroft Memoir, Aug. 1984; Ashcroft to me, Nov. 10, 1987). The one time Fania Marinoff met Yolande Jackson, she described her as "very lovely" (FM to CVV, July 18, 1932, CVV Papers, NYPL/Ms. Div.). Essie's prior knowledge of the affair with Yolande is evident in a cryptic reference in her diary on the day she found the Ashcroft letter: "Found a letter from Peggy at the flat. Exactly like the one from Yolande last year. . . . I dare not think of it till I get away from here—my nerves are too far gone" (ER Diary, Sept. 1, 1930, RA). Alberta Hunter's description is in an interview with Sterner; Rebecca West's comments are in an interview with me, Sept. 1, 1982. Marie Seton, in our interviews of Aug./Sept. 1982, added a few details. Seton met Yolande once or twice in the early thirties; she found her uncommunicative and politically conservative. Seton's point of contact with Yolande was Gwen Hammond, a Canadian whose father was proprietor of the *Fortnightly Review* and who had acted in a play with Yolande. Hammond's impression "was that Paul was really profoundly in love with Yolande."

39. Interviews with Uta Hagen, June 22–23, 1982 ("great love"); ER to CVV and FM, Dec. 19, 1930, Yale: Van Vechten; ER Diary, Dec. 27, 1930, RA; ER to Grace Nail Johnson (Mrs. James Weldon), Dec. 19, 1930, Yale: Johnson. The breakdown must have been immediate; as early as Sept. 8, 1930, Essie wrote to Harold Jackman, "I have been very ill with a nervous breakdown" (Yale: Johnson).

40. The Robesons had first met Noel Coward in 1926, when they went backstage after seeing his play *The Vortex:* "The play was trash," Essie wrote in her diary, "but he emanated a sweetness and personality right over the footlights" (ER Diary, Jan. 30, 1926, RA). ER to CVV and FM, Dec. 19, 1930, Yale: Van Vechten. Judging from the half-dozen letters from Jean Forbes-Robertson to the Robesons, they had a polite, rather distant friendship. Forbes-Robertson later married André Van Gyseghem, who within a few years was to be Robeson's director.

41. ER Diary, Dec. 27, 1930, RA.

42. ER Ms. Auto., RA ("Frederick Douglass"); interview with G. Foster Sanford, Jr., April 12, 1983. Bricktop, in her autobiography, claims that at the urging of C. B. Cochran, the English theatrical producer, she told Paul that he would be "ruined if he'd married that white Englishwoman"; "I don't know if I influenced him or not," she writes, "but a few years later Essie told her, "Bricky, thanks so much. You saved my life" (*Bricktop,* pp. 128–29). For more on Bricktop, see note 4, p. 618.

43. At a showing of the film *Hallelujah,* Essie decided to let the "very attractive Frenchman" who happened to sit

next to her caress her hand and then place it on his thigh until, breathing heavily, he had an orgasm. "I thought I would see just what these nudging men do," Essie wrote in her diary—"It was remarkable." ER Diary, Dec. 28, 1930–Jan. 25, 1931, RA; ER to CVV and FM, postcard, Jan. 26, 1931; ER to CVV and FM, Feb. 4, 1931, Yale: Van Vechten (illnesses). The night before Paul left for the States, he and Essie went to see Josephine Baker at the Casino de Paris. "She is as beautiful as ever," Essie wrote in her diary (Dec. 20, 1930, RA), "beautiful body, but is doing the same things she did five years ago. [For more on Baker and the Robesons, see p. 93 and note 8, p. 754]. The show was cheap dirty and stupid, and we were profoundly bored. We could only sit through half the show." While Essie was in Paris, Clarence Cameron White, director of the School of Music at Hampton Institute, played her parts of his opera about Haiti, *Owanga*. Two years later, White wrote to Robeson about the possibility of his playing the role of Dessalines in the opera, offering to rewrite it "to suit your voice" (C. C. White to PR, Oct. 10, 1932, RA). Shortly before, Essie had heard the score of *Owanga* played and thought it "marvellous, thrilling, and wonderful rhythm" (ER Diary, Sept. 27, 1932, RA).

44. CVV to ER, Jan. 12, 1931, RA (Carnegie); ER to LB, March 7, 1931, NYPL/Schm: Brown. Judging from the programs in RA, PR added the following "art songs" (as the press called them) to his repertory: Beethoven's "Die Ehre Gottes," Mozart's "O Isis," Schumann's "Two Grenadiers" and "What Care I Now," Purcell's "Passing By," Borodin's "A Dissonance," and Gretchaninov's "The Captive."

45. "R. W." [Roy Wilkins], "Talking It Over," Kansas City *Call*, Feb. 13, 1931; Wilkins, *Standing Fast*, p. 104 ("bumpers") PR to ER, Jan. 27, 1931, RA. Earlier, Robeson had also complained to Ethel Mannin that interviewers "get it all wrong" when he talked to them (Mannin, *Confessions*, pp. 158–59). The promoters of the Kansas City concert found themselves short of Robeson's guaranteed fee of two thousand dollars per concert.

Robeson, not wanting to disappoint the audience, finally insisted on singing (Pittsburgh *Courier*, Feb. 21, 1931). Robeson stayed with the Fairfax family in Kansas City, who often played host to visiting black artists (since hotels wouldn't take them). He took time to listen to a talented young woman, Etta Moten, sing for him in the Fairfax living room and encouraged her to continue with her career (she later toured for years in the role of Bess in *Porgy and Bess*, and became the wife of Claude Barnett, head of the Associated Negro Press). Comparing vocal ranges with Etta Moten, he said to her, "I only have an octave, but it's the right octave" (phone interview with Etta Moten Barnett, April 18, 1985).

46. ER Diary, Dec. 15, 1930, RA (birthday). There are several short notes from Coward to ER in RA, none revelatory.

47. PR to ER, Jan. 27, 1931, RA; CVV to ER, Jan. 12, 1931, RA; ER to CVV and FM, Dec. 19, 1930, Feb. 4, 1931, Yale: Van Vechten.

48. *Harlem Home Journal*, April 11, 1931; ER Diary, March 4–April 14, 1931, RA. In her diary Essie refers to possibly having a gynecological procedure performed in New York (for the pertinent entry, see note 15, pp. 578–79). In regard to her friendship with Noel Coward, Essie wrote, "We had begun back in December in London, when I was all upset with Paul. Noel Coward had been marvelous to me, had come often to the flat to talk with me, dine with me, and I had been out with him. . . . When Paul finished his tour of the provinces and came into town, Noel invited him to the theatre with me and out to supper afterwards. We had a lovely talk, and Paul was impressed" (ER Diary, April 18, 1931, RA). After 1931, Essie's friendship with Coward cooled, but she did go backstage after seeing *Design for Living* in New York in 1933 and recorded that she and Coward had "a nice chat" (ER Diary, Feb. 13, 1933). I have found no evidence of a sexual affair. Graham Payn, Coward's longtime lover and the editor of his diaries, which start in the 1940s, has gone through the earlier material and recalls no reference to Essie Robeson (phone interview with Payn,

Sept. 3, 1982). Nonetheless, the oblique reference in PR's letter (Jan. 27, 1931, RA) leaves the matter in doubt.

49. ER Diary, April 15, 1931, RA; ER to PR, "pencil draft," Nov. 1931, RA; ER to CVV and FM, April 20, 1931, Yale: Van Vechten; ER to Grace and James Weldon Johnson, April 18, 1931, Yale: Johnson.

50. *Era* (London), May 27, 1931 (rehearsals); ER Diary, May 10, 1931, RA. O'Neill first had the idea of PR's doing Yank (Light to ER, n.d.; O'Neill to ER, April 10, 1930, RA) and was enthusiastic enough about it to make sure the Gate Theatre in London, which had done an earlier production of the play, did not revive it at a time and in a manner that might conflict with Robeson's production (O'Neill to Bright, June 12, 1930, UCLA: Bright).

51. A mixed review for Robeson appeared in *New Age*, May 21, 1931, and the two negatives were in *The Lady* (never a fan of Robeson's), May 21, 1930, and the *Sun Dispatch*, May 17, 1930: "Cannot Paul Robeson control that lovely voice of his? If he uses it as abandonedly in the future as he did on Monday night, it means that every part he takes will seem like the tragedy of an opera singer, who has missed his vocation, rather than the author's conception of any other human character." The *Graphic* comment on his physique is in May 23, 1931. The many negatives for the play include *The Times*, May 12, 1930; the *Daily Express*, May 12, 1930; *Stage*, May 14, 1930; *News-Chronicle*, May 12, 1930; *Star*, May 12, 1930 ("splendidly vital"); "racial consciousness"); also on the racial dimension, *Daily Express*, May 12, 1931; *Morning Post*, May 12, 1931; *Star*, May 12, 1931; *Reynolds News*, May 17, 1931; *Sunday Times*, May 17, 1930 ("expressionism"); ER Diary, May 11, 1931, RA.

52. ER to CVV and FM, May 23, 1931, Yale: Van Vechten.

53. Ethel A. Gardner to LB, May 21, 27, 1931, NYPL/Schm: Brown; ER Diary, May 15, July 27, 30 (Gambs), 1931, RA; *Daily Herald*, May 22, 1931 (no acting); *Daily Express*, May 11, 1931 (repertory theater); *The Observer*, May 10, 1931

(Africa, Russia). An editorial in the *Evening Standard* (May 22, 1931) expressed concern over Robeson's announced plans to sing Russian music: "Something more than mere voice or even the greatest artistry is required. For to sing a gypsy song one must be able to interpret the longings and desires of a highly complex, if somewhat savage, nation."

54. ER to PR, "pencil draft," Nov. 1931, RA. In her Guggenheim application (RA), Essie described her purposes in going to Africa as a wish to study "the relation between the modern American Negro and the African, and to learn [to] how great an extent our original racial characteristics have been submerged by western culture and transplantation. I hope to find material for a Negro-African play and novel."

55. ER to LB, March 7, 1931, NYPL/Schm: Brown.

56. ER to CVV and FM, Sept. 6, 1931, Yale: Van Vechten (PR's concerts); ER to Grace Nail Johnson, Sept. 6, 1931, JWJ Papers, Yale (Africa); ER Diary, June 11 (hemorrhage), June 15 (nursing home), Aug. 19 (ill), 1931, RA; PR to Dr. Lowinger, Aug. 5, 1931, RA. Essie described living arrangements in Kitzbühel, and also Pauli's governess, in detail in ER to Noel Sullivan, Sept. 29, 1931, BLUC. Essie left for Austria on Aug. 7. Judging from the full schedule she maintained between Aug. 5 and 7, it seems unlikely she had an abortion while still in London. After entering the sanatorium in Austria, she wrote in her diary (Aug. 19, 1931), "They know what its all about!"—implying, though not specifying, an abortion. One suggestion that she and Paul slept together is in her diary, June 17, 1931, which reads, "Paul came to dinner, and we had a very pleasant afternoon. He remained all night, and we had a delightful talk about many things." She saw Michael Harrison with particular frequency (ER Diary, June 2, 11, 18, 21, July 25, Aug. 5, 1931, RA).

PR's occasional concerts during these months did not meet with notable favor, though he did some further experimenting—including readings from the "Uncle Remus" stories, using local trios to perform instrumental music, adding a few Russian songs, and continuing to sing some lieder. In regard to the latter, *The Observer*'s critic (Oct. 4, 1931) commented: "Sterner control over rhythm is needed in these more formal songs. The improvisatory method of the spiritual is not stable enough to give them complete expression." On the other hand, Ethel A. Gardner sent Larry Brown encouraging reports of the tour—good houses, with Paul "improving all the time" (EG to LB, July 14, 1931, NYPL/Schm: Brown; also June 18, 30, July 6, 21, 28, Aug. 14, 25, Sept. 8, 15, 21, Oct. 1, 6, 12, 23, 27, 1931). Gardner made some new records with Robeson (including "Daniel") and accompanied him during six radio broadcasts, arranging some new songs for him.

57. PR to ER, Aug. 27, 1931, RA; ER to CVV and FM, Sept. 6, 1931, Yale: Van Vechten; ER Diary, "September 1931," RA; ER to Grace Nail Johnson, Sept. 6, 1931, Yale: Johnson.

58. PR to Freda Diamond, Sept. 7, 1931, courtesy Diamond; ER Diary, Oct. 5, 7 (divorce), 28 (Ashcroft), 1931, RA.

59. ER Diary, Nov. 8 ("strangely"), 10 ("degenerating"), 1931, RA.; EG to LB, Oct. 10, 1931, NYPL/Schm: Brown (cancellation). Robeson gave the Albert Hall concert a month later, but it was not well received. The *Daily Sketch* (Dec. 14, 1931) complained that he seemed "in difficulty with his upper notes," and *The Times* (Dec. 14, 1931) felt "Mr. Robeson's voice was not in its best condition." (EG to LB, Oct. 10, 1931, NYPL/Schm: Brown).

60. ER to PR, "pencil draft," Nov. 1931, RA.

61. Robeson had employed Andy at least as early as 1930 (ER Diary, "October, 1930," RA). They probably met through Larry Brown; in any case, the Andy–Larry Brown friendship predated the Andy-Robeson one (Andrews to Helen Rosen, May 15, 1967, courtesy of Rosen). Helen Rosen confirms that Essie "hated" Andy and strongly suspected that he arranged many of Robeson's assignations (multiple interviews with Rosen). For more on Andy, see pp. 476, 496.

62. ER to PR, "pencil draft," Nov. 1931 RA. Edwina Mountbatten's biographer records that she was "extremely fond" of "Hutch" (Leslie Hutchinson) and gave him "a gold cigarette case engraved with her name and a loving message, and it would have been extraordinary for Leslie Hutchinson not to show this with some pride to his friends" (Richard Hough, *Edwina, Countess Mountbatten of Burma* [Weidenfeld and Nicolson, 1983], p. 125).

63. ER to PR, "pencil draft," Nov. 1931, RA.

64. Ibid.

65. ER Diary, Nov. 29, 1931, RA; ER to CVV and FM, Dec. 20, 1931, Yale: Van Vechten.

66. ER Diary, Dec. 5, 8, 10, 23, 29, 30, 1931, RA. For *Uncle Tom's Cabin* she tried to enlist Larry Brown as composer, and hoped to interest Jerome Kern and Ziegfeld (ER to LB, March 7, 1931, NYPL/Schm: Brown).

CHAPTER 9   THE DISCOVERY OF AFRICA *(1932–1934)*

1. New York *Sun, Times, Herald Tribune*—all Jan. 19, 1932; New York *Post*, Jan. 28, 1932 (Russian); Goldman to Berkman, Feb. 5, 1933, IISH (courtesy of Paul Avrich); ER Diary, Jan. 20, 1932, RA ("keen").

2. Boston*Globe*, Jan. 27, 1932 ("excellent"); Boston *Herald*, Jan. 27, 1932 ("untutored"); Des Moines *Register*, Feb. 5, 1932 ("blues"); PR to CVV, postcard, postmarked Feb. 5, 1932, Yale: Van

Vechten; *Gazette* (Montreal), Feb. 29, 1932.

3. Prince Touvalou to ER, April 27, 1932, RA (Guitry); Jannett Hamlyn to Larry Brown, May 21, 1932, NYPL/Schm: Brown (Guitry); ER Diary, March 15, 22, 25, April 8, 1932, RA; ER to George Horace Lorimer, May 6, 1932; ER to Brown, March 7, 1932, NYPL/Schm: Brown. Essie completed *Uncle Tom's Cabin* in May, showed it to various

friends (including Buddy Herring and Tony Butts), who encouraged her, and sent it in mid-May to the Theatre Guild, to Cochran, the London producer, and to Fox Films in New York (ER Diary, March 17, April 3, 4, 11, 18, 28, 29, May 17, 23, 1932, RA). ER to CVV, June 2, 1932, Yale: Van Vechten *(Uncle Tom)*. At around the same time, Essie got rather daunting news from her editor at Harper & Brothers, Eugene F. Saxton, who let her down gently about the "ineffectiveness" of her novel, *Black Progress*, which she had submitted to him. Essie then tried to persuade Saxton that it was really intended as a "travel book" about Harlem, not as a novel, but when he dutifully reread it in that light, his judgment remained negative. She accepted the final rejection in good spirits and even with magnanimity, writing Saxton that he was "a peach" for having responded so thoughtfully and in so much detail (Saxton to ER, March 28, May 5, 1932; ER to Saxton, April 10, May 17, 1932, RA).

4. ER Diary, April 8, May 27, 31, June 4, 6, 25 (journalism), 1932, RA. ER, Ms. "I Believe in Divorce" (from which the first quotation comes) and "Divorce," both in RA. During her trip to Paris, Essie met and got friendly with Bricktop, the singer–nightclub owner. Bricktop told her she had expected not to like her, since "she heard I didn't bother with niggers, and was high hat," but in fact they "got on beautifully." Bricktop sent her car to take Essie out to her house at St. Cloud a few days after they first met and ended up, according to Essie, "thick as thieves" (ER Diary, June 10, 13, 17, 1932, RA). On another trip to Paris, a few months later, Essie met Marcel Duchamp through the actress Rita Romilly, saw him nearly every day during her week-long stay, and suggested in her diary that the two had been romantically drawn to each other (ER Diary, Sept. 26, 29, Oct. 1, 2, 4, 1932, RA).

5. N.Y. *Daily Mirror*, May 2, 1932. The *Mirror*'s story was widely circulated: e.g., New York *Amsterdam News*, May 4, 1932; Philadelphia *Tribune*, May 5, 1932. Cunard's stylish part of the story is stylishly told in Anne Chisholm, *Nancy Cunard* (Knopf, 1979), pp. 194–96.

6. The *Daily Mirror* story of May 2, 1932, does not, in fact, quote Robeson at all—let alone use the word "insult"; Cunard to PR, Dec. 10, 1930 (*Negro* invitation), May 2, 1932 ("amazing"); Dabney to Schomburg, May 5, 1932; McKay to Schomburg, June 15, 1933; Smith to Schomburg, May 7, 1932, NYPL/Schm. Albert A. Smith was, along with Henry O. Tanner, one of two blacks in the American Professional Artists League (Paris). The anonymous threat to Cunard, signed "X22" and dated May 2, 1932, is in UT: Cunard.

7. *Daily Mirror*, May 20, 1932; *The New York Times*, May 20, 1932; New York *Herald Tribune*, May 20, 1932; Ferber to Woollcott, as quoted in *The Portable Woollcott* (Viking, 1946), pp. 162–63; James Weldon Johnson to PR, June 2, 1932, Yale: Johnson. Ferber told much the same opening-night story to the Robesons themselves (ER Diary, Jan. 5, 1932, RA), saying it was "one of the great moments in the theater, for her."

8. ER Diary, May 31, 1932, RA; *The New York Times*, June 26, 1932 ("ennui"); New York *American*, June 26, 1932 ("separation"); *Sunday News*, June 26, 1932 ("leave forever").

9. ER Diary, June 22, July 9, 1932, RA; interviews with Marie Seton, Aug./Sept. 1982. The black press covered the proceedings fully: Chicago *Defender*, July 2, 1932; New York *Amsterdam News*, Oct. 26, 1932; Pittsburgh *Courier*, July 2, 1932; New York *Age*, July (?) 1932. A summary of the libel hearing is in the *Star* (London), July 8, 1932. Lord Mountbatten's most recent biographer, Philip Ziegler, who has had access to the family's private papers (including Edwina's diary; the quote from the diary in the text is taken from Ziegler, p. 114), wholly dismisses the veracity of the story (Ziegler, *Mountbatten* [Knopf, 1985]). But if Edwina Mountbatten had "never met" Robeson when she wrote that claim in her 1932 diary, she met him very soon thereafter. John Krimsky, coproducer of the film version of *The Emperor Jones*, came to London to talk with Robeson early in 1933 and, on going to his suite at the Dorchester, where he was entertaining, was introduced to Robeson's guests—among

them, he distinctly recalls, Lord and Lady Mountbatten (John Krimsky, "The Emperor Jones—Robeson and O'Neill on Film," *The Connecticut Review*, April 1974, pp. 94–99). Further confirmation that Edwina Mountbatten and Robeson were acquainted, despite the denial in her private diary, comes from Edwina's biographer, Richard Hough. "Their friendship was widely known in Society," Hough writes, "and many people today remember him at Brook House parties" (*Edwina*, p. 124). But Hough includes no documentation for his statement, and his chief—perhaps sole—source seems to have been Marie Seton. Hough also insists (though again without citing evidence) that Edwina instituted the suit only because of pressure from the Palace, was herself "outraged at the whole business, its covertness, hypocrisy and censoriousness," "never forgave the Palace," and "was virtually barred from the Court during the remainder of George V's reign" (p. 127). For a followup on Edwina and Robeson, see note 37, p. 727. Right in the midst of these proceedings, the unflappable Essie went to see Peggy Ashcroft perform in *The Secret Woman*. "Peggy is definitely a good actress," she wrote in her diary (June 25, 1932, RA).

10. FM to CVV, July 18, 1932, CVV Papers, NYPL/Ms. Div.; ER Diary, July 11, 1932, RA; ER to CVV, July 13, 1932, Yale: Van Vechten.

11. PR to ER, Aug. 2, 1932, RA. PR's Rutgers citation is in RA. He called the honorary M.A. in 1933 "the greatest hour of my short life"—it was the first time Rutgers "had paid such a tribute to an artist, black or white, and I was certainly the youngest man Rutgers had ever chosen for such a distinction" (PR in *John Bull*, May 13, 1933). His *Show Boat* broadcast and Lewisohn Stadium appearance were widely reported: e.g., *Brooklyn Eagle*, June 12, 1932 (broadcast); *World-Telegram*, Aug. 1, 1932 (Sanborn), *Musical Courier*, Aug. 6, 1932.

12. PR to ER, Aug. 2, 1932, RA; *Telegraph*, June 28, 1932 (Aid Society); *The New Yorker*, Aug. 5, 1932 (Duranty).

13. ER to Jackman, Aug. 30, 1932, Yale: Van Vechten; ER to CVV and FM, Dec. 20, 1931, Yale: Van Vechten; ER

Diary, March 17 (Woolf), 25 (Teichner), 1932, RA; A. O. Bell, ed., *Diary of Virginia Woolf* (Hogarth Press, 1982), vol. IV, pp. 84–85.

For more on Plomer (a considerable figure in English literary circles), see A. O. Bell, ed., *Diary of Virginia Woolf*, vol. IV, pp. 84–85; P. N. Furbank, *E. M. Forster: A Life* (Harcourt, 1977), pp. 178–79; *Autobiography of William Plomer* (Cape, 1975).

There were other indications of ER's mounting interest in Africa: ER to George Horace Lorimer, ed. of the *Saturday Evening Post*, May 6, 1932, RA, suggesting a series of articles on the Negro, including several on Africa; ER Diary, Feb. 25, May 21, 25, 1932, RA—including letting her hair go "native" (ER Diary, March 4, 1932, RA). Yet when Barrett Brown, the principal of Ruskin College at Oxford, asked her to have a look at an African student who had had a mental breakdown, Essie described her as "pure nigger in every possible way; no trace of refinement or culture, awful hair, smelled, was untidy, domineering, and completely impossible. I told the authorities frankly that I thought she was too primitive for their kind of education, culture and civilization and thought the strain of trying to live up to it had been too great, and I thought the best thing was to send her straight back to Africa, among her own people" (ER Diary, Feb. 21, 1932, RA).

14. PR to ER, Aug. 2, 1932, RA; ER Diary, June 6–13 (fittings), Sept. 16, 1932, RA; PR to Larry Brown, n.d. (1932?), NYPL/Schm: Brown.

15. ER Diary, Sept. 27, Oct. 7, 8, 12, 15, 23, 1932, RA; Jannett Hamlyn to Larry Brown, Nov. 15, 1932 (engagement), NYPL/Schm: Brown; Nancy Wills to me, Dec. 11, 1983; Pat Gregory (Stitt) to me, Oct. 18, 1985 (lost nerve). Though Seton (interviews, Aug.-Sept. 1982) urged on me with some insistence that Yolande's father disliked people of color, Rupert Hart-Davis, who was actually a guest in the Jackson house frequently in the late twenties and early thirties, has written me (June 30, 1987) that "although old Jackson never appeared until dinner in the evening, when he wore a

cloth cap and a dressing-gown, he must have known that black visitors frequently came. It is the only house I've ever been in where there seemed to be *no* colour-bar." According to Marie Seton, the Jackson family enlisted the help of Frank Benson (of the famed Benson Shakespeare Co.) to help break up the romance. Benson, in turn, solicited the help of the actor Henry Ainley in the effort to discredit Paul with Yolande. Ainley's recent *Hamlet* in London had not been a success—Gielgud's *Hamlet* being much preferred by the critics—and, according to Seton, Ainley agreed to help out of "unadulterated, green-eyed jealousy" of Paul (whom he didn't know personally) for having been successful playing Othello. (The back-to-back *Hamlet*s had been performed in London in the spring of 1930. The Robesons saw them both. Essie thought Ainley "dreadful" and Gielgud "fine" [ER Diary, April 25, May 7, 1930, RA]). In a follow-up comment to our interviews, Seton wrote me, "Paul was *vulnerable* to hurt because he was more sincere than sophisticated" (Seton to me, Nov. 23, 1982). Rupert Hart-Davis, however, once again disputes Seton's account. He feels it is "certain" that Yolande "wouldn't have consulted her parents" if she had been contemplating marriage to Robeson (Hart-Davis to me, June 30, 1987). Moreover, if Robeson knew of the role Frank Benson purportedly played in alienating Yolande, it did not keep him from attending a luncheon over which Benson presided to celebrate the fortieth anniversary of the old Temple Shakespeare and to inaugurate the publication of the new version (*Morning Post* [London], April 28, 1934). According to Pat Gregory (Stitt) [see note 43 for more on her], "Paul told me he had actually left home expecting that they would go away together. . . . He took it hard" (Stitt to me, March 5, 1985). In Dec. 1932, less than three months after their breakup, Essie recorded in her diary that Yolande had telephoned "and said that if Paul wasn't in Paris that night [where Yolande was], she would catch a plane over to London. So I helped Paul pack a bag, gave him all my cash, and wished him Godspeed" (ER Diary, Dec.

6, 1932, RA). Three weeks later she wrote, "We discussed Yolande at great length, and I advised him how best to get her off his back" (ER Diary, Dec. 31, 1932, RA). It may be that was just the impression Paul wished Essie to have about his feelings for Yolande.

16. ER Diary, Oct. 29 (stop divorce), Nov. 2, 3, 7, 8, 20 (new life), 22, 24, 26, 28, 30, Dec. 1, 2, 1932, RA; interviews with Marie Seton, Aug.-Sept. 1982; multiple interviews Freda Diamond; Nancy Wills, *Shades of Red* (Communist Arts Group [Australia], 1980), p. 91; Nancy Wills to me, Dec. 11, 1983. Even later, writing in *Freedom,* Robeson described how "one day I heard one of these Aristocrats talking to his chauffeur in much the same way as he would to his dog. I said to myself, 'Paul, that is how a southerner in the United States would speak to you'" (Ms. dated Feb. 23, 1949, RA).

17. The quotes are from Payne to Brown, April 19, 1950, May 17, 1950, Yolande Jackson to Payne, May 13, 1950, NYPL/Schm: Brown. Other letters in the correspondence from Payne to Brown are dated Dec. 20, 1932, June 3, 1945, Feb. 2, 1947, June 3, 5, 1949, March 26, 1950, April 17, 19, May 12, 19, 1950, June 12, July 5, 1950—all in NYPL/Schm. Payne was seventy-eight years old in 1950 and had taken to writing somewhat in shorthand; I have made minor grammatical and punctuation changes to make the quotations readable.

18. The four letters from Yolande Jackson to Larry Brown in NYPL/Schm: Brown are dated July 10, 1949 (Monte Carlo); Sept. 5, 1950 (Sussex); n.d. (Sussex, 1950?—"stolen hours"); n.d. (London, 1950—"rules are hard").

19. Jackson to Rockmore, April 22, 1950, RA (the only Yolande Jackson letter in RA); Jackson to Brown, n.d. (1950), NYPL/Schm: Brown.

20. Rupert Hart-Davis to me, June 6, 7, 1987, enclosing four letters from Yolande Jackson to him (March 24, April 8, 11, 29, 1953), from which the quotations have been taken. Among the Yolande Jackson–Larry Brown letters in NYPL/Schm, hers are postmarked "Worthing," and thereby hangs one last installment of the Yolande Jackson story. An old friend

of mine, Terence Higgins, has long been the member of Parliament from Worthing. When I discovered the Worthing postmark, I enlisted Terry's help in trying to track down Yolande Jackson's later history. After digging up the deed for "50 Broomfield Avenue, Worthing," Terry reported back that Yolande Chervachidze had indeed lived there with her parents and a sister—but not a husband—until they sold the house in 1955. Rupert Hart-Davis, however, doubts if Yolande ever lived with her parents as an adult, though in her "wild, wandering life" it may have been "an asset to have one fixed address"—and so she used the Worthing one as long as her family owned the house there (Hart-Davis to me, June 30, 1987). Terry Higgins's wife, Rosalyn (my still older friend), and their son Daniel nobly joined the search, looking through Public Records Office materials, trying to discover Yolande's later whereabouts. But their search yielded no further information. In a last-ditch effort, I hired the genealogist Michael S. de L. Neill to try to find current members of the Jackson or Chervachidze clans. He did locate Lady Richard Jackson—who denied me additional information on Yolande, saying "all that was in the past"—but otherwise came up empty-handed.

21. ER to LB, Dec. 24, 1932, NYPL/ Schm: Brown; ER Diary, Dec. 15, 25, 1932, RA; ER interview with T. R. Poston, New York *Amsterdam News*, Feb. 8, 1933. Essie told Poston that she and Paul were once again "terribly happy" together. She also made (unless Poston misquoted her) some obtuse remarks about the current economic depression: "In London many people who have enjoyed large fortunes and estates have lost almost everything. They are being forced to move into small quarters, and are constantly worried by the lack of space and other inconveniences. But do they talk about it—lament aloud? Of course not. But here, everyone talks about the depression. We who are only a generation removed from the washtubs—and who can go back to the tubs if need be—are loudest in our lamentations. Over there, the situation is much worse. Lady So-and-so cannot very well apply for a job as someone's maid." Essie seems not to have followed through with her plans to take acting and playwriting courses, though there is one mention in her diary (Feb. 24, 1933, RA) of taking "my first private lesson at the Repertory Theatre, with Mr. and Mrs. Gellendre . . . one in improvisation, and one in lines. Think I did well. I was surprised at myself, and interested."

22. PR, "Notes: December 5, 1932," RA; Manchester *Guardian*, Nov. 14, 1932.

23. PR, "Notes: 1932," RA ("favorite part"); Malcolm Page, "The Early Years at Unity," *Theater Quarterly*, vol. 1, no. 4 (Oct.-Dec. 1971); André Van Gyseghem, "British Theatre in the Thirties: An Autobiographical Record," *Culture and Crisis in Britain in the Thirties*, ed. Clark, Heinemann, Margolies, and Snee (Lawrence and Wishart, 1979), pp. 209–18. Van Gyseghem went on to have a distinguished theatrical career as both actor and director. He remained firmly pro-Soviet in his views until his death in 1979. ER to CVV and FM, Dec. 25, 1932, Yale: Van Vechten; Sterner interview with Van Gyseghem; my interview with Flora Robson (PR, Jr., participating), September 1982.

24. Sterner interview with Van Gyseghem; my interview with Robson (PR, Jr., participating) September 1982; *The Observer*, March 19, 1933. A wide spectrum of the British press wrote in comparable terms ("the most superb exhibition of histrionics that London has seen for years": *Daily Express*, March 14, 1933). Flora Robson received no negative reviews, Robeson only a few: *The Spectator*, March 17; *Sketch*, March 22, *The Lady*, March 23. On the other hand, O'Neill fared poorly. Among the many reviews that called his play to task, the Manchester *Guardian*'s is representative: "It is not a well-made play, and its first half is seriously inadequate."

25. The film was produced by John Krimsky and Gifford Cochran and directed by Dudley Murphy (best known for his work on the Bessie Smith vehicle *St. Louis Blues*). The contract, with Krimsky and Cochran, dated Feb. 24, 1933, is in RA, *Screenland*, Oct. 1933. Fritz Pollard, the black football star and an old friend of Robeson's, had a tiny part in the film,

assisted Krimsky in casting, and served as Robeson's dresser. *Jones* also had J. Rosamond Johnson as musical director and an able supporting cast that included Dudley Digges, Fredi Washington, Frank Wilson, and Ruby Elzy. DuBose Heyward was hired to write an opening segment for the film designed to provide background events leading up to the point where O'Neill's play began, prompting the *New Statesman* critic later to write, "The people who made this film would adapt *King Lear* to show you the birth of each of his three daughters, or *Hamlet* to show his father and mother courting" (*The New Statesman*, clipping date illegible, 1933), ER to CVV, postmarked June 24, 1933, Yale: Van Vechten. According to Krimsky, considerable pressure was put on him and his partner, Gifford Cochran (like Krimsky, twenty-five years old), to cast Lawrence Tibbett in the leading role, but Eugene O'Neill made it clear that he would give them the film rights only if Robeson was cast in the part (Krimsky, "The Emperor Jones," pp. 94–95). In high spirits over accompanying Paul to the States, Essie wrote Harold Jackman (April 19, 1933, Yale: Van Vechten), "I've got some gorgeous new clothes—yes, more of them—which my lord and master has just bought for me— and I'm a hussey in them." After spending an afternoon alone with Van Vechten during her stay, Essie wrote him: "I always feel I like to 'report' our progress to you, as you are a sort of Godfather to us both. Especially when the report is good news, as it is these days" (ER to CVV, postmarked June 24, 1933, Yale: Van Vechten).

26. "Interview: William Lundell and Paul Robeson," *Screenland*, Oct. 1933. O'Neill had "dug down into my racial life," Robeson added, "and has found the essence of my race. Every word he wrote for 'The Emperor Jones' is true to the Negro racial experience."

27. New York *Amsterdam News*, Sept. 27, 1933; Philadelphia *Tribune*, Nov. 2, 1933; Muse to Barnett, Nov. 22, 1933, CHS: Barnett. Two contemporary film critics who have written with special sympathy for the "breakthrough" aspects of *The Emperor Jones*, despite all its limita-

tions as stereotype, are Thomas Cripps, "Paul Robeson and Black Identity in American Movies," *The Massachusetts Review*, Summer 1970, and Richard Dyer, "Paul Robeson: Crossing Over," ms. courtesy of Dyer (subsequently published as *Heavenly Bodies* [St. Martin's, 1987]). New York *Evening Post*, Sept. 20, 1933; *Daily Express*, March 18, 1934 (too civilized). Samples of favorable reviews for Robeson are: *Daily News, The New York Times*, New York *Journal-American*, New York *Sun*—all Sept. 20, 1933; *The Film Weekly*, March 16, 1934; *Cinema*, Jan. 31, 1934. Among the many damning reviews of the film are: *The Observer*, May 18, 1934; *The Times* (London), Feb. 19, 1934; *The Tatler*, March 28, 1934; *New Britain*, March 28, 1934. The film, according to Peter Noble (*The Negro in Films* [Arno reprint, 1970], p. 57), was a financial failure, in part because of distribution problems encountered in the Southern states.

Most of the criticisms expressed in the white press had to do with cinematic, not racial values and are aptly summed up in a letter from Frank Merlin, managing director of the Little Theatre in New York, to Essie: "It definitely has helped Paul in introducing him to a new audience, but it's a damn shame that Paul was not helped by those around him. He is good in spite of his director, and this, of course, should not be so. The photography is not good. The trick camera work is obvious, and old-fashioned. . . ." Essie was at that time suggesting scripts to Merlin—including bringing over John Gielgud in *Richard of Bordeaux*—who was expanding his theatrical organization with the hiring of Eleanor Fitzgerald (Fitzi) of the Provincetown Players, as his general manager. Essie also passed along Countee Cullen's *Leavin' Time*, which (so she wrote Cullen, Sept. 23, 1934, RA), "was definitely good theatre, and had an authentic folk quality. . . . It was such a relief to read a play about Negroes which didn't call upon the (by now) very tired audience to get up and sympathize with the poor downtrodden black. . . ." She added that she'd told Merlin "I'd like very much to read the part of Della, and if I was any good, to play her." Essie told

Merlin exactly what she had written Cullen, adding (in regard to both *Leavin' Time* and Wallace Thurmond's *Jeremiah, the Magnificent*), "I was so surprised and glad to read Negro plays by Negroes, which were not about lynching and all the wrongs of the poor black man, that perhaps I am over generous. But I really think "Leavin' Time' is good" (ER to Merlin, Sept. 17 [1934], RA).

Bess Rockmore, recently divorced from Bob and remarried to Motty Eitingon was also involved with Merlin and the Little Theatre. The Eitingons were generous people (at one point they gave Essie the present of a silver-fox fur) who were devoted to Paul (and Bess always remained friendly to Essie). Bess Eitingon's opinions about both the Robesons, cited throughout, have struck me as unusually insightful (interview with Bess Eitingon [PR, Jr., participating], March 30, 1982). The half-dozen letters between Essie, Bess, and Merlin in RA not only detail Essie's intense activity for a time as a kind of play-reader and scout for Merlin, but also reveal her often shrewd assessments of theatrical properties and players.

28. *Star*, Aug. 3, 1933 ("doubtful"); New York *World-Telegram*, June 13, 1933 ("subtleties"); *The Film Weekly*, Sept. 1, 1933 (Hollywood).

29. *The Film Weekly*, Sept. 1, 1933 (Negro culture; "trifle exaggerated"); *Daily Express*, Aug. 4, 1933 ("a great race"; "modern white American"); interview in *Tit-Bits*, May 27, 1933 ("essentially an artist").

30. PR, "The Culture of the Negro," *The Spectator*, June 15, 1934. A letter in RA from Mrs. Manet Harrison Fowler, president and founder of Mwalimu, School for the Development of African Music and Creative Art, to ER, April 7, 1934, is in response to her inquiry about "the possibility of Mr. Robeson's continuing his work in an African language of the West Coast of Africa here in New York." PR's registration card in the School of Oriental Studies (University of London) shows him enrolled in two courses only during 1933–34: Phonetics in the first term and Swahili in the second.

31. ER to CVV and FM, April 5,

1934, Yale: Van Vechten ("our people"); Zora Neale Hurston to ER, April 18, 1934, RA (I've corrected the typos in Hurston's hastily typed letter [e.g., "steaedily" to "steadily"]; Du Bois to ER, March 27, 1934; ER to Du Bois, April 22, 1934 (U. Mass.: Du Bois). Ultimately, Essie studied more than two years at LSE with, among others, Malinowski, Firth, and W. J. Perry (ER to E. Franklin Frazier, Oct. 10, 1943, MSRC: Frazier Papers. For Padmore, see note 34, p. 634.

32. His 1927 comments on Hayes and Cullen are in *Wisconsin Literary Magazine*, Nov. 1927. He himself refers to "discovering" Africa while in London in *Freedom*, June 1953. For a 1920s reference to the "artistic stature" of ancient Africa, see p. 72.

33. Walter White, "The Strange Case of Paul Robeson," *Ebony*, Feb. 1951.

34. Robeson's notes for 1934 in RA are in four sections, totaling eight to ten thousand words. One of the four sections, about one-fifth of the whole, consists of technical philological notes—the position of the tongue in making particular sounds, the use of phonemes, assorted language groupings, etc. The other four-fifths is in the form of jottings, a mix of half-thoughts and fully developed sentences. For the sake of simplicity I'll use the abbreviated citation "PR, Notes, 1934, RA," in the rest of this section to designate all four batches of material.

35. For more on the group around the *Menorah Journal*, see Alan M. Wald, *The New York Intellectuals: The Rise and Decline of the Anti-Stalinist Left from the 1930s to the 1980s* (University of North Carolina Press, 1987), especially ch. 2.

36. It is necessary to differentiate here between what one can call Nationalism (with a capital "N")—i.e., political separatism—and cultural nationalism (with a small "n")—i.e., an identification with the folkways, institutions, special historical experience and perspective, etc., of one's group. PR, Jr., told me (interview, March 3, 1984) that his father had "no use at all" for the Garvey movement or for the Nation of Islam. "You will never find a single instance of his seeking

out, relating to, talking about, having a good word to say about any Nationalist movement in the United States. He saw them as reactionary to varying degrees. . . . Paul Robeson was not a Nationalist (with a capital "N") . . . and made it plain he wasn't." Yet, even as regards cultural nationalism, Robeson should not be overly categorized; even at the height of his cultural nationalism in the 1930s, his sympathies were more broadly gauged. Freda Diamond recounts a telling episode: hearing from Freda that Paul, Jr., had described him on a television program in the early seventies as first and foremost a black nationalist, Paul, Sr., said to her, "Has he cut me down to *that* size?" She told the anecdote during the question period of a panel on PR [with both PR, Jr., and me participating] at the annual meeting of the Society of American Archivists on Sept. 5, 1987.) The chief proponent of the theory of PR as black nationalist is Sterling Stuckey (*Slave Culture* [Oxford, 1987], pp. 303–58).

37. PR, Notes, 1934, RA; Levy, *Johnson*, pp. 65–70 (Johnson's support of eventual assimilation).

38. PR, Notes, 1934, RA; PR, "The Culture of the Negro," *The Spectator*, June 15, 1934 ("Confucius"); Stuckey, *Slave Culture*, p. 334 (de-emphasizing tribal differences).

There is a letter in RA from Essie to Dr. Ronald Moody, who had apparently solicited assistance for his brother Harold's League of Coloured Peoples, then surveying Africans living in London with a view toward ameliorating their condition (see note 59). In responding, Essie claimed she and Paul had talked the matter over and "He has definitely said No, and I agree with him. . . . We are really not interested at all in any Negroes who have decided to stay in this country, whether accidentally or no. We feel they are of no importance whatever, in comparison to the major problem, which is the Negroes, 150,000,000 of them, in Africa. The Negroes here are separated from their natural background. . . . We feel they really don't belong here at all, and shouldn't be here. . . . Many of them are not even interested in themselves, but in white people's ideals and ideas, and

many of them are trying hard to fit into a white world and a white future. That is their affair, not ours" (March 3, 1934, RA).

But this may have been one of the times Essie wrongly believed (or deliberately set out to create the false impression) that she and Paul were of one mind on an issue. On Seton's ms. of *Robeson* (lent to me by Seton), Robeson, in reference to another event in 1934, scrawled: "I was at a meeting called by League of which Ronald Moody's brother was President. Many Africans & West Indian students were discussing Africa. . . ." So apparently Robeson did lend his name and presence to a league of whose purposes Essie (at least in 1934) disapproved. Robeson possibly shifted between both views, sometimes identifying with "displaced" Westernized Africans, sometimes scorning their "debasement." As another example, Seton quotes him in 1934 as saying to her, ". . . if necessary, I will die for Africa, but what should Africans care about American Negroes when most of them are Americans in culture? Can one expect a Chinese in China to be as concerned about the Chinese in San Francisco as about his own neighbors?" (Seton, *Robeson*, p. 87.)

39. PR, Notes, 1934, RA.

40. PR, Notes, 1934, RA. It may be a comment on the low state of American Indian studies at the time, and the general contempt with which Native Americans were held, that Robeson did not use that culture to draw analogies with the black one, although wisdom for the Indian also consists in not trying to reduce behavior to "logic," regarding the spiritual dimension as the pre-eminent one. Five years later he *had* made the connection, referring to the "many analogies with American Indian cultures" (PR, Notes, 1939, RA).

41. PR interview with *The Observer*, July 29, 1934. Arnold Toynbee, for one, congratulated Robeson on his "intuition of the malady which a Late Modern Western Society had inflicted on itself," for "putting his finger on the difference between an integrated and a disintegrated culture," and for perceiving "that the

structural and the spiritual disintegration of culture are two aspects of a single process" (*Study of History* [Oxford University Press, 1954], vol. 8, p. 501).

42. PR, Notes, 1934, RA; *Pearson's Weekly*, Oct. 20, 1934.

43. *Star*, Dec. 13; *Evening Times* (Glasgow), Jan. 26; Oxford *Mail*, March 9; *Journal of Living and Learning*, March—all 1934. Along with interviews, Robeson published several articles in 1934–36 on these same themes. The most important were collaborations with Leonora (Pat) Gregory (now Stitt), a young Australian-born journalist he met in 1934. In a series of letters to me (1985–86), Pat Gregory has outlined in detail her relationship with Robeson and has generously sent me as well the draft outline of a book she at one point was preparing to write with him, as well as the ms. for her own unpublished book, *New Ways*. The three articles she co-authored with Robeson were "Negroes—Don't Ape the Whites," *Daily Herald*, Jan. 5, 1935; "Want Negro Culture, Says Paul Robeson," *News-Chronicle*, May 30, 1935; "Primitives," *The New Statesman and Nation*, Aug. 6, 1936. Gregory has asked me to state, if I mentioned these articles, that "the ideas and nearly all the words were wholly Paul's" and that she merely "organised" the material. In one of her letters (Oct. 18, 1985), Gregory emphasized Robeson's need to find someone—as he did in her—to whom he could speak freely without fear that his confidences would be broken; he was so widely known and admired in London that he had trouble finding any protective anonymity. Among the confidences he related to Gregory was that of his broken love affair with Yolande Jackson, though without ever naming her (see note 15). When Gregory found herself in financial difficulty in 1937, Robeson insisted on making her an allowance so she could get on with her writing; he continued to help her financially until he returned to the States in 1939. She saw him again in 1949–50 and visited him backstage at the Stratford *Othello* in 1959 ("The other friends wondered why he took me by the hand and kissed me. I never told them": Gregory to me, Feb. 21, 1985).

44. *Daily Herald*, Jan. 3, 1935 (Nig-

eria); *Star*, Dec. 13, 1934 ("lonely"); *Daily Mail*, Dec. 11, 1934 ("companions"). In a letter in RA from Tohekedi Khama to Dr. Roseberry T. Bokwe (June 21, 1934), in response to an inquiry about the Robesons' possible trip to South Africa, he promises them "a hearty welcome to the Bechuanaland Protectorate. If you know them and they are your friends, I do not require any further particulars."

45. *Daily Mail*, Dec. 11, 1934 ("some day"); *The Spectator*, June 15, 1934 ("vocal genius"); Huddersfield *Examiner*, Dec. 4, 1934 ("Wagner"); *Film Pictorial* Feb. 27, 1934 ("Wagner").

46. Sheffield *Daily Telegraph*, March 14, 1930 ("High Water"); Yorkshire *Herald*, Feb. 14, 1930 ("spiritual significance"); *Evening News* (London), Feb. 13, 1930; Huddersfield *Examiner*, Dec. 4, 1934; Sheffield *Telegraph*, Feb. 21, 1935; Newcastle *Journal*, Feb. 25, 1935; Sheffield *Independent*, Feb. 21, 1935; Dundee *Courier and Advertiser*, March 27, 1935; Lewis, *Harlem in Vogue*, p. 173 (Harlem elite); *Melody Maker*, July 19, 1958 ("most important"); PR, Notes 1950s, RA ("Savoy"). In his Music Notes (n.d., 1960s?, RA), PR wrote, "The jazz scale is a new and significant development in the history of music in general and American music in particular . . . [there is] a unique immediacy, a direct communication here and now—from the living to the living—which jazz seems to provide." In her diary entry for July 19, 1932, Essie wrote, "Went to Louis Armstrong's opening, at the Palladium, this afternoon, and was terribly disappointed. I thought he was awful. I saw him in his dressing room afterwards, and thought he was worse. He may be alright on records, but he's a mess on the stage and in person." On the other hand, PR wrote in his Notes, 1934 (RA), "Ellington-Calloway have appeared and showed how shallow was all that went before, almost too late—for having received the synthetic, public hardly knows real—when it sees or hears it." And when Cab Calloway came to London, Essie wrote the Van Vechtens that she and Paul "lived at the Palladium, listening to his Hi-de-hi-de-ho, and pretending we were in Harlem. He was handled very badly here, which is a shame" (ER to CVV

and FM, April 5, 1934, Yale: Van Vechten).

47. Sheffield *Telegraph*, Feb. 21, 1935 ("decadent"); *Star*, May 20, 1936 ("genuine"); *Daily Collegian* (Pennsylvania State University), Dec. 10, 1940 ("St. Louis Blues"); interview with John Hammond, Aug. 8, 1985 (joined by Basie's biographer, Albert Murray, who corroborated Hammond's version). The "King Joe" record had verses by Richard Wright. Robeson, Wright, and Basie gathered at Okeh for the recording session, along with a group of reporters, photographers, and friends (including Max Yergan and Walter White). Clearly the record was widely regarded as a major event. In evaluating the special qualities of PR's musical gifts, my interviews with John Hammond (Aug. 8, 1985), Pete Seeger (July 4, 1986), and Earl Robinson (Aug. 17, 1985) were especially helpful. Additionally, I found the insights in Levine's *Black Culture and Black Consciousness* and Richard Dyer's *Heavenly Bodies: Film Stars and Society* particularly useful.

48. Perth *Advertiser*, Jan. 20, 1934 (Hebridean, etc.); Gambs to ER, April 18, 1934, RA (Russian); Glasgow *News*, March 18, 1934 (folk songs); Glasgow *Exhibitor*, Jan. 3, 1934 (Jews); *Jewish Transcript*, Nov. 22, 1935. Marie Seton describes Robeson as late as 1933 as innocent and uninformed on the Jewish question and at first reluctant ("I'm an artist, I don't understand politics") to play a special matinee of *All God's Chillun* to benefit Jewish refugees. Seton claims he agreed after she helped clarify the parallels between the persecution of the Jews in Germany and the blacks in the United States, and further claims that "In later years he referred to this matinee as the beginning of his political awareness." That event may have been contributory, but in my reading does not bear the heavy weight Seton puts on it (Seton, *Robeson*, pp. 66–69).

49. Birmingham *Post*, April 20, 1934. Among the other notices that expressed doubts about his ability to carry off his new repertory were: *The Times*, April 18, 1934; Oxford *Mail*, May 5, 1934; Yorkshire *Telegraph*, Jan. 23, 1934; Liverpool *Post and Mercury*, Jan. 19, 1934; East-

bourne *Gazette*, Aug. 15, 1934; *Irish Times*, Dec. 18, 1934.

50. *The Observer*, July 29, 1934; F. C. Schang (Metropolitan Musician Bureau) to PR, Aug. 24, 1934, RA (Amonasro). Robeson was paid two thousand pounds for appearing in *Sanders*, plus 5 percent of the gross in excess of eighty thousand pounds. The contract, dated June 25, 1934, is in RA; also B. Bleck (Contracts Dept., London Film) to ER, July 3, 1934, RA.

51. *The Observer*, July 29, 1934.

52. *The Era*, Sept. 12, 1934 ("accurate"); *World-Telegram*, Oct. 5, 1935 (port towns); ER to CVV and FM, Jan. 6, 1936, Yale: Van Vechten.

53. New York *Amsterdam News*, Oct. 5, 1935; Freda Diamond ms. comments. The advertising for *Sanders* is in Cripps, "Paul Robeson and Black Identity," p. 480.

54. Jeremy Murray-Brown, *Kenyatta* (E. P. Dutton & Co., 1973; 2nd ed., 1979), p. 217; *Jewish Chronicle*, Nov. 4, 1938 ("Fascist"). Robeson and Kenyatta struck up a friendship on the set, which was to continue. During the filming Robeson told Leslie Banks, who played Sanders, that in the role of Bosambo he felt he had "accomplished a lifelong desire—to show negroes on the screen as human beings" (Banks, *Film Pictorial*, April 6, 1935). Flora Robson (Sterner interview) relayed an anecdote relating to *Sanders:* Robeson "wore a leopard-skin and he was ticked off by a prince of the Ashanti who was up at Oxford who said what do you wear a leopard-skin for, so he said well what do you wear in Africa, tweeds? And the prince said Yes, we do."

55. *Daily News*, June 27, 1935; *Sunday Times*, April 7, 1935; *The Times*, April 3, 1935; New York *Herald Tribune*, June 27, 1935 ("melodrama"); New York *World-Telegram*, June 27, 1935 ("sacredness"); *The Sketch*, April 10, 1935 ("punctilious").

56. Yorkshire *Post*, April 3, 1935 ("sophisticated"); *Picturegoer*, April 20, 1935 *("Vagabond")*; unidentified news clipping, 1935 (Beery); *New Theatre*, July 1935 (Stebbins). Melville J. Herskovits, specialist on Africa and an acquaintance of Robeson's (for more on their relation-

ship see p. 198 and note 36, pp. 634–35), wrote him that he "didn't like the 'white man's burden' plot" in *Sanders* (MH to PR, Dec. 11, 1935, Herskovits Papers, Northwestern University (henceforth NUL: Herskovits).

57. ER to Ma Goode, Jan. 20, 1935, RA.

58. Frances Williams interview with Kim Fellner and Janet MacLachlan, June 8, 1982, transcript courtesy of Fellner (part of the interview has been printed in *Screen Actor*, Summer 1982); New York *Amsterdam News*, Oct. 5, 1935; PR interview with Ric Roberts, Pittsburgh *Courier*, Aug. 13, 1949 ("hate the picture"). Further evidence of Robeson's later regret at having made *Sanders* is in an exchange of letters with Anne Cohen, a librarian at the 136th Street Harlem branch of the New York Public Library. Cohen wrote him in 1944 to invite him to a screening of *Sanders* that she had arranged at the Harlem branch. Robeson wrote back to ask her to try to substitute *Desert Sands, Song of Freedom*, or *King Solomon's Mines* for *Sanders*—"I personally am sorry about doing *Sanders*" (Cohen to PR, Jan. 27, 1944; PR to Cohen, Jan. 31, 1944, RA). In her book *Robeson*, Marie Seton (p. 97) claims that he—"a tower of ice-bound fury"—walked out of the Leicester Square Theatre in protest on the first-night showing of the film. The evidence will not support this claim. Though the press covered the opening extensively, no mention was made in it of such a protest—as surely there would have been had it occurred. Robeson *may* have slipped out briefly, the result of nerves (as reported in *Daily Mirror*, April 5, 1935), but if so he definitely returned. Indeed, at the close of the premiere he made a speech to the audience, one that the publicity manager for London Films, producers of *Sanders*, thought "was quite the best speech that has been made on such occasions for years"—an opinion he would hardly have entertained had Robeson included in it any statement of protest (John B. Myers to ER, April 11, 1935, RA). Since Robeson cooperated with Seton on her book and went over the ms., it's possible he himself, in a retroactive fit of anger, fed her the tale of having walked

out on opening night. Interestingly, though, the ms. (lent to me by Seton) has the sentence about his "ice-bound fury" crossed out—though by whom is not known, nor why the sentence reappeared in the printed version. Seton's ms. also has written on it, in Robeson's hand, this sentence: "All money earned from Sanders went to help Africa"; the business records in RA show that Robeson received royalties from *Sanders* through the early forties.

Another possible version of what happened at the Leicester Square Theatre on opening night is found in a *Daily Express* report (Oct. 18, 1937) and in an interview Ben Davis, Jr., did with Robeson in the *Sunday Worker* (May 10, 1936). Both items suggest that Robeson was sufficiently angry on opening night to refuse to perform when a piano was pushed onto the stage after the screening. As he told Davis, ". . . when it was shown at its premiere in London and I saw what it was, I was called to the stage and in protest refused to perform." In other words, if Robeson's account to Davis is accurate, he *did* let his displeasure be known on opening night—but it took the form of refusing to perform, not (as tradition has it) leaving the theater.

59. Eisenstein to PR, undated (1934), RA; Seton's undated letter (1934) to PR, introducing Eisenstein ("You both have a thousand interests beyond your immediate work") is in RA. Seton had originally met Eisenstein in 1932, when she carried some books to him in Moscow from Maurice Dobb the Marxist economist (interviews with Seton, Aug.-Sept. 1982). Eisenstein's letter was one, but not the only, triggering event that led to Robeson's first trip to Russia. On the ms. of Seton's *Robeson*, he wrote this comment in the margin next to the text describing how and why the trip came about: "I thought I told you . . . [at a political meeting filled with African and West Indian students] in the audience were many English 'Liberals.' Suddenly a man got up in the back of the Room and told us all to stop our mouthing. 'If we were honest' he said, 'we would be interested in the African Peasants and Workers. And in the Soviet Union.' Why didn't

I go there. I accepted the challenge. His name was Ward."

Subsequent to his trip to the U.S.S.R., Robeson several times referred to its having been triggered by a Dec. 12, 1934, meeting of Harold Moody's League of Coloured Peoples at which he spoke. Moody had founded the league in 1931 to provide social services for West Indian and African students resident in London. Its moderate Pan-Africanism contrasted with the more militant group surrounding George Padmore and C. L. R. James (Judith Stein, *The World of Marcus Garvey: Race and Class in Modern Society* [Louisiana State University Press, 1986], pp. 268–69). Since the Dec. 12 meeting of the league was a mere eight days before Robeson's departure for Moscow, it is impossible that it carried the importance in his decision that he subsequently assigned it. Indeed, at the meeting itself, he referred to the fact that he was about to visit the U.S.S.R. (*West Africa*, Dec. 22, 1934), and no contemporary account of the meeting refers to any interruption by questioning (e.g., *Daily Telegraph*, Dec. 13, 1934). Marie Seton (interviews, Aug.-Sept. 1982) confirmed that Robeson "didn't go plunging in," that his trip to Moscow was preceded by a good deal of study and planning. The black U.S./Soviet actor Wayland Rudd later reminisced in a letter to Robeson about an "all night conversation" prior to his first trip to the U.S.S.R. "when you told me that your knowledge of your duty before our People, and your love for the Soviet Union compelled you to postpone pending Contracts and make your long intended first visit to Moscow in the Spring following! I'll never forget the ring in your voice, Paul, when you said: 'Way I'll come!' Man of your word, that you are, you came" (Rudd to PR, n.d. [1959?], RA). (And he had already attended a reception at Harrington House given by the Soviet Ambassador and Madame Maisky [*The Times*, April 3, 1934; *The Tatler*, April

4, 1934].) Robeson was never, by temperament, a "plunger"—he made the important decisions in his life only after careful, deliberate reflection. Seton also thought she remembered—but wasn't sure—that William Patterson had been pushing the idea for some time that Robeson ought to visit the U.S.S.R.

Although Robeson's connection with the League of Coloured Peoples seems to have been minimal, the whole issue of his relationship with West Indian and African students and organizations in London is short on documentation. Future scholars pursuing more evidence on this question will want to note two possible leads from the RA. The first is a letter from W. A. Domingo (chairman of the Planning Committee of the West Indies National Emergency Committee) to PR, July 29, 1940, in which he refers to ". . . your magnificent assistance in the cause of West Indians two years ago in London. . . ." The second is a passage in a 1973 statement by Michael Manley (then Prime Minister of Jamaica) on the occasion of Robeson's seventy-fifth birthday: "I was once, as a young student in London, privileged to spend a quiet evening with Paul Robeson. Our host was Errol Barrow, now the Prime Minister of Barbados. I was warmed by his kindness, humbled by his simplicity, and inspired by his vision. It was a milestone in my life—such was the power of the man."

60. Sergei M. Eisenstein, *Immoral Memories: An Autobiography*, trans. Herbert Marshall (Houghton-Mifflin, 1983); Seton, *Robeson*, pp. 78–80; Marie Seton, *Sergei M. Eisenstein* (The Bodley Head, 1952; rev. Dennis Dobson, 1978), pp. 316–34; Jay Leyda, *Kino: A History of the Russian and Soviet Film* (Princeton University Press, 1960, 1973, 1983), p. 299; interviews with Marie Seton, Aug.-Sept. 1982; interview with Jay Leyda and Si-lan Chen, May 26, 1985; interview with Ivor Montagu (PR, Jr., participating), Sept. 7, 1982.

CHAPTER 10 BERLIN, MOSCOW, FILMS *(1934–1937)*

1. ER Diary, Dec. 21, 1934, RA; Seton, *Robeson*, pp. 81–82.

2. ER Diary, Dec. 21, 1934, RA; Seton, *Robeson*, pp. 83–84; *Berliner Zei-*

tung, June 21, 1960, an interview with Robeson—apparently a condensation of a longer interview he gave Kláus Ullrich for *Neues Deutschland*—in which he reminisced about his visit to Berlin in 1934. I have followed Robeson's own version of events on the platform rather than the one in Seton—which has struck me as suspiciously elaborate and pat.

3. ER Diary, Dec. 22, 23, 24, 1934, RA. ER to Ma Goode, Jan. 5, 1935, RA. For more on the Afinogenovs and on Wayland Rudd and other black Americans living in the U.S.S.R., see Langston Hughes, *I Wonder As I Wander* (Hill and Wang, 1956), chs. 3–5. ER to CVV and FM, Jan. 6, 1939, Yale: Van Vechten. Returning to Harlem after three years in the Soviet Union, John Goode gave an interview to the Pittsburgh *Courier* (April 3, 1937) in which he said "social discrimination as practiced in America is unknown in Russia." According to the Afro-American toolmaker Robert Robinson, who lived in the U.S.S.R. from 1930 to 1964, John Goode later became disillusioned but his brother Frank remained in the Soviet Union (interview with Robinson, May 18, 1988). In Homer Smith's *Black Man in Red Russia* (Johnson Publishing Co., 1964), pp. 196–201, there is a poignant description of Frank Goode's difficult life in the U.S.S.R. during World War II. Following the war, he lived on a wrestler's pension in Gorky, his lot somewhat improved. According to Robert Robinson (interview, May 18, 1988), Frank Goode enlisted his sister Essie's help in trying to get an apartment in Moscow, but her efforts to that end failed.

4. ER Diary, Dec. 23, 1934, RA; Moscow *Daily News*, Dec. 24, 1934; Chatwood Hall article on Robeson's arrival in U.S.S.R., Chicago *Defender*, Jan. 12, 1935 (comment on Soviet theater); *The Observer*, April 28, 1935 (Uzbekistan). According to Hall, Robeson told the reporters that "The whole future of the Race is tied up with conditions in [Russia, Soviet Asia, Africa, and Soviet China] . . . especially the Chinese situation, which is much like the situation in Africa."

5. ER Diary, Dec. 24, 25, 31, 1934,

RA; ER to Ma Goode, Jan. 20, 1935, RA.

6. ER Diary, Dec. 24, 1934 (she further described Litvinov as "nice, pleasant, homely" and Ivy, "who pays no attention to clothes, or her personal appearance," as "a curious woman—downright, gruff"); ER to "Mama," Jan. 20, 1935, RA; interviews with Marie Seton, Aug.-Sept. 1982. For more on PR and Ivy Litvinov, see note 12, p. 659. Essie was very fond of Coates ("as fat and as jolly, and soft as ever; full of fun"), and the Robesons saw him fairly often in Moscow, attending one of his concerts at the Conservatory, pleased at the enthusiasm it produced (ER Diary, Dec. 24, 29, 30, 1934).

7. ER Diary, Dec. 24, 28, 1934, RA; Seton, *Robeson*, pp. 91–92; interviews with Seton, Aug.-Sept. 1982. In his autobiography *(The Man Who Cried Genocide)* Patterson makes no reference to this episode. PR several times in later years credited Patterson with helping along his political education (e.g., *Freedom*, Aug. 1951). In a letter to her mother (Jan. 20, 1935, RA), ER refers to three visits to Pat, though her diary accounts for only two. "Pat was very pleased and flattered that we came so often to see him," she wrote Ma Goode. She thought he "seemed better, but I think he has botched up some business of the Government, and is not in too high favor at the moment." Shortly before PR had left for Moscow, he had sent a check for fifteen pounds to the Negro Welfare Association to be used for the defense of the Scottsboro boys (Reginald Bridgman to PR, Nov. 24, 1934, RA). According to Robert Robinson, Essie "intensely disliked" Patterson. So did Robinson, who in our interview of May 18, 1988, made some serious allegations about Patterson's role in the fall from official favor of Lovett Fort Whiteman, another Afro-American resident of the U.S.S.R. For more on Whiteman, see Robinson, *Black on Red* (Acropolis, 1988), p. 361, and Homer Smith, *Black Man in Red Russia*, pp. 77–83.

8. ER Diary, Dec. 24, 25 (women), 26 (hospitals), 29, 30 (Luria), 31, Jan. 1 (nurseries), 2 (Luria), 1935, RA; Seton,

Robeson, pp. 87–88; interviews with Seton. Aug.-Sept. 1982; ER to CVV and FM, Jan. 6, 1936, Yale: Van Vechten. On her return, Essie sent Luria a packet of books (Luria to ER, March 20, 1935, RA). Essie several more times in her diary referred to the "roughness" of the Russian temperament and then, toward the end of her stay, isolated another side of the Russians she "didn't like"—"the maudlin sentimentality, and introspection . . . the ineffectuality, and tiresomeness" (ER Diary, Jan. 6, 1935, RA).

9. ER Diary, Dec. 25 (primitives), 1934, RA. Toward the end of their stay, the Robesons spent a few days in Leningrad (ER Diary, Jan. 8, 1935, RA), which is where he came into contact with the Samoyeds (tape of PR's speech in Perth, courtesy of Lloyd Davies, is the source for PR's comments on the Samoyeds).

Whereas much is disputed among specialists about the actual extent of Moscow's sympathy for ethnic diversity (in the thirties and since), there seems general agreement that the Soviets marked an advance over the czars in regard to respecting national minorities and providing for "ethnic enclaves" and for the preservation of minority languages and literature in the schools (though *not* for separate political organizations). This was especially true during the years immediately following the Bolshevik revolution—and even in 1986 the official Soviet publishing agency printed textbooks in fifty-two languages to serve its disparate minorities, and the state radio broadcasted in sixty-seven languages (*The New York Times*, Dec. 28, 1986).

10. ER Diary, Dec. 27 (Tairov), 28 (Children's Theater), 1934, Jan. 2, 1935, RA; ER to Ma Goode, Jan. 5, 1935, RA; PR, Notes, 1938, RA (little boy); ER to CVV and FM, Jan. 6, 1935, Yale: Van Vechten. The Robesons went to see Tairov's production of *All God's Chillun*.

11. Interview with Si-lan Chen Leyda and Jay Leyda, May 26, 1985; Si-lan Chen Leyda, *Footnote to History* (Dance Horizons: 1984), ed. by Sally Banes, pp. 196–97. According to Louis Fisher, the Moscow public which had earlier gone "wild" over Chen's Spanish fan dance, "frowned" on her effort to "dance Marx-

ism"—"For an interpretation of the theory of surplus value one does not go to Terpsichore" (*Men and Politics*, Duell, Sloan and Pearce, 1941, p. 156).

12. Robinson, *Black on Red*, p. 311; interview with Robinson, May 18, 1988; ER Diary, Dec. 27, 1934, Jan. 3, 1935, RA; Seton, *Robeson*, p. 88; William Lundell interview with PR, 1933, transcript in RA; Ben Davis, Jr., interview with Robeson, *Sunday Worker*, May 10, 1936. The black actress Frances Williams, who was in Moscow at the time of Robeson's visit in 1934, also recalls how impressed he was with the conditions he found there (Williams interview with Kim Fellner and Janet MacLachlan, June 8, 1982, transcript courtesy of Fellner). Frances Williams was later administrative secretary of the American Youth Congress (Williams to PR, July 15, 1941, RA). Homer Smith, an Afro-American resident of the U.S.S.R. until 1946, reports that at least until the first purge trials, efforts at racial equality were abundantly evident in the Soviet Union (*Black Man in Red Russia*, especially ch. 8). Robert Robinson, however, in his bitterly anti-Soviet book, *Black on Red*, disputes the "myth" of Soviet racial egalitarianism even for the period of the thirties (see especially ch. 25).

13. PR, Notes, 1938, RA (Pauli); ER Diary, Jan. 1, 2, 4, 5, 10, 1935, RA; ER to Ma Goode, Feb. 6, 1935, RA; ER, *PR, Negro*, pp. 138, 140 (manners).

14. ER Diary, Dec. 23, 24, 25, 26, 28, 31, 1934, RA; ER to the Bollings, Jan. 5, 1935, RA; ER to Ma Goode, Jan. 20, 1935, RA. *Picturegoer Weekly*, Oct. 26, 1935, for PR's comment on *General Line;* interview with Si-lan Chen Leyda and Jay Leyda, May 26, 1985; Vladimir Nizhny, *Lessons with Eisenstein*, trans. and ed. Ivor Montagu and Jay Leyda (Hill & Wang, 1963), pp. 27, 170–71). According to Leyda, Eisenstein thought Robeson was physically too large for the Toussaint role. Leyda thinks *Black Majesty* "was probably doomed even before it became a subject for discussion," because of the hostility of Film Commissar Shumyatsky—a great pity, in Leyda's view, since the two men would have "worked together wonderfully" (interview, May 26, 1985). For other projects: *Evening*

Standard, Sept. 19, 1936; Chicago *Defender*, Jan. 12, 1935; Amdur to ER, Dec. 30, 1935, RA. In 1937 discussion centered on a film about the war in Spain. In July (?), Eisenstein's wife, Pera Attasheva, wrote Ivor Montagu: "What do you think about Robeson playing the part of a Morocco soldier in Spain—that is the new idea, instead of 'Black Majesty' (sweet dreams! while Shumyatsky sleeps!)" (as printed in Jay Leyda and Zina Voynow, *Eisenstein at Work* [Pantheon Books/The Museum of Modern Art, 1982], p. 95). Although there is no mention of Mikhoels in Essie's diary, which is detailed for the trip to Moscow, Robeson later said he met Mikhoels during his first visit to Moscow, in 1934. "First in the film CIRQUE, his entrance with little 'Jimmy' was electrifying and very moving" (PR to Dolinsky and Chertok, Feb. 28, 1958, RA).

15. Seton, *Robeson,* pp. 94–95 ("human dignity"). In the *Daily Rundschau* (Berlin), June 17, 1949, PR refers to his 1934 visit as the first time he felt "the sympathy of a whole people for me, a Negro." The notion that Robeson may have been bisexual, and had an affair with Eisenstein, has gained some currency (see, e.g., *WIN* magazine, Sept. 1, 1981). I have found absolutely no evidence to support these suggestions, and my sources have included an interview with a gay man, Bernard Koten, who lived in Moscow in the thirties and knew Robeson there. Eisenstein's sister-in-law, Zina Voynow (interview Feb. 1987), also scoffed at the idea of Robeson having an affair with Eisenstein—though she did not deny Eisenstein's homosexuality. (Silan Chen and Jay Leyda, as well as Herbert Marshall and Fredda Brilliant, have also confirmed that Eisenstein was homosexual—contrary to Marie Seton's wholly unpersuasive argument that he was not in her *Serge M. Eisenstein.*) Also utterly without corroboration is the rumor that Guy Burgess once "revealed" that PR had had affairs with men. My futile efforts to trace it led me to this passage from a BBC TV show (aired in New York City, April 14, 1983, script courtesy of PBS): " 'Now listen Guy,' he said, 'when you get to Washington, remember three things: don't be too aggressively left wing, don't get in-

volved in race relations, and make sure there aren't any public homosexual incidents.' 'I see,' [Burgess] said, 'what you mean is I mustn't make a pass at Paul Robeson.' "

16. *Record* (Glasgow), Feb. 1, 1935; ER to Patterson, March 22, 1938, MSRC: Patterson. In an unpublished interview enclosed in a letter from J. Steinberg to ER, Jan. 23, 1936 (RA), PR is said to have deplored violence against blacks and to have commented that "Even Soviet-Russia which is now connected with America economically and politically will not protest either against these murders"; the quote seems garbled, yet does convey another instance of Robeson's continuing to express doubt in 1935 about Soviet intentions. *The New York Times* published a curious article (Jan. 2, 1935) reporting that "high officials" in Soviet radio had been dismissed for broadcasting a Robeson recording of "Steal Away to Jesus."

Maisky to PR, Jan. 6, 1936, RA. For a lively picture of Ivan Maisky and his "gay, confident" wife, Agnes, see Victor Gollancz, *Reminiscences of Affection* (Gollancz, 1968), pp. 132–33. As for Stalin's forced collectivization programs, the Soviet expert Edward Allsworth has put it to me this way: "In 1934 almost *anyone* would have missed what Robeson did."

17. ER to Ma Goode, Feb. 8, 1935, RA; FM to CVV, June 3, 1935, CVV Papers, NYPL/Ms. Div.; ER to CVV and FM, Feb. 17. 23, 1935, Yale: Van Vechten; Cunard to Schomburg, Aug. 4, 1930, NYPL/Schm.

18. ER to Ma Goode, Feb. 21, 1935, RA.

19. *Soviet Russia Today,* Nov. 1935. The concert manager in Belfast reported that in "thirty years experience he never remembered such a pressing demand for seats at any celebrity or other concert" (Belfast *Telegraph,* Feb. 16, 1935). As for audience response, there are newspaper reports of enthusiastic calls for encores, favorites being shouted up from the crowd, cheering applause, and half the audience staying to clap twenty minutes after the last encore (e.g., Manchester *Daily Dispatch,* March 4, 1935; Aberdeen *Press and Journal,* March 26, 1935). A dif-

ferent, politically noteworthy kind of reception was the party thrown for the Robesons by some twenty-five black university students in Dublin (*Irish Press*, Feb. 21, 1935), during which Robeson talked about the problems of race. To whites as well, Robeson reiterated his intertwined new themes of racial and musical integrity. He told reporters that his recent studies had further convinced him that the "basic melody" of all national folk music was the same, that "peasants and labourers of all races and nationalities think alike up to a point, and this brings about a basic similarity of their music, which is their form of self expression. If the Hebridean fisher folk and the African fisher folk are doing precisely the same work, under conditions which are very similar, they express themselves similarly" (*Northern Whig*, Feb. 8, 1935; Edinburgh *Evening Dispatch*, March 16, 1935). His contention was that "differences between civilisations disappear in folk-music," and that folk music, "being melodic, is also particularly congenial to his race, to which melody has always meant more than harmony" (Manchester *Guardian*, Feb. 31, 1935).

As an example of the contradictory critical reception, *The Scotsman* (March 18, 1935) complained that "this born artist" did not extend "the bounds of his repertory," while the *Evening Express* complained that, when he moved beyond the black spirituals, his "inimitable genius" failed him (or, as the Birmingham *Post* declared, "Mr. Robeson thrilled us with familiar echoes rather than with new tunes" [March 21, 1935]). Similar comments are in the Belfast *News Letter*, Feb. 18, 1935; the Glasgow *Bulletin*, March 19, 1935; and the *Northern Whig*, Feb. 19, 1935. More technical criticism of Robeson's musical qualities mentioned a "phrase-moulding" that was "too level in tone-amount" (*Glasgow Herald*, March 19, 1935), "a slight break in his voice," an occasionally unattractive "tremolo" (Glasgow *Times*, March 19, 1935), and a tendency to be "over-weighted with considerations of tone-quality and sostenuto" (Leicester *Mercury*, March 22, 1935).

20. Margaret Webster was in the cast of *Basalik* and came away with the best set of reviews (e.g., the *Morning Post* and the *Daily Sketch*, April 8, 1935). Coral Browne, as the governor's wife, also did well, winning applause for her "cool and stylish" performance (*The Observer*, April 14, 1935). In calling the play "thin and unsatisfying," the *Daily Telegraph* (April 8, 1935) struck the representative note. The contract for *Basalik* in RA reveals that the author was an American woman, Norma Leslie Munro (she adopted the pseudonym Peter Garland, and her identity was kept secret). She granted Robeson exclusive rights to the play for six months.

21. *The New York Times*, April 29, 1934; Seton, *Robeson*, pp. 99–101. Just before opening night, Essie wrote Ma Goode, "I think it will be a success, and am only worried for fear they will get riled over its revolutionary speeches" (ER to "Mama," May 6, 1935, RA). Both the secretary for the Theatre Union, Margaret Larkin, and the director of its *Stevedore* production, Michael Blankfort, wrote Robeson prior to his opening in the play in London. Blankfort sent him general enthusiasm and good wishes; Larkin sent him photos, prompt script, staging and light cues, music, and reviews of the New York production (Larkin to PR, Aug, 8, 1934, Blankfort to PR, n.d., Herbert Marshall Papers, Morris Library, Southern Illinois University at Carbondale, henceforth SIU).

22. *Sunday Times*, May 12, 1935. Several critics singled out Van Gyseghem's production as misguided (e.g., *New English Weekly*, May 16, 1935; *The Observer*, May 12, 1935). The Tory press expressed some fear that the play was an inflammatory bit of Bolshevik propaganda (*Daily Herald*, May 10, 1935). Nancy Cunard's review is in *The Crisis*, Aug. 1935. Larry Brown also got good reviews (e.g., *West Africa*, May 11, 1935).

23. Pabst to PR, Aug. 6, 1935; Antheil to PR, Aug. 6, 1935; Pabst to ER, Oct. 3, 1935; Antheil to ER, Oct. 3, 1935, RA. Munsell, business manager of Theatre Guild, to PR, Feb. 21, 1934; Gershwin to ER, April 25, 1934; Heyward to PR, June 21, Aug. 19, 1935, RA; ER to

CVV and FM, April 5, 1935, Yale: Van Vechten. The role of Porgy went to Todd Duncan.

24. The half-dozen telegrams and letters relating to the Edinburgh offer are in RA.

25. James's play was one of four on various aspects of the Haitian revolution that Robeson had been considering (ER to CVV and FM, Feb. 23, 1935, Yale: Van Vechten; Carl Laemmle, Jr., to ER, Oct. 8, 1935, RA). The novelist Waldo Frank sent Robeson an outline for yet another possible play about Toussaint and, when Robeson didn't respond, sent Essie a testy letter, complete with a glowing account of having met Richard Wright: "Beautiful deep brilliant . . . You two dont know what you're missing spending your life in a stagnant eddy (swiftly turning into a sewer) like England. Yes, there is struggle here, and hope—and beauty. And a whole younger generation of Negroes second to none in value. I am happy to find these young men close to my own work" (Frank to PR, Sept. 18, 1935; Frank to ER, Dec. 4, 1935, RA).

26. ER to Ma Goode, Feb. 14, March 29, 1935; there are some dozen other letters from Essie to her mother in 1935, all in RA. There is also a typed ms. by Ma Goode of roughly twelve thousand words in RA entitled "The Education of My Grandson," in which she details her strict theories of pedagogy, as well as numerous anecdotes about Paul, Jr.'s upbringing—and especially the kind of incidents involving racial discrimination that contributed to the decision to educate him in the Soviet Union.

27. ER to PR, Jr., April 20 ("sissy"), Sept. 14 ("nigger"), 1935, RA. There are some half-dozen other letters from ER to PR, Jr., during 1935.

28. ER to CVV and FM, Nov. 21, 1935, Yale: Van Vechten; Hammerstein to PR, Oct. 17, 1935, RA; CVV to Knopf, Sept. 30, 1935, UT: Knopf (Van Vechten also passed on the rumor that Robeson was to do *Green Pastures*); ER to Hattie Bolling, December 12, 23, 1935, RA.

Along with her series of portraits "of interesting Negroes wherever we go," with an eventual book in mind (ER to Harold Jackman, July 23, 1935, Yale: Van Vechten), Essie had a variety of her own projects. She continued her studies at LSE, where Bronisław Malinowski was one of her professors, and in the summer of 1935 had enrolled in a six-week course of theater studies at the Malvern Festival (ER to Harold Jackman, March 9, 1935, Yale: Van Vechten; Malinowski to ER, March 13, 1935, RA; ER to Jackman, July 23, 1935, Yale: Van Vechten). She greatly enjoyed the drama-school course at Malvern: "It is giving me exactly the kind of information and experience I need," she wrote her mother, still hoping and intending to apply the knowledge toward forging a career as actress and playwright (ER to Ma Goode, Aug. 12, 16, Sept. 12, 1935, RA). In addition, in line with her temperamental drive to keep busy, Essie had a two-hour massage every other day, did fifteen minutes of exercise every night and morning, attended dancing class once a week, and took up horseback riding (ER to Ma Goode, Feb. 8, 1935, RA).

29. ER to Hattie Bolling, Dec. 12, 1935, RA; ER to CVV, Dec. 17, 1935, Yale: Van Vechten; ER to Jackman, Dec. 26, 1935, Yale: Van Vechten. Robeson apparently surprised the sound engineers by moving in from the standard ten-foot distance to less than two feet from the microphone, singing in an intimate, less-than-full-volume style, which allowed him to keep his voice projection even and unstrained and to repeat a song twenty-five times with the same phrasing—which in turn allowed for nearly perfect synchronization (Los Angeles *Times*, Jan. 1, 1936; *The Referee*, March 8, 1936; *Picturegoer Weekly*, Jan. 2, 1937).

30. For the elaborate and hectic logistics: New York *Evening Journal*, May 9, 1936; Sidney Skolsky in the *Daily News*, May 16, 1936; *Picturegoer Weekly*, Jan. 2, 1937; New York *Herald Tribune*, May 24, 1936 (which reports on special makeup problems in "aging" Robeson). The Robesons nonetheless managed to get to Mexico for Thanksgiving, and Paul also found time to do a radio broadcast for Alexander Woollcott (Woollcott to Robesons, two telegrams, Dec. 25, 30,

1935, letter to ER, Dec. 18, 1935, RA); ER to Hattie Bolling, Dec. 12, 23, 1935, RA; ER to CVV and FM, Dec. 30, 1935; ER to Jackman, Dec. 26, 1935, Yale: Van Vechten.

31. Whale to PR, April 28, 1936; Hammerstein to PR, Feb. 25, 1936, RA; Hammerstein to ER, May 25, 1936, RA.

32. *Sunday Times,* March 1, 1936 ("Wordsworth"); *The Observer,* March 22, 1936 ("careful"); *Daily Herald,* March 17, 1936; *The Times,* March 17, 1936; *Evening Standard,* March 17, 1936.

Before beginning rehearsals, PR gave a few recitals, including one at the Albert Hall. The most significant element in the critical response was the nearly uniform opinion that the group of Russian songs he offered was unsuccessful. Robeson's voice, the Manchester *Guardian* wrote, "has nothing in it of the real Russian sonority and dark timbre," and his singing of Gretchaninov's songs deprived them "of what little national character they possess" (Jan. 20, 1936). The same opinion was echoed in the *Daily Telegraph* (Jan. 20, 1936) and the *Morning Post* (Jan. 20, 1936).

Robeson continued to consider material about the Haitian revolution as a vehicle. A year after the James play, Essie wrote an aspiring writer that they had read fifty books and some hundred plays and scenarios about Christophe, Dessalines, and Toussaint. "All have been strangely disappointing save one, which we actually did produce here in London at a special experimental theatre. Even that didn't prove good enough. We feel the history, and the characters are too good to spoil in a poor play, and so we are continuing to read manuscripts" (ER to Downing, Oct. 23, 1937, UT).

33. Interview with C. L. R. James, Nov. 1983 (the interview was conducted by Jim Murray, then assisting James in archival work, after I first forwarded a set of questions to James for his consideration). The single line about "great gentleness" is not from the interview, but from James, "Paul Robeson: Black Star," *Black World,* Nov. 1970, p. 114.

34. James interview, Nov. 1983; Seton, *Robeson,* pp. 75–76 (detachment).

Elaborating further on Robeson's "reserve," James described him as "a figure, but Padmore was a reality." PR and Padmore were acquainted, but no more than that. On the ms. of Seton's book on him, PR wrote in the margin at one point, "I never talked with Padmore & would not know him if I saw him" (ms. courtesy of Seton).

35. Emma Goldman to ER, Dec. 16, 1935, IISH (courtesy of Richard Polenberg); multiple interviews with Freda Diamond. By 1937 Goldman did believe that Robeson had committed himself to the Communists; commenting on the political mood in Britain, she wrote Rudolf Rocker that "95% of the intellectuals have been caught in the Communist trap including so great a mind as Paul Robeson" (Dec. 30, 1937, as quoted in David Porter ed., *Vision on Fire: Emma Goldman on the Spanish Revolution* [Commonground Press, 1983], p. 306). In his note 51, p. 326, Porter reports that Robeson appeared at a fund-raising event Goldman organized (even though the Communists "had organized a competing affair for the same date") and also gave a strongly supportive public statement to a meeting Goldman and others sponsored that same year (even though the *Daily Worker* had refused to accept an advertisement for the event). Porter confirmed this information in a letter to me of Sept. 23, 1982. Moreover, Richard Drinnon, one of Goldman's biographers, reports that earlier, in 1933, when the English edition of her autobiography, *Living My Life,* appeared, Robeson had sung two songs at a "literary luncheon" in her honor (Drinnon, *Rebel in Paradise* [Beacon, 1961], p. 274); that event is confirmed in *Daily Sketch,* March 2, 1933. Three years later, however, when Goldman asked PR to appear on a platform with her, Essie wrote back, ". . . his managers have forbidden him by contract to speak about anything, even vaguely connected with politics, etc." Goldman replied, "Indeed I understand Paul's position, Not for worlds would I ever want to embarrass him" (ER to EG, March 6, 1936, EG to ER, March 8, 1936, IISR).

36. ER to CVV and FM, April 27,

1936, Yale: Van Vechten (Webbs); Herskovits to PR, Nov. 11, 1935; ER to the Herskovitses, Dec. 1, 1935, NUL: Herskovits. Jean Herskovits, their daughter, is the source for her father's and Robeson's having roomed together; Herskovits's biographer, however, makes no mention of the fact, printing instead a recollection by Margaret Mead in which she recalls that the sociologist Malcolm Willey was Herskovits's roommate before his 1924 marriage (George Eaton Simpson, *Melville J. Herskovits* [Columbia University Press, 1973], pp. 2–3). The Robesons and Herskovitses stayed in touch and occasionally socialized at least through 1938, judging from the additional correspondence between them in the Herskovits Papers, NUL (Melville J. Herskovits to ER, Dec. 11, 1935; ER to Herskovitses, n.d. [1937]; MH to ER, Aug. 18, 1938). In the late forties, however, there seems to have been a polite political falling-out. PR invited Herskovits to join the National Non-Partisan Committee to defend the rights of the twelve leaders of the CP under indictment. Herskovits replied that the request "leaves me cold" (PR to Herskovits, July 26, August 31, 1949, Herskovits to PR, July 28, 1949, Herskovits Papers, NYPL/Schm); *West Africa*, Nov. 7, 1936 ("applause"); Charles S. Johnson to PR, June 21, Sept. 27, 1935; Hughes to PR, Jan. 7, 1936, RA; ER to ? ("race war").

37. Leys's *Kenya* was first published in 1924 and reissued in its fourth edition in 1973 (Frank Cass [London], with an introduction by George Shepperson). For a full discussion of Leys's life and work, see the Introduction by John W. Cell to *By Kenya Possessed: The Correspondence of Norman Leys and J. H. Oldham 1918–1926*, ed. John W. Cell (University of Chicago Press, 1976). Robeson's remarks about "decadent," etc., are from PR, Notes, 1936, RA. Leys sent a copy of his June 11, 1935 letter to Leonard Barnes (PR ambivalences) to the Robesons as well (June 14, 1935) to be sure he hadn't misrepresented their views. There is no evidence that they found Leys's characterizations of their opinions inaccurate (also Jane Leys to ER, March 9, 1935;

Norman Leys to PR, June 12, 1935, RA). The Robesons stayed in the Leyses' house in Brailsford, Derbyshire, "on a number of occasions" (Alan Newland to me, July 1, 24, 1988).

38. PR, Notes, 1936, RA.

39. Ibid.; Leys to Barnes, June 11, 1935, copy to the Robesons (RA). Leys's remark about "vague and confused" is repeated in a letter from Winifred Holtby to William Ballinger (the 1935 letter, undated, is in the Ballinger Papers, University of Cape Town Archives, courtesy of Tim Couzens, African Studies Institute, University of the Witwatersrand). For more on the interaction of these people with PR, see p. 205.

40. Leys to Barnes, June 14, 1935, copy to the Robesons (RA).

41. In this and the following paragraph I am quoting directly from PR's own Notes, 1935, as sent to the journalist Marcia de Silva. Despite her efforts, these were neither included in the article as published in *Nash's* (Dec. 1935) nor subsequently printed as a corrective in the letter she wrote to the editor (a truncated version of her letter *is* in *Nash's* for Jan. 1936). De Silva explains all this in a letter to PR of Nov. 16, 1935, RA.

42. PR, Notes, 1935, and Notes, 1936, RA; *Nash's*, Dec. 1935. In his Notes, 1939 (RA), PR continues to speak of the Afro-American as "essentially African in his cultural heritage." For one example of Robeson being mislabeled an "African nationalist" in this period, see Fischer, *Men and Politics*, p. 192. Fischer met Robeson soon after *Sanders* and, visiting him at home, found him "immersed in Black Zionism, and the rooms were filled with African masks, weapons, trophies and jungle knickknacks." Fischer claims to have predicted that "Moscow would cure him of his African nationalism" and claims, too, to have suggested Robeson go there. Although Robeson would not, after the thirties, often sound in public the themes of cultural nationalism, his reaffirmation in PR, *Stand*, p. 35, and the reference in a statement he drafted in 1957 suggest they continued to exert at least some hold over him: "As for me, my proudest heri-

tage is the knowledge of the richness and depth of the age-old African culture from which I and my people spring" (ms. statement in response to article in *The Worker*, Jan. 23, 1957, RA).

43. PR, Notes, 1935, and Notes, 1936, RA.

44. James, "Paul Robeson: Black Star," p. 112.

45. The various drafts of the prologue to Best's film are in RA, along with Best to PR, May 26, June 2, 1936; Best to ER, May 28, Sept. 4, 1936; *The Worker*, April 12, 1937. Ten years later Joseph Best sent Robeson an account of the film's subsequent history, also revealing that Robeson had invested £250 in it. According to Best, the film was well received in the trade papers, but he "soon found that there was a dead set against it originating from S. Africa House." He was asked to cut out "many references," but refused. When the film failed to get many bookings, Best withdrew it and then put out a shorter version under the title *Africa Sings*. This got a "fair showing," and he "managed just to recoup" expenses and to draw "about even" (Best to PR, Feb. 18, 1944, RA).

46. Telegram, Carl Laemmle, Jr., to Universal, Sept. 20, 1935, RA; New York *Tribune*, May 15, 1936; *The Tatler*, June 17, 1936; New York *Amsterdam News*, June 20, 1936; California *Eagle*, May 8, 1936 ("shiftless moron"); *The Black Man* (London), Jan. 1937; Robinson to ER, Aug. 26, 1936, RA; Emma Goldman to PR, Oct. 21, 1935, IISH, courtesy of Richard Polenberg; Eisenstein to PR and ER, Feb. 1, 1937, RA. The *Show Boat* reviews are also summarized in Beulah Livingstone (Universal Pictures) to ER, May 22, 1936, RA, and ER to CVV and FM, May 25, 1936, Yale: Van Vechten.

47. ER to CVV and FM, April 27, 1936, Yale: Van Vechten; Pittsburgh *Courier*, May 20, 1937.

48. Interview with Elizabeth Welch, Sept. 6, 1982 (PR, Jr., participating); Pittsburgh *Courier*, May 20, 1937; Hughes to ER, July 16, 1938, RA. The white press was largely favorable—e.g., "A thoroughly entertaining film" (*The Era* [London], Aug. 19, 1936); "Robeson comes into his own" (*Film Pictorial*, March

6, 1937). However, there were some decided negatives—e.g., *Picturegoer*, March 6, 1937; *The Spectator*, Sept. 26, 1936, and *The Bystander*, Sept. 30, 1937, which called the film "sentimental, over-coloured and unreal."

49. PR, Jr., ms. comments (authorities opposed), as borne out by an editorial in *The Cape Times* (Feb. 1, 1935) expressing the hope that "if Paul Robeson comes to South Africa it will be to confine himself [to the] field of music, and not to indulge in the fanciful suggestions given to the Press." ER's remark was made in a newspaper interview she gave to a South African newspaper (the *Argus*, undated clipping in RA); ER to CVV and FM, May 25, 1936, Yale: Van Vechten.

50. Interviews with Seton, Aug.-Sept. 1982. The remaining information about the Leys circle comes from Tim Couzzens of the African Studies Institute, University of the Witwatersrand, the product of his research into the Winifred Holtby Papers at Hull Central Library and the William Ballinger Papers at the University of Cape Town Archives (research he has generously shared with me). The quotations are from the following documents: ER to Holtby, n.d. (1935), Holtby Papers; Holtby to Margaret Ballinger, April 16, 1935; Holtby to the Ballingers, May 20, 1935; Holtby to Leys, April 17, 1935, Ballinger Papers. Tim Couzzens also generously put in my hands a copy of the novel *Wild Deer* by Ethelreda Lewis. The leading character in *Wild Deer* is a black American singer of international renown, and the novel recounts his experiences when visiting Africa. Lewis wrote PR to say, "The central figure . . . is not Paul Robeson," but it is probably based on a composite of Robeson and Roland Hayes (Lewis to PR, Oct. 31, 1932, RA). This entire backlog of events may help to explain Essie's caution with the Cape Town reporters when responding to questions about Paul's political plans.

51. ER to CVV and FM, May 25, 1936, RA; the letters of introduction are in RA; ER to CVV and FM, postcard, June 6, 1936, Yale: Van Vechten; ER to PR, June 4, 1936, RA. I. Schapera (professor

of anthropology at Cape Town University), Dr. Bokwe, Max Yergan, Dr. James Moroka (later president-general of the African National Congress), and Rheinallt Jones of the South African Institute of Race Relations in Johannesburg were especially helpful (e.g., Jones to ER, June 12, 1936, RA).

52. ER to PR, June 4, 17, 21, 23, 1936, RA; ER to Marie Seton, July 28, 1936, courtesy of Seton; ER, *African Journey* (John Day Co., 1945) passim; Cape Town *Argus*, n.d., (clipping in RA); Johannesburg *Sunday Times*, July 5, 1936 (interview with ER); New York *World-Telegram*, Sept. 11, 1936 (report on trip). C. L. R. James was also of the opinion "that people were looking to Paul to start . . . a movement." (James, "Paul Robeson") ER to Jackman, Oct. 6, 1936, Yale: Van Vechten ("grand dreams"). Jackman had begun to edit *Challenge* with Dorothy West, and in the issues of Jan. and June 1936 had published Essie's "Black Paris" in two parts. Arthur Schomburg, for one, was acid about the new journal: "It does not seem to challenge anything," he wrote Nancy Cunard (Schomburg to Cunard, June 9, 1936, NYPL/Schm).

53. PR referred to his Aug. 1936 vacation in the U.S.S.R. in the five-page ms. Notes, 1938, RA, subsequently published as "Why I Left My Son in Moscow," *Russia Today*, Feb. 1938. Robert Robinson, who again saw PR during his 1936 visit, found him more fully committed to the Soviet Union than he had been in 1934 (interview with Robinson, May 18, 1988). Peggy Dennis told me about the consultation over Pauli (interview, April 1982 [PR, Jr., participating]). She has also written about it in *The Autobiography of an American Communist* (Westport, 1977), pp. 119–20.

54. New York *Amsterdam News*, July 1, 1938; Pittsburgh *Courier*, Aug. 14, 1937. The negative critics were particularly harsh about the artificial placement of the songs and the foolishness of their lyrics (e.g., *The Spectator*, July 30, 1937). Robeson did not have the contractual power to veto the anachronisms, but he seems to have had enough informal clout to bring about some changes in the plot line: a handwritten note by Essie appended to

the screen treatment (RA) registers objection to indiscriminate scenes of killing: "No blood orgies. OK one or 2 killed in melee . . . but no general killing." PR was paid eight thousand pounds for ten weeks (Harold Holt to ER, Dec. 14, 1935, RA). For a persuasive reading of *King Solomon's Mines* as a defense of the British Empire, see Jeffrey Richards, "Patriotism with Profit: British Imperial Cinema in the 1930s," *British Cinema History*, ed. James Curran and Vincent Porter (Barnes and Noble, 1983).

55. Interview with Elizabeth Welch, Sept. 6, 1982 (PR, Jr., participating); *Picturegoer Weekly*, Oct. 26, 1935 (comic part); ER to "Ann," postcard, Jan. 3, 1937, Yale: Van Vechten. "We are both so proud of you," Van Vechten wrote ER on hearing about her movie role, knowing well her need for acknowledgment as an independent person (CVV to ER, June 22, 1937, RA). Hearing the news that Essie was going to act, Flora Robson wrote to congratulate her: "I hope you'll love it and succeed, and get where you want to—the production side" (FR to ER, Dec. 30, 1936, RA).

56. Fenn Sherie (one of the two scriptwriters) and "Arthur" to J. Edgar Wills, Oct. 14, 1936, RA (script; title). Welch and Essie did not get along well: "Essie didn't care for me. Essie didn't care for a lot of ladies. She was nervous of Paul, you see. . . . She had no humor. I mean, she may have had some in her own way, but she didn't have any of ours" (interview with Welch, Sept. 6, 1982).

57. ER to CVV and FM, Feb. 9, 1937, postcard, Yale: Van Vechten; Moscow *Daily News*, Dec. 20, 1936; also Moscow *News*, Dec. 30, 1936. The Dec. 1936 *Workers' Moscow* review was translated for me (as well as much other Russian-language material) by Eisenstein's sister-in-law Zina Voynow; she characterized the Eisenstein review as typical of his style "when he was not doing real criticism." Ma Goode's ms., "The Education of My Grandson" (RA), details both the discrimination young Pauli had already faced and his contentment at the contrasting atmosphere of the Soviet school.

58. ER to "Ann," Jan. 3, 1937, postcard, RA; ER to CVV and FM, Feb. 9,

1937, postcard, Yale: Van Vechten; *Sunday Worker*, May 10, 1936 (Davis). On Stalin's collectivization policies, see Robert Conquest, *The Harvest of Sorrow* (Oxford, 1986); however, for exaggerations in Conquest's account, see Jeff Coplan, "In Search of a Soviet Holocaust," the *Village Voice*, Jan. 12, 1988, and also the follow-up letters in the *Voice*, Feb. 2, 10, 1988.

59. *Film Pictorial*, May 10, 1937 ("mix"); ER to CVV and FM, Feb. 9, 1937, postcard, Yale: Van Vechten.

60. California *Eagle*, May 21, 1937; *Picture Show*, May 15, 1937; New York *Amsterdam News*, n.d. (1937) (Kalsoun); Egyptian *Gazette*, Feb. 6, 1937 (cinema); *Evening News*, April 13, 1937: "My voice is embarrassingly delicate. I simply can't afford to play tricks with it."

61. Interview with Henry Wilcoxon (PR, Jr., participating), Sept. 1982. Wilcoxon and Essie seem to have gotten along well despite his finding her "sharp"; there are several chatty (undated) letters from him to her in RA.

62. Wilcoxon interview, Sept. 1982.

63. *Evening Standard*, Dec. 22, 1936 (Kouka); *The New York Times*, Aug. 17, 1938. *The Times* (London), Nov. 11, 1937, ran a representative English review: "This film begins admirably . . . then declines into the commonplace." In a reverse of the usual reception, Washington *Afro-American*, Aug. 20, 1938, praised Robeson more highly than did any of the white reviewers: ". . . in 'Dark Sands,' he is permitted to redeem himself completely." On the commercial failure of *Jericho*, see Ernest Betts, *Inside Pictures* (Cresset, 1960), pp. 11–14.

64. Pablo Azcarate (Spanish Ambassador) to PR, April 26, 1937, Jan. 19, 1938; Yergan to PR, May 25, 1937, RA. The program for the Victoria Palace concert is in RA; among the patrons listed are Dame Sybil Thorndike, Rebecca West, Havelock Ellis, John Gielgud, and John Cowper Powys.

65. ER to CVV and FM, May 30, 1937, Yale: Van Vechten; Moscow *Daily News*, May 15, 1937; E. C. Goode ("Ma" Goode), "The Education of My Grandson," ms., RA. Jean Blackwell Huston (interview, Sept. 21, 1983) told me an anecdote about meeting PR in Moscow in

1937 that bears repeating for its insights into his personality: "I was walking along the street, and I was wearing the homespun clothing that they wore, which I had acquired by exchanging with some people I met going south on a train. . . . However, I was still wearing my American shoes. And when Robeson saw me, he thought he must be seeing somebody from home. . . . So he followed me. You know, he had a wonderful sense of humor. . . . I remember then I turned around and he said, 'Is you is or is you ain't?'. . . Then he walked along and showed me the sights of Moscow. . . . I think this was characteristic of him—that he would forget where he was supposed to be and just impulsively be kind and cordial to a person."

66. ER to CVV and FM, May 30, 1937, Yale: Van Vechten. The quotes expressing Paul's views in this and the following paragraphs are taken from two of his statements, "National Culture and the Soviet Union" (written for the *Sunday Worker*, Oct. 10, 1937; ms. in RA) and an untitled four-page ms. in RA, there given the title "Soviet Worker, 1937." Years later, recalling his 1937 attendance at the Uzbek National Theater (and writing for a pro-Soviet journal), Robeson described the performance as "national in form, socialist in content," and the Uzbek people as "quite comparable to some of the tribal folk of Asia—quite comparable to the proud Yoruba or Basuto of West and East Africa, but now their lives flowering anew within the socialist way of life" (*New World Review*, April 1953).

67. The three-page typescript of PR's speech, dated June 24, 1937, is in RA. The account of threats to ban or jam his broadcast is drawn from: Manchester *Guardian, Daily Mirror, Daily Worker*—all June 25, 1937; *News-Chronicle*, June 19, 1937; *Daily Herald*, June 24, 1937. The *News-Chronicle*, June 25, 1937, is among the papers reporting his speech as "the most striking." The program of the event, listing the sponsors, is in RA. Yvonne Kapp, the principal organizer of the rally, called Robeson's speech "the finest an artist has ever made," and Hilda Browning, of the National Joint Committee for Spanish Relief, credited Robe-

son's personal appearance with the sell-out crowd. John McMillan, of the publishing firm of William Heinemann Ltd., was so enamored of his "magnificent speech" that he tried (unsuccessfully) to persuade him to broaden it into a book (Kapp to PR and ER, Browning to ER, McMillan to PR—all June 25, 1937, RA).

68. T. H. Lee to PR, Nov. 7, 1937, RA; Gollancz to PR, Sept. 22, 1937, RA (there are three versions of a blurb PR gave, at Gollancz's request, for Edgar Snow's *Red Star Over China*, written in ER's hand on the Gollancz letter); A. C. Thomas to ER, Nov. 8, 1937, RA (Friends U.S.S.R.); Agnes Maisky to ER, Jan. 16, 1938, RA; *Daily News-Chronicle* (London), Nov. 7, 1937 ("aspirations"); *Reynolds News*, Oct. 10, 1937 ("decadent"); *Daily Worker*, Nov. 22, 1937; Cripps to PR, Oct. 12, Dec. 4, 1937; Cripps to ER, Nov. 25, 1937, RA. For more on Robeson's connection with Unity Theatre, see pp. 223–24. Ambassador Azcarate invited the Robesons to dinner on Nov. 18, 1937, to meet Pablo Casals. Programs for PR's benefit concerts are in RA. At the Nov. 6, 1937, Queen's Hall meeting in support of China, PR shared the platform with the

Dean of Canterbury, P. J. Noel Baker (Master of Balliol), and Ellen Wilkinson, MP. Robeson told the black press he was sick and tired of playing Uncle Tom roles, admitting that those who had earlier attacked his acceptance of such parts had been justified in their protests. He vowed for the future to avoid portraying caricatures (New York *Amsterdam News*, undated, 1937; Philadelphia *Tribune*, May 20, 1937).

69. For more on the changes in lyrics, see note 14, pp. 604–05. The programs for PR's benefit appearances are in RA. Newspaper accounts of the Albert Hall rally include the *Daily Herald* and *News-Chronicle*, both Dec. 20, 1937. During this same period PR's gift of $250 initiated a fund-raising drive for the Negro People's Ambulance to Republican Spain, a cause whose sponsors came to include such black luminaries as Channing Tobias, A. Philip Randolph, William Pickens, Langston Hughes, and Richard Wright; the mimeographed report on the ambulance's Eastern tour is in RA. Finally, Robeson made a record in aid of the Basque Refugee Children's Fund for His Master's Voice.

CHAPTER 11   THE SPANISH CIVIL WAR AND EMERGENT POLITICS *(1938–1939)*

1. ER to William Patterson, March 22, 1938, MSRC: Patterson; ER Diary, 1938, and her eighty-page reworking of it (entitled "We Go to Spain")—the two mss. are in RA and are hereafter cited together as ER, "Spain"; ER to CVV and FM, Jan. 21, 1938, Yale: Van Vechten.

2. On the visa problem: James E. Parks (American Consul, London) to PR, Dec. 21, 28, 1937; Parks to ER, Jan. 7, 1938, RA. Robeson may have decided to go to Spain with Charlotte Haldane after he had sung at a benefit concert for the International Brigade (Dependents and Wounded Aid Committee) at Shoreditch Town Hall; Charlotte Haldane was hon. secretary of the group (CH to PR, Jan. 3, 1938, RA).

3. The Guillén interview was originally published in the radical Cuban journal *Mediodía*, reprinted in a translation by Katheryn Silver in *World Magazine*, July

24, 1976; Manchester *Guardian*, Feb. 2, 1938.

4. *News-Chronicle*, Feb. 4, 1938; *Scotsman*, Feb. 4, 1938.

5. ER, "Spain," RA; ER Diary, January 23, 1938, RA (Minor).

6. ER, "Spain," RA.

7. PR, Notes, 1938, "My Impressions of Spain," nine ms. pp., RA; ER, "Spain," RA (black soldiers). In the documentary film *The Good Fight*, Tom Page, another black American in the brigade, is quoted as saying, "For the first time in my life I was treated with dignity." Langston Hughes, who was in Spain the year before Robeson and friendly with Guillén, also reported that "All the Negroes, of whatever nationality, to whom I talked, agreed that there was not the slightest trace of color prejudice in Spain" (*I Wonder As I Wander* [Hill & Wang, 1956], p. 351; the Hughes volume has considerable infor-

mation on blacks who served in Spain). Additional detail on the experiences of black Americans including information on Gibbs, Mitchell, and Pringle, is in James Yates, *Mississippi to Madrid: Memoirs of a Black American in the Spanish Civil War 1936–1938* (Shamal, 1986).

8. PR, Notes, 1938. "My Impressions of Spain," RA; *Daily Herald*, Feb. 4, 1938 (film). PR expressed the same sentiments to Nicolás Guillén about "big capital" controlling the film industry and insisting on "a caricature image of the Black, a ridiculous image, that amuses the white bourgeoisie, and I am not interested in playing their game. . . ." When Guillén asked him if that meant he was abandoning films, Robeson purportedly replied, "No, not that. What I won't do any more is work for the big companies, which are headed by individuals who would make me a slave, like my father, if they could. I need to work with small independent producers" (Guillén interview with Robeson, as reprinted in *World Magazine*, July 24, 1976). For more on Oliver Law, including a description of his death, see Steve Nelson, James R. Barrett, and Rob Ruck, *Steve Nelson: American Radical* (University of Pittsburgh, 1981), pp. 205–18.

9. ER, "Spain," RA; Sterner interviews with George Baker and Tommy Adlam. Charlotte Haldane published a series of brief notes in the *Daily Worker* (London) describing the trip to Spain. In *The Worker* for Feb. 15, 1938, she paid tribute to Essie as "one of the most gifted women I have had the pleasure of knowing" and made some affectionate fun of her recent obsession—much in evidence during the Spanish trip—of snapping pictures. Essie had taken up photography with her usual enthusiasm; on returning from Spain she took a course for a time with Marcel Sternberger (ER to CVV and FM, April 4, 1938, Yale: Van Vechten). She gave some of the Spanish photographs to William Patterson to publish and was annoyed when he captioned some of them inaccurately (ER to Patterson, April 5, 1938, PR Coll., NYPL/Schm).

10. ER, "Spain," RA.

11. ER, "Spain," RA; ER Diary, Jan. 30, 1938, RA; *Daily Worker*, Jan. 29, 1938.

12. ER, "Spain," RA. Apparently Robeson also met Hemingway, who was in Spain as a war correspondent for the North American Newspaper Alliance and was undergoing his own political metamorphosis. According to Norberto Fuentes (*Hemingway in Cuba* [Lyle Stuart, 1984], pp. 148, 187), Hemingway and Robeson were together at least twice (there is no mention of such meetings in Essie's diary or elsewhere), one time at La Moraleja, the palace of the Loyalist supporter, the Duchess of Aldama, on the outskirts of Madrid, where Hemingway drank too much and fell asleep.

13. ER Diary, Jan. 30, 1938, RA; Manchester *Guardian*, Feb. 15, 1938 (Gols).

14. ER Diary, Jan. 30, 1938, RA; ER, "Spain," Jan. 1947, RA ("barrier").

15. PR, *Stand*, p. 53; PR, Notes, 1938, "My Impressions of Spain, RA; Worthing *Herald*, Sept. 23, 1938 ("murdered"); ER, "Spain," RA; ER to CVV and FM, April 4, 1938, Yale: Van Vechten (Cortez; Moscow); Madeleine Braun (Paris) to PR, Feb. 11, 1938, RA; ER to Patterson, March 22, 1938, MSRC: Patterson. The importance of the Soviet role in Spain in cementing loyalty to the U.S.S.R. for many others besides Robeson is well documented (see, for example, Steve Nelson, *The Volunteers* [Masses and Mainstream, 1953], and John Gates, *The Story of an American Communist* [Chilton, 1961]). There are a half-dozen letters from Castillo in RA. *L'Humanité*, Feb. 7, 1938; *Ce Soir*, Feb. 12, 1938. ER to CVV and FM, April 25, 1939, Yale: Van Vechten (Ruiz). In 1947 Castillo and his family were living in exile in Mexico (ER, "Spain," Jan. 1947, RA). When Rockmore declined his help with the exhibition, Freda said to Paul, "Rockmore may be your lawyer but he's not your friend"—causing Paul "to roll on the floor with laughter" (multiple interviews with Diamond; ER to Freda Diamond, April 11, 15, 21, 1939, courtesy of Diamond). According to Freda Diamond, Paul showed up at the New York opening of Cristobal's paintings as a surprise, carrying under his arm a portrait Cristobal had done of Pauli.

16. ER to Kaye, March 21, 1938, RA (return to States); ER to Patterson, March 22, 1938, MSRC: Patterson; ER to Patterson, April 5, 1938, NYPL/Schm, PR Coll.

17. The interview with Ben Davis, Jr., is in the *Sunday Worker,* May 10, 1936; multiple interviews with Marie Seton, Aug.-Sept. 1982; Hugh Thomas, *John Strachey* (Harper & Row, 1973), p. 159. According to PR, Jr., his father told him in 1938 "that because he [Paul] had developed a close friendship with Kazakov, Kazakov's arrest and the absurd charges against him had been an important factor in fueling his [Paul's] doubts about the charges leveled in the 1937 trials" (PR, Jr.'s written comments on ms.). I have found no evidence in specific support of this claim, but one fragment of general evidence has emerged in Lia Golden's reminiscences, "Black Americans' Uzbek Experiment," *Moscow News,* Sept. 20-27, 1987. Golden reports that in the summer of 1937 the Robesons vacationed at Kislovodsk with her parents, Oliver John and Bertha Golden, and she, Lia (age four), remembers "the adults discussing something and arguing heatedly. During that trip Paul Robeson could not find many of his friends. My father too lost many of his acquaintances. . . . Later I found out that Paul Robeson had made official inquiries regarding his arrested friends, trying to help them. In reply, one of them was brought from prison. . . ." The latter statement may be a garbled version of the PR-Feffer incident in 1949 (see pp. 352–53). Robert Robinson believes that PR knew almost nothing of the purges (which to Robinson were familiar from disappearances within his own factory), and ascribes PR's comparative ignorance to his unwillingness to talk at length with other blacks resident in the U.S.S.R. who might have disabused him of his growing faith in the Soviet system (interview with Robinson, May 18, 1988). On the other hand, PR may have been concerned about Robinson's already well-developed anti-Soviet sentiments (on account of which, apparently, he decided not to help Robinson get permission to leave the U.S.S.R.) and may simply have decided not to discuss the purge trials

with *him* (Robinson, *Black on Red,* esp. pp. 313–17).

18. ER to CVV and FM, April 4, May 18, July 16, 1938, Yale: Van Vechten; Ma Goode, ms., "The Education of My Grandson," RA; Ma Goode to the Associated Negro Press, Feb. 20, 1942, CHS: Barnett ("we left Moscow in tears"); *News-Chronicle,* Jan. 25, 1938 ("Russian children"). There is a letter full of veiled references about the situation in the U.S.S.R. and the inadvisability of keeping Pauli in school there ("I am telling you this strictly privately. . . . The idea of bringing Pauli up in Russia was originally a good one, but according to reliable information—circumstances have changed") in RA from Kurt Shafer of the International Relief Association for Victims of Nazism to PR, April 26, 1938. Interviewed after his return to London, Pauli told a reporter he had had many friends in Russia and hoped to go back there to school (*Soviets Today* [Australia], Oct. 1, 1938). Because of the Spanish and Russian visas on Essie's passport, the Germans had already confiscated it once (ER to Patterson, April 5, 1938, PR Coll., NYPL/Schm). Not wanting anyone "to believe that we have taken him out," the Robesons at first explained Pauli's reappearance in London as merely a holiday visit (ER to Patterson, April 5, 1938, PR Coll., NYPL/Schm).

19. Philip Noel Baker to PR, Feb. 9, 1938 (IPC); Nancy E. Bell to PR, Feb. 14, 1938 (IPC); E. E. Brooke to ER, April 12, 1938 (Basque); Marian Wilbrahan to PR, May 10, 1938 (BYPA); Trent to ER, April 2, 1938 (music); Walter Starkie to ER, April 26, 1938 (music); Eisenstein to ER, April 9, 1938—all RA; Leyda, *Kino,* p. 360 (roadblocks). The preliminary draft of a proposal to the Rockefeller Foundation for an International Theatres Foundation is in RA, along with a letter from Ambrose to PR, Jan. 5, 1938, making reference to earlier discussions.

20. Holt to PR, June 10, 1938, RA; ER to CVV and FM, April 4, 1938 (Albert Hall), Yale: Van Vechten. For the 1937–38 season, Holt, in his advertising, had placed Robeson's name alone, above all the others, in a star-studded list that included Gigli, Richard Tauber, Kreisler,

Yehudi Menuhin, Lawrence Tibbett and Rachmaninoff (placard courtesy of Freda Diamond). The critics of the Albert Hall concert were less ecstatic than the audience (e.g., *Evening News* and *Daily Mail*, April 4, 1938). *Daily Worker*, June 16, 1938 (anthem); Mary Atherton to PR, June 13, 1938; Judith Todd to PR, June 27, 1938, RA. In signing a contract with Roman Freulich of Los Angeles to make a film, PR insisted on a clause guaranteeing him final cut—and when Freulich failed to come up with a script that met his approval, he canceled the deal. However, it was probably not for political reasons but for musical ones—his antipathy to appearing in opera, even one by an old friend—that at this same time Robeson turned down an offer to appear in Gertrude Stein and Virgil Thomson's *Four Saints in Three Acts*, recommending Todd Duncan as a replacement. The contract with Freulich, dated Feb. 1938, is in RA; ER to CVV and FM, May 18, 1938, Yale: Van Vechten (film refusal); ER to Mrs. Kaufman, June 9, 1938, RA *(Saints)*.

21. *The Cine Technician*, Sept.-Oct. 1938; *Daily Record* (Chicago), Feb. 28, 1939; *Daily Express*, June 9, 1938, and PR ms., "The English Theater," n.d. (1938), RA ("inside turned"; "talented tenth").

22. Malcolm Page, "The Early Years at Unity," *Theater Quarterly*, Oct.-Dec. 1971, pp. 60–66; Raphael Samuel, *Theaters of the Left 1880–1935* (Routledge & Kegan Paul, 1985), pp. 59–64, 94–95. The Program for Unity Theatre (RA) contains its statement of purpose; interview with Herbert Marshall and Fredda Brilliant, July 20, 1985. Robeson also lent his name to Unity Theatre's fourteen-person General Council, along with (among others) Sean O'Casey, Harold Laski, Stafford Cripps, Victor Gollancz, Tyrone Guthrie—and Maurice Browne, the producer of the 1930 *Othello*; but Robeson did not actually attend the council's meetings (interview with Herbert Marshall and Fredda Brilliant, July 20, 1985). At the inaugural ceremonies for Unity, on Nov. 25, 1937, Gollancz spoke, Robeson sang, and O'Casey sent a message of support.

23. Page, "Early Years"; interview with Marshall and Brilliant, July 20, 1985.

The program for *Plant* (RA) does indeed omit the names of the actors, but a contemporary photograph of the Unity Theater (*Weekly Illustrated*, June 25, 1938) reveals a large placard over the building's entrance prominently advertising PR's name immediately underneath the play's title. Herbert Marshall (interview, July 20, 1985) recalled that Robeson lent him money during the run of *Plant* but begged Marshall not to let Essie know.

24. *Time and Tide*, July 16, 1938; Unity Theater, "Press Statement," 1938, RA.

25. Beste's recollections are in a 1979 letter to Ann Soutter (who had also been a member of Unity), as copied and sent to PR, Jr., May 14, 1985, courtesy of PR, Jr. In her covering letter, Soutter recalled Essie as "a real watchdog, and needed to be, for Paul was very soft hearted. She would send a taxi to pick him up after the performance. . . . If he wasn't home in time she would telephone to know the reason why." Sterner interview with Alfie Bass.

26. Haemi Scheien, "Paul Robeson Becomes an Amateur," *Drama*, July 1938 ("drying up"); *Weekly Review*, June 23, 1938 ("compact"); *Evening Standard*, July 25, 1938 ("gentle strength"); Manchester *Guardian*, June 16, 1938.

27. The ms. of PR's speech at the Jamaica meeting (Town Hall, July 17, 1938) is in RA; Marie Seton, *Panditji: A Portrait of Jawaharlal Nehru* (Taplinger, 1967), pp. 94–97. Seton, who was working on a biography of Krishna Menon before her death, recalled (in our interviews of Aug.-Sept. 1982) that Menon and Robeson had very much liked each other.

28. *Daily Worker*, June 29, 1938 (Dutt); two-page typed notes of PR's welcoming remarks, RA.

29. Nehru to ER, July 7, 21 ("delight"), Oct. 13, 1938, Jan. 27, 1939; Vijaya Lakshmi Pandit to ER, Sept. 15, 1938, RA; ER to Richard Wright, April 19, May 31, 1939, Yale: Johnson; ER to CVV, July 16, 1938, Yale: Van Vechten ("thrilled to death" with Wright's *Children*). Four versions of the introduction Robeson wrote to *Uncle Tom's Children* are in RA (all contain the sentence quoted).

When Wright's theatrical adaptation of *Native Son*, written in collaboration with Paul Green, opened on Broadway two years later, PR telegraphed him, "You have advanced the cause of your people immeasurably and doubly strengthened your place in American letters. Congratulations and thanks!" (March 24, 1941, Yale: Johnson). Contrary to PR, Van Vechten thought *Native Son* "an overrated book if there ever was one" (CVV to Harold Jackman, Feb. 8, 1941, Bruce Kellner, ed., *Letters of CVV*, p. 176. When imprisoned in 1941, Nehru asked Essie to send him more books, enclosing a list of thirteen titles, which included Reinhold Niebuhr, Ortega y Gasset, Carl Becker, Admiral Mahan, and Upton Sinclair (Nehru to ER, Aug. 2, 1941, RA). Harold Leventhal, the theatrical agent who served as a GI in India during World War II, recalls meeting Nehru soon after his release from prison; almost his first question was "How is Paul Robeson?" The very next week, according to Leventhal, he met Gandhi—who asked him exactly the same question (phone interview with Leventhal, Oct. 13, 1983).

30. Nehru's remarks about Essie are in a letter to "Betty," Oct. 12, 1943, as published in S. Gopal, ed., *Selected Works of Jawaharlal Nehru* (Orient Longman Ltd., 1980), vol. 13, pp. 255–56. For a time in 1938, Robeson was thinking of visiting India as a stopover on his way to Australia—but the tour was canceled. Seton (interview, Aug. 31, 1982) told me she was convinced not just that Nehru was available for an affair with Essie but that she backed off because of the "cultural divide" between them.

31. Essie's U.S. trip is most fully reported in the New York *Amsterdam News*, Aug. 6, 1938. While in New York she saw, as always, a lot of theater, including Langston Hughes's *Don't You Want to Be Free?* Hughes had written her to suggest she read the play, even while doubting it was "anything Paul could do abroad," since he had written it "expressly for a Negro theater" (i.e., Negro audiences) (Hughes to ER, July 16, 1938, RA). Descriptions of PR's tour are from: Eastbourne *Gazette*, Aug. 10, 1938; South Wales *Evening Post* (Swansea), Aug. 13,

1938; *Herald and Express* (Torquay), Aug. 22, 1938; *The Scotsman*, Sept. 2, 1938; *Daily Mail*, Jan. 14, 1939; Aberdeen *Express*, Jan. 18, 1939; *Express and Star*, Jan. 23, 1939. Preparations and arrangements for the tour are recounted in a series of letters from H. M. Horton (of Harold Holt Ltd.) to Larry Brown, May-July 1939, in NYPL/Schm: Brown. At Glasgow, Robeson sang in aid of a food ship's being sent to Spain, and just before he stepped onto the platform, the mother of two little boys, George and Eric Park, brought them to him in an anteroom to show him an autograph book belonging to their father, which Robeson had signed in Spain—just days before their father was killed. Robeson was deeply moved by the encounter and referred to it "in the quietest of voices" when he took the platform (Glasgow *Bulletin*, Aug. 19, 1938). In September 1938, Robeson further demonstrated his commitment to the Loyalist cause by taking supper with thirty Manchester members of the International Brigade and singing at a Merseyside meeting to commemorate the Brigade's fallen members (Manchester *Guardian*, Sept. 19, 29, 1938). *Star*, Nov. 16, 1937; *Daily Mail*, Nov. 24, 1938 (poll).

32. Mark Naison, *Communists in Harlem During the Depression* (University of Illinois, 1983), pp. 198–99; Barnett to PR, July 19, 1938, Barnett Papers, Chicago Historical Society (hereafter CHS: Barnett). The American Red Cross in Washington, D.C., felt the need to censor part of an article on Robeson that referred to his pro-Soviet sympathies, to avoid having "many readers in this country condemn him" (Charlotte Kett, author of the article, to ER, June 27, 1939, RA).

33. *Daily Telegraph*, Nov. 1, 1938; *News-Chronicle*, Nov. 2, 1938; PR interview with J. Danvers Williams, "Why Robeson Rebelled," *Film Weekly*, Oct. 8, 1938. At this time a potential film deal fell through with British National Films Ltd., though the main reason seems to have been financial rather than ideological (John Cornfield to ER, Nov. 14, 1938, RA). Robeson sought legal advice in successfully breaking an earlier contract agreement with Walter Futter, who had produced *Jericho*, to make another picture

with him (Crane to PR, Feb. 14, 1939; the agreement with Futter, dated Feb. 10, 1937, is in RA).

34. *Jewish Chronicle*, Nov. 4, 1938 (cinemas); Cambridge *Daily News*, Dec. 1, 1938; *News-Chronicle*, Dec. 23, 1938; *Daily Herald*, Dec. 24, 1938; *Answers* (London), April 8, 1939 (fees).

35. Edney to PR and Hannington to PR, both Dec. 29, 1938 (NUWM), RA; Fred Copeman to PR, Jan. 10, 1939 (NMF); Monica Whately to PR, Feb. 17, 1939 (League); J. R. Cox to PR, Feb. 20, 1939 (Coloured), RA; *The Times* (London), May 1, 1939 (SCR). In these same months, Robeson also adopted a hundred Spanish children for a month, was signatory to a letter urging the American government to lift the embargo against Republican Spain, and was invited to become a vice-president of the Society for Cultural Relations . . . British Commonwealth and the U.S.S.R. (SCR) (Judith Todd to PR, Oct. 13, 1938). When S. I. Hiung solicited a statement from him to be sent to the Chinese people, Robeson replied with this message: "Greetings to the Chinese people who are so heroically defending the liberties of *all* progressive humanity" (Hiung to PR, Oct. 16, 25, 1938; PR to Hiung, n.d. [1938], RA).

36. *Western Mail*, Dec. 8, 1938; Arthur Horner, *Incorrigible Rebel* (Macgibbon & Kee, 1960) (Welsh hunger marches in 1927, 1929); Mark A. Exton, "Paul Robeson and South Wales: A Partial Guide to a Man's Beliefs," M.A. thesis, University of Exeter, Oct. 1984; Sterner interviews with Tommy Adlam and William Paynter.

37. ER to Harold Jackman, April 12, 1939, Yale: Van Vechten (Australia); Seton, *Robeson*, p. 119 (anti-Nazi); Rockmore to Larry Brown, Feb. 21, 1938, RA. The New York *Post*, June 20, 1939, called the revival of *Jones* "magnificent," and the New York *World-Telegram*, June 22, 1939, thought Robeson "in brilliant form." Luretta Bagby Martin, a student at Pennsylvania State University, when Robeson gave a concert there in 1939, asked an employee at the Nittany Lion Inn, a college property, whether the college "honored the non-discrimination rule in the dining room. He reported that Robeson took his meals in his room" (Martin to me, June 1, 1985). Robeson was also in contact with the radical labor organizer, Ella Reeve Bloor ("Mother" Bloor) during his stay in the States (the references are in letters from Mother Bloor to her children, in Bloor Papers, Sophia Smith Collection, Smith College (henceforth SSC: Bloor).

38. *Sunday Worker*, June 4, 1939; Woollcott to PR, May 28, 1939, RA; Yergan to PR, June 2, 1939, RA; Walter White to PR, two letters June 15, 1939, one marked Special Delivery ("I have been trying to reach you for several days without success"); Parkinson to White, June 14, 1939; White to Parkinson, June 15, 1939, LC: NAACP; ER to PR, May 31, June 2, 1939, RA; ER to CVV and FM, July 19, 1939, Yale: Van Vechten.

39. CVV to FM, Aug. 2, 4, 1939, Kellner, ed., *Letters CVV*, pp. 167–68; FM to CVV, Aug. 3, 1939, CVV Papers, NYPL/Ms. Div.

40. *The Worker*, Sept. 1, 1964 (met in Harlem early twenties); PR to Ben Davis, n.d. (1954–55), courtesy of Nina Goodman (Mrs. Ben Davis); Herndon to "My dear Paul" (suggesting prior acquaintance), June 17, 1939, RA; accompanying Herndon's letter is a news clipping from the Birmingham *World*, describing the activities of the Negro Youth Congress. In 1934 Herndon had written his own appeal for justice, *You Cannot Kill the Working Class*, and then, in 1937, a second book, *Let Me Live*, which credited the Communists as being the most effective rallying point against white supremacy. For more on Herndon, see Naison, *Communists in Harlem*.

41. Dorothy Heyward to PR and ER, May 3, 1939; ER to PR, June 25, 1939 (Vesey), RA; for PR's interest in the Heyward play during the forties, see note 47, p. 665. Anderson's letter to PR (March 3, 1939) is reprinted in Laurence G. Avery, ed., *Dramatist in America: Letters of Maxwell Anderson* (University of North Carolina Press, 1977), pp. 84–86, which also refers to ER to Anderson, March 29, 1939, in which she cites PR's refusal to perpetuate a stereotypic image of blacks. In 1941–42 Robeson was marginally involved in abortive negotiations by Clarence Muse

for an all-black production of Brecht and Weill's *Threepenny Opera*. In a letter to Essie, Weill characterized the contract Muse offered him as "the most shameful proposition that has ever been made to me," and in response Essie expressed relief that Weill had held on to his rights— "We feel the idea of a Negro Theatre is a splendid idea, but I must say the actual workings of it at the moment are not so splendid!!" (ER to Kurt Weill, March 22, July 15, 1942; Weill to ER, June 11, 1942, Kurt Weill Foundation for Music [henceforth KWF].) For the subsequent history of *Eneas Africanus,* and the renewed possibility in 1945 that Robeson might become available to perform in it, see Ronald Sanders, *The Days Grow Short: The Life and Music of Kurt Weill* (Holt, Rinehart and Winston, 1980). In turning down the script, ER wrote Anderson a long and revealing explanation, an attempt to blend diplomacy with self-respect.

You may perhaps know, that the general public has taken it for granted that Mr. Robeson REPRESENTS to some extent, the Negro race, the Negro thought, and the Negro behavior. This is extremely inconvenient for us, as it limits our scope a great deal. It is also very unfair and unreasonable and irritating. If he plays a drunk, then Negroes are drunkards; if [he] plays Ol' Uncle Tom, then all Negroes are "handkerchief heads" and don't want to be free. It is ridiculous, of course, but there it is.

We both feel very deeply about our problems as a race; while we are not at all sensitive, we are deeply conscious—which is another matter altogether. Mr. Robeson feels that one of the reasons for the almost universal prejudice against our race is the fact that very few people know anything about us (as a race). The ignorance is largely deliberate, we feel. The general public's idea of a Negro is an Uncle Tom, an Aunt Jemima, Ol' Mammy, and Jack Johnson.

These types have always been sold to the public deliberately. Well, now they don't exist any more except in the sentimental minds of credulous people, and we feel that we certainly must not do anything in any way, to prolong their non-existent lives!!! We feel Mr. Robeson must play a Negro who does exist, who has something to do with reality. That's all he asks. . . .

She added that she herself had "loved the story" in Anderson's play, and thought it "very funny, very folky and very touching." Paul did not agree. But Essie thought that perhaps later on, when he "doesn't have to consider it merely as a vehicle for himself, he too will find it amusing and interesting" (ER to Anderson, March 29, 1939, UT).

42. Hughes to ER, July 25, 1939, RA; Naison, *Communists in Harlem*, p. 209; ER to PR, June 25, 1939, RA. The following year Robeson was again briefly tempted by a possible Langston Hughes project (Charles Leonard to PR, Nov. 26, 1940, RA). PR stayed abreast of the activities of the Harlem Suitcase Theatre; an eleven-page description of its "Summer Season and Activity—1939" is in RA, along with a covering letter (James H. Baker, Jr., to PR, Oct. 6, 1939). During his New York trip PR made himself more accessible to the black press than the white. Interviews with him and articles about him appeared in the New York *Amsterdam News,* May 20, 1939 (plus an editorial on May 29 that seconded his decision to educate his son in the U.S.S.R. to avoid racial prejudice, saying his statement "just about sums up the feeling of most Negroes today: it isn't Communism that they are seeking, but equal opportunities"); the Chicago *Defender,* May 27, June 17, 1939; and the Pittsburgh *Courier,* May 27, 1939. The *Defender* (June 17) quotes him as praising the Roosevelt administration for having rebuked the DAR after it refused Marian Anderson permission to sing in its hall. PR also gave an interview to the *Sunday Worker* (June 4, 1939) in which he's quoted as saying, "I feel that it is now

time for me to return to the place of my origin. . . ." Robeson did agree to appear, while in New York, in behalf of Spanish Intellectual Aid (Spanish Culture in Exile), singing at its meeting in the grand ballroom of the Roosevelt Hotel (Jane Sherman to PR, June 30, 1939, RA).

43. *News Review*, June 1, 1939 (Balcon); Hampstead and St. John's Wood *News and Advertiser*, June 1, 1939 (Tennyson). Pen Tennyson had made a promising directorial debut at age twenty-seven with *There Ain't No Justice*, a boxing exposé; he was killed early in the war, having completed only three films (George Perry, *The Great British Picture Show* [Hill & Wang, 1984], p. 85).

44. ER to CVV and FM, July 18, 1939, Yale: Van Vechten.

45. Leonard Lyons's column, "The Lyons Den," New York *Post*, Dec. 26, 1940, printed PR's letter to Lyons ("in no way whatsoever") denying Lyons's earlier report in his column that the Nazi-Soviet pact had produced a change in Robeson's sympathies; four-page typewritten ms., "The Foreign Policy of the Soviet Union," undated (1940?), RA (pact).

46. ER Diary, Sept. 1–30, 1939, RA; ER to CVV and FM, Sept. 22, 1939, Yale: Van Vechten; Walter Legge (of His Master's Voice) to PR, Aug. 10, 1939 (recordings); Sterner interviews with people in Wales (Rachel Thomas, Dilys Thomas, Evelyn Jenkins, Clifford Evans, Roderick Jones, W. J. Davies, Dai Francis) who either acted in *The Proud Valley* or got to know Robeson during the filming. The interviewees all agree in their profound admiration for PR, all echoing in different words the view of Rachel Thomas quoted in the text. My own interview with Herbert Marshall and his wife, Fredda Brilliant (July 20, 1985), who together had written the original script for *The Proud Valley* especially for Paul, elicited the additional information that an American cameraman on the picture had to be removed because of his racist views. Finally, there is the testimony gathered by Mark A. Exton ("Paul Robeson and South Wales"), including interviews with Rachel Thomas, Martha Edwards, and Annie Powell, of the uniformly high esteem in which the Welsh held Robeson. The original script of *The Proud Valley* had a group of unemployed miners defying the owners by opening up the pit themselves and operating it as a co-operative—a strong left-wing statement with obvious appeal to Robeson. That ending, however, was ultimately changed; Balcon, the producer, decided it was not sufficiently "tactful," given the wartime call for greater production (Balcon, *Michael Balcon Presents* [Hutchinson, 1969], p. 126).

47. At first they gave some thought to leaving Pauli in school in London, but decided it was too dangerous (ER to Harold Jackman, Aug. 12, 1939, Yale: Johnson). In her diary (Sept.-Oct. 1939, RA) Essie noted with pleasure the warmth of their reception from the dining-room staff on the ship home (the S.S. *Washington*). The truth of that reception has emerged in a phone interview with Ted Rolfs (Feb. 17, 1987). Rolfs, then a dining-room steward on the ship and a trade-union activist, witnessed the Robesons being "placed in a very undesirable area near the galley." He informed the chief steward who Robeson was, and the steward said to him, "Well, if you think so much of him, give up the captain's table [where Rolfs had been the waiter] and serve him." Rolfs did. Thereafter the rest of the dining-room staff became "unctuous and oily" to Robeson. He refused a request to sing to the passengers—"He was hurt"—but accepted Rolfs's request to sing to the crew at a union meeting. Rolfs and Robeson maintained contact (see note 17, p. 701, and note 19, p. 710).

CHAPTER 12   THE WORLD AT WAR (*1940–1942*)

1. ER Diary, "End of October" 1939, RA (docking); PR's ms. statement is in RA; PR's remarks are from an interview with the New York *Amsterdam News*, Oct. 21, 1939; PR, Notes, 1939, RA (Goering). Essie noted in her diary that they paid no

77. Robeson addressing the Paris Peace Conference at the Salle Pleyel, April 20, 1949

78. Walter White

79. Cartoon in the *Afro-American*, published July 19, 1949, after Jackie Robinson's appearance before HUAC, with the caption: "DROP THAT GUN, JACKIE! The leading player in the National Baseball League is only a tyro as a big-game hunter."

80. Robeson in Moscow, June 1949, speaking in front of a portrait of Pushkin at the celebration of the 150th anniversary of the poet's birth

81. (ABOVE) Welcome-home
rally for Robeson at the
Rockland Palace in Harlem,
June 19, 1949

82. (LEFT) In a confrontation
with news photographers,
after leaving Paul, Jr., and
Marilyn Robeson's wedding
with Marilyn's mother,
June 19, 1949

PEEKSKILL, SEPTEMBER 4, 1949

83. (ABOVE) Robeson and Larry Brown
performing, guarded by union members,
at Peekskill concert

84. (RIGHT) Robeson hung in effigy in
the town of Peekskill

85. (ABOVE) The WWI black veteran aviator, Eugene Bullard, being knocked down and beaten in the riot

86. (RIGHT) "Wake Up America, Peekskill Did!"

87. (BELOW) Police in the middle between pro-Robeson and anti-Robeson factions at Peekskill

88. & 89. Sam and Helen Rosen, 1940s

90. With his sister,
Marian Forsythe,
and his brother Ben,
pastor of Mother
A.M.E. Zion Church,
in the Harlem
parsonage, 1950s

91. (LEFT) In a concert
at his brother's Mother
A.M.E. Zion Church
in Harlem, 1956

92. (BELOW) Eslanda
Robeson testifying before
Joseph McCarthy's
Senate Investigating
Committee, July 7, 1953

93. Ben Davis, Jr., in 1958

94. With Eugene Dennis on May Day, 1950

95. Robeson leaves Washington District Court in August 1955 after a federal judge refused to order the State Department to grant him a passport. With him are William L. Patterson (left) and Lloyd L. Brown.

96. (ABOVE) Robeson
testifying before the
House Committee on
Un-American Activities,
June 12, 1956
(His attorney, Milton
Friedman, is at left.)

97. (RIGHT) Leaving
from Idlewild Airport
for London, July 10,
1958, after restoration
of his passport

98. With African and Asian students at the World Youth Festival
in Vienna, 1959

99. On a visit to the V. I. Lenin Artek Pioneer Camp, September 1958

100. The Robesons with Nikita Khrushchev at Yalta, 1958

101. With Sam Wanamaker and Mary Ure in Stratford during the run of *Othello*, 1959

102. In Prague, 1959   103. Essie, 1959

104. The Robesons with Nnamdi Azikiwe of Nigeria
in London, 1960

105. With Prime Minister Jawaharlal Nehru of India in New York, 1957

106. Robeson receiving the Star of
Friendship of Nations from Walter Ulbricht
in East Berlin, October 1960

107. Robeson holding a portrait of
Patrice Lumumba at Lumumba Friendship
University in Moscow, March 1961

108. Robeson in East Berlin, December 1963, during his stay at the Buch Clinic, with his doctor, Alfred Katzenstein (left), and Harry Francis (right)

109. Met by Paul, Jr., and Marilyn Robeson on arrival at Kennedy Airport in New York, December 22, 1963

110. At the funeral service for playwright Lorraine Hansberry, January 1965
(From left are Ruby Dee, Shelley Winters, Robeson, Leo Nemiroff, and Diana Sands)

111. At his sister
Marian's house in
Philadelphia, 1970s

112. The coffin of Paul Robeson being taken from Mother Zion
A.M.E. Church on January 27, 1976

duty on their enormous number of bags, the customs inspectors showing interest in nothing except the heads Jacob Epstein had done of both Pauls and the African artifacts from her trip. (There are a number of letters in RA during 1938–39 from Epstein discussing the two sculptures.)

2. Hannen Swaffer, *World's Press*, March 14, 1940; New York *Post*, Feb. 1, 1940 (Laski, etc.). Additional interviews with PR from which the above statements are drawn are in the *Daily Worker*, Dec. 12, 23, 1939 (interview with Ben Davis, Jr.); the Philadelphia *Record*, Dec. 11, 1939; and the *Evening Public Ledger* (Philadelphia), Dec. 8, 1939. Four-page typewritten ms. entitled "The Foreign Policy of the Soviet Union," undated (1940?), RA (peace pact). In an article on PR in the *Sunday Worker*, 1940, his career is said to have been seriously damaged as a result of his refusal to defend Finland (" . . . no manager would dare rent an auditorium to Robeson"), to be rescued only by the huge success of "Ballad for Americans"; but I have found only minor evidence of any career setback. After the war Swaffer and Robeson renewed contact, and with considerable cordiality (e.g., Swaffer to PR, Dec. 13, 1961, RA).

3. New York *World-Telegram*, Jan. 20, Feb. 1, 1940 ("real democracy"); the black letter-writer was Cyril W. Stephens (New York *Amsterdam News*, Dec. 23, 1939); a similar rebuke to Robeson is in the Winnipeg *Free Press*, Feb. 14, 1940; McKay, *The New Leader*, Jan. 20, 1940. McKay's criticism of Robeson was later echoed in the assessment of Shostakovich in his *Testimony* (see note 42, p. 690). For a detailed exposition of official CPUSA reaction to international issues in this period, see Maurice Isserman, *Which Side Were You On?: The American Communist Party During the Second World War* (Wesleyan University Press, 1982).

4. New York *Post*, Feb. 1, 1940; New York *World-Telegram*, Feb. 1, 1940; *Daily Worker*, Oct. 26, 1939; CVV to White, Dec. 14, 1939, CVV to Noel Sullivan, Feb. 13, 1940, CVV to Peterson, Dec. 3, 1939—all in Kellner, ed., *Letters CVV*, pp. 169, 171–72.

5. ER Diary, "End of October," "End of November," 1939, RA.

6. *Time*, Nov. 20, 1939 (background on "Pursuit"); interview with Earl Robinson, Aug. 17, 1986.

7. Interview with Earl Robinson, Aug. 17, 1986. Later in life, PR wrote, ". . . now I always try to pitch my songs in the range of my speaking voice. Therefore practically all of my songs have to be transposed to lower keys, since my natural voice is a deep bass" (music notes, n.d. 1960s?, RA).

8. Liner notes inside cover of Victor recording; interview with Earl Robinson, Aug. 17, 1986; Norman Corwin to PR, Nov. 8, 1939, RA; Atkinson to PR, Dec. 29, 1940 (Atkinson was writing in response to the Victor recording, not the broadcast); Robert Minor to PR, Dec. 31, 1939 (Lydia Minor wrote him separately, also raving about "Ballad," n.d.)—all RA.

9. Luther Davis and John Cleveland, "And You Know Who I Am" (profile of John LaTouche), *Collier's*, Oct. 19, 1940 (convention, "Boy scouts"). *Time*, July 8, 1940, reported that Robeson's Victor recording of "Ballad" was "the popular number most in demand at the R.C.A. exhibit at the New York World's Fair." *Time* also reported that the Republicans had considered inviting Robeson to sing "Ballad" but had decided against it because of his color. But Earl Robinson (interview, Aug. 17, 1986) insists that the Republicans *did* invite Robeson to sing at their 1940 convention, but he had to turn them down because of a prior engagement in New York. When *The New Yorker* asked Robinson for his reaction to the Republicans' doing "Ballad," he said, "Fantastic!—we wrote the Ballad for everyone."

10. Seton to ER, Jan. 5, 1951; interview with Earl Robinson, Aug. 17, 1986.

11. ER Diary, "End of December," 1939, "End of January," 1940, RA; *Daily Worker*, Oct. 26, 1939 (Ben Davis); interviews with Bayard Rustin, March 25, April 20, 1983; ER to CVV and FM, Dec. 15, 1939; postcard, Jan. 6, 1940, Yale: Van Vechten. Essie's warning to him about the Bradford script is in ER to PR, June 25, 1939, RA. A sample of the mixed-to-negative out-of-town reviews:

Variety, Dec. 13, 1939; Philadelphia *Inquirer*, Dec. 12, 1939; *Evening Public Ledger*, Dec. 16, 1939; Boston *Herald*, Jan. 4, 1940. A sample of the New York reviews: *Herald Tribune*, New York *World-Telegram*, *The New York Times*, all Jan. 11, 1940. Only the *Telegram* was strongly favorable to the play, but almost all the reviewers liked Robeson's performance—"a man of magnificence who ought to be on the stage frequently in plays that suit him," Brooks Atkinson wrote in the *Times*; and in a letter, PR's friend Jimmy Sheean said, "I thought your performance . . . one of great power and beauty. It's hard luck that the play itself didn't rise to the height of that performance" (Sheean to PR, Jan. 11, 1940, RA). Because of a dispute between the producer and the theater manager, a financial brouhaha developed, and Robeson had trouble securing his salary for a time (New York *World-Telegram*, Jan. 20, 1940; ER Diary, "End of January," 1940, RA; Sterner interview with Leonard de Paur, who supervised the show's music). Two organizations, the Harlem Cultural Conference and the Negro People's Committee for Spanish Refugees, took over the house for one performance of *John Henry* (Yergan to ER, Dec. 8, 1939, RA).

12. ER Diary, Jan. 21, 1940, RA; PR, ms., "Notes on speech at Hamilton College," RA; Woollcott to PR, May 25, 1940, RA. When Woollcott died in Jan. 1943, Robeson read the Twenty-third Psalm at his memorial service (*The New York Times*, Jan. 29, 1943; Utica *Observer Dispatch*, Jan. 22, 1940). Oumansky to ER, Dec. 11, 1939, RA; ER Diary, Jan. 28, July 18, 1940, RA.

13. Rudolph Polk to Fred Schang, Jan. 18, 1941 (Kraft); Moses Smith to PR, May 9, 1941 (Columbia); Schang to Rockmore, Feb. 1, 1941—all RA; *Hearings Special Comm.* (Dies) *UnAmerican Activities*, May 22, 1941, 60 (in hearings three years later, Matthews again cited the *SRT* article against PR, falsely claiming that in it he had "stated categorically that communism was the only way": Sept. 29, 1944, p. 10337.

14. A. Philip Randolph to Walter White, Feb. 6, 1941, LC: NAACP. White forwarded Randolph's criticisms to Gilbert Josephson, director of the World Theatre (Feb. 13, 1941, LC: NAACP). *The Proud Valley* was released in 1940 in Britain, 1941 in the United States. Several of the British reviewers liked the film (*Listener*, March 21, 1940; *Picturegoer*, May 18, 1940; *Scotsman*, April 1, 1940), but the majority found it, in the words of the Manchester *Guardian* (March 7, 1940), "undistinguished" (see also *Punch*, March 27, 1940; *The Times*, March 11, 1940; *New Statesman*, March 9, 1940; *The Observer*, March 10, 1940). A radio-broadcast version of *The Proud Valley* was given before the actual release of the film (*The Times*, London, March 7, 1940). The American reviews were marginally more favorable; the New York *Daily News* (May 17, 1941) seems representative: "roughly made . . . fine Welsh music . . . The plot is a routine affair. . . . Robeson's magnificent voice is one of the picture's chief attractions. . . ." *The Afro-American* (May 24, 1941) hailed the film as "a triumph for Robeson, and for the British motion picture makers as well" because of its unorthodox casting.

15. Los Angeles *Examiner*, Los Angeles *News*, Los Angeles *Times* (responsive); Los Angeles *Evening Herald and Express* (ovation)—all May 14, 1940. Betty L. Richardson, 1982 interview with Edwin Lester (producer of the Civic Light Opera), under auspices of Oral History Program, UCLA (Bertha Powell). In the interview Lester also reports that he had to let Helen Morgan go because of her drinking problem. He recounts, too, an aborted effort to present PR in the role of Porgy at the Civic Light Opera. According to Lester, PR initiated the idea, and Lester went along with it, though warning him that he thought the role lay too high for his voice. Robeson was at first confident he could sing it (and Lester proceeded to make tentative production plans), but he subsequently backed out, afraid his voice would not stand up under the strain.

16. New York *Sun*, June 26, 1940; New York *Amsterdam News*, July 6, 1940; *Time*, July 8, 1940; ER Diary, June 24, 1940, RA. *Time* reported, "Last week Mrs. Robeson, who chaperones her husband in interviews, shushed him on poli-

tics, said 'there is a witch hunt on in America now.' Asked if Communism is compatible with the U.S. Constitution, the Robesons declined to reply."

17. Chicago *Journal of Commerce*, July 29, 1940 (Cassidy); on Aug. 31 Robeson performed "Ballad" again in Chicago, this time under the baton of the black conductor James A. Mundy (Pittsburgh *Courier*, Sept. 14, 1940); New York *World-Telegram*, Aug. 6, 1940 *(Jones);* Langner to O'Neill, Aug. 20, 1940, RA; Langner to PR, Aug. 15, Sept. 13, 1940; Rockmore to Langner, Aug. 29, Sept. 11, 16, 1940 —all in Yale: Langner. (Langner also tried, unsuccessfully, to interest Robeson in appearing in a new play, *Not on Friday.*) There is a letter from PR to O'Neill, July 31, 1940 (Yale: O'Neill) requesting permission to use a special Hammond Organ for offstage sound effects in the *Jones* production; perhaps O'Neill denied the request, since the reviews don't refer to such effects.

During Aug. PR also found time to sing at Camp Wo-Chi-Ca, an interracial camp for the children of workers that had declared Paul Robeson Day (Hacketts-town *Gazette*, Aug. 16, 1940)—for more on the camp, see p. 254— and also to sing at a benefit for the monthly journal *Equality*, prompting Lillian Hellman to write him, "It is a fine thing to *hear you sing,* and like all really decent art, it makes you feel sad and happy and good" (Hellman to PR, Aug. 12, 1940, RA).

Robeson had somewhat less than full success in his first indoor New York City concert in nearly five years in Carnegie Hall in early Oct. 1940; it was enthusiastically greeted by the audience, but somewhat less so by the critics (New York *Herald Tribune, Sun, World-Telegram,* and *Times*—all Oct. 7, 1940—expressed varying degrees of reservation). When he returned to sing in New York two months after that Carnegie Hall concert, Robeson was again treated with politeness rather than acclaim by the critics—at least in comparison with the thunderous welcome he got on tour; as in Britain, his provincial receptions were more enthusiastic than his cosmopolitan ones (New York *Herald Tribune, Sun, Times, World-Telegram, PM*—all Dec. 18, 1940;

the *Sun* review seems representative: "... Robeson's richly sonorous but somewhat monotonous voice ..."). During the war years, Robeson gradually expanded his concert repertoire. He added a number of Russian songs, especially by Mussorgsky (including "The Death Scene" and "Varlaam's Ballad" from *Boris Godunov*), and also a number of popular English ballads ("Oh No, John!" became a great audience favorite, though its trivial, arch nature was hardly well suited either to Robeson's voice or his temperament). The programs for PR's concerts in 1939–45 are in RA.

18. Chicago *Defender*, Aug. 3, 1940; interview with Earl Robinson, Aug. 17, 1986. Robeson flew to Hollywood; it was his first time on a plane and, according to Essie, he "loved the trip" (ER Diary, June 5, 1940, RA).

19. Multiple interviews with Freda Diamond.

20. Multiple interviews with Freda Diamond; ER to Toni Strassman, June 6, 1938; ER to Nan Pandit, Aug. 15, 1951; ER to Nehru, Sept. 17, 1957, RA. Many entries in PR's datebook for 1941 (RA) list appointments with Freda.

21. The executed documents turning over control to Rockmore are in RA. Interviews with Clara Rockmore, April 26, 1983, March 17, 1984; ER Diary, June 5 (Columbia), 9, 12, 1940, RA; Frances Taylor Patterson (who taught Essie film at Columbia) to ER, May 20, 1940, RA *(Black Progress);* David Bader to ER, June 1, 7, 1940 *(Uncle Tom),* RA; Nehru to ER, July 10, 1940, RA. In Erik Barnouw's recollection, Essie registered for his class because "She wanted to develop a formula for a series to present her husband on the air" (Shannon Shafly and Mark Langer interview with Barnouw, 1975, Columbia University Oral History Project). ER's trip to Central America is fully documented in her diary for Aug. 1940 and in the several long letters she wrote to Pauli and to her mother (all in RA). No letters were sent directly to Paul, nor do the other letters make any mention of him— which cannot have been an accident. Paul also signed up at Columbia—for nine credits in Russian and Chinese—but there is no record of his attending classes.

In the years immediately preceding their return to the States, tension between Paul and Essie had receded but not disappeared. In 1938, for example, she wrote the Van Vechtens, "Paul actually came out on the tender to meet me at Southampton when I returned. I was so astonished. I never expected anything like that and never even looked. Idly watching the tender arrive, I noted a very big lump of brown, and it was Paul!! Well, well" (ER to CVV and FM, Aug. 17, 1938, Yale: Van Vechten).

22. Theodore Ward (president, Negro Playwrights) to ER, May 30, 1940; Ward to ER, June 25, 29, 1940, RA; *Daily Worker*, July 27, 1940 (inaugural); *Sunday Worker*, Sept. 15, 1940 (Davis); the Pittsburgh *Courier* (Sept. 14, 1940) and the New York *Amsterdam News* (Sept. 14, 1940) also carried articles about the opening; Richard Wright, Langston Hughes, Andy Razaf, Hazel Scott, Gwendolyn Bennett, and Morris Carnovsky (of the Group Theatre) were among the other participating celebrities.

23. *PM*, Sept. 17, 1940 (Spanish songs); Jessica Smith to PR, July 5, 1941, March 26, 1942, MSRC: Jessica Smith Papers. At the same time, a film PR made while in Spain was recovered (William Pickens to PR, Oct. 22, 1940, RA, enclosing a statement from Nancy Cunard about the film); George Gregory to PR, Oct. 12, 1940, RA (Harlem); Madame Sun Yat-sen to PR, Sept. 1940, RA (China); Frederick V. Field to "Brother Robeson," Sept. 20, 1940 (conscription); Dreiser to PR, May 14, 1940, RA; *Herald*, March 30, 1941; *Daily Province* (Vancouver), Oct. 31, 1940; Jane Swanhuysen to Marcantonio, Nov. 11, 1940, NYPL, Ms. Div.: Marcantonio (Emergency Peace Mobilization).

24. Interviews with Clara Rockmore, April 26, 1983, March 17, 1984.

25. Interviews with Clara Rockmore, April 26, 1983, March 17, 1984. "Paul's attitude to me is really touching," Clara Rockmore wrote her husband (n.d. [1940s]); also PR to Bob Rockmore, Nov. 3, 1944—both courtesy of Clara Rockmore.

26. Interviews with Clara Rockmore, April 26, 1983, March 17, 1984. PR's popularity with college audiences is amply attested to in the local and campus reviews of his concerts. *Daily Home News* (New Brunswick), Oct. 10, 1940: "tumultuous applause by 3,600"; Hamilton *Republican*, Oct. 17, 1940: "established a record for the largest attendance at a non-athletic event in Colgate history"; *Daily Cardinal* (University of Wisconsin), Oct. 22, 1940: "a tremendous ovation"; Seattle *Times* (University of Washington), Nov. 7, 1940: "turbulent applause." Clara and Larry Brown were very fond of each other; there's a letter in NYPL/Schm: Brown, Nov. 5, 1940, from Bob Rockmore to Brown expressing his gratitude for "all your kindness and consideration to Clara."

27. Interviews with Clara Rockmore, April 26, 1983, March 17, 1984; followup phone interview with Revels Cayton, May 30, 1987 (Vanessi's); the incident at Vanessi's is also described in the San Francisco *People's World*, Nov. 15, 1940, *The New York Times*, Nov. 10, 1940, and the *Sunday Worker*, Nov. 17, 1940; the lawsuit in the Chicago *Defender*, Nov. 30, 1940, which reports that damages in the sum of $22,500 were being sought. In a lighter vein, Leonard Lyons reported in his gossip column, "The Lyons Den" (New York *Post*, Dec. 4, 1940), that, when Robeson was dining on a Chicago-bound train with Oscar Levant and Marc Connelly, a Pullman waiter approached Robeson for an autograph. He obliged, and the pleased waiter left—without asking Levant or Connelly for their autographs. Robeson purportedly smiled and said, "No offense—it's just racial solidarity."

28. Interviews with Clara Rockmore, April 26, 1983, March 17, 1984; multiple interviews with Helen Rosen (rage).

29. Interviews with Clara Rockmore, April 26, 1983, March 17, 1984. In some of the quotes from Rockmore I have removed ellipses between comments she made at different points in our interviews, combining them to avoid endless diacritical marks. Of course, as Alan Bush, who accompanied PR in the later fifties, pointed out to me: "There's no such thing as natural singing. If there is, it's unbearable to listen to. People who

think they sing by the light of nature, you would never wish to hear them a second time. Now, he was a developed singer, very highly developed technically, but he sounded absolutely natural. And so you would think he was born to sing. . . . He had relative pitch" (interview with Alan Bush, PR, Jr., participating, Sept. 3, 1982).

Toward the end of the tour, Robeson started to cup a hand behind his ear in order to hear himself better; he retained the habit of ear-cupping thereafter. He also participated, during this same period, in an experiment with an electronic device ("Synthia") developed by Prof. Harold Burris-Meyer, theater sound-research director at the Stevens Institute of Technology, to enable a singer to hear his own sound without producing acoustical distortions or amplification in the concert hall (papers, newspaper articles, and correspondence surrounding the experiment are in RA).

30. ER to PR, Nov. 3, 5, 9, 1940, RA; ER to CVV, Nov. 7 (weight), 9 (parents' functions), 1940; ER to CVV and FM, Nov. 15, 1940, Yale: Van Vechten. "We've been hanging around for months, doing nothing, since 'John Henry' closed, and were beginning to get restless," Essie wrote John P. Davis, describing her own turmoil more than Paul's (ER to Davis, April 20, 1941, National Negro Congress Papers—henceforth NYPL/Schm: NNC).

31. Hartford *Courant*, April 2, 1941 (worker); ER to CVV and FM, Nov. 27, 1941 ("Big Paul"), RA; PR to ER, Aug. 29, 1941, RA; Freda Diamond ms. comment (scaffold). Essie bombarded Bob Rockmore with itemized bills and enthusiastic reports about the detailed adventures of settling in. Various friends —including Minnie Sumner, Hattie Bolling, Bert and Gig McGhee, Sadie Sumner, Essie's brother John Goode, Freda Diamond, and Walter White's son, Pidgy White (to visit Pauli)—came up for a look at the new place, and all expressed enthusiasm (e.g., ER to Rockmore, June 16, July 13, 23, Aug. 10, 25, 1941, RA). Rockmore periodically showed his exasperation with Essie's nest-building ex-

penditures, writing her that until the last of the renovations and improvements were finally finished, there would "be no peace on earth for anybody" (Rockmore to ER, Aug. 12, 1941, RA).

32. Of special value in understanding the Popular Front years (though it is concerned primarily with the leadership, not the rank and file of the CP) is Harvey Klehr, *The Heyday of American Communism* (Basic Books, 1984).

33. It's impossible to cite with any thoroughness the large literature on these issues, but I found of special value (along with Klehr, *Heyday*) Raymond Wolters, *Negroes and the Great Depression* (Greenwood, 1970), Bert Cochran, *Labor and Communism* (Princeton, 1977), John B. Kirby, *Black Americans in the Roosevelt Era* (University of Tennessee, 1980), and, above all, Naison's indispensable *Communists in Harlem*.

The Robesons were never more than marginally acquainted with the Ralph Bunches. In 1932 Essie interviewed Bunche for a book she was planning at the time on prominent black figures and found him "attractive and very, very interesting" (ER Diary, Sept. 26, 1932, RA). A telling anecdote about Robeson and Bunche was told to me by Jean Herskovits, daughter of Melville Herskovits: The family had recently returned from Trinidad where Jean (age four) had picked up fluent pidgin English. Robeson was the first black man Jean had seen since Trinidad, and when he swept her up in his arms on arriving at the Herskovits house, she enthusiastically greeted him in pidgin. Robeson and Jean's parents burst out laughing. "Thank God she didn't do that with Ralph [Bunche]!" Paul said. In 1949, when Robeson was under fire from the established black leadership, Bunche is quoted as saying, "I have always admired Mr. Robeson's singing more than his social philosophy" (as quoted in Gilbert Ware, *William Hastie: Grace Under Pressure* [Oxford, 1984], p. 229). Subsequently, Robeson apparently made a disparaging remark about Bunche (Corliss Lamont to PR, Dec. 1, 1950, NYPL/Schm: PR Coll.).

34. ER to Davis, April 20, 1941, NYPL/Schm: NNC; Rajni [Patel] to ER,

April 26, 1940, RA (India); PR joined Theodore Dreiser in cabling his support of the British People's Convention (Jan. 4, 1941), hailing its struggle against imperialist war aims—both men's statements are in RA. Alphaeus Hunton served as a chairman of the NNC's Labor Committee, and Doxey Wilkerson headed its Civil Affairs Committee. Both men subsequently moved to the Council on African Affairs, and Hunton became a close Robeson associate. John P. Davis resigned from the NNC early in 1943; at that time the national office closed, though the Council continued to function for a while longer in New York before folding into the Civil Rights Congress (Dorothy Hunton, *Alphaeus Hunton: The Unsung Valiant* [privately printed by Dorothy Hunton, 1986]).

35. *Daily Worker*, Feb. 1, Oct. 1, Dec. 16, 18, 1941 (Browder), March 25, 1942 ("anti-fascist"); Citizen's Letter to Free Earl Browder, 1941–42 (PR was one of the Sponsors of the National Conference to Free Earl Browder), NYPL: Marcantonio. Gurley Flynn's statement about PR's expenditures in Browder's behalf was reported in War Dept., March 15, 1943, FBI 100-26603-1067, p. 2. The March 17, 1941, mass "Free Browder" rally was formally billed as a sixtieth birthday celebration for William Z. Foster, general secretary of the CPUSA. Browder himself appeared at the rally and received an ovation; as did Robeson when introduced by Robert Minor, then acting secretary of the CPUSA. In tribute to Foster, Robeson sang Marc Blitzstein's "The Purest Kind of Guy." Other speakers included the black Communist leader James W. Ford and Israel Amter, New York State chairman of the Party. Theodore Dreiser sent a telegram.

36. In a commencement speech he gave at the Manual Training School on June 10, 1943, PR advised blacks to "view the whole struggle within the Labor Movement as *our* struggle. We must fight for our rights inside our *labor organizations*—for here are, for the most part, our *real allies*—those who suffer as we, subject to the same disabilities as we. Organizations as N.M.U.—militant sections of C.I.O.—prove point" (typed ms. in RA).

He reiterated the theme yet again in accepting an honorary degree from Morehouse College in 1943 (the typed ms. is in RA). For a full discussion of Robeson's role with the UAW, see Charles H. Wright, *Robeson: Labor's Forgotten Champion* (Balamp, 1975), pp. 83–103. In the general discussion which follows of CP-CIO interaction, I am heavily indebted to Mark Naison's study *Communists in Harlem*, especially pp. 261–73. A sympathetic view of the relationship between the CP and the CIO is ably argued in Harvey A. Levenstein, *Communism, Anticommunism, and the CIO* (Greenwood Press, 1981). In Levenstein's estimate, as many as eleven of the CIO's thirty-three affiliates during World War II had substantial Communist leanings (including the UEW, the ILWU and the NMU). For the contribution of the CP to industrial unionism in Detroit, see Roger Keeran, *The Communist Party and the Auto Workers Union* (Indiana University Press, 1980). For a less favorable interpretation of the CP's influence on trade-unionism, see Nelson Lichtenstein, *Labor's War at Home* (Cambridge University Press, 1982). See also p. 419, and note 33, p. 712.

37. In his brilliant discussion of Communism's failure to ignite the black working class, from which many of my own views derive, Naison additionally suggests that the CP's "artificially imposed interracialism" made working-class blacks, who preferred the coherence and integrity of their own fraternal and social institutions, uncomfortable; similarly, the demands the Party placed on the skills of verbal dialectics alienated the many blacks who were recent rural migrants (Naison, *Communists in Harlem*, especially pp. 279–83).

38. *Daily Worker*, Dec. 17, 1941; *Ford Facts*, May 17, 1941; *News of Connecticut*, Aug. 1, 1941 (hailing the CIO's stand against discrimination). The program for "The Negro in American Life"—which was repeated—is in RA, along with newspaper accounts of the event and an enthusiastic thank-you letter from Dave Greene (executive secretary of the IWO) to PR, April 4, 1941. Fort Wayne *U.E. Herald*, April 1, 1943.

39. Lucy Martin Donnelly to PR,

April 23, 1941 (PR's concert for Chinese scholarships at Bryn Mawr, April 18, 1941), with enclosures, RA; Frank Kai-ming Su (China Aid Council) to ER, Feb. 5, 1941, RA; *PM*, March 30, 1941 (DAR). Anson Phelps Stokes, who had been a canon of the cathedral in Washington when the Marian Anderson issue arose and had helped spearhead the protest, sent PR his deep regrets over the DAR's latest refusal, along with a copy of the pamphlet *Art and the Color Line*, which he had written in response to the Anderson protest (Stokes to PR, April 19, 1941, RA).

40. Press release of the Associated Negro Press, CHS: Barnett.

41. Press release of the Associated Negro Press, CHS: Barnett; Cornelia Pinchot to Eleanor Roosevelt, April 13, 1941, along with ms. drafts of her press release, Roosevelt Papers, Hyde Park (hereafter FDR). On Aug. 7, 1941, Zola Ardene Clear, who had been publicity director of the Washington Committee for Aid to China, gave extended testimony about the incident before the Dies Committee in which she accused the NNC of Communistic duplicity throughout (House *Hearings* concerning Un-American Propaganda Activities, 1941, pp. 2366–79).

42. NNC press release, CHS: Barnett; Pinchot to Roosevelt, April 13, 1941, FDR. Pinchot's statement to the papers about her reasons for withdrawing, and also a separate statement she released to the black press, are printed in full in House *Hearings* concerning Un-American Propaganda Activities, 1941, pp. 2374–76.

43. The program for the April 25, 1941, Uline Arena concert is in RA. It did list Dr. Hu Shih as an "Honorary Sponsor"—apparently he changed his mind—and contains a printed "commendation" from the NNC to the Washington Committee for Aid to China for its "excellent work." Apparently Robeson sang the Chinese Communist "Cheelai" ("March of the Volunteers") for the first time, of what would become many, at the Uline concert (Liu Liang-mo to ER, April 11, 1941, RA, containing the words to "Cheelai" and a piano accompaniment,

as PR had requested). Newspaper accounts of the concert are in the Washington *Post*, April 26, 1941, the *Times-Herald*, April 26, 1941 ("Willkie"), and the Philadelphia *Inquirer*, May 3, 1941. Letters of thanks from Muriel Koenigsberg (executive secretary, WCAC) to PR and to ER, both April 30, 1941, and from Frank Kai-ming Su to PR, Sept. 5, 1941, are in RA.

44. Klehr, *Heyday*, p. 399.

45. *Daily Worker*, July 4, 23, 1941; *Sunday Worker*, July 6, Nov. 2 (masses), 1941; Vancouver *News-Herald*, Vancouver *Sun*, Nov. 22, 1941; Chicago *Defender*, Nov. 1, 1941; Rose N. Rubin to PR, May 1, 1941; Harriet L. Moore (American Russian Institute), May 2, 1941, RA; *PM*, April 30, 1941 (Benny Goodman); Hewlett Johnson letter dated Oct. 17, 1941, RA. Two weeks after Pearl Harbor, Robeson, in a single five-day period, sang before a record crowd at the Civic Auditorium in San Francisco, gave a benefit concert in Oakland for Medical Aid to Russia, and participated in the Russian War Relief concert in San Francisco (*People's World*, Dec. 18, 1941); programs in RA.

46. These examples of the shift in American opinion about the Soviet Union are quoted in Irving Howe and Lewis Coser, *The American Communist Party* (Da Capo Press, 1974), pp. 431–33.

47. R. P. Bonham, District Director, to FBI Special Agent in Charge (hereafter SAC), Seattle, FBI Main 100-12304-1 ("reputedly"); R. B. Hood, SAC, to Director, April 3, 1942, blurred file number 100-12304-?; "Summary of Chinese Writing in Brown Notebook," by Harold L. Child, April 24, 1942, FBI Main 100-12304-5; Hoover to SAC L.A., May 27, 1942, file number blurred; Foxworth to Director, Sept. 19, 1942, FBI Main 100-12304-6 (Wo-Chi-Ca). According to Mother Bloor, Robeson "helped a lot to build one of the finest music rooms in the country" at Camp Wo-Chi-Ca: "It is like a temple" (Bloor to "My dear Family," Sept. 28, 1947, SSC).

For a discussion of the provenance and substance of the FBI files used here (and throughout the rest of the book) see my Note on Sources, p. 557. The year

1941 saw a general increase in FBI activity regarding "the threat of Communism." Its efforts remained somewhat episodic until early 1946, when the Bureau inaugurated a formal strategy of "educating" the public by a variety of devices, including the selective leaking of confidential files to "friendly" newspaper columnists like Walter Winchell, Drew Pearson, and George Sokolsky (Kenneth O'Reilly, "The FBI and the Origins of McCarthyism," *Historian,* vol. XLV [May 1983], pp. 372–73).

48. Hoover to Lawrence M. C. Smith, Chief, Special War Policies Unit, Jan. 12, 1943, FBI Main 100-12304-8 (custodial detention); Guy Hottel, SAC, to Director, Aug. 26, 1943, FBI Main 100-12304-10 ("leading"); Office of Naval Intelligence memo, Jan. 14, 1942, FBI NY 100-25857-3A; War Department letter, March 15, 1943, 100-26603-1067, p. 2, NY 100-25857-8.

49. Interviews with Uta Hagen, June 22–23, 1982, Sept. 28, 1984.

50. The typed mss. of PR's speeches at Morehouse and to the *Herald Tribune* Forum are in RA. In a radio address over WEAF on Jan. 2, 1944, PR decried the continuing denial of full citizenship to blacks (typed ms. of speech, RA).

51. Typed ms. of speech delivered at the commencement of the Manual Training School on June 10, 1943, RA.

An encyclopedic listing of Robeson's nonstop round of appearances during this period would be tediously repetitive, and I've decided instead to cite only a few of the more significant: At a "Defend America Rally" in Los Angeles on Dec. 22, 1941, called by the NNC in conjunction with "100 leading Negro citizens," he encouraged the full mobilization of the black community (*People's World,* Dec. 22, 26, 1941). In Dec. 1941 he gave a brief concert for the inmates at San Quentin Prison (*The Other Side of the Inside!,* December 25, 1941; *Daily Worker,* Dec. 27, 1941). His appearances at war-bond rallies included one in Boston (Boston *Post,* Aug. 12, 1942) as well as the first interracial bond rally in Detroit, in which he was joined by Supreme Court Justice Murphy, Marian Anderson, Joe Louis, Olivia De Havilland, and Bill (Bojangles)

Robinson (Detroit *Evening News,* June 1, 1942). His work for the troops included a radio broadcast, "Salute to the Champions," for which Secretary of War Henry L. Stimson sent him a letter of thanks (Oct. 1, 1941, RA). The following year Henry Morgenthau, Jr., Secretary of the Treasury, sent him a gold-embossed citation (dated May 17, 1942, RA) "In recognition of distinguished and patriotic service to our Country"—namely, a recital at West Point (Alvin D. Wilder, Jr., to PR, Jan. 12, 1942, RA), and a "Salute to Negro Troops," a pageant celebrating black war heroes held at the Cosmopolitan Opera (New York *Amsterdam Star News,* Jan. 17, 1942). On March 22, 1942, PR was the guest of honor at a dinner "in tribute to Anti-fascist fighters" held at the Hotel Biltmore, chaired by Dorothy Parker and attended by a thousand people, including a large turnout of celebrities (Dorothy Parker to ER, March 17, 1942; New York *Amsterdam Star News,* March 28, 1942). Another dinner, however, was attacked as "Communist-inspired." Also held at the Biltmore, it was a dinner-forum in behalf of exiled writers interned in French concentration camps, with Lillian Hellman and Ernest Hemingway as cochairs. Seven hundred people attended, but Governor Herbert H. Lehman and others withdrew after the *World-Telegram* attacked the event as "Communist-inspired." At the dinner, Hellman protested the accusation. *PM* quoted her as saying (Oct. 10, 1941), "I am damn sick and tired of these attacks; I am sick of their ignorance, their irresponsibility, and their malice and their cowardice." In her invitation to PR to attend, Hellman wrote, "It will make me feel much better to have you there, and it will make everybody else feel better, too" (Hellman to PR, Sept. 29, 1941, RA). Hellman would have felt sicker still had she seen the FBI report characterizing the Biltmore dinner as in reality designed to raise funds "for the transportation of Communists to Mexico and other Latin-American countries," branding participants Erskine Caldwell and Margaret Webster as "of course close to the Communist Party" and describing Benny Goodman as having "long been an ardent Communist sympathizer" (report from San Antonio, Texas, dated March 16, 1942; the file number, FBI Main, is blurred but appears to be 100-12304-2).

52. Chicago *Defender*, Feb. 21, 1942; *People's World*, March 5, 1942; Kansas City *Times*, Feb. 18, 1942 ("stronger feeling"). A month before the Kansas City episode, while traveling by train across New York State, Robeson found himself seated alone at a table in the crowded dining car because no whites were willing to sit next to a black man. The incident—hardly the first such that Robeson had experienced—may have helped to fuel his anger in Kansas City (Judith Green, *The Columbia Law Alumni Observer*, April-May 1982; David W. Meltzer to Judith Green, July 16, 1982, courtesy of Green).

53. Albuquerque *Journal*, Feb. 18, 1942; Bluford to PR, Feb. 21, 1942, RA; Pittsburgh *Courier*, Feb. 28, 1942. Fred Schang, PR's agent at the Metropolitan Musical Bureau, which booked the tour, applauded Robeson's position and promised to redouble vigilance in the future when booking his concerts (Schang to PR, Feb. 18, 1942, RA). The following year PR canceled an appearance in Wilmington when he learned of discriminatory policies there against blacks; he had been reluctant to fill the engagement from the first after receiving a letter from the president of Wilmington Concerts Association that sought to "allay" his fears about segregation by assuring him, "There is not segregation because there are no negro members of our Association. . . . We have not discriminated against negroes becoming members of our Association since none applied for membership" (Harold W. Elley to PR, Dec. 28, 1942, RA). Robeson also, during a Robin Hood Dell concert in Philadelphia, refused to honor a request to sing "De Glory Road," declaring it "an insult to the colored race" (*The Afro-American*, Aug. 1, 1942). Jacques Wolfe, the author of the ballad, wrote a letter to *Variety* (Aug. 12, 1942) protesting that he himself had played "Glory Road" for Robeson back in 1928 and Robeson had not only expressed approval of the song but had also recommended it to Schirmer's for publication. Wolfe ex-pressed puzzlement as to why a song Robeson found acceptable in 1928 "now suddenly becomes 'an insult to the entire Negro race.' " But it was no puzzle. Robeson's view of what was "acceptable" had undergone radical transformation in the intervening fourteen years.

54. Yergan to PR, Feb. 18, 1942, RA; Yergan to PR, Feb. 10, 18, 1942, RA, are examples of Yergan's itemizing and suggesting a calendar of political events for PR to attend. In his new capacity as Robeson's political aide, Yergan tried to use the Kansas City incident as an opening to President Roosevelt. He telegraphed Roosevelt's secretary, Stephen T. Early, requesting "an immediate appointment to confer on the larger aspects of 'Negroes and the War,' " including its international ramifications. Yergan subsequently sent a proposed agenda (as the President's office requested), using the occasion to plead as well for the release of Earl Browder, still confined in the Atlanta penitentiary. But the only response was a last-minute invitation to Robeson and Earl Robinson to sing Robinson's new *Roosevelt Cantata* at the White House, which Robeson's schedule prevented him from accepting. Yergan to PR, Feb. 18, 1942; PR to Watson, April 2, 1942; PR to FDR, April 2, 1942, RA; Earl Robinson to ER, April 5, 1942, RA.

55. The original members of the Council of twelve people included seven black Americans, among them Hubert T. Delany, Channing Tobias, Ralph Bunche, and Mordecai Johnson, but the latter two soon resigned because (according to the FBI) "the organization was 'too left.' " The FBI also reported that black CP leader James Ford had been active in helping to form the Council and that the "Communist leaders" became "increasingly active in controlling the organization" (FBI Report of SA, Oct. 20, 1950, 100-19377-545). At the time when E. Franklin Frazier was invited to join the Council late in 1941, it had only fourteen members, including officers; along with Frazier, eleven others were issued invitations in 1941, of whom five accepted (including Earl Dickerson and Dr. R. T. Bokwe of the Union of South Africa). By 1945 membership had grown to twenty-

seven, and in 1946 was augmented to seventy-two, 20 percent white, mostly politically radical Jewish intellectuals (Yergan to Frazier, Oct. 3, 1941, Jan. 29, 1946, MSRC: Frazier). Additional details on the early years of CAA, its membership, financing, and goals, is in Hollis R. Lynch, *Black American' Radicals and the Liberation of Africa: The Council on African Affairs 1937–1955* (Cornell University Press, 1978), especially pp. 17–28. For the background discussion of Pan-Africanism (along with the definition quoted), I have relied centrally on Mark Solomon's fine "Black Critics of Colonialism and the Cold War," in T. G. Paterson, ed., *Cold War Critics* (Quadrangle, 1971), pp. 205–11, and on Wilson Jeremiah Moses, *The Golden Age of Black Nationalism, 1850–1925* (Archon Books, 1978), especially ch. 10. My interview with Doxey Wilkerson on May 7, 1984 (PR, Jr., participating) was also helpful. Hunton's quote is from an appendix he wrote to PR's *Stand*, pp. 117–19 ("A Note on the Council on African Affairs").

56. FBI 100-28627-70, p. 22.

57. The previous year, Walter White had tried to get Robeson to give a concert at the First Congregational Church (White's family church) in Atlanta. Because "Paul has told me at various times about his unwillingness to go South," White enlisted Essie in the project, but she wrote back, "No, no south so far" (Eugene Martin to White, April 7, May 1941; White to Martin, May 6, 1941; White to ER, April 16, 1941; ER to White [appended to a letter from ER to Martin], April 29, 1941—all in LC: NAACP). Later that year, Robeson did venture to the all-black North Carolina College for Negroes where he sang "Ballad for Americans" and had "a grand time" (PR to ER, Oct. 7, 1941, RA).

58. Interview with Howard "Stretch" Johnson, March 5, 1985; interview with Junius Scales, March 10, 1986. The quote is from the ms. of Scales's autobiography, which he kindly showed me (since published as Junius Irving Scales and Richard Nickson, *Cause at Heart* (University of Georgia Press, 1987], pp. 164, 166).

59. Klehr, *Heyday*, pp. 276–78

(SCHW); *National Negro Congress News*, April 24, 1942; "The Reminiscences of Harry L. Mitchell," interview by Donald F. Shaughnessy, 1956–57, Oral History Project, Columbia University; Eleanor Roosevelt, "My Day," *New York World-Telegram*, April 22, 1942; Virginia Foster Durr, *Outside the Magic Circle* (University of Alabama Press, 1985), pp. 154–55, also has a brief account of PR's appearance at SCHW. H. L. Mitchell sent me the list of a dinner committee "from the late 1930s" for the Committee for a Democratic Far Eastern Policy, which includes among its sponsors both Robeson and Ronald Reagan (Mitchell to me, July 13, 1985). The year following SCHW, Mary McLeod Bethune wrote Robeson, "It gives me a thrill to know you and to know that you are a part of us" (Bethune to PR, Nov. 10, 1943, RA). In 1944 Robeson lunched with Mrs. Roosevelt at Hyde Park, along with Judge Delany, Mrs. Pratt, and the Laskers, to discuss the Wiltwyck School for Boys, which Mrs. Roosevelt had founded (Claude Brown, author of *Manchild in the Promised Land*, was among its graduates). Subsequent to the luncheon, Robeson spent a day at Wiltwyck and offered to give a benefit concert for the school (Eleanor Roosevelt to PR, June 2, Sept. 23, 1944; PR to Roosevelt, June 30, 1944, RA).

60. Pittsburgh *Courier* interview, Sept. 26, 1942 (rural poor); *The Worker*, Sept. 24, 1942; Deseret *News*, Sept. 23, 1942.

61. Dan Burley's review in the New York *Amsterdam Star News*, Oct. 3, 1942, hailed the film as "the most powerful indictment of the absentee landlord and sharecropping system in the South I have ever seen on the screen"—though it was that same paper, two months earlier (Aug. 15, 1942), that had headlined the negative review; *PM*, Sept. 25, 1942; *Amsterdam Star News*, Aug. 29, 1942 (Anderson meeting); Pittsburgh *Courier*, Sept. 5, 12, 1942 (Muse). "Many persons," Walter White later wrote, "wondered why he had not been perceptive enough to understand what he was doing while the picture was being filmed" (Walter White, "The Strange Case of Paul Robeson," *Ebony*, Feb. 1951).

62. Associated Negro Press, Oct. 1, 1942; *PM*, Sept. 22, 1942; Pittsburgh *Courier*, Sept. 26, 1942; *People's World*, Sept. 22, 1942. The film's opening grosses were the highest recorded that week—topping *Mrs. Miniver* (*Variety*, Aug. 12, 1942). To some extent PR's script suggestions *were* heeded (Boris Morros to Larry Brown, Nov. 22, 1941, NYPL/Schm: Brown). Boris Morros, producer of *Tales of Manhattan*, later became a counterspy for the FBI (*My Ten Years as a Counterspy* [Dell, 1959]). PR's stage prospects could not have appeared any more appealing than filmic ones for a while: Vincent Burns (author of *I Am a Fugitive from a Chain Gang*) professed excitement about a play he was writing for PR that "begins in a chain gang and ends in heaven, with a chorus singing on the balcony of heaven" (Burns to ER, Jan. 25, 1943, RA).

63. Phone interview with Sidney Poitier, Oct. 20, 1986; Cripps, "Paul Robeson and Black Identity," p. 484. The New York *Daily News* (Oct. 13, 1942) outright called Robeson "a Communist or anyway a fellow traveller." In 1945 Robeson was again tempted to make a film, this time on the life of Félix Eboué (the Guyanese-born Governor General of French Equatorial Africa during W.W. II), but the project never took off (ER to Larry Brown, Aug. 14, 1945, NYPL/Schm: Brown).

In assessing PR's abilities as an actor, Poitier characterized him as "a very strong presence and a capable actor. I would go so far as to say he was a good actor." Agreeing that Robeson was not in a class with those few extraordinary performers who can both transcend the particular acting style of their own day and subordinate their own personality to the demands of a role, Poitier added, "But Robeson's character was bigger than any he would have to create" (interview, Oct. 20, 1986). Donald Bogle has offered a much less generous estimate of PR's film career in *Toms, Coons, Mulattoes, Mammies and Bucks* (Viking, 1973). He credits PR with conveying a view of black males far removed from the usual servile caricature, but further (and inexplicably) describes PR's image as lacking "gen-

tleness, an overriding interest and sympathy in all of mankind. No matter how much producers tried to make Robeson a symbol of black humanity, he always came across as a man more interested in himself than anyone else" (p. 70). I find this characterization far off the mark.

64. A thorough account of Frontier Films and the making of *Native Land* is in Russell Campbell, *Cinema Strikes Back: Radical Filmmaking in the United States 1930–1942* (UMI Research Press, 1982). See also William Alexander, *Film on the Left* (Princeton University Press, 1981), ch. 6. At the time of its release, a number of reviewers hailed the film as pioneering and powerful (e.g., Bosley Crowther in *The New York Times*, May 13, 1942, and Joy Davidman in *New Masses*, May 19, 1942); the *Daily News* (May 13, 1942) was among those expressing doubt over timing. Sterner interview with Leo Hurwitz for the information about Robeson's fee. In the interview Hurwitz also spoke of what an "absolute joy" it was to work with Robeson—he was free of vanity, a hard worker, and a man of "tremendous gentleness." Later on Hurwitz and PR planned to make a film based on Howard Fast's *Freedom Road*, but the onset of the Cold War made it impossible to raise money (interview with Howard Fast, Nov. 21, 1986). The FBI report (Main 100-12304-7) also labeled Frontier Films "a Communist instrumentality."

65. Stretch Johnson, whose sister married "Stepin Fetchit" (Lincoln Perry) in 1937, has urged the point that even Perry was not widely resented for playing stereotypical roles. "The black community understood that that was the only way to succeed, and most black performers had to make that adaptation in order to function on the American stage or in American movies. . . . Robeson was regarded, despite the pro–British imperialist character of *Sanders of the River*, as a successful black artist who had much more dignity from the point of view of the roles that he played, even in imperialist films, than Stepin Fetchit. And even Stepin Fetchit was not regarded as a bad guy" (interview, March 5, 1985).

CHAPTER 13   THE BROADWAY *Othello* (*1942–1943*)

1. MW and PR discuss *Othello* on a tape, n.d., in RA; Webster, "Paul Robeson and Othello," *Our Time*, June 1944. Even before Webster's proposal, Lillian Baylis, manager of the Old Vic, had sounded Robeson out about the possibility of playing Othello to Laurence Olivier's Iago—but there is no known follow-up to the suggestion (Baylis to PR, Nov. 13, 1936, RA).

2. Margaret Webster, *Don't Put Your Daughter on the Stage* (Knopf, 1972), pp. 107–8.

3. Born in 1905, Margaret Webster was an actress as her first career. In the 1920s she played the gentlewoman in John Barrymore's *Hamlet*, and performed at the Old Vic in London in the early thirties under Harcourt Williams's direction. His influence on her, and that of Harley Granville-Barker, is detailed in Margaret Webster, *Shakespeare Without Tears* (McGraw-Hill, 1942; rev. ed., World, 1955), and Ely Silverman, "Margaret Webster's Theory and Practice of Shakespearean Production in the United States (1937–1953)," New York University, Ph.D. thesis, 1969. Webster's successes as a director had included *Richard II* (1937), *Hamlet* (1938), and *Macbeth* (1941), all with Maurice Evans, and a 1940 production of *Twelfth Night* with Helen Hayes as Viola. Interviews with Uta Hagen, June 22–23, 1982, Sept. 28, 1984. See also Susan Spector, "Uta Hagen, the Early Years: 1919–1952," Ph.D. thesis, New York University, 1982.

4. Interviews with Hagen, June 22–23, 1982, Sept. 28, 1984; Webster, *Daughter*, pp. 109–11; the fantasy about Ben Davis was told to me by PR, Jr.

5. Interviews with Hagen, June 22–23, 1982, Sept. 28, 1984.

6. Boston *Post*, Aug. 11, 16, 1942; *Christian Science Monitor*, Aug. 11, 28, 1942; Boston *Herald*, Boston *Daily Globe*, Boston *Evening American*, Boston *Traveler*—all Aug. 11, 1942; *Harvard Crimson*, Aug. 12, 14, 1942; *Variety*, Aug. 12, 1942; *The New York Times*, June 12, Aug. 16, 1942; Flora Robson to Webster and Whitty, Aug. 15, 1942, LC: Margaret Webster. Flora Robson confirmed her view in our interview of Sept. 1982 (PR, Jr., participating).

7. Boston *American, Post, Globe, Herald*—all Aug. 11, 1941; *The New York Times*, Aug. 16, 1942; *Variety*, Aug. 12, 1942. The *Times* review praising PR's performance was signed "E.N."—almost certainly Elliot Norton of the Boston *Post*. *Time* magazine's review (Aug. 24, 1942) voiced misgivings over Robeson's "overacting"—he sometimes "throbbed awkwardly"—but on balance thought he gave a performance "that even at its worst was vivid and that at its best was shattering."

8. *PM*, Aug. 13, 1942; *Variety*, Aug. 12, 1942; see also Boston *Post, Traveler, Globe*—all Aug. 11, 1942.

9. Webster, "PR and Othello"; Webster, *Daughter*, p. 113; Langner, *Magic Curtain;* Sterner interview: Marshall.

The program for the McCarter engagement at Princeton of Aug. 17–22, 1942, is in ARC: Fredi Washington Papers. For that production, the black press was represented by the Pittsburgh *Courier*. Its correspondent reported (Sept. 5, 1942), "We sat in McCarter's theater . . . and watched this whole scene bewildered . . . a Negro artist who courts, kisses, marries and kills a white woman. . . . A short time ago the whites would have advanced a thousand objections. . . . But today the audience and press applauded. . . . We were buoyant when we left the theater . . . the day of our redemption had not yet dawned, [but] the darkest part of the night has passed!"

A black man recalled years later ("Discussion at Old People's Meeting in Princeton," Sterner) that his mother, who "worked in several of the homes in the university," would overhear at parties after the tryout performances "much discussion about the fact that in the McCarter Theater Paul Robeson kissed a white woman. . . . It was a play but they could not accept that and they showed their Southern upbringing and their Southern attitudes. . . ." Also on the

Princeton production: Jean Muir to PR, Dec. 31, 1942, RA; ER to CVV and FM, Aug. 18, 1942, Yale: Van Vechten.

10. A description of the India rally is in the *Daily Worker*, Aug. 29, 1942, and *The Chronicle*, Sept. 12, 1942; the transcript of PR's speech is in RA. Apparently his speech was recorded in a somewhat sketchy fashion (Diane Sommers, Yergan's secretary at the CAA, to ER, Nov. 23, 1942, RA). *New Masses*, Oct. 20, 1942; Lin Liang-mo, Pittsburgh *Courier*, Sept. 19, Nov. 7, 1942; FBI 100-25857-1875, Referral Doc #16.

11. *People's World*, Sept. 10, 17, 19, 1942; *Labor Herald*, Sept. 17, 1942; *Daily Worker*, July 28, Sept. 19, 20, 1942; transcript of Oct. 19, 1942, New. Orleans speech, RA.

12. Robeson's itineraries and datebooks are in RA. Throughout the tour he shared the platform with the pianist William Schatzkammer. Mansfield *Times*, April 6, 1942; the many other reviews of the tour are in RA and are too numerous to cite. Robeson had to cancel his March 17 recital in Tacoma because of illness (Tacoma *News Tribune*, April 9, 1943). Apparently he was also ill in Nov. 1942, seriously enough to prompt a letter from Earl Browder: "Reports of your health give me much concern. May I urge you not to overexert yourself, nor assume too many responsibilities" (Browder to PR, Dec. 1, 1942, RA). The FBI agent who attended the Detroit concert reported that "Communist literature in the form of pamphlets and leaflets was distributed following the conclusion of the concert" (Detroit Report, 4/14/43, 100-9292-211A, p. 3).

Robeson occasionally interrupted the concert tour to attend political rallies of special importance to him (e.g., *Daily Worker*, April 19, May 20, 1943; North to Marcantonio, Jan. 18, 1943, NYPL Ms. Div.: Marcantonio). In Nov. 1942 he returned to New York to appear at a mass rally in Madison Square Garden, "Salute to Our Russian Ally," where, according to the FBI agent who covered the gathering, "Robeson received the greatest ovation of the afternoon when he read a letter of a Soviet soldier and sang Russian war songs in English and Russian" (FBI New York 100-39062-17). For his continuing work with the Joint Anti-Fascist Refugee Committee, a group that had attracted the support of innumerable non-Communist liberals, Robeson was denounced by an FBI informant as "undoubtedly 100% Communist." As proof, the informant adduced the further information of having "seen him in company with Madame LITVINOFF [sic] alone in a theatre" (FBI New York, 10/15/42, 62-7713-4, p. 2). He was again linked with Ivy Litvinov the following year when misquoted as saying, "America gives her minority groups more of a chance than just about any country on earth." Robeson immediately issued a statement denying that he had been quoted accurately, and Mrs. Litvinov wrote a letter to *PM* asserting the U.S.S.R.'s total lack of segregated facilities. The Robesons had been entertained by the Litvinovs in the U.S.S.R. in 1934 (see p. 186) and in denying the quotation PR added that on his visits to the U.S.S.R. from 1934 to 1938 he had "found the real solution of the minority and racial problem, a very simple solution—complete equality" (Chicago *Defender*, Sept. 25, 1943).

13. *Daily Worker*, April 24, 28, May 4, 1943; Atlanta *Daily World*, June 2, 1943; Chicago *Defender*, June 5, 1943; *The Chronicle*, June 12, 1943; the Morehouse program is in RA. In February 1943 Robeson had received another distinguished award. The Schomburg Collection of Negro Literature (NYPL) named him among the twelve black and six white individuals, organizations, or institutions that had done the most to improve race relations in the preceding year (*The New York Times*, Feb. 7, 1943). Among the others named were Wendell L. Willkie, Dr. Franz Boas, Lillian Smith, Duke Ellington, Dr. George Washington Carver, Judge William H. Hastie, Dr. Channing Tobias, Margaret Walker, and Dr. Alain Locke.

14. *PM*, July 1, 2, 1943 (Lewisohn); *The New York Times*, July 2, 1943 (Lewisohn); Chicago *Defender*, July 31, 1943 (Apex); *Apex Alloyer*, Aug. 1943; *Daily Worker*, Aug. 28, 1943 (CIO speech). Robeson's speech in Chicago on July 24, 1943, is printed in "The Metal and

Human Engineering Magazine," the *Apex Alloyer,* Aug. 1943. The FBI kept PR under surveillance during his California trip, its agents dutifully reporting his activities, including his visit with the actor Clarence Muse, a car ride with Louise Bransten ("a wealthy woman, extremely active in Communist Party Front organizations and a heavy contributor to the JAFRC"), and a party attended by local left-wingers, such as Harry Bridges of the CIO and Revels Cayton. The FBI was again in close attendance when Robeson flew back out to Chicago in mid-Sept. to address a rally dedicated to "winning the war and peace." He did so on the direct appeal of Vice-President Henry A. Wallace. Although by then in rehearsal for *Othello,* he let himself be persuaded and, along with giving a speech to the rally, attended various functions in honor of Wallace—with whom he would soon be closely associated in the Progressive Party (FBI New York 100-25857-1875; 100-47315-1053, 2459; 100-4931-3645, 3645, 3677). Already an admirer of Wallace, Robeson wrote to congratulate him on his "great speech . . . Everyone is still excited and grateful for your clear and beautiful exposition of the practical working plan for the World of the Common Man" (PR to Wallace, Nov. 12, 1942, RA).

15. MW to May Whitty, Aug. 1943, LC: Webster. Additional details are in Spector, "Hagen," and Webster, *Daughter.* The prestigious Theatre Guild was led by Lawrence Langner and Theresa Helburn. The Guild agreed to raise the money, manage the business affairs, and serve as the official producer of *Othello*—but artistic control remained with Webster, Robeson, and their stage manager, John Haggott. In her interview with Sterner, Langner's wife, Armina Marshall, says that the directors of the Guild "were around the rehearsal all the time," but she, too, portrays their role as essentially a back-seat one, recalling their care in giving their "notes" to Webster rather than directly to members of the cast or crew. The Robesons had been frequent guests in the Marshall-Langner household during the 1920s. For PR's

help with Ferrer's draft status, see note 5, p. 707.

16. Multiple interviews with Freda Diamond.

17. References to the original contract are made in MW's Feb. 28, 1944, contract with the Guild (RA); MW to May Whitty, Aug. 25, 1943, LC: Webster; Janet Barton Carroll, "A Promptbook Study of Margaret Webster's Production of *Othello,*" unpublished Ph.D. thesis, LSU, 1977, as quoted in Spector, "Hagen," p. 207 (Schnabel contract); MW to May Whitty, Feb. 17, 1944, LC: Webster, for the later dispute over billing for the tour—when MW did resign her role, Edith King (who had been playing Bianca) replaced her; MW, *Daughter,* p. 116 ("sweet, unassuming"; "Svengali").

18. Interviews with Uta Hagen, June 22–23, 1982, Sept. 28, 1984.

19. John K. Hutchens, "Paul Robeson," *Theatre Arts,* Oct. 1944.

20. As early as 1924, Essie recorded in her diary Paul's frequent acting lessons from Koiransky, the Russian critic and Stanislavski's collaborator: "They will go over 'Othello' together, Koiransky suggesting and Paul learning the part" (ER Diary, Aug. 27, 1924). Similarly, she recorded frequent vocal coaching from the great teacher Proschowsky in 1926 (e.g.: "Found him absolutely marvelous. Showed him all his faults and showed him how to correct them and how to sing right" [March 16, 1926]; "Paul's progress is remarkable. . . . We are confident now" [March 17, 1926]). In his own diary for 1929 Paul enthusiastically recorded working on his "soft-voice problem" with Miss Armitage, whom he found a "really wonderful" help (Nov. 11, 1929, RA). On Uta Hagen's suggestion, Robeson consulted with her own singing coach, Jerry Swinford, and off and on studied with him for nearly three years (interviews with Hagen).

21. The fellow director, Edgar Reynolds, is quoted in Silverman, "Margaret Webster's Shakespearean Production," p. 161. "What the old boy meant" is in a *New Yorker* profile of MW by Barbara Heggie (May 20, 1944). MW took pained exception to that profile in her

book *Don't Put Your Daughter on the Stage,*
p. 87.

22. Webster, *Daughter,* pp. 109–11.
23. Ibid.
24. Interviews with Uta Hagen, June
22–23, 1982, Sept. 28, 1984. A very different version is in an effusive exchange
of letters between Essie and Dame May
Whitty. Initially, during the 1942
rehearsals, Robeson was enthusiastic
about Webster's directorial skills: "We
had a couple of swell rehearsals Webster
& I," he wrote to Essie. "She's going to
be wonderful, exactly what I had hoped.
. . . She's going to get me to do plenty—
and she'll fill in the gaps. I'm really excited and encouraged" (PR to ER, n.d.
[1942], RA). Twenty years later Webster
told an interviewer that Robeson's
"innate dignity" and "sweetness" could
not compensate for the fact that he "was
not an experienced actor," with the result
that in a few scenes she had "to construct
a cradle around him, a production structure that would sustain him and mask his
weaknesses" (Ely Silverman interview
with Margaret Webster, Jan. 26, 1962,
printed as "Appendix C" in Silverman's
"Margaret Webster's Shakespearean Production"). Another cast member, James
Monks, the young actor playing Cassio,
in retrospect puts a far higher estimate
on Webster's directorial skills—though
Monks's recollections of everyone tend to
be uniformly beneficent (Sterner interview with Monks). Flora Robson, writing
to Webster's parents, decidedly gilded
the lily: "They [PR and ER] are tremendously grateful to Peggy and Paul believes in her implicitly" (Robson to
Webster and Whitty, Aug. 15, 1943, LC:
Webster). According to PR, Jr., his father
never—either publicly or privately—had
an unkind word for Webster. A sample of
PR's public praise for her is in an interview with the *Princetonian,* Aug. 17, 1943.
At the end of the *Othello* tour, Webster
wrote PR, ". . . since we started to work
. . . there have been a lot of ups &
downs—way ups & way downs . . . but
let's remember only the heights" (June
11, 1945, RA).

25. Interviews with Hagen, June 22–
23, 1982, Sept. 28, 1984; phone interview

with Sanford Meisner, April 12, 1985.
Meisner, unlike Hagen, feels that enough
good teachers were then available to have
helped Robeson. Meisner saw the Broadway *Othello* and in his view Robeson was
"no actor," but he "could have been
helped." Though he had a "singer's
voice," it was a "beautiful" one and he
could have been shown "how to use
it better, so as not to sound too ama-
teurish."

26. Sterner interview with John
Gerstadt.
27. Ibid.
28. Sterner interviews with Monks
and Gerstadt.
29. Sterner interview with Gerstadt;
phone interview with Joseph Gould,
March 17, 1985 ("powerfully cool").
Gould met PR in 1947 when they
worked together on a film version—ultimately aborted—of Howard Fast's *Freedom Road.*
30. P. L. Prattis's column, "The Horizon," Pittsburgh *Courier,* Nov. 18, 1944
(for similar statements, see Jerome
Beatty's quotes from an interview with
PR, "America's No. 1 Negro," *The American,* May 1944); interviews with Uta
Hagen, June 22–23, 1982, Sept. 28, 1984.
31. "Negro warrior" is in Beatty,
"America's No. 1 Negro"; PR, "Some
Reflections on *Othello* and the Nature of
Our Time," *The American Scholar,* Autumn
1945. Robeson's views on the importance
of putting Othello's jealousy on a cultural
basis are from an interview with Otis L.
Guernsey, Jr., *Herald Tribune,* Oct. 17,
1943.
32. Beatty, "America's No. 1
Negro."
33. John Lovell, Jr., "Shakespeare's
American Play," *Theatre Arts,* June 1944.
My discussion of the historical back-
ground of *Othello* is also indebted to Ar-
thur Colby Sprague, *Shakespeare and the
Actors* (Harvard University Press, 1948);
Margaret Webster's program notes,
"The Black Othello" (and her *Tears* and
Daughter); William Babula, *Shakespeare in
Production* (Garland, 1981); and Errol
Hill, *Shakespeare in Sable: A History of Black
Shakespearean Actors* (University of Massa-
chusetts Press, 1984). The Maryland

woman, Mary Preston, is as quoted in Webster, *Daughter,* p. 112.

In the decade immediately preceding Robeson's *Othello,* serious black actors, when able to secure work at all, had been allowed to appear on Broadway in stereotypical roles only, and plays by black writers were nonexistent (except for the 1935 production of Langston Hughes's *Mulatto,* in a production heavily doctored—without Hughes's consent—so as to emphasize the lurid and underplay the social commentary). For more on the history of *Mulatto,* see Faith Berry, *Langston Hughes: Before and Beyond Harlem* (Lawrence Hill and Co., 1983), pp. 241–43, and Arnold Rampersad, *The Life of Langston Hughes* (Oxford, 1986), vol. I, pp. 311–16. More common were casual references to "niggers" in several first-run plays of the period. Gerald Weales, "Popular Theatre of the Thirties" (*Tulane Drama Review,* summer 1967), is the best summary of black theater in the period; his conclusion is that ". . . the Negro exists in the popular plays of the 1930's—if at all—as a background figure who gets no special comment." To some limited extent, the decade of the thirties contrasts unfavorably with the preceding decade of the twenties and the *comparatively* greater platform it offered for the "black voice" to be heard (e.g., see Johnson, *Black Manhattan,* chs. xv–xvii in the 1968 Atheneum reprint).

34. In "Shakespeare's American Play," *Theatre Arts,* June 1944, John Lovell, Jr., lists several professional stage productions with a black Othello—including the B. J. Ford Company in the 1880s, the Fine Arts Club of Denver in 1938, and the Lafayette Players in 1916 (Benjamin Brawley, *The Negro in Literature and Art in the United States* [Duffield and Co., 1930], p. 130, refers to this performance as having been given by the Edward Sterling Wright Players—and having "made a favorable impression"). Howard Barnes (New York *Herald Tribune,* Oct. 31, 1943) refers to "a dozen or more correspondents" who wrote in correcting his early statement that Robeson was the first black to play Othello, citing productions that went back to the nineteenth century. Errol Hill, in *Shakespeare in Sable,* has documented a considerable number of black Othellos, dating back at least to 1880 (see especially pp. 38–39, 45–47, 53–57, 82, 101–2, 110). Among Robeson's predecessors was Wayland Rudd, hired by Jasper Deeter to play Othello at the Hedgerow Theatre in 1930. Rudd later became a Soviet citizen and was part of the welcoming committee when Robeson arrived for his first visit to Moscow in 1934 (see note 3, p. 629). Robeson also knew William Marshall, the black actor who performed *Othello* in 1953 at Mother Zion A.M.E. (brother Ben's church). Marshall played the role again in 1955 for the Brattle Street Players, and when PR's passport problems temporarily cast doubt on his ability to fill a Stratford, England, engagement, director Glen Byam Shaw hired Marshall as a replacement; he gracefully bowed out after Robeson's passport difficulties cleared up. For PR's acquaintance with Ira Aldridge's daughter, Amanda Ira Aldridge, in London during the twenties, see p. 91.

35. Webster, *Tears,* pp. 236–37. See also her article—appearing in *The New York Times* on the day the play opened on Broadway—"Pertinent Words on His Moorship's Ancient," *The New York Times,* Oct. 19, 1943. The black writer J. A. Rogers (in his Pittsburgh *Courier* column, "Rogers Says," for Nov. 13, 1943) provides a learned and persuasive case for believing Shakespeare precisely meant to portray Othello as a Negro—and chides Margaret Webster for muddying the issue by saying in the New York *Herald Tribune* (Oct. 31, 1943) that "Othello was a black man, a blackamoor. Oh, we know the Moors aren't Negroes, but Shakespeare either didn't know or didn't care." On the contrary, Rogers argues, Shakespeare did know—Negroes in his day were called "Moors."

36. PR interviews in *The American* (May 1944), the Philadelphia *Record* (Oct. 5, 1943), and the Rochester *Times-Union* (Oct. 3, 1944). Laurence Olivier also felt Othello was the most difficult role Shakespeare ever wrote (Webster, *Daughter,* pp. 87, 109).

37. Pearl Bradley, "Robeson Questionnaire," 1944, twelve-page ms., RA (interview for Bradley's M.A. thesis).

Margaret Webster's own exhausting schedule is recounted in an undated letter to Essie (RA): "I have been in the theatre from 8 a.m. to 3 a.m. without any break for the past three days!"

38. Uta Hagen as quoted in Spector, "Hagen," p. 210. The superlatives were "F. R. J." in the New Haven *Journal-Courier;* Paul Daniel Davis in the Chicago *Defender,* Oct. 9, 1943; Helen Eager in the Boston *Traveler,* Sept. 21, 1943; Jerry Gaghan in the Philadelphia *Daily News,* Oct. 5, 1943; Robert Sensenderfer in the Philadelphia *Evening Bulletin,* Oct. 5, 1943. Only two years before Robeson appeared in Philadelphia, Langston Hughes's *Mulatto* had been prevented from opening when the commissioner of licenses rejected it as an "incitement to riot" (*The People's Voice,* Oct. 23, 1943).

39. Elinor Hughes, Boston *Herald,* Sept. 22, 26, 1943; Elliot Norton, Boston *Sunday Post,* Sept. 26, 1943; Spector, "Hagen," p. 210 ("thumbs"). Leo Gaffney's review in the Boston *Daily Record* (Sept. 22, 1943) also came down hard on Robeson, giving the acting palm to Ferrer, and revealing something of a racist bias: ". . . his Moor is too black. . . . The tragedy of miscegenation comes into disquieting prominence. . . ." Judging from one newspaper account, the opening-night audience in Boston sided with Elinor Hughes: "Hundreds cheered and the curtain kept doing a St. Vitus dance to accommodate the curtain-calls" (Boston *Evening American,* Sept. 21, 1943). The Philadelphia reviews were also mixed: Philadelphia *Record* (Oct. 5, 1943), Philadelphia *Inquirer* (Oct. 5, 1943).

Offstage, Robeson was widely interviewed and hailed during the tryout. In Boston he was fêted at the Ritz Hotel, was presented by Mayor Maurice Tobin with the first key to the city since the outbreak of World War II, and received a letter of apology from Governor Leverett Saltonstall for having had to depart early from a luncheon held in Robeson's honor at the Tavern (*The Afro-American,* Oct. 2, 1943; New York *Amsterdam News,* Oct. 9, 1943; Pittsburgh *Courier,* Oct. 2, 1943; *The Worker,* Oct. 3, 1943; Saltonstall to Robeson, Oct. 4, 1943, RA).

40. Interviews with Uta Hagen, June 22–23, 1982, Sept. 28, 1984; Webster, "Paul Robeson and Othello," *Our Time,* June 1944. Mrs. Roosevelt, too, caught the excitement; on Oct. 16 she sent a note to the Shubert management in advance of her intended visit to the theater on November 4 to make sure PR would be performing that night (note dated Oct. 16, 1943, RA).

41. *Newsweek,* Nov. 1, 1943; *World-Telegram,* Oct. 20, 1943; Uta Hagen to her parents, quoted in Spector, "Hagen," p. 212; MW to May Whitty, Oct. 20, 1943, LC: Webster; interview with Uta Hagen, June 22–23, 1982; V. Rogov, "Othello in the American Theatre," translated from *Literatura i Iskustvo,* February 9, 1944, RA; multiple interviews with Freda Diamond. Accounts of what Webster said in her "speech" vary from a choked "thank you" (Webster, *Daughter,* p. 114) to (turning to Robeson), "Paul, we are all very proud of you tonight" (*Christian Science Monitor,* Oct. 20, 1943). MW's later memories of opening night (in *Daughter,* pp. 113–14) closely parallel the feelings she expressed at the time. As she wrote (*Our Time,* June 1944) about the opening-night ovation, "I have never, in any theatre in the world, heard a tribute so whole-hearted, so tremendous, so deeply moving. . . ."

42. New York *Daily Mirror, Journal-American, World-Telegram*—all Oct. 20, 1943.

43. Lewis Nichols in *The New York Times,* Oct. 20, 24, 1943; Howard Barnes in the New York *Herald Tribune,* Oct. 20, 24, 1943; John Chapman in the New York *Daily News,* Oct. 20, 24, 1943; Wilella Waldorf in the New York *Post,* Oct. 20, 1943; Ward Morehouse in the New York *Sun,* Oct. 20, 1943. Waldorf, Chapman, and Morehouse expressed the three reservations about Robeson. The critics especially admired the punchy quality of Webster's staging—her rich melodramatic sensibility, so suited, they felt, to the play's central tone (see especially Wilella Waldorf's review, Oct. 20, 1943). Lewis Nichols in the *Times* and Howard Barnes in the *Tribune* both registered some minor reservations about the production, but Nichols called it "the best interpretation of 'Othello' to be seen

here in a good many years," and Barnes called Webster's rendering "a triumphant handling of the tragedy." Sanford Meisner (phone interview, April 12, 1985) thought "the good performance in that production was José Ferrer." Uta Hagen agrees: ". . . probably the finest Iago that ever was"; in her opinion Ferrer couldn't then or ever sustain the quality of his performance: "He hates long runs. . . . It got more and more tricks, and outer gimmicks, or vocalizations," but "initially . . . he was sensational. . . . He was the only actor on stage. . . . I *know* I wasn't good. . . . It was shape without content— borrowed outer form, conventional and traditional in the worst sense. Everyone whose opinion I really respected did not like me as Desdemona—'nice quality but conventional' " (interviews with Hagen, June 22–23, 1982).

44. Kronenberger, *PM*, Oct. 20, 1943; Gibbs, *The New Yorker*, Oct. 30, 1943; Young, *The New Republic*, vol. 109, pp. 621–62; Speaight (*SOS*, p. 231); Marshall (*The Nation*, vol. 157, pp. 507–8. Writing much later, George Jean Nathan appended to a column of his the only entirely negative (and irreducibly succinct) verdict *Othello* got; his one-line notice read: "One of the very few virtues of Margaret Webster's production of *Othello* is that it contains no ballet" (Nathan, "Such Stuff as Dreams Aren't Made On," *American Mercury*, May 1945). The Robesons had met Nathan at least once, back in 1925, at a party given by the Knopfs. In her diary Essie had described Nathan as "the nicest little spic and span fellow." *Time* echoed exactly the views expressed by the other weekly critics: "Robeson did not bring to the part poetry and drama so much as sculpture and organ music. He was not so much Othello as a great and terrible presence" (Nov. 1, 1943).

45. Interviews with Uta Hagen, June 22–23, 1982, Sept. 28, 1984; phone interview with Sanford Meisner, April 12, 1985. Earle Hyman, who in 1953 was to be the next black actor to portray Othello in New York, had a very different view. He saw Robeson's performance ten times and pronounced it "magnificent." Hyman further recalls that in 1953 Robeson came backstage to congratulate him on

his performance (aware that Robeson was in the audience that night, Hyman froze and gave, in his view, one of his worst shows). A photographer backstage wanted to take a picture of Hyman and Robeson together, but Robeson, at the time widely denounced for his "Communist leanings," waved the photographer away: "No, don't do that. It won't do this young man any good" (Sterner interview with Hyman).

"Impressive emptiness" is, curiously, precisely the defining quality F. R. Leavis and subsequent critics have seen in the character of Othello. That interpretation of the role began with T. S. Eliot's essay "Shakespeare and the Stoicism of Seneca" (1927) and was then elaborated by Leavis in "Diabolic Intellect and the Noble Hero," *The Common Pursuit* (Salem House Publications, 1984). Leavis refers to Othello as "self-centered and self-regarding," far more interested in his own "heroic self-dramatization" than in Desdemona; he sees his life in operatic terms and is given to stentorian speechifying about it. I am grateful to Seymour Kleinberg for introducing me to this interpretation—one that Olivier took as his own in both his stage and film versions of the role. Robeson never saw Olivier's version, but when Freda Diamond described it to him he expressed disbelief that so great an actor would lend himself to so "distorted" a version of the role (multiple interviews with Freda Diamond).

46. Interview with James Earl Jones, *The New York Times*, Jan. 31, 1982.

47. Fredi Washington, *The People's Voice*, Oct. 23, 1943. For other accounts in the black press, all stressing the racial issue, see the Pittsburgh *Courier*, Oct. 30, 1943; New York *Amsterdam News*, Oct. 30, 1943; the Chicago *Defender*, Oct. 30, 1943 (far more sanguine than Fredi Washington in its reference to the effect of Robeson's *Othello* in "sweeping aside" "whatever silly racial prejudices New Yorkers may have had in the past"). Along with Howard Barnes in the *Tribune*, the only other white reviewer to make any reference at all to the *cultural* aspect of race, to which Robeson had directed his efforts, was the anonymous critic for *Cue*

magazine, and in that instance the reference was compromised by the description of a "primitive" Othello being "bewildered by the effete products of 16th century Venetian civilization" (Oct. 30, 1943).

Though Robeson's *Othello* was never made into a film, it was recorded. Nobody, however, was happy with the results. Margaret Webster and the Theatre Guild were outraged at Robeson and José Ferrer for agreeing to a recording contract without consulting the producers, but "decided it would be wisest to acquiesce rather than imperil the tour by a fight with Paul." Webster took some consolation in the fact that "The records were not good," but regretted that they would "be considered a fair representation of the production" (*Daughter*, p. 117). Uta Hagen, to this day, thinks the recording so bad that "I can't hear it—I just find it embarrassing." As Hagen remembers it, the recording sessions had been done "with great care" over an extended six-week period, but, "having

played it, there was a sense of compensating for what couldn't be seen . . . a kind of deliberate overemphasis on every line that to me is agonizing" (interviews with Hagen, June 22–23, 1982). To my contemporary ear, Webster and Hagen's judgment is sound, though perhaps exaggerated.

Three years later Fredi Washington took the lead in a public campaign to persuade Robeson to accept the role of the insurrectionary leader Denmark Vesey in Dorothy Heyward's play about him, *Set My People Free*. Washington wrote two "Open Letters" to him in *The People's Voice* (June 1, Aug. 17, 1946). She was joined by the columnist Earl Conrad (*Chicago Defender*, July 6, 1946), and the *Afro-American* publisher, Carl Murphy, who wrote directly to Robeson, asking him to consider the role (Murphy to PR, June 12, 1946, ARC: Fredi Washington). Judging from an FBI phone tap (March 9, 1946), Rockmore strongly discouraged Robeson's initially favorable response to the script (see p. 230).

CHAPTER 14   THE APEX OF FAME *(1944–1945)*

1. FBI 100-6393-1A 181 (Red Army); FBI 100-26603-1271, p. 3 (Loyalist); FBI 100-28715-150, p. 24 (common man); FBI New York 100-25857-1875 Referral Doc. #18 (wealthy woman); FBI 100-7518-699 (serfs); FBI 100-47315-2573, p. 36 (Anthem); FBI 100-47315-2252 (high officials); FBI 100-28715-150 (100%).

2. Dawson to PR, Nov. 23, 1943, RA; Uta Hagen to her parents, Oct. 25, 1943, as quoted in Spector, "Hagen," p. 213 (advance sale); CVV to ER, Nov. 22, 1943, RA; White to Langner, Nov. 24, 1943, Yale: Theatre Guild; Coward to PR, Dec. 31, 1942, RA; Du Bois to PR, Jan. 5, 1944, U. Mass.: Du Bois *(Phylon)*. Among some of the other noteworthy letters of congratulation were those from Clarence Cameron White to PR, Oct. 27, 1943, Arthur Judson (president of Columbia Concerts) to PR, Nov. 23, 1943, and Franklin P. Adams, Feb. 2, 1944—all in RA.

3. *The New York Times*, Oct. 29, 1944;

New York *Herald Tribune*, Oct. 31, 1944 *(Scholar)*; Associated Negro Press, May 20, 1944 (Gold Medal). The Donaldson Awards were set up by *Billboard* and were arrived at by a poll of theater people, including actors, critics, stagehands, producers, and technicians. Robeson won in the category "Outstanding lead performance (actor)"—José Ferrer and Elliott Nugent were the runners-up (*PM*, July 5, 1944). Dreiser to Mencken, June 28, 1944, in Thomas P. Riggio, ed., *Dreiser-Mencken Letters* (University of Pennsylvania Press, 1986), vol. II, p. 713. PR was a guest of Dreiser's in California in 1944–45 and in the latter year Dreiser suggested he do an interview with PR about his views on how to advance the black race (Dreiser to PR, Feb. 15, 1945, Riggio, ed., *Dreiser Letters*). According to a third party, Dreiser himself "disclaimed godhood, though he thought Paul Robeson might qualify" (Ish-Kishor to W. A. Swanberg, as quoted in Swanberg, *Dreiser* [Scribner's, 1965], p. 418).

4. *ILWU Dispatcher,* Nov. 19, 1943; New York *Herald Tribune,* Jan. 7, 8, 12, June 8, 1944; *World-Telegram,* Oct. 13, 1943; *The New York Times,* Jan. 19, 1944 (equity). In 1944 Robeson was made an honorary member of the Fur and Leather Workers union at its biennial convention (*Daily Worker,* May 17, 1944).

5. There are dozens of letters in RA requesting various favors from him. The log of PR's conversation with Yergan on Nov. 23, 1944, as recorded by the FBI, is Main 100-12304-25. Even before the pressure created by the election, Robeson wrote Van Vechten, "I've been a little worn and rushing about doing benefits, etc. . . . The matinee days are so wearing" (postmarked May 24, 1944, Yale: Van Vechten).

Robeson always kept a retreat to which he could repair when feeling overwhelmed, or simply in need of privacy. During his London years he had sometimes used producer Earl Dancer's place (for more on Dancer, performer and nightclub owner, see Ethel Waters, *His Eye Is on the Sparrow,* [Pyramid, 1967], especially pp. 172 ff.). In New York in the early forties, Jean Blackwell Hutson remembers that in order to locate him she had to "penetrate some personal hideaway of his own" (interview with Hutson, Sept. 21, 1983). For more on PR's "retreats," see note 19, p. 710.

6. New York *Herald Tribune,* Nov. 17, 1943, April 4, 1944 (Africa); *Daily Worker,* Aug. 28, 1943; Chicago *Defender,* July 24, 1943; Pittsburgh *Courier,* Dec. 25, 1943, Jan. 8, 1944 (hurt); PR speech, Jan. 2, 1944, radio station WEAF, several versions, RA; transcript of the radio program for the Entertainment Industry Emergency Committee, May 19, 1944, RA (black resentment); telegram signed by Walter White and PR soliciting additional signatures to protest lack of funding appropriation for the FEPC, June 10, 1944, LC: NAACP; PR's opening statement to the "Africa—New Perspectives" conference called by the Council on African Affairs, April 14, 1944 (Soviets; new imperialists), transcript in RA; the agenda and program for the CAA conference on Africa are in NYPL/Schm: NNC, as is the call for the Aug. 8, 1943, San

Francisco Conference on Racial and National Unity in Wartime, at which PR spoke; transcript (RA) of broadcast interview, WHN, by William S. Gailmor with PR, April 1944, for the quote about black patriotism (the style is not PR's but the sentiment is).

Robeson also continued his activities in behalf of the war effort, appearing at bond rallies and participating in programs for the Office of War Information and the War Production Board (e.g., Silverman to PR, Feb. 3, 1944; Baren to PR, Feb. 15, 1944; Nelson to PR, June 7, 1944; Betz to PR, June 13, 1944; Smith to PR, Aug. 27, 1944—all RA). During the outbreak of race riots in Detroit, he sent a confidential memo to Roosevelt suggesting that "the tension is being fostered deliberately by anti-administration and anti-war elements" among white reactionaries (PR to Roosevelt, June 21, 1944; Jonathan Daniels to PR, June 27, 1944, RA).

7. Interviews with Ishmael Flory, July 1–2, 1986; *Daily Worker,* Dec. 4, 1943; New York *Amsterdam News,* Dec. 11, 1943. On the career of Landis, see Jules Tygiel, *Baseball's Great Experiment: Jackie Robinson and His Legacy* (Random House, 1983), pp. 30–43. Ben Davis, Jr., records what seems to be a later (1945) meeting with the club owners and also notes that he and Robeson attended a small reception for Jackie Robinson after the Dodgers had signed him (*Communist Councilman from Harlem* [International, 1969], pp. 133–34).

8. *Daily Worker,* Oct. 23, 1943, Nov. 11, 1943; Wilson to PR, Nov. 1, 1943, RA; Naison, *Heyday,* p. 313; Ben Davis, Jr., to ER, April 27, 1943, RA ("membership"); FBI Main 100-12304-13 (Robeson for Congress). According to Howard "Stretch" Johnson, Ellsworth "Bumpy" Johnson, head of the "Black Mafia" and later a protector of Robeson's "contributed heavily" to Davis's campaign (interview with Johnson, March 5, 1985); for more on Bumpy Johnson and Robeson, see p. 312 and note 17, p. 695. Davis's record as a city councilman is discussed in Edwin R. Lewison, *Black Politics in New York City* (Twayne Publishers, 1974), especially pp. 76–79. Davis moved actively

against segregated housing, police brutality, and inadequate fire-department services in Harlem. He was also known for being available to his constituents.

9. Interviews with Barney Josephson, March 23, 1982, April 2, 1985; *In Person: Lena Horne*, as told to Helen Arstein and Carlton Moss (Greenberg, 1950), pp. 180–85; Pearl Primus interview, *The New York Times*, March 18, 1979; *metro-Newark!*, Oct. 1979 (Vaughan). John Hammond recounts a similar incident in *On Record* (Summit, 1977), pp. 261–62. Interviews with Uta Hagen. Hagen also remembers one unhappy occasion when she and Paul went backstage to congratulate Billie Holliday after she had just given a "spectacular, totally controlled" performance—and found her crawling around on all fours, far gone on drugs.

10. The many letters and telegrams are in RA, including a letter from Lillian Hellman (April 7, 1944) that she sent out to solicit greetings. In declining to serve as a sponsor for the event, Eleanor Roosevelt described Robeson as a man "whom I greatly admire" but added, "I wonder however, if your group would not be better off without my name this year when everything I do brings the cause criticism?" (Roosevelt to Yergan, March 3, 1944, FDR.) After seeing *Othello*, Mrs. Roosevelt wrote Joseph Lash, "Robeson is moving in it because the lines might be said by him today!" She added, however, that "the character is never quite convincing and all of a piece . . . to me" (as quoted in Joseph Lash, *A World of Love* [Doubleday, 1984], p. 84).

11. *The New York Times*, April 17, 1944; *Daily Worker*, April 10, 18, 1944; *PM*, April 17, 1944. The following year Robeson in turn paid his respects at the celebration for Mary McLeod Bethune's seventieth birthday (New York *Amsterdam News*, July 19, 1945).

12. Department of the Army, File No. 100-25857-63. PR had sent Roosevelt a letter protesting a deportation order issued against Raissa Browder (*Daily Worker*, Dec. 14, 1943); the FBI was aware of the letter.

13. Theresa Helburn (Theatre Guild) to PR, June 30, 1944 (closing), Yale: Theatre Guild. The previous re-

cord-holders for Shakespeare on Broadway had been a tie at 157 performances each for Jane Cowl in *Romeo and Juliet* in 1923 and Orson Welles's *Julius Caesar* in 1937.

14. Interviews with Uta Hagen, June 22–23, 1982, Sept. 28, 1984. All Hagen quotations hereafter in this section, unless other sources are cited, are from my interviews with her.

15. PR to ER, Aug. 29, 1941, n.d. (1942), RA.

16. Sadie Davenport Shelton, who knew PR back in his undergraduate days, recalls, "He always liked light-skinned women" (interview, March 26, 1985, PR, Jr., participating). Skin color, of course, was not the sole variable in determining his preference. Sustained attraction for him seems to have hinged on a woman's being forceful, tough-minded, motherly, and loyal—an indomitable earth mother.

17. Spector, "Hagen" (hate mail). Robeson later remarked that in Cincinnati he felt the climate was especially tense and in the performance that night "I was careful how close I got to Desdemona" (remark on "A Closer Look," aired in 1979).

18. Langston Hughes, for one, roundly applauded Robeson's refusal to play segregated houses, contrasting his attitude, in print, with Bill Robinson's: when Robinson's *Hot Mikado* hit segregated Washington, D.C. (a town Robeson refused to play), and blacks were denied admittance to the theater, Robinson "defended himself by saying that he was making $2,500 a week out of it. And he went right on playing" (Hughes, Chicago *Defender*, July 22, 1944, reprinted in *Negro Digest*, Sept. 1944).

19. Another moment of hilarity had come while the show was still playing on Broadway. In saying his line "Since these arms of mine had seven years pith," Robeson accidentally said "piss" instead of "pith." Hagen, who had just turned upstage, shook with laughter, and they collapsed all over again later when Robeson added, "How would you feel if you'd been pissing for seven years?" (Sterner interview with James Monk.)

20. Richardson to PR, April 6, 1973, courtesy of Paulina Forsythe. Richard-

son had been elected to the state legislature in Indiana in 1932, during the height of KKK influence, and later won the first public-housing desegregation case (Indianapolis *Recorder,* Dec. 16, 1972). According to Earl Dickerson, a postperformance party in Chicago lasted until 6:00 a.m., with Etta Moten Barnett singing and Duke Ellington playing the piano (1969 tape, courtesy of Terkel; interview with Dickerson, July 2, 1986).

21. Interview with Studs Terkel, June 30, 1986. The pertinent Chicago reviews are: Chicago *Daily Tribune,* Chicago *Sun,* Chicago *Herald-American,* Chicago *Times*—all April 11, 1945—and Chicago *Sun* and Chicago *Herald-American,* April 15, 1945. A large batch of other tour reviews are in RA. Though Hagen thought PR's performance on the tour was better, it was on the political platform that she felt he was without peer—his marvelous voice, his personal magnetism, and his profound conviction blending to produce "remarkable impact." During *Othello*'s six-week engagement in Chicago, Robeson made a number of political appearances. He was featured at United Nations Day (sponsored by the United Packinghouse Workers/CIO), attended a membership meeting of the United Auto Workers/CIO (Local 453 made him an honorary member), sang and spoke at a meeting sponsored by American Youth for Democracy, at a large event organized by the Chicago Council on African Affairs, at two synagogues, and at a hundred-dollar-a-couple dinner to benefit the Abraham Lincoln School (of which William Patterson was assistant director). Robeson sat for a portrait by Edward Biberman while in Los Angeles on tour and Biberman has provided a vivid account of Robeson's hectic schedule: ". . . we were never alone. He would always make several appointments here for the time that he was posing. Earl Robinson would be sitting at this piano banging away a new tune that he wanted Paul to hear, and somebody would be reading a script, and somebody else would be interviewing him" (Emily Corey interview with Biberman in 1977 for UCLA: Special Collections; Biberman to me, July 31, 1982).

22. ER to PR, Dec. 1, 1946, RA; ER to Larry Brown, July 15, 1945, NYPL/Schm: Brown.

23. ER to CVV and FM, July 15, Aug. 12, Sept. 9, Nov. 14, 1943, April 26, Aug. 18, Sept. 15, Oct. 3, 31, Dec. 14, 1944—all Yale: Van Vechten; ER to PR, Jr., Jan. 28, 1947, RA (Ma Goode); CVV to ER, Nov. 22, 1943, RA; ER to E. Franklin Frazier, Oct. 10, 1943, MSRC: Frazier (summarizing her work at Hartford). The Robesons had known Frazier as far back as the twenties (Frazier to ER, Oct. 21, 1932, MSRC: Frazier). As students, Pitt and Robeson had often sat together because of the alphabetical listing of names, and became friendly. I am grateful to Pitt's widow, Mrs. Juliet Pitt, for sending me the Robeson-Pitt correspondence, which suggests some marginal contact over the years. The correspondence consists of three letters from ER to Pitt from the forties (April 6, July 25, 1942, Sept. 9, 1945) and one (n.d. [probably 1931]) in which she apologizes for having spent one evening in London "burdening you with my troubles." There is also one letter from Malcolm to Paul (March 30, 1942). When Shirley Graham published her largely imagined biography of Robeson in 1946 (*Paul Robeson: Citizen of the World* [Julian Messner, Inc.]), Pitt wrote to Robert C. Clothier, the president of Rutgers, to express his "discomfort" over Graham's "fictionalized" version of his undergraduate friendship with Robeson (Pitt to Clothier, July 11, 1946; Meder to Pitt, July 22, 1946, RUA).

24. Herman Shumlin to ER, Oct. 5, 1944 (pronouncing *Goodbye Uncle Tom* on the "ponderous side"); ER to Shumlin, Oct. 16, 1944 (accepting his verdict with grace); Owen Dodson to ER, Nov. 2, 1944 (liking the play); Arthur S. Friend to ER, April 8, 1945; ER to Friend, July 19, 1945—all RA. She sent a film treatment to Kenneth Macgowan, then at Paramount Pictures (Macgowan to ER, Dec. 14, 1945, Jan. 2, 1946, RA). ER to Earl Browder, April 18, 22, July 11, Sept. 28, Nov. 7, 1944, Browder Papers, Syracuse University (henceforth SU: Browder); Browder to ER, May 29, 1944, RA; ER to CVV and FM, Aug. 9, 1945, Yale: Van Vechten (Paul's phone call). She was also

delighted at a call from Paul, Jr., saying that the whole campus at Cornell was talking about her book; he encouraged her to forget about attending his athletic events so dutifully if they stood in the way of her accepting lecture dates (ER to CVV and FM, Aug. 12, 1945, Yale: Van Vechten). Essie liked to remind Paul that she went to many more of Paul, Jr.'s athletic events than Paul did, even mentioning to Earl Browder how much Paul, Jr., would have liked it if his father could have attended more often (ER letters to Browder, 1944–45, SU: Browder). Apparently Essie's old friend Minnie Sumner was hired to prepare maps for the book (Day Co. to ER, Aug. 3, 1945, RA).

25. ER to Larry Brown, Aug. 14, 1945 (enclosing two reviews), NYPL/Schm: Brown; ER to CVV and FM, Aug. 9, 12, 1945, Yale: Van Vechten; Viola V. Boyd ("Vie") to Larry Brown, n.d. (1946); Rockmore to Brown, April 20, 1946, NYPL/Schm: Brown. Mary McLeod Bethune to ER, Feb. 27, 1946, RA (NCNW selection). RA contains many other letters congratulating Essie on the effectiveness of her lectures. The mss. of Essie's lectures during the 1944–46 period are in RA. The typed ms. of one talk is a stenotype and clearly demonstrates her effectiveness in question-and-answer exchanges. "I took off 20 pounds," Essie exuberantly wrote Paul's sister, Marian, "exercised myself hard and flat, and have cleared my face out and have just had my hair done. What do you know? I think the big boy will be quite pleased. I'm at my best. And now is the time!!!!!" (ER to Marian Forsythe, April 4, 1945, courtesy of Paulina Forsythe.) Essie wrote this letter just a few days before her disastrous trip to see Paul in Chicago.

26. The transcript of PR's WHK talk is in RA; ER letters to Earl Browder, 1944–45, SU: Browder; ER to Ben Davis, Jr., July 27, 1944; Davis to ER, July 27, Nov. 18, 1944, Feb. 17, March 30, 1945, RA. Essie wrote Mrs. Roosevelt about her electioneering, enclosing a copy of one of her speeches (ER to Mrs. Roosevelt, Nov. 1, 1944; Mrs. Roosevelt to ER, Nov. 6, 1944, RA). Hubert T. Delany congratulated Essie on her role in the campaign (Delany to ER, Nov. 10, 1944, RA).

27. According to Revels Cayton, "The Party just railed at his 'exploits,' you know, his personal life . . . but they never had him up on the carpet about it, I don't think. . . . I guess Ben spoke to him some" (interview with Cayton, April 29, 1982).

28. James M. Nabrit, Jr., to PR, April 20, 24, 1945, RA (Howard); *Howard University Bulletin,* Oct. 1, 1945, for the Howard citation to PR, delivered at the ceremony by President Mordecai Johnson. Acting Sec. NAACP (Wilkins) to Spingarn Medal Award Committee, March 21, 1943, LC: NAACP; interview with John H. Hammond, Aug. 8, 1985. The only written ballot I've found in the NAACP papers from absent committee members is Langston Hughes's. He voted, in order of preference, for Robeson, Joe Louis, and Tobias (Hughes to Wilkins, March 24, 1945, LC: NAACP). It was also in April 1945 that Robeson won an award from the Negro Newspaper Publishers Association (Frank L. Stanley to PR, April 18, 1945, RA). PR crossed out this passage from the Seton ms. of *Robeson:* ". . . it had become a custom during the war years for Walter White to suggest someone other than Paul Robeson for the Springarn [sic] Medal. It had, in fact, reached the proportion of a Robeson family joke with everyone guessing as to whom Walter White would come up with this time. But in the summer of 1945 there wasn't anyone, so, at last, Robeson had to get the Medal."

CHAPTER 15   POSTWAR POLITICS *(1945–1946)*

1. His optimistic views are reflected in interviews with the Vancouver *News-Herald,* Jan. 11, 1945; Victoria (Canada) *Daily Times,* Jan. 13, 1945; Chicago *Defender,* Feb. 24, April 14, 1945.

2. Robeson's activity, through the CAA, in preparing for the San Francisco conference was known in detail to the FBI, including an effort made to include the African leaders Nnamdi Azikiwe, Ban-

kole (president of the Nigerian Trade Union Congress), and Esua (general secretary of the Nigerian Union of Teachers) in a broadcast dealing with the upcoming UN conference (FBI New York 100-25857-90). The FBI noted ominously (after tracking telephone conversations between Yergan and Rockmore) that PR had made a one-thousand-dollar contribution to the CAA in 1941 and, in response to Yergan's special plea, an additional thousand in 1944 (FBI Main 100-12304-25, 27). *New Africa*, vol. 4, nos. 4–7 (May, June, July ["low ebb"], 1945). The CAA retained hope somewhat longer in the potential restraining power of the United Nations, a hope bolstered in 1946 by the successful passage in the General Assembly of a resolution introduced by Nan Pandit, chief of the Indian delegation, objecting to racial discrimination against Indians in South Africa. The Soviet Union supported the Indian resolution and the United States and Great Britain opposed it (*New Africa*, vol. 5, no. 11) [Dec. 1946]. I am grateful to my friend Rosalyn Higgins, the international law expert, for reading over this section on the United Nations.

3. *New Africa*, June 1945 (PR telegram); Stettinius to PR, June 6, 25, 1945, Jan. 19, 1946, NYPL/Schm: PR; Dulles to PR, Dec. 7, 1946, RA. Other Council members were also urged to telegraph Truman et al. (Hunton to E. Franklin Frazier, May 21, 1945, MSRC: Frazier).

4. New York *Amsterdam News*, June 16, 1945; Larry Brown to ER, Aug. 8, 1945; Abe Lastfogel (president, USO Camp Shows) to PR, Oct. 1, 1945; Chicago *Defender*, Aug. 25, 1945. FBI Main 100-25857-88 and 89 refer to attempted negotiations through Archibald MacLeish (then an assistant secretary with the State Department) for the *Othello* tour to Europe. Typical of the bizarre combination to be found in FBI documents of the arcanely well informed and the abysmally unfounded, the informant in FBI NY 25857-89 was unable to identify the "Joe" mentioned in the phone log as Joe Ferrer—though the *Othello* tour was currently in progress—but did at least suggest that "Joe" might "possibly [be] associated with Paul Robeson's

show." A confidential informant reported to the FBI that Max Yergan, a "known active Communist" who exerted "considerable influence" over Robeson, had given him a going-away party on July 25, 1945, at his home, attended by "two Communist Chinese delegates to the San Francisco Conference" (FBI Main 100-12304-40, April 5, 1946).

5. FBI New York 100-25857-112 (disturbed); the quote about the "Sudeten soldiers" is from PR's testimony before the Senate Judiciary Committee in 1948 (transcript in RA) in which he looked back to his views in 1945.

6. FBI New York 100-25857-112, 116, 120 (Yergan), 121, 123, 129; FBI Main 100-12304-40. Diane Sommers, Yergan's secretary (and Ben Davis, Jr.'s lover), was another focal point of tension within the CAA office, since she was known to reproach Yergan for his "lavish personal expenses" paid for with CAA funds (Freda Diamond, ms. comments). FBI New York 100-25857-135, which is the log of a phone conversation between two unidentified people, reports their shared view that "Paul doesn't know what's going on [in terms of tension over Diane Sommers] so he would be rooting for her," adding that Essie wasn't aware of developments within the office, either; the log also contains the view of the two callers that Alphaeus Hunton and Doxey Wilkerson, the two respected, dignified, dedicated men who worked alongside Yergan in the CAA office, were temperamentally unsuited to deal with the tension, characterizing Hunton as a "guy [who] knows just one thing—his job. With all his guts he just sits there and pushes his pencil away . . . and [is] absolutely uninterested in anything else." In 1948 Robeson joined Louise Bransten, Barney Josephson, Howard Fast, and Blackie Myers and Ferdinand Smith of the NMU in hosting a dinner for Frederick Field in "appreciation of his response whenever a progressive cause needed help" (PR to Corliss Lamont, April 21, 1948, courtesy of Lamont).

7. Robeson's expressions of fear about the roles the U.S. State Department and Churchill were playing are also in *The Afro-American*, June 9, 1945, and

the Boston *Chronicle*, Aug. 4, 1945. For confirmation of James F. Byrnes's control of foreign policy during the last half of 1945, see Robert L. Messer, *The End of an Alliance: James F. Byrnes, Roosevelt, Truman, and the Origins of the Cold War* (University of North Carolina Press, 1982).

8. *New Africa*, vol. 2, no. 1 (Aug. 1943) (Labour conference); Robeson's cable to Attlee is in the Manchester *Guardian*, Sept. 27, 1945.

9. *New Africa*, vol. 4, no. 8 (August–September 1945), no. 9 (October 1945).

10. Wilkins telegram to White, May 12(?), 1945; White memo of Aug. 24, 1945 (Rockmore's suggestions); White memo to Wilkins, Sept. 5, 1945 (Welles, etc.)—all LC: NAACP; FBI NY 100-25857-10 (Clara Rockmore). Both Rockmore and Essie sent White lists of people to invite (RR to WW, Aug. 24, 1945; ER to WW, Aug. 25, 1945, LC: NAACP).

11. The text of Marshall Field's remarks is in RA.

12. Pittsburgh *Courier*, Sept. 22, 29, Oct. 27, 1945; the FBI document quoting PR is a blurred Xerox, the file date Nov. 28, 1945, the file number illegible. The Spingarn dinner is also reported in FBI Main 100-12304-40.

13. White, "The Strange Case of Paul Robeson," *Ebony*, Feb. 1951.

14. The four-page typed ms. of PR's speech at the World Freedom Rally on Nov. 14, 1945, and the six-page ms. of his talk at the Institute on Judaism, Nov. 25, 1945, are in RA. FBI reports on preparations for the Nov. 14 event, including a phone tap between Yergan and Robeson, are in New York 100-25857-124, 133. A month later, continuing to emphasize the same themes, Robeson gave a statement to *The People's Voice* stressing that "the domestic fascists . . . have boldly stepped forward to take up the battle . . . are powerful and influential. Their influence extends up to the very top of our government." He expressed continuing optimism that although "the enemy is powerful . . . the masses of peoples are more powerful," and if they stood together would "win the struggle" (two-page ms. statement is in RA).

As a result of the appearance of PR and several other actors at a Madison Square Garden rally late in Sept. to aid the victims of the Franco regime—at which Harold Laski attacked the Catholic Church for its support of Franco—the Catholic actor Frank Fay formally protested to Actors' Equity (the dispute is detailed in FBI phone taps, New York 100-25857-110, 115, 116, 129). PR wrote Equity a blistering letter in response to Fay, defending his right to appear and expressing the hope of finding Fay someday "on the side of the great forces of anti-fascists—Catholic and non-Catholic" (PR to Equity Council, Oct. 2, 1945, Actors' Equity Association Records, NYU: Wagner). The Constitutional Educational League published a thirty-two-page pamphlet, *The Fay Case* (RA) by Joseph P. Kamp, portraying Fay as "an old fashioned American," all those connected with the Madison Square Garden rally as "Communists," and Robeson himself as "Mr. Moscow."

FBI Main 100-12304-23 (for the report that PR had joined the CP—while on a tour in England, inspired by Harry Pollitt the British Communist leader); FBI Main 100-12304-34 ("definitely classify"). The FBI had also been investigating Essie—triggered, apparently, by the report she "has mailed several letters addressed to Nehru" (FBI Main 100-12304-10?) but, after lengthy investigation, concluded that there was "no known Communist activity" on her part (FBI Main 100-12304-21), although she was "vitally interested in the matter of racial discrimination" (FBI Main 100-12304-14). Still, the FBI issued a "security index card" for her (FBI Main, June 10, 1944, file number blurred; additional reports on ER: FBI Main 100-12304-15 and 17).

15. Duclos's "On the Dissolution of the Communist Party of the United States" is reprinted in *Political Affairs*, July 1945. Of the secondary works covering the Browder crisis, I've found Joseph R. Starobin, *American Communism in Crisis, 1943–1957* (Harvard University Press, 1972), particularly useful.

16. FBI Main 100-12304-29 (June 9, 1945). In FBI Main 100-12304-40 (April 5, 1946), a confidential informant advised that Ben Davis, Jr., and PR had talked over the import of the Duclos article and

"Robeson expressed himself as thinking that William Z. Foster was correct in his thinking about the matter."

17. Pittsburgh *Courier*, July 6, 1946; Seton, *Robeson*, pp. 168–72. Because of the voluminous number of newspaper reviews in RA—and their repetitive nature, adding little to Larry Brown's succinct summary quoted above—I have decided against specific citations from the reviews here.

Difficulties developed between PR and "Willie" Schatzkammer, the pianist who often appeared as an associate artist on PR's concert programs; for a while (according to Rockmore) Robeson felt Larry Brown was allied with Schatzkammer, and Rockmore warned Brown that he was likely to become the brunt of "a great deal of hostility" because of this. In his letter to Brown (March 4, 1947, NYPL/Schm: Brown) Rockmore never specified the nature of the Robeson-Schatzkammer dispute and referred to it only cryptically, but he advised Brown not to take sides openly with Schatzkammer for fear of alienating Paul. He closed his letter on a more light-hearted note, saying that all this would one day be "grist" for Larry's "memoirs" of his life on stage with "La Hayes [Roland Hayes] and Le Robeson." Rockmore asked Brown "to tear this letter up after you have read it." FBI Main 100-12304-40 (JAFRC). Robeson's endorsement of Quill was the subject of a separate report, FBI New York 100-25857-126 (Nov. 5, 1945). Revels Cayton received many requests for a Robeson appearance (they are in NYPL/Schm: NNC), but he reported that Paul's singing schedule was so tough he didn't "have the heart to ask him to do something for the Congress" [NNC] while he was out in California (Cayton to Matt Crawford, Jan. 14, 1946, NYPL/Schm: NNC).

18. In my discussions of foreign policy, I've found myself leaning (strongly) in the direction of the revisionist historians and have found Marty Jezer's *The Dark Ages: Life in the United States 1945–1960* (South End Press, 1982) consistently useful. The following have also been significant resources: John Lewis Gaddis, *The United States and the Origins of the Cold War* (Columbia University Press, 1972); Lloyd C. Gardner, *Architects of Illusion* (Quadrangle, 1970); Thomas M. Patterson, *Soviet-American Confrontation* (Johns Hopkins Press, 1973); Richard Freedland, *The Truman Doctrine and the Origins of McCarthyism* (Knopf, 1972). For a summary of Churchill's unrelentingly anti-Soviet views and his insistence on maintaining British ascendancy in the Mediterranean, see Fraser J. Harbutt, *The Iron Curtain: Churchill, America, and the Origins of the Cold War* (Oxford University Press, 1986). Harbutt argues that the new Labour Foreign Secretary, Ernest Bevin, worked with Churchill behind the scenes to shape a British anti-Communist consensus and that, in his Feb. 1946 visit to the United States, Churchill succeeded in recruiting a previously wavering Truman. In his impressive study, *American Intervention in Greece, 1943–1949* (Columbia University Press, 1982), Lawrence S. Wittner concludes that the Soviet government took no direct action to aid the Greek left and that U.S. dealings with postwar Greece "are not very pretty" (see especially ch. 2).

19. FBI New York 100-25857-156 (March 21, 1946); California *Eagle*, March 14, 1946; *Daily People's World*, March 26, 1946.

20. FBI New York 100-25857-156 (March 21, 1946).

21. Ibid. The FBI believed PR had "apparently increasingly come under the control of Max Yergan," himself described as "a leader in Communist front activities," and accurately characterized Robeson as being "reticent in giving his approval to send the [original] letter over signature" (Main 100-12304-40, April 5, 1946). Other prominent blacks, along with significant portions of the black press, protested Churchill's speech (Mark Solomon, "Black Critics of Colonialism and the Cold War," in T. G. Paterson, *Cold War Critics* (Quadrangle, 1971), pp. 217–19.

22. *The People's Voice*, March 30, 1946; *New Africa*, Jan. 1946 (famine); Yergan to Du Bois, Jan. 17, 1946, reports on the success of the famine campaign (U.Mass.: Du Bois); program on the April Win the

Peace Conference and typed ms. of Temple Israel speech, RA; FBI New York 100-25857-158 (telephone log of PR phoning his Win the Peace speech).

23. The Win the Peace program is in RA. A "Big Three Unity for Colonial Freedom" rally held on June 6, 1946, in Madison Square Garden is a further example of the wide variety of prominent Americans in attendance: among others, Mary McLeod Bethune, Norman Corwin, Judy Holliday, Lena Horne (Louise Hopkins to PR, April 25, 1946, RA). Nehru was among those who sent cables in support of the meeting (Nehru to PR, May 16, 1946, RA). Stettinius to PR, May 24, 1946, RA.

During 1946 Robeson made dozens of political appearances in addition to those cited above. He contributed to half a dozen Win the Peace rallies from coast to coast. He lent his presence both to organizational conferences and to mass meetings sponsored by the National Negro Congress and the Council on African Affairs. And he put in single appearances in behalf of such causes and commemorative celebrations as the Veterans of the Lincoln Brigade, the *New Masses* magazine, the 3rd American Slav Congress, the Oust Bilbo Dinner (at the Hotel Pennsylvania in New York) and the Southern Youth Legislature (at Columbia, South Carolina). Because the sentiments he expressed on these occasions are already summarized in the detailed account above of several of his appearances in 1946, I have refrained from unnecessary duplication. One additional appearance, however, is worth special mention. On Dec. 29, 1946, PR spoke to the Convention of Alpha Phi Alpha, the leading black fraternity, which was *not* known as outspokenly political, and did not trim his sentiments to his audience. He deplored the role of the U.S. government "in extending loans and credits and even guns to the powers which are trying to maintain their empires," hailed the role India and the U.S.S.R. had played in the United Nations in thwarting the attempt by General Smuts of the Union of South Africa to annex South-West Africa, applauded "the new democratic states which have been born in Central Europe

since the end of the war: Poland, Czechoslovakia, Yugoslavia. . . ." In regard to domestic policy, he called for a determined effort to get the new Congress to pass antilynching legislation, create a permanent FEPC, and end poll-tax discrimination. "If the Democratic party and the Republican party cannot do this job," he said, prefiguring the role he was soon to play in the Progressive Party campaign, "then it will be necessary for the people to form a new party of their own" (ms. of the talk is in RA).

24. Several versions of PR's Sept. 12, 1946, speech at the Garden are in RA; a summarizing Associated Negro Press release is in CHS: Barnett. In the speech, Robeson singled out Gov. Thomas E. Dewey of New York for excoriation because of his whitewash of a Long Island policeman who had killed two black veterans. The black political cartoonist Ollie Harrington helped make Isaac Woodward's blinding into a major NAACP case. Harrington invited only foreign correspondents to a press conference and presented Woodward, along with his doctors, to them. At a second press conference, Harrington recalls Robeson and Yergan looking reproachfully at him from the audience, as if to say, "This case belongs to *us*." Harrington deeply admired Robeson but thought this attitude unworthy of him—"It was the saddest moment in my relation with Robeson" (interview with Harrington, July 29, 1986). Walter White asked Harrington to become public-relations director for the NAACP, but as red-baiting pressures mounted, he decided to live in Europe.

25. Robeson's telegram to Du Bois asking him to join the call, dated Aug. 30, 1946, is in U.Mass.: Du Bois.

26. White to PR, Sept. 10, 1946; Gloster B. Current (NAACP director of branches) to Edward M. Swan (executive secretary, Detroit branch of NAACP), special delivery, Sept. 20, 1946; memo from Franklin H. Williams to White, Sept. 17, 1946, denouncing the American Crusade as "irresponsible"; White to Du Bois, Sept. 19, Oct. 2, 1946; Du Bois to White, Sept. 23, 1946—all in LC: NAACP. The Rev. Charles A. Hill, president of the Detroit branch of the

NAACP, like Du Bois denied that he had ever been told of the "broadly representative" National Emergency Committee Against Mob Violence; now that he had belatedly been informed, he wrote White, he was nonetheless going to attend the Robeson gathering—"I will go representing my church. ... If there is not a good showing . . . the reflection will be on all of the liberal forces" (Hill to White, Sept. 18, 1946, LC: NAACP). Revels Cayton, in line with the policy of the National Negro Congress to challenge the NAACP for leadership of black workers, urged attendance at the American Crusade gathering (Cayton to Jack Bjoze, executive secretary, Abraham Lincoln Brigade, Aug. 30, 1946, NYPL/Schm: NNC).

In June 1946 the NNC had presented a petition to the UN calling for action in behalf of the oppressed black citizens of the United States. The list of the United Nations Campaign Committee is in NYPL/Schm: NNC and does not include a single member of the NAACP hierarchy (or that of any other mainstream black organization). It does include the names of many leading CP and left-wing figures, black and white, among them Robeson, Ben Davis, Jr., Du Bois, Frederick Field, Doxey Wilkerson, Albert Kahn, Ben Gold, Michael Quill, Irwin Potash, Lawrence Reddick, Ferdinand Smith, Henry Winston, and, among the "publicists," Langston Hughes. In response to Yergan's appeal for support of the petition drive, Mary McLeod Bethune wrote him, ". . . there is a question in our minds as to whether the approach to the existing conditions here in our own United States should come through the United Nations, whose problems for consideration are international rather than national" (Bethune to Yergan, Nov. 20, 1946, NYPL/Schm: NNC).

27. *The People's Voice,* Sept. 28, 1946. Robeson also spoke on MBS radio on Sept. 23, 1946, denouncing lynching (the text of the talk is in RA; there was a lengthy excerpt in *The People's Voice,* Jan. 11, 1947). The limited success of the Crusade meetings is described in the papers of the NNC (letter from Nellie Zakin to participants, NYPL/Schm), along with letters of thanks to the contributors, who included, among others, Roger de Koven, Mercedes McCambridge, and Jan Minor; memo from Gloucester Current to Walter White, Sept. 24, 1946, LC: NAACP.

28. *The New York Times,* Sept. 24, 1946; Philadelphia *Tribune,* Sept. 24, 1946; New York *World-Telegram,* Sept. 23, 1946; Chicago *Sun,* Sept. 24, 1946; *The People's Voice,* Sept. 28, 1946 (which listed the delegates as [besides Robeson] Dr. Charlotte Hawkins Brown, Palmer Memorial Institute, Sedalia, N.C.; Mrs. Harper Sibley, president of the Council of Church Women; Rev. W. H. Jernagin, National Baptist Convention; Dr. Joseph L. Johnson, dean of the Howard University School of Medicine; Dr. Max Yergan; and Aubrey Williams, editor of the *Southern Farmer*). Additionally, the Chicago *Defender* (Sept. 28, 1946) lists Metz T. P. Lorchard, editor-in-chief of the *Defender;* Rabbi Irving Miller, American Jewish Congress; and an "H. Murphy of Chicago" as being part of the delegation. The several FBI reports (New York 100-25857-188, 196) headed "Re: American Crusade to End Lynching," have nearly their entire contents inked out. Apparently the decision to go from the meeting to the White House was spur-of-the-moment. Later recounting the event, George B. Murphy, Jr. (the left-wing scion of the family that owned the *Afro-American*), wrote, ". . . on the platform . . . the question came up about going down to the White House to picket. . . . Dr. Jernagin began to caution 'restraint': 'Why Dr. Jernagin,' [Paul said,] 'it looks to me like these folks want us to lead them down to the White House and I think that is what we should do.' Presto, Dr. Jernagin got his hat and went right along with Paul to do just that" (Murphy to Du Bois, Aug. 31, 1956, U.Mass.: Du Bois).

29. The complete transcript of Robeson's testimony before the Tenney Committee was printed in a California newspaper, the Westwood Hills *Press,* Oct. 18, 1946; unless otherwise cited, the quotations in the following paragraphs come from that source. Additional detail on the committee can be found in Edward

L. Barrett, Jr., *The Tenney Committee* (Cornell University Press, 1951).

30. Cayton to Yergan, Oct. 11, 1946, NYPL/Schm: NNC.

31. As early as 1941, Robeson wrote of having been with "my friend Revels Cayton" (PR to Freda Diamond, Aug. 1941, courtesy of Diamond). Yergan to William Schneiderman, Aug. 23, 1945; Yergan to Jeanne Pastor, Dec. 12, 1945, NYPL/Schm: NNC; interviews with Revels and Lee Cayton (PR, Jr., participating), April 27–28, 1982; separate interview with Revels Cayton, April 29, 1982; follow-up phone interviews with Cayton, 1987–88. There is an additional and revealing group of letters in NYPL/Schm: NNC concerning Cayton's arrival at NNC and the need to reorient the Congress's purpose (e.g., Thelma M. Dale to William L. Patterson, Sept. 26, 1945; Patterson to Cayton and Matt Crawford, July 2, 1945; Yergan to Cayton, Aug. 23, 1945; Cayton to Crawford, Jan. 3, 14, Feb. 1, 1946; Cayton to James Hunter [CIO], Jan. 10, 1946). In explaining his attraction to the Party, Cayton sounded a note close to Robeson's own: "I found a new world . . . a kind of equality with whites, within the Party, that I'd never known before. And it was attractive" (interview, April 29, 1982). Similar sentiments can be found in two other books by or about black Communists: Nell Irvin Painter, *The Narrative of Hosea Hudson* (Harvard University Press, 1979); Harry Haywood, *Black Bolshevik: Autobiography of an Afro-American Communist* (Liberator Press, 1978). As an example of the personal closeness between the two men, Robeson talked to Cayton (and to few others) about his relationship with Lena Horne, telling Cayton that she broke up with him when he refused to marry her. Horne's own (platonic) version of the friendship is in *In Person: Lena Horne*, pp. 181–87. She reiterated her denial of a love affair in our phone interview of Sept. 8, 1987: "It would never have occurred to me to be physical with him—he was too mythic."

32. Yergan to Cayton, Aug. 23, 1945, NYPL/Schm: NNC (reorientation of NNC). Cayton correspondence, NYPL/Schm: NNC; interviews with Revels and Lee Cayton, April 1982; follow-up phone interviews with Revels Cayton, 1987–88.

33. Interview with Revels Cayton, April 29, 1982. Addie Wyatt, who worked with the Packinghouse Union in the early 1950s, also emphasized to me Robeson's concern about unity among black and white workers in the trade-union movement (interview with Wyatt, Jan. 7, 1986). According to Annette Rubinstein, who worked closely with Vito Marcantonio in the American Labor Party, "Marc very much distrusted and disliked Ben Davis." Marcantonio and Doxey Wilkerson were both "horrified" to learn that during the war Davis knew and kept quiet about the Party's sanctioning segregated meetings in the South (interview with Rubinstein, Dec. 5, 1983). Angus Cameron recalls once asking Ben Davis directly what he thought about the question of whether American blacks constituted a nation. Davis's reply was (according to Cameron): "The Party was wrong when it held that blacks in America were a nation, and also when it held they were not a nation" (Cameron to me, April 25, 1987).

34. Interviews with Cayton, April 1982; follow-up phone interviews 1987–88; Cayton to Yergan, Oct. 11, 1946, NYPL/Schm: NNC. Another description of Cayton and Robeson in action together, this time at the tenth-anniversary celebration of the NNC on May 31, 1946, in Detroit, is in *New Masses*, June 18, 1946, written by Abner W. Berry, the black Communist. For a negative view of the NNC, strongly "anti-Communist" in bias, see Wilson Record, *Race and Radicalism* (Cornell University Press, 1964).

Speaking to the delegates to the Longshore and Shipsclerks' caucus at their convention in San Francisco in August 1943, Robeson had saluted Harry Bridges as a "courageous leader" (*The Dispatcher*, Sept. 3, 1943). And when Bridges, who was foreign-born, was being threatened with deportation in 1945, Robeson had written in his defense directly to President Roosevelt, stating that "Bridges has stood steadfastly against discrimination." Bridges's record was better than that of Mike Quill of the Transport Workers Union, but privately Robeson would argue with him about the need to wage a stronger fight against racial discrimination in the ILWU. Bridges later came to resent the movement for black caucuses, insisting the effort would split his union (*The Dispatcher*, March 9, 1945; *The Pilot* [NMU], March 16, 1945). On the other hand, Bridges's reputation as a champion of black rights remained high enough for the National Negro Labor Council to pass a special resolution in support of his fight against deportation at its second annual convention, in 1952 (*The Dispatcher*, Dec. 5, 1952).

35. Interviews with Uta Hagen, June 22–23, 1982, Sept. 28, 1984. Unless otherwise cited, the quotations in the account that follows are from these interviews.

36. Perhaps adding to PR's concern, the following exchange took place at just this time during the House Hearings Regarding the Communist Infiltration of the Motion Picture Industry:

> Richard Nixon: "Have you any other tests which you would apply which would indicate to you that people acted like Communists?"
>
> Adolphe Menjou: "Well, I think attending any meetings at which Mr. Paul Robeson appeared and applauding or listening to his Communist songs in America, I would be ashamed to be seen in an audience doing a thing of that kind" (*Hearings*, Oct. 1946, p. 104).

PR, Jr., is the source for the information about the relationship between Ellsworth "Bumpy" Johnson and his father (see also note 17, p. 695). For more on Bumpy Johnson, see Helen Lawrenson, *Stranger at the Party* (Random House, 1972), ch. 9. Tension in the CP over relationships between black men and white women went back at least to the thirties (see Naison, *Heyday*, pp. 136–37; George Charney, *A Long Journey* [Quadrangle, 1968], p. 102). Freda Diamond has told me (multiple interviews) that, at one point in the mid-forties, Ben Davis, Jr., came to her on behalf of the CP and asked that she pointedly let Paul know that his relationship

with Uta was causing a lot of talk. She refused.

37. "The Midnight Raid of José Ferrer," *Confidential*, Sept. 1955.

38. Several members of Robeson's inner circle share a version of one aspect of the breakup at odds with Hagen's (and which they say Paul himself told them). According to this version, Hagen was so distraught at Paul's attempt to disentangle himself that she swallowed a quantity of sleeping pills. Sensing something was wrong, this version continues, Robeson hastened to her apartment, found her comatose, walked her around, got her medical treatment, "saved her life." Hagen hooted with derision when I ran that version by her. "I've never been in a coma. I took eight sleeping pills when my mother died in 1939, about five years before I met Paul, and I was walked around a room in St. James Hotel in Philadelphia by my brother and Joe Ferrer. . . . It sounds like a combination of two stories. . . . I'm sure I told Paul about what I did in Philadelphia when my mother died." (A not-incidental reason for taking the pills in 1939, she added, was to get out of going on tour with the Lunts.) What a shame, she said—"The relationship was so phenomenal all by itself, there's nothing to lie about." I should add that I believe Hagen's version, on the grounds that in all other ways I found her candid and forthcoming. Hagen last caught sight of Robeson sometime in the fifties; he was coming out of the Astor Theater surrounded by bodyguards, and she had the impulse to run and embrace him but resisted it (interviews with Hagen).

39. RA contains itineraries for Essie's extensive lecture tours plus a number of letters extolling her abilities on the platform (e.g., A. Ritchie Low to PR, April 11, 1947: "I heard Mrs. Robeson give a wonderfully fine lecture in San Francisco"). She applied to the Carnegie Corporation for funding on yet a third book—"a comprehensive SURVEY OF BLACK AFRICA"—but was turned down with the explanation that Carnegie was already funding Lord Hailey "to look at the scene with European eyes" (ER to Devereux C. Josephs, Nov. 22, 1946; Whitney H. Shepardson to ER, Dec. 23,

1946, RA). Essie wrote a pamphlet that the Council on African Affairs published in 1946 in which she was critical of U.S. policy on Africa, and predicted that the continent would soon be in the forefront of international politics. For further discussion of ER's views on Africa, see Barbara Ransby, "Eslanda Goode Robeson, Pan-Africanist," *Sage*, 3:2 (Fall 1986). Essie described her African trip to the Van Vechtens as "fabulous" (ER to CVV and FM, postcard, Sept. 12, 1946, Yale: Van Vechten). The background on Paul, Jr.'s finances is in ER to PR, Jr., Nov. 30, 1946, RA.

Essie's lecture dates are partly detailed in a brief diary she kept for Feb. 1946, which also records some interesting encounters she had. In St. Louis, her "old beau from Indiana U," Elmer Mosee, came to see her. In 1946 Mosee was the superintendent of the People's Hospital in St. Louis (in Jan. 1947 Robeson sang in St. Louis under the hospital's sponsorship), and Essie described him as the "closest Negro to Truman"; as such he gave her "all the low down," describing Truman as "loyal, stubborn, devoted to his mother, honest, conservative, grass roots, cautious, firm. Says he removed a secretary on Elmer's complaint" (ER Diary, Feb. 4, 1946, RA). In Pennsylvania she had a talk with Congressman Francis E. Walter, a "wonderful man, liberal, interesting, friendly, sound. Tells me Rankin is really mental case. Bilbo just a career politician with one item to sell—discrimination" (ER Diary, Feb. 15, 1946, RA). This same Francis Walter was later co-author of the infamous McCarran-Walter Act and a tormentor of Robeson—see pp. 440–42. In Philadelphia Essie saw the play *Jeb* and disliked it but thought Ossie Davis "gave a beautiful performance" (ER Diary, Feb. 16, 1946, RA). Back in New York, between lectures, she saw Bess Eitingon for dinner (the two had decided to write a play together on the atom bomb), along with Clifford Odets and his wife and Marc Blitzstein. She found Odets "insufferable. We got into a terrific row over [the play] *Deep Are the Roots*. I was so furious at his pompous stupid criticism I could have killed him.

Marc is nice" (ER Diary, Feb. 19, 1946, RA). In the dining car of a train outside of Columbus, Ohio, she talked "with a white passenger at table who is opposite me in the sleeper. After he left I told the waiter—Negro of course—It's some job educating these white folks. He said dont waste your time. You cant educate them. Why a guy came in the diner for breakfast this morning—white man—and asked one of the boys—Say why dont you smile? The waiter said—dead pan—Did you come in here to eat or to see me smile. He was so angry. The white man was furious. All the waiters froze up on him and he didn't know what to do. Said he'd report the waiter. So all the waiters gave him bad service. White folks!! It never occurs to them we do double shift, long hours, what have we got to smile about?" (ER Diary, Feb. 25, 1946, RA.)

40. ER to PR, Jr., Nov. 30, 1946, RA.

41. ER to PR, Dec. 1, 1946, RA. Essie angrily threatened never again to communicate directly with Paul if he passed on to Rockmore the contents of her letter. Yet Essie herself made it all but certain Rockmore would learn of her angry discontent. When H. Lee Lurie, a partner in Rockmore's law firm, was assigned to do Essie's taxes and sent her a query about her checkbook stubs, she replied, "Honey, where would I get a checkbook, and for what? I havent had a checkbook since I arrived in this country, in 1939, and Bobby took over our personal affairs. Not only have I not had a checkbook, but I haven't had an adequate housekeeping allowance since then. . . . I realize that I have had to live down a reputation for extravagance. I am still trying to figure out how I have been extravagant. . . . Paul has been living at the regular rate he used to, but I have been living on the rock bottom level. . . . Before then, abroad, Paul and I lived on the same level and hence, I daresay, I was considered extravagant" (Lurie to ER, Dec. 21, 1946; ER to Lurie, Jan. 3, 1947, RA).

42. ER to PR, Jr., Nov. 30, 1946, Jan. 28, 1947, RA.

43. ER to Revels Cayton, Jan. 6, 1947, NYPL/Schm: NNC. Essie made the

comment about not being told anything specifically in reference to Cayton's efforts, with Robeson's support, to launch a national trade-union department in the NNC, but it seems to me to have broader applicability. Information on establishing the Labor Department is in Cayton's correspondence for this period in NYPL/Schm; one letter particularly refers to "an extremely successful banquet for Paul Robeson" for that purpose, held in Detroit (Cayton to Max Perlow, secretary-treasurer of the Furniture Workers of America, Jan. 21, 1947, NYPL/Schm: NNC).

CHAPTER 16   THE PROGRESSIVE PARTY *(1947–1948)*

1. For background information on the inception of the Progressive Party, I've found three works of special value: Curtis D. MacDougall, *Gideon's Army* (Marzani & Munsell, 1965), 3 vols.; Allen Yarnell, *Democrats and Progressives* (University of California Press, 1974); and Norman D. Markowitz, *The Rise and Fall of the People's Century* (The Free Press, 1973). The two groups that sponsored Wallace's Sept. 1946 speech were the Independent Citizens Committee of the Arts, Sciences and Professions (ICC-ASP) and the National Citizens Political Action Committee (NC-PAC). As early as Feb. 1946 Robeson spoke for the Minnesota ICC (Samuel A. Cordon to PR, Feb. 4, 1946, RA), and the month before that the nominating committee of ICC-ASP unanimously chose him to stand for election as a vice-chairman (Jo Davidson, national chairman, to PR, Jan. 17, 1946, RA; minutes of the We Want Wallace Committee of Harlem, Feb. 10, 1945, NYPL/Schm: NNC).

2. For information on the Win the Peace bannings, I'm grateful to Abbott Simon and Freda Diamond for a memo on the subject. *The New York Times*, Jan. 27, 1947 (St. Louis); FBI Main 100-12304-52, Jan. 29, 1947 (St. Louis); Philadelphia *Inquirer*, March 19, 1947 ("sing what I please"); Pittsburgh *Courier*, Feb. 1, 1947. The car was being driven by Elmer Mosee, superintendent of the People's Hospital of St. Louis; his son Elmer Mosee, Jr., and Larry Brown were the other passengers. Mosee had known the Robesons a long time (ER Diary, Feb. 4, 1946, RA). For more on Mosee, see note 39, p. 677. Hearing about PR's announcement that he was leaving the concert stage, Bob Rockmore expressed annoyance at not having been consulted (Rockmore to PR, April 11, 1946, NYPL/Schm: Brown).

3. FBI Main 100-12304-50 (Hoover); Los Angeles *Times*, March 20, 1947 (Hopper); San Francisco *Progress*, April 4, 1947. At the same time, the FBI withdrew the Security Card Index on Essie, having decided "there is no evidence that Mrs. Robeson is presently active in Communist Party affairs" (FBI Main 100-12304-60 and 61, April 10, 1947).

4. Strong to Lawrence J. Campbell, April 22, 1947, NYPL/Schm: Brown.

5. I've drawn this account of the Peoria incident from a large number of sources. The most significant have been: *PM*, April 20, 1947; Hartford *Courant*, April 18, 1947; Chicago *Sun*, April 20, 1947; FBI Main 123405-65 and 72 (Patterson), with a number of enclosures including the important five-page "The People's Side of the Robeson Incident" (which is also in the NYPL/Schm: CRC). Yergan, who had accompanied Robeson to Peoria, wrote Essie: "It was a nasty situation and is the clearest evidence of fascist tyranny dominating an entire city" (Yergan to ER, April 22, 1947, RA). Ferdinand C. Smith, secretary of the CIO National Maritime Union, wired a protest to the Peoria City Council against the ban on Robeson, and Frank Kingdon and Jo Davidson, cochairs of the Progressive Citizens of America (PCA), spoke out against it. The Cultural Division of the NNC also took an active role in protesting the ban (Vivian L. Cadden to "Dear Friend," April 23, 1947, NYPL/Schm: NNC). The FBI agent in Springfield, Illinois, reported that Mayor Triebel "was deluged with correspondence from all over the United States censuring him and

requesting that Paul Robeson be permitted to appear" (FBI New York 100-25857-468). Roy Wilkins, on behalf of the NAACP, was among those who protested abrogating "the cherished American right of freedom of speech" (Wilkins telegram to Triebel, May 1, 1947, LC: NAACP). Thomas J. Fitzpatrick, president of District Six, United Electrical, Radio, and Machine Workers of America, wrote Mayor Triebel (May 2, 1947, NYPL/Schm: CRC), "Robeson is a threat, it is true, to the Thomas-Rankin Committee on Un-American Activities—a threat to all reactionary thought in America." Milton Kaufman of the NNC wrote to Interior Secretary Ickes (April 30, 1947, NYPL/Schm: CRC) charging that "the industrial interests representing the Caterpillar Tractor plant" had worked behind the scenes to prevent Robeson's appearance, a charge corroborated by Mary Sweat of the United Farm Equipment and Metal Workers of America (to Milton Kaufman, April 26, 1947, NYPL/Schm: CRC), who reported that, although some FE-CIO locals had passed resolutions condemning the mayor's action in Peoria, "the large Caterpillar Tractor Local 105-FE-CIO has yet to take action." She reported, too, that "we were unable to buy space in the newspapers" for an ad they had taken out protesting Robeson's barring, "and were refused time on the air."

6. The two clippings from the local press in RA are dated 1947 but are otherwise without identifying headings; Chicago *Sun*, April 20, 1947; Hartford *Courant*, April 18, 1947 ("fight"). The Ministerial Association in Peoria did issue PR an invitation "at some future date" to return, guaranteeing the use of a church (FBI Main 100-12304-65).

7. FBI Main 100-12304-77 (includes the Legion resolutions and the Dirksen correspondence). Hazelwood's name has been inked out of all the FBI documents, but I have been able to deduce it from corollary accounts in the Peoria press about his public statements and his Legion/NAACP affiliations.

8. Chicago *Sun*, April 20, 1947.

9. *PM*, May 4, 1947; New York *Tribune*, April 25, 26, May 7 (Bookstein), May 11 (concert); Army Intelligence (War Department) to FBI, May 13, 1947, 100-25857-2891. Hazel Ericson (Dodge), Robeson's friend from Somerville school days, was among those in the audience, she and her husband attending "as a gesture of support"—for which she was subsequently followed by the FBI (interview with Hazel Ericson Dodge, Nov. 7, 1983; see ch. 1 for more on her). A number of individuals and groups outside Albany joined the protest, including the National Lawyers Guild and the Civil Rights Congress (*PM*, April 29, 1947; telegram from George Marshall, chairman of CRC, to PR, April 25, 1947, NYPL/Schm: CRC). Norman Corwin wrote Essie, "A dozen more fighters like Paul in this country, and reaction would not be winning so many bouts" (Corwin to ER, May 10, 1947).

10. Toronto *Daily Star*, May 19, 20, 1947; in an editorial on May 19, the *Star* reported that, "to enforce its order, the police commission had sent police to his concert—police with notebooks. Such is freedom of speech in Toronto." PR's typed CAA speech, dated April 25, 1947, is in RA. Edward Rettenberg, who had been in law school with Robeson, told me (phone interview, Dec. 10, 1982) that around this same time PR stopped calling on him, explaining that he "would be in trouble" if known to be a friend; FBI agents did subsequently visit Rettenberg.

11. *Newsweek*, May 12, 1947; *Times Herald*, May 22, 1947 (Sokolsky); FBI Main 100-12304-76 (Hoover). By then Robeson had further inflamed opinion against himself by appearing on May 8 at a V-E Day Encampment rally of Communist veterans of World War II (Washington *Post*, May 9, 1947). First Army Headquarters reported to the War Department (which passed the information along to the FBI) that Robeson and Howard Fast "are expected to announce at the Encampment conference their intentions of joining the Communist Party" (FBI New York 100-25857-287). An FBI report dated March 10, 1947, quotes black Party leader Henry Winston telling Roy Hudson, the District 5 Party leader, ". . . It is time that a lot of people begin to speak out. . . . Thus the ball can be

started rolling again by getting Paul Robeson and Howard Fast to publicly join the Party. . . . This will burn up the wires. . . ." They did not, but the Encampment may have marked the first public appearance Robeson made at an avowedly Communist-sponsored event, and, in the retroactive opinion of the ex-CPUSA leader John Gates, "The embrace was too tight" (interview with Gates, June 8, 1982). Reading the Sokolsky-like attacks in England, Joseph Andrews ("Andy"), Robeson's valet and friend from his London days, expressed fear that "you may be fouled" (Andrews to PR, Aug. 29, 1947, RA). He expressed much the same sentiments to Larry Brown (May 27, 1947, NYPL/Schm: Brown). In another letter to Brown, Andy also expressed some resentment toward Robeson: "I was hoping to go home for the Sun this winter, and asked Paul to help toward this, but have heard not a word, so shall have to hold on here" (Jan. 8, 1948, NYPL/Schm: Brown). Since Robeson was never accused of a lack of generosity—except by Essie, who alternately accused him of extravagance toward *others*—the problem here was almost certainly Paul's familiar failure as a correspondent and not as a friend. Harold Holt had offered Robeson an English tour, but Robeson turned it down (Rockmore to Holt, April 10, 1946, NYPL/Schm: Brown).

12. FBI Main 100-12304-69, 70, 73, 75, 77 (Canal Zone). PR's Miami speech is summarized in an ANP release dated June 9, 1947 (CHS: Barnett). Apparently U.S. officials General F. T. Hines, General McSherry, and others initially promised to attend the Robeson concert (Edward Cheresh, UPWA-CIO, to Tom Richardson, April 28, 1947, NYPL/Schm: PR). FBI New York 100-25857-382(7?) (scholarship fund). The letter from PR, Du Bois, Bass, and Howard soliciting support for the Committee to End the Jim Crow "Silver-Gold" System in the Panama Canal Zone, dated Aug. 31, 1948, is in U.Mass.: Du Bois. Several letters from Panama in NYPL/Schm: Brown comment (in the words of one) "on the good your party has done for our community" (Sydney C. Fuller [a jeweler] to

LB, June 30, 1947). In undated (1947) handwritten notes in RA, PR accounted it a "privilege" to have visited his "brothers and sisters" in Panama and the West Indies. "Your struggle is our struggle," he wrote. Ewart Guinier has made reference (in "The Paul Robeson That I Knew," *The Black Scholar*, March 1978, p. 45) to working with Robeson on "organizing non-white workers on the Panama Canal Zone and in Hawaii" (where Robeson went in 1948) while he, Guinier, was international secretary-treasurer of the United Public Workers (1946–53). More of this relationship and the organizing work the two men did together will become known once the Ewart Guinier Papers, currently held privately by Mrs. Guinier, are made available to scholars.

13. *Look*, June 24, 1947 (Gallup); Boston *Chronicle*, June 28, 1947; *PM*, July 20, 1947 (Lewisohn); FBI New York 100-25857-337, 341, 345; MacDougall, *Gideon's Army*, p. 199 (Wallace). The FBI recorded a phone conversation between two members of JAFRC in which one argued that Robeson was being misused by progressive organizations because they were failing to coordinate their efforts, thereby scattering Robeson's energies (FBI New York 100-25857-346, Oct. 29, 1947). Among other notable events to which Robeson lent his presence were the Madison Square Garden rally celebrating the seventeenth anniversary of the Jewish People's Fraternal Order and the sixth biennial convention of the NMU (New York *Fraternal Outlook*, Aug.-Sept. 1947; *Tribune*, Sept. 30, 1947).

14. Yarnell, *Democrats and Progressives*, pp. 17–24; MacDougall, *Gideon's Army*, chs. 7, 9; Markowitz, *Rise and Fall*, chs. 7–8. Late in March 1947 Truman had issued Executive Order 9385, requiring a loyalty oath of all civil-service employees (it was later extended to all workers in defense industries); the oath had contributed to the alienation of organized labor.

15. Starobin, *Crisis*, ch. 7; Lichtenstein, *Labor's War*, ch. 12; Markowitz, *Rise and Fall*, ch. 6.

16. Essie's transcribed notes from the Oct. 6 and Nov. 8 meetings, along with the form letter of invitation and a list

(of more than one hundred names) of those invited, are all in RA. Essie asked Walter White to join in sending out the invitation to the Nov. 8 meeting, but he did not sign the call, even though Essie again stressed in writing to him that the plan was "to bring together a powerful group of Negro leaders . . . without creating any new organization" (ER to White, Oct. 16, 1947, LC: NAACP). Initially, Hubert Delany, Channing Tobias, and Mary McLeod Bethune had told Essie they would attend the Oct. 6 meeting (ER to Du Bois, Oct. 1, 1947, U.Mass.: Du Bois). Du Bois told her he would have attended had not another meeting held him up, and he advised her that one stumbling block to unification would be the difficulty of weighing how much influence to parcel out to participating organizations (Du Bois to ER, Oct. 8, 1947, U.Mass.: Du Bois); to which Essie replied that the focus was on uniting powerful individuals, not organizations (ER to Du Bois, Oct. 16, 1949, U.Mass.: Du Bois).

17. Richard Dalfiume, "The Forgotten Years of the Negro Revolution," in Bernard Sternsher, ed., *The Negro in Depression and War* (Quadrangle, 1969).

18. White to ER, Oct. 22, 1947, LC: NAACP. White suggested Essie show his letter to Paul and offered apologies for having "missed his telephone calls at the office and at the house."

19. Quotes are from ER's notes on Oct. 6 and Nov. 8 meetings, RA. All the participants felt that a promising base on which to place their demands was the progressive recommendations of the President's Committee on Civil Rights ("To Secure These Rights") and the NNC initiated petition to the UN to investigate racism in the United States. Du Bois believed Walter White had dragged his feet in giving NAACP support to the petition (Gerald Horne, *Black and Red: W. E. B. Du Bois and the Afro-American Response to the Cold War, 1944–1963* [State University of New York Press, 1986]).

20. The flier for the June 2, 1948, event, along with a statement of purpose and a list of cosponsors, is in RA. Walter White to Comm. Adm., Jan. 24, 1948; WW to NAACP staff, Feb. 25, 1948, March 13, 1948, LC: NAACP. When the

NAACP, in coordination with other national organizations, organized a National Civil Rights Mobilization to be held in Washington, D.C., in Feb. 1950, William L. Patterson, executive secretary of the Civil Rights Congress, requested that the CRC be allowed to participate. Roy Wilkins turned Patterson down (Wilson Record, *Race and Radicalism*, pp. 154–55).

21. Springfield *Republican*, Jan. 18, 1948 (Chicago); MacDougall, *Gideon's Army*, pp. 301, 512. The other cochairs elected with Robeson were the sculptor Jo Davidson, the New Deal "brain truster" Rex Tugwell, the Progressive Party financial angel Anita McCormick Blaine, and Albert J. Fitzgerald, president of the CIO-UE union. During the campaign James Barfoot, the Progressive candidate for governor of Georgia, publicly stated that he "would like to see Paul Robeson secretary of state. No two nations of the world would go to war if he were" (New York *Amsterdam News*, Oct. 16, 1948). Again relating to public office, an FBI agent reported that the "Communist Party has given serious consideration to the possibility of running Paul Robeson for Congress against Adam Clayton Powell Jr." (FBI New York 100-25857-368). In 1949 the *Amsterdam News* (Sept. 17, 1949) printed a rumor that the American Labor Party might run Robeson as its candidate for the U.S. Senate, and the Baltimore *Afro-American* reported that he was eying a run for Adam Clayton Powell, Jr.'s seat in Congress (Nov. 22, 1949).

Essie served on the platform committee of the Progressive Party's national convention, and campaigned widely for the ticket in Connecticut, Massachusetts, and New York, though feeling ill much of the time. The FBI kept tabs on her activities. Quoting the Stamford *Advocate* for July 30, 1949, the FBI cited her as having said that Truman's order concerning the armed forces "does not abolish Jim Crow—all it does is set up another committee." It further quoted her as saying, "I am not a Communist. . . . It's really not important anyway. If we lynched all the Communists in this country or sent them to Moscow, that would not solve the major problem of inflation or the housing shortage. The only way to solve them is to build for peace and not for war" (FBI Main 100-12304-182, Dec. 28, 1949). The day after the election, Essie went to Washington, D.C., for a full checkup. Dean Joseph Johnson of the Howard University Medical School—a strong supporter of the Progressive Party who had worked with Essie on the platform committee—arranged for her to be seen by Dr. Kelly Brown, who kept her in the hospital for three weeks, then diagnosed her as "suffering from prolonged chronic exhaustion." He related her spastic colitis to amoebic dysentery contracted in Africa, but found her free of amoebic infection. He warned that a stellate tear of the cervix made when Paul, Jr., was born was often a precancerous condition and advised her to have it attended to. Paul, Jr., in his senior year at Cornell, came down to Washington to bring her home from the hospital (ER Diary, Sept. 18, Oct. 31, Nov. 2, 28, 1949, RA).

22. Yarnell, *Democrats and Progressives,* ch. 3 (Clifford), 6 (ADA). Red-baiting the Progressive Party has continued well into the present, and among "objective" scholars as well as more consciously committed ideologues. As one example, Irving Howe and Lewis Coser, in their 1957 study, *The American Communist Party: A Critical History* (Da Capo Press, 1974), pp. 475, 478, refer to the Communists' being "in full organizational command" of the Progressive Party's founding convention and, in the arch, dismissive tone characteristic of their entire discussion of the Progressives, say of its final disintegration, "and still another Stalinist adventure had come to an end." In the same vein, Michael Straight, who was centrally involved in the Progressive campaign but whose politics subsequently took a different course, has written in his memoirs, without qualification, that the Progressive Party "was created by the Communist Party" and that, when Wallace asked Straight in 1947 if Robeson was a Communist, Straight had replied, "I'm afraid so" (Michael Straight, *After Long Silence* [W. W. Norton, 1983], pp. 220, 222). When I interviewed Straight (April 3, 1985), I asked him what evidence he had

for calling Robeson a Communist. He offered none.

23. Starobin, *Crisis,* ch. 7; David A. Shannon, *The Decline of American Communism* (Harcourt Brace, 1958), p. 175.

24. Yarnell, *Democrats and Progressives,* ch. 5, and the books previously cited by Gaddis, Gardner, Patterson and Freedland. As a corrective to the view of Truman's deliberately inciting an anti-Soviet policy, see Alonzo Hamby, *Beyond the New Deal* (Columbia University Press, 1973).

25. MacDougall, *Gideon's Army,* pp. 652–83.

26. Robeson's account of his trips south on behalf of the Progressive Party, including the episodes described in the next two paragraphs, is on a tape in RA. The typed mss. of several of his speeches during the campaign are also in RA, along with many newspaper accounts of his appearances. The West Virginia Library Commission removed Shirley Graham Du Bois's *Paul Robeson, Citizen of the World* (aimed at young adults) from its list of books recommended for children, leading her to protest the action to the book's publisher, Julian Messner (Shirley Graham Du Bois to Kathryn Messner, n.d., U.Mass.: Du Bois). Annette Rubinstein passed on to me (interview, Dec. 5, 1983) the anecdote about Robeson's travels in the South, as told to her by George Murphy. Theodora Peck, who headed the Progressive Party's speakers' bureau, told me (interview, April 8, 1982) that she had had few reports of hostility toward Robeson during his speaking engagements. According to MacDougall (*Gideon's Army,* pp. 671, 676–77), Robeson, "a deeply sentimental person" with an "emotional nature," was so "elated over his Memphis triumph" that "he hired a cab and drove, first into Mississippi and then into Arkansas, in order to set foot in two states where he knew his public appearances would be unwelcome."

27. Detroit *Free Press,* April 10, 1948 ("known Communist"); FBI Main 100-12304, three reports dated March 18, April 10, 13, 1948, but only one file number (108 for March 18) is legible. Interview with Theodora Peck, April 8, 1982 (St. Louis); phone interview with Mrs.

Harry White (her husband headed the Wallace campaign in Indiana), May 21, 1983 (Indianapolis). Robeson did speak just off the Ohio State campus to a gathering of some one thousand students and that evening addressed twenty-five hundred people in Columbus (FBI New York 100-25857-436).

28. Hoover to SAC, Honolulu, March 18, 1948, FBI Main 100-12304-103; SAC, Honolulu, to Hoover, June 2, 1948, FBI Main 100-12304-? (illegible); interview with Earl Robinson, Aug. 17, 1986. According to another FBI report (FBI Main 100-12304-126), on arriving in Honolulu, Robeson "was greeted by a number of prominent local Communists" and at a press conference prior to his departure on March 21, 1948, remarked that "he was a real Socialist, a 'strong Wallace man,' but one who goes beyond Wallace's thinking on progressive capitalism.'" One of fifteen concerts Robeson gave was at a leper colony: he sang tirelessly to the audience, later telling Jean Seroity, a Progressive Party stalwart whom he saw soon after returning from the tour, "That was the most inspiring audience I ever had" (interview with Jean Seroity [PR, Jr., participating], May 3, 1982). On labor unrest in the islands during the years immediately preceding Robeson's tour, see Charles H. Wright, *Robeson: Labor's Forgotten Champion* (Balamp Publishing, 1975), pp. 49–55. According to Wright, the widows of the murdered labor leaders Jesus Mendenez and Manuel Joven each received checks for $1,250 from the territorial ILWU as a result of proceeds from Robeson's tour.

29. Excerpts from Charles P. Howard's diary are printed in MacDougall, *Gideon's Army*, pp. 672–76.

30. Ibid., pp. 410–12.

31. The full transcript of Robeson's testimony before the Senate Judiciary Committee is in RA. The remaining quotations in this section are from the transcript, unless otherwise cited.

32. The Pittsburgh *Courier* reported that, after Robeson gave his testimony, there was some talk on the Senate Judiciary Committee of citing him for contempt—an action not taken, primarily out of concern about alienating the black

vote in the upcoming presidential election. *Afro-American*, June 10, 1948; Springfield (Massachusetts) *Union*, June 1, 1948; FBI New York 100-25857-493 (pickets at White House); Pittsburgh, *Courier*, June 12, 1948 ("impressive"); *Time*, June 14, 1948.

33. Granger as quoted in MacDougall, *Gideon's Army*, p. 655.

34. Interview with Doxey Wilkerson (PR, Jr., participating), Dec. 3, 1983.

35. I've pieced together this account of the struggle within the CAA from a large collection of documents in RA and elsewhere—too many to cite in full. As the account proceeds, I will specifically cite only the most important documents.

36. Du Bois to Yergan (same letter went to PR), March 5, 1948; two letters from Hunton to Council members, both dated March 7, 1948; Yergan to Council members, March 13, 1948—all in RA; Hunton to E. Franklin Frazier, March 19, 1948, MSRC: Frazier.

37. The minutes of the March 25 meeting are in RA; *The New York Times*, April 6, 1948; New York *Herald Tribune*, April 6, 7, 1948; Dean Albertson interview with William Jay Schieffelin, 1949, for Oral History Project: CU ("unfair"). Dorothy Hunton, wife of Alphaeus Hunton, has written disparagingly of Yergan's "non-collective, one man rule" at the Council (Dorothy Hunton, *Alphaeus Hunton: The Unsung Valiant*, privately printed, 1986). In 1951 Hunton was jailed for six months for contempt of court for refusing to turn over the records of the Civil Rights Bail Fund. John Hammond, who was a member of the CAA in 1948, has told me that he, Judge Hubert Delany, and Thomas Russell Jones (then on the legal staff of the Civil Rights Congress, later to be a judge in Brooklyn) constituted a committee to look into the charges of financial misappropriation against Yergan. Hammond and Delany concluded that Yergan "was sloppy but he was not guilty of any malfeasance," but to their surprise Tom Jones, "on orders from the Party," filed a minority report accusing Yergan of malfeasance (interview with Hammond, Aug. 8, 1985).

38. Robeson's statement to the press is in RA.

39. The telegram of protest from PR to Yergan, dated April 15, 1948, is in RA; ER's letter to her fellow Council members, dated April 8, with a subsequent version—little changed—dated April 17, is also in RA. Robeson sought and got a private meeting with E. Franklin Frazier to relay "certain important bits of information." Frazier voted with Robeson and remained on the Council (PR to Frazier, April 3, 1948; Frazier to PR, April 6, 1948, MSRC: Frazier). Robeson, on behalf of the executive board, sent out a letter to the Council members, dated April 15, 1948, in which he asked that the meeting Yergan had called for April 21 be postponed for a few days, since he had an engagement in Philadelphia within two hours of the scheduled meeting time and since he had previously asked Yergan to consult him before fixing on a date. Yergan refused to postpone (PR to council members, April 15, 1948, RA).

40. Press release dated April 21, 1948; letter from PR to all Council members, April 26, 1948, RA.

41. Minutes of the Sept. 17, 1948, meeting and PR's press release of Sept. 28, 1948, are in RA, as well as a letter sent to "friends" of the Council on Oct. 7, 1948, declaring, "The long disruption of the Council's work is at an end." Essie was among the litigants; she brought suit against Yergan for the return of various African art objects and mss. that she had lent the Council for exhibition (Thomas Russell Jones to ER, April 27, 1948; ER to Yergan, April 28, 1948, RA).

42. An FBI report advised that Robeson had had a series of conferences with Mrs. Bethune. He supposedly "requested that Mrs. Bethune divorce herself from the Yergan faction," promising that if she did he would sing a series of benefits for Bethune-Cookman College—and if she refused he "would fight her as he is fighting Yergan." Internal evidence suggests (but does not prove) that the FBI informant was Yergan himself (FBI New York 100-25857-467A, June 11, 1948). Mrs. Bethune also resigned from the Civil Rights Congress; in response to her resignation, Patterson wrote her in reproach, dismayed at how many were being "intimidated" by fear of the Attor-

ney General's reprisals, and added, provocatively, that in earlier periods of our history some women, "like Harriet Tubman and Sojourner Truth," had preferred to confront their enemies and had "spat upon them" (Bethune to Patterson, Sept. 14, 1948; Patterson to Bethune, Sept. 15, 1948, NYPL/Schm: CRC). Robeson's brother Rev. Ben Robeson was among the new members on the reconstituted Council (minutes of the Council's Feb. 9, 1949, meeting, RA). Du Bois was elected vice-chairman and moved his office to the council at 23 West 26th St. Additional information on the CAA can be found in Lynch, *Black American Radicals*. It is likely that at least some of the enigmas of Max Yergan's life and the role he played on the CAA will be more fully resolved by the materials in MSRC: Yergan; these papers are currently closed to scholars.

43. *U.S. News & World Report*, May 1, 1953 (Yergan article); PR column in *Freedom*, May 1953 (response to Yergan; also Dr. Z. K. Matthews's response in *Freedom*, June 1953, and CAA press release, May 12, 1953). For a harsh evaluation of Yergan's entire career ("All his life he merely sought gold for himself"), see Ben Davis, Jr., *Communist Councilman from Harlem* (International, 1969), pp. 199–203. For Yergan's career in the sixties, see the summary in Carl T. Rowan, *The Evening Star*, Feb. 23, 1966. Joe Louis provided some unexpected outside support for Robeson. Appearing with him at a "Tribute to Negro Veterans" held at Uline Arena, in Washington, D.C., on June 26, Joe Louis issued a statement praising PR as "my friend and a great fighter for the Negro people. . . . There are some people who don't like the way Paul Robeson fights for my people. Well, I say to that that Paul is fighting for what all of us want, and that's freedom to be a man. . . . We're with you, Paul, in the fight to the end" (*Daily Worker*, June 29, 1948). The June 26 Uline program, containing a strong printed statement condemning both Truman and Congress, is in RA.

44. The letter and statement, dated July 28, 1948, are in U.Mass.: Du Bois; the press release, dated Aug. 23, 1948, listing the signatories, is in RA.

45. For a discussion of the widespread protest against Du Bois's firing in the black community, see Horne, *Black and Red,* pp. 105–111.

46. The text of Robeson's speech and the typescript of the Oct. 29 broadcast are in RA.

CHAPTER 17   THE PARIS SPEECH AND AFTER *(1949)*

1. The characterization of the *National Guardian* as "Stalinist" was made in a 1949 report of the California Committee on Un-American Activities (FBI Main 100-12304-408). The *Guardian* first appeared on the stands in Oct. 1948, edited by James Aronson and Cedric Belfrage. Their eloquent book, *Something to Guard* (Columbia University Press, 1978), recounts the central role their newspaper played in political life during the next two decades. FBI Main 100-12304-112; Jamaica *Times,* Nov. 13, 1948; *Sunday Gleaner,* Nov. 21, 1948; *National Guardian,* Nov. 15 (reaction), Dec. 20 ("fresh air"), 1948; Dec. 6, 1948; ANP press release, CHS: Barnett (Kingston); Adele Glasgow to Marilyn Alexander, Aug. 25, 1953 (Little Carib); Adele Glasgow to PR, Aug. 26, 1953 ("hero worship"), NYPL/Schm: PR; George B. Murphy, Jr., to Carl Murphy, n.d., MSRC: Murphy, for a crowd estimate of seventy-two thousand. Many years later, on the occasion of Robeson's seventy-fifth birthday, Prime Minister Michael Manley of Jamaica issued a statement recalling how his 1948 visit "filled our hearts with pride" (statement in RA).

2. *Liberator* (organ of Civil Rights Congress), March 1949 (Trenton Six); *Life,* Dec. 6, 20, 1948; FBI Main 100-12304-? (illegible); the New York office responded with a fifteen-page report (FBI Main 100-12304-126). A War Department memo to the FBI (FBI New York 100-25857-506, Nov. 12, 1948) refers to Robeson, without qualification, as the "well known Communist leader." Bob Rockmore, far more conservative politically than Robeson, took the occasion of Levi Jackson's election to write Larry Brown that if so conservative a school as Yale could manage to elect a black football captain, he was willing to be hopeful about the "American species of democratic process" (Rockmore note on a letter from Clara Rockmore to LB, Nov. 23, 1948, NYPL/Schm: Brown).

3. *National Guardian,* Jan. 24, 1948. At another meeting on behalf of the Trenton Six, held in Trenton itself, Robeson said, "I know what's been done to these boys could have been done to my own boy" (*National Guardian,* Feb. 7, 1949).

4. FBI Main 100-12304-126. George W. Crockett, Ben Davis, Jr.'s lawyer, has said, "Paul Robeson gave definition to the meaning of friendship. . . . I met frequently with Ben Davis to prepare our defense, and in several of those meetings Paul was there" (Crockett speech as printed in *World Magazine,* 1973).

5. Telegram, dated Jan. 29, 1949, U.Mass.: Du Bois; Michael R. Belknap, *Cold War Political Justice: The Smith Act, the Communist Party, and American Civil Liberties* (Greenwood Press, 1977), ch. 3. Belknap (p. 78) points out that the jury finally chosen in March contained seven women and three blacks. Robeson joined in a further protest of the jury selection process at a rally at St. Nicholas Arena on Feb. 3, 1949 (FBI New York 100-25857-534).

6. Robeson described these events in a talk at the People's Songs Conference in New York City on Aug. 13, 1949 (RA).

7. LB to ER, March 4, 24, 1949, RA. The importance of Desmond Buckle's role in helping to manage PR's affairs on tour is confirmed in Stockwell (of Harold Fielding agency) to LB, May 31, 1949, NYPL/Schm: Brown, and in Buckle to Patterson, March 21, 1949, NYPL/Schm: CRC. Robeson of course had his detractors, political objections merging into artistic ones. One of Larry Brown's friends wrote of the Albert Hall concert, "I was able to take in my stride Paul's haughty take-it-and-like-it attitude with his Soviet music and the other esoteric pieces that he sings to please himself. I still think he has more charm in his little finger than

most other men I've ever known, but I greatly miss the old, gentle, 'genial giant' aura that surrounded Paul in the old days" (Jannett Hamlyn to LB, May 28, 1949, NYPL/Schm: Brown). Another correspondent, a Dr. Millard (apparently a West Indian physician), attacked Robeson more angrily, pronouncing a meeting called to protest the Trenton Six case in which Paul had participated in England a "failure" because he had not explained the case to the audience, instead "making himself a buffoon. He sang 'Water Boy' like a 3rd rate comedian and I am just a bit tired of Negroes who seek sympathy, pity and tolerance from whites by referring to the fact that their fathers or grandfathers were slaves. . . . I am no longer interested in him. Moreover he prefers the company of whites and his courtesies are reserved only for whites" (Millard to LB, July 3, 1949, NYPL/Schm: Brown).

8. PR to Helen Rosen, n.d. (March-April 1949), courtesy of Rosen.

9. Multiple interviews with Helen Rosen; *The Autobiography of Samuel Rosen* (Knopf, 1973). Henry Wallace was among those who commented on Helen's being the driving political force (Dean Albertson interview with Wallace, 1950–51, Oral History, Columbia University).

10. The quotes are from three of PR's 1949 letters from Europe to Freda Diamond and are courtesy of Diamond.

11. Ben Davis, Jr., to Blackman, Oct. 6, 1949, courtesy of Blackman via PR, Jr. Blackman told PR, Jr., that Paul, Sr., had helped him out financially (interview, Sept. 8g, 1982, transcript PR, Jr.).

12. *Daily Worker*, March 31, 1949; *Leader Magazine*, March 12, 1949; *Inkululeko* (English-language weekly, London), April 9, 1949; Valentine Elliott in the June-August 1949 issue of *Makerere*, published at Makerere College in British East Africa; Manchester *Guardian*, April 21, 1949. For more on U.S. relations with South Africa, see Thomas J. Noer, *The Cold War & Black Liberation: The United States and White Rule in Africa, 1948–1968* (University of Missouri Press, 1985), especially ch. 2 for the contrast between Roosevelt and Truman. Desmond Buckle, in an article in *New Africa*, vol. 8,

no. 4 (April 1949), reported on another of PR's political appearances: a speech at Friends' House in which he blasted Premier Malan of South Africa, predicted this would be his last tour for some time ("This is no time to go about the world singing pretty songs. I want to use my voice like tonight with you"), sang the "Song of the Warsaw Ghetto," and recited Langston Hughes's "Freedom Train." Robeson also found time—as George Padmore reported favorably in his column in the Chicago *Defender* (May 7, 1949)—"to give encouragement to the Colored Theatre Group founded by the West Indian baritone, Edric Connor, of Trinidad" and to pay "generous tribute to . . . [the] promising West Indian musicians and actors" he had found everywhere in his recent tour of the Caribbean. (For more on Robeson and Edric Connor, see note 16, p. 725; note 48, p. 750.) Robeson was also invited to the wedding of Nehru's niece (and that of Nan Pandit's daughter), Chandralekha Pandit, to Ashok Mehta on April 14 (the invitation is in RA).

13. CAA News Release, April 13, 1953 ("brothers and sisters"), LC; Tambo to PR, Nov. 1954, PR to African National Congress, Dec. 4, 1954, NYPL/Schm: PR. Additional PR activities in behalf of South Africa are in *Daily Worker*, April 7, 1952; *Spotlight on Africa* (CAA newsletter), April 14, 1952; PR telegram to *Advance* (Cape Town newspaper), April 15, 1943, NYPL/Schm.

14. New York *Herald Tribune*, April 24, 1949; *New Africa*, vol. 8, no. 5, (May 1949); *The New York Times*, April 26, 1949.

15. The quotes in the text are taken from Alphaeus Hunton's translation from the French (transcript in RA). Because there is controversy on this point, Ivor Montagu (a British delegate to the Congress) sent me the printed transcript in French (source uncited), in which the relevant phrases are: *"Et nous ne voulons pas de ces imbécillités hystériques parlant de nous faire partir en guerre contre qui que ce soît. Nous avons, nous, la ferme volonté de combattre pour la paix. (Applaudissements) Nous ne voulons pas partir en guerre pour n'importe qui et contre n'importe qui. (Acclamations) Nous ne voulons pas partir en guerre contre L'Union*

Soviétique. (Nouvelles acclamations)" The only full and unimpeachable record of what Robeson said in Paris is on a film of the event that is known to exist but has so far resisted all efforts at recovery; unless it can be found, Robeson's actual words cannot be verified.

16. The full transcript of the AP dispatch is in RA. In his testimony on the Mundt-Nixon Bill on May 31, 1948, Robeson had openly expressed sentiments close to those falsely ascribed to him in Paris a year later—but with the important difference that he claimed to be speaking only for himself: "Question: Would you fight for America if we were at war with Russia? Answer: That would depend on the conditions of war with Russia, how the war came up and who is in power at the time, etc. . . . That's just too hypothetical. . . . I would like to say that I would be on the American side to have peace. I would struggle for peace at all points. . . . If the American government would be a Fascist government, then I would not support it. . . . I am an anti-Fascist, and I would fight Fascism whether it happens to be the German, the French or American species. . . . I would do it under the banner of being an American and protecting the Democratic rights of the American people."

17. In an interview with me (Sept. 7, 1982 [PR, Jr., participating]), Ivor Montagu, who heard Robeson's speech, said he recalled nothing untoward or unexpected in it—nothing like the inflammatory words the AP dispatch ascribed to him. Randolph is quoted in Patrick S. Washburn, *A Question of Sedition: The Federal Government's Investigation of the Black Press During World War II* (Oxford University Press, 1986).

18. INS memos, April 25–May 6, 1949, FBI 56275-730.

19. Marilyn Smith (State Department) to Walter White, April 21, 1949, LC: NAACP, enclosing a copy of the story she wrote for release to the news media following their phone conversation of that morning, along with a copy of the statement Mary McLeod Bethune had given to her over the phone ("Mr. Robeson's remarks . . . chilled my blood. I just cannot understand it"). White's com-

ments were widely dispersed by the State Department—Voice of America, European Regional File, Middle East File, Wireless Bulletin, Mission Services, Far East File—and in various forms appeared in the press (e.g., New York *Herald Tribune,* May 1, 1949). For confirmation that the State Department had initiated White's statement, see "Secretary to Mr. White" (not otherwise identified) to Mark Stanley Matthews, May 20, 1949, LC: NAACP: "Immediately upon receiving word of Mr. Robeson's statement, the State Department called on Mr. White for a statement." Earl Brown, "Once Over Lightly," New York *Amsterdam News,* April 29, 30, 1949.

20. Interviews with Bayard Rustin, March 25, April 20, 1983.

21. Ibid.

22. Columbia, South Carolina, *Record,* April 26, 1949; *The New York Times,* April 24, 25, 26, Nov. 7 (Randolph), 1949; New York *Amsterdam News,* April 29, 30, 1949; Detroit *Tribune,* April 30, 1949; Pittsburgh *Courier,* April 30, 1949; Chicago *Defender,* April 30, 1949 (editorial headlined "Nuts to Mr. Robeson," attacking him for having gotten "so far away from the race" that he had lost his "moorings"); New York *Age,* April 30, May 7, 1949; *Christian Science Monitor,* May 3, 1949 (summary); Du Bois, *Negro Digest,* March 1950 (Morgan). Bethune also devoted a full column (Chicago *Defender,* April 30, 1949) to attacking Robeson's "presumption" and to declaring that she "thoroughly disagreed with such an expression of disloyalty. . . ." Predictably, the conservative black columnist George S. Schuyler roasted Robeson for "brushing aside . . . the well-known brutalities, injustices and calculated fiendishness of Red concentration camps which have been filled largely with minority groups of the Soviet Union and the satellite countries" (Pittsburgh *Courier,* May 7, 1949). Less predictably, Fritz Pollard, Robeson's old football buddy, offered a more-in-sorrow comment: "Paul's at it again, playing Emperor Jones. . . . Sometimes he thinks he's the Negro island liberator, Henri Christophe. Despite his spectacular popoffs, he's no Commie, in his heart" (New York *Age,* April 30,

1949). There are in LC: NAACP a half-dozen letters congratulating Walter White on his remarks, in language more intemperate than any White himself had used (e.g., Robeson "has not ever bothered to take the pulse of a race he presumes to represent": Capt. Leonard L. Bruce, April 22, 1949).

23. Interviews with Bayard Rustin, March 25, April 20, 1983. William Pickens III corroborates Rustin's view that (in Pickens's words) "Down deep the black leadership had a warm spot for Paul Robeson"—they had no intention of falling behind him as "the leader," but were nonetheless pleased that "somebody was raising the issues of fundamental racism in American life" (interview with Pickens, Oct. 3, 1983).

24. Mark Solomon, "Black Critics of the Cold War"; Modjeska (Mrs. Andrew W.) Simkins (executive committeewoman of the Republican Party of South Carolina and prominent in the S.C. NAACP; she was to take part in the Welcome Home rally for PR on June 19, 1949, at Rockland Palace) to the Columbia *Record*, May 2, 1949; Durham, N.C., *Times*, April 30, 1949; Pittsburgh *Courier*, June 25, 1949.

25. Max Yergan's letter is in the New York *Herald Tribune*, April 23, 1949.

26. Abner Berry, New York *Age*, May 21, 1949. "As We See It," *Daily Worker*, May 2, 1949; Benjamin J. Davis, Jr., *Daily Worker*, May 8, 1949; Du Bois's letter is in the Norfolk *Journal and Guide*, May 28, 1949, and the New York *Amsterdam News*, May 21, 1949.

27. The typescript of ER's speech is in RA.

28. Multiple conversations with PR, Jr. (PR's anger); Patterson to PR, May 17, 1949, NYPL/Schm: CRC; Charles P. Howard to ER, May 10, 1949, RA; Vito Marcantonio to ER, April 29, 1949, NYPL: Marcantonio; *Congressional Record*, April 28, 1949.

29. *The Crisis*, May 1949, p. 137. The black California *Eagle* editorially protested the *Crisis* article (June 2, 1949). In his autobiography, *Standing Fast*, Wilkins backhandedly admits to having written the editorial (pp. 205–6). Yet, when Robeson died, in 1976, Wilkins wrote,

"Anything to spread black culture and manhood was his lifelong doctrine. . . . Any Negro who protested the treatment of the black citizens was called a communist or worse." Unless Wilkins was merely paying perfunctory homage to the recently dead, this statement amounts to a complete retraction of his 1949 *Crisis* editorial.

30. Ben Davis, Jr., to ER, May 25, 1949, RA; Davis to White, May 28, 1949, LC: NAACP. In an article Davis wrote before the *Crisis* editorial appeared, he had already set Walter White apart from the "political street-walker Max Yergan," the "foxy old reformist Channing Tobias," and "Rep. Adam Powell with his double-talk," as "more nearly reflect[ing] the feelings of the Negro people" (*Daily Worker*, May 8, 1949).

31. Howard to Wilkins, May 26, 1949, CHS: Barnett. Howard not only sent Barnett (the head of the Associated Negro Press) a copy but also sent one to Alphaeus Hunton and another to Dr. Louis Wright (Howard to Wright, May 27, 1949, LC: NAACP); and he sent a form letter to key members of the Progressive Party soliciting letters of protest to Wilkins (Howard to Barnett, May 27, 1949, CHS: Barnett; Howard to "Dear Friend," May 27, 1949; Howard to Hunton, May 26, 1949; Ben Davis, Jr., to Hunton, May 28, 1949, RA). C. B. ("Beanie") Baldwin, executive secretary of the Progressive Party, was among those who wrote in: "I regard [Robeson] as one of the world's great human beings"; he "happens to believe that the struggle for democratic rights for the Negro people cannot be separated from the struggle for peace" (Baldwin to Wilkins, June 2, 1949, RA). Larkin Marshall, cochairman of the Progressive Party in Georgia, was another who responded (Marshall to Hunton, May 28, 1949, enclosing a copy of a pro-Robeson editorial Marshall wrote for the Macon *World*, RA).

32. Memo from White to Wilkins, June 3, 1949; memo from Wilkins to White, June 6, 1949, LC: NAACP.

33. Wilkins, *Standing Fast*, pp. 205–6; AP dispatch, July 13, 1949 (NAACP convention), RA. (Mary Church Terrell to Hunton, June 6, 1949, RA).

34. *The New York Times*, April 25, 1949; *Christian Science Monitor*, May 2, 1949 (Stockholm); PR to Diamond, May 1, 1949, RA. FBI Main 100-12304-126 reports that during the Stockholm concert the trouble started when Robeson "sang a Russian anthem. The first verse, sung in Russian, was greeted quietly; however, when he sang the second verse in English, which most of the audience understood, a demonstration started, which for a time drowned out the singer. Anti-Communists answered with loud cheers and frantic applause. Following the anthem, Robeson stepped to the microphone and told the audience he could no longer draw the line between his art and his political convictions. He said he wanted universal peace, but above all peace with the Soviet Union." FBI NY 100-25857-646A Referral Document #2 ("beyond control") also reports PR as saying, "I can assure you they [blacks] will never fight against either the Soviet Union or the Peoples Democracies." An indication of how PR addressed criticism of his pro-Soviet stance before a predominantly *black* audience is in a speech he gave at the Golden Gate Ballroom in Harlem on Aug. 30, 1949: "What did Soviet Russia ever do for me? (Laughter) I said, Just a minute now. One thing they did for you—in destroying fascism; you remember, you better remember this Hitler again. He destroyed six million Jewish people—burned six million Jewish people up. He was just hoping to get hold of ten or fifteen million Negroes to burn up. Well, the reason he couldn't get hold of them happened to be because ten to twenty million Russians took him" (tape recording of speech, RA).

35. *National Guardian*, May 2, 1949; Chicago *Defender*, May 21, 1949; Norfolk *Journal and Guide*, May 2, 1949; press release from the CAA, May 11, 1949, RA (second denial). The full text of the Copenhagen interview with Robeson is in RA.

36. *The Times* (London), April 23, 1949 (Copenhagen); Ulf Christensen, "Paul Robeson's Visit to Oslo," June 6, 1949, RA. Apparently somewhat apprehensive, Rockmore wrote Larry Brown, "Thanks for your two notes from Oslo

immediately before and after the concert. I breathed a sigh of relief with you" (Rockmore to Brown, May 6, 1949, NYPL/Schm: Brown).

37. John Payne to Larry Brown, May 6, 1949, NYPL/Schm: Brown; PR, Jr., interview with Bruno Raikin, Sept. 8, 1982, transcript courtesy of PR, Jr.

38. *National Guardian*, June 13, 1949 (Prague reception); Pittsburgh *Courier*, June 4, 1949; Baltimore *Afro-American*, June 7, 1949; Josef Škvorecký, "Red Music," in *The Bass Saxophone* (Knopf, 1977), p. 19. Škvorecký was speaking generally; he didn't mean, he later explained, that PR was in Prague at the exact time of Horáková's execution (Škvorecký to Barbara Bristol, Sept. 9, 1987, courtesy of Bristol). In fact, Horáková was executed on June 27, 1950. *The New York Times* (Dec. 7, 1949) and *Time* (Dec. 19, 1949) reported that in Prague, Harry James's music was much preferred to Robeson's.

39. PR, Jr., interviews with Raikin (Sept. 8, 1982) and Blackman (Sept. 9, 1982), transcripts courtesy of PR, Jr.; Seton, *Robeson*, pp. 201–02.

40. Richard Yaffe, in *The Jewish Week–American Examiner*, Feb. 1–7, 1976, recalls Robeson singing "Zog Nit Kaynmal," the song of the Warsaw ghetto fighters, during his 1949 Warsaw concert, but Yaffe's article contains a number of inaccuracies and it is probable, nearly thirty years after the event, that he confused Robeson's Warsaw performance with the concert that followed in Moscow. PR, Jr., interview with Peter Blackman, Sept. 9, 1982, transcript courtesy of PR, Jr. In an article for the Polish newspaper *Trybuna Ludu*, June 2, 1949, Robeson expressed his belief that "the strength of the progressive camp in America is greater than during the elections in 1948" and his conviction that "the reign of capitalism and imperialism will end." The optimism may have been for the consumption of a particular audience, may have marked yet another resurgence of hopefulness—or may have been manufactured or misquoted by whoever ghost-wrote the article.

41. FBI NY 100-25857-646A Referral Document #2; PR, Jr., interviews with Blackman, Sept. 9, 1982, and Raikin,

Sept. 8, 1982 (transcripts courtesy of PR, Jr.); *The New York Times*, June 8 (Scandalize), 15, 1949. The FBI had begun to entertain the possibility that Robeson had taken out Soviet citizenship (FBI New York 100-23857-557, report from the Immigration and Naturalization Service).

42. *Daily Worker*, July 4, 8, 1943; *Morning Freiheit*, Feb. 19, 1948 (memorial); PR, Jr., "How My Father Last Met Itzik Feffer, 1949," *Jewish Currents*, Nov. 1981; Lloyd Brown, "Setting the Record Straight," *Daily World*, Dec. 24, 1981; "Paul Robeson Jr. Refutes Lloyd Brown," *Jewish Currents*, Feb. 1982; Lloyd L. Brown to Morris U. Schappes (editor, *Jewish Currents*), Dec. 14, 1981; PR, Jr., to Schappes, Dec. 30, 1981, RA; Blackman interview with PR, Jr., Sept. 9, 1982, transcript courtesy of PR, Jr. In their 1943 visit to the States, Mikhoels and Feffer had been representing the Jewish Anti-Fascist Committee. For additional background on the two men, as well as on the fate of other Jewish writers and cultural functionaries, see Benjamin Pinkus, *The Soviet Government and the Jews, 1948–1967* (Cambridge University Press, 1984).

There are several variant versions of the meeting between Robeson and Feffer. Mikhoels's daughter published an account very close to PR, Jr.'s version, except that she places the meeting in 1951, which is clearly inaccurate, since Robeson's passport had by then been lifted (Natalya Mikhoels-Vovsi, *Vremya i mwi*, no. 3 [Tel-Aviv, 1976], p. 190). Esther Markish, in her book *The Long Journey* (Ballantine paperback, 1978), pp. 171–72, asserts that Feffer dutifully performed the role demanded of him by the Soviet secret police and said nothing to Robeson about the purges. Yet a third version is in Dmitri Shostakovich, *Testimony* (Harper & Row, 1979), pp. 188–89), who places the meeting in a restaurant, with Feffer accompanied by police agents. Shostakovich angrily denounces Robeson for maintaining silence after returning to New York: "Why don't these famous humanists give a damn about us, our lives, honour, and dignity?"

43. Multiple conversations with PR, Jr. Partial documentation—confirming

the reception of the Warsaw Ghetto song—is in the Polish newspaper *Kurjer Codzienny*, June 10, 1949: "He was given an unusually cordial reception. . . . The song about the Warsaw Ghetto was enthusiastically received by the audience." *The New York Times* (June 15, 1949) and *New Times* (June 22, 1949) alike refer to the outpouring of acclaim for Robeson during his Moscow visit, without specific reference to the reception of the Warsaw Ghetto song. For another example of Robeson's publicly protesting Soviet anti-Semitism, see note 44, p. 736.

44. "Paul Robeson's Soviet Journey," an interview by Amy Schechter, *Soviet Russia Today*, Aug. 1949. At exactly this same time, the conservative black columnist Willard Townsend was arguing in the Chicago *Defender* (June 16, 1949) that "the open revival of anti-semitism in new forms is proceeding today at a rapid pace behind the formidable Iron Curtain."

45. The serious consideration in U.S. government circles of a pre-emptive strike against the U.S.S.R. is documented in Gregg Herken, *The Winning Weapon: The Atomic Bomb in the Cold War, 1945–1950* (Knopf, 1980). Robeson went from Moscow to Stalingrad, where he sang at a tractor factory and where a survivor of the battle of "Mamaev's Hill" took off the ring that only survivors of that battle were entitled to wear and put it on Robeson's finger. The ring was inscribed "To Paul Robeson, the American Stalingrader." Robeson responded by referring to Stalingrad as "the very spot where our civilization was saved" (PR's handwritten notes, RA).

46. *The New York Times*, June 17, 1949; FBI New York 100-25857-575, 616 (report from U.S. Customs Service); news release from the Council on African Affairs, June 16, 1949, RA; ER to Larry Brown, June 9, 14, 1949, NYPL/Schm: Brown.

47. Hunton to ER, n.d. (June 1949), RA; New York *Amsterdam News*, June 18, 1949; *The New York Times*, June 17, 1949; *Daily Compass*, June 17, 1949. On leaving the airport, a banner-decked cavalcade of five cars carried Robeson to Harlem; the FBI reported that the motorcade

"received no ovation or recognition from Harlemites" (FBI Main 100-12304-? [illegible]). Testifying in opposition to the North Atlantic Treaty at a hearing of the Senate Foreign Relations Committee on May 13, 1949, Hunton had given a rather fiery accounting of his own, not only strongly condemning the treaty but referring to Great Britain as "a prison-house of colored peoples" (his testimony is in RA).

48. Interviews with Marilyn Robeson, Dec. 18, 1983, Jan. 4, 1984, Jan. 7, 15, 1985; New York *Herald Tribune*, June 20, 1949. Rather than making a scene, which was not his style, Marilyn's father had withdrawn into silent opposition. Neither Paul, Sr., nor Essie, to Marilyn's knowledge, showed any sense of insult or grievance. The accounts in the *Daily Compass* (June 20, 1949) and the New York *Amsterdam News* (June 25, 1949) do not contain any reference to Robeson's supposed remark about the Soviet Union; the *Compass* did report that he "shook his fist at one photographer and moved a pace toward him, but was blocked by the crowd." Essie's comment is in an undated handwritten note (possibly for a future speech), RA; she also wrote, "I felt like strangling them. . . . I was so angry I was calm." Although the black press was generally friendly, the headline in *The Afro-American* (June 25, 1949) referred to "Junior's Socialite Bride."

49. CVV to ER, July 6, 1949; ER to CVV, July 10, 1949, Yale: Van Vechten. Essie's gracious letter included an extended thank-you to Carlo for having helped them get started back in the 1920s. "The fight then," she explained, "was intellectual, artistic, and social. We Negroes were trying to be heard, to get started, to participate. . . . Now, I think this fight today is another phase of that same fight. . . . Now it is political. At least Paul and I think it is political."

Marilyn Robeson, in our interview of Dec. 18, 1983, described Essie as having been "very firm and very determined and very incensed also" during the wedding-party fracas; several newspaper accounts confirm this, with both the *Daily Compass* (June 20, 1949) and the *Amsterdam News* (June 25, 1949) referring to Essie's ef-

forts to ward off the news media. As well, Essie wrote an article, "Loyalty—Lost and Found," in which she described her anger with the press (the article was enclosed for distribution in carbon letters to Hunton, George Murphy, and Charles Howard, June 22, 1949, RA). Soon after, Essie enlisted the help of Murphy and Howard in circulating a packet of her articles, including "Loyalty," to the 108 chapters of her sorority, Delta Sigma Theta: "I think Deltas are reasonably influential in their communities. . . . Sort of slow infiltration, what?" (ER to Murphy and Howard, July 12, 1949, NYPL/Schm: CRC.) Essie's five-page covering letter to her sorority sisters (dated Aug. 4, 1949) is in NYPL/Schm: PR. In it she said point-blank, ". . . for the record, I am NOT A COMMUNIST," but added that what needed questioning at the moment was not the loyalty of blacks to the country, but "THIS COUNTRY'S LOYALTY TO THE NEGRO." Widely reprinted (e.g., *Daily Compass*, July 14, 1949; even *Time* printed excerpts, July 25, 1949), the "Loyalty" article prompted a warm letter of support from William Patterson to Essie, praising her for her "uncompromising" stand. Because of the underlying —but acknowledged—antipathy between them (see p. 187), Patterson sent his letter with some trepidation, lest Essie take "offense"; but he reminded her that he was well aware that they were both "on the same side of . . . the barricades" (Patterson to ER, July 7, 1949, NYPL/Schm: CRC). In her lengthy reply, Essie wrote, "It most definitely occasioned no offense. How on earth could it? . . . I consider praise from the Old Guard is praise indeed." She went on to describe herself in general terms as someone who, when disagreeing, "open[s] up my big mouth and say[s] so—often far too vehemently I admit"; then, in specific terms, she referred to her past disagreements with Pat: ". . . I am unduly biased and sensitive on the matter of Big Paul, because I do think that everybody is very prone to exploit him. Me, I'm against exploitation,—not only of the masses, but also of individuals, especially of friends." Polite though the tone, ER's letter amounts to a considerable indictment of how the CP (the "Old Guard") in her view "used" her husband. "As a peace token" ER sent Pat a copy of *American Argument*, the book she had co-authored with Pearl Buck (ER to Patterson, July 9, 1949, NYPL/Schm: CRC).

50. Pearl Buck to ER, June 26, 1949, RA; Springfield *Union*, June 28, 1949 (Roosevelt); New York *Amsterdam News*, June 25, 1949; the dozens of hate letters are in RA. Ma Goode's frequent letters to Essie during this period (e.g., June 27, 28, 30, July 7, 9, 11, 13, Aug. 7, Sept. 4, 30, Oct. 2, 17, 1949, RA) are full of demands and directives; she may have been partly senile. Late in Oct. 1949 Ma Goode had to be shifted for ten days from Resthaven to the Boston State Hospital for observation. At that point Essie described her as "rambling and wholly inattentive when I was there" (circular letter, n.d., apparently to family members, RA). Essie summed up her mother's recent behavior, over a period of many years: "The moment I go away . . . she has made the most terrific scenes, stretched out in violent temper when she could not have her way instantly, and threatened suicide" (Dorothy Livingston of the Resthaven home to ER, June 24, 1949; ER to Mr. Benjamin, Nov. 1, 1949, RA).

51. The Du Bois and Howard speeches, excerpted in news releases from the CAA, are in RA, along with a full listing of speakers (others included Hunton, Ben Davis, Jr., Vito Marcantonio, and Louis Burnham, former executive secretary of the Southern Negro Youth Congress and currently Southern director of the Progressive Party, who would be centrally involved with Robeson politically in the future). Among those sending welcoming messages were Clifford Odets, the cast of *Detective Story* (Lee Grant, Alex Scourby, Joan Copeland, Lou Gilbert), and Henry Wallace (all are in RA).

52. The transcript of PR's speech is in RA.

53. Interview with Kay Pankey, July 26, 1986. For more on Robeson and the Pankeys, see pp. 426, 518–19. For the wedding party, the married couple drew up the small guest-list, which consisted mostly of their own friends plus such fam-ily standbys as Minnie Sumner, Buddy and Hattie Bolling, Bert and Gig McGhee, Ben Davis, Jr., and Paul, Sr.'s sister, Marian Robeson Forsythe, who came up from Philadelphia with her husband, Dr. James Forsythe.

54. *The New York Times*, June 20, 1949; Boston *Advertiser*, June 26, 1949; *Congressional Record*, June 27, 1949; Pittsburgh *Courier*, June 25, 1949.

55. New York *Herald Tribune*, June 20, July 15, 1949 (Truman); *The Afro-American*, June 25, 1949; New York *Amsterdam News*, June 25 ("richest artist"), June 25 (Granger), 1949; The California *Eagle* defended him (July 7, 1949). In his column in the Chicago *Defender* for July 2, 1949, A. N. Fields quoted Richard Wright (who had left the CP some five years previously) as disapproving of Robeson's political activities and taking "sharp issue" with his statement in Paris. Dozens of letters suggesting Robeson leave the country are in RA (e.g., this telegram from the American Legion Post in Sayre, Oklahoma: "Our attitude toward you is the same as yours toward this country. Why stay?"). In an article in the *National Guardian* (June 27, 1949), reporter Yvonne Gregory decided to sample opinion in "the poorest parts" of Harlem and found that with few exceptions people were "reluctant to talk," fearful of "getting mixed up in any politics"—"I've got enough trouble already"; "I don't know nothing about these Communists." But one woman told her, "My sons wouldn't talk much when they came home from the war. . . . They were jealous and mad when they found we colored people still didn't have our freedom." The day after the Rockland Palace rally, the black conductor Dean Dixon and the graphic artist Raphael Soyer, on behalf of the CAA, hosted a private reception for Paul, Sr., to welcome him home (the invitation is in RA).

56. Madison S. Jones, Jr. (NAACP administrative assistant) to Wood, July 12, 1949; Wood to Jones, July 12, 1949, LC: NAACP.

57. *Hearings Regarding Communist Infiltration of Minority Groups*, July 13–18, 1949 (U.S. Govt. Printing Office, D.C.); *The New York Times*, July 15, 1949; New

York *Herald Tribune,* July 15, 1949; Boston *Post,* July 14, 1949; *New Age,* July 23, 1949; Chicago *Defender,* June 23, 1949; Pittsburgh *Courier,* Sept. 17, 1949 (PR on Stalin). On Manning Johnson, see Victor Navasky, *Naming Names* (Viking, 1980), pp. 14-15, 39, 68, 191. During the thirties, Johnson had been a trade union official of the Restaurant Workers and a district organizer from Buffalo for the CPUSA (Naison, *Depression,* pp. 135, 261, 294). The New York *Amsterdam News* reported (July 30, 1949) that Robeson "is alleged to have expressed his desire to be heard in the Nation's capital" to "refute the charges made against him by Manning Johnson," but the committee "has refused to permit Robeson to appear, because one member said, 'Robeson only wants to use the Committee as a sounding board.'" I haven't found any confirmation of Robeson's alleged attempt to appear before HUAC.

58. *Hearings Regarding Communist Infiltration,* July 13–18, 1949 (U.S. Govt. Printing Office, D.C.). Young insisted that "Negro publishers, almost to a paper, completely repudiated Robeson's statement" and in addition recounted an Alpha Phi Alpha smoker in October 1947 in Norfolk, Virginia, at which Robeson had purportedly said, "If this country ever went to war against Russia and my son took up arms to fight against Russia, he would no longer be my son." Chicago *Defender,* June 23, 1949. The full text of Lester Granger's statement to HUAC (July 14, 1949) is in LC: NAACP. Sandy F. Ray, chairman of the Social Service Commission of the National Baptist Convention and himself a minister, made a strong statement—and without attacking Robeson—about American racism (July 14, 1949, full text in RA).

59. *Hearings Regarding Communist Infiltration of Minority Groups,* July 13–18, 1949 (U.S. Govt. Printing Office, D.C.); PR to Robinson, July 11, 1949, RA, enclosing a copy of his Rockland Palace speech so he could "acquaint yourself with the true statements made by me"; *New Age,* July 23, 1949; Norfolk *Journal and Guide,* July 23, 1949 (VFW).

60. *The New York Times,* July 19, 1949;

Roosevelt, "My Day," Nov. 2, 1949; New York *Amsterdam News,* July 23, 1949.

61. CAA press release, July 13, 1949, RA; Carolina *Times,* July 23, 1949; *The Afro-American,* July 19, 1949. Robeson wrote Carl J. Murphy, president of the Afro-American Company, to thank him— a rare example of his commenting on a newspaper mention of himself, pro or con, and by that much perhaps a gauge of his concern about reaction in the black community; PR to Murphy, July 14, 1949, RA. *The Afro-American* followed up (Aug. 20, 1949) with an article entitled "What's Wrong with Paul Robeson?" by Ralph Matthews, which concluded, "There is nothing really wrong with Paul Robeson. He is quite sane and purposeful." He was not anti-American, but "pro-peace." To him America was not "the small clique of financial despots, the small one per cent who control the wealth"; he was "loyal to that large portion of America which wants to remain at peace with the world." Robeson, *The Afro-American* concluded, spoke "not for the insignificant 15 million [black] Americans struggling for crumbs in a predominantly white America where they will always be a minority, but . . . for the hundreds of millions of black people in Africa and other sections of the world with whom he feels a kinship." J. A. Rogers, Pittsburgh *Courier,* July 30, Oct. 15, 1949; *New Age,* July 23, 1949; New York *Age,* July 23, 1949 (Bill of Rights conference). The statement by the black delegates is in NYPL/Schm: CRC. A tape recording of PR's speech at the June 28, 1949, Civil Rights Congress is in RA. *The Afro-American* (July 30, 1949) reported, though, that Robeson met with a mixed reception, having to cross a picket line of forty white and black veterans to get into the Mosque Theatre; George Stevens, Essex County commander of the Veterans of Foreign Wars, had issued a call for members of all forty-six posts to meet in front of the theater (FBI Main 100-12304-184). Even Earl Brown, the conservative *Amsterdam News* columnist, called "the whole show before the Committee . . . ridiculous and unnecessary" (July 23, 1949).

62. *The Afro-American,* July 30, 1949; New York *Amsterdam News,* July 23, 1949;

text of statement issued to the AP from the CAA office by Robeson, dated July 20, 1949, RA; Jackie Robinson, *I Never Had It Made* (Putnam's Sons, 1972), p. 98. For more detail on Robinson's later political views and activities, see Jules Tygiel, *Baseball's Great Experiment.*

63. The Knoxville incident was reported in the Pittsburgh *Courier,* Aug. 20, 1949.

CHAPTER 18   PEEKSKILL (1949)

1. A tape recording of Robeson's People's Songs Conference speech is in RA.

2. *Daily Worker,* July 24 (Davis), Aug. 6 (Bureau of Engraving), 7 (Clark), 8 (Winston), 1949; New York *Herald Tribune,* Aug. 5 (White House), 1949. A confidential informant of the FBI reported on two street meetings in Winston's behalf (FBI Main 100-12304-184, Jan. 9, 1950). FBI Washington Smith Act Prosecution File 100-3-74-4351,4917 (income tax). Hoover had already sent for Robeson's law-school, selective-service, and passport records (FBI Main 100-12304-135, 136, 137; New York 100-25857-673).

3. The Peekskill *Star* items, plus reports of subsequent developments, are conveniently and chronologically summarized in the privately printed *Eyewitness: Peekskill, U.S.A.,* a documentary report prepared by the Westchester Committee for a Fair Inquiry into the Peekskill Violence.

4. Multiple interviews with Helen Rosen. I'm also grateful to her for contacting Sydney Danis in order to clarify certain details.

5. Multiple interviews with Helen Rosen; New York *Herald Tribune,* Aug. 29, 1949. The burning cross Helen had seen (Paul had, too) was confirmed as real in the subsequent grand-jury report (copy in RA)—though the report ascribed it to "an unfortunate prank by a few teen-age boys" bearing "no relation to the Ku Klux Klan or any other anti-social or anti-religious organization."

6. Interviews with Ruth Jett (who introduced PR at the Hotel Theresa conference), April 2, 1982; Clara Rockmore, April 26, 1983, March 17, 1984, Dec. 13, 1985; New York *Herald Tribune, The New York Times,* Aug. 29, 1949; New York *Amsterdam News,* Sept. 3, 1949 (press conference); press release of Civil Rights Congress, Aug. 28, 1949, RA.

7. Multiple interviews with Helen Rosen; the FBI got a full report of the meeting at the Rosens' (FBI New York 100-25857-747).

8. *Daily Mirror,* Aug. 29, 1949; *Daily Worker,* Aug. 29, 1949; FBI New York 100-25857-743-746.

9. New York *Herald Tribune,* Aug. 29, 31, 1949; *The New York Times,* Aug. 29, 30, 31, 1949; *Eyewitness: Peekskill, U.S.A.*

10. RA contain dozens of tapes of radio broadcasts and eyewitness accounts, as well as a large file of newspaper reports. It is impossible to cite this bulky material in any detail. Among the most useful accounts summarizing the various statements are: New York *Herald Tribune,* Aug. 29, 31, 1949; *The New York Times,* Aug. 31, 1949; New York *Sun,* Aug. 31, 1949. From my reading of the press accounts, I would say *Time* magazine (Sept. 5, 1949) is a representative example of national press response: the Peekskill riot, it wrote, was "an example of misguided patriotism and senseless hooliganism." FBI New York 100-25857-753 for the pro-Robeson list.

11. New York *Sun,* Aug. 31, 1949.

12. New York *Daily Compass,* Aug. 31, 1949; New York *Amsterdam News,* Sept. 3, 1949; Washington *Star,* Aug. 31, 1949; FBI New York 100-25857-750. A tape recording of PR's speech is in RA. The quotations are from that tape.

13. Interview with Howard "Stretch" Johnson, March 5, 1985.

14. New York *Daily Compass,* Aug. 30, 1949; *Eyewitness: Peekskill, U.S.A.;* interviews with Helen Rosen; FBI Main 100-12304-184; FBI New York 100-25857-754, 771 (which includes a Furriers' Union circular), 760 ("Communists"). James Rorty and Winifred Raushenbush, "The Lessons of the Peekskill Riots,"

Commentary, Oct. 1950, pp. 309–53, concluded that at Peekskill "the Communists unveiled . . . a strategical formula by which they hope to increase civil strife, to inflame the racial and religious passions and antagonisms that are already this country's shame. . . ."

15. *The New York Times,* Sept. 4, 5, 1949; New York *Herald Tribune,* Sept. 5, 6, 1949; *Daily Compass,* Sept. 5, 1949; *Daily News, Daily Mirror,* Sept. 5, 6, 1949.

16. Interview with Revels Cayton, April 29, 1982. The details of how Robeson was taken out after the concert are from PR, Jr., as told to him by his father. At the time of Peekskill, Essie and Freda Diamond were together at a Peace Conference in Mexico City; while there, they visited with the resettled Fernando Castillo, who had been the Robesons' escort in Spain, and his family (multiple interviews Diamond).

17. *The New York Times,* Sept. 5, 1949; New York *Herald Tribune,* Sept. 5, 6, 1949; *Daily Worker,* Sept. 5, 1949; *The Afro-American,* Sept. 10, 1949; *Daily Compass,* Sept. 5, 1949; *Eyewitness: Peekskill, U.S.A.;* Howard Fast, *Peekskill USA* (Civil Rights Congress, 1951); interview with Howard Fast, Nov. 21, 1986; FBI 100-25857-764 (list of injured and arrests), 773 (Fanelli); Dean Albertson interview with Henry Wallace, 1950–51, for Oral History Project, CU: by the time he gave the interview, Wallace had come out in support of Truman's intervention in Korea, and he characterized the decision to return to Peekskill as a "serious mistake"—though certain that many of those attending were not Communists and while holding the townspeople "completely" responsible for the violence. Pete Seeger had felt confident there would be no violence and had brought along his two babies, his wife, and his father-in-law to the concert. On the ride home two stones shattered his car windows, spraying glass into the children's hair; Seeger cemented the stones into a chimney he was building (phone interview with Pete Seeger, July 4, 1986). According to PR, Jr., Ellsworth "Bumpy" Johnson, the "Black Mafia" leader, offered that night to take a group of armed men back up to Peekskill to rescue the guards temporarily trapped in the

hollow; news came that they were safe and Bumpy wasn't needed. The son of the Peekskill chief of police and the son of an American Legion official were briefly detained for "malicious mischief" in throwing rocks, but were released. Among those injured was Eugene Bullard, a black aviator in World War I who had won the Croix de Guerre. Stephen Szego, owner of the grounds on which the concert had been held, subsequently had shots fired at his house; an attempt at arson was also made. Dozens of affidavits and statements by people who attended the Peekskill concert and experienced some form of injury to body or property are in the NYPL/Schm: CRC.

18. New York *Compass,* Sept. 6, 15, 1949; *New Age,* Sept. 10, 1949; Washington *Post,* Sept. 6, 1949; *People's Voice,* Sept. 15, 1949; *The New York Times,* Sept. 6 (tears), 15, 1949.

19. *National Guardian,* Sept. 19, 1949; *Daily Compass,* Sept. 8, 15, 1949; New York *Amsterdam News,* Sept. 10, 1949; New York *Herald Tribune,* Sept. 11, 15, 1949; *The Dispatcher* (ILWU), Sept. 16, 1949; *Daily Worker,* Sept. 11, 14, 16, 1949; *Newsweek,* Sept. 12, 1949; *People's Voice,* Sept. 15, 1949; FBI New York 100-25859-809; *Eyewitness: Peekskill, U.S.A.; Life,* Sept. 26, 1949; *Newsweek,* Sept. 12, 1949. *The New York Times* (Sept. 8, 1949) challenged the accuracy of the Fanelli report, saying it was sharply at variance with photographs, eyewitness accounts, and the arrest record. The Fur and Leather Workers Union, the United Electrical, Radio and Machine Workers CIO, the International Longshoremen's Union, the American Jewish Labor Council, and the New York State CIO were among the labor groups calling for an investigation. ACLU Director Roger Baldwin called Peekskill "the most shocking of all incidents aroused by the current anti-Communist hysteria." And among the many protests was one signed by sixty artists, including Bette Davis, Ruth Gordon, Lee J. Cobb, Leonard Bernstein, Charles Chaplin, and Oscar Hammerstein II. Dewey's charge to the grand jury is printed in its twenty-six-page typed report (a copy is in RA).

20. Rosen describes the problems he

had with his medical practice after Peekskill in *The Autobiography of Samuel Rosen*, pp. 72–74. Interviews with Helen Rosen; *Eyewitness: Peekskill, U.S.A.*; New York *Daily Compass*, Oct. 18, 20, 1949; FBI New York 100-25857-779A.

Three years later, Peekskill D.A. Fanelli and two carloads of police knocked on the door of the Rosens' Katonah kitchen on an early Sunday morning. "We've found the head and have been looking in the field all night for the body," he announced to Helen portentously. Swallowing her surprise—and then her amusement—Helen let Fanelli into the kitchen, made herself some tea, and did not invite him to sit down. The "head" was "Jonesy"—as the Rosen family dubbed one of the half-dozen specimens Dr. Sam kept in formaldehyde jars in the root cellar. The gardener, it turned out, had told his policeman brother about "Jonesy," and the brother had conveyed the news to D.A. Fanelli. After Sam explained his "scientific arrangement" with a New York morgue, a disappointed Fanelli finally realized he was not going to be able to nab the "Commies" after all. "You know, Doc," he said as he left, "what you've done is illegal, and I could pull you in if I wanted to, even if it isn't for murder" (multiple interviews with Helen Rosen). The Rosens did not finally sell their house in Katonah until 1971.

The local informer turned up again in 1965, when the Robesons were in California (see note 23, p. 757). Recognizing him, Essie made sure that people on the left knew his history (interview with Claire "Micki" Hurwitt, May 14, 1982). In Jan. 1950 leaders of veterans' organizations in the Peekskill area held the first in what was planned to be a series of meetings "to arouse America to the danger of Communism." It was addressed by former Rep. Hamilton Fish, whose isolationist views had cost him his congressional seat during the war; he called for outlawing the Communist Party and preparing for a war with Russia (New York *Daily Compass*, Jan. 23, 1950). The *National Guardian* reported (Oct. 3, 1949) that in defense of the Cortlandt ordinance a Legion spokesman said, "It may be unconstitutional, but when the Consti-

tution was written it was never considered what would happen later—people trying to overthrow the government."

21. The full transcript of the grand-jury report is in RA. The New York *Daily Compass* (Oct. 24, 1949) reported on the rigged proceedings during the grand-jury investigation—including the withholding or cropping of crucial photographic evidence. In response to Dewey's Sept. 14 statement, the CAA circulated an open letter to President Truman—the sixty-odd signatories included C. B. Baldwin, Charles Chaplin, Dean Dixon, E. Y. Harburg, Charles P. Howard, John Howard Lawson, and Rockwell Kent—declaring that the state of New York could "not be relied on to protect the basic constitutional rights of its citizens" and appealing to the federal government for an investigation. Truman did not respond, but he had earlier said that he agreed with Mrs. Roosevelt in deploring the lawlessness at Peekskill.

22. New York *Herald Tribune*, Dec. 16, 1949; New York *Daily Mirror*, Dec. 19, 1949 (Winchell); New York *Daily Compass*, Dec. 20, 1949, March 1, 1950; *The New York Times*, Dec. 16, 1949, Nov. 11, 1950, Jan. 24, 1952 (dismissal); New York *Amsterdam News*, March 24, 1951. O. John Rogge, a former assistant U.S. attorney general who had subsequently become active in the Progressive Party—and later became a conservative anti-Communist—headed the group of lawyers handling the action. One of the youthful lawyers was Bella Abzug; her extensive correspondence with William Patterson is in NYPL/Schm: CRC. In other subsequent developments, one of the rioters was appointed a police officer in Yorktown Heights, and Superintendent Gaffney admitted before a Senate crime-investigating committee that he had covered up a report on gambling in Saratoga (*Daily Worker*, Jan. 19, 1950, March 19, 1951).

23. New York *Herald Tribune*, Sept. 9, 1949.

24. New York *Herald Tribune*, Sept. 21, 1949; New York *Amsterdam News*, Sept. 24, 1949; Hartford *Courant*, Sept. 21, 1949; *The Afro-American*, Oct. 1, 1949; FBI New York 100-25857-740 (shouldn't have called Robeson). On Oct. 10 PR

joined sixty others in a signed appeal to Attorney General J. Howard McGrath to quash the Foley Square indictment; McGrath refused to meet with the delegation (*Daily Worker*, Oct. 11, 1949). Belknap, *Cold War Political Justice*, pp. 106–7, states that "the singer had no knowledge of any facts relevant to the case and . . . his appearance was just a publicity stunt"; the comment seems gratuitous. The verbatim transcript of PR's testimony is contained in a special agent's report to Hoover, Sept. 22, 1949, FBI Main 100-12304-? (illegible).

25. Pittsburgh *Courier*, Sept. 17, 1949. In a separate column accompanying the interview, Graves expressed his annoyance at the difficulty he had had in getting to PR and the fact that once he did, "The interview . . . was monitored by the inner circle of party dialecticians who had all the facile answers straight out of the book, in case Paul needed any help. Robeson, who knows the handbook very well himself, didn't need much help. . . . One cannot escape the feeling that this man is deeply sincere in his desire to do something about the degrading humiliations and indignities suffered by Negroes in this country. . . . Whether Robeson is or is not a Communist (and there can be little doubt that he is in the minds of those who listen to him), the racial injustices which he so vigorously protests are real, not fancied."

26. *Congressional Record*, Sept. 21, 1949, p. 13375; New York *Amsterdam News*, Oct. 1, 1949.

27. Four-page typed copy of Gwinn's Sept. 23, 1949, remarks, RA. The AP reports are in *Eyewitness: Peekskill, U.S.A.*, which also remarks that in the week following the concert the Klan received 722 letters of application from people in Westchester County.

28. *The Afro-American*, Oct. 1, 1949. ER had just (Sept. 1949) returned from the Continental Peace Conference in Mexico—"The Boss," she wrote Larry Brown, had sent her down to take his place (ER to LB, postcard, Sept. 11, 1949, NYPL/Schm: Brown). PR had apparently intended to attend the Congreso Nacional Por la Paz y La Democracia in Havana as well, but finally had to decline

because (as he telegraphed) "Presence here imperative" (Edith García Buchaca telegram to PR, July 13, 1949; Louise T. Patterson to Buchaca, July 14, 1949; Patterson to Dr. Ortiz, July 25, 1949; PR telegram to Buchaca, Aug. 1, 1949—all in RA). The FBI had followed PR's Mexican plans (FBI New York 100-25857-752). In Nov. Essie went to peace conferences in Moscow and Peking. "This has been a marvellous experience," she wrote Larry Brown from Peking, "which still seems like a terrific and wonderful dream" (Dec. 26, 1949, NYPL/Schm: Brown). The full transcript of the conference of women in Moscow is in RA; in it ER is quoted as emphasizing "the necessity for unity of the efforts of women throughout the world in the struggle for peace." During this entire period ER continued to work hard at her writing, polishing yet again her novel about a black girl passing for white (which she now called *Color*), and writing Oscar Hammerstein II that she thought her ms. "may be the idea for a musical play" (*South Pacific* had just opened) and inquiring about the script *Goodbye Uncle Tom* she had earlier sent him (ER to Hammerstein, n.d. [Oct. 1949], RA). On at least one occasion, an effort was also made to block ER from speaking in public (at a Progressive Party meeting in Trenton, N.J. [*Daily Worker*, Oct. 21, 1949]).

29. "My Day," Sept. 7, 1949. Mrs. Roosevelt wrote two other "My Day" columns relating to Peekskill, on Sept. 3 and Sept. 6, showing herself in the first one to be misinformed in her reference to the Peekskill meeting's being sponsored by the ACLU (she apologized in the column of Sept. 6) and in saying that "Paul Robeson left this country and took his family to the U.S.S.R. until the coming of the war." In Atlanta to attend a conference of Southern churchwomen on Sept. 8, she termed the recent violence at Peekskill "perfectly outrageous" and added that the North was "quite as bad" in its racial discrimination as the South (Boston *Daily Record*, Sept. 9, 1949). The ACLU statement, with a covering letter to Mrs. Roosevelt from John Haynes Holmes and Arthur Garfield Hays (Sept. 26, 1949), along with Mrs. Roosevelt's reply (Sept.

30, 1949), is in the FDR Library. In one other reference to PR in a "My Day" column (Jan. 19, 1950), Mrs. Roosevelt wrote, in regard to his Paris Peace Conference remark, "It seems strange to me that Mr. Robeson does not refute that statement. I cannot believe that he made it, since his own son served brilliantly in World War II. [PR, Jr., in fact served in the Army Air Force in 1946–7, just after World War II, and was not sent overseas.] Also, I think he knows his own people too well really to believe that they [would] . . . refuse to defend this soil of ours." *The New Yorker*, comparably, declared that when Robeson "mixes Ol' Man River with Ol' Man Marx he is being unfair to the Mississippi and is playing fast and loose with the Negro race, for whom he purports to speak. Robeson lost 'the people' as an audience when he began to make pronouncements that were largely unpopular" (Sept. 24, 1949).

30. Randolph's letter, dated Sept. 30, is in *The New York Times*, Oct. 9, 1949; the text of Frazier's remarks, which were made at a meeting in Washington, D.C., on Oct. 13, 1949, is in RA. PR wrote Frazier to thank him (Oct. 27, 1949, MSRC: Frazier). Alice Dunnigan letter, n.d. (1949), CHS: Barnett (Hughes).

31. New York *Daily Compass*, Sept. 25, 1949; Larry Adler, *It Ain't Necessarily So* (Grove, 1984), p. 130; *The New York Times*, Sept. 8, 1949 (Pittsburgh rally); Pittsburgh *Press*, Sept. 29, 1949 (cancellation); *The Afro-American*, Sept. 24, 1949 (Ohio); letter (Sept. 15, 1949) and statement from the Cincinnati Committee to Welcome Paul Robeson are in RA, as in the "Official Statement of the Cleveland Committee on the Oberlin Incident," which contains PR's rationale for cancellation; Chicago *Defender*, Oct. 15, 1949 ("cold feet") (*Newsweek*, Oct. 17, 1949, took the same tack); *Daily Worker*, Oct. 12, 1949 (Cleveland); FBI New York 100-25857-904 (Cleveland).

32. Interviews with Ishmael Flory, July 1–2, 1986, and Rev. Louis Rawls, July 1, 1986; *National Guardian*, Oct. 3, 1949; (White Sox) Chicago *Sunday Times*, Oct. 8, 1949 (Sherman); Rawls was related to Claude Lightfoot, the Chicago

CP leader, and was approached by Flory, also a CP activist.

33. *Daily Worker*, Sept. 26, 1949 (Walls); Chicago *Defender*, October 1, 1949 (overflow); FBI Main 100-12304-(illegible); *The Afro-American*, Oct. 1, 1949 (disturbances).

34. FBI Main 100-12304-172; FBI New York 100-25857-895A; San Francisco *Voice*, Sept. 29, 1949; *National Guardian*, Oct. 3, 1949; California *Eagle*, Sept. 22, 29, Oct. 5, 6, 13, 1949. Director Sam Wood, founder of Alliance of American Ideals, had decreed in his will that no beneficiary except his widow could collect his inheritance without first filing an "anti-Communist" affidavit with the probate court; the contents of Wood's will were released to the press on the eve of PR's concert.

35. *National Guardian*, Oct. 3, 1949; California *Eagle*, Sept. 29, Oct. 3, 13, 1949; Los Angeles *Mirror*, Oct. 1, 1949; *Daily Worker*, Oct. 4, 1949; *The Afro-American*, Oct. 15, 1949.

36. FBI Main 100-12304-161; FBI New York 100-25857-914A; Detroit *News*, Sept. 25, 1949; *Daily Worker*, Oct. 10, 12, 1949; *The Afro-American*, Oct. 29, 1949. Back in June, Dean Joseph L. Johnson had written to PR to say, "I want you to know that, in spite of all these attacks and smears, I have seen or heard nothing that I am willing to accept as evidence of disloyalty to our country, the United States of America. Your outstanding achievements and your courage, in my way of thinking, are still a credit both to yourself and your people" (June 14, 1949, RA).

37. Washington *Star*, Oct. 1, 1949; *Christian Science Monitor*, Oct. 14, 1949 (Strout); Washington *Post*, Oct. 19, 1949; PR to Frazier, Oct. 27, 1949, MSRC: Frazier.

38. Swami Avyaktananda to PR, Oct. 14, 1949 (World Religions); Curie telegrams to PR, Oct. 14, Nov. 11, 1949; PR to Jean Lafitte, Oct. 19, 1949 (Curie); Louise T. Patterson to Curie, Nov. 11, 1949; John Takman to PR, Sept. 13, 1949 (Sweden); telegram to PR, Oct. 17, 1949 (All-India); Nan Pandit to ER, Sept. 26, 1949—all in RA. PR, Jr., feels that another reason his father refused to see

Nehru is that he was convinced the "secret" meeting would not remain secret (PR, Jr., ms. comments). While Nehru was away, Acting Prime Minister Patel apparently hinted to U.S. officials that he might take responsibility for refusing PR (who had been rumored to be making a trip to India) a visa (FBI Main 100-12304–176, 180).

Paul's reaction to Nehru's 1949 visit is from Seton (interviews, Aug.-Sept. 1982), as told to her directly by ER. But Annette Rubinstein recalls a somewhat different version, also told to her by ER. According to Rubinstein, Essie solved the dilemma of Paul's refusing to see Nehru by scheduling a dinner party for a night when Paul would be out of town. She then sent Nehru a telegram in PR's name expressing his regret at not being able to attend (interview with Rubinstein, Dec.

5, 1983). According to Geri Branton, Robeson later told her that he regretted his snub of Nehru—"I think it's probably the only time I ever heard him say that—that there was a certain act he had regretted" (interview with Branton [PR, Jr., participating], April 2, 1982).

39. Ben Davis's reaction to sentencing is in Ware, *Hastie,* p. 228.

40. New York *Post Home News,* Nov. 2, 6, 1949; New York *Daily News,* New York *Daily Mirror,* New York *Telegram,* New York *Journal-American,* New York *Sun*—all November 4, 1949; FBI New York 100-25857-895; interview with Ollie Harrington, July 29, 1986; interview with Revels Cayton, April 29, 1982; Cayton to me, May 30, 1988 (giant); interview with Dorothy Healey (PR, Jr., participating), May 1, 1982 ("use us").

CHAPTER 19   THE RIGHT TO TRAVEL *(1950–1952)*

1. New York *Daily Compass,* Oct. 13, 1949 (UN debate). The Council of American-Soviet Friendship was originally set up with Edward Smith, former chairman of the NLRB, as its first executive director. After relations between the two countries soured, Richard Morford, a Christian Marxist, took over as director. PR was active in the Council from its inception (interview with Abbott Simon, March 27, 1982; Corliss Lamont to PR, March 4, 1946; Muriel Draper to PR, Dec. 18, 1947, RA).

2. The typescript of PR's Nov. 10, 1949, speech at the Waldorf is in RA. The speech was reprinted as a pamphlet: Paul Robeson, *The Negro People and the Soviet Union.*

3. *The New York Times,* July 19, 1949; *National Guardian,* July 25, 1949.

4. Conversations with PR, Jr.; interview with Wilkerson (PR, Jr., participating), Dec. 3, 1983.

5. New York *Amsterdam News,* Dec. 31, 1949; FBI New York 100-25857-888; *The Afro-American,* March 7, 1950 (surveillance).

6. New York *Daily Compass,* Feb. 21, 1950 (preliminaries); *Daily News,* June 2, 1950 (Tito); *National Guardian,* March 8,

1950 (Wallace); New York *Post Home News,* Feb. 27, 1950; two different versions of PR's speech to the convention are in RA. According to Seton (*Robeson,* p. 222), PR moved from the white Croydon hotel in Chicago, where the Progressive Party convention was taking place, to the Evans Hotel in the black South Side, explaining his action to her this way: "I'm no longer going to stay in downtown white hotels where Negroes have to come and see me where they cannot live. Any of my white friends who want to see me here can come to the South Side and see me, or if they are afraid to come I never wish to see them again."

7. Multiple interviews with Helen Rosen; PR, "Here's My Story," *Freedom,* May 1951 (applauding China's new government).

8. *National Guardian,* March 22, 1950; New York *Journal-American,* March 13, 1950; David M. Oshinsky, *A Conspiracy So Immense: The World of Joe McCarthy* (The Free Press, 1983), pp. 100–106; J. Fred MacDonald, *Blacks and White TV: Afro Americans in Television Since 1948* (Nelson-Hall, 1983), pp. 50–57.

9. Press releases from the Associated Negro Press, March 20, 22, 1950, CHS:

Barnett; *Daily Worker,* March 21, 1950 (PR on Roosevelt); the "private citizen" was Mrs. Ethel Hykin, who kindly sent me a copy of Mrs. Roosevelt's reply to her, dated March 27, 1950.

10. *Daily Worker,* March 17, 1950 (PR statement); FBI Main 100-12304-190 (Mrs. Roosevelt); *The Afro-American,* March 25, 1950; J. Fred MacDonald, *Black and White TV,* pp. 54–55; New York *Amsterdam News,* March 18, 1950 (Smith); Louise T. Patterson to William H. Gray, Jr. (editor-manager, Philadelphia *Afro-American*), March 29, 1950; Carl Murphy to PR, May 8, 1950; ER to Murphy, May 14, 1950 (Honor Roll), RA; statement by C. B. Baldwin, Progressive Party, March 13, 1950, NYPL/Schm: PR; memo from Henry Lee Moon to Wilkins, March 23, 1950, LC: NAACP; New York *Telegram-Sun,* March 1950. The following year a Conference on Equal Rights for Negroes (in which PR participated) spelled out some additional statistics on discrimination: the largest movie union, IATSE, had no black members; only thirty-six of the twenty thousand persons employed in advertising were blacks, and most of them held menial jobs; almost no blacks were employed in the symphonic-music field, in the editorial or business departments of the large newspapers, or in the production or technical side of television and radio (*Daily Worker,* Nov. 14, 1951).

11. Some of the letters containing invitations are in RA, others in NYPL/Schm: PR; I will not attempt to cite them individually. The following newspaper accounts detail Robeson's various speeches and appearances: *Daily Worker,* March 17, 23, May 2, 18, 24, 25, 1950; *Morning Freiheit,* April 15, May 22, 1950; San Francisco *Chronicle,* May 16, 1950; also, Charlotta A. Bass to PR, March 31, 1950, NYPL/Schm: PR. Special-agent reports to the FBI contain additional details: FBI Main 100-12304-193, 195, 196, 198; FBI New York 100-25857-1043, 1075 (describing PR's appearance at the funeral of Moranda Smith, leader of the tobacco workers in Winston-Salem, N.C., who had died in her mid-thirties of a cerebral hemorrhage).

12. PR, Jr. (multiple conversations),

is the source for PR's distrust of ER's speaking for him. The details of ER's national speaking tour are documented in a diary she kept during 1950 (RA) and in an exchange of letters with Louise Thompson Patterson (as well as between Patterson and some of Essie's hosts), which are also in RA. The FBI St. Louis report is in FBI Main 100-12304-188, the reference to the Security Card in FBI New York 100-25857-1151. The typed mss. of ER's speeches, including "Communism" and "Women and Progressive America," are in RA. The description of the black ministers in Detroit is from ER to Charles Howard and George Murphy, March 10, 1950, NYPL/Schm: PR (in which she also denounces Herbert Hill). On Muriel Draper's death in 1952, Essie was elected national co-chair (along with Virginia Epstein) of the Women's Division of the National Council of American-Soviet Friendship, and Jessica Smith was elected vice-chair, a position Freda Diamond had already held (Richard Morford to Patterson, Dec. 9, 1952, NYPL/Schm: CRC).

13. *Daily World,* June 2, 1950; *Daily Worker,* June 6, 1950; Shaw to PR, June 13, 1950, RA. At the conference Robeson joined the majority in voting against the readmission of delegates from Yugoslavia, telling the press that "Yugoslavia has tied itself firmly to the capitalist camp. . . ." (*Time,* June 12, 1950).

14. Interviews with Chatman Wailes, July 1, 1986, and Ishmael Flory, July 1–2, 1986; Seton, *Robeson,* pp. 225–27; the typescript of Robeson's speech is in RA. The Harlem Trade Union Council published Robeson's speech, under the title *Forge Negro-Labor Unity for Peace and Jobs,* as a pamphlet in August 1950. Annette Rubinstein has contrasted Robeson's attitude when traveling in behalf of left-wing causes in 1949–50 with that of some of the prima donnas in the progressive movement. One well-known writer threw a scene when told he would only have a berth rather than a private room during a scheduled train trip. By contrast, Paul—whose large bulk really did require something more than a berth—said that money for a roomette for him was better spent on organizational work (interview, Dec. 5, 1983).

15. The issues involved in the Korean War have divided scholars for decades. The two most recent accounts, less polemical than much of the preceding scholarship, are: James Irving Matray, *The Reluctant Crusade: American Foreign Policy in Korea, 1941–1950* (University of Hawaii Press, 1985), and Rosemary Foot, *The Wrong War: American Policy and the Dimensions of the Korean Conflict, 1950–1953* (Cornell University Press, 1985).

16. The typescript of Robeson's June 28, 1950, speech in Madison Square Garden is in RA.

17. FBI Main 100-12304-204; FBI New York 100-25857-1107, 1109, 1111. Revels Cayton had been urging Robeson to show himself more in Harlem, and in Aug. 1950 Louise Patterson found a one-room apartment for Paul at 270 Saint Nicholas Avenue. Essie sent down some furniture for it from Enfield. He shifted residences back and forth, sometimes staying with the Rosens or the McGhees, often taking meals at Lee and Revels Cayton's apartment. Lee Cayton recalls that he was "very sensitive to the fact that we had limited funds" and insisted on giving her money each week for food (Patterson to Rockmore, Aug. 10, 1950; ER to Rockmore, Aug. 8, 1950, RA; interview with Lee Cayton, April 1982). Freda Diamond has stressed to me that Robeson *always* had a second place to retreat to. For the thirties in London, see note 5, p. 666. For the forties, Ted Rolfs has confirmed one hideaway on Saint Nicholas Avenue, to which Robeson gave him a key (Garber interview, Feb. 4, 1983, plus my follow-up phone interview, Feb. 17, 1987; Rolfs had known Robeson for about ten years—see note 47, p. 646, and note 19, p. 710); and the FBI claimed to have uncovered another "hide-out" (as they put it) on West 10th Street in Greenwich Village (FBI New York 100-25857-7871, Sept. 16, 1949).

18. Warren Hall Saltzman, "Passport Refusals for Political Reasons: Constitutional Issues in Judicial Review," *Yale Law Journal*, Feb. 1952, for the historical dimensions of the dispute.

19. FBI Main 100-12304-204; FBI New York 100-25857-1107, 1109, 1111; Witt to Acheson, Aug. 1, 1950; Shipley to Witt, Aug. 7, 1950; Witt to Shipley, Aug. 11, 1950; Willis H. Young (acting passport chief) to Witt, Aug. 17, 1950—all in RA. Prior to the State Department action, the American Consul General in Trinidad had reported that the acting governor of the island requested advance notice of PR's rumored intention to make speeches in Trinidad "in support of leftist candidates," with an eye to trying to prevent such activity; it was also reported that "The British Security Forces in the Caribbean Area are obviously not anxious to have Robeson visit British possessions because of his Communistic activities" (FBI Main 100-12304-? [illegible], March 22, 1950, 201, 214 [British]). According to the FBI, Witt had briefly been a member of the CPUSA in the mid-thirties (FBI Main 100-12304-255).

20. The unnumbered State Department "Memorandum for File," released under the FOIA, contains a firsthand account of the meeting; the version in the *Daily Worker*, Aug. 25, 1950, closely parallels the official memo; Patterson to Clyde Jackman, Jan. 31, 1951, NYPL/Schm: CRC. The three other lawyers attending PR were Judge James A. Cobb, Dean George A. Parker of the Terrill Law School, and George E. C. Hayes, a former member of the Washington, D.C., Board of Education and a Howard University trustee. The prestigious law firm of Cobb, Hayes and Howard (Perry Howard, GOP national committeeman from Mississippi) representing PR had been in existence for two decades and had a conservative reputation; it clearly felt uneasy about PR's political radicalism (Pittsburgh *Courier*, April 28, 1951, in which Judge Cobb stresses his rock-ribbed Republican credentials and resents the suggestion of "pinkish leanings")—which may be why PR soon shifted to another firm. ER's comment is in an "open letter" she sent to the House Lobby Investigation Committee, Aug. 10, 1950, NYPL/Schm: CRC. She sent a copy of the letter to Vito Marcantonio, who replied, "I fully agree with you" (Marcantonio to ER, Aug. 19, 1950, NYPL: Marcantonio). In a speech on Oct. 24, 1950 (text in RA), PR made a critical reference to William Dawson, the black Representative from Chi-

cago, in regard to the Patterson episode: he "might have spoken, but he chose to keep quiet—possibly because Mr. Lanham of Georgia is a member of his Committee on Executive Expenditures, a little plum which Mr. Dawson received for years of faithful service to the corrupt machine bosses of Chicago and Washington." Oppositely, PR praised Marcantonio for having spoken out against Lanham's attack on Patterson: "Marcantonio did not choose to remain silent. His voice resounded in the halls of Congress in defense of the Negro people as he has done so many times in the past. . . ." Marcantonio was defeated in his bid to be returned to Congress in 1950.

21. *Daily Worker*, Aug. 9, Sept. 4, 8, 11, 1950; California *Eagle*, Aug. 11, Sept. 14, 1950; *Daily People's World* (West Coast CP paper), Aug. 9, 1950; *Daily Compass*, Aug. 10, 1950; sample protests from abroad are John Takman to PR, Aug. 19, 1950, and J. Chore to Du Bois, Sept. 7, 1950—both in RA; statement on Madison Square Garden issued by Hunton (CAA), Aug. 31, 1950, RA; FBI New York 100-25857-1148 (Garden).

22. The typescript of PR's Harlem speech is in RA. The Harlem Trade Union Council had held its first convention in June 1950, opening with a concert by PR. The Council before that had been a body of delegates from various unions; after the convention it became a delegate-and-membership body. The National Negro Labor Council consisted of delegates from ten black labor councils throughout the nation, the New York City unit being the Harlem Trade Union Council, which in July 1951 changed its name to the Greater New York Negro Labor Council (*Daily Worker*, June 3, 1950, May 18, June 4, 1951. For more on NNLC, see note 47, p. 714). In all its manifestations, the FBI labeled it "A Communist Party front organization" (FBI Main 100-12304-255).

23. According to a Naval Intelligence report, at the Hands Off Korea rally on July 3 Robeson "blistered the United States" (FBI New York 100-25857-1800); interview with Annette Rubinstein, Dec. 5, 1983. Not even in Harlem were all Robeson's streetcorner rallies well at-

tended; if *Collier's* (Oct. 28, 1950) can be believed, one rally for "peace, freedom and jobs" drew a mere two hundred.

24. CVV to Donald Angus, July 20, 1950, in Kellner, ed., *Letters CVV*, p. 242. In this same period CVV gave a party for Edith Sampson, the black UN delegate who was generally viewed on the left as an apologist for the U.S. State Department (CVV to Brion Gysin, Dec. 16, 1950, in Kellner, ed., *Letters CVV*, p. 244). Ruark's syndicated column is dated Oct. 3, 1950. Pittsburgh *Courier*, Aug. 19, 1950 (Cayton).

25. Boston *Traveler*, Aug. 12, 1950 (Moscow); the Soviet play *John—Soldier of Peace* was written by Yuri Krotkov, starred the distinguished Soviet actor M. Nazvanov, and played more than a hundred times (Nazvanov to PR, March 8, 1952, RA). Pittsburgh *Courier*, Sept. 9, 1950 (Josh White); Navasky, *Naming Names*, pp. 192–93 (Belafonte); interview with Revels Cayton, April 27, 1982; *Rolling Stone*, March 1976 (Gillespie); phone interview with Sidney Poitier, Oct. 20, 1986. Pete Seeger confirms that Josh White told Robeson about his HUAC appearance in advance, and also Robeson's lack of bitterness over it—but has it happening over the phone rather than in person (interview with Seeger, July 4, 1986). When Seton was preparing her book on PR, he asked her "to cut down on quotes of fellow Black Americans who testified against him, because, as he said, he understood the predicament of the pressures they were put under 'to clean [sic] their skirts.' There was a total absence of mean or vindictive mindedness in Paul" (Seton to Geoffrey Baines, Nov. 30, 1978, courtesy of Seton).

26. *Christian Science Monitor*, Oct. 11, 1950; Boston *Post*, Oct. 6, 11, 12 (editorial), 14, 1950; Boston *Herald*, Oct. 11, 12, 1950; Associated Negro Press releases, Nov. 6, 18, 1959, CHS: Barnett; Washington *Star*, Nov. 8, 1950 (Soviet party); New York *Amsterdam News*, Nov. 18, 1950; *Life*, Nov. 20, 1950. Reports on the Second World Peace Conference are in New York *Herald Tribune*, Nov. 17, 23, 1950; *Daily Worker*, Nov. 10, 20, 24, 1950; *Morning Freiheit*, Nov. 18, 1950. When Dorothy Bushnell Cole returned from the

peace conference, a special FBI agent, "through the cooperation of the U.S. Customs Inspector," photographed material in her baggage relating to the conference (FBI New York 100-25857-1800, Referral Doc. #3 from U.S. Customs, Department of Treasury, to FBI). When the International Peace Prize was presented to PR at a rally on Dec. 11, 1950, Army Intelligence was present and reported that Robeson once again spoke out against the U.S. presence in Korea (FBI New York 100-25857-1800, Referral Doc. #21 from G-2 to FBI). The State Department also monitored the activities of PR, Jr., who had by then become active in the Labor Youth League (PR, Sr., had addressed its founding convention at Stuyvesant Casino on Nov. 24, 1950; the typescript of PR's address is in RA). In December, PR, Jr., was part of a group of two hundred young people who staged a peace demonstration in the main lobby of the UN headquarters; they cheered Mrs. Roosevelt when she walked through the lobby, but after she remonstrated with them, the cheers turned to boos (ANP release, Dec. 6, 1950, CHS: Barnett).

27. A summary of Du Bois's Senate race can be found in Horne, *Black and Red*, ch. 13. Bishop Walls wrote Ben Robeson that he regarded Paul as "a Christian and a race hero" (Walls to B. C. Robeson, March 8, 1950, RA).

28. *Daily Worker*, Oct. 6, 1950; FBI New York 100-25857-1800; Referral Doc. #20 from Army Intelligence (G-2); *The New York Times*, Oct. 27, 1950; the typescripts of PR's two speeches, Oct. 5, 24, 1950, are in RA. Robeson attended a number of rallies protesting Du Bois's indictment (*Daily Worker*, Feb. 6, 1951; New York *World-Telegram and Sun*, Feb. 22, 1951; FBI Main 100-12304-255).

29. Interviews with Alice Childress, Sept. 19, 1983, Oct. 9, 1984. It was also in 1950 that Alice Childress and Clarice Taylor decided to start a theater in Harlem. They went to John Barone, owner of Club Baron, a bar and grill at 132nd Street and Lenox Avenue, and got free space from Mondays to Thursdays. When they asked Robeson for the use of his name, he readily agreed, but he warned the two women—as he did so many others—that association with him would not necessarily be an asset. For their first production, in 1950—Childress's *Just a Little Simple*, adapted from Langston Hughes's "Simple Speaks His Mind"—PR dropped by, brought in people, and even appeared at fund-raisers at Wells' Chicken Shack in Harlem. He also wrote a personal check for five hundred dollars. (interviews with Alice Childress, Sept. 19, 1983, Oct. 9, 1984; interview with Ruth Jett, April 2, 1982; Sterner interview with Ellsworth Wright). The theater managed to struggle along for a few years (in 1952 it performed Childress's *Gold Through the Trees*, directed by Clarice Taylor), but, according to Ruth Jett (interview, April 2, 1982), some of its own committee members "panicked" under McCarthyite pressure and padlocked the door.

30. Interviews with Alice Childress, Sept. 19, 1983, Oct. 3, 9, 1984; Alice Childress to me, Aug. 23, 1984; *Daily Worker*, Oct. 23, Nov. 20, 1950; Burnham to ER, Nov. 15, 1950; assorted Freedom Associates memos from Burnham, RA; FBI Main 100-12304-255 ("front"); PR's lengthy (twenty-seven handwritten pages) ms. for his first column, the early section containing valuable information on his youth, is in NYPL/Schm: PR, which also has a two-page outline of purpose of the Freedom Fund, and the minutes of the meeting of Freedom Associates, Feb. 12, 1952, which set up the Freedom Fund and organized a PR tour in its behalf.

31. Copies of all the pertinent legal documents are in RA, as is Ruark's column with the Hoover comment; the panic over the "Robeson" sailing is summarized in FBI Main 100-12304-220.

32. New York *Herald Tribune*, Jan. 3, 1951; Ernest Thompson wrote an answer to Sugar Ray Robinson in the Pittsburgh *Courier*, Jan. 20, 1951; "The Strange Case of Paul Robeson" is in the Feb. 1951 issue of *Ebony*.

33. Roger P. Ross, public-affairs officer, to State Department, Jan. 9, 1951 (the only legible file number on the document is from DC/R Central Files: 511.45K21/1-951).

34. The typescript of ER's "The Not So Strange Case of Paul Robeson" is in

RA (it was printed in the California *Eagle*, April 5, 1951); Ben Burns (executive editor, *Ebony*) to ER, Jan. 22, 1951; ER to John Johnson, Feb. 1, 1951. Seton, too, was furious at White's "snide utterly dishonest" article and wrote in protest to *Ebony* (Seton to ER, Jan. 5, 25, 1951, RA). Pearl Buck, on the other hand, replied coolly to Essie: "I suppose basically the trouble is that Walter thinks that Paul has given his major allegiance to a foreign power. I wish Paul could disprove this, publicly, for his own sake" (Buck to ER, Feb. 5, 1951, RA). Pearl Buck's husband, Richard J. Walsh, president of the John Day publishing company, had earlier written in disagreement to ER about Korea: "I still can't take it when it is charged that anybody other than the North Koreans started the aggression" (Walsh to ER, Aug. 17, 1950, RA).

35. William H. Brown to "Wilkinson" [sic], July 9, 1951; Wilkins to Brown, July 11, 1951, LC: NAACP; PR, Jr., ms. comments; *The Crisis*, Nov., Dec. 1951.

36. *The Afro-American*, Jan. 26, 1952; San Francisco *Voice*, Feb. 15, 1952; ER to Hicks, Jan. 29, 1952, RA; Du Bois, *Negro Digest*, March 1950. When George Wood, Jr., the popular manager of the Red Rooster, died in 1955, PR sang at his funeral (*The Afro-American*, Sept. 24, 1955). Du Bois's comment was part of a debate he had with Walter White in the pages of the *Negro Digest* on the question "Paul Robeson: Right or Wrong?" The debate preceded the appearance of White's article in *Ebony* by nearly a year, and in this earlier article White took issue with PR in more measured tones, avoiding any insinuation about his supposed neuroticism or his inadequate prior contribution to the black struggle, and confining himself to questioning Robeson's "uncritical" acceptance of Soviet accomplishments. In reply, Du Bois denied that Russia was an aggressor nation and argued eloquently that Robeson in fact spoke more for blacks than the Walter Whites liked to believe, chastising those who attacked PR for being "deathly afraid to act or talk or even think in any way which is in opposition or can be interpreted as opposing the current hysteria."

37. FBI Main 100-12304-230; *The New York Times*, April 13, 1951 (Bastian).

38. Patterson to Clyde O. Jackson, Jan. 31, 1951 (Martinsville), NYPL/Schm: CRC; Al Richmond, *A Long View from the Left: Memoirs of an American Revolutionary* (Houghton Mifflin, 1972), pp. 295–99 (second-echelon); PR led a delegation to the UN to protest the Martinsville case (*Daily Worker*, Feb. 4, 8, 1951); Gaunzetta Mitchell to PR, Feb. 7, 1951, NYPL/Schm: PR (Martinsville); *Morning Freiheit*, Feb. 23, 1951 (Foster); New York *Amsterdam News*, March 24, May 26, 1951 (McGee); *Daily Worker*, Feb. 12, 1951 (McGee); FBI New York 100-25857-1321 (McGee); *Daily Worker*, April 12, 1951 (Hollywood Ten); ER to CVV and FM, May 24, 1951 (David Paul), Yale: Van Vechten; *Daily Worker*, May 7, 30, 1951 (HTUC), Aug. 21, 26 (Patterson); *Amsterdam News*, May 26, 1951 (HTUC). Though the National Maritime Union revoked Robeson's honorary membership (Neal Hanley to PR, Feb. 26, 1951, RA), he continued to believe in the trade-union movement as a source for progressive social action; in the June 1951 issue of *Freedom*, he devoted his entire column to describing a trip to California with Revels Cayton to talk with trade-unionists, and he placed particular faith in the black union leaders Joe Johnson, Charles Nichols, Al Thibodeaux, and Bill Chester, as well as in surviving progressive unions like the United Cafeteria and Restaurant Workers in D.C. (Oliver Palmer to PR, Nov. 10, 1951, RA) and the National Union of Marine Cooks and Stewards (MCS), which was 40 percent black and had been expelled by the CIO in 1949. *Daily Worker*, Feb. 1, March 18, 1951; *The New York Times*, Feb. 1, 1951 (American Peace Crusade). The APC attracted many distinguished figures, including Robert Morss Lovett, Prof. Philip Morrison of Cornell, and Prof. Henry Pratt Fairchild. Acheson denounced the APC as a "Communist front organization" (*Herald Tribune*, Feb. 21, 1951). Alvah Bessie, another of the Hollywood Ten, still imprisoned in the Federal Correctional Institution at Texarkana, Texas, wrote a touching poem about Paul (Bessie to PR, June 21, 1951, RA). The above

events hardly cover the full spectrum of PR's activities during these months. To but mention several others, he helped launch the *New World Review,* he marched in the May Day parade, he joined the plea to Truman not to provide U.S. military aid to Franco, and he was active in the National Committee to Defend Du Bois (*Daily Worker,* May 2, 17, 1951; Alice Citron to PR, May 29, 1951; Vincent Sheean to PR, April 10, 1951, RA). Essie, too, remained active, writing frequently in *New World Review* (e.g., July 1951) and elsewhere (e.g., *Freedom,* July 1951) about colonialism and the role of women, but in June 1951 she took seriously ill with a combination of spastic colitis and phlebitis and was hospitalized in Washington, D.C., for a month (her old friends Minnie and Sadie Sumner, along with Nan Pandit, then India's Ambassador to Washington, were particularly attentive: ER to Robert Rockmore, July 12, 1951, RA; ER to Vito Marcantonio, June 13, 1951, NYPL: Marcantonio).

39. *Daily Worker,* June 28, July 2, 1951 (Chicago); *Masses and Mainstream,* Aug. 1951, and FBI New York 100-25857-1409 for Chicago remarks; interview with Chatman Wailes, July 1, 1986 (Wailes had gotten to know PR when he came through Gary, Indiana, in 1949, where Wailes was then living). The Chicago rally was a considerable event. The *National Guardian* (July 4, 1951) estimated that five thousand peace delegates attended. Among the sidelights, a poem, "Paul Robeson" by Beulah Richardson, recited at the convention, proved a minor sensation (Patterson to Richardson, Aug. 1, 1951, NYPL/Schm: CRC, which also contains the text of the poem).

40. The typescripts of PR's statements in regard to Malik (June 26, 1951) and Austin (June 12, 1951) are in RA, along with surrounding letters and telegrams. (PR reprinted his letter to Austin in his column, "Here's My Story," for the July 1951 issue of *Freedom.*) Additionally, NYPL/Schm: PR has memo drafts of the Robeson–Willard Uphaus report to U.S. members of the World Council for Peace of the meeting with Malik, and a letter from PR to Malik thanking him, in the name of the World Council of Peace

(Burnham—"For Paul Robeson"—to Malik, June 29, 1951). CU: Minor has a letter to Dr. Henry A. Atkinson (Church Peace Union) dated June 23, 1951, and cosigned by PR and Willard Uphaus, asking him to be an observer for the June 26 presentation at the UN.

41. Patterson, *Man Who Cried Genocide,* chs. 12, 13. NYPL/Schm: CRC contains considerable documentary material on the petition drive; of particular interest is Patterson's letter to *The New York Times* (Nov. 26, 1951) chastising the paper for prominently reporting a call to investigate genocide charges against the Soviet Union while ignoring the genocide charges against the United States. Essie was one of the signatories to the final petition. Patterson recounts his disappointment with the genocide campaign ("It neither got the support nor recognition which I believed it deserved") in WP to George B. Murphy, Jr., March 7, 1957, MSRC: Murphy. The 1951 petition to the UN on behalf of black Americans was in fact the third such. The first, presented by the NAACP, asked for a redress of grievances for black people in the United States and was edited by Du Bois. The second, presented by Yergan for the NNC, was initially drafted by Patterson. Both failed to secure a hearing in the Commission of Human Rights (Patterson to Oakley C. Johnson, June 10, 1952, NYPL/Schm: CRC).

42. Krishan Chandar to PR, June 11, 1951, RA (Bombay); *Daily Worker,* July 3, 1951 (Paris); Lynford Joel Concertato, telegram, August 28, 1951 (British tour); Peter Blackman to Patterson, Sept. 19, 1951 NYPL/Schm: CRC (London), which also sounds the frequent complaint among Robeson associates that "he must answer letters or otherwise nobody knows what he wants done"—for this same complaint see also Earl Robinson to Hunton, Nov. 18, 1949, RA; Michael Hamburger to PR, July 10, 1951 (Aberdeen); Warren Brody to PR, May 9, 1951 (Harvard), both in NYPL/Schm: PR; FBI Main 100-12304-233 (sample opposition to PR); Isidore M. Cohen to PR, June 11, 1951, NYPL/Schm: PR. An additional batch of foreign invitations are in RA for the first few months of 1952. By that time

Robeson's lawyers and friends were making something of a concerted effort to solicit such invitations as a vehicle for challenging the State Department's ban; as Essie wrote in response to one such invitation, "Thank you. . . . Every invitation is of great importance for us. For each one, we go again to the State Department for a passport" (ER to C. Bogdan, Rumanian legate, Feb. 15, 1952, RA; see also, D. N. Pritt to Patterson, Dec. 14, 1951, NYPL/Schm: CRC). PR to Lionel Kenner, Oct. 28, 1951, RA (common search). His brief Christmas message for 1950 had similarly stated, "Peace depends on the friendly, though competitive co-existence of different systems" (RA).

43. The number of memos, teletypes, and instructions relating to the Vancouver incident in RA are too numerous to cite individually. PR had attended a reception for Harry Bridges and had spoken out in his defense after the longshoremen's leader was convicted of perjury in a federal district court in California for denying under oath at the time of his naturalization that he had ever been a CP member (FBI Main 100-12304-255), a conviction subsequently reversed by the Supreme Court.

44. Bellingham *Herald,* Jan. 31, 1952; *Freedom,* March 1952 (PR's own account of Vancouver); Vancouver *Daily Province,* Jan. 29, Feb. 1, 12, 1952; Vancouver *Sun,* Jan. 31, Feb. 8, 9, 1952.) Jerry Tyler, one of four union men who helped Robeson find accommodations in Seattle—he "wanted to get a room in the Negro community"—and to arrange a press conference, described the hours he spent with Robeson as a "thrill and inspiration. . . . How can you paint a word picture of the impact on yourself of a man so full of warmth and love that he stands like a giant, yet makes you feel, without stooping to you, that you too are a giant and hold the power of making history in your own hands as well?" (Tyler to Eddie Tangen, secretary-treasurer, National Union MCS, Feb. 3, 1952, NYPL/Schm: PR.)

45. *Morning Freiheit,* Feb. 12, 1952 (miners' convention); *People's World,* Feb. 8, 1952 (PR's speech); FBI Main 100-

12304-253; FBI New York 100-25857-1548.

46. John Gray, field representative for the United Freedom Fund, who accompanied PR on much of the tour, wrote Louis Burnham and business manager Bert Alves (May 22, 1952, NYPL/Schm: PR), "Mobilization on this side of the border was non-existent, although some 1000 or so were there thru no special effort. Concert was *tops.* Response *grand.*" Bellingham *Herald,* May 19, 1952; Pacific *Tribune,* May 23, 1952; Vancouver *Sun,* May 10, 1952; FBI Main 100-12304-262, 263; a transcript of PR's brief remarks at the Arch are in RA. There was some disagreement between Harvey Murphy, regional director of the miners' union, and John Gray over what percentage of the money raised at the concert should go to the Freedom Fund and what percentage toward paying back union expenses (Murphy to Gray, May 30, 1952, NYPL/Schm: PR, which also contains statements itemizing income and expenses from the tour and correspondence about making the Peace Arch concert an annual event).

47. Pettus to PR, Feb. 19, 1952; Murphy, Jr., to Pettus, April 14, 1952; Pettus to *Freedom,* April 16, 1952; Murphy, Jr., to Lester Catlett, April 18, 1952—NYPL/Schm: PR.

48. Murphy to Catlett, April 18, 1952; Pettus to *Freedom,* April 26, 1952; Eleanor Nelson to Murphy, May 1, 1952, NYPL/Schm: PR.

49. Pacific *Tribune,* May 16, 1952; Seattle *Post-Intelligencer,* May 8, 1952; *Daily People's World,* Northwest Edition, May 9, 1952; Seattle *Times,* May 8, 1952.

50. Gray to Burnham and Alves, May 22, 1952; Pettus to Robeson and Gray, May 24, 1952, NYPL/Schm: PR; *Daily People's World,* May 16, 1952 (which reported that two local newspapers had refused ads for the concert).

51. San Francisco *Examiner,* April 25, 1952; New York *Daily Compass,* May 23, 1952; *The Nation,* June 7, 1952 (Berkeley); *Morning Freiheit,* June 13, 1952; *Daily People's World,* April 25, 1952; San Francisco *Chronicle,* April 23, 1952; Chester to Murphy, Jr., April 23, 25, 1952; Murphy, Jr., to Chester, April 27, 28, 30, 1952;

Alves to Chester, June 2, 1952; Murphy, Jr., to Coleman Young, April 20, 1952; John Gray to *Freedom,* May 25, 1952—all NYPL/Schm: PR.

52. Hershel Walker to Bertram Alves, May 28, 1952 (St. Louis); Mike Walter to Alves, May 20, 1952 (Milwaukee), NYPL/Schm: PR; two-page typed report, unsigned, on the University of Minnesota, RA; Pittsburgh *Courier,* June 14, 28, 1952; FBI office memos, June 6, 9, 1952, and Main 100-12304-

266X; *Daily Worker,* April 29, 1952 (birthday).

53. John Gray to Maurice Travis, July 17, 1952; Edith Roberts to Coleman Young, July 30, 1952, NYPL/Schm: PR. Robeson's income-tax returns in RA demonstrate that his financial situation was not acute, but PR was so indifferent to money matters that at one point Rockmore had to hound him for information about his tax returns (Rockmore to PR, Sept. 5, 1951, RA).

CHAPTER 20   CONFINEMENT *(1952–1954)*

1. Oshinsky, *Conspiracy So Immense,* passim. In March 1952 Robeson sent a message to the World Peace Council excoriating the continuing U.S. involvement in Korea: "The enormity of this crime"—he was apparently specifically referring to rumors that the United States had used bacteriological warfare—"against the brave Korean & Chinese People should bring down the wrath of all decent humanity upon the heads of the military & shapers of this genocidal policy" (draft, March 21, 1952?, NYPL/Schm: PR). As newly released documents have revealed, high-level discussion and planning took place during the Eisenhower administration for deploying nuclear weapons against North Korea and Communist China (the revelations are reported in *The New York Times,* June 8, 1984).

2. Horace Alexander to PR, Feb. 24, 1952; Thelma Dale to PR, Feb. 26, 1952 (Progressive nominations), NYPL/Schm: PR; FBI New York 100-25857-1597 (convention); Horace Alexander to PR, n.d. (1952), NYPL/Schm: PR (California); interview with Annette Rubinstein, Dec. 5, 1983 (Bass remark); PR speech to NNLC convention, Cleveland, Nov. 21, 1952, RA ("fateful year"). I'm grateful to David Randall Luce, who was present in Ann Arbor, for his recollections, as well as pertinent Michigan state police documents, of that event (Luce to me, Sept. 19, 1982, plus enclosures).

3. In PR's speech at the NNLC convention on Nov. 21, 1952 (ms. RA) he added: "Professor Mathews's son is one

of those arrested in Capetown for his defiance of unjust laws. I ask you now, shall I send my son to South Africa to shoot down Professor Mathews's son on behalf of Charles E. Wilson's General Motors Corporation? . . ."; PR's column, Aug. 1952, *Freedom* (optimism).

4. Copies of the minutes of the Progressive Party national-committee meeting of Nov. 29–30, 1952, and the secretary's report on the election are in RA.

5. Both RA and NYPL/Schm: PR contain batches of congratulatory messages, mostly from abroad. The Kent telegram is in RA; Ferrer's statement is printed, among many other places, in the Pittsburgh *Courier,* Jan. 3, 1953. According to an FBI phone tap (FBI New York 100-25857-89), during World War II Robeson intervened to get a draft deferment for Ferrer, arguing that his presence in the cast was essential for the continuing run of *Othello.* Rockmore successfully sued in court to get the Stalin Prize money for Robeson tax-free because, like the Nobel, it was a "prize" (the five-year battle is described in the *Herald Tribune,* Feb. 5, 1959).

6. PR's April 1952 Detroit speech, RA. Robeson's lawyers had made appeals for the return of his passport in Sept. and Dec. 1951 and March and Aug. 1952. A large amount of documentation connected with these appeals, and the one in Dec. 1952, is in RA, NYPL/Schm: PR, NYPL/Schm: CRC, and assorted FBI files. The documentation is too extensive to warrant detailed citation here. Several

additional points emerging from the documentation do, however, need to be stressed. First, PR's European supporters, as mentioned earlier, deliberately worked to get him invitations for commercial engagements so that (in the words of Desmond Buckle) they could "give real point to our demand for the restoration of your passport" (Buckle to PR, Sept. 14, 1951, RA). Second, a Provisional Committee to Restore Paul Robeson's Passport was formed late in 1951 to build up grass-roots support (Burnham/Patterson correspondence, NYPL/Schm: PR and CRC).

7. An especially persuasive analysis of the shaky assumptions behind the Government's case is I. F. Stone in the *National Guardian,* March 14, 1952; *Daily Worker,* April 6, 1952; *Freedom,* April 1952.

8. Both ER and PR wrote effusive eulogies of Stalin in *New World Review,* April 1953; and on March 26, 1953, PR spoke at a memorial meeting under the auspices of the National Council of American-Soviet Friendship about Stalin's "magnificent leadership" (FBI Main 100-12304-677). Among the accounts of PR's efforts in behalf of the Rosenbergs, are: *The New York Times,* Oct. 15, 1952; *National Guardian,* Nov. 6, 1952; *The Worker,* Nov. 9, 1952, Jan. 12, 14, 1953; FBI 100-38128-9; FBI Main 100-12304-677. RA contains a typescript of PR's remarks at the Rosenberg Theatre Rally on Nov. 19, 1952. Among the many accounts of PR's continuing efforts to bring about an end to the Korean War are: *The Worker,* Sept. 28, Oct. 7, Nov. 16, Dec. 4, 1952; FBI New York 100-25857-1612, 1622; *Freedom,* Dec. 1952 (PR speech at NNLC convention).

9. Multiple interviews with Helen Rosen.

10. Ibid.

11. Multiple conversations with PR, Jr.

12. Multiple interviews with Helen Rosen. According to PR, Jr., they sometimes recorded in people's living rooms, or alternately at Nola and Esoteric Studios, where the owner's stood their ground even though FBI agents were all over them. Herbert Biberman, one of the Hollywood Ten, had earlier tried to form a company "to move into a number of cultural projects," of which the first was expected to be a PR recording, but nothing further came of the plan (Biberman to PR, July 14, 1951, RA). Robeson frequently saw Biberman and his wife, the blacklisted actress Gale Sondergaard, when he was in California. At around the same time, Howard Da Silva, Sam Wanamaker (who would play Iago to PR's Othello in 1959), PR, and others had some notion of forming a theater-and-film group, but that, too, failed to materialize (Da Silva to PR, May 15, 1951, RA; Cleveland *Herald,* July 15, 1950; FBI Main 100-12304-255).

13. The itemization of the earnings from *Robeson Sings* is in PR, Jr., to Rockmore, Oct. 6, 1953, RA. *The New York Times* complained that *Robeson Sings* was "cheapened by slickly commercial orchestral backgrounds" (Feb. 7, 1954). Another Robeson album, *I Came to Sing,* a recording of his 1952 Peace Arch concert, was released in 1953 by the Mine, Mill union (Canadian *Tribune,* March 23, 1953, May 4, 1954). Although the IRS audited Robeson repeatedly, it never found anything untoward. Thanks to Rockmore, PR even had enough money to set up Bruce Liggins, husband of his niece Marian, in medical practice, and to pay for his daughter-in-law Marilyn's school tuition. He also periodically lent money to Ben Davis and to his own brother Ben. PR's voluminous financial records are in RA.

14. Dale to Crawford, April 6, 1953; Alves to Gray, July 1, 1953, NYPL/Schm: PR; J. Maceo Green, San Francisco *Sun,* June 13, 1953; interview with Thelma Dale Perkins, Nov. 11, 1986; interview with Stretch Johnson, March 5, 1985. Pete Seeger (phone interview, July 4, 1986) is the source for the NAACP story (having heard it from a member of the Oberlin NAACP chapter).

15. Interviews with Dr. Aaron Wells, Jan. 8, April 23, 1983, multiple interviews with Rosen (Hellman). Bishop Clinton Hoggard, in an interview with Sterner, recalled a similar episode involving the Alpha Phi Alpha chapter in Washington, D.C., late in the fifties. PR had asked "to

meet with some of the brothers"; Hoggard had passed the word around but encountered considerable resistance: "They were very hesitant, especially those who were in government employ—'Well, I can't be in a room where he is.' " As an example of another kind, Langston Hughes, in three of the children's books he published during the McCarthy years—*First Book of Negroes* (1952), *Famous American Negroes* (1954), and *Famous Negro Music Makers* (1955)—omitted all mention of Robeson (and Du Bois as well). Attempting to justify his action ten years later, Hughes cited pressure from his publishers (Hughes to William G. Horne, Oct. 25, 1965, RA).

16. This analysis of local black reactions to PR's tour is based on material in NYPL/Schm: PR, especially on the correspondence of Herschel Walker (St. Louis), Rev. Charles A. Hill (Detroit), John Gray (his letters back home to *Freedom* while on the road making tour arrangements), and Bernard Alves (particularly his letters from Atlanta and Cleveland when he was canvassing concert possibilities). A copy of McGowan's speech, printed as a pamphlet by the National Committee to Defend Negro Leadership, is in RA.

17. *Daily Worker*, April 28, 1953; Rev. Charles A. Hill to John Gray, Nov. 30, 1953, NYPL/Schm: PR (Detroit); Bellingham *Herald*, Aug. 17, 1953; Vancouver *Sun*, Aug. 18, 1953 (Blaine); *Freedom*, May 1953. George Murphy, Jr., recalled "the plight we got into with Salem Methodist, even after the tickets were printed," when the minister "got cold feet because of the pressure of some of his parishioners" (Murphy to ER, Feb. 22, 1958, MSRC: Murphy Papers). The Canadian organizers had predicted to Robeson that he would get a turnout of fifty thousand in Canada and five to ten thousand in the States (PR to Judy Rosen Ruben, July 28, 1963, courtesy of Rosen). According to *The Afro-American* (July 18, 1953), PR's appearance at the Lawndale Baptist Church in Chicago attracted only 200 people because "a number of persons were 'intimidated' not to show up," but he drew a large crowd for an outdoor concert in Washington Park. *The Afro-*

American also reported that in Chicago "None of his activities received newspaper publicity; most of them received word of mouth notice or handbill announcement."

18. Seattle SA report, Oct. 12, 1953, FBI Main 100-12304-? (blurred) (Seattle); FBI New York 100-25857-1556a ("hideout"), 2617 (Pettus); telephone interview with Chief Jim Richards, Enfield, Feb. 1, 1985. PR's activities in behalf of the Smith Act defendants are too numerous to itemize. Some of the major rallies are described in *The Worker*, Feb. 24, March 17, 18, May 16, 1952, Feb. 11, 1953; important correspondence relating to plans for defense and protest are in NYPL/Schm: PR and CRC. Essie had also taken a highly visible role in the nationwide committee to aid the families of the Smith Act victims, which further persuaded the FBI that it had been right to reclassify her as a Communist (FBI Main 100-12304-297). In his autobiography, Junius Scales recalls that in the 1956–57 period, when the initial furor over the Smith Act trials had passed and funds were increasingly difficult to raise, PR came to the aid of his Defense Fund. He simply appeared one night when Scales (in his words) "was boring an audience of about a hundred or so in a wretched hall in the Bronx," spoke eloquently of their common heritage as Southerners fighting against racism, and helped raise three or four times the sum Scales had hoped for. Moreover, that was the first of several appearances PR made in Scales's behalf (ms. of Scales autobiography, courtesy of Scales; since published as *Cause at Heart* [University of Georgia]).

19. RA contains a multisided correspondence—between Essie and Rockmore, Rockmore and Julius Meltzer (the real-estate agent), and Bert McGhee and Rockmore (about rent)—relating to the Enfield sale in particular and PR's finances in general; it is too bulky to cite in detail. It should be noted, though, that Rockmore occasionally wrote directly to Robeson admonishing him about his continuing indifference to his financial affairs (e.g., Rockmore to PR, Sept. 5, 1951, June 24, 1953, RA). The asking price on Enfield is in *The New York Times*, July 21,

1953. For a time Robeson himself seems to have agreed to Essie's purchase of a building lot in the progressive residential area of Norwalk called Village Creek Colony (PR to Judy Rosen Ruben, July 28, 1953, courtesy of Rosen). In regard to PR's finances, the black actress-activist Frances Williams has recorded a touching anecdote. Hearing that he was in bad straits, she told him, " 'Paul, I don't want you to worry about that because, damn it, if we all have to stand on corners with cups, we'll get enough money so you can keep going.' He sat there and cried. I can see the tears coming down his face. He said, 'Oh, baby you don't have to worry about me and money. . . .' This great man crying. Can you see me standing on the corner with a cup? I loved him. He was a great, great man" (Williams interview, 1981, with Kim Fellner and Janet Mac-Lachlan, transcript courtesy of Fellner). At this same time, the early fifties, PR had kept at 188 West 135th Street. The union activist Ted Rolfs (in an interview conducted for me by Eric Garber, Feb. 4, 1983, and my follow-up phone interview with him on Feb. 17, 1987) described the apartment as having a gigantic bed and floor-to-ceiling bookshelves, along with iron protective guards on special windows and an iron floor-bolt on the front door. PR allowed Rolfs, who had been named a security risk, to stay in the apartment, but Rolfs described how difficult PR's black neighbors in the building made it for him until they were finally persuaded he was not there to do Paul any harm. (For more on Rolfs, see note 47, p. 646, and note 17, p. 701.) PR sometimes stayed in this period at Ben Davis's apartment and also at the Pettis Perry family's apartment. A little later (around 1955) he used William Patterson's apartment at 409 Edgecomb Avenue when Patterson was away.

20. The quotations in this and the following paragraphs come from the stenographic transcript of the hearing in RA, which also has the handwritten notes Essie made after the hearings to set down her second thoughts—all those "brilliant things" she wished she had said at the time; among them was this imaginary question to the Senator: "Are you or are you not married? Why not?"

21. Stenographic transcript, RA; ER to Seton, July 14, 1953, RA. In her typed statement to the press, July 9, 1953, RA, Essie referred to McCarthy's insistence that all Americans were equal in their citizenship as "that old American Party Line."

22. PR to Judy Rosen Ruben, July 28, 1953, PR to Helen Rosen, Dec. 14, 1953, courtesy of Rosen.

23. The many letters of invitation from overseas are in RA. The offer to do *Othello* was from Leslie Linder. Robeson telegraphed his acceptance, pending receipt of a passport (Linder to PR, June 15, 1953; PR to Linder, n.d., RA). NYPL/Schm: PR contains considerable correspondence on both the ASP and Hartford incidents; some newspapers accounts have also been useful in reconstructing those events, particularly the Hartford *Times*, Nov. 17, 1952 (PR's reaction to reporters); *The Afro-American*, Nov. 29, 1952; and *The New York Times*, Nov. 11, 12, 18, 1952.

24. The plight of the CAA can be traced in two memos it issued (Oct. 23, Dec. 17, 1953), copies in LC: NAACP. *Freedom* fell four months behind in its publication schedule and when it finally reappeared, in Feb. 1954, ran a front-page appeal for support: "The existence of the paper is at stake." Interviews with Alice Childress, Sept. 19, 1983, Oct. 9, 1984 (money problems at *Freedom*); *Amsterdam News*, Feb. 19, 1954. The FBI report on PR's "heart trouble" has no legible serial number but is dated (from L.A.) Dec. 1, 1953. PR to Helen Rosen, Dec. 14, 1953, courtesy of Rosen.

25. The two FBI memos dated Jan. 13, 1953, and April 27, 1954, do not have legible file numbers; a third (FBI New York 100-25857-1976) also refers to his "changing his views." The *Jet* article appeared Jan. 28, 1954. When Cliff W. Mackay printed a story in his Jan. 23, 1954, column for *The Afro-American*—the black paper that had most consistently supported Robeson—that PR had taken out an ad in *Pravda* to extend New Year's greetings to the Soviet people, Robeson wrote Mackay that *Pravda* did not accept

ads and that the greetings in question had been in response to the paper's request for "a message about the attitudes of the American people toward peace" (PR to Mackay, Feb. 9, 1954, NYPL/Schm: PR). An exchange of letters between Rev. J. Spencer Kennard, Jr., and PR contains a firm denial by PR of the Drew Pearson report (Kennard to PR, May 3, 1954; John Gray to Kennard, May 19, 1954, NYPL/Schm: PR). George B. Murphy, Jr., general manager of *Freedom* Associates, who had been an editor of the Washington *Afro-American* (and was a member of the family that owned the paper), had arranged a meeting in Baltimore a few years previously between Robeson and Carl Murphy, president of the *Afro-American* newspaper chain. (The chain had the largest circulation among blacks of any weekly in the country, reaching, on the basis of three or four persons reading one copy, some six hundred thousand each issue. The Pittsburgh *Courier* chain, about equal in influence to *The Afro-American*, had taken a more staunchly anti-Communist line in its editorial policy, and was therefore less sympathetic to Robeson's plight.) His four-hour meeting with Carl Murphy went splendidly, and *The Afro-American* stopped taking snide potshots at PR and published a half-dozen favorable articles on him (Murphy to Du Bois, Aug. 31, 1956, U. Mass.: Du Bois). As one sign of *The Afro-American*'s esteem, its assistant managing editor, Josephus Simpson, asked PR (along with other prominent figures) to reflect for *The Afro*'s readers on the events of 1953 and to forecast what lay ahead in 1954—and also to nominate "the outstanding American." In his response, PR rejoiced that the issue of segregation in education had reached the Supreme Court, but warned that "the whole civil rights program" had been "scuttled by the Eisenhower administration in the President's successful bid for Southern support." Further, he characterized the administration as "largely a political vehicle for the giant corporations and entrenched greed" and pilloried it for embracing McCarthyism. As the two most significant achievements of 1953 he listed "the ending of the bloodshed in Korea" and "the

further awakening of the colonial peoples, particularly our brothers in Africa, and now in the West Indies and Latin America." He nominated two "outstanding Americans"—W. E. B. Du Bois and Dr. Mary Church Terrell, who at age ninety had been leading picket lines to desegregate the capital's lunchrooms and had gone to Georgia to plead for clemency for Rosa Lee Ingram, a sharecropper accused of killing a white man (Simpson to PR, Dec. 14, 1953; PR to Simpson, Dec. 19, 1953, NYPL/Schm: PR). When Mary Church Terrell died, seven months later, PR hailed her as one of America's "great daughters" (handwritten draft, July 27, 1954, NYPL/Schm: PR).

26. The ms. of PR's lengthy reply is in NYPL/Schm: PR. His formal statement through *Freedom* Associates, dated May 3, 1954, is in RA.

27. Interview with Stretch Johnson, March 5, 1985; PR, "Their Victories for Peace Are Also Ours," *New World Review*, Nov. 1955; *The New Statesman and Nation*, Sept. 24, 1955.

28. ER to Seton, Aug. 11, 1952, RA. When the president of the Yale chapter of the NAACP invited Robeson to participate in a debate on "Is American fit to be the leader of the world?" or "Is the American Government moving toward equality and civil rights?" he wrote on the invitation, "This question not debateable—willing to come, speak & answer questions—no debate" (NYPL/Schm: PR).

29. Conversations with PR, Jr. (20th Congress); but PR does seem to have discussed Khrushchev's revelations later with Harry Francis (see pp. 505–06). On the need to distinguish between the visionary Bolshevism of the twenties and the authoritarian Stalinism that replaced it—a distinction few American Sovietologists have been willing to make—see Stephen F. Cohen's illuminating discussion in *Rethinking the Soviet Experience: Politics and History Since 1917* (Oxford University Press, 1985). According to PR, Jr., his father "had deep concern about the 1952 frame-up trial and execution of the leading Jewish cultural figures in the U.S.S.R.," but when Paul Novick of *Frei-*

heit approached him in 1957 to sign a public statement on the matter, Robeson declined. Novick spoke to him again in Moscow in 1958 "about what was going on in the Soviet Union and the Jewish question and whatnot, and Dad was under no illusions about what had happened, and what was happening then, as a matter of fact" (multiple conversations with PR, Jr.; PR, Jr., to Morris U. Schappes, Dec. 30, 1981; PR, Jr., ms. comments).

30. Interview with Sam Parks, Dec. 27, 1986. (For more on Parks and PR, see p. 457.)

31. Interview with Peggy Dennis, April 27, 1982; letter from Dorothy Healey to me, June 22, 1982; multiple conversations with Helen Rosen. A California friend, Geri Branton, offered the same caution against making the CPUSA "all that important" in Robeson's life (interview, April 2, 1982). One gauge of Robeson's *un*involvement in CP organizational affairs is that he goes wholly unmentioned by Party memoirists of the period as having participated in factional struggles or daily routine. My analysis of Robeson's relationship with the CPUSA and the Soviet Union is drawn from many sources, but has been especially enriched by personal interviews—with Peggy Dennis (April 27, 1982), John Gates (June 8, 1982, Feb. 13, 1984), Rose Perry (April 27, 1982), Dorothy Healey (May 1, 1982), Stretch Johnson (March 5, 1985), Junius Scales (March 10, 1986), Carl Marzani (March 11, 1986), Ollie Harrington (July 29, 1986), and Sam Parks (December 27, 1986).

32. Interviews with Healey (April 1982), Gates (June 8, 1982, Feb. 13, 1984). Echoing Gates's formulation, PR was reported in the undergraduate newspaper at Swarthmore as telling the students during a visit to that campus in 1955 that he "did not accept the opinion of the U.S. press about the degree of freedom within the USSR. For working class people," he stated, "there is a great deal of freedom"; the reported slave-labor camps in the U.S.S.R., he supposedly went on to say, "were used for no other purpose than for the improvement [sic]

in our sense of the word," a necessity given the "historical background of the present State" and "the fact that the Western powers have been trying to destroy the USSR since its inception" (Swarthmore *Phoenix*, May 3, 1955).

33. For more details on these aspects of Soviet and CPUSA policy, see Isserman, *Side*, especially pp. 137–41, 215–16, 246–47. As Isserman points out (pp. 141–43), the CPUSA did continue to fight hard within CIO unions like the NMU and the TWU for better employment opportunities and high union posts for blacks.

34. Interviews with Stretch Johnson (March 5, 1985), Rose Perry (April 27, 1982). The Pettis Perry papers, consisting of some 250 letters to his wife Rose as well as various notes and speeches, have recently (1987) been acquired by NYPL/Schm, and I am grateful to the staff for allowing me access before the materials were fully catalogued. Perry (b. Jan. 4, 1897) was an almost exact contemporary of PR and was somewhat close to him during the fifties. Perry had been born in poverty on a tenant farm near Marion, Alabama, had learned the trade of moulding at a pipe foundry in Tuscaloosa and during the Scottsboro trial had joined the International Labor Defense, serving as its Executive Secretary from 1934–36. He became a CP Section Organizer in 1936 and was ultimately elected to the National Committee. Indicted among the New York Smith Act defendants, he was jailed from 1955–57.

35. Interviews with John Gates, June 8, 1982, Feb. 13, 1984.

36. Interview with Peggy Dennis, April 1982; Peggy Dennis to me, March 24, 1984, Feb. 16, 1987.

37. Ibid. PR admired Foster as a theoretician, though he did not feel especially close to him as a man; in notes dated April 30, 1956 (RA), he referred to Foster as "that master of Marxist theory and practice. . . ." The sympathy and depth of Foster's views on black issues is best sampled in Foster's own book, *The Negro People in American History* (International Publishers, 1954), especially chs. 42, 43, 48; Foster admiringly refers to PR several times in the book.

38. Multiple conversations with PR, Jr. PR turned down Patterson's request that he appear at the eighth-anniversary celebration of the Civil Rights Congress (Patterson to PR, March 16, 1954; John Gray to Patterson, March 25, 1954, NYPL/Schm: PR). From prison, Ben Davis, Jr., wrote Patterson a guarded but decipherable complaint about the Party's racial obtuseness: ". . . There were missteps on our side that never should have occurred. . . . One cannot be satisfied that the groundwork for an assault on my 60 day contempt was not laid ahead of time. . . . I would be less than candid if I did not point out that the absence of certain counteractive measures left a deep and painful impression on me. Nor will I go into this; but I want you to think about it. And I want that this shall not be repeated with Pete [Pettis Perry] and above all with the great and horribly brutalized Claudia [Claudia Jones]"—Perry and Jones being black Communist leaders who had been arrested under the Smith Act (Davis to Patterson, n.d. [1954–56?], NYPL/Schm: PR). Robeson shared Davis's concern and admiration for Claudia Jones, supporting the move in behalf of her parole after a year in prison, her health compromised (James W. Ford to PR, May 4, 1955, RA; FBI New York 100-25857-2397); and when she was deported in late 1955, he sent "heartfelt greetings" to a gathering in her honor (dated Dec. 7, 1955, RA).

39. Multiple conversations with PR, Jr.

40. Interviews with John Gates (June 8, 1982 and Feb. 13, 1984).

41. Multiple conversations with PR, Jr. The story about "toning down" was Ben Davis's, who told it to Robeson, who told it to PR, Jr.

42. *The Afro-American*, March 13, 1954; Patterson to John Gray, Feb. 25, 1954; Richard Greenspan to Gray, March 8, 1954, NYPL/Schm: PR (Guatemala); PR telegram to Neruda, July 12, 1954, RA (Guatemala); FBI New York 100-25857-1950? (Guatemala), 1981 (McCarran); minutes of the Formation of Kenya Aid Committee, NYPL/Schm: PR; Hunton to "Dear Friends," May 18, 1954 (Conference in Support of African Liberation), LC: NAACP; *Daily Worker*, April 27, 1954

(subversive). In the March 1954 issue of *Freedom*, PR also wrote presciently about Vietnam in an article entitled "Ho Chi Minh Is the Toussaint L'Ouverture of Indo-China": "Vast quantities of U.S. bombers, tanks and guns have been sent against Ho Chi Minh and his freedom-fighters; and now we are told that soon it may be 'advisable' to send American GI's into Indo-China in order that the tin, rubber and tungsten of Southeast Asia be kept by the 'free world'—meaning White Imperialism."

43. The large number of letters, cables, minutes, and memos relating to the spring 1954 passport campaign—as well as messages of thanks from PR—in both RA and NYPL/Schm: PR are too numerous for detailed citation. Additional sources for piecing together the story of the campaign are issues of the *National Guardian*, May–June 1954, and *Bulletin of the World Peace Council*, July, Aug., Sept., Oct. 1954.

44. Interview with Diana Loesser, July 29, 1986. The Jewish-owned business concern NAHUM offered free space for future meetings, and the local Jewish paper, *Jewish Chronicle*, provided strong editorial support.

45. The "Salute" did not bring out the number of blacks that had been hoped for: ". . . it was not what we wanted by any means as to composition" (John Gray to Mary Helen Jones, June 9, 1954, NYPL/Schm: PR); interviews with Alice Childress, Sept. 19, 1983, Oct. 9, 1984.

46. Details of the Chicago incident are in correspondence between Ishmael P. Flory, secretary of the Committee for African Freedom (the sponsoring group), and John Gray, field representative of the *Freedom* Fund, NYPL/Schm: PR. Flory gave me additional details in our interviews of July 1–2, 1986, including the information that an alternate concert at a black church in Chicago was "packed," with people "standing all along the walls." Another left-wing Chicagoan, Norman Roth, told me (phone interview, June 26, 1986) that he witnessed black policemen forming a gauntlet for PR and telling him (while looking over their shoulders at their white officers), "Good work, Paul; good work, Paul." The corre-

spondence between Gray and James T. Wright, also at NYPL/Schm, details the hiring of Wright and Boudin. I am greatly indebted to Leonard Boudin for turning over to me his complete files on the Robeson passport case.

47. Celia L. Zitron to PR, June 16, 1954 (Smith Act); Mary Helen Jones to John Gray, Nov. 17, Dec. 19, 1954; Jessica Smith to ER and PR, June 1, 1954 *(New World Review)*—all in NYPL/Schm: PR; (Essie served as editorial consultant on black and colonial questions for *NWR*); FBI New York 100-25857-2074, 2124 *(New World* dinner); *Daily Worker,* Oct. 20, 1954 (for PR on Essie's contributions); Jessica Smith to "Dear Friend," Aug. 11, 1954, MSRC: Smith Papers. There is a large correspondence in RA relating to the business affairs and recording arrangements of Othello Recording Company; in 1954 Othello issued a new PR album, *Let Freedom Sing,* and in 1955, *Solid Rock: Favorite Hymns of My People,* and entered into arrangements to send special language matrices to Hungary, the U.S.S.R., Czechoslovakia, and Poland, bringing in for Robeson some needed funds (in Jan. 1955, for example, Paul, Jr., was able to send Rockmore a royalty check for PR's account for $3,451.25, and in May another for nearly $3,000). Robeson paid tribute to Marcantonio, both in a private telegram to his widow (Aug. 10, 1954, NYPL/Schm: PR) and in an article for *Freedom* (Aug. 1954). Through *Freedom* Associates, he hailed him as "the Thaddeus Stevens of the first half of the 20th century" and "the foremost spokesman for the rights of man the Congress of the United States has produced in the 20th century" (the statement, dated Aug. 12, 1954, is in RA).

The National Negro Labor Council had been officially launched in a convention in Cincinnati in 1951 as a mass organization to fight against limited job opportunities and Jim Crow and to build unity between black and white workers. PR was given honorary membership in the Council and was present at its inaugural convention, speaking and singing to the delegates (his speech is reprinted in the *Daily World,* April 8, 1976). He remained active in the NNLC, playing a

particularly dramatic role at the second annual convention, in Cleveland in 1952, when he brought the delegates to their feet with a resounding declaration that black youth should not participate in "shooting down the brave people of Kenya" *(Daily Worker,* May 7, 1951, June 16, 1952; Pittsburgh *Courier,* Nov. 10, 1951; New York *Amsterdam News,* Dec. 3, 1951; *Freedom,* Jan., Dec. 1952). At the third annual convention, in Chicago in 1953, he reiterated yet again the sentiments of his 1949 speech in Paris: "No one has yet explained to my satisfaction what business a black lad from a Mississippi or Georgia sharecropping farm has in Asia shooting down the yellow or brown son of an impoverished rice farmer"; the audience, according to *Freedom* (Oct. 1953), responded "with a thunderous cheer." At the 1954 convention, in New York, he gave a powerful speech assailing the U.S. government for refusing to trade with China, Eastern Europe, and the Soviet Union while fostering trade with fascist Spain and with Malan's South Africa: "If politics is to be the yardstick in international trade it means that the U.S. government is saying to 15,000,000 Negroes that it approves the politics of the most oppressive racist dictatorship on the face of the globe today" (ms. of speech in RA). PR did not engage in behind-the-scenes strategy sessions but, rather, "came in more or less as a great man" to sing and talk (interview with Oscar Brown, Jr., Dec. 27, 1986; Brown was especially active at the 1952 convention in Cleveland). PR, Jr., insists to the contrary that his father attended and spoke at committee sessions and met privately with the top leadership group (PR, Jr., ms. comments).

48. George B. Murphy, Jr., to Du Bois, Aug. 31, 1956, U. Mass.: Du Bois; New York *Age,* July 30, 1949; interview with Kay Pankey, July 26, 1986. Essie's two-hundred-dollar monthly allowance was apparently provided in addition to her hotel bills and other standing expenses, leading Rockmore once again to warn Paul about "the monthly drain that goes on ceaselessly" (Rockmore to PR, May, 1954, RA). A confidential FBI informant reported that another reason pro-

pelling PR's move was that McGhee was "at present, very ill and under doctor's care" (FBI Main 100-25857-2273). The informant also claimed that until the move PR had visited his brother Ben only infrequently because the two "do not get along too well." In fact it was Essie who did not get along with either Ben or his wife, Frankie.

49. My view of Robeson's family culture and also the particular environment of the parsonage is especially indebted to insights from multiple conversations with Marilyn Robeson, and from my interview with Marian Liggins, Ben and Frankie Robeson's daughter (Nov. 21, 1982).

50. Interview with Howard Fast, Nov. 21, 1986; multiple interviews with Helen Rosen.

51. Spottswood to PR, Feb. 16, 1955, RA. When Frances ("Frankie") Robeson died, in 1957, Paul attended the services along with A.M.E. Zion Bishops Rt. Rev. William J. Walls, Spottswood, and Brown (Chicago *Defender,* Dec. 21, 1957; Pittsburgh *Courier,* Dec. 28, 1957).

CHAPTER 21   BREAKDOWN *(1955–1956)*

1. Ms. of PR article for *Liberation* (Paris), dated June 19, 1954, RA; FBI New York 100-25857-2063 (Ben Gold), 2108 (ALP), 2142 (Lightfoot); FBI Main 100-12304-316 (Patterson and Davis); Muriel Symington to John Gray, Nov. 20, 1954, NYPL/Schm: PR (Patterson). A handwritten speech by Robeson in Patterson's behalf is in MSRC: Patterson (n.d. [c. August 1954]); in it, Robeson reiterated his view that "When the Americans know the truth—the simple truth—they'll put a fast end to many of these present fascist-like absurdities, an end to the blatant destruction of our Constitutional rights." When the London *Daily Herald* asked Adam Clayton Powell, Jr., to write a thousand-word profile on PR, he protested directly to the *Herald* on the basis of Powell's support of "the aggressive war policy of the Republican government" and the "cold-war policy of the preceding Democratic administration. Though his 'bipartisan' political conformity qualifies Rep. Powell for a passport, I cannot see that it qualifies him in any way to present an objective report on me to your readers" (Powell to PR, July 16, 1954; PR to *Herald,* Sept. 11, 1954, RA). FBI New York 100-25857-2284 ("specific information").

2. *The New York Times,* Feb. 24 (Hammett), 25, 26 (Robeson testimony); New York *Herald Tribune,* Feb. 24 (Hammett), 26 (editorial). For a particularly smooth bit of savagery against Robeson that appeared at this very time, see the ch. entitled "George" in Murray Kempton's *Part* *of Our Time* (Simon and Schuster, 1955). Among other claims, Kempton insists that the character of Sebastien Cholmondley (a fatuous, pretentious, self-deceived black man) in Evelyn Waugh's 1928 novel *Decline and Fall* was meant as a portrait of Robeson.

3. PR to Josephus Simpson (assistant managing editor, *The Afro-American*), Dec. 19, 1953 ("magnificent"); *Freedom,* Feb. 1955; Swarthmore *Phoenix,* May 3, 1955. Robeson also used his involuntary idleness to further his musical studies and to return to the study of languages and cultures which had so preoccupied him twenty years earlier. In a short article in *Spotlight on Africa* (February 1955), he reiterated the familiar themes of his 1934–36 notes, i.e., the similarities between many African languages and other cultures such as Chinese, especially in their structures and in the "thinking" behind the language.

4. There is considerable correspondence in NYPL/Schm: PR, especially between John Gray and Lynne Childs, Mary Helen Jones, Matt Crawford, Rev. Stephen H. Fritchman, and Horace Alexander, detailing the plans and difficulties of arranging a California tour for Robeson in 1955 ("We're going to keep banging away," Mary Helen Jones wrote Gray in a letter of Oct. 19, 1954, "because if we do give up the concert idea then Mr. Charlie will really know he's got us down"). Robeson's comments while in L.A. are from the *Daily People's World,* March 17, 1955. Whether the car episodes repre-

sent a deliberate attempt to harm Robeson cannot be conclusively decided from the evidence, but both Paul Robeson, Jr., and Lloyd L. Brown believe that they did (*Daily World*, Oct. 25, 1979 [PR, Jr., interview]; Lloyd L. Brown, "Did They Try to Kill Paul Robeson?," ms. in RA). In a similar vein, PR, Jr., asserts that he has "credible evidence that in the middle 1950's and early 1960's the CIA considered the possibility of assassinating Robeson" (ms. comments), but if so he has not shared it with me. Having carefully studied all the *currently available* evidence, I do not find PR, Jr.'s assertion persuasive.

5. Patterson to U Nu, Oct. 21, 1955, MSRC: Patterson; *The Afro-American*, May 21, 1955; *The New York Times*, April 23, 1955; New York *Amsterdam News*, May 14, 1955. Powell did, however, speak out several months later for the return of PR's passport (London *Daily Worker*, Sept. 22, 1955). Two years later Essie wrote another blast at Powell, in relation to the violence against school integration at Little Rock High, Arkansas. When Louis Armstrong reacted to Little Rock by saying, "The Government can go to Hell; it's getting almost so bad a colored man hasn't got any country," most of black America rejoiced (not least over the fact that Armstrong, who had long continued to play before segregated audiences, had at last spoken out). But Adam Clayton Powell, Jr., appearing on the TV program "Youth Wants to Know" on Sept. 19, 1957, said that Armstrong didn't understand international affairs, that he was just a musician. Soon after that, in a sermon on Little Rock to his congregation at the Abyssinian Baptist Church, Powell said the President could not send federal troops to Little Rock without making "a confession of our moral decadence," precipitating "a second civil war and sending democracy down the drain for at least a generation and maybe forever." On all these counts, ER excoriated Powell ("Daniel Louis 'Satchmo' Armstrong, Spokesman," *International Life*, Oct. 1957). PR's remarks at Swarthmore are from *Freedom*, May–June 1955. The earlier move to bar him from CCNY is reported in the Pittsburgh *Courier*, Dec. 1,

1951, and *Campus*, Dec. 6, 1951. A confidential memo to Walter White (dated Nov. 28, 1951) in LC: NAACP reports a conversation with Dr. Kenneth Clark, then chairman of the committee in charge of the use of the Great Hall at CCNY, in which Clark said he "would like to be in a position to recommend that if the Hall is opened to Robeson it should be in a forum type of affair with a representative of our Association, preferably you, so that both sides of the question would be presented." Walter White appended to the memo, "As there is a possibility that I shall be out of the country on January 10 [the suggested date for the forum] it is impossible for me to attend."

6. The surveillance, monitoring, and phone taps have already been documented many times over in these pages; for evidence of PR's mail's being opened, see FBI New York 100-25857-3118, 3147. Among the informants cooperating with the FBI in this period was Noble Sissle, the partner of Eubie Blake, and a man who had known Robeson at least since the days of "Shuffle Along" in the early twenties (FBI Main 100-12304-405, 62-65252).

7. Dave Curtis to PR, March 3, 1955; PR to Curtis, March 7, 1955 (Workers' Sports Association); Jacob Ori to PR, Jan. 26, 1955 (Tel Aviv); Sergei Yutkevich to PR, March 15, 1955 (Mosfilm). Once again, the documentation with regard to the passport case is too bulky to cite with any completeness. Suffice it to say that in this and the following paragraphs I have relied on the press releases of the Provisional Committee to Restore Paul Robeson's Passport in RA; the complete files of the case Leonard Boudin turned over to me; detailed reports of the battle in the *Daily Worker* (especially Jan. 24, May 30, June 2, 3, 8, 1955) and *The New York Times* (especially Jan. 14, June 2, 3, 4, 7, 15, July 15, 1955); and private correspondence in both RA and NYPL/Schm: PR. A good summary of the issues in the case is in Boudin, "The Constitutional Right to Travel," *Columbia Law Review*, Jan. 1956. For a historical overview arriving at a pro–State Department position see Louis L. Jaffe, "The Right to Travel: The Passport Problem," *Foreign Affairs*, Oct. 1956.

8. PR, Jr., to Dave Curtis, Ferdinand C. Smith, Will Sahnow—all July 28, 1955, RA; Atlanta *Daily World,* July 28, 1955; *The Afro-American,* July 3, 30, 1955; *Daily Worker,* July 24, Aug. 14, 1955. The officials present at the meeting were Under-Secretary of State Loy W. Henderson (who as U.S. Ambassador to Iran had helped to engineer the overthrow of the democratic Mossadegh government two years earlier), Frances G. Knight (director of the Passport Division), Security Chief Scott McLeod, and Raymond Yingling, assistant legal adviser to the State Department. Just two weeks before PR's passport conference in Washington, *The New York Times* had run an editorial recommending more cultural exchanges between the U.S. and the U.S.S.R. In welcoming the *Times*'s suggestion, *Pravda* cited the "humiliating procedures" prescribed for Soviet visitors to the States and also protested the refusal of the U.S. government to allow Robeson to travel. Shortly before that exchange, the *Times* reported that the Soviets, having earlier named a mountain after Robeson, had now named the main street in a new state farm settlement after him as well (*Times,* April 3, 1955). Since the *Times* in this period reported no news of PR other than his passport case and his assorted Soviet ties, the paper directly contributed to the already firm public image of him as "a dangerous subversive." Mount Paul Robeson is the highest peak in the Ala-Tau range in the Kirghiz Republic. A bronze bust of Robeson by Olga Manuilova is placed on top of the mountain. (See Thelma Dale Perkins, "A Letter to Paul Robeson on Our Visit to Mt. Robeson," *New World Review,* 4th quarter 1973.)

9. *The New York Times,* Aug. 17, 1955; New York *Herald Tribune,* Aug. 17, 1955; PR, Jr.'s handwritten notes on the Aug. 16 meeting ("this man"), at which he had been present, are in RA; *U.S. News & World Report,* Aug. 26, 1955 (an excerpted transcript of the proceedings); interview with Leonard Boudin, July 14, 1982.

10. Pittsburgh *Courier,* Aug. 17, 1955; the New York *Amsterdam News,* Sept. 10, 1955; PR's press release (Oct. 1955) is in RA.

11. See p. 407 for the State Department's 1952 assertion; Rover's testimony is reprinted in *U.S. News & World Report,* Aug. 26, 1955; PR's statement is reprinted in the Philadelphia *Tribune,* Oct. 18, 1955.

12. The powerful historical argument in the *amicus curiae* brief was prepared by Milton Friedman, William Patterson, and Ralph Powe and then circularized (mostly among black Americans) for signatures. Essie took an active role in writing to potential signers. Du Bois, Alphaeus Hunton, and Rev. Charles Hill were among those who signed. Benjamin E. Mays, president of Morehouse College, was among those who refused (". . . it would have been better to have argued the case for Mr. Robeson," he wrote Patterson, "without indicting Mr. Dulles" [Mays to Patterson, March 1, 1956, NYPL/Schm: PR]). In explaining the reluctance of Judge W. C. Huston to sign, George B. Murphy, Jr., wrote Essie (March 6, 1956, NYPL/Schm: PR) that he "apparently never . . . recovered from the effect of his having signed a statement which he wrote himself, on the basis of his convictions in the Rosenberg case, which caused him some difficulties in the State of Michigan with the Elks State Association there. . . . [He] asked me to say to you and Paul that if there is something else he can do he will be happy to help" (see also March 5, 1956).

At the time of Emmett Till's murder, PR sent a telegram to A. Philip Randolph (Sept. 24, 1954, RA) calling for black unity "in militant resistance to terror and oppression." It was one of several gestures PR made in 1954–55 to reach out in common cause with the established black leadership. (He also telegraphed "greetings to the officers and delegates of the NAACP convention," June 24, 1955, RA.)

13. Interviews with Dr. Aaron Wells, Jan. 8, April 23, 1983; multiple conversations with PR, Jr., and Helen Rosen; interview with Annette Rubinstein, Dec. 5, 1983 (making out a will); PR's reference to himself as a "prisoner" is from the London *Daily Herald,* Oct. 21, 1955.

14. Interview with Lee Cayton, April 28, 1982. Helen Rosen recalls that her

husband, Sam, had tried to persuade Robeson to go to a surgeon at Mt. Sinai, where Sam was on staff, but other friends persuaded him that "he must have a black doctor do it, and it has to be done uptown." She also recalls that Sam was "absolutely furious" that the operation was done in two steps, an older surgical technique, thereby exposing Paul to a double dose of pain and anxiety (multiple conversations with Helen Rosen). According to PR, Jr., his father told him he didn't want a downtown white doctor or a CP doctor and went on his own to Wells and Wiles—though agreeing to let Ed Barsky, the physician for several CP leaders, watch the operation at Sydenham. The FBI had a report on Robeson's hospitalization from an unnamed source at Sydenham (FBI New York 100-25857-2518). Among the many get-well letters in RA is one from Eugene Dennis (Oct. 12, 1955) and one from Mike Gold (Oct. 18, 1955), who wrote, *"We need you as we need sunlight!"* PR's hospital bills, revealing his private nursing care, are in RA. His medical expenses, totaling over two thousand dollars, put another dent in an income that (according to the official estimate on his 1955 tax returns in RA) for the year 1955 amounted to a gross of $12,751.90. Essie's income for that year totaled a mere three hundred dollars, for three articles in *New World Review* (ER to Rockmore, Feb. 13, 1956, RA). PR's finances got a boost the following year when he received a check for ten thousand dollars "as a fee for your records sold in the Soviet Union" (Yuri I. Gouk [cultural attaché, U.S.S.R. Washington Embassy] to PR, undated [enclosed check is dated June 7, 1956], RA).

15. For an understanding of why Paul returned to Essie, I'm especially grateful for the insights Marilyn Robeson provided in our several talks. The historians Judith Mara and Herbert Gutman got to know the Robesons fairly well during the 1950s (because of their close friendship with Paul, Jr., and Marilyn) and stressed to me, during an informal conversation on June 7, 1985, that they had found ER an unusually well-informed, astute political observer. In regard to Essie and the CPUSA, Rose Perry recalls that

Essie "was always at loggerheads with some of the people in the Party," and PR, Jr., adds, "She was very critical of Foster and Ben" (interview with Perry, April 27, 1982 [PR, Jr., participating]). The FBI, in 1955, was citing Essie as "active on behalf of numerous Communist fronts" (FBI Main 100-12304-317, 318). The FBI received information that Ben Davis, Jr., after completing a conditional-release sentence on Feb. 24, 1956, "possibly will live with" Robeson, having asked a friend to get him a larger apartment for that purpose (FBI Main 100-12304-360).

16. Interview with Thelma Dale Perkins, Nov. 11, 1986 (parachute); ER to "Nana," Jan. 11, 1956, RA; talks with Marilyn Robeson. When the United Nations Department of Public Information gave Essie temporary accreditation, USUN Warren M. Chase suggested to the Justice Department in a confidential memo that "steps be taken" to have her credentials canceled. Since the department had a policy of not objecting to the accreditation of U.S. correspondents to the UN, Chase suggested that she be watched to see if she introduced herself in a status other than as a correspondent for a "Communist monthly," and that if she did the department "might be asked to make an investigation directed at this specific point" (FBI Main 100-12304-336). The special agent in New York reported soon after that "no info has come to the attention of the NYC indicating that subject has misused her accreditation to the UN" (FBI Main 100-12304-353). Samples of ER's political writings for *New World Review* are in the issues of June and Aug. 1956 (respectively, favorable reactions to Sukarno of Indonesia and Krishna Menon of India), May 1957 ("The Changing Face of the UN"), and June 1957 ("China and the UN"). ER suggested to Claude Barnett, head of the Associated Negro Press, that from time to time she send along from her UN post stories of special interest to black readers, for syndication by Barnett. But he replied that the material "really does not suit our needs" (ER to Barnett, Oct. 18, 1957; Barnett to ER, Nov. 15, 1957, CHS: Barnett). In a notebook in RA marked "1957 some notes

and appointments," Essie wrote regarding her UN job: "Be very careful, during debate, not to laugh or sneer or make any expression."

17. Interview with Dr. Morris Perlmutter, March 7, 1983. *Mine-Mill Herald*, Feb. 1956; *The Telegram* (Canada), Feb. 13, 1956; Canadian *Tribune*, Feb. 20, 1956; Toronto *Daily Star*, Feb. 13, 1956; ER to Lloyd L. Brown, Jan. 29, 1959, RA. The ms. of PR's Sudbury speech is in RA. In his Toronto speech PR also congratulated the city on having banned *Little Black Sambo* from the public schools; his support of the ban reflected both the limits of his civil-libertarian stand and the campaign against "white chauvinism" that had been gathering strength—and wreaking havoc—within the Communist Party. Six months before, PR had gotten a letter from Neruda, telling him, "I am speaking about you and your case in a great meeting for public freedom, here in Santiago in 15th August. . . . I send you my best regards, and the love and admiration of all my people" (Neruda to PR, July 2, 1955, RA).

18. For additional discussion of PR's reaction to the Khrushchev revelations, see pp. 416–17; also, interviews already cited with Peggy Dennis, Dorothy Healey, John Gates, Stretch Johnson. The fate of the March 1956 passport appeal is traced in newspaper accounts (*The New York Times*, Jan. 1, 21, Feb. 12, March 9, 1956; *Daily Worker*, March 9, 1956; *The Afro-American*, March 10, 1956) and in correspondence from Robeson's lawyers, Boudin and Wright, in NYPL/Schm: PR. Warren E. Burger, then Assistant Attorney General, Civil Division, for the Justice Department, was one of the lawyers arguing the case against Robeson.

19. Interviews with Dr. Morris Perlmutter (March 7, 1983), Freda Diamond (liturgy), PR, Jr.; my interviews with Pete Seeger (July 4, 1986, phone) and Earl Robinson (Aug. 17, 1986) were especially useful in regard to the pentatonic scale. RA contains voluminous Music Notes in PR's hand, written from 1955–57. In them, he sometimes speculates on the *two* pentatonic scales of the piano (e.g., Notes of Jan. 15, 1957) and far from claiming absolute originality for his theories, cites a large number of scholarly sources for them, including Béla Bartók, Hugo Leichtentritt, J. Rosamond Johnson, Marshall Stearns, F. M. Hornbostel, Marion Bauer, and Harold Courlander.

Though depressive symptoms were not manifest in 1956, they may have dominated earlier mood swings; Seton, for example, referred in our interviews of Aug.-Sept. 1982 to PR's "always having the curtains closed" when she visited him at the McGhees' apartment (though she was uncertain about the dates). There are almost no additional references in the surviving evidence to PR's having sharp mood swings prior to 1956, except for an occasional elusive reference such as an AP report of March 16, 1951, that had PR "sweating profusely and gesticulating wildly" while addressing a mass rally for peace. But it would be unwarranted to attach much "medical" significance to the AP's words, since (in the general context of its report) they seem designed as a political commentary, a strategy for discrediting his "tirade."

20. Multiple conversations with Helen Rosen.

21. Interviews with Dr. Aaron Wells, Jan. 8, April 23, 1983; Dr. Morris Perlmutter, March 7, 1983; PR, Jr. (multiple); Helen Rosen (multiple). I have also benefited from discussion with Dr. Robert Millman, who went over some of the medical records with me and offered his observations.

22. ER to Rockmore, April 30, 1956, RA. Another new stress factor impeding recovery was receipt of the news in mid-April that Canada's Department of Immigration had refused him a visa for a thirty-eight-day concert tour that had been in the planning stages, citing as the reason its sponsorship by a "Communist" booking agency. Details of the controversy, which included questions in the Canadian Parliament, are in the Toronto *Daily Star*, April 10, 11, 1956; the Canadian *Tribune*, April 16, 1956; *The Globe and Mail*, April 12, 1956; the *National Guardian*, May 7, 1956; correspondence from John Boyd of the Jerom Concert Bureau (sponsors of the tour), RA, and Boyd to Lloyd L. Brown, April 13, 1956 (copy), MSRC: Patterson. I got some additional

details from my interview with Sylvia Schwartz (Jan. 16, 1983), who was active in protesting the visa cancellation. In William Patterson's opinion, Canada's refusal of a visa was "a heavy blow" (Patterson to Sylvia Schwartz, May 4, 1956, NYPL/Schm: PR). The American Consul General in Montreal kept the State Department closely informed about the fate of PR's Canadian tour (FBI New York 100-25857-2668, 2673).

23. Wiles, "To Whom It May Concern," May 25, 1956; Wells, "To Whom It May Concern," May 26, 1956; Richard Arens (director, HUAC) to Friedman, May 31, 1956 (postponement); Wells to Friedman, June 8, 1956—all in RA; FBI memo from L. B. Nichols to Clyde Tolson, May 31, 1956, FBI Main 100-12304-? (illegible).

24. Phone interviews with Milton Friedman, Aug. 27, Nov. 29, 1982. Freda Diamond (multiple interviews) is the source for Essie's fainting scheme. The prepared statement is in RA. In it PR listed the more important of the many invitations he'd had to perform all over the world, declared it "would be more fitting for me to question Walter, Eastland and Dulles than for them to question me, for it is they who should be called to account for their . . . truly un-American activities"—claiming that he, in contrast, had "won friends for the real America before the millions before whom I have performed"—and defiantly refused to back down one inch in "continuing the struggle at home and abroad for peace and friendship with all of the world's people, for an end to colonialism, for full citizenship for Negro Americans, for a world in which art and culture may abound. . . ."

25. The transcript of the hearing is in RA. For Manning Johnson's previous testimony on PR, see p. 359. It was referred to during the hearing, and Boudin angrily protested the tainted source (Boudin to Frances Knight, July 29, 1957, RA).

26. Transcript of the hearing, RA; Essie's remark is in an article she wrote about the day, "Paul Robeson Goes to Washington," ms., RA.

27. Transcript of the hearing, RA. In the summer of 1955 Sen. Eastland, as chair of a Senate Judiciary subcommittee, had issued subpoenas to some three dozen journalists, two dozen of whom were current or former staff members of *The New York Times,* for hearings on the alleged influence of the CPUSA on U.S. newspapers. The *Times* management threatened to fire any employee pleading the Fifth Amendment, substituting private confessionals within the *Times'* own "family." For a history of the episode, see James Aronson, *The Press and the Cold War* (Bobbs-Merrill, 1970) and his "The Fifth Remembered," *The Nation,* Dec. 27, 1986–Jan. 3, 1987.

28. Transcript of the hearing, RA.

29. Transcript of the hearing, RA; phone interviews with Milton Friedman, Aug. 27, Nov. 29, 1982.

30. Washington *Evening Star,* June 12, 1956; New York *Amsterdam News,* June 13, 1956; *Daily Worker,* June 13, 1956; *The Afro-American,* June 23, 1956; Pittsburgh *Courier,* June 23, 1956.

31. FBI New York 100-25857-2729 (Davis phone call); Davis to PR, June 24, 1956, RA; Du Bois to PR, June 30, 1956, U.Mass.: Du Bois; Mary Helen Jones to PR, June 14, 1956; Aronson to PR, June 21, 1956; Williams to PR, June 14, 1956—all in RA; *The Afro-American,* June 16, 1956; San Francisco *Sun Reporter,* June 23, 1956; Pittsburgh *Courier,* July 7, 1956. Robeson was especially grateful for the sympathetic story Alice A. Dunnigan filed with the Associated Negro Press (PR and ER to Claude Barnett, June 20, 1956; Barnett to Dunnigan, June 16, 1956; Barnett to PR, June 27, 1956—all in CHS: Barnett). The most scathing negative voice in the black press was, predictably, that of George S. Schuyler (Pittsburgh *Courier,* June 23, 1956), a voice echoed more frequently in the white press (e.g., the New York *Journal-American,* June 13, 1956: "Robeson's performance was a combination of tirade and weaseling evasion"). On the other hand, Edward P. Morgan, a staunch anti-Communist, chided HUAC in his ABC broadcast of June 14, 1956, for having behaved "with all the punitive bravery of a school principal making a public spectacle of thrashing an ornery child" (transcript of his broadcast, RA).

32. The New Jersey visit is detailed in FBI Main 100-12304-377X; ER to Rockmore, Aug. 5, 1956, RA; FBI New York 100-25857-2815; *Daily Worker*, Oct. 12, 1956 (Newark). It was a sign of the changing times that Rep. James Tumulty, who had been a strong supporter of Sen. Joseph McCarthy, spoke publicly in favor of PR's right to sing at Newark (*Daily People's World*, Oct. 16, 1956). During the visit to New Jersey, Robeson felt well enough to give an interview to the local paper (Orange *Transcript*, Aug. 2, 1956), in which he once more declared himself "optimistic about the future." At this same time, when Ernest Thompson was expressing dismay over how the CP had misused Robeson, an FBI agent reported that an unidentified informant claiming acquaintance with PR had declared that during a conversation PR had said "he realizes now that the CP is not 'following through' on trying to break the interracial barrier which exists between the negroes and white people," though he continued to believe "that the CP was sincerely interested in tearing down the interracial barrier" (FBI New York 100-25857-2775). But if Robeson had indeed expressed such doubts, they did not represent any generalized disillusion with socialism. In a lengthy handwritten ms. (undated [July 1956?]) in RA, in which he returned to the basic themes of his 1930s notes on African culture, he responded to a *New York Times* article of July 15, 1956, by Stuart Preston on African sculpture, first by taking issue with Preston for having asserted that African art had "nothing in common" with art in the West, despite its manifest influence on artists like Picasso; and then going on to hail "The triumphant emergence of new powers and of revolutionary socialism in Asia," a development that revealed "that the Western led and capitalist phase of modern industrial civilization is rapidly giving way to an Eastern-led and Socialist phase. . . ."

33. Washington *Post*, Nov. 8, 1956.

34. *The New York Times*, New York *Post*, New York *Daily Mirror*, New York *Herald Tribune*, New York *Journal-American*, New York *Daily News*—all Nov. 14, 1956; FBI Main 100-12304-393, FBI New

York 100-25857-2821; Foster to PR, Nov. 27, 1956, RA. It was in an interview with *The Afro-American* three days later (Nov. 17, 1956) that Robeson referred to the "somebody" at work. The ms. of his prepared remarks to the meeting made only one possible and indirect reference to Hungary: referring to the Soviet Union, he said, ". . . you have leaped forward time and again when civilization was in danger." For comparable views on Hungary from PR's friend Pettis Perry ("it is an attempt to bring back into Hungary a reactionary regime"), see Perry to Rose Perry, Nov. 20, Dec. 25, 1956, Perry Papers: NYPL/Schm.

35. Pittsburgh *Courier*, Jan. 12, 1957; San Francisco *Sun Reporter*, Jan. 5, 1957.

36. *The Afro-American*, Nov. 17, 1956. According to Essie (ER to George Murphy, Jr., Nov. 23, 1956, MSRC: Murphy), PR was "immensely pleased" with the *Afro* interview, largely the work of George B. Murphy, Jr.

37. *The Afro-American*, Nov. 17, 1956. The Patterson quote is from a letter he wrote protesting the Supreme Court decision, as printed in both the Pittsburgh *Courier*, Dec. 1, 1956, and *The Afro-American*, Nov. 24, 1956. *The New York Times*, Nov. 6, 1956, and the *National Guardian*, Nov. 19, 1956, contain accounts of the Supreme Court decision against Robeson.

Following Judge Mathews's Aug. 1955 ruling against Robeson in the passport case, William Patterson had taken charge of trying to raise additional support in the States, while a number of groups overseas, and particularly in England, had redoubled their efforts in PR's behalf. Patterson's correspondence in regard to the passport fight is in NYPL/Schm: PR. RA contains the large number of invitations from overseas. The notable activity in PR's behalf in Britain included an appeal sent directly to President Eisenhower from twenty-five prominent musicians (Sir Adrian Boult, Rutland Boughton, Humphrey Searles, Alan Rausthorne, Lennox Berkeley, etc.), a petition from Scotland with over three thousand signatures (including a dozen MPs), protests in the press (for example, Tom Driberg in *Reynolds News*), and a Let

Paul Robeson Sing Rally in Manchester addressed by Manchester MPs Will Griffiths and Konni Zilliacus; Liberal barrister Vaughan Davis; Foundry Workers Union President and member of the Labour Party National Executive R.A. Cassasola; and black former British middleweight boxing champion Len Johnson (*Daily Worker,* Feb. 22, 1956; *National Guardian,* March 12, 26, 1956). Cedric Belfrage, coeditor of the *Guardian,* who had been deported from the States, wrote that "Among British workers the fight to liberate Robeson is taking on a new emphasis, as the central symbolic expression of their concern over American thought-control" (*Guardian,* Sept. 26, 1955); also, interview with Belfrage, May 29, 1984. For a time Diana and Franz Loesser played a particularly prominent role in organizing the National Paul Robeson Committee in London (Loesser to PR, May 31, Oct. 20, 1956; Loesser to ER, Oct. 27, 1956; Belfrage to PR, June 3, 1956—all in RA; interview with Diana Loesser, July 29, 1986). The success of a large rally the Loessers organized in Manchester in Dec. 1956, which included a showing of *The Proud*

Valley and a concert by the Welsh Miners' Choir, is described in Loesser to ER and PR, Dec. 18, 1956, and Marie Seton to PR, Dec. 7, 1956 (Seton attended), RA. USIA/London reported to USIA/Washington on the "renewed attention" being given the Robeson passport case in Britain. The report stressed that, although the case had long been "exploited at intervals by the Communist press in Britain," currently numerous non-Communists were adding their voices, including members of "the Bevanite wing" of the Labour Party (FBI Main 100-12304-358). Summarizing the contrasting response to the passport fight from overseas and at home, Patterson wrote that the Europeans had "responded magnificently," but the minimal reaction at home had been emblematic of the general American failure to fight "to safeguard constitutional liberties" (Patterson to Sylvia Schwartz, May 4, 1956, NYPL/Schm: CRC). A comparable view, citing the failure of the left to put up a fight for PR, is in James W. Ford to PR (citing Ferdinand Smith's opinion to that effect), Oct. 27, 1956, RA.

CHAPTER 22   RESURGENCE (*1957–1958*)

1. The classic account is Richard Kluger, *Simple Justice: The History of "Brown v. Board of Education": Black America's Struggle for Equality* (Knopf, 1976). Harvard Sitkoff's *The Struggle for Black Equality, 1954–1980* (Hill and Wang, 1981) is a reliable shorter summary.

2. Los Angeles *Herald Dispatch,* July 4, 1957 (King). Essie described the Montgomery bus boycott as "magnificent" and hailed the "new young brilliant courageous Negro leaders" who had emerged in an article for the Czechoslovak News Agency, Feb. 11, 1957 (ms. in RA). She expressed much the same sentiments in her Sept. 19, 1957, article for *The Afro-American,* "Passive, Massive Resistance" (ms. in RA). PR's statement on Little Rock, dated Sept. 12, 1957, is in RA. *The Afro-American* carried it in the issue of Sept. 21, 1957; a brief summary appeared

in the New York *Amsterdam News* that same day.

3. Phone interview with Anne Braden, May 5, 1985; FBI New York SAC to Hoover, Dec. 19, 1957–Jan. 8, 1958, FBI New York 100-25857-3186. Oscar Brown, Jr., puts it this way: "He stayed off on this left tangent. . . . He had gone so far out on that limb, there was no way he could get back, psychologically even" (interview, Dec. 27, 1986).

4. ER to Murphy, Easter Sunday 1957, MSRC: Murphy. In a private letter Essie referred to the Prayer Pilgrimage as "one of the most important events of our time here in this country" (ER to Zamiatin, May 25, 1957, RA). The FBI knew of the Robesons' presence in Washington for the Pilgrimage (FBI New York 100-25857-2917). PR subsequently recalled that during the Pilgrimage, "Many

Negroes came to me and said, 'Paul, we might not be on these steps [of the Lincoln Memorial] today, but for certain of the things you have stood by and fought for your people' " (transcript of passport hearings, May 29, 1957, RA). The assertion that Robeson was testing the waters for an NAACP takeover was ascribed to Newell Johnson, PR's public-relations manager during his 1957 California trip (SA, San Francisco, to N.Y., Dec. 19, 1957; then N.Y. to Hoover, Jan. 8, 1958, FBI New York 100-25857-3186); FBI New York 100-25857-3204, also 3210 (CPUSA).

5. He also began work on a never-to-be-completed book on his musical theories (ER to Diana Loesser, March 8, 1957, PR Archiv, GDR). PR's notes, Aug.-Sept. 1957, RA, attest to his continuing absorption in pentatonic musical theory, and the surrounding scholarship on the subject. In a set of notes entitled "re: article by A. Medvedev on Aram Khachaturyan, *USSR* (No. 12)," Robeson gave a succinct version of his research design: " . . . there is a world body, a universal body of basic folk themes from which all folk music is derived, and is directly or indirectly related. Interested as I am in the universality of mankind—in the fundamental relationship of all peoples to one another—this idea of a universal body of folk music intrigued me, and I pursued it along many fascinating paths. Confirmation came from many diverse sources. . . ."

6. Los Angeles *Tribune*, July 3, 1957; ER to George Murphy, Jr., May 30 (Cayton), Aug. 26, 1957, MSRC: Murphy. In the latter letter, ER characterized the Lomax article as "a dog" and claimed she had told Paul, "That'll learn you to keep your big mouth shut long enough for some other people to get in a few words edgewise." She also claimed that "Paul laughed when I suggested that, and admitted it was true." Something of the same ramblingly immodest tone had characterized PR's remarks during the May 29, 1957, hearing on his passport application in Washington; he described himself as "one of the great artists of the contemporary period" and referred to his recent

recording as "some of the greatest singing I have done in the last 20 years" (transcript in RA). The possibility that Robeson may have experienced recurrent emotional trouble in California is hinted at in a letter from ER to Cedric Belfrage (May 30, 1957, RA) just before he left on the trip: "He is beginning to feel very tired, so we are going to curtail all his activities. When he returns from the coast, we will try to persuade him to take a long holiday, and get some real rest and relaxation." She expressed the same doubts to the radical clergyman Rev. Stephen H. Fritchman, one of PR's hosts in L.A.: "I don't want him tied up to a wearing program even before he starts out. I have no idea whether he will be able to stand up to it or not" (May 2, 1957, RA).

Carlton Goodlett, the left-wing black physician and publisher in San Francisco, credits Rev. F. D. Haynes of the Third Baptist Church (the largest black church in San Francisco) for PR's breakthrough singing engagement. Following that concert, the Baptist Ministers Union of Alameda County obtained the use of the Oakland Municipal Auditorium from the Oakland City Council for a Robeson concert—the first time since 1952 that a civic building had been made available to him. There was vigorous protest from right-wing groups, but the black community "developed a counterforce" and the City Council held firm. Despite torrents of rain on the day of the concert, the auditorium was filled to overflowing one hour before PR's performance began. The Oakland police, Alameda County sheriff, and federal officers took down the license-plate numbers of those parked outside (Carlton Goodlett, ms. reminiscences of PR, in the PR Archiv, GDR). In L.A., Robeson gave two concerts at the progressive First Unitarian Church (Stephen H. Fritchman was its minister) to help the church defray the costs of raising additional tax monies resulting from its refusal to abide by California loyalty oaths. He was also sponsored in L.A. by the Committee for Protection of the Foreign Born, on the Attorney General's "subversive" list, and by the Los Angeles Committee to Secure

Justice for Morton Sobell, in prison on Alcatraz Island as a result of the Rosenberg case. While in L.A., PR stayed with black friends, Frankie and George Sims, both active in the L.A. National Negro Labor Council, and was guest of honor at a private dinner at the home of Dalton Trumbo, the blacklisted screenwriter. The Los Angeles *Herald Dispatch* (July 4, 1957) described him editorially as "the man best fitted, by virtue of sincerity, integrity and courage, to give leadership to the Negro people in this day"—though at the same time it expressed the hope that he had "learned a lesson" about the "left progressives" he had surrounded himself with for fifteen to twenty years and who had "failed to give him the proper support"; they had "isolated [him] from his own people," so that the "Negro masses (had also) failed to rise to support him because they were unfamiliar with his activities." This affirmation from the black community, however tempered, gave PR a real boost: "a very happy experience," is how ER described it (ER to Rev. Riley, Aug. 6, 1957, RA). Details of PR's activities and the concert reviews are in: Los Angeles *Herald Dispatch*, July 4, 1957; California *Jewish Voice*, June 21, 1957; *People's World*, June 29, Aug. 3, 10, 1957; California *Eagle*, July 4, 1957; San Francisco *Sun Reporter*, July 20, Aug. 31, 1957; FBI Main 100-12304-408, FBI New York 100-25857-2965, 3021.

7. Statements of support from many people were published in a pamphlet, *Let Robeson Sing*, put out by the London Robeson Committee (a copy is in RA). Flora Robson and J. Dover Wilson wrote supporting letters to the London *Times* (May 4, 10, 1957). Driberg's column is in *Reynolds News*, May 12, 1957. The British Equity resolution and the debate surrounding it are described in the Manchester *Guardian*, April 20, 1957, and the London *Times*, April 29, 1957. The actor Adolphe Menjou told the New York columnist Hy Gardner he was "incensed" at British Equity (*Herald Tribune*, May 14, 1957). According to Cedric Belfrage (interview, May 29, 1984), Laurence Olivier was one of the few in England to refuse to lend his name. PR also valued an invitation to appear at the International

Music Festival Prague Spring (Vilein Pospisil to PR, Jan. 25, 1957; PR to Pospisil, March 16, 1957, RA).

8. The two fullest accounts are Cedric Belfrage's article in the *National Guardian*, May 27, 1957, and the detailed report he wrote ER, May 27, 1957, RA. Additional details are in Belfrage to ER, May 1, 10, 20, 28, 30, 31, 1957; ER to Belfrage, May 13, 30, June 5, 17, 1957—all in RA.

9. Belfrage to ER, May 27, 1957, RA; Manchester *Guardian*, May 28, 1957; ER to Belfrage, May 30, June 5, 1957, RA. In his May 27 letter Belfrage reported that "One thing that was particularly good was the number of Negroes in the concert audience—I should think at least 150. We also had mainly African and West Indian students as ushers." Taking a page from Belfrage's book, the South Wales miners arranged for a transatlantic transmission for the Eisteddfod in Oct. 1957 (Dilwyn Jones to PR, Oct. 25, 1957; Paynter and Evans to PR, October 7, 1957, RA).

10. Boudin to PR, with enclosed copies of correspondence with the Passport Division, Jan. 22, Feb. 19, March 15, May 10, 1957, RA; interview with Boudin, July 14, 1982; Boudin passport-case files, courtesy of Boudin.

11. The full transcript of the hearing is in FBI New York 100-25857-1A88; FBI Main 100-12304-403 ("wash out").

12. ER to Mr. Evans, Aug. 29, 1957 (perjury fear); Knight (Passport Division) to PR, Aug. 9, 1957; Boudin to PR, Aug. 13, 1957. FBI Main 100-12304-427 (Trinidad). The Jagans had met and corresponded with the Robesons (e.g., Janet Jagan to ER, Oct. 2, 1957, RA).

13. Shaw to PR, Oct. 16, 1957, RA. Shaw had first sounded out PR about the possibilities of *Pericles* in Jan. 1957 (ER to Paul Endicott, Jan. 15, 1957, RA); the formal invitation and announcements ten months later were aimed at public relations. Boudin to PR, Nov. 7, 1957; Boudin to John Abt (who had joined as PR's counsel; Abt was known as the lawyer for the CPUSA), Dec. 6, 1957, enclosing draft letter to Frances G. Knight; Boudin to Knight, Dec. 10, 1957—all in RA.

14. ER to Shaw, Nov. 15, 1957; ER and PR to Shaw, Nov. 26, 1957; Shaw to

ER and PR, Nov. 22, 1957; Tony Richardson to PR, three notes, n.d.—all in RA.

15. *Daily Herald,* Jan. 15, 1958. Harold Davison to PR, Jan. 14, 31, 1958; Richardson to ER and PR, n.d.; Frances G. Knight to Boudin, Jan. 17, 1958; Boudin to Loy Henderson, Jan. 31, 1958; Boudin to PR, Feb. 3, 19, 1958; Boudin to ER, Feb. 7, 25, 1958; ER to Richardson, Feb. 1, 1958—all in RA. *Daily Express,* Jan. 31, 1958; see pp. 233–34 for the earlier incidents referred to. Less predictably, the Oxford *Mail* wrote (Jan. 30, 1958), "He has made some most insulting remarks about Britain, but obviously does not mind taking British money"; but the *Mail* did not want to keep him out of Britain—to do that "would be to punish a man for his opinions."

16. ER to Shaw, Feb. 22, 1958; Shaw to ER, March 8, 1958, RA. Edric Connor, the West Indian singer and actor, replaced Robeson as Gower, thereby becoming the first black to appear in a Shakespeare season at Stratford. According to the London *Daily Herald* (July 8, 1958), PR had suggested Connor as a replacement. For more on Robeson and Connor, see note 12, p. 686; note 48, p. 750.

17. FBI New York 100-25857-2921 ("losing courage"), 2927 ("supers"), 3184 (1957 activities); FBI Main 100-12304-428 (1957 activities); ms. of PR's Carnegie Hall speech, Nov. 10, 1957, RA; PR's many New Year's Day greetings are in RA; the Albanian one is dated Feb. 25, 1958.

18. ER to Richardson, Feb. 1, 1958; Pollard to ER and PR, Jan. 29, 1958; Daisy Bates to PR, Jan. 24, 1958; ER to Bates, Feb. 22, 1958; Archie Moore to PR, Jan. 26, 1958, telegram April 5, 1958—all in RA. Another telegram from Archie Moore to PR, dated Dec. 31, 1958, reads: "One punch was in your behalf. I'm sure you understand me" (RA).

19. Sacramento *Union,* Oct. 27, 1957; San Francisco *Chronicle,* Feb. 5, 1958; Oregon *Journal* and *The Oregonian,* March 17, 1958. Pleased though he was to have renewed requests for his appearance, PR turned down a tentative invitation for a concert at the Metropolitan A.M.E. Church in Washington, D.C., un-

less (in ER's paraphrase) it "should be backed by the NEGRO COMMUNITY, not just one church, in order to insure that the concert will be properly supported by a wide section of the community, and not become involved in fears and rivalries and uncertainties of individuals or small groups" (George Murphy, Jr., to ER, Feb. 22, 1958; ER to GM, Jr., Feb. 28, 1958, MSRC: Murphy).

20. FBI Main 100-12304-465, 501, 511, 515.

21. FBI Main 100-12304-465 (Perry), 511 (left prominence). Hoover decided not to survey PR's residence for "installation of a tesur," since his continuing travels would prevent "sufficient day-to-day coverage" of his activities (FBI Main 100-12304-501, May 28, 1958). Interview with Rose Perry, April 27, 1982; ER to Pettis Perry, Nov. 16, 1957, NYPL/Schm: Perry Papers. When SAC, New York, later recommended to Hoover that PR "be removed from the Key Figure list of the NYO" (FBI Main 100-12304-545, Oct. 17, 1958), Hoover replied that "The Bureau does not concur with your recommendation. . . . Robeson continues to be of sufficient importance and potential dangerousness from an internal security standpoint to require his immediate apprehension in the event of an emergency. . . . Robeson's current activities and freedom to travel enhance his value to the communist movement. It is, therefore, felt that his potential dangerousness to the internal security of the United States is increased" (Hoover to SAC, New York, Oct. 28, 1958, FBI Main 100-12304-545). PR, Jr., ms. comments (accident). For more on the St. Louis and Los Angeles incidents, see pp. 317 and 431.

22. Oakland *Tribune,* Feb. 10, 1958 ("velvety"); San Francisco *Chronicle,* Feb. 10, 1958 ("greatest basso"); FBI New York 100-25857-3502; FBI Main 100-12304-515 (effective). PR billed his 1958 concerts as "informal recitals," combining songs with his reflections on "the origins of, and relations between, folk music"—meaning theories on the pentatonic scale (PR press release, RA). Geri Branton (interview, April 2, 1982 [PR, Jr., participating]) confirmed PR's enthusi-

astic reception in the black community.

23. Pittsburgh *Courier*, April 12, 19, 28, 1958. The FBI kept fully posted on the events in Pittsburgh (FBI Main 100-12304-512). Rosalie to Marian Forsythe, April 22, 1958, courtesy of Paulina Forsythe.

24. ER to Burroughs, March 22, 1958; ER to Bennett, March 22, 1958; ER to Ishmael Flory, March 23, 1958—all in RA; interview with Oscar Brown, Sr., July 2, 1986. By the time of the Alpha Phi Alpha national convention the following year, Ishmael Flory, who attended, found "attitudes towards both Du Bois and Robeson very high, very high" (interviews with Flory, July 1–2, 1986).

25. Interview with Margaret Burroughs, July 1, 1986; interview with Julia Lorchard, July 2, 1986. Mrs. Lorchard has recently (1986) given her husband's papers to Du Sable Museum in Chicago, and I found them a rich source. Also useful was a 1969 tape Studs Terkel played for me made with various prominent blacks in the Chicago area, including Margaret Burroughs (for a full description of the tape, see note 7, p. 577.

26. Interview with Sam Parks, Dec. 27, 1986, plus follow-up phone discussion, Dec. 30, 1986.

27. Ibid.

28. Interviews with Ishmael Flory, July 1–2, 1986; interview with Oscar Brown, Sr., July 2, 1986; *Jet*, April 17, 1958; Murphy to ER, April 10, 1958, RA; MacDonald, *Black and White TV*, pp. 56–57 (local TV). According to Flory, the establishment of the Afro-American Heritage Association was the direct result of PR's 1958 visit to Chicago. A number of people had asked Robeson what they could do to help, and he had suggested they direct their energies toward disseminating information about the Afro-American past. Flory described the Heritage Association as "an effort to build local heritage associations for the purpose of stressing the Negro's past history in communities of Negro population of 2000 or over" (Flory to Pettis Perry, May 30, 1958, NYPL/Schm: Perry Papers).

29. The quotations in this and the following paragraph are from PR, *Stand*, pp. 1–2, 38–40. The 1958 edition of *Here*

I Stand was issued by Othello Associates and was dedicated to ER (a rather impersonal acknowledgment of her political labors). Angus Cameron, the radical editor at Knopf who had known PR in the Progressive movement, had been trying since the 1940s to get him to write an autobiography; he believes PR did not submit *Here I Stand* to him for possible publication because he wanted to keep "full control" in his own hands (interview with Cameron, July 15, 1986). The 1971 edition (Beacon Press) contains an informative preface by Lloyd L. Brown about the book's initial reception and a brief Afterword (dated Aug. 28, 1964) by PR in which he takes pleasure in noting recent "transformations" that had changed his 1958 emphasis on the "power of Negro action" from "an idea into a reality that is manifesting itself throughout our land. The concept of mass militancy, of mass action, is no longer deemed 'too radical' in Negro life." There was open displeasure among some in the CPUSA over PR's emphasis in *Here I Stand* on the need for blacks themselves—rather than the Party—to serve as the vanguard in the black struggle.

30. *Stand*, pp. 98–99, 103.

31. *The Afro-American*, Feb. 22, March 15, May 3, 1958; Pittsburgh *Courier*, Feb. 22, March 29, 1958; Chicago *Crusader*, March 8, 1958; *Herald Dispatch*, May 8, 1958; *The Crisis*, March 1958; "Summary Financial Statement" as of May 31, 1959, RA. Continuing his campaign to mend fences, PR sent an inscribed copy of the book to Ralph Bunche, who acknowledged it politely (Bunche to PR, Feb. 14, 1958, RA). The FBI also took an interest in the book, following its publication history and sales closely (FBI New York 100-25857-3266). In a bugged conversation between Lloyd Brown and Ben Davis, FBI SAC New York reported to J. Edgar Hoover (Sept. 15, 1958, FBI Main 100-12304-541) that Brown felt a recent speech by A. Philip Randolph was "right out of the book on the subject of white allies" and that "even" Adam Clayton Powell was "red-baiting less and less"; Davis responded with the assertion that *Here I Stand* "is going to be like Tom

Paine's *Common Sense* as far as Negroes are concerned." *The Afro-American* serialized *Here I Stand* in nine weekly installments in the spring of 1958, as arranged for by George Murphy, Jr. (GM, Jr., to ER, Dec. 20, 1957, Jan. 13, 1958; GM, Jr., to Carl Murphy, Dec. 20, 1957, MSRC: Murphy).

32. *Ebony*, Oct. 1957; transcript of the Oct. 2, 1957, NBC program is in RA. In response to a question about whether Robeson was ill, Rowan said, "I noticed no signs of physical illness when I interviewed him." George Murphy, Jr., to ER, n.d. (1957); in a letter to his brother Carl, Murphy characterized the Rowan piece more moderately (GM, Jr., to CM, Sept. 30, 1957, MSRC: Murphy). In a long letter to *Ebony*, Essie expressed gratification that "the Negro press has taken the initiative in raising the Curtain of Silence with which official America has tried for seven years to cut Paul Robeson off from the American public" (ER to *Ebony*, Sept. 16, 1957, RA).

33. ER to Peggy Middleton and Cedric Belfrage, Feb. 5, 1958, RA; ER to George Murphy, Jr., Feb. 28, 1958, MSRC: Murphy. *Equity*, June 1958, has selections from the debate over the Robeson resolution; the resolution was not, however, passed by the Equity Council, to which it was automatically sent (*The New York Times*, New York *Herald Tribune*, April 1, 10, 1958). Nat Hentoff sat in on one of the Vanguard recording sessions and wrote a piece about it (*The Reporter*, April 17, 1958) in which he quoted the "grinning" president of Vanguard, Maynard Solomon, as saying, "It's a real schmaltzy album."

34. The correspondence between Peggy Middleton and Essie, in RA, is full of details of the birthday celebrations; additionally, Middleton's correspondence with "Schlicting" (G. F. Alexan) in the GDR, copies of which are in RA, and Alexan's with PR, are particularly rich in information about the East European celebrations. Also useful has been Akira Iwasaki to PR, March 16, 1958; ER to Iwasaki, March 30, 1958; L. Kislova to PR, April 19, 1958—all in RA; FBI Main 100-12304-490 (Port-au-Prince). RA also has a bulky collection of messages of greeting

to PR from around the world, including one from Soong Ching-ling (Madame Sun Yat-sen), March 31, 1958. Earl Robinson (interview, Aug. 1986) said the GDR paid him ten thousand dollars to make the film on Robeson. PR himself was in Chicago on the actual day of his birthday and celebrated at a public party for him in the Masonic Temple.

35. A copy of Nehru's widely publicized statement is in RA, dated March 6, 1958. *The New York Times* announced it on March 21, then in its edition of April 9 headlined "Nehru Soft Pedals Words on Robeson." The New York *Post*, among other publications, characterized the Indian celebration as run by "Indian Communists" (March 25, 1958), and *Blitz* (London) reported the diplomatic flurry (April 12, 1958).

36. The full packet of Indian press clippings and pertinent State Department documents are in RA and too numerous to cite. The critical documents are: Bunker telegram to Dulles, March 26, 1958; Chargé Turner to State, telegram, March 20, 1958; Department of State memoir of talk with Mehta, March 21, 1958; Bunker to Dulles, telegram, March 22, 1958; Dulles to Bunker, telegram, March 24, 1958. A stirring defense of PR by Chagla is in *Blitz*, April 19, 1958.

37. ER to Nehru, March 31, 1958; ER to Indira Gandhi, March 31, 1958 (RA). Details on the celebrations in India are in the Delhi *Times of India*, May 10, 1958; The Hindustan *Times*, April 7, 1958; *National Herald*, April 10, 1958; The Hindu *Weekly Review*, April 14, 1958. Turner reported to Dulles that Alub D. Gorwala had suggested to him that "Nehru's backing this movement stems from Lady Mountbatten who is admirer of Robeson" (telegram, March 21, 1958, 791.-001/3-2058); for the earlier contact between Mountbatten and PR, see pp. 160–61. In an untaped interview granted me, PR, Jr., and Marilyn Robeson in Aug. 1982, Indira Gandhi expressed anger at the attempted interference of the American authorities in the celebration and confirmed that her father, for diplomatic reasons, had stayed aloof from the detailed planning after issuing his initial statement. Late in her life Indira Gandhi

described PR as "a remarkable man. It is tragic that his country tried to denigrate and belittle him" (Gandhi to Marie Seton, Aug. 22, 1982, courtesy of Seton).

38. *The Afro-American,* May 17, 1958; *National Guardian,* May 19, 1958; New York *World-Telegram,* May 10, 1958 ("lost glow"); New York *Herald Tribune, The New York Times,* May 10, 1958; New York *Post,* May 11, 1958; New York *Amsterdam News,* May 17, 1958; *Newsweek* (the sourest review), May 19, 1958; *DownBeat,* May 29, 1958 ("vigor"); *The Saturday Review,* May 24, 1958. The latter review, by the respected Irving Kolodin, chided PR for announcing the "basic musicological truth" about the affinity between the different folk musics of the world as if it was "a revelation"— aided by his "histrionic talent for vivifying a commonplace by an inflection of speech, a thrust of head...." The FBI tapped a phone conversation with Ben Davis in which PR spoke of "new vistas" (FBI Main 100-12304-? [illegible], May 26, 1958). The second concert is described in an interview with Marvel Cook (who helped distribute the tickets) by Mike Wallington and Howard Johnson for their 1986 BBC program on Robeson (tapes courtesy of Wallington and Johnson); interview with Edith Tiger, June 17, 1985. The tape of the concert at Mother A.M.E. Zion is in RA. George Murphy, Jr., played a key role in arranging the A.M.E. Zion concert (GM, Jr., to Ben Robeson, March 3, 1958, MSRC: Murphy).

39. FBI Main 100-12304-516, 524; ER to Paul Endicott, June 19, 1958, RA; *Daily Worker,* June 28, 1958; interview with Leonard Boudin, July 14, 1982; *New York Times,* June 17, 27, 1958; *National Guardian,* June 23, 1958; *The Afro-American,* May 31, 1958; ER to Glen Byam Shaw, June 30, 1958, RA. Corliss Lamont, who, unlike PR, had been at liberty to travel in the Western Hemisphere, got his passport back at the same time. Originally passports had been denied both men on the ground that their travel was contrary to the "best interests" of the nation. Later the ground was shifted to stress their refusal to sign "non-Communist" affidavits, a rationale entirely removed as a result of the court's denial

that the State Department had a right to inquire into the political beliefs or associations of those applying for passports. The court did not, however, give a definitive ruling on the constitutional question of whether *Congress* had the right to withhold passports on the basis of an applicant's politics. As a result, there was an immediate move, spearheaded by President Eisenhower himself, to pass explicit enabling legislation. On July 7, 1958, Eisenhower asked Congress to give the government "clear statutory authority" to refuse passports to known Communists and to those subject to CP domination, claiming it was "essential" that the Secretary of State have such authority to maintain "national security." Eisenhower stressed the "urgency" of the matter: "each day and week that passes without it exposes us to great danger." A bill embodying the President's wishes was immediately introduced in both the House and the Senate. (*The New York Times* came out editorially against such a bill [July 8, 9, 1958]; the New York *Herald-Tribune* came out for it [June 18, July 9, 1958].) Eisenhower's call for speed prompted a sardonic editorial in the Washington edition of *The Afro-American* (July 12, 1958): he "proved again this week that his advocacy of patience is a commodity which he reserves especially for a minority clamoring for civil rights. . . . Eisenhower does not think that it is important to rush matters where the interests of colored citizens are concerned. . . ."

40. Shaw telegram to PR, June 28, 1958; Patrick O'Donovan to PR, June 28, 1958 *(The Observer);* Neruda to PR, July 1958; Alexan to Middleton, July 6, 1958; Iwasaki to PR, July 2, 1958; ER to Shaw, June 30, 1958; ER to Indira Gandhi, June 30, 1958—all in RA. Multiple interviews with Freda Diamond ("applause"). Not wanting to cause Nehru any political embarrassment, ER wrote Indira Gandhi, in regard to a visit to India, "You are to be absolutely frank with me, because we want to become, wherever it is possible, a UNIFYING force, not in any way a divisive or controversial force. We women have to by pass diplomatic nonsense and be practical." After the Robesons were set-

tled in London in July, Indira Gandhi arrived in England for a visit and asked Essie to meet her at the airport and "had a good talk"; it was apparently at that time that Mrs. Gandhi okayed a visit to India (ER to Freda Diamond, July 22–27, 1958, RA). To a Soviet friend (Mrs. Kislova), ER wrote (June 30, 1958, RA) that Paul thought probably the first thing he would want to do on a visit to the Soviet Union would be "something with the Soviet children, who have sent him so many letters of love and encouragement. . . ."

According to an FBI report—based apparently on a phone tap—PR called the passport decision "an important political victory" and called the offers coming in from overseas "fantastic" (FBI New York 100-25857-3842).

41. Interview with James Aronson, May 31, 1983.

42. Essie's two pages of notes are in RA.

43. *Daily Mail*, June 28, 1958; Pittsburgh *Courier*, July 5, 1958; *World-Telegram and Sun*, July 9, 1958 (Ruark).

CHAPTER 23   RETURN TO EUROPE (1958–1960)

1. Interviews with Cedric Belfrage (May 19, 1984) and Harry Francis (Aug. 1982); *National Guardian*, July 21, 1958; West Indian *Gazette*, Aug. 1958; *Sunday Times*, July 13, 1958; *News Chronicle*, July 12, 1958; *Reynolds News*, July 13, 1958; *Daily Mail*, July 12, 1958; *Daily Sketch*, July 12, 1958. In its welcoming issue of July 11, 1958, the *Daily Worker* printed greetings to PR from, among others, the bandleader Johnny Dankworth, the actor Bernard Miles, and Dame Sybil Thorndike ("We welcome him to England with all our hearts and wish him a triumphal success once more").

2. *Daily Express*, July 6, 1958; *News Chronicle*, July 12, 1958 ("most remarkable"); *Daily Sketch*, July 12, 1958 ("royal personage"); *Reynolds News*, July 13, 1958 (Driberg); New York *Herald Tribune*, July 14, 1958; interviews with Cedric Belfrage (May 29, 1984) and Harry Francis (Aug. 1982). Both dailies quoted Robeson as making the same later statement, thereby increasing the likelihood that it was reported accurately (Edinburgh *Evening News*, *The Bulletin*, both Nov. 10, 1958). Bernard Levin, the highly regarded critic, chided PR for constantly saying people of color were "walking in freedom" in the Soviet Union: "In the Soviet Union no man, whatever his colour, can walk or carry out his task freely" (*The Spectator*, Aug. 29, 1958).

3. James Aronson, "Notes on a Reunion," *National Guardian*, Aug. 25, 1958; interview with Aronson, May 31, 1983.

4. A typed schedule of PR's appearances is in RA; the many letters of invitation from organizations, ambassadors, and friends are also in RA. The *Daily Telegraph* (July 14, 1958) reported that PR's ITV fee was "believed to be the largest ever paid to an American performer for three appearances." The Nigerian dinner is described in a report from AmConGen, Lagos, to State Department, July 30, 1958. Nigerian Premier Azikiwe himself wrote PR (Aug. 23, 1958, RA) to welcome him to London.

5. PR, Jr., interview with Bruno Raikin, Sept. 8, 1982; interview with Alan Bush (PR, Jr., participating), Sept. 3, 1982; ER to Brown, Aug. 6, 1958; ER (with appended PR note) to Freda Diamond, July 22–27, 1958, RA; London *Times*, July 28, 1958; also *Variety*, Aug. 6, 1958; *Sunday Dispatch*, July 27, 1958; *The Stage*, July 31, 1958. Soon after his television debut, PR sang at the National Eisteddfod of Wales. Introduced by Aneurin Bevan and his wife, Jennie Lee, Robeson was given a rousing, heartwarming reception by the miners and their families. Though the reunion was emotional, Rachel Thomas, who had appeared with him in *The Proud Valley*, did not think he was in particularly good voice (Sterner interview with Thomas).

6. Larry Brown had apparently answered the call to London reluctantly (Rockmore to LB, Aug. 4, 8, Sept. 17, 1958; Marie Dokens to LB, Aug. 6, 1958, NYPL/Schm: Brown), and once he arrived was apparently as nervous about the concert as PR (ER to Lloyd Brown,

Aug. 6, 1958, RA). While in London, Brown negotiated with Dennis Dobson for a "Paul Robeson Song Book," which never saw print, though the projected table of contents can be found in Dobson to Brown, Aug. 14, 1958, NYPL/Schm: Brown. LB stayed with the Robesons for a while when he first arrived in London. PR, Jr., interview with Raikin, Sept. 8, 1982; *Telegraph and Morning Post, News Chronicle,* London *Times, Evening News, Daily Mail*—all Aug. 11, 1958; *News Chronicle,* Aug. 14, 1958 (backstage with Belafonte). Beaverbrook's *Daily Express* printed a savagely negative review (Aug. 11, 1958): ". . . a sad shock . . . dull and monotonous"; *Reynolds News,* Aug. 19, 1958; also *Daily Mirror,* July 12, 1958; *National Guardian,* Aug. 25, 1958 (Belafonte). Yet, the following year, in the *Herald* (Dec. 19, 1959), Belafonte is quoted as saying, "I disagree violently with Paul Robeson. He's always giving out with that stuff about 'the Africans are on the march.' He makes me think sometimes that his influence might start a Negro movement that could get out of hand. And he would regret that."

7. Along with an official "Moscow tour" schedule, there is a ten-page typed itinerary, with comments by Essie, in RA. The opening-day reception is described in the Moscow *News,* Aug. 16, 20, 1958; the *Daily Worker,* Aug. 16, 18, 1958; the *Daily Telegraph and Morning Post* (London), Aug. 16, 1958. ER to family, completed Aug. 31, 1959; this letter and several others were found in duplicate in CIA files, proof that the Robesons' mail was intercepted.

8. David E. Mark, first secretary of Embassy, to State Department, Aug. 18, 1958, FBI Main 100-12304-(no file number), and distributed, as marked on the dispatch, to the CIA, the USIA, and intelligence units of the army, navy, and air force. The account of PR's TV show in the *National Guardian* (Sept. 8, 1958) also has him saying that "things are better for the Negroes in America."

9. *Pravda* (the only Moscow paper appearing on Monday morning) devoted a four-column spread with photographs to Robeson's Lenin Stadium appearance (Aug. 18, 1958, issue); *Daily Worker,* Aug.

18, 1958; Moscow *News,* Aug. 20, 1958; Washington *Post,* Aug. 18, 1958. *The New York Times* did report (Feb. 4, 1959) that the Soviets were making a film about PR, adding with a hint of derision that it would show him as an "unbending peace champion."

10. Typed ms. of ER's "Southern Hospitality (Soviet Style)," RA, published as the first of a two-part series by Essie in *The Afro-American,* Oct. 11, 18, 1958. Later, in Tashkent, the Robesons spent time with Bertha and Lillie Golden, wife and daughter of the deceased John Golden, the black American from the Tuskegee Institute who had helped the Russians with their fledgling cotton industry.

11. Vasily Katanian's recollections (recorded about 1978) were made available to me by PR, Jr. All the quotes are from Katanian's memoir, except the one about Robeson's dancing, which is from ER's typed ms. "Paul Robeson Jitterbugs in Middle Asia," dated August 20, 1958, RA. Katanian (in a letter to me, May 1987) has approved the accuracy of the quotations from his memoir. *Soviet Weekly* (October 2, 1958) reported PR's visit to the collective.

12. ER's annotated schedule, RA; Katanian's memoir; ER, article on the boat trip, San Francisco *Sun Reporter,* Nov. 8, 1958; ER to family, completed Aug. 31, 1959, RA.

13. Phone interview with Sally Kent Gorton, Sept. 28, 1986; Gorton to me, Oct. 1, 1986; Konstantin Kudrov, "Paul Robeson: A Russian Remembrance," *Rutgers Alumni Magazine,* Winter 1974, pp. 26–27 (Yalta). Ivan S. Koslovski, ms. reminiscence of Robeson—including singing with him at Yalta—in the PR Archiv, GDR; Katanian's memoir; Moscow *News,* Sept. 17, 1958 (Chekhov). RA contains a film script by Paul Delmer, *Caravan in Russia,* which he sent along to the Robesons, asking for their help in promoting it.

14. ER to family, completed Aug. 31, 1959, RA; ER's ms. "Kill The Umpire!!! U.S.A. and U.S.S.R.," RA (Khrushchev joke). PR also recorded several songs especially for Katanian's film; when he couldn't remember the words, Essie

wrote them in chalk on a blackboard in large letters. On Aug. 31, 1958, *The New York Times* printed a captioned picture of the two men, "Khrushchev Receives Robeson," but with no accompanying article. In the Aug. 31 letter home ER described Mrs. Khrushchev as "delightful, very motherly and warm." PR told the *Soviet News Bulletin* (a publication of the press office of the U.S.S.R. Embassy in Canada), Sept. 18, 1958, that on meeting Khrushchev he had been "greatly impressed by his penetrating mind, a clear understanding of the affairs all over the world, and his concern and sincere striving for the further development and prosperity of the Soviet Union, for an all-round increase in the welfare of his people"; he commented, too, on Khrushchev's "cheerful disposition and optimism . . . his good-heartedness and hospitality, his subtle racy humor. . . ."

In a news conference in Moscow about his visit to the United States, First Deputy Premier Anastas J. Mikoyan charged that the Voice of America was "the chief spokesman of the cold war" and said its broadcasts were "not pleasing to our ears." Paul Robeson, he added, was "also a voice of America and he is pleasing to our ears" (*The New York Times* international ed., Jan. 26, 1959). When Khrushchev was in the States in Sept. 1959, he made comments much like Mikoyan's at a dinner of the Economic Club of New York. Asked why the Russian people were not allowed to listen to American broadcasts, he replied that they were anti-Soviet in content, and inquired why the voice of Paul Robeson, which was *not* unfriendly, had been "jammed" by Robeson's government (*The Afro-American*, Sept. 26, 1959). Essie's friend from the UN, Ruth Gage Colby, went up to Khrushchev at the Togo reception for him at the UN and on behalf of the Robesons offered their greetings of welcome and affection. According to Colby, Khrushchev thanked her profusely (Colby to ER, Sept. 22, 1960, RA).

15. RA contains a large collection of tour reviews; almost uniformly positive and nearly uniform in their descriptions, they would be redundant to cite individually. PR, Jr., interview with Raikin, Sept.

8, 1982. Halfway through the concert tour, PR again came down with a cold, and some of the dates had to be canceled (ER to Rajni Patel, Jan. 29, 1959, RA).

16. Ernest Bradbury in *The Yorkshire Post and Leeds Mercury* (Oct. 9, 1958) had this comment on Robeson's musical theories: "Robeson has discovered—afresh if not for the first time—the international language of folk songs, and he is caught up in the idea of universality in music . . . and demonstrated the mystery of the pentatonic scale with all that seriously boyish enthusiasm which is so much part of his charm." *The New York Times*, Sept. 22, 1958; Essie's rebuttal is in *The Afro-American* (Nov. 22, 1958); Carl Murphy to ER, Nov. 20, 1958, RA. About the only political comment made on tour—at least as reported by the press—was to criticize U.S. policy on Formosa (*The Scotsman*, Sept. 23, 1958); he also described himself as "perhaps a little to the left of the British Labour party" (*Daily Telegraph*, Sept. 28, 1958) and expressed the view that recent race riots in Nottingham and Notting Hill "do not typify the general feeling in this country" (Leicester *Evening Mail*, Sept. 25, 1958). The Boston *Evening News* (Sept. 22, 1958) reflected the minority reaction to PR's announcement about staying in London by commenting that, if he claims "the greatest measure of freedom" is to be found in the Soviet Union, "isn't it surprising" that he should have decided to seek refuge in Britain instead.

17. London *Times, Daily Mirror, Daily Herald, News Chronicle,* Manchester *Guardian*—all Oct. 13, 1958; ER's ms. "Paul Robeson Sings in St. Paul's Cathedral," RA (reprinted in the San Francisco *Sun Reporter*); Peggy Middleton typed ms. "Paul in St. Paul's," Oct. 13, 1958, RA (reprinted in the *National Guardian*).

18. The invitation to attend the Accra conference (which is in RA) had actually been to Paul, and he sent a message (also in RA) with "warmest greetings" expressing his deep disappointment at being held in England by tour commitments. Marie Seton's book, *Paul Robeson* (Denis Dobson, 1958), has been referred to and commented on at several points in this text, and I will not

undertake a repetitive assessment here. I would only add in general that the book, though valuable in places for its firsthand recollections, is sketchy overall and in details frequently inaccurate, suffering from a lack of archival sources. At the time it appeared, Robert Rockmore wrote Larry Brown regretting that it "was not more accurate and less 'slanted' " (Sept. 8, 1958, NYPL/Schm: Brown).

Claude Barnett and his wife, Etta Moten, were also at Accra and seemed so impressed (so Essie described it) "with the respect and affection the Africans paid me—all of them—and also the way Nkrumah treated me," that Barnett decided to syndicate her articles (ER to Freda Diamond, Dec. 12, 1958, Feb. 8, 1959; ER to Tamara, Feb. 3, 1959; Barnett to ER, Jan. 19, 1959, RA). The notes Essie took during the UN sessions and the Accra convention are in RA. She hailed the conference in her articles as opening "a new page of history for the African Continent," chided Western press representatives for trying to pit Nasser against Nkrumah, and complained that "the women of Africa were not adequately represented" (only ten of the two hundred delegates were women, and only two addressed the plenary, Shirley Du Bois being one). One of ER's articles on Accra, in which she had written that Africans "are no longer passive (because the situation seemed hopeless) under foreign domination" and advising the white minority that "if they are sensible" they would find themselves "well treated," was reprinted in the West Indian *Gazette*, a London monthly, and alarmed the American Embassy. In a confidential dispatch to the State Department, the Embassy characterized ER's piece as "a most devastatingly destructive article, calculated as it obviously is to stir Africans and Asians alike against Westerners" (Francis J. Galbraith, first secretary of Embassy, to State Department, Jan. 27, 1959, FBI Main 100-12304-566).

19. Memo of Washington-Herter phone call, plus Skofield to Oulashin reporting it, Dec. 9, 1958, no file number, State Department. Consul General Turner in Bombay reported to Dulles that the same individuals who had organized PR's birthday celebration were behind his visit and that therefore "we may confidently predict strong anti-American propaganda along color lines."

20. Bunker to Dulles, Dec. 10, 1958, Jan. 8, 1959; memo Dec. 24, 1958, of State Department meeting involving Val Washington and Kenneth Bunce "to counteract communist exploitation of visit of Paul Robeson to India"; Dulles to Bunker, Jan. 12, 1959; Turner to Dulles, Jan. 20, 1959; CIA dispatch, Jan. 6, 1959—no file numbers listed.

21. ER, ms., "Purely Personal," dated Jan. 14, 1959, RA (also the source for the following paragraph).

22. *Daily Worker*, Aug. 21, 1958; ER to Lloyd Brown, Aug. 6, 1958, RA. Du Bois sat for the sculptor Lawrence Bradshaw while staying in the Robeson apartment, and ER was later asked to present the finished head as a gift to the People's Republic of China (Shirley Graham to George Murphy, Jr., Oct. 20, 1959, MSRC: Murphy).

23. Shirley Graham Du Bois, Pittsburgh *Courier*, June 20, 1959; Shirley Graham Du Bois, ms. reminiscences of PR, PR Archiv, GDR. While in Moscow, PR also saw the Stratford Company perform *Hamlet* and *Romeo and Juliet*; according to Essie, he thought Michael Redgrave "simply marvelous" (ER to Glen Byam Shaw, Jan. 13, 1959, RA).

24. ER to PR, Jr., Jan. 12, 1959; ER to Rajni Patel, Jan. 29, 1959; ER to Seton, March 12, 1959; ER to Glen Byam Shaw, Jan. 13, 1959—all in RA.

25. ER to Glen Byam Shaw, Jan. 13, 1959, RA ("duty idea"); ER to Marilyn and PR, Jr., Jan. 12, 16, 1959, RA.

26. ER to Marilyn and PR, Jr., Jan. 16, 1959, RA.

27. ER to Marilyn and PR, Jr., Jan. 14, 16, 18, 1959; ER to Freda Diamond, Feb. 8, 1959; ER to Rajni Patel, Jan. 29, 1959, RA. Nehru expressed his personal disappointment at the cancellation of PR's trip to India (Nehru to ER, Nov. 30, 1959, RA). In her letter to Patel, Essie refers to the doctors' diagnosing "a slight strain on the heart due to exhaustion." She also mentioned, in a letter to Glen Byam Shaw (Jan. 20, 1959, RA), that the doctors were "not at all satisfied with his

heart condition." PR himself later told a reporter, "The doctors thought I had heart trouble" (*News Chronicle,* March 10, 1959). Rumors that Paul had had a heart attack, or possibly even cancer, prompted his sister, Marian Forsythe, to telephone him for reassurance (*The Afro-American,* Feb. 14, 1959). Marian's husband, Dr. James Forsythe, had died in January 1959; Paul, from the hospital, wrote her one of his rare letters (PR and ER to Marian Forsythe, January 31, 1959, RA). In a phone conversation between two unidentified people (tapped by the FBI), a woman told her caller that she had recently received a letter from the Robesons and that they were "very upset and nervous. . . . She added that he had not been well since he had that business a couple of years ago" (FBI New York 100-25857-650, March 3, 1959).

28. ER to Marilyn and PR, Jr., Jan. 16, Feb. 6, 1959, RA; ER to Shaw, Jan. 20, 1959; Shaw cable to PR, Feb. 4, 1959, RA.

29. Alphaeus Hunton to George Murphy, Jr., April 9, 1959 (weight), MSRC: Murphy; ER to PR, Jr., Feb. 6, 1959; PR and ER cable to Shaw, Feb. 5, 1959; ER to Shaw, Feb. 6, 1959; Shaw to ER, Feb. 13, 1959; Shaw to PR, Feb. 13, 1959—all in RA. On Feb. 21 and March 3, PR felt strong enough to attend a meeting of the World Peace Council in Moscow (ER to family, Feb. 28, 1959, RA). He also consulted with the Russian film crew on the documentary. Katanian organized a special showing for Essie, of whom he was very fond, in the hospital (Katanian memoir). PR gave a speech to the World Peace Council on Feb. 21, 1959 (ms. in RA). It is notable for his repeated references to the "deep-seated will and desire of the American people" (as opposed to "a powerful minority") for "lasting peace." Even more significant, PR attended a special evening to honor Shalom Aleichem; according to ER, he "was pleased to make this gesture on the ticklish question of Jewish culture" (ER to family, March 4, 1959, RA).

30. ER to Rosens, March 14, 1959 (courtesy of Rosen); ER to family, Feb. 28, March 4, 1959, ER to Rosens, March 1959, RA; *News Chronicle,* March 10,

1959; *Daily Herald,* March 10, 1959. *Time* magazine (March 24, 1959), predictably sardonic when discussing PR, commented that he had had "predictable praise" for the Kremlin Hospital. Essie was so enthusiastic about Soviet medicine that she wrote an article on it ("Robesons Participate (As Patients) in Soviet Medicine," ms. in RA), taking special care to point out that medical care in Russia was free and that some of their doctors had been women.

31. For more on Andy, see pp. 478, 496 and note 61, p. 617. Interview with Andrew Faulds, Sept. 7, 1982 (PR, Jr., participating); Faulds to me, Oct. 30, 1984. Faulds credits Robeson with having inspired his own subsequent career as a member of Parliament. Watching the Oct. 1959 election returns on television, Faulds bemoaned the return of the Conservatives to power. "Paul made a very simple observation in that very rich voice of his, saying something like 'You have no right to complain about these things, because you are not politically involved!' And I thought, 'My God, he's absolutely right.'" The very next day Faulds joined the Stratford-on-Avon Labour Party and was later elected to Parliament.

32. London *Times,* Manchester *Guardian, Daily Herald, Evening Dispatch, Daily Mirror, The New York Times,* New York *Herald Tribune, News Chronicle, Daily Express, Daily Mail*—all April 8–12, 1959; *The New Statesman,* April 18, 1959; *The Tatler,* April 22, 1959. According to Sylvia Schwartz (interview, Jan. 16, 1983), PR found Mary Ure "cold" and did not enjoy acting opposite her. Nor did he have high opinions of Richardson and Wanamaker, although, typically, he barely alluded (even in private) to his discontent with them.

33. ER to Freda Diamond, April 18, 1959, RA; multiple interviews with Helen Rosen (in one she said, "He did *Othello* on sheer guts," it being her feeling that he "was never quite the same" after his 1955 prostate operation. "It had done something to his psyche, upset his feeling of . . . strength or invulnerability or something"). Peggy Ashcroft to me, Aug. 28, 1984, enclosing the memoir she was kind enough to write for me, which includes

her impressions of the 1959 *Othello*. A note from Vanessa Redgrave, apparently written to PR on opening night, is in RA: ". . . We are all very proud and thrilled that you are with us playing Othello." Among Robeson's other opening-night messages were telegrams from Olivier, Gielgud, Edith Evans, Sean O'Casey, and a number of voices from his past: André Van Gyseghem, Turner Layton—and his Rutgers sweetheart, Gerry Bledsoe. Alphaeus Hunton was among those in the audience on opening night and wrote an article about it (Hunton to George Murphy, Jr., April 9, 1959, enclosing typescript of article, MSRC: Murphy).

34. RA contains a typed list, apparently made by ER, of PR's schedule on a near-daily basis, along with a few words of comment by her. In an interview in *The New York Times* (April 26, 1985), Roy Dotrice recalls occasional baseball games between the Stratford players and a nearby U.S. Air Force base, Robeson playing first base. ER to Freda Diamond, April 18, May 8, July 21, Sept. 17, 1959, RA; Report of SA New York, Nov. 16, 1959, FBI Main 100-12304-689-? (illegible) (separation). Shirley Graham wrote up her enthralled impressions of PR as Othello in an article that appeared in the Pittsburgh *Courier* (June 20, 1959); she had seen the 1930 *Othello* and "beyond all question" thought his performance at Stratford superior. In her ms. reminiscences of PR in the PR Archiv, GDR, she recalled Paul's going up to London with the Du Boises on a train the morning after they had seen him in *Othello*. Besieged during the ride by fans and well-wishers, Robeson turned toward Du Bois and said, "Now I want you to meet a really great man," and then "boomed on about Du Bois."

35. ER to Katanian, May 17, 1959, RA; interview with Ashcroft, Sept. 9, 1982 (PR, Jr., participating); Ashcroft Memoir. A painful knee—stumbling at the theater, he reactivated an old football injury—added to his discomfort. When, several months later, PR and Ashcroft appeared together at the Youth Theatre Festival in Bristol, Ashcroft remembers "again being amazed at the rapturous acclaim that he had from the young people.

It was quite marvelous." That same season at Stratford—before the appearance at Bristol—Robeson agreed to join Ashcroft at a poetry reading for the Apollo Society, which she had started in 1943, with Larry Brown accompanying them; she remembers that Paul read "marvelously"—"he surprised by his mastery of so many other poets—Byron, Blake, Browning, etc."

36. Mimeo, "Excerpts of Speech of Paul Robeson," June 27, 1959 (*Gazette*), RA; Claudia Jones, "The Robeson Legend," West Indian *Gazette*, June 1959; Elizabeth Gurley Flynn to Pettis Perry, Nov. 3, 1958 ("do something"), NYPL/Schm.: Perry Papers; John Ebert to PR and ER, April 21, 1959, RA (Africa Day); Whitney to State Department, telegram, April 23, 1959, no file number (Africa Day); *Daily Express*, April 20, 1959. At the end of March, PR appeared at a private subscription dinner for the *Daily Worker* in London (ER to Freda Diamond, March 8, 1959, RA), and also accepted election as vice-president of the British-Soviet Friendship Society (*The New York Times*, May 11, 1959). Robeson's private socializing likewise had a considerable admixture of—though it was not confined to—left-wing friends; he lunched, for example, with Miroslav Galuska, the Czechoslovak Ambassador, greeted a group from the Chinese Embassy backstage, and saw Shirley and W. E. B. Du Bois with some frequency, including a dinner in Du Bois's honor at the Chinese Embassy (outline of daily schedule, RA).

37. *Daily Worker*, April 25, 1959; *News Chronicle*, June 29, 1959; Manchester *Guardian*, June 29, 1959; Jim Gardner (British Peace Committee) to PR, July 1, 1959; Prague *News Letter*, June 27, 1959; Josef Ullrich to ER, July 28, 1959; ER to Freda Diamond, July 21, 1959; Heinz Altschul to PR, July 17, 1959—all in RA; FBI Main 100-12304-575, FBI New York 100-25857-4172; *The New York Times*, Aug. 4, 11, 1959. While at the festival, PR used the occasion of a visit to the GDR tent to tell reporters that he "believes the future of the whole world rests on socialism" (*National Abend*, Aug. 4, 1959).

38. Essie wrote Katanian (June 14, 1959, RA) that in Prague Paul met with

his "Soviet friends and had a wonderful time." *The New York Times*, Aug. 4, 11, 1959. Inger McCabe Elliott, a member of the American delegation to the Vienna Youth Festival, describes the ongoing conflict within the delegation as a "brawl," with the anti-Communist "Chicago group" eventually losing out in its struggle to gain control over the election of officers (interview, Oct. 14, 1986). The anti-Communist version can be read in detail in Gloria M. Steinem et al., *Report on the Vienna Youth Festival* (Cambridge: 1960).

39. A translation of PR's interview in *Nepszabadsag*, Aug. 22, 1959, is in RA; a tape recording of his comments to the Budapest crowd, transcribed by PR, Jr., is also in RA.

40. The assorted telegrams, memos, and letters involved in this episode are in the FBI files for 1959–60, and too numerous to cite in detail. In the middle of the dispute, and probably further prejudicing his case, PR appeared at a festival sponsored by the Communist newspaper *L'Humanité* at Meudon, a suburb of Paris (*L'Humanité*, Sept. 5–7, 1959). The American legate in Paris, on behalf of the FBI, asked for and received help from the Prefecture of Police and the Renseignements Généraux, general-investigative section of the Sûreté Nationale, in gathering information on PR (FBI Main 100-12304-579, 581). The ms. of an essay PR wrote for *L'Humanité*, mostly on musical theory, is in RA.

41. ER to Helen Rosen, Oct. 5, 1959; Huw Wheldon (BBC) to PR, April 14, 1959—both in RA; *The New Statesman*, Nov. 7, 1959; ER to Freda Diamond, Sept. 25, 1959, RA (Menuhin); ER to Mrs. Beard, July 5, 1959, RA (rest); Bill Worsley to PR, Dec. 18, 1959, RA (new series); RA contains dozens of letters from fans about his broadcasts; Pittsburgh *Courier*, Oct. 31, 1959; *Daily Worker*, Feb. 15, 1960 (reprint of part of PR-Menuhin broadcast). Though the white press did not report on PR's triumphs (except for *Othello*), William Weinstone of the New York State CP committee, at its meeting on Nov. 6–7, 1959, in New York City, told the gathering that he had talked to PR on the phone while in

Prague and was delighted to report that he was "an immense figure" everywhere he went in Europe (FBI New York 100-25857-4204).

42. ER to Claude Barnett, Oct. 13, 24, Dec. 2, 1959; Barnett to ER, Oct. 21, 1959, CHS: Barnett; ER to Rosens, Oct. 24, 1959; ER to Helen Rosen, Nov. 13, 1959, courtesy of Rosen. Helen Rosen described the "polite" nature of her relationship with ER in our multiple interviews. Only once, she said, did Essie visit them in Katonah—after she had expressed interest in seeing the place "Paul is so fond of."

43. ER to Freda Diamond, Nov. 14, Dec. 1, 1959, RA; Glen Byam Shaw to PR, Nov. 26, 1959, RA; PR to Helen Rosen, November 16, 23, 28, 1959, courtesy of Rosen. Robeson's final performance coincided with Shaw's retirement as director of Stratford (to be replaced by Peter Hall), and there was a farewell on stage, with all the stars of the hundredth season joining in (Birmingham *Post*, Nov. 30, 1959)..

44. ER to Marilyn and PR, Jr., Jan. 24–29, 1960, RA. ER to Marilyn and PR, Jr., Jan. 24, 29, 1960, RA; U.S. Embassy in Moscow to State Department, Feb. 18, 1960, FBI Main 100-12304 (no file number).

Robeson's appearance at State Ball Bearing Plant #1 involves an episode of crucial if clouded importance. The State Ball Bearing Plant was where the black American toolmaker Robert Robinson had long worked. Robinson had been a reluctant resident of the U.S.S.R. for decades (see the account in his book *Black on Red* [Acropolis, 1988]), had known PR since his first visit to the U.S.S.R. in 1934 (see pp. 188–89; note 3, p. 629; notes 7 and 12, pp. 629 and 630; note 53, p. 641; note 17, p. 634), and had unsuccessfully been trying to enlist PR's assistance in getting out of the Soviet Union (*Black on Red*, pp. 313–17). In his book Robinson claims that he arranged for Robeson to give a concert at State Ball Bearing Plant #1 in 1961 and he prints two photos of PR at the plant (pp. 315–16) which he dates "July 1961." But that dating cannot be accurate; in July 1961 PR was confined in poor health at Barveekha Sanitarium.

Moreover, the photos show PR with the beard he *did* have during his January 1960 visit to Moscow but (according to Helen Rosen's distinct recollection) he was no longer wearing when she saw him in March 1961 in London, just prior to his trip to the U.S.S.R. Since Robinson's book contains several other serious mis-datings (notably on p. 319, where he is off by several years on PR's vacation meeting with Khrushchev and on his medical treatment in the GDR), I pressed him during our interview (May 18, 1988) about his choice of dates for the PR photograph in his book. Robinson insisted that he dated (with the year, not the month) all his photographs at the time he took them, and the evidence I marshalled above persuaded him only that "July" on the photo might be inaccurate—he continued to insist that the year 1961 was not. However, a photo I found in the Sovfoto Archives (New York) of PR singing at State Ball Bearing Plant #1 is clearly dated "Jan. 1960."

The importance of all this is in how it affects an evaluation of the dating and veracity of the additional testimony Robinson offers on PR, both in his book and in our interview. In *Black on Red* (pp. 318–19) Robinson records his surprise—since he had long since decided that PR was blinkered to the harsh realities of Soviet life—when, during his concert at the ball bearing plant, he included "a mournful song out of the Jewish tradition that decried their persecution through the centuries." Robeson sang it, in Yiddish, with such "a cry in his voice," such a seeming "plea to end the beating, berating, and killing of Jews," that Robinson concluded PR had made a conscious choice to protest Soviet anti-Semitism (a conclusion confirmed in Robinson's mind after he checked with PR's interpreter and learned that he had also chosen to sing the Jewish song during several of his other concert appearances in Moscow). A week or so later, according to Robinson, a rumor began to circulate that PR had had "an unpleasant confrontation with Khrushchev." In our interview, Robinson claimed to have heard the rumor from five different people, none of whom knew each other and all of whom were "within the Party structure." According to the rumor, Robeson purportedly had asked Khrushchev if stories in the Western press about Soviet anti-Semitism were true, and Khrushchev had purportedly blown up and accused Robeson of trying to meddle in Soviet internal affairs. Robinson claimed as further confirmation of the rumored confrontation the fact that he never again heard Robeson's records broadcast over Radio Moscow (as they had previously been on a regular twice-weekly basis) and "never read another word about him in the Soviet press."

In our interview, Robinson staunchly stood by the accuracy of the *content* of his account and wavered only insofar as he was willing to say that the Ball Bearing concert (and Robeson's purported subsequent confrontation with Khrushchev) may have taken place in March rather than in July 1961. If that confrontation did take place in March 1961—though I have found no evidence that PR saw Khrushchev at all on that visit—it might shed some light on PR's attempted suicide in that month (see p. 498) or his seeming terror when later passing the Soviet Embassy (see p. 502). But as I have argued above, the weight of evidence far more strongly supports the date of January 1960 as the correct one for PR's appearance at Ball Bearing Plant #1.

But although the dating of Robinson's account can be proven unreliable, that does not automatically discredit the content of his testimony. In the present state of the evidence (perhaps more will surface in the future), the accuracy of Robinson's reporting cannot be definitively gauged. During our interview, I found his manner to be earnest and impassioned, and his memory, though inconsistent, seemed vivid and detailed. But on the other hand, I found portions of his book so heavy-handedly anti-Soviet, and the circumstances surrounding its writing and publication so thick with cloak-and-dagger innuendo, as to suggest some sort of "official" sponsorship.

45. PR to Helen Rosen, March 1, 11, 1960, courtesy of Rosen.

46. Birmingham *Post*, Feb. 29, 1960; Leicester *Mercury*, Feb. 24, 1960; Nottingham *Evening News*, April 7, 1960;

Yorkshire *Evening News*, April 29, 1960 (thin audiences). Rockmore to ER, April 29, 1960 ("expenditure"); PR telegram to Rockmore, July 3, 1960; Rockmore to Harold Davison, May 4, 1960; Davison to Rockmore, March 31, April 29, May 10, June 16, 28, 1960—all in RA.

47. *Daily Worker*, March 14, 1960; American Consulate to State Department, May 3, 1960 (May Day; Sterner interview with Stern). The day after he returned to London he participated in a ban-the-bomb rally in Trafalgar Square (*Daily Worker*, May 16, 1960; the London *Times*, May 16, 1960; the rally also called for admitting China to the UN). The May Day affair was apparently marred by a poor amplification system (Glasgow *Herald*, May 2, 1960). Interview with Andrew Faulds (PR, Jr., participating), Sept. 7, 1982. Just before leaving on tour, Robeson told a *Daily Worker* interviewer (Jan. 14, 1960), "I feel I have reached the beginning of another stage in my life. . . . It is something that reaches beyond art. I feel that a battle has been fought and won. Now I feel that I can relax." He still had enough political verve to denounce the resurgence of anti-Semitic outrages in West Germany, and the American government for propping up the Adenauer regime.

48. Interview with Diana Loesser, July 29, 1986; Franz Krahl (*Neues Deutschland*) to PR, June 22, 1960, FBI Main 100-12304-622; PR to Helen Rosen, May 16, 1960, courtesy of Rosen; Faulds interview (PR, Jr., participating), Sept. 7, 1982.

49. PR to Helen Rosen, March 6, 7, 1960, courtesy of Rosen.

50. PR to Helen Rosen, May 10, 16, 1960, courtesy of Rosen; FBI New York 100-25857-4248 ("permanent"); Washington *Post*, June 21, 1960; PR's speech in Melbourne, Australia, Nov. 1960 ("my folks"), tape courtesy of Lloyd L. Davies.

51. Earl Robinson to PR, Sept. 12, 1959; Willard Uphaus to Robesons, Nov. 8, 1959, RA; also the positive report in George Murphy, Jr., to ER, Jan. 29, 1961, MSRC: Murphy. PR wrote A. Philip Randolph that he had "avidly followed" plans for the creation of a Negro Trade Union Congress and paid him the conciliatory

compliment—despite Randolph's long-standing and outspoken hostility toward Communism—of having "so wisely led" the Pullman Porters. In the same letter PR applauded the "courageous activity" and "growing unity of Negro and white American Youth in breaking down the tottering walls of segregation and discrimination," and also expressed his pleasure that "all sections of the Negro People" were "drawing together," despite "some differences of opinion in some spheres, particularly that of International Relations." Finally, Robeson expressed the poignant hope of being "able to greet you in person in the near future" (PR to Randolph, July 22, 1960, RA). There is no known reply from Randolph.

52. ER to Freda Diamond, July 17, 1960, RA. In another letter to Freda Diamond (June 27, 1960, RA), ER contrasted the unpromising U.S. scene with developments abroad: "the picture this side looks better and better. War and nuclear policies are being repudiated everywhere, tactfully, but quietly and very firmly. I think the U.S. is going to have to take low. Will be healthy." PR's remark on Kennedy is as quoted in the *National Guardian*, Oct. 1960. In a postelection estimate of Kennedy, John Pittman wrote the Robesons from Moscow: ". . . he will at least begin by trying to emulate some of FDR's statesmanship. He will undoubtedly bring many Negroes into the project of 'saving Africa from communism.' . . . Under such a banner, he is sure to have the support of the right-wing labor bureaucracy, including Mr. Randolph" (Pittman to the Robesons, Dec. 10, 1960, RA).

53. ER to Freda Diamond, June 27, July 7, 17, Aug. 19, 1960; ER to Ruth Gage Colby, Sept. 10, 1960, RA. During the summer PR also completed the second series of ten radio broadcasts and a special Christmas program for the BBC, as well as a long-playing, stereophonic album for EMI (with a fifty-fifty royalty split). Though the trip to Ghana never came off, it involved considerable preliminary planning and correspondence, including letters between ER and President Nkrumah (A. W. Ephson to PR, Feb. 23, March 25, April 6, 23, 1960; K. A. Gbede-

mah to PR, April 23, 1960; Nkrumah to ER, July 29, Aug. 10, Sept. 7, 1960—all in RA). Hearing of PR's difficulties in getting his passport renewed, Nkrumah suggested he become a citizen of Ghana—as W. E. B. Du Bois was soon to do.

54. Roucaute to PR, June 29, 1960; ER to Roucaute, July 18, 1960; Leschemelle to ER, July 22, 1960, RA; FBI Main 100-12304-603, 608; *L'Humanité*, Sept. 1–6, 1960; *Daily Worker*, Sept. 25, 1960; ER to Direktor, Interkonzert, Aug. 14, 1960, RA (Budapest). He spent a lot of time in Paris with his brother Ben, who had come overseas for a World War I reunion (ER to Rockmore, Sept. 9, 1960, RA). For more on Fajon, see Edward Mortimer, *The Rise of the French Communist Party, 1920–1947* (Faber and Faber, 1984).

55. Diana Loesser, the wife of Franz Loesser, handled most of the details of the Robesons' visit to the GDR, and her correspondence with Essie about arrangements is in RA. Also pertinent are Walter Friedrich (president of the Peace Council) to PR, Aug. 29, 1960; George Spielmann to ER and PR, August 2, 1960, RA (Peace Medal); *Neue Zeit*, Oct. 7, 1960 (interview with PR in which he said, "I will tell the peoples of other countries that I have seen the true Germany"); *Neues Deutschland*, Oct. 9, 1960 (PR press conference); *Morning Freiheit*, Oct. 23, 1969 (Graham); Brigitte Boegelsack, "Paul Robeson's Legacy in the German Democratic Republic," *Arbeitschefte* (Paul Robeson For His 80th Birthday), (Akademie der Kunste [Berlin], 1978); and the English-language "souvenir book," *Days with Paul Robeson* (Der Deutsche Friedensrat, 1961). The latter records one additional honor given Robeson during his stay: honorary membership in the German Academy of Arts. The American legate in Bonn requested U.S. Army Intelligence and the Office of Special Investigation (OSI) "to furnish any information coming to their attention" regarding PR's "activities" while in Berlin, but the agencies "indicated that they had no information" (Bonn to Hoover, Nov. 22, 1960, FBI Main 100-12304-618). Essie had been to the GDR the previous year as well, to help celebrate its tenth anniversary (Paul had been unable to go, because of his *Othello* commitments). During her trip Essie visited the site of the Nazi camp at Ravensbrück and helped dedicate a monument to the women who died there. She was accompanied by the GDR Minister Toeplitz, the Deutsches Theater actress Mathilde Danegger, and Erica Buchmann, the Communist Party member who had been imprisoned in Ravensbrück from 1934 to 1945. Buchmann introduced Essie to Rosa Thalmann, widow of the German Communist leader (interview with Diana Loesser, July 29, 1986, who is also the source for the story about the medals).

56. PR to Clara Rockmore, Sept. 9, 1960, courtesy of Rockmore; the contract for the New Zealand–Australia tour is in RA; R. J. Kerridge to Harold Davison, Sept. 30, 1960 (TV fees); ER to Freda Diamond, July 7, 1960, RA). The offer was put together by Kerridge who was the owner of the largest chain of motion-picture houses in New Zealand and the sponsor of all Soviet-bloc performers in the country, along with the well-known Australian impresario D. D. O'Connor, who sponsored PR's tour.

57. Sydney *Morning Herald*, Oct. 13, 1960; *Telegraph*, Oct. 13, 1963; *Sunday Truth* (Brisbane), Oct. 16, 1960; ER to Diamond, Nov. 13, 1960, RA.

58. Nancy Wills to me, Nov. 12, 1983. In 1987 Wills wrote a theater piece on PR's life, which was produced in Brisbane (*The Age*, Sept. 18, 1987).

59. ER to Freda Diamond, Nov. 13, 1960, RA; D. D. O'Connor to ER, Oct. 24, 1960, RA (Hobart).

60. The Sydney *Morning Herald*, Nov. 8, 1960 (platform manner); PR postcard to Clara Rockmore, Nov. 29, 1960, postmarked Feb. 12, 1961 (Maori), courtesy of Rockmore. Comparing New Zealand with Australia, ER wrote, "America is here, all over the place. But much more in Australia than in New Zealand. So, as you can imagine, we by far prefer New Zealand, which we found very beautiful, and very friendly. Australians are much more like Americans" (to Freda Diamond, Nov. 13, 1960, RA). A sample of PR's excellent musical reviews in New Zealand is the *Evening Post* (Wellington),

Oct. 21, 1960: "The voice, even at the age of 62, is the remembered voice of the records, of no great range nor sophisticated cultivation but with a rich vibrant sonority." I have not detailed the musical reviews of the tour because they are so repetitive and also so much of a piece with the kinds of reviews PR got throughout his career: they were largely positive and often glowing ("a great entertainment by a great man"—Melbourne *Sun*, Nov. 17, 1960), emphasizing the richness of his personality over the richness of his art, though an occasional critic complained about the narrow range of his voice and his selections (Melbourne *Nation*, Nov. 19, 1960; Adelaide *Advertiser*, Nov. 28, 1960) or the "naivete" of his interpolated political references (Sydney *Sun*, Nov. 8, 1960; Sydney *Daily Mirror*, Nov. 8, 1960). Janetta McStay, the young New Zealand pianist who was the assisting artist for the tour, also got her share of excellent notices—as did Larry Brown.

61. New Zealand *Woman's Weekly*, Nov. 2, 1960; New Zealand *Herald*, Oct. 18, 1960; *People's Voice*, Oct. 19, 26, Nov. 2, 1960 (Maori Centre); Christchurch *Star*, Oct. 24, 1960; Otago *Daily Times*, Nov. 3, 1960; ER to Freda Diamond, Nov. 13, 1960, RA; *The Press* (New Zealand), Oct. 27, 1960 (sample ER interview); ER to Rosens, Nov. 26, 1960, courtesy of Helen Rosen. Perhaps Robeson's most notable contact with workers in Australia was his appearance, by invitation of the Building Workers' Industrial Union, on the job site for the construction of the Sydney Opera House. PR sang to the workers, they presented him with a hard hat with his name on it, and, to great applause, he autographed the cuffs of their working gloves (correspondence of P. Clancy, secretary of BWIU, to PR, RA; also Australian TV interview with Miriam Hampson, transcript courtesy of Sterner).

62. James P. Parker, American Consul in Auckland, to State Department, Nov. 7, 1960, FBI New York 100-25857-4294. Although there was no civic reception, the mayor of Auckland, D. M. Robinson, did entertain the Robesons at a private morning tea, and in Wellington, the seat of government, Prime Minister Nash and the Minister of the Interior and Culture received them in their offices. PR did a "Spotlight" television show, arranged to include three sympathetic interviewers, in which he was "friendly and gay (not angry)" and which had "a very fine effect" (ER to PR, Jr., Dec. 15, 1960). She sent a duplicate letter to Mikhail Kotov of The Soviet Peace Committee (same date, RA), designed to fulfill a promise to Tass for an article. There is considerable correspondence in RA concerning invitations and arrangements in regard to social occasions and public appearances; the letters from Flora Gould (New Zealand Peace Council), Rona Bailey (New Zealand), and William Morrow (New South Wales Peace Committee) contain especially important details.

63. I'm grateful to Lloyd L. Davies of the Aboriginal Legal Service of Western Australia, who saw a newspaper "call" of mine for information on PR and responded with anecdotes of his own about PR's visit to Australia and sent two tapes of speeches PR gave while there (one of which, at Paddington, is quoted above). Davies subsequently placed a "call" of his own in the Australian press, which reaped an additional trove of letters and photos, which he then forwarded to me (one of them is a letter from Faith Bandler, May 11, 1983, but the Bandler quotation above is in fact from an interview she gave to Australian television about PR—the transcript courtesy of Sterner). In regard to the Australian press, PR is quoted on the aborigines in the *Sunday Mirror* (Sydney), Nov. 13, 1960; *Truth* (Brisbane), Nov. 13, 1960; and the Melbourne *Age*, Nov. 16, 1960. In his book *Broad Left, Narrow Left* (Alternative Pub. Coop.), Len Fox has an account of PR seeing the aboriginal film that corroborates the Faith Bandler version (Fox to Davies, May 16, 1983, courtesy of Davies). The Perth newspaper *The West Australian* (Dec. 1, 1960) described PR as so wound up during his press conference that it was "difficult for anyone else to get a word in edgeways." He began by protesting the treatment of the aborigines and ended by warning that anyone who tried to get tough with Russia "could get hurt, and they have plenty to hurt you with."

64. Lloyd L. Davies to me, Jan. 14, June 24, 1983. In her letter to Davies of May 11, 1983, Faith Bandler points out that PR "did not have many opportunities to meet Aborigines while here," though he did meet Charles Leon and several of his friends at a reception in Paddington Town Hall. Another of Davies's correspondents, Vic Bird (letter of June 18, 1983), recalls an occasion, in the Collingwood-Fitzroy area of New South Wales when Mr. and Mrs. Jack Lynch, peace activists, arranged at the Robesons' request for them to meet two aboriginal women at the home of Mr. and Mrs. Sam Goldbloom; according to Vic Bird, who was a guest at the Goldblooms' that evening, Robeson left the group of some forty to fifty people in order to go off to an anteroom and have a talk with the two women. It's possible that Judy Ingles was the woman who arranged the meeting between PR and the two aborigines (Ingles to Robesons, Nov. 24, 1960, RA, along with enclosure about her work on the aborigines). The Bandler and Bird letters were kindly forwarded to me, along with much other material, by Lloyd L. Davies. I'm also grateful to Annette Cameron of Maylands, Western Australia, who sent me her own brief memoir (Cameron to me, June 25, 1983), which includes an account of a union committee at Midland Trailway Workshops arranging an outdoor event for Robeson after management had refused to let him inside to sing. The tape of PR's speech to the West Australian Peace Council is courtesy of Lloyd L. Davies. Though PR continued to speak out in Western Australia and also in Adelaide, South Australia, the press and public seemed more indifferent to his politics than in New South Wales and Victoria. John C. Ausland, the American Consul in Adelaide, explained it this way: ". . . they are eager for novelty and, for the most part, completely indifferent to international politics"; Ausland was speaking of Australians in general (Ausland to State Department, Dec. 15, 1960, FBI New York 100-25857-4306).

65. PR to Clara Rockmore, Dec. 6, 1960, courtesy of Rockmore; ER to Freda Diamond, Dec. 15, 1960, RA ("strain");

ER to George Murphy, Jr., Dec. 16, 1960, Jan. 23, 1961, Murphy Papers, MSRC. Essie was not only preparing a new book, but still trying to resuscitate an old film script (ER to David Machin, March 16, 1961, RA).

As part of his musical research, PR corresponded with Edinburgh critic Christopher Grier (PR to Grier, Jan. 29, March 1, 1961; Grier to PR, Feb. 19, 1961, RA) and visited the musicologist Dennis Gray Stoll (Stoll to Robesons, Jan. 12, 1961; ER to Stoll, Jan. 23, 1961, RA). Robeson sent Grier some of his writing on the pentatonic scale. In his response (Feb. 19, 1960, RA) Grier expressed agreement with Robeson's high evaluation of Bartók but thought "it was too late" for "a return to the basic roots of a world universal folk pentatonic modal musical mother tongue" which PR had apparently called for; moreover, Grier felt "a return to 'grass roots' is only valid in countries which have lacked or been outside the main stream of Western European musical culture." On the other hand, Willie Ruff, the bassist, French-horn player, and professor of music at Yale, credits Robeson's insistence that the folk music of widely disparate countries has a common source, and his recognition of Bartók's importance, for having opened his own ears to musical interconnections (*The New Yorker*, April 23, 1984).

66. PR, Jr.'s notes of his talk (not taped) with Harry Francis, Sept. 1982, courtesy PR, Jr. The FBI got wind of PR's invitation to visit Cuba, apparently as the personal guest of Castro, and Justice Department memos flew (FBI Main 100-12304-619, FBI New York 100-25857-4310). In the Soviet weekly, *Ogonek*, no. 14, April 1961, Robeson is quoted as saying about his future plans (which included possible trips to Ghana and Guinea): "I received an invitation to visit Cuba. . . . I don't see how I can do it all."

67. PR to Clara Rockmore, Jan. 30, Feb. 12, 13, 1961, courtesy of Rockmore; ER to Freda Diamond, Feb. 19, March 25, 1961, RA; PR to Helen Rosen, Feb. 11, 27, 1961, courtesy of Rosen; Claude Barnett to ER, April 14, 1961, CHS: Barnett; ER to George Murphy, Jr., Feb. 25, 1961,

MSRC: Murphy. Both Essie and Paul wrote letters in support of Kenyatta to the Release of Jomo Kenyatta Committee, Jan. 22, 1961, RA; A. Oginga-Odinga (vice-president of the Kenya African National Union) to PR, Dec. 22, 1960; Ambu H. Patel (organizing secretary of "Release" Committee) to Robesons, March 1, 1961, RA. Harry Francis remembered "how deeply affected" Robeson was by Lumumba's murder (Francis to PR, Jr., June 10, 1968, RA). The thirty-first birthday celebration of the *Daily Worker*, at the Albert Hall on March 5, 1961, at which Robeson sang and spoke, heard Communist Party General Secretary John Gollan protest the jailing of Kenyatta and the murder of Lumumba (*Daily Worker*, March 6, 1961). Paul had already left for Moscow, but Essie spoke at the big Trafalgar Square Anti-Apartheid rally to commemorate the Sharpeville Massacre, along with Anthony Wedgwood Benn, Barbara Castle, and Rev. Michael Scott (ER to Freda Diamond, March 25, 1961; Martin Ennals to ER, Feb. 24, 1961, RA). While still in Australia, the Robesons had been invited by Nnamdi Azikiwe personally to attend his inauguration on Nov. 16, 1960, as Governor-General and Commander-in-Chief of the Federation of Nigeria (Azikiwe to Robesons, Oct. 26, 1960, RA). The script of "This Is Your Life, Flora Robson" is in RA (Robeson praised her work with him in *All God's Chillun* but penciled out the portion of the prewritten script that talked about her being "better" than Mary Blair in the American production); "thank-you" note from Flora Robson to PR, Feb. 18, 1961, RA; interview with Flora Robson, Sept. 1982.

68. Interview with Herbert Marshall and Freda Brilliant, July 20, 1985; Neil Hutchinson to PR, Robeson, Nov. 15, 1960 *(Othello)*; Herbert Marshall to Robesons, Dec. 25, 1960; Tony Richardson to ER, Feb. 8, 16, 27, 1961; Lewenstein to ER, Feb. 16, 1961; ER to Richardson, Feb. 22, 1961; ER to Lewenstein, Feb. 22, 1961—all in RA.

69. PR to Clara Rockmore, Sept. 9, 1960 (HUAC), Jan. 30, 1961 (lengthy), Feb. 12, 13, 27, 1961, courtesy of Rockmore. Abe Moffat (president, National Union of Mine Workers) to ER, March 29, 1961, RA; ER to Kotov, Feb. 24, 1961, RA; Marie Matejkova to PR, Oct. 7, 1960; ER to Matejkova, Feb. 17, 1961; Walter Friedrich to Robesons, Feb. 16, 1961; ER to Friedrich, March 4, 1961—all in RA. Robeson had been set to participate in the Africa Freedom Day concert on April 16 in London and had also accepted an invitation to join the Tagore Conference, part of the Centenary Celebrations in London on May 5 (John Eber to PR, March 13, 1961; Omeo Gooptu to PR, March 20, 1961—both in RA).

70. PR to Helen Rosen, Feb. 11, 1961, courtesy of Rosen.

71. PR to Helen Rosen, Feb. 11, 24, 27 (twice), 1961, courtesy of Rosen; multiple conversations with Helen Rosen.

72. Multiple conversations with Helen Rosen.

73. *Neue Zeit*, April 27, 1961; Moscow *News*, April 1, 1961; *Ogonek*, no. 14, April 1961; *Izvestia*, March 24, 1961; *Bechernyaya Moskva*, March 21, 1961; *Trud*, April 2, 1961 (Zavadsky); Chernyshev to PR, March 24, 1961; McVicker (U.S. Embassy in Moscow to State Department), March 31, 1961, FBI Main 100-12304-(no file number); ER to PR, March 24, 1961, RA.

CHAPTER 24   BROKEN HEALTH *(1961–1964)*

1. The sketchy details of PR's suicide attempt are primarily derived from interviews with PR, Jr. (multiple), Helen Rosen (multiple), Dr. Alfred Katzenstein (July 26, 1986), and Dr. Ari Kiev (Dec. 14, 1982). According to PR, Jr. (ms. comments), "[I] asked to see two top-level Soviet officials with whom [I] discussed the entire matter of [my] father's collapse. When [I] asked them whether a blood test showed any evidence that Paul had been drugged, they answered in the negative and with considerable concern gently suggested that perhaps [I] had been under excessive strain and ought to get some rest. But when [I] asked them

Notes for pages 499–500

about the party at the hotel, they became visibly agitated, saying that although many of the people at the party 'were not Soviet people' (i.e., disloyal Russians), there was not concrete evidence against any of them. As for the party, everyone had assumed it was Robeson's party, so despite many complaints, no one had intervened." Interview with Lord Ivor Montagu (PR, Jr., participating), Sept. 1982; PR, Jr., interview with Harry Francis (notes courtesy of PR, Jr.); interview with Dr. Alfred Katzenstein, July 26, 1986 ("conflict"); Harry Francis was surprised (and hurt), because he had increasingly become a trusted go-between for Robeson (ER to Jerry Sharp, Aug. 30, 1961, RA). There are various versions of the overcoat incident: that Robeson pushed it away, that he accepted it and later returned it, that the overcoat belonged to an American art dealer or to Montagu himself. Unable to reconcile the sketchy memories involved, I have settled here for a "best guess." Essie, too, seems to have believed the overcoat incident had been significant. In my interview with Jay and Si-lan Chen Leyda (May 26, 1985), they recalled meeting ER accidentally in a GDR airport (they thought the year was 1963 but were not positive; a letter from ER to family, Nov. 26, 1963, courtesy of Paulina Forsythe, reporting on meeting the Leydas, confirms that the year was 1963, and the place Leipzig). Upset, Essie had sat the Leydas down, said she "had to talk," and proceeded to describe how in an airplane someone—"she thought an American"—had put a heavy coat over Paul's shoulders on seeing he didn't have one. "He was never the same thereafter," the Leydas quote ER as telling them; startled at the gesture, he had reacted as if (in Jay Leyda's words) "chase and capture— and some sort of revenge" were at stake. What seems to have been meant as an act of kindness was apparently mistaken for the opposite by Robeson. Significant as a triggering event, the overcoat episode does not, of course, account for Robeson's underlying and pre-existing anxiety.

2. The translated Russian medical report (dated April 4, 1964, RA) is an overall evaluation but makes specific ref-

erence to the 1961 period. PR, Jr.'s recollections are on a tape he made for me and in his ms. comments. Cedric Belfrage and his then wife, Jo Martin, are among those who saw Robeson with some frequency in the months before his departure for Moscow and did not detect any overt symptoms of disturbance. But Jo Martin, now a therapist herself, stressed the unpredictability of depressive mood swings; she feels certain of only one diagnosis: Robeson did not have the serious memory losses associated with the early stages of Alzheimer's disease, as others have suggested to me (interviews with Cedric Belfrage, May 29, 1984, and Dr. Josephine Martin, June 5, 1984).

3. Several people who knew PR only casually have voiced the view that he collapsed "from conscience," from disillusion with the Soviet Union. Herbert Marshall, in Moscow at the time but denied access to Robeson, is the strongest proponent of that view, and quotes Pera Attasheva, Sergei Eisenstein's widow and a friend of Robeson's since his first visit to Moscow in 1934, to the effect that "the full knowledge of what had been happening in the Soviet Union crashed in on him" (interview with Herbert Marshall and Fredda Brilliant, July 20, 1985). But Zina Voynow told me that her sister, Pera Attasheva, warned her that Marshall was not a reliable witness (conversation with Voynow, March 1987). Angus Cameron (interview, July 15, 1986) and Marie Seton (interviews, Aug.-Sept. 1982) are among those who have argued the broader view of disillusion with the historical process, Seton adding as causative the accumulated stress Robeson felt at being alienated from the black struggle at home, and from living with Essie on a daily basis. Interview with Sam Parks, Dec. 27, 1986 (moorings).

4. Multiple conversations with PR, Jr.

5. ER to Jessica Abt, April 19, 1961; ER to Ben Robeson, May 6, 1961 ("Feeling much better"); ER to Freda Diamond, May 9, 14, 1961 ("fell flat"); ER to Prof. Friedrichs, May 29, 1961; PR, Jr., to Marilyn Robeson, April 13, 27, May 5, 10, 1961; PR, Jr., to Ben Robeson, May 4,

1961—all in RA. PR, Jr., to Marian Forsythe, May 4, 1961; ER to Marian Forsythe, May 5, 1961—both courtesy of Paulina Forsythe. Larry Brown, too, wrote Helen Rosen that he was feeling "a little happier" after getting "a very cheerful letter" from ER (April 29, 1961, courtesy of Rosen), and ER's own chatty letter to Helen about how well both Pauls were doing was no more informative (April 28, 1961, courtesy of Rosen).

6. PR, Jr., to Marilyn Robeson, May 5, 10, 1961; ER to Marilyn Robeson, May 31, 1961; ER to Diana Loesser, May 29, 1961—all in RA. Between medical duties, Essie kept busy writing articles and doing occasional broadcasts over Radio Afrika (Moscow). The mss. of her articles—including "Cuba Libre," full of praise for Castro's revolution—are in RA. "So every dog has his day," Essie wrote Freda Diamond (May 14, 1961, RA) in summary of her numerous activities—the phrase suggestive of psychological gratification beyond mere article-writing. To add to her pleasure, she received word in Aug. that the GDR had awarded her the Clara Zetkin Medal in honor of her "great merits in the struggle for peace." "I am very proud of it," she wrote Peggy Middleton (Rudolf Dolling to ER, Aug. 4, 1961; ER to Middleton, Aug. 17, 1961, RA). She accepted the medal in person two years later (see p. 518).

7. ER to Helen Rosen, June 15, 1961, courtesy of Rosen; Nkrumah to PR, May 10, June 21, 1961, RA; Cheddi Jagan to PR, June 14, 1961, RA; Shirley Du Bois to Freda Diamond, Oct. 9, 1961, courtesy of Diamond. Soon after, Nnamdi Azikiwe of Nigeria, responding to a letter from Essie, wrote to express his sorrow "to learn of the indisposition of my hero, Paul" (Azikiwe to ER, July 15, 1961, RA). Hearing that Robeson was back at Barveekha, Nkrumah, who was himself on a visit to Moscow, wrote again ("Dear Uncle Paul") to express regret at not having any room in his schedule to visit him (Nkrumah to PR, July 25, 1961, RA). Predictably, the State Department was displeased when it learned of Nkrumah's offer of a professorship (Accra Embassy to Secretary of State Dean Rusk, April 5, 26, 1962; Rusk to Accra, April 19, 1962,

reporting that Robeson was ill with "a nervous disorder" in Moscow, implying it was unlikely he would be able to assume the appointment). For the return to Moscow: ER to Ruth Gage Colby, July 4, 1961; ER to Shirley Du Bois, July 2, 1961; Du Bois to PR, July 25, 1961; ER to PR, Jr., and Marilyn, July 7, 1961; ER to Rockmores [May 1961], July 10, 1961—all in RA. In the middle of July, Essie came down with an attack of gallstones and was herself hospitalized for two weeks; deciding against surgery, the doctors put her on a restricted diet (ER to PR, Jr., and Marilyn, July 29, 1961; ER to Ed Barsky, Aug. 11, 1961—both in RA).

8. ER to Helen and Sam Rosen, July 31, 1961, courtesy of Rosen; ER to PR, Jr., and Marilyn, Aug. 18, 19, 1961, RA; multiple conversations with Helen Rosen. Alphaeus and Dorothy Hunton also visited the Robesons briefly at Barveekha, along with John Pittman and his wife, Margrit; they had all come to attend the funeral of William Z. Foster in Moscow (ER to PR, Jr., and Marilyn, Sept. 5, 1961, RA). Shortly before he died, Foster had been at Barveekha for treatment (ER to Freda Diamond, May 14, 1961, RA).

9. ER to Rosens, Sept. 5, 1961, RA; multiple conversations with Helen Rosen. In a letter to family, et al., ER later confirmed that it was Davison's doctor, Philip Lebon, who had put her in touch with the Priory (ER to family, et al., January 28, 1963, RA).

10. Multiple interviews with Helen Rosen.

11. The comments on Ackner were made to me by Dr. Max Fink, the ECT specialist (at the State University of New York, Stony Brook). Ackner to Perlmutter, Jan. 9, 1964; John Flood to Perlmutter, Jan. 17, 1964; Ackner to Dr. Baumann, Aug. 24, 1963, RA. Of the Priory doctors, Essie (at least in the beginning) was especially keen on John Flood. "HE is our man," she wrote Helen Rosen enthusiastically. "He is Paul's choice, and he and Dr. A. [Ackner] are the ONLY ones he talks to" (Dec. 19, 1961, courtesy of Rosen). Although ECT treatment was not so benign a procedure then as currently, Helen Rosen says that Paul was "always highly sedated before being given one

and afterwards remembered nothing" (multiple interviews with Rosen). That Robeson did suffer at least some short-term memory problems from the ECT treatments is confirmed in ER to Helen Rosen, Dec. 14, 19, 1961, courtesy of Rosen. Apparently Robeson also got at least a few insulin treatments (ER to Rosens and Rubens, Oct. 11, 1962, courtesy of Rosen). Dr. Robert Millman and Dr. Theodore Tyberg helped me to evaluate Robeson's general medical history. Two phone conversations (June 1985) with Dr. Max Fink, of SUNY, Stony Brook, helped clarify the ECT specifics. "Attitudes today are different towards ECT," Fink said, "but not dosage particularly." Fink added, in a follow-up letter to me of July 4, 1986, that "in today's classification, the history and description of Paul Robeson's condition would most likely fit that of a patient with a delusional depressive disorder, probably bipolar disorder—for which condition convulsive therapy remains the most effective treatment." The most recent reviews of the literature on ECT are Raymond R. Crowe, "Electroconvulsive Therapy—A Current Perspective," *New England Journal of Medicine* (July 19, 1984); Philip G. Janicak, et al., "Efficacy of ECT: A Meta-Analysis," *American Journal of Psychiatry*, March 1985; Richard Abrams, *Electroconvulsive Therapy* (Oxford 1988); A. J. Frances and R. E. Hales, eds., *Review of Psychiatry* (APA, 1988), pp. 431–532. The current debate is conveniently summarized in "Electroconvulsive Therapy: An Exchange," *The New York Review of Books*, May 30, 1985, in which William H. Nelson argues for the conclusion that "ECT is clearly superior to all other available forms of treatment of severe depression" and is especially impressive in achieving results with patients who had previously failed to respond to drug or psychological therapy. Nelson cites a survey of three thousand randomly selected psychiatrists (*Task Force Report #14: Electroconvulsive Therapy* [APA Press, 1978]) in support of his claim that two-thirds share his favorable disposition to ECT, and only 2 percent totally oppose the treatment. He acknowledged, though, that ECT "remains a controversial treatment," and

in answering him Marilyn Rice and Israel Rosenfield reiterate the opposing view that "proper testing" (in Rosenfield's words) will eventually reveal that ECT treatment does produce permanent brain damage even though it is useful in treating severe depression. According to Dr. Max Fink, the arguments presented by Rice and Rosenfield "have been assessed repeatedly, and rejected; the latest is by the 1985 NIH Consensus Conference on Electroconvulsive Therapy" (Fink to me, July 4, 1986). Even today, according to Fink, the "efficacy rate" for a condition like Robeson's is higher with convulsive therapy (greater than 75 percent in controlled studies) than with an alternative drug regimen ("The combination of an antidepressant drug like imipramine or amitriptyline and an antipsychotic drug like perphenazine or fluphenazine" has an efficacy rate of less than 65 percent). As regards psychotherapy, a major study released in the spring of 1986 concludes that some forms are as effective as drugs in treating depression (*The New York Times*, May 14, 1986)—an option not used with PR except peripherally in 1965. The study, however, is based on a small sample and involves ambulatory, non-psychotic, and mildly depressed individuals; at the time he was admitted to the Priory, Robeson's illness was more acute. According to Dr. Max Fink (letter to me, July 4, 1986), "There is no study suggesting that any form of psychotherapy is even moderately successful with patients with bipolar disorder, or with major depressive disorders with delusions." For a less positive view on ECT than Fink's (though it cites him as a leading authority), see the popularized account in Mark S. Gold, *The Good News About Depression* (Villard Books, 1987), especially pp. 231–32. Gold's exultant listing of the promising new drug therapies currently available makes for poignant reading in relation to the limited treatment options in Robeson's day.

12. PR, Jr., believes that the shock treatments and drug therapies at the Priory were a part of "a deliberate attempt to 'neutralize' Robeson, traceable to the CIA and its British counterpart MI-5," but no direct evidence has surfaced to

substantiate this conclusion. PR, Jr.'s views were expressed to me in multiple conversations and in his ms. comments. For more on this issue, see note 27, p. 747. A number of Essie's friends have suggested to me that although she may have acted imperfectly, she did so with Paul's interests foremost in her mind.

13. From the limited records available to him, Dr. Max Fink concluded that the treatment Ackner prescribed "seems to have been entirely appropriate for the time. ECT was the most effective treatment for Robeson's condition" (phone interviews; letter of July 4, 1986). The Priory doctors did attempt to treat Robeson with many of the drugs then available—including Paratlin, Nardil, Tofranil, Tryptizol, Marsalid, and Meprobamate. Marsalid was a new, well-regarded drug, since replaced in the medical arsenal because it can cause liver-function disturbances, as indeed it did with Robeson. He also got the standard side effects of dry mouth and breathing difficulties from Tofranil and Tryptizol. In the words of Dr. John Flood, "the only treatment which had any effect, albeit temporary, was ECT" (Flood to Perlmutter, Jan. 17, 1964, RA). Ackner's comparable phrase, "without much benefit," is in Ackner to Baumann, Aug. 24, 1963, RA. That Robeson derived some immediate (but not lasting) benefit from ECT treatment is documented in ER's letters to Sam and Helen Rosen, Dec. 20, 1961, Feb. 19, 26, March 1, 5, Nov. 27, 1962, courtesy of Rosen.

14. Multiple interviews with Rosen.

15. ER to Rose Rubin, Oct. 5, 1961; ER to Peggy Ashcroft, Oct. 12, 1961; ER to Freda Diamond, Oct. 13, 1961; Rockmore to ER, no date (Oct. 1?), 1961, carbon to PR, Jr., along with note about "furious," Oct. 11, 1961; ER to Rockmore, Oct. 15, 29, 1961—all in RA; ER to Revels Cayton, Dec. 24, 1961, courtesy of Cayton. John Abt, the lawyer for the CPUSA, had been allowed to visit PR, and this fact, plus the account of Robeson's debilitated condition Abt gave on his return to the States, partly accounted for the Rockmores' concern and anger.

16. ER to PR, Jr., Oct. 5, 7, 13, 29, 30, 1961; Shirley Du Bois to ER, Oct. 29,

1961—all in RA. In her Oct. 30 letter to PR, Jr., Essie reported that she and Big Paul had watched Martin Luther King, Jr., on the TV program "Face to Face"; she thought King "very good, but . . . a bit on the quiet side . . . a bit uninspired. . . ." As an example of Essie's "upbeat" accounts, the unusually detailed "REPORT" (four typed pages, RA) for Oct. 12–13, 1961, begins with how she found Big Paul "with relief nurse in garden on bench, happy, welcoming," continues with his discussing the unsuitability of John Gielgud for the role of Othello (Zeffirelli's production had just opened, with Peggy Ashcroft playing Emilia), then has PR having a "nice chat" with a woman who approached them (she turned out to be the first wife of Beerbohm Tree), and ends with her expressing some slight concern about his inability to sleep and the high dose of medication being given him at night.

17. ER to Rockmores, Oct. 29, 1961 (Gracie Fields); ER to Freda Diamond, Dec. 24, 1961—both in RA; ER to Helen Rosen, Dec. 8, 19, 1961, courtesy of Rosen.

18. ER to Helen Rosen, Dec. 8, 1961 (courtesy of Rosen).

19. PR, Jr., ms. comments (suicidal); interview with Harry Francis, 1971, cassette courtesy of PR, Jr.

20. ER to Helen Rosen, Nov. 18 (two letters, same date), Dec. 24, 1961, courtesy of Rosen.

21. ER to Sam and Helen Rosen, Feb. 9, 1962, courtesy of Helen Rosen.

22. ER to Rosens, Feb. 11 (Robinson), 19, 26, March 1, 5, 1962, courtesy of Rosen; ER to Marian Forsythe (with copies to PR, Jr., the Rosens, and Bob Rockmore), March 16, 1962; also a note from PR to Marian, March 1, 1962, reassuring her that he was "feeling much, much better"—both courtesy of Paulina Forsythe; PR to Clara and Bob Rockmore, March 1, 1962, courtesy of Clara Rockmore.

23. Interview with Katzenstein, July 26, 1986; Ackner to Baumann, Aug. 24, 1963; ER to Janet Jagan, Feb. 5, 1962; ER to Larry Brown, Oct. 3, 1962—all in RA; Andy to Larry Brown, Nov. 19, 1962, NYPL/Schm: Brown. Hearing from

Charles Howard about his visit to Paul, Ralph Bunche wrote Essie a note saying how sorry he was "to learn that Paul is incapacitated. . . . Although over the years Paul and I have not seen eye to eye on political matters, I have great affection for him and I send him warm personal regards." ER wrote back how "VERY pleased" Paul was "to have your warm greetings" (Bunche to ER, Aug. 22, 1962; ER to Bunche, Aug. 25, 1962, RA).

24. ER to Helen Rosen, Dec. 4, 14, 1961; ER to Rosens, April 10, 1962; ER to Rosens and Rubens, Oct. 11, 1962 (Larry's music, last visit)—all courtesy of Helen Rosen. PR's public tribute to Brown was during his Aug. 30, 1949, Rockland Palace speech (tape, RA). When Louise Bransten was in London in late 1961, she also was allowed to visit.

25. ER to "Dear Friends," March 24, 1962 (soliciting greetings), MSRC: Murphy. The many letters, cards, and telegrams are in RA; Nkrumah's letter is dated April 3, 1962; Helen Rosen's comment on the phone call is in Helen Rosen to PR, April 9, 1962, RA. They also named a new youth singing club in the GDR for Robeson (Deckert to PR, Aug. 17, 1962; PR to Deckert, Aug. 25, 1962, RA). The black militant Julian Mayfield wrote a glowing tribute to him in the Ghana *Evening News*, April 18, 1962. Nkrumah continued with his efforts to entice Robeson to settle down in Ghana, as Shirley and W. E. B. Du Bois had done (they were joined by Dorothy and Alphaeus Hunton in the spring of 1962 to work with Du Bois on the *Encyclopedia Africana*, sponsored by the Ghana Academy of Sciences [Hunton to Robesons, May 14, 1962, RA]). To meet Paul's needs, Nkrumah converted his original offer of a chair at the University of Ghana to a visiting professorship, but, although Paul willingly and gratefully agreed to have his name associated with the university, he made it clear (through Essie) that he had no idea whether he would again be able to work, and if so how much. It was a deep sorrow to him. (E. C. Quist-Therson, secretary to Nkrumah, to PR, April 10, 1962; ER to Nkrumah, March 4, May 24, 1962—all in RA). He was then invited to become an honorary fellow of the Institute of African Studies at the University of Ghana (Thomas Hodgkin to PR, Dec. 11, 1962; ER to Hodgkin, Feb. 17, 1963—both in RA).

Essie was unable to get back to work on the two books (one on the Congo, the other on politics) she had hoped to write, but between visits to the Priory she kept her hand in. She participated in the birthday rally for the *Daily Worker* (reading a few words of greeting from Paul), maintained an active political correspondence with Janet Jagan on developments in British Guiana, with Russian friends about the possible translation and publication of her work (Boris Polevoi had become editor-in-chief of the magazine *Youth*, and Mikhail Kotov assisted from several angles), and in the fall of 1962 covered the Commonwealth prime-ministers' conference for the Associated Negro Press, deeply engaged by the British debate over Common Market versus Commonwealth. (*Daily Worker:* George Matthews, editor, to ER, Feb. 9, March 1, 1962, RA; *London Daily Worker,* March 5, 1962; PR's brief remarks to the rally are in RA. British Guiana: ER to Jagan, Feb. 3, April 13, Aug. 27, 1962; Jagan to ER, July 2, 1962. Russia: ER to Kotov, Feb. 19, June 22, 1962. Commonwealth Conference: ER to Larry Brown, Oct. 3, 1962; ER to Freda Diamond, Oct. 26, 1962; ER to Indira Gandhi, September 19, 1962; ER to Nehru, September 19, 1962—all in RA.)

26. ER to Rosens, May 10, 27, June 20, 1962; ER to Helen Rosen, May 31, 1962 (rise in PR's spirits)—all courtesy of Rosen. William Wolff to PR, May 14, 1962; Hille to PR, June 4, 1962; PR's brief ms. of Hille greetings and also the preface to George Cunelli's book, *Voice No Mystery* (dated July 19, 1962, and, judging from the style, written by Essie)—all in RA. A dozen years later Cunelli's book had still not been published. The way Cunelli explained it to Robeson, "The publishers . . . put some obstacles in my way, asking diminished admiration for Soviet achievements in visual art and vocal problems, and could I ask my past pupil, Laurence Olivier, to write a Preface instead of Paul Robeson.

I refuse this opportunist proposition" (Cunelli to PR, June 3, 1974, courtesy of Paulina Forsythe). Essie thought that writing the preface to the book had been important in getting Paul a labor permit (ER to Rosens and Rubens, Oct. 11, 1962, courtesy of Rosen).

27. FBI New York 100-25857-4379, March 5, 1962 (Key Figure); FBI Main 100-12304-641 (passing). Robeson was finally deleted from the Key Figures list at the New York Office in January 1963. As early as April 1961, shortly after PR's suicide attempt, an FBI memo speculated that "the death of Robeson would be much publicized . . . his name and past history would be highlighted . . . in propagandizing on behalf of the international communist movement" (FBI Main 100-12304-621).

Both in print and in private discussion, PR, Jr., has strenuously argued the possibility that the U.S. government deliberately "neutralized" his father, perhaps by slipping him the hallucinogen BZ (which the United States is on record as using elsewhere) in Moscow in March 1961, perhaps by playing a role in the course his medical treatment took, particularly in the administering of a protracted series of ECT. I have done everything I could think of—including a lawsuit against the FBI for the release of Robeson files denied me under the Freedom of Information Act—to unearth the evidence that would allow for a conclusion one way or the other on PR, Jr.'s speculations. So many of the government documents forwarded to me under the FOIA (or extracted by lawsuit) are inked over that I have found it impossible to say for sure that there is *nothing* to his charges (especially since PR's Priory records are apparently lost; after a prolonged search, the deputy hospital director informed me that she was unable to locate the "relevant medical notes." [Alison Boyle to me, March 29, 1988]). So little of even a circumstantial nature has surfaced to support PR, Jr.'s case that I have had to draw the conclusion, tentative though it must remain for now, that the case is unproved.

28. ER to the Rosens; ER to the Rockmores; ER to PR, Jr., and Marilyn—all May 27, 1962, RA. The Rockmores were on their way to the U.S.S.R. and were able to visit with Paul—separately, to avoid undue strain—three times at the Priory and four times at the flat. Essie reported to the Rosens (May 27, 1962, RA) that before they came "He had been going down toward depression. . . . I think the stimulation of their visit postponed the depression, arrested it. . . . After they left on the Monday, he slowly went down." Dr. Ackner agreed that he was "way down." He had begun ECT again on May 19 (the last previous treatment had been April 19), and in the following week he got ECT three times, the series of eleven (for a total to date of thirty-five) extending through October 15, 1962 (Ackner to Baumann, Aug. 24, 1963). It was not unusual in those days to have repeated courses of ECT. On this round, he came out of the first three treatments at "a much higher level" (according to Essie), but he almost always did improve immediately afterward, only to relapse once again. Essie asked the Rockmores to report fully to the Rosens, "and to Pauli fully, but cautiously." PR, Jr.'s own health was much improved, but still not entirely secure. "Have had my own little ups and downs but the *average* has been steadily *up,*" he wrote his father on April 4, 1962 (RA); seven months later he was still reporting "feeling pretty good these days. . . . I'm getting stronger and more confident quite rapidly. I was not upset too much even by the events of the last couple of weeks [the Cuban missile crisis]. . . . I seem to be well on my way now and getting steadily stronger and more confident" (PR, Jr., to ER and PR, Nov. 4, 1962, RA).

29. ER to John Abt and Ben Davis, Jr., July 13, 1962; Bailey to ER, July 10, 1962; American Embassy to State Department, July 12, 1962, along with ER's affidavit—all in RA. FBI Main 100-12304-657.

30. ER to John Abt and Ben Davis, Jr., July 13, 1962, RA. According to an FBI report, Robeson was additionally upset at this time by PR, Jr.'s alleged "expulsion" from the CPUSA (Director to SAC Chicago, Jan. 3, 1963, FBI Main 100-12304-[illegible]).

31. Abt to Robesons, July 17, 1962, RA. Robeson once again managed a trip to the U.S. Embassy to sign, this time supported by Essie, Harry Francis, and the British lawyer D. N. Pritt.

32. ER to Rosens, May 27, 1962 ("hopeless"); ER to Mikhail Kotov, June 22, 1962 ("wither away"); Helen Rosen to PR, April 9, 1962 (planned trip); ER to Sam Rosen, Sept. 1, 1962; ER to Judy Ruben, Sept. 1, 1962; ER to Freda Diamond, Aug. 25, 1962 ("end of nightmare")—all in RA. Helen Rosen told me that in her actual presence she never heard Paul threaten suicide. Dr. Ackner thought Robeson was "morbidly preoccupied about his inability to sleep and about his loss of weight" (Ackner to Baumann, Aug. 24, 1963, RA). The *Daily Herald*, Oct. 26, 1962, reported Harold Davison "hotly" denying the rumor that Robeson had decided to retire; all he had to do, Davison is quoted as saying, is "to slow down his pace a little," and he had "a great deal of artistry" left "to offer the world." At just this time, Peggy Middleton was writing Cedric Belfrage, "Paul is still in and out of his nursing home. I have had tea with him. That's all I can say without being depressing" (Oct. 13, 1962, courtesy of Belfrage).

33. ER to family, et al., Jan. 28, 1963, RA; Middleton to Belfrage, Jan. 27, 1963, courtesy of Belfrage.

34. ER to Rosens, Feb. 5, March 27, 1963, courtesy of Rosen; ER to Clara Rockmore, Feb. 17, March 19, 1963, RA; PR to Clara Rockmore, March 18, May 30, 1963, courtesy of Clara Rockmore. In his May 30 letter to Clara, PR wrote to her as if for the first time about Rockmore ("Just heard today about our beloved Bobby"), sadly suggesting his confused state of mind.

35. ER to Clara Rockmore, March 19, 1963; "Dear Dear Friends," March 17, 1963—both in RA.

36. The many letters and telegrams of greetings on his sixty-fifth birthday are in RA. Walter Ulbricht of the GDR was one of those who cabled good wishes, and Paul signed a thank-you letter Essie composed in response (PR to Ulbricht, June 2, 1963, RA). Among the other celebrations was a Radio East Berlin broadcast, an article on him by Martha Dodd (" 'I Am A Folk-Singer': Paul Robeson," ms. in RA) in the Cuban paper *Hoy*, and a radio talk in Ghana by Reba Lewis (transcript in RA). ER to Helen Rosen, April 7, 1963, courtesy of Rosen ("so angry"); ER to Freda Diamond, April 27, 1963 ("damn thing"), RA.

37. *The National Insider*, Jan. 6, 13, 1963. The FBI gave some thought to using the articles in its Counterintelligence Program, but abandoned the idea: the *Insider* was too obviously a sleaze publication, the articles themselves contained too much "anti-American sentiment on the racial issue," and no confirming evidence of Robeson's supposed change of heart could be found (FBI New York 100-25857-4407, 4408). The Pittsburgh *Courier* (Jan. 26, 1963) was among the publications reprinting the rumor of Robeson's break with Russia (as filtered through the syndicated labor columnist Victor Reisel). In Europe, *Le Figaro* published the story on May 2, 1963, but was swiftly rebutted by the Communist paper *L'Humanité* on May 3 (FBI Main 100-12304-677).

38. ER to PR, Jr., et al., April 28, 1963; Pritt to ER, May 2, 1963; PR, Jr., to ER, May 17, 1963—all in RA. ER's draft and final statement are also in RA. Claude A. Barnett to ER, May 29, 1963, and ANP release are in CHS: Barnett; Middleton to Belfrage, "Christmas '63," courtesy of Belfrage. ER ms. in RA (further statement); *Time*, Sept. 6, 1963 ("Eslandic").

It was around this same time, curiously, that Alfred Knopf asked Carl Van Vechten to have a look at a proposal he'd received for a biography of PR: "I think it a very poor idea myself, but I am, as always, willing to sit at the feet of the master." Van Vechten read the proposal and wrote Knopf, "I see no point in a book about Paul Robeson now *unless* James Baldwin can be persuaded to write it. He would assuredly take an intransigent point of view and might even attack Robeson. Anyway anything Baldwin writes sells and *is read*." Knopf wrote back, "I certainly wouldn't want to chance a book on Robeson by Baldwin. In fact, as I wrote you, I wasn't very keen myself about the whole idea, and I gather that you are not exactly excited." The idea died there. (The proposal was submitted in a memo to Knopf from H. Cantor on Dec. 26, 1962; Knopf to Van Vechten, Dec. 27, 1962, Jan. 2, 1963; Van Vechten to Knopf, Dec. 29, 1962, all in UT: Knopf.)

39. Middleton to Belfrage, Aug. 7, 1963, courtesy of Belfrage; ER to Kotov, June 22, 1962, RA; ER to ? (no salutation or date; [Oct. 1962?]) (reporters at Priory), courtesy of Helen Rosen. In regard to the missile crisis, Essie had herself written, "I have always been glad that Castro is a Man what takes no tea for the fever, as we Negroes say" (ER to Rosens and Rubens, Nov. 1, 1962, courtesy of Helen Rosen).

40. Peggy Middleton to Cedric Belfrage, Aug. 7, Sept. 4, 1963, and "Christmas '63," courtesy of Belfrage. In the Aug. 7 letter she wrote, ". . . I have broken through at last and he will be going elsewhere soon. I could write a book about all this. . . . The whole thing is a kind of 20th Century nightmare." Middleton claimed that the Priory had been so "interested in the mind that they do not notice what is happening to the body" and had been indifferent to Paul's "physical state." Helen Rosen considers that untrue: Paul had regular and frequent physical examinations—though perhaps the results were not sufficiently attended. Interview with Micki Hurwitt (PR, Jr., participating), May 14, 1982; interview with Cedric and Mary Belfrage, May 29, 1984; ER to Rosens, June 27, July 14, 1963 (Hurwitt), courtesy of Helen Rosen. Hurwitt was very drawn to Essie, finding her charming, accomplished, and complex, a "feminist," a "woman of great pride who had her own interests and wouldn't take any shit of certain kinds from Paul," though she was entirely willing to front for him and protect him: she was willing to "be 'a dragon' so he could be his beautiful self."

41. Middleton to Belfrage, Aug. 7, Sept. 4, 1963, courtesy of Belfrage; interview with Hurwitt, May 14, 1982; interview with Katzenstein, July 26, 1986. Dr. Ackner had used paraldehyde in Feb. 1962, after Robeson became "very de-

pressed," in order to put him "on modified narcosis for three days"; he interspersed the paraldehyde with sodium amytal. He also prescribed paraldehyde for sleeping, believing that "the combination which appeared to benefit him most was "Paraldehyde drachms 3 with Nembutal gr. 3 and Largactil mg. 100" (Ackner to Baumann, Aug. 24, 1963, RA).

42. Middleton to Belfrage, Sept. 4, 1963, courtesy of Belfrage.

43. *Sunday Telegraph,* Aug. 25, 1963; interview with Diana Loesser, July 29, 1986.

44. ER to Marie Seton, Sept. 12, 1963, courtesy of Seton; interview with Hurwitt, May 14, 1982; typed ms. of Essie's "Kidnapped!! A True Short Story," RA, serialized in *The Afro-American,* Nov. 2, 9, 16, 1963. Hurwitt remembers that Nick Price went to the apartment first and brought the key back to her, reversing Essie's version in "Kidnapped"; I have gone with Essie's version because it was written immediately afterward, whereas the Hurwitt interview took place twenty years later; the discrepancy, in any case, is not over a significant point; on all major elements in the story the three accounts are in agreement. Hurwitt recalled that at least one of the Priory doctors was hostile to Paul's removal, sarcastically asking her, "What will you do if a man of that size goes berserk on the plane?" Nick Price was the son of Branson Price, an expatriate left-wing American woman who had known Paul during the Progressive Party campaign.

45. ER, "Kidnapped," RA; interview with Hurwitt, May 14, 1982; ER to Marie Seton, Sept. 12, 1963, courtesy of Seton; *Punch,* Sept. 4, 1963.

46. ER, "Kidnapped," RA; interview with Hurwitt, May 14, 1982; ER to Seton, Sept. 12, 1963, courtesy of Seton.

47. ER, "Kidnapped," RA; ER to Seton, Sept. 12, 1963, courtesy of Seton. *The New York Times,* in fact, carried a more restrained account than appeared in much of the British press, quoting Harry Francis to the effect that it was "sheer nonsense" to talk of Robeson's being "smuggled" out (Aug. 26, 1963). In contrast, the *Daily Sketch* talked of a "deepen-

ing" mystery, and the *Daily Mirror* head-lined "Rumors of Plot" (both Aug. 26, 1963). The New York *Daily News*, on the other hand, matched British sensational-ism with its statement (Aug. 30, 1963) that "some of us suspect Paul Robeson never again will emerge from behind the Iron Curtain." The FBI was more cau-tious in evaluating the rumors, deciding to let the whole matter "die [a] natural death" (FBI Main 100-12304-309, 310). USIA London reported to USIA Wash-ington on Aug. 30, 1963, that "The Em-bassy's Legal Attaché says he has no evidence whatsoever that Robeson had changed his views about Communism or had a desire to recant" (FBI Main 100-12304-240).

48. ER, "Kidnapped," RA; interview with Hurwitt, May 14, 1982; ER to Seton, Sept. 12, 1963, courtesy of Seton; *Tele-graph*, Aug. 26, 1963. In a second *Tele-graph* article (Aug. 27, 1963), Osman quoted a GDR Peace Council spokesman to the effect that Robeson had come for a thorough medical examination. He also revealed that John Peet had been on the Polish Airways flight to East Berlin. Peet was a former British journalist who had "gone over" to the GDR more than a decade earlier and edited the English-language *Democratic German Report*. A few days after the flight, Peet sent Essie an extract from *The New Statesman* of Aug. 30 which hurtfully took her to task for refus-ing to cooperate with the press and for creating "a mountain of suspicion and mistrust out of what may have been only a mole-hill of gossip," thereby injuring "her husband's reputation and his life's cause" (Peet to ER, Aug. 31, 1963, RA). Harry Francis wrote a lengthy response to *The New Statesman* (Sept. 2, 1963), de-nying that PR's illness was in any degree linked to his purported "discovery" of racial discrimination within the U.S.S.R. When Robeson returned to Europe in 1958, Francis wrote, "it was clear that he was already a sick man," and he had then proceeded to overtax himself further in *Othello* ("I personally feared that he was due for a crack-up in health before the end of that year"), compounded by a difficult tour of Australia during which "he found himself in argument, often

quite violent, with sections of the Aus-tralian press who showed themselves to be even less subtle than their counter-parts in Britain." Robert G. Spivak wrote an article in the New York *Herald Tribune* that tried to keep alive the flames of sus-picion, both about Robeson's "disillu-sionment" and his "kidnapping," and quoted the West Indian actor Edric Con-nor as yet another voice of doubt (for more on Connor and PR, see note 12, p. 686, and note 16, p. 725.

49. Interview with Dr. Katzenstein, July 26, 1986. For a detailed discussion of the recent literature on ECT, see note 11 of this chapter. Curiously, Dr. Katzen-stein (who was a clinical psychologist, not a physician) does not seem, in his ses-sions with PR, to have encouraged him to talk about his private life. In our inter-view, Katzenstein told me, "I didn't even go into too much on personal questions," and he had never even heard the names of Clara or Bob Rockmore. (However, PR did tell Katzenstein that he and Lena Horne had been "in love." For more on Horne and PR, see note 31, p. 675.) Kat-zenstein further said, remarkably, that he did not know that Robeson had had a breakdown in 1956, although he claims that Robeson did "always answer" his questions about political matters: "I didn't see any evidence of his having 'dis-loyal' thoughts about the Soviet Union. On the contrary, he immediately became angry if anybody thought this sort of thing."

According to Micki Hurwitt, "One of the first things that Katzenstein said to me in regard to the ECT Paul had been given was, 'They would never have done this to him in the States'" (interview, May 14, 1982). According to PR, Jr. (in conversa-tions with me), the Soviet team of doctors, led by Dr. Snezhnevsky, had also said, in 1961, that ECT was not indicated in PR's case. Dr. Larry Kerson, the last neurolo-gist to treat Robeson (in Philadelphia, 1974–75), and cautious in general about the use of ECT, believes there is a possi-bility—no more than that—that the ECT treatment given Robeson may have ac-celerated a degenerative process that might have happened anyway. Even so, Kerson agrees that, given the state of the art in 1961, ECT would have been the logical treatment choice for Robeson (phone interview, March 1987).

50. ER to Dorothy and Alphaeus Hunton, Oct. 5, 1963; ER to Shirley Du Bois, Oct. 5, 1963; ER to Freda Diamond, Nov. 5, 1963; Elliott Hurwitt to ER, Sept. 20, 1963—all in RA; multiple interviews with Helen Rosen (Sam's reaction); ER to Helen Rosen, Oct. 4, 15, 1963, courtesy of Rosen. Micki Hurwitt (interview, May 14, 1982) was impressed that the Buch doctors *believed* Paul when he said he couldn't sleep; in the Priory they had told him he was "morbidly preoccupied" with the issue, and in fact slept more than he thought he did (Ackner to Baumann, Aug. 24, 1963, RA).

A lengthy, remarkably detailed report on Robeson is contained in Dr. Baumann to Dr. Barsky, Dec. 14, 1963, RA (the report is in German; Michael Lipson translated it for me). Among its findings, the report refers to "heart activity" being in "the normal range," but "Hemodynamically, there is a much-too-low rate of recuperation of the heart" and some limited "myocardial damage." The Buch doctors treated the heart problem with Ceglunat (Lanatosid C) and also, "for improvement of myocardial metabolism," injections of Atriphos and Vitamin B_{12}; "the tendency to (Hyptomie) responded well to pholedrin medication 30 g." They treated his intestinal difficulties with prednisone and a broad range of antibiotics. "The checkup rectoscopy showed clear improvement."

For PR's sleeping problem, the doctors at Buch began "autogenous training," with "great emphasis" on the patient's maintaining a set daily schedule, including daily massage, gymnastic exercises, a walk morning and afternoon, as well as a one-and-a-half-hour nap at noon; PR "responded well at first, so that it was possible with the help of this technique to bring about four to six hours of sleep per night. Further lengthening of sleeping time proved difficult."

As for Paget's disease, the contemporary (1986) medical textbooks (supported by Dr. Lawrence Mass, Dr. Theodore Tyberg, Dr. Robert Millman, and other physicians I questioned on the matter) do not list any psychiatric consequences resulting from the disease. Yet the Buch clinicians, in apparent disagreement, concluded in PR's case, "Even the sleep disturbances and the past circumstance of attacks of depression could be seen as results of this disease." In our personal interview (July 26, 1986), however, Dr. Katzenstein confirmed the view of my American medical consultants that the Paget's finding was strictly secondary and had no psychiatric significance.

The Buch doctors made only one other formal comment on Robeson's psychological state: "This altogether intelligent, sensitive, and strong-willed patient, at a time of life in which purely for reasons of age a certain lessening of his capacities was natural, suffered a serious psychological trauma as a result of a suite of extremely burdensome circumstances [that] . . . brought with it a diminished capacity for achievement and for self-consciousness, and in its wake led to a suite of psychological crises"—in other words, a social rather than an organic explanation for Robeson's problems. The difficulty with that explanation lies in its all-encompassing vagueness and in its inability to account for the renewed onset of psychological problems at a time when his artistic outlets had once more been restored. The Buch clinicians felt that Robeson made "relatively good progress" in his "general psychological condition" through Librium treatment ("Depressive tendencies were no longer present as often, and the patient once again began to take an interested part in the events of his environment"), and recommended that Librium be continued "for some time," in combination with "intensive psychotherapeutic conversations." The latter never became part of PR's treatment, though in 1965–66 he did occasionally (perhaps half a dozen times in all) talk with the New York psychiatrist Dr. Ari Kiev (see pp. 533–34.)

Katzenstein also told Sam Rosen that PR had Paget's. Seeming to confirm that such a diagnosis was made, Peggy Middleton wrote Cedric Belfrage, "As I always, admittedly only intuitively, insisted, it has turned out to be a physical defect," adding, "the prognosis is not good. I suppose he could live quite a while, but he is a shadow of the man he was, both physically and mentally, or perhaps I should say spiritually, because he is quite sane, but so tired mentally that sustained conversation is difficult for him." Middleton relayed the gist of a phone call she had had the day before with Harry Francis in which "we both said to each other how we wished we had been more successful earlier . . . to have saved Paul the 58 [four more than the 54 listed by Ackner] shock treatments and all the unnecessary medication"; but Essie had been entirely in control, and neither Peggy, who had questioned the treatment, nor Harry, who apparently had not, had had any real influence over her (Middleton to Belfrage, "Christmas '63," courtesy of Belfrage). Dr. Pearlmutter's notes provide additional confirmation of the diagnosis of Paget's disease; when admitting PR to Gracie Square Hospital in June 1965, Perlmutter wrote on his chart: ". . . also has Paget's disease of the skull" (Gracie Square Hospital records, courtesy of PR, Jr.).

51. ER to the Huntons, Oct. 5, 1963; ER to Shirley Du Bois, Oct. 5, 1963; ER to Freda Diamond, Nov. 5, 1963; ER to Colin Sweet, Nov. 15, 1963; ER to family, Nov. 18, 1963—all in RA; ER to family, Nov. 16, 21, 1963, courtesy of Paulina Forsythe. Harry Francis also told me that Dr. Katzenstein had said PR would have to live quietly (untaped interview, Aug. 30, 1982). *Neues Deutschland,* Sept. 7, 1963 (Zetkin "peace" medal).

According to Dr. Katzenstein, Essie had earlier sensed that her illness was terminal, and the feeling was confirmed when the Buch clinicians decided not to operate on her. According to Ursula (Mrs.) Katzenstein, Paul "wasn't concerned with Essie's problems"; he didn't want to believe she was seriously ill, because "his physical well-being depended on her." Essie wrote in a similar vein to the family: "First, he was a bit scared when I went down, but fortunately he missed the worst part. . . . After that I was able to maintain a cheerful front while he was in my room. . . . By the time he was disarmed and relieved, I began really to feel better. . . . What is really encourag-

ing, he began to wait on me. . . . All very new for him. And he seemed to really take an interest, and enjoy being useful, without any reminder. It was sweet, and quite a departure" (ER to family, Sept. 23, 1963, courtesy of Paulina Forsythe). The Katzensteins were amazed when one day Essie casually took out the breast prosthesis she'd recently gotten and showed it off to them, delighting in how good it looked and how well it was made (interview with the Katzensteins, July 26, 1986).

While in the GDR, Essie also stayed busy with writing and putting in occasional public appearances. One especially notable one was a seminar on "The Negro and the USA" that she led at Humboldt University. Taking advantage of the presence in East Berlin of Helen and Scott Nearing, Kay Cole (wife of Lester Cole, the blacklisted writer, and herself active in Women Strike for Peace), Rev. Stephen Fritchman, and Earl Dickerson, she formed a panel that ran for nearly three hours and was apparently a great success (". . . Scott got up and delivered a BLAST about the oligarchy of money and power and the takeover by Fascism of everything, including the means of communication, Etc!!! Boy, Oh Boy, he just stood up and blasted, with no introduction, no anything, militant, fighting, terrific" [ER to family, Dec. 5, 1963, RA]) (interview with Earl Dickerson, July 2, 1986).

52. Interviews with Katzenstein (July 26, 1986) and Diana Loesser (July 29, 1986); ER to family, Nov. 18, 1963, RA; ER to family, Oct. 27, Nov. 2, 16, 21, 26, Dec. 1, 1963, courtesy of Paulina Forsythe. He also had a brief phone interview with *Sovietskaya Rossiya* (April 31, 1963). Back in 1954 PR had recorded a song for Joris Ivens's film *The Song of the Rivers,* with a score by Shostakovich, lyrics by Bertolt Brecht, screenplay and commentary by Vladimir Pozner (Pozner to PR, July 22, 1954; PR to Pozner, telegram, July 27, 1954, NYPL/Schm: PR).

53. Interviews with Kay Pankey, July 26, 1986, and Ollie Harrington, July 29, 1986; PR to Aubrey Pankey, May 24, 1963; ER to Pankeys, Nov. 6, 30, 1963—courtesy of Kay Pankey. For more on PR and the Pankeys, see pp. 358, 426. Dr.

Katzenstein confirms that, although PR talked little, he "understood fully" (interview, July 26, 1986).

54. ER to family, Nov. 18, 1963, RA; ER to family, Nov. 16, 21, 1963, courtesy of Paulina Forsythe.

55. PR to Ben Robeson, Nov. 10, 1963, courtesy of Paulina Forsythe; interview with Dr. Katzenstein, July 26, 1986; ER to family, Nov. 18, 1963, RA; ER to family, Nov. 16, 21, 1963, courtesy of Paulina Forsythe. Paul and Essie had watched the March on Washington on television (ER to George Murphy, Jr., Oct. 4, 1963, MSRC: Murphy).

56. ER to family, Nov. 18, 1963, RA. Essie strongly implied that letters seconding the opinion of the doctors were needed from family and friends. Responding to ER's query whether Paul would be "accepted" back in the States, George Murphy, Jr., suggested he could profitably busy himself in two ways: working to establish a repertory theater in Harlem and helping to set up a Du Bois Foundation (Murphy to ER, Dec. 7, 1963,

RA). Katzenstein advised him against making public appearances but, recognizing Paul's need to feel useful, suggested he "might be visited for strategy and advice" (interview with Katzenstein, July 26, 1986).

57. ER to family, Dec. 5, 7, 13, 1963, RA; interview with Katzenstein, July 26, 1986. On Dec. 15, two days before the Robesons left the GDR, the Katzensteins had them to dinner to celebrate Essie's birthday. In their guest book that night, Robeson wrote, "... And thanks so much for taking me into your lovely family—integrating me, so to speak. ..." At the bottom of the page he added, "Thanks *so* much. Grateful remembrances. All best possible" (guest book courtesy of Katzensteins). Even while at the Priory, Robeson had sometimes talked about wanting to go home (ER to Rosens, May 17, 1963, courtesy of Helen Rosen), and had once appended a note to one of Essie's letters to Helen: "I'm terribly lonely and miss home" (ER to Helen Rosen, May 31, 1963, courtesy of Rosen).

CHAPTER 25   ATTEMPTED RENEWAL (1964–1965)

1. New York *Post*, New York *Daily News*, *The New York Times*, all Dec. 23, 1963. The New York *Herald Tribune* characterized Essie as a "hovering shield" (Dec. 23, 1963), and described PR as suffering "a physical breakdown" as the result of "a severe circulatory condition" (Dec. 20, 1963).

2. New York *Amsterdam News*, Jan. 4, 1964; *Post, News*, and *Times*—all Dec. 23, 1963; F. G. Dutton to Mailliard, Jan. 23, 1964, RA; FBI Main 100-12304-674, 691 (press); FBI New York 100-25857-4453.

3. New York *Herald Tribune*, Dec. 25, 1963. The *Journal-American* made similar remarks.

4. Paul Jarrico letter in *Herald Tribune*, Paris ed., Dec. 28, 1963; Pittsburgh *Courier*, Jan. 11, 1964 (J. A. Rogers); Joseph North in *The Worker*, Jan. 5, 1964, also protested the *Trib* editorial; ER to Davison, Sept. 7, 1964, RA. The ms. of a brief tribute to Du Bois, dated Aug. 29

(which the Robesons sent Shirley Du Bois), is in RA.

5. Interview with Perlmutter, March 7, 1983; Perlmutter to Ackner, June 15, 1964 (drugs), and nearly identical letter to Dr. Baumann at the Buch Clinic, same date, RA. Requests for interviews are in William Longgood to PR, Jan. 7, 8, 1964; Allan Morrison (Johnson Publishing) to PR, Sept. 8, 1964; Bob Lucas to PR, June 14, 1964 (saying *Life* was interested)—all in RA. He also got an invitation from the Student Council at Rutgers to speak (Leo Ribuffo to PR, Feb. 3, 1964, RA).

6. ER to George Murphy, Jr., Jan. 31, May 31, 1964, MSRC: Murphy; Multiple interviews with Freda Diamond. Rockmore had made money for PR in the stock market and had assured him, "your finances are in such a condition that if you decided to take it easy ... you can get by without too much effort" (Rockmore to PR, Sept. 22, 1961, RA). Multiple interviews with Marilyn Robeson; ER to "Joe

753

and Mary" North, March 5, 1964; ER to Loessers, Sept. 6, 1964, PR Archiv, GDR. Helen Rosen and Marilyn Robeson had spent a week, along with two cleaning men, scouring the Jumel house; unoccupied for years, it had been filthy.

7. ER to George Murphy, Jr., March 4, 1964, RA. Murphy had had dinner with the Robesons soon after their return and wrote his brother Carl, publisher of *The Afro-American,* "Carl, Paul is a sick man!" and suggested that an interview in *The Afro-American,* whenever Paul felt able, might help to perk him up (GM, Jr., to CM, Dec. 31, 1963; GM, Jr., to ER, Jan. 18, 1964, MSRC: Murphy). Essie's tribute to Du Bois was printed in the San Francisco *Sun Reporter,* March 7, 1964, and favorably commented on in the press (Philadelphia *Afro-American,* March 7, 1964) and by friends (Herbert Biberman to Robesons, Feb. 24, 1964, RA). The FBI also monitored the Du Bois event (FBI New York 100-25857-4531).

8. ER to George Murphy, Jr., May 21, June 2, 1964 (baseball), MSRC: Murphy; ER to Ben Davis, Jr., March 7, 1964, courtesy of Nina Goodman (Mrs. Ben Davis, Jr.); Aptheker to ER, April 21, 25, 1964, RA; *National Guardian,* March 28, 1964; ER to Claude Barnett, June 1, 1964, CHS: Barnett (Marian). When the British Peace Committee, through Harry Francis, arranged a concert in honor of Paul, and *The Worker* celebrated its anniversary, Essie wrote out messages of greetings for Paul to sign (Harry Francis to ER, Jan. 20, Feb. 12, 18, 28, March 26, 1964, RA; the messages are in RA). At the *Guardian* luncheon Essie had strong praise for the current civil-rights struggle, a theme she often sounded in her articles, particularly in "Long Hot Summer" and "Dialogue Between White and Black Americans at the Town Hall" (typed mss. in RA). She was sympathetic to the radical wing of the movement and defended Malcolm X for talking about the need for self-defense ("What could be more reasonable?" she wrote Carlton Goodlett [April 1, 1964, RA], "What with all the dogs, and bombs, and dynamite around!"). During the four months at the Buch Clinic, Essie had also completed a new book, tentatively entitled *Determined to Be an American,* but it was turned down by U.S. publishers (Walter Bradbury, Harper & Row, to ER, April 14, 1964, RA). In July, Essie went to London to cover the Commonwealth meetings; her articles on them are in RA. After seeing Josephine Baker's show one night, Essie went backstage for a chat. "Surrounded by practically all of New York, when she heard my name she left everybody, backed me into a corner and said: My Dear, how is our Paul? Bless her. I gave her our phone number and address and she was on the telephone bright and early. . . . She talked with Paul. . . . [He] was VERY pleased and touched" (ER to Goodlett, May 1, 1964, RA). All the doctors Pearlmutter contacted responded with pleasure to the news of Robeson's improvement: copies of letters from Drs. Snezhnevsky, Ackner, and Katzenstein are in RA; Dr. Baumann wrote the Robesons, "It also gives me pleasure to hear that Paul is doing quite well again and that the process of healing that we set under way here has made continual progress since then" (Sept. 18, 1964, RA, translated from the German by Michael Lipson).

9. A copy of Pearlmutter's medical records is in RA; interview with Pearlmutter, March 7, 1983. ER to George Murphy, Jr., March 4, 1964 ("feels he isn't"); ER to Bass, May 24, 1964 (limited energy); ER to Kotov, June 14, 1964 (idleness); ER to "Dear Dear Friend," Sept. 19, 1964 (reduced medication)—all in RA; ER to Rosens, April 10, 1964, courtesy Rosen.

10. An account of PR's appearance at the Davis funeral is in *The Worker,* Sept. 1, 1964. Elizabeth Gurley Flynn had also recently died; though she and Robeson were not close, shortly before her death she had written an admiring column about him (*The Worker,* April 19, 1964) and he in turn sent a message on the occasion of a memorial tribute to her (Grace Hutchins to PR, Sept. 30, 1964, RA). New York *Amsterdam News,* Sept. 5, 1964 (scene at funeral); the typescript of PR's brief eulogy is in RA.

11. The typed ms. of PR's statement to the black press (dated Aug. 28, 1964) is in RA. Several black papers reprinted the statement, including the *Sun-Reporter,*

the New York *Amsterdam News,* and *The Afro-American* (both on Sept. 5, 1964). Essie had wanted to hold a press conference exclusively for the black press, with the socialist press and maybe "a Tass man" included, but Paul decided on issuing a statement instead (ER to family, Sept. 23, 1963, courtesy of Paulina Forsythe).

12. Rinzler to PR, June 23, Nov. 16, 1964; Rinzler to ER, April 27, June 3, 1965; ER to Rinzler, May 5, 1965; ER to "Dear Dear Friend," Sept. 19, 1964; ER to Harold Davison, Sept. 7, 1964—all in RA; phone interview with Alan Rinzler, May 5, 1986; interview with Earl Robinson, Aug. 17, 1986.

13. ER to George Murphy, Jr. (appended to copy of ER to Clifford McKay, Nov. 16, 1964), MSRC: Murphy. Copy of Pearlmutter's medical notes on PR in RA, as is the typescript of PR's Carnegie Hall remarks; Richard Morford (executive director of American-Soviet Friendship), Nov. 6, 24, 1964; Joe North to PR, Oct. 8, 1964; Joe North to ER, Oct. 8, 1964 (Lawson); *The Worker,* Nov. 16 (Carnegie), 22 (Lawson), 1964; Lawson to Robesons, Nov. 29, 1964; ER to Kotov, Nov. 22, 1964—all in RA. Predictably, the FBI was also present at the Carnegie Hall event (FBI New York 100-25857-4608).

14. Copy of Pearlmutter's medical notes on PR are in RA; ER to Kotov, Nov. 22, 1964, RA ("exhausted"); John Henrik Clarke (associate editor of *Freedomways*) to PR, Oct. 6, 1964, RA. The seven-page typescript of PR's article on Du Bois—by far the most extensive writing he had attempted in some time—is in RA. Esther Jackson to PR, March 25, 1965, RA; New York *Amsterdam News,* April 10, 1965 (ovation). In PR's own hand is the brief statement he wrote for *American Dialog,* the replacement for *Mainstream* (which had folded in Aug. 1963), edited by his friend Joseph North; in the statement Robeson hailed "the gallant new chapter in American history" written by the recent Selma-to-Montgomery March (*American Dialog,* May-June 1965). Yet another death in this period was that of Lil Landau, a close associate of Vito Marcantonio's and friendly with the Robesons since Progressive Party days; the ms. of

ER's brief tribute to her, dated March 6, 1965, is in RA.

15. The arrangements for Claudia Jones's funeral produced some incidental friction. Her associate, A. Manchanda ("Manu"), publicly announced that Robeson had agreed to serve as honorary chairman of the memorial committee, when in fact he had not. Harry Francis was indignant about Manchanda's role (Francis to Robesons, Jan. 18, 1965; Francis to Manchanda, Jan. 17, 1965; "Manu" to Robesons, Jan. 20, 1965 [misdated 1964]—all in RA, along with a transcript of PR's tape recording). On the Hansberry funeral: *The New York Times,* New York *Herald Tribune,* both Jan. 17, 1965, plus PR's brief eulogy, partly written in his hand, RA. ER had put Hansberry's mother in touch with Hubert Delany for legal advice and had visited Lorraine in the hospital twice during her last days (ER to George Murphy, Jr., Dec. 24, 1964, MSRC: Murphy. PR in early 1965 also put in a surprise appearance at the Jan. 15 Statler-Hilton dinner to mark the double celebration of Alexander Trachtenberg's eightieth birthday and the fortieth anniversary of International Publishers, which he had founded (*National Guardian,* Jan. 23, 1965; James S. Allen [president of International Publishers] to PR, Jan. 6, 18, 1965; ms. of PR's tribute, partly in his hand—all RA). The FBI also attended (FBI New York 100-25857-4635). Several weeks later PR spoke briefly at a party to raise money for the Upper West Side W. E. B. Du Bois Club, a Marxist youth group of the New Left (Frieder to PR, Feb. 6, March 1, 1965, RA).

16. Conversations with PR, Jr. Malcolm X's comment on Robeson is quoted in *The Afro-American,* Nov. 30, 1963; the occasion was an attack Malcolm was making on Jackie Robinson for having criticized the Muslims, during which he alluded to Robinson's earlier assault on Robeson. Essie wrote a sympathetic account of Malcolm X's funeral (*The Afro-American,* March 16, 1964), though it's possible to read hostility toward the Muslims in general in a cryptic comment she makes about them in a letter to Henry Winston (Dec. 12, 1964, RA); moreover,

she had earlier written the Rosens that she found Muslim influence in the United States "very frightening. . . . Brother, it's bad enough with the Arabs!!" (ER to Rosens, May 6, 1963, courtesy of Helen Rosen.) RA contains the typescript of an interview with PR by Jack O'Dell and Esther Jackson, editors of *Freedomways*, in which Robeson is described as having "great respect" for the Muslims' "emphasis on the development of economic power among Negroes, discipline, responsibility and pride." But according to PR, Jr., who was present at the interview, the editors of *Freedomways* added so much extraneous material that, in consultation with his father, PR, Jr., denied permission for the interview to be published.

There are several other versions (besides PR, Jr.'s) of the Muslims' approach to Robeson. According to an article in the *Amsterdam News* (May 1, 1965) reporting the *Freedomways* salute to Robeson on April 22, Ossie Davis recalled in front of the audience that Malcolm X "had asked him after Miss Hansberry's funeral to help arrange a meeting with Mr. Robeson whom Malcolm had come to admire." Davis repeated the same version in his interview with Sterner. According to Chuck Moseley and Homer Sadler, Robeson's bodyguards during his May-June 1965 trip to California, a delegation from the Muslims came to them with greetings from Elijah Muhammad as well as an invitation to meet (interview with Moseley and Sadler [PR, Jr., participating], May 3, 1982).

17. Davis/Baldwin/Killens to Jessica Smith, March 3, 1965, MSRC: Smith Papers; Young to Ossie Davis, April 6, 1965; Lawson to *Freedomways*, April 7, 1965; Wilkins to Davis, April 8, 1965; Susskind to *Freedomways*, April 2, 1965—all in RA.

18. The program for the Americana Hotel salute is in RA. The fullest accounts of the event are in *The Worker*, May 2, 1965; the *Amsterdam News*, May 1, 1965 (audience four-fifths white); and Charles P. Howard in the Washington *Afro-American*, May 8, 1965. Among the transcribed speeches and greetings in RA is a letter hailing Robeson's "enormous courage and his complete devotion to his fellow-

men" signed by fifty members of the House of Commons (Julius Silverman, the organizer, to PR, April 3, 1965), as well as congratulatory messages from Compton MacKenzie, Benjamin Britten, Stefan Heym, Cedric Belfrage, Konstantin Simonov—and PR's Somerville classmate Hazel Ericson (Dodge). Rev. Walter Fauntroy, at his June 4, 1965, commencement address at Howard University, praised Robeson as a "cultural giant," though declaring, "He holds political views that are unpalatable to all of us" (the address was sent by Elizabeth Cardozo to ER, July 10, 1965, RA). In the seven hundred tapes and transcripts about the civil-rights movement at Howard University, there is not a single mention of Robeson—a devastating gauge of the generation gap. James Farmer records being taken to meet Robeson at his home in 1965, and inviting him to attend some CORE rallies. When he didn't, Farmer checked back and asked why: "Jim," Robeson purportedly said, "I felt that you had enough problems without being embarrassed by my presence" (James Farmer, *Lay Bare the Heart* [Arbor House, 1985], p. 297).

19. The text of PR's speech is in RA. The FBI, having long since decided that *Freedomways* (to say nothing of Robeson) was avowedly Marxist, conducted a "physical surveillance" of the Americana (FBI New York 100-25857-4704). PR's remarks, along with the speeches by Hope R. Stevens and John Lewis, were published in the Summer 1965 issue of *Freedomways;* the editors excerpted PR's comments.

20. Joe North to Robesons, n.d., RA ("inspiring"); Norma Rogers to PR, May 6, 1965, RA ("memorable"); phone interview with Alan Rinzler, May 5, 1986; *Liberator*, June 1965. The quote from Azikiwe is in a letter to Alphaeus Hunton (Feb. 25, 1958, RA), which was apparently passed on to PR. In a letter to PR himself—the salutation is "My dear Hero"—Azikiwe expressed the fear that "we are now on the verge of realising our dreams, and I do hope that we shall not have dreamt and fought in vain. I say this because as I near my 54th milestone I begin to become disillusioned and I

begin to appreciate the aphorism: things are not always what they seem" (Aug. 23, 1958, RA).

21. Multiple conversations with PR, Jr.; interviews with Alice Childress, Sept. 19, 1983, Oct. 9, 1984.

22. ER to Rosens, May 19, 1965, courtesy of Helen Rosen; ER to family, May 19, 1965, RA; Los Angeles *Times,* May 16, 1965; *People's World,* May 22, 1965; the ms. of PR's speech at the church is in RA—it was also recorded; interview with Chuck Moseley and Homer Sadler (PR, Jr., participating), May 3, 1982. Essie also gave a short speech (*Morning Freiheit,* May 27, 1965). Frankie Lee Sims had been treasurer of the Los Angeles Negro Labor Council in the early fifties, and her husband, George Sims, had been active in the AFL Carpenters Local; both were devout Baptists (*Freedom,* Dec. 1952). In Dorothy Healey's view, to rely on Fritchman and his church as sponsors for Robeson's one major appearance was tantamount to admitting that he had failed to "get a major black response. . . . You do that when it's your last refuge and you have to show a big audience, and there's no question he would . . . pack the church . . . but it wouldn't be packed with black people" (interview, April 1982). Geri Branton (interview, April 2, 1982) confirms that he was not enthusiastically received "in the white *or* the black community."

23. Interviews (PR, Jr., participating) with Geri Branton, April 2, 1982; Dorothy Healey, April 1982; Rose Perry, April 27, 1982. According to Essie, Gus Hall was brought to the Simses' house for a visit by Bill Taylor only "after respectfully obtaining permission . . . didn't stay long. Nice visit . . . All cordial" (ER to family, May 31, 1965, RA). Some of Essie's protectiveness seemed justified when the local Peekskill informer (see p. 371) reappeared in California. Somehow he had ingratiated himself with George and Frankie Lee Sims, and they recommended him to Robeson, who immediately remembered him and refused to get in a car he was driving (interviews with Helen Rosen).

24. ER to family, May 19, 1965, RA. In that letter, Essie reported that Paul had been induced to sing by a woman in the audience who said "she would like to hear Paul sing 8 bars of Go Down Moses. Paul laughed, hesitated, then said, 'O.K., I'll try. I don't know if it will come out, but I'll try'. He then proceeded to sing it right through, beautifully, really beautifully, and the people went wild, and then the lady got up and said: 'I just wanted to prove to you that you could do it'. And Paul said, 'Well, you did!' And the people were delighted."

25. ER to family, May 31, 1965, RA; multiple conversations with PR, Jr; phone interviews with Ruby Silverstone, Feb. 23, March 1, 1987.

26. Phone interviews with Ruby Silverstone, Feb. 23, March 1, 1987; ER to family, May 31, 1965. Transcripts of Robeson's various brief remarks at *People's World,* etc., are in RA.

27. Multiple conversations with PR, Jr. The June 4 Salute to Paul Robeson came off despite his absence and was well attended and enthusiastic (Alvah Bessie to PR, June 6, 1965; James Herndon [chairman] to ER, June 30, July 19, 1965; Mary Helen Jones to ER, July 7, 1965; ER to Herndon, July 8, 1965—all in RA; San Francisco *Sun Reporter,* May 22, June 12, 1965; Canadian *Tribune,* July 19, 1965, reprinting Alvah Bessie's tribute). On June 13 a Musical Tribute to Robeson also came off as planned, sponsored by the San Francisco Negro Historical and Cultural Society; Ethel Ray Nance, who had been an important figure in the Harlem Renaissance, was the chair of the library committee (the program is in RA; *Sun Reporter,* June 12, 1965).

28. It is Paul, Jr.'s belief that in the days preceding the Gracie Square admission Kline had prescribed amphetamines for his father, which were discontinued only because PR, disliking their effect, refused to take them. Dr. Kline had agreed to turn his records on PR over to me, having previously denied to Paul, Jr., that he still had them, but his sudden death intervened. In the absence of those records, the possibility of amphetamines' being used can be neither confirmed nor denied. Pearlmutter to PR, Jr., Oct. 31, 1979 (referral to Kline); interview with

Perlmutter, March 7, 1983; Gracie Square Hospital records (all courtesy of PR, Jr.) for the quotes about "scissors" and "difficulty," recorded by a Dr. Robins when he took PR's history from Essie on the day of admission. In his first entry under "Progress Notes" in the Gracie Square records, Perlmutter refers to the suicide attempt of the previous evening as having been made "with a double-edged razor blade."

29. The physicians' reports and the nurses' comments are all from the Gracie Square Hospital records, courtesy of PR, Jr.

30. In the nurses' notes for June 19, 1965 (Gracie Square Hospital), R.N. Paul Jones recorded, "He said many people felt that he was taking an active part in left wing organizations and this turned them against him."

31. Interview with Dr. Alfred Katzenstein (Buch Clinic), July 26, 1986. Dr. Katzenstein's view that Robeson should have had intensive psychotherapy immediately following his ECT treatments—indeed, his view that ECT is only useful when done in conjunction with analysis—is not shared by most ECT specialists (see note 11, pp. 743–44). At any rate, Robeson never had rigorous psychoanalytic treatment.

32. Interview with Dr. Ari Kiev, Dec. 14, 1982; follow-up phone discussion, Nov. 1, 1986; Du Bois, *Negro Digest*, March 1950.

33. Interview with Dr. Ari Kiev, Dec. 14, 1982; follow-up phone discussion, Nov. 1, 1986.

34. Ibid.

35. Essie's medical records are in RA; multiple conversations with PR, Jr., and with Helen Rosen.

36. Multiple conversations with Helen Rosen.

37. Multiple conversations with Helen Rosen and with PR, Jr.; Gracie Square Hospital records, courtesy of PR, Jr.; interview with Dr. Ari Kiev, Dec. 14, 1982. PR, Jr., ms. comments. Apparently Robeson was no longer on Librium, though it is not clear when he was taken off. Since that medication had worked so well, its withdrawal could alone account for his deterioration.

38. Physicians' reports and nurses' notes are part of the Gracie Square Hospital records, courtesy of PR, Jr.; Essie's medical records are in RA.

39. Physician reports and nurses' notes are from Gracie Square Hospital records, courtesy of PR, Jr. Dr. Kiev has indicated (in follow-up conversations of Nov. 11, 1986, and June 11, 1987) that, although it was contrary to his usual practice to put a patient on Valium *and* Thorazine, he felt the combination was indicated in Robeson's case. Thorazine, then and since, is the most widely used of the major tranquilizers, and the amount Robeson got was below the recommended dosage. He received no more than three hundred milligrams on any one day (and probably less), while for "Hospitalized Patients: Acutely Agitated, Manic, or Disturbed," the *Physicians' Desk Reference* suggests that "500 mg. a day is generally sufficient" and "gradual increases to 2,000 mg. a day or more may be necessary" (*PDR* [Medical Economics Oradell, 1987], p. 1934). Moreover, the dosages used in clinical practices tend to run higher than what are generally viewed as the conservative estimates of the *PDR*.

40. Multiple conversations with PR, Jr.

41. Nachtigall's report, along with the other medical data, is in the Gracie Square Hospital records, courtesy of PR, Jr.; multiple conversations with Helen Rosen and with PR, Jr.; confirming phone interview with Richard Nachtigall, March 10, 1987.

42. University Hospital (NYU) medical records, courtesy of PR, Jr. In my interview with him (March 7, 1983), Dr. Pearlmutter confirmed that "some toxic reaction to the medication" apparently did play a role. He reiterated, too, that after the complications from pneumonia and drug toxicity were resolved, Robeson's degenerative arteriosclerosis may have remained a complicating organic factor in his continuing depression. In a phone interview (March 10, 1987) with Dr. Nachtigall, he confirmed his earlier view that Robeson's high fever was a response to the combination of drugs he had been given. He also said, "It is

theoretically possible that brain damage could result from such a high fever reaction," but "doubted very much" that had been the case with Robeson.

43. ER to Franz Loesser, Oct. 23, 1965, PR Archiv, GDR ("What happened?"); multiple conversations with PR, Jr.; ER's statement is in RA; New York *Journal-American*, Oct. 18, 1965; New York *World-Telegram* and *The New York Times*, Oct. 19, 1965; the Presbyterian and University hospital records are in RA. In the weeks before Robeson disappeared he had been to Dr. Pearlmutter's office for a checkup and Pearlmutter had increased his Valium dosage (Pearlmutter's medical records on Robeson, copy in RA); conceivably, the higher dosage contributed to his confusion.

44. Essie's medical records are in RA; multiple conversations with PR, Jr. The two fullest newspaper obits are: *The New York Times*, Dec. 14, 1965, and *National Guardian*, Dec. 18, 1965. *Freedomways* (Fourth Quarter 1965) put out a special supplement, "Tribute to Eslanda Robeson," containing selections from her writings and reminiscences from friends (including the comments of Ruth Gage Colby, Essie's U.N. friend). Essie died intestate; a statement in Surrogate's Court to that effect, dated Feb. 18, 1966, and signed by PR, Sr., is in RA, which also contains many letters of condolence. Shortly before she died, Essie wrote to Peggy Middleton in London asking her to clean out the Connaught Square flat. Reporting on that to Cedric Belfrage, Middleton went on to make this mysterious comment: "I suspect I shall find that the housekeeper has been told to burn the letters. I'm not in favour of muck-raking biographies, but I somehow feel that all that stuff ought not to be destroyed. I'll take a bet that it is though . . . I should be reluctant myself to set fire to it" (Middleton to Belfrage, Oct. 4, 1965, courtesy of Belfrage). Middleton may have been referring to letters from women to Essie that Paul, Jr., told me he destroyed because he considered them to be love letters.

When near death, Essie had still managed, in the last few months of her life, not only to arrange for the disposition of the London Connaught Square flat, but also to convey approval for the formal establishment of a Paul Robeson Archiv in the GDR (ER to Harold Davison, Oct. 2, 1965; Peggy Middleton to Marilyn Robeson, Aug. 1, 1965; ER to Dr. Ossinger, Nov. 14, 1965; Diana Loesser to ER, Aug. 30, 1965; Victor Grossman to PR, Dec. 24, 1965; Alfred Katzenstein to PR, April 2, 1965—all in RA; Peggy Middleton to Cedric Belfrage, Oct. 4, Dec. 29, 1965, courtesy of Belfrage [Middleton, Harry Francis, and D. N. Pritt were suggested by ER as the English nominees for the Archiv committee; Middleton favored linking Robeson and Du Bois in one archive]).

CHAPTER 26   FINAL YEARS *(1966–1976)*

1. According to Mrs. Gertrude Cunningham, a family relative who lived across the street, Paulina "was furious at all the attention Marian gave to her brother" (interview, Aug. 17, 1982).

2. Lee Lurie to Harold Davison, Jan. 7, 1966 ("pretty rough"); Marian Forsythe to Lurie, Jan. 12, 18, plus an undated letter, 1966—all in RA; Marian to Larry Brown, undated Christmas card (1965?); letter, Jan. 12, 1966—both NYPL/Schm: Brown.

3. Multiple conversations with Helen Rosen, with PR, Jr., and, separately, with Marilyn Robeson; interview with James Aronson, May 31, 1983; Carl Marzani to PR, March 25, 1966, RA; interview with Marzani, March 11, 1986 ("laid out").

4. George B. Murphy, Jr., to PR, Dec. 2, 1966 (Patterson); William J. McKenna, Jr., to PR, Oct. 27, 1966 (Rutgers); Thomas McDonough to PR, Nov. 30, 1966 (film); A. Philip Randolph to PR, June 22, 1966; Dr. Karel Duda to PR, Oct. 18, 1966 (Czechoslovak Ambassador); PR, Jr., to Duda, Oct. 26, 1966—all in RA. The FBI comment is in a Dec. 8, 1966, New York Office report, no file number; also FBI New York 100-25857-477 for New York Office's fur-

nishing data on Robeson to Philadelphia.

5. Anna Louise Strong to Fritchman, Sept. 20, 1966; Fritchman to PR, Oct. 17, 1966—both in RA. Helen Rosen (in multiple conversations) supports Strong's view that Robeson was upset over the Sino-Soviet split and leaned toward the Chinese. According to PR, Jr. (multiple conversations), his father told him in London in 1959, "In my head I'm still with the Russians but with my heart I'm with the Chinese"—though PR, Jr., has subsequently insisted, "That was with reference to a specific [unspecified] issue involving the third world, not an overall position." Yet, when *Newsweek* printed a rumor in 1963 that Paul had been invited to China and was considering the invitation, Essie reassured the Soviet Ambassador to the GDR that it was "a malicious rumor out of whole cloth, just to aggravate" (ER to family, Nov. 16, 1963, courtesy of Paulina Forsythe).

6. Multiple interviews with Marilyn Robeson; Marian Forsythe to Lee Lurie, Nov. 7, 11, 1966; Lurie to Forsythe, Nov. 9, 1966; Alvin I. Goldfarb to John Rockmore, Oct. 20, 1966—all in RA.

7. Marian Forsythe to Lee Lurie, Nov. 7, 1966, April 24, July 2, 1967, RA; the closing statement on the Jumel Terrace sale is also in RA. The piano teacher-friend was Charlotte Turner Bell. She has published an account of her visits that, measured against a variety of other reports, seems exaggeratedly cheerful—e.g., see note 18 (Charlotte Turner Bell, *Paul Robeson's Last Days in Philadelphia* [Dorrance & Co., 1986]).

8. Joseph Martindale to PR, Nov. 14, 1967. As late as 1967, Robeson's picture was absent from the gallery of football players in the Rutgers gym, and when students questioned it, university athletic officials replied that Robeson had failed to send his picture in; besides, "We do not brag about him." His picture was finally hung in the late sixties, but the university continued to refuse to sponsor him for the National Football Hall of Fame (whose home was at Rutgers). Indeed, the 1950 reference work *College Football* listed a *ten*-man All-American team for 1918, omitting Robeson; PR, Jr., "Paul Robeson: Black Warrior," *Freedomways*, First Quarter 1971).

9. Philadelphia *Evening Bulletin*, Dec. 22, 1967; New York *Post*, Dec. 23, 1967; FBI 100-38128-162; FBI Main 100-12304 (no file number), December 8, 1967; Middleton to Belfrage, Feb. 1, 1968, courtesy of Belfrage. Visiting him in the hospital, Charles Blockson found Robeson's "handshake firm and his eyes clear" (interview with Blockson, April 10, 1988). The newspaper accounts of Robeson's illness prompted a number of letters from fans and friends (all in RA), expressing pleasure at having had some news of him, however unpleasant, and wishing him well.

10. *The Worker*, April 7, 1968; Patterson's speech was printed up for distribution by the CPUSA (a copy is in RA), with the appended remarks by Lightfoot and Mitchell. Citation for the establishment of the Paul Robeson Archive in the GDR is in note 44, p. 759.

11. Franz Loesser to PR, Jr., and Marilyn, May 27, 1968 (GDR); *Morning Star*, March 9, 28, April 10, 1968; *Stage*, March 14, April 10, 1968; the program for the London event is in RA, complete with a list of sponsors, including Oliver Tambo (also O. R. Tambo to June Purdie, Dec. 30, 1967)—all in RA.

12. In 1968, when a new student-union building was under construction at Rutgers, the Black Student Union asked that it be named in Robeson's honor. The question was left to a vote of the student body, which defeated the suggestion by a vote of 753 to 478; a second such proposal lost by fewer than two hundred votes (Rutgers *Daily Targum*, Nov. 15, Dec. 11, 1968). A year later, however, the Paul Robeson Arts and Music Lounge was dedicated in the student building; feeling the event had been allowed to take place without adequate ceremony, the eastern-region branch of Alpha Phi Alpha (Robeson's fraternity) and the Student Center Board rededicated the lounge in April 1970. In 1971 the Harambee Organization, a black student group at the Newark campus of Rutgers, proposed to the board of governors that the Newark Student Center be named after Robeson; the nomination was supported

by thirty-seven other campus and community groups and passed by the Board (Philip Hoggard to PR, March 11, 1970, RA; *Daily Home News*, April 4, 1970; the New York *Amsterdam News*, April 18, 1970; Harambee to Board of Governors, Dec. 9, 1971; Karl E. Metzger [Board] to PR, Feb. 15, 1972—both in RA). In 1975 a proposal was made at Rutgers to change the name of Livingston College to Paul Robeson College. The faculty divided on the issue and the proposal was rejected (Rutgers *Daily Targum*, Nov. 14, Dec. 2, 4, 1975; *Rutgers Alumni Magazine*, Feb. 1976). Interview with Robert Sherman, March 21, 1983 (WQXR). The CBC broadcast produced hundreds of letters and phone calls, but Paul, Jr., angrily protested it; feeling it was now up to him to protect his father's public image as well as his personal privacy, he accused the broadcasters (accurately, in my view) with having minimized his father's contributions to black liberation and the colonial struggle, and with having perpetuated the falsehood that his father had lived in *exile* from the United States (PR, Jr., to Eleanor Fischer, March 29, May 1, 1971; Eleanor Fischer to PR, Jr., April 16, 1971—all in RA). On the Black Academy of Arts and Letters: C. Eric Lincoln to PR, April 21, 1970; Julia Prettyman to PR, May 14, June 3 ("immeasurable"), 1970—all in RA; NYPL/Schm has the BAAL Papers, and they document the unsuccessful effort to compile a film on PR as part of the awards ceremony, because of the refusal of film companies and network-television news broadcasters to cooperate in releasing material on him (see especially Julia Prettyman to Franz Loesser, June 23, Sept. 4, 1970; NYPL/Schm: BAAL also contains a transcript of the proceedings at the award dinner, along with surrounding correspondence about its preparation). Ossie Davis, Ruby Dee, Pete Seeger, Mary Travers, and Hattie Winston were among those participating in Local 1199's tribute to PR (program is in RA; *1199 News*, Feb. 1971; Moe Foner [executive secretary] to Lurie, Oct. 25, 1971, RA; interview with Moe Foner, Oct. 24, 1983). At the GDR celebration, planned to coincide with PR's seventy-third birthday, William L. Patterson made the keynote speech and Angela Davis sent greetings from her prison cell. On the various awards given Robeson 1970–72: Josephine C. Macauley to PR, Feb. 8, 1970 (Negro History); Boston *Globe*, May 4, 1972 (Black Psychiatrists); Mahlon T. Puryear to PR, Aug. 22, 1972 (Urban League); Junius Griffin to PR, telegram, Nov. 9, 1972 (NAACP)—all in RA. The *Ebony* article appeared in its Aug. 1972 issue, and *The New York Times* piece, by Loften Mitchell (a reprint from *Equity* magazine), on Aug. 6, 1972. Also in the years 1970–72, Dizzy Gillespie presented a Tribute to Paul Robeson and Black Culture in the Princeton University Chapel on Dec. 7, 1971 (Ernest Gordon to PR, Dec. 1, 1971, RA); he was also one of thirty outstanding black instrumentalists and singers given the Ellington Medal in 1972 by Yale in honor of Duke Ellington (*The New York Times*, Oct. 9, 1972). Actors' Equity Association passed a resolution setting up a committee to suggest "some suitable recognition" of his work (Fredrick O'Neal to PR, Jr., July 20, 1971, RA), and it eventually decided upon an annual award in his name in recognition of his "commitment to the struggle for a decent world"; as a special tribute, Robeson himself was named the first honoree (*Labor Chronicle*, June 1974). Columbia Records issued *Paul Robeson in Live Performance* in the spring of 1971 (*Daily World*, Nov. 1971).

13. Interviews with Helen Rosen (multiple), Clara Rockmore (March 17, 1984).

14. Interviews with Robert Sherman (March 21, 1983), Sylvia Schwartz (Jan. 16, 1983), Bayard Rustin (March 25, 1983). Rustin had sent greetings to Robeson soon after his return to the States late in 1963, but according to Paul, Jr., his father said he wanted nothing to do with him, that Rustin had become "a stooge for American foreign policy" (multiple conversations with PR, Jr.).

15. Phone interview with Dr. Herbert E. Cohen, March 17, 1987 (Cohen kindly retrieved all of Robeson's hospital records and read me parts of them, including Dr. Good's "semivegetative" description); multiple interviews with Helen Rosen; Lee Lurie to Morris Pearlmutter,

Aug. 27, 1969 (considering shock); Lloyd Brown to Lurie, Sept. 25, 1969—both in RA. Again in 1971, when writing to Robeson's Soviet friend Katanian, Brown said, "it's been years since I've seen him so happy" (June 22, 1971, RA). During his 1969 hospitalization for depression, *The New York Times* reported that he was suffering from a heart ailment (Aug. 6, 1969), but the FBI was better informed, describing him as "under psychiatric care because of 'depression' " (FBI Main 100-12304-721, 724).

16. Marian Forsythe to Lee Lurie, Jan. 23, 1969, Feb. 23, May 5, Dec. 8, 1971, March 26, 1972, RA.

17. Other examples of "good news being trumpeted abroad" about PR's condition are: the Watkinses to PR, April 12, 1971; Harry Francis to PR, Jr., July 26, 1971—both in RA. The summer of 1972, indeed, was apparently a relatively long "up" period for Robeson, since even Lee Lurie, who knew his actual prognosis well, wrote Harold Davison in London that "at the last visit with Paul Sr., it was heartwarming in the respect that he was almost his old self albeit that his exposure to the public is as yet completely counter-indicated" (July 2, 1971, RA). Evidence that Marian *did* occasionally let in an unexpected or uncertified caller is in my interviews with Edith Tiger (June 17, 1985), Hazel Dodge (Nov. 7, 1983), and Theodora Peck (April 8, 1982); also in Percy La Bohne to Marian Forsythe, April 10, 1973, thanking her "for permitting Rosalie to bring me by," and a postcard from Leila McKenzie to PR, n.d., in which she writes, "Do hope no harm was done to you by my unexpected visit" (the letter and card are courtesy of Paulina Forsythe, plus pictures taken by a Rose Kricheff, showing her sitting with Paul on a couch in Marian's living room); Louise Oswell to PR, June 29, 1971, also refers to a visit (courtesy of Paulina Forsythe). Occasionally, an unannounced out-of-town friend of genuine reliability was kept away, the oversight too late to rectify; Chuck Moseley, for example, who had been Robeson's bodyguard in California, tried unsuccessfully to get through to him

while passing through Philadelphia (interview with Moseley and Homer Sadler, May 3, 1982).

18. Interview with Robert Sherman, March 21, 1983; *New York Times*, April 16, 1973; interview with Edith Tiger, June 17, 1985. A transcript of PR's taped message is in RA. On the day of his birthday, Marian filled the house with flowers and invited in a number of old friends and relatives (Bell, *Last Days*, p. 12). Bell's account of Robeson enjoying "every minute" and "chatting quietly" is contradicted by Gertrude Cunningham's recollection that she had to grab his hand to prevent him from putting it absentmindedly into the birthday cake (interview with Cunningham, April 1982).

19. *The New York Times*, April 16, 1973.

20. The large batch of tributes, spoken and written, are in RA, along with the souvenir program of the Carnegie Hall event. Among the many others who expressed their admiration were Soviet Ambassador Anatoly Dobrynin, Zebbediah M. Gamanya (chief representative of FROLIZI, the Front for the Liberation of Zimbabwe), Jorge Amado, nineteen members of the House of Commons (including Harold Wilson, Roy Jenkins, James Callaghan, Barbara Castle, Denis Healey, Anthony Wedgwood Benn, Tom Driberg, Anthony Crosland, and Andrew Faulds), Cesar Chavez, Robert Ryan, Leonard Bernstein, Linus Pauling, Eugene Carson Blake (past president of the National Council of Churches)—and Chief Justice Warren E. Burger ("We often recall your magnificent performance of Othello . . . and we continue to enjoy your recordings"). The following year the Congressional Black Caucus gave Robeson its Special Award of Merit, and Congressman John Conyers, Jr., from Michigan read into the *Congressional Record* his remarks at a special salute to PR at a Detroit high school, as well as a Washington *Star* review of a PBS "Interface" documentary on Robeson's life (Charles B. Rangel and Walter E. Fauntroy to PR, n.d., RA [Merit]; Conyers to PR, Jr., June 20, 1975, RA; *Congressional Record*, June 19, 1975).

21. The Rutgers *Daily Targum* (April 10, 1973) reports "a noted lack of excitement" and a small turnout for the tribute to PR; Branson to PR, March 14, April 10, 1973 (Lincoln); Acklyn Lynch to PR, Jr., May 11, July 14, 1973 (U. Mass.); Allan P. Barron to PR, July 13, 1973 (Black Sports); FBI New York 100-38128-244. The National Football Foundation and Hall of Fame continued to be a holdout to the general trend of honoring Robeson. Rutgers's president, Edward J. Bloustein, and its head football coach, Dr. John F. Bateman, joined forces in securing a belated Rutgers nomination, but the Hall of Fame continued to turn it down. Bateman protested angrily to Vincent Draddy, chairman of the Hall's honors committee, and another Robeson supporter, Sam Woldin, carried the protest to Jimmie McDowell, the Hall's executive director. McDowell's laconic response was that "Loyalty to America is involved. The National Football Foundation honors men who honor the game and who honor the country" (Bateman to Committee, June 23, 1970; Bateman to Draddy, Sept. 23, 1970; Woldin to Foundation, Oct. 1, 1971; McDowell to Woldin, Oct. 12, 1971; Woldin to McDowell, Oct. 19, 1971 —copies in RA; *The Afro-American*, Dec. 12, 17, 1970). As if to prove its claim that "only" politics and not race was involved in the decision to reject Robeson, the Hall in 1970 elected Bill Willis, a black player from Ohio State, and dug back into the early 1900s to elect an obscure black Minnesota player named Bobby Marshall. The Memorial Concert program for Larry Brown is in RA; the text of PR's message (a brief, formal tribute) is printed in the *Daily World*, Feb. 20, 1973. In what was probably his last letter to them, Larry Brown sent Paul and Marian New Year's "Greetings from God's Town" [Harlem] and wishing them good health "if you . . . can get it" (Dec. 29, 1971, courtesy of Paulina Forsythe). Yergan to PR, Nov. 4, 1974, RA.

22. Fritchman to Marian Forsythe, Sept. 28, 1975, enclosing a copy of his remarks about Robeson to the First Unitarian Church, courtesy of Paulina Forsythe; multiple interviews with Freda Diamond; Lloyd L. Brown, "Paul Robeson Today" and "Paul Robeson Rediscovered," copies in RA.

23. Phone interview with Dr. Herbert E. Cohen, March 17, 1987; Philadelphia *Evening Bulletin*, Jan. 23, 1976 (spokesman); multiple conversations with Helen Rosen and with PR, Jr.

24. The headline and editorial are from the New York *Amsterdam News*, Jan. 31, 1976; the poem from Bil [sic] Brown, enclosed in a letter to Judge George W. Crockett, Nov. 6, 1977, RA. I will not attempt to cite separately the huge number of personal messages and public obituaries collected in RA.

25. New York *Amsterdam News*, Jan. 31, 1976; *Daily World*, Jan. 29, 1976; *Newsday*, Jan. 29, 1976. Gerry Bledsoe and her daughter Geraldine had visited Paul several times at Marian's specific invitation. She had written Gerry to encourage her to come by, thinking it might stimulate Paul to see old friends from his early years. However, Gerry found him "a sick man," essentially unresponsive (as described in several letters, 1983–85, from Gerry Bledsoe to me).

26. The full text of the eulogy and tributes is in RA. Both Paul and Eslanda Robeson are buried in Ferncliff Cemetery, Hartsdale, New York.

Index

TEXTUAL ACKNOWLEDGMENTS

Grateful acknowledgment is made to the following for permission to reprint previously published material:

Edward Burns: Excerpts from letters of Carl Van Vechten and Gertrude Stein from *The Gertrude Stein—Carl Van Vechten Letters: 1913–1946*, edited by Edward Burns. Copyright © 1986 by Columbia University Press. Reprinted by permission of Edward Burns.

Columbia Pictures Publications and *Fred Fisher Music Co., Inc.:* Excerpt from "Ballad for Americans" by John LaTouche and Earl Robinson. Copyright 1939, 1940. Renewed 1966, 1967 by Robbins Music Corp. & Fred Fisher Music Co., Inc. Rights of Robbins Music Corp. assigned to SBK Catalogue Partnership. All rights for SBK Catalogue Partnership controlled and administered by SBK Robbins Catalog Inc. All rights reserved. International copyright secured.

Yale University Press: Excerpts from letters of Carl Van Vechten from *Letters of Carl Van Vechten,* selected and edited by Bruce Kellner. Copyright © 1987 by Yale University. Reprinted by permission of Yale University Press.

Special thanks to all those who granted permission to use the following previously unpublished material:

Excerpts from letters by W. Bryher are reprinted by permission of the Estate of W. Bryher courtesy of Schaffner Agency, Inc.; excerpts from letters by Pearl S. Buck and Richard J. Walsh are reprinted by permission of the Pearl S. Buck Family Trust, Edgar S. Walsh, Trustee; excerpt from a letter by Countee Cullen, copyright 1928 by Countee Cullen, copyright renewed 1956 by Ida M. Cullen, are reprinted by permission of G.R.M. Associates, agents for the Estate of Ida M. Cullen; excerpts from letters by Nancy Cunard from the Schomburg Center for Research in Black Culture, The New York Public Library, Astor, Lenox and Tilden Foundations, are reprinted by permission of the Estate of Nancy Cunard, courtesy of Patrick Seale Associates; excerpts from a letter by Ben Davis are reprinted by permission of Nina Davis Goodman; excerpt from a letter by H. D., copyright © 1988 by Perdita Schaffner, are reprinted by permission of New Directions Publishing Corporation, agents for the Estate of H. D.; excerpt from a letter by Dr. Max Fink is reprinted by permission of Max Fink, M.D., Professor of Psychiatry, SUNY at Stony Brook; excerpts from letters by Emma Goldman are reprinted by permission of the Estate of Emma Goldman, courtesy of Ian Ballantine, Executor; excerpts from a letter by Oscar Hammerstein II, copyright © 1989 by the Estate of Oscar Hammerstein II, are reprinted by permission of the Estate of Oscar Hammerstein II; excerpts from letters by Lillian Hellman are reprinted by permission of The Literary Property Trustees Under the Will of Lillian Hellman; excerpts from letters by Langston Hughes are reprinted by permission of Harold Ober Associates Incorporated, agents for the Estate of Langston Hughes; excerpt from a manuscript by Lincoln Kirstein from the Knopf Library at the University of Texas is reprinted by permission of Lincoln Kirstein; excerpts from letters by Alfred A. Knopf are reprinted by permission of Helen N. Knopf; excerpts from letters by Claude McKay from the Paul Robeson Archives at the Moorland-Spingarn Research Center, Howard University, Washington, D.C., are reprinted by kind permission of Hope McKay Virtue; excerpts from letters by Fania Marinoff are reprinted by permission of the Estate of Fania Marinoff; excerpts from letters by Eugene O'Neill and excerpts from his diary are reprinted by permission of the Collection of American Literature, Beinecke Rare Book and Manuscript Library,

Yale University; excerpt from a letter by Louis Sheaffer is reprinted by permission of Louis Sheaffer; excerpts from letters by Carl Van Vechten are reprinted by permission of the Estate of Carl Van Vechten, Joseph Solomon, Executor; excerpt from a letter by Margaret Webster is reprinted by permission of Diana Raymond for the Estate of Margaret Webster; excerpt from a letter by Glenway Wescott is reprinted by permission of Harold Ober Associates Incorporated, agents for the Estate of Glenway Wescott; excerpts from letters by Walter White are reprinted by permission of Jane White Viazzi; and excerpts from letters by Max Yergan from the Paul Robeson Archives at the Moorland-Spingarn Research Center, Howard University, Washington, D.C., are reprinted by permission of his daughter Mary Y. Hughes.

PHOTOGRAPHIC ACKNOWLEDGMENTS

The following photographs are courtesy of Paul Robeson, Jr.: 1, 2, 4, 6, 7, 8, 13, 14, 15, 16, 17, 20, 24, 29, 31, 32, 33, 34, 35 *(photo by Raphael)*, 36, 41, 48, 49, 50, 52, 53, 55 *(photo by Eslanda Robeson)*, 63 *(photo by Eslanda Robeson)*, 65, 68 *(photo by Eslanda Robeson)*, 70, 71, 90, 93, 100, 103 *(photo by Lotte Meitner-Graf)*

These photographs are courtesy of the following individuals and institutions:

Courtesy of *The Afro-American:* 79

Courtesy of Akademie der Künste der DDR/Nationale Forschungs- und Gedenkstätten, Paul Robeson Archiv: 3, 42, 104, 106 *(photo by Paskowiak, Berlin)*, 108

© by Paramount Pictures. Courtesy of MCA Publishing Rights, a Division of MCA Inc., and the American Museum of the Moving Image *(photo by Jack Shalitt)*: 39, 40

Courtesy of AP/Wide World Photos: 58, 77, 83, 94, 96, 97

Courtesy of The Bettmann Archive: 84

Courtesy of The Bettmann Archive/BBC Hulton: 27, 43

Courtesy of Revels Cayton: 67

Courtesy of Columbia Law School Library: 12

Courtesy of the Czechoslovak News Agency: 102

Courtesy of Freda Diamond *(photo by Hilda Kassell)*: 64

Courtesy of the Thyra Edwards Papers, Mss. Department, Chicago Historical Society: 56

Courtesy of Paulina Forsythe: 111

Courtesy of Uta Hagen *(photo by Eileen Darby, Graphic House)*: 59

Courtesy of International Museum of Photography at George Eastman House: 28

Courtesy of International Museum of Photography at George Eastman House; bequest of Edward Steichen by direction of Joanna T. Steichen *(photo by Edward Steichen)*: 25

Courtesy of the Julius Lazarus Collection: 98, 101 *(photo by T.F. Holte)*

Courtesy of Julius Lazarus *(photos by Julius Lazarus)*: 69, 73, 74, 76, 91

Courtesy of Harold Leventhal and of Paul Robeson Archives, Inc.: 105

Courtesy of *Life* magazine, © 1943 Time Inc. *(photo by Herb Gehr)*: 61, 62

Courtesy of Life Picture Service: 22

Courtesy of Moorland-Spingarn Research Center, Howard University: 75, 78

Courtesy of *The New York Times:* 112

Courtesy of Paul Robeson Archives, Inc. *(photo by Ira Rosenberg)*: 81

Courtesy of The Billy Rose Theatre Collection, The New York Public Library at Lincoln Center, Astor, Lenox and Tilden Foundations: 18, 21, 26, 37 *(photo by J.W. Debenham)*, 46, 47, 57

Courtesy of Helen Rosen: 88, 89

Courtesy of Special Collections and Archives, Rutgers University Libraries: 5, 11

Courtesy of the Schomburg Center for Research in Black Culture, The New York Public Library, Astor, Lenox and Tilden Foundations: 45, 60, 66, 72, 85 *(Daily World photo)*

Courtesy of Sadie Davenport Shelton: 9, 10

Courtesy of Sovfoto: 80, 99 *(photo by V. Sasiukov)*, 107 *(Tass photo)*

Courtesy of Springer/Bettmann Film Archive: 51, 54

Courtesy of UPI/Bettmann Newsphotos: 44, 82, 86, 87, 92, 95, 109, 110

Courtesy of the Estate of Carl Van Vechten, Joseph Solomon, Executor; and of Paul Robeson, Jr. *(photo by Carl Van Vechten):* 38

Courtesy of the Estate of Carl Van Vechten, Joseph Solomon, Executor; and of The Rose McClendon Memorial Collection, Moorland-Spingarn Research Center, Howard University *(photo by Carl Van Vechten):* 30

Courtesy of The Yale Collection of American Literature, Beinecke Rare Book and Manuscript Library, Yale University *(photo by Doris Ulmann):* 19

Courtesy of The Yale Collection of American Literature, Beinecke Rare Book and Manuscript Library, Yale University; and of the Estate of Carl Van Vechten, Joseph Solomon, Executor *(photo by Carl Van Vechten):* 23